SAP ABAP

Hands-On Test Projects with Business Scenarios

Sushil Markandeya

Kaushik Roy

Apress®

SAP ABAP: Hands-On Test Projects with Business Scenarios

ISBN-13 (pbk): 978-1-4302-4803-3

ISBN-13 (electronic): 978-1-4302-4804-0

Managing Director: Welmoed Spahr
Lead Editor: Robert Hutchinson
Technical Reviewer: Alistair Rooney
Editorial Board: Steve Anglin, Gary Cornell, Louise Corrigan, Jonathan Gennick, Robert Hutchinson, Michelle Lowman, James Markham, Matthew Moodie, Jeff Olson, Jeffrey Pepper, Douglas Pundick, Ben Renow-Clarke, Dominic Shakeshaft, Gwenan Spearing, Matt Wade, Steve Weiss
Coordinating Editor: Mark Powers
Copy Editor: Karen Jameson
Compositor: SPi Global
Indexer: SPi Global
Artist: SPi Global
Cover Designer: Anna Ishchenko

Distributed to the book trade worldwide by Springer Science+Business Media New York, 233 Spring Street, 6th Floor, New York, NY 10013. Phone 1-800-SPRINGER, fax (201) 348-4505, e-mail `orders-ny@springer-sbm.com`, or visit `www.springeronline.com`. Apress Media, LLC is a California LLC and the sole member (owner) is Springer Science + Business Media Finance Inc (SSBM Finance Inc). SSBM Finance Inc is a Delaware corporation.

For information on translations, please e-mail `rights@apress.com`, or visit `www.apress.com`.

Apress and friends of ED books may be purchased in bulk for academic, corporate, or promotional use. eBook versions and licenses are also available for most titles. For more information, reference our Special Bulk Sales–eBook Licensing web page at `www.apress.com/bulk-sales`.

Any source code or other supplementary material referenced by the author in this text is available to readers at `www.apress.com/9781430248033`. For detailed information about how to locate your book's source code, go to `www.apress.com/source-code/`.

To all of my trainees from whom I have learned.

Contents at a Glance

Contents

About the Authors

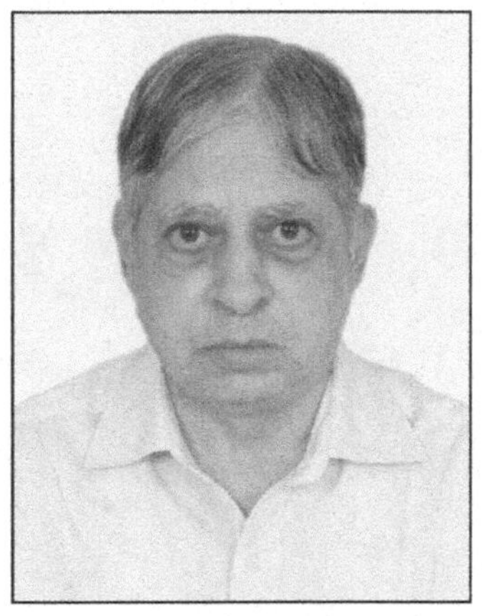

Sushil Markandeya is a B.E. from Osmania University (1973) and a M.E. (Electrical Engineering) from B.I.T.S., Pilani (1975). In 1977 he shifted to I.T. He was always involved in business application software on various platforms.

Since 1999, he has been associated with training on ERP software. On SAP, on ABAP; on 'Oracle Applications' on the functional side (financial modules: General Ledger, Fixed Assets Management, Accounts Receivable, Accounts Payable, and Cash Management). Since July 2006, he has been doing corporate training in SAP ABAP for people just out of college. The corporate clients he has trained for are: Accenture India Pvt. Ltd, Wipro Group (Wipro Technologies Ltd., Wipro Infotech. Ltd), Sony India Pvt. Ltd. Mphasis Pvt. Ltd. (part of HP), ITC Infotech Ltd, ITM – Saudi Arabia, Hyundai Motor India Ltd, and Godrej Info Tech. Ltd. To date, he has trained more than 1000 people in these corporations.

Kaushik Roy is involved in requirement definition, design and development of business components, testing, performance tuning and QA related activities. He is a Technical Consultant and is part of a team of highly efficient software professionals. He has solid experience in object oriented analysis and design, UML, user interface design using ABAP, HANA, data modeling and performance tools like HP diagnostics and TPTP. He also has advanced knowledge of the Business Objects tool which is used to develop secured applications.

He has been part of the core team that developed the applications for several clients. He understands the implementation processes very well and has the knowledge to successfully design, develop and implement. He possesses a sound understanding of the end customer's business processes. He has been awarded a Bachelors of Engineering in Computer Science from Uttar Pradesh Technical University in India. He is based out of Detroit, Michigan, USA.

About the Authors

About the Technical Reviewer

Alistair Rooney has over 30 years development experience. After a short military career in the Air Force, he started as an operator while studying and moved into programming in the early 80's. Alistair has been a programmer, analyst, project manager, architect and IT manager, but still keeps diving into code. Alistair has been working for SAP since 2002 as both a contract and permanent employee. In 2010 he worked for SAP Research developing leading edge mobile apps. He currently heads up the Data team for a large implementation at a major bank and is, once again, an SAP contract employee. He is married with two teenage children and is based near Durban, South Africa. He is the author of *Foundations of Java for ABAP programmers*, another Apress publication.

Acknowledgments

Author Sushil Markandeya acknowledges that but for his co-author, Kaushik Roy's initiative and zeal; this book would not have progressed beyond just an idea and a notion.

Acknowledgements are due to the technical reviewers: Shreekant Shiralkar and Alistair Rooney.

Acknowledgements are also due the Apress editorial personnel: Jeffrey Pepper (editorial director), Robert Hutchinson and Mark Powers (coordinating editor).We have had interaction with the above mentioned Apress personnel through internet and email. Our regular face-to-face interaction was with Saswata Mishra (acquisitions editor). Saswata Mishra has been very collaborative and has put up with all of our eccentricities and idiosyncrasies. The technical reviewers and the Apress editorial personnel have put in tremendous efforts and have imparted form to the amorphous manuscripts submitted to them. Finally, acknowledgement is due to the Springer and Apress personnel who worked behind the scenes to produce this book.

—Sushil Markandeya

Writing a book of this sort requires a sustained obsession over a single topic. I owe a great deal of thanks to all those who not only tolerated but indulged my obsession. It would be impossible to mention everyone who contributed to the work related to this book. Some who deserve special mention, are greatest strengths my loving Mom and Dad.

Above all I want to thank my lovely wife, Poonam and the heartbeat of my entire family, Kinshuk, Rahul, Rupsi, Rishan, Rusheel, Achintya, and Rachit who supported and encouraged me in spite of all the time it took me away from them.

Special thanks to the consulting clients from whom I've learned so much about how to crystallize the challenge & then implement it. This Book really "belongs" to all those friends, believers, enthusiasts, and supporters. I beg forgiveness of all those who have been with me over the course of the years and whose names I have failed to mention.

—Kaushik Roy

Introduction

ABAP (Advanced Business Application Programming) is the programming language and the platform on which the entire SAP software has been developed. Originally, a procedure oriented language, OOP constructs and features were added to it more than a decade back. Though, its core constructs remain the same, it underwent many enhancements over the last decade. The ABAP platform is used during both the customization and implementation phases of the SAP software in the enterprise.

Target Audience

The book addresses people who want to learn ABAP afresh and people working with ABAP for a few years (0-4 years). People with experience in ABAP will find this book useful as a reference for hands-on examples, from the context of doing meaningful things.

Target Audience Pre-requisites

The target audience must have a fair exposure to OOP language/s like C++, Java, etc. They must be exposed to the basic features of OOP including encapsulation, inheritance, polymorphism, etc.

They must also have a good exposure to RDBMS basics like RDBMS tables, table columns, relationships, primary key, foreign key, cardinality, entity, attribute and table metadata. An exposure to RDBMS SQL, especially the data retrieval statement, is required.

Book's Approach

The whole of the book's thrust is on the doing something meaningful part: to be able to create programs and objects required as per a defined context or scenario.

The book uses a scenario oriented presentation style. Concepts, commands and statements are communicated through illustrative examples and scenarios. Wherever possible, small business scenarios are used to communicate concepts, commands and statements.

Shorn of weighty theoretical treatment and preoccupations with language syntax, the book is a completely practical approach, demonstrating and conveying the language's commands, features through hands-on examples.

Definitions, descriptions, syntax, etc. are introduced even as you set about implementing a scenario.

The presentation of the features is scenario oriented: most of the features are demonstrated in terms of small business scenarios. The book's scenario descriptions along with source program resource containing the ABAP program source enable the reader to create all objects related to the scenario and run or execute them. The underlying concepts of a feature/command are totally conveyed through execution of these hands-on programs.

The demonstrating/illustrating objects, including the programs, rely on some of the SAP functional module tables being populated (the term functional module is explained in Chapter 1). This is assured if the reader is logged on to an IDES (internet demonstration & evaluation server) server or system. The IDES server is briefly described in Chapter1. An IDES server is now a de facto system for all SAP training related activities. Specifically SAP functional module tables used for illustration and hands-on exercises in the book are the basic tables of sales and purchase. Most people with nil or little to no exposure to the business, and commercial world relate to the business areas of sales and purchase.

All of the hands-on exercises in the book are performed using SAP sales and purchase functional module tables. The IDES server is used ensuring substantial data in the SAP functional module tables. Details of the SAP functional module tables used in the hands-on exercises are to be found in Appendix A. The authors strongly advise you to go through the appendix describing the functional module tables used in the hands-on exercises of the book. You can visit this Appendix A before you commence the reading of a chapter from Chapter 5 onwards (when you start using the SAP functional module tables).

The book also uses a "carry forward" approach for the hands-on exercises. Where ever possible, a hands-on exercise performed in earlier chapters is carried forward to subsequent chapters, with additions and enhancements carried out to it. This involves re-usability of created objects again and again.

Chronology and order of presentation of topics and sub topics is related to pre requisites required for the presented topics and sub topics. At some places, topics and sub topics are introduced on a preview basis to make the current hands-on exercise more meaningful. Subsequently the topics and sub topics introduced on a preview basis are formally presented.

The authors strongly insist that you perform the hands-on exercises as you read a chapter and encounter the hands-on exercises—do not defer performing them until after reading a chapter or the book. It should not be just reading, but reading and simultaneously performing the hands-on exercises.

Resources

The book is supplemented with an E-resource or source program resource.

The E-resource or source program resource contain the hands-on exercises source programs. Most source programs in the E-resource are also listed in the book. Some source programs of the E-resource are partially listed in the book and some are not listed in the book. This is indicated in the respective chapters. The E-resource is downloadable and each of the hands-on exercise source programs can be opened as a separate file in Windows Notepad. While performing the hands-on exercises, you can copy and paste an entire source program from the E-resource, or manually enter the source program by referring to the source program lines of the E-resource. Manual entry of source programs will get you a feel of the syntax of statements. If you are copying and pasting, remember to replace the 'REPORT. . .' statement line from the E-resource program into the created ABAP program in the ABAP workbench environment. You will be introduced to the ABAP workbench environment in Chapter 1.

In addition to the book and the supplementary E-resource, you will use the following additional resources:

You must have connectivity to SAP, preferably a SAP IDES server. Your log-in user id must be able to create, edit and delete objects in the ABAP workbench environment. Your log-in user id must be able to access data from SAP functional module tables. Apart from book reading, some extra reading is required such as:

You will need to read extra theory and description not exposited in the book. You need to refer to some detailed information not provided in the book.

You will need to read up the detailed tutorial or documentation related operations in the ABAP workbench environment not described in the book.

You will likely refer to and read the detailed properties, methods and events, etc. of some SAP supplied classes.

The material for most of the above mentioned readings is available in freely downloadable PDF documents from the following link `http://www.easymarketplace.de/online-pdfs.php`. You will not violate any copyright law downloading the documents from this link. These are PDF documents of SAP version 4.6C. Though the documents are older versions; they will largely serve your purposes.

Download the following PDF documents from the link: `http://www.easymarketplace.de/online-pdfs.php`.

ABAP Programming (BC-ABA)	BCABA.pdf
ALV Gird Control (BC-SRV-ALE)	BCSRVALV.pdf
BC - ABAP Dictionary	BCDWBDIC.pdf
BC ABAP Workbench Tools	BCDWBTOO.pdf
BC ABAP Workbench Tutorial	BCDWBTUT.pdf
SAP List Viewer (ALV): Classic	CAGTFLV.pdf

You will need to refer (not read) to these documents for information during your reading of this book. Preferably, you won't read these documents during your chapter reading. Read these documents between chapters. At what stage, which of these documents are to be read or referred is indicated in the book's chapters.

So, on to stimulating reading. Not just readings though, the hands-on exercises should be performed simultaneously with your reading. The documents mentioned above will also be available for download on `http://www.apress.com/9781430248033`.

CHAPTER 1

ERP and SAP Overview

ERP Overview

Enterprise Resource Planning (ERP) software products are business application, packaged software. They are used to run large- to medium-sized business enterprises. The ERP software suppliers claim that their software can cater to every business activity of every category of business enterprise. In most cases, an enterprise relies on multiple databases to maintain its operations: to facilitate the migration, the ERP software supports multiple databases for interaction and input but relies primarily on a centralized database for storing all function module data. The ERPs integrate the different business activities of a business enterprise. They support multiple currency handling, an essential feature for business enterprises operating globally. The ERPs also have the feature of consolidation, which facilitates the consolidation or accumulation of the accounting numbers of transnational business enterprises having a large number of subsidiaries around the world. The ERP software suppliers claim that all advances in hardware and software technologies are incorporated in their newer upgrades or versions. Quite a few phrases and terms have been used in this attempt at defining an ERP. Explanations of these terms and phrases follow.

Business Enterprises

A language dictionary meaning of business enterprise does not help in the present context. A definition is being attempted from the point of view of law or statute. The users of ERP software are large- and medium-sized business enterprises. Such business enterprises have to be registered or incorporated companies. Any group of people wanting to start a business enterprise should apply for registration or incorporation. Business enterprises are also called companies, enterprises, firms, or organizations. Any of these synonymous terms will be used. In the ERP world, the registered companies are also called 'legal entities.' Once a company is registered, it can commence business operations. The registered company must, as per law, publish its audited financial results once a year, and unaudited financial results every three months or quarter. Audited means the financial results generated by the company would be cross-checked and verified for its accuracy, or authenticity, by an independent audit company. These are statutory financial results as required by law distinct from financial results the company would produce for its own internal purposes. The statutory financial results must be reported in the currency of the country where the company is registered. Hence, companies registered in the United States would produce their financial results in U.S. dollars. This currency, in which a company has to produce financial results, as per law, could be termed 'operating currency of the company.'

A company registered in one country, generally, will not directly operate a full-scale business in another country. A company 'ABC U.S.' registered in one country, say the United States, wanting to conduct a full-scale business in another country, say the United Kingdom, will register a local company in the United Kingdom, such as 'ABC U.K.'. This company in the United Kingdom, 'ABC U.K.,' is designated as a subsidiary of the parent company 'ABC U.S.'. A parent company can own 100% of a subsidiary or less. A parent company can have any number of subsidiaries around the world. A subsidiary company can, in turn, have many subsidiaries.

Business enterprises are categorized based on their prime activity. Figure 1-1 shows the categories of business enterprises.

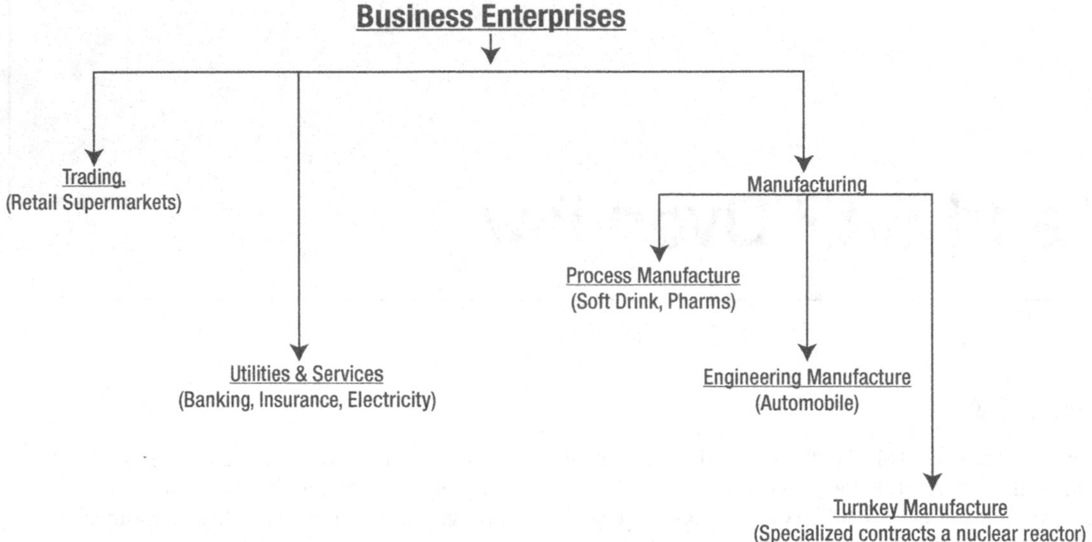

Figure 1-1. *Business Enterprise Categories*

The first category of business enterprise, 'Trading,' does not involve producing or manufacturing any goods. Such enterprises buy goods and sell them. A very common example of this subcategory is 'Retail Trading,' such as supermarkets. The second category of business enterprise is 'Utilities & Services' ('Electric Energy Distribution,' 'Banking') and do not do any manufacturing. Though electricity is produced, it is not a good in the normal sense of the word, so it is categorized under 'Utilities.'

The third category of business enterprise is 'Manufacturing.' This category is further subcategorized into 'Process,' 'Engineering,' and 'Turnkey.' The subcategories reflect the production or manufacturing characteristic. In the first subcategory 'Process,' ingredients pass through a process, and the product at the end of the process is frequently packaged in different modes. Once ingredients and processes are fixed, this is repetitive in nature. The most common examples of 'Process' manufacturing are the soft drink companies and the pharmaceutical companies. One other example of the subcategory 'Process' would be an oil refinery company. The crude oil passes from one fractional distillation process to another, producing various petroleum products at each stage of fractional distillation.

In the second subcategory of manufacture, 'Engineering,' components or parts are produced and/or procured in the first stage. Then these components are assembled to produce the final product. Before the assembly stage, all the required components should be available if the assembly is to be carried out successfully. So in the 'Engineering Manufacture,' to produce a certain number of finished products, components required before the assembly stage are to be ascertained. This is called 'Requirement Planning,' a major exercise to be performed in 'Engineering Manufacture.' In fact, a set of software called 'Material Requirement Planning' – MRP – were predecessor to the ERP. The most common example of this subcategory is a business enterprise manufacturing automobiles. It is to be noted that once the specifications of, for example, a car model are finalized, the process of production, procurement, and assembly is repeated over and over again, a kind of routine process to produce that model of the car. Components could be manufactured within the business enterprise: for example, an engine is manufactured within the business enterprise from some raw materials. Ready-made components could be procured (outsourced) components: for example, headlights and tail lights are procured from other business enterprises. Therefore, in the assembly stage, there could be a mix of produced components and procured components.

The third subcategory of 'Manufacture' is 'Turnkey Manufacture.' This subcategory is similar to the subcategory 'Engineering Manufacture' to the extent that components are produced first and then subsequently assembled. But in 'Turnkey Manufacture,' unlike the 'Engineering Manufacture,' there is a degree of non-repetitiveness in the process. Some parts of the process could be repetitive, but some parts would be non-repetitive.

Though each of the business enterprise categories is complex in its own way, as shown in Figure 1-1, the complexity of business increases in relative terms as you move from left to right. So 'Services' are perceived as relatively more complex than 'Trading,' 'Manufacture' more complex than 'Services,' 'Engineering Manufacture' more complex than 'Process Manufacture,' and so on.

There could also be more categories of business enterprises. Try to think whether packaged software companies such as SAP, Oracle, and Microsoft would fit into these categories or require a new one. Similarly, think about whether 'Real Estate' business enterprise (selling houses) fits into an existing category in the diagram or not.

The categories of business enterprises in the diagram might not be complete. The subcategories of manufacturing business enterprises might not pass muster from a fastidious production planning professional. But the objective here of describing the categories and subcategories is to give a feel for the complexities of business enterprises that ERP software has to address to people having their first exposure to business in a commercial world.

Business Activities

Within a business enterprise, different business activities are performed. These business activities are 'Accounting' or 'Finance,' 'Sales,' 'Material Accounting' or 'Material Management,' 'Production Planning,' 'HR,' etc. Some of these business activities could be common to categories of business enterprises such as 'Finance' ('Finance' is the heart of every business, and every business enterprise must perform this business activity); 'Sales'; 'HR'; or 'Material Management.' Some of the business activities could be specific to certain categories of business enterprises. The business activity 'Material Management' is relevant to the categories of 'Manufacturing' and 'Trade' but not to the category 'Services.' Similarly, the business activity 'Production Planning' is not relevant to the categories 'Trade,' 'Services,' and so on. These business activities could be viewed as departments performing a specific function in a business enterprise. In ERP parlance, these departments are termed business functions or functional modules, and each functional module caters to a specific business function. Henceforth, you will refer to the business activities as functional modules.

ERP Concept, Its Evolution

Pre ERP Business Application Software Scenario: Before the advent of the ERP concept — in the mid-1970s and earlier (a long time ago) – business application software used to be created around each business function. The accounting or finance functional module would have its set of programs or software and data; the sales would have their own software and data to run the application. The data of the different functional modules was maintained separately, not in a centralized database. The software of different functional modules was running in a segregated manner (i.e., there was no integration – a major hallmark of the ERP software). Moreover, the software was the so-called tailor-made software. At that time there was no concept of packaged, off-the-shelf software that is available today. Business application software used to be created much like the tailor-made shirt. Every time you want a shirt, you go to the tailor with the requisite cloth, give measurements, and specify the shirt's features (for example, how many pockets?). Are the pockets flapped? Are they full or half sleeved? In an analogous fashion, to create new business application software for a functional module of a business enterprise, personnel designated as 'systems engineers' or 'systems analysts' would interact with the functional modules' personnel of the business enterprise, study the functional module's processes and systems, do a conceptual design and a data design, write programs, test programs, and implement and maintain the programs. Next time that software for the same functional module is to be produced for a different business enterprise, the same gamut of activities would be completed, maybe involving repetition of some or most of these activities.

Pre ERP Technology Scenario: In the 1970s, the computer industry was in its nascent stage. The level and scale of hardware and software features available were nowhere close to what is available today.

To give a bare idea of what was conspicuously not available in hardware, consider this list: (i) No microprocessors. (ii) No distributed processing, only centralized processing represented by the mainframes and mini computers. (Mini computers subsequently vanished.) (iii) No semiconductor RAM. RAM sizes were of the order of kilobytes and a few megabytes. Disk sizes of the order of 10s of megabytes. (v) Very little networking, almost to the extent of nonexistence (i.e., no connectivity).

Here is now an idea of what was conspicuously not available in software: (1) No Graphical User Interface - GUI. (2) No networking operating systems. (3) No OOPS technology. (4) The operating systems were rudimentary; even a task like disk and file space management was performed by the end user. (5) RDBMS was in a very nascent stage.

And all of this cost lot of money, millions of dollars. The computers could only be afforded by the Fortune 500 companies!

The 'Pre ERP Business Application Software Scenario' and 'Pre ERP Technology Scenario' descriptions have been included because ERP software carries a legacy relating to these scenarios, and exposure to this helps relate to the legacies in the ERP software.

Major Attributes of ERP Software

Centralized Database

In ERP software, all the data relating every functional module is stored in one centralized database. The next attribute, integration, is possible only with a centralized database.

Integration

The term 'integration' has been introduced in the context of ERP software. Let this integration be illustrated by a simple business need. Consider the instance of business enterprise payroll processing. Every week/month (depending on the payment period), an enterprise has to generate the pay sheet of its employees. For each employee, a pay sheet has to be created detailing the various earnings - basic salary, house allowance, conveyance allowance, etc.; and the various deductions - provident fund, health insurance, etc. Each employee will receive his or her respective pay sheets through an e-mail or by some other mode. The functional module responsible for the pay sheet (perhaps HR) will maintain the pay sheet data.

Now, since the pay sheet involves money payment, the finance functional module should be notified. This is a basic need of any business. Any activity involving payment or receipt of money will invariably involve this notification to the finance functional module. But the finance functional module requires the pay sheet information in a different fashion. They do not want the detailed information of every employee. Instead, they want summary information for each functional module: the total of every type of earning and deduction. Tables 1-1 and 1-2 elaborate this scenario.

Table 1-1. *Employee Pay Sheet*

Functional Module/ Department	Employee No.	Basic	House Allowance	Conveyance Allowance	Provident Fund	Health Insurance
HR	500001	20000	4000	2000	1600	1000
HR	500010	30000	6000	3000	2400	1500
HR	500015	25000	5000	2500	2000	1250
Total - HR		75000	15000	7500	6000	3750
Sales	500030	50000	10000	5000	4000	2500
Sales	500035	40000	8000	4000	3200	2000
Total - Sales		90000	18000	9000	7200	4500

Table 1-2. *Functional Module Wise Pay Sheet Summary*

Functional Module Department	Basic	House Allowance	Conveyance Allowance	Provident Fund	Health Insurance
Total - HR	75000	15000	7500	6000	3750
Total - Sales	90000	18000	9000	7200	4500

For illustrative purposes, only three employees for the first functional module have been considered, and only two employees for the second functional module. In a real-life scenario, there could hundreds and thousands of employees in a functional module, and there would be quite a few functional modules, not just two. What is to be understood is the way the functional module of finance should receive the pay sheet data.

In the ERP software, this facility of summarizing the data and sending the data from HR to finance is built in. The sending and receiving of data in technical terms obviously means transfer of data from HR tables to finance tables of the centralized ERP database.

Multiple Currency Handling

Business enterprises conduct business around the globe. They buy goods and services from suppliers in countries other than the country of their registration, so they may have to pay in the currencies of the countries where the suppliers are located. Similarly, they sell goods and services to customers located in countries other than the country of their registration, so they may raise bills in the currencies of the countries where the customers are located. But as per the law of the land, ultimately everything has to be converted into the currency of the country where the business enterprise is registered. So the element of conversion from one currency to another comes into play. The conversion rate to convert from one currency to another is called the exchange rate. The issue of conversion is complicated by requirements of the laws. Most countries' laws require that different exchange rates be adopted in different contexts. This entails maintenance of a large number of exchange rates to be used and assigned in different contexts as prescribed by laws. Let these concepts be again explained with a simple business scenario.

Assume that there is a software services company 'ABC Ltd.' operating in India; its operating currency is Indian rupees. 'ABC Ltd.' has provided services (probably implemented SAP) to a customer company located in the United States. For the services provided, 'ABC Ltd.' presents a bill of 5,000,000 U.S. dollars. As per the law, this figure needs to be converted to Indian rupees to incorporate this into the book of accounts of 'ABC Ltd.' The issue is what exchange rate to adopt. This is a context of sales (i.e., software services have been sold). Suppose the law states that in the context of sales, the exchange rate (U.S. dollar vis-à-vis Indian rupee) prevailing on the last trading day of the month on the money market in which the sales bill was raised should be adopted. Suppose this rate was 1 U.S. dollar = 55.00 Indian rupees. [There is a money market, where money of different currencies is sold and purchased like a commodity]. Hence the figure of 5,000,000 is taken into 'ABC Ltd.' account books as 275,000,000. This is the end of this transaction. This was a simple scenario of currency conversion and multiple currency handling.

The issue of multiple currency handling is a complex one. The ERP software has built-in features to enable the handling of this issue.

Consolidation

This feature is required by business enterprises having subsidiaries around the globe. When the financial statements are prepared for these business enterprises (parent companies) having a number of subsidiaries around the world, the financial statements must incorporate the numbers of all the subsidiaries as well. This flow of numbers from the subsidiaries to the parent is called consolidation. The process of incorporating subsidiaries' numbers is complicated by two factors: (a) When the numbers of the subsidiaries flow to the parent company, they should be converted to the currency of the parent company, as the parent company and its subsidiaries will be operating in different currencies.

The multiple currencies factor is again operating. (b) The parent company's ownership is not direct but through other subsidiaries, and ownership might be less than 100%. The ERP software addresses these issues and has built-in features to enable consolidation.

Figure 1-2 attempts to graphically convey the consolidation of a simple scenario.

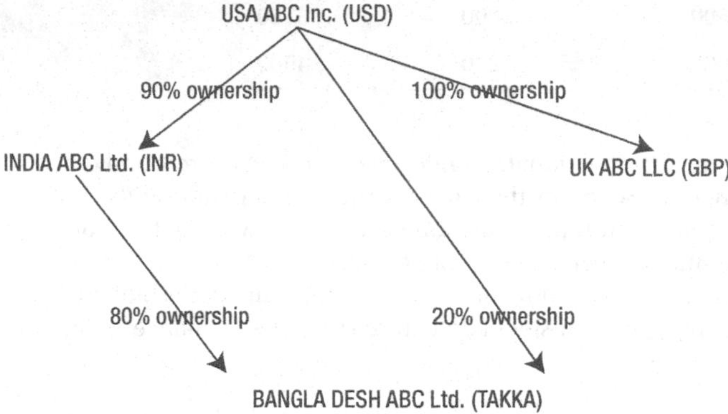

Figure 1-2. *Parent & Subsidiary Companies*

In the graphic hierarchal representation, the parent company USA ABC Inc. has subsidiaries INDIA ABC LTD. (90% ownership), UK ABC LLC (100% ownership), and BANGLA DESH ABC Ltd. (20% ownership). USA ABC Inc. also owns BANGLA DESH ABC Ltd. through subsidiary INDIA ABC Ltd. (80% ownership). The currencies of these countries are indicated in parentheses.

When figures of parent company USA ABC Inc. are prepared, the numbers of its subsidiaries should flow in the manner shown in Table 1-3.

Table 1-3. *Flow of Numbers from Subsidiary Companies to Parent Company*

From Company	Currency Conversion	% Ownership	To Company
INDIA ABC Ltd.	INR to USD	90	USA ABC Inc.
UK ABC LLC	GBP to USD	100	USA ABC Inc.
BANGLA DESH ABC Ltd.	TAKKA to USD	20	USA ABC Inc.
BANGLA DESH ABC Ltd.	TAKKA to INR	80	INDIA ABC Ltd.
INDIA ABC Ltd.	INR (from TAKKA) to USD		USA ABC Inc.

This is a small illustrative scenario. A real-life scenario would involve more subsidiaries and more complex parent vis-à-vis subsidiary relationships. The ERP software is equipped to deal with the consolidation process.

Technology Advances

Every major ERP supplier/vendor has a technical tie-up with every other hardware and software supplier/vendor. These major ERP suppliers claim they introduce and incorporate features of technology advances into their newer release/versions.

Multiple Lingual Support

Business enterprises conduct business in their respective native language: business enterprises located in China conduct business in Mandarin, business enterprises located in Germany conduct business in German, and so on. The ERP software supports multiple languages. At the user login stage or a process of setup, a language is input. In the ERP operating environment, the messages, labels, and texts, etc. will then appear in the logged language.

SAP Overview

SAP - *Systems, Applications, and Products in Data Processing* – is the name of the company as well as the product. The company was later renamed as SAP A.G. It is headquartered in Germany and was started by five engineers who were then employed with IBM. At IBM they performed the task of creating tailor-made business application software. At that time every single computer supplier supplied everything related to computers such as all hardware (processors and memory devices), operating systems, development tools such as language compilers, and tailor-made business application software. When the five engineers left IBM and started their own company, they persuaded IBM to subcontract the *business-application-software* part to their company, probably the first instance of outsourcing in the IT industry. Wherever IBM delivered mainframe hardware and accompanying deliverables, except the business application software, SAP created this business application software.

SAP came out with product SAP R/1 in 1972. In this product specification, 'R' signified real time. Real time was then a hot technology feature like cloud computing is today. The simplest example of real time is when your airline tickets are booked, the seat availability for booked flight/s of the specific day/s are updated instantly. The '1' signified one or single-tier architecture; the database, application, and presentation resided on a single system.

In 1979, SAP released the multiuser SAP R/2 with the following features:

- Supported on IBM Mainframe
- 'R' indicated 'Real Time'
- '2' indicated 2-tier architecture: (1) Database+Applications layer (2) Presentation layer
- Most of the common modules, such as Finance, Sales, Material Management, Manufacturing, and HR were offered

Until mid-1992, when SAP R/3 was released, the number of SAP installations ≈ 300.

In mid-1992, SAP released the SAP R/3 product with the following features:

- '3' indicated a 3-tier architecture: (1) Database (2) Applications layer (3) Presentation layer
- Supported on (1) popular flavors of UNIX: IBM, HP, Sun Solaris; (2) OS/2, Windows
- Supported the following databases: (1) ADABAS now called SAP MaxDB (2) Oracle (3) Informix (4) IBM DB2 (5) MS SQL Server (when it was released)
- SAP as of now supports the following additional databases: (1) Sybase ASE (2) HANA

No other ERP suppliers or vendors could match this multi-platform offering of SAP at that time. Because of a drastic reduction in hardware and software licensing costs in following years (more and companies could afford it), SAP witnessed an exponential growth in these years. Its installed base crossed 100,000 in 2010. It is now the third largest software company.

SAP followed up the SAP R/3 product with MySAP Business Suite (with integration through the Internet), E.C.C. 5.0 (E.C.C. - ERP Core Component), and E.C.C. 6.0. The latest version at this time of writing is E.C.C. 6.0 EHP6 (Enhancement package 6).

Client Server Architecture

At this stage, it is sufficient to have only a basic idea about the client server architecture, which is the software view of SAP architecture. An SAP installation consists of a database server, typically on a UNIX-based machine/system; one or more application server/s, each typically on a UNIX-based machine/system (maybe a maximum of six); and many window-based presentation servers or systems. The database server is meant to provide the services of data maintenance and data access. Programs are loaded into the application server/s and executed in the application server/s' RAM. Presentation servers are for user access, operation, interaction, and dialogue.

In typical window-based SAP training environments, the database server and application servers are located on a single system/machine. If you install SAP software on a laptop or a desktop and work on it, all three servers (i.e. database, application, and presentation) are located on the same system or machine.

SAP NetWeaver

SAP NetWeaver is an integration framework. It was designed to operate in *service-oriented architecture* **(SOA)**. It constitutes cooperative technologies that integrate SAP functional modules and also provide connectivity to external systems. The NetWeaver is a successor to SAP R/3. The first NetWeaver version 6.2 was released in 2003. The latest NetWeaver version is 7.3 at the time of this writing. The NetWeaver version is distinct from The SAP software version (E.C.C. 6.0). The SAP NetWeaver has components, tools, and applications.

The application server is a component of the SAP NetWeaver and also part of the software view of SAP architecture. The application server has a complex architecture. The application server is called the NetWeaver Application Server (SAP NW AS). The NetWeaver application server has a five-tiered architecture: presentation, business, integration, connectivity, and persistence. The NetWeaver application server consists of an application server ABAP (AS ABAP) and an application server Java (AS JAVA).You can install either one or both.

Other components of NetWeaver: business warehouse, business process management, business rules management, process integration, master data management, mobile, portal, Auto-ID Infrastructure, identity management, and information life-cycle management.

SAP Functionalities

The SAP business suite consists of five components:

Enterprise Resource Planning - ERP

Customer Relationship Management -CRM

Supply Chain Management - SCM

Supplier Relationship Management - SRM

Product Life-Cycle Maintenance - PLM

The ERP component, in turn, consists of the various functional modules. The functional modules are referred by the short forms: FI for finance, SD for sales and distribution, and so on.

A partial list of functional modules with their names and their short forms:

1.	Accounting/Finance	FI
2.	Control(Cost)	CO
3.	Sales & Distribution	SD
4.	Material Management	MM
5.	Production Planning	PP

6.	Human Resources	HR
7.	Quality Maintenance	QM
8.	Plant Maintenance	PM
9.	Project System	PS
10.	Treasury	TR

SAP Implementation Overview

The SAP implementation is a substantial exercise and involves large high-skill manpower resources and time resources. The cost of SAP implementation exceeds the combined cost of hardware and software licensing. Generally the company planning to use the SAP software does not implement the software; they would not have the requisite know-how. The implementation for the most part is done by third parties. These third parties are SAP-authorized implementation partners. The SAP implementers form implementation teams at the commencement of implementation. There is a team from the implementer side and another team from the company that will use the SAP software. A company planning to use SAP will not implement all the SAP functional modules. They will only implement functional modules relevant or required by them. Even the functional modules to be implemented by a company need not be implemented in one phase. The implementation could be done in phases, with a time gap between the phases. A typical SAP implementation time period is 18 months.

A SAP implementation involves configuration, customization, enhancement, and modification. Modification involves modifying SAP-provided objects - not advisable except in rare situations.

A typical configuration activity will involve creation of a company code: assigning a chart of accounts and business area to the company code, etc.

A simple example of customization: on a SAP-provided data entry screen, disabling fields not required by the enterprise.

An example of enhancement: addition of fields required by the enterprise to a SAP-delivered table.

Implementation Team Composition

An implementer side team will have a hierarchy such as project managers, project leads, team leaders, team members, and so on. The team from the implementer side consists of three main categories of consultants. They are:

I. The Basis consultants
II. The Functional consultants
III. The ABAP/Technical consultants

Implementation Environments

The SAP implementation is carried out in well-defined controlled environments. Different stages of implementation are carried out in different environments segregated from each other. The typical implementation environments are (i) development and (ii) testing and quality assurance. The outcome of these two environments will flow to the third environment, which is the live environment (a typical implementation has at least three stages, which are discussed here).

End-user training is a very critical activity of SAP implementation that commences after configuration, customization, and enhancement stages are complete. It deals with training of staff at the customer site in usage of software to carry out their day-to-day tasks.

Objects would be created by an ABAP consultant in the development environment. These would be moved - or to use the SAP terminology - transported to the testing and quality assurance environment. Once they pass testing and quality assurance, they will be transported to the live environment.

Similarly, a functional consultant will create functional components (like company codes, charts of accounts, etc.) in the development environment. These would be transported to testing and quality assurance. Once they pass testing and quality assurance, they will be transported to the live environment.

Suppose, in another scenario, testing and quality assurance are two separate environments. Then, objects/components would be transported from development to testing, from testing to quality assurance, and from quality assurance to live environment.

Now how an object/component travels is determined by the transport layer that gets associated with the object/component. The transport layer and transportation of objects/components are part of a feature, 'Central Transport System,' which is the purview of the Basis consultant.

In today's hardware and software scenario, you can have different systems for different environments (a three-system 'Landscape'). You can have one Windows-based system assigned to the development environment. (Windows can support a few hundred users without any performance or response bottlenecks.) Similarly another Windows-based system is assigned to testing and quality assurance. The end-user training usually resides on one of these two systems. On the other hand, a UNIX-based system is assigned to a live environment. The systems are connected to each other through network for transporting objects and data from one environment to another as per transport layer specification. The objects and data in these environments are segregated from each other because they are residing physically on different systems. This is called the three-system landscape. This description is represented in Figure 1-3.

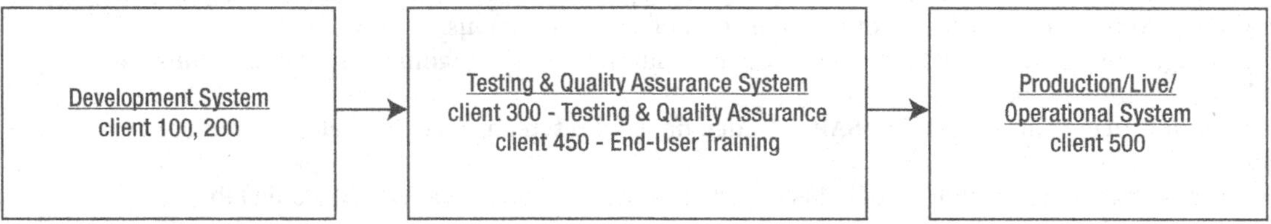

Figure 1-3. *Three-System Landscape*

The 'Clients' are explained in the section entitled 'Client Code Perspectives.'

Now, consider this case in the SAP R/2 mainframe system. A separate mainframe could not have been assigned for each environment (development, testing and quality assurance, live). All the environments had to reside on a single mainframe system. Yet these environments needed to exist in a segregated manner. The segregation was obviously implemented through a logical means. The means of logical segregation is a legacy carried by the subsequent and latest version of SAP software.

The segregation is essential. Whatever is being done in the development environment should not be visible and available in other environments and vice versa. There is a separate environment for end-user training. To train an end user in the procedure and process of creation of customer data, dummy customers are created in the end-user training. These dummy customers must not appear in the live environment or other environments. There would normally be no transport of objects and data from end-user training environment to other environments.

Overview of SAP Login, SAP GUI, ABAP Workbench

You are advised to use the SAP IDES server. (The IDES server has been elaborated in the section entitled 'SAP IDES Server and use of SAP IDES Server for Trainings.) All the hands-on exercises in this book have been performed on the IDES server.

It is assumed you have access to a SAP server, preferably to an IDES server. The front-end software has been installed, connectivity established, and you are ready with the login pad.

SAP Login

When you click on the SAP login pad on your system, the SAP Login screen will look like the one in Figure 1-4.

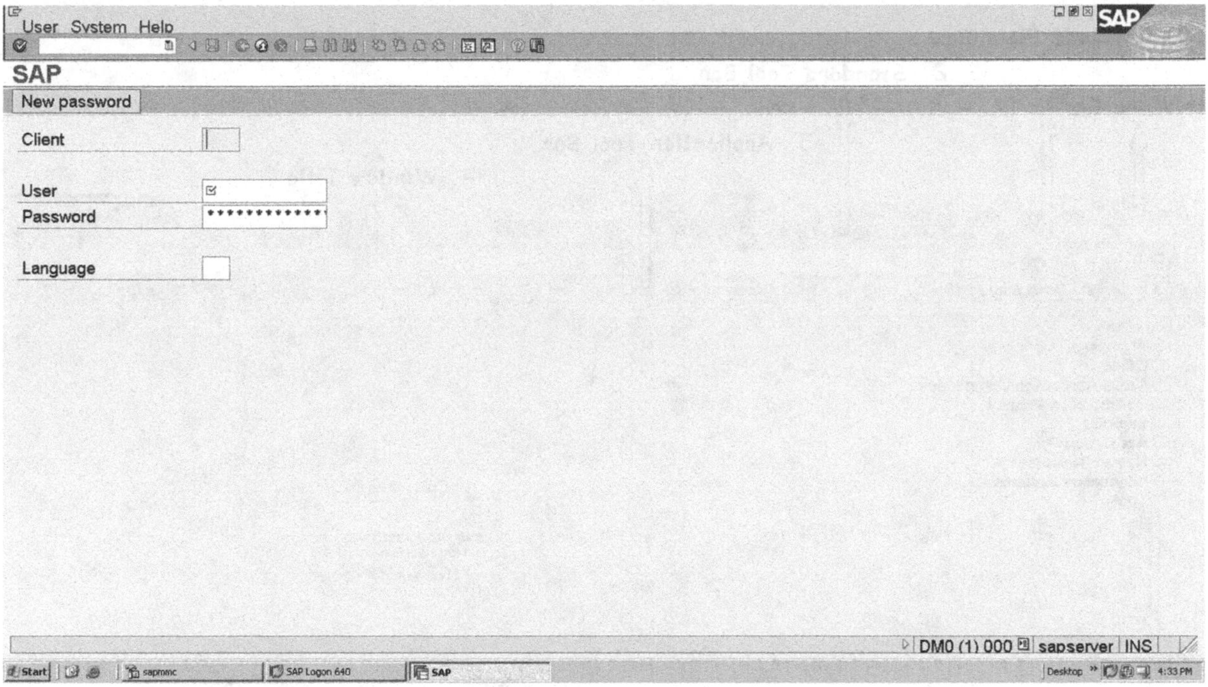

Figure 1-4. *SAP Login*

The SAP login screen (Figure 1-4) prompts for four fields of information:

1. Client
2. User
3. Password
4. Language

1. The Client, a three-digit number, is one of the parameters through which environment segregation (development, testing & quality assurance, et al.) is implemented. In the section entitled 'Client Code Perspectives,' this has been discussed.

2 & 3 Userand.Password - essential in any multiuser system.

4. A language code ('EN' for English, 'DE' for German et al.) is to be input here. Language code field in the SAP tables is a single character, but while presented on screen, appears as two characters. This is the typical situation prevailing in the SAP environment. The internal storage of data fields in the tables is different from the manner in which it presented on the screen and printer. During SAP installation, you can specify a default language for the installation. You can also specify the language/s to be installed. (All the languages supported by SAP need not be installed.) The German language ('DE') gets installed mandatorily. You cannot omit its installation. If you leave the Language field blank on the login screen, login will occur with the default language.

The User and Language are case insensitive. The Password is case sensitive.

SAP GUI

After the entries on this screen have been accepted, the SAP opening screen appears called the SAP Easy Access. (Figure 1-5)

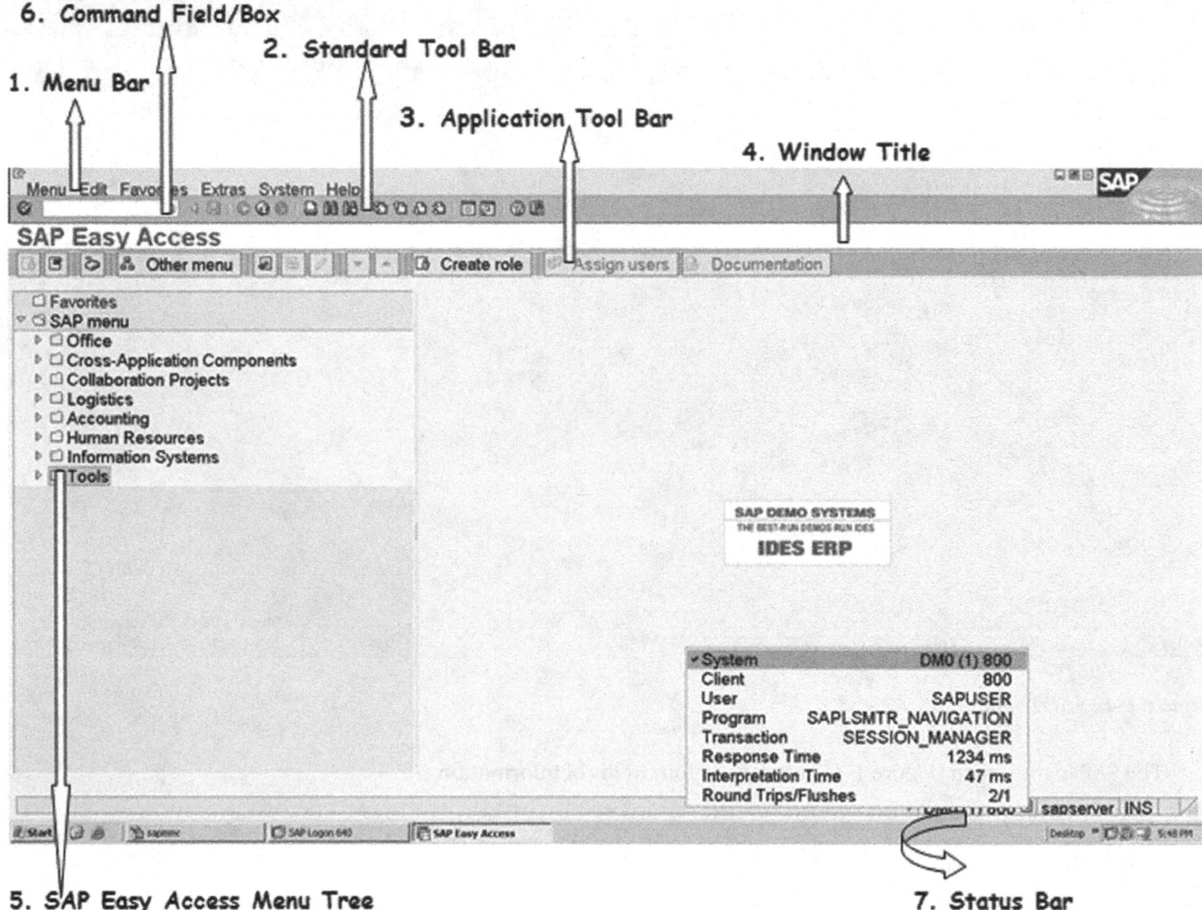

Figure 1-5. *SAP Easy Access Screen*

In the SAP Easy Access screen, the following areas, indicated by arrows in Figure 1-5, need to be recognized:

1. Menu Edit Favorites Extras System Help.

   The SAP Menu Bar, Menu Options: This will vary screen to screen except for the last two bars, System and Help.

2\.

The Standard Tool Bar: The buttons or icons appearing in this area are the same from screen to screen. Buttons or icons are enabled or disabled depending on the context. The button is for saving. On the opening SAP Easy Access screen, this is in a disabled state, as there is nothing to save on this screen.

3\. SAP Easy Access

The Window Title: This contains the title of the window.

4\.

The Application Tool Bar: The buttons or icons on the Application Tool Bar vary from screen to screen.

5\.

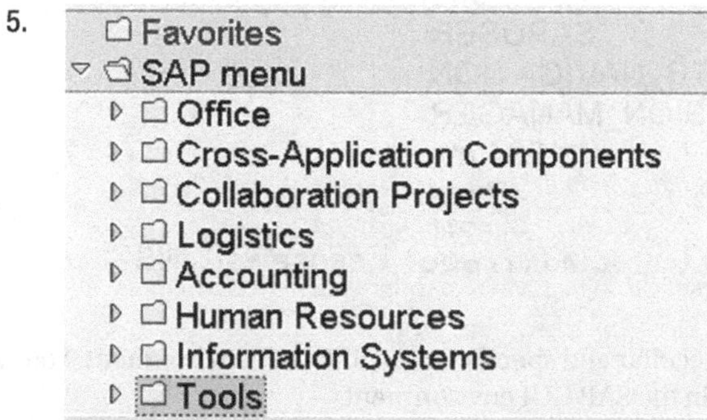

SAP Easy Access Menu Tree: In the *SAP GUI environment*, you need to navigate to different screens to carry out different tasks. One way of navigating to different screens is to use the menu tree. Clicking on or expanding the nodes of the menu tree will give access to subnodes and to the innermost subnode; clicking on this innermost subnode will enable you to navigate to different screens to carry out the various tasks. If you wanted to create an ABAP program, you will (1) click on the node 'Tools' (at the bottom), and subnodes will appear. (2) Click on the subnode 'ABAP Workbench,' and further subnodes will appear. (3) Click on the subnode 'Development,' and further subnodes will appear. (4) Click on the last level of subnode 'ABAP Editor.' This will take you to the screen supporting the ABAP program maintenance. This is the ABAP editor screen. This sequence of nodes/subnodes will appear, provided nobody has customized the SAP Easy Access screen from its initial default. In this manner the user can navigate to various screens to carry out different tasks.

6\.

Command Field: Using the command field is another way of navigating to screens to carry out various tasks by the SAP user. One mode has been described under SAP Easy Access Menu Tree. The other shorter mode is to enter the transaction code in the command field and press the <Enter> key. For instance, again, you want to navigate to the ABAP editor screen. The transaction code to navigate to the ABAP editor screen is 'SE38.' You enter SE38 in the command field and press <Enter>. If you want to navigate to the ABAP dictionary screen, the transaction code is 'SE11.' These are predefined transaction codes provided by SAP. You can also create your own transaction codes.

You will create your own transaction code during in the Chapter14 entitled 'Screen Programming'. There are more than 100,000 predefined SAP provided transaction codes available in the *SAP GUI environment*. You will be familiar with around 15 transaction codes by the time you finish reading this book. The command field can be made to appear/disappear through the button at the right.

7.

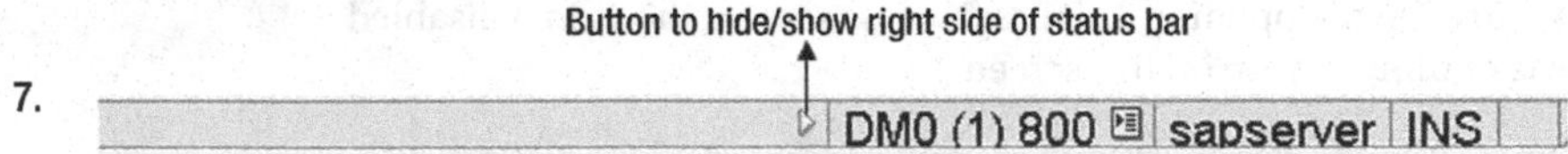

Status Bar: This is at the bottom of the screen. In the right side area of the status bar, system-related information such as 'system id', 'system no', log-in client, application server name and status of keyboard INS key on/off is presented. The left side of the status bar is used for notifications to the user through messages during program execution. If the button appearing on the status bar after 'system id', 'system no' and log-in client is clicked; a pop-up like the one shown below appears. You get to know the program, transaction code getting executed, and login client et al.

Most of the icons in the SAP GUI environment are peculiar and specific to the SAP GUI environment. You will get familiar with them and what they signify as you operate in the SAP GUI environment.

Function keys can be used in the SAP Workbench environment to perform operations. A partial list is available in Table 1-4.

Table 1-4. *Function Keys Operations*

Function Key	Operation
F1	When the cursor is on a screen field, help text for the screen field pop-ups. When the cursor is on an ABAP program keyword, ABAP documentation for the ABAP program keyword in a new session pop-ups.
F2	Mouse Double Click.
F3	Goes to previous screen.
F4	Selection List pop-ups.
F5	To create a new object.
F6	To edit or change an existing object.
F7	To display an existing object.
F8	To execute a program.

SAP External Sessions, Sessions' Control

In a standard tool bar, the [button is to create new external sessions. Alternatively, you can select the menu option 'System' and select the sub-option 'Create Session' to do the same. The system creates a new task or window. In this manner, a single SAP logged-in user can create a maximum of 16 windows, which are called external sessions. The Basis administrator can reduce this limit to less than 16. This limit of 16 is excluding the external sessions the system spawns when a nonclassical debugger is used and when the function key F1 is pressed on the keyword of an ABAP program. These are external sessions (simply different windows operating system tasks)and there is the concept of internal sessions. The difference between the two will be known when the concept of internal sessions is introduced in Chapter 7.

A developers' work involves handling of multiple objects like ABAP program, ABAP dictionary objects, screens, GUI status etc. One way of carrying out the developmental work involving multiple objects is to have multiple windows or external sessions. In one external session, the developer would be operating the ABAP editor; in a second, operating ABAP dictionary; in a third, the screen painter; in a fourth, the menu painter and so on.

The external sessions can be manipulated through the command box. Table 1-6 summarizes this:

Table 1-6. *SAP Sessions' Handling*

Command Box Content	Explanation
/NXXXX	This terminates the current transaction and starts Transaction XXXX (example: /NSE38).
/N	This terminates the transaction. This generally corresponds to pressing F15 to go back.
/NEND	This terminates all separate sessions and logs off (corresponds to System - Logoff).
/NEX	This terminates all separate sessions and logs off immediately (without any warning!).
/NOXXXX	This opens a new session and starts transaction XXXX in this session.
/O	This lists existing sessions and allows deletion or opening of a new session.
/I	This terminates the current session (corresponds to System End).

Perform each of the commands in the table as an exercise.

ABAP Workbench

ABAP - Advanced Business Application Programming is SAP's propriety language, earlier called ABAP/4: '/4' signified a fourth-generation language and has been dropped now that most of the languages are fourth-generation languages. In the SAP environment, except for very few kernel programs, (like login screen) every other program is an ABAP program, and the entire SAP ERP software has been written in ABAP. When you click on the [button on the status bar of SAP GUI screen, the name of the ABAP program in execution is available. Refer to SAP GUI 7. ABAP is not just a language. It is a full-fledged developmental platform with a plethora of tools. The whole gamut of developmental tools such as ABAP editor, ABAP dictionary, Function module (general purpose, generic subroutines) builder, Class builder, Screen painter, Menu painter et al. constitute the ABAP Workbench. As the chapters of this book unfold, these workbench tools will be introduced: how to access them (transaction codes), how to operate them, and settings, etc. will be elaborated.

In this book, the focus is on the creation of workbench objects as per scenarios. The operations required to create these objects is described. For more elaborate descriptions of workbench operations, you can refer to the downloaded documents: BC ABAP Workbench Tools and BC ABAP Workbench Tutorial.

Client Code Perspectives

In the SAP login section, you have seen that the first field on the login screen is the client or client code. It is a three-digit number. When a new user is created by the Basis administrator, client code will be part of it; a user cannot be created without a client code. And the client associated with a user has to exist on the system. It was mentioned that the client code is one of the parameters used to implement the segregation of SAP environments: development, quality, testing and live. You will then get a clearer picture of the environment segregation. A functional consultant will view the client code very differently; a basis administrator will perceive a client differently than a functional consultant. You, as an ABAP consultant or an aspiring ABAP consultant, will view the client code from a technical and developer perspective.

When SAP software is installed, the SAP database gets created automatically as part of the installation process. This database (in version E.C.C. 6.0) contains more than 70,000 tables. Almost all of these tables will be empty after installation. A few of the tables envisaged contain the universal nature of data such as country codes and names; states/provinces/regions of countries; and currency codes and names will be populated with data after SAP installation.

Every developmental object that a developer creates inside SAP such as programs, screens, and ABAP dictionary objects, etc. are stored in tables of SAP database.

A majority of the 70,000+ tables of SAP database will store the functional module data. To mention simple examples: data relating to customers; suppliers or vendors; business documents data such as customers' bills, purchase orders, etc. The tables storing the functional module data invariably contain in the table structure a field of ABAP dictionary type 'CLNT' as the first field. ABAP dictionary supports its own 20 odd data types; 'CLNT' is one of them. The next chapter (Chapter 2) will introduce these 20 odd data types. Most often the name of this first field of type 'CLNT' is 'MANDT'.

All tables containing in its structure the first field of type 'CLNT' are termed client dependent tables. Tables not containing this field as the first field in the structure are termed client independent tables. Shown below in Figure 1-6 is a partial structure of a functional module (client dependent) table and in Figure 1-7, a partial structure of a client independent table.

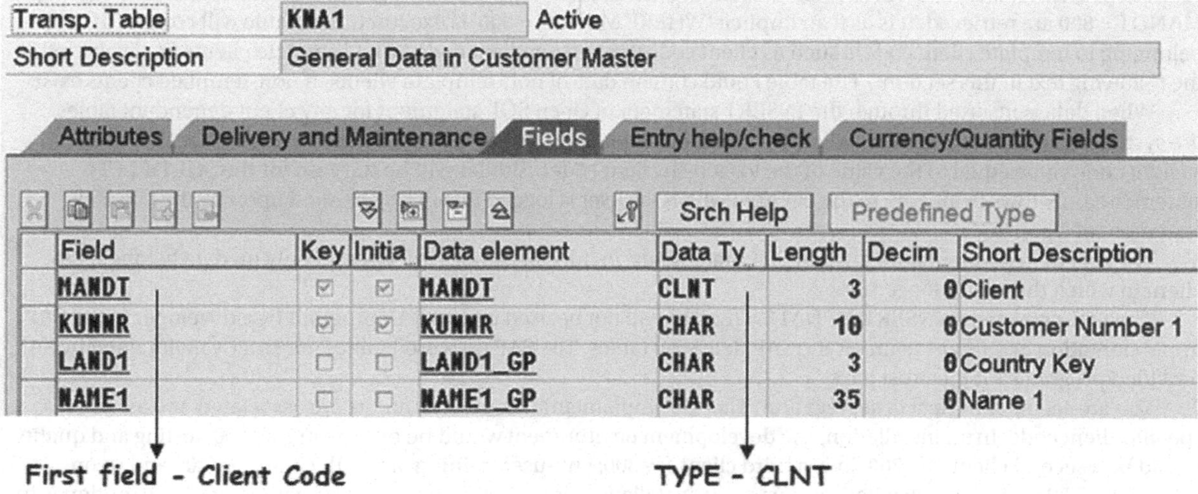

Figure 1-6. *Table KNA' Structure – Client Dependent*

Attributes | Delivery and Maintenance | Fields | Entry help/check | Currency/Quantity Fields

Srch Help | Predefined Type

Field	Key	Initia	Data element	Data Ty	Length	Decim	Short Description
PGMID	☑	☑	PGMID	CHAR	4	0	Program ID in Requests and Tasks
OBJECT	☑	☑	TROBJTYPE	CHAR	4	0	Object Type
OBJ_NAME	☑	☑	SOBJ_NAME	CHAR	40	0	Object Name in Object Directory
KORRNUM	☐	☐	TRKORR_OLD	CHAR	10	0	Request/task up to and including Re

First field TYPE 'CHAR' not 'CLNT'

Figure 1-7. *Table TADIR Structure – Client Independent, first field not TYPE CLNT*

It has been mentioned earlier that SAP supports different database brands: Oracle, MS SQL server, Informix, ADABAS, and IBM DB/2. You can have any one of these installed. (Database brand can be specified during SAP software installation time. Installation of database software forms part of SAP software installation.) This creates an ABAP program portability problem. Suppose you have created an ABAP program using Oracle SQL statements. This program would run as long as the installed database of SAP installation is Oracle. If the installed database is other than Oracle, the source program needs to be modified. SAP got over this portability problem by introducing its own SQL called the 'Open SQL.' If programs are written using Open SQL statements, they are portable across all the supported brands of databases. The ABAP language supports Open SQL as well as the SQL of the supported database brands. In practice, invariably the Open SQL is used; the use of database SQL is rare and infrequent.

When data is retrieved or updated through SELECT or UPDATE statements using Open SQL statement for any of the functional module tables (i.e., the client dependent tables), the system will retrieve or update only data belonging to the client code with which user has logged in. To explain in specific terms: A user has logged into client 800. Once logged in, user executes an ABAP program using Open SQL SELECT statement to retrieve data from a client dependent table, say TCURC (table containing the currency codes, data of universal nature); only rows having MANDT = 800 are retrieved. It is as if an implicit 'WHERE MANDT = 800' is executed. The table will contain data belonging to template client code/s such as client code 000 and/or client code 001. (Template clients are explained in the following text in this section.) The table could contain data of non-template clients, if non-template clients exist.

When data is inserted through the INSERT statement of Open SQL statement for any client dependent tables, the system will automatically assign logged-in client values to the client code fields (i.e., a row will be inserted with a client code value equal to the value of the logged-in client code). Similar will be the case for the SQL DELETE statement; only rows belonging to the client in which the user is logged in will be operated upon by the DELETE statement of Open SQL.

With client dependent tables, Open SQL statements, in normal course, will operate only on data belonging to client in which the user is logged in.

The SQL commands INSERT, UPDATE, DELETE will not be used in an ABAP program by a developer in the SAP implementation or support team on the SAP delivered tables. The SAP delivered tables are strictly maintained by SAP provided programs for the most part.

You are seeing the effect of segregation. The SAP implementation environments are associated and assigned a specific client code. In an installation, the development environment would be one client, say 100; testing and quality would be a second client, say 200; live, a third client say 300; end-user training, a fourth client, say 400 and so on.

When SAP software is installed, as part of the installation process, template client/s gets created. The option is to either create 000 or 001 or both. These are classified as template clients. The template clients are not to be operated in. The template clients are copied into the environmental clients such as developmental, testing/quality, and live. For example, suppose you decide to have client 100 for developmental environment, 200 for testing/quality, 300 for live. Then these would be derived by making copies of 000/001 into 100, 200, and 300. The process of copying (template or even non-template) clients is a task carried out by the basis administrator.

The difference between the template clients 000 and 001 is that the client 001 contains the special functionalities of Euro sales tax VAT. (Value Added Tax). If Euro VAT functionalities are required (implementation or support is being done for a customer located in European Union), 001 needs to be copied to non-template/operational clients, or else 000 needs to be copied to non-template/operational clients. One can, of course, copy one non-template to another non-template client.

There is one other client that gets created as part of SAP software installation. This is client 066 called the 'early watch system.' When SAP is installed initially in an enterprise, it could face performance and response time issues. The SAP On-line Support System - OSS - offers its services to help fix these issues. For this, the SAP OSS requires login into the enterprise SAP system. They would log through client 066. After all, the SAP OSS should not access the enterprise data.

SAP IDES (Internet Demonstration & Evaluation System) Server and Usage of IDES Server for Trainings

When SAP software is installed, as has been mentioned earlier, except for the few tables containing data of universal nature, such as countries, states/provinces/regions, currencies et al., all other functional module tables will be empty. It has also been mentioned that the SAP functional module tables are populated through SAP provided ABAP programs that perform rigorous validation before data is accepted and inserted into the said tables.

Also, data can be inserted into functional module table, (through SAP provided ABAP programs) provided the functional modules have been configured and customized by the functional consultants. To give one scenario, if you want to create a new customer (i.e., insert data into customer tables), the SD (Sales and Distribution) or FI (Accounting/Finance) module should have been configured and customized by the respective functional consultants.

When SAP software is installed, no module is configured and customized. If this were so, there would be no need for the costly exercise of implementation through functional consultants.

Since the SAP functional module tables are maintained by SAP provided ABAP programs, ABAP consultants implementing and supporting SAP projects are absolved of this task of maintaining data of SAP tables. One of the major tasks required to be performed by ABAP consultants implementing and supporting SAP is retrieving data (SQL SELECT statements) and presenting data (reports).

To get good exposure to the data retrieval aspect, you need to do fairly complex exercises in data retrieval. With no data in the SAP functional module tables of bare SAP installed software, this would be impossible. Even if modules were configured and customized, it would require some skills to manually enter data. And manually you can't be creating too much of data: data running into thousands of rows. Not everybody can have access to SAP installation with substantial data in functional module tables.

The IDES server is preconfigured and customized for a number dummy business enterprises and contains lo of dummy data in functional module tables.

As its name suggests, SAP initially intended the IDES server for demonstration of software to prospective buyers. But now it is being used everywhere for training, especially for functional modules' trainings. To those undergoing training in the functional modules, the preconfigured dummy data of more than a dozen companies is a very handy reference.

Most ABAP trainings, including the certification training, use SAP provided tables of 'Flight Data System' for exercises. These tables have been specially created and provided for ABAP trainings. But these are small tables. (Small in terms of number of fields, small in terms of number of tables, less than a dozen.) These tables are available in all servers. They can be populated by data through executing an ABAP program. They are of hypothetical nature.

But why use hypothetical tables when the real-world ones are available? You will use a few tables of sales and purchase in your exercises. People not exposed to the business and commercial world can easily relate to the basic sales and purchase functionalities. Though these tables on an average contain more than 100 fields, you will be restricted to using a few fields, maybe 15-20. But you will get the feel and exposure of the SAP real-world tables while doing the exercises with these tables.

Typically, the IDES server installed with default and not custom options creates four clients: 800, 810, 811, and 812. The client 800 could be used as it contains substantial dummy data. Typically, it contains:

- Data of more than 15 companies' codes.
- More than 7,000 customers.
- More than 1,500 suppliers or vendors.
- More than 30,000 billing documents.
- More than 10,000 purchasing documents.

Terminology Clarification

The functional modules have been described. In the ABAP Workbench, there is an object 'Function Module'. The 'Function Modules' are general purpose routines existing in the library area. They can be called from multiple ABAP programs (Reusability). The function modules are the most powerful construct of the procedure-oriented ABAP. This will be covered in Chapter 7 entitled 'Modularization'. The two similar sounding terms - functional modules and function modules - should not be confused. Sometimes, functional consultants refer to functional modules as function modules!

The word *company* refers to a business enterprise. In the SAP environment, the word company has a different meaning. In the SAP environment, the word company is used to refer to a business group. For instance, suppose there is a business group called 'Super Group'. This business group operates a number of registered companies or business enterprises such as 'Super Iron & Steel Co. Inc.', 'Super Motors Inc.', and 'Global Beverages Inc.'. The registered companies in the SAP environment are termed as company codes. It is important to know this terminology.

Conclusion

In this chapter, you learned the basics of ERP, SAP, and SAP GUI environments. You have also learned about client code and have been apprised of the suitability of SAP IDES server for SAP trainings. In the forthcoming chapters you will be learning technical aspects of the ABAP developmental platform. In the next two chapters, you will be learning about the *SAP ABAP dictionary* or *data dictionary* (DDIC) as it is popularly known.

CHAPTER 2

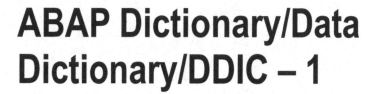

ABAP Dictionary/Data Dictionary/DDIC – 1

ABAP Dictionary, data dictionary, dictionary, and *DDIC* are synonymous terms. *DDIC* — a contraction of *data dictionary* — will be used throughout this book. The DDIC is a multifaceted facility that is a substantial feature of the ABAP Development Workbench environment.[1]

Any developmental activity invariably uses DDIC objects. This chapter and the next one list and identify DDIC objects that will be covered in subsequent chapters. This chapter also describes the major attributes of the DDIC, introduces the DDIC Data Types, and teaches the reader to create Domains, Data Elements, and Transparent Tables through hands-on exercises framed in a simple business scenario.

Note The word *object* is used in this book in its natural language meaning of thing. *Object* will not be used in the context of OOP unless explicitly stated.

ABAP Dictionary: Initial Screen

To navigate to the screen for maintaining and viewing DDIC objects from the SAP Easy Access screen, enter the transaction code SE11 in the command field. Alternatively, you can always navigate from the SAP Easy Access menu tree. A screenshot of the ABAP Dictionary: Initial Screen is shown in Figure 2-1. (The term *ABAP Dictionary* is used here to match the window title in Figure 2-1. Throughout this book, the term *DDIC* will be used by default).

[1]For a detailed theoretical treatment of the DDIC, download *BC – ABAP Dictionary* from `http://help.sap.com/printdocu/core/print46c/en/data/pdf/bcdwbdic/bcdwbdic.pdf`.

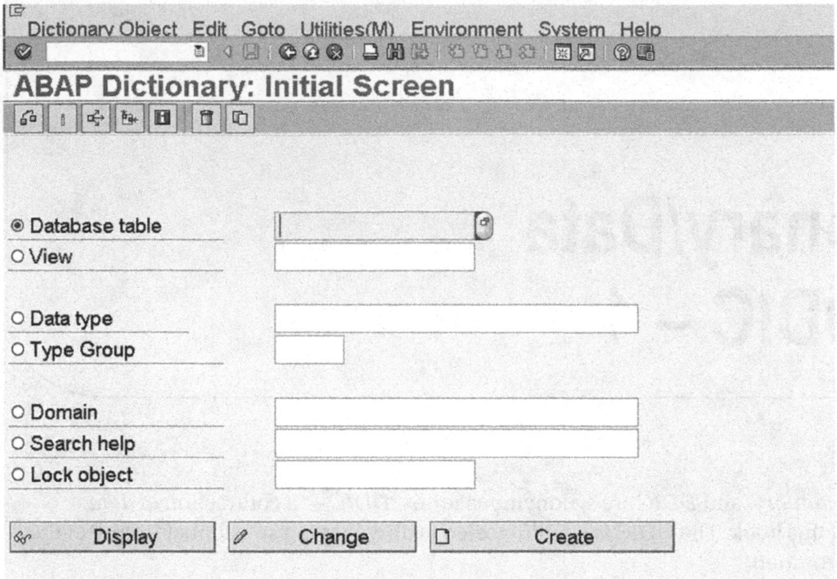

Figure 2-1. *ABAP Dictionary: Initial screen*

A complete list of DDIC objects follows. The non-struck items in the list are covered in this chapter and the next one. The struck-out items in the list will be covered in subsequent chapters as detailed below, after the reader has acquired prerequisite knowledge.

- Database table
  - Transparent
  - Pooled
  - Cluster
- View
  - Database
  - Projection
  - Maintenance (Chapter 7)
  - Help
- Data type
  - Data element
  - Structure (Chapter 6)
  - Table type (Chapter 6)
- Type group (Chapter 4)
- Domain
- Search help
- Lock object (Chapter 14)

View Table Structure Definitions of the SAP Delivered VBRK and VBRP Tables

You will be using the VBRK and VBRP tables frequently in the hands-on programming exercises, so let's view the structure of these table definitions as a first exposure to the DDIC object database table. To view the VBRK structure definitions, click on the Database Table radio button, enter the table name VBRK, and click on the Display button or function key F7. The structure definitions of the VBRK database table are displayed as shown in Figure 2-2.

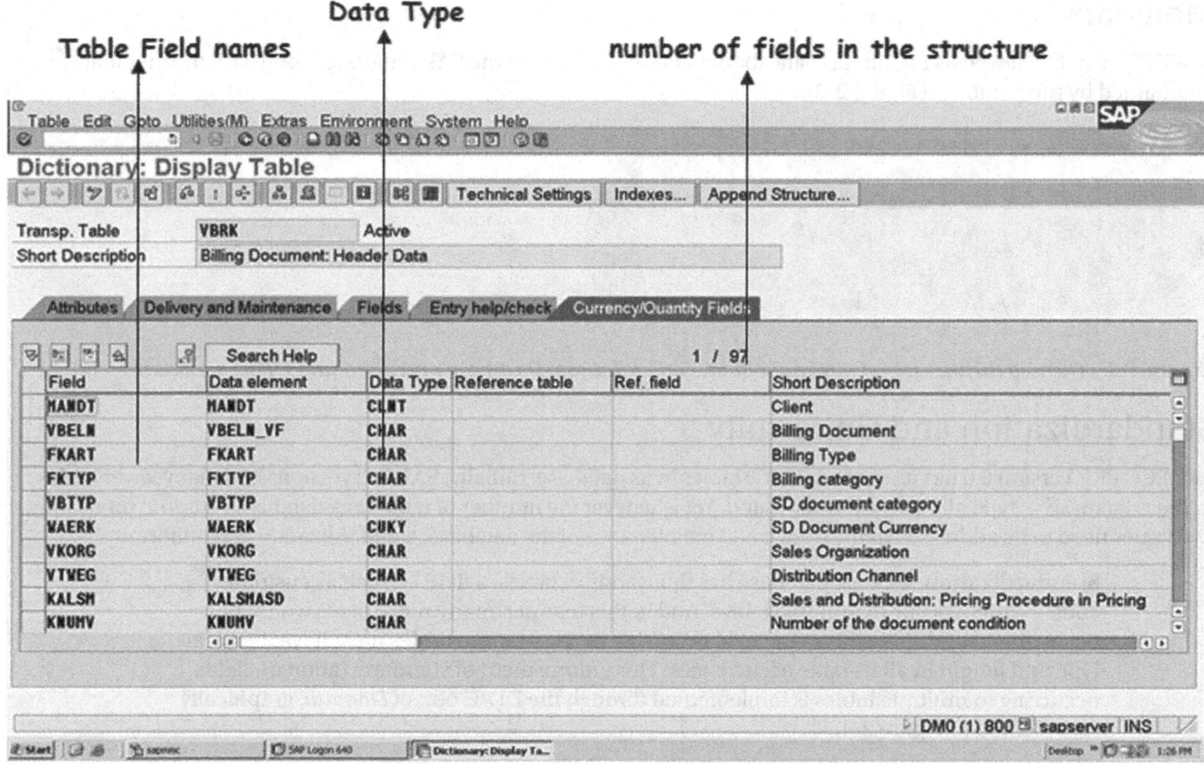

Figure 2-2. *Structure definitions of the VBRK database table*

The VBRK table consists of 97 fields. The VBRP table consists of 190 fields. You can locate a field by its name by using the Find button. Functional module tables in the SAP environment typically consist of more than 100 fields.

These tables store data of customer bills. A single bill might consist of 1 or n number of items. The bill (called Billing Document in SAP parlance) information is located in two tables. One table, designated the *header table*, contains the header information of the bill, with one row for each bill. The second table, designated the *item table*, contains the item information of the bill, with as many rows as the number of items in each bill.

DDIC Attributes

The prime attributes of the DDIC are described in the following sections.

Metadata

The DDIC can be viewed as metadata (data about data) that resides in the SAP database along with the metadata maintained by the database (Figure 2-3).

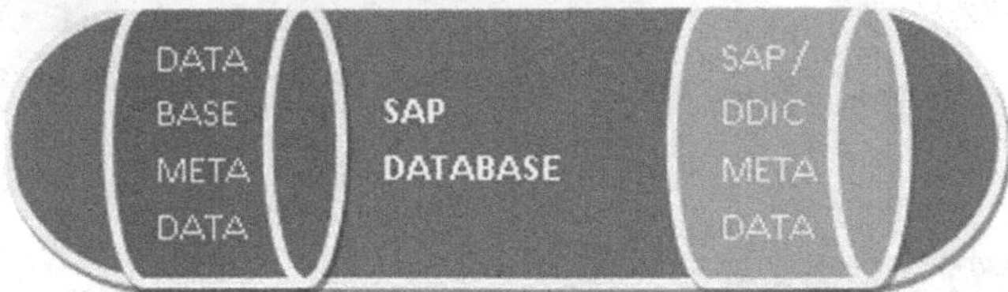

Figure 2-3. *The two distinct sets of metadata in the SAP database: Database metadata and DDIC metadata*

Standardization and Uniformity

SAP ECC ERP Version 6.0 has more than 70,000 tables in its database. Initially, SAP R/2 versions had many fewer tables in their database — typically only a few thousand. Yet whenever the number of tables in a database runs into thousands, two issues need to be addressed in the design and maintenance of the database: standardization and uniformity.

> **Standardization:** When a database has thousands of tables, a field — such as customer code — might occur in multiple tables. And in this manner, many more fields would be occurring in multiple tables. Any field occurring in two or more tables must have identical type and length in all its table occurrences. This enforcement of standardization on fields occurring in multiple tables is implemented through the DDIC object *Domain*, graphically represented in Figure 2-4.

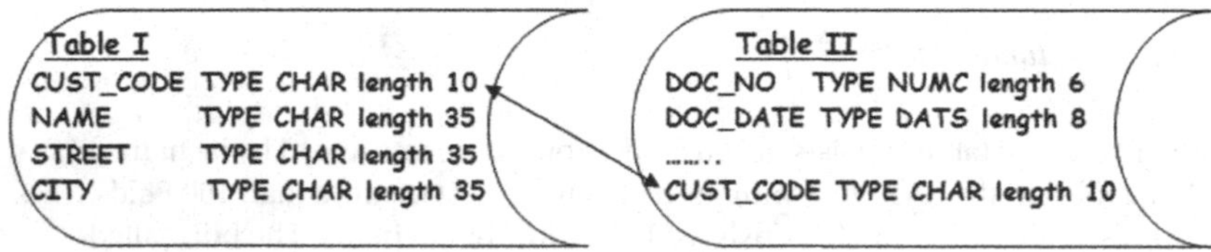

Figure 2-4. *A field occurring in two tables should have identical data type and length in both*

> **Uniformity**: The name of a field in a table is the technical name for it used by technical personnel and developers. It is not expected to make sense to an end user. When a field appears on a screen, however, it must carry a field label that will make sense to the end user.

An example: The field name of a customer code in the SAP database table KNA1 is KUNNR, which would mean nothing to end users. For a user logged in English, the field KUNNR should appear on the screen with a label such as Customer Code — and similarly for users who are logged in in other languages. When a given field appears on multiple screens, care must be taken to ensure that the label is uniform across screens for a given login language. These requirements are implemented through the DDIC object *Data Element* (Figure 2-5).

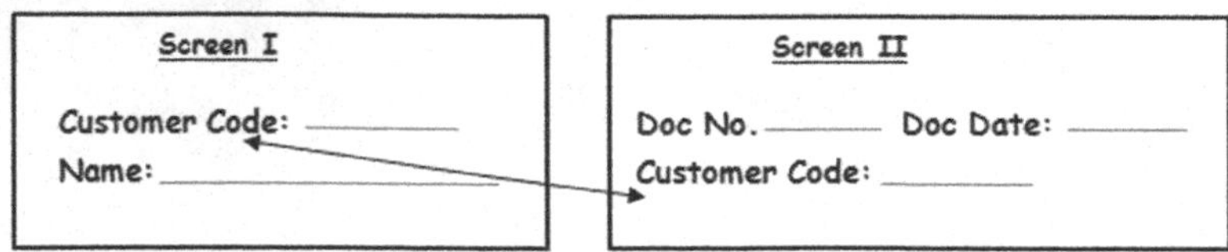

Figure 2-5. *Field names should appear identically across different screens*

Open SQL and the Data Definition Language

SAP supports the following databases, among others: Oracle, Microsoft SQL Server, Informix, ADABAS, IBM DB/2, and Sybase ASE. In the ABAP programs, SQL commands are commonly written in SAP Open SQL rather than in the respective databases' SQL languages. As mentioned in the Client Code Perspectives section of Chapter 1, Open SQL enables portability. Open SQL uses the DDIC as an interface and reference. For Open SQL to operate on a table, a table structure definition must exist in the DDIC. If a table exists in the database as database metadata but no definition exists in the DDIC as DDIC metadata, the table is nonexistent to Open SQL. In the ABAP Workbench, table definitions are not created using the SQL script of the respective database, such as CREATE TABLE. The DDIC provides an interface to create and define database tables. When a DDIC table structure definition is activated for the first time, the objects created in the ABAP Workbench environment are activated such that a database table definition is automatically created at the back-end database, resulting in two definitions for the given table — one related to the DDIC and the other to the back-end database's own metadata. Likewise, views (including database views and projection views) do not have to be created with SQL script because interfaces exist in the DDIC environment to create them. The DDIC also has interface to create secondary indexes. All these tasks are handled in a typical database environment such as Oracle through the *data definition language* (DDL). In this context, one might view the DDIC as serving the function of the DDL.

DDIC Object References in ABAP Programs

Various objects in the DDIC environment can be referenced in ABAP programs. The DDIC is called the *global area.* The objects in the DDIC are global to all ABAP programs. Data in ABAP programs can be declared by reference to DDIC global objects. The declared data in ABAP programs referring to DDIC objects inherit the attributes of these DDIC objects. DDIC objects that can be referenced in ABAP programs to declare data are (1) tables, (2) views, (3) structures, (4) table/view/structure fields, (5) table types, (6) type groups, and (7) data elements. The use of DDIC objects to declare data in ABAP programs will be demonstrated in the coding of ABAP programs beginning in Chapter 4.

Data Control Language

In the SAP environment, an entity and transaction data reside in multiple tables. Suppose, for instance, that customer information resides in 20 tables. If a user is operating on a customer by insertion or update, the rows corresponding to this customer in all the 20 tables need to be locked to users other than the one who initiated the insert or update operation. Any database supports only locking or unlocking at table level; automatic locking or unlocking at an entity level where data resides in multiple tables is not supported. To accommodate the automatic locking or unlocking of rows in multiple tables, SAP offers its own locking or unlocking mechanism through the DDIC object: Lock Object. The DDIC thereby serves as a *data control language* (DCL).

Search Helps/Pop-up Selection Lists

In the SAP environment pop-up lists are available at appropriate screen fields for the user to make a selection from the list instead of manually entering field data. These pop-up selection lists can be created as Search Help objects in the DDIC. Otherwise these pop-up selection lists would have to be provided through program code. Also the pop-up selection lists or Search Helps created in the DDIC environment can be used on fields of multiple screens. The DDIC circumvents the necessity of writing program code and enables the reusability of Search Help objects (Figure 2-6).

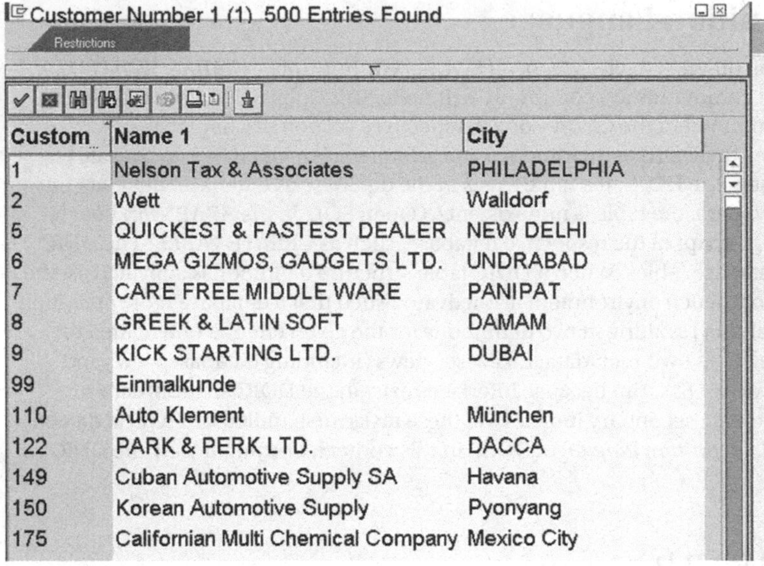

Figure 2-6. *Search Help pop-up list*

Data Types in the DDIC

The predefined DDIC data types available are listed in Table 2-1.

Table 2-1. *DDIC Data Types*

Data Type	Description	Initial Value
ACCP	Account posting period (YYYYMM, fixed length 6 bytes)	ASCII zeroes
CHAR	Character string, can store 1 character/byte in non-Unicode and 1 character/two bytes in 16 bit Unicode(length can vary 1-255)	Spaces
CLNT	Client code(3 digit number in 3 bytes)	ASCII zeroes
CUKY	Currency code/key, referenced by type CURR fields (fixed length 5)	Spaces
CURR	Currency field, internal storage & output same as type DEC	Binary zeroes
DATS	Date field (YYYYMMDD, fixed length 8 bytes)	ASCII zeroes
DEC	Numeric field with comma, decimal, and sign in output.	Binary zeroes
FLTP	Floating point, maximum accuracy up to 16 digits Exponent range. From 10^{+307} to 10^{-308} Fixed length of 8 bytes	Binary zeroes
INT1	1-byte integer, unsigned number (value 0 - 255)	Binary zeroes
INT2	2-byte integer, to be used only for length field before fields of types LCHR & LRAW	Binary zeroes
INT4	4-byte integer, integer number with sign. Can store numbers between -2177483647 to -2177483648	Binary zeroes

(*continued*)

Table 2-1. *(continued)*

Data Type	Description	Initial Value
LANG	Language code/key (1 byte)	Spaces
LCHR	Long character string, requires a preceding INT2 type field	Cannot be set
LRAW	Long byte string, requires a preceding INT2 type field	Cannot be set
NUMC	Character string with only digits 0-9 (length can vary 1 - 255 bytes) Normally should be used for codes (employee code etc.)	ASCII zeroes for length < 33. Length > 32, cannot be set
PREC	Precision of a QUAN type field	Binary zeroes
QUAN	Quantity field, internal storage & output same as type DEC	Binary zeroes
RAW	Un-interpreted sequence of bytes	Cannot be set
RAWSTRING	Byte String of Variable Length	N/A
SSTRING	Short Character String of Variable Length	N/A
STRING	Character String of Variable Length	N/A
TIMS	Time field (HHMMSS), (Fixed length of 6 bytes)	ASCII zeroes
VARC	Long character string, not supported from Rel. 3.0 onwards	N/A
UNIT	Unit key referenced by QUAN fields (length 3)	Spaces

All the Data Types listed in Table 2-1 with the descriptions are self-explanatory. Data Types DEC, CURR, and QUAN are further elaborated upon below.

The Initial Value column indicates what is stored, if no value is assigned to a field.

Data Type DEC

- Two decimal digits are stored in one byte. (Like maximum 99 in a byte)
- Half a byte is reserved for storage of sign.
- A maximum of 31 decimal digits (digits before + after decimal) are supported.
- The length can vary between 1–16 bytes.
- The number of digits after decimal can be specified, by default is 0.
- A maximum of 16 digits after decimal is allowed.
- Decimal (.) is not stored separately, but will appear during output. Thousand separators (i.e., commas after thousand, million and billion) will appear by default during output like for other numeric types (i.e., CURR, FLTP, INT4, and QUAN). Commas are made to appear with numeric Data Types to enable them to be discerned easily. Consider the number 1000000 vis-à-vis 1,000,000 with million, thousand separator “ , ”. The latter is visually easier to discern.

Data Types CURR, QUAN

Fields with DDIC Data Type CURR are used to store currency amounts. The internal storage of Data Type CURR is identical to Data Type DEC. The currency amounts are incomplete information. Whether the amount or figure is U.S. Dollars, Euros, Great Britain Pounds, etc., is to be included to make the information complete. (What currency?)

In the DDIC Data Type CUKY the currency key or code can be stored. So DDIC Data Types CURR, CUKY goes together. If a DDIC structure definition contains a field of Data Type CURR, this field must point to the corresponding CUKY field (called reference field in DDIC environment). How Data Types CURR, CUKY go together is simplified below:

Amount (Data Type CURR) 10000 Currency (Data Type CUKY) USD

Internal storage of DDIC Data Type QUAN is identical to Data Type DEC. On similar and parallel lines of DDIC Data Types CURR & CUKY, the DDIC Data Types QUAN and UNIT will exist together. Inventory quantities are stored in Data Type QUAN fields. The quantities being incomplete information, whether the quantities are numbers, dozens, kilograms, tons, etc. (unit of measure or UOM for short) will have to be incorporated to make the information complete. The unit of measure information (unit code) is contained in a field Data Type UNIT. If a DDIC structure definition contains Data Type QUAN, this field must point to the corresponding UNIT field. A simplification is given below:

Quantity (Data Type QUAN) 100 UOM (Data Type UNIT) TON

To see an example of the CURR, CUKY & QUAN, UNIT fields in the DDIC environment, you can navigate to the table structures of SAP functional module tables VBRK (billing document - header) and VBRP. (Billing document - items).

VBRK Table

The header table - VBRK - contains the document's header information (document No., document date, document type, customer code, Net Value in Document Currency (Data Type CURR field), document currency (Data Type CUKY field), etc. In the table structure, select the tab Currency/Quantity Fields.

In the table VBRK, the Net Value in Document Currency field (Data Type CURR) is NETWR. The columns Reference Table, Reference Field of this field contain VBRK and WAERK respectively. It means that the corresponding CUKY field is in the table VBRK and the field name is WAERK. The table name where DDIC Data Type CUKY field is located is contained in Reference Table, and field name is contained in Reference Field.

VBRP Table

The item table - VBRP - contains the document's items information (material code, sale quantity (Data Type QUAN), sales unit of measure (Data Type UNIT), amount for the item (Data Type CURR field), etc.

In the table VBRP, the item amount field (Data Type CURR) is NETWR; this is the amount for each item, whereas the field NETWR in the table VBRK is the total amount for all items in the document. The columns Reference Table, Reference Field of this field contain VBRK and WAERK respectively. It means that the CUKY field for Data Type CURR field NETWR (in table VBRP) is in the table VBRK and the field name is WAERK.

In the table VBRP, the sales quantity field is FKIMG (Data Type QUAN). The columns Reference Table, Reference Field of this field contain VBRP and VRKME respectively. It means that the corresponding UNIT field is in the table VBRP and the field name is VRKME.

The coverage each of the DDIC objects: domain, data element, and transparent table follow.

DDIC Object Domain

Domains are for enforcement of standardization on fields occurring in multiple tables. Theoretically, any two or more table fields having same Data Type and length can share or be assigned the same domain. (Ensure fields occurring in multiple tables having same Data Type & length).

View or Examine an SAP Delivered Domain

The predefined domain selected for viewing is ECN_COLOR. On the SE11 screen, click the Domain radio button, enter the name ECN_COLOR and click the display button.

The screen shot for domain with the three tabs Properties, Definition, Value Range is shown:

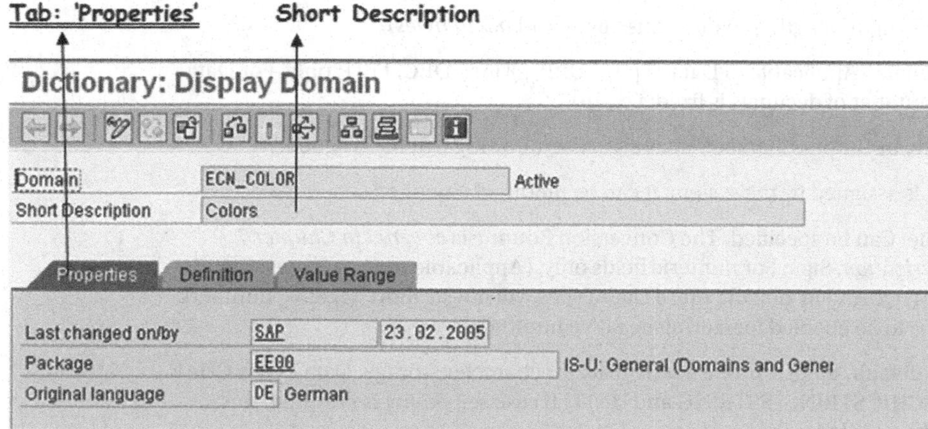

Figure 2-7. *Domain – tab Properties*

There are hundreds of thousands of predefined domains being used in SAP delivered tables in the DDIC.

The Short Description is to be mandatorily entered for any object created in ABAP Workbench. The Properties tab fields are controlled and inserted by the system except for the Package, which is assigned by the user creating the object.

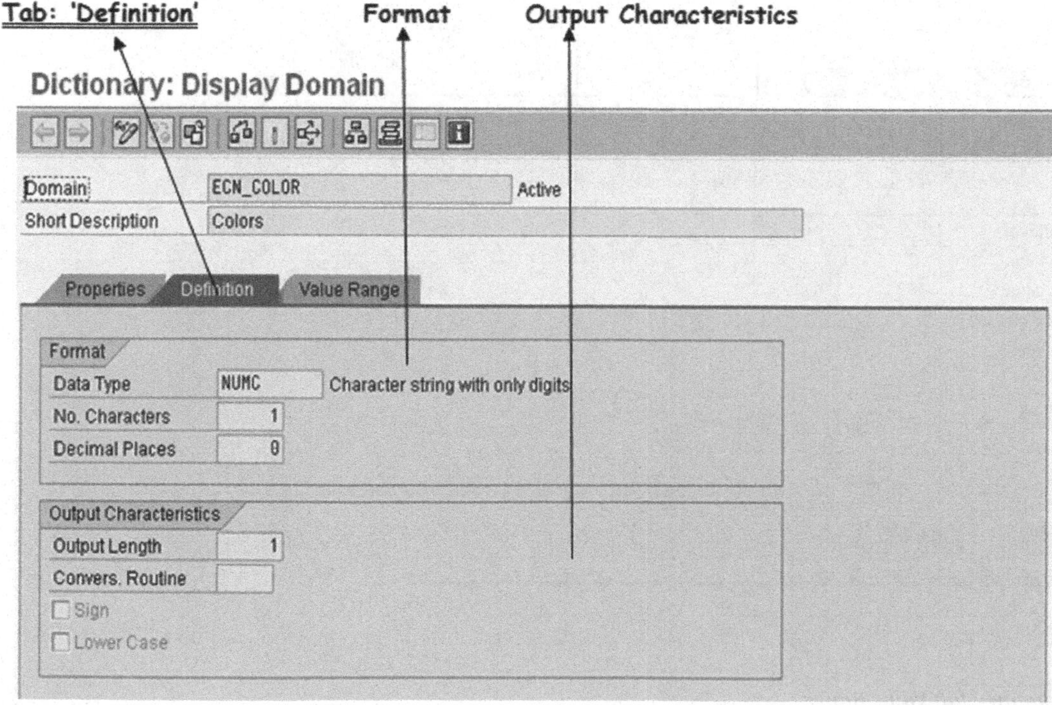

Figure 2-8. *Domain – tab Definition*

Under the Definition tab, in the Format area, the following are assigned:-

1. Data Type: DDIC Data Type, (refer to Table 2-1 under DDIC Data Types)
2. No. Characters: Length (length is in positions/digits and *not in bytes*)
3. Number of decimals. (Applicable to Data Types CURR, QUAN, DEC, FLTP, only. For Data Type FLTP the number of decimals is fixed: i.e., 16)

Under the Definition tab, in Output Characteristics area, the following can be assigned:-

1. Output Length: Is assigned by the system, it can be modified if needed.
2. Convers. Routine: Can be specified. The Conversion Routine is *covered in Chapter 7 entitled Modularization.* Sign: For numeric fields only. (Applicable to Data Types: CURR, DEC, FLTP, INT4, QUAN) By default, these Data Types will not support negative numbers. This check box is to be enabled for storing negative numbers.
3. Lower Case: By default, there is no case sensitivity for character storage. Data Types CHAR, CUKY, LANG, LCHR, STRING, SSTRING and UNIT) If case sensitivity is required, this check box is to be enabled.

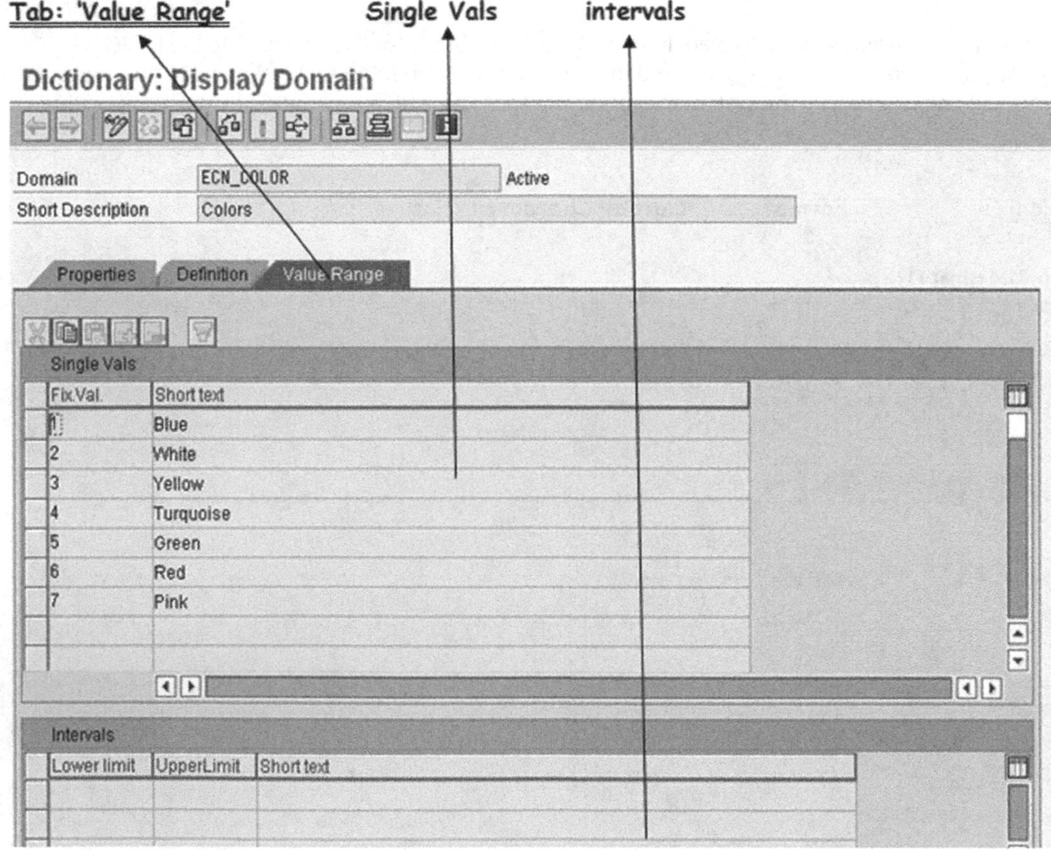

Figure 2-9. *Domain - tab Value Range*

In the Value Range tab, under Single vals, you can enter values (fixed Values & Short text) as is shown for the SAP provided domain ECN_COLOR. Ideally, values should be entered here when (a) there are few entries (less than 32), and (b) these values do not change or change very infrequently.

The implication of entering values here is as follows: when this domain is assigned to a data element, this data element is assigned to a table field, a field appearing on a screen is referring to this table field automatically, and a pop-up list facility is available for this screen field to the user. The pop-up list will display the values entered here; when a user makes a selection, the Fixed Value selected will be assigned to the screen field.

Under the Value Range tab, in Intervals, you can enter valid values and valid ranges of values. When this domain is assigned to a data element, this data element is assigned to a table field; a field appearing on a screen is referring to this table field, the values which can be entered for the field will have to be in the range of values entered here.

DDIC Object Data Element

(Ensure field appearing on multiple screens has the same field label).

Data elements are for enforcement of uniformity, ensuring that a field occurring on multiple screens has the same label.

View or Examine an SAP Delivered Data Element

You will view a predefined data element: ECN_COLOR.

On the SE11 screen, click the Data type radio button, enter the name ECN_COLOR, and click the display button.

The screen shot for data element with the four tabs Attributes, Data Type, Further Characteristics, and Field label is shown:

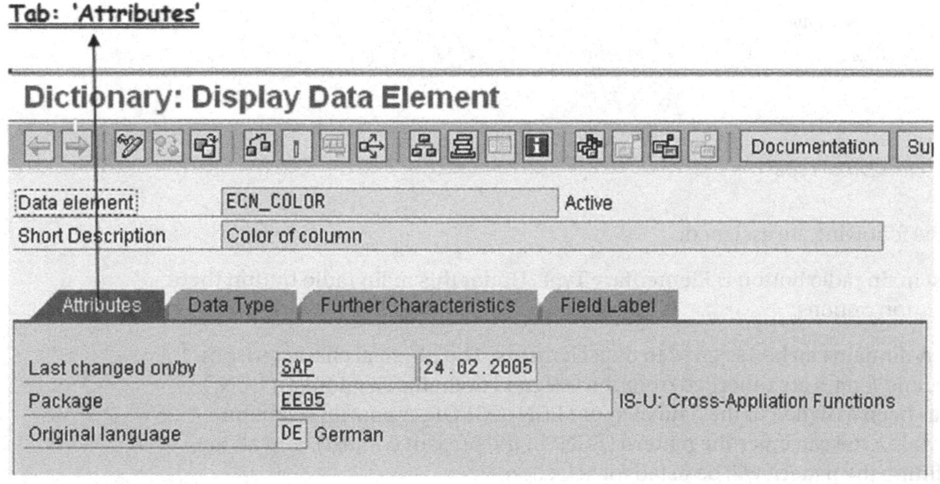

Figure 2-10. *Data element - tab Attributes*

This is the display of SAP provided Data element ECN_COLOR.

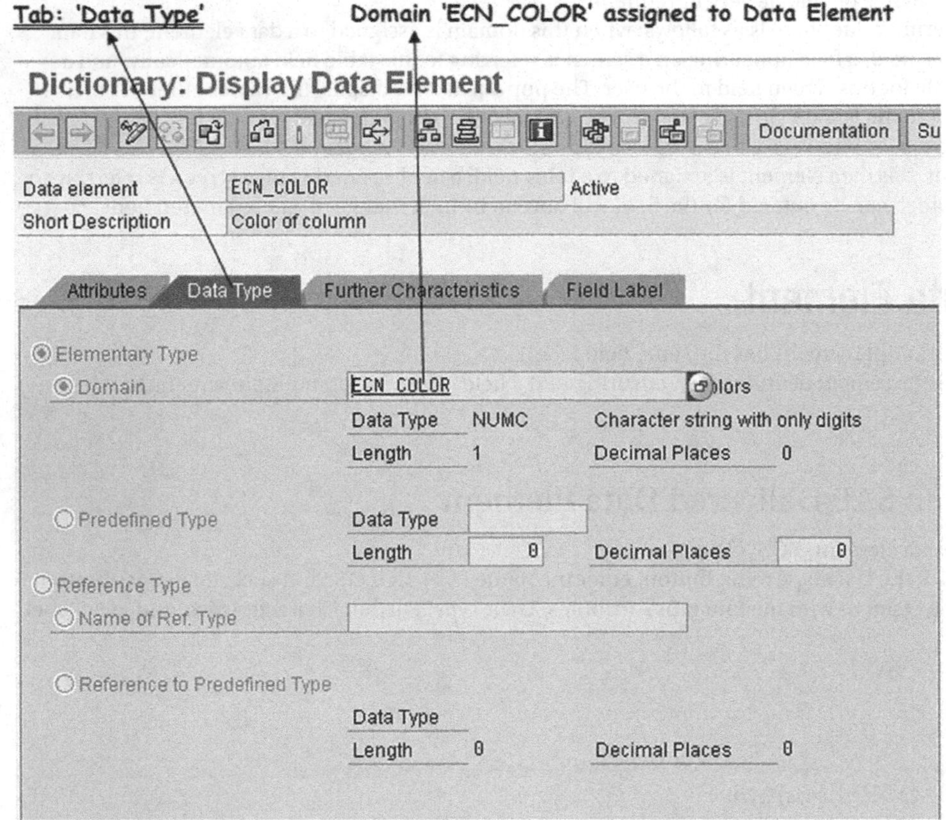

Figure 2-11. *Data element - tab Data Type*

In the Data Type tab, the following are assigned:

1. The default first main radio button is Elementary Type. Under this main radio button there are two radio button options:

    a. Domain - A domain can be assigned to data elements. The physical characteristics, Data Type, and length are inherited from the assigned domain. The domain ECN_COLOR has been assigned to the data element ECN_COLOR. A pop-up selection list is available. One can enter the pattern (ECN* in the present context), and all the domains fitting the pattern will be listed for selection.

    b. Predefined Type - This is just like in domain. A DDIC Data Type can be assigned here (refer to Table 2-1 under DDIC Data Types). This is equivalent to short circuiting the domain, not using the domain facility, and assigning DDIC Data Type to the data element. This option is rarely used.

2. The second main radio button is Reference Type. Under this there are two radio button options:

   a. Name of Ref Type - A built-in class, interface can be assigned here

   b. Reference to Predefined Type - Again a DDIC Data Type can be assigned here. (Refer to Table 2-1 under DDIC Data Types.)

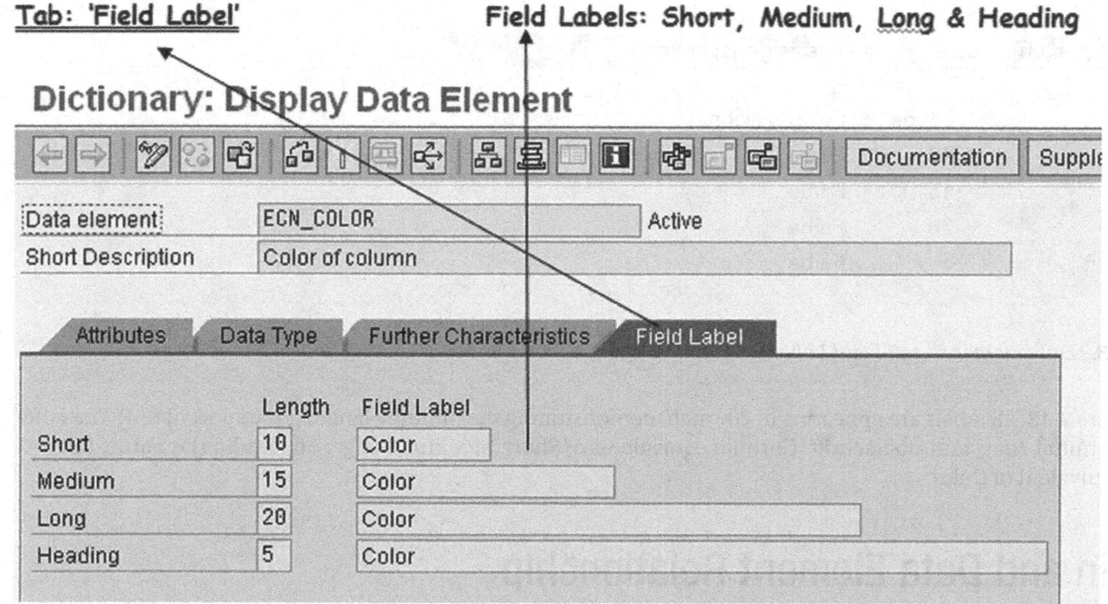

Figure 2-12. Data element - tab Field Label

Field labels or text can be maintained here in multiple languages. Four types of labels can be entered: Short, Medium, Long, and Heading. These texts will appear as labels when the table field associated with this data element appears on screen. By default a label entered in the field Medium will appear but can be overridden. The label in the field Heading will appear when the table field associated with this data element appears in a list or report.

In this Data Element ECN_COLOR, the same text Color has been entered in all the four fields (i.e., Short, Medium, Long, and Heading).

The same screen logged in the German language - DE - is shown in Figure 2-13.

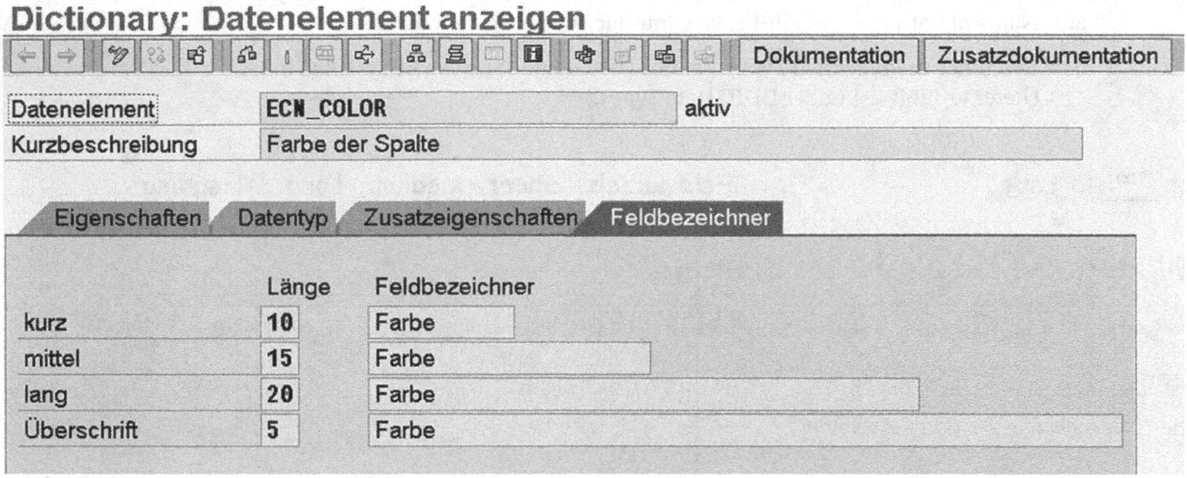

Figure 2-13. *Data element - tab Field Label [logged in language DE]*

In Figure 2-13, all labels are appearing in German, demonstrating the multiple language support of SAP. The label in the kurz, mittal, lang, and Überschrift (German equivalents of Short, Medium, Long, and Heading) is Farbe, the German equivalent of Color.

Domain and Data Element Relationship

An example (demonstrative but somewhat contrived) to bring out the relationship between domains and data elements: Let it be assumed that an enterprise wants to standardize in the payroll application the amounts related to allowances. (Various allowances paid to employees such as house allowance, conveyance allowance, etc.) Suppose they fix the type and length of allowance amounts as DDIC Data Type DEC and length 5, 2. (Five digits before decimals and two digits after decimals and a total length of 7 digits or 4 bytes.) So a domain can be created with DDIC Data Type DEC and length 5, 2. This same domain can serve for house allowance, conveyance allowance, etc.
In the context of data elements, separate labels are required such as House Allowance, Conveyance Allowance, etc., for house allowance and conveyance allowance respectively. Hence as many data elements need to be created as the number of allowances. All these data elements would be assigned the same domain created with DDIC Data Type DEC length 5, 2. So a domain can be assigned to one or more data elements. The relationship is shown here diagrammatically:

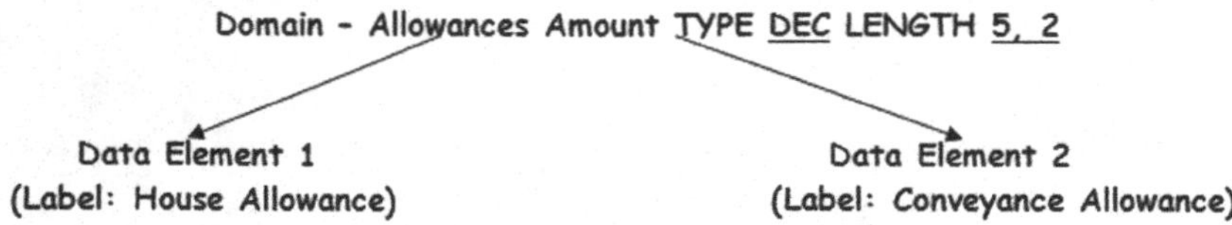

Figure 2-14. *Domain, Data Element relationship*

DDIC Object Table

There are three types of tables supported in the DDIC environment: the transparent table, the pooled table, and the clustered table. For the present, our detailed coverage is confined to the transparent tables. The pooled and clustered tables are mentioned in passing.

For a pooled table, many random table definitions in the DDIC will go as one definition in the database metadata. A pool consisting of many pooled tables will go as one table definition in the database metadata.

The clustered tables principle is similar to that of pooled table (many tables) except that the many clustered table definitions residing in a cluster are not on a random basis. For all the clustered tables to reside in one cluster, the clustered tables must have part of their primary key field/s in common.

For the pooled and clustered tables, the special mode of storage and retrieval technology is SAP's propriety technology. With Open SQL, pooled and clustered tables can be used in the same way as transparent tables – SELECT.., INSERT..., UPDATE..., DELETE with some constraints.

A table pool or table cluster is used exclusively for storing internal control information (screen sequences, program parameters, temporary data, and continuous texts such as documentation). *All business/commercial data are stored exclusively in transparent tables.*

For a transparent table, for every table definition in the DDIC, there will be exactly one corresponding table definition in the installed database metadata.

Transparent Tables

The table structures are defined or created in the DDIC. When a DDIC table structure definition is activated for the first time, a table definition is automatically created in the respective database installed on the database server (Oracle, MS SQL Server et al.). There are two definitions of any table in a SAP database: one corresponding to the DDIC and the other corresponding to the respective installed database. The additional definition of a table accrues benefits and advantages. One benefit has already been mentioned: Open SQL affording portability of ABAP programs. Open SQL uses DDIC as a reference and interface. The table structures defined in DDIC offer extra features such as CURR CUKY & QUAN UNIT fields check, table buffering, Search Help attachment, delivery class, etc. The standardization, uniformity (domain & data element) is also implemented through the DDIC table metadata. In the following text, transparent tables will be referred as tables (transparent is implicit).

Domain, Data Element, and Table Relationship

The relationship of a domain data element has been explained earlier. When table fields are specified during a table definition, a data element is to be assigned to every table field. In this way, a field occurring in multiple tables would be assigned the same data element, thus ensuring the same label for the field on multiple screens. Also, since a domain is assigned to a data element, a field occurring in multiple tables would be assigned the same domain ensuring Data Type and length to be the same. The relationship is shown here diagrammatically in Figure 2-15.

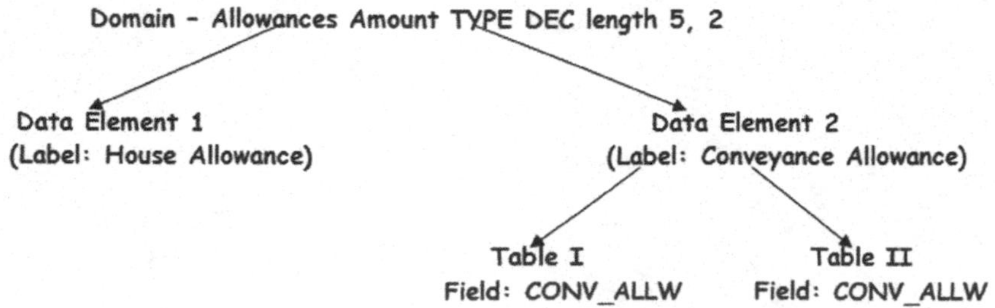

Figure 2-15. *Domain, Data Element, and Table relationship*

View, Examine an SAP Delivered Table

SAP delivered domains and data elements were examined and viewed. You will view an SAP delivered table: T005T. It stores the texts of different countries. The texts of the countries are stored in all the SAP supported natural languages.

Display Table – the tabs

On the SE11 screen, click the Database table radio button, enter the name T005T, and click the display button. The screen shot for a table with the five tabs Attributes, Delivery and Maintenance, Fields, Entry help/check, and Currency/Quantity Field are shown in Figures 2-16 and 2-17.

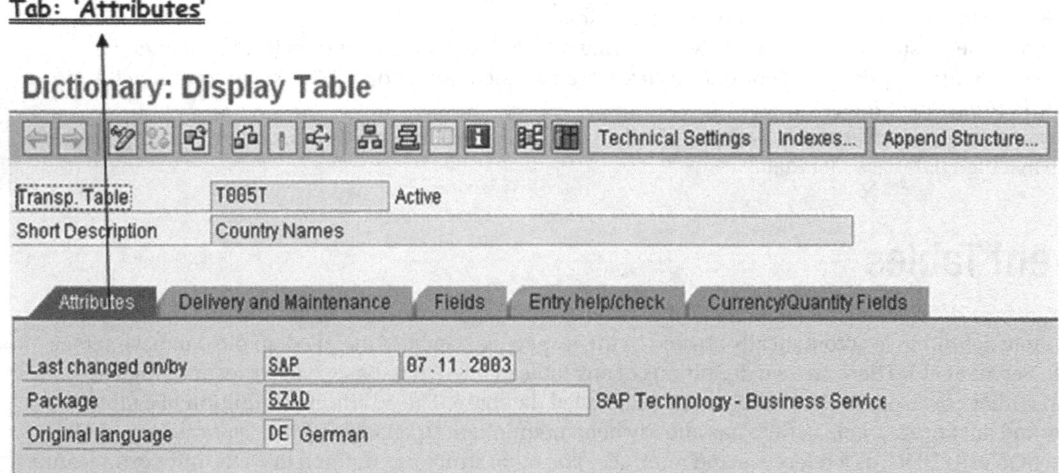

Figure 2-16. *Table – tab Attributes*

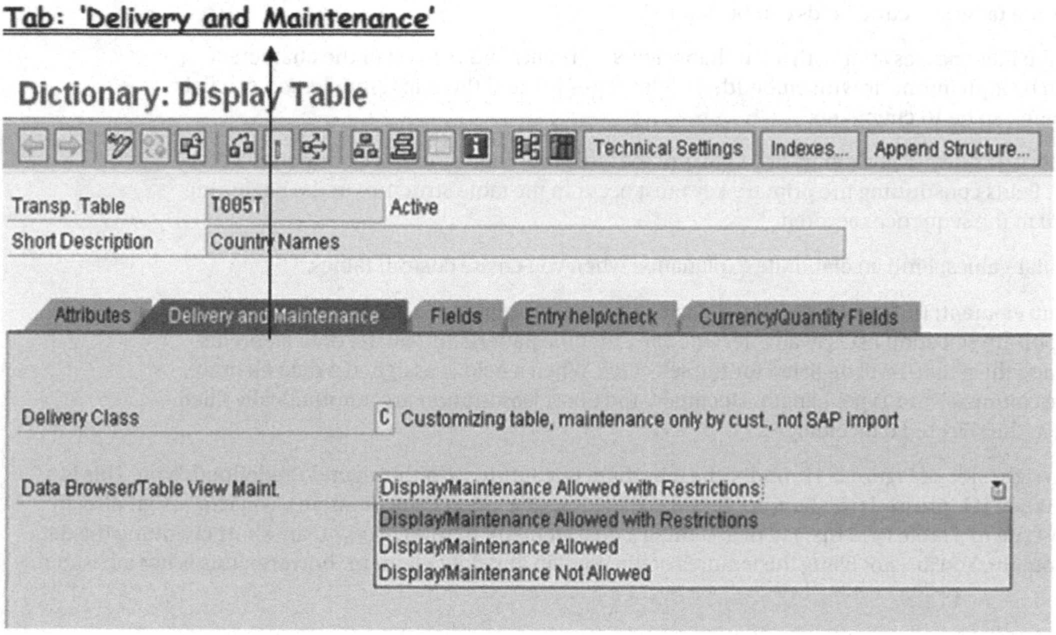

Figure 2-17. Table – tab Delivery and Maintenance

In the Delivery and Maintenance tab, the following are assigned:

1. Delivery Class: This controls the transport of table data during installation, upgrade, client copy, and transportation between customer systems. It is also used in the extended table maintenance.

2. Data Browser/Table View Maint.: Three options are available:

    a. Display/Maintenance Allowed with Restrictions: When this option is operative, new entries/rows cannot be created in the table, existing entries cannot be edited or deleted through the table maintenance dialog or maintenance view. The table maintenance dialog is automatically generated when the table is activated.

    b. Display/Maintenance Allowed: When this option is operative, new rows can be created through the table maintenance dialog or maintenance view. Existing entries can be edited, viewed, and deleted through the table maintenance dialog or maintenance view.

    c. Display/Maintenance Not Allowed: When this option is operative, the table maintenance dialog is not generated when the table is activated. New entries cannot be created, and existing entries cannot be viewed.

In this tab, the table structure fields can be entered.

1. Field: Field names start with an alphabet letter normally and the rest of the characters can be alphanumeric with embedded underscores (_), and the maximum length of a field name can be 16 characters.
2. Check box Key: The primary key field/s of the table must have this check box enabled. All the fields constituting the primary key must occur in the table structure in the beginning and in the sequence required.
3. Initial Values: Find an elaborate explanation when you create custom tables.
4. Data element: In this column, the data element to be assigned to the field is to be entered. A pop-up selection list is available. One can enter the pattern and all the data elements fitting the pattern will be listed for the selection. When a field is assigned a data element, the columns Data Type, Length, Decimals, and Short Description are automatically filled from the selected data element.

On the top right side of Figure 2-18, under the tabs there is a button with the legend Predefined Type. This is a toggle button. When it is pressed (the button pressing changes its legend to Data Element), you can assign directly the DDIC Data Type to a table field instead of assigning a data element. In this case, you are short circuiting the data element and domain. You are not using the features of the domain and data element; however, this is not advisable.

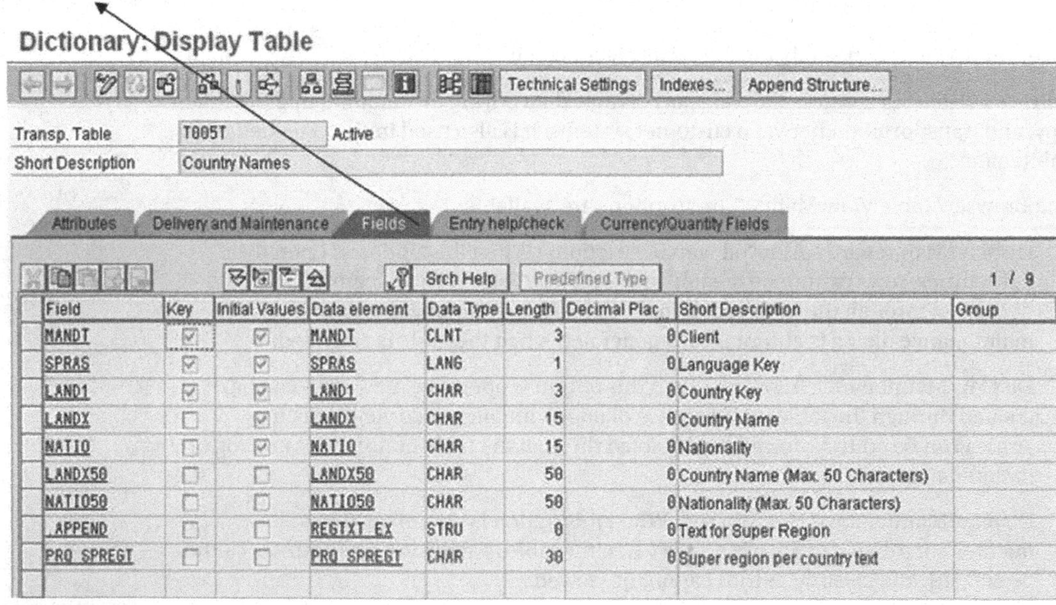

Figure 2-18. *Table - tab Fields*

Tab: 'Entry help/check'

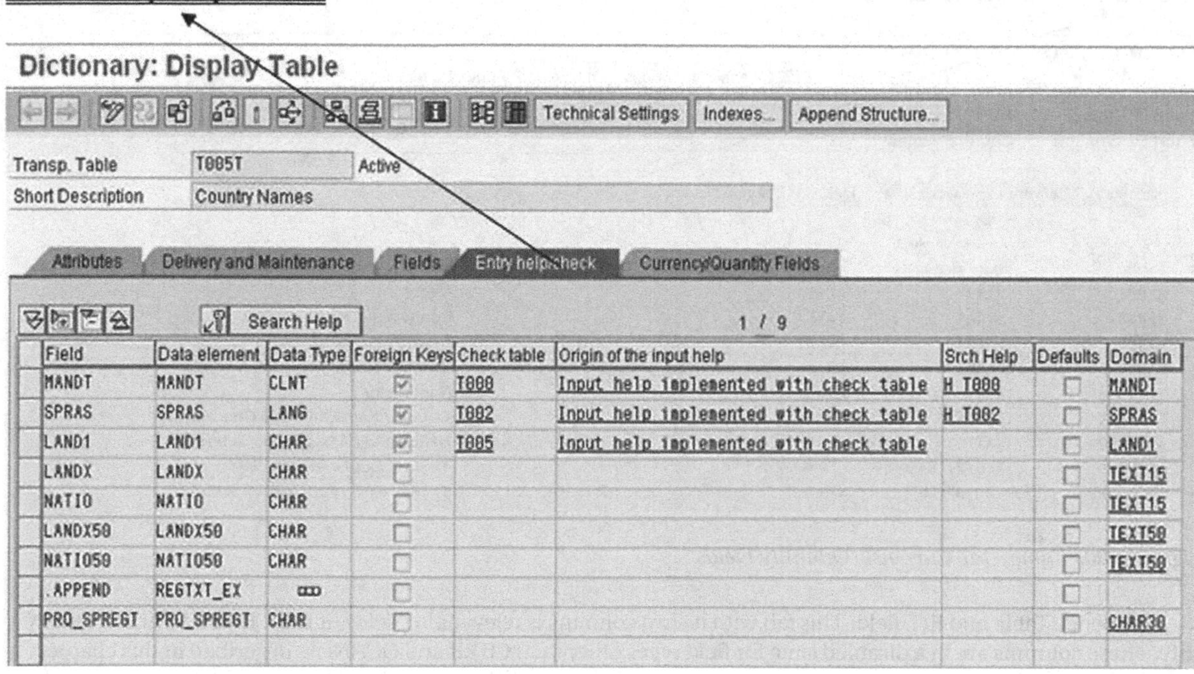

Figure 2-19. *Table – tab Entry help/check*

All the columns under this tab are entered and controlled by the system.

1. Foreign Keys (check box): This check box, when in enabled state, indicates the field to be a foreign key or part of foreign key (fields can be declared as foreign key or part of foreign key).

2. Check table: If the field is a foreign key or part of foreign key, then the check or primary table name is automatically entered by the system in this column (i.e., Check table). Check table and primary table are synonymous. You will use the term Check table.

3. Origin of the input help: This refers to the origin of a pop-up list for this field when this field is appearing on the screen. This will be covered with in the DDIC topic Search Help in the next chapter.

4. Srch Help: The column entry like all columns under this tab is controlled by the system; the name of the search help if assigned appears here. It will be covered in the DDIC topic Search Help in the next chapter.

5. Defaults: Check box that indicates whether the set of values of a domain is restricted through entry of fixed values.

6. Domain: The name of the domain derived from the data element assigned to the field is entered by the system.

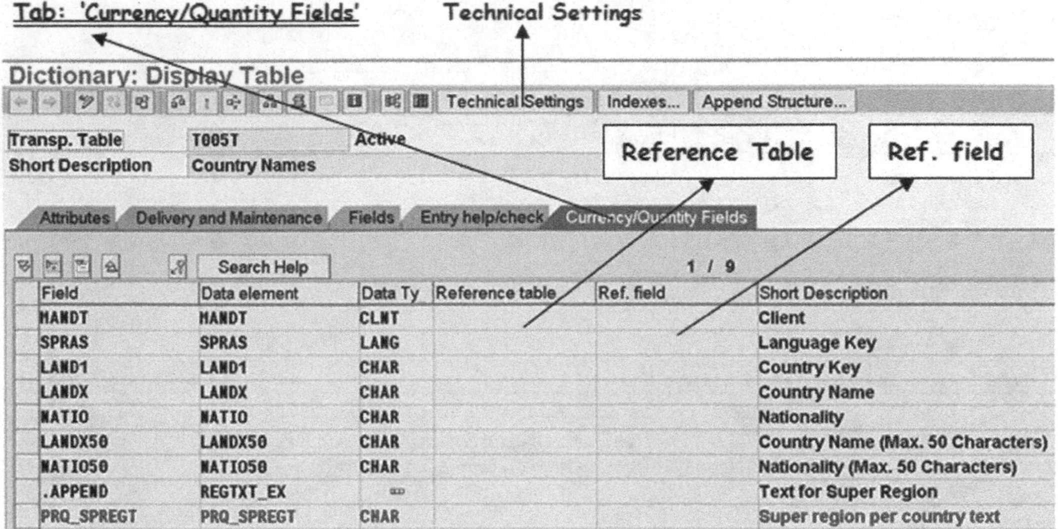

Figure 2-20. *Table - tab Currency/Quantity Fields*

Reference Table and Ref. field: This tab with its two columns is relevant for fields of Data Type CURR and QUAN only. These columns are in a disabled state for field types other than CURR and QUAN. As described in this chapter, these types store the currency amount or quantity numbers respectively.

Whenever there is a field of type CURR in a table structure or structure definition, the column Reference table for a type CURR field will have to be filled up with the name of the table structure or structure where the type CUKY field is occurring. And the column Ref. field will have to be filled with the name of the type CUKY field.

Similarly, the column Reference table for a type QUAN field will have to be filled up with the name of the table structure or structure where the type UNIT field is occurring. And the column Ref. field will have to be filled with the name of the type UNIT field.

Display Table – Technical Settings

This is part of a table definition. You get to the screen by clicking the application toolbar button Technical Settings. The technical settings screen looks like Figure 2-21.

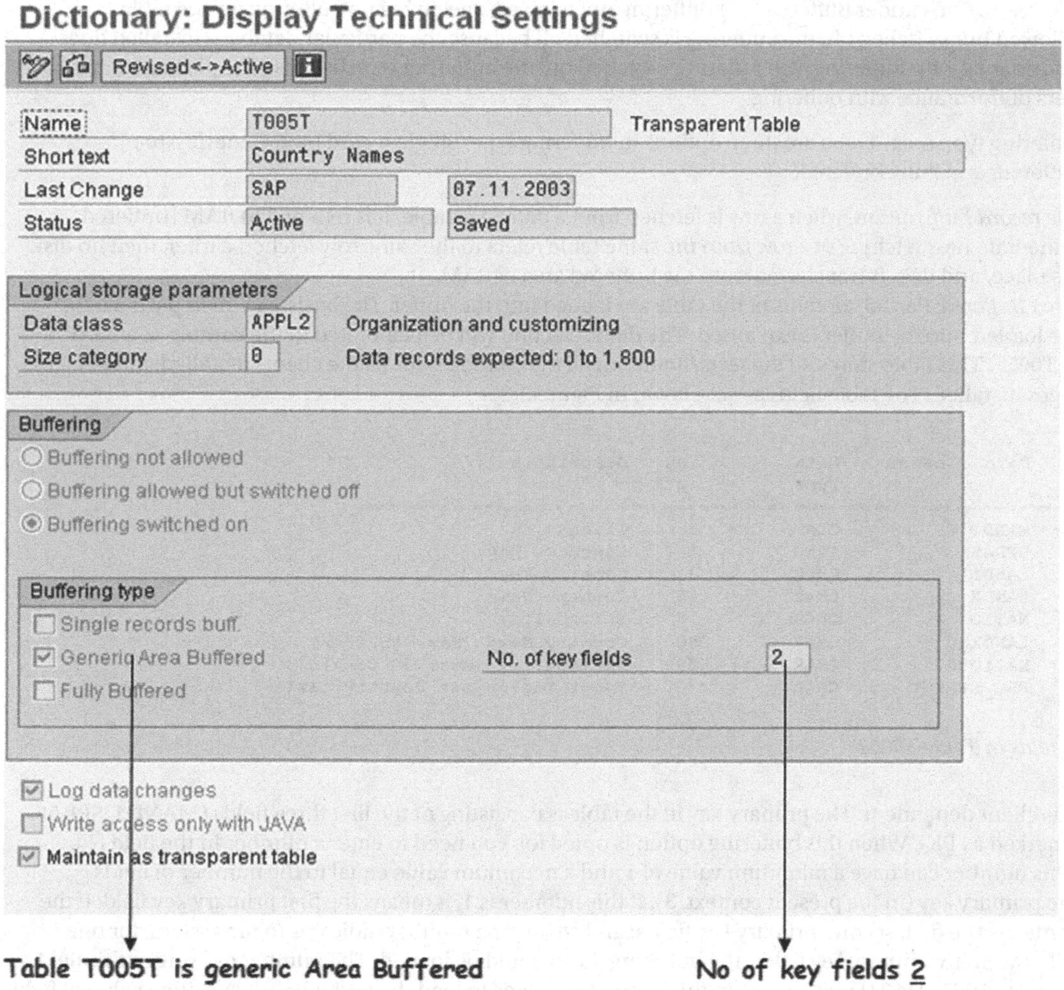

Dictionary: Display Technical Settings

Revised<->Active

Name T005T Transparent Table
Short text Country Names
Last Change SAP 07.11.2003
Status Active Saved

Logical storage parameters
Data class APPL2 Organization and customizing
Size category 0 Data records expected: 0 to 1,800

Buffering
Buffering not allowed
Buffering allowed but switched off
Buffering switched on

Buffering type
Single records buff.
Generic Area Buffered No. of key fields 2
Fully Buffered

Log data changes
Write access only with JAVA
Maintain as transparent table

Table T005T is generic Area Buffered **No of key fields 2**

Figure 2-21. *Table - Technical Settings*

- In the Logical storage parameters area of Figure 2-21:
  - Data class: The data class has relevance only for ORACLE and INFORMIX database systems. It defines the physical area of data base in which the table is logically stored. Typical values to be assigned when you are creating a table in Y/Z name space are USER, USER1, USER6, and USER7.
  - Size Category: The assigned size category will determine the initial probable space requirement for a table in the database.
- Buffering area: Buffering (selective disk data is maintained in RAM) is available with Open SQL to improve performance. An ideal table for buffering would be small sized (a few KB), very frequently accessed, and rarely updated. Not all database brands deliver performance improvement with buffering.

There are three options under Buffering: (1) Buffering not allowed, specifying no buffering for the table. (2) Buffering allowed but switched off; the buffering is switched off because the particular database installed does not deliver performance with buffering. (3) Buffering switched on; the buffering is on because the particular database installed delivers performance with buffering.

- Buffering type area: There are three options in buffering type: Single record buff, Generic Area Buffered, and Fully Buffered.

With *Single record buff.* option, when a row is fetched from a database table, it is retained in RAM (buffered area). If the immediate next fetching of a row from the same table refers to the same row fetched earlier, then no disk operation takes place, and data is transferred from the buffered area of RAM.

Generic Area Buffered: Partial contents of the table are loaded into the buffer. The basis on which partial data is selected to be loaded into the buffer is explained. The data selection will be elaborated in the context of an SAP provided table T005T. This table stores all the texts/names of all the countries for all the clients installed and in all the natural languages installed. The table fields are as shown in Figure 2-22.

Field	Data element	Data Type	Len -gth	Description
MANDT (PK)	MANDT	CLNT	3	Client
SPRAS (PK)	SPRAS	LANG	1	Language Key
LAND1 (PK)	LAND1	CHAR	3	Country Key
LANDX	LANDX	CHAR	15	Country Name
NATIO	NATIO	CHAR	15	Nationality
LANDX50	LANDX50	CHAR	50	Country Name (Max. 50 CHAR)
NATIO50	NATIO50	CHAR	50	Nationality (Max. 50 CHAR)
PRQ_SPREGT	PRQ_SPREGT	CHAR	30	Super region per country text

Figure 2-22. *Fields in Table T005T*

The table is client dependent. The primary key in the table is consisting of the first three fields (MANDT, SPRAS, and LAND1 - marked as PK). When this buffering option is opted for, you need to enter a number in the field No. of key fields. This number can have a minimum value of 1 and a maximum value equal to the number of fields constituting the primary key (in the present context, 3). If this number is 1, it means the first primary key field; if the number is 2, it means the first, second primary key fields; and so on. The number indicates to the system, for one unique value of how many primary key fields, the buffering data should be loaded. The number existing in this field for the chosen table (T005T) is 2 (Figure 2-21). In this context, it means to load the buffer with a specified value of field MANDT (first field) and a specified value of field SPRAS (second field). If you are logged into client 800 and language E, the buffer will be loaded with rows belonging to client 800, and language E, though the table is containing rows belonging to clients 000, 001 (one of these or both depending on the installation option), 810, 811, 812, and language codes A, B, C, D, and so on. The total number of rows in this table (for all client codes, all language codes) on our system is 22,608. The number of rows in this table for client = 800 and language code = E on our system is 248. All this is based on the assumption of working on a typical IDES server.

With the *Fully Buffered* option, all the rows of the table (full table) are fetched into the buffered area. All subsequent retrieval of row/s will be from the buffered area.

The buffers are loaded on the application server/s.

- Log data changes check box: If enabled, changes to the data rows of this table are logged.
- Write access only with JAVA check box: If enabled, contents of the table can be changed from within Java only.
- Maintain as transparent table check box: This flag indicates that a table should be transparent and that this attribute should be kept even after a change of release or an upgrade.

Display Table - Setting up Foreign Key Relationships

From the Technical Settings screen, navigate back to the normal table maintenance screen by clicking the standard tool bar button or alternatively pressing function key F3.

For all the table field/s that are foreign keys (these fields are primary key fields in the check tables), the foreign key relationships are established. The foreign key relationships of a table field can be established or viewed by positioning the cursor on that field and clicking on the button (under the tabs). (See Figure 2-23).

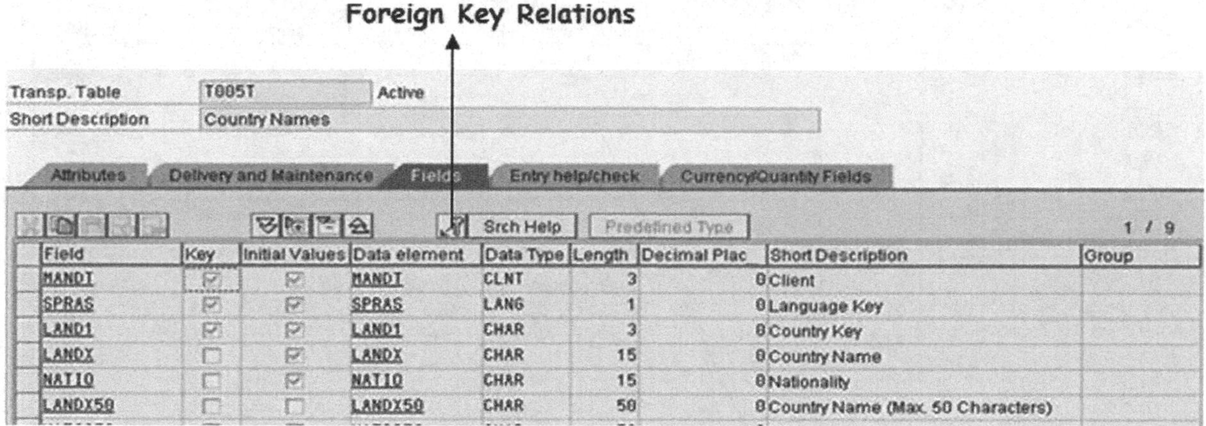

Figure 2-23. *Table - Proceed to Foreign Key Relationship*

For the selected table T005T, you can view the foreign key relationship for the field SPRAS (language code). The screen would look like that in Figure 2-24.

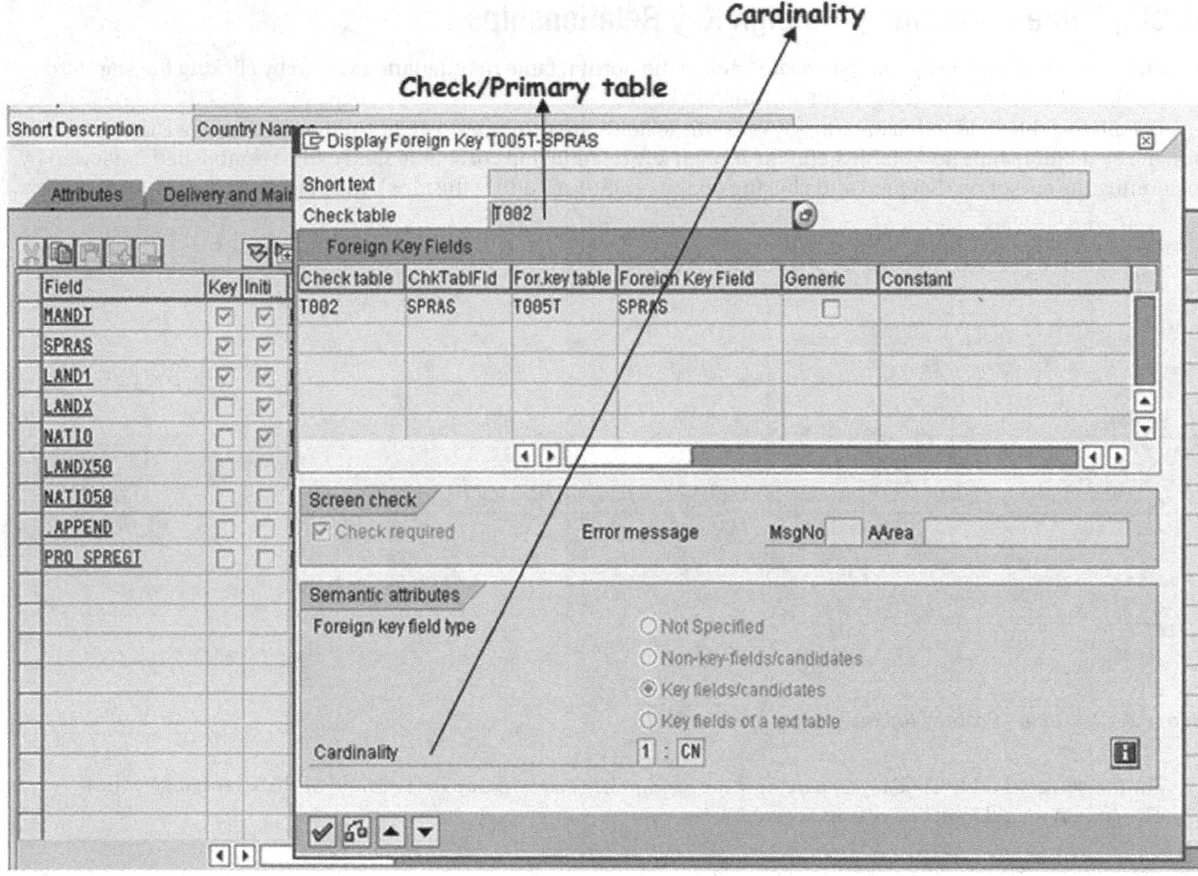

Figure 2-24. *Table - Foreign Key Relationship*

The check table for the field SPRAS is T002. When the Check required check box is enabled, values entered in this field in the secondary table will be checked for existence in the check table. Values not existing in the check table will trigger an error condition.

The Cardinality entries operate as follows:

The cardinality (n:m) describes the foreign key relationship as regards the number of possible dependent rows involved (rows of the foreign key table) vis-à-vis referred rows (rows of the check table).

1. For the left side of the cardinality signifying the check table:
    a. If n = 1 then, for each dependent row there is exactly one row in the check table.
    b. If n = C then, there can be rows in the foreign key table that do not reference any row of the check table (orphan dependent rows can exist).
2. For the right side of the cardinality signifying the foreign key table:
    a. If m = 1, for each row in the check table there is exactly one dependent row.
    b. If m = C then, for each row in the check table there is, at most, one dependent row.
    c. If m = N then, for each row of the check table there is at least one dependent row.
    d. If m = CN then, for each row of the check table there are any number of dependent rows.

You have examined and viewed existing DDIC objects domain, data element, and transparent table. The DDIC metadata is much more complex than database metadata. But then, DDIC table definition is addressing issues of standardization (domain) uniformity, (data element) providing facilities such as OPEN SQL portability, table buffering, search help attachment, and check for CURR & CUKY; QUAN & UNIT fields, etc.

Scenario for Hands-on Exercise on Domain, Data Element, and Table

When SAP is installed, the database tables and other objects that get created as part of the installation are called SAP delivered tables or objects. Post installation, further database tables or objects created by developers are called custom tables or objects.

You will create your own or custom DDIC objects: domains, data elements, and transparent tables. The possibility, in a real-life situation for creation of custom tables is rare, unless one is developing a new application on an ABAP platform or doing a large enhancement entailing creation of new tables.

The objective of creating custom tables here is for better understanding of the SAP table definitions, becoming familiar with the DDIC table definitions, and being able to relate to SAP delivered tables.

Let there be a business scenario for creating custom tables. A simple everyday scenario: Probably every one of you has walked into a casual restaurant. And you have received and paid the bill at the end of your meal.

A rough format of a typical restaurant bill is presented in Figure 2-25.

Burgers & Pizzas...
321, M.G. Road, Bengaluru

Bill No.: 1234 Bill Date: 01/07/2013
Table No.: 10 Waiter's No.:03

Item Code	Item Description	Rate	Qnan-tity	Amount
0005	Vegetarian Supreme Medium	275.00	02	550.00
0010	Barbeque Chicken Regular	175.00	02	350.00
1005	Special Lemonade	100.00	01	100.00

Total: 1000.00
VAT Amount @ 12.5%: 125.00
Net Amount: 1125.00

Thank You. Visit again!

Figure 2-25. *A typical restaurant bill*

Map this bill (business document) and its related information into RDBMS tables, and the fields in the tables. This is being done here in an intuitive, manual way. In a real-life situation, with complex and involved scenarios (many database tables and many fields), you will use some data designer or data modeler tool.

You will call this storage of restaurant bills and its related information "a restaurant billing system."

A list of very commonly used icons or buttons (on the system and application tool bars) is available in Table 1-5.

Table 1-5. *Very Commonly Used Icons or Buttons*

Icon or Button	Description
s	Equivalent to pressing <enter> key. The <enter> key has a different meaning in the SAP GUI environment. When you are finished with a screen, you press the <enter> key. To navigate forward from one field to another, use the [tab] key; to navigate backwards between fields use the [shift]+ [tab] key combination.
	Universal Save
	Navigate to previous screen [F3]
	Exit screen
	Cancel operation
	Find
	Create session
	Execute [F8]
	Create object [F5]
	Display object [F7]
	Change or Edit object [F6]
	Delete

Table and Table Fields

First, the restaurant bill data will have to reside in two database tables:

(1) Database Table 'Bills - Header' will contain the bills' header Information:-

Bill No.
Bill Date
Table No.
Waiter No.
Total
VAT Amount
Net Amount

(2) Database Table 'Bills - Items' will contain the bills' item information:-

Bill No.
Serial No.
Item Code
Quantity
Rate
Amount

The two database tables will be related through Bill No. and Bill No. will be a foreign key in the database table Bills – Items.

You will have two more database tables storing information connected to the restaurant billing: Item Master storing Item information and Waiter Master storing Waiter information.

(3) Database table 'Item Master' will contain the following information:-

Item Code
Item Description
Rate

(4) Database table 'Waiter Master' will contain the following information:-

Waiter No.
Title (Mr. Ms. et al)
Name
Street
City

Waiter No will be a foreign key in database table Bills – Header. Item Code will be a foreign key in database table Bills – Items.

Entity Relationship Diagram – Restaurant Billing System

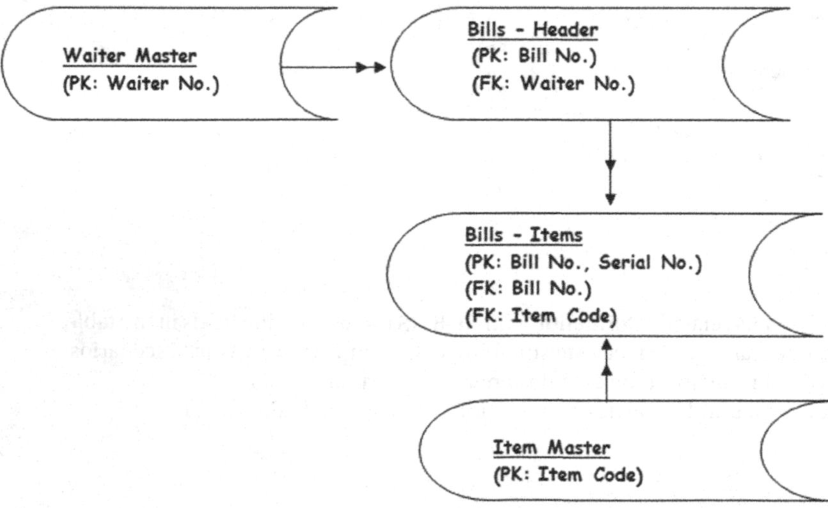

Figure 2-26. *Four-table ER diagram. PK – Primary Key. FK- Foreign Key*

Assigning DDIC Data Types and Lengths to Table Fields

Assigning DDIC Data Types and lengths to these fields is the next step. You are assigning Data Type DEC to the amount and quantity fields. A restaurant does not raise bills in multiple currencies, so the currency can be implicit. This restaurant is serving and delivering only in numbers (i.e., a number of pizzas and burgers, etc.). So the unit of measure for the quantity is also implicit. The tables and fields with Data Type and lengths are shown in Tables 2-2, 2-3, 2-4, and 2-5:

Field Description	Data Type	Length
Bill No. (PK)	NUMC	4
Bill Date	DATS	8
Table No.	NUMC	2
Waiter No.(FK)	NUMC	2
Total	DEC	6,2
VAT Amount	DEC	5,2
Net Amount	DEC	6,2

Table 2.2 (Bills - Header)

Field Description	Data Type	Length
Bill No. (PK) (FK)	NUMC	4
Serial No. (PK)	NUMC	3
Item Code (FK)	NUMC	4
Quantity	DEC	3,0
Rate	DEC	5,2
Amount	DEC	6,2

Table 2.3 (Bills - Items)

Field Description	Data Type	Length
Item Code (PK)	NUMC	4
Item Description	CHAR	30
Rate	DEC	5,2

Table 2.4 (Item Master)

Field Description	Data Type	Length
Waiter No. (PK)	NUMC	2
Title	CHAR	10
Waiter Name	CHAR	35
Street	CHAR	35
City	CHAR	35

Table 2.5 (Waiter Master)

The notation 6, 2 for Data Type DEC is 6 digits before the decimal point and 2 digits after the decimal (a total length of 8 digits or 5 bytes). This is not standard notation; this is custom notation.

The Data Types and lengths have been assigned to fields by experience.

Summary of Data Types, Lengths, and List of Tables' Entities and Attributes

A summary of Data Types and lengths in the four tables (with the fields):

1. NUMC	4	Bill No., Item No.
2. DATS	8	Bill Date
3. NUMC	2	Table No., Waiter No.
4. DEC	6,2	Total, Net Amount, Amount
5. NUMC	3	Serial No.
6. DEC	3,0	Quantity
7. DEC	5,2	Vat Amount, Rate
8. CHAR	30	Item Description
9. CHAR	10	Title
10. CHAR	35	Waiter Name, Street, City

To create table definitions for the four tables, you need to create a minimum of 10 domains. Recall that domain is related to Data Type and length. Two or more fields having the same Data Type and length may or may not be assigned the same domain. In the four-table scenario, two or more fields sharing same Data Type and length are:

Field	Type	Length
Bill No.	NUMC	4
Item Code	NUMC	4
Table No.	NUMC	2
Waiter No.	NUMC	2
Total	DEC	6,2
Net Amount	DEC	6,2
Amount	DEC	6,2
VAT Amount	DEC	5,2
Rate	DEC	5,2
Waiter Name	CHAR	35
Street	CHAR	35
City	CHAR	35

Let the same domain be assigned for fields of the same Data Type and length. (This is an arbitrary decision).

A *summary list of all fields* in the four-table scenario (entities & attributes):

1. Bill No
2. Bill Date
3. Table No
4. Waiter No
5. Total
6. VAT Amount
7. Net Amount

8. Serial No.
9. Item Code

10. Quantity
11. Rate
12. Amount

13. Item Description

14. Title (Mr. Ms. et al)
15. Name
16. Street
17. City

As each of these fields must have a label when appearing on the screen, you need to create 17 data elements, 1 for each of these fields.

You have to create 10 domains, 17 data elements, and 4 tables for the restaurant billing system.

Creation of Domains, Data Elements, and Tables

Objects Naming Convention, Listing of Objects

Before you commence the creation of custom DDIC objects, let a naming convention be adopted for the objects to be created in the ABAP Workbench. Most of the objects created in the ABAP Workbench environment (not SAP delivered) have to start with the letters Y or Z. In the DDIC environment, except for lock objects, all other custom object names start with Y or Z. Hence, the objects you are planning to create (domains, data elements, tables, and others) will have the starting letter as Y or Z. This practice of starting the object names with letters Y or Z is a basic procedure to ensure separation of SAP delivered objects that exist just after SAP installation and the objects created by SAP customers or other users of the SAP development platform. It ensures there is no conflict of object names, and the separation ensures that the objects created by SAP customers (or you) remain intact during a version upgrade. You will be creating all objects in the ABAP Workbench environment starting with prefix YCL. Next you will identify an object with a two-digit chapter number such as CH01, CH02 ... Next you give some meaningful suffix – for example, when you are creating a domain of Data Type NUMC and length 4, you would give it a name YCL_CH02_NUMC4. You will name custom objects in this manner.

The DDIC objects you create should start with Y/Z; the rest of the characters in the names can be any combination of alphanumeric characters (A-Z & 0-9) with embedded underscores (_). The names are case insensitive. This is so with all of the objects in the ABAP Workbench. Normally, a developer after logging into SAP set the Caps

Lock key on. The name space (maximum characters allowed in the object name) varies from object to object. For tables it is 16; for domains and data elements it is 30.

A list of the 10 domains as they would be named as per the naming convention is given in Table 2-6:

Table 2-6. *Domains List*

No.	Domain Name	Data Type	Len
1	YCL_CH02_NUMC4	NUMC	4
2	YCL_CH02_DATS	DATS	8
3	YCL_CH02_NUMC2	NUMC	2
4	YCL_CH02_DEC62	DEC	6,2
5	YCL_CH02_NUMC3	NUMC	3
6	YCL_CH02_DEC30	DEC	3,0
7	YCL_CH02_DEC52	DEC	5,2
8	YCL_CH02_CHAR30	CHAR	30
9	YCL_CH02_CHAR10	CHAR	10
10	YCL_CH02_CHAR35	CHAR	35

A list of data elements as they would be named as per the naming convention is given in Table 2-7:

Table 2-7. *Data Elements List*

Na	Data Element	Label	Domain to be assigned
1	YCL_CH02_BILL_NO	Bill No	YCL_CH02_NUMC4
2	YCL_CH02_BILL_DATE	Bill Date	YCL_CH02_DATS
3	YCL_CH02_TAB_NO	Table No	YCL_CH02_NUMC2
4	YCL_CH02_WAIT_NO	Waiter No	YCL_CH02_NUMC2
5	YCL_CH02_TOTAL	Total	YCL_CH02_DEC62
6	YCL_CH02_VAT_AMT	VAT Amount	YCL_CH02_DEC52
7	YCL_CH02_NET_AMT	Net Amount	YCL_CH02_DEC62
8	YCL_CH02_SRL_NO	Serial No.	YCL_CH02_NUMC3
9	YCL_CH02_ITEM_CODE	Item Code	YCL_CH02_NUMC4
10	YCL_CH02_QNTY	Quantity	YCL_CH02_DEC30
11	YCL_CH02_RATE	Rate	YCL_CH02_DEC52
12	YCL_CH02_AMOUNT	Amount	YCL_CH02_DEC62
13	YCL_CH02_ITEM_DESC	Item Description	YCL_CH02_CHAR30
14	YCL_CH02_TITLE	Title (Mr. Ms. et al)	YCL_CH02_CHAR10
15	YCL_CH02_NAME	Name	YCL_CH02_CHAR35
16	YCL_CH02_STREET	Street	YCL_CH02_CHAR35
17	YCL_CH02_CITY	City	YCL_CH02_CHAR35

A list of the tables with fields, Data Types & lengths, data elements and domains is shown in Tables 2-8, 2-9, 2-10, and 2-11. All the DDIC objects have been given names as you would in the ABAP Workbench environment.

1. Database Table Description: Bills - Header Name: YCL_CH02_BILLH

Table 2-8.

Field Description	Field Name	Data Type	Length	Data Element	Domain
Bill Number (PK)	BILL_NO	NUMC	4	YCL_ CH02_BILL_NO	YCL_CH02_NUMC4
Bill Date	BILL_DATE	DATS	8	YCL_ CH02_BILL_DATE	YCL_ CH02_DATS
Waiter No. (FK)	WAIT_NO	NUMC	2	YCL_ CH02_WAIT_NO	YCL_ CH02_NUMC2
Table No.	TABL_NO	NUMC	2	YCL_ CH02_TAB_NO	YCL_ CH02_NUMC2
Total	TOTAL	DEC	6,2	YCL_ CH02_TOTAL	YCL_ CH02_DEC62
VAT Amount	VAT_AMT	DEC	6,2	YCL_ CH02_VAT_AMT	YCL_ CH02_DEC52
Net Amount	NET_AMT	DEC	6,2	YCL_ CH02_NET_AMT	YCL_ CH02_DEC62

2. Database Table Description: Bills - Items Name: YCL_CH02_BILLI

Table 2-9.

Field Description	Field Name	Data Type	Length	Data Element	Domain
Bill Number (FK, PK)	BILL_NO	NUMC	4	YCL_ CH02_BILL_NO	YCL_ CH02_NUMC4
Serial No. (PK)	SRL_NO	NUMC	3	YCL_ CH02_SRL_NO	YCL_ CH02_NUMC3
Item Code (FK)	ITEM_CODE	NUMC	4	YCL_ CH02_ITEM_CODE	YCL_ CH02_NUMC4
Quantity	QNTY	DEC	3,0	YCL_ CH02_QNTY	YCL_ CH02_DEC30
Rate	RATE	DEC	5,2	YCL_ CH02_RATE	YCL_ CH02_DEC52
Amount	AMOUNT	DEC	6,2	YCL_CH2_AMOUNT	YCL_CH02_DEC62

3. Database Table Description: Waiter Master Name: YCL_CH02_WAITM

Table 2-10.

Field Description	Field Name	Data Type	Length	Data Element	Domain
Waiter No. (PK)	WAIT_NO	NUMC	2	YCL_ CH02_WAIT_NO	YCL_ CH02_NUMC2
Title	TITLE	CHAR	10	YCL_ CH02_TITLE	YCL_ CH02_CHAR10
Waiter Name	WAIT_NAME	CHAR	35	YCL_ CH02_NAME	YCL_ CH02_CHAR35
Street	STREET	CHAR	35	YCL_ CH02_STREET	YCL_ CH02_CHAR35
City	CITY	CHAR	35	YCL_ CH02_CITY	YCL_ CH02_CHAR35

4. Database Table Description: Item Master Name: YCL_CH02_ITEMM

Table 2-11.

Field Description	Field Name	Data Type	Length	Data Element	Domain
Item Code (PK)	ITEM_CODE	NUMC	4	YCL_ CH02_ITEM_CODE	YCL_ CH02_NUMC4
Item Description	ITEM_DESC	CHAR	30	YCL_ CH02_ITEM_DESC	YCL_ CH02_CHAR30
Rate	RATE	DEC	5,2	YCL_ CH02_RATE	YCL_ CH02_DEC52

Start creating the DDIC objects: 10 domains, 17 data elements, and 4 tables. You have to create domains, data elements, and tables in that order.

Create Domains

From SAP Easy Access, get to the DDIC maintenance screen; SE11, etc.

Select the radio button for domain (fifth radio button from the top).

Enter the name of first domain (i.e., YCL_CH02_NUMC4). The initial screen will look like the one shown in Figure 2-27.

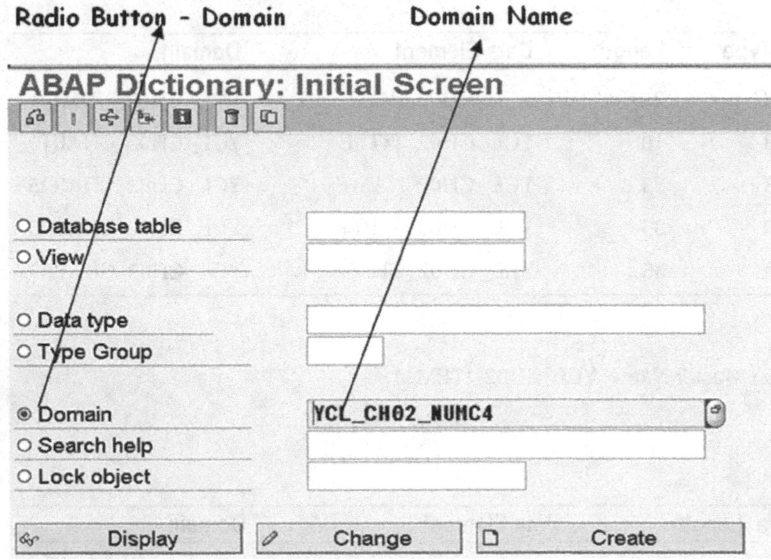

Figure 2-27. *Create Domain - Initial SE11 Screen*

After clicking on the Create button or pressing the function key F5, the screen with the Definition tab enabled is opened.

The entered fields are (1) Short Description with Data Type NUMC, LEN 4, (2) Data Type with NUMC, and (3) No. Characters with 4. Do not enter any value in the field Output Length; it will be generated by the system. Other fields on this screen are not applicable.

Field Data Type has been assigned value through the pop-up selection list appearing by pressing function key F4 or pressing the button on the field. The pop-up selection list is appearing on the right side with all of the 24 DDIC Data Types. Wherever pop-up selection lists are available, it is good practice to assign value through a selection list rather than manually entering data. To make a selection either double-click on the selected row or choose the row by single click (chosen row appears in yellow, orange color), then click on the button.

This is shown in Figure 2-28.

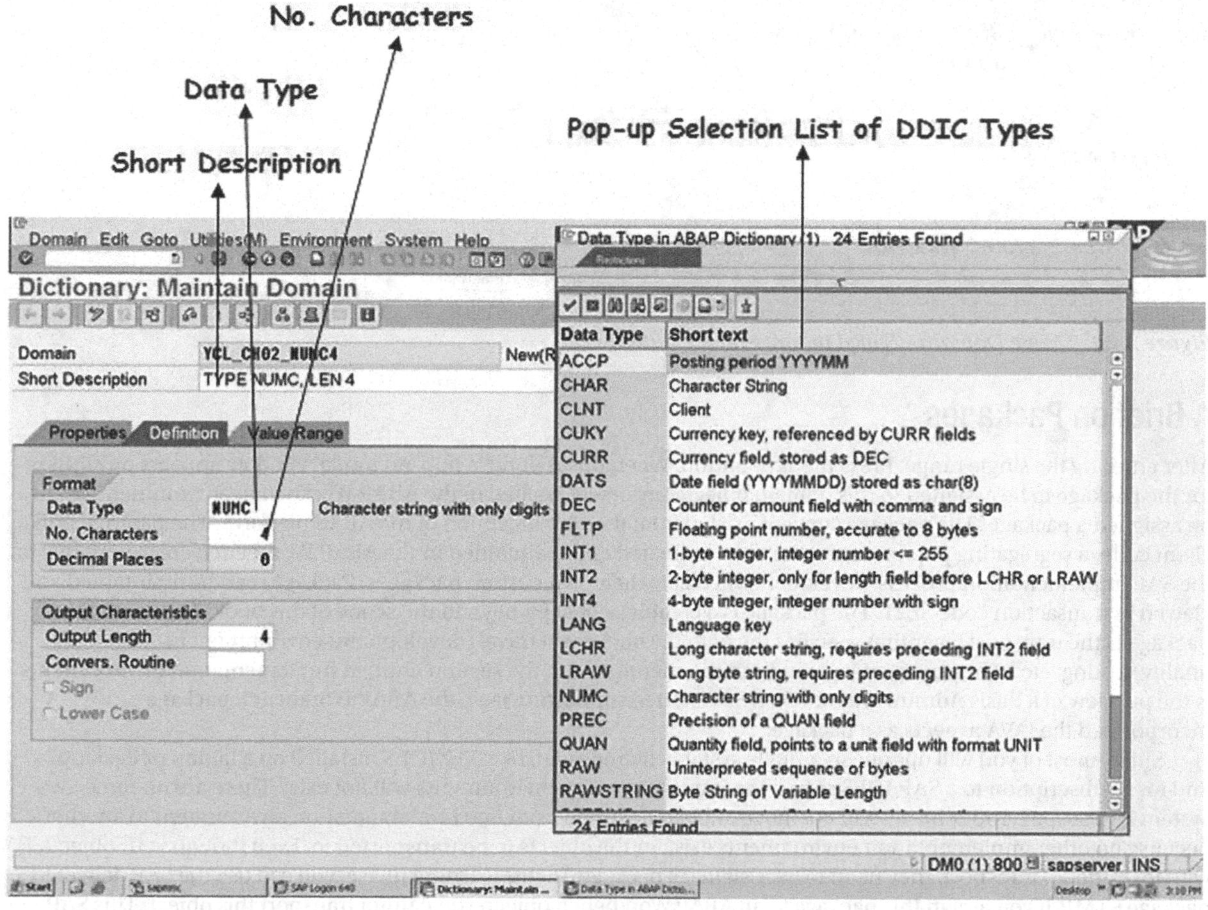

Figure 2-28. *Create Domain – tab 'Definition' with fields entered*

Click the Value Range tab. You are entering a single value range her, (i.e., 0001–5000) under the Intervals area of the screen (bottom area of the screen, see Figure 2-29). When a field associated with this domain will appear on screen, it automatically checks the entered value, and values outside the range will trigger an error condition. You have entered only one range for the purpose of illustrating the feature rather than a practical necessity. In a real-life situation, multiple ranges of values in this area can be entered as warranted by a scenario requirement.

Do not enter anything in this Intervals area for other domains.

Under the Intervals area, there is a field Value Table as shown in Figure 2-29. You can enter a DDIC table name here. When you assign this domain to a data element, assign this data element to a table field, and this table field is to be made into a foreign key field through a foreign key relationship; then the system will propose this table as the default check table.

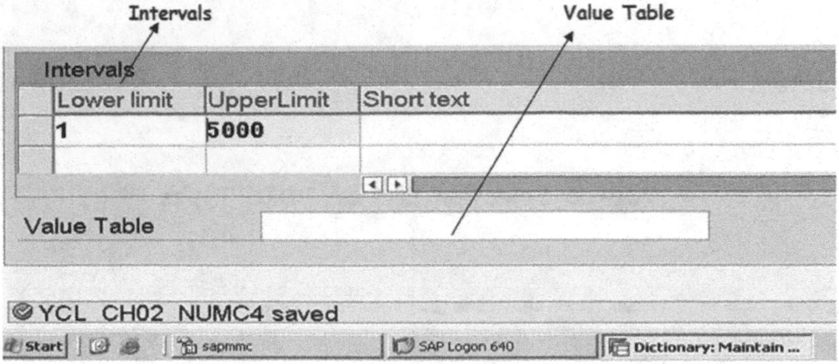

Figure 2-29. Create Domain - Saved message on the status bar

A Brief on Packages

After entering the single range, press the save button. When this is done, a pop-up modal window appears prompting for the package to be assigned to this domain object. Any object created in the ABAP Workbench environment has to be assigned a package. The package concept existed from the very inception of the ABAP platform. The package is like client code: a segregating parameter for the objects created and maintained in the ABAP Workbench environments. In the SAP implementation process, developers will create their own custom packages. Packages can be maintained and viewed in transaction code SE21. The package is a complex concept, beyond the scope of this book. The core of the package is the transport layer that specifies the path the object will travel (development environment to quality/testing, etc.).The transport layer as has been mentioned in the section entitled Implementation Environments is the purview of a Basis Administrator. When SAP started supporting Java, the ABAP Workbench package incorporated the JAVA aspects as a package.

Since, most of you will operate in a single system environment, like SAP IDES installed on a laptop or desktop, and for a subscription to a SAP IDES server, the implementation environments will not exist. There are no three/two system landscapes. Your objects will not move or be transported from one implementation environment to another because no other implementation environments exist for the objects to be transported to. Even though your objects will not undergo transport, they need to be assigned a package. In this learning phase, you can use the SAP delivered package $TMP. If you assign this package to an ABAP Workbench object, you cannot transport this object. This SAP delivered package $TMP is designated as a package to be assigned to local objects (i.e., the objects are local to the environment where they are created and cannot be transported to other environments).

Domain Creation Continued

On the modal dialog box prompting for the package, click on the **Local Object** button. The system will assign the SAP delivered package $TMP to the domain. The screen shot appears as in Figure 2-30.

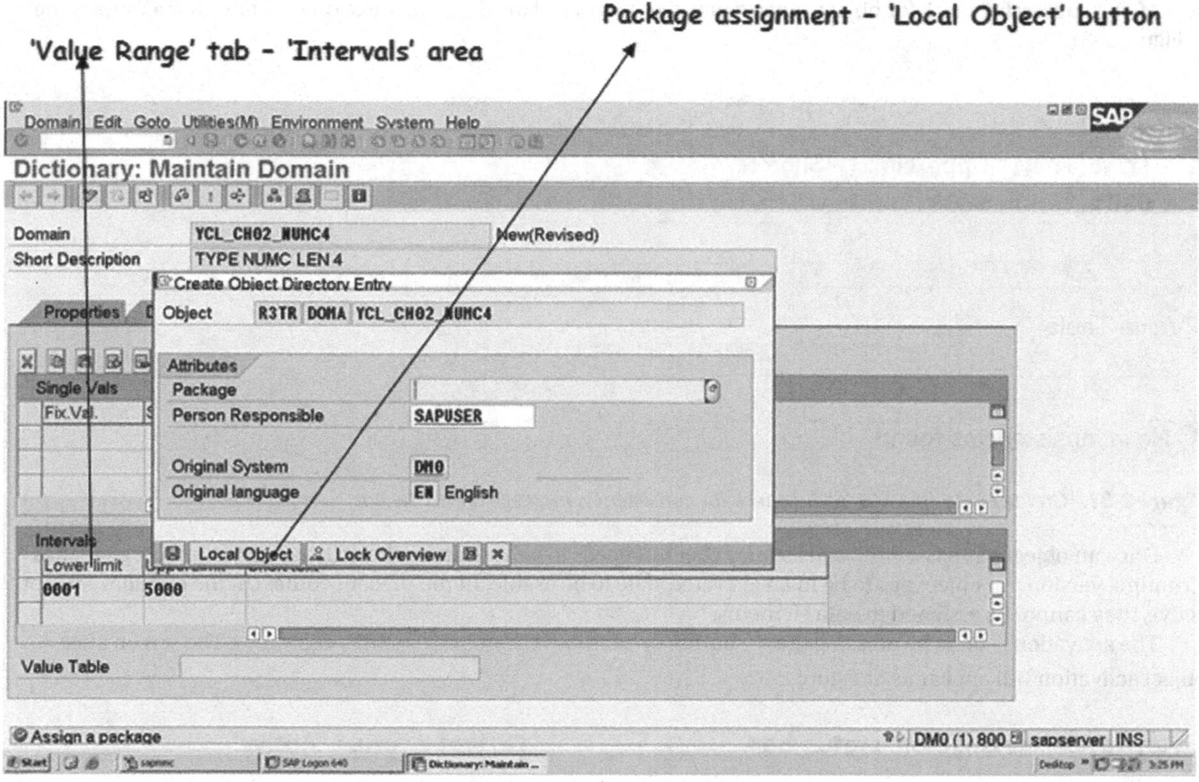

Figure 2-30. *Create Domain – Enter Value Range Intervals, assign package $TMP*

An ABAP Workbench object whenever it is created and if subsequently changed or edited will be checked for inconsistencies. You can do this by clicking the button on the application tool bar or alternatively pressing <Ctrl>+<F2> keys (combination of Ctrl & F2 keys, + indicating combination). If inconsistencies exist in the object, this will throw an error message on the status bar. This should be investigated and fixed. For instance if you had entered a number in the domain field Decimal Places, it would have displayed an error message. Decimals places are not applicable to the DDIC Data Type NUMC.

After a successful check for object consistency, the system will display a message on the status bar as appearing in Figure 2-31.

Intervals

Lower limit	UpperLimit	Short text
0001	5000	

Value Table

No inconsistencies found

Figure 2-31. *Create Domain - Successful check for consistency, message on status bar*

Once an object has passed the consistency check, it needs to be activated. The activation of an object generates a runtime version. An object has to be in an activated state to be usable. In the present context, if the domains are not active, they cannot be assigned to data elements.

The activation is done by pressing the button or alternatively pressing <Ctrl>+<F3> keys. The screen after object activation will appear as in Figure 2-32.

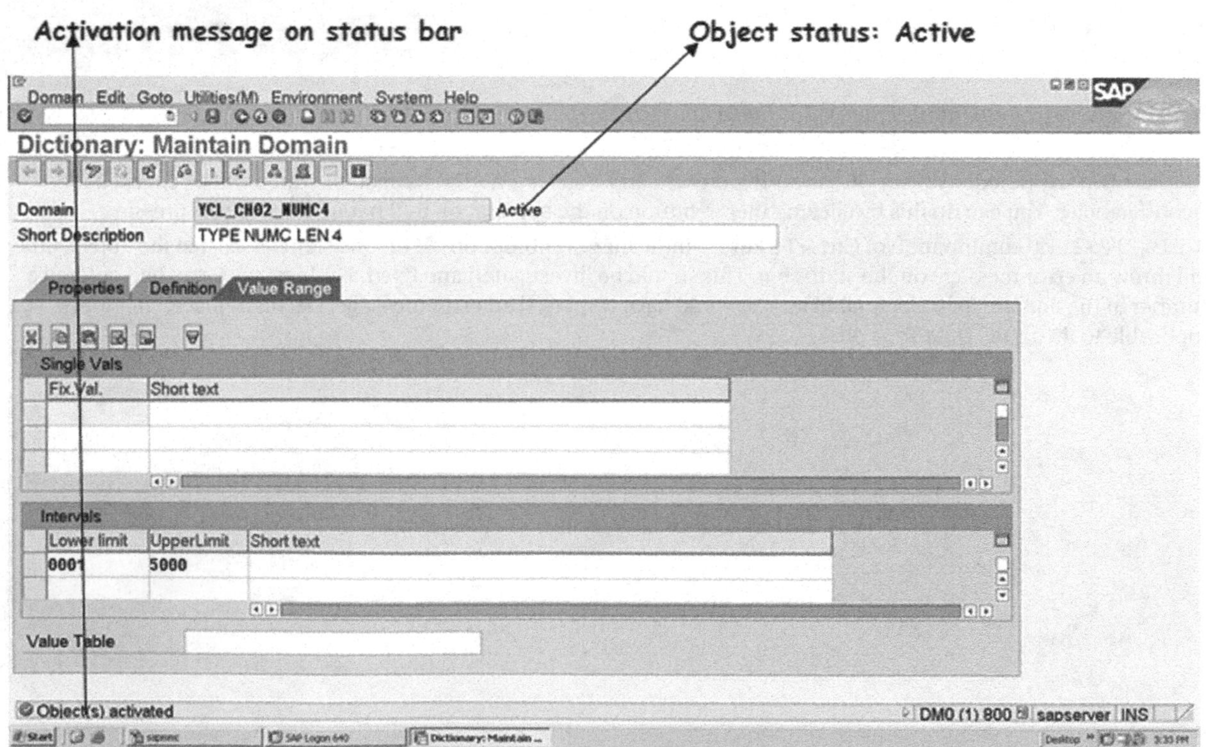

Figure 2-32. *Create Domain - Activation*

In a similar manner, you can create the nine other domains of a restaurant billing system.

When creating domains of DDIC Data Type DEC, remember for DEC 6, 2, there will a total of 8 digits: 6 digits before decimal position and 2 digits after decimal position. So in the fields on the domain screen: No. Characters 8 should be entered; Decimal Places 2 should be entered.

For domains of DDIC Data Type CHAR, if case sensitivity is desired (i.e., storage of both upper, lower case of alphabets), click on the check box with label Lower Case on the domain screen.

For the field TITLE, in the corresponding domain, you will use the Single Vals Area of the Value Range tab. The restaurant billing system is making provision for waiters as well as waitresses. When the data for them is stored, the TITLE field can contain values such as MR., MS., MRS., etc., you will enter these possible values in Single Vals area of the Value Range tab of domain. When the TITLE field appears on the screen, the user has the facility of a pop-up selection list. This pop-up selection list will display all the values entered in this Single Vals area of Value Range tab. Ideally you should enter values in this area when the number of entries are few (less than 32) and the entries do not change over time or change rarely. In the present context, the titles by which people are addressed in English language are not going to change in foreseeable future. A screen shot of the Value Range tab for the domain YCL_CH02_CHAR10 (domain for field TITLE) is shown in Figure 2-33.

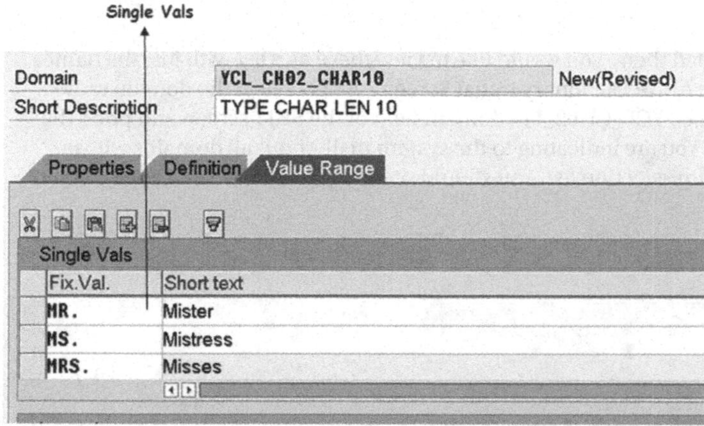

Figure 2-33. *Create Domain- Single Vals*

You will be making multiple row entries in many situations of ABAP Workbench objects' maintenance. In all these situations, you will have the facility of this user interface that enables you make one or more row/s selection, copy, cut, paste, and delete with the buttons shown in the Figure 2-34. You can insert rows as well; a row will be inserted where your cursor is positioned.

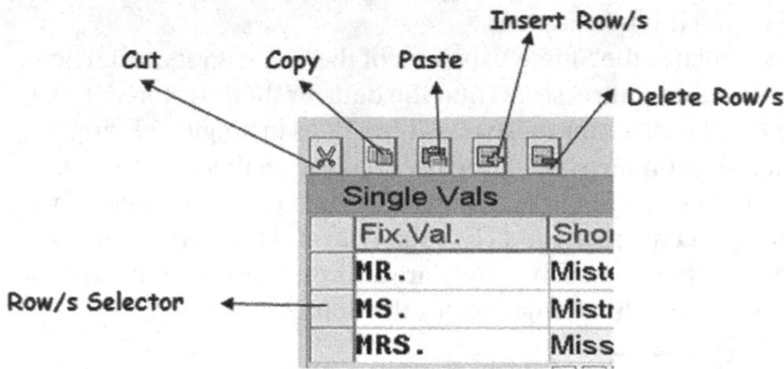

Figure 2-34. *Multiple Row Manipulation*

If you have created all 10 domains and activated them, you would like to view these as a list with just the names of domains appearing in the list. For this, go to the ABAP Dictionary Initial Screen - SE11. Select the domain radio button. Enter the pattern of your domain names (i.e., YCL_CH02_* in domain field of the SE11 screen and press the function key F4). This is appearing in Figure 2-35. You are indicating to the system to filter out all domains whose names start with YCL_CH02_ and produce a pop-up selection list. You should see a screen like the one appearing in Figure 2-36.

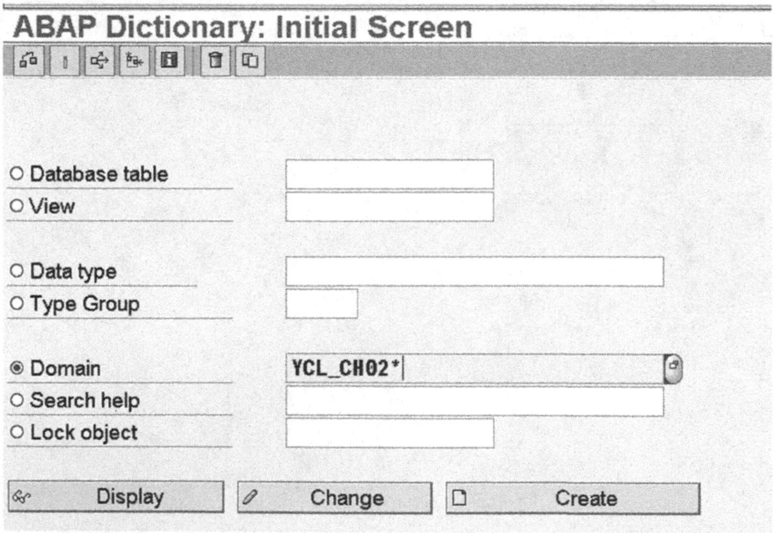

Figure 2-35. *Create Domain - Get overview of domains created*

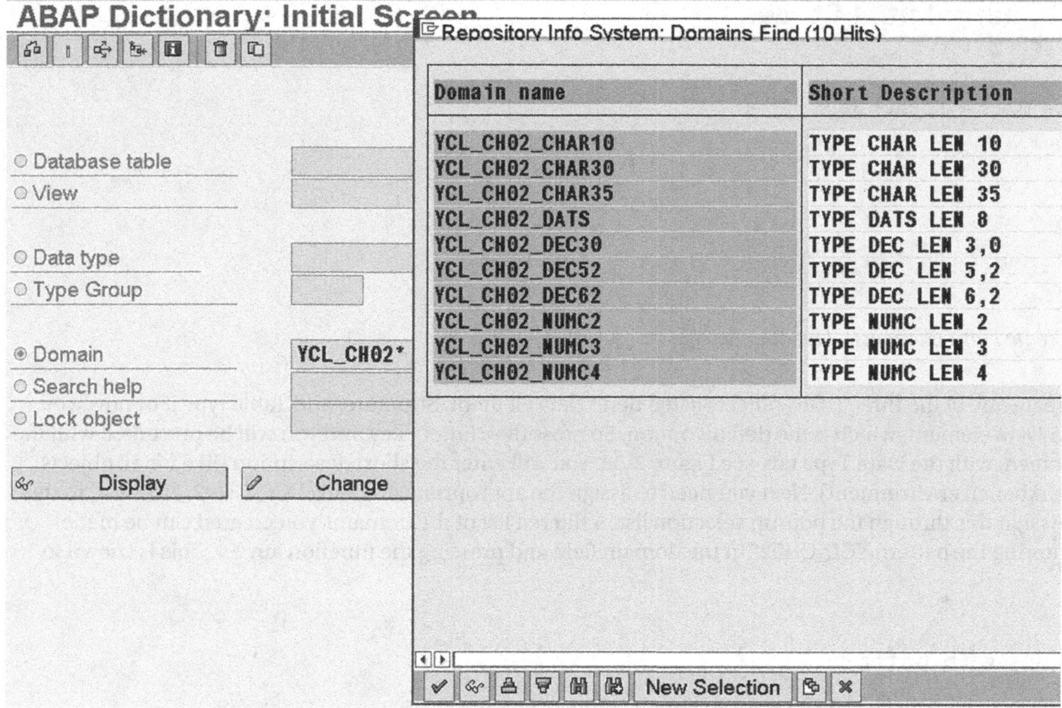

Figure 2-36. *Create Domain - Overview of domains created*

The list appears with a name and short description. If the short description is appearing as blank, the corresponding domain is in an inactive state. The List appears in alphabetic ascending order.

Editing/Changing domains

If you need to perform any changes to domains, you can do so by selecting the Domain radio button and entering the name of the domain you want to change in the Domain field. (Alternatively, you can get the list of domains you created by entering the pattern in the Domain field, pressing function key F4, and making a selection from the list). Click on the Change button or press function key F6. Perform the changes, save, and reactivate the domain. After editing any object, the changed version of the object is in an inactive mode. The changed version needs to be activated to enable its usage. Take care to do this.

Create Data Elements

On the SE11 ABAP Dictionary: Initial Screen, select the radio button Data type (third radio button from the top). Enter the name of the first data element to be created (i.e., YCL_CH02_BILL_NO.). (Table 2-7 is a list of data elements to be created with the respective labels and assigned domains.) Press the Create button or function key F5. The following screen will appear:

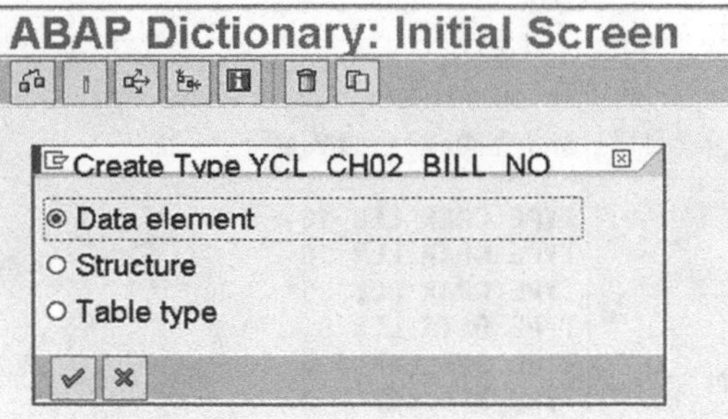

Figure 2-37. *Create Data Elements – Opening Screen*

You can create one of the three DDIC objects listed here: Data element, Structure, and Table type. For now, you want to create a Data element, which is the default option. So press the <Enter> key and you will be presented with the data element screen, with the Data Type tab, see Figure 2-38. You will enter the short description (like for all objects in the ABAP Workbench environment). Next you need to assign the appropriate domain (YCL_CH02_NUMC4) to this data element. Assign this through the pop-up selection list. A filtered list of the domains you created can be made to appear by entering the pattern YCL_CH02* in the domain field and pressing the function key F4. This is shown in Figure 2-38.

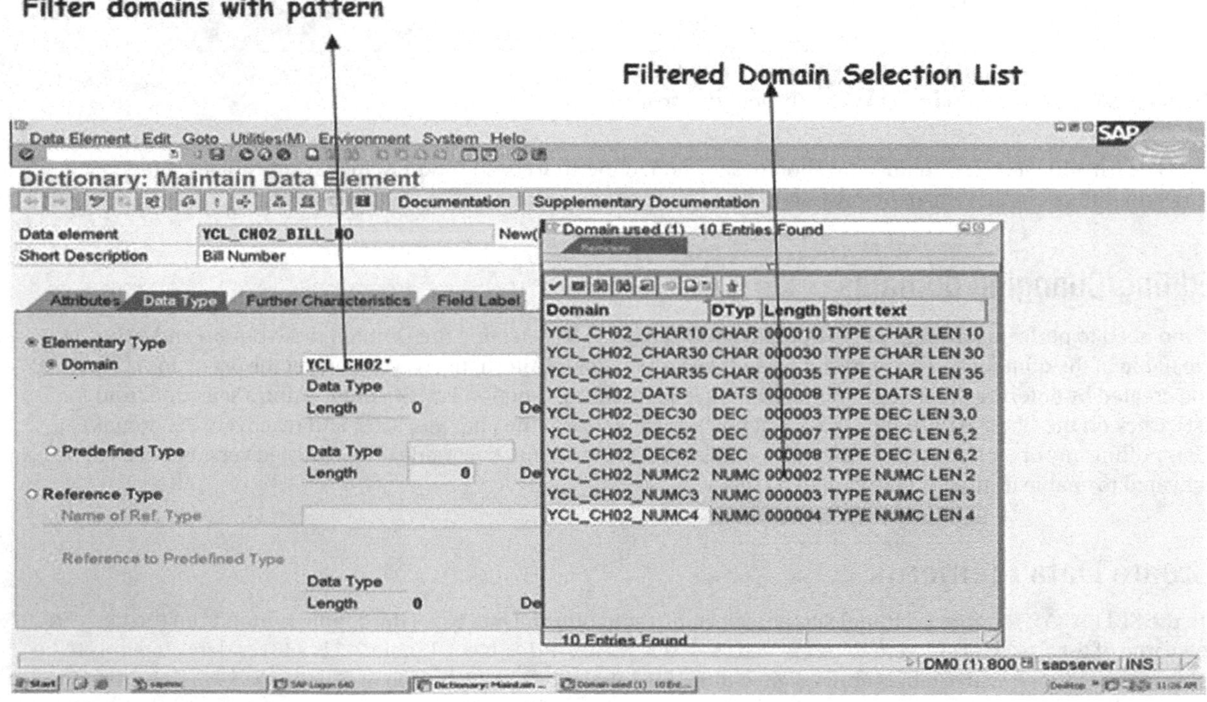

Figure 2-38. *Create Data Element – Tab: 'Data Type'*

Having assigned the domain, click on the Field Label tab. (You are by-passing the Further Characteristics tab.)

In the Field Label tab, you need to enter the screen labels for the field to which this data element will be assigned in the tables subsequently when you create tables. There is a provision for four labels (i.e., Short, Medium, Long, and Heading. You must make a distinction between the first three and the last. The first three will

Bill No.: 1234

In case of Heading Field value will appear under field label. The Heading serves as column or field heading when this field is output on screen or printer like

Bill No.

1234

In this context, when the data length is very small (like in the case of Waiter No. or Table No. of length 2), the label in the heading should not be too long. There should be an attempt to make the label for heading cryptic.

For most part (even in the SAP delivered data elements), the same label is entered in all the three (i.e., Short, Medium, and Long). Let the same label be entered in these three fields: Short, Medium, and Long as well as the heading.

The screen shot with entered labels is shown in Figure 2-39.

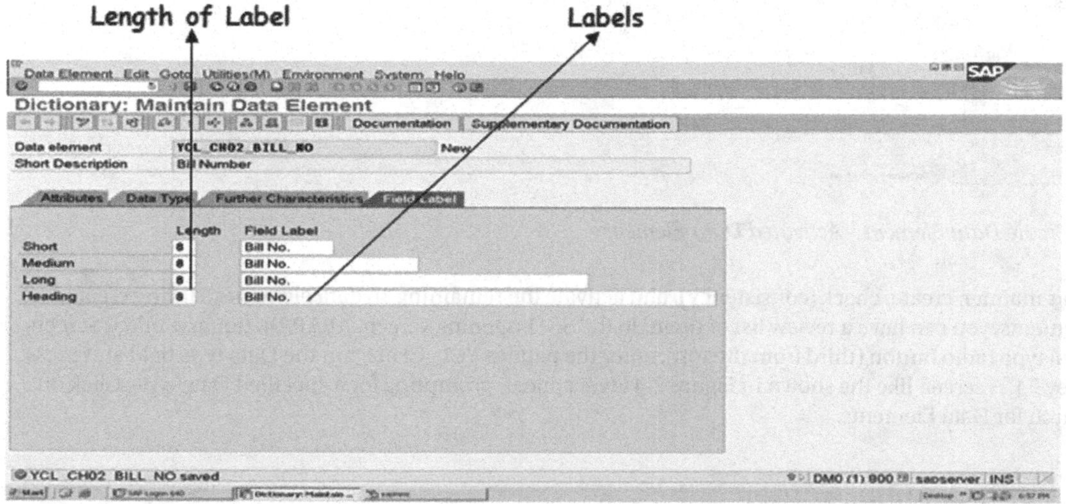

Figure 2-39. *Create Data Element - tab Field Label*

There are two set of fields: Length and Field Label. Do not enter any values in the Length field. The system generates the lengths automatically after you enter the labels and save them. Subsequently, if you want to change a label resulting in an increase in label length, then you have to manually adjust the Length field (not very user friendly).

You can create labels in other languages by clicking on menu bar option Go to and suboption Translation.

When you are finished with the label entry, click the save button. The system will prompt for package assignment. Assign the SAP delivered package $TMP or click on the Local Object button.

Perform a consistency check by clicking on the button or press <Ctrl>+<F2> keys. If the consistency check is without errors, activate the data element by clicking the button or pressing the keys <Ctrl>+<F3> keys.

A screen shot of activated data element YCL_CH02_BILL_NO is shown in Figure 2-40.

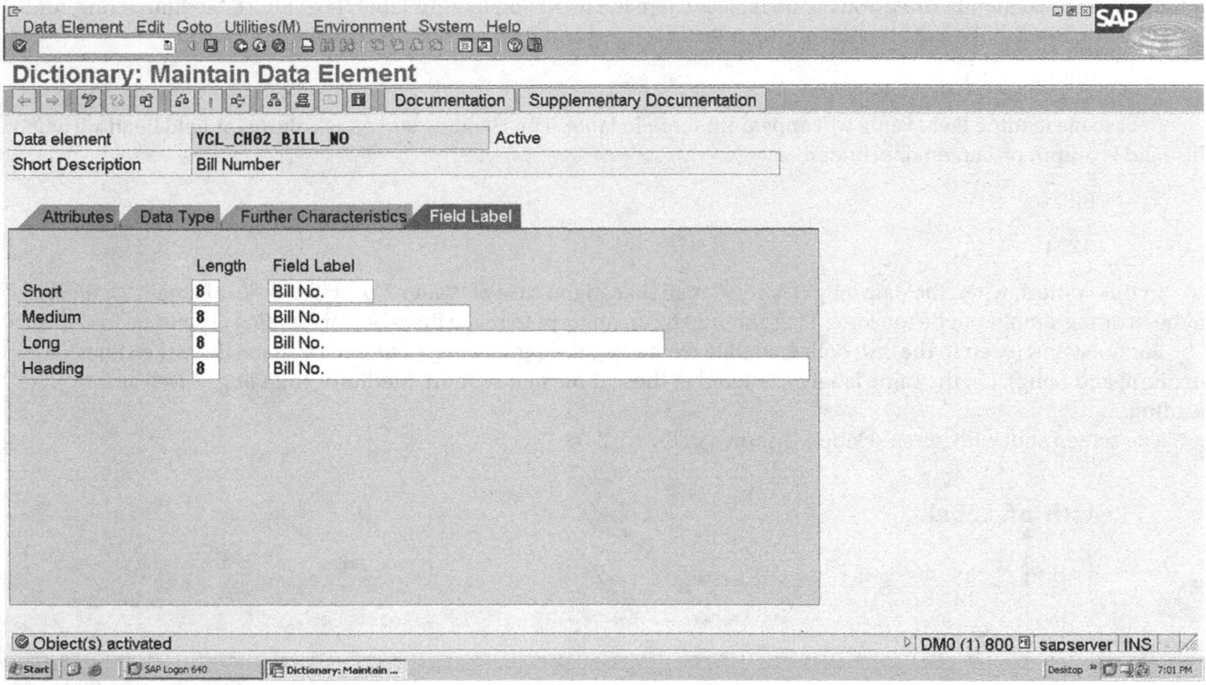

Figure 2-40. Create Data Element – Activated Data Element

In a similar manner, create, check (consistency), and activate the remaining 16 data elements. Having created all the 17 data elements, you can have a review list of them. In the SE11 opening screen, ABAP Dictionary: Initial Screen, enable the Data type radio button (third from the top); enter the pattern YCL_CH02_* in the Data type field and press the function key F4. A screen like the shown in Figure 2-41 will appear, prompting for a specified Data type. Click on the button Search for Data Elements.

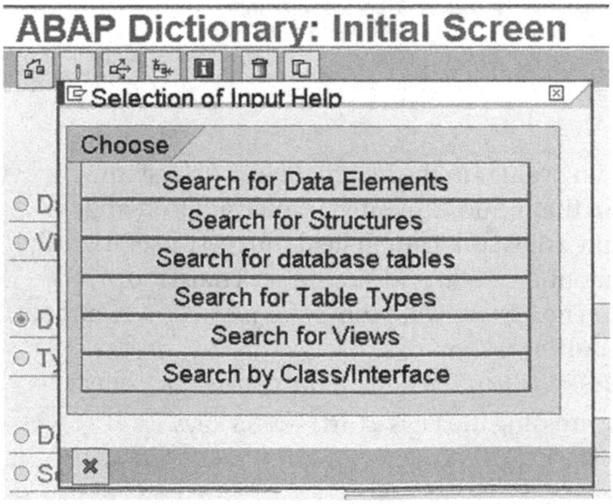

Figure 2-41. Create Data Element – Prompt for selection of Data type of list

A list like the one in Figure 2-42 will appear. The list is appearing with name and short description. If the short description is appearing blank, the corresponding data element is in an inactive state. The List is appearing in alphabetic ascending order.

Repository Info System: Data Elements Find (17 Hits)

Data element	Short text
YCL_CH02_AMOUNT	Amount
YCL_CH02_BILL_DATE	Bill Date
YCL_CH02_BILL_NO	Bill number
YCL_CH02_CITY	C i t y
YCL_CH02_ITEM_CODE	Item Code
YCL_CH02_ITEM_DESC	Item Desc
YCL_CH02_NAME	Name
YCL_CH02_NET_AMT	Net Amount
YCL_CH02_QNTY	Quantity
YCL_CH02_RATE	Rate
YCL_CH02_SRL_NO	Srl No.
YCL_CH02_STREET	Street
YCL_CH02_TAB_NO	Table No.
YCL_CH02_TITLE	Title
YCL_CH02_TOTAL	Total
YCL_CH02_VAT_AMT	VAT Amount
YCL_CH02_WAIT_NO	Waiter No.

Figure 2-42. *Create Data Element - Review List*

Editing or Changing data elements: If you need to perform any changes to data elements, you can do so by selecting the Data type radio button and entering the name of the data element you want to change in the Data type field. (Alternatively, you can get the list of data elements you created by entering the pattern in the Data type field, pressing function key F4, and making a selection from the list.) Click on the Change button or press function key F6. Perform the changes; save and reactivate the data element. After editing any object, the edited version of the object is in an inactive mode. The edited version needs to be activated to enable its usage.

Create Tables

Now that you have the required domains and data elements created and activated for the four tables, you are ready to create your custom tables. You will first create the tables without the foreign keys (i.e. Waiter Master: YCL_CH02_WAITM, Item Master: YCL_CH02_ITEMM). You will then create Bills - Header: YCL_CH02_BILLH and Bills - Items: YCL_CH02_BILLI.

Tables 2-8, 2-9, 2-10, and 2-11 can be referred while creating them.

In the SE11 opening screen - ABAP Dictionary Initial Screen: click on the Database table radio button. Enter the table name YCL_CH02_WAITM, press button Create or function key F5. The *Delivery and Maintenance* tab screen will appear as shown in Figure 2-43.

In the field Delivery Class, press the function key F4 for a pop-up selection list. Select the value G, the most appropriate and protected against SAP upgrade. The assigned value G signifies an SAP customer table that will not be overwritten or disturbed when the SAP version upgrade takes place.

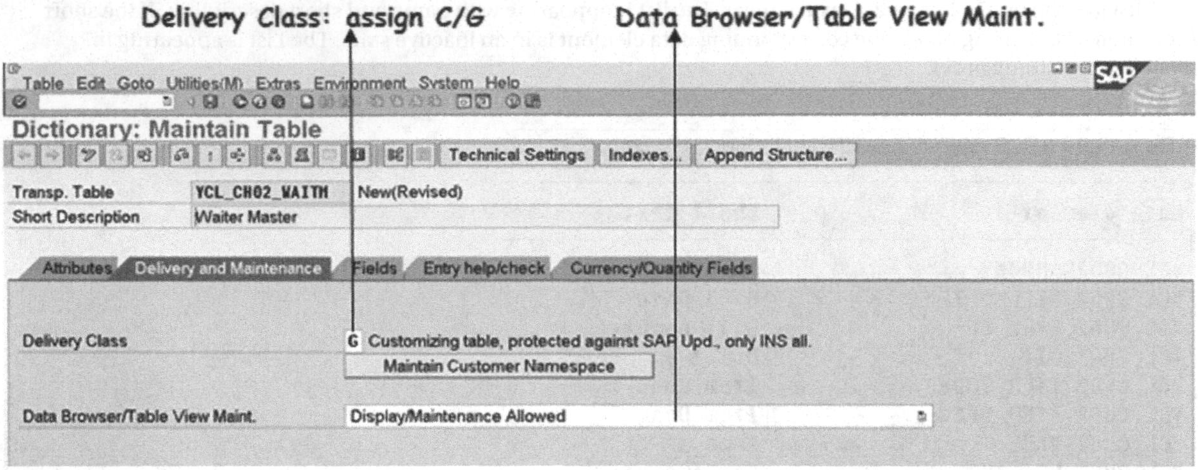

Figure 2-43. Create Table - tab Delivery and Maintenance

In the field Data Browser/Table View Maint., a drop-down list is available. Select the option Display Maintenance Allowed. With this option you can create, edit, delete, and view data in the table through an automatically generated dialog box or a maintenance view. (SAP DDIC supports four types of views. One of them is maintenance view.) If you look up this field of any SAP delivered table such as VBRK, etc., this field is assigned the value Display Maintenance Allowed with Restrictions. This means that the table data can be viewed, but creation, editing, and deletion operations cannot be performed on the table data through the automatically generated dialog box or a maintenance view. For the custom created tables, you would like to be able to create, edit, delete, and view data. Hence the option: Display Maintenance Allowed.

Next, Click on the *Fields* tab. Here you need to enter the name of the fields and assign the corresponding data elements. The fields' Data Type and lengths are derived from the corresponding domains assigned to the data elements. Refer to the section entitled Domain, Data Element, and Table Relationship.

The fields in a table are not DDIC objects. They are part of the objects. So normally they need not start with the letters Y or Z. In a specific context they should start with the letters Y or Z. This specific context is not explicitly covered in this book. The field names have to start with an alphabet, subsequent positions can be a combination of alphanumeric characters with embedded underscores (_). The maximum length of a field name is 16 characters.

The primary key fields have to appear at the beginning. The check box under Key is to be enabled to make a field as a primary key field.

So fill in the field names starting with WAITER_NO. Enable the check box field Key to designate this field WAIT_NO as a primary key field.

When you populate a table and do not enter data in some fields, the system automatically incorporates initial values in these fields (i.e., the system takes care of the null value issue). The initial value is dependent on the DDIC Data Type of the field. Refer to the last column of Table 2-1. To give examples: if one of the fields is of Data Type NUMC and no data is entered in this field, ASCII zeroes (ASCII code for zero is 01100100 or 64) is stored.

The initial check box for primary key fields is controlled by the system. Whether you enable it or disable it, it gets enabled when you activate the table. This system is allowing one initial value for primary key field/s. Considering the context of the table YCL_CH02_WAITM, you can omit entering values in the primary key fields; a row will be created with primary key fields equal to initial value/s. In the table YCL_CH02_WAITM, the system will allow creation of one row with field WAIT_NO equal to 00.

The enabling or disabling of the initial check box for non-primary key fields has relevance in the context of modification of the table structure subsequently on insertion of new fields. If this check box is enabled, the system will fill the fields with initial values or else they will be null values in such fields.

Assign the data element YCL_CH02_WAIT_NO. Do not key in these data elements manually. Instead key in the pattern YCL_CH02*' in the field Data element and press function key F4 for a selection list. This is shown in Figure 2-44.

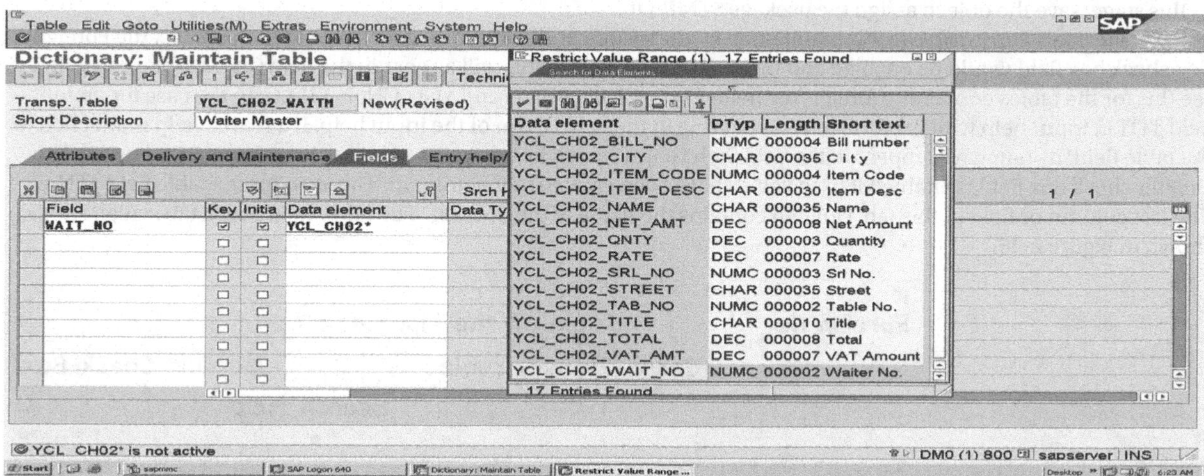

Figure 2-44. *Create Table – Assigning Data Element to a Field from Selection List*

In a similar manner, enter the other fields, and assign data elements to them. After all the fields have been entered and data elements assigned to them, the screen will appear like that in Figure 2-45.

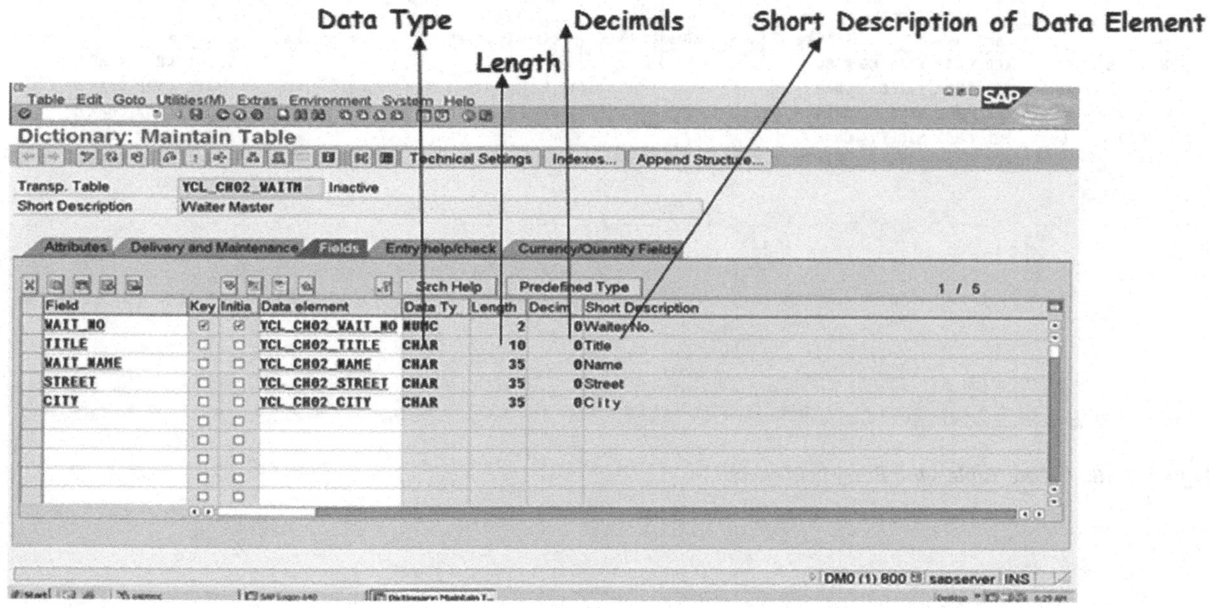

Figure 2-45. *Create Table – Fields with Data Elements assigned*

For each field, The Data Types, lengths, and decimals are appearing automatically, derived from the domain assigned to the corresponding data element.

Some older SAP versions might show these lengths to be zero. The lengths will appear only after table activation. At this stage, save the object, assign the package $TMP, etc.

The next tab *Entry help check* is maintained by the system. If a field is a foreign key field in this table, the Foreign Key check box field would be enabled and the name of the check table will appear in the field Check table. You will see this for the tables containing foreign key fields (YCL_CH02_BILLH and YCL_CH02_BILLI). In the case for table field TITLE, input help with fixed values is appearing in the field Origin of the input help. If a search help is attached to the table field, its name will appear in the field Srch Help. (Search help is covered in the next chapter, Chapter 3) The Default check box field is enabled if fixed values have been created in the domain. This is so for the table field TITLE. The last column or field in this tab, Domain contains the name of the domain. The Entry help check tab screen shot is shown in Figure 2-46.

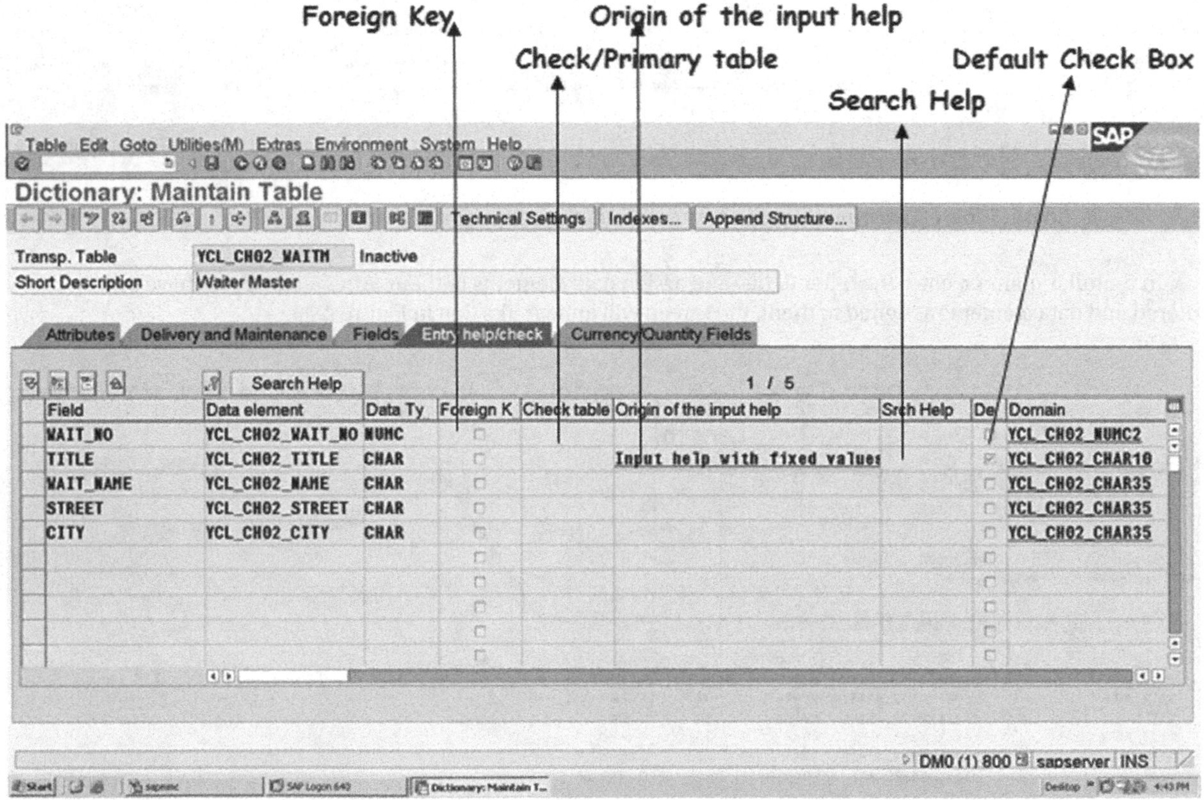

Figure 2-46. *Create Table - tab Entry help check*

The last tab on the screen *Currency/Quantity Fields* is meant to assign a reference table and reference field to the DDIC Data Types CURR and QUAN fields. As you do not have any table fields of DDIC CURR and QUAN in the restaurant billing system, you will not be using this tab.

Table Technical Settings: You need to assign technical settings next. Click on the application toolbar button Technical Setting or from the menu bar Go to, and select the option Technical Setting. The Technical Setting screen is shown in Figure 2-47.

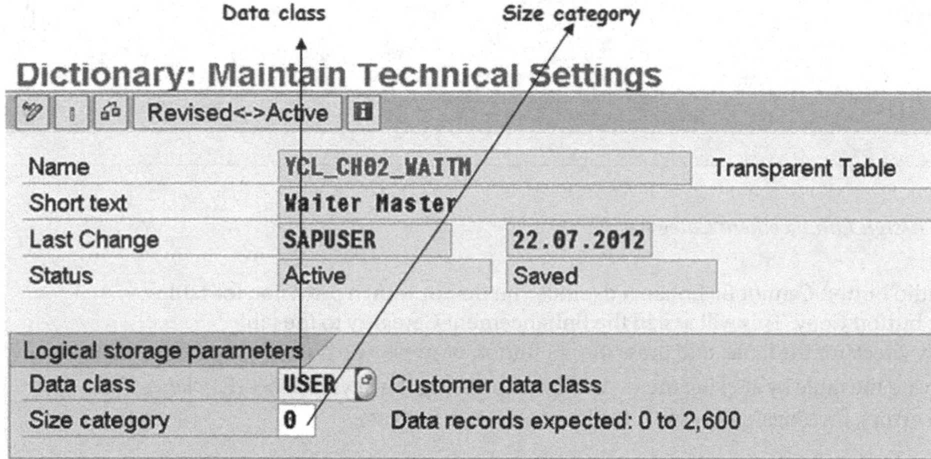

Figure 2-47. *Create Table - Technical Settings*

You are assigning values to two fields. The Data class signifies a physical area in the database. Press the function key F4 and assign values of pattern USER*, and the physical area for users of SAP.

The field Size category is for initial allocation of disk space. Assign the value 0 from the pop-up selection list available. Do not plan to create too many entries or rows in the tables: the value 0 will suffice. Save the Technical Settings.

Enhancement Category

You need to perform one more tasks before you can activate your table; this is specifying the enhancement category. It is not advisable to modify structure definitions of the SAP delivered tables. Fields can be added to SAP delivered tables through the concept of Enhancements. This is an advanced topic not covered in this book. The four tables you are creating are custom tables. You can modify their structure definitions as you want, subject to some constraints. So you need not provide for future enhancement of the tables. This is to be indicated to the system. From menu bar Extras, select the option Enhancement Category. An information message pop-up will appear, and then press <Enter>. Next, a pop-up screen will appear like the one in Figure 2-48.

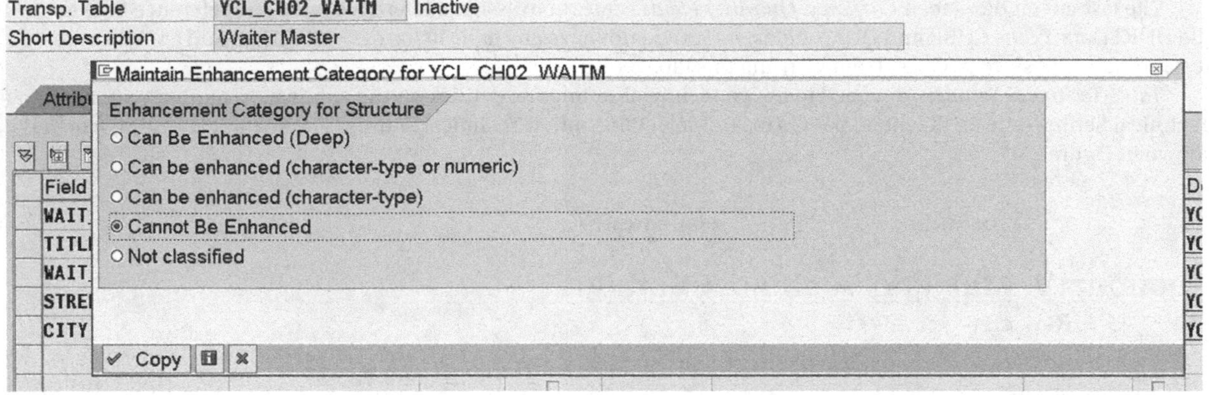

Figure 2-48. Create Table - Assign Enhancement Category

Select or click on the radio button Cannot Be Enhanced (since you do not want a provision for tables' enhancement). Click on the button Copy. This will assign the Enhancement Category to the table.

Perform the consistency check for the table, and press the button or press <Ctrl>+<F2> keys. If the consistency check is without errors, activate the table by clicking the button or pressing the keys <Ctrl>+<F3> keys. If the consistency check results in errors, investigate the errors, fix them, and then activate.

Database Metadata

When a DDIC table definition is activated for the very first time, the system will create the table definition in the database. The table definition then is ready for creation or insertion of data.

In a similar manner create the tables YCL_CH02_ITEMM, YCL_CH02_BILLH.

Creating Foreign Key Relationship - Table: YCL_CH02_BILLH, Field WAIT_NO

Create the table YCL_CH02_BILLH, fill in all the tabs, create Technical Settings; then assign Enhancement Category and save.

In the table YCL_CH02_BILLH, the field WAIT_NO is a foreign key field, and for this field, this is the foreign key table. So you need to establish a relationship between the tables YCL_CH02_WAITM and YCL_CH02_BILLH.

On the Fields tab, position the cursor on the field WAIT_NO (you want to establish the foreign key relationship for this field); then click on the Foreign Keys button (just above the data element column), and a pop-up dialog box appears as shown in Figure 2-49.

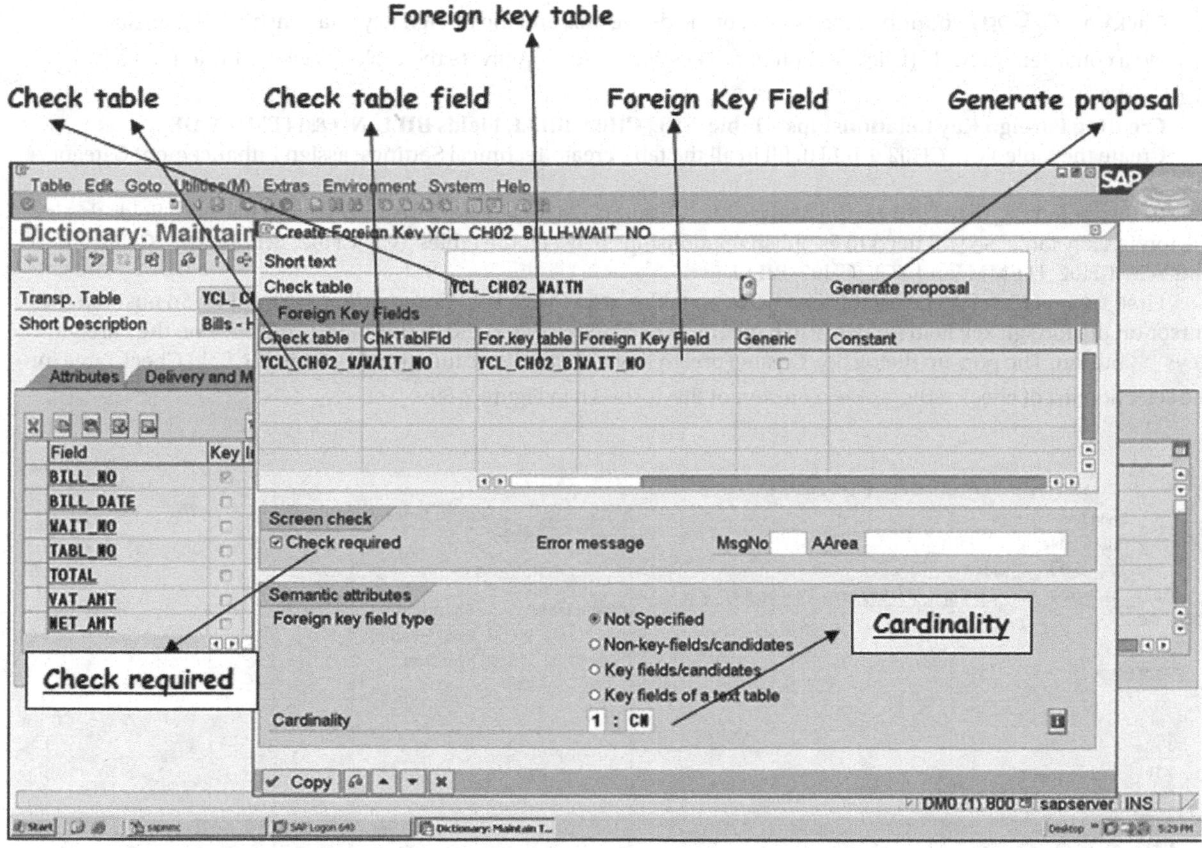

Figure 2-49. Create Table – Establish Foreign Key Relationship for field WAIT_NO

Fill in the following fields in this pop-up dialog box:

- Short text with meaningful text. For once this is optional. You are leaving it blank.
- In the Check table field, press function key F4. A list will appear with a single entry YCL_CH02_WAITM and the name of the check table with which you want to establish a relationship. This table YCL_CH02_WAITM is appearing on the basis of the common domain of field WAIT_NO in both the tables YCL_CH02_WAITM and YCL_CH02_BILLH (YCL_CH02_NUMC2).
- After the field Check table is filled with the value from the single entry of the selection list, click on the button Generate Proposal. This will fill up the columns Check table, Chk Tab Fld, For key table, and Foreign Key Field (i.e., which field/s in the check table relate with which field/s in the foreign key or secondary table).
- In the Screen check area, enable the check box Check required. This will prevent the creation of row/s in the foreign key table without a corresponding row in the check table. (No orphan rows are allowed in the foreign key table.)
- Next, fill in the cardinality – 1: CN. This means for every row in the check table, there can be any number of corresponding rows (including 0) in the foreign key table.

Click on ✔ Copy button at the bottom of the dialog box, and the foreign key relationship is established.

Do a consistency check. (Click button or keys <Ctrl>+<F2>)Activate the table. (Click button or keys <Ctrl>+<F3>)

Creating Foreign Key Relationships – Table: YCL_CH02_BILLI, Fields BILL_NO & ITEM_CODE

Create the table YCL_CH02_BILLHI, fill in all the tabs, create Technical Settings; assign Enhancement Category and save.

In the table YCL_CH02_BILLI, the fields BILL_NO and ITEM_CODE are foreign keys, and for these fields this is the foreign key table. So you need to establish relationships between the tables YCL_CH02_BILLH, YCL_CH02_BILLI and YCL_CH02_ITEMM, and YCL_CH02_BILLI.

First, let a relationship be established between tables YCL_CH02_BILLH and YCL_CH02_BILLI. So position the cursor on the foreign key field (which also happens to be a primary key field in this table), and click on the Foreign Keys button. The pop-up dialog box Create Foreign Key appears. Press function key F4 in the field Check table for the selection list of check table/s. A screen shot of this is shown in Figure 2-50.

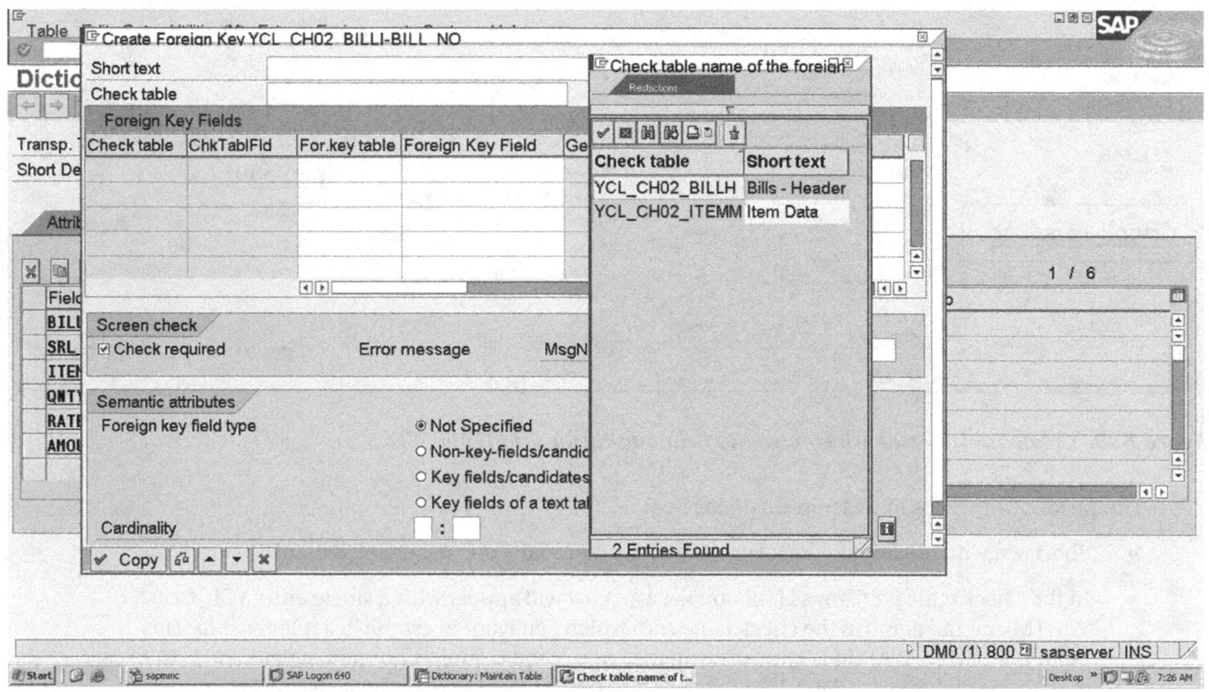

Figure 2-50. Create Table – Foreign Key Relationship for field BILL_NO, Check Table List

The system is proposing two check tables: YCL_CH02_BILLH and YCL_CH02_ITEMM. This is obviously erroneous.

The system is doing so because the key fields of these tables BILL_NO and ITEM_CODE are sharing the same domain (i.e., YCL_CH02_NUMC4. This has been done deliberately to highlight this issue. Key fields that have the same DDIC Data Type and length should not share the same domain.

For now, you know that you should select the table YCL_CH02_BILLH as the check table, as the foreign key field for which you are establishing relationship now is BILL_NO.

After selecting the check table *YCL_CH02_BILLH*, click on the button Generate Proposal.

The columns under Foreign Key Fields will be filled up.

Ensure the Check required check box is enabled (and to ensure no orphan rows are in the foreign key table).

Enter cardinality 1: CN. (One row in check table can have 0 to many rows in foreign key table.

The Create Foreign Key dialog box for the field BILL_NO with the required fields filled up is shown in the Figure 2-51. Clicking on the Copy button will establish the foreign key relationship for the field BILL_NO.

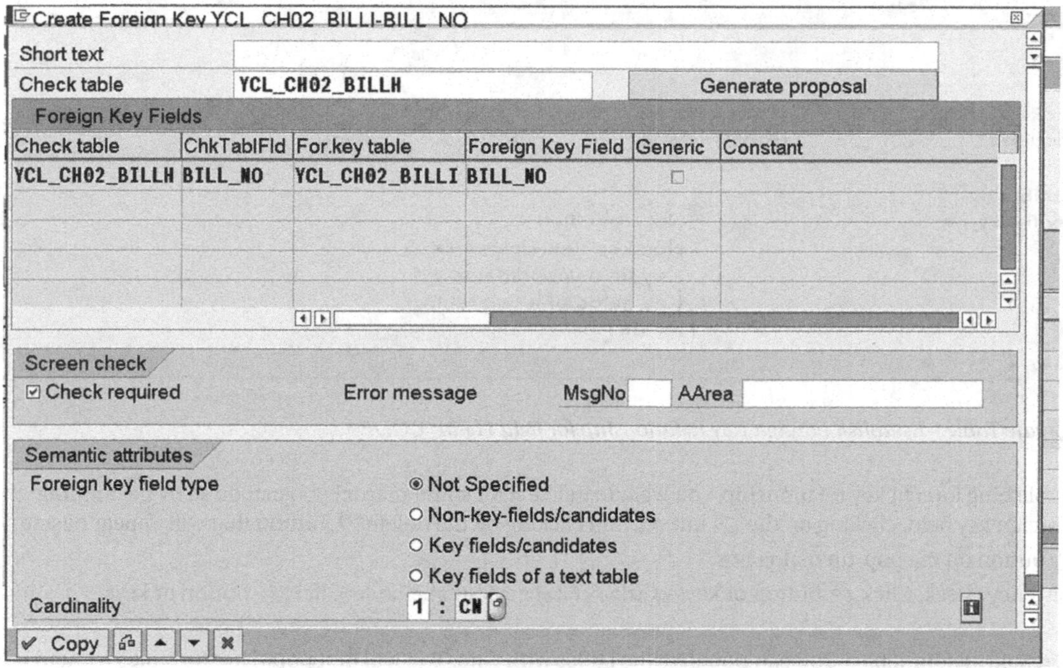

***Figure 2-51.** Create Table – Establish Foreign Key Relationship for field BILL_NO*

On similar lines position the cursor on the field ITEM_CODE and carry out the creation of foreign key relationship for the field ITEM_CODE. The filled-up dialog box for foreign key relationship of field ITEM_CODE is shown in Figure 2-52.

Clicking on the ✔ Copy button will establish the foreign key relationship for the field ITEM_CODE.

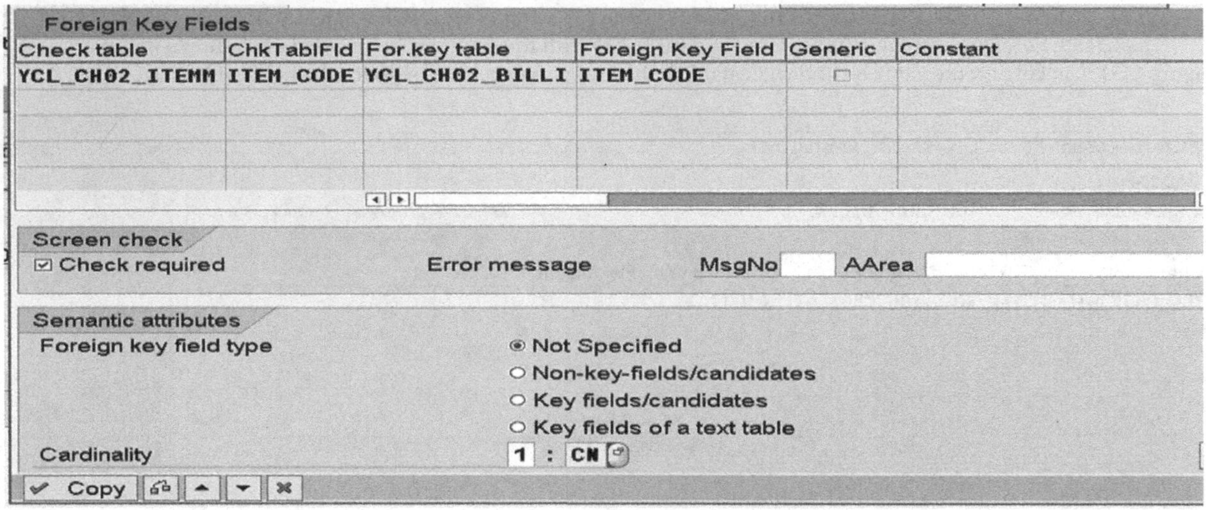

Figure 2-52. *Create Table - Establish Foreign Key Relationship for field ITEM_CODE*

If after establishing foreign key relationship, you want to delete it for some reason; you can do so by positioning the cursor on foreign key field, clicking on the button, and clicking on the delete button that will appear beside the Copy button on the pop-up dialog box.

Do a consistency check. Click button or keys <Ctrl>+<F2>) Activate the table. Click button or keys <Ctrl>+<F3>

You have created all four tables. You can populate the tables with data. You will first populate the tables without the foreign keys, so that when you create entries in the tables with foreign keys, data is available in the check tables.

Create Data in Tables

Data in Table YCL_CH02_WAITM

Let the data entry be started with the table YCL_CH02_WAITM. In the ABAP Dictionary Initial Screen, select the Database table radio button. Enter the table name (i.e., YCL_CH02_WAITM). Click on the Display button. The Dictionary: Maintain Table screen appears. From the menu bar Utilities, select Table Contents -> Create Entries path.

A screen shot of data creation for the table YCL_CH02_WAITM is shown in Figure 2-53.

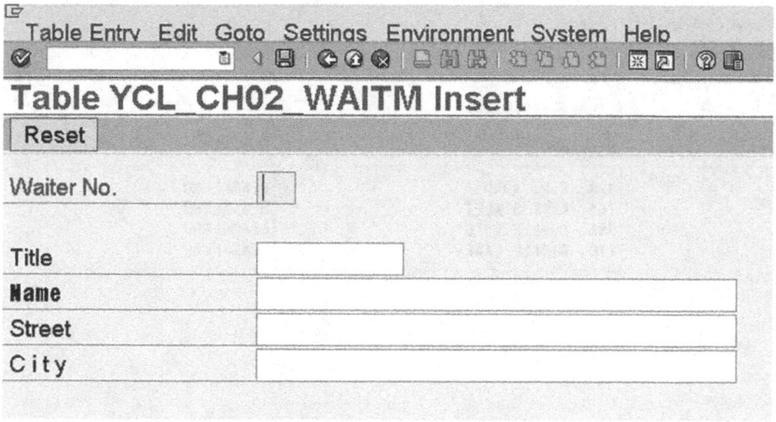

Figure 2-53. *Create Data in Table YCL_CH02_WAITM*

Notice that the data element labels are appearing with the fields. If this is not happening and you are getting table field names like WAIT_NO, etc., then click on the menu bar Settings ➤ User Parameters. A User Specific Settings dialog box pops up as shown in Figure 2-54. Ensure that the radio button Field Label is enabled (at the very bottom).

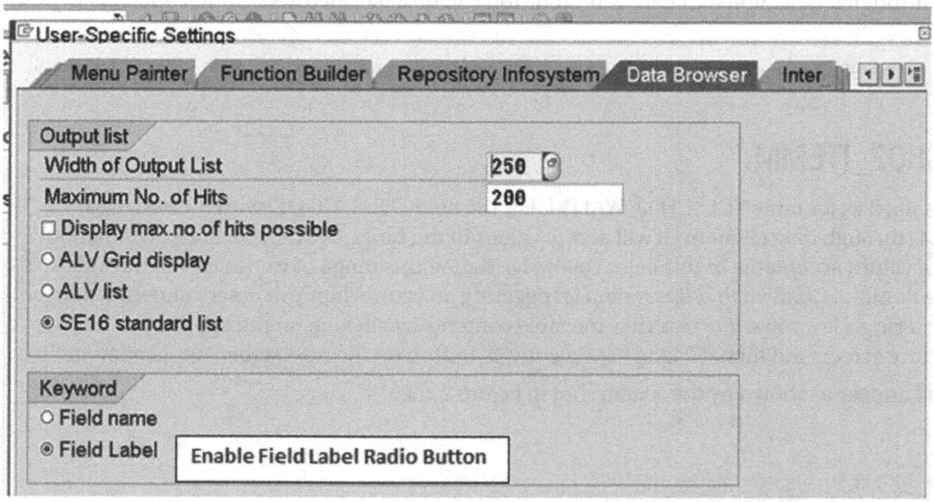

Figure 2-54. *User Specific Settings*

Enter data. There is a pop-up selection list available for the field TITLE. This list's source of data is the fixed values of the domain associated with the field TITLE. You can test that the system will not accept any other values than those of the selection list.

After entering all fields, press the save button on the standard tool bar. Press the Reset button on the application tool bar to clear the fields for the next row.

Enter three/four waiters' data. You can exit by pressing the button (back/previous screen) on the standard tool bar or by pressing function key F3. This brings you to the structure screen. You can see or view the table contents by clicking on the application tool bar button, then clicking the execute button on the next screen application tool bar. The contents of the table will appear as shown by screen shot in Figure 2-55.

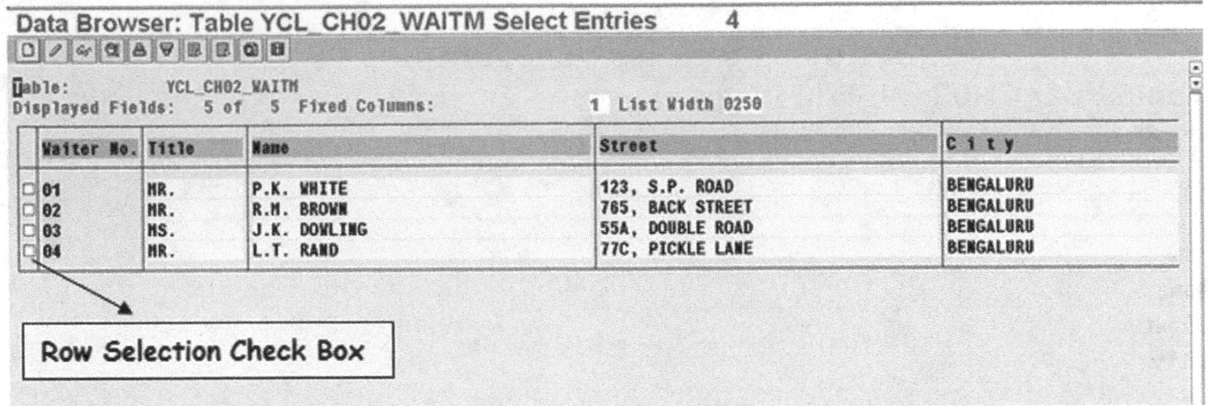
Data Browser: Table YCL_CH02_WAITM Select Entries 4

Table: YCL_CH02_WAITM
Displayed Fields: 5 of 5 Fixed Columns: 1 List Width 0250

Waiter No.	Title	Name	Street	City
01	MR.	P.K. WHITE	123, S.P. ROAD	BENGALURU
02	MR.	R.M. BROWN	765, BACK STREET	BENGALURU
03	MS.	J.K. DOWLING	55A, DOUBLE ROAD	BENGALURU
04	MR.	L.T. RAND	77C, PICKLE LANE	BENGALURU

Figure 2-55. *View and Manipulate Data in Table YCL_CH02_WAITM*

You can select rows by clicking on the Row Selection Check Boxes. You can then view the rows one row at a time: through application tool bar button, change contents one row at a time; through application tool bar button, delete selected rows by clicking on the menu bar Table Entry and using Delete options. You can create new rows (Waiters) by clicking on the application toolbar button.

You can select all rows through application tool bar button. You can deselect all rows through application toolbar button.

If you want to navigate to the SE11 opening screen, then press button three times.

Data in Table YCL_CH02_ITEMM

The same procedure is to be used as for table YCL_CH02_WAITM. For the field ITEM_CODE, with the assigned domain YCL_CH02_NUMC4 (through data element) it will accept values in the range 0001-5000. Pressing function key F4 will show the range of values acceptable in this field. You had assigned this range of values in the Intervals area of the Value Rang' tab of the domain. Confirm that the system is triggering an error when you enter values outside the range of 0001-5000. After entering a few rows, you can view the table contents by clicking on the application tool bar button in the table structure screen and then clicking the execute button on the next screen application toolbar. The contents of the table will appear as shown by the screen shot in Figure 2-56.

Table Entry Edit Goto Settings Utilities(M) Environment System Help

Data Browser: Table YCL_CH02_ITEMM Select Entries 4

Table: YCL_CH02_ITEMM
Displayed Fields: 3 of 3 Fixed Columns: 1 List Width 0250

Item Code	Item Desc	Rate
0005	Vegetarian Supreme Medium	275.00
0010	Barbeque Chicken Regular	175.00
0015	Barbeque Chicken Medium	320.00
1005	Special Lemonade	100.00

Figure 2-56. *View and Manipulate Data in Table YCL_CH02_ITEMM*

The screen shows the four created rows. This data can be manipulated through the display, change, create, etc., buttons on the application toolbar.

Data in Table YCL_CH02_BILLH

Let the data be created in this table by a different procedure. If an end user (nondeveloper) was entering data into a table, he would not have access to the DDIC object maintenance screens. Such users can enter data into tables through transaction code SE16. So enter /NSE16 in the command box and press the <Enter>/ button. The screen shot of SE16 Data Browser: Initial Screen is shown in Figure 2-57.

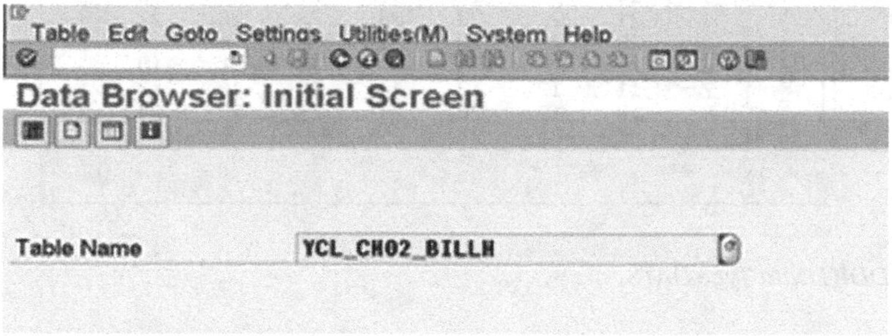

Figure 2-57. *SE16/Data browser: Initial Screen - Data in Table YCL_CH02_BILLH*

The screen prompts for the table name. The table name YCL_CH02_BILLH has been entered. Press the application toolbar button to create entries. The screen shot of the data entry screen is shown in Figure 2-58.

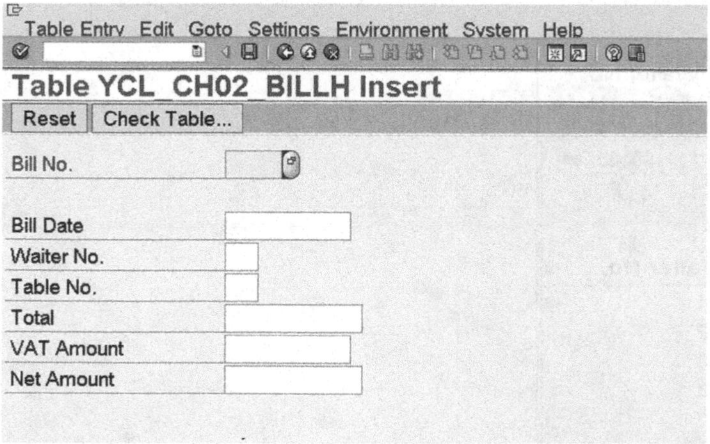

Figure 2-58. *Create Data in Table YCL_CH02_BILLH [SE16]*

The field BILL_NO was assigned the domain YCL_CH02_NUMC4. It will accept values in the range 0001-5000. For the field BILL_DATE, which is DDIC Data Type DATS, pressing function key F4 pops up a calendar, and you can assign a date from this calendar. You get this facility for DDIC Data Type DATS. This is shown in Figure 2-59.

Table YCL_CH02_BILLH Insert

Reset | Check Table...

Bill No.	1
Bill Date	01.01.2013
Waiter No.	01
Table No.	01
Total	1,000.00
VAT Amount	125.00
Net Amount	1,125.00

Calendar

01.01.2013

	WN	Mo	Tu	We	Th	Fr	Sa	Su
2012/11	45	5	6	7	8	9	10	11
	46	12	13	14	15	16	17	18
	47	19	20	21	22	23	24	25
	48	26	27	28	29	30	1	2
2012/12	49	3	4	5	6	7	8	9
	50	10	11	12	13	14	15	16
	51	17	18	19	20	21	22	23
	52	24	25	26	27	28	29	30
2013/1	1	31	1	2	3	4	5	6
	2	7	8				12	13
	3	14	15				19	20
	4	21	22	23	24	25	26	27
	5	28	29	30	31	1	2	3
2013/2	6	4	5	6	7	8	9	10
	7	11	12	13	14	15	16	17
	8	18	19	20	21	22	23	24

Tuesday, January 01, 2013

Figure 2-59. *Calendar for Date Selection - DDIC Data Type DATS*

If you press function key F4 in the foreign key field WAIT_NO, a pop-up list appears displaying the primary key values from the corresponding check table (YCL_CH02_WAITM). This is shown in Figure 2-60. You can make a selection from this list. This facility is available for any foreign key field on the screen. The pop-up list with primary key values is a rudimentary selection list. You would have preferred, in the present context, for the name of the waiter to appear in the selection list. This will be possible through the DDIC object Search Help. If you enter a value in the field WAIT_NO other than the values in the pop-up list (values in the check table), an error condition is triggered. This is so because you had enabled in the foreign key dialog box the check box Check required.

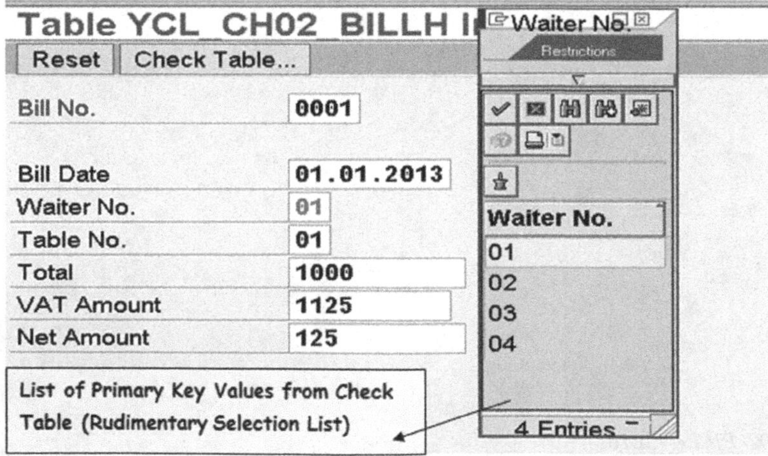

Figure 2-60. *Pop-up List of Primary Key Values for Foreign Key Fields*

After entering data into all the fields, save. Press the Reset button to clear fields. Create a few rows. When you are finished, click the button (back/previous screen) on the standard tool bar or press function key F3 to return to the SE16 opening screen.

Click the application toolbar button to review the entered data. A screen shot of the entered data is shown in Figure 2-61.

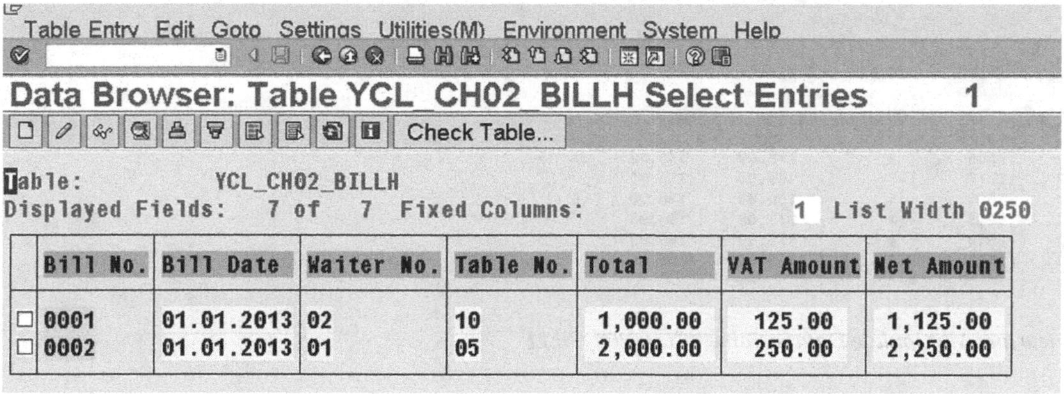

Table Entry Edit Goto Settings Utilities(M) Environment System Help

Data Browser: Table YCL_CH02_BILLH Select Entries 1

Check Table...

Table: YCL_CH02_BILLH
Displayed Fields: 7 of 7 Fixed Columns: 1 List Width 0250

Bill No.	Bill Date	Waiter No.	Table No.	Total	VAT Amount	Net Amount
0001	01.01.2013	02	10	1,000.00	125.00	1,125.00
0002	01.01.2013	01	05	2,000.00	250.00	2,250.00

Figure 2-61. *View and Manipulate Data in Table YCL_CH02_BILLH*

Data in Table YCL_CH02_BILLI

Create data in this table through transaction code SE16.

The screen prompts for the table name. Enter the table name YCL_CH02_BILLI. Press application tool bar button to create entries. The screen shot of data entry screen is shown in Figure 2-62.

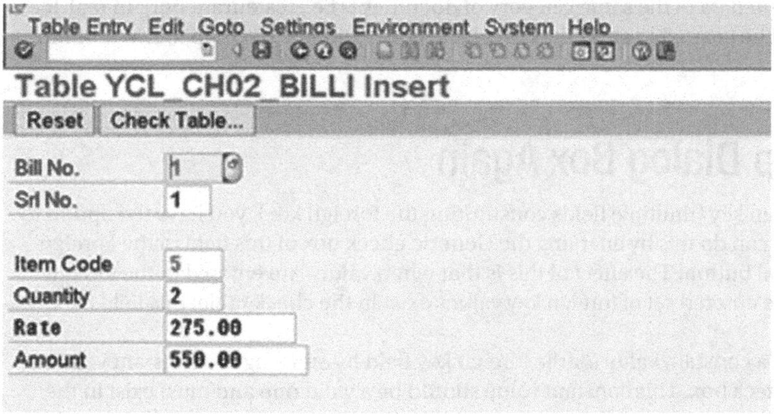

Table Entry Edit Goto Settings Environment System Help

Table YCL_CH02_BILLI Insert

Reset Check Table...

Bill No.	1
Srl No.	1
Item Code	5
Quantity	2
Rate	275.00
Amount	550.00

Figure 2-62. *Create Data in Table YCL_CH02_BILLI [SE16]*

After entering data into all the fields, save. Press the Reset button to clear fields. If you enter BILL_NO and ITEM_CODE in the foreign key fields a value other than the values in the pop-up list (values in the check tables), an error condition is triggered. Create a few rows. When you are finished, click the button (back/previous screen) on the standard tool bar or press function key F3 to return to the SE16 opening screen.

Click the application toolbar button to review the entered data. A screen shot of the entered data is shown in Figure 2-63.

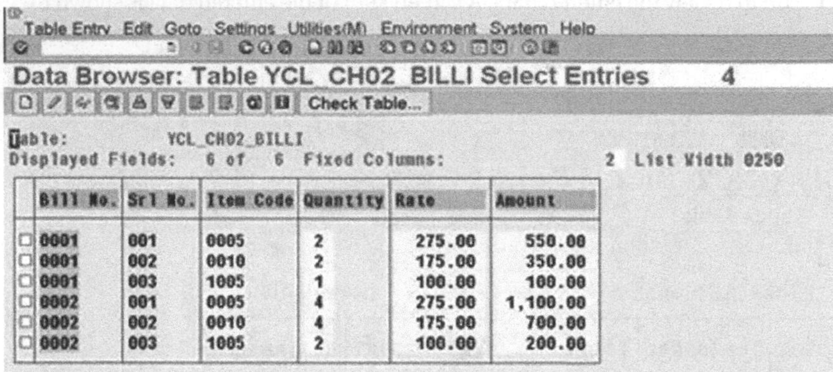

Bill No.	Srl No.	Item Code	Quantity	Rate	Amount
0001	001	0005	2	275.00	550.00
0001	002	0010	2	175.00	350.00
0001	003	1005	1	100.00	100.00
0002	001	0005	4	275.00	1,100.00
0002	002	0010	4	175.00	700.00
0002	003	1005	2	100.00	200.00

Figure 2-63. *View and Manipulate Data in Table YCL_CH02_BILLI*

There are two foreign key fields in the table YCL_CH02_BILLI (i.e., BILLI_NO and ITEM_CODE. In each of these fields, when you press function key F4, a pop-up list will appear (rudimentary selection list) displaying the primary key field from the respective check tables. When you make a selection, the primary key value from the list is returned to the foreign key field on the screen.

In the case of the field BILL_NO, it would be desirable to have a selection list that displays BILL_NO, BILL_DATE, WAIT_NO, or TABL_NO instead of just the BILL_NO.

And in the case of the field ITEM_CODE, it would desirable to have a selection list that not only displays ITEM_CODE, ITEM_DESC, and RATE, but assigns the value of RATE field from the list of the selected ITEM_CODE to the screen field. This will be implemented when the DDIC object search help in the next chapter (Chapter 3) is covered.

You are now entering the data for the two tables YCL_CH02_BILLH and YCL_CH02_BILLi separately through separate dialog boxes. The two tables contain data of the same category of document (i.e., restaurant bill). In real-life scenarios, a complex ABAP program would be created to enter data of business documents that map to two or more RDBMS tables.

Foreign Key Relationship Dialog Box Again

When you establish a field as part of a foreign key (multiple fields constituting the foreign key), you have the option to omit field/s from the check procedure. You can do this by enabling the Generic check box of this field in the Foreign Key Fields area under the Generate proposal button. The effect of this is that when values are entered in the foreign key fields, a check is performed whether the entered set of foreign key values exist in the check table; this field is omitted in the check.

Similarly, you have the option to enter a constant value for the foreign key field by entering the constant value in the field Constant, next to the Generic check box. This constant value should be a valid one and must exist in the check table

In the Foreign Key relationship dialog box Semantic attributes area, (at the bottom), there are the four radio buttons:

- **Not Specified**
- **Non-key-fields/candidates** **(The foreign key fields are not part of the primary key in the current table)**
- **Key-fields/candidates** **(The foreign key fields are part of the primary key in the current table)**
- **Key fields of a text table** **(If the primary key of the current table differs from the primary key of the Check table only in terms of an additional language code field, this radio button needs to be enabled)**

The enabling of one of these radio buttons along with the cardinality serves documentary purposes only except in two contexts:

1. In a text table, for the code field, the radio button Key fields of a text table should be enabled. This is one indication to the system that this is a text table apart from the DDIC Data Type LANG field preceding the code field and forming part of the primary key.
2. In case of the table being used in maintenance, help view, the information of cardinality and the semantic attributes is used by the system.

A table with a generic key field could be located. A table with a constant key field was not able to be located. The above descriptions are in the screen shot (Figure 2-64).

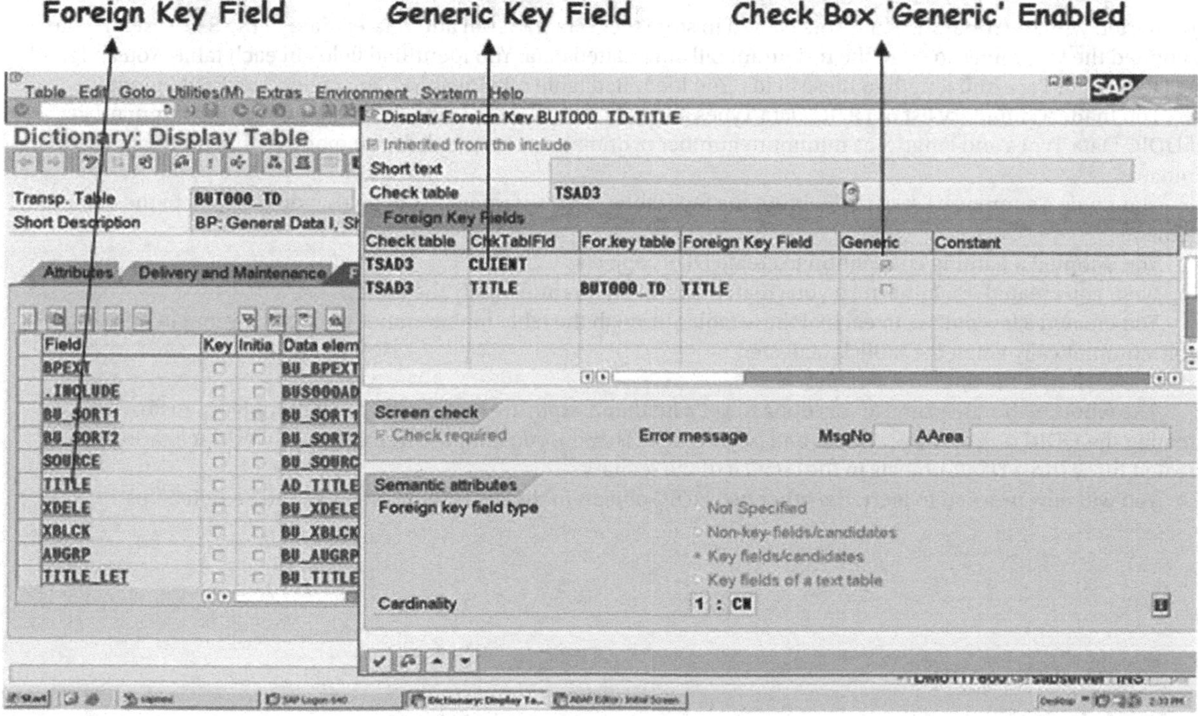

Figure 2-64. *Table: 'BUT000_TD' with Generic Key Field 'CLIENT'*

Text Tables

Short texts (text length <= 255 characters) are required to be maintained in the SAP functional modules tables and related tables. Some very common instances: texts of currency names (table TCURT), texts of country names, (table T005T), texts of state/province/region names (table T005U), material descriptions (table MAKT), and so on. These tables storing texts are called text tables. The texts have to be maintained in multiple languages. Thus the language code has to be a part of the primary key of the text tables. The language code field is assigned the DDIC Data Type LANG. Most of the text tables have the language code field of Data Type LANG named as SPRAS. And most of the text table names end with the letter T.

These text tables are foreign key tables to the respective check tables where the codes are stored: currency codes, country codes, state/province/region codes, material codes, etc. These code fields are foreign key fields as well as part of the primary key in the text tables. The primary key fields in the text tables are in the order MANDT, <language code field>, and <code field1> [<code field2>.]. There can be more than one code field like in table T005U (LAND1 & BLAND). Only client dependent tables are being considered.

You can confirm this with the tables mentioned earlier: TCURT, T005T, T005U, and MAKT.

You can confirm one other thing. When you browse the data of the check table of these text tables: TCURC/T005/T005S/MARA (either in SE11 or SE16), the texts or descriptions appear in the logged-in language automatically.

You could face a problem with table T005. The texts might not appear. If this is so, in the restrictive or filter dialog box preceding the data browser window, enter a value >=1000 in the field Width of Output List above the field Maximum No. of Hits. By default the values in these two fields is 250 and 200 respectively. By default the width of output is 250 columns, and the maximum number of rows output is 200. The number of fields in the table T005 are many - also (65) field titles are very long, hence you need the output width to be >=1000 columns.

Recapitulation: Domains, Data Elements, and Tables

You started with the restaurant bill. You wanted to store the restaurant bill and related data in the SAP system. You identified the four tables to store the restaurant bill and related data. You identified fields in each table. You assigned the DDIC Data Type and length to these fields. You identified table relationships. You created an ER diagram.

You made a summary list of DDIC Data Types and lengths in the four tables. You identified this summary list of DDIC Data Types and lengths as minimum number of domains to be created. You mapped this summary list to domains.

You made a summary list of the fields in the four tables. This summary list of fields, you mapped to the data elements.

You adopted a naming convention to create DDIC objects.

First, you created domains; next you created data elements and finally the tables.

You created a few entries in each of these tables through the table maintenance dialog box generated for each table automatically when the table is activated.

You reviewed the data in the tables.

The whole elaborate exercise was done to get a firsthand exposure to these three DDIC objects. Instead of creating the DDIC objects in a random and hypothetical fashion, you adopted a simple real-world scenario and created these three DDIC objects in the context of the scenario.

You will now proceed to learn the other two DDIC objects in the next chapter: Views and Search helps.

CHAPTER 3

ABAP Dictionary/Data Dictionary/DDIC – 2

Creation of custom DDIC objects continues in this chapter. You will create DDIC objects: views and search helps. You will create views and search helps using custom tables as well as the SAP delivered tables. The search helps using the SAP delivered tables are tested using ABAP programs. ABAP programming is introduced in this chapter on a preview basis.

DDIC Objects Views

In the DDIC, you can create the following four types of views:

1. Database
2. Projection
3. Maintenance
4. Help

In this chapter, the view types 1and 2 will be created and demonstrated; the view type 3 will be described. View type 4 will be covered in Chapter 7 entitled Modularization.

Database Views

- A database view can consist of one or more tables. Mostly it is multiple tables.
- Database views consisting of multiple tables implement an inner join. That is, when you consider two tables at a time, a row has to exist in both the tables for it to appear in the result. The view is a cross product of the two tables. The joining condition is generally with the primary key fields in one table and foreign key fields in the other table, but it need not be so. A join condition can be established on non-key fields as well.

If you consider the scenario of creating a database view with your custom tables YCL_CH02_WAITM and YCL_CH02_BILLH, and the field WAIT_NO joining the two tables, you will get a result where only the waiters have bills. Of course, a waiter having multiple bills will appear that many times in the result (cross product). The waiters having no bills will not appear in the result. Your first hands-on exercise will implement this scenario.

- If the database view consists of multiple tables, it is designated as a read-only view, and the participating tables of database view cannot be updated (insert, update, delete) through the view. If the database view consists of a single table, this table can be updated (insert, update, delete) through the view.
- When you activate a DDIC database view for the first time, a view is created in the database metadata.
- A database view can consist of only transparent tables.
- The database view can be used in the Open SQL SELECT statement just like a table.
- A database view (in fact, all the four types of views) can be referred to declare data in an ABAP program.
- With the plethora of tables in the SAP environment, data required in an ABAP program is spread across many tables. An efficient way of retrieving this data spread across many tables is to create database view/s and retrieve data with simple SELECT statements instead of using complex SELECT statements implementing the inner joins - a simple process of data gathering. The database view also serves the purpose of reusability. A single database view could be used in multiple ABAP programs.
- A database view just like the tables has technical settings. So buffering can be set up if desired.
- Database view retrieval will perform faster than the retrieval with individual tables.

Database Views – Inner Join

It is better to explain the inner join (that a database view uses) with a simple example involving your custom tables:-

Suppose the data in the table YCL_CH02_WAITM is as follows: (5 rows)

```
WAIT_NO ...
01...
02  ...
03
04
05
```

The data in the table YCL_CH02_BILLH is as follows (10 rows)

WAIT_NO	BILL_NO	WAIT_NO	BILL_NO
02	1234	02	1239
04	1235	05	1240
05	1236	02	1241
04	1237	05	1242
04	1238	04	1243

You perform an inner join on the two tables using the field WAIT_NO. This field is a primary key in YCL_CH02_WAITM and a foreign key in the table YCL_CH02_BILLH. The result of the inner join will be to drop the WAIT_NO values 01 and 03 originating from table YCL_CH02_WAITM in the result as they do not have any corresponding row in the table YCL_CH02_BILLH. The 10 rows from the table YCL_CH02_BILLH will appear in the result. Waiters having no bills will not appear in the result.

This was hypothetical data contrived for explanation. The tables do not contain this data.

Now let a database view be created with these very tables in DDIC. The interface of the database view creation is peculiar and has to be understood.

Create Database View with Tables YCL_CH02_WAITM and YCL_CH02_BILLH

In the SE11 opening screen, select the radio button View. Enter the name of the view to be crested. (Name space, like tables, are 16 characters.) Let the name of the database view be YCL_CH03_WBH. Click on the Create button or press function key F5. The system will prompt for the view type to be created as shown in Figure 3-1.

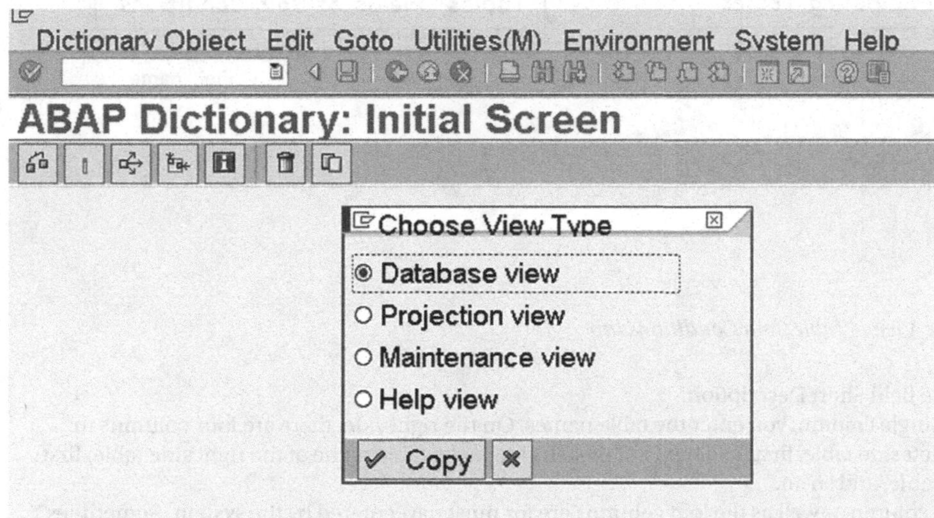

Figure 3-1. *Create Database View - Choose View Type*

Select the database view, which is also the default, and press the ✔ Copy button. The screen to create database view, as shown in Figure 3-2, appears.

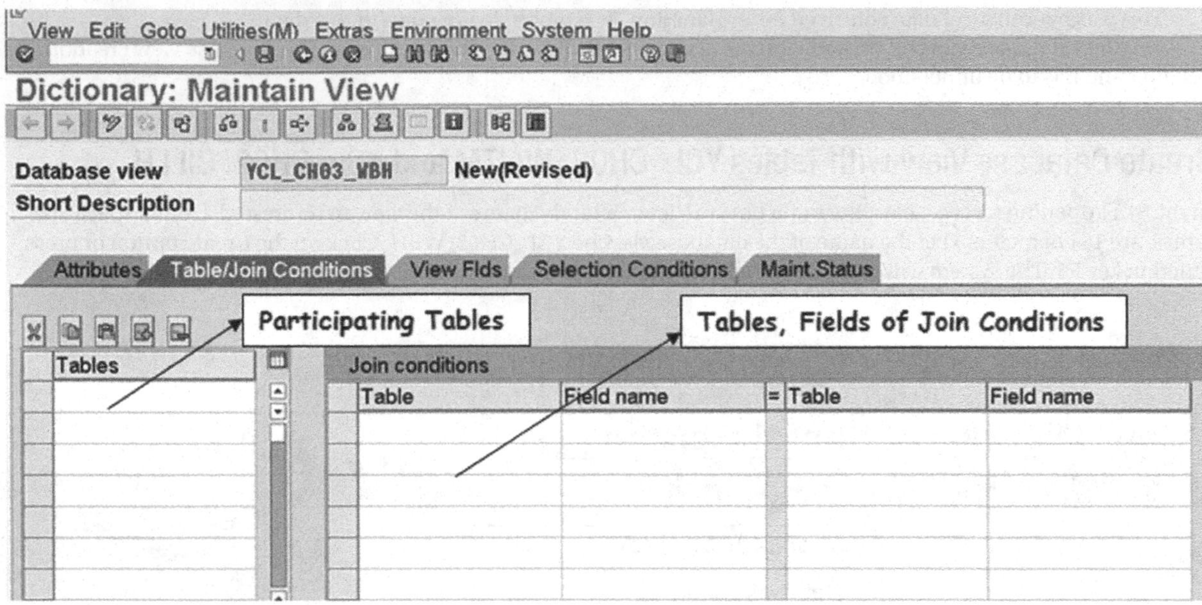

Figure 3-2. *Create Database View – Table/Join Conditions tab*

Enter suitable text in the field Short Description.

On the left side, in the single column, you enter the table names. On the right side, there are four columns to enter the table name of the left side table, first field name of the left side table; table name of the right side table, first field name of the right side table, and so on.

The entries in the table column as well as the join columns are for most part entered by the system. Sometimes they are entered manually.

In the present scenario the entries should look like this:

```
YCL_CH02_BILLH          YCL_CH02_WAITM       WAIT_NO         YCL_CH02_BILLH         WAIT_NO
```

YCL_CH02_WAITM The present exercise is of a very simple scenario: only two tables; only one field in the join condition. A real-world scenario would consist of more than two tables and more than one field in a join condition. In such situations, it is always better to define a hierarchy. Of course, in a hierarchy, at a time you are tackling two tables for an inner join condition. In an inner join condition of two tables, it is immaterial which table appears on the left side of join condition and which table appears on the right side. But it is a good practice to follow the RDBMS hierarchy where possible.

In the present hands-on exercise, the table YCL_CH02_WAITM is the check table, and the table YCL_CH02_BILLH is the foreign key table. So you will have the table YCL_CH02_WAITM on the left side of the join condition and the table YCL_CH02_BILLH on the right side of the join condition.

There are five tabs including the Attributes tab, which is maintained by the system. You are on the Table/Join Conditions tab. You need to enter the participating tables and the join conditions.

When you want the join condition to be generated by the system, the procedure is to enter the name of the foreign key table under the column Table, and click on the button Relationships, which is at the bottom. The system will extract the check table/s from the foreign key relationship you defined when creating the table definitions and list out these with a prompt as shown in Figure 3-3.

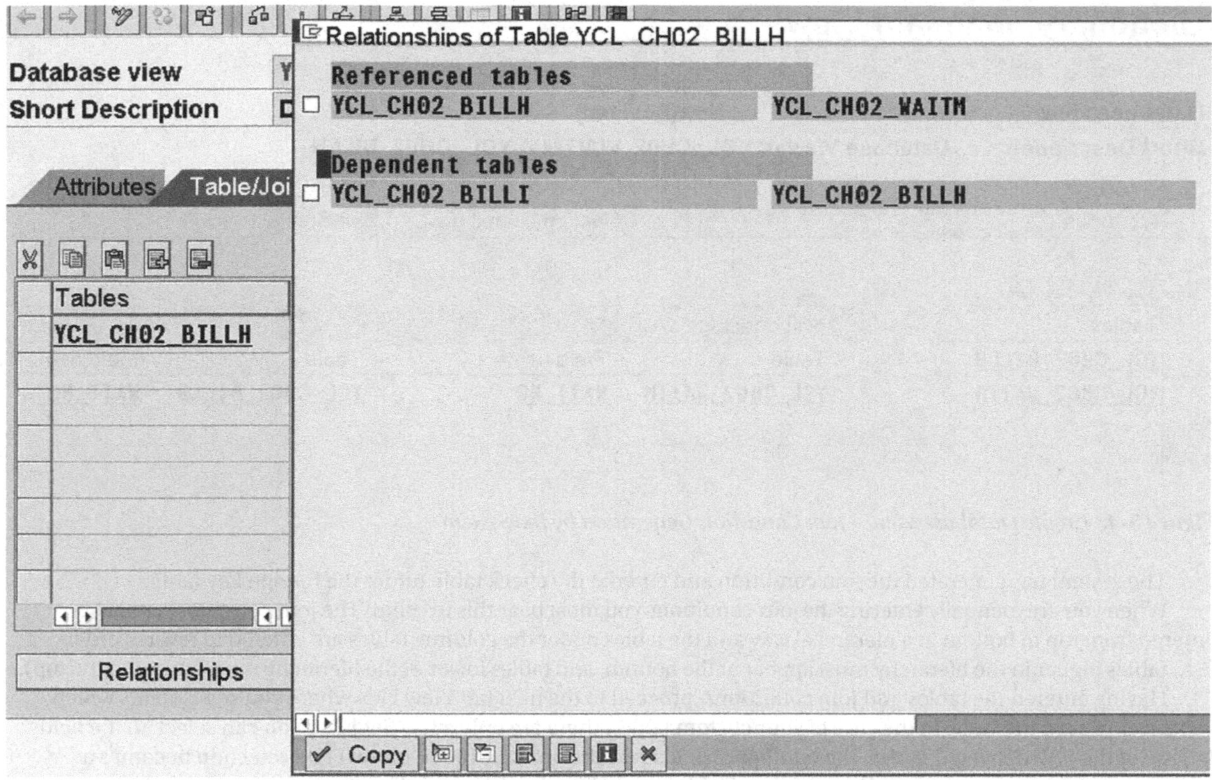

Figure 3-3. *Create Database View – Relationships of Table YCL_CH02_BILLH*

There is one entry under Referenced tables. In this dialog box, the table on the left (YCL_CH02_BILLH) is the foreign key table, and the table on the right is the check table (YCL_CH02_WAITM).

Under the Dependent tables, there is one entry. The table on the left again is the foreign key table (YCL_CH02_BILLI), and the table on the right is the check table (YCL_CH02_BILLH).

The entries under the heading Referenced tables are of interest to you. The table YCL_CH02_BILLH you entered under the column Tables of the Tables/Join Conditions tab is a foreign key table, and in clicking the button Relationships, you are seeking the check table, which is the table YCL_CH02_WAITM. Enable the check box of this row and press the ✔ Copy button. The screen will look like that in Figure 3-4.

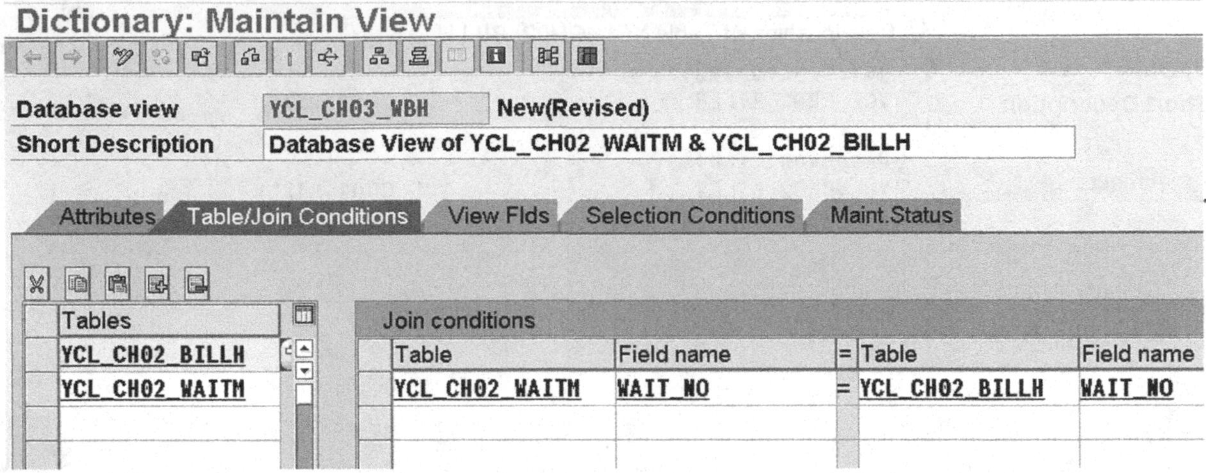

Figure 3-4. Create Database View – Join Condition Generation by the System

The system has generated the join condition and entered the check table under the foreign key table.

When you are manually entering the join conditions you must bear this in mind: The join conditions must be entered from top to bottom in a hierarchal way and the tables under the column Tables are entered in reverse order (i.e., tables higher in the hierarchy must appear at the bottom, and tables lower in the hierarchy must appear at the top).

Having entered the tables and join conditions, proceed to the next tab View Flds where you select fields which should appear in the view. In the case of your custom tables, there are only a few fields, so you can select all the fields. In case of the SAP delivered tables, the number of fields is of the order of 100 or more. Field selection becomes a necessary exercise; you cannot select all fields. Fields should be selected depending on the scenario requirements.

The View Flds tab screen is shown in Figure 3-5.

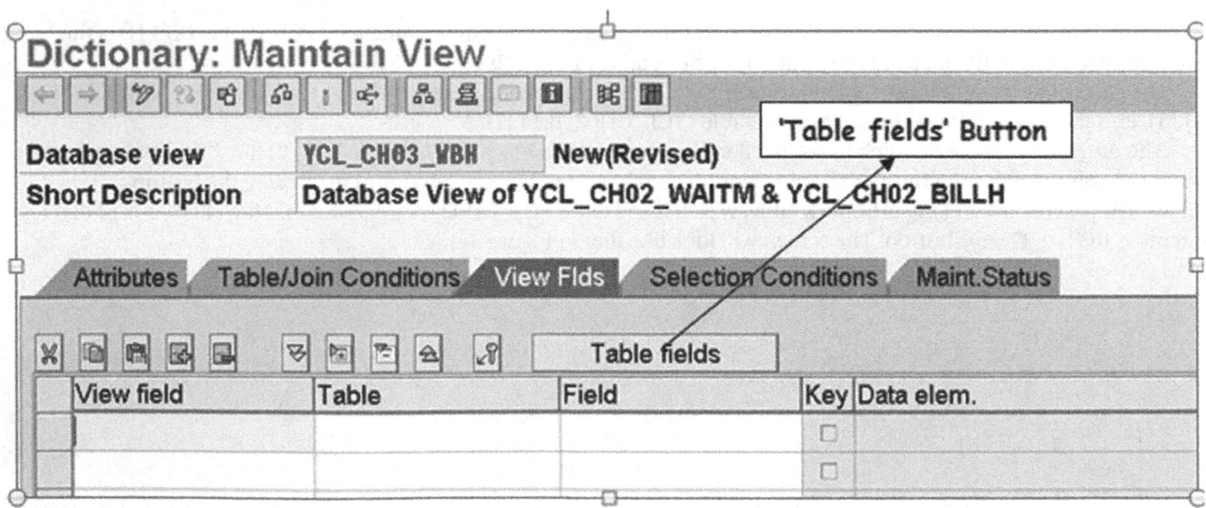

Figure 3-5. Create Database View – View Flds tab

You can manually fill in the fields, but a better way is to select them from lists. The fields' names in the view can be different from their corresponding names in the tables, but it is better to retain field names of tables in the view. To select fields, click on the Table fields button. A pop-up dialog box as shown in Figure 3-6 appears.

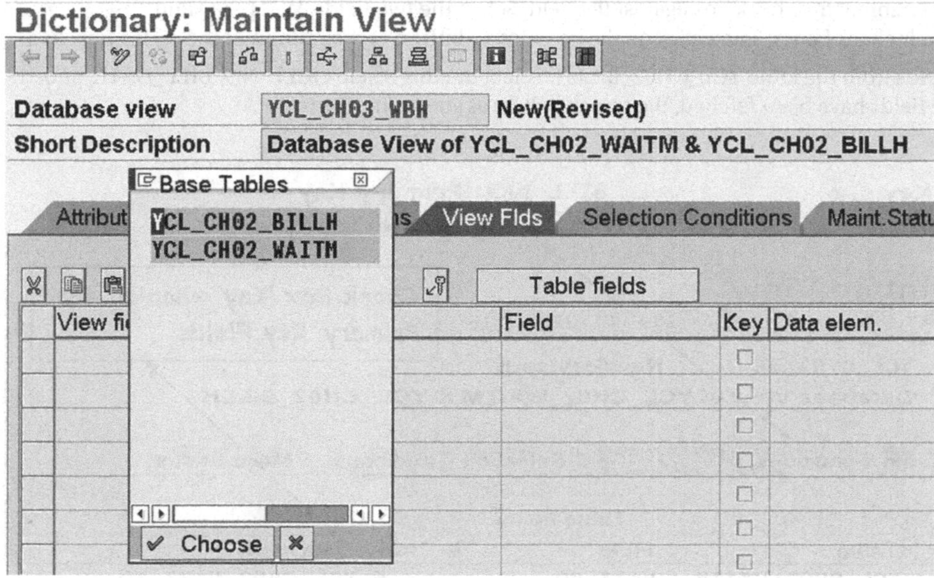

Figure 3-6. *Create Database View – Choose Table for Field Selection*

You have to select the table from which to make field selections. Proceed in a hierarchal manner. You select YCL_CH02_WAITM first. So either double-click on that table name or position the cursor on the table name and click on the Choose button. The field selection screen as shown in Figure 3-7 appears.

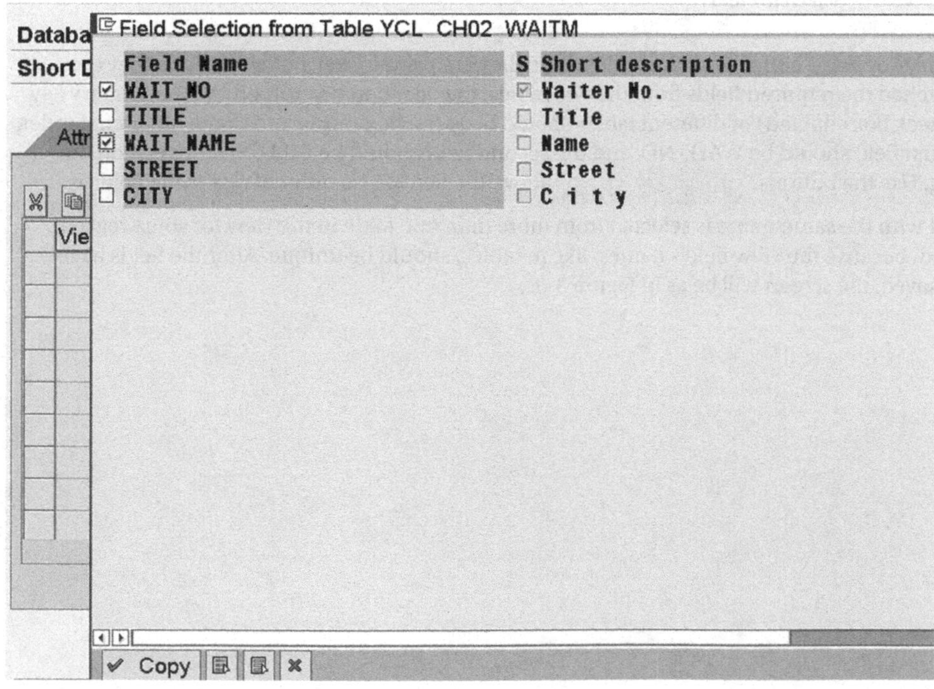

Figure 3-7. *Create Database View – Field Selection from Table YCL_CH02_WAITM*

You can select fields by enabling the check box against the field. Select the two fields, WAIT_NO and WAIT_NAME by enabling their check boxes. Then click on the ✔ Copy button at the bottom of the dialog box. In a similar manner select the fields from the table YCL_CH02_BILLH. Select the three fields BILL_NO, BILL_DATE, and NET_AMT. After these three fields have been fetched, the screen will be as shown in Figure 3-8.

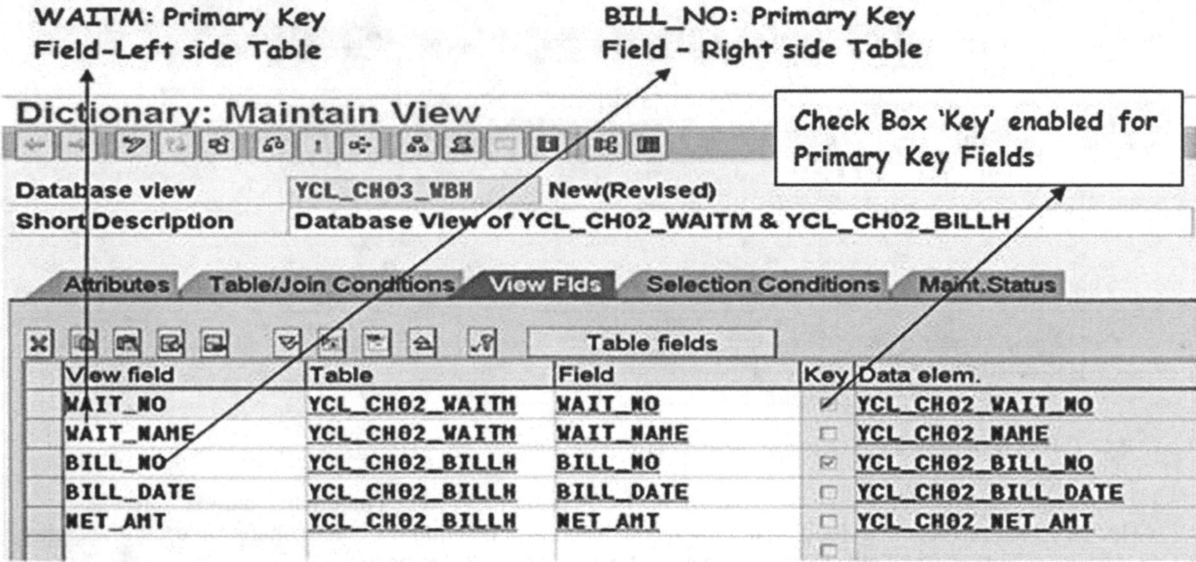

Figure 3-8. *Create Database View – Selected Fields*

Always select the primary key fields either from the table where they are primary key fields or where they are foreign key fields. Having fetched the required fields from the two tables, they need to be ordered. All the primary key fields (fields with the Key check box enabled) of different tables should be at the beginning and in the hierarchal order. In the present context, the first field should be WAIT_NO, and the second field should be BILL_NO. Reposition the fields by cutting and pasting. Use the buttons: above the fields. The order of rest of the fields is immaterial. If the same field with the same name is selected from more than one table in the view for some reason, the fields should be renamed, because the view field's names, like in tables, should be unique. After the fields have been ordered and the view saved, the screen will be as in Figure 3-9.

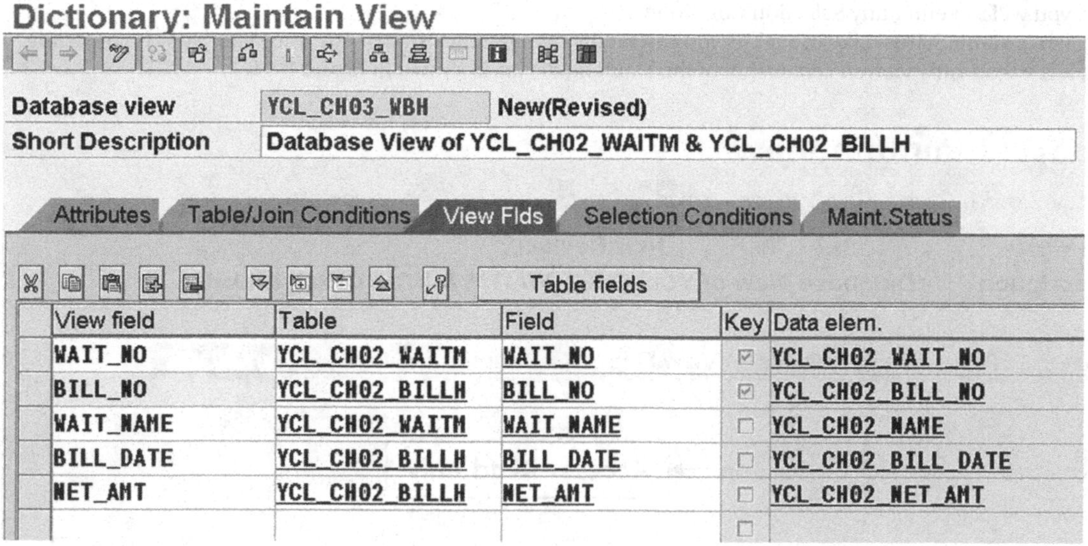

Dictionary: Maintain View

Database view: YCL_CH03_WBH New(Revised)
Short Description: Database View of YCL_CH02_WAITM & YCL_CH02_BILLH

Attributes | Table/Join Conditions | View Flds | Selection Conditions | Maint.Status

Table fields

View field	Table	Field	Key	Data elem.
WAIT_NO	YCL_CH02_WAITM	WAIT_NO	☑	YCL_CH02_WAIT_NO
BILL_NO	YCL_CH02_BILLH	BILL_NO	☑	YCL_CH02_BILL_NO
WAIT_NAME	YCL_CH02_WAITM	WAIT_NAME	☐	YCL_CH02_NAME
BILL_DATE	YCL_CH02_BILLH	BILL_DATE	☐	YCL_CH02_BILL_DATE
NET_AMT	YCL_CH02_BILLH	NET_AMT	☐	YCL_CH02_NET_AMT

Figure 3-9. *Create Database View – Primary Key Fields ordered hierarchically*

Click the Selection Conditions tab of the view. You can enter simple, compound (with logical operators AND/OR) WHERE conditions to filter data. One constraint is that the value on the right side of the WHERE condition has to be a literal (No run-time decision). A screen shot of the Selection Conditions tab appears in Figure 3-10.

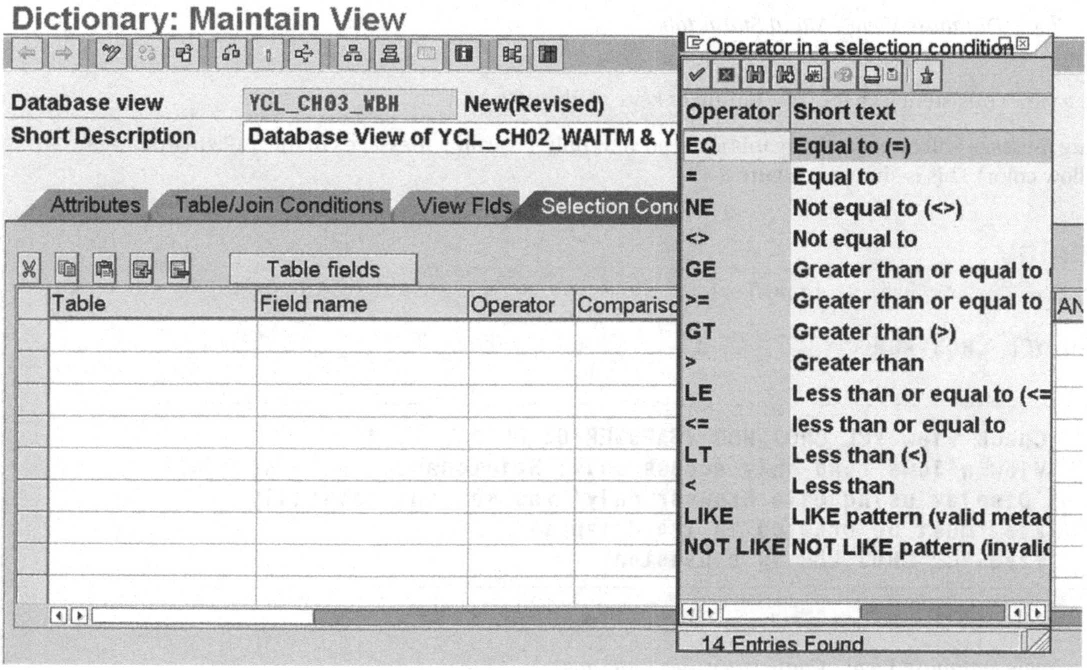

Dictionary: Maintain View

Database view: YCL_CH03_WBH New(Revised)
Short Description: Database View of YCL_CH02_WAITM & Y

Attributes | Table/Join Conditions | View Flds | Selection Conc

Table fields

Table	Field name	Operator	Compariso

Operator in a selection condition

Operator	Short text
EQ	Equal to (=)
=	Equal to
NE	Not equal to (<>)
<>	Not equal to
GE	Greater than or equal to
>=	Greater than or equal to
GT	Greater than (>)
>	Greater than
LE	Less than or equal to (<=
<=	less than or equal to
LT	Less than (<)
<	Less than
LIKE	LIKE pattern (valid metac
NOT LIKE	NOT LIKE pattern (invalic

14 Entries Found

Figure 3-10. *Create Database View – Selection Conditions tab*

For now, you will not enter any Selection Condition.

The next tab is Maint.Status. Like in a table, you can set the maintenance status. But since your view is consisting of two tables, it is a read-only view. A screenshot of the Maint.Status tab is shown in Figure 3-11.

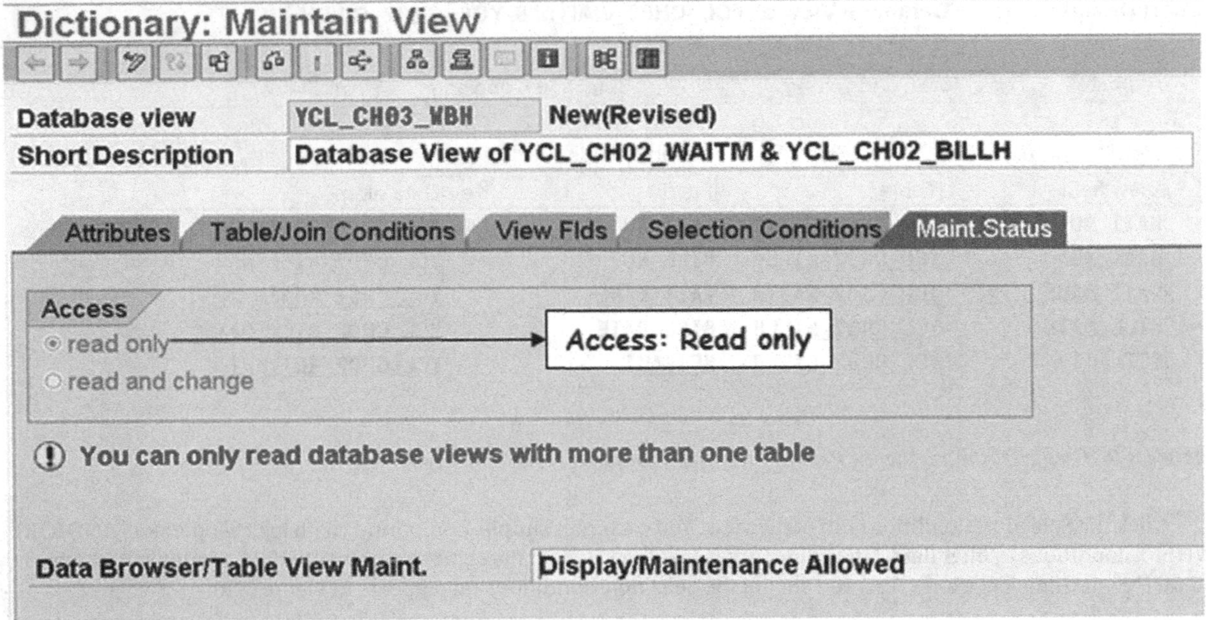

Figure 3-11. *Create Database View – Maint.Status tab*

Perform a view consistency check (Button or keys <Ctrl>+<F2>).

A warning message will appear stating this is a read view only. (Warning messages in the SAP environment appear in Yellow color) This is shown in Figure 3-12.

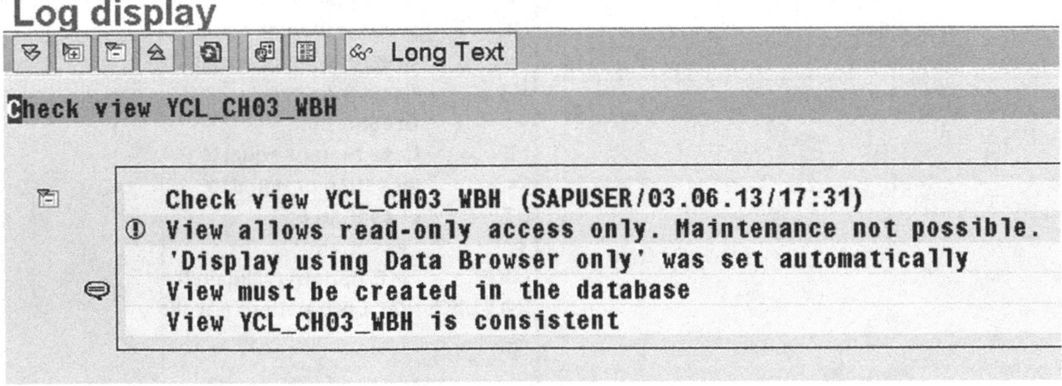

Figure 3-12. *Create Database View – Consistency Check Message*

If any other error/s occurs; troubleshoot and fix them.
Activate the database view (Button or keys <Ctrl>+<F3>).

You can display the contents of the view by clicking on the application toolbar button, then pressing function key F8 (execute) in the Selection Screen. The data in the participating tables YCL_CH02_WAITM and YCL_CH02_BILLH is available in Figures 3-13 and 3-14. The contents of the view are shown in Figure 3-15.

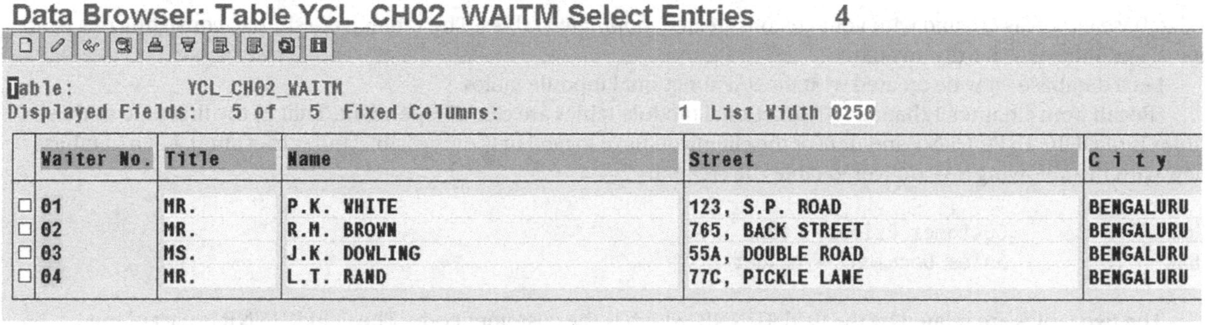

Data Browser: Table YCL_CH02_WAITM Select Entries 4

Table: YCL_CH02_WAITM
Displayed Fields: 5 of 5 Fixed Columns: 1 List Width 0250

Waiter No.	Title	Name	Street	C i t y
01	MR.	P.K. WHITE	123, S.P. ROAD	BENGALURU
02	MR.	R.M. BROWN	765, BACK STREET	BENGALURU
03	MS.	J.K. DOWLING	55A, DOUBLE ROAD	BENGALURU
04	MR.	L.T. RAND	77C, PICKLE LANE	BENGALURU

Figure 3-13. *Table Contents – YCL_CH02_WAITM*

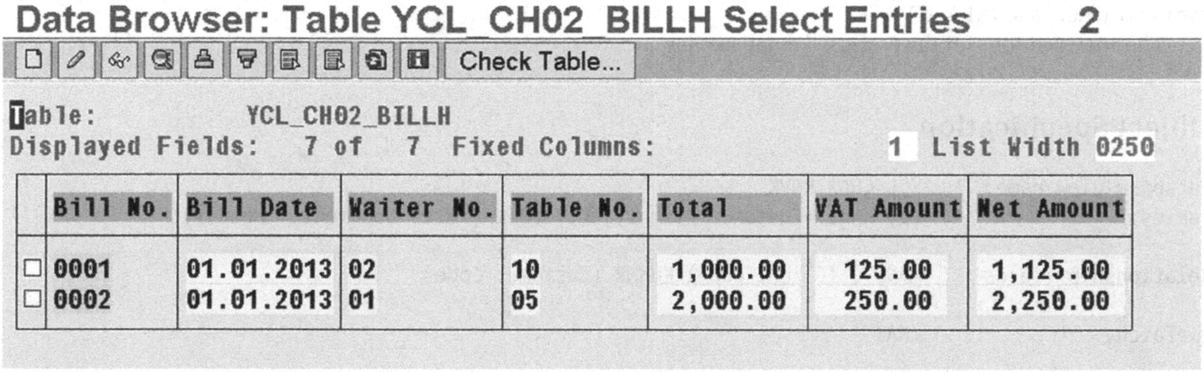

Data Browser: Table YCL_CH02_BILLH Select Entries 2

Check Table...

Table: YCL_CH02_BILLH
Displayed Fields: 7 of 7 Fixed Columns: 1 List Width 0250

Bill No.	Bill Date	Waiter No.	Table No.	Total	VAT Amount	Net Amount
0001	01.01.2013	02	10	1,000.00	125.00	1,125.00
0002	01.01.2013	01	05	2,000.00	250.00	2,250.00

Figure 3-14. *Table Contents - YCL_CH02_BILLH*

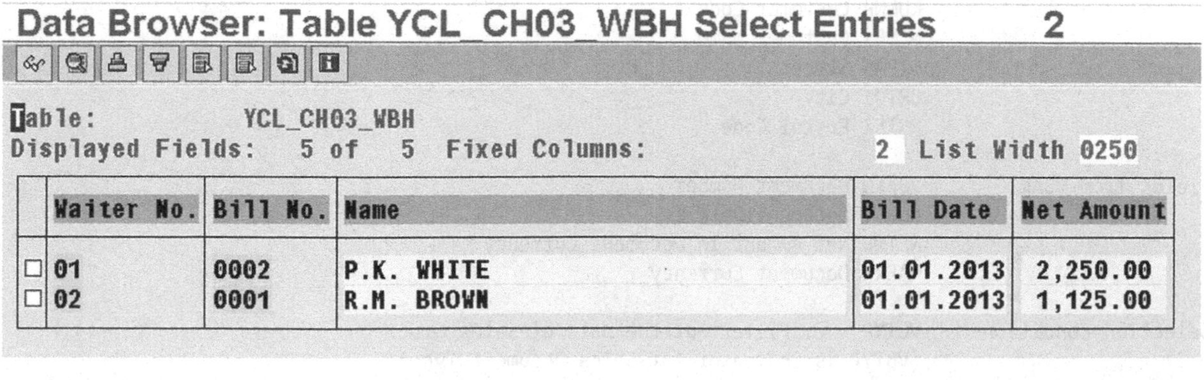

Data Browser: Table YCL_CH03_WBH Select Entries 2

Table: YCL_CH03_WBH
Displayed Fields: 5 of 5 Fixed Columns: 2 List Width 0250

Waiter No.	Bill No.	Name	Bill Date	Net Amount
01	0002	P.K. WHITE	01.01.2013	2,250.00
02	0001	R.M. BROWN	01.01.2013	1,125.00

Figure 3-15. *Database View Contents - YCL_CH03_WBH*

There are 4 rows in table YCL_CH02_WAITM: WAIT_NO values = 01,02,03,04.

There are 2 rows in YCL_CH02_BILLH: WAIT_NO values = 02, 01.

In the database view YCL_CH03_WBH WAIT_NO values = 01, 02 appear. WAIT_NO = 03, 04 are dropped, as there are no bills for these values of WAIT_NO.

Create Database View with SAP delivered Tables KNA1and VBAK

A database view was created with your custom created, populated tables. The tables were simple, consisting of a few fields, and there was hardly any data.

Let a database view be created with the SAP functional module tables.

(Recall from Chapter 1 that all SAP functional module tables are client dependent. That is, the first field in these tables is of DDIC TYPE CLNT and data of the client you have logged in is only visible and retrievable). Let a database view with the following SAP delivered tables be created:

```
KNA1            Customer Primary table
VBAK            Sales Document - header
```

The two tables are related by the field KUNNR, which is the customer code. The field KUNNR is part of the primary key in table KNA1 and it is a foreign key in the table VBAK. Check this out in SE11.

The customer information is contained in multiple tables; KNA1 is the primary table for customer information.

Table VBAK contains Sales Document header data. There is a Sales Document – item table: VBAP. You will only use the two tables KNA1 and VBAK.

The specifications for the proposed database view:

Object Specification

```
Database view name:     YCL_CH03_KNVK
Tables:                 (1) KNA1 (Customer Primary) (2) VBAK (Sales Document - Header)

Relationship fields     MANDT, (Client Code) KUNNR (Customer Code)

Hierarchy:              KNA1
                         |
                        VBAK

Fields from KNA1        MANDT Client code
                        KUNNR Customer Code
                        NAME1 Customer Name
                        STRAS Street
                        ORT01 City
                        PSTLZ Postal Code

Fields from VBAK        VBELN Document Number
                        AUDAT Document Date
                        NETWR Net Amount in Document Currency
                        WAERK Document Currency

Selection Condition     VBTYP = C. Filter out the data of Sales Order
                        (VBTYP is indicator for Sales Document Type)
```

Object Creation

On the SE11 opening screen, select the radio button for View.

Enter the view name YCL_CH03_KNVK. Click the Create button or press function key F5. Select the Database view (default) on the Choose View Type screen and click on the ✔ Copy button. You will get to the Table/Join Conditions tab. Enter Short description. Under the Tables, enter the name of your foreign key table VBAK. Click on the button Relationships. The screenshot of the dialog box is shown in Figure 3-16.

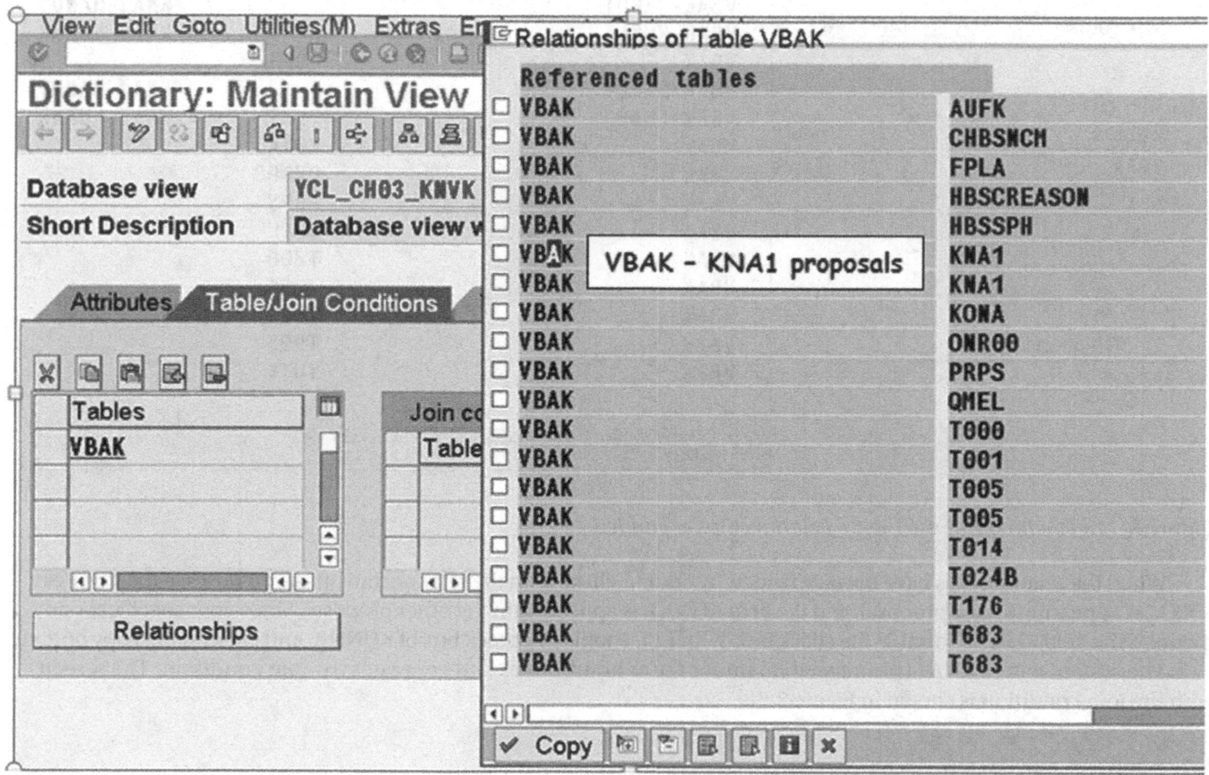

Figure 3-16. Create Database View – Relationships

A relationship involving KNA1 and VBAK is appearing twice in the list. Which one is to be selected? Double-click on both and the screen as shown in Figure 3-17 will appear.

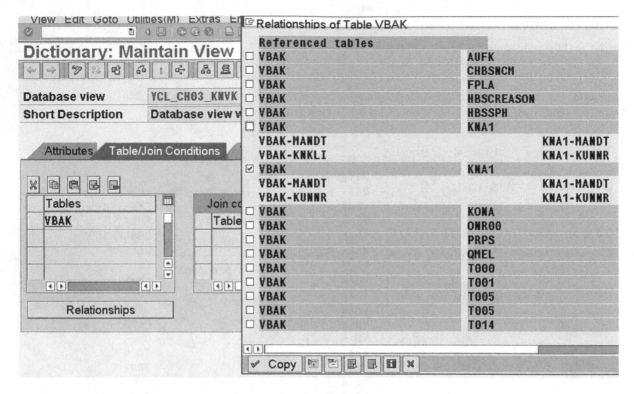

Figure 3-17. *Create Database View – Relationships expanded*

When the relationships have been expanded by double-clicking on the relationship lines, you observe that the field KNKLI is appearing in one proposal, and the field KUNNR is appearing in the other proposal. Since your specifications mention the field KUNNR, disable the check box of KNKLI, enable the check box of KUNNR, and click on the copy button.

The system enters KNA1 (primary table) under the column Tables and generates the join condition. The screen with the join condition is shown in Figure 3-18.

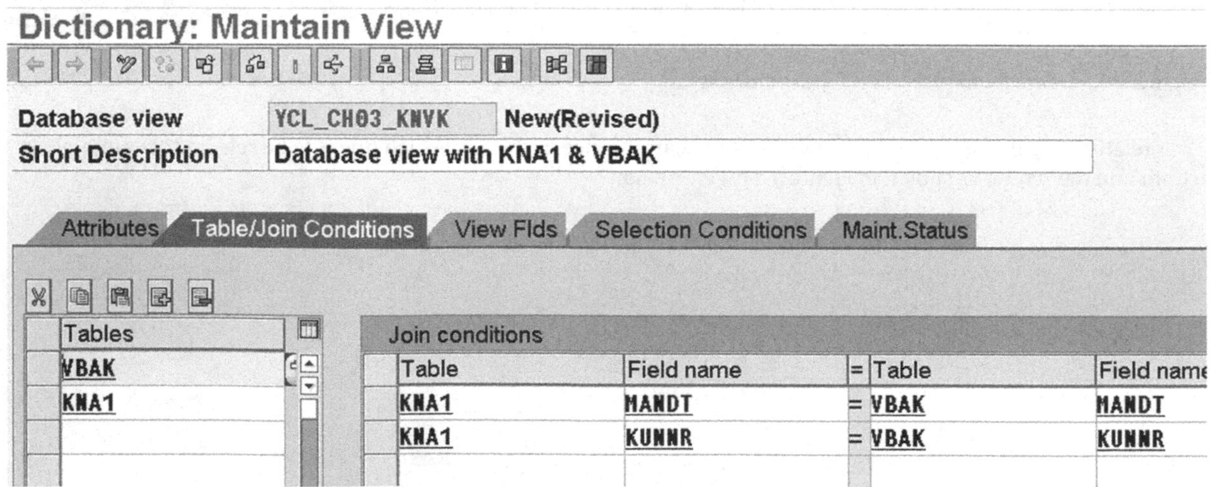

Figure 3-18. *Create Database View – Join Conditions*

Notice that the DDIC TYPE CLNT field MANDT is on the first line of join condition, because the field MANDT is the first field in every client dependent table. When entering the join condition manually, bear this in mind.

With the join condition in place, proceed to the View Flds tab. Select the fields as per the specifications. Recall from the previous exercise that you have to use the Table fields button to select the table and then select the fields of the chosen table.

Recall from the previous exercise that fields have to be ordered. The primary key fields (with the Key check enabled have to be located at the beginning and should be in order of table hierarchy. The order of primary keys should be as follows:

MANDT

KUNNR

VBELN

The rest of the fields can be in any order.

Notice that you can select the field KUNNR from either one of the tables KNA1 or VBAK. If you select the field from the table KNA1 where it is part of primary key, it will have the Key check box enabled in the view; if you choose KUNNR from the table VBAK, where it is a foreign key, it will have the Key check box disabled in the view. If you have selected KUNNR from table KNA1, you need to put the first three fields in the order mentioned above. If you have selected KUNNR from table VBAK, then the first two fields should be:

MANDT

VBELN

You have selected the field KUNNR from table KNA1.A screenshot of the selected fields as per the specifications and ordered as expected by interface is shown in Figure 3-19.

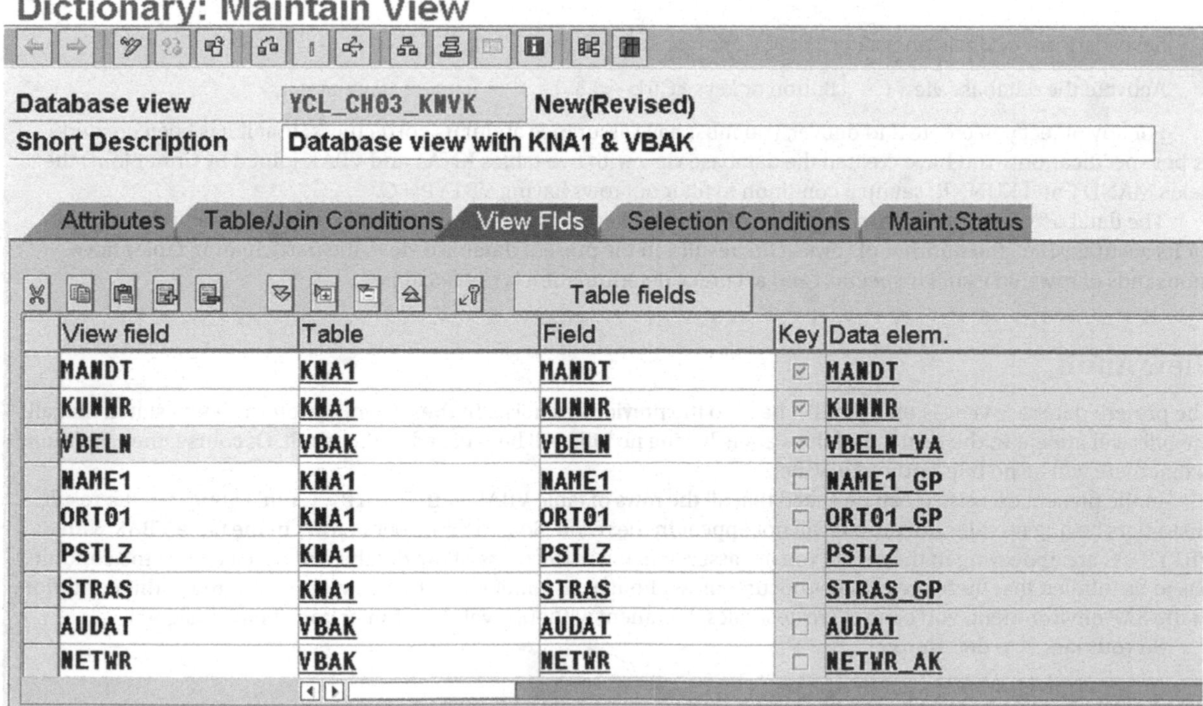

Figure 3-19. *Create Database View – Fields Selected, Ordered*

Next, click on the Select Conditions tab. According to the specifications, you have to enter a condition as to filter out rows in which the field VBTYP = C. The field VBTYP is in the table VBAK. Table VBAK contains different types or kinds of sales documents. The field VBTYP (DDIC TYPE CHAR & length 1) contains 1 character code for each document type. It contains C for sales orders. When a customer of an enterprise places an order, a sales order is generated. In the present database view, you will filter out rows where VBTYP = C (sales orders).

Use the button Table fields to select the table (VBAK) Field (VBTYP). Select the relational operator from the list (function key F4) - EQ/=. Under the Comparison Value column enter 'C'. (Enclose C within single quotes. Recall C is the code for sales orders). A screenshot of the Selection Conditions tab after the fields are entered is shown in Figure 3-20.

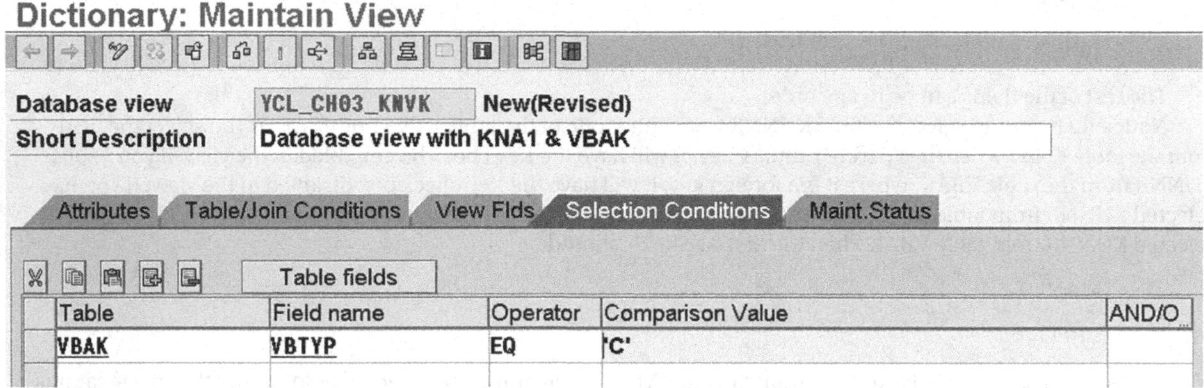

Figure 3-20. *Create Database View - Selection Conditions*

Save. Perform a consistency check (Button or keys <Ctrl>+<F2>).

Activate the database view (Button or keys <Ctrl>+<F3>).

For any object you create and deliver, you must have assurance about its correctness: that it has been created as per specifications. You have created the database view with two tables KNA1 and VBAK joined by (inner join) the fields MANDT and KUNNR; set up a condition to filter out rows having VBTYP = C.

The database view you created earlier had very little data in its participating tables, so you visually checked it for its accuracy (i.e., the number of rows in the result). In the present database view, the participating tables have thousands of rows, so visual inspection and accuracy determination is not feasible.

View Audit

The present database view is on a parallel basis to the previous exercise. In the previous exercise, it was stated that all the bills will appear in the result, and the waiters having no bills will be omitted in the result. Of course, the condition is that there will be no bills without a waiter.

In the present exercise it can be stated that all the rows of table VBAK with VBTYP = C must appear in the result, customers having no sales document will not appear in the result. So if the number of rows in the table VBAK with VBTYP = C are appearing in the result, you are assured of the correctness of the database view. Of course the condition has to be fulfilled that there are no sales documents without a customer code. In fact, you are assured of this condition. In the SAP environment, you cannot create a sales document without a valid customer code being assigned.

So your task is to determine:

a. The number of rows in the table VBAK with VBTYP = C.

b. The number of rows in your database view.

If these two match, your database view is correct. If they do not match, you have to troubleshoot. When join conditions are not generated by the system but entered manually, this is one area prone to errors.

Now let the number of rows in the database view YCL_CH03_KNVK be determined. Click on the button of the Database view application toolbar. The screen Data Browser: Table YCL_CH03_KNVK: Selection Screen will appear. On this screen there is a button Number of Entries on the application toolbar. Click on this button. The system will display the number of rows in the database view. This is shown in Figure 3-21.

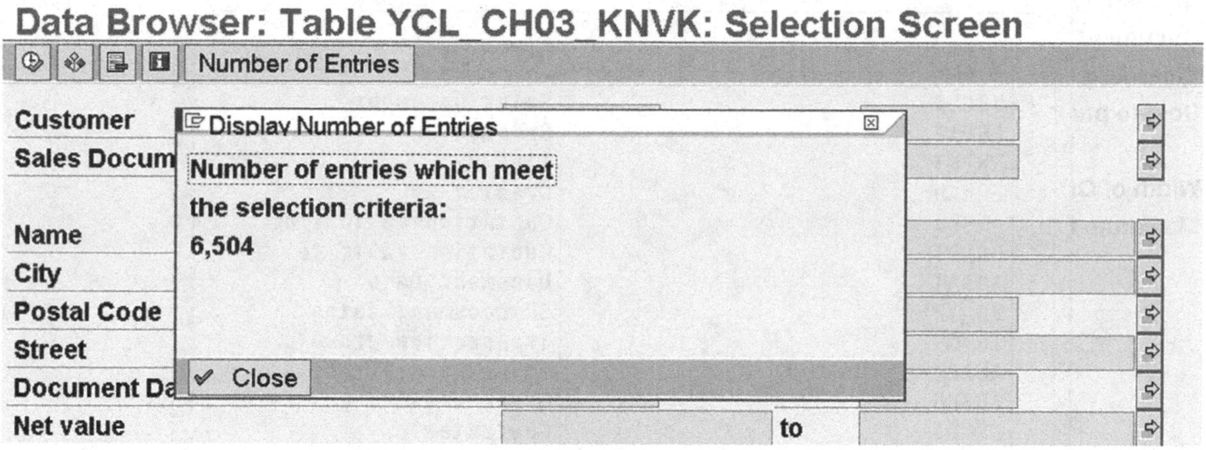

Data Browser: Table YCL_CH03_KNVK: Selection Screen

Customer			
Sales Docum			
Name			
City			
Postal Code			
Street			
Document Da			
Net value		to	

Display Number of Entries

Number of entries which meet the selection criteria:
6,504

Close

Figure 3-21. Database View - Selection Screen: Determine number of rows

The number of rows in the database view is 6504.

Now determine the number of rows in the table VBAK with field VBTYP = C. Navigate to the transaction code SE16 screen; enter the table name as VBAK. Click on the table of contents button. The screen Data Browser: Table VBAK: Selection Screen will appear. You have to filter out rows with VBTYP = C. For this, click on the menu bar Settings ➤ Fields for Selections. A dialog box will appear with the fields of tables and check boxes as shown in Figure 3-22.

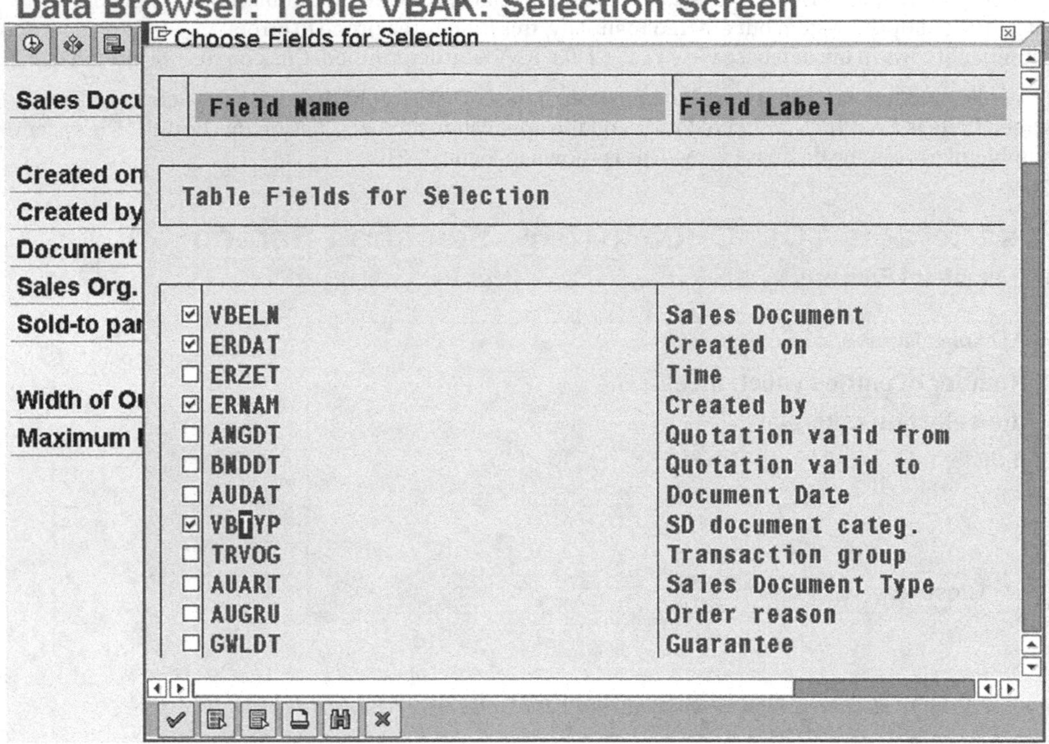

Figure 3-22. *Table VBAK - Selection Screen: Choose Fields for Selection*

Ensure the check box for the field VBTYP is enabled, and click on the ✔ button.

In the Document cat. field enter C (just the letter C) and click on the application toolbar button Number of Entries. The system will display the number of rows in the table VBAK where VBTYP = C. This is shown in Figure 3-23.

Data Browser: Table VBAK: Selection Screen

Number of Entries

Sales Document

Created on

Created by

Document cat. C

Sales Org.

Sold-to party

Width of Output List 250

Maximum No. of Hits 200

Display Number of Entries

Number of entries which meet the selection criteria:

6,504

Close

Figure 3-23. *Table VBAK - Selection Screen with VBTYP = C: Number of Rows/Entries*

The number of rows in the table VBAK with VBTYP = C is 6504. This is matching with the number of rows in the database view.

The Selection Screen (where you entered C in the field Document cat. /VBTYP is a sophisticated feature, which will be covered when prerequisites are in place. For now you can take it that initially if this field was not on the Selection Screen, you made it appear on the Selection Screen through Settings ➤ Fields for Selections, etc. Once it was on the Selection Screen, you entered the value C (for sales document type sales order) the system filtered data as per this value (i.e., it fetched and counted rows with VBTYP = C).

Making the Database View Client Independent

In the database view YCL_CH03_KNVK, the first field is the client code field MANDT of DDIC TYPE CLNT. As the first field is DDIC TYPE CLNT, your view is client dependent. Let the position of this field be changed and its repercussions observed. As shown in Figure 3-24, the field MANDT has been shifted to the second position. Since the first field is no longer DDIC TYPE CLNT, your view now will be client independent; that is, the data of clients other than the logged in client is also retrieved.

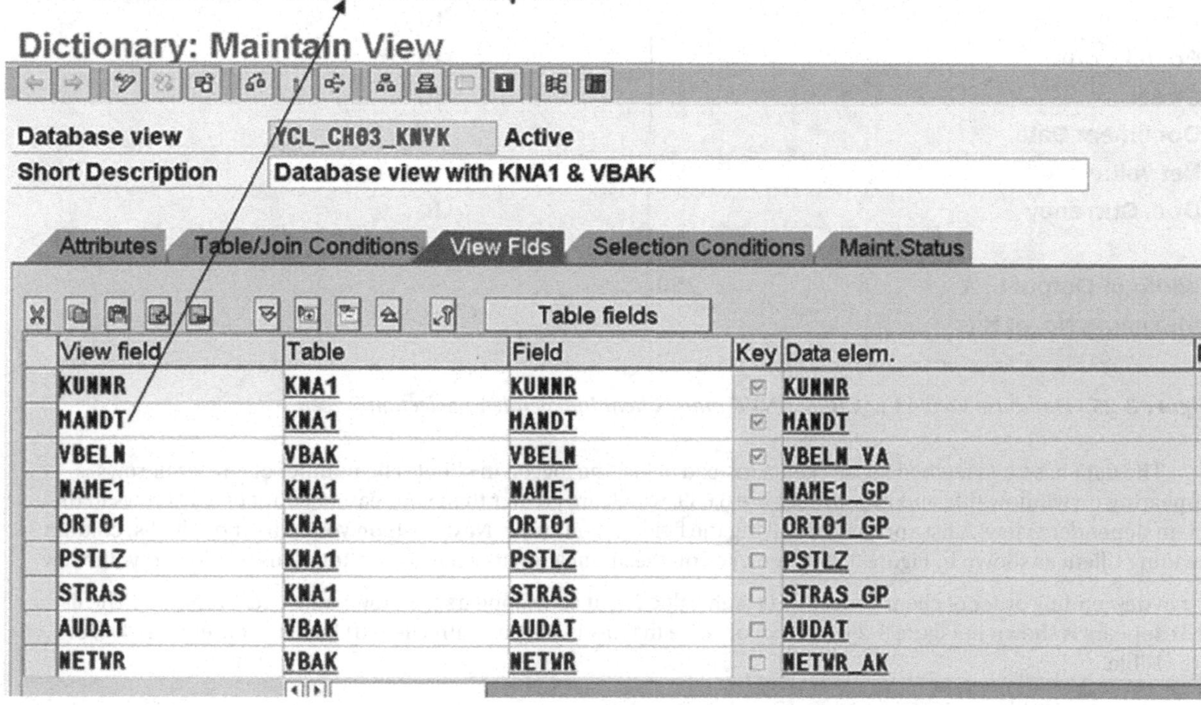

View field	Table	Field	Key	Data elem.
KUNNR	KNA1	KUNNR	☑	KUNNR
MANDT	KNA1	MANDT	☑	MANDT
VBELN	VBAK	VBELN	☑	VBELN_VA
NAME1	KNA1	NAME1	☐	NAME1_GP
ORT01	KNA1	ORT01	☐	ORT01_GP
PSTLZ	KNA1	PSTLZ	☐	PSTLZ
STRAS	KNA1	STRAS	☐	STRAS_GP
AUDAT	VBAK	AUDAT	☐	AUDAT
NETWR	VBAK	NETWR	☐	NETWR_AK

Figure 3-24. *Database View YCL_CH03_KNVK - Shift MANDT to Second Position: The View Becomes Client Independent*

After making this change, do an object consistency check. The system will highlight two warnings: (a) View access is read only, and (b) View is client independent.

Activate the object. Click on the contents button. The selection screen appears. In the field Maximum No. of Hits (at the very bottom), change the value to 9999. Normally, as per default settings, the value here is 200 (i.e., it lists a maximum of 200 rows). In your present situation, the number of rows in your view is > 6,500. So you have changed the value to 9999 (i.e., display a maximum of 9999 rows). This is shown in Figure 3-25. Press function key F8 or the execute button.

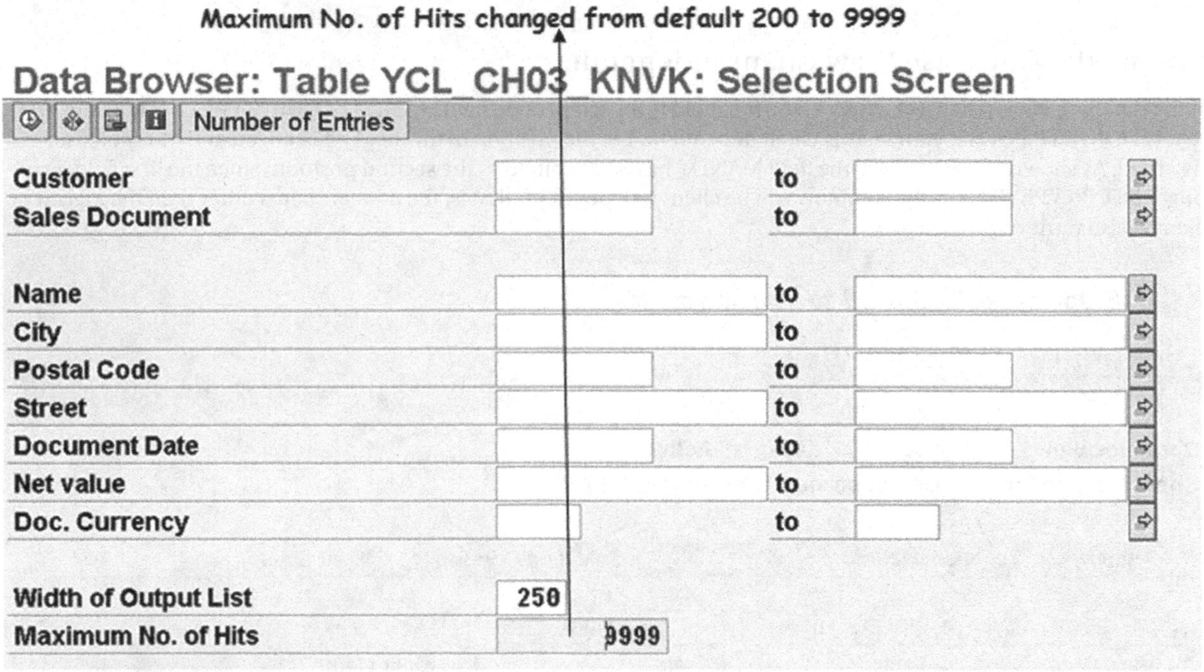

Figure 3-25. *Database View YCL_CH03_KNVK made Client Independent: Selection Screen*

The data has been fetched for all clients instead of just the logged in client. The number of entries or rows is appearing on window title and in your case are 6,639, which are greater than your earlier count of 6,504 rows in the client dependent view. A list appears displaying the fields of your view. Next position your cursor on the list column heading Client as shown in Figure 3.26. Then click on the application tool bar button. This would sort your view list in descending order of client code: that is high value client code appears first, low value client next, etc. The list that appears is shown in Figure 3-26. You can observe that list is starting with client 811; clients other than 800, etc., are visible.

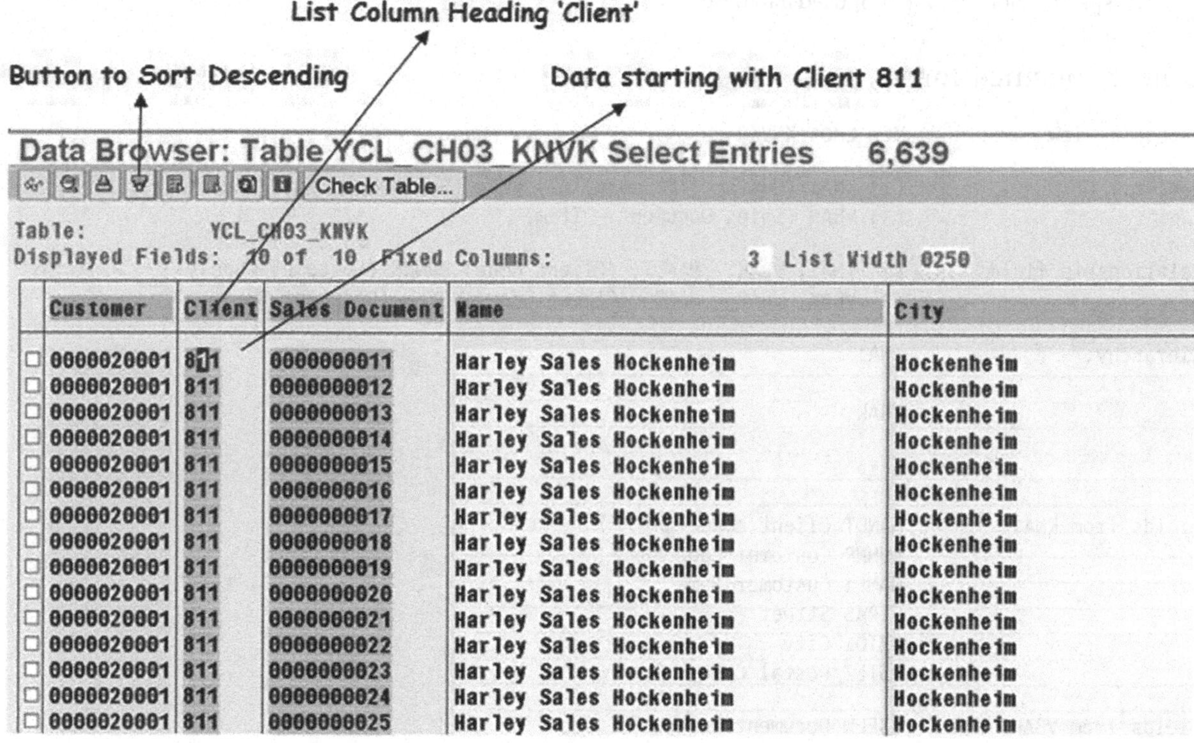

List Column Heading 'Client'
Button to Sort Descending
Data starting with Client 811
Data Browser: Table YCL_CH03_KNVK Select Entries 6,639
Check Table...
Table: YCL_CH03_KNVK
Displayed Fields: 10 of 10 Fixed Columns: 3 List Width 0250
Customer | Client | Sales Document | Name | City
0000020001 | 811 | 0000000011 | Harley Sales Hockenheim | Hockenheim
0000020001 | 811 | 0000000012 | Harley Sales Hockenheim | Hockenheim
0000020001 | 811 | 0000000013 | Harley Sales Hockenheim | Hockenheim
0000020001 | 811 | 0000000014 | Harley Sales Hockenheim | Hockenheim
0000020001 | 811 | 0000000015 | Harley Sales Hockenheim | Hockenheim
0000020001 | 811 | 0000000016 | Harley Sales Hockenheim | Hockenheim
0000020001 | 811 | 0000000017 | Harley Sales Hockenheim | Hockenheim
0000020001 | 811 | 0000000018 | Harley Sales Hockenheim | Hockenheim
0000020001 | 811 | 0000000019 | Harley Sales Hockenheim | Hockenheim
0000020001 | 811 | 0000000020 | Harley Sales Hockenheim | Hockenheim
0000020001 | 811 | 0000000021 | Harley Sales Hockenheim | Hockenheim
0000020001 | 811 | 0000000022 | Harley Sales Hockenheim | Hockenheim
0000020001 | 811 | 0000000023 | Harley Sales Hockenheim | Hockenheim
0000020001 | 811 | 0000000024 | Harley Sales Hockenheim | Hockenheim
0000020001 | 811 | 0000000025 | Harley Sales Hockenheim | Hockenheim

Figure 3-26. *Database View YCL_CH03_KNVK made Client Independent: List*

This is rarely done in a practical world; that is, making a view consisting of a functional module table's client independent. It has been done here to highlight and demonstrate the client dependency feature. Restore the view to its original configuration.

Exercise: Create Database View with SAP delivered Tables KNA1, VBAK, VBAP

Extend the two table database view to three table database views:

```
KNA1        Customer Primary table
VBAK        Sales Document - header
VBAP        Sales Document - item
```

The two tables KNA1 & VBAK are related by the field KUNNR, which is the customer code. The field KUNNR is part of the primary key in table KNA1 and it is a foreign key in table VBAK.

The two tables VBAK and VBAP are related by the field VBELN, which is the Document Number. The field VBELN is part of the primary key in table VBAK, and it is a foreign key in table VBAP as well as part of the primary key. Check this out in SE11.

The specifications for the proposed database view:

Object Specification

Database view name:	YCL_CH03_KNVKP
Tables:	(1) KNA1 (Customer Primary) (2) VBAK (Sales Document - Header) (3) VBAP (Sales Document - Item)
Relationship fields	(1) KNA1, VBAK - MANDT, (Client Code) KUNNR (Customer Code) (2) VBAK, VBAP - MANDT (Client Code) VBELN (Document No.)
Hierarchy:	KNA1 | VBAK | VBAP
Fields from KNA1	MANDT Client code KUNNR Customer Code NAME1 Customer Name STRAS Street ORT01 City PSTLZ Postal Code
Fields from VBAK	VBELN Document Number AUDAT Document Date NETWR Net Amount in Document Currency WAERK Document Currency
Fields from VBAP	POSNR Sales Document Item (Serial No.) MATNR Material No ZMENG Target Quantity ZIEME Target Unit of Measure
Selection Condition	VBTYP = C. Filter out the data of Sales Order (VBTYP is indicator for Sales Document Type)

Tables	Join Conditions			
VBAP	KNA1	MANDT	VBAK	MANDT
VBAK	KNA1	KUNNR	VBAK	KUNNR
KNA1	VBAK	MANDT	VBAP	MANDT
	VBAK	VBELN	VBAP	VBELN

Fields	Table
MANDT	KNA1
KUNNR	KNA1
VBELN	VBAK
POSNR	VBAP
NAME1	KNA1
STRAS	KNA1

```
ORT01         KNA1
PSTLZ         KNA1
AUDAT         VBAK
NETWR         VBAK
WAERK         VBAK
MATNR         VBAP
ZMENG         VBAP
ZIEME         VBAP

Selection Conditions

VBAK         VBTYP         EQ         C
```

After creation, a perform consistency check and activate the database view. Test and ascertain that the number of rows in the database view is as per the inner joins expectations.

This concludes the database views.

Projection View

- A projection view is used to restrict access to only certain fields of a table.
- A projection view consists of exactly one database table.
- A projection view can use pooled, clustered tables.
- Selection Conditions are not available for projection views.
- A projection view can be used with an Open SQL SELECT statement.
- A projection view can be referred to declare data in an ABAP program.
- Table data can be maintained through the projection view (insert, update, delete).

Create Projection View with SAP delivered TableKNA1

Object Specification

```
Projection view name:     YCL_CH03_KNA1_PJ

Table:                    KNA1 (Customer Primary)

Fields from KNA1          MANDT Client code
                          KUNNR Customer Code
                          NAME1 Customer Name
                          STRAS Street
                          ORT01 City
                          PSTLZ Postal Code
```

Object Creation

In the SE11 opening screen, select the radio button View. Enter the name of the view to be crested YCL_CH03_KNA1_PJ. Click on the Create button or press function key F5. The system will prompt for the view type to be created as shown in Figure 3-27.

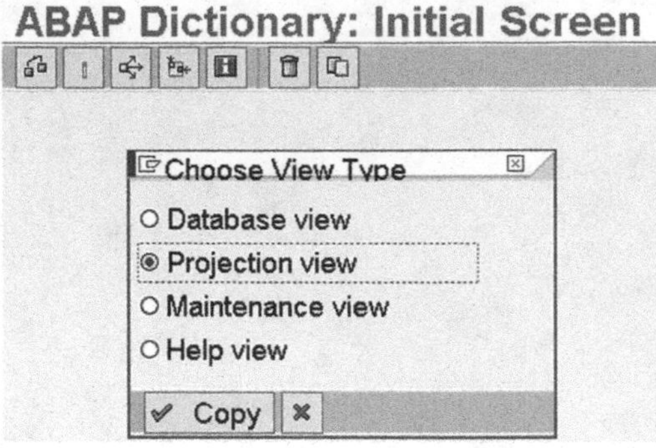

Figure 3-27. *Create Projection View – Choose View Type*

Select the Projection view on the Choose View Type screen and click on the Copy button. You will be prompted with an information message like the one shown in Figure 3-28.

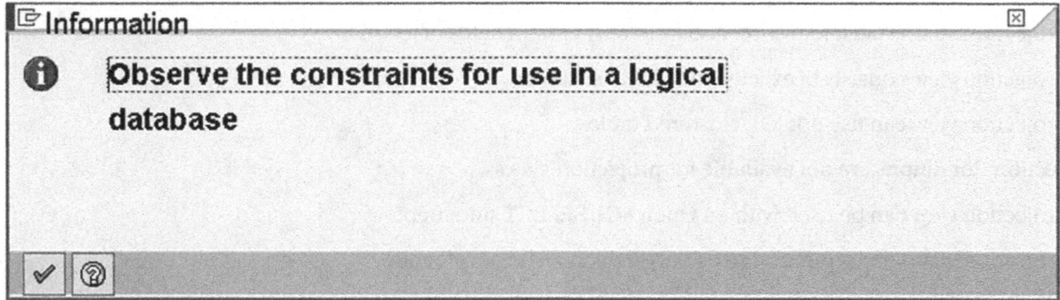

Figure 3-28. *Create Projection View – Information Message*

Information messages have the icon . They are notifying messages. This one reminds you to Observe constraints for use in Logical database. The Logical database is a feature in the ABAP Workbench somewhat obsolete now (HR functional module uses it). The Logical database is not covered in this book. Press <Enter> on the information message. You are on the View Fields tab. Enter Short description. Enter the table name KNA1 in the field Base Table. Click on the button Table fields. The system pop ups the Field Selection from Table KNA1 window as shown in Figure 3-29.

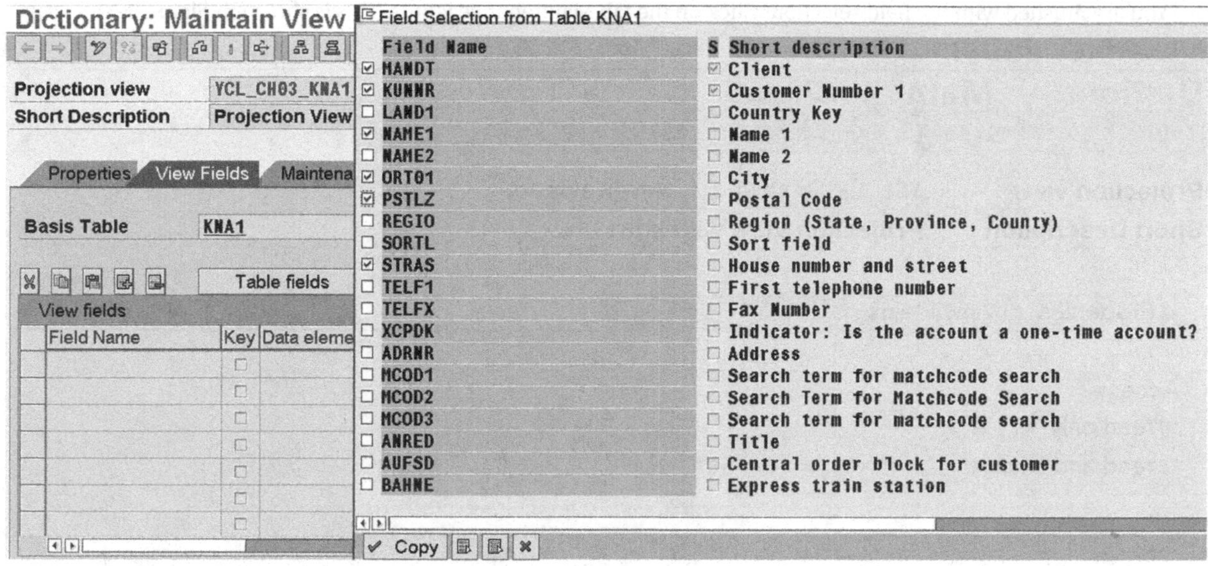

Figure 3-29. *Create Projection View – Field Selection from Table KNA1*

Select the fields as per the object specifications and click on the ✔ Copy button. The screen shot with the selected fields is shown in Figure 3-30.

Dictionary: Maintain View

Projection view YCL_CH03_KNA1_PJ New(Revised)

Short Description Projection View with kna1

Properties | View Fields | Maintenance Status

Basis Table KNA1

Table fields

View fields

Field Name	Key	Data element	Mod	DTyp	Length	Short description
MANDT	☑	MANDT	☐	CLNT	3	Client
KUNNR	☑	KUNNR	☐	CHAR	10	Customer Number 1
NAME1	☐	NAME1_GP	☐	CHAR	35	Name 1
ORT01	☐	ORT01_GP	☐	CHAR	35	City
PSTLZ	☐	PSTLZ	☐	CHAR	10	Postal Code
STRAS	☐	STRAS_GP	☐	CHAR	35	House number and street

Figure 3-30. *Create Projection View – Selected Fields*

You are finished with the field selection. Click on the tab Maintenance Status. This is shown in Figure 3-31.

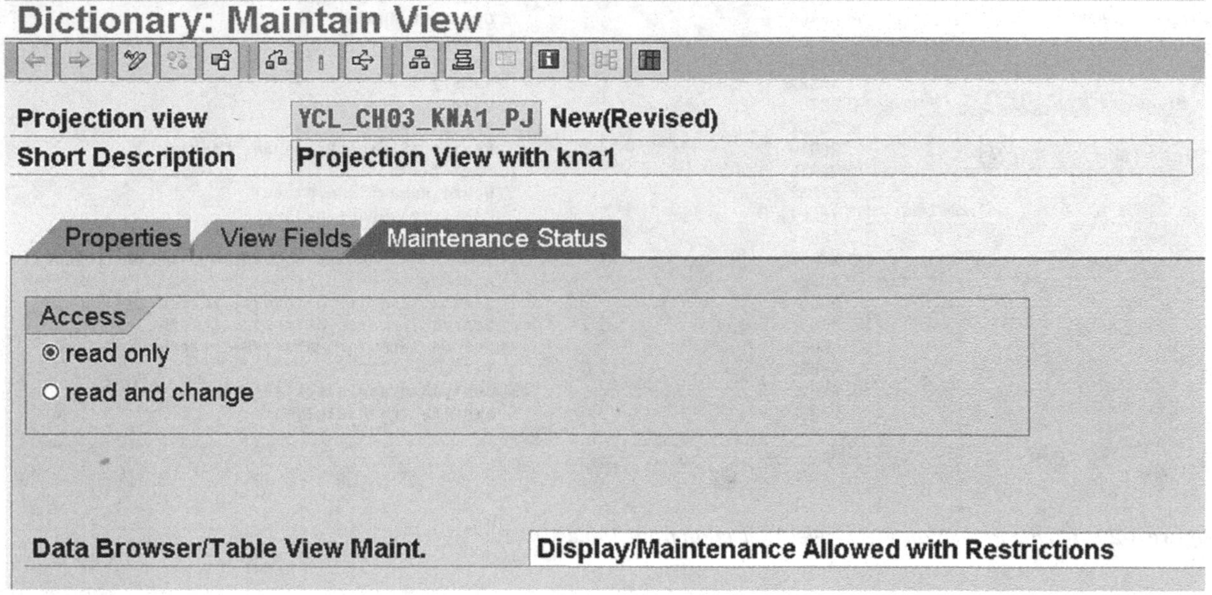

Figure 3-31. *Create Projection View – Maintenance Status tab*

You should not intend to operate on the data of KNA1 (insert, update, delete). Operating on the data of SAP delivered functional module tables is not advisable. Click on the radio button "read only" in the Access area. Select Display/Maintenance Allowed with Restrictions option from the drop-down list of the field Data Browser/Table View Maint.

Save the projection view. Perform the consistency check. This should produce the screen shown in Figure 3-32.

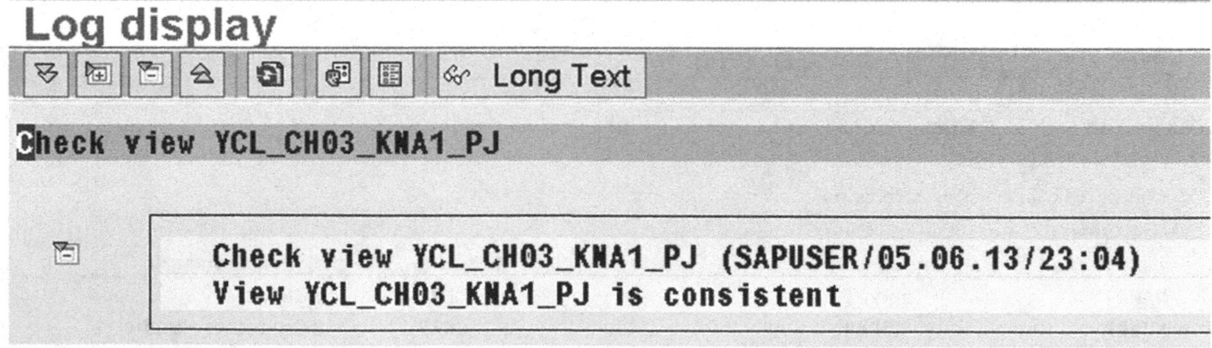

Figure 3-32. *Create Projection View – Consistency Check Message*

From the Log display screen, press function key F3 or the standard toolbar button. Activate the Projection view. Let the contents of the projection view be examined. On one of the projection view tabs, click on the button. The selection screen will appear. Enter A* in the field Name to retrieve and display customer names starting with A, and change field Maximum No. of Hits from default 200 to 9999. This is shown in Figure 3-33.

Data Browser: Table YCL_CH03_KNA1_PJ: Selection Screen

Number of Entries

Customer		to	
Name	A*	to	
City		to	
Postal Code		to	
Street		to	
Width of Output List	250		
Maximum No. of Hits	9999		

Figure 3-33. *Projection View - Selection Screen*

Press function key F8 or the ✔ button. The projection view contents are appearing in Figure 3.34 (only customers; names starting with A).

Data Browser: Table YCL_CH03_KNA1_PJ Select Entries 536

Check Table...

Table: YCL_CH03_KNA1_PJ
Displayed Fields: 6 of 6 Fixed Columns: 2 List Width 0250

Client	Customer	Name	City	Postal Code	Street
800	0000000110	Auto Klement	München	81737	Bert-Brecht-Alle
800	0000000261	Andrew Williams	ALBUQUERQUE	87104	1030 1030 Rio Gr
800	0000000470	Alex Lynch	PHILADELPHIA	19143	Spring Garden St
800	0000000472	Agnes Varda	CHEYENNE	82009	1765 Dell Range
800	0000000473	Albert Brooks	COLORADO SPRINGS	80914	456 456 Paine St
800	0000000512	Anne Anderson	LOS ANGELES	90042	156 156 Lincoln
800	0000000540	Agnes Iams	CHEYENNE	82009	1236 1236 Dell R
800	0000000541	Albert Fisher	COLORADO SPRINGS	80914	521 521 Paine St
800	0000000565	Andrew Webber	NEW YORK	10025	20 20 100th St
800	0000001012	Autohaus Franzl GmbH	Muenchen	80939	Schwarzhauptstra
800	0000001191	ALDO Supermarkt	Stuttgart	70563	Lindenstrasse 23
800	0000001360	Amadeus	Muenchen	81373	Faberstrasse 45
800	0000001400	A.I.T. GmbH	Koeln	50997	Landsbergerstras
800	0000001470	Aircraft Products	Slough	SL1 4UY	185 Farnham Road
800	0000001550	Adam Baumgarten und Söhne	Brandenburg	14776	Postdamer Strass

Figure 3-34. *Projection View - Contents*

You are finished with the Views for now. You will proceed to the next DDIC object, Search Help.

DDIC Objects Search Helps

The DDIC object search help enables users to make a selection from a selection list (also called the *hit list*) to assign value to a screen field instead of manually entering the value, which is tedious and error prone.

You have already seen the search help in operation when you assigned domains to data elements in the section entitled Create Data Elements, and assigned data elements to table fields in the section entitled Create Tables in Chapter 2. The selection list's appearance is generally preceded by a dialog box called the restrictive or filter dialog box. In this book, it is being referred to as a restrictive dialog box. The restrictive dialog box contains fields, and the user can enter values or patterns in these fields. The search help will filter out the data as per value/s, pattern specification in the restrictive dialog box fields, so that the resulting selection list is small and manageable. This is true of situations where the unrestricted selection lists contain large amounts of data.

Out of the hundreds of thousands of domains, you could filter out your 10 domains into a selection list; out of the hundreds of thousands of data elements, you could filter out your 17 data elements into a selection list.

Search helps are of two types: (a) elementary search help, and (b) collective search help. A collective search help consists of multiple elementary search helps. The search help can be attached to a primary key table, a table field (usually a foreign key field), a data element, or a screen field, etc.

You will perform hands-on exercises to create elementary as well as collective search helps. Search help creation will be scenario based. At first, you will create search helps using your custom tables. You will follow this up by creating search helps using SAP delivered tables.

Search Help with Custom Tables

Create Search Help: Scenario of Elementary Search Help with Custom Table

In your table YCL_CH02_BILLI, the field ITEM_CODE is a foreign key, and the check table for this field is YCL_CH02_ITEMM.

When you are entering data in this table (i.e., YCL_CH02_BILLI in the Data Browser, and SE16/SE11, etc.), when you press the function key F4 on the foreign key field ITEM_CODE, a list of primary key field values from the check table YCL_CH02_ITEMM is displayed. And when a user makes a selection by double-clicking, etc., the value of the primary key is assigned to the screen field. See Figure 3-35.

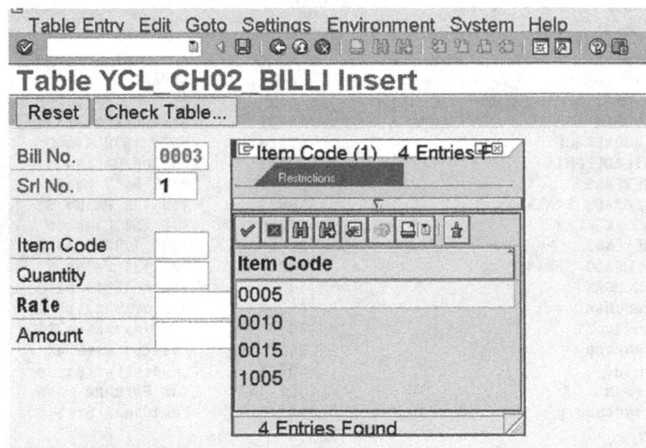

Figure 3-35. Create Data in Table YCL_CH02_BILLI, Press F4 key in Field ITEM_CODE

This is not very user friendly. First, you want a description of the item and rate (fields ITEM_DESC, RATE) to be displayed on the list along with ITEM_CODE. Next, you would like the field RATE value to be assigned from the list to the screen field RATE along with the field ITEM_CODE.

To achieve this, you are going to create an elementary search help, attach this search help to the foreign key field ITEM_CODE in the table YCL_CH02_BILLI, and test the attachment of the search help.

Create Elementary Search Help with Table YCL_CH03_ITEMM - Object Specification

```
Search Help name:                   YCL_CH03_ITEMS_SH

Database Table:                     YCL_CH02_ITEMM (source of data)

Attachment:                         Table - YCL_CH02_BILLI
                                    Field - ITEM_CODE (Foreign Key)
Selection List Fields:              ITEM_CODE - LPos = 1.
                                    ITEM_DESC - LPos = 2.
                                    RATE    - LPos = 3.

Restrictive Dialogue Box Fields     ITEM_CODE - Spos = 1.
                                    ITEM_DESC - Spos = 2.

Export Fields:                      ITEM_CODE - Export = X.
                                    RATE- Export = X

Import Fields:                      None
```

- You are creating an elementary search help YCL_CH03_ITEMS_SH (maximum name space 30 characters). This search help's source of data is the table YCL_CH02_ITEMM. The source of data can either be a *table, a projection view, a database view, or a help view.*
- You will attach this search help to the foreign key field ITEM_CODE of table YCL_CH02_BILLI (Bills -Items).
- The fields that will be displayed in the pop-up selection list are ITEM_CODE, ITEM_DESC, and RATE - Lpos values.
- The fields that will be displayed in the restrictive dialog box are ITEM_CODE and ITEM_DESC - Spos values.
- The screen fields that will be assigned values from the selection list fields of table YCL_CH02_ITEMM are ITEM_CODE and RATE - check box Export.
- There are no import parameters. The concept of search help import parameters will be explained and demonstrated with real-life type scenario in Chapter 14, entitled Screen Programming.

In the context of search help, export parameters means what the search help selection list sends values to the screen fields on the screen when the user has made a selection.

In the context of search help, import parameters means what the search help restrictive dialog box fields receives from the screen fields where user presses the function key F4.

Create Elementary Search Help YCL_CH03_ITEMS_SH with Table YCL_CH02_ITEMM, to be attached to field ITEM_CODE of table YCL_CH02_BILLI

In the SE11 opening screen, select the radio button for Search help. Enter the name of the search help to be created. The name as per your object specification is YCL_CH03_ITEMS_SH. Click on the Create button or press function key F5. The system will prompt for the search help type to be created as shown in Figure 3-36.

ABAP Dictionary: Initial Screen
Create Search Help YCL_CH03_KNA1_SH1
Elementary search help
Collective search help

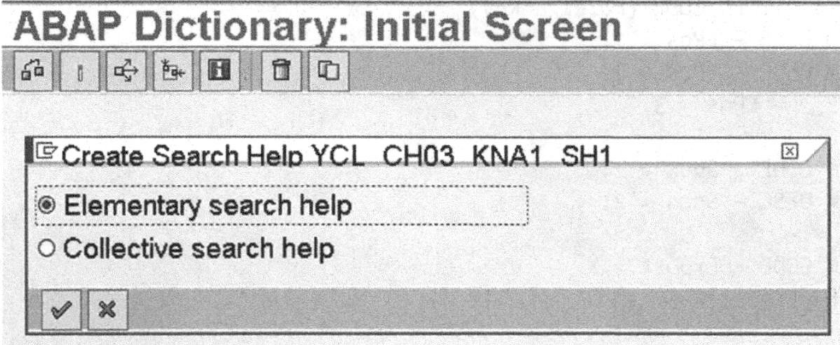

Figure 3-36. *Create Search Help – Select Search Help Type*

Select the Elementary search help, which is the default; press the ✔ button. The screen to create elementary search help as shown in Figure 3-37 appears.

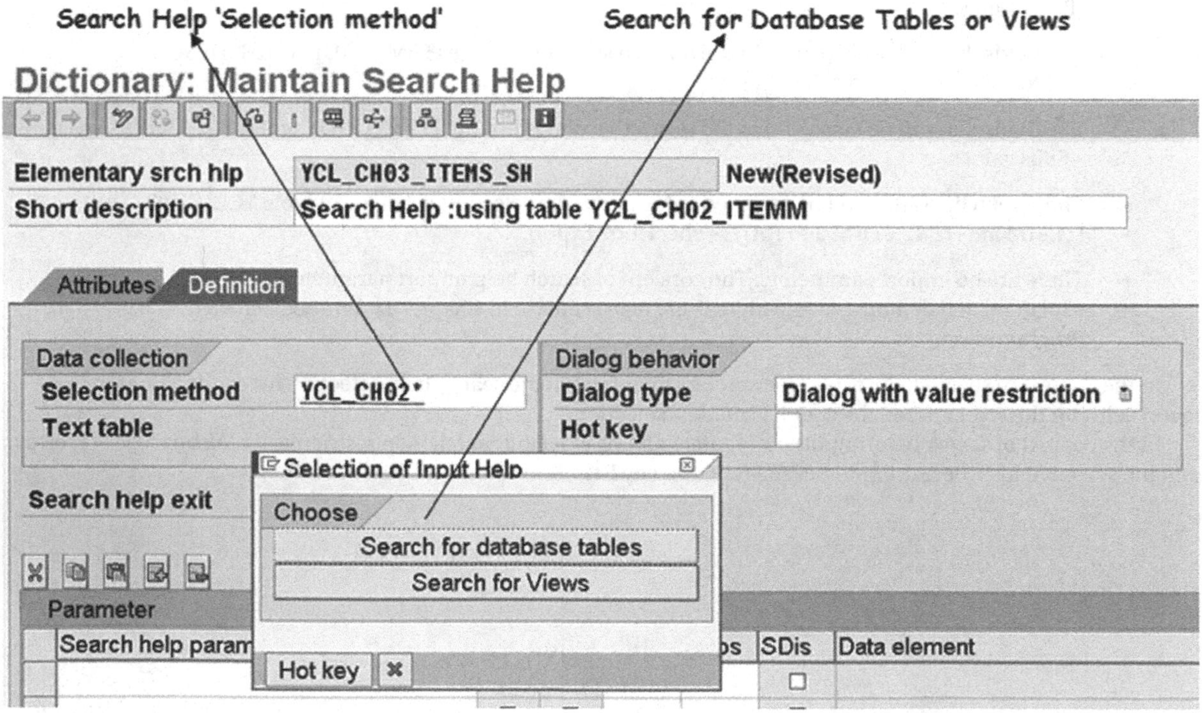

Search Help 'Selection method'
Search for Database Tables or Views
Dictionary: Maintain Search Help
Elementary srch hlp
YCL_CH03_ITEMS_SH
New(Revised)
Short description
Search Help :using table YCL_CH02_ITEMM
Attributes
Definition
Data collection
Selection method
YCL_CH02*
Text table
Dialog behavior
Dialog type
Dialog with value restriction
Hot key
Selection of Input Help
Choose
Search for database tables
Search for Views
Hot key
Search help exit
Parameter
Search help param
SDis
Data element

Figure 3-37. *Create Search Help – Selection Method*

In the selection method, you have to indicate first whether your source of data is a table or a view. (Database, projection and help views are acceptable.) In your case it happens to be a table. The table is YCL_CH02_ITEMM. It is selected from a selection list as shown in Figure 3-38.

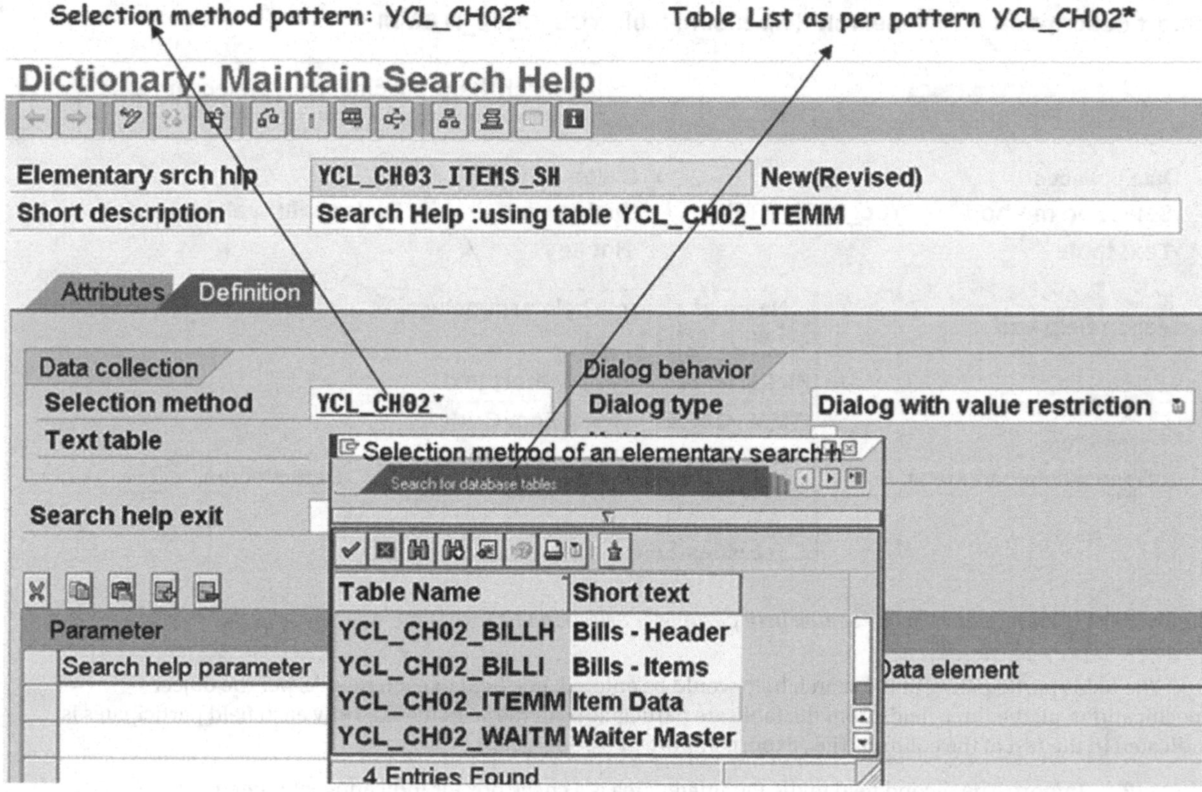

Figure 3-38. Create Search Help – A Selection List on Selection Method

After the selection method is entered, the next field is the Dialog type. This controls the appearance of the restrictive dialog box, whether it appears immediately on the user pressing function key F4 or not. There is a drop-down list with three options. You will select the third option: Dialog with value restriction. This option pops up the restrictive dialog box first, and next the selection list makes its appearance. You can try out the other options as an exercise.

The Search help exit is an advanced feature beyond the scope of this book.

Next is the parameter area. In this area there are nine column fields. For each Search help parameter or field these column fields have to be entered as per requirements. Explanation for these column fields follows:-

1. Search help parameter: This is a field from the source of data. A F4 pop-up (search help) facility is available. The fields from the table or view are listed in the selection list. With your source of data, the table YCL_CH02_ITEMM; its three fields ITEM_CODE, ITEM_DESC and RATE appear in the selection list as shown in Figure 3-39. One of these fields is entered in this column.

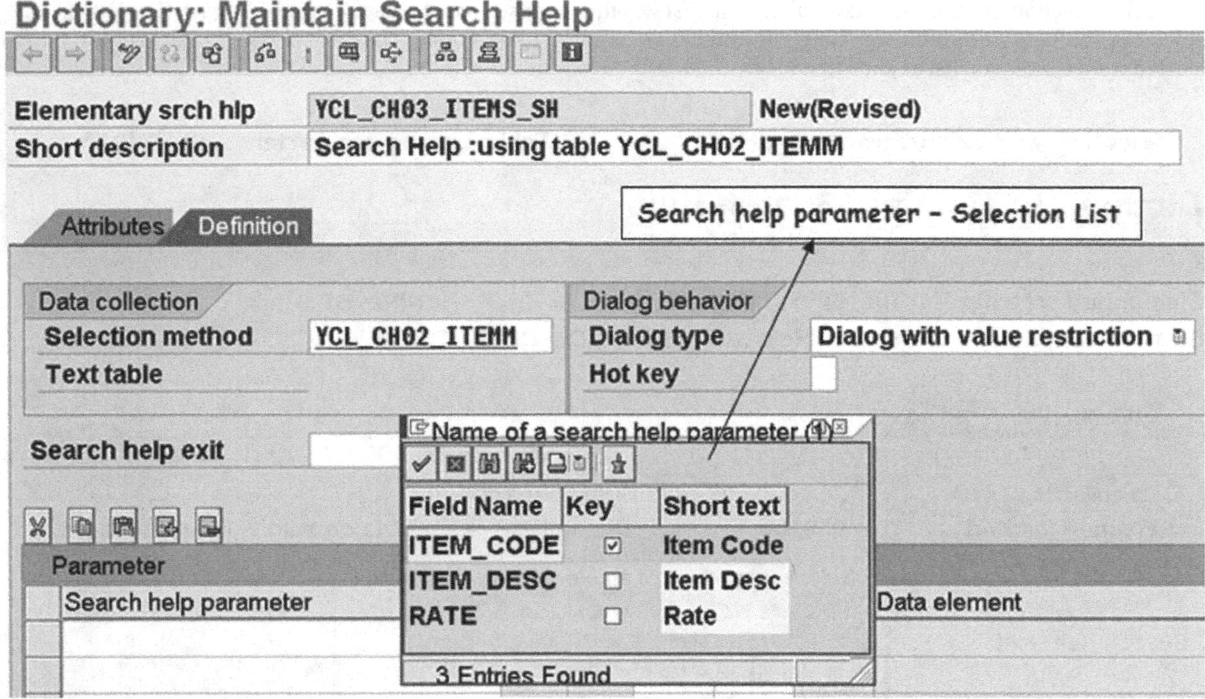

Figure 3-39. Create Search Help – Search help parameter Selection List

The fields participating in the search help would be entered, one field in each row. As per the object specifications, all the three fields from the table are participating in the search help. How each field participates is indicated in the rest of the columns (i.e., export, import, LPos, Spos, etc.).

2. Import: The second field in the Parameter area is a check box for indicating whether a Search help parameter is an import parameter. The export or import is with reference to the search help. The import will be of value/s from screen field/s to one or more of the restrictive dialog box field/s. As has been stated earlier, the import parameter feature will be demonstrated in Chapter 14 entitled Screen Programming.

3. Export: The third field in the Parameter area is a check box for indicating whether a Search help parameter is an export parameter. The export will be transfer of field values from the selection list to screen fields. As per the object specifications, you are exporting two fields such as ITEM_CODE and RATE.

4. LPos: This is the fourth field in the parameter area. Its value controls the physical position of Search help parameter or field in the selection list. If you enter a value 1, the field will appear in the first position in the selection list and so on. If you don't enter any value, this field will not appear in the selection list.

5. SPos: This is the fifth field in the parameter area. It controls the physical position of Search help parameter or field in the restrictive dialog box. If you enter a value of 1, the field will appear in the first position in the restrictive dialog box and so on. If you don't enter any value, this field will not appear in the restrictive dialog box. As per the object specification, the field RATE will qualify for this; you don't want it to appear in the restrictive dialog box.

6. SDis: The sixth field, the SDis, is a check box; it goes with the check box import and so will be covered along with the import. Refer to item 2 for a description.
7. Data element name & Modified check box: (seventh and eighth fields). Every Search help parameter or field by default is assigned a data element that was assigned to it in the source of data (Table or View). This data element name appears in display mode. If for some reason, you want to assign some other data element, then you enable the check box Modified. When you enable this check box, the data element column switches from display to edit mode and you can assign another data element of your choice. The data element and check box Modified go together.
8. Default value: This goes with the check box import and will be covered along with the import.

As per the object specifications, three rows with the appropriate values have been entered in the parameter area, and this is shown in Figure 3-40.

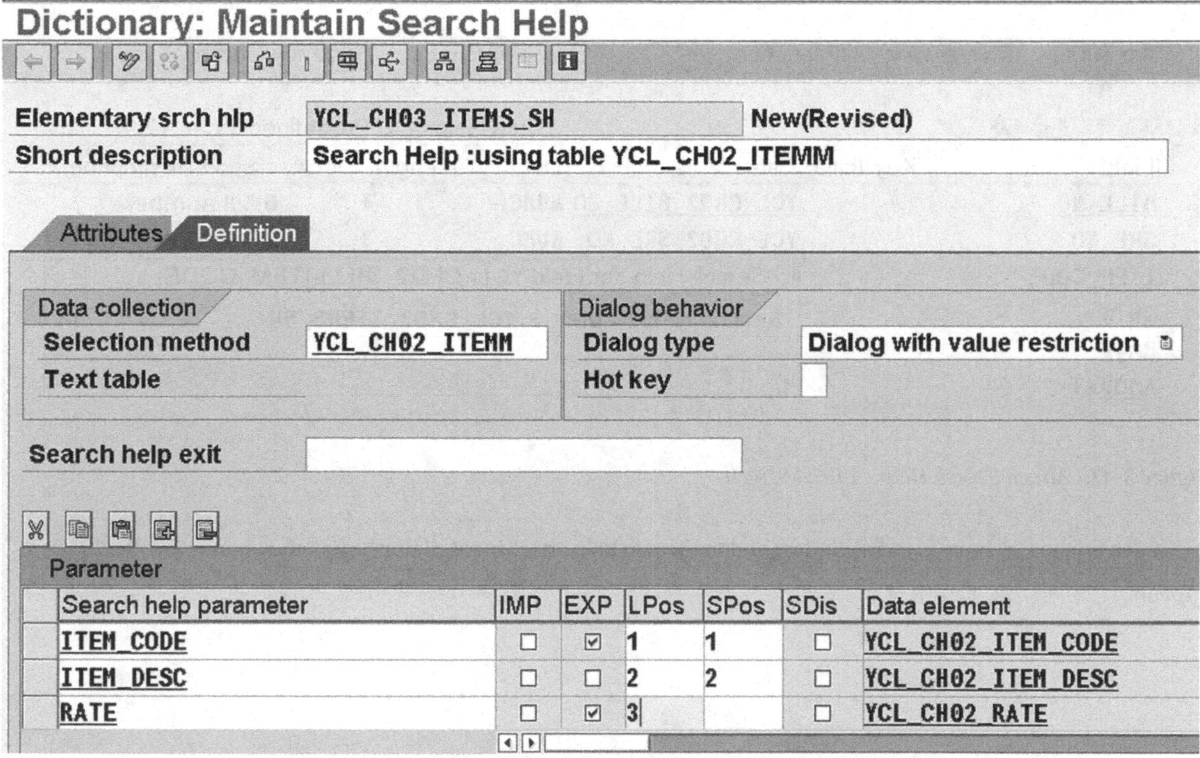

Figure 3-40. *Create Search Help – All Fields filled up as per Object Specification*

Perform a consistency check (button or keys <Ctrl>+<F2>).

Activate the search help (button or keys <Ctrl>+<F3>).

Once the search help is activated, it is ready for attachment to the field ITEM_CODE of table YCL_CH02_BILLI.

Attach Search Help YCL_CH03_ITEMS_SH to Table YCL_CH02_BILLI, Field ITEM_CODE

In attaching a search help to a table field, you will be basically modifying a DDIC table definition.

To attach a search help to a table, in the SE11 opening screen, click on the Database table radio button, enter the name of the table YCL_CH02_BILLI. (Alternatively, you can make a selection from the selection list by entering the pattern YCL_CH02_* and pressing F4, etc.) Click on the Change button or press the function key F6. You will be presented with the table definition screen. On this screen position the cursor on the field to which you want to attach search help: that is, ITEM_CODE (the foreign key field), and click on the Srch help button, next to the foreign key relationship button just above the fields. A dialog box prompting for the search help name will pop up. Enter the name or select the search help from the selection list. The dialog box with the search help name is shown in Figure 3-41.

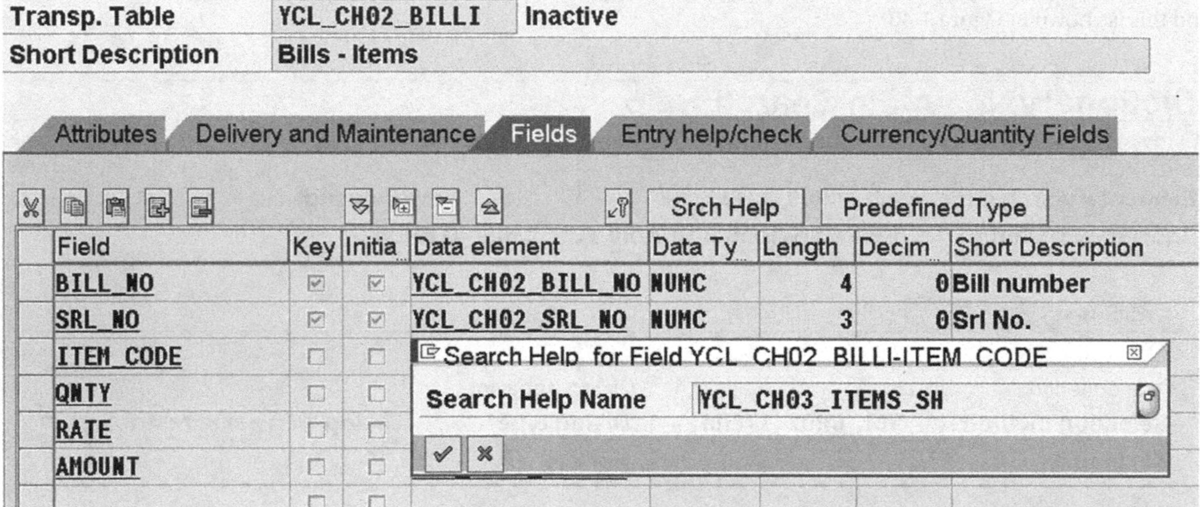

Figure 3-41. Attach Search Help – Initial Screen

Click on the button and a window and the search help attachment dialog box as shown in Figure 3-42 appears.

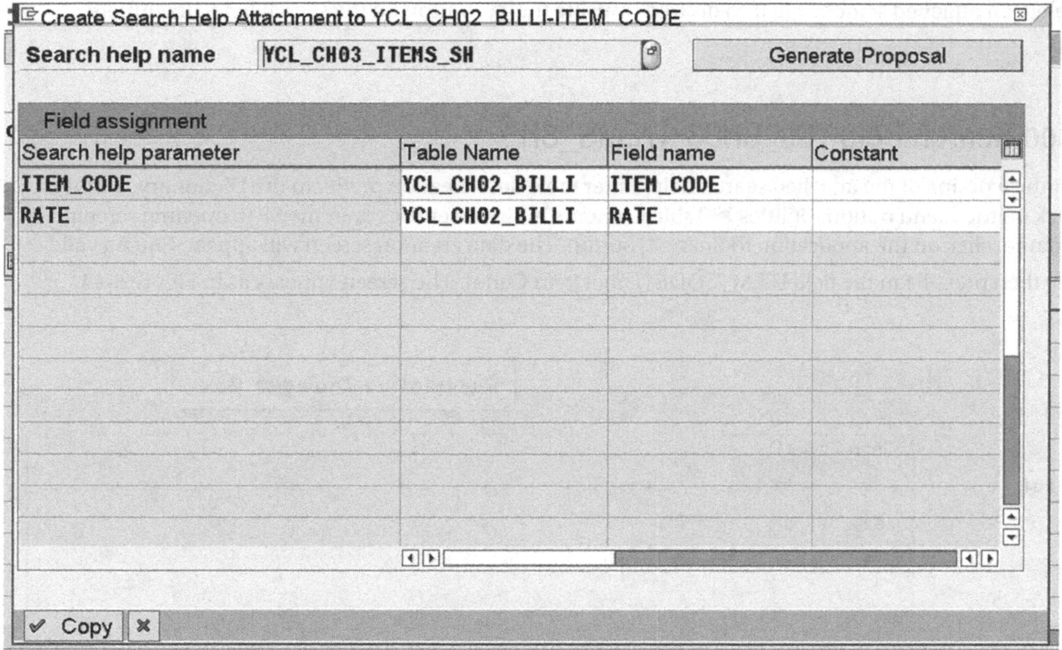

Figure 3-42. *Attach Search Help – Field Assignment*

All the import, export parameters are listed here. Your two export parameters will appear in the Field assignment area. If the fields are not appearing, click on Generate Proposal Button at the top right corner. Click on the Copy button to copy search help.

Save the table changes. Perform a consistency check: button or keys <Ctrl>+<F2>. Activate the table button or keys <Ctrl>+<F3>.Click on the Entry help/check tab on the table maintenance screen, and you will see the search help entry under the Srch Help column for the field ITEM_CODE as shown in Figure 3-43.

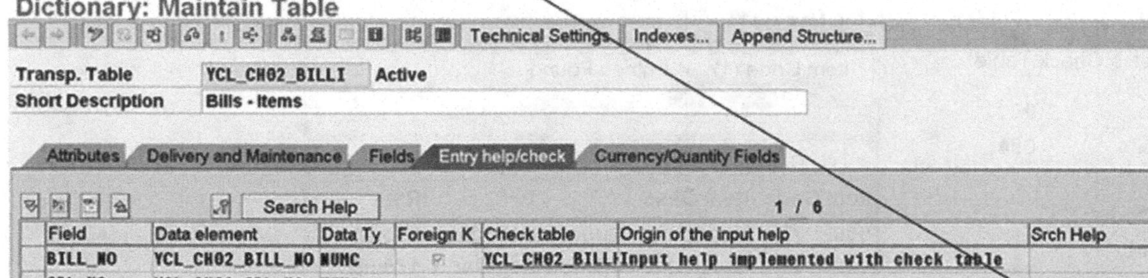

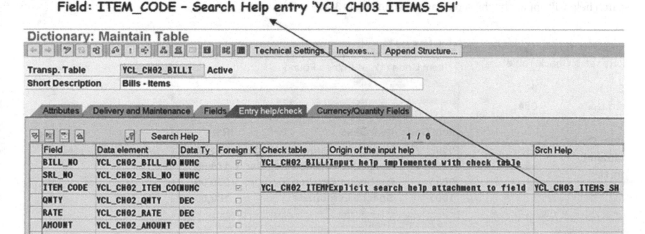

Figure 3-43. *Attach Search Help – Entry in Srch HELP*

You can delete an attached search help if so desired by using the button on the search help attachment dialog box.

Test Attached Search Help YCL_CH03_ITEMS_SH

You need to test the working of the attached search help. Enter table data creation mode. In the Dictionary: Maintain Table screen click on the menu option: Utilities ➤ Table Contents ➤ Create entries or in the SE16 opening screen, enter the table name, click on the application toolbar button. The data creation screen will appear. Enter a valid bill no, serial no; then press F4 in the field ITEM_CODE (Label Item Code). The screen appears as in Figure 3-44.

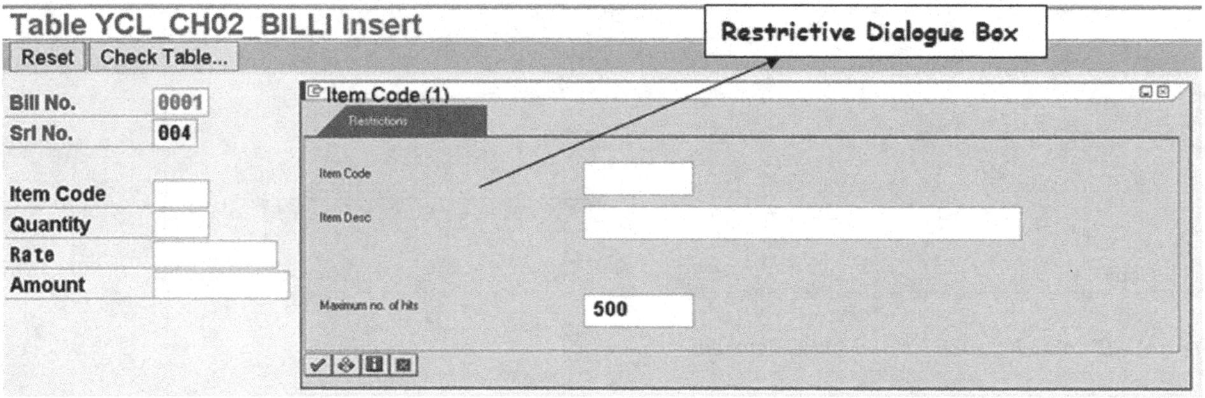

Figure 3-44. *Test Search Help – Restrictive Dialogue Box*

You are viewing the search help restrictive dialog box with the two fields ITEM_CODE and ITEM_DESC. SPos values for these two fields were 1 and 2 respectively, and they appear in the first and second position in the restrictive dialog box. You can enter some value/s or pattern/s in these fields in the dialog box and data will be filtered as per the value/s, pattern/s in the selection list. If you do not enter any value and press <Enter>, all the rows (up to the Maximum of Hits) will appear in the selection list. Press <Enter> in the restrictive dialog box. The selection list of the search help will appear on the screen as shown in Figure 3-45.

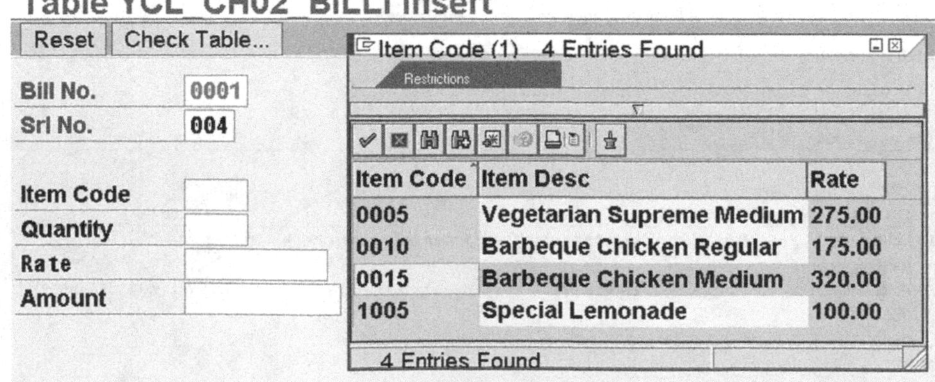

Figure 3-45. *Test Search Help – Selection List*

The search help selection list is displaying ITEM_CODE in the first position, ITEM_DESC in the second position, and RATE in the third position as per the object specification; LPos value assignments to these fields are 1, 2, and 3. Select an item in the selection list by double-clicking on it or selecting the row and clicking on the button (the Button is used for cancellation and exit of selection list). Select ITEM_CODE value 0015 with RATE value 320.00. The search help exports the two fields' ITEM_CODE and RATE values from the selection list fields to the respective screen fields. This is shown in Figure 3-46.

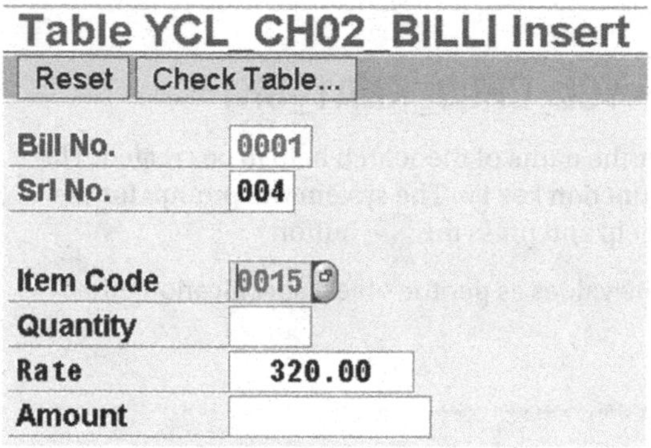

Table YCL_CH02_BILLI Insert
Reset | Check Table...
Bill No. 0001
Srl No. 004
Item Code 0015
Quantity
Rate 320.00
Amount

Figure 3-46. *Test Search Help – Export from Selection List to Screen Fields*

You have fully tested the search help and it is operating as per the object specifications.

Search Helps with SAP delivered Tables

Scenario of Elementary Search Help with SAP Delivered Table

You will create search helps using the SAP customer primary table KNA1. You will not be able to attach this search help to a SAP table field (no modification of SAP delivered objects); you will test the search through an ABAP program. ABAP program writing is being introduced in a preview manner. It will be formally introduced in the Chapter 4.

The object specification for this search help follows in the next section:

Create Elementary Search Help with Customer Primary Table KNA1 - Object Specification

```
Search Help name:           YCL_CH03_KNA1_SH1

Table:                      KNA1 (source of data)

Test:                       ABAP Program


Selection List Fields:      KUNNR - LPos = 1.
                            NAME1 - LPos = 2.
                            ORT01 - LPos = 3.
                            LAND1 - Lpos = 4. (Country Code)
```

```
Restrictive Dialogue Box Fields    KUNNR - SPos = 1.
                                   NAME1 - SPos = 2.
                                   ORT01 - SPos = 3.
                                   LAND1 - SPos = 4. (Country Code)

Export Fields:                     KUNNR - Export = X.

Import Fields:                     None
```

Create Elementary Search Help with Table KNA1 - YCL_CH03_KNA1_SH1

In the SE11 opening screen, select the radio button Search help. Enter the name of the search help to be created. The name is YCL_CH03_KNA1_SH1. Click on the Create button or press function key F5. The system will prompt for the search help type to be created. Select the default Elementary search help and press the ✔ button.

The screen to create elementary search help will appear. Fill in the values as per the object specification. After filling in the values, the screen will appear as shown in Figure 3-47.

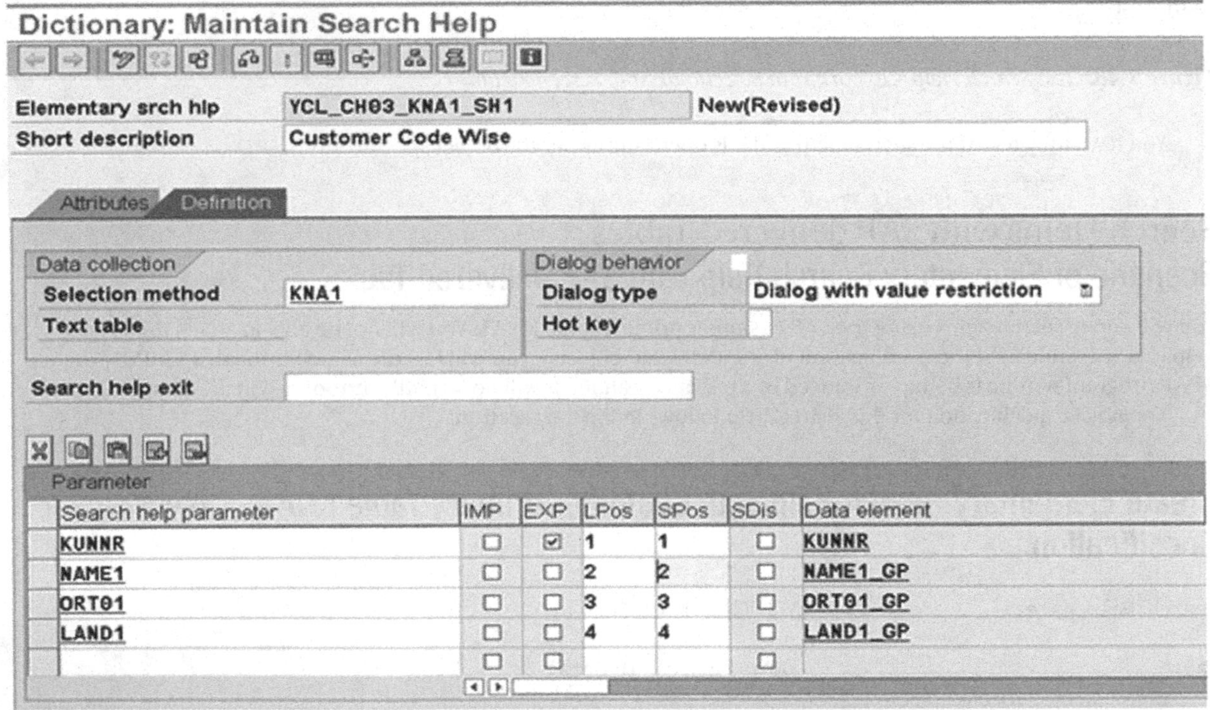

Figure 3-47. Create Search Help -YCL_CH03_KNA1_SH1

Save and perform a consistency check and activate.

Test Elementary Search Help YCL_CH03_KNA1_SH1 in its environment

There is a mode of testing a search help within the search help environment. Select menu option Search Help ➤ Test. A window appears as shown in Figure 3-48.

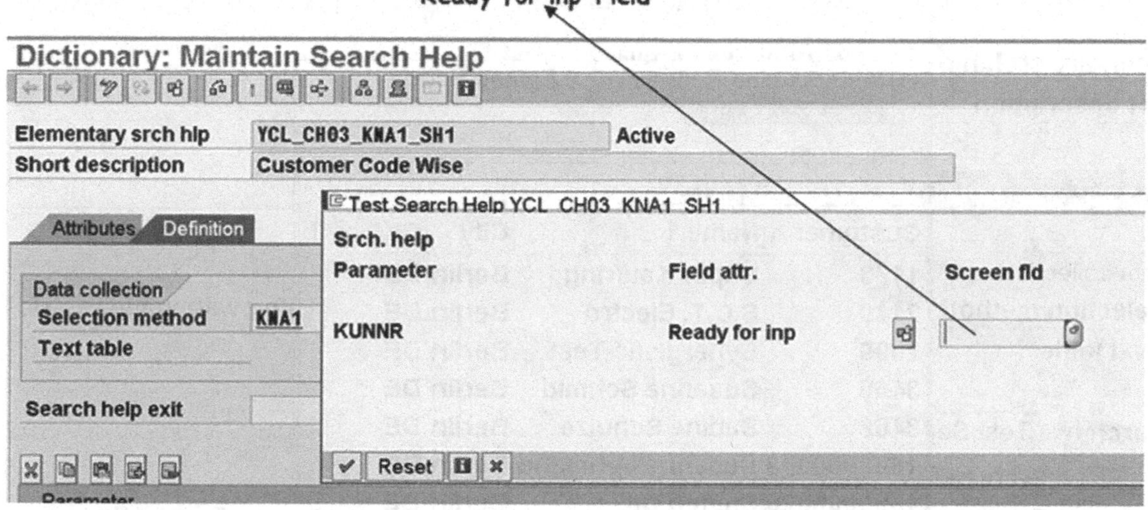

Figure 3-48. Test Search Help - YCL_CH03_KNA1_SH1 in Search Help Screen

Click in the field Ready for inp and press F4. The restrictive dialog box as shown in Figure 3-49 appears.

Dictionary: Maintain Search Help
Elementary srch hlp YCL_CH03_KNA1_SH1 Active
Short description Customer Code Wise
Test Search Help YCL_CH03_KNA1_SH1
Restrict Value Range (1)
Restrictions
Customer
Name S*
City Berlin
Country
Maximum no. of hits 500
Parameter
Search help parar
KUNNR
NAME1
ORT01

Figure 3-49. Test Search Help - YCL_CH03_KNA1_SH1 Restrictive Dialogue Box

Enter S* in the Name1 field and Berlin in ORT01 field. That is, fetch all customers of Berlin starting with the letter S. This produces the selection list as shown in Figure 3-50.

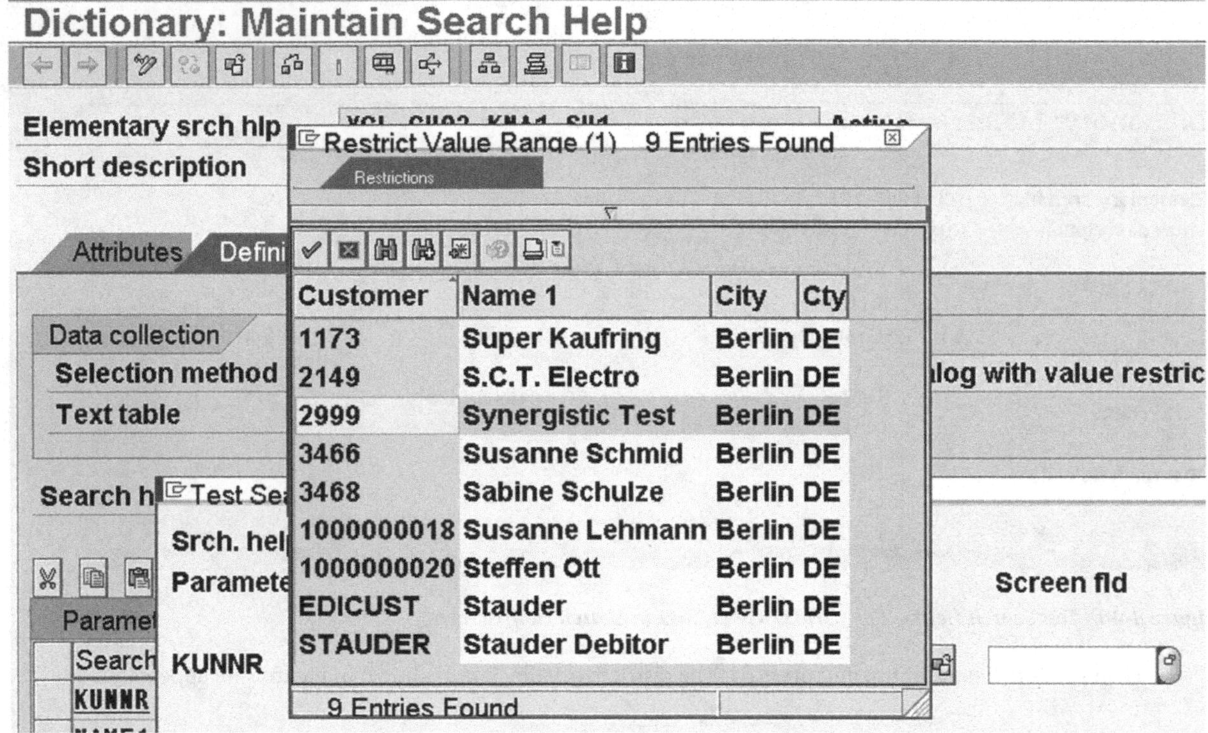

Figure 3-50. *Test Search Help - YCL_CH03_KNA1_SH1 Selection List*

If you select a customer, the customer code field KUNNR value should be exported from the selection list to the screen field. Select the customer code 2999. When you double-click on this, it is returned to the screen field. This is shown in Figure 3-51.

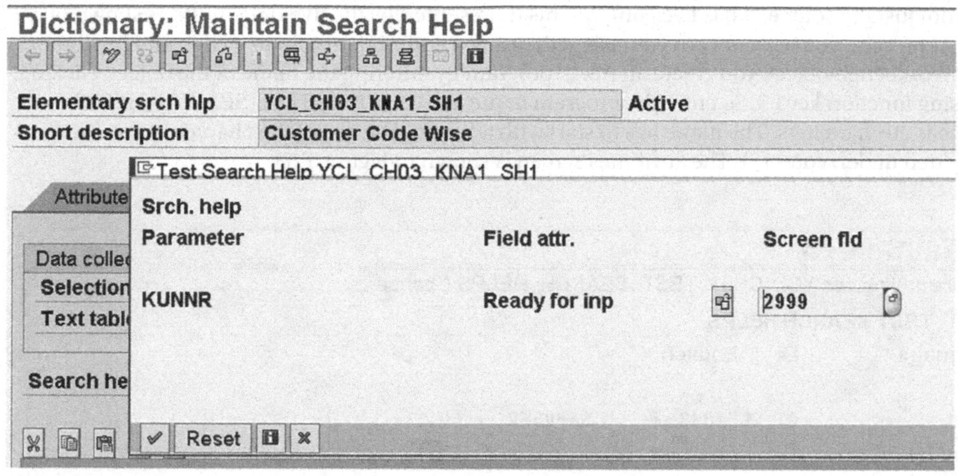

Figure 3-51. *Test Search Help - YCL_CH03_KNA1_SH1 Export*

This search help is as per the object specification. It has four fields in the restrictive dialog box in the order specified by SPos values. It has the same four fields in the selection list in the order specified by LPos values. It is returning the value of KUNNR from the selection list to the screen field.

Test Elementary Search Help YCL_CH03_KNA1_SH1 with an ABAP Program

Create an ABAP program. The transaction code for ABAP program maintenance is SE38. The SE38 opening screen is shown in Figure 3-52.

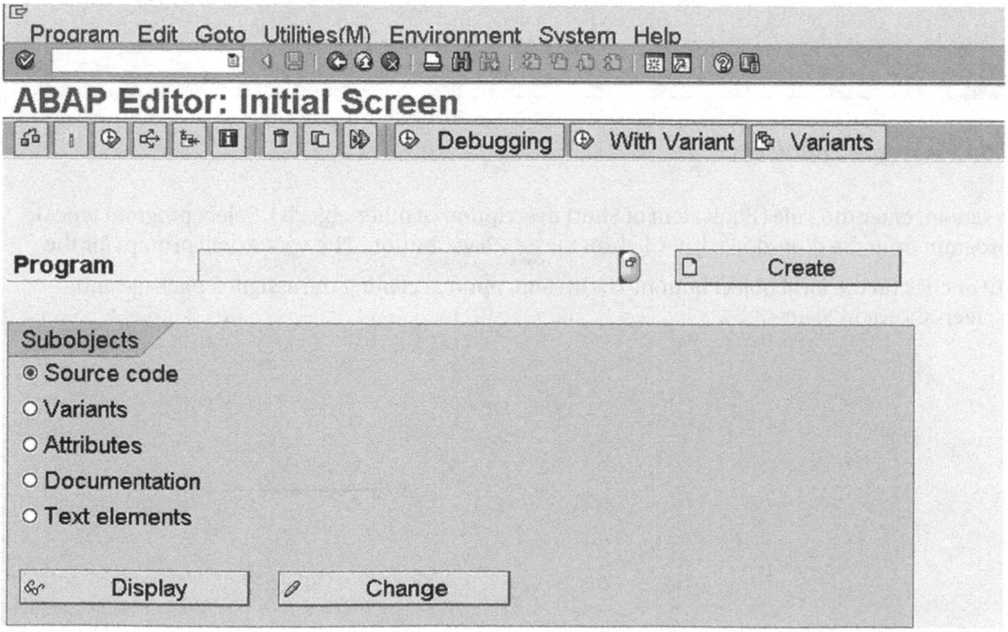

Figure 3-52. *ABAP Editor - Opening Screen*

An ABAP program is not just the source. It has five components represented by the five radio buttons shown on the screen of Figure 3-52. At present, you will concern yourself with just two components: Source code and Attributes.

Like any other ABAP Workbench object, you create an ABAP program by entering the name of the object, clicking the Create button or pressing function key F5. So enter the program name as YCL_CH03_TEST_SEARCH_HELPS. The maximum name space is 30 characters. The name has to start with a Y or Z. The rest of the characters can be alphanumeric with embedded underscores (_). The attributes screen is shown in Figure 3-53.

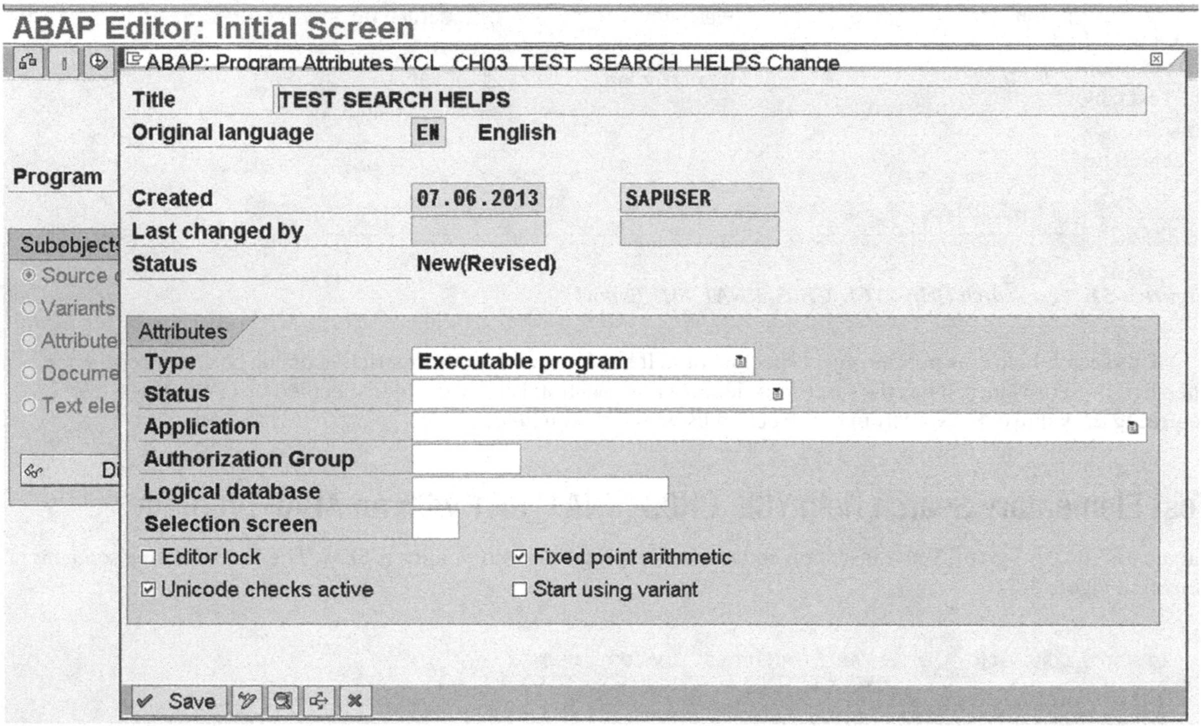

Figure 3-53. *ABAP Editor - Program Attributes*

In the Attributes screen, enter the Title (Equivalent of Short description of other objects). Select program type or Type as Executable program from the drop-down list. Click on the ✔ Save button. The system will prompt for the package. Assign $TMP or click on the local object button. The system, upon accepting the assigned package and saving, presents the screen shown in Figure 3-54.

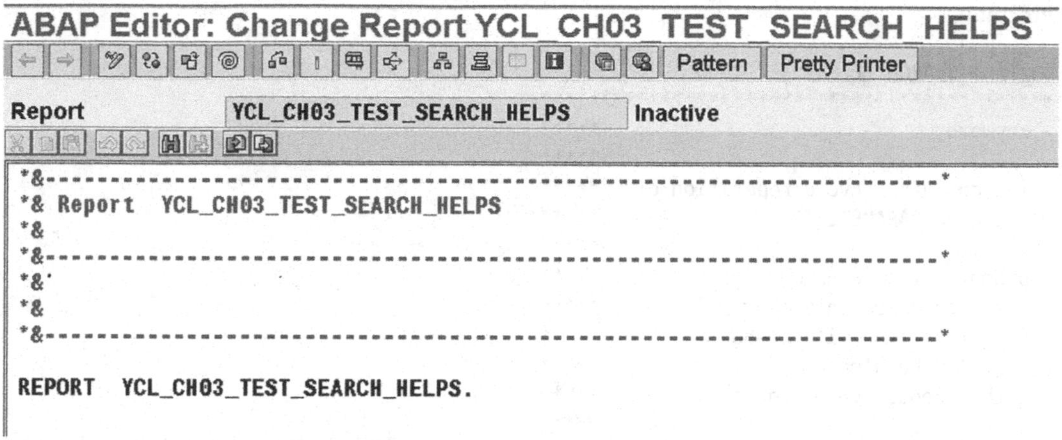

ABAP Editor: Change Report YCL_CH03_TEST_SEARCH_HELPS

Pattern Pretty Printer

Report YCL_CH03_TEST_SEARCH_HELPS Inactive

```
*&---------------------------------------------------------------------*
*& Report  YCL_CH03_TEST_SEARCH_HELPS
*&
*&---------------------------------------------------------------------*
*&
*&
*&---------------------------------------------------------------------*

REPORT  YCL_CH03_TEST_SEARCH_HELPS.
```

Figure 3-54. *ABAP Source Text Editor*

The ABAP text editor has all the facilities to create and maintain source text. Its features will be covered in detail when ABAP is introduced formally in Chapter 4.

If a line has an asterisk or * in the first column, the entire line is treated as a comment line.

If a line has a double quote or “, the rest of the line to the right of double quote “”’is treated as a comment.

When you create a program, the system generates seven lines of comments, as well as the REPORT statement for an executable program (the executable program is the program type assigned on the attribute screen). The REPORT is a key word and is followed by the name of a program and is terminated by a period (.). All statements except the chained ones are terminated by a period. Chained statements are separated by commas (,) with the last statement in the chain again terminated by a period.

The convention is to create ABAP source in upper case.

The following lines have been entered in the editor. There is elaborate comment at the beginning of program. Read this comment carefully. The PARAMETER statement is somewhat like the scanf of C. It creates a screen prompt. You are attaching the search help to the prompt variable with the key phrase MATCHCODE OBJECT. The prompt variable is referring to the DDIC field KUNNR of table KNA1. The prompt variable will derive its TYPE, length, etc., from the TYPE length of field KUNNR in the table KNA1. The notation KNA1-KUNNR denotes field KUNNR of table KNA1.

The ABAP Program:

```
REPORT YCL_CH03_TEST_SEARCH_HELPS.
********************************************************
* PARAMETERS - keyword                            *****
*                                                 *****
* :          - for chaining (Avoid repetition of  *****
*              key word PARAMETERS)               *****
*                                                 *****
* CUST_CD1   - prompt variable name.              *****
*              Variable name can 8 char           *****
*              long, starting with alpha          *****
*              rest can be alphanumeric           *****
*              with embedded underscores          *****
*                                                 *****
* TYPE       - key word                           *****
*                                                 *****
* KNA1-KUNNR - TYPE, LENGTH of CUST_CD1           *****
*              same as TYPE, LENGTH OF            *****
*              KNA1-KUNNR                         *****
*                                                 *****
* MATCHCODE  - key phrase to attach               *****
* OBJECT       search help                        *****
*                                                 *****
* YCL_CH03_KNA1_SH1 - name of search help         *****
********************************************************
PARAMETERS:
     CUST_CD1 TYPE KNA1-KUNNR MATCHCODE OBJECT YCL_CH03_KNA1_SH1
```

Perform a program syntax check (the button or keys <Ctrl>+<F2>).

Activate the program (the button or keys <Ctrl>+<F3>).

Execute the program by clicking on the button or pressing the function key F8. A screen prompt will appear as shown in Figure 3-55.

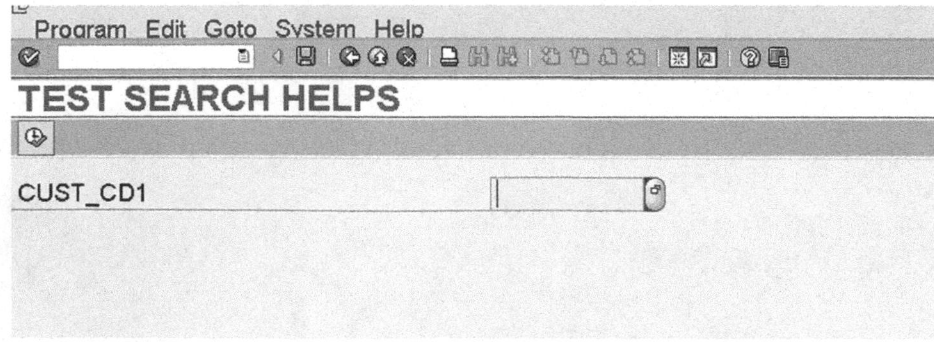

Figure 3-55. *PARAMETERS Variable with Search Help Attached*

On pressing the function key F4 on this prompt variable, the restrictive dialog box as shown in Figure 3-56 pops up.

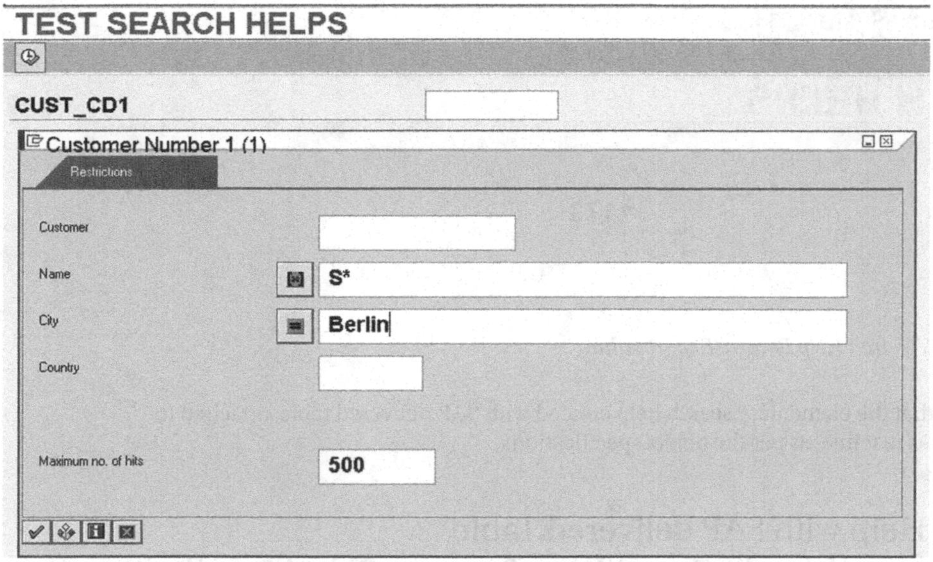

TEST SEARCH HELPS

CUST_CD1

Customer Number 1 (1)

Restrictions

Customer

Name S*

City Berlin

Country

Maximum no. of hits 500

Figure 3-56. PARAMETERS Search Help Restrictive Dialogue Box

Entering the S* pattern in Name field and Berlin in the City field will fetch all customers' names starting with S of City Berlin, and these will appear in the search help selection list as shown in Figure 3-57.

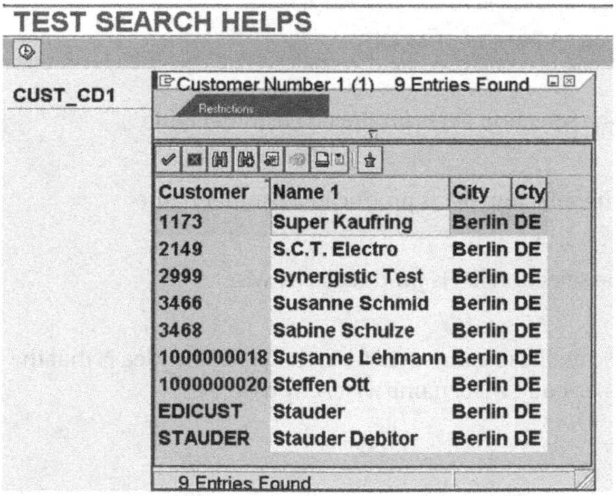

TEST SEARCH HELPS

CUST_CD1

Customer Number 1 (1) 9 Entries Found

Restrictions

Customer	Name 1	City	Cty
1173	Super Kaufring	Berlin	DE
2149	S.C.T. Electro	Berlin	DE
2999	Synergistic Test	Berlin	DE
3466	Susanne Schmid	Berlin	DE
3468	Sabine Schulze	Berlin	DE
1000000018	Susanne Lehmann	Berlin	DE
1000000020	Steffen Ott	Berlin	DE
EDICUST	Stauder	Berlin	DE
STAUDER	Stauder Debitor	Berlin	DE

9 Entries Found

Figure 3-57. PARAMETERS Search Help Selection List

On double-clicking on the customer 1173, this is returned or exported to the screen prompt variable. This is shown in Figure 3-58.

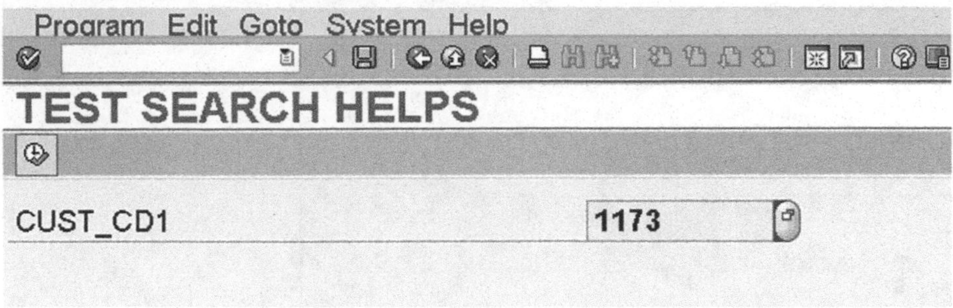

Figure 3-58. PARAMETERS Search Help Return/Export value

So you have observed that the elementary search help created with SAP delivered table, attached to PARAMETERS variable works just fine, as per the object specifications.

Collective Search Help with SAP delivered Table

Create Collective Search Help with Table KNA1 –Scenario, Object Specification

You will create a collective search help with SAP delivered with table KNA1. A collective search help consists of a collection of elementary search helps. In the elementary search help YCL_CH03_KNA1_SH1, the first field in the selection list is KUNNR for which LPos = 1. The selection list by default is produced in ascending order of the first field in the selection list (i.e., the field for which LPos = 1).

Let two more elementary search helps be created: (a) YCL_CH03_KNA1_SH2 in which LPos for NAME1 = 1, and (b) YCL_CH03_KNA1_SH3 in which LPos for ORT01 = 1.

Both these elementary search helps will have the same export parameter KUNNR.

Finally you will have three elementary search helps:

- YCL_CH03_KNA1_SH1 – field KUNNR, LPos = 1. The selection list is produced customer code wise ascending. Export parameter - KUNNR.
- YCL_CH03_KNA1_SH2 – field NAME1, LPos = 1. The selection list is produced customer name wise ascending. Export parameter - KUNNR.
- YCL_CH03_KNA1_SH3 – field ORT01, LPos = 1. The selection list is produced city wise ascending. Export parameter – KUNNR.

You will create a collective search help in which you will locate these elementary search helps. The idea is that the same information of customers is presented in different ways (i.e., code wise, name wise, city wise).

Create Two Elementary Search Helps to be included in collective search helps

Create the elementary search help YCL_CH03_KNA1_SH2. The filled-in values of the search help screen are shown in Figure 3-59.

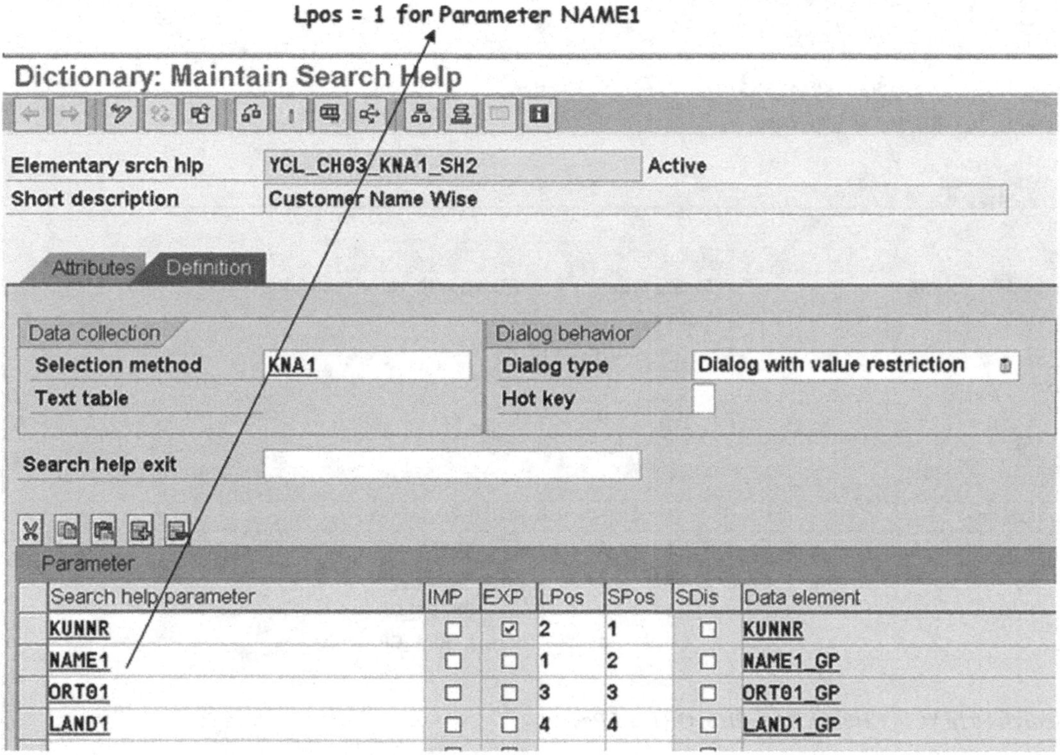

Figure 3-59. *Search Help YCL_CH03_KNA1_SH2, NAME LPos = 1*

Perform a consistency check and activate.
Test the elementary search help in the search help environment.

Create the elementary search help YCL_CH03_KNA1_SH3. The filled-in values of the search help screen are shown in Figure 3-60.

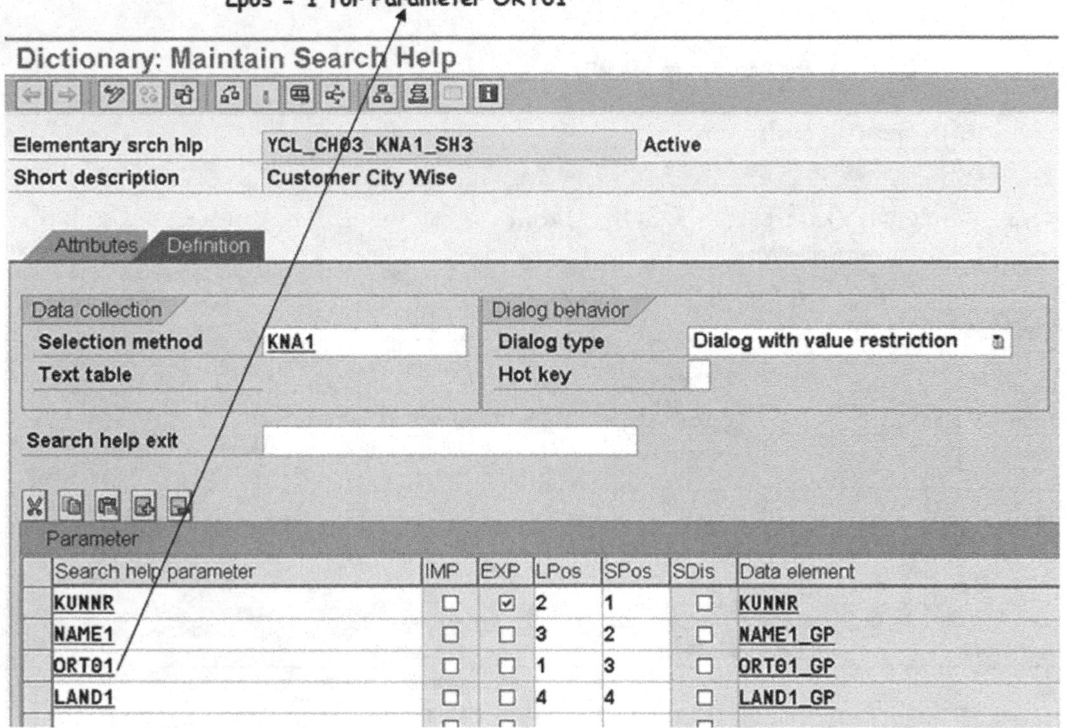

Figure 3-60. Search Help YCL_CH03_KNA1_SH3, ORT01 LPos = 1

Perform a consistency check and activate.
Test the elementary search help in the search help environment.

Create, Test Collective Search Help

In the SE11 opening screen, select the radio button Search help. Enter the name of the search help to be crested: YCL_CH03_KNA1_CSH. Click on the Create button or press the function key F5. The system will prompt for the search help type to be created. Select this time the collective search help radio button, and press the ✔ button.

The screen to create collective search help appears as shown in Figure 3-61.

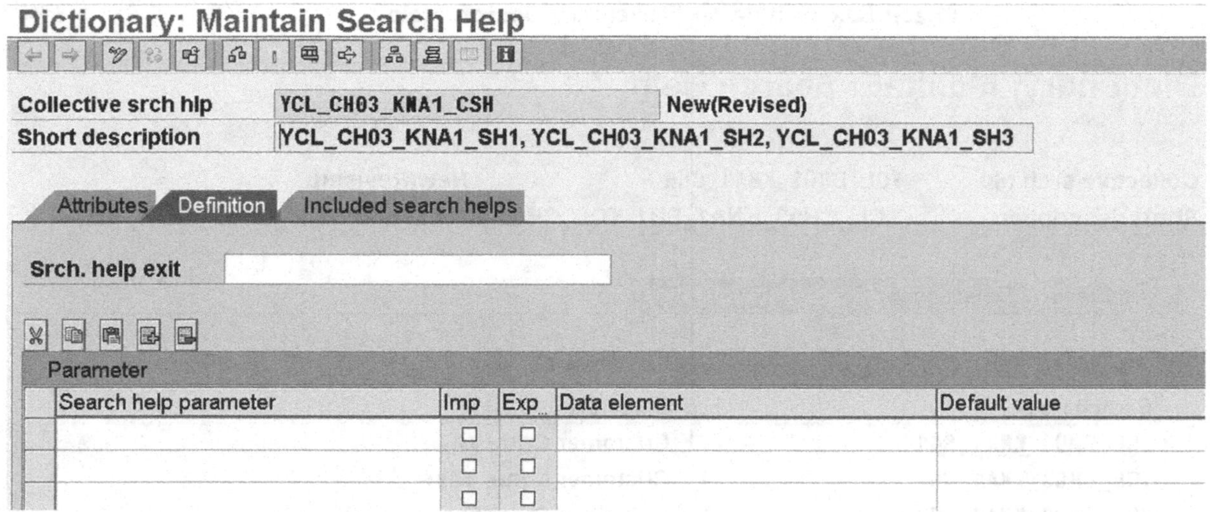

Figure 3-61. *Create Collective Search Help – Definition tab*

Click on the Included search helps tab. The second tab under the first column Search Help, you have to incorporate the elementary search helps, one in each row. Enter the pattern YCL_CH03* and press F4. A selection list to choose an elementary search help appears as shown in Figure 3-62.

Dictionary: Maintain Search Help

Collective srch hlp YCL_CH03_KNA1_CSH New(Revised)

Short description YCL_CH03_KNA1_SH1, YCL_CH03_KNA1_SH2, YCL_CH03_KNA1_SH3

Attributes | Definition | Included search helps

Param. assignment

Search Help: YCL_CH03_KNA1* | Hid

Search help included in a collective search help (2) 3 Entries

Srch Help	HKy	el	Short text
YCL_CH03_KNA1_SH1	H	☑	Customer Code Wise
YCL_CH03_KNA1_SH2		☑	Customer Name Wise
YCL_CH03_KNA1_SH3		☑	Customer City Wise

3 Entries Found

Figure 3-62. *Create Collective Search Help – Included search helps tab*

Assign each of the three elementary search helps YCL_CH03_KNA1_SH1, YCL_CH03_KNA1_SH2, and YCL_CH03_KNA1_SH3. The check box to hide an elementary search help is in the context of enhancing an SAP delivered collective search help. The screen with the assigned elementary search helps is shown in Figure 3-63.

Check Box to hide an Elementary Search Help

Dictionary: Maintain Search Help

Collective srch hlp	YCL_CH03_KNA1_CSH New(Revised)
Short description	YCL_CH03_KNA1_SH1, YCL_CH03_KNA1_SH2, YCL_CH03_KNA1_SH3

Attributes | Definition | Included search helps

Param. assignment

Search Help	Hid	Short text
YCL_CH03_KNA1_SH1	☐	Customer Code Wise
YCL_CH03_KNA1_SH2	☐	Customer Name Wise
YCL_CH03_KNA1_SH3	☐	Customer City Wise
	☐	

Figure 3-63. Create Collective Search Help –Enter elementary search helps

Click the Definition tab. Now, on this tab, you have to manually enter all the export and import parameters of all the elementary search helps included in the collective search help. In your scenario, you have only one export parameter KUNNR for all your three elementary search helps and no import parameter. Enter this export parameter under the column Search help parameter, and enable the export check box; enter the data element name for KUNNR, which is KUNNR itself. (Verify from the KNA1 table definition, the data element name for the field KUNNR). After entering parameter KUNNR, enabling the export check box, entering the data element KUNNR; the screen is as shown in Figure 3-64.

Dictionary: Maintain Search Help

Collective srch hlp	YCL_CH03_KNA1_CSH New(Revised)
Short description	YCL_CH03_KNA1_SH1, YCL_CH03_KNA1_SH2, YCL_CH03_KNA1_SH3

Attributes | Definition | Included search helps

Srch. help exit

Parameter

Search help parameter	Imp	Exp	Data element	Default value
KUNNR	☐	☑	KUNNR	
	☐	☐		

Figure 3-64. Create Collective Search Help – Enter parameters in Definition tab)

Click again on the Included search helps tab. You have to assign export and import parameters to each of the included elementary search helps. To do this, position the cursor on each of the elementary search help rows in turns (YCL_CH03_KNA1_SH1 and so on) and click on the button Param. assignment. A message prompt appears asking whether the system should propose parameter assignment. Click on the button Yes. This is shown in Figure 3-65.

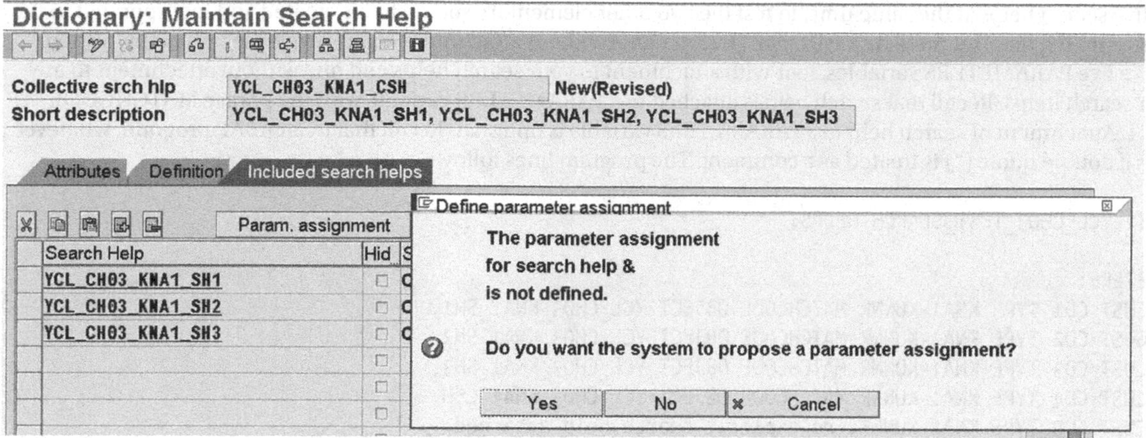

Figure 3-65. Create Collective Search Help – parameters assignment message prompt

On clicking the button Yes, the parameter assignment system proposal window will appear as shown in Figure 3-66.

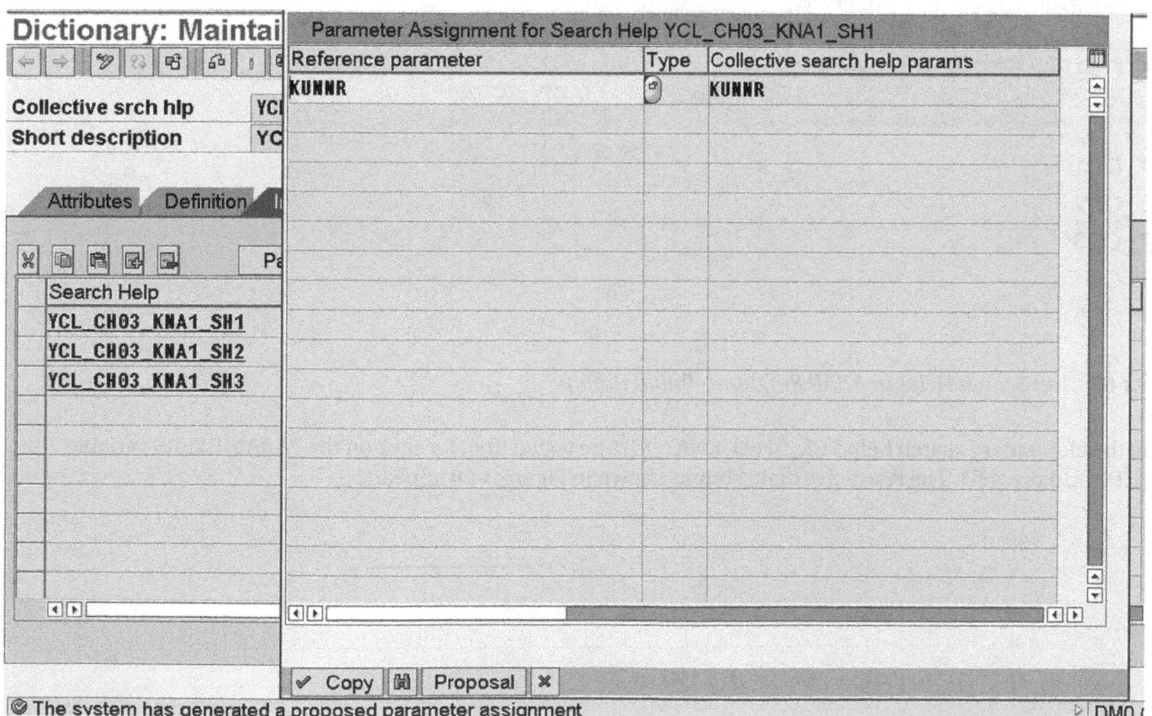

Figure 3-66. Create Collective Search Help – parameters assignment System Proposal

Click on the ✔ Copy button. Repeat this procedure for remaining two elementary searches helps (i.e., YCL_CH03_KNA1_SH2 and YCL_CH03_KNA1_SH3).

Perform a consistency check. Activate the collective search help.

You are ready to test the collective search help. Let it be done in the ABAP program. Modify your program that you used to test the elementary search help. Write a statement to have the PARAMETERS variable to attach the collective search help. At the same time, to test the two other elementary search helps created and incorporated in the collective search help, let there be a PARAMETERS variable without attachment of any of your search helps. So you will have five PARAMETERS variables, four with attachment to your search helps and one without attachment to any of your search helps. Recall that search help is attached to a PARAMETERS variable with the phrase MATCHCODE OBJECT. Attachment of search help to a PARAMETERS variable is optional. Recall that in an ABAP program, whatever follows a double quote (") is treated as a comment. The program lines follow:

```
REPORT  YCL_CH03_TEST_SEARCH_HELPS.

PARAMETERS:
     CUST_CD1 TYPE KNA1-KUNNR MATCHCODE OBJECT YCL_CH03_KNA1_SH1,
     CUST_CD2 TYPE KNA1-KUNNR MATCHCODE OBJECT YCL_CH03_KNA1_SH2,
     CUST_CD3 TYPE KNA1-KUNNR MATCHCODE OBJECT YCL_CH03_KNA1_SH3,
     CUST_CD4 TYPE KNA1-KUNNR MATCHCODE OBJECT YCL_CH03_KNA1_CSH,
     CUST_CD5 TYPE KNA1-KUNNR. no explicit search help attached
```

After the modifications have been carried out, perform syntax check, troubleshoot syntax errors and fix them if any; activate the program, and execute it (F8 /). The screen will be as shown in Figure 3-67.

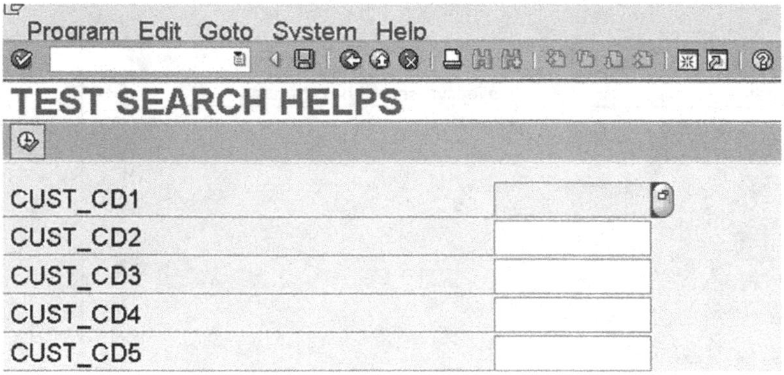

Figure 3-67. *Test Search Helps in ABAP Program - Initial Prompt*

Let the elementary search help YCL_CH03_KNA1_SH2 be tested first. So click on the PARAMETERS variable CUST_CD2 and press F4. The restrictive dialog box as shown in Figure 3-68 appears.

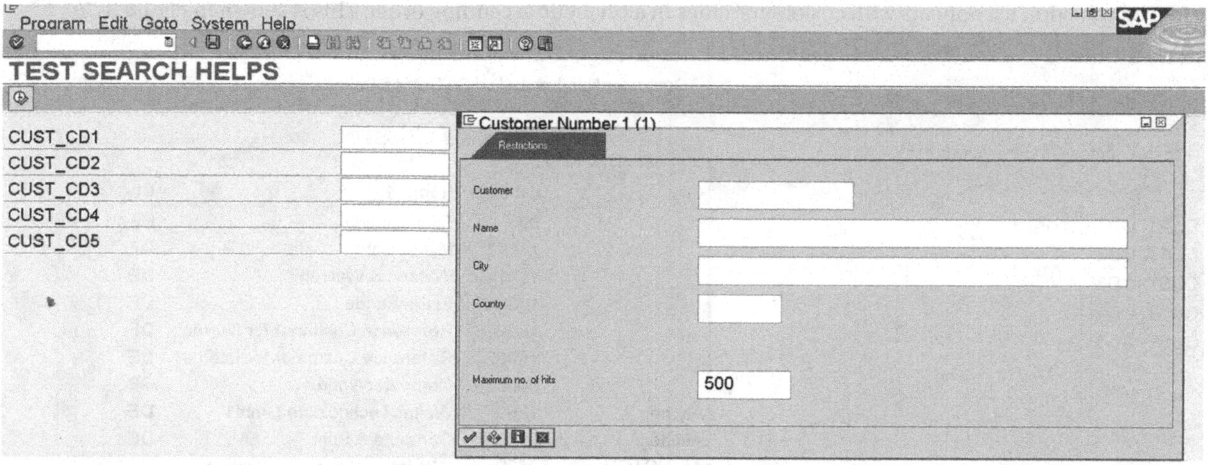

Figure 3-68. *Test Search Helps in ABAP Program – CUST_CD2-Restrictive Dialogue Box*

Press <Enter>. The selection list appears with customers' names in alphabetic ascending order. This is shown in Figure 3-69.

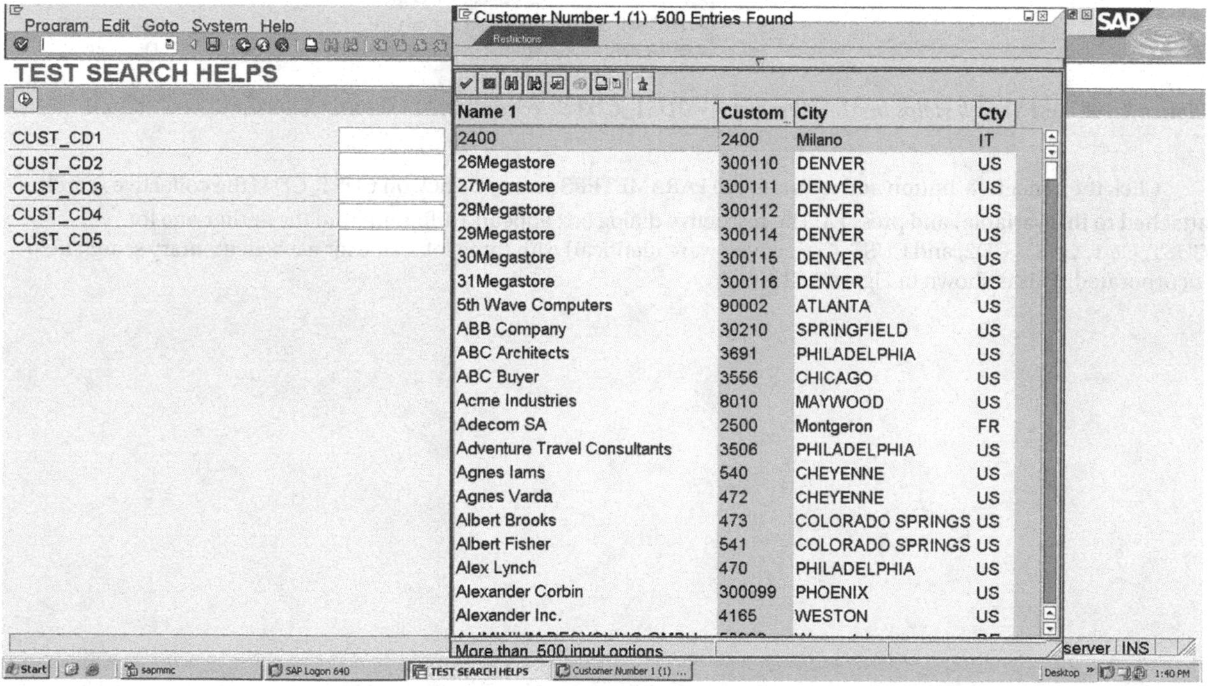

Figure 3-69. *Test Search Helps in ABAP Program – CUST_CD2-Selection List*

Click the cancel [✔ Save] button and return to the PARAMETERS prompt. Click on CUST_CD3 and press F4. The restrictive dialog box appears, which is the same as for CUST_CD2. Press <Enter>.

The selection list appears with customers' cities in alphabetic ascending order. This is shown in Figure 3-70.

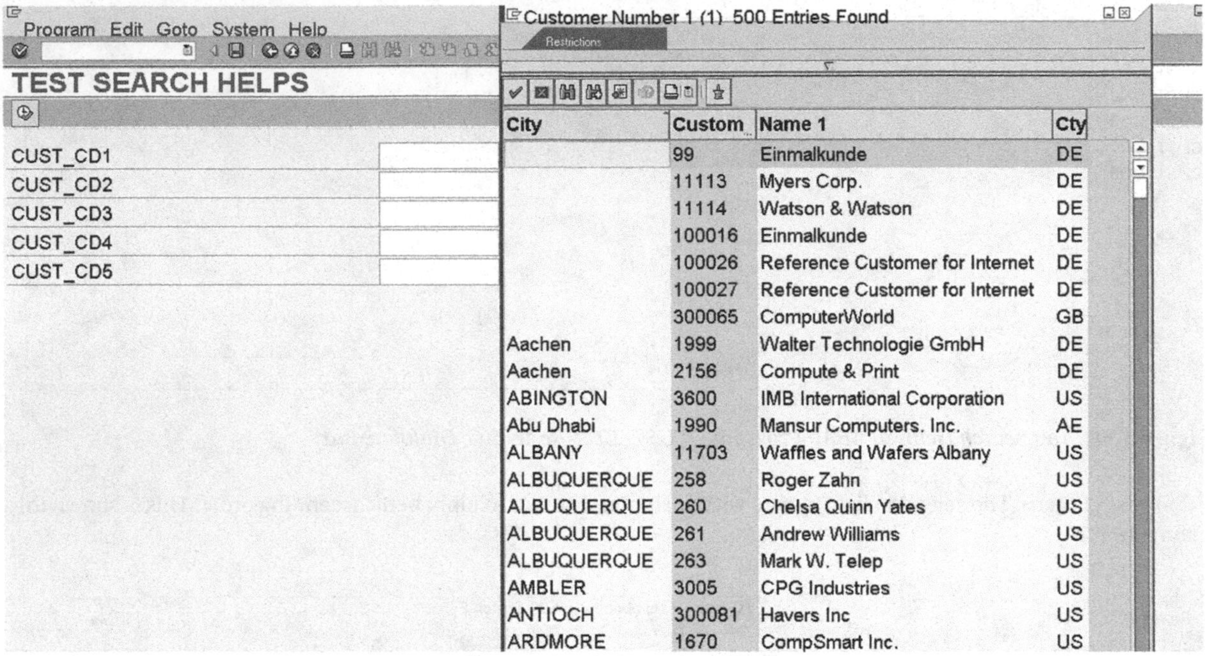

Figure 3-70. Test Search Helps in ABAP Program - CUST_CD3-Selection List

Click the cancel button and return to the PARAMETERS prompt. Click on CUST_CD4 (the collective search attached to this variable) and press F4. The restrictive dialog box appears (different from the earlier one for CUST_CD1, CUST_CD2, and CUST_CD3, which were identical) with three tabs, one for each elementary search help incorporated. This is shown in Figure 3-71.

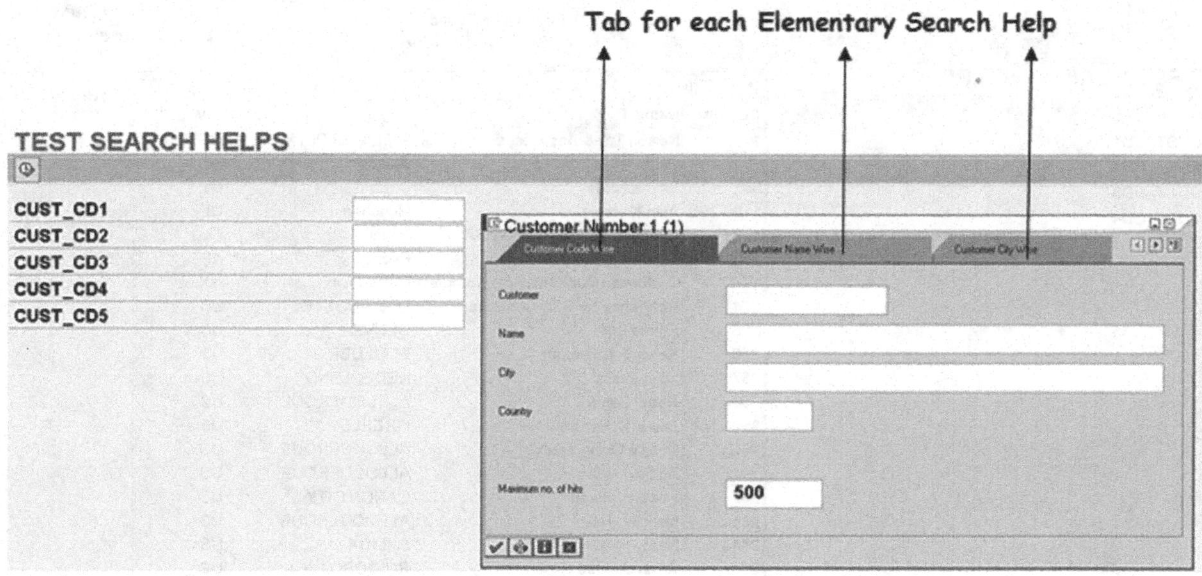

Figure 3-71. *Test Collective Search Help in ABAP Program - CUST_CD4-Restrictive Dialogue Box*

The three tabs for Customer Code Wise, Customer Name Wise, and Customer City Wise correspond to each of the elementary search helps. For simplicity, your restrictive dialog box is the same for all the elementary search helps (i.e., the SPos values are identical for all the elementary search helps). The texts Customer Code Wise, etc., are picked up from the short description of the respective elementary search helps.

You are now on the Customer Code Wise tab, and when you press <Enter>, customer code wise selection list appears as shown in Figure 3-72.

Program Edit Goto System Help

TEST SEARCH HELPS

CUST_CD1
CUST_CD2
CUST_CD3
CUST_CD4
CUST_CD5

Customer Number 1 (1) 500 Entries Found

Code Wise | Name Wise | City Wise

Custom	Name 1	City	Cty
1	Nelson Tax & Associates	PHILADELPHIA	US
2	Wett	Walldorf	DE
99	Einmalkunde		DE
110	Auto Klement	München	DE
149	Cuban Automotive Supply SA	Havana	CU
150	Korean Automotive Supply	Pyonyang	KP
175	Californian Multi Chemical Company	Mexico City	MX
224	Reference for B2C Customer	LOS ANGELES	US
255	Emma Bull	DENVER	US
256	Kenny A Chadburn	BOULDER	US
257	John Evans	NEDERLAND	US
258	Roger Zahn	ALBUQUERQUE	US
259	Laurel K. Hardin	GREELEY	US
260	Chelsa Quinn Yates	ALBUQUERQUE	US
261	Andrew Williams	ALBUQUERQUE	US
262	Robert Jensen	CANON CITY	US
263	Mark W. Telep	ALBUQUERQUE	US
264	Nancy Hagan	SALIDA	US
265	Kevin Strauss	RUIDOSO	US
266	Charles Scott	TORREY	US
267	Patricia Kress	TONOPAH	US

More than 500 input options

Figure 3-72. *Test Collective Search Help in ABAP Program – CUST_CD4-Selection List*

If you click on the Customer Name Wise tab, the restrictive dialog box for it appears (identical to the restrictive dialog box of the Customer Code Wise tab) as shown in Figure 3-73.

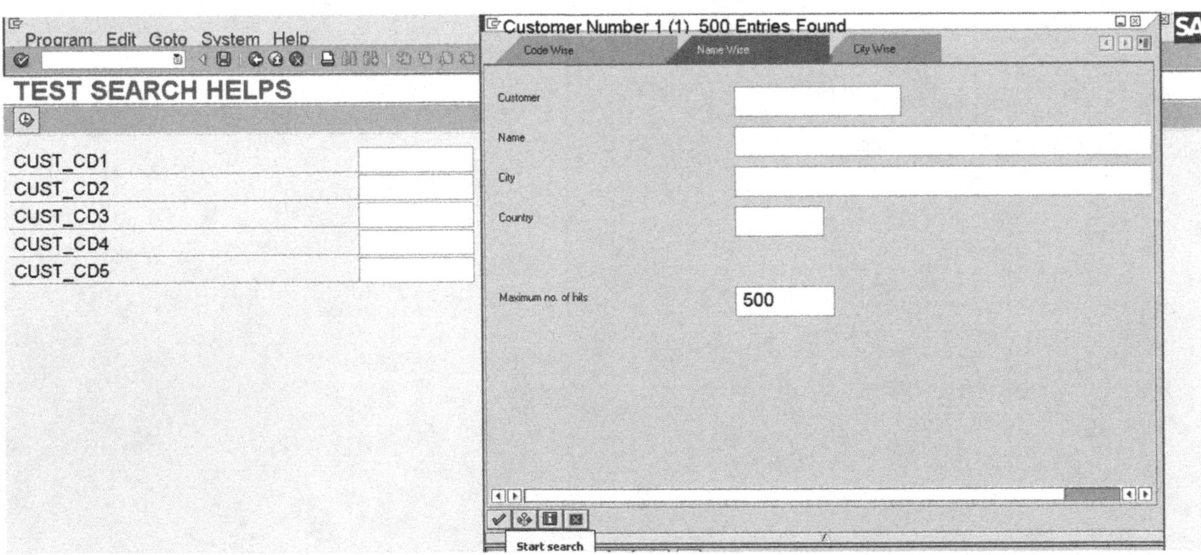

Figure 3-73. *Test Collective Search Help in ABAP Program – CUST_CD4-Restrictive Dialogue Box*

When you press <Enter> on this restrictive dialog box, the Customer name wise selection list appears. Similarly, you can press Customer City Wise tab, press <Enter> and get the city wise selection list.

In this manner, the end user can get the same information presented in a different manner. It is a requirement when your data is very large. Different people relate to different presentations in different situations.

In the collective search help, the restrictive dialog box can be different for every elementary search help. The export and import parameters can be different for every elementary search help. This would depend on the requirement and scenario. In your scenario, to keep things simple, you are using an identical restrictive dialog box, with one export parameter for all elementary search helps located in the collective search help.

Let the last of the PARAMETERS prompt variables CUST_CD5 be tested to which you have not attached explicitly any search help through the phrase MATCHCODE OBJECT. Click on the variable, and press F4. It presents the screen shown in Figure 3-74.

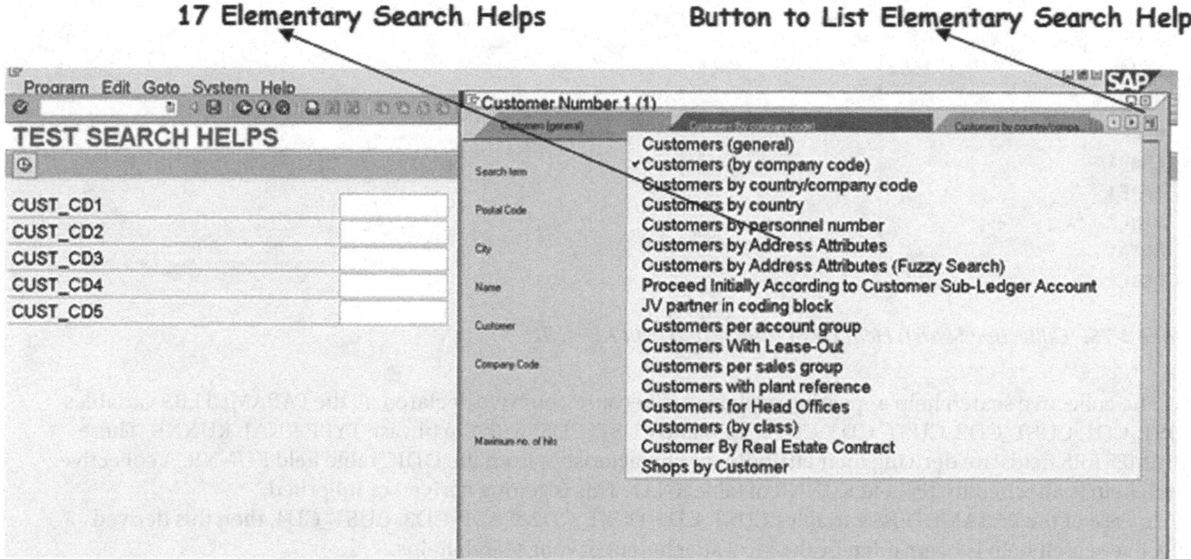

Figure 3-74. *Test Search Helps in ABAP Program - CUST_CD5-Restrictive Dialogue Box*

A collective search help is implicitly attached to the PARAMETERS variable CUST_CD5. If the number of elementary search helps is very many, like in the present case of 17 elementary search helps, all the tabs corresponding to these elementary search helps cannot appear horizontally. A button at the top right corner of the restrictive dialog box is provided as shown in the Figure 3-75. Clicking on this toggle button, you make the elementary search help list appear and disappear and make selection of a particular tab, or you can horizontally scroll across the tabs.

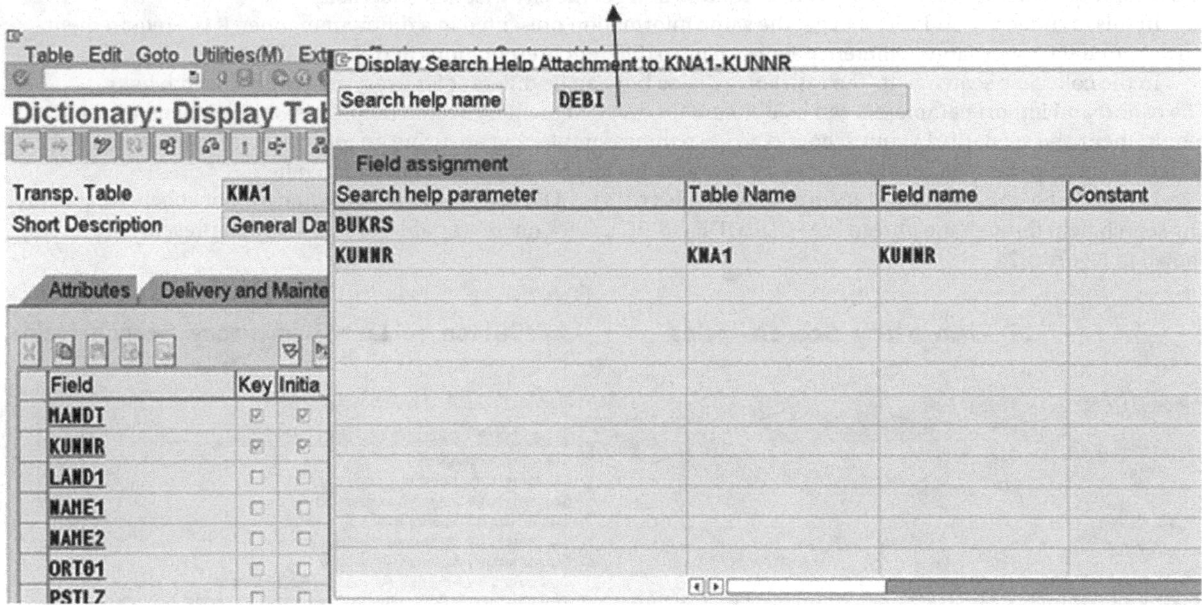

Figure 3-75. *Collective Search Help DEBI attached to field KUNNR*

The collective search help appearing by default is because you have declared all the PARAMETERS variables (CUST_CD1, CUST_CD2, CUST_CD3, CUST_CD4 and CUST_CD5) with the phrase TYPE KNA1-KUNNR. These PARAMETERS fields are deriving their attributes or characteristics from the DDIC table field KUNNR. A collective search help is attached to the field KUNNR of table KNA1. This is getting derived or inherited.

In case of the PARAMETERS variables CUST_CD1, CUST_CD2, CUST_CD3, CUST_CD4, then this derived collective search help is overridden by the local attachment of your search helps.

So you are witnessing the power of DDIC. A reference to a DDIC object in an ABAP program will have the local data object inheriting all the characteristics of the DDIC objects.

Confirm an attachment of collective search help to the KUNNR field of table KNA1. On the SE11 opening screen, select the Database table radio button, enter KNA1 in the field, and click on the Display button or F7.

In the table structure, position the cursor on the field KUNNR, and click on the button Srch Help. The screen appears as in Figure 3-75.

You can explore and view this collective search help DEBI as an exercise. You can do so by double-clicking on the search help name on this screen. The system will navigate to the DEBI collective search help screen. In the ABAP Workbench environment, you have this facility. If you double-click on an assigned object, the system will navigate to that object screen.

Like, for example, if you double-click on the data element assigned to a table field, it will navigate to that data element screen as if you opened that object in change or display mode. If you double-click on the domain assigned to a data element, the system will navigate to the screen of that domain.

If on double-clicking on an assigned object, if the object exists, the system will navigate to the object screen; if the object does not exist, the system message prompts whether you want to create the object.

Search Help Attachments

The search helps can be attached to table fields. In the coverage of search help, you have two instances of this: (1) attaching elementary search help to the field ITEM_CODE (foreign key field) of your custom created table YCL_CH02_BILLI, and (2) the collective search help DEBI attached to KUNNR (primary key field) field of table KNA1.

You can attach search helps to a primary table. This has been done in the SAP functional module table LFA1, which is the Vendor/Supplier primary table. Look this up as an exercise. In the LFA1 table structure definition, click on the menu Extras ➤ Search Help for Table. The collective search help is attached to the table as KRED.

You can attach a search helps to a data element. You can do this in the Further Characteristics tab, Search Help area. You can attach a search help to a data element, provided the search help has one export parameter, because there is a provision for one parameter only in the Search Help area of the data element.

Search helps can be attached to screen fields like you have seen in the ABAP program. More of this search helps attached to screen fields, and you will see this in Chapter 14 entitled Screen Programming.

Search Help with Help View

A help view implements a left outer join. If you create a help view with the tables KNA1 and VBAK, you will obtain in the result all the rows from the table VBAK as well as the customers having no corresponding rows in the VBAK table. You can try this out as an exercise. Create a help view using tables KNA1 and VBAK. Using this help view, create a search help. The result of a left outer join is sometimes required in business scenarios.

DDIC Tit Bits

In the DDIC opening screen, there is a provision to copy objects. Use the application toolbar *copy* button to do this. The copied object will not be in an active state. To use the copied object, you need to activate it.

You can delete DDIC objects, provided they are not in use. You cannot delete a domain that has been assigned to ata element/s. You cannot delete an object referred to in an ABAP program. Use the application toolbar *delete* button to do so.

You should also be aware of the *where used* button. Using this button, you can derive the information of *where all* DDIC objects are being used. A domain has been assigned to *what all* data elements; and a data element has been assigned to *what all* table fields and referred in *what all* ABAP programs, etc. A data element can be referred to in an ABAP program to declare data.

Conclusion

In the forthcoming chapters, you will find multiple references to DDIC objects to declare data in ABAP programs. You will learn about business scenarios that warrant creation of DDIC objects, notably database views, structures, table types, type groups, search help, and data elements.

DDIC is ubiquitous as regards the ABAP developmental platform.

CHAPTER 4

ABAP Language Basics

Introduction

Advanced Business Application Programming (ABAP), the proprietary language of SAP, has basically procedure oriented constructs. When it was created (in the 1970s), there was no OOP technology application. The OOP constructs in ABAP were incorporated sometime in the beginning of the millennia. It is an interpreter driven language. And its limited repertoire of statements and features at the time SAP R/3 release (in 1992) have grown considerably.

The ABAP source programs are stored in the SAP database. The complied runtime version, much akin to the Java byte code, is also stored in the SAP database. The maintenance of ABAP source programs can be done only in the SAP environment: that is, you have to be logged into SAP to create, edit, and syntax check ABAP programs.

The ABAP programs can only be executed in the SAP environment. The execution of ABAP requires the ABAP runtime environment, only available when you are logged into SAP. An ABAP runtime code is extracted from the database, loaded onto the RAM of an application server, and executes in the application server and presentation server for interaction with the end user.

The ABAP runtime environment is part of the work processes, and the work processes are, in turn, components of the application server, which is called the NetWeaver Application Server (AS) ABAP. The NetWeaver AS ABAP has the complete technology and infrastructure to run ABAP applications.

The work processes (components of NetWeaver AS ABAP) execute individual dialog steps of ABAP application programs. The work processes are constituted by the ABAP processor, the screen processor, and the database interface. The ABAP processor takes care of the processing logic of ABAP programs, and the screen processor takes care of the screen flow logic and the database interface to provide all the database related services (DDIC is part of this database interface).

Almost the entire SAP ERP application has been developed in ABAP. Every screen in the SAP environment is an ABAP program. If you click on the button on the right side of the status bar, you get ABAP program information. The SE11 transaction operations you performed in the last two chapters are coded in ABAP.

The ABAP language is used by ABAP implementation consultants to customize interfaces and reports and to perform enhancements of SAP provided functionalities.

In this chapter, the ABAP language basic elements are covered: data types available, data declarative statements, arithmetic operations, string handling, data movement, condition testing, and repetitive process - looping. These elements are part of all computer languages. Most of you are already familiar with these. You will learn how these elements, which are common to all computer languages, exist and operate in ABAP.

For a detailed theoretical treatment of ABAP programming, you can refer from time to time to the document **ABAP Programming (BC-ABA)**, downloadable from the link given in the introduction to the book.

ABAP Data Types

In Chapter 2, you were introduced to the DDIC data types. Shown in Figure 4-1 are the data types available in ABAP programs called the ABAP types.

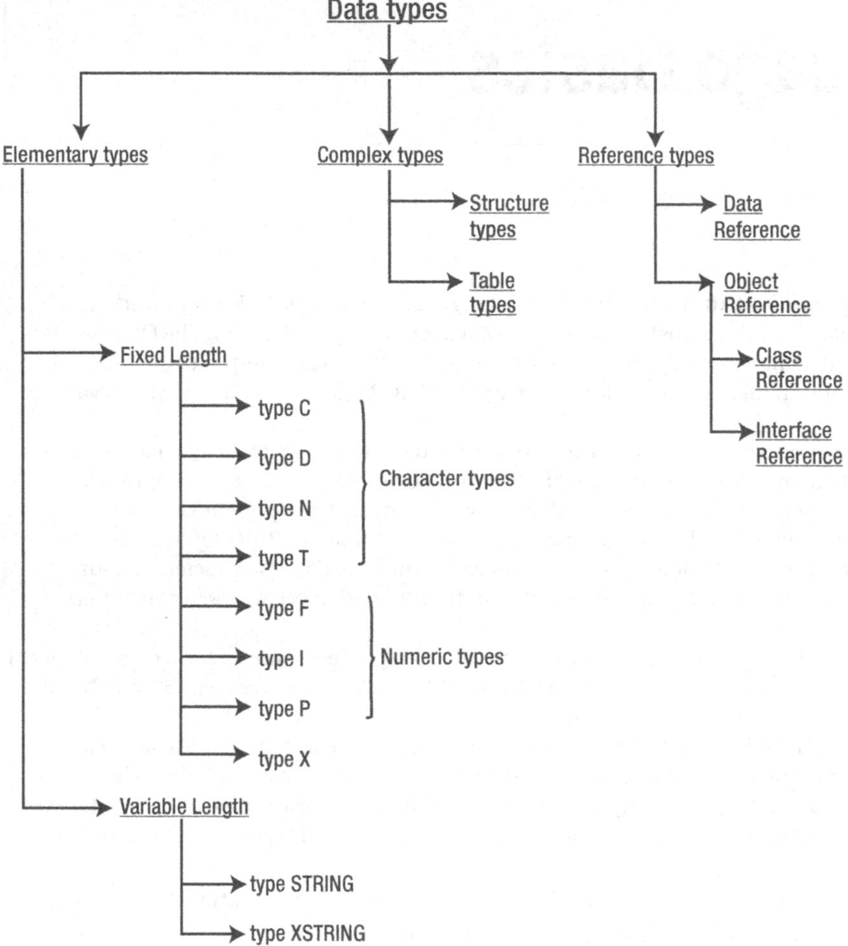

Figure 4-1. *Data types in an ABAP Program*

Elementary Types

In elementary types, the 'Fixed Length' (types C, D, N, T, F, I, P, and X) means that either the length of this type is inherently fixed (TYPES D, F, I, or T) or while declaring a data item; length in bytes or characters is specified for that data item, and the length of this data item remains fixed all through its existence.

In 'Variable Length,' (types STRING and XSTRING), the length of a data item is not specified while declaring it: it varies during the execution of a program as you assign data to it.

The bunching of elementary types as 'Character types' is for the types that store one ASCII character/byte (in a 16-bit Unicode system, 2 bytes/character). The bunching as 'Numeric types' is for the types on which you can perform normal arithmetic operations. You can perform arithmetic operations on elementary type N, but it is not very advisable. You can perform date arithmetic on elementary type D and time arithmetic on elementary type T.

Table 4-1 describes the *elementary* data types that are predefined in ABAP. (The valid size and initial size are given in bytes or characters.) The mapping to DDIC data types is also specified.

Table 4-1. *ABAP Elementary Data Types*

Data Type	Initial Size	Valid Size	Initial Value	Description	DDIC Data Type
C	1 Character	1-65,535 Characters	SPACE	Text, Characters (Alphanumeric Characters)	CHAR
N	1 Character	1-65,535 Characters	Character Zeroes	Will accept only digits 0-9. Used for assigning codes like employee code, etc. Normally not used in arithmetic operations	NUMC
D	8 characters	8 Characters	Character Zeroes	Date: YYYYMMDD	DATS
T	6 characters	6 characters	Character Zeroes	Time: HHMMSS	TIMS
X	1 Byte	1-65535 Bytes	Binary Zeroes	Hexadecimal: stores two Hexadecimal digits per Byte	-
P	8 Bytes	1-16 Bytes	Binary Zeroes	Like the DDIC Data Type DEC. Up to 14 digits allowed after the decimal	DEC CURR QUAN
I	4 Bytes	4 Bytes	Binary Zeroes	Integer / Whole Number. Range 2^{31-1} to -2^{31}	INT4
F	8 Bytes	8 Bytes	Binary Zeroes	Like the DDIC Data Type FLTP. The maximum accuracy is up to 15 digits after decimal depending upon the hardware platform	FLTP
STRING	0 Characters			Like type C, length varies at runtime with the amount of data stored	STRING
XSTRING	0 Characters			Like type X, length varies at runtime with the amount of data stored	

The data types D, F, I, and T are predefined in all respects including the size, but the data TYPES C, N, P, and X can have additional specifications. For example, you can specify the size of these data types in the program in bytes or characters, when data is declared. For type F and P, you can specify the number of decimals with the data declaration.

The 'Initial Size' column specifies the default length, a data item will assume, if its length is not specified while declaring a data item.

Complex Types

The *complex types* are categorized into the (a) structure types and (b) table types.

a. In the *structure types*, elementary types, structure types (structure embedded in a structure) are grouped together. You will consider only the grouping of elementary types. The grouping involving structures (structure/s embedded in a Structure - nested structures) are an advanced feature beyond the scope of this book. You must be aware of the facility or availability of nesting of structures. When the elementary types are grouped together, the data item can be accessed as a grouped data item or the individual elementary type data items (fields of the structure) can be accessed.

b. The *table types* are called arrays in other programming languages. Arrays can either be simple or structure arrays. The arrays are called internal tables in ABAP. In ABAP, the internal tables can be declared and operated upon in many more ways than in other programming languages. An entire chapter, Chapter 6, entitled 'Internal Tables' is devoted to the declarations and operations of internal tables.

Reference Types (Discussion Is in OOP Context)

The *reference types* are used to refer to instances of classes, interfaces, and runtime data items.

The ABAP OOP Run Time Type Services (RTTS) enables declaration of data items at run time. A reference variable of type '\\Data Reference'\\\ is used to refer to instances of the runtime data items.

When an instance of a class is created, a reference variable of type 'Class Reference' is used.

When an instance of an interface is created, a reference variable of type 'Interface Reference' is used.

Either of the reference variables, 'Class Reference' or 'Interface Reference', will be categorized as 'Object Reference'.

The discussion of OOP context is over!

Data Objects in ABAP Programs

In an ABAP program, you can work with four kinds of data objects:

Internal Data Objects

Internal data objects are declared in a particular ABAP program. They do not have any existence outside the particular program. Internal data objects are assigned RAM. Internal data objects further categorization:

- Literals (constants defined as part of an ABAP statement or command)
- Variables
- Constants

External Data Objects

External data objects exist independent of ABAP programs. You cannot work with them directly, but you can copy them to internal data objects and write them back when you have finished. External data objects can be used globally throughout the system environment.

ABAP stores external data objects in tables defined in the DDIC. To access this data from within a program, you declare the tables in the program with the *TABLES* or *DATA* statement.

System-defined Data Objects

Besides user-defined data objects, some data objects are defined automatically by the system. Some of the system defined data objects - SPACE, SY-SUBRC, SY-DATUM, SY-UZEIT and SY-TCODE.

Special Data Objects

ABAP also includes some data objcts with special features, namely:

`- PARAMETERS`

PARAMETERS are variables that are linked to a selection screen. They can accept values after an ABAP program is started (input).

`- Selection criteria - SELECT-OPTIONS`

Selection criteria are special internal tables used to specify value ranges. They are also linked to a selection screen. Set of values are accepted after a program is started (ranges of values input).

All *data objects* you want to work with in the programs (except system *data objects* and literal *data objects*) have to be declared. While declaring *data objects,* you must assign attributes to them. The most important of these attributes is the *data type* (except for *data object* declared with keyword 'TABLE'). In ABAP, you can either use predefined data types similar to other programming languages, or user-defined data types.

The user-defined *data types* in ABAP provide you with a powerful tool since they allow for great flexibility in programming. They range from elementary types (e.g., character strings of a given length) to very complex structures (e.g., nested structures).

Assigning user-defined *data types* to *data objects* allow you to work with precisely the *data objects* you require. User-defined *data types* can be used in the same way as predefined *data types*. You can declare them locally within a program or store them globally in the ABAP Dictionary (DDIC object: Type Group).

There are three hierarchical levels of *data types* and objects:

- Program-independent data, defined in the ABAP Dictionary
- Internal data used globally in one program
- Data used locally in a procedure (subroutine, function module)

ABAP Program Components

ABAP programs are maintained with *transaction code SE38.*

An ABAP program consists of five subobjects (see SE38 screen radio buttons):-

1. Source code (source lines)
2. Variants (will be covered in Chapter 9 entitled 'SELECTION-SCREEN' and require knowledge of 'Internal Tables' and 'SELECTION-SCREEN'
3. Attributes (mandatory: Title, Type, (program type) and Package (local object/$TMP)
4. Documentation (You will not create separate documentation in the course of your exercises. You will comment your program source lines profusely, making them self-documentary as well as self-explanatory)
5. Text elements, which, in turn, consist of: (i) Text Symbols, (ii) Selection Texts (will be covered in Chapter 9), and (iii) List Headers (will be covered in Chapter 5)

The attributes (item 3) of an ABAP program consists of:

- 'Title', equivalent of short description you were entering when creating DDIC objects
- 'Original language', logged-in language code when the program was created (maintained by the system)
- 'Created', date of program creation, user id.(maintained by the system)
- 'Last changed by', last date of change, user id. (maintained by the system)
- 'Program Attributes' area
    - 'Type': program type is mandatory. A drop-down list is available with the following options:
        - Executable program – A program that can be executed.
        - Include Program – The lines of these programs can be incorporated in other programs.
        - Module Pool – It contains screen flow logic modules.
        - Function group – It contains function modules, which are generic routines. Cannot be created in the ABAP editor. (SE38) Is to be created in SE37, SE80.
        - Subroutine Pool – It contains external subroutines.
        - Interface pool – It contains interfaces. Cannot be created in the ABAP editor. (SE38) Is to be created in SE24.
        - Class pool – It contains classes. Cannot be created in the ABAP editor. (SE38) Is to be created in SE24.
        - Type Pool – It contains user-defined TYPES. Cannot be created in the ABAP editor. (SE38) Is to be created in SE11.
        - XSLT Program. Cannot be created in the ABAP editor. (SE38) Is to be created in SE80.
    - 'Status': This is an optional program categorization. A drop-down list is available with the following options:
        - SAP Standard Production Program
        - Customer Production Program
        - System Program
        - Test Program
    - 'Application': An optional entry. You can assign a program to an application. A drop-down list is available.
    - 'Authorization Group': An optional entry. Authorization is a security feature. A pop-up (F4) list is available.
    - 'Package': Any object created in the ABAP Workbench environment is to be assigned a package. You are designating all your objects as local (i.e., not transportable to other implementation environments). You are assigning the SAP delivered package $TMP.

- 'Logical database': An optional entry. Logical database is basically a data retrieval reusable object. A Logical database created can be used by multiple programs (programs that are retrieving similar data from almost the same database tables), saving the effort of data retrieval in the programs using the Logical database. Works slow. Still used in the HR Module.
- 'Selection screen': An optional entry. Maintained by the system or goes along with the 'Logical database'. Will be covered in Chapter 9 entitled 'SELECTION-SCREEN'.
- 'Editor lock' check box: Enabling this prevents other user ids from editing the program.
- 'Fixed point arithmetic' check box: Enabled by default. In business applications, you perform mostly fixed point arithmetic, not floating point arithmetic.
- 'Unicode checks active' check box: To enable the program syntax checks relating to Unicode.
- 'Start using variant' check box: Will be covered in Chapter 9 entitled 'SELECTION-SCREEN'.

A screenshot of ABAP program attributes is shown in Figure 4-2.

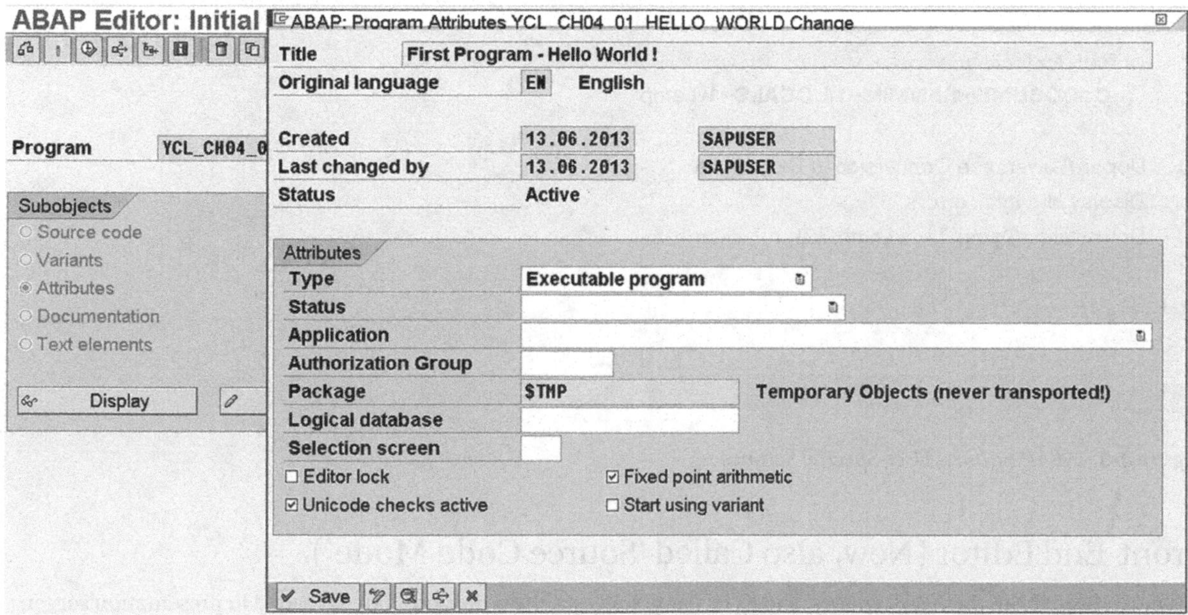

Figure 4-2. *ABAP Program Attributes*

ABAP Editors

There are three types of ABAP editors you can choose from: (i) Front-End Editor (New), (ii) Front-End Editor (Old), or (iii) Back-End Editor. To choose an ABAP editor, on the SE38 'ABAP Editor: Initial Screen,' select the menu option: Utilities(M) ➤ Settings. . . This menu selection pops up the screen as shown in Figure 4-3.

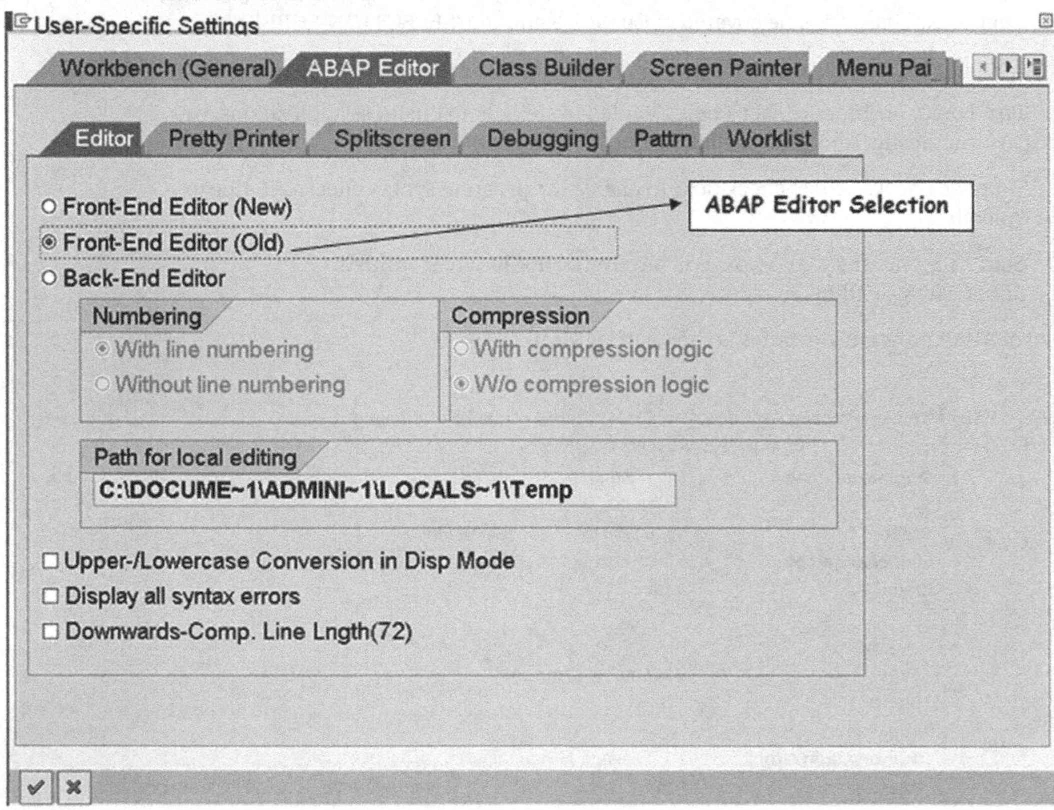

Figure 4-3. *ABAP Editor – User-Specific Settings*

Front-End Editor (New, also Called 'Source Code Mode')

It is most recent from the ABAP editors, and as its name suggests, the editor program is loaded in presentation server. The program line numbers appear; keywords appear in a separate color, when the first few letters of keyword are entered; and the system proposes the keyword. Even as you enter program lines, the editor interacts. It has a host of formatting facilities. You can select font, etc. specifically for editor environment separate from SAP environment. It should be the preferred choice for those starting to learn ABAP programming.

Front-End Editor (Old, also Called 'Plain Text Mode')

It is the predecessor of the new front-end editor. The editor program is loaded in presentation server. The program line numbers do not appear. It is a simple text editor; there is no action by the editor when you enter program lines (i.e., no interactiveness).

Back-End Editor (also Called 'Line Based Mode')

This is more like a line editor than a text editor. Selecting multiple source lines involves extra effort. You have the option to make program line numbers appear and disappear. It is recommended to be used when handling large programs in a wide access network.

The three modes of the ABAP editor are interchangeable and completely compatible.

This is bare outline overview of the three ABAP editor modes that is ample to get you started.

Common Features of the Three ABAP Editor Modes

The ABAP source is case insensitive: you can code in upper or lower case. The convention is to use upper case. In your hands-on source programs, you are coding the statements in upper case and using lower case for comments with keywords in comments in the upper case.

The usual text editor features: navigation, selection, copy, cut, paste, delete, undo, redo, save, etc. are implicit. They are not listed here. The features listed here are for a beginner and non-advanced ABAP programmer.

The ABAP editor offers the following prime functions and features:-

Table 4-2. *ABAP Editor Prime Features*

Feature	Menu Path/Keys/Button
Pretty Printer - Standardization of Program layout	Edit ➤ Pretty Printer <Shift>+<F1> Pretty Printer Button
Pattern - To autogenerate code lines, especially when calling a function module, a method.	Edit ➤ Pattern <Ctrl>+<F6> Pattern Button
Find, Find and replace text	Edit ➤ Find/Replace <Ctrl> + F Button
Block/Buffer X,Y,Z In addition to O.S. clipboard, ABAP editor offers every logged-in user three other buffers designated as X, Y, Z. These are non-volatile buffers. Their contents are saved in the SAP database when the user logs off/server is shut down and restored when user logs in again. These buffers contents can be edited as well.	Utilities(M) ➤ Block/Buffer
Upload/Download - You can upload text files on the presentation server into your ABAP programs and download your ABAP source lines onto a text file on a presentation server	Utilities(M) ➤ More Utilities ➤ Upload/Download
Comment/De-comment Selected Block of Source Lines. If you want to convert a block of lines into comment lines or vice versa, use this function. In ABAP a line with asterisk (*) in the first column is treated as a comment.	<Ctrl>+< to comment <Ctrl>+> to de-comment

(continued)

Table 4-2. (*continued*)

Feature	Menu Path/Keys/Button
Check Program Syntax	Program ➤ Check ➤ Syntax <Ctrl>+<F2> / button
Extended Program Check	Program ➤ Check ➤ Extended Program Check
Code Inspector	Program ➤ Check ➤ Code Inspector
Activate Program	Program ➤ Activate <Ctrl>+<F3> / button
Test/Run/Execute Program	Program ➤ Test ➤ Direct Processing <F8> / Button
Toggle between Edit/Change Mode & Display Mode	Program ➤ Display ➤ Change <Ctrl>+<F1> button

You can use the context menu (mouse right click) as well for most of these operations.

There is also a very sophisticated *debugger*, a *runtime analysis* facility and an *online help* (ABAP documentation) available in the ABAP developmental environment.

ABAP Program Structure

An ABAP program consists of the following two parts:

Declaration Part- Global Data, Selection Screens, and Local Classes

- All global data declaration statements (global in the context of a program). Global data is accessible in all internal processing blocks. You define it using declarative statements that appear before the first processing block, in dialog modules, or in event blocks. You cannot declare local data in dialog modules or event blocks.
- All selection screen definitions.
- All local class definitions (CLASS DEFINITION statement).
- Data declaration statements made in procedures (methods, subroutines, function modules) form the declaration part for local data in those processing blocks. This data is only existent, accessible in the procedure in which it is declared.

Container for Processing Blocks

The second part of an ABAP program contains all of the processing blocks for the program. The following types of processing blocks exist:

- Dialog modules (no local data area, whatever data declared treated as global)
- Event blocks (no local data area, whatever data declared treated as global)
- Procedures (methods, subroutines, and function modules with their own local data definitions)

The dialog modules and procedures are enclosed in the ABAP keywords that define them. There are keywords for start of modules, procedures and corresponding keywords for end of modules and procedures. Event blocks are introduced with event keywords and conclude implicitly with the beginning of the next processing block.

All ABAP statements (except declarative statements in the declaration part of the program) are part of a processing block. Non-declarative ABAP statements, which occur between the declaration of global data and a processing block is automatically assigned to the START-OF-SELECTION event or processing block by the ABAP processor.

Calling Processing Blocks

You can call processing blocks either from outside the ABAP program or using ABAP statements that form part of a processing block. Dialog modules and event blocks are called from outside the ABAP program by the ABAP runtime environment. Procedures are called using ABAP statements in ABAP programs.

Calling event blocks is different from calling other processing blocks for the following reasons:

An event block call is triggered by an event. User actions on selection screens, lists, and the runtime environment trigger events that can be processed in ABAP programs. You only have to define event blocks for the events to which you want the program to react (whereas a subroutine call, for example, must have a corresponding subroutine). This ensures that while an ABAP program may react to a particular event, it is not mandatory to do so.

ABAP Statement Structure

An ABAP source program will consist of comments and ABAP statements.

Comments

A comment can be incorporated by

i. Starting a line with an asterisk (*). The asterisk has to be in the very first column of the line. An asterisk in the first column will make the entire line comment. Like:-

```
* This is the Hello World program
```

ii. By using a double quote ("). Whatever follows the double quote is treated as comment. This is a right side comment; you can incorporate comments on the right side of an ABAP statement. If a line starts with a double quote, the entire line is treated as comment. A line could have an ABAP statement followed by a comment. Like:-

```
WRITE / 'Hello World'."this will output the string literal Hello World
```

You can always have blank lines in the source code.

ABAP Statements

ABAP statements begin with an ABAP keyword and are terminated by a period (.) or a comma (,) when they are within a chain and not the last statement in the chain. The last statement in a chain must terminate with a period. ABAP statements can run into multiple lines; or a line may contain multiple ABAP statements. Enterprise convention is not to code lines with multiple ABAP statements.

A statement running into multiple lines:

```
DATA COMPANY_NAME(50) TYPE C  VALUE
'NO BIG DEAL Inc.'.
```

A line with multiple statements: (two statements)

```
DATA EMPLOYEE_CODE(5) TYPE N. DATA EMPLOYEE_NAME(25) TYPE C.
```

In this last line of ABAP code, the keyword DATA is repeated. The keyword DATA is used to declare variables (one type of internal data objects) in an ABAP program. A real-world program would have many variables declared; each of these declarations must start with the keyword DATA. The ABAP editor provides a means to avoid the repetition of word/s through the feature of *chaining* statements.

In the chaining feature, whatever word or words repeating on the left side of ABAP statements will be chained and the repetition is avoided. The above code rewritten with chaining will be:

```
DATA: EMPLOYEE_CODE(5) TYPE N, EMPLOYEE_NAME(25) TYPE C.
```

The keyword DATA is followed by a colon (:) to signify chaining. The first statement is not terminated by a period but by a comma; and the last statement in the chain is terminated by a period. Another example of chaining:

```
WRITE /5: 'FIRST', 'SECOND', 'THIRD', 'FOURTH'.
```

Unchained version of this:

```
WRITE /5 'FIRST'. WRITE /5 'SECOND'. WRITE /5 'THIRD'. WRITE /5 FOURTH'.
```

ABAP Statements and Keywords

The first element of an ABAP statement is an ABAP keyword. The keyword determines the category of the statements. The different statement categories are:

Declarative Statements

These statements declare user-defined data types or declare internal data objects that are used by the other statements in a program or routine.

Examples of declarative keywords:

```
TYPES, DATA, TABLES
```

Modularization Statements

The modularization statements define the processing blocks in an ABAP program.

The modularization keywords are further categorized into:

- Event Keywords

You use event keywords in statements to define event blocks. There are no statements to signify the conclusion of processing blocks - they end when another processing block is defined.

Examples of event keywords:

```
INITIALIZATION, AT SELECTION SCREEN, START-OF-SELECTION, END_OF_SELECTION
```

- Defining keywords

You use statements containing these keywords to define subroutines, function modules, dialog modules, and methods. You conclude these processing blocks using the corresponding END statement.

Examples of definitive keywords:

```
FORM.....ENDFORM.
FUNCTION... ENDFUNCTION.
MODULE. ... ENDMODULE.
```

Control Statements

You use the control statements to control the ABAP program flow within a processing block according to conditions.

Examples of control keywords:

```
IF ... ENDIF, WHILE ... ENDWHILE, CASE ... ENDCASE.
```

Call Statements

You use the call statements to call processing blocks that you have already defined using modularization statements. The blocks you call may be located in the same or a different ABAP program.

Examples of call keywords:

```
PERFORM, CALL, MODULE
```

Operational Statements

The keywords operate on the data that you have defined with declarative statements.

Examples of operational keywords:

```
WRITE
MOVE
CONCATENATE
```

Database Statements

The statements use the database interface to access the tables in the SAP database system. Examples of database keywords are:

```
SELECT and INSERT
```

Now, that you have had a review of ABAP program components, ABAP editor, ABAP program structure, and ABAP statement structure, you are ready to code your first program.

First ABAP Program

You will create the proverbial Hello World program. You will, though, create it with a multilingual facility. You will program it in a way that the user can see the text is output in the logged-in language, using the multilanguage support feature of SAP. And you will be introduced to the ABAP program feature that will enable this: maintain multilingual texts.

You will use a 'WRITE' statement to output the text. The 'WRITE' statement is being introduced in a preview manner. The 'WRITE' statement is formally introduced in chapter 5 entitled 'WRITE Statement (Classical Reporting)'.

On the SE38 screen, enter the program name YCL_CH04_01_HELLO_WORLD. The name space of an ABAP program is a maximum of 30 characters and must start with letters Y or Z, but the rest can be alphanumeric with embedded underscores. (_)

Click on the Create button or press function key F5. The program attributes screen appears. Enter a suitable program title. Select the Executable program in the program type. Click the save button on the dialog box. The system will prompt for a package. Assign your usual package $TMP. The system will generate the REPORT statement and enter into the ABAP editor mode.

In the ABAP program environment, you can create and maintain multilingual text through the 'Text Symbols' sub component of the program component 'Text elements'. The 'Text elements' are attached to ABAP programs and can be accessed from within that program only. Of course 'Text elements' can be copied from one program to another (Transaction code SE32).

You will create a 'Text Symbol' to contain the Hello World text. The 'Text Symbols' can be assigned a three-character alphanumeric identification and be referred to by that identification.

To create 'Text Symbols' from within the ABAP editor, select the menu option Goto ➤ Text Elements ➤ Text Symbols. The screen with the created text is shown in Figure 4-4.

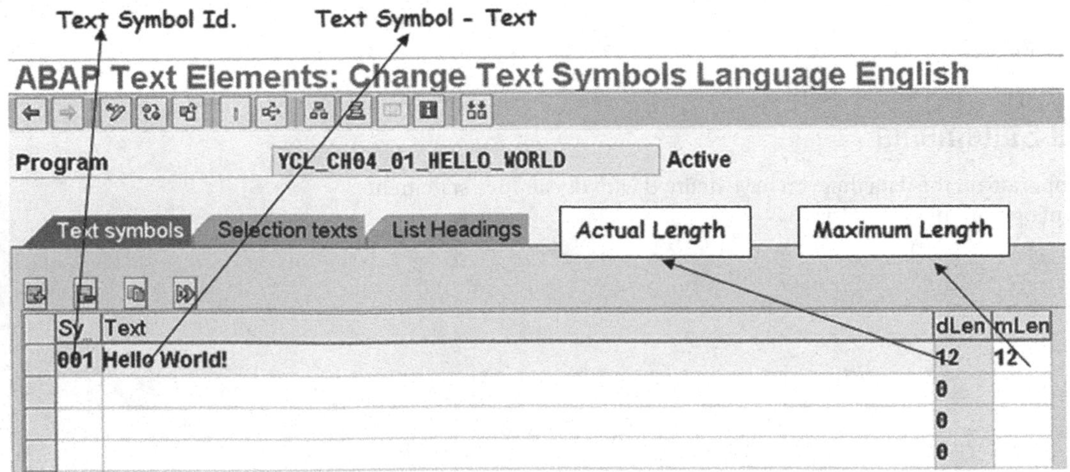

Figure 4-4. *Maintaining Text Symbols - Information Message on Saving*

The defined length is the length of the entered string. The maximum length by default is the defined length. If you entered text in a text symbol id.: for example, 001 and want to subsequently add more text to it, you will have to manually adjust the maximum length to be able to add more text to the text symbol id 001. This is just like it was in the DDIC data element label environment: not very user friendly.

Manually create the German equivalent text of 'Hello World'. To do so, select the menu option Goto ➤ Translate. A prompt will appear for source and target languages. Enter 'EN' as the source and 'DE' as the target languages, then click on the continue button. A screen as shown in Figure 4-5 appears.

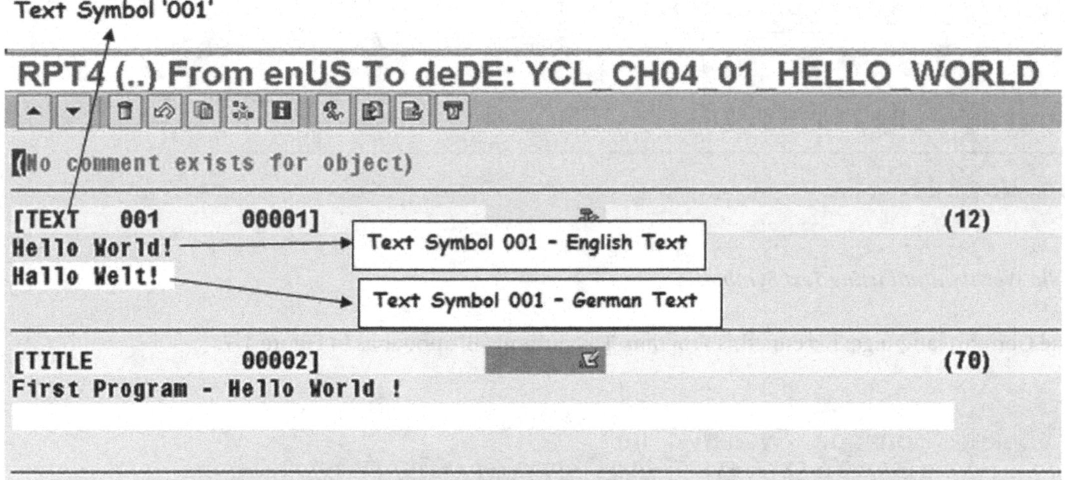

Figure 4-5. *Text Symbols – Maintaining Language Texts*

All the text associated with a program appears on this screen. In the present context, you have only two text items associated: the program title and a single text symbol.

The German equivalent of Hello World 'Hallo Walt' has been manually entered.

There is procedure of automatic translation by the system translator. It is a bit complex and a digression for the scope of this book.

Press the save button and go back to text element – text symbol screen and activate the text symbol. Activation of the text symbol is separate from activation of the ABAP source program.

Return to the ABAP source editor screen. Your program will look like:-

```
REPORT  YCL_CH04_01_HELLO_WORLD.

***********************************
* Hello World ! - Use Text Symbol *
***********************************

WRITE /5 TEXT-001. " / - start output on new line. 5 - start output
                   " from 5th column.
                   " text symbols are addressed with pre-fix TEXT,
                   " followed by the text symbol three character
                   " identification
```

The WRITE statement outputs data objects on the screen. The output on the screen can be printed, spooled, etc. The program comments explain the syntax of the WRITE statement.

Save the program, perform a syntax check, and activate. Execute the program. The output will appear as in Figure 4-6.

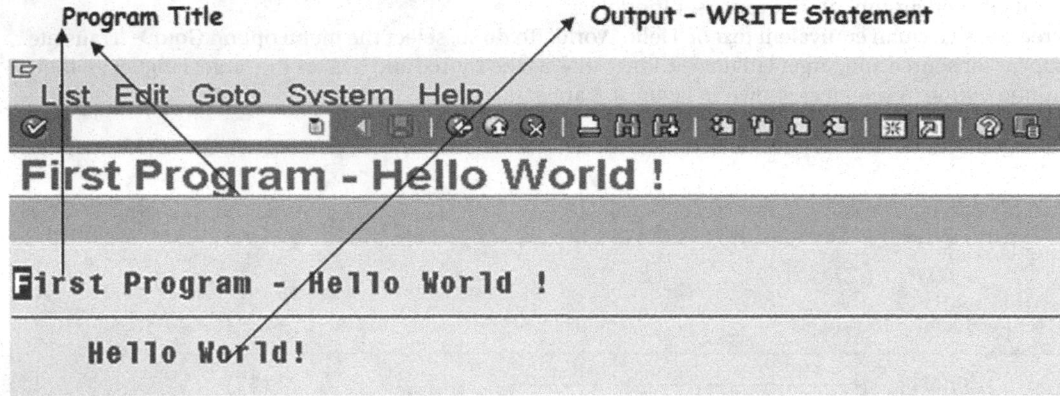

Figure 4-6. *Hello World output using Text Symbols*

Log into the German language. Execute this Program. The output will appear as in Figure 4-7.

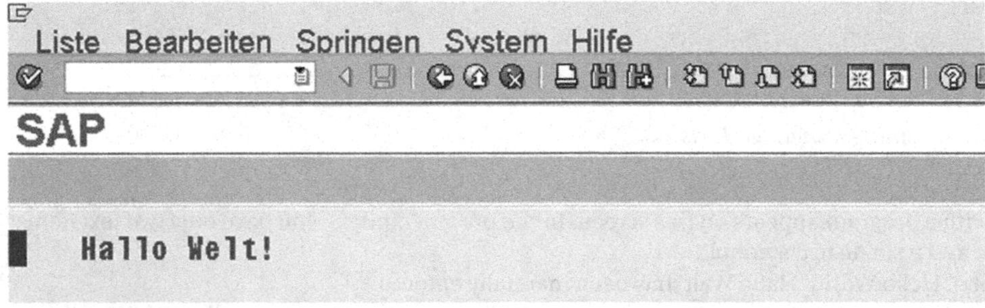

Figure 4-7. *Hello World output - Logged in German using Text Symbols*

Observe that the program title is not appearing above the output of the WRITE statement, even as it is not appearing in the window title. This is because you have not created any German text for the program title.

ABAP Program – Output a Few System Fields

System Fields

One of the data objects in an ABAP program is the system data object. The system data object consists of the system fields or variables. There are more than one hundred system fields. The system fields make available to the ABAP developer, information related to the ABAP runtime environment. For instance, there are system fields that give logged-in information: user, client, language. There is a system field that provides the developer with the success or failure information of an operation.

You will find a complete list of the system fields in the PDF document **ABAP Programming (BC-ABA)** under System Fields, downloadable from the link given in the Introduction of this book. The system fields are listed alphabetically as well as theme wise in this manual.

The system fields start with the prefix SY-. There are five categories of these system fields. The category of the system field is identified by icon flags as follows:

✔ This category of system fields is set by the runtime environment. The developer can interrogate the field for its value.

✔✎ These are set by the runtime environment; you can change their value in a program. It will affect the runtime behavior of the program.

✎ These should be set in the ABAP program. They will be used by the runtime environment and in the program 🔒 For SAP internal use.

🗑 Obsolete.

The system fields will be introduced as and when their context arises.

You should also be aware of the system field DDIC Data Type and length. This is available in the list. You will find that the Data Type and length of the very first system field SY-ABCDE is CHAR, 26 - to accommodate the 26 alphabet letters of the English language.

Thirteen system fields are introduced right now. In this program, you output the values of the 13 system fields listed in Table 4-3.

Table 4-3. *System Fields*

System Field	Description
SY-ABCDE	English Alphabet Set
SY-DATUM	Date of Application Server on which the Program is Executing (YYYYMMDD)
SY-DBSYS	Installed Database
SY-HOST	Host name of Application Server on which the Program is Executing
SY-LANGU	Logged-in language
SY-MANDT	Logged-in client
SY-OPSYS	Application Server Operating System on which the Program is Executing
SY-REPID	Name of the Program which is Executing/Current Program
SY-SAPRL	NetWeaver Version
SY-SYSID	Application Server System Id.
SY-TCODE	Current Transaction Code
SY-UNAME	Logged in User Name/Id.
SY-UZEIT	Time on Application Server on which the Program is Executing (HHMMSS)

Create the following program, perform a syntax check, and activate.

```
REPORT  YCL_CH04_02_LIST_SYS_FIELDS.

**************************
* Output System Fields  **
**************************

WRITE:/5 'SY-ABCDE', SY-ABCDE, " / start output on new line
      /5 'SY-DATUM', SY-DATUM, " 5 start the output from 5th column
      /5 'SY-DBSYS', SY-DBSYS, " : & , are for chaining i.e. avoiding
                               " repetition of the key word WRITE
      /5 'SY-HOST ', SY-HOST,  " text literals enclosed in single quotes
      /5 'SY-LANGU', SY-LANGU,
      /5 'SY-MANDT', SY-MANDT,
      /5 'SY-OPSYS', SY-OPSYS,
      /5 'SY-REPID', SY-REPID,
      /5 'SY-SAPRL', SY-SAPRL,
      /5 'SY-SYSID', SY-SYSID,
      /5 'SY-TCODE', SY-TCODE,
      /5 'SY-UNAME', SY-UNAME,
      /5 'SY-UZEIT', SY-UZEIT.
```

When you execute this program, the following output is generated.

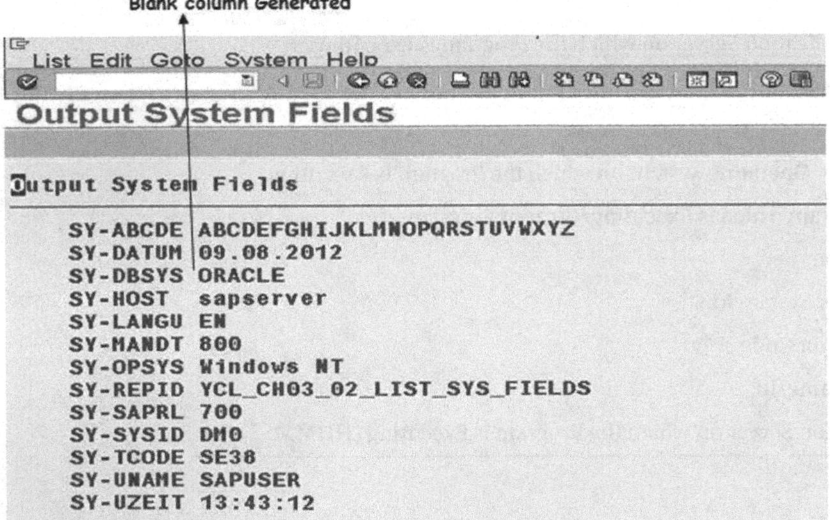

Figure 4-8. *Output of Program: YCL_CH04_02_LIST_SYS_FIELDS*

In the preceding code, WRITE is the keyword to output, and / is to start the output on a new line: 5 to start output from column 5 onwards. Chaining has been used to avoid repetition of the keyword WRITE.

For the first WRITE statement, starting on a new line, from column 5 onwards, the literal 'SY-ABCDE' and its value are output on the same line one beside the other with a blank column between them. Similarly for the succeeding WRITE statements, a total of 13 lines are output.

You are using 13 string or text literals ('SY-ABCDE' etal.) in this program.

String literals must be avoided in the ABAP programs. Instead, enter the literals in the text symbols (that is what they are meant for with multilingual support). But in the teaching, training paradigm that you are in, this profuse use of literals occasionally can be excused.

Internal Data Objects (Elementary) Declarations

Internal data objects (variables, constants, literals):

- Data objects are physical units that a program uses at runtime.
- Each data object has a specific data type assigned to it.
- Each data object occupies some space in memory.
- ABAP processes a data object according to its data type.

There are three hierarchical levels of data types and objects:

1. Program-independent data, defined in the ABAP Dictionary
2. Internal data used globally in one program
3. Data used locally in a procedure (subroutine, function module)

Variables

A variable is used to store and reference data under a certain name and in a certain format. Variables can differ in:

- name
- type
- length
- structure

You declare variables in your program with the DATA statement.

Naming a Variable (internal data objects' name, special data objects' name)

The variables and constants names of internal data objects may be up to 30 characters long and special data objects up 8 characters. You can use any alphanumeric characters except:

Plus sign + or a period . or a comma , or a colon : or parentheses ( )

Do not use a name consisting entirely of numeric characters.

ABAP Program: Declare Internal Data Objects – Variables (with VALUE) - Output

The program declares each of the 10 elementary types of data objects and assigns appropriate, applicable lengths and decimals. It assigns each of these data objects starting values through the VALUE clause. (Except XSTRING, which disallows this.)

The program outputs the value of these data objects through the WRITE statement already introduced.

Create the program, perform a syntax check, and activate.

```
REPORT  YCL_CH04_03_ELEM_DATA_OBJECTS.

*******************************************************************
* declare elementary DATA objects, assign values with declaration *
* output data objects                                             *
*******************************************************************
*********************************************************************
* key word DATA used to declare data (variables)                   **
*                                                                  **
* : & , used for chaining i.e. avoid repetition of key word DATA.  **
*                                                                  **
* variable TYPE is specified with the key word TYPE followed by    **
* C/D/F/I/N/P/T/X/STRING/XSTRING. if TYPE not specified, assumes   **
* default TYPE as C.                                               **
*                                                                  **
* length to be specified  for TYPES C,N,P,X in parenthesis. length **
* is in bytes for P & X. if length not specified for TYPES C,N,P,X **
* it assumes the default length.(see table 4-1) lengths of TYPES   **
* D,F,I,T is fixed. TYPES STRING, XSTRING length varies at run time **
*                                                                  **
* the VALUE clause is to assign a starting value. it is optional.  **
*                                                                  **
* decimals for TYPE F,P are specified with key word DECIMALS       **
* followed by the number of decimals                               **
*                                                                  **
* if single quote required as part of literal string,single quote  **
* should be entered twice like 'ABC''' is for string ABC'          **
*********************************************************************

DATA: CNAME(25)      TYPE C
      VALUE 'MPHASIS - an H.P. Company', " length in parenthesis
                                         " VALUE is optional

      TODAY          TYPE D
      VALUE '20130101', " numeric literals not containing any sign
                        " & decimal can be enclosed in single quotes
                        " numeric literals containing sign or decimal
                        " should be enclosed in single quotes

      FNUM           TYPE F VALUE '12345.6789',
      COUNT          TYPE I VALUE 987654321,
      ECODE(7)       TYPE N VALUE 2191778,
      BASIC_SAL(4)   TYPE P DECIMALS 2 VALUE 20000,
      NOW            TYPE T VALUE '094500', "give value in quotes
      HEXA(8)        TYPE X VALUE '0123456789ABCDEF',
      STRNG          TYPE STRING VALUE 'MORGAN''S GATE', "single quote
                                                         "as part of string
```

```
    XSTRNG         TYPE XSTRING." XSTRING does not take VALUE addition
************************************************************************
WRITE:/5 'TYPE C        :', CNAME,
      /5 'TYPE D        :', TODAY,
      /5 'TYPE F        :', FNUM,
      /5 'TYPE I        :', COUNT,
      /5 'TYPE N        :', ECODE,
      /5 'TYPE P        :', BASIC_SAL,
      /5 'TYPE T        :', NOW,
      /5 'TYPE X        :', HEXA,
      /5 'TYPE STRING :', STRNG.
```

The output will appear as:

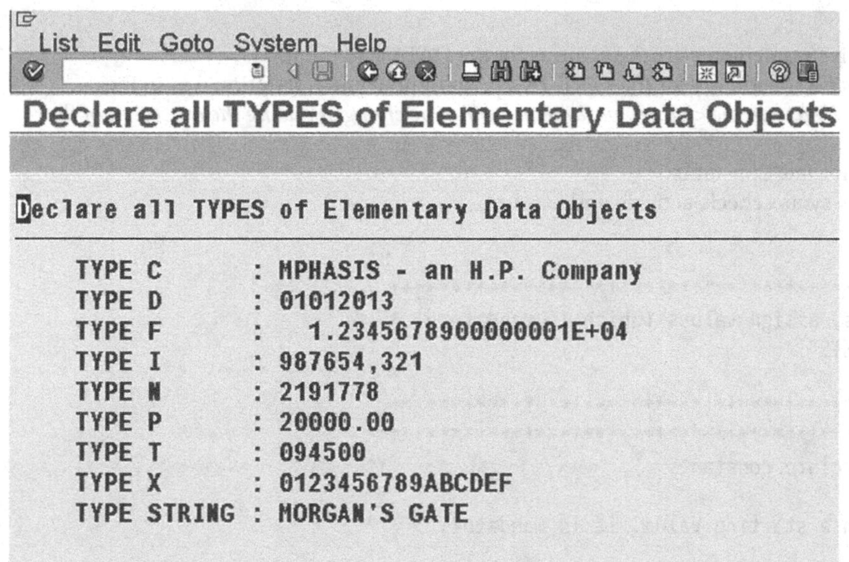

Figure 4-9. *Output of Program: YCL_CH04_03_ELEM_DATA_OBJECTS*

In the output, *type D* is output as DDMMYYYY (internal storage is YYYYMMDD) without the separator character between date & month and between month & year. The separator character was appearing when you output the system field SY-DATUM in the previous program. This issue will be addressed in Chapter 5 entitled 'WRITE Statement (Classical Reporting)'.

Type F is output in normalized form. Type F is output by the WRITE statement in 22 columns by default including 1 column for the sign. TYPE F is used rarely in business applications. Type F will not be discussed further.

Type I is output with only one thousand separators, (thousand separator comma [,]) when it should have been appearing with two thousand separators: one after millions and one after thousands like 987,654,321 instead of 987654,321. The type I by default outputs through a WRITE statement in 11 columns with one column reserved for the sign on the right. So there was scope for only one comma. This issue will be addressed in Chapter 5 entitled 'WRITE Statement (Classical Reporting)'.

Type P by default is output by the WRITE statement in columns twice the number of bytes plus one specified in its declaration. (In your present context 9.) These columns include one column for decimal (.) and one column for sign on the right. In your present case with the value stored in the data object (20000.00), there is no scope for a thousand separator. This issue will be addressed in Chapter 5 entitled 'WRITE Statement (Classical Reporting)'.

Type T is output without the separator character between hours & minutes and between minutes & seconds. The separator character was appearing when the system field SY-UZEIT in the previous program was output.

Type X, XSTRING (hexadecimal) is not used in business applications, and no more reference will be made to these types.

ABAP Program: Declare Internal Data Objects - Constants - Output

If you use a constant frequently in a program, you can declare it as a fixed value variable with the CONSTANTS statement.

The *CONSTANTS* Statement syntax:

```
CONSTANTS:
<constant name> TYPE <type>[(<length>)] [DECIMALS <decimals>] VALUE <value>,
......
```

The parameters of the CONSTANTS statements are the same as for the DATA statement.

The use of the <value> parameter is mandatory for the CONSTANTS statement and not optional as in the DATA statement. The *start value specified with the <value> parameter cannot be changed during the execution of the program.*

A program to declare and output a few Constants:

Create the program, perform the syntax check, activate and execute.

```
REPORT  YCL_CH04_04_CONSTANTS.
********************************************************************
* declare Constant data objects, assign values (which is mandatory) *
* declarative statement CONSTANTS                                 . *
* output constant data objects                                      *
********************************************************************
**********************************************************************
* key word CONSTANTS used to declare constants                      **
*                                                                   **
* the VALUE clause is to assign a starting value. it is mandatory   **
*                                                                   **
**********************************************************************

CONSTANTS: INDIAN_REPUBLIC_DAY     TYPE D VALUE '19500126',
           AMERICAN_INDE_DAY       TYPE D VALUE '17760704',
           ZERO                    TYPE I VALUE IS INITIAL.

WRITE:/5 'INDIAN_REPUBLIC_DAY', INDIAN_REPUBLIC_DAY,
      /5 'AMERICAN_INDE_DAY', AMERICAN_INDE_DAY.
```

The output is shown in Figure 4-10.

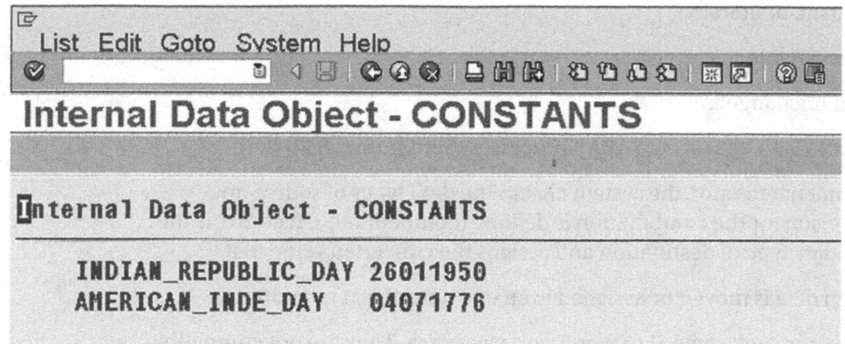

Figure 4-10. *Output of Program: YCL_CH04_04_CONSTANTS*

Literals

A literal is a fixed value. ABAP distinguishes between text literals and number literals.

Text literals.

Text literals are sequences of alphanumeric characters enclosed in single quotation marks.

```
'SAP AG Germany'
'ABAP WORKBENCH'
```

Text literals can be up to 254 characters long. If a text literal contains a quotation mark, you must repeat it to enable the system to recognize the contents as a text literal and not as the end of the literal.

To ensure that the programs offer multilingual support, do not use text literals. Instead, create them as text symbols as you did in the HELLO WORLD program.

Number literals:

Number literals are sequences of digits that may contain a leading sign. They can contain up to 15 digits like:

```
123, -321, +456
```

If you need a noninteger value or a longer number, you must use a text literal, which is converted to the correct type automatically, such as:

```
'12345678901234567890', '+0.58498', '-8473.67'
```

Elementary Data Objects - Assigning Values or Data Movement

The *MOVE* statement or the assignment operator (=) is used to assign a value to a data object.

Syntax

```
MOVE <f1> TO <f2>.
<f2> = <f1>.
<f4> = <f3> = <f2> = <f1>.
```

- f1 can be a variable, constant, or literal.
- f2, f3, f4 have to be to be a variable.
- The contents of f1 remain unchanged.
- In the multiple assignment <f4> = <f3> = etc., ABAP processes them from right to left.
- For each MOVE or assignment operator, the system checks the data types of source and destination. If type conversion for the combination is defined (compatibility), it converts the contents of source to the data type of destination and assigns the converted value to it.
- There are two issues when data is moved or assigned from one data object to another:
    - Compatibility. You cannot move type D to type T and vice versa. They are not compatible with each other. Such assignments will result in syntax error.
    - Convertibility. Suppose you have source data object as type C and destination as type N. This is accepted by the compiler. As long as the source is containing 0 to 9 numerals and blanks, the assignment or movement from source to destination is successful. If the source contains characters other than 0 to 9 or blanks, the assignment or movement fails, source data is not convertible and a runtime error occurs. This is the issue of convertibility.

In the real world, with so much control on the type and length of data objects (domains etc.), the possibility of such scenarios is rare. The SAP ABAP help documentation discusses these issues elaborately.

Elementary Data Objects - Assignment or Movement with Offsets and Lengths (Types C, D, N and T)

For the elementary predefined types C, D, N, T; which store one character oriented, assignment or movement statement can access individual characters.

Let this be demonstrated with an example. When you output type D or type T, the date or time is output by WRITE statement without the separator characters. Date was output as DDMMYYYY.

Let your requirement be that the date should be output as MM-DD-YYYY (US requirement). The separator character is a hyphen (-). You will output the date in this format with the MOVE statement using offsets and lengths.

In Figure 4-11, what is available in the type D as on the left, needs to be transformed to the form as shown on the right. Type D length is 8 characters. The transformed date as on the right will require 10 characters (2 extra characters for separators).

```
 Source-Offsets        Destination-Offsets
0 1 2 3 4 5 6 7        0 1 2 3 4 5 6 7 8 9
----------------      ---------------------
|Y|Y|Y|Y|M|M|D|D|      |M|M|-|D|D|-|Y|Y|Y|Y|
----------------      ---------------------
```

Figure 4-11. *Source, Destination for Date Transformation*

The offset datum (first character) starts as 0, not 1.

The operations required for transformation will be as follows:

```
Move offset 4, length 2 from source (MM) to offset 0, length 2 in destination.
Move '-' to offset 2, length 1 in destination(Separator character).
Move offset 6 and length 2 from source (DD) to offset 3, length 2 in destination.
Move '-' to offset 5, length 1 in destination.(Separator character).
Move offset 0 and length 4 from source (YYYY) to offset 6, length 4 in destination.

ABAP program:to transform type D from YYYYMMDD to MM-DD-YYYY and output:

REPORT  YCL_CH04_05_TRANSF_DATE_MOVE.

**************************************************
* Date Transformation with MOVE Offset & Length **
* convert YYYYMMDD to MM-DD-YYYY                **
**************************************************
*********************************************
*  Source-Offsets      Destination-Offsets *
*  0 1 2 3 4 5 6 7     0 1 2 3 4 5 6 7 8 9 *
* -----------------   --------------------- *
* |Y|Y|Y|Y|M|M|D|D|   |M|M|-|D|D|-|Y|Y|Y|Y| *
* -----------------   --------------------- *
*********************************************

DATA: SOURCE     TYPE D VALUE '20130116',
      DESTIN(10) TYPE C.
*****************************************
MOVE SOURCE+4(2)  TO DESTIN+0. "MOVE MM to DESTIN
MOVE '-'          TO DESTIN+2. "MOVE '-' TO DESTIN

MOVE SOURCE+6(2)  TO DESTIN+3. "MOVE DD to DESTIN
MOVE '-'          TO DESTIN+5. "MOVE '-' TO DESTIN

MOVE SOURCE+0(4)  TO DESTIN+6. "MOVE YYYY to DESTIN

WRITE:/5 'SOURCE-DEFAULT OUTPUT     (DDMMYYYY)    :', SOURCE,
      /5 'DESTIN-TRANSFORMED OUTUT (MM/DD/YYYY)  :', DESTIN.
```

The execution of the program will generate the output shown in Figure 4-12.

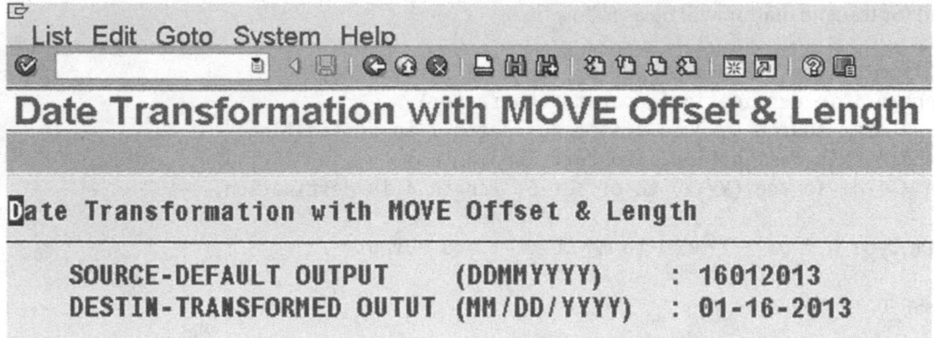

Figure 4-12. *Output of Program: YCL_CH04_05_TRANSF_DATE_MOVE*

Structured Data Objects, Own Data Types

A structured data object is a group or collection of internal fields in a program. The structured data object can be accessed as a single entity; and individual fields in the structure can be accessed as well. You use the DATA statement and mark the beginning and the end of the group of fields with BEGIN OF and END OF statements. The syntax is as follows:

```
DATA: BEGIN OF <structure name>,
<field1>.....,
           ..............
      END OF <structure name>.
```

A structured data object can contain elementary data objects as well as complex data objects (i.e., another structured data object or internal table). A structured data object containing complex data object is not discussed in this book.

Structured Data Object–ABAP Program: Access Individual Fields

```
REPORT YCL_CH04_06_STRU_DATA_OBJ.

******************************************************
* Structured Data Objects: Access Individual Fields **
******************************************************

**************************************************
* declare structured data object. Assign       **
* starting values to fields in the structured  **
* data object. output these fields by accessing **
* the individual fields.                        **
**************************************************
```

```
DATA: BEGIN OF CONTACT_MODES," CONTACT_MODES-name of struc data object

  NAME(25)          TYPE C VALUE 'SURAJ NAIR',
  LAND_LINE(12)     TYPE N VALUE '009126960021',
  CELL_NO(14)       TYPE N VALUE '00919502102377',
  EMAIL             TYPE STRING VALUE 'snair23@gmail.com',

END OF CONTACT_MODES.

   WRITE :/5 'Name          :', CONTACT_MODES-NAME,
          /5 'Land Line No. :', CONTACT_MODES-LAND_LINE,
          /5 'Cell No.      :', CONTACT_MODES-CELL_NO,
          /5 'Email Address :', CONTACT_MODES-EMAIL.
```

In this program, a structured data object has been declared using BEGIN OF..END OF.. notation to indicate the beginning and ending of the structured data object declaration. The four fields inside the structure have been declared in the usual manner. When you refer to the individual fields in the structure, you have to specify the structure name hyphen followed by the field name. The field is inside the structure.

The following output is generated upon this program execution.

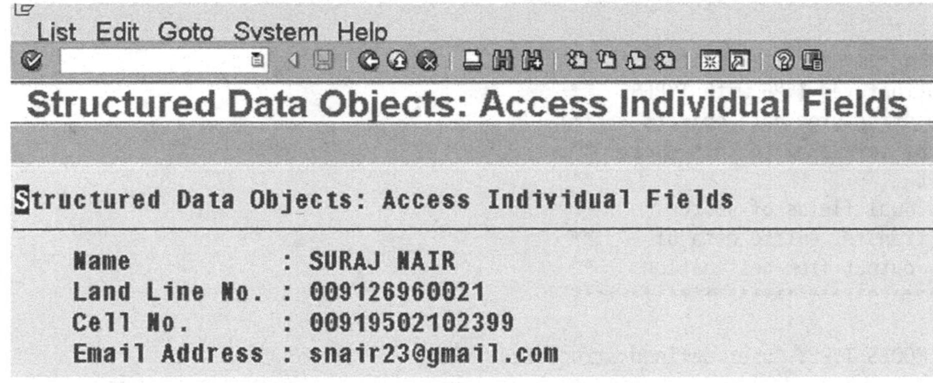

Figure 4-13. *Output of Program: YCL_CH04_06_STRU_DATA_OBJ*

Structured Data Object: Access Complete Structure

To access a complete structure, let there be a context. Let there be two identical structures: that is, having the same fields in the same order, and each of the corresponding fields in the structures identical in type length, etc. You will move data from one structure to another by referring to the structure and not individual fields.

User Defined Structure Types

You have to declare two identical structures. In declaring these structures, another ABAP feature is introduced: the user defined types. The user defined types can be declared in an ABAP program and used to refer to these types to declare data objects within that program. The user defined types can also be declared in the DDIC object 'Type Group,' the fourth radio button on the SE11 opening screen. The user defined types declared in the DDIC object 'Type Group' can be referred to in multiple ABAP programs to declare data objects or types.

When you declare user defined types in an ABAP program, they are just definitions. They are not data objects, and they do not occupy memory. You cannot operate on them (i.e., assign values, etc.). They can only be referred to declare data objects. The data objects declared by referring to them will have the attributes (type, length etal.) of the referred types.

User defined types are declared in an ABAP program with the keyword 'TYPES'. Other notations used in declaring user defined types are same as when declaring data with the keyword 'DATA'.

In your present context you needed to declare a user defined structured type. You can declare an elementary user defined type, a table user defined type, and so on.

Structured Data Object in an ABAP Program: User Defined Type in ABAP Program, Access Complete Structure

Your ABAP program will have a user defined structured type. Two identical structured data objects will be declared by referring to this user defined structure type.

```
REPORT YCL_CH04_07_STRU_DATA_TYP_OBJ1.

************************************************************
* User Defined TYPE, Reference to Structured Data Object  **
************************************************************

******************************************************
* declare user defined structured TYPE with TYPES    **
* statement. declare two structured data objects     **
* (source, destination) by referring to this user    **
* defined structured TYPE                            **
* assign values to individual fields of source       **
* use MOVE statement to transfer entire data of      **
* source to destination. output from destination     **
******************************************************

TYPES: BEGIN OF CONTACT_MODES_TYPE, "user defined structured TYPE

         NAME(25)          TYPE C,
         LAND_LINE(12)     TYPE N,
         CELL_NO(14)       TYPE N,
         EMAIL             TYPE STRING,

       END OF CONTACT_MODES_TYPE.

DATA: CONTACT_MODES_SRCE TYPE CONTACT_MODES_TYPE,
      CONTACT_MODES_DEST TYPE CONTACT_MODES_TYPE.

CONTACT_MODES_SRCE-NAME         = 'ATUL VASAN'.
CONTACT_MODES_SRCE-LAND_LINE    = '00912696008'.
CONTACT_MODES_SRCE-CELL_NO      = '00919502102355'.
CONTACT_MODES_SRCE-EMAIL        = 'atulvs@yahoo.co.in'.

MOVE CONTACT_MODES_SRCE TO CONTACT_MODES_DEST. "MOVE stru to stru
```

```
WRITE: /5 'Name           :', CONTACT_MODES_DEST-NAME,
       /5 'Land Line No. :', CONTACT_MODES_DEST-LAND_LINE,
       /5 'Cell No.       :', CONTACT_MODES_DEST-CELL_NO,
       /5 'Email Address :', CONTACT_MODES_DEST-EMAIL.
```

You might very well ask, why assign values to fields of CONTACT_MODES_SRCE, move the data of this structure to CONTACT_MODES_DEST and output? Why not directly assign values to fields of CONTACT_MODES_DEST and output? Well! This is a demonstrative program. In the real world, data is fetched into structured data objects from database tables. Data is rarely assigned to literals as has been done here.

This was a demonstration: (a) to declare data by referring to user defined types, and to (b) MOVE operation on an aggregate of fields or structure.

The output of this program is shown in Figure 4-14.

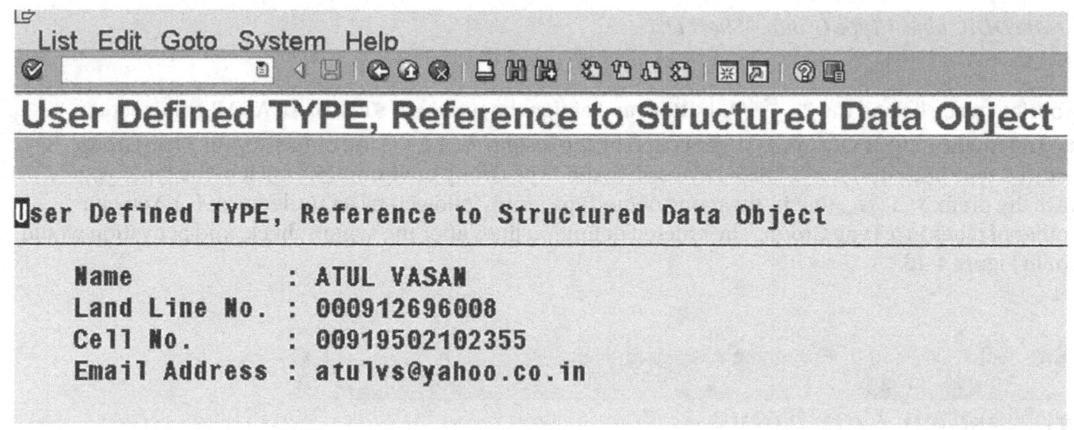

Figure 4-14. *Output of Program: YCL_CH04_07_STRU_DATA_TYP_OBJ1*

User Defined Type in DDIC

You will code the previous program by shifting the user defined structured type from the program to the DDIC 'Type Group'. You need to create a 'Type Group' and locate your user defined structured type in it.

On the SE11 opening screen, click the 'Type Group' radio button, and enter a name for the 'Type Group' as YCLG1 (Name space only 5 characters). Click on the Create button or press F5. The following screen appears prompting for Short text.

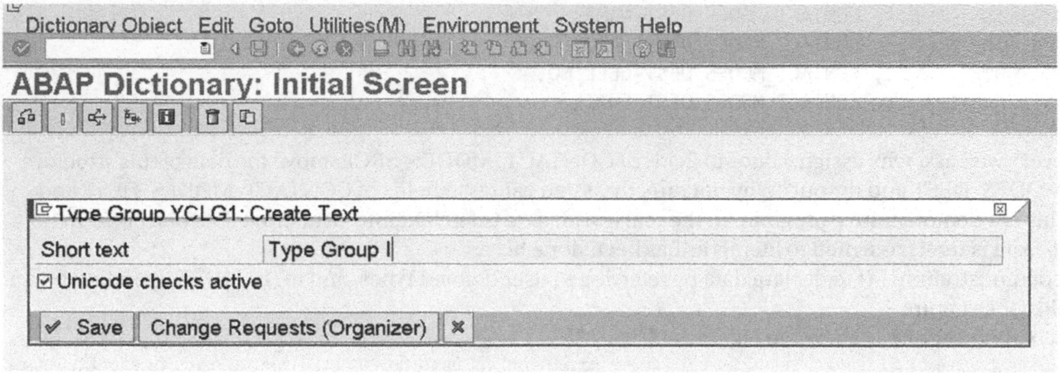

Figure 4-15. Create DDIC object Type Group – Short text

Enter appropriate text, click on the ✔ Save button, and assign the package ($TMP). An ABAP editor screen appears with the statement TYPE-POOL YCLG1 generated by the system. YCLG1 is the name of your Type Group. Enter your structured type lines under a 'TYPES' keyword. In the Type Group environment, each of the types you declare must have the prefix YCLG1_: that is, the name of the Type group followed by an underscore (_). You can declare any number of types in a Type Group. The entered definition lines after the syntax check, and activation would appear as shown in Figure 4-16.

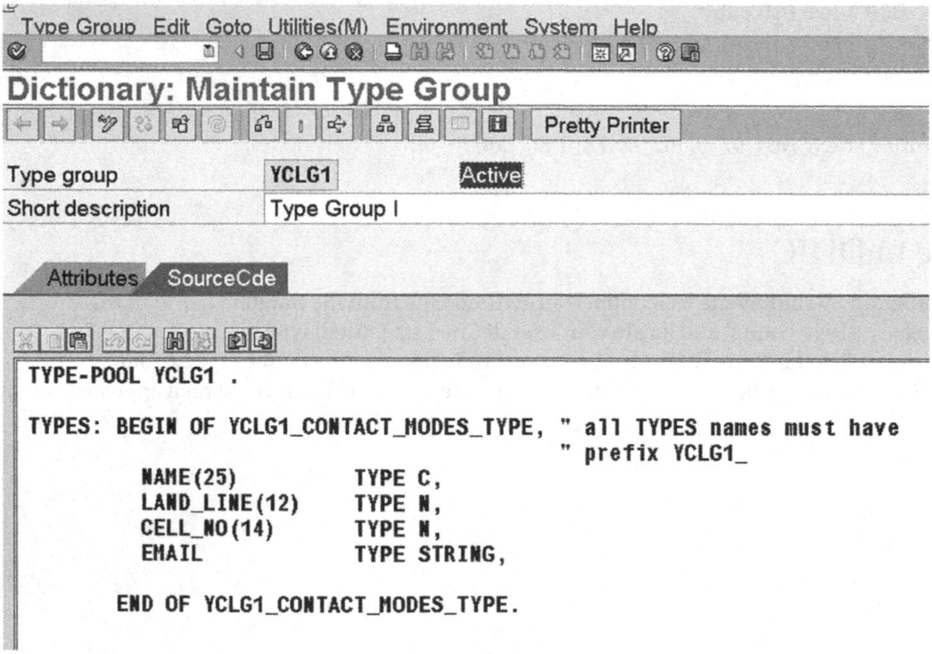

```
TYPE-POOL YCLG1 .

TYPES: BEGIN OF YCLG1_CONTACT_MODES_TYPE, " all TYPES names must have
                                          " prefix YCLG1_
         NAME(25)         TYPE C,
         LAND_LINE(12)    TYPE N,
         CELL_NO(14)      TYPE N,
         EMAIL            TYPE STRING,

       END OF YCLG1_CONTACT_MODES_TYPE.
```

Figure 4-16. Define user defined TYPES in Type Group – YCLG1

Structured Data Object in an ABAP Program Referring to DDIC Type Group

The ABAP program must contain a statement to list the Type Groups used in the program starting with the key phrase TYPE-POOLS. You are using only one Type Group (i.e., YCLG1). The two structured data objects have been declared, referring to the structured type you defined in the Type Group. The rest of the program is the same as the previous one.

```
REPORT YCL_CH04_08_STRU_DATA_TYP_OBJ2.

*****************************************************************
* User Defined TYPE in DDIC, Reference to Structured Data Object **
*****************************************************************

****************************************************
* declare two structured data objects            **
* (source, destination) by referring to structured **
* TYPE defined in DDIC Type Group               **
* assign values to individual fields of source     **
* use MOVE statement to transfer entire data of    **
* source to destination. output from destination   **
****************************************************
TYPE-POOLS YCLG1. "list Type Group you are using in this program

DATA: CONTACT_MODES_SRCE TYPE YCLG1_CONTACT_MODES_TYPE,
      CONTACT_MODES_DEST TYPE YCLG1_CONTACT_MODES_TYPE.

CONTACT_MODES_SRCE-NAME         = 'AGHA SHEIK'.
CONTACT_MODES_SRCE-LAND_LINE    = '00912696010'.
CONTACT_MODES_SRCE-CELL_NO      = '00919502102350'.
CONTACT_MODES_SRCE-EMAIL        = 'asheik41@yahoo.co.in'.

MOVE CONTACT_MODES_SRCE TO CONTACT_MODES_DEST. "MOVE stru to stru

WRITE: /5 'Name           :', CONTACT_MODES_DEST-NAME,
       /5 'Land Line No. :', CONTACT_MODES_DEST-LAND_LINE,
       /5 'Cell No.      :', CONTACT_MODES_DEST-CELL_NO,
       /5 'Email Address :', CONTACT_MODES_DEST-EMAIL.
```

After the syntax check, activation, and execution, the output appears as in Figure 4-17.

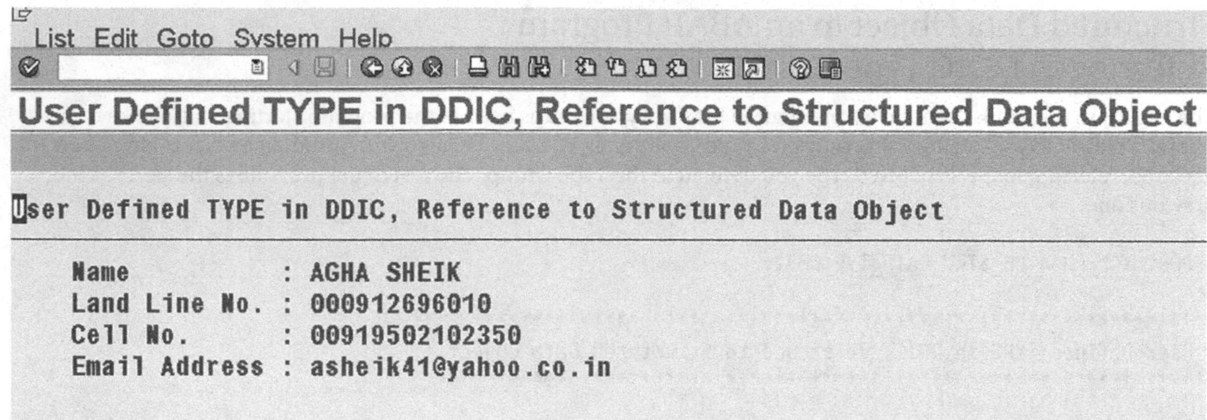

Figure 4-17. *Output of Program: YCL_CH04_08_STRU_DATA_TYP_OBJ2*

Structured Data Objects: MOVE Statement – Source, Destination Not Identical

In the preceding programs involving data movement from one structured data object to another, you had identical structures: the source and destination contained the same number of fields, the order of the fields was same, and each of the fields in the source was identical to the corresponding field in the destination as far as TYPE, length, etc. The MOVE statement, when operated on structured types, treats an entire aggregate of fields in the structure as one field of TYPE C; the bytes in the source are transferred to the corresponding byte nos. in the destination.

This identicalness of source and destination structured data objects might not always be so. In such a case, you should not operate the MOVE command at the structure level. Perhaps you could issue a MOVE statement for individual fields. If there are 10 fields to be transferred from one structure to another, issue 10 MOVE or assignment statements.

There is a variation of a MOVE statement that lets you copy the fields of a source structure to the fields of a destination structure. The transfer of data is based on the names of the fields of source and destination being identical. The contents of fields in destination whose names do not match with names in the source have their contents undisturbed. The data movement is field wise.

Syntax

```
MOVE-CORRESPONDING <structure1> TO <structure2>.
```

Figure 4-18 represents this graphically. There will be no data transfer for LAND_LINE since there is no field with this name in the destination. Also, the field CELL_NO length is 14 bytes in source and 12 bytes in destination. The data movement for TYPE N is right to left; the leading first two digits '00' will get truncated in the destination.

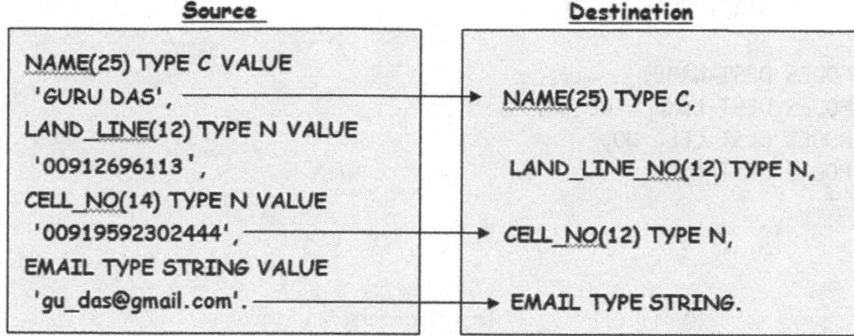

Figure 4-18. *Operation of MOVE-CORRESPONDING in Structured Data Objects*

The ABAP program for this scenario is

```
REPORT YCL_CH04_09_STRU_MOVE_CORR.

*************************************************
* Structured Data Objects - MOVE-CORRESPONDING **
*************************************************

*******************************************************
* declare two structured data objects with one field **
* name differing in source & destination             **
*                                                    **
* assign values to individual fields of source and   **
* destination                                        **
*                                                    **
* use MOVE-CORRESPONDING statement to transfer from  **
* source to destination. output from destination     **
*******************************************************

DATA: BEGIN OF CONTACT_MODES_SRCE,
       NAME(25)          TYPE C VALUE 'GURU DAS',
       LAND_LINE(12)     TYPE N VALUE '00912696113',
       CELL_NO(14)       TYPE N VALUE '00919592302444',
       EMAIL             TYPE STRING VALUE 'gu_das@gmail.com',
      END OF CONTACT_MODES_SRCE,

      BEGIN OF CONTACT_MODES_DEST,
       NAME(25)          TYPE C VALUE 'ZZZZZZZZ',
       LAND_LINE_NO(12) TYPE N VALUE '999999999999',
       CELL_NO(12)       TYPE N VALUE '999999999999', " length differs from source
       EMAIL             TYPE STRING VALUE 'ZZZZZZZZZZZZZZZZ',
      END OF CONTACT_MODES_DEST.
```

```
MOVE-CORRESPONDING CONTACT_MODES_SRCE TO CONTACT_MODES_DEST.

WRITE: /5 'Name           :', CONTACT_MODES_DEST-NAME,
       /5 'Land Line No. :', CONTACT_MODES_DEST-LAND_LINE_NO,
       /5 'Cell No.      :', CONTACT_MODES_DEST-CELL_NO,
       /5 'Email Address :', CONTACT_MODES_DEST-EMAIL.
```

The output is shown in Figure 4-19.

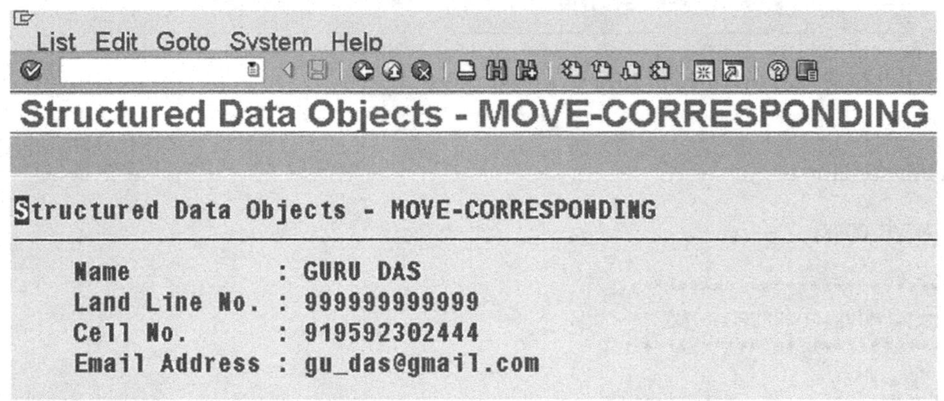

Figure 4-19. *Output of Program: YCL_CH04_09_STRU_MOVE_CORR*

Date, Time Arithmetic

You can perform some basic arithmetic operations on types D and T. You add days to a date to derive a future date, subtract days from a date to derive a past date, and derive the difference in days between two dates. Similarly, you can add seconds to a time to derive advanced time, subtract seconds from a time to derive a time in the past and the difference in seconds between two times.

Date Arithmetic – ABAP Program

An ABAP program demonstrating date arithmetic is coded.

```
REPORT YCL_CH04_10_DATE_ARITHM.

********************
* Date Arithmetic **
********************
**************************************************
* input of two dates DATE1 DATE2 through        **
* PARAMETERS statement (special data object)    **
* the DEFAULT clause with PARAMETERS assigns    **
* starting value to the prompt variables just like **
* VALUE for data objects in DATA statement      **
*                                               **
```

```
* input of DAYS (TYPE I)                            **
*                                                   **
* calculate & output difference between DATE1,DATE2**
* calculate & output date by adding DAYS to DATE2   **
* calculate & output the last day of month of DATE1**
*                                                   **
* bit of jugglary code to calculate last day of     **
* month. you are first deriving the date as of      **
* first day of next month, next subtracting 1 from **
* that date. (there would be better ways)           **
*                                                   **
* the IF statement has not been introduced, but     **
* should not be a problem                           **
*                                                   **
* VAR is TYPE I, outputs in 11 columns by default. **
* (5) sigifies the output must appear in 5 columns **
*                                                   **
* when you output TYPE D data objects, you are      **
* specifying the clause DD/MM/YYYY for separator.   **
* you are not able to output separator of your      **
* choice. the period (.) as separatr is appearing   **
* from global setting / master record               **
*****************************************************
*****************************************************
* when you press F8 system will prompt for input    **
* DATE1, DATE2, DAYS. when you finished with input **
* press F8 again to obtain output.                  **
* press F3 to return from output to input screen    **
* press F3 to return from input screen to program   **
*****************************************************

DATA: VAR      TYPE I,
      DATE     TYPE D,
      YEAR(4)  TYPE N,
      MONTH(2) TYPE N,
      DAY(2)   TYPE N.
PARAMETERS: DATE1   TYPE D DEFAULT '20131025',
            DATE2   TYPE D DEFAULT '20121125',
            DAYS    TYPE I DEFAULT 100.

*************************************************
VAR = DATE1 - DATE2. "difference between DATE1,DATE2

WRITE:/5 'Diff. between Dates:', DATE1 DD/MM/YYYY,
        DATE2 DD/MM/YYYY, '=', (5) VAR.

DATE = DATE2 + DAYS. "the date ahead/behind of DATE2 by DAYS

WRITE:/5 DATE2 DD/MM/YYYY, '+', (5) DAYS, '=', DATE DD/MM/YYYY.

YEAR  = DATE1+0(4). "offset & length used
MONTH = DATE1+4(2).
```

```
IF MONTH < 12.
 MONTH = MONTH + 1.
ELSE.
 MONTH = 1.
 YEAR = YEAR + 1.
ENDIF.

DATE+0(4) = YEAR. "get to first day of next month
DATE+4(2) = MONTH.
DATE+6(2) = '01'.

DATE = DATE - 1. "subtract 1 from first day of next month
                 "for last day of month

DAY = DATE+6(2).

WRITE:/5 'Last day of month date', DATE1 DD/MM/YYYY, '=', DAY.
```

When you execute the program with the default values, the output in Figure 4-20 is generated.

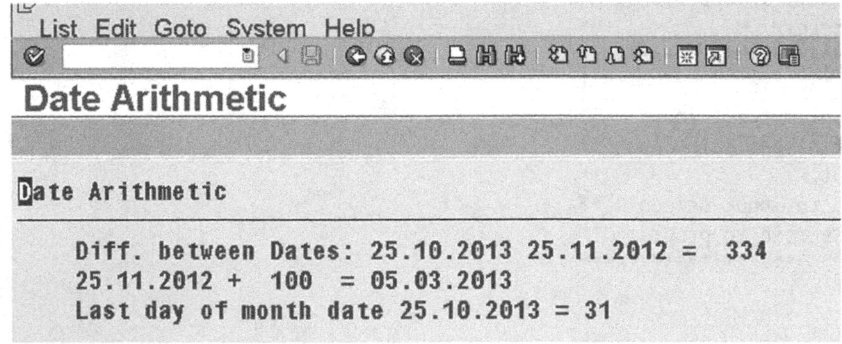

Figure 4-20. *Output of Program: YCL_CH04_10_DATE_ARITHM*

You can attempt an exercise with TYPE T on a parallel basis.

Arithmetic - Numerical Operations

Basic Arithmetic Operations/Operators

- **Addition** +
- **Subtraction** -
- **Multiplication** *
- **Division** /
- **Integer Division** DIV
- **Remainder of Integer Division** MOD
- **Exponentiation** **

The arithmetic assignment statement has the syntax

```
[COMPUTE] <n> = <expression>.
```

The word COMPUTE is optional.

- The field <n> is assigned to the result of the arithmetic expression.
- The numerical precision is defined by the operand of the numerical operation that has the highest hierarchy level. The system treats the target field <n> and the floating point functions as operands. The order of the hierarchy levels is I, P, and F. ABAP converts all numbers of a numerical operation into its hierarchically highest data type that occurs in the operation. Then the system executes the operation with the converted numbers.

The order or precedence of operations or evaluation is as follows:-

- Expressions in parentheses
- Functions
- ** Exponentiation
- * / MOD / DIV (Multiplication, division, & MOD)
- + - (additions & subtractions)

When writing arithmetic expressions and statements, you must leave a blank before an = sign and after an equal sign. You must also leave a blank between an operator and operand like:

```
TAX = (TAX_RATE / 100) * TAX_AMOUNT.
```

In addition to the mathematical operators, you can use the ADD, SUBTRACT, MULTIPLY, DIVIDE. . . statements. The usage of these is rare. Most people stick to mathematical operators.

Functions Common to All Numeric Data Types

Table 4-4. *Numeric Functions*

Function	Description
ABS(X)	Absolute value of the argument
SIGN(X)	= 1 if X > 0; = 0 if X = 0; = -1 If X < 0
CEIL(X)	Smallest integer value not smaller than the argument
FLOOR(X)	Largest integer value not larger than the argument
TRUNC(X)	Integer part of argument
FRAC(X)	Fraction part of argument

Floating Point Functions

There are floating point functions. You can refer to the PDF document **ABAP Programming (BC-ABA)** under Basic Statements ➤ Numerical Operations ➤ Mathematical Functions. However, these are not of much significance in business applications.

Arithmetic Operations on Structures

Similar to a MOVE-CORRESPONDING statement involving identical field names in *Structures*, you can perform arithmetic operations on fields of two structures having identical field names and *type numerical*:

- ADD-CORRESPONDING
- SUBTRACT-CORRESPONDING
- MULTIPLY-CORRESPONDING
- DIVIDE-CORRESPONDING

You will not have any exclusive hands-on programs for arithmetic operations. Most of you will have already be exposed to these concepts. The arithmetic operations in ABAP are very similar to that in other computer languages. You will be performing arithmetic operations in the subsequent chapters, when and as a scenario demands it.

String Operations

You are creating and executing a half dozen hands-on programs to cover the major features of string operations or statements.

An ABAP Program Demonstrating *TRANSLATE*. UPPER CASE/LOWER CASE is Coded

```
REPORT YCL_CH04_11_TRANSLATE.

***************************************
* TRANSALATE: UPPER CASE, LOWER CASE **
***************************************
************************************************
* take a string input through PARAMETERS      **
* variable ISTRING                            **
*                                             **
* in the PARAMETERS statement the phrase      **
* LOWER CASE enables input in LOWER as well   **
* as UPPER case.(case sensitivity) by default **
* the PARAMETERS statement accepts only UPPER **
* case i.e. even if you enter lower case it   **
* is converted to UPPER case.                 **
*                                             **
* the ISTRING is assigned to OSTRING. the     **
* TRANSALATE.. TO UPPER CASE is performed on  **
* OSTRING. OSTRING is output                  **
*                                             **
* the ISTRING is assigned to OSTRING. the     **
* TRANSALATE.. TO LOWER CASE is performed on  **
* OSTRING. OSTRING is output                  **
************************************************
```

```
DATA: OSTRING(50) TYPE C.
PARAMETERS: ISTRING(50) TYPE C LOWER CASE DEFAULT
 'MpHasIS - An H.p. CoMPanY'.

OSTRING = ISTRING.
TRANSLATE OSTRING TO UPPER CASE.

WRITE:/5 'Original String  :',ISTRING,
      /5 'UPPER CASE STRING:',OSTRING.

OSTRING = ISTRING.
TRANSLATE OSTRING TO LOWER CASE.
WRITE:/5 'lower case string:',OSTRING.
```

The program with the DEFAULT value of ISTRING will generate the output in Figure 4-21.

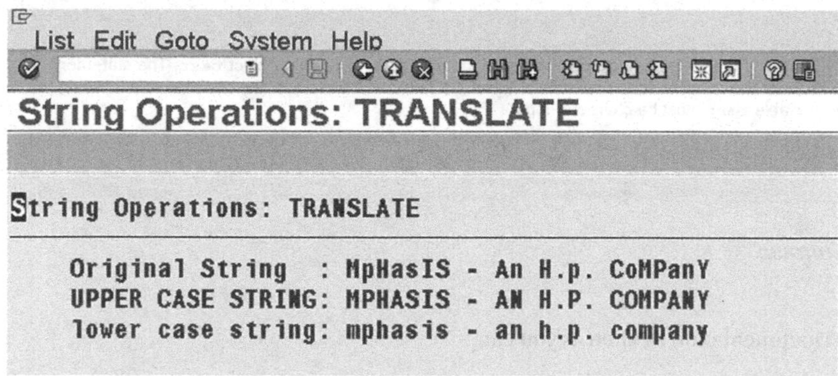

Figure 4-21. *Output of Program: YCL_CH04_11_TRANSLATE*

In the ABAP editor, when you position the cursor on a keyword and press F1, the system opens a new window. The new window displays 'the ABAP Keyword Documentation' for the keyword on which F1 was pressed. If you pressed F1 on the keyword TRANSLATE in the ABAP program, then the screen shown in Figure 4-22 is displayed.

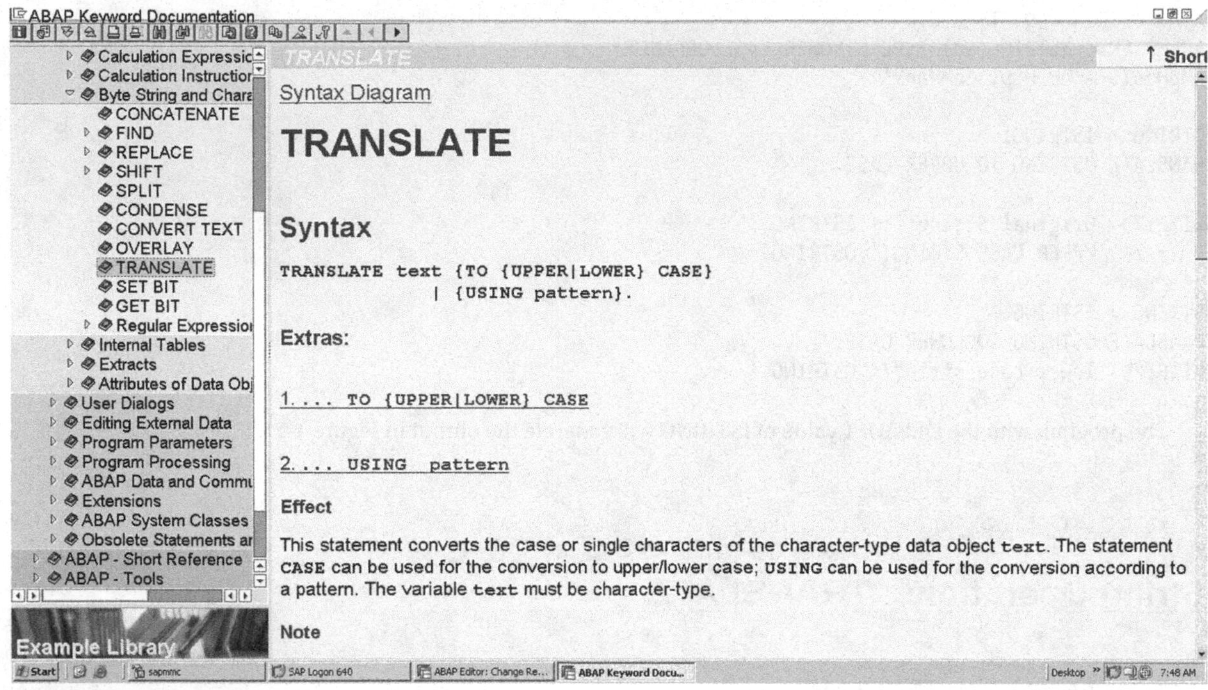

Figure 4-22. *ABAP Keyword Documentation*

Keep visiting the ABAP Keyword Documentation as often as you can.

An ABAP Program Demonstrating *CONCATENATE* is Coded

The CONCATENATE statement has been used to transform the date from YYYYMMDD to MM/DD/YYYY format and output. Earlier you had used the MOVE statement to implement this. As you will observe, this is a better option. The CONCATENATE statement joins multiple source strings into one destination string with an optional separator character string.

If the destination string is insufficient for accommodating the result, truncation will occur on the right side and no runtime error occurs.

```
 Source-Offsets      Destination-Offsets
0 1 2 3 4 5 6 7      0 1 2 3 4 5 6 7 8 9
----------------     --------------------
|Y|Y|Y|Y|M|M|D|D|    |M|M|-|D|D|-|Y|Y|Y|Y|
----------------     --------------------
```

```
REPORT YCL_CH04_12_CONCATENATE.

*****************************************************
* CONCATENATE - Join Multiple Strings Into One String *
*****************************************************
*****************************************
* input a date IDATE through PARAMETERS    **
* use CONCATENATE statement to join MM     **
* [IDATE+4(2)] '/' DD [IDATE+6(2)] '/'     **
* YYYY [IDATE+0(4)] in CDATE. CDATE will   **
* will contain MM/DD/YYYY.                 **
* Output IDATE and CDATE                   **
*                                          **
* repeat the CONCATENATE statement by      **
* specifying separator string/character    **
* Output IDATE and CDATE                   **
*****************************************

DATA: CDATE(10) TYPE C.
PARAMETERS IDATE TYPE D DEFAULT '20130116'.

CONCATENATE IDATE+4(2) '/' IDATE+6(2) '/' IDATE+0(4) INTO CDATE.
WRITE:/5 IDATE, CDATE.

CONCATENATE IDATE+4(2) IDATE+6(2) IDATE+0(4) INTO CDATE
 SEPARATED BY '/'. "use of separator character
WRITE:/5 IDATE, CDATE.
```

The program with the DEFAULT value of IDATE will generate the following output:

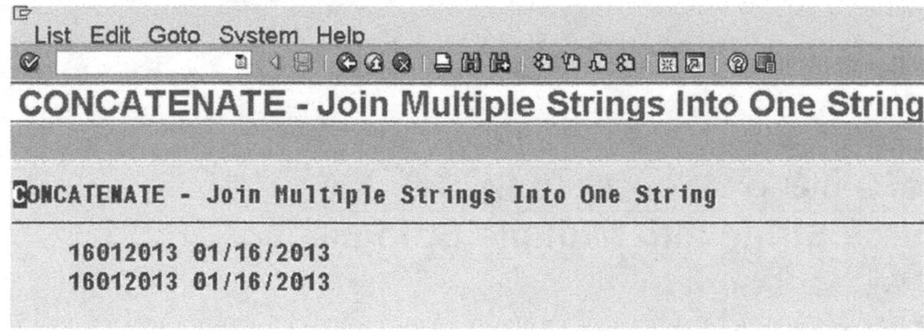

Figure 4-23. *Output of Program: YCL_CH04_12_CONCATENATE*

An ABAP Program Demonstrating *SPLIT*, the Reverse of CONCATENATE is Coded

The SPLIT statement breaks one source string into multiple destination strings. You have to specify a separator string/character that determines the splitting. If is blank or SPACE is specified, this will split a sentence into its constituent words.

If there are not enough destination strings, the residual string after the last split will go into the destination string variable appearing last in the statement. If the last variable in the statement is insufficient for accommodating the residual string, truncation will occur on the right side and no runtime error occurs.

```
REPORT YCL_CH04_13_SPLIT.

**********************************************************
* SPLIT - Break One Source String Into Multiple Strings *
* (Break Into Words)                                     *
**********************************************************
*****************************************************
* take input string as ISTRING through PARAMETERS  **
* 5 destination variables provided                 **
* operate the SPLIT statement on ISTRING AT SPACE  **
* output destination variables                     **
*****************************************************
DATA:STR1(10)  TYPE C,
     STR2(10)  TYPE C,
     STR3(10)  TYPE C,
     STR4(10)  TYPE C,
     STR5(10)  TYPE C.
*************************************************
PARAMETERS: ISTRING(50) TYPE C DEFAULT 'NIGHT AT THE MUSEUM'.

SPLIT ISTRING AT SPACE INTO STR1 STR2 STR3 STR4." SPACE is a System Data
                                                " Object - blank/s

WRITE /5: STR1,
          STR2,
          STR3,
          STR4.
```

The program with the DEFAULT value of ISTRING will generate the following output:

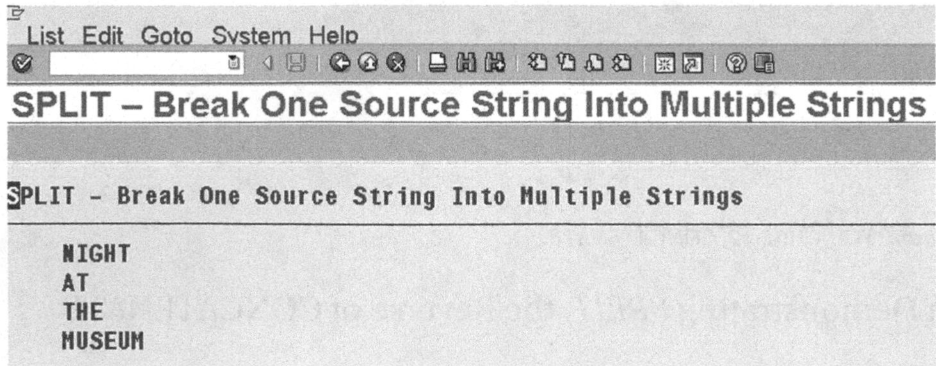

Figure 4-24. *Output of Program: YCL_CH04_13_SPLIT*

A variation of this statement that returns the destination strings in an array is mostly used. This variation will be covered in Chapter 6 entitled 'Internal Tables'.

An ABAP Program Demonstrating the Function *STRLEN( )* is Coded

The STRLEN( ) function returns the length of a string variable. The leading blanks are counted and the trailing blanks are not counted in the length.

```
REPORT YCL_CH04_14_STRLEN.

*********************************************************
* STRLEN() - returns the length of a string variable    *
*********************************************************

DATA: LEN(2) TYPE P DECIMALS 0.

PARAMETERS: ISTRING(50) TYPE C DEFAULT ' ABAP WORKBENCH '.

LEN = STRLEN( ISTRING ).

WRITE AT :/5 'String Length of:', (LEN) ISTRING, (2) LEN.
```

The program with the DEFAULT value of ISTRING will generate the output as in Figure 4-25.

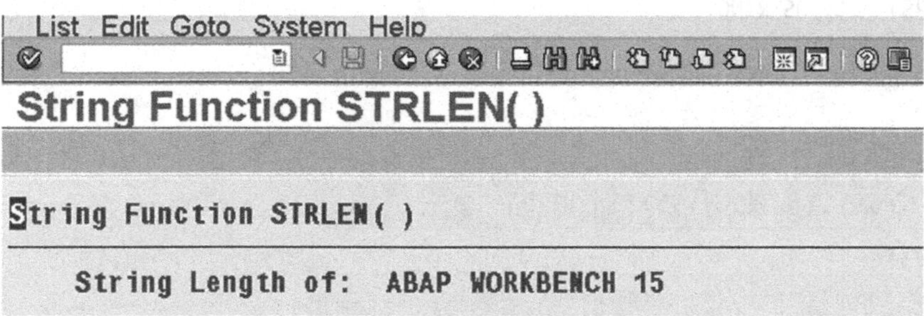

Figure 4-25. *Output of Program: YCL_CH04_14_STRLEN*

An ABAP Program Demonstrating the Statement *CONDENSE* is Coded

The CONDENSE statement removes the leading/left side blanks and reduces the embedded blanks to one or zero.

```
REPORT YCL_CH04_15_CONDENSE.

***********************
* CONDENSE Statement **
***********************

***************************************************************
* take input string as ISTRING through PARAMETERS           **
*                                                           **
* assign ISTRING to OSTRING. operate CONDENSE on OSTRING.   **
* output OSTRING                                            **
*                                                           **
```

```
* assign ISTRING to OSTRING. operate CONDENSE on OSTRING with **
* NO-GAPS. output OSTRING                                      **
*                                                              **
* CONDENSE statement operation:                                **
* (a) removes all leading/left side blanks. (b) it reduces     **
* embedded blanks to one blank. (c) if the addition NO-GAPS    **
* is specified, it reduces embedded blanks to zero i.e.        **
* embedded blanks will be removed totally                      **
****************************************************************

DATA OSTRING(50) TYPE C.
PARAMETERS: ISTRING(50) TYPE C DEFAULT
 '    ABAP    LANGUAGE BASICS'.

MOVE ISTRING TO OSTRING.
CONDENSE OSTRING.
WRITE:/5 'Original String           :', ISTRING,
      /5 'Condense String           :', OSTRING.

MOVE ISTRING TO OSTRING.
CONDENSE OSTRING NO-GAPS.
WRITE:/5 'Condense String(NO-GAPS)  :', OSTRING.
```

The program with the DEFAULT value of ISTRING will produce an output as in Figure 4-26.

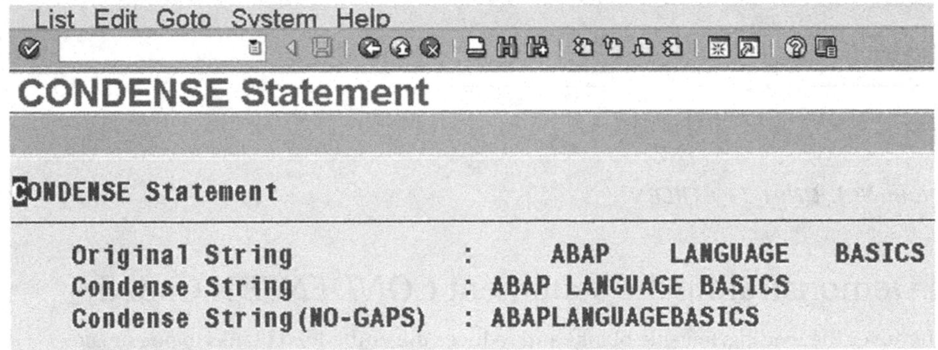

Figure 4-26. *Output of Program: YCL_CH04_15_CONDENSE*

Not all string operators are covered here. Any string operator you might need in a scenario would be introduced in the scenario context.

Program Internal Flow Control

Like in any other programming language, ABAP also executes statements sequentially one after another. This sequential execution is broken by the so-called flow control statements. ABAP, like any other fourth-generation language is event driven. In ABAP there are two types of flow control statements: (i) Internal Control and (ii) External Control.

The *internal flow control* consists of the following categories of statements:-

Table 4-5. *Internal Flow Control Statement Categories*

Condition Testing	IF, ELSE, ELSEIF, ENDIF
Single variable equality testing	CASE, WHEN, ENDCASE
Unconditional looping or repetitive procedures	DO, ENDDO
Conditional looping or repetitive procedures	WHILE, ENDWHILE
Modularization, calling external procedures	PERFORM, CALL

The *external flow control* consists of events. Events will be introduced in Chapter 5 entitled 'WRITE Statement (Classical Reporting)'.

Conditions, Conditional Operators

The internal flow of programs is controlled with conditions. To construct a condition, logical expressions are used that compare data fields as follows:-

```
. . . <f1><conditional operator><f2> . . .
```

The expression compares two fields (operands) <f1>, <f2>. These fields can be database fields, program data objects, literals, or constants. Structured data types can also be used as operands. Structures are compared component by component, and nested structures are broken down into elementary fields. The ABAP supports the following conditional operators.

Conditional Operators

Operator	Meaning
EQ =	EQUAL TO
NE <>><	NOT EQUAL TO
LT <	LESS THAN
LE <=	LESS THAN OR EQUAL TO
GT >	GREATER THAN
GE >=	GREATER THAN OR EQUALTO
BETWEEN	BETWEEN
IS INITIAL	IS INITIAL

If fields of different data types are compared, they must be convertible. Before performing the comparison, the system executes an automatic conversion. The conversion is according to the following hierarchical rules:-

- If one of the operands is a floating point number (type F), the system converts the other operands also to type F.
- If one of the operand is a packed decimal number (type P,) the system converts the other operand also to type P.

- If one of the operands is a date field type (type D) or a time field (type T), the system converts the other operands to type D or T. Comparison between date and time fields are not allowed.
- If one of the operands is a character field (type C) and the other is a hexadecimal field (type X), the system converts type X to type C.
- If one of the operands is a character field (type C) and the other is a numeric string (type N), the system converts both the operands to type P.

ABAP also supports special comparison pattern operators for TYPES C, D, N, and T. Look in the PDF document 'ABAP Programming (BC-ABA)' under Basic Statements ➤ Logical Expressions ➤ Comparing Strings.

Logical Operators

```
AND
OR
NOT
```

The IF Condition Statement

Syntax & some variations

- ```
  IF <condition>.
    <statement block>
  ENDIF.
  ```
- ```
  IF <condition>.
    <statement block>
  ELSE.
    <statement block>
  ENDIF.
  ```
- ```
  IF <condition>.
    <statement block>
  ELSEIF <condition>.
    <statement block>
  ELSEIF <condition>.
    <statement block>
  ELSE.
    <statement block>
  ENDIF.
  ```
- ```
  IF <condition>.
    <statement block>
    IF <condition>.
      <statement block>
    ENDIF.
    <statement block>
  ENDIF.
  ```

ABAP allows unlimited nesting of IF - ENDIF statement blocks, but they must terminate within the same processing block. So an IF - ENDIF block cannot contain an event keyword.

Conditional Branching with CASE

Syntax & some variations

To execute different mutually exclusive statement blocks depending on the contents of a particular data object, you can use the CASE statement as follows:

```
CASE <f>.
   WHEN <f1>.
<statement block>
   WHEN <f2>.
<statement block>
   WHEN ...
   ......
   WHEN OTHERS.
<statement block>
ENDCASE.
```

The system executes the statement block after the WHEN statement if the contents of <f> equals the contents of <fi>, it and continues processing after the ENDCASE statement. The statement block after the optional WHEN OTHERS statement is executed if the contents of <f> are not equal any of the <fi> contents. The last statement block must be concluded with ENDCASE.

The Unconditional Loops: DO - ENDDO

Repetitive execution of a statement block is achieved by the unconditional loop statement DO.

Syntax

```
DO [<n> TIMES] [VARYING <f> FROM <f1> NEXT <f2>].
<statement block>
ENDDO.
```

- The system processes the statement block between DO & ENDDO repeatedly until it finds an EXIT, STOP statement.
- The number of times the loop should perform repeatedly can be optionally specified by the TIMES option. The parameter <n> can be a literal or variable. If <n> is zero or less than zero, the system does not process the loop.
- Each time the execution proceeds from the start to the end of the loop, it is called a *loop pass*. The system field *SY-INDEX* contains the value of the loop pass of the current loop being executed.
- It should be ensured that the loop is executed endlessly or infinite times.
- Loops can be nested one inside another any number of times. The unconditional loop DO can be combined in the nesting with the other type of loop, the conditional loop statement: WHILE - ENDWHILE.
- The VARYING option is used infrequently, but its operation can be referenced in the manual **ABAP Programming (BC-ABA)** under Basic Statements ➤ Loops.

Three statements: EXIT, CONTINUE, and CHECK operate inside the loop as follows:-

- EXIT (Terminate Loop) is for exiting and coming out of the current loop altogether.
- CONTINUE (Terminate Loop Pass Unconditionally) is for bypassing the current pass of the loop and starting the execution of the next pass, if any.
- The CHECK (Terminate a Loop Conditionally) statement if true allows the statement block following it to be executed. If the check statement evaluates to be false, the statement block following it is not executed, and it is equivalent to the rest of loop statements being bypassed for that pass of the loop.

The Conditional Loops: - WHILE - ENDWHILE

Conditional repetitive execution of a statement block is achieved by the conditional loop statement WHILE.

Syntax

```
WHILE <condition>  [VARYING <f> FROM <f1> NEXT <f2>].
<statement block>
ENDWHILE.
```

- The <condition> can be a simple condition or a compound condition like in IF statements.
- The system processes the statement block between WHILE & ENDWHILE repeatedly until it finds an EXIT or STOP statement or the <condition> evaluates as false.
- The VARYING option works the same way as for unconditional loop DO - ENDDO.
- Also the CONTINUE and CHECK statements work the same way as for the unconditional loops.

The internal flow control statements in ABAP is simple, and you are not performing any specific hands-on programs on these. In the forthcoming chapters, you will have the occasion to use these.

You will though have one hands-on program demonstrating the behavior of the system field SY-INDEX associated with looping constructs. This system field assumes the value of the pass number of the current loop.

An ABAP program coded for demonstrating the behavior of system field SY-INDEX in a two-level loop nesting.

```
REPORT YCL_CH04_16_SY_INDEX.

******************************************************
* Demonstrate the Behavior of System Field SY-INDEX **
******************************************************

*************************************************************
* SY-INDEX contains the pass no of current loop           **
*                                                         **
* if you are in the outer loop, it will contain pass no of  **
* outer loop. if you are in the inner loop, it will       **
* contain pass no of inner loop                           **
*                                                         **
* the inner loop will perform twice (IF SY-INDEX > 2. EXIT.) **
* for every pass of outer loop. the outer loop will       **
* perform thrice (IF SY-INDEX > 3. EXIT.)                 **
*                                                         **
```

```
* the WRITE statement in outer loop outputs starting from     **
* column 5. SY-INDEX is TYPE I. TYPE I outputs by default in **
* 11 columns. SY-index is being output in two columns        **
* (its value never excedding 3 in this program)              **
*                                                             **
* the WRITE statement in inner loop outputs starting from     **
* column 10.                                               **
***************************************************************

  DO.
   IF SY-INDEX > 3.
    EXIT.
   ENDIF.

   WRITE:/5 'Outer Loop:', (2) SY-INDEX.

   DO.
    IF SY-INDEX > 2.
     EXIT.
    ENDIF.

    WRITE:/10 'Inner Loop:', (2) SY-INDEX.
   ENDDO.
  ENDDO.
```

The program will produce an output as in Figure 4-27.

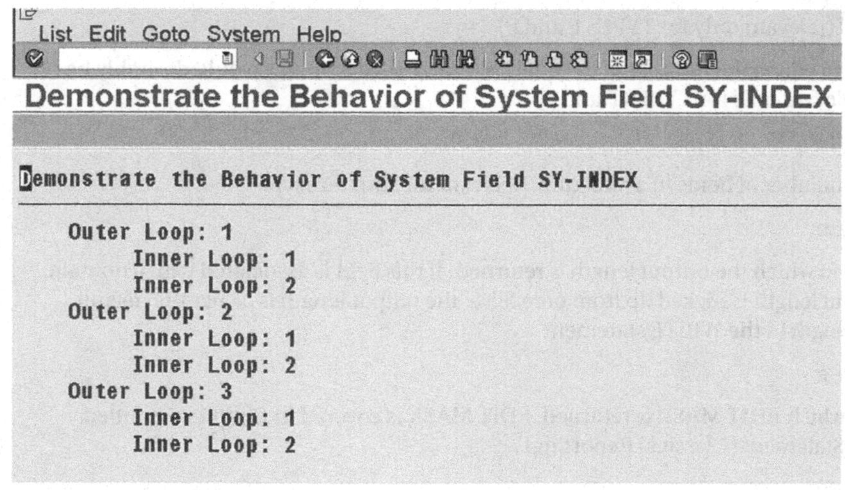

Figure 4-27. *Output of Program: YCL_CH04_16_SY_INDEX*

Determine Attributes of Data Objects

Sometimes, you need to determine in a program, the attributes of a data object declared by reference to a DDIC object. The attributes that can be determined are type (elementary types: C, D, F, I, N, P, T, X, STRING, XSTRING; Reference types; Complex types: Structure or Table), length, decimals, output length, etc.

The DESCRIBE FIELD statement is available to ascertain the attributes of a data object. The syntax of the DESCRIBE FIELD statement:

```
DESCRIBE FIELD <field name> [TYPE <type>] [LENGTH <length>IN {BYTE|CHARACTER} MODE ]
[DECIMALS <decimals>] [COMPONENTS <components>]
[OUTPUT-LENGTH<output length>] [EDIT MASK<edit mask>] [HELP-ID <help-id>].
```

DESCRIBE FIELD	Key phrase
<field name>	Name of data object whose attributes are to be determined
TYPE	Keyword
<type>	Variable in which the type will be returned. <type> should be type C and the appropriate length (see Table 4-6 for the different types returned)
LENGTH	Keyword
<length>	Variable in which the length is returned as number of characters / bytes <length> desirably be type I
IN CHARACTER MODE	Key Phrase. Length is returned in Character Count. This should be given for TYPES C, D, N, and T Only
IN BYTE MODE	Key Phrase. Length is returned in Byte Count. This can be given for elementary and structure TYPES
DECIMALS	Keyword (relevant only for TYPES F and P)
<decimals>	Variable in which the number of decimals is returned.<decimals> would desirably be of type I(relevant only for TYPES F and P)
COMPONENTS	Key Phrase
<components>	Returns number of fields in a structure. Relevant for structure type
OUTPUT-LENGTH	Key Phrase
<output length>	Variable in which the output length is returned. If this field is associated with a domain, the output length is picked up from here. Else, the output length is as per the default output length in the WRITE statement
EDIT MASK	Key Phrase
<edit mask>	Field in which EDIT MASK is returned. EDIT MASK is covered in Chapter 5 entitled 'WRITE Statement (Classical Reporting)'.
HELP-ID	Key Phrase
<help-id>	Field in which HELP-ID is returned HELP-ID is covered in Chapter 9 entitled 'SELECTION-SCREEN'

The different types returned by the DESCRIBE FIELD statement (other than the elementary types that are returned as 'C', 'D', 'F', 'I', 'N', 'P', 'T', 'X', 'STRING', and 'XSTRING) are listed in Table 4-6.

***Table 4-6.** DESCRIBE FIELD: TYPE Return Values*

Description	Return Type Value
Elementary ABAP TYPE STRING	g
Elementary ABAP TYPE XSTRING	Y
Object Reference	r
Data Reference	l
DDIC INT1	b
DDIC INT2	s
Flat structure (structure with no embedded structure or table)	u
Deep Structure (structure with embedded structure or table)	v
Internal Table	h

An ABAP program coded for demonstrating the DESCRIBE FIELD statement:

```
REPORT YCL_CH04_17_DESCRIBE_FIELD.

*******************************************************
* DESCRIBE FIELD: Determine Attributes of Data objects *
*******************************************************

**********************************************************************
* declare elementary data objects referring to DDIC table fields     **
* declare elementary data object referring to DDIC data element      **
* declare structure data object referring to DDIC table definition   **
* declare elementary TYPE STRING                                     **
*                                                                    **
* use DESCRIBE FIELD statement to determine attributes               **
* output attributes                                                  **
*                                                                    **
**********************************************************************

DATA: NAME1          TYPE KNA1-NAME1, "DDIC table field
      FKDAT          TYPE VBRK-FKDAT, "DDIC table field
      NETWR          TYPE VBRK-NETWR, "DDIC table field
      TEXT1          TYPE TBOOKSHOP-TEXT1, "DDIC table field
      LENGTH         TYPE TBOOKSHOP-LENGTH, "DDIC table field
      WAERS          TYPE WAERS, "reference to data element
      INT1           TYPE MCSAPINT1, "reference to data element
      VBRK           TYPE VBRK, "reference to table structure
      STRNG          TYPE STRING,
```

```
      TYP(1)         TYPE C,
      LEN            TYPE I,
      OLEN           TYPE I,
      DECI           TYPE I,
      COMPO          TYPE I.

**************************************************************************
DESCRIBE FIELD NAME1 TYPE TYP.

IF TYP = 'C' OR TYP = 'D' OR TYP = 'N' OR TYP = 'T'.
 DESCRIBE FIELD NAME1 LENGTH LEN IN CHARACTER MODE.

ELSE.
 DESCRIBE FIELD NAME1 LENGTH LEN IN BYTE MODE.

ENDIF.

WRITE:/5 'KNA1-NAME1 TYPE & LENGTH                        :', TYP,
 (3) LEN.
*********************************************************************
DESCRIBE FIELD FKDAT TYPE TYP.

IF TYP = 'C' OR TYP = 'D' OR TYP = 'N' OR TYP = 'T'.
 DESCRIBE FIELD FKDAT LENGTH LEN IN CHARACTER MODE.

ELSE.
 DESCRIBE FIELD FKDAT LENGTH LEN IN BYTE MODE.

ENDIF.

WRITE:/5 'VBRK-FKDAT TYPE & LENGTH                        :', TYP,
 (3) LEN.
**********************************************************************
DESCRIBE FIELD NETWR TYPE TYP.

IF TYP = 'C' OR TYP = 'D' OR TYP = 'N' OR TYP = 'T'.
* DESCRIBE FIELD NETWR LENGTH LEN IN CHARACTER MODE.

ELSE.
 DESCRIBE FIELD NETWR LENGTH LEN IN BYTE MODE.

ENDIF.

IF TYP = 'F' OR TYP = 'P'.
 DESCRIBE FIELD NETWR DECIMALS DECI.

ENDIF.
DESCRIBE FIELD NETWR OUTPUT-LENGTH OLEN.
WRITE:/5 'VBRK-NETWR TYPE, LENGTH OUTPUT-LENGTH & DECIMALS :', TYP,
 (3) LEN,  (2) OLEN, (2) DECI.
**********************************************************************
```

```
DESCRIBE FIELD TEXT1 TYPE TYP.

IF TYP = 'C' OR TYP = 'D' OR TYP = 'N' OR TYP = 'T'.
 DESCRIBE FIELD TEXT1 LENGTH LEN IN CHARACTER MODE.

ELSE.
 DESCRIBE FIELD TEXT1 LENGTH LEN IN BYTE MODE.

ENDIF.

WRITE:/5 'TBOOKSHOP-TEXT1 TYPE & LENGTH                    :', TYP,
 (4) LEN.
**********************************************************************

DESCRIBE FIELD LENGTH TYPE TYP.

IF TYP = 'C' OR TYP = 'D' OR TYP = 'N' OR TYP = 'T'.
* DESCRIBE FIELD LENGTH LENGTH LEN IN CHARACTER MODE.

ELSE.
 DESCRIBE FIELD LENGTH LENGTH LEN IN BYTE MODE.

ENDIF.

WRITE:/5 'TBOOKSHOP-LENGTH TYPE & LENGTH (DDIC TYPE INT2)  :', TYP,
 (3) LEN.
********************************************************************
DESCRIBE FIELD WAERS TYPE TYP.

IF TYP = 'C' OR TYP = 'D' OR TYP = 'N' OR TYP = 'T'.
 DESCRIBE FIELD WAERS LENGTH LEN IN CHARACTER MODE.

ELSE.
 DESCRIBE FIELD WAERS LENGTH LEN IN BYTE MODE.

ENDIF.

WRITE:/5 'CURRENCY CODE WAERS TYPE & LENGTH                :', TYP,
 (3) LEN.
*********************************************************************
DESCRIBE FIELD INT1 TYPE TYP.

IF TYP = 'C' OR TYP = 'D' OR TYP = 'N' OR TYP = 'T'.
* DESCRIBE FIELD INT1 LENGTH LEN IN CHARACTER MODE.

ELSE.
 DESCRIBE FIELD INT1 LENGTH LEN IN BYTE MODE.

ENDIF.
```

```
WRITE:/5 'DDIC TYPE INT1 & LENGTH (REF. TO DATA ELEMENT)    :', TYP,
 (3) LEN.

*********************************************************************
DESCRIBE FIELD VBRK TYPE TYP COMPONENTS COMPO LENGTH LEN IN BYTE MODE.

WRITE:/5 'VBRK TYPE, LENGTH & CMPONENTS                    :', TYP, (4)
 LEN, (3) COMPO.
*********************************************************************

DESCRIBE FIELD STRNG TYPE TYP.

IF TYP = 'C' OR TYP = 'D' OR TYP = 'N' OR TYP = 'T'.
* DESCRIBE FIELD STRNG LENGTH LEN IN CHARACTER MODE.

ELSE.
 DESCRIBE FIELD STRNG LENGTH LEN IN BYTE MODE.

ENDIF.

WRITE:/5 'LOCALLY DEFINED TYPE ''STRING'' TYPE & LENGTH      :',
 TYP, (3) LEN.
```

The program output will appear like this:

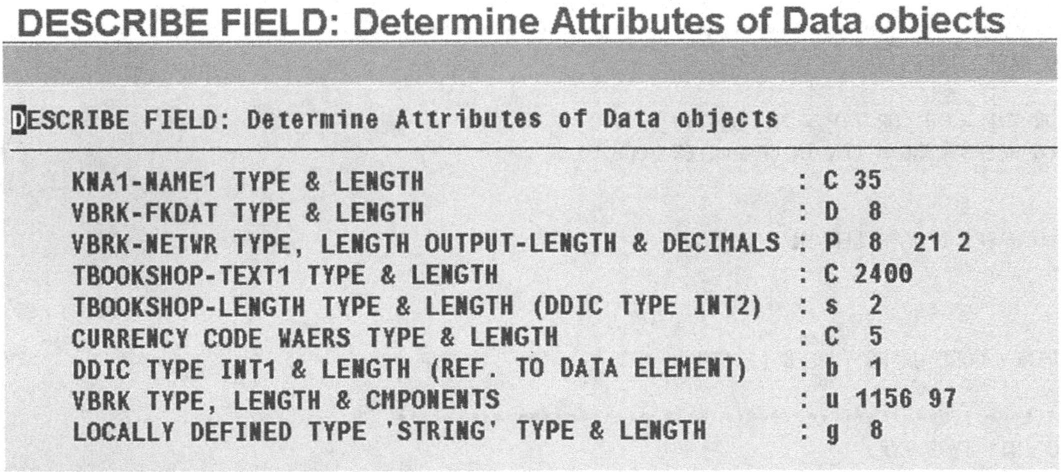

```
DESCRIBE FIELD: Determine Attributes of Data objects

DESCRIBE FIELD: Determine Attributes of Data objects

    KNA1-NAME1 TYPE & LENGTH                          : C 35
    VBRK-FKDAT TYPE & LENGTH                          : D  8
    VBRK-NETWR TYPE, LENGTH OUTPUT-LENGTH & DECIMALS  : P  8  21 2
    TBOOKSHOP-TEXT1 TYPE & LENGTH                     : C 2400
    TBOOKSHOP-LENGTH TYPE & LENGTH (DDIC TYPE INT2)   : s  2
    CURRENCY CODE WAERS TYPE & LENGTH                 : C  5
    DDIC TYPE INT1 & LENGTH (REF. TO DATA ELEMENT)    : b  1
    VBRK TYPE, LENGTH & CMPONENTS                     : u 1156 97
    LOCALLY DEFINED TYPE 'STRING' TYPE & LENGTH       : g  8
```

Figure 4-28. *Output of Program: YCL_CH04_17_DESCRIBE_FIELD*

You can cross-check the output length of domain NETWR as 21. The length of TYPE STRING is appearing as 8, which is the initial allocation of RAM to it.

The length for TYPES C, D, N, and T can be determined either in characters or bytes. So you can give either of the options: IN CHARACTER MODE/IN BYTE MODE. With 16-bit Unicode in operation (2 bytes), the length returned in bytes will be twice the length returned in characters.

For the TYPES other than C, D, N, and T, the length will be returned in bytes and hence the option 'IN BYTE MODE' is acceptable syntactically. During the compilation, the ABAP compiler checks the DDIC data object references and also determines the TYPE and syntactically rejects the *'IN CHARACTER MODE'* option if the TYPES are other than C, D, N, and T. That is the reason you have commented on the lines where this syntax error is highlighted. You will be able to tackle this syntax error after learning *subroutines* in the forthcoming Chapter 7: 'Modularization'.

Conclusion

You have learned the basic elements of the ABAP language. A few programs, mostly involving string operations, were coded. These programs were small and simple. You were also introduced to the 'WRITE' statement used for getting output. This was used to visually see the result of our operations in the programs.

From the next chapter onward, you are going to retrieve data from database tables. In business applications - notably SAP - data retrieval from database tables forms a major task.

CHAPTER 5

WRITE Statement (Classical Reporting)

Part of any business application programming involves retrieval and presentation of data (reporting or reports). Data in typical situations is retrieved from diverse multiple sources (database tables) and presented in character and/or graphic form. With any object oriented reporting tools (Crystal Reports), graphic interface, objects drag and drop, properties, methods, and events will take care of every reporting requirement.

WRITE Statement

In the ABAP environment, the WRITE statement is used to output data (produce lists or reports). It was conceived and created before OOP technology was an option. There are a few events associated with the WRITE statement. The one simple conspicuous feature absent in the WRITE statement from that of the OOP reporting tools is that one cannot impart specific styling (font type, font size, bold, underline, and italic) to specific areas of a report. With the WRITE statement, the entire report is generated with a single font type and size. When the styling feature is available as in the current reporting tools, one has to deal with physical dimensions in the areas of the report: inches, centimeters, points, and so on. When using the WRITE statement, physical dimensions are not used as such; instead you deal with columns and rows (not to be confused with columns and rows in the context of a database). A specific field to be output occupies a certain number of characters or column positions; all the fields being output on a line occupy a certain number of characters or column positions; and how many lines or rows are output in a page(for a specific type of page: for example, 'A3,' 'A4,' and so on).

A partial syntax of the WRITE statement is as follows:-

```
WRITE: [/][col1][(len1)] <dobj1> [color specification1]
 [<format specification1>],
       [/][col2][(len2)] <dobj2> [color specification2]
 [<format specification2>], ...
```

Where

- [] has the usual meaning - Anything enclosed in this is optional.
- *WRITE* is the keyword. ':' and ',' combination is for avoiding the repetition of the keyword *WRITE* (i.e., the process of chaining).
- / (optional) is for the output to start on a new line.
- *Col1, col2.* (Optional) to indicate the absolute column position at which output should start.

- *(len1), (len2),* (optional) for output to appear in *len1, len2* column length positions.
- *<dobj1>, <dobj2>* - data objects.(they can be variables/constants/literals).
- *<format specification1>* .. to output the field in a specified format.
- *<color specification1>* .. to impart color to the data object output.

The WRITE statement will not accept a function as an output item. This is a constraint of the WRITE statement. You cannot issue a statement like this:

```
WRITE:/5 ABS( AMOUNT ).
```

WRITE statement - a simple syntax example:

```
REPORT YCL_CH05_01_LIST_SYNTAX.
DATA: FLD1(20) TYPE C VALUE 'Message I :-',
      FLD2(20) TYPE C VALUE 'Message II:-'.

WRITE:/10(12) FLD1, 'Hello World',
      /,
      /15 FLD2, 'Hello U.S.A.'.
```

- FLD1 and FLD2 contain 12 characters of actual data.
- `WRITE:/10(12) FLD1` – means
  - / ... start output on a new line.
  - 10 ... start output from column position 10.
  - (12) ... output FLD1 in 12 column positions (not 20 column positions).
  - FLD1 ... output the data object FLD1 value.
- `'Hello World'` outputs the literal 'Hello World' on the same line as the variable data object FLD1. By default there will be one column position gap between the two data objects variable FLD1 and the literal 'Hello World.'
- / will generate a blank line.
- `/15 FLD2` will start output of FLD2 from the 15th column position on a new line, and FLD2 output will appear in 20 column positions (length of data object).
- `'Hello U.S.A.'` will output the literal 'Hello U.S.A.' on the same line. By default there will be one column position gap between the two data objects variable FLD2 and literal 'Hello India.'

The output would appear like this:-

```
Message I :-          Hello World

Message II:-          Hello U.S.A.
```

Terminology: You will refer to the output of WRITE statements as list or lists; this is the SAP terminology. The output of WRITE statements is also called a report or reports.

You will learn, in this chapter, how to produce output from data retrieved from a database. To retrieve data from a database, the *Open SQL* basic looping construct is introduced in the chapter on a preview basis. You will produce page headers and page footers. In this context, the events START-OF_SELECTION, TOP-OF-PAGE, END-OF-PAGE are introduced and program flows are described. The features of imparting color to outputs are to ensure part of the output to appear on a page, enclosing output in boxes, and make sure that freezing columns on the left, etc., are covered. This chapter is concluded with the WRITE statement's miscellaneous features and output formatting options.

WRITE Statement: Hands-on Exercise - A Simple Customer List

You will execute a hands-on exercise using the WRITE statement with data from a database table. Output of 'Hello world' in a few lines is a bit frivolous. You will want to output not only multiple lines, but also multiple pages. Since the focus is on the WRITE statement, data retrieval will be kept simple at this stage. You will use the *Open SQL* SELECT statement to retrieve data from a single database table. The *Open SQL* is formally covered in the Chapter 8 entitled 'Open SQL: Data Retrieval.' In the present chapter, it is an informal introduction to Open SQL. The simplest form of the SELECT statement is a *looping procedure* and has the following syntax:-

```
    SELECT <field list> FROM <source> INTO <destination structure>.
....<statements>
    ENDSELECT.
```

Each pass of this loop fetches one row of data from fields specified in <field list> from a table or view specified in <source> into the structure specified in <destination structure>. The next row fetched with the next pass of the loop will overwrite the existing contents of the structure specified in <destination structure>. This repetitive process goes on until all the rows have been fetched from the <source>. At the end of the loop process, the program control goes to the statement following the statement ENDSELECT (if there is a statement else exit in the program). The statements located between the looping statements SELECT ... ENDSELECT will be executed *as many times as the number of times the loop is executed or the number of* rows fetched. A graphical representation of the looping process is shown in Figure 5-1.

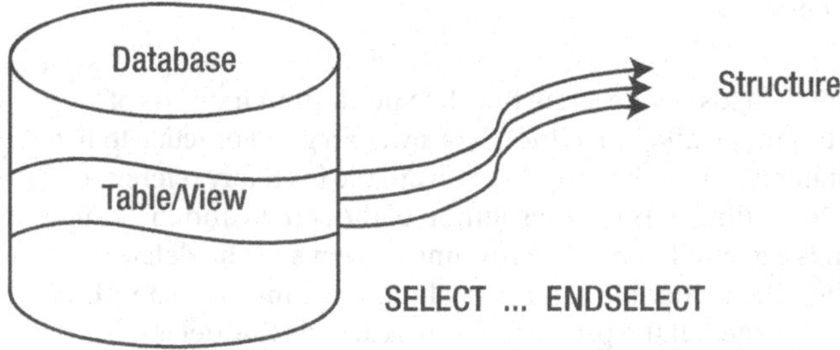

Figure 5-1. *SELECT.. ENDSELECT Process*

You will use this form of SELECT...ENDSELECT and the WRITE statement to generate a simple customer list for data retrieved from the primary customer table KNA1. The KNA1 table contains one row for each customer. Each line in the list will have information for one customer. You will output the following fields from the KNA1 table:-

Field Name	DDIC type, length		Description
KUNNR	CHAR	10	Customer Number/Code
NAME1	CHAR	35	Customer Name
STRAS	CHAR	35	Street
ORT01	CHAR	35	City Name
PSTLZ	CHAR	10	Postal Code

This kind of a list should be output with a serial number. You can declare a numeric data object in the program, increment it before the WRITE statement, and output it as the first item within the WRITE statement. If a system field avails you, this is unnecessary. The system field that serves your purpose in the present context is SY-DBCNT. Within the SELECT...ENDSELECT loop, this system field will contain the number of the current row fetched or the number of the loop pass.

The output layout with column positions will be as follows:-

Field Name	Column Positions	Description
SY-DBCNT	5-9(5)	Serial No
	10	BLANK
KUNNR	11-20 (10)	Customer Number/Code
	21	BLANK
NAME1	22-56(35)	Customer Name
	57	BLANK
STRAS	58-92(35)	Street
	93	BLANK
ORT01	94-128(35)	City Name
	129	BLANK
PSTLZ	130-139(10)	Postal Code

BLANK indicates a blank column between two adjoining fields on the same line. So your output in terms of total number of columns positions is 139 (139 is the last column position in a line). It is always a good practice to list out fields to be output in this manner. When the WRITE statement is coded, this list is available for ready reference. You need to know the total number of columns in a line. Depending upon the resolution of the screen and the font end setting of a presentation server on which the program is executed; the ABAP runtime system sets the default maximum number of columns in a line (i.e., the line width). The higher the screen resolution, the more the number of columns in a line. The default line width can be reset or changed. If the program output exceeds this default line width, the output appears in an embarrassing word wrap fashion. To ensure that the word wrap output does not appear, the line width can be set by an addition in the REPORT statement (when an executable ABAP program is created, the REPORT statement is generated by the system). The line width is set in the following manner by modifying the REPORT statement.

```
REPORT YCL_CH05_02_CUST_LIST01 LINE-SIZE 140.
```

The addition LINE-SIZE 140 sets the line width to 140 columns. The actual line width has been rounded to 140. The line width is available in the system field SY-LINSZ. The maximum value of LINE-SIZE can be 1023.

The source code for generating the customer list is:-

```
REPORT YCL_CH05_02_CUST_LIST01 LINE-SIZE 140.

********************************
* WRITE - Simple Customer List **
********************************
**********************************************
* KUNNR LIKE KNA1-KUNNR - the field KUNNR of **
* our declared structure CUST_STRU has same  **
* attributes as the field KUNNR of DDIC table**
* definition KNA1. here either the key word  **
* LIKE or TYPE can be used. difference       **
* LIKE & TYPE will be discussed subsequently **
*                                            **
* like wise for NAME1, STRAS, ORT01, PSTLZ   **
**********************************************

DATA: BEGIN OF CUST_STRU,
       KUNNR LIKE KNA1-KUNNR, "referring to a DDIC table field
       NAME1 LIKE KNA1-NAME1,
       STRAS LIKE KNA1-STRAS,
       ORT01 LIKE KNA1-ORT01,
       PSTLZ LIKE KNA1-PSTLZ,
      END OF CUST_STRU.
****************************************
SELECT KUNNR NAME1 STRAS ORT01 PSTLZ FROM KNA1 INTO CUST_STRU.
 WRITE:/5(5) SY-DBCNT, CUST_STRU-KUNNR USING NO EDIT MASK,
 CUST_STRU-NAME1, CUST_STRU-STRAS, CUST_STRU-ORT01, CUST_STRU-PSTLZ.
ENDSELECT.
```

1. The field order KUNNR NAME1 STRAS ORT01 PSTLZ in the SELECT statement should be in the same order as in the structure CUST_STRU definition. The structure should not contain any other fields. The fields in the structure should be of the same type and length as in the database table. You are ensuring this by referring to the database table fields while defining the fields in structure CUST_STRU. You must adhere to these rules in all situations where you are fetching data from database table/s or view/s and specifying the fields in the SELECT statement into structure/s.

   You have seen that a typical SAP functional table consists of fields of the order of hundreds. Your fields of interest will mostly be few of these. So the SELECT * (fetch all fields) should be used discreetly, only when the number of fields are few in a data source (table/view) or you are fetching only a few rows of data.

2. WRITE is a keyword.

3. ':' and ',' are as usual for chaining (i.e., avoid repetition of the keyword WRITE).

4. '/' is to get the output on a new line (each customer's information on one line).

5. '5' to have the output starting from column position 5 (4 blank column positions on the left as a left margin).

6. '(5)' to have the output of SY-DBCNT occupy 5 column positions. The system field SY-DBCNT is DDIC Data Type INT4 (integer 4 bytes) or ABAP type I. The output of ABAP type I by default occupies 11 column positions including a column on the right for sign. You know the number of customers to be less than 10000 (5 column positions). If output length is not specified with (5), it would generate a large gap between the fields SY-DBCNT and CUST_STRU-KUNNR. In business applications, the output should be clear, crisp, and attractive. To compress this unnecessarily large gap, you have specified the output length as (5) for field SY-DBCNT.

7. The addition 'USING NO EDIT MASK' with CUST_STRU-KUNNR (customer number/code) is to enable the leading zeroes for the field to appear; by default they are suppressed.

8. By default, a blank column will be generated between two adjoining fields in a line. So the information of a customer in a line will appear with a blank column between fields.

The output will appear like Figure 5-2.

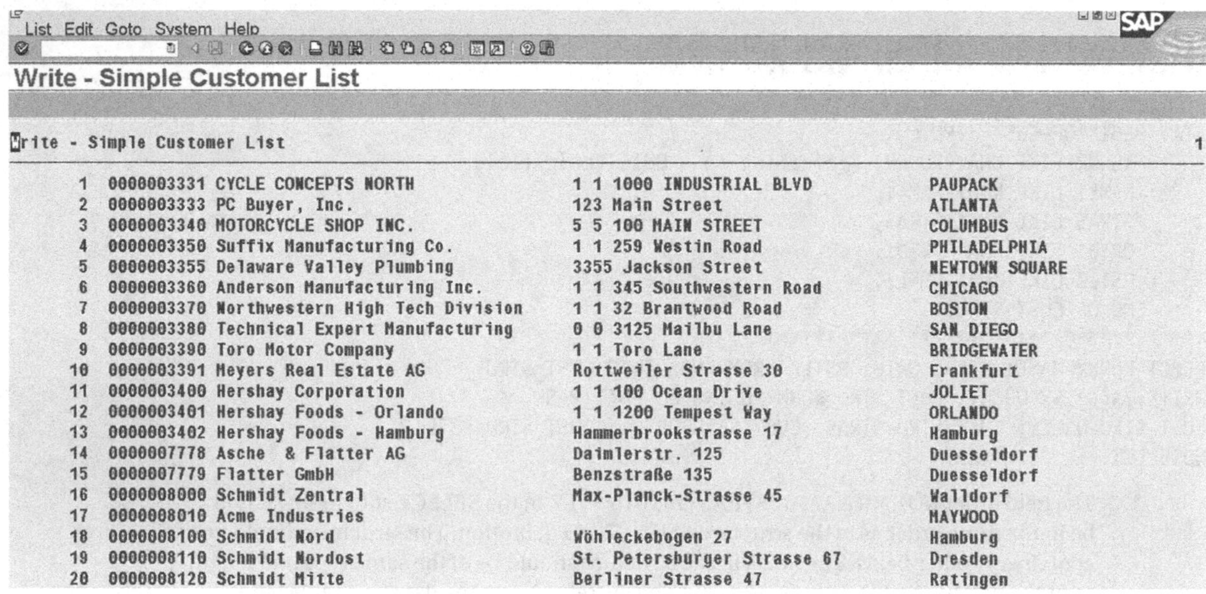

Figure 5-2. *Output of Program YCL_CH05_02_CUST_LIST01*

The output obtained by executing the program can be redirected from the screen to printer spool, SAP folder, reporting tree, and desktop software: Rich text (Word file), Excel spreadsheet, HTML file, Notepad file, and Clip board. The menu path for redirection to desktop software from a generated list is System ➤ Lists ➤ Save ➤ Local File. The desktop files (Word, Excel, etc.) are saved on the presentation server. The facilitation of redirection of output is through the list processor, part of the *ABAP runtime environment*.

When the output is viewed, an end user will not be able to make out what the information is about. Obviously the list should contain a header for the output mentioning what this list is (list of customers) and must contain headings for each of the output fields (Serial no, Customer code, Customer Name, and so on). So the list needs a list or report header and field headings. The field heading is referred to in standard documentation as *Column heading*; so you will refer to it as *Column heading* though you are always referring to data objects as fields. The *List header* and the *Column heading* can be implemented using one of two methods: (a) Creating, using an ABAP program *text element's List Headings*. This is referred to as a *Standard Page Header*; or (b) Triggering the event TOP-OF-PAGE, coding, or programming for the *List header* and the *Column heading*. This is referred to as a *nonstandard page header*.

The first method requires no programming; the second requires programming. You will execute a hands-on exercise for each of these.

WRITE Statement: Hands-on Exercise - A Simple Customer List with *Standard Page Header* or *List Headers*

The *List Headers* or *List Headings* is one of the components of a *Text element*. The other two are: *Text symbols* and *Selection texts*. You used *Text symbols* in Chapter 4 (the Hello World program).

List Headers can be created from the ABAP editor opening screen (transaction code SE38) by selecting the *Text elements* radio button (the last radio button), clicking the Create/Change push button, and selecting the *List Heading*' tab. It can also be created from inside the source program editor by selecting the 'Goto' menu option and selecting the *Text elements* option and further selecting the *List Headings* sub-option. *List Headers* can also be created with transaction code SE32.

When the *List Headers* screen appears, you can see that there can be only one line for *List header*, and the maximum length of this can be 70 characters or column positions.

For the *Column heading*, you can have a maximum of 4 lines. The maximum width of *Column heading* can be 255 characters. The width of the list cannot exceed 255 columns with a *Standard Page Header*.

If your list output exceeds 255 columns, you have to use the *nonstandard page header*.

In the *List header* and *Column heading* area, multiple language texts can be entered and maintained just like in the DDIC data element field label area and the ABAP program *text symbol*. The language texts appear as per the logged-in language. The *List Headers* also allow variable or runtime information to be incorporated. This is achieved through the concept of placeholders and 10 special system fields. The placeholders (where variable information, determined at runtime, will sit) are indicated by place holders &0 &1 &2 &3 &4 &5 &6 &7 &8 &9. The corresponding 10 system fields are SY-TVAR0 to SY-TVAR9. Wherever &0 is placed in the *List Headers* area, it will be replaced by the contents of the system field SY-TVAR0 at run time. In a similar manner, &1 will be replaced by the contents of SY-TVAR1 and so on. It should be ensured in the program that the desired value is assigned to the system field SY-TVAR0 so that it appears in place of &0 in the *List Headers* area. You can use none or one or two up to a maximum of ten place holders. The placeholders &0 and so on and system field SY-TVAR0 can be used arbitrarily (i.e., you need not start from &0 only). The ABAP type of SY-TVAR0 to SY-TVAR9 is type 'C' and length 20.

In your *List header*, let the application server system date SY-DATUM be output. The value of SY-DATUM is determined at run time. You will use the feature of placeholder (&0 to &9) and one of the system fields (SY-TVAR0 to SY-TVAR9) to implement this.

Your *List header* area will be like this: List of Customers as on &1........

The *List Headers* screen will look like Figure 5-3.

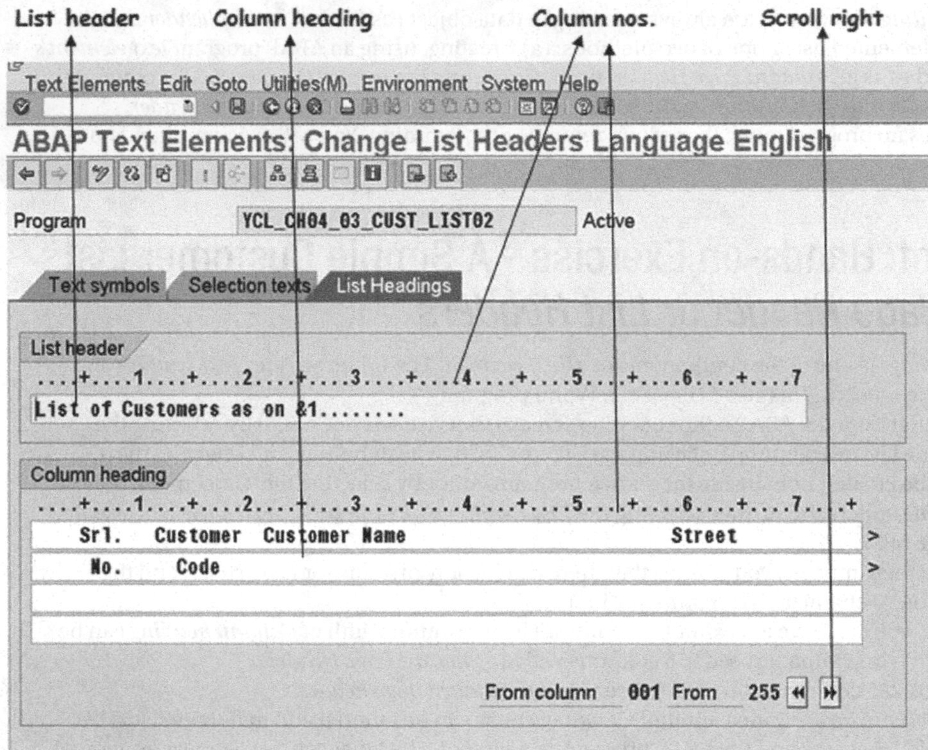

Figure 5-3. *Text Element: List Headers*

You are using the '&1' placeholder. The '&1' is followed by eight periods (full stops). The periods are used to indicate the width of output. You intend to output the SY-DATUM with a separator character in the form DD/MM/YYYY (&1 and 8 periods indicate a length of 10). The periods are necessary because if they are missing, it will assume an output length of 2, only the day DD will be output, and the rest of the data will be truncated. You have to assign the value of SY-DATUM with the separator character '/' into the system field SY-TVAR1. You do this by using the CONCATENATE statement:

```
CONCATENATE SY-DATUM+6(2) SY-DATUM+4(2) SY-DATUM+0(4)
 INTO SY-TVAR1 SEPARATED BY '/'.
```

The source code for generating the customer list with *List Headings*:-

```
REPORT YCL_CH05_03_CUST_LIST02 LINE-SIZE 140 LINE-COUNT 60.

*************************************************
* WRITE - Simple Customer List With List Headings**
* (STANDARD HEADER)                              **
*************************************************
```

```
DATA: BEGIN OF CUST_STRU,
       KUNNR LIKE KNA1-KUNNR, "referring to a DDIC table field
       NAME1 LIKE KNA1-NAME1,
       STRAS LIKE KNA1-STRAS,
       ORT01 LIKE KNA1-ORT01,
       PSTLZ LIKE KNA1-PSTLZ,
      END OF CUST_STRU.
************************************************************
CONCATENATE SY-DATUM+6(2) SY-DATUM+4(2) SY-DATUM+0(4)
 INTO SY-TVAR1 SEPARATED BY '/'.

SELECT KUNNR NAME1 STRAS ORT01 PSTLZ FROM KNA1 INTO CUST_STRU.
 WRITE:/5(5) SY-DBCNT, CUST_STRU-KUNNR USING NO EDIT MASK,
 CUST_STRU-NAME1, CUST_STRU-STRAS, CUST_STRU-ORT01, CUST_STRU-PSTLZ.
ENDSELECT.
```

The CONCATENATE statement has already been explained. The data is stored in SY-DATUM in the form YYYYMMDD (8 characters). Using the CONCATENATE statement, it is converted and stored in the system field SY-TVAR1 in the form DD/MM/YYYY (10 characters).

Create, perform the syntax check, activate, execute, and observe the results of the ABAP program YCL_CH05_03_CUST_LIST02. The output will appear like Figure 5-4.

List Edit Goto System Help

Write - Simple Customer List With List Headings(STANDARD PAGE HEADER)

List of Customers as on 16/08/2012 1

Srl. No.	Customer Code	Customer Name	Street	C i t y
50	0000001990	Mansur Computers. Inc.	486 Corniche Avenue	Abu Dhabi
51	0000001991	Reserv.f.Kreditprozess	Theodor-Stern-Kai 10	Frankfurt
52	0000001992	IDES UK		London
53	0000001993	IDES US	1 Baker Street	SCHENECTADY
54	0000001997	Royal Bank of Great Britain	8 New Square	Feltham
55	0000003403	Hershay Foods - Frankfurt	Bockenheimer Landstrasse 42	Frankfurt
56	0000003410	Feralloy	1 State Rd.	ARDMORE
57	0000003411	Delta Steel	1 BakerStr.	HOUSTON
58	0000003412	AP Steel	London Rd.	Birmingham
59	0000003413	Schneider & Söhne	Muenchener Strasse 95	Nuernberg
60	0000003414	Ancofer	Reichspräsidentenstrasse1-25 21	Muelheim an der Ruhr
61	0000003415	Metallexport	Puskin Ul.	Petersburg
62	0000003443	Computer Specialists, Inc.	444 North Park Ave	NEW YORK
63	0000003450	Norbert Neumann	Lyoner Strasse 125	Frankfurt
64	0000003451	Anna Ahrens	Lyoner Strasse 144	Frankfurt
65	0000003452	Karin Keller	Lyoner Strasse 10	Frankfurt
66	0000003453	Susanne Schenk	Lyoner Strasse 222	Frankfurt

Figure 5-4. *Output of Program YCL_CH05_03_CUST_LIST02*

The list is output with *List header*, run date, and *column heading*. The *List header* and *Column heading* have been output (without any program coding) using ABAP program's *text element's List Headings* feature.

Realignment of *Column Heading* from the Output:

If after the output is generated, you realize that *Column heading* needs shifting or realignment, you can go back to ABAP editor mode and go to *text elements, List Headings,* and make the corrections. There is also a simpler way to shift and realign the *Column heading* from the output screen itself.

On the output screen, click on menu options System ➤ List ➤ List Header like it is shown in Figure 5-5:

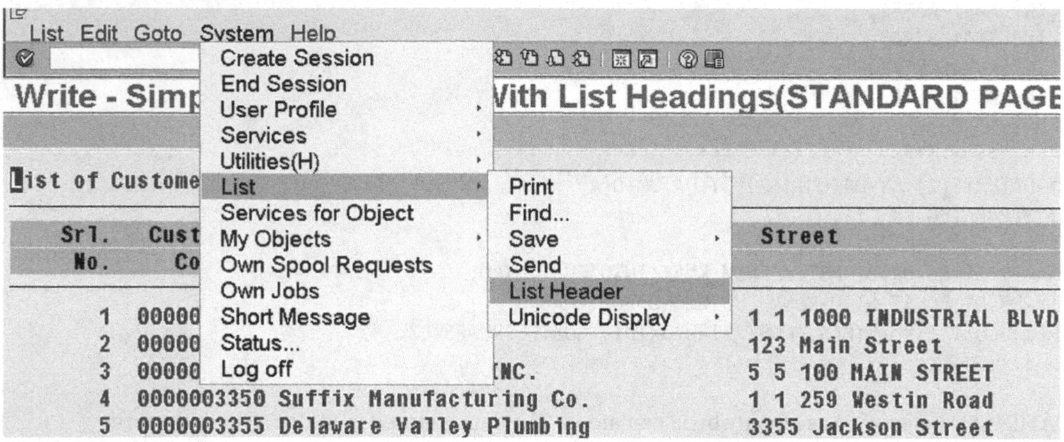

Figure 5-5. *List Heading – Navigate for Realignment of Column Heading from Output*

When you make the menu selections as shown in Figure 5-5, the following screen will appear:

On this screen (Figure 5-6), you can move, shift, and realign your *List header* and *Column heading*. When you are finished with this realignment exercise, save your changes. Re-execute the program for the changes to be reflected in the output.

```
Program Edit Goto Development System Help
Write - Simple Customer List With List Headings(STANDARD PAGE HEADER)

List of Customers as on &1........

   Srl.  Customer  Customer Name                     Street                         C i t y
   No.     Code

     1  0000003331 CYCLE CONCEPTS NORTH              1 1 1000 INDUSTRIAL BLVD       PAUPACK
     2  0000003333 PC Buyer, Inc.                    123 Main Street                ATLANTA
     3  0000003340 MOTORCYCLE SHOP INC.              5 5 100 MAIN STREET            COLUMBUS
     4  0000003350 Suffix Manufacturing Co.          1 1 259 Westin Road            PHILADELPHIA
     5  0000003355 Delaware Valley Plumbing          3355 Jackson Street            NEWTOWN SQUARE
     6  0000003360 Anderson Manufacturing Inc.       1 1 345 Southwestern Road      CHICAGO
     7  0000003370 Northwestern High Tech Division   1 1 32 Brantwood Road          BOSTON
     8  0000003380 Technical Expert Manufacturing    0 0 3125 Mailbu Lane           SAN DIEGO
     9  0000003390 Toro Motor Company                1 1 Toro Lane                  BRIDGEWATER
    10  0000003391 Meyers Real Estate AG             Rottweiler Strasse 30          Frankfurt
```

Figure 5-6. *List Heading – Realignment of Column Headings from Output*

On the line of the *List header* 'List of Customers as on 18/08/2012' is appearing, on the extreme right a number '1' is output. This is the page number. The entire list of 7000+ customers is appearing on a single page!

If a hard copy is to be produced from this screen output, you need to take into account the physical size of the stationery (page size) used for the hard copy. When using a WRITE statement to output, you specify the page size not in physical dimensions such as inches/centimeters/millimeters, etc., but in terms of maximum number of lines available on a page (line count). The line count is set in the REPORT statement in the following manner:

```
REPORT YCL_CH05_03_CUST_LIST02 LINE-COUNT 60.
```

The addition of LINE-COUNT 60 sets the page size to a maximum of 60 lines. The line count is available in the system field SY-LINCT. So your REPORT statement with LINE-SIZE and LINE-COUNT will be:

```
REPORT YCL_CH05_03_CUST_LIST02 LINE-SIZE 140 LINE-COUNT 60.
```

Executing the program YCL_CH05_03_CUST_LIST02 with the LINE-COUNT 60 in the REPORT statement, output will look like Figure 5-7.

```
List  Edit  Goto  System  Help
Write - Simple Customer List With List Headings(STANDARD PAGE HEADER)

List of Customers as on 16/08/2012                                                                   1

   Srl.   Customer  Customer Name                        Street                             C i t y
    No.      Code

     50  0000001990 Mansur Computers. Inc.               486 Corniche Avenue                Abu Dhabi
     51  0000001991 Reserv.f.Kreditprozess               Theodor-Stern-Kai 10               Frankfurt
     52  0000001992 IDES UK                                                                 London
     53  0000001993 IDES US                              1 Baker Street                     SCHENECTADY
     54  0000001997 Royal Bank of Great Britain          8 New Square                       Feltham
     55  0000003403 Hershay Foods - Frankfurt            Bockenheimer Landstrasse 42        Frankfurt

List of Customers as on 16/08/2012                                                                   2

   Srl.   Customer  Customer Name                        Street                             C i t y
    No.      Code

     56  0000003410 Feralloy                             1 State Rd.                        ARDMORE
     57  0000003411 Delta Steel                          1 BakerStr.                        HOUSTON
     58  0000003412 AP Steel                             London Rd.                         Birmingham
     59  0000003413 Schneider & Söhne                    Muenchener Strasse 95              Nuernberg
     60  0000003414 Ancofer                              Reichspräsidentenstrasse1-25 21    Muelheim an der Ruhr
```

***Figure 5-7.** Output of Program YCL_CH05_03_CUST_LIST02 with LINE-COUNT*

Observe that 55 lines are output in the list body; and 5 lines consumed by the *List header* and *Column heading*, including two horizontal lines enclosing the *Column heading*.

The default value of SY-LINCT is zero. In this case, the entire output appears on a single page. The maximum number of lines that can appear on this single page is 60,000.

An Introduction to Events in ABAP Programs

Event - START-OF-SELECTION

The kinds of program structures you have created until now (in Chapters 3, 4, and the current chapter) have consisted of:

- Declarative statements - DATA, TYPES, CONSTANTS, PARAMETERS
- Control statements (internal flow control) - DO ENDDO, IF ENDIF
- Operational statements - MOVE, WRITE, TRANSLATE, CONCATENATE et al.
- Database statements- SELECT ENDSELECT

You have not used any event keywords to code for events. Events have not been introduced. You must recall that in ABAP (from Chapter 4) there are event keywords to indicate when an event code starts, but there are no keywords to indicate the conclusion of an event in the code. The conclusion of an event in the code is when you begin the code for another event (i.e., an implicit event conclusion). You are being introduced to the event START-OF-SELECTION. The first thing to understand about an event is to know when an event is triggered: that is, when program control jumps to the code under an event.

Scenario-I

If there are no PARAMETERS statements in a program, pressing the function key F8 will begin the execution of the program starting from the first nondeclarative statement in the program. Refer to any of the programs up to this point in this chapter.

Scenario-II

If there is a PARAMETERS statement/s in a program, when you execute such a program (function key F8, etc.), the input prompt/s of the PARAMETERS statement/s appears on the screen. When you press F8 on the input prompt screen, other nondeclarative program statements start getting executed. Refer to programs YCL_CH04_11_TRANSLATE and YCL_CH04_12_CONCATENATE of Chapter 4.

The START-OF-SELECTION event will be explained in the context of these two scenarios described and extended to other scenarios. In the scenario-I (no PARAMETERS statement/s) when the program is executed, control jumps to the event START-OF-SELECTION. In scenario-II, when the user presses F8 on the input prompt screen, control jumps to the event START-OF-SELECTION. In scenario-II, if you are validating the inputs, invalid inputs will trigger error conditions, and you will remain on the input prompt screen. An F8 key press for valid inputs will make the control jump to START-OF-SELECTION.

In Chapter 4, under the heading, “Container for Processing Blocks,” it was mentioned that all Nondeclarative ABAP statements, which occur between the declaration of global data and a processing block, are automatically assigned to the START-OF-SELECTION event by the ABAP processor (i.e., implicit assignment of statements to this event). This has been happening to all your programs coded up to now; before now, you have never explicitly defined the event START-OF-SELECTION. All the nondeclarative statements were getting assigned to this event implicitly by the ABAP processor.

Henceforth, all your ABAP programs will have an explicit coding of the START-OF-SELECTION event.

WRITE Statement: Hands-on Exercise - Simple Customer List with the *Nonstandard Page Header*

TOP-OF-PAGE Event

If you do not want to be bound by the limits of *List Headers* and you wish to have full control over the *list header* and *column heading*, you have to resort to the *nonstandard page header*. The *nonstandard page header* is implemented using the event TOP-OF-PAGE. This event is triggered in two situations:

a. When the WRITE statement is encountered for the very first time during the program execution. In this situation, the program does not generate the output for the WRITE statement; instead, control jumps to the event TOP-OF-PAGE and executes statements in this event. After executing all the statements in this event, control jumps to the WRITE statement that triggered the TOP-OF-PAGE event and generates output of this statement.

b. When the WRITE statement is encountered and the number of lines output on the current page is equal to the value of the system field SY-LINCT set in the REPORT statement through the addition of LINE-COUNT (current page is full), in this situation the program again jumps to the event TOP-OF-PAGE, starts a new page and executes statements in this event. After executing all the statements in this event, control jumps to the WRITE statement that triggered the TOP-OF-PAGE event and generates output of this statement.

Let a customer list be generated with a *nonstandard page header*.
A rough layout with the list header and column heading:

```
List of Customers as on DD/MM/YYYY                                        Page No.: XXX
----------------------------------------------------------------------------------------
Srl.    Customer      N a m e                 S t r e e t            C i t y     Postal
No.       Code                                                                     Code
----------------------------------------------------------------------------------------
```

Text Element Component Text Symbols

In the *Text elements* component *List Header*, the environment supported the maintenance of multilanguage texts. Now, in the *nonstandard page header*, you will have to issue WRITE statements to output the list header ('List of Customers as on '), etc. For the column heading, you will have to issue WRITE statements ('Srl No,' 'Customer Code'), etc. You can't be using literals; you will be unable to support multiple languages. You will be using the *Text Symbols* component of *text elements* to store texts of the list header and column heading.

From inside the source program editor click the 'Goto' menu bar, and select the *Text elements* option and further select the *Text symbols* suboption. Figure 5-8 is a screenshot of *text symbol* with the text for the list header and column heading.

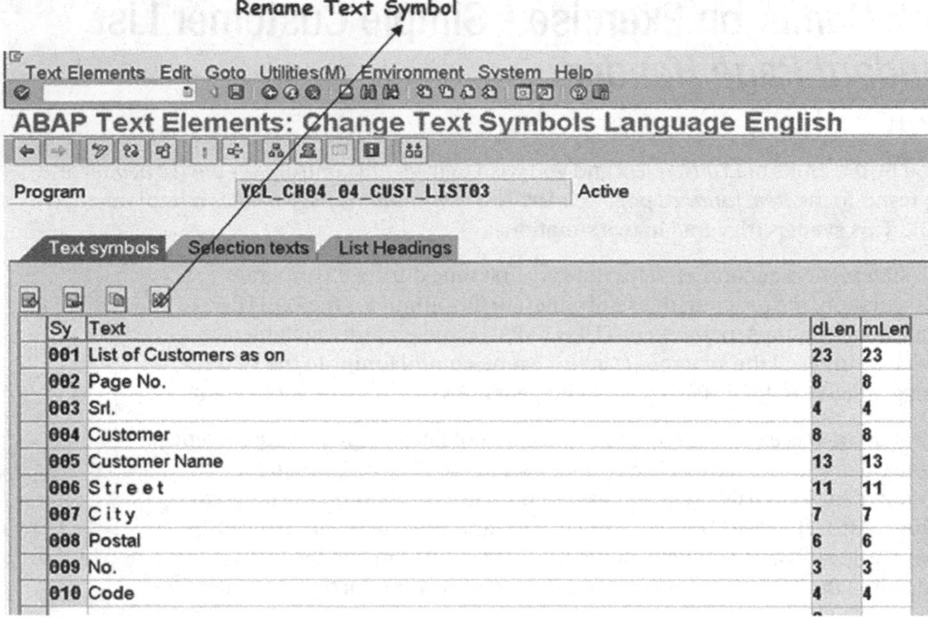

Figure 5-8. *Program YCL_CH05_04_CUST_LIST03 - Text Symbols*

The source code for generating the customer list with a nonstandard page heading:-

```
REPORT YCL_CH05_04_CUST_LIST03 LINE-SIZE 140 LINE-COUNT 60
 NO STANDARD PAGE HEADING.

*****************************************************
* Simple Customer List With NON STANDARD PAGE HEADER **
*****************************************************

DATA: BEGIN OF CUST_STRU,
       KUNNR LIKE KNA1-KUNNR,
       NAME1 LIKE KNA1-NAME1,
       STRAS LIKE KNA1-STRAS,
       ORT01 LIKE KNA1-ORT01,
       PSTLZ LIKE KNA1-PSTLZ,
      END OF CUST_STRU,
      DATE_CHR(10) TYPE C .
*******************************************************************
TOP-OF-PAGE.
WRITE:/5 TEXT-001, DATE_CHR, 130 TEXT-002, 137(3) SY-PAGNO.
SKIP 1.
WRITE:/5(135) SY-ULINE.
WRITE:/6 TEXT-003, 12 TEXT-004, 23 TEXT-005, 60 TEXT-006,
 96 TEXT-007, 130 TEXT-008.
WRITE:/6 TEXT-009, 13 TEXT-010, 131 TEXT-010.
WRITE:/5(135) SY-ULINE.
********************************************************************
```

```
START-OF-SELECTION. " event triggered in this program, when user
                    " presses F8 i.e. control will jump to the
                    " statement next to START-OF-SELECTION and
                    " execution of statements starts

CONCATENATE SY-DATUM+6(2) SY-DATUM+4(2) SY-DATUM+0(4)
INTO DATE_CHR SEPARATED BY '/'.

SELECT KUNNR NAME1 STRAS ORT01 PSTLZ FROM KNA1 INTO CUST_STRU.
 WRITE:/5(5) SY-DBCNT, CUST_STRU-KUNNR USING NO EDIT MASK,
  CUST_STRU-NAME1, CUST_STRU-STRAS, CUST_STRU-ORT01, CUST_STRU-PSTLZ.
ENDSELECT.
```

Source Program, the Program Flow

The flow of the program will be as follows:-

When the function key F8 is pressed or the button is pressed, control jumps to the statement following the event START-OF-SELECTION: that is, the CONCATENATE statement. This statement will convert the SY-DATUM contents into the form DD/MM/YYYY and assign it to the data object DATE_CHR. Next the SELECT ENDSELECT looping procedure will commence. The first row from table KNA1 will be fetched into the structured data object CUST_STRU.

- With the first row fetched, the WRITE statement is being encountered for the first time in the program execution. The control will jump to the statement following the event TOP-OF-PAGE.
- The WRITE statements in the TOP-OF-PAGE event will be executed and will generate 6 lines of list header and column heading.
- After the list header and column heading is output, control will return to the WRITE statement. The WRITE statement within the SELECT ENDSELECT loop will execute 54 times to output 54 customers. Recall, your LINE-COUNT is set to 60 in the REPORT statement (i.e., a maximum of 60 lines in a page). When 54 customers (54 lines) are output on a page, the total number of lines output on the page is 60 (54 customers lines + 6 lines of list header and column heading). When the WRITE statement is encountered for the 55th customer, before the 55th customer is output, control again jumps to the TOP-OF-PAGE event. The WRITE statements in TOP-OF-PAGE event will again generate a 6 line list header and column heading on a new page. Then the 55th customer will be output. This process will go on. After every 54 customers, before the next customer is output, the control will jump to TOP-OF-PAGE event. When all the customers have been output, the SELECT...ENDSELECT loop and the program are exited.

The addition in the REPORT statement, NO STANDARD PAGE HEADING, suppresses the standard header if any. By default, the *program title* entered as part of the *program attributes* along with a horizontal line and appears on every page as part of the *standard page header*. When the list is output with the *nonstandard page header*, you want these two lines to be suppressed. Hence the addition: NO STANDARD PAGE HEADING.

The *Text symbols* are referred as TEXT-001, TEXT-002, and so on, and the prefix TEXT- with *Text symbol* identification.

The system field SY-PAGNO contains the value of the current page number. You can readily use this to output the page number on the list header.

The SKIP statement generates blank lines. Either a variable or a literal number can be specified with the SKIP statement. As many blank lines will be generated as the value of the variable and literal. A simple SKIP statement will generate one blank line.

The system field SY-ULINE outputs horizontal lines. You are enclosing the column heading in horizontal lines (see the rough layout of a list header and column heading).

The command WRITE:/5(135) SY-ULINE will output a horizontal line, starting on a new line, starting from column position 5, length of 135 column positions. The rest of the program statements are self-explanatory.

Create, perform the syntax check, activate, execute, and observe the results of the ABAP program YCL_CH05_04_CUST_LIST03. The output will appear like Figure 5-9.

List Edit Goto System Help

Simple Customer List With NON STANDARD PAGE HEADER

List of Customers as on 16/08/2012 Page No 1

Srl. No.	Customer Code	Customer Name	S t r e e t	C i t y	Postal Code
1	0000003331	CYCLE CONCEPTS NORTH	1 1 1000 INDUSTRIAL BLVD	PAUPACK	18451
2	0000003333	PC Buyer, Inc.	123 Main Street	ATLANTA	30301
3	0000003340	MOTORCYCLE SHOP INC.	5 5 100 MAIN STREET	COLUMBUS	43206
4	0000003350	Suffix Manufacturing Co.	1 1 259 Westin Road	PHILADELPHIA	19113
5	0000003355	Delaware Valley Plumbing	3355 Jackson Street	NEWTOWN SQUARE	19073
6	0000003360	Anderson Manufacturing Inc.	1 1 345 Southwestern Road	CHICAGO	60611
7	0000003370	Northwestern High Tech Division	1 1 32 Brantwood Road	BOSTON	02210
8	0000003380	Technical Expert Manufacturing	0 0 3125 Mailbu Lane	SAN DIEGO	92121
9	0000003390	Toro Motor Company	1 1 Toro Lane	BRIDGEWATER	08807
10	0000003391	Meyers Real Estate AG	Rottweiler Strasse 30	Frankfurt	60327
11	0000003400	Hershay Corporation	1 1 100 Ocean Drive	JOLIET	60432
12	0000003401	Hershay Foods - Orlando	1 1 1200 Tempest Way	ORLANDO	32821
13	0000003402	Hershay Foods - Hamburg	Hammerbrookstrasse 17	Hamburg	20097
14	0000007778	Asche & Flatter AG	Daimlerstr. 125	Duesseldorf	40235
15	0000007779	Flatter GmbH	Benzstraße 135	Duesseldorf	40235
16	0000008000	Schmidt Zentral	Max-Planck-Strasse 45	Walldorf	69190
17	0000008010	Acme Industries		MAYWOOD	60153
18	0000008100	Schmidt Nord	Wöhleckebogen 27	Hamburg	21035
19	0000008110	Schmidt Nordost	St. Petersburger Strasse 67	Dresden	01069
20	0000008120	Schmidt Mitte	Berliner Strasse 47	Ratingen	40880
21	0000008200	Schmidt Sued	Adolf-Kolping-Strasse 16	Ismaning	85737
22	0000008210	Schmidt Suedwest	Bahnhofstrasse 46	Freiburg	79117
23	0000008500	Supplies Group Pty Ltd	23 Miller Street	North Sydney	2060

Figure 5-9. *Output of Program YCL_CH05_04_CUST_LIST03*

You could have located the TOP-OF-PAGE event after START-OF-SELECTION. In this case, you could remove the event statement START-OF-SELECTION (a case of an implicit START-OF-SELECTION). But from now on, no implicitness and no leaving matters to the ABAP processor. You will code all programs with an explicit START-OF-SELECTION.

On the other hand with the TOP-OF-PAGE event before the START-OF-SELECTION like in the present program, if you comment or remove the event statement START-OF-SELECTION, all the statements that were under START-OF-SELECTION will now be under the TOP-OF-PAGE event. The ABAP processor will not find any statements to assign to START-OF-SELECTION. Executing this program will not generate any output.
Please try this out: commenting out the START-OF-SELECTION statement and execution.

WRITE Statement: Hands-on Exercise - Simple Customer List with the *NonStandard Page Header*, Footer

A list often needs a footer on every page. With the WRITE statement, a list footer can be generated with the event END-OF-PAGE. For generating a footer, footer lines need to be reserved. The footer lines are reserved with the addition of LINE-COUNT in the REPORT statement. Suppose you wanted to reserve 5 lines for the footer out of the total 65 lines in a page (LINE-COUNT 65), then the statement will look like this:

```
REPORT YCL_CH05_05_CUST_LIST04 LINE-COUNT 65(5).
```

The '5' within parentheses is for reserving 5 lines for the footer. The footer lines need to be reserved in this manner if the footer is to be output. If the footer lines are not reserved, then even though the END-OF-PAGE event would have been triggered with WRITE statements to output the footer, no footer will appear, as no footer lines were reserved.

The END-OF-PAGE event is triggered every time the number of lines output on a page is the total lines in a page less the lines reserved for the footer. So in this example, with the total lines in a page being 65 (LINE-COUNT 65), 5 lines are reserved for the footer, and the END-OF-PAGE event will be triggered every time 60 lines are output on a page.

Let the customer list with the *nonstandard page header* and footer be output. Let one line of the footer be output on each page. The footer line would just indicate the list being continued on the next page. So the footer at the bottom of the first, second, third... pages will appear like this:

```
Continued on page 2
Continued on page 3
...
```

For the hands-on exercise, let there be a LINE-COUNT of 60, let 3 lines be reserved for the footer, 1 blank line between the list body and list footer, 1 line for the 'Continued on page xx' text, and 1 blank line after the footer text. There will be 6 lines for the *nonstandard page header*. So there will be 60-6-3 = 51 lines for the body of the list: that is, 51 customers will output on each page.

The source code for generating the customer list with *nonstandard page header* and footer is:-

```
REPORT YCL_CH05_05_CUST_LIST04 LINE-SIZE 140 LINE-COUNT 60(3)
       NO STANDARD PAGE HEADING.

************************************************************
* Simple Customer List - NON STANDARD PAGE HEADER & FOOTER **
************************************************************

DATA: BEGIN OF CUST_STRU,
       KUNNR LIKE KNA1-KUNNR,
       NAME1 LIKE KNA1-NAME1,
       STRAS LIKE KNA1-STRAS,
       ORT01 LIKE KNA1-ORT01,
       PSTLZ LIKE KNA1-PSTLZ,
      END OF CUST_STRU,
      DATE_CHR(10) TYPE C,
      NXT_PAGE(3)  TYPE N. "to store next page, increment current page

**********************************************************************
TOP-OF-PAGE.
```

```
WRITE:/5 TEXT-001, DATE_CHR, 130 TEXT-002, 137(3) SY-PAGNO.
SKIP 1.
WRITE:/5(135) SY-ULINE.
WRITE:/6 TEXT-003, 12 TEXT-004, 23 TEXT-005, 60 TEXT-006, 96
 TEXT-007, 130 TEXT-008.
WRITE:/6 TEXT-009, 13 TEXT-010, 131 TEXT-010.
WRITE:/5(135) SY-ULINE.

***************************************************************
END-OF-PAGE.
NXT_PAGE = SY-PAGNO + 1.
SKIP 1.
WRITE:/60 TEXT-011,(3) NXT_PAGE.
***************************************************************

START-OF-SELECTION.

CONCATENATE SY-DATUM+6(2) '/' SY-DATUM+4(2) '/' SY-DATUM+0(4)
 INTO DATE_CHR.
SELECT KUNNR NAME1 STRAS ORT01 PSTLZ FROM KNA1 INTO CUST_STRU UP TO 51 ROWS.
 WRITE:/5(5) SY-DBCNT, CUST_STRU-KUNNR USING NO EDIT MASK,
  CUST_STRU-NAME1, CUST_STRU-STRAS, CUST_STRU-ORT01, CUST_STRU-PSTLZ.
ENDSELECT.
```

The program statements are self-explanatory. After the program creation, you can copy the *text symbols* of program YCL_CH05_04_CUST_LIST03 into the current program with the transaction code SE32. Add one *text symbol* 011 as 'Continued on'. Save. Activate the *text symbols*. The text in this will be used for the *nonstandard page header* and footer. The *text symbols* screen will appear like Figure 5-10.

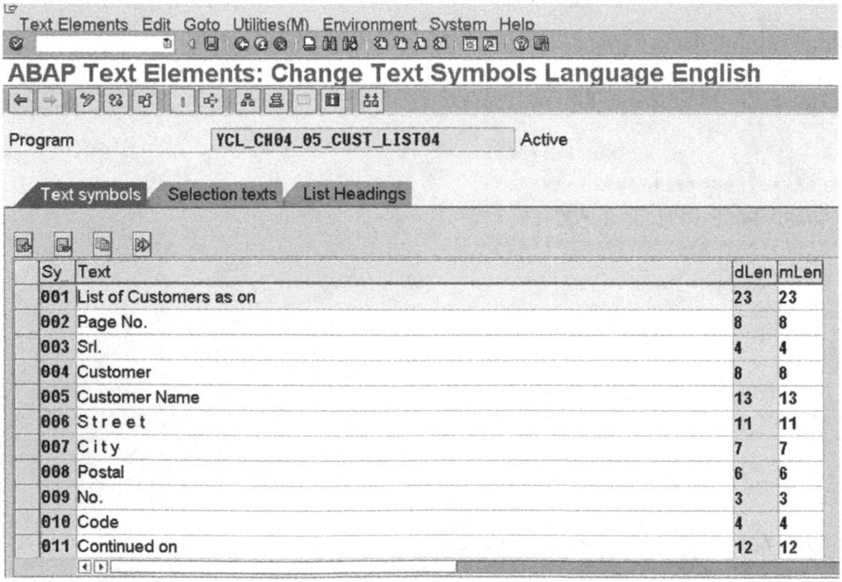

Text Elements Edit Goto Utilities(M) Environment System Help

ABAP Text Elements: Change Text Symbols Language English

Program YCL_CH04_05_CUST_LIST04 Active

Text symbols | Selection texts | List Headings

Sy	Text	dLen	mLen
001	List of Customers as on	23	23
002	Page No.	8	8
003	Srl.	4	4
004	Customer	8	8
005	Customer Name	13	13
006	Street	11	11
007	City	7	7
008	Postal	6	6
009	No.	3	3
010	Code	4	4
011	Continued on	12	12

Figure 5-10. *Text Symbol Screen – Program YCL_CH05_05_CUST_LIST04*

The output will appear like Figure 5-11.

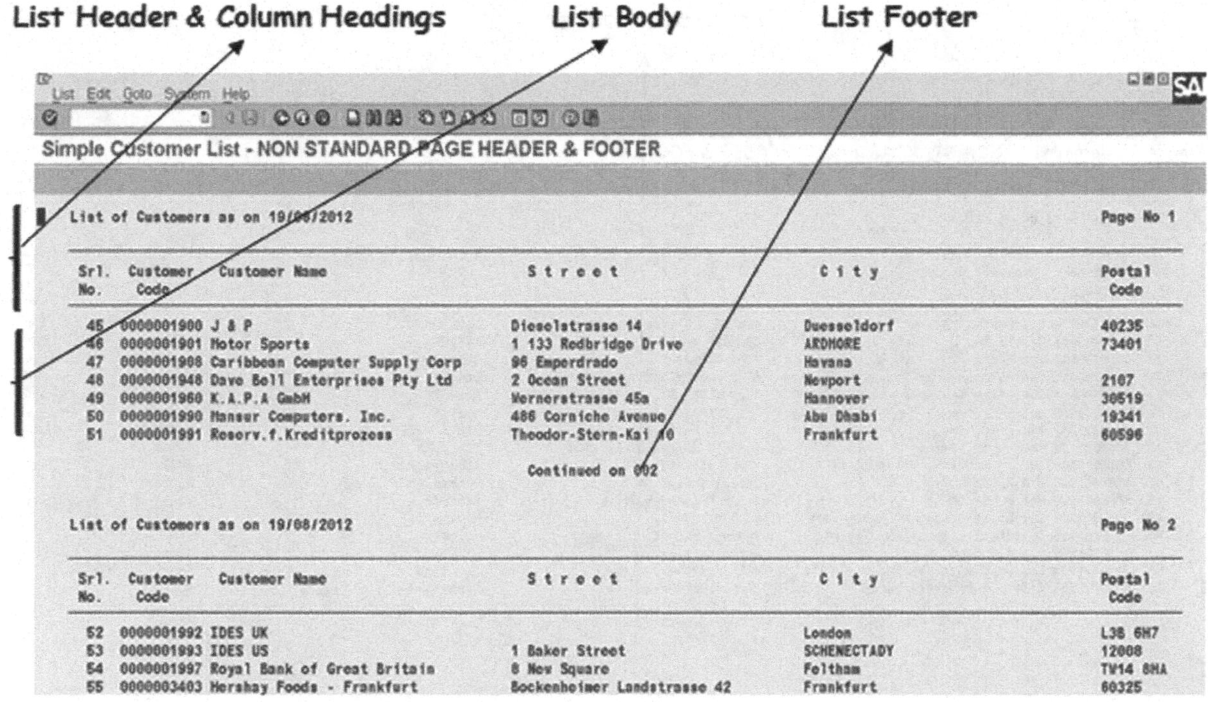

Figure 5-11. *Output of Program YCL_CH05_05_CUST_LIST04*

There is no output beyond the last page and the footer on the last page 'Continued on Page xxx' is not only redundant but erroneous. In most contexts, the footer would be required on the last page. It is only in your present context that the footer is not required on the last page.

The footer is output by the event END-OF-PAGE. This event is triggered in your context only when 57 lines (list header + column heading + body) are output on a page or 51 customers (body) are output on a page. So only if the last page of your list has 51 customers, will the footer line 'Continued on Page xxx' appear on the last page. Or else there will be no footer on the last page.

The problem of the footer being output on the last page is simulated by retrieving a multiple of 51 rows by addition in the SELECT command:

```
SELECT KUNNR NAME1 STRAS ORT01 PSTLZ FROM KNA1 INTO CUST_STRU
 UP TO 51 ROWS.
  ....
ENDSELECT.
```

The output, when a multiple of 51 customers is retrieved will appear like this:-

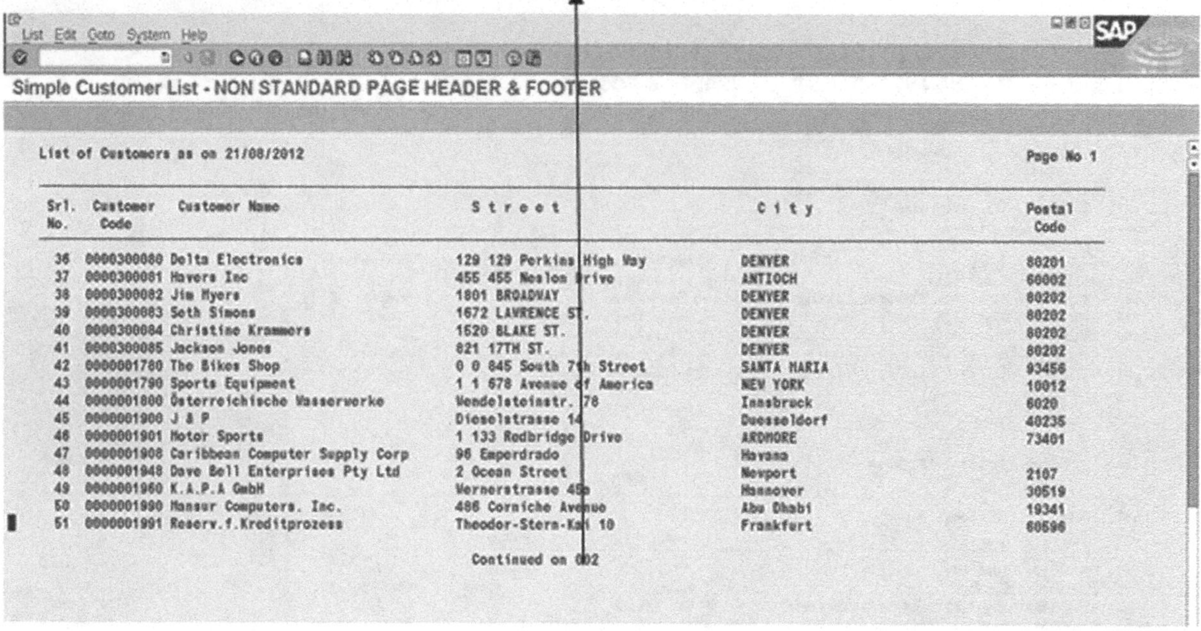

Figure 5-12. *Output of Program YCL_CH05_05_CUST_LIST04 – 51 Rows Only*

This is a latent program bug, the bug manifests itself only if a particular condition occurs in the program; and the number of rows fetched is a multiple of the number of lines output on a page in the list body.

To overcome this problem, you have to have an insight into the flow of the program: that is, when the last time (for the last page) the event END-OF-PAGE is triggered. The event END-OF-PAGE is triggered for the last page only after execution of statements (if any) following the ENDSELECT statement. Presently, there are no statements following the ENDSELECT statement in the program. Since END-OF-PAGE is triggered for the last page only after execution of statements following the ENDSELECT statement (you are getting the control before the footer is output on the last page), you can control the contents of a FLAG or SWITCH type variable and make the footer output conditional on the contents of this variable. You will make the following changes in the program:

1. Declare a variable FLAG of TYPE C, length 1, in the DATA declarative statement.

2. The footer is now output conditionally on this FLAG variable being blank (i.e., IF FLAG = ' ', with the corresponding ENDIF).

3. At the end of the SELECT...ENDSELECT loop, after the ENDSELECT statement, assign the variable FLAG a non-blank value (i.e., FLAG = 'X').

The revised program code will be as follows:-

```
REPORT YCL_CH05_05_CUST_LIST04 LINE-SIZE 140 LINE-COUNT 60(3)
       NO STANDARD PAGE HEADING.
```

```
**************************************************************
* Simple Customer List - NON STANDARD PAGE HEADER & FOOTER **
**************************************************************

DATA: BEGIN OF CUST_STRU,
       KUNNR LIKE KNA1-KUNNR,
       NAME1 LIKE KNA1-NAME1,
       STRAS LIKE KNA1-STRAS,
       ORT01 LIKE KNA1-ORT01,
       PSTLZ LIKE KNA1-PSTLZ,
      END OF CUST_STRU,
      DATE_CHR(10) TYPE C,
      NXT_PAGE(3)  TYPE N, "to store next page, increment current page

      FLAG(1)      TYPE C. "initially this will be blank
                           "on exiting SELECT.. ENDSELECT loop
                           "you are assigning it a non-blank value
                           "footer will be outputted on the
                           "condition FLAG = ' '

************************************************************************
TOP-OF-PAGE.

WRITE:/5 TEXT-001, DATE_CHR, 130 TEXT-002, 137(3) SY-PAGNO.
SKIP 1.
WRITE:/5(135) SY-ULINE.
WRITE:/6 TEXT-003, 12 TEXT-004, 23 TEXT-005, 60 TEXT-006, 96
 TEXT-007, 130 TEXT-008.
WRITE:/6 TEXT-009, 13 TEXT-010, 131 TEXT-010.
WRITE:/5(135) SY-ULINE.

***************************************************************
END-OF-PAGE.
IF FLAG = ' '.   " footer outputted conditionally on FLAG = ' '.
 NXT_PAGE = SY-PAGNO + 1.
 SKIP 1.
 WRITE:/60 TEXT-011,(3) NXT_PAGE.
ENDIF.
***************************************************************

START-OF-SELECTION.

CONCATENATE SY-DATUM+6(2) '/' SY-DATUM+4(2) '/' SY-DATUM+0(4)
 INTO DATE_CHR.
SELECT KUNNR NAME1 STRAS ORT01 PSTLZ FROM KNA1 INTO CUST_STRU UP TO 51 ROWS.
 WRITE:/5(5) SY-DBCNT, CUST_STRU-KUNNR USING NO EDIT MASK,
  CUST_STRU-NAME1, CUST_STRU-STRAS, CUST_STRU-ORT01, CUST_STRU-PSTLZ.
ENDSELECT.

FLAG = 'X'. " control will jump to END-OF-PAGE after executing this
            " statement
```

The output will appear like Figure 5-13.

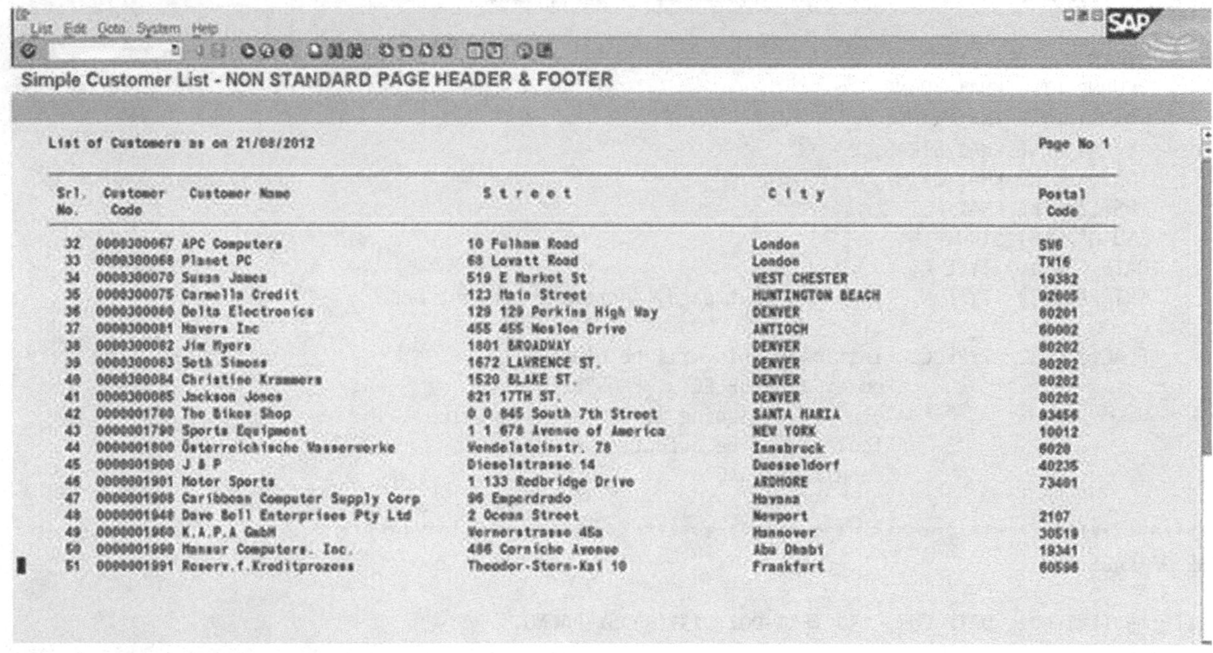

Simple Customer List - NON STANDARD PAGE HEADER & FOOTER

List of Customers as on 21/08/2012 Page No 1

Srl. No.	Customer Code	Customer Name	Street	City	Postal Code
32	0000300067	APC Computers	10 Fulham Road	London	SW6
33	0000300068	Planet PC	68 Lovatt Road	London	TW16
34	0000300070	Susan James	519 E Market St	WEST CHESTER	19382
35	0000300075	Carmella Credit	123 Main Street	HUNTINGTON BEACH	92605
36	0000300080	Delta Electronics	129 129 Perkins High Way	DENVER	80201
37	0000300081	Mavers Inc	455 455 Neslon Drive	ANTIOCH	60002
38	0000300082	Jim Myers	1801 BROADWAY	DENVER	80202
39	0000300083	Seth Simons	1672 LAWRENCE ST.	DENVER	80202
40	0000300084	Christine Krammers	1520 BLAKE ST.	DENVER	80202
41	0000300085	Jackson Jones	821 17TH ST.	DENVER	80202
42	0000001700	The Bikes Shop	0 0 845 South 7th Street	SANTA MARIA	93456
43	0000001790	Sports Equipment	1 1 678 Avenue of America	NEW YORK	10012
44	0000001800	Österreichische Wasserwerke	Wendelsteinstr. 78	Innsbruck	6020
45	0000001900	J & P	Dieselstrasse 14	Duesseldorf	40235
46	0000001901	Motor Sports	1 133 Redbridge Drive	ARDMORE	73401
47	0000001908	Caribbean Computer Supply Corp	96 Emperdrado	Havana	
48	0000001948	Dave Bell Enterprises Pty Ltd	2 Ocean Street	Newport	2107
49	0000001960	K.A.P.A GmbH	Wernerstrasse 45a	Hannover	30519
50	0000001990	Mansur Computers. Inc.	486 Corniche Avenue	Abu Dhabi	19341
51	0000001991	Reserv.f.Kreditprozess	Theodor-Stern-Kai 10	Frankfurt	60596

Figure 5-13. *Output of Program YCL_CH05_05_CUST_LIST04 - 51 Rows Only*

The problem of the footer appearing on the last page if the number of rows fetched is a multiple of the number of lines in the list body has been resolved.

WRITE Statement: Hands-on Exercise - Simple Customer List Using COLOR Options

There is a facility to impart colors to the lists. The color options operate as follows:

1. Either the foreground color (INVERSE or INVERSE ON) or background color (INVERSE OFF) can be controlled at a time, not both. By default, output is in the background color. (INVERSE OFF).

2. When controlling the background color, there is an option to have deeper or sharper shades (INTENSIFIED ON) or paler shades. (INTENSIFIED OFF) By default INTENSIFIED ON is operative.

3. Color can be specified with the FORMAT statement. The output will appear as per the color specification in the FORMAT statement. Color can also be specified with the field in the WRITE statement. Color specified with the field in the WRITE statement overrides the color specified in the FORMAT statement. The statement FORMAT RESET restores the default colors. The FORMAT statement is operative in a particular event: START-OF-SELECTION, TOP-OF-PAGE, END-OF-PAGE, etc.

4. Eight colors are supported. Colors can be specified by color codes (0-7) or color names.
5. A quick reference to how the colors operate, the color codes, and names are shown in Figure 5-14.

CO -DE	INTENSIFIED ON (BACKGROUND)	INTENSIFIED OFF (BACKGROUND)	INVERSE ON (FOREGROUND)
0	COL_BACKGROUND	COL_BACKGROUND	COL_BACKGROUND
1	COL_HEADING	COL_HEADING	COL_HEADING
2	COL_NORMAL	COL_NORMAL	COL_NORMAL
3	COL_TOTAL	COL_TOTAL	COL_TOTAL
4	COL_KEY	COL_KEY	COL_KEY
5	COL_POSITIVE	COL_POSITIVE	COL_POSITIVE
6	COL_NEGATIVE	COL_NEGATIVE	COL_NEGATIVE
7	COL_GROUP	COL_GROUP	COL_GROUP

Figure 5-14. *WRITE Statement Output - Color Options*

You are generating the same customer list using color options. Create program YCL_CH05_06_LIST05. Copy the appropriate lines from the previous program. Copy *text symbols* from one of the earlier programs for the *nonstandard page header* you are going to have in this program. Use transaction code SE32 to copy the *text symbols*. Activate the *text symbols*.

The source code for generating the customer list with color options: -

```
EPORT YCL_CH05_06_CUST_LIST05 LINE-SIZE 140 LINE-COUNT 60
 NO STANDARD PAGE HEADING.

*****************************************
* Simple Customer List - Usage of COLOR **
*****************************************

************************************************************
* (1) color can be specified with FORMAT statement. all WRITE **
*     statements will be output as per the color specified in **
*     FORMAT statement                                        **
* (2) but if color is specified for field/s in the WRITE      **
*     statement,this will override specification of FORMAT    **
*     statement                                               **
* (3) FORMAT RESET will restore default colors                **
* (4) only 8 colors are supported                             **
* (5) either the foreground(INVERSE ON) or the background     **
*     color(INVERSE OFF) can be controlled at a time, not     **
*     both. by default INVERSE is OFF                         **
* (6) background color can be sharp(INTENSIFIED ON) or faint  **
*     (INTENSIFIED OFF) by default INTENSIFIED is ON          **
* (7) colors can be specified by color code 0,1,2,3,4,5,6,7   **
*     or name see color table                                 **
************************************************************
```

```
DATA: BEGIN OF CUST_STRU,
       KUNNR LIKE KNA1-KUNNR,
       NAME1 LIKE KNA1-NAME1,
       STRAS LIKE KNA1-STRAS,
       ORT01 LIKE KNA1-ORT01,
       PSTLZ LIKE KNA1-PSTLZ,
      END OF CUST_STRU,
      DATE_CHR(10) TYPE C .
*******************************************************************

TOP-OF-PAGE.

FORMAT RESET. "header in default color

WRITE:/5 TEXT-001, DATE_CHR, 130 TEXT-002, 137(3) SY-PAGNO.
SKIP 1.
WRITE:/5(135) SY-ULINE.
WRITE:/6 TEXT-003, 12 TEXT-004, 23 TEXT-005, 60  TEXT-006, 96 TEXT-007, 130 TEXT-008.
WRITE:/6 TEXT-009, 13 TEXT-010, 131 TEXT-010.
WRITE:/5(135) SY-ULINE.
*******************************************************************
START-OF-SELECTION.
CONCATENATE SY-DATUM+6(2) '/' SY-DATUM+4(2) '/' SY-DATUM+0(4) INTO DATE_CHR.

FORMAT INVERSE ON COLOR COL_POSITIVE. "foreground green

SELECT KUNNR NAME1 STRAS ORT01 PSTLZ FROM KNA1 INTO CUST_STRU.
 WRITE:/5(5) SY-DBCNT INVERSE OFF COLOR = 4, CUST_STRU-KUNNR USING NO
 EDIT MASK, CUST_STRU-NAME1 INVERSE ON COLOR COL_GROUP, CUST_STRU-STRAS,
  CUST_STRU-ORT01, CUST_STRU-PSTLZ.
ENDSELECT.
```

- The FORMAT RESET statement appearing in the TOP-OF-PAGE event will make the heading appear in the default color set by the system.
- The statement `FORMAT INVERSE ON COLOR COL_POSITIVE` appearing before the WRITE statement inside the SELECT...ENDSELECT loop will make the output appear in the color COL_POSITIVE (green) in the foreground (INVERSE ON).
- The color specification for the field SY-DBCNT (INVERSE OFF COLOR = 4) will override the color specification of the FORMAT statement.
- The color specification for the field CUST_STRU-NAME1 (INVERSE on COLOR COL_GROUP) will override the color specification of the FORMAT statement.

The output will appear like Figure 5-15.

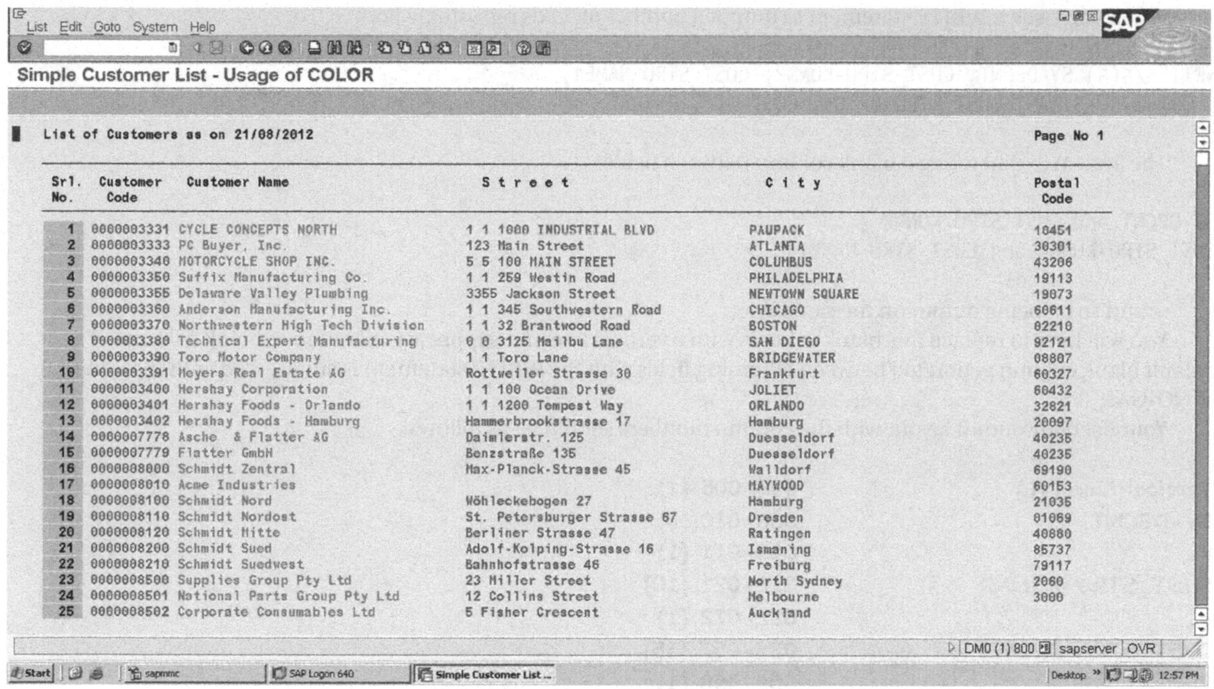

Srl. No.	Customer Code	Customer Name	S t r e e t	C i t y	Postal Code
1	0000003331	CYCLE CONCEPTS NORTH	1 1 1000 INDUSTRIAL BLVD	PAUPACK	18451
2	0000003333	PC Buyer, Inc.	123 Main Street	ATLANTA	30301
3	0000003340	MOTORCYCLE SHOP INC.	5 5 100 MAIN STREET	COLUMBUS	43206
4	0000003350	Suffix Manufacturing Co.	1 1 259 Westin Road	PHILADELPHIA	19113
5	0000003355	Delaware Valley Plumbing	3355 Jackson Street	NEWTOWN SQUARE	19073
6	0000003360	Anderson Manufacturing Inc.	1 1 345 Southwestern Road	CHICAGO	60611
7	0000003370	Northwestern High Tech Division	1 1 32 Brantwood Road	BOSTON	02210
8	0000003380	Technical Expert Manufacturing	0 0 3125 Malibu Lane	SAN DIEGO	92121
9	0000003390	Toro Motor Company	1 1 Toro Lane	BRIDGEWATER	08807
10	0000003391	Meyers Real Estate AG	Rottweiler Strasse 30	Frankfurt	60327
11	0000003400	Hershay Corporation	1 1 100 Ocean Drive	JOLIET	60432
12	0000003401	Hershay Foods - Orlando	1 1 1200 Tempest Way	ORLANDO	32821
13	0000003402	Hershay Foods - Hamburg	Hammerbrookstrasse 17	Hamburg	20097
14	0000007778	Asche & Flatter AG	Daimlerstr. 125	Duesseldorf	40235
15	0000007779	Flatter GmbH	Benzstraße 135	Duesseldorf	40235
16	0000008000	Schmidt Zentral	Max-Planck-Strasse 45	Walldorf	69190
17	0000008010	Acme Industries		MAYWOOD	60153
18	0000008100	Schmidt Nord	Wöhleckebogen 27	Hamburg	21035
19	0000008110	Schmidt Nordost	St. Petersburger Strasse 67	Dresden	01069
20	0000008120	Schmidt Mitte	Berliner Strasse 47	Ratingen	40880
21	0000008200	Schmidt Sued	Adolf-Kolping-Strasse 16	Ismaning	85737
22	0000008210	Schmidt Suedwest	Bahnhofstrasse 46	Freiburg	79117
23	0000008500	Supplies Group Pty Ltd	23 Miller Street	North Sydney	2060
24	0000008501	National Parts Group Pty Ltd	12 Collins Street	Melbourne	3000
25	0000008502	Corporate Consumables Ltd	5 Fisher Crescent	Auckland	

Figure 5-15. *Output of Program YCL_CH05_06_CUST_LIST05 - Color in Lists*

WRITE Statement: Hands-on Exercise - Simple Customer List with Fields Enclosed in Boxes

Figure 5-16 is an output of the WRITE statement (program). You can enclose each field being output in a box to impart good appearance to the output. You use the horizontal and vertical lines generated by the system fields SY-ULINE (already used in earlier programs) and SY-VLINE respectively. The output must look like this:

List of Customers as on 21-08-2012 Page No 1

Srl. No.	Customer Code	Customer Name	S t r e e t	C i t y	Postal Code
1	0000003331	CYCLE CONCEPTS NORTH	1 1 1000 INDUSTRIAL BLVD	PAUPACK	18451
2	0000003333	PC Buyer, Inc.	123 Main Street	ATLANTA	30301

Figure 5-16. *Sample Box enclosed Output*

When you issue a WRITE statement to output a number of fields on a single line:

```
WRITE:/5(5) SY-DBCNT, CUST_STRU-KUNNR, CUST_STRU-NAME1,
 CUST_STRU-STRAS, CUST_STRU-ORT01, CUST_STRU-PSTLZ.
```

The system is generating a blank column between fields:

```
SY-DBCNT and CUST_STRU-KUNNR
CUST_STRU-KUNNR and CUST_STRU-NAME1
```

... and so on being output on the same line.

You will have to replace this blank column with a vertical line and suppress generation of blank columns. The default blank column generated between adjoining fields with the WRITE statement is suppressed with the addition of NO-GAP.

Your list body output layout with the column numbers should be as follows:

```
Vertical Line (VL)          005-005 (1)
SY-DBCNT                    006-010 (5)
VL                          011-011 (1)
CUST_STRU-KUNNR             012-021 (10)
VL                          022-022 (1)
CUST_STRU-NAME1             023-057 (35)
VL                          058-058 (1)
CUST_STRU-STRAS             059-093 (35)
VL                          094-094 (1)
CUST_STRU-ORT01             095-129 (35)
VL                          130-130 (1)
CUST_STRU-PSTLZ             131-140 (10)
VL                          141-141 (1)
```

You need to have a horizontal line above and below (before and after the fields are output in a line). You should have an identical layout for the list column heading. Except for the first line, the bottom horizontal line for one set of field values will serve as the top horizontal line for the next set of field values.

The following code will generate the customer list with field values and *Column Headings* in boxes:

```
REPORT YCL_CH05_07_CUST_LIST06 LINE-SIZE 145 LINE-COUNT 60
 NO STANDARD PAGE HEADING.

****************************************************
* Simple Customer List - Fields Enclosed in Boxes **
****************************************************

DATA: BEGIN OF CUST_STRU,
       KUNNR   TYPE KNA1-KUNNR,
       NAME1   TYPE KNA1-NAME1,
       STRAS   TYPE KNA1-STRAS,
       ORT01   TYPE KNA1-ORT01,
       PSTLZ   TYPE KNA1-PSTLZ,
      END OF CUST_STRU.
```

```
*************************************************
TOP-OF-PAGE.

WRITE :/5 TEXT-001, SY-TVAR9, 132 TEXT-002, 139(3) SY-PAGNO.
SKIP.

WRITE :/5(137) SY-ULINE.

WRITE :/5 SY-VLINE NO-GAP, TEXT-003 NO-GAP, 11 SY-VLINE NO-GAP,
 TEXT-004 NO-GAP, 22 SY-VLINE NO-GAP, TEXT-005 NO-GAP, 58
 SY-VLINE NO-GAP, TEXT-006 NO-GAP, 94 SY-VLINE NO-GAP, TEXT-007
 NO-GAP, 130 SY-VLINE NO-GAP, TEXT-008 NO-GAP, 141 SY-VLINE NO-GAP.

WRITE :/5 SY-VLINE NO-GAP, TEXT-009 NO-GAP, 11 SY-VLINE NO-GAP,
 TEXT-010 NO-GAP, 22 SY-VLINE NO-GAP, 58 SY-VLINE NO-GAP, 94
 SY-VLINE NO-GAP, 130 SY-VLINE NO-GAP, TEXT-010 NO-GAP, 141
 SY-VLINE NO-GAP.

WRITE :/5(137) SY-ULINE.
**************************************************************
START-OF-SELECTION.

CONCATENATE SY-DATUM+6(2) SY-DATUM+4(2) SY-DATUM+0(4) INTO SY-TVAR9
SEPARATED BY '-'.

SELECT KUNNR NAME1 STRAS ORT01 PSTLZ FROM KNA1 INTO CUST_STRU.

 WRITE :/5 SY-VLINE NO-GAP, (5) SY-DBCNT NO-GAP, 11 SY-VLINE NO-GAP,
  CUST_STRU-KUNNR USING NO EDIT MASK NO-GAP, 22 SY-VLINE NO-GAP,
  CUST_STRU-NAME1 NO-GAP, 58   SY-VLINE NO-GAP, CUST_STRU-STRAS
  NO-GAP, 94 SY-VLINE NO-GAP, CUST_STRU-ORT01 NO-GAP, 130 SY-VLINE
  NO-GAP, CUST_STRU-PSTLZ, 141 SY-VLINE NO-GAP.

WRITE :/5(137) SY-ULINE.

ENDSELECT.
```

Copy the appropriate lines from previous programs. Use transaction code SE32 to copy *text symbols* from previous programs. Activate the *text symbol.*

When executed, the program will generate the output in Figure 5-17.

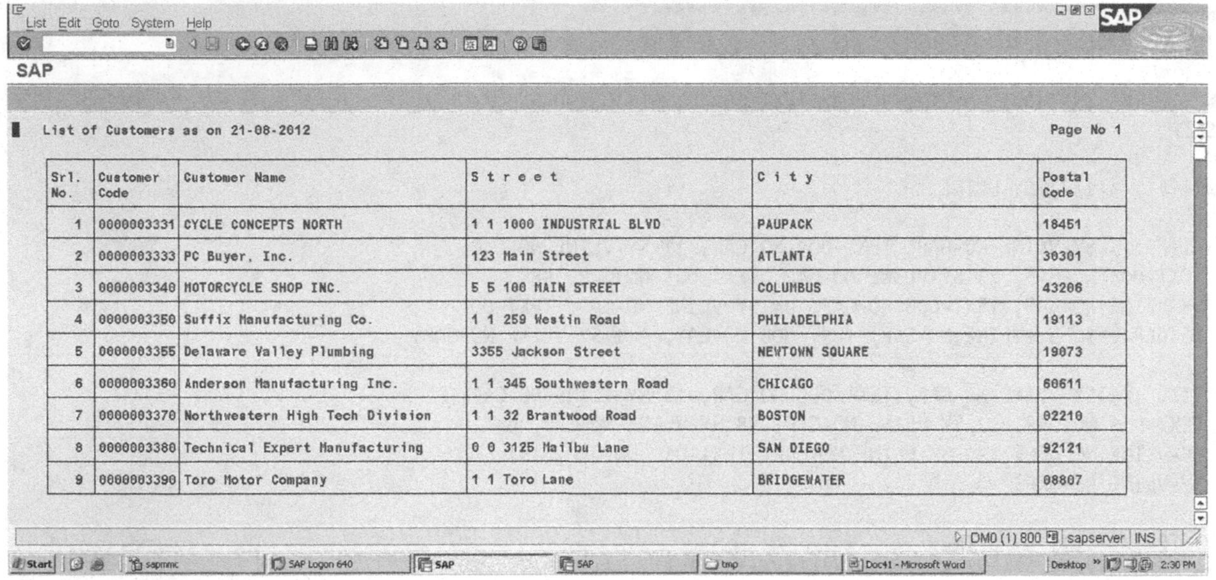

List of Customers as on 21-08-2012 Page No 1

Srl. No.	Customer Code	Customer Name	S t r e e t	C i t y	Postal Code
1	0000003331	CYCLE CONCEPTS NORTH	1 1 1000 INDUSTRIAL BLVD	PAUPACK	18451
2	0000003333	PC Buyer, Inc.	123 Main Street	ATLANTA	30301
3	0000003340	MOTORCYCLE SHOP INC.	5 5 100 MAIN STREET	COLUMBUS	43206
4	0000003350	Suffix Manufacturing Co.	1 1 259 Westin Road	PHILADELPHIA	19113
5	0000003355	Delaware Valley Plumbing	3355 Jackson Street	NEWTOWN SQUARE	19073
6	0000003360	Anderson Manufacturing Inc.	1 1 345 Southwestern Road	CHICAGO	60611
7	0000003370	Northwestern High Tech Division	1 1 32 Brantwood Road	BOSTON	02210
8	0000003380	Technical Expert Manufacturing	0 0 3125 Mailbu Lane	SAN DIEGO	92121
9	0000003390	Toro Motor Company	1 1 Toro Lane	BRIDGEWATER	08807

Figure 5-17. *Output of Program YCL_CH05_07_CUST_LIST06 - Boxed Output*

WRITE Statement: Hands-on Exercise - List of Billing Documents of a Specified Company Code

Your next hands-on exercise will list or output a few prime fields from the SAP billing documents header table VBRK for a specified company code. The company code field in the table VBRK is BUKRS. You will input a company code through a PARAMETERS statement and have a WHERE condition in the SELECT statement to retrieve only the data for the input company code of the PARAMETERS statement. Recall, the company code in a SAP environment is for a registered or incorporated company.

In this list, you will want to incorporate the customer name and customer city available in the customer primary table KNA1. You will create a database view of these tables and access fields from it. You will output the amount field from table VBRK (i.e., NETWR). The amount in the billing document header can be in different currencies. But you will convert the different currencies to the operating currency of the company code for which you are producing the list. You can do this by multiplying the amount field with the exchange rate field in the VBRK table KURRF.

In the list heading, (*nonstandard page header*) you will output the company code, the name of the company code and currency of the company code. The name and currency of the company code are available in table T001. (Fields: BUTXT Data Type CHAR length 25 and WAERS Data Type CUKY length 5).

You can retrieve the fields BUTXT and WAERS for a company code with a SELECT SINGLE... statement.

Output - Rough Format
A rough layout of your list:

```
Billing Documents of XXXX/XXXXXXXXXXXXXXXXXXXXXXXXX   Curr: XXXXX

-----------------------------------------------------------------------
Srl. Doc No. Doc Date Customer     N a m e        C i t y        Amount
 No.                  Code
-----------------------------------------------------------------------

XXXX                                   - BUKRS
XXXXXXXXXXXXXXXXXXXXXXXXX              - BUTXT
XXXXX                                  - WAERS
```

Output - Fields
On an overall basis, you will have the fields in Table 5-1 in the output.

Table 5-1. *List of Fields in the Output*

Field	Table	DDIC Data Type & Length	Description	Output Area
BUKRS	T001	CHAR 04	Company Code	Header
BUTXT	T001	CHAR 25	Company Code Name	Header
WAERS	T001	CUKY 05	Company Code Currency	Header
SY-DBCNT	System Field	INT4	For Serial No.	Body
VBELN	VBRK	CHAR 10	Billing Document No.	Body
FKDAT	VBRK	DATS 08	Billing Document Date	Body
KUNNR	KNA1	CHAR 10	Customer Code	Body
NAME1	KNA1	CHAR 35	Customer Name	Body
ORT01	KNA1	CHAR 35	Customer City	Body
NETWR	VBRK	CURR 15,2	Billing Document Net Value/Amount in Document Currency. Multiply this with the field KURRF and output	Body

Output Body - Layout

The output body will have the following layout:

Table 5-2. Output Body Layout

Field Name	Table Name	Description	Column Positions
SY-DBCNT	System Field	Serial No.	005,009 (5)
			010
VBELN	VBRK	Billing Document No.	011,020 (10)
			021
FKDAT	VBRK	Billing Document Date	022,031 (10)
			032
KUNNR	KNA1	Customer Code	033-042 (10)
			043
NAME1	KNA1	Name	044-078 (35)
			079
ORT01	KNA1	City	080-114 (35)
			115
NETWR	VBRK	Billing Document Net Value (Converted to Company Code Currency)	116-132 (17)

The field NETWR (CURR) is output in 17 columns. This includes 3 column positions for commas of billion, million, thousand; 1 column position for decimal and 1 column position for the sign on the right side. That leaves you with 12 digit positions: 10 digits before the decimal and 2 digits after the decimal. With 10 digits, you can have a maximum figure of 9 billion, 999 million, 999 thousand, 999, etc. Good enough for your present context.

Output Data Source - Database View

Create a database view YCL_CH05_VBRKKNA with the tables KNA1 and VBRK. The tables and join conditions will be like this:

```
VBRK
KNA1                          KNA1    MANDT  =  VBRK     MANDT
                              KNA1    KUNNR  =  VBRK     KUNAG
```

The view fields:

```
View field          Table            Field
----------------------------------------
 MANDT              KNA1             MANDT
 KUNNR              KNA1             KUNNR
 VBELN              VBRK             VBELN
 NAME1              KNA1             NAME1
 ORT01              KNA1             ORT01
 PSTLZ              KNA1             PSTLZ
 STRAS              KNA1             STRAS
 FKDAT              VBRK             FKDAT
 KURRF              VBRK             KURRF
 BUKRS              VBRK             BUKRS
 NETWR              VBRK             NETWR
```

Source Program

The source code for billing document list:

```
REPORT YCL_CH05_08_BILL_DOCS_LIST LINE-SIZE 135 LINE-COUNT 60
       NO STANDARD PAGE HEADING.

*******************************************************************
* List of Billing Documents of a Specified Company Code with Total **
*******************************************************************

* Billing Documents of XXXX/XXXXXXXXXXXXXXXXXXXXXXXXX   Curr: XXXXX
* -----------------------------------------------------------------
* Doc No. Doc Date Customer     N a m e       C i t y       Amount
*                    Code
* -----------------------------------------------------------------
*     SY-DBCNT      005 - 009  **
*     VBELN         011 - 020  **
*     FKDAT         022 - 031  **
*     KUNNR         033 - 042  **
*     NAME1         044 - 078  **
*     ORT01         080 - 114  **
*     NETWR         116 - 132  **
********************************
*****************************************************************
* database view with tables KNA1 (customer primary)            **
* YCL_CH05_VBRKKNA          VBRK (billing docs-header)         **
*                                                              **
*   VBRK                    KNA1    MANDT = VBRK    MANDT      **
*   KNA1                    KNA1    KUNNR = VBRK    KUNAG      **
*                                                              **
* View field      Table    Field                               **
*                                                              **
*  MANDT          KNA1     MANDT                               **
*  KUNNR          KNA1     KUNNR                               **
*  VBELN          VBRK     VBELN                               **
*  NAME1          KNA1     NAME1                               **
```

```
* ORT01          KNA1     ORT01                             **
* PSTLZ          KNA1     PSTLZ                             **
* STRAS          KNA1     STRAS                             **
* FKDAT          VBRK     FKDAT                             **
* KURRF          VBRK     KURRF                             **
* BUKRS          VBRK     BUKRS                             **
* NETWR          VBRK     NETWR                             **
*                                                           **
**************************************************************
TABLES: YCL_CH05_VBRKKNA, " creates a local structure having all
                          " fields of view YCL_CH05_VBRKKNA
       T001.              " local structure with all fields of T001

DATA: STRNG     TYPE STRING,
      TOTAL     TYPE VBRK-NETWR.

PARAMETERS CCODE  TYPE VBRK-BUKRS DEFAULT 3000 VALUE CHECK.
                  " the clause VALUE CHECK will check values
                  " in the primary table of this foreign key field
****************************************************************
TOP-OF-PAGE.

WRITE :/5 STRNG, 129(3) SY-PAGNO. " STRNG - refer CONCATENATE sttement in
                                  " START-OF-SELECTION
SKIP 1.
WRITE:/5(127) SY-ULINE.
WRITE:/5 TEXT-003,11 TEXT-004, 22 TEXT-005, 33 TEXT-006, 46 TEXT-007,
        83 TEXT-008, 126 TEXT-009.

WRITE:/6 TEXT-010, 35 TEXT-011.
WRITE:/5(127) SY-ULINE.

*****************************************************************
START-OF-SELECTION.

SELECT SINGLE * FROM T001 WHERE BUKRS = CCODE." fetches a single row, no
                                              " loop construct SELECT
                                              " ENDSELECT

CONCATENATE TEXT-001 CCODE '/' T001-BUTXT TEXT-002 T001-WAERS INTO STRNG.

SELECT * FROM YCL_CH05_VBRKKNA WHERE BUKRS = CCODE.
 YCL_CH05_VBRKKNA-NETWR = YCL_CH05_VBRKKNA-NETWR *
  YCL_CH05_VBRKKNA-KURRF.

 WRITE:/5(5) SY-DBCNT, YCL_CH05_VBRKKNA-VBELN, YCL_CH05_VBRKKNA-FKDAT,
             YCL_CH05_VBRKKNA-KUNNR, YCL_CH05_VBRKKNA-NAME1,
             YCL_CH05_VBRKKNA-ORT01, (17) YCL_CH05_VBRKKNA-NETWR.

 TOTAL = TOTAL + YCL_CH05_VBRKKNA-NETWR.
```

```
ENDSELECT.
*******************************

END-OF-SELECTION.
SKIP 1.

WRITE: /(17) TOTAL UNDER YCL_CH05_VBRKKNA-NETWR. " the field TOTAL will
                                                " be outputted
                                                " UNDER NETWR. no need
                                                " to count columns
                                                " for alignment
```

Text Symbols

For the *nonstandard page header*, you require text. Create the *text symbols* and activate it. It will look like Figure 5-18.

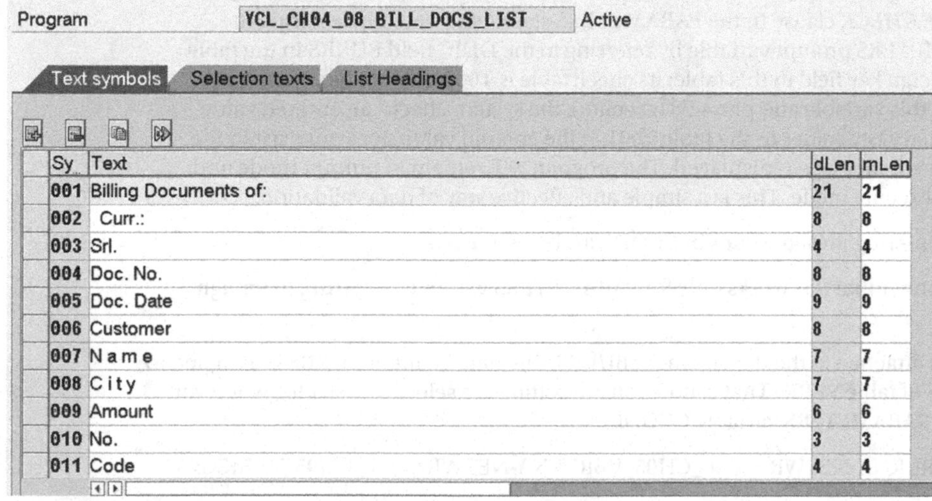

Sy	Text	dLen	mLen
001	Billing Documents of:	21	21
002	Curr.:	8	8
003	Srl.	4	4
004	Doc. No.	8	8
005	Doc. Date	9	9
006	Customer	8	8
007	N a m e	7	7
008	C i t y	7	7
009	Amount	6	6
010	No.	3	3
011	Code	4	4

Figure 5-18. *Text Symbols - Program YCL_CH05_08_BILL_DOCS_LIST*

Source Program– New Features

- The *TABLES* statement. You declare structured data objects by referring to DDIC objects: (a) tables, (b) views (any of the four type of views), and (c) structure. The ABAP compiler checks the entries against existence of DDIC tables/views/structures. If no entries exist with the name, it is a syntax error. If an entry exists, a structure of this name gets defined in the program (internal data object); the fields in this structure are the same as the fields in the corresponding DDIC table/view/structure.

  In the present program, you have declared with the TABLES statement two internal data objects:

  YCL_CH05_VBRKKNA is reference to a DDIC view. A structure of this name with the same fields as the DDIC view YCL_CH05_VBRKKNA gets defined in the program. This is the structure into which you are fetching a row of data repeatedly through the SELECT statement from the database view. In the earlier programs you defined the structure in the DATA statement with BEGIN OF... END OF...

T001 is reference to the DDIC transparent table. A structure with this name gets defined in the program. This structured internal data object has the same fields as the DDIC T001 table definition.

The DATA statement equivalent of the TABLES statement in this context will be:

```
DATA :    YCL_CH05_VBRKKNA        TYPE YCL_CH05_VBRKKNA,
          T001                    TYPE T001.
```

Though this notation throws a compiler warning/s, it works the same way as the TABLES statement.

The TABLES statement is not supported in an OOP environment and so is not recommended to be used except with dynpro programming - Chapter 14. The DATA statement equivalent of the TABLES statement can be used to declare a structured data object referring to DDIC objects and carrying the same name as the DDIC object.

Let's continue our discussion of the code:

Note the *VALUE CHECK* clause in the PARAMETERS statement. You are declaring the CCODE PARAMETERS prompt variable by referring to the DDIC field BUKRS in the table VBRK. It is a foreign key field in this table; its check table is T001. At runtime, when you enter a value in this variable and press F8 (execute), the system checks an entered value against the primary key values in the table T001. If the entered value does not exist in the T001 table, an error message is displayed. The program will remain in prompt mode and will not go into execute mode. This is a simple and effective way of data validation.

You can try by entering invalid values in CCODE and pressing F8.

You must remember that this works only for PARAMETERS variables referring to foreign key fields.

- A search help is attached to the data element BUKRS. The data element BUKRS is assigned to the field BUKRS of table VBRK. That is how you are getting the selection list, etc., when you press F4 on the PARAMETERS variable CCODE.

- YCL_CH05_VBRKKNA-NETWR = YCL_CH05_VBRKKNA-NETWR * YCL_CH05_VBRKKNA-KURRF.

  You are multiplying the field NETWR of structure YCL_CH05_VBRKKNA with the field KURRF of structure YCL_CH05_VBRKKNA and assigning it back to the field NETWR of structure YCL_CH05_VBRKKNA. All this is happening in RAM. You are not disturbing the database tables. You are losing the original value of NETWR in which you are not interested after the conversion/multiplication.

- SELECT SINGLE... This is to fetch a single row. You require the name of the company code and its currency from the table T001 corresponding to the single value of the company code entered in CCODE. In Table T001, the company code is the primary key (in addition to the client code MANDT). For a logged-in client, each value of the company code will be unique; your prior RDBMS exposure is tested.

- The event END-OF-SELECTION. This event is triggered when all the statements in the event START-OF-SELECTION have been executed. You could have done without this event in the present context. The idea was to introduce this event. This event is more relevant in the context of *logical databases*.
- WRITE...UNDER... In the WRITE statement for TOTAL in the END-OF-SELECTION event, you have used the clause UNDER YCL_CH05_VBRKKNA-NETWR. It means the output variable TOTAL is aligned with or under the previously output variable YCL_CH05_VBRKKNA-NETWR. This is one of the formatting features of a WRITE statement.

When you execute the program, the output will look like that in Figures 5-19 and 5-20.

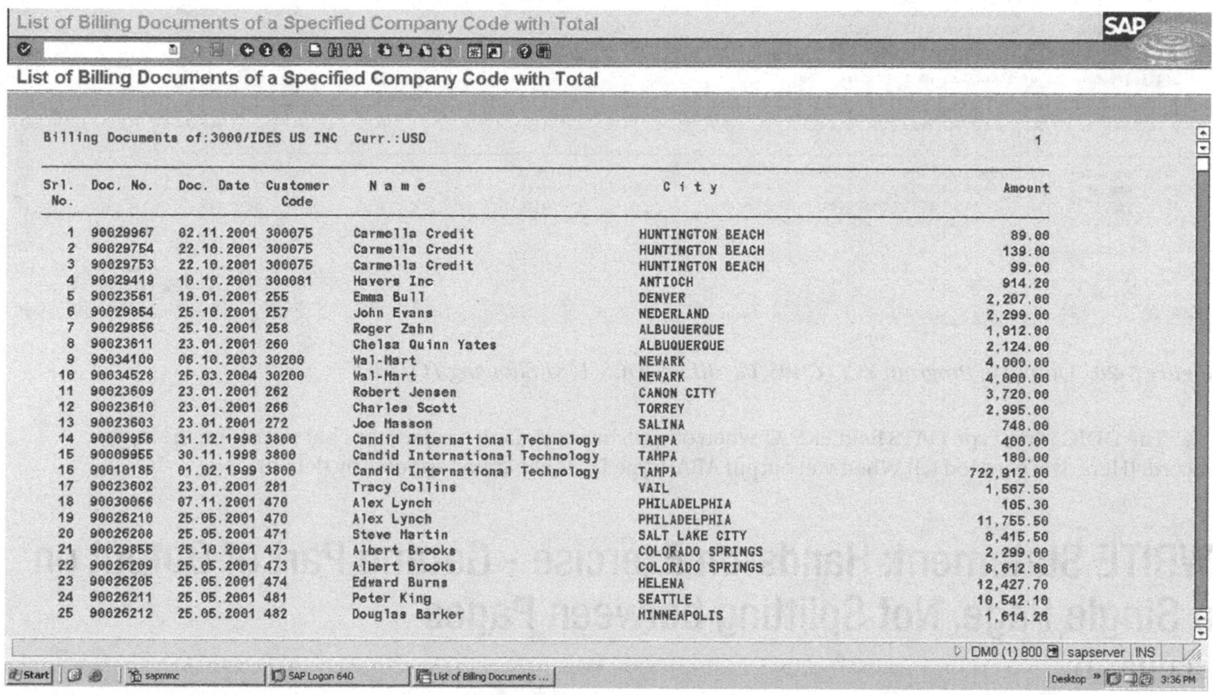

Srl. No.	Doc. No.	Doc. Date	Customer Code	N a m e	C i t y	Amount
1	90029967	02.11.2001	300075	Carmella Credit	HUNTINGTON BEACH	89.00
2	90029754	22.10.2001	300075	Carmella Credit	HUNTINGTON BEACH	139.00
3	90029753	22.10.2001	300075	Carmella Credit	HUNTINGTON BEACH	99.00
4	90029419	10.10.2001	300081	Havers Inc	ANTIOCH	914.20
5	90023561	19.01.2001	255	Emma Bull	DENVER	2,207.00
6	90029854	25.10.2001	257	John Evans	NEDERLAND	2,299.00
7	90029856	25.10.2001	258	Roger Zahn	ALBUQUERQUE	1,912.00
8	90023611	23.01.2001	260	Chelsa Quinn Yates	ALBUQUERQUE	2,124.00
9	90034100	06.10.2003	30200	Wal-Mart	NEWARK	4,000.00
10	90034528	25.03.2004	30200	Wal-Mart	NEWARK	4,000.00
11	90023609	23.01.2001	262	Robert Jensen	CANON CITY	3,720.00
12	90023610	23.01.2001	266	Charles Scott	TORREY	2,995.00
13	90023603	23.01.2001	272	Joe Masson	SALINA	748.00
14	90009956	31.12.1998	3800	Candid International Technology	TAMPA	400.00
15	90009955	30.11.1998	3800	Candid International Technology	TAMPA	180.00
16	90010185	01.02.1999	3800	Candid International Technology	TAMPA	722,912.00
17	90023602	23.01.2001	281	Tracy Collins	VAIL	1,567.50
18	90030066	07.11.2001	470	Alex Lynch	PHILADELPHIA	105.30
19	90026210	25.05.2001	470	Alex Lynch	PHILADELPHIA	11,755.50
20	90026208	25.05.2001	471	Steve Martin	SALT LAKE CITY	8,415.50
21	90029855	25.10.2001	473	Albert Brooks	COLORADO SPRINGS	2,299.00
22	90026209	25.05.2001	473	Albert Brooks	COLORADO SPRINGS	8,612.80
23	90026205	25.05.2001	474	Edward Burns	HELENA	12,427.70
24	90026211	25.05.2001	481	Peter King	SEATTLE	10,542.10
25	90026212	25.05.2001	482	Douglas Barker	MINNEAPOLIS	1,614.26

Figure 5-19. *Output of Program YCL_CH05_08_BILL_DOCS_LIST*

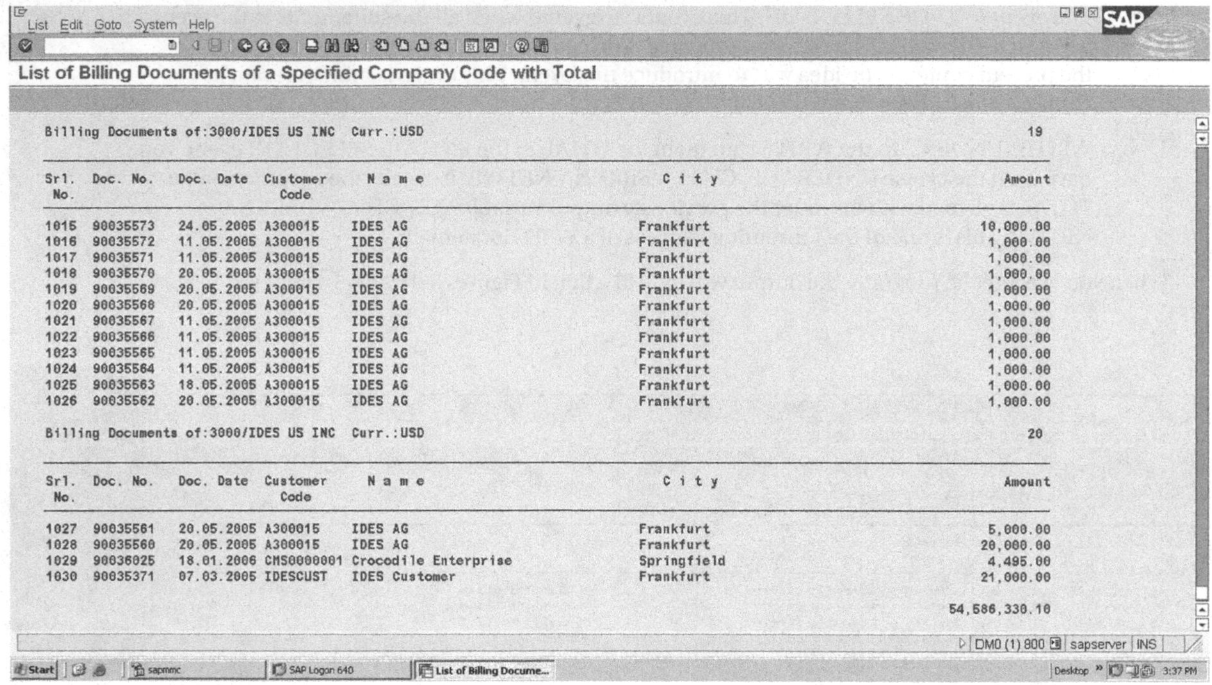

Figure 5-20. *Output of Program YCL_CH05_08_BILL_DOCS_LIST Showing TOTAL*

The DDIC Data Type DATS field FKDAT when output, has by default a separator character from the master record. [Here, it is a period (.)] When you output ABAP type D, no separator appears by default.

WRITE Statement: Hands-on Exercise - Getting Part of Output on a Single Page, Not Splitting between Pages

Scenario:

Consider the customer primary table KNA1. You want to output the following fields from it:

```
KUNNR          Customer Code/Number
NAME1          Name
STRAS          Street
ORT01          City
PSTLZ          Postal Code
LAND1          Country Code
```

Suppose, instead of the country code field LAND1, you need to output the country name. The country name is available in the language dependent text table T005T. The fields of table T005T are:

```
MANDT          Client Code
SPRAS          Language Key/Code
LAND1          Country Code
LANDX          Country Name
```

```
NATIO           Nationality
LANDX50         Country Name (Max 50 Characters)
NATIO50         Nationality (Max 50 Characters)
PRQ_SPREGT      Super region per country text
```

So, you need to create a database view to be able to fetch all the required fields from a single data source.

When you create a database view with tables KNA1 and T005T, if you join the two tables with the fields MANDT (client code) and LAND1, (country code) you will end up fetching country names in all the installed languages. However, you do not need the country names in all the installed languages.

```
KNA1    MANDT           T005T           MANDT
KNA1    LAND1           T005T           LAND1
```

The customer primary table KNA1 also contains the language key or code field SPRAS. This signifies the language key or code in which the customer communicates. This field is in the Vendor/Supplier primary table LFA1 as well. An enterprise needs to maintain this information - in what language the business partners (customers and vendors) communicate.

If you include the SPRAS field in the join condition, you will end up fetching country names in different languages (i.e., country names will be fetched in the respective language of customers).

```
KNA1    MANDT           T005T           MANDT
KNA1    LAND1           T005T           LAND1
KNA1    SPRAS           T005T           SPRAS
```

On the other hand, if you do not include the SPRAS field in the join condition, but specify a single language key or code value in the Selection Conditions of the database view, you will be fetching country names in a single language for all the customers.

Your output requirements will determine which of these options to choose. If you are communicating with the customers, you will include the language key or code SPRAS in the join condition. If you are producing a list for the enterprise internal purpose (the enterprise will be operating in a specific language), you can resort to the second of the options described.

Let it be assumed that your present output is for internal purposes. So create a database view with the tables KNA1, T005T. Join conditions would include the fields MANDT and LAND1. In the Selection Conditions, include an equal condition for the SPRAS field:

```
T005T   SPRAS   EQ              'E'
```

Take care to enter the language key or code value in upper case, enclosed in single quotes.

The *View Flds* tab will look like this:

```
MANDT           KNA1            MANDT
KUNNR           KNA1            KUNNR
SPRAS           T005T           SPRAS
LAND1           T005T           LAND1
NAME1           KNA1            NAME1
ORT01           KNA1            ORT01
PSTLZ           KNA1            PSTLZ
STRAS           KNA1            STRAS
LANDX           T005T           LANDX
```

Save, then perform a consistency check; activate and audit the database view.

Strictly, in formal terms you should reach the text table T005T through the country code master table T005 in the view. In your database view, you have resorted to a shortcut and reached it directly. Your output's rough format will be:

```
KUNNR
NAME1
STRAS
ORT01
PSTLZ
LANDX
```

Each field is output on a separate line, a total of 6 lines for each customer.

Your requirement is that each customer's information must not split between two pages, with certain fields of a customer appearing in one page, and remaining fields appearing in the next page:

```
KUNNR
NAME1
STRAS

--------------------- Page boundary

ORT01
PSTLZ
LANDX
```

Each customer's information is output in 6 lines. So if 6 lines are not available on the current page, the system must automatically go to the next page to output the customer. This is achieved with the RESERVE LINES feature. The previous output with RESERVE 6 LINES:

```
--------------------- Page boundary

KUNNR
NAME1
STRAS
ORT01
PSTLZ
LANDX
```

In the program YCL_CH05_09_RESERVE_LINES, you are implementing this. Source lines of this program:

```
REPORT YCL_CH05_09_RESERVE_LINES LINE-COUNT 55 LINE-SIZE 50
       NO STANDARD PAGE HEADING.

***************************************************************
* Part Of Output Not Splitting Between Pages - RESERVE LINES **
***************************************************************

TABLES: YCL_CH05_KNAT5T.

TOP-OF-PAGE.
WRITE:/40 'Page:', (5) SY-PAGNO.
```

```
****************************************************************
START-OF-SELECTION.

SELECT * FROM YCL_CH05_KNAT5T UP TO 1000 ROWS.

 RESERVE 6 LINES. " checks 6 lines are available in the current page
                  " if 6 lines available, it outputs
                  " else goes to next page and outputs

 WRITE /5: YCL_CH05_KNAT5T-KUNNR USING NO EDIT MASK,
           YCL_CH05_KNAT5T-NAME1,
           YCL_CH05_KNAT5T-STRAS,
           YCL_CH05_KNAT5T-ORT01,
           YCL_CH05_KNAT5T-PSTLZ,
           YCL_CH05_KNAT5T-LANDX.
 SKIP 1.

ENDSELECT.
```

Execute the program first with RESERVE 6 LINES commented. Next, de-comment the RESERVE 6 LINES and execute.

The program outputs without RESERVE LINES and with RESERVE LINES would appear like Figure 5-21.

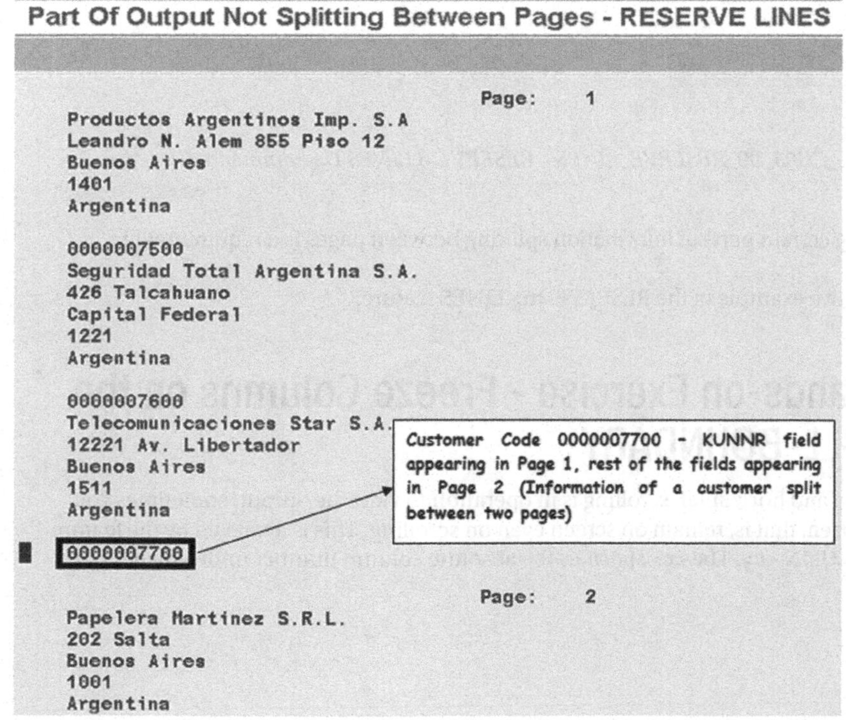

Figure 5-21. *Output of Program YCL_CH05_09_RESERVE_LINES - RESERVE 6 LINES Commented*

```
Part Of Output Not Splitting Between Pages - RESERVE LINES

                                      Page:     1
   Leandro N. Alem 855 Piso 12
   Buenos Aires
   1401
   Argentina

   0000007500
   Seguridad Total Argentina S.A.
   426 Talcahuano
   Capital Federal
   1221
   Argentina

   0000007600
   Telecomunicaciones Star S.A.
   12221 Av. Libertador
   Buenos Aires
   1511
   Argentina


                                      Page:     2
   0000007700
   Papelera Martinez S.R.L.
   202 Salta
   Buenos Aires
   1001
   Argentina
```

Customer Code 0000007700 - All the fields appearing in Page 2 (Information of a customer not split between two pages)

Figure 5-22. *Output of Program YCL_CH05_09_RESERVE_LINES - RESERVE 6 LINES De-commented*

This requirement of not allowing certain parts of information splitting between pages is a requirement in business applications.

This was a contrived demonstrative example of the RESERVE <n> LINES feature.

WRITE Statement: Hands-on Exercise - Freeze Columns on the Left: SET LEFT SCROLL-BOUNDARY

When an output on the screen is wide and horizontal, scrolling is in operation to view the output; sometimes you want information on the left to be frozen: that is, remain on screen even on scrolling. This is achieved by the feature SET LEFT SCROLL-BOUNDARY COLUMN <c>. The <c> specifies the absolute column number until which the information is to be frozen.

Let the database view YCL_CH05_KNAT5T be an input again, and let the six fields - KUNNR, NAME1, STRAS, ORT01, PSTLZ, LANDX be listed in one line along with the serial number (SY-DBCNT). This would make the output line wide enough to create scope for horizontal scrolling. The output layout:

```
SY-DBCNT                            005,009 (5)
                                    010
YCL_CH05_KNAT5T-KUNNR               011-020 (10)
                                    021
YCL_CH05_KNAT5T-NAME1               022-056 (35)
                                    057
YCL_CH05_KNAT5T-STRAS               058-092 (35)
                                    093
YCL_CH05_KNAT5T-ORT01               094-128 (35)
                                    0129
YCL_CH05_KNAT5T-PSTLZ               130-139 (10)
                                    140
YCL_CH05_KNAT5T-LANDX               141-155 (15)
```

Let the statement SET LEFT SCROLL-BOUNDARY COLUMN <c> be used to freeze the serial number (SY-DBCNT) and customer code YCL_CH05_KNAT5T-KUNNR. These two fields reach up to column 20. (Your output starts from column 5, SY-DBCNT is 5 columns, 1 intermediate blank column between SY-DBCNT and YCL_CH05_KNAT5T-KUNNR, 10 columns for YCL_CH05_KNAT5T-KUNNR, 2 blank columns to make freezing more apparent.) So set the left scroll boundary to column 22.

The source program of this hands-on:

```
REPORT YCL_CH05_10_LEFT_SCROLL_BNDRY LINE-SIZE 160.

****************************************
* SET LEFT SCROLL-BOUNDARY COLUMN <c> **
****************************************

TABLES: YCL_CH05_KNAT5T.

****************************************
START-OF-SELECTION.

SELECT * FROM YCL_CH05_KNAT5T.
 SET LEFT SCROLL-BOUNDARY COLUMN 22.
 WRITE:/5(5) SY-DBCNT, YCL_CH05_KNAT5T-KUNNR USING NO EDIT MASK, YCL_CH05_KNAT5T-NAME1,
  YCL_CH05_KNAT5T-STRAS, YCL_CH05_KNAT5T-ORT01, YCL_CH05_KNAT5T-PSTLZ,
  YCL_CH05_KNAT5T-LANDX.
ENDSELECT.
```

The outputs before and after a horizontal scroll will look like Figure 5-23.

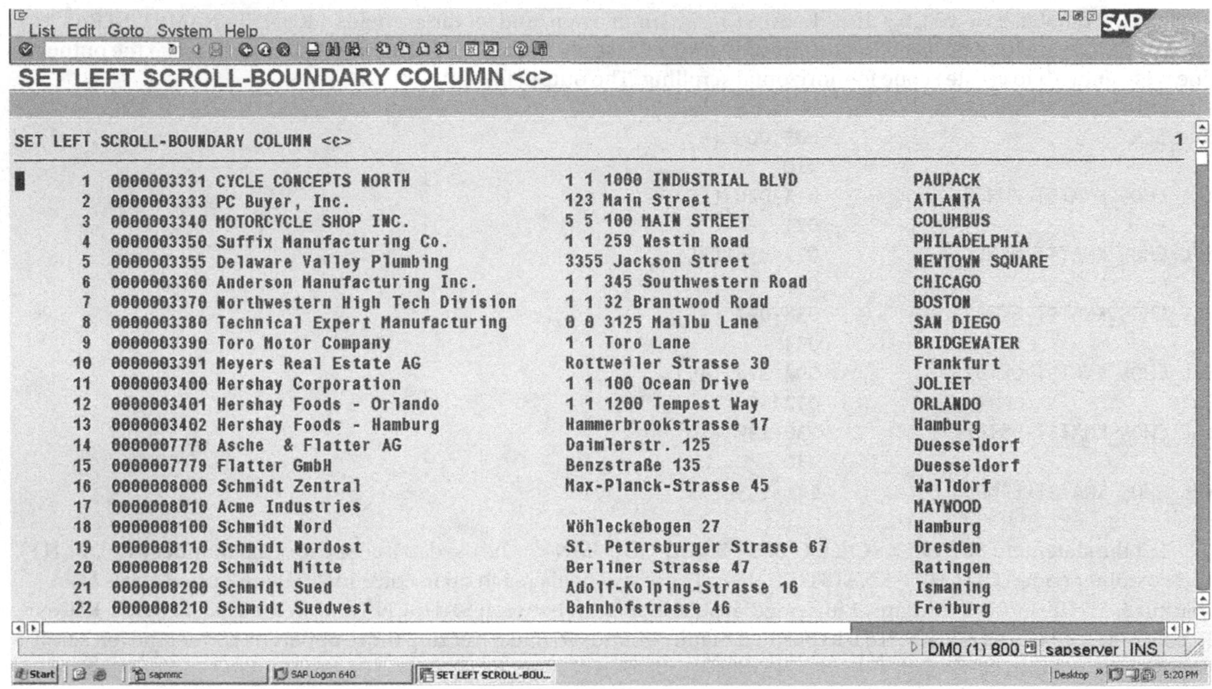

Figure 5-23. *Output of Program YCL_CH05_10_LEFT_SCROLL_BNDRY: Pre-scroll*

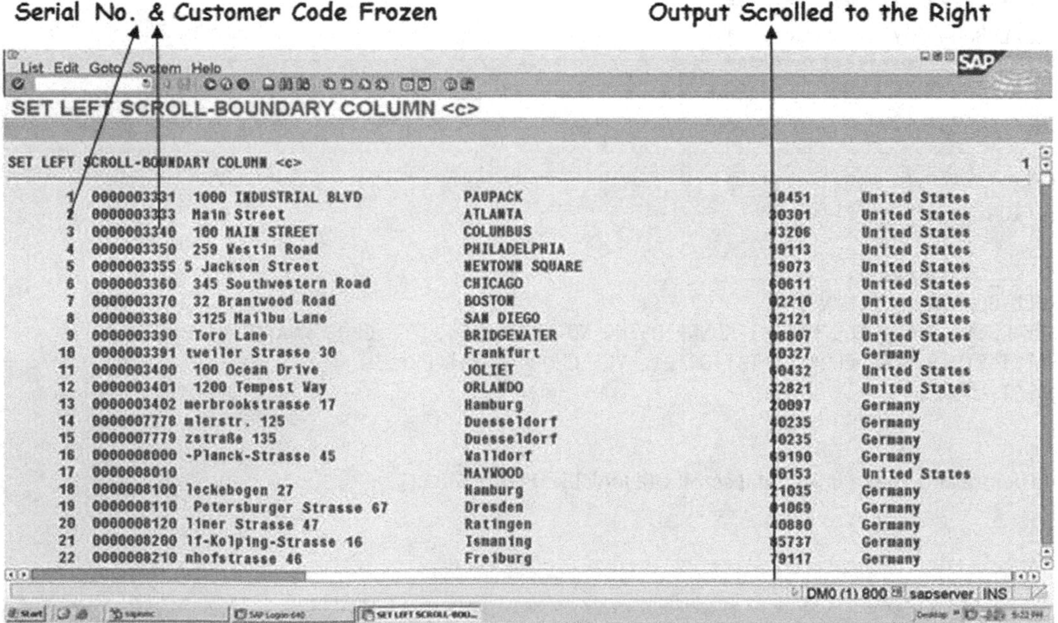

Figure 5-24. *Output of Program YCL_CH05_10_LEFT_SCROLL_BNDRY: Post-scroll*

WRITE Statement: Miscellaneous Features, Statements

WRITE Statement - Features

Output Blank Lines with WRITE: By default, blank lines are not output with the WRITE statement (you generated blank lines with the SKIP statement). If you want blank lines to be output with the WRITE statement, you need to give the following SET statement:

```
SET BLANK LINES ON.
```

By default, BLANK LINES is OFF.

Output Icons: There are more than 1100 icons in the SAP GUI environment. The definitions and particulars of these icons are stored in the SAP table ICON. Icons are identified by names such as ICON_CREATE, ICON_CHANGE, ICON_DISPKAY... et al. The icon definitions and particulars are also stored in the DDIC TYPE GROUP ICON. So a program in which icons are to be output with a WRITE statement, the statement TYPE-POOLS ICON should be included. Icons can be output with the WRITE statement in the following manner:

```
TYPE-POOLS ICON.
...

WRITE <icon name> AS ICON.
```

Output Symbols: The symbol definitions and particulars are stored in the DDIC TYPE GROUP SYM. So a program in which symbols are to be output with the WRITE statement, the statement TYPE-POOLS SYM should be included. Icons can be output with the WRITE statement in the following manner:

```
TYPE-POOLS SYM.
...

WRITE <symbol name> AS SYMBOL.
```

Output HOTSPOTS: You can output fields and lines in the WRITE statement as HOTSPOTS. When you output fields and lines as a HOTSPOT, when the mouse pointer is positioned on these fields and lines, a hand symbol will appear as a mouse pointer instead of the normal mouse pointer. A HOTSPOT can be set to for instance, COLOR, with the FORMAT statement or at the individual field level of the WRITE statement:

```
FORMAT HOTSPOT. "no specification: ON"
FORMAT HOTSPOT OFF.

WRITE XXX HOTSPOT.
```

HOTSPOT has significance in the context of Interactive Lists; see Chapter 10.

Output CHECKBOX: You can output the enable/disable check box with a WRITE statement. This has meaning and significance in Interactive lists in Chapter 10. The variable associated with the checkbox can be any. If it is number oriented (TYPE D, F, I, N, P, T, X, XSTRING), it will store 0 for disabled and 1 for enabled. For character oriented data (TYPE C, STRING), it will store X for enabled and SPACE for disabled. You should preferably declare a check box variable as TYPE C and length 1.

The program YCL_CH05_11_MISC is implementing these miscellaneous features. Source lines of this program:

```
REPORT YCL_CH05_11_MISC.

*********************************************
* WRITE STATEMENT - MISCELLANEOUS FEATURES **
*********************************************

TYPE-POOLS: ICON,  "TYPE GROUP for icon definitions
            SYM.   "TYPE GROUP for symbol definitions

DATA CBOX(1)  TYPE C. "for check box

START-OF-SELECTION.

*********** outputting blank lines ************************
SET BLANK LINES ON. "blank lines outputted on with this setting
SKIP 2.

WRITE:/10(25)  ' ' INTENSIFIED ON COLOR COL_TOTAL.
WRITE:/10(25)  ' ' INTENSIFIED ON COLOR COL_KEY.
WRITE:/10(25)  ' ' INTENSIFIED ON COLOR COL_POSITIVE.
WRITE:/10(25)  ' ' INTENSIFIED ON COLOR COL_NEGATIVE.
WRITE:/10(25)  ' ' INTENSIFIED ON COLOR COL_GROUP.

*********** output icons **********************************
SKIP 1.
WRITE: /10 'ICON_SYSTEM_SAVE', ICON_SYSTEM_SAVE AS ICON,
       /10 'ICON_CHECK      ', ICON_CHECK       AS ICON.

*********** output symbols ********************************
SKIP 1.
WRITE: /10 'SYM_FOLDER    ', SYM_FOLDER      AS SYMBOL,
       /10 'SYM_DOCUMENTS ', SYM_DOCUMENTS   AS SYMBOL.
*********** output HOTSPOT ********************************
SKIP 1.

 " HOTSPOT like COLOR can be specified with
 " (1) FORMAT statement like
 "     FORMAT HOTSPOT = <ON/OFF>. subsequent output will support
 "     HOTSPOT
 "
 " (2) it can be specified in a field of WRITE statement like
 "     WRITE XXX HOTSPOT.

WRITE /10: 'This is HOTSPOT output' HOTSPOT,
           'This is NORMAL output '.
*********** output check box *******************************
SKIP 1.
 " checkbox variable to be TYPE C, preferable length 1
 " can assume only two values i.e. X     when enabled
 "                                 SPACE when disabled
```

```
" if number oriented TYPE D, F, I, N, P, T, X: values 1     when enabled
"                                                     0     when disabled

WRITE: /10 'Check Box:', CBOX AS CHECKBOX. " this phrase AS CHECKBOX
                                            " to make output check box
```

When the program is executed, the output will look like Figure 5-15.

```
SET COUNTRY <c>.
```

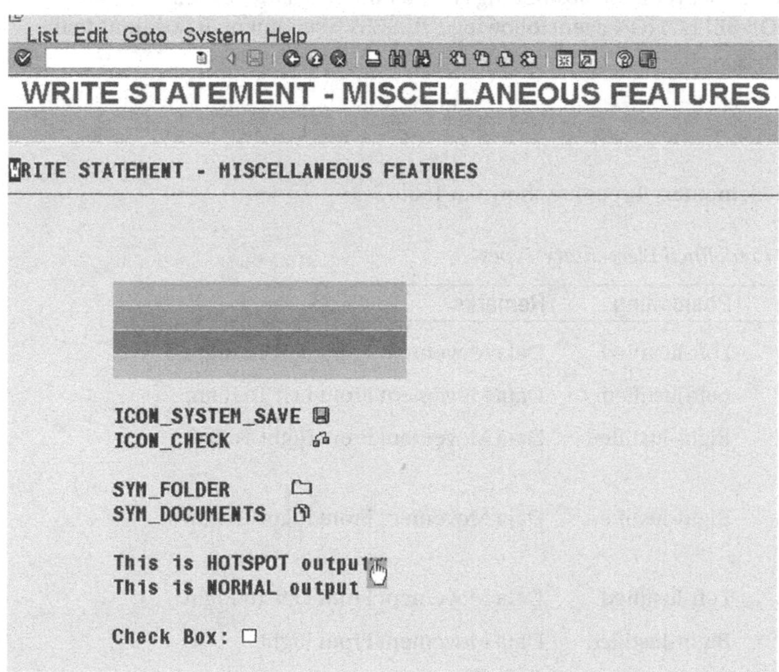

Figure 5-25. *Output of Program YCL_CH05_11_MISC*

The table T005X contains output settings for countries. There are two output settings in this table: one for period/decimal (.) and comma (,) and the other for date. For the country code 'DE,' Germany, they use a comma (,) to separate the integer and fraction parts of a number [where you use a period/decimal (.). They use a period/decimal (.) as a thousand separator [where you use a comma (,)]. If this statement is given, the output for numeric data and date will appear as per the entry of that country code in table T005X.

WRITE Statement – Associated Statements

NEW-PAGE: This statement is used to skip to a new page. You will deal with this in detail in Chapter 10, entitled 'Interactive Lists.'

NEW_LINE: To start a new line.

ULINE: To output horizontal lines, it is an alternative to WRITE SY-ULINE, etc. The horizontal line generated with ULINE statement will always start from a new line.

POSITION <column>: (absolute horizontal positioning) this is another way to start output from a specified column. The system field SY-COLNO is set to the <column> value after this statement. The system field SY-COLNO contains the current column number.

SKIP TO <line no>: (Absolute vertical positioning) This statement will skip to the absolute <line no>. The system field SY-LINNO is set to this value. The system field SY-LINNO contains the current line number. The SKIP statement skips line/s forward relative to current line number. The line number starts from 1 up to a maximum of value in SY-LINCT.

BACK: If this statement is given in the START-OF-SELECTION event, not following a RESERVE statement, it positions to the line after the header (i.e., the first line of the list body).

If this statement is given in the TOP-OF-PAGE event, the positioning is under the standard header.

If this statement is given in the START-OF-SELECTION event following a RESERVE statement, it positions to the first line after the RESERVE.

Output Formatting Options

Default Output Format of ABAP Predefined Elementary Types are shown in Table 5-3.

Table 5-3. *Default Output Format of ABAP Predefined Elementary Types*

Data Type	Output Length	Positioning	Remarks
C	Field Length	Left-Justified	Data Movement From Left To Right
D	8 Columns	Left-Justified	Data Movement From Left To Right
F	22 Columns Including Sign	Right-Justified	Data Movement From Right To Left
I	11 Columns Including Sign	Right-Justified	Data Movement From Right To Left
N	Field Length	Left-Justified	Data Movement From Left To Right
P	2 * Field Length In Bytes + 1 Including Sign	Right-Justified	Data Movement From Right To Left
T	6 Columns	Left-Justified	Data Movement From Left To Right
X	2 * Field Length In Bytes	Left-Justified	Data Movement From Left To Right
STRING	Length Of Data	Left-Justified	Data Movement From Left To Right
XSTRING	2 * Length Of Data In Bytes	Left-Justified	Data Movement From Left To Right

Output Formatting Options available For ABAP Predefined Elementary Types:

Table 5-4. *Output Formatting Options for All Types*

Formatting Option	Description
LEFT-JUSTIFIED	Output LEFT-JUSTIFIED If By Default Output Is RIGHT-JUSTIFIED, Requirement Is LEFT-JUSTIFIED
CENTERD	Output CENTERED
RIGHT-JUSTIFIED	Output RIGHT-JUSTIFIED. If By Default Output Is LEFT-JUSTIFIED, Requirement Is RIGHT-JUSTIFIED
UNDER <field>	Output Aligned With , Under Previously Output Field <field>
NO-GAP	The Default Blank Generated Between Two Fields Suppressed
USING EDIT MASK <mask>	Output Using The Format Template <mask>. Will be elaborated in Chapter 7.
USING NO EDIT MASK	Suppresses DDIC Format Template When Output. Will be further elaborated in Chapter 7.
NO-ZERO	Zeroes Are Replaced By Blanks In The Output. In TYPE C, N Fields, The Leading Zeroes Are Replaced By Blanks

Try out LEFT-JUSTIFIED, RIGHT-JUSTIFIED, CENTERED, and NO-ZERO as exercises.
Output Formatting Options available For Numeric ABAP Predefined Elementary Types: (TYPE F, I, P).

Table 5-5. *Output Formatting Options for Numeric Types – F, I, P*

Formatting Option	Description
NO-SIGN	Sign Is Not Output
DECIMALS <d>	The Number Of Decimals To Appear In The Output
EXPONENT <e>	For TYPE F, The Exponent Is Defined In <e> Normalize mantissa as per this value
ROUND <r>	For TYPE P, Multiplication Is Done By (10** -<r>) And Then Rounding Is Performed
CURRENCY <c>	Format AS Per The Entry Of Currency <c> In Table TCURX
UNIT <u>	The Number Of Decimal Places In The Output Is Fixed According To The Unit <u> In in Table T006 For Type P

Try out each one of these as exercises. For CURRENCY <c>, you should make the figure a whole number before it is output. In most SAP functional area tables, the amount fields (DDIC TYPE CURR: field NETWR in table VBRK) contain two digits after the decimal. For instance, suppose you want to output an amount figure as per Kuwaiti Dinar currency, with three digits after the decimal. You will multiply the DDIC TYPE CURR with 1000 or 10 to the power of the number of decimal digits in the currency you want to output and then output it. The following code communicates this description:

```
DATA: NETWR  TYPE VBRK-NETWR VALUE
              '123456.78', " VBRK-NETWR has two digits after decimal
      AMT(5) TYPE P . " in TYPE P, by default no of decimals is 0
*************************************
AMT = NETWR * 1000.

WRITE AMT CURRENCY 'KUD'. " Kuwaiti currency code, has entry in TCURX
```

This will generate the following output (three decimals digits as per 'KUD' record in table TCURX):

```
123456.780
```

Output Formatting Options available For ABAP Predefined Elementary Type D:

Table 5-6. *Output Formatting Options for Type D*

Formatting Option	Description
DD/MM/YY	Separator Character As Defined In User's Master Record
MM/DD/YY	Separator Character As Defined In User's Master Record
DD/MM/YYYY	Separator Character As Defined In User's Master Record
MM/DD/YYYY	Separator Character As Defined In User's Master Record
MMDDYY	No Separator Character
DDMMYY	No Separator Character
YYMMDD	No Separator Character

For ABAP predefined elementary TYPE D, you have used the CONCATENATE statement to format output in a much more flexible manner.

Conclusion

These are the major features of the WRITE statement used to generate classical lists (outputs). This is not all as there are 'Interactive Lists' in Chapter 10, also using the WRITE statement. In every other chapter, whenever you want to visually see the results of your operations, you will resort to the WRITE statement to produce them.

Chapters 12 and 13 will cover the deployment of OOP built-in classes to produce outputs - ALV reports (Lists).

CHAPTER 6

Internal Tables

Internal tables are complex data objects distinct from elementary data objects in an ABAP program. The earlier complex data objects covered were structures. An internal table is what is called a structured array in other platforms. Like its name suggests, it can store multiple rows of data, and it can grow and shrink dynamically during program execution. It exists only during the program's execution. An internal table can be a structured array or a simple array. Most often, it would be a structured array. In the SAP R/3 client server architecture, data will be retrieved and loaded from the database tables in large chunks into the internal tables (application server RAM) and processed from these internal tables. The database server should not be burdened with application processing. The database services are to be requisitioned selectively and infrequently for data maintenance, management, and retrieval. That is why retrieval of large chunks of data is preferred instead of frequent retrieval of small amounts of data; all of this is for better performance. The internal tables fit into this scenario.

The internal tables can be declared in many different ways, and the number of operations you can perform on the internal tables are a lot more compared to the structured arrays of the other platforms.

The internal tables are sometimes referred to as just "tables," but this should not cause confusion. The context will make it apparent that when the word "table" is used, the reference is to an internal table.

In this chapter, the internal table types and declarations are covered. You will learn the different ways to fill or load internal tables, how to process internal table data sequentially, and how to retrieve a row randomly. You will further learn how to change or update existing data in internal tables and how to delete data in internal tables. The use of internal tables to generate a multilevel summary is explained. The chapter concludes with statements to derive internal table attributes and initialize internal tables.

You will also know how to create and use the DDIC objects *structure* and *Table type*.

DDIC Object: Structure

You will be creating a DDIC structure first. Its usage is subsequently required in this chapter.

You can maintain DDIC structure through the third radio button on the SE11 *ABAP Dictionary* opening screen: the same radio button you used to maintain data elements. A third DDIC object the *Table type* is also maintained through this radio button. A DDIC structure or simply a structure, like its name suggests, is a bare definition. Unlike the DDIC table definition, this does not create any definition in the database metadata on activation. So it cannot be populated with any data.

It serves the purpose of being used in DDIC table definitions and other DDIC structures, *Table type* definitions, and referenced in ABAP programs.

You can check this out (DDIC structure used in DDIC table definitions) in the customer primary table KNA1. When you scroll down the fields in the KNA1 table, you will see the '.INCLUDE' as a field name under the column 'Field' and 'SI_KNA1' under the column 'Data element' (double-click on 'SI_KNA1' and view this structure). This is an instance of fields from a DDIC structure incorporated in a DDIC table definition. The incorporated fields appear in a blue color against the local fields (fields defined in the table definition) appearing in black. Through this concept of incorporating structure fields into a table definition, SAP customers can incorporate their own fields into SAP delivered tables. When SAP customers incorporate such fields into SAP delivered tables, it is an instance of enhancement (i.e., enhancement of SAP delivered objects). Like tables, most SAP delivered objects in the ABAP Workbench environment can be enhanced. However, enhancements are not covered in this book.

DDIC structure definitions are assigned to DDIC *Table type* (internal table) definitions. This will be apparent in the forthcoming topic 'Create DDIC Internal Table Type' of this chapter.

A DDIC structure definition is very similar to a DDIC table definition. A DDIC structure has no *Delivery and Maintenance* tab, and no *Technical Settings* button - these two relate to data. The DDIC structure definition can have search help attached to fields, have foreign key fields, and reference table and reference field columns for currency quantity fields.

Apart from being used in other tables, structure definitions and *Table type* definitions, a DDIC structure can be referenced to declare internal data objects in the ABAP programs. The SAP functional module entity data normally resides in multiple tables. The fields of the multiple tables can be included in one composite DDIC structure definition. This composite structure can be used to declare structured data in ABAP programs. This facilitates screen programming involving multiple tables and multiple screens.

Let's create a DDIC structure YCL_CH06_CUST_STRU consisting of the following customer data fields:

KUNNR	Customer Code
NAME1	Name
STRAS	Street
ORT01	City
PSTLZ	Postal Code

The entered fields with the data elements will appear as shown in Figure 6-1.

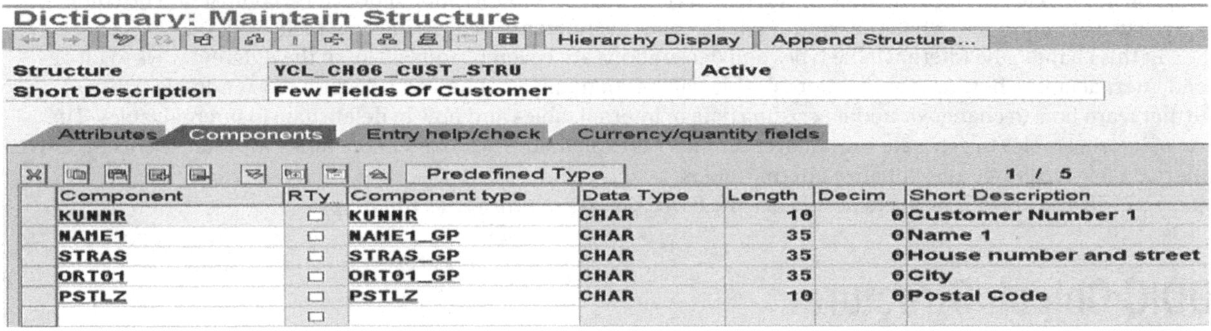

Dictionary: Maintain Structure

Hierarchy Display | Append Structure...

Structure: YCL_CH06_CUST_STRU — Active
Short Description: Few Fields Of Customer

Attributes | Components | Entry help/check | Currency/quantity fields

Predefined Type — 1 / 5

Component	RTy	Component type	Data Type	Length	Decim	Short Description
KUNNR	☐	KUNNR	CHAR	10	0	Customer Number 1
NAME1	☐	NAME1_GP	CHAR	35	0	Name 1
STRAS	☐	STRAS_GP	CHAR	35	0	House number and street
ORT01	☐	ORT01_GP	CHAR	35	0	City
PSTLZ	☐	PSTLZ	CHAR	10	0	Postal Code
	☐					

Figure 6-1. *DDIC Object Structure YCL_CH06_CUST_STRU*

You can use some other field names, but it is good practice to stick to the SAP standard names. The standard data elements have been assigned to these structure fields.

Set *Enhancement Category* to *Cannot Be Enhanced*, perform a consistency check, and activate the structure. You have now created a DDIC structure.

Internal Tables Declarations

You have two broad ways of declaring internal tables. First, the way internal tables were declared until SAP R/3 version 3.X (i.e., version 3 and all its subversions) and the way internal tables are declared from SAP R/3 version 4.0 onward. You will call the internal table declarations in the 3.X mode and 4.x mode of declaration. You are advised to use the 4.X mode of internal table declaration. In fact, within the ABAP OOPS environment (class definitions and implementations), the 3.X mode of internal table declaration is not supported. The 3.X mode of internal table declaration will be introduced first, so that you are exposed to it. You will then switch over to the 4.X mode of declaration and use the 4.X mode of declaration throughout the rest of the book.

Internal Tables – 3.X Mode of Declarations

The internal tables declared in 3.X mode are called the standard tables. What follows are different ways of declaring internal tables in 3.x mode. The roman numerals signify this.

Declaring the Internal Table and Structure Together

The simplest way of declaring an internal table in 3.X mode:

```
DATA: BEGIN OF <internal table name> OCCURS <number>,
       <field1>.........,
       <field2>.........,
        .....................
      END OF <internal table name>.
```

OCCURS <number>: The above declaration is somewhat like the way you declared structures in your programs until now, except that there is the addition OCCURS <number>. This addition is what makes it an internal table. The word 'OCCURS' is a reserved keyword. The <number> can be any small integer value, even zero. The <number> will determine the initial RAM allocation when the program starts execution. The internal table, of course, grows dynamically. The <number> also determines the incremental block of RAM allocated every time the internal table grows.

Two Data Objects with the Same Name: The declaration made above creates two data objects of the same name (i) a structure and (ii) an internal table. With two data objects with the same name, the issue of ambiguity arises. When a reference is made with this name, how do you know whether this is a reference to the internal table data object or to the structured data object? Most of the time, the system will resolve this ambiguity by context (i.e., certain ABAP statements operate only on the internal table while certain statements operate only on the structure). When statements are common to both types of data objects, you should add brackets ([]) after the data object name if you mean to refer to the internal table data object. A name without the brackets refers to the structure.

Example:

```
DATA: BEGIN OF CUSTOMER_TAB OCCURS 5,
        KUNNR TYPE KNA1-KUNNR,
        NAME1 TYPE KNA1-NAME1,
      END OF CUSTOMER_TAB.
```

This declaration creates an internal table and a structure using the same name: CUSTOMER_TAB.

You Declare an Internal Table by Referring to a Local/Global Structured TYPE or Local/Global Structure

(a global structure includes a database table and all kinds of views).

```
DATA <internal table name> {TYPE|LIKE} <structure name> OCCURS <number>.
```

```
<structure name> is either
```

a. A structured TYPE declared locally with the TYPES key word. The key word TYPE not LIKE should be used when referring to it.

Example:

```
* Internal table declared by referring to
* a local structure TYPE
TYPES: BEGIN OF CUSTOMER_STRU_TYPE,
         KUNNR TYPE KNA1-KUNNR,
         NAME1 TYPE KNA1-NAME1,
       END OF CUSTOMER_STRU_TYPE.

DATA: CUSTOMER_TAB TYPE CUSTOMER_STRU_TYPE OCCURS 5.
```

b. A structured TYPE declared in the DDIC object Type Group. The key word TYPE not LIKE should be used when referring to it.

Example:

```
* Internal table declared by referring to
* a DDIC structure TYPE in Type Group

TYPE-POOLS YCLG1.
DATA: CUSTOMER_TAB TYPE YCLG1_CUSTOMER_TYPE OCCURS 5.
```

A TYPE YCLG1_CUSTOMER_TYPE has been created in the Type Group YCLG1 as shown in Figure 6-2.

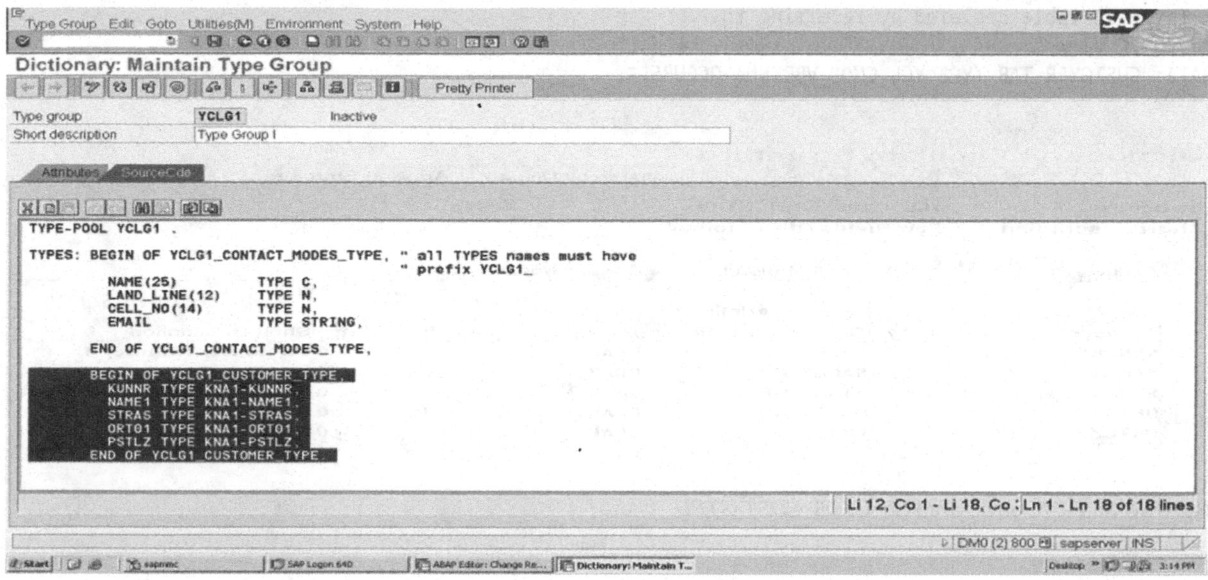

Figure 6-2. *{TYPE YCLG1_CUSTOMER_TYPE in Type Group YCLG1 [highlighted]*

c. A structure declared locally. The key word LIKE, not TYPE, should be used when referring to it.

Example:

```
* Internal table declared by referring to
* a local structure
DATA:  BEGIN OF CUSTOMER_STRU,
         KUNNR TYPE KNA1-KUNNR,
         NAME1 TYPE KNA1-NAME1,
       END OF CUSTOMER_STRU.

DATA: CUSTOMER_TAB LIKE CUSTOMER_STRU OCCURS 5.
```

Next let's look at a structure created in a DDIC data type or a database table or a view. The key words TYPE or LIKE can be used when referring to it.

Examples:

```
* Internal table declared by referring to
* a DDIC structure
DATA: CUSTOMER_TAB TYPE YCL_CH06_CUST_STRU OCCURS 5.
```

A DDIC type structure YCL_CH06_CUST_STRU is shown in Figure 6-3.

```
* Internal table declared by referring to
* a DDIC table definition
DATA: CUSTOMER_TAB TYPE KNA1 OCCURS 5.
```

```
* Internal table declared by referring to
* a DDIC view
DATA: CUSTOMER_TAB TYPE YCL_CH05_VBRKKNA OCCURS 5.
```

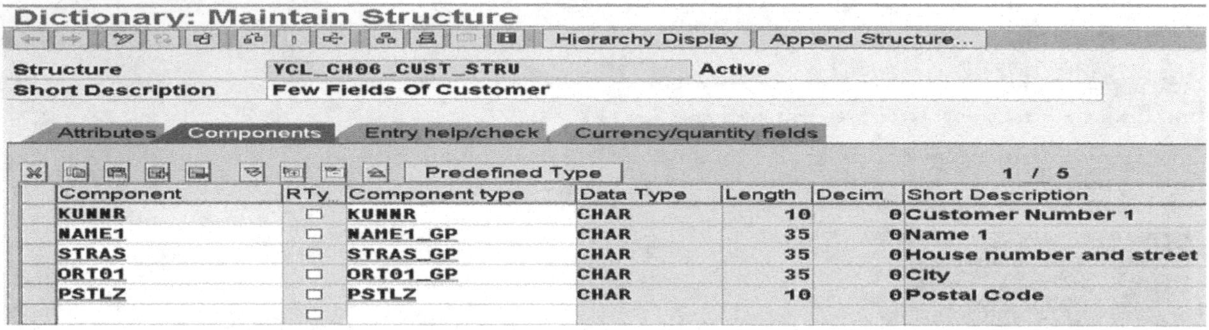

Dictionary: Maintain Structure

Hierarchy Display | Append Structure...

Structure: YCL_CH06_CUST_STRU — Active

Short Description: Few Fields Of Customer

Attributes | Components | Entry help/check | Currency/quantity fields

Predefined Type — 1 / 5

Component	RTy.	Component type	Data Type	Length	Decim.	Short Description
KUNNR	☐	KUNNR	CHAR	10	0	Customer Number 1
NAME1	☐	NAME1_GP	CHAR	35	0	Name 1
STRAS	☐	STRAS_GP	CHAR	35	0	House number and street
ORT01	☐	ORT01_GP	CHAR	35	0	City
PSTLZ	☐	PSTLZ	CHAR	10	0	Postal Code
	☐					

Figure 6-3. *DDIC Structure YCL_CH06_CUST_STRU*

Declaring Both an Internal Table and a Structure by Referring to a Structured Local/Global TYPE or Local/Global Structure

(global structure includes a database table and all kinds of views)

All considerations of II apply here except that you are creating two data objects of the same name (i) an internal table and (ii) a structure:

```
DATA <internal table name> {TYPE|LIKE} <structure name> OCCURS <number>
WITH HEADER LINE.
```

WITH HEADER LINE is a reserved key phrase. The addition of this phrase creates a structure. A declaration without this phrase as in II creates only an internal table. The ambiguity issue is resolved in the same way as in I.

Examples:

You could add the phrase *WITH HEADER LINE* to the examples of II and derive examples for this mode of internal table declaration.

Declaring Nonstructured Internal Tables (Simple Arrays)

The nonstructured internal tables can be declared by referring to elementary data type (local/global), data object (local/global), and data element.

Examples:

```
* non-structure internal table referring to local TYPE
TYPES STR_TYPE(10) TYPE C.
DATA STR_TAB TYPE STR_TYPE OCCURS 5 WITH HEADER LINE.

* non-structure Internal table declared by referring to
* a DDIC structure TYPE field in Type Group
```

```
TYPE-POOLS YCLG1.
DATA: STR_TAB TYPE YCLG1_CUSTOMER_TYPE-KUNNR OCCURS 5.

* non-structure internal table referring to local data object
DATA: STRNG(10) TYPE C,
      STR_TAB LIKE STRNG OCCURS 5.

* non-structure internal table referring to global data object
DATA: STR_TAB LIKE KNA1-KUNNR OCCURS 5 WITH HEADER LINE.

* non-structure internal table referring to DDIC data element
DATA: STR_TAB TYPE KUNNR OCCURS 5. " KUNNR is data element
```

Declaring a Structure by Referring to an Internal Table

Example:

```
* a structure declaration by referring to
* an internal table
TYPES: BEGIN OF CUSTOMER_STRU_TYPE,
        KUNNR TYPE KNA1-KUNNR,
         NAME1 TYPE KNA1-NAME1,
       END OF CUSTOMER_STRU_TYPE.
DATA: CUSTOMER_TAB  TYPE CUSTOMER_STRU_TYPE OCCURS 5,
CUSTOMER_STRU LIKE LINE OF CUSTOMER_TAB.
```

CUSTOMER_STRU is declared by referring to the internal table CUSTOMER_TAB. The phrase LIKE LINE OF here means LIKE the structure of internal table. The declared structure will have the same fields as the internal table structure.

The structures used with internal tables are often referred to as work areas. A structure with the same name as an internal table is often referred to as a header line.

Hands-On Exercise: List of Billing Documents of a Specified Company Code

You will repeat the exercise of Chapter 5 that used the SELECT...ENDSELECT loop with the view YCL_CH05_VBRKKNA. This view contains fields from the tables KNA1 and VBRK. Now, you will load date from this view into an internal table and process from the internal table.

You will declare an internal table with the notation BEGIN OF...OCCURS... END OF.... (Internal table and structure are created with this declaration). You will load this internal table with data from the view with a variation of the SELECT statement. As you are not fetching one row at a time from the view, this will not be a looping repetitive construct of the SELECT statement.

Once the internal table is loaded with data, you have to fetch data row by row from the internal table into a structure and output it from structure fields using the WRITE statement.

The process of loading an internal table from a database table/view and processing it row by row from the internal table into a structure is represented in Figure 6-4.

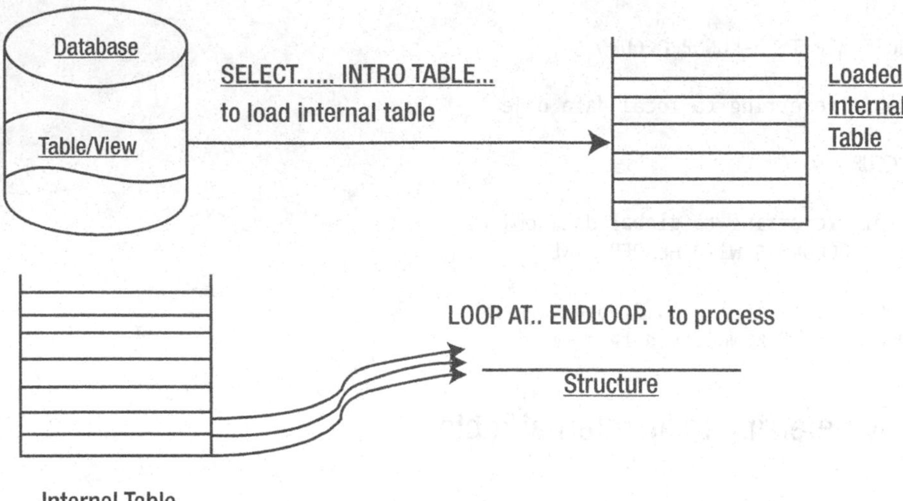

Figure 6-4. *Load Internal Table from Database Table/View & Process in LOOP..ENDLOOP Construct*

An internal table construct LOOP AT...ENDLOOP somewhat a parallel to the SELECT...ENDSELECT is available for a row by row processing. A simple syntax of this internal table construct is like:

```
LOOP AT <internal table name> into <structure name>.
 <statement block>
ENDLOOP.
```

Your output body will have the layout in Table 6-1 (from Chapter 5).

Table 6-1. *Output Body Layout*

Field Name	Table Name	Description	Column Positions
SY-TABIX	System Field	Serial No.	005,009 (5)
			010
VBELN	VBRK	Billing Document No.	011,020 (10)
			021
FKDAT	VBRK	Billing Document Date	022,031 (10)
			032
KUNNR	KNA1	Customer Code	033-042 (10)
			043
NAME1	KNA1	Name	044-078 (35)
			079
ORT01	KNA1	City	080-114 (35)
			115
NETWR	VBRK	Billing Document Net Value (Converted to Company Code Currency)	116-132 (17)

You have declared the internal table with only the required fields: that is, the fields appearing in the output and the field KURRF (exchange rate) to convert all amounts to the operating currency of the company code. You don't need the field BUKRS (company code) from the view, though you are specifying it in the WHERE condition of the SELECT statement.

The data is transferred from view to internal table with the SELECT statement variation. You are using the key phrase INTO TABLE and specifying the internal table name next.

The LOOP AT statement fetches one row at a time from the internal table into the structure starting from the first row, then the second row overwriting the existing contents of the structure, and so on until all the rows have been fetched from the internal table. When all rows are fetched, the control will fall to the statement next to the ENDLOOP statement if any, or else it will exit the program. There are few variations in the LOOP AT statement. You can specify a WHERE condition and you can specify a starting row to fetch from and an ending row to conclude the fetching. You need not fetch a row into a structure as you can directly refer to the data in a row.

When the internal table name and the destination structure name (following the INTO key word) are the same, the INTO <destination/structure name> can be dropped and the destination is implicit. Inside classes this implicitness is disallowed. And it is a good practice to mention the destination explicitly.

The order of the fields in the SELECT statement and the internal table structure must be identical. The internal table structure must not contain any other fields. Each of the fields in the table structure must be identical to the corresponding field in the SELECT statement <result> in terms of type, length, etc.

You were using in your Chapter 5 program the system field SY-DBCNT in the SELECT...ENDSELECT loop. This contained the current number of the row of data fetched. You can no longer use this. You are now processing row by row from an internal table in a LOOP...ENDLOOP construct. In your present program, you are loading the internal table from the view in one go. The system field SY-DBCNT after the SELECT...INTO TABLE...has been executed will contain the total number of rows loaded into the internal table.

You need a serial number for the list. You can always declare a numeric data object (type I, N, P) and increment it before the WRITE statement and output it, but you have a system field relating to internal table operations parallel to the SY-DBCNT. This is the system field SY-TABIX. Within the LOOP...ENDLOOP construct, it contains the number of the row fetched. So you can use this to output the serial number. The system field SY-TABIX is of type I.

Copy and activate the text symbols from the Chapter 5 program into the current program using the transaction code SE32.

The rest of the code is same as in Chapter 5. The source code for generating the Billing Document list using an internal table:

```
REPORT YCL_CH06_ITAB01 LINE-SIZE 135 LINE-COUNT 60
      NO STANDARD PAGE HEADING.

*****************************************************************
* List of Billing Documents of a Specified Company Code with Total **
*****************************************************************
****************************************************************
* declare internal table in 3.X mode:BEGIN OF <itab> OCCURS <n>. **
*                                ..                            **
*                               END OF ,itab>                  **
*                                                              **
* PARAMETERS CCODE TYPE VBRK-BUKRS VALUE CHECK DEFAULT 3000    **
* to select company code                                       **
*                                                              **
* get BUTXT WAERS from T001 - SELECT SINGLE etc.               **
*                                                              **
* load the internal table from the view  YCL_CH05_VBRKKNA      **
* with SELECT <fields> from YCL_CH05_VBRKKNA INTO TABLE <itab>  **
*      WHERE BUKRS = CCODE.                                     **
*                                                              **
```

```
*  set LOOP AT <itab> into <itab>.                                  **
*     calculate amount in operating currency of chosen CCODE        **
*     WRITE...                                                      **
*     build total                                                   **
*    ENDLOOP.                                                       **
*                                                                   **
*  output total                                                     **
*                                                                   **
*********************************************************************
TABLES: T001. " local structure with all fields of T001

DATA: BEGIN OF BILL_DOCS_TAB OCCURS 5,
       VBELN  TYPE YCL_CH05_VBRKKNA-VBELN,
       FKDAT  TYPE YCL_CH05_VBRKKNA-FKDAT,
       KUNNR  TYPE YCL_CH05_VBRKKNA-KUNNR,
       NAME1  TYPE YCL_CH05_VBRKKNA-NAME1,
       ORT01  TYPE YCL_CH05_VBRKKNA-ORT01,
       NETWR  TYPE YCL_CH05_VBRKKNA-NETWR,
       KURRF  TYPE YCL_CH05_VBRKKNA-KURRF,
      END OF BILL_DOCS_TAB,

      STRNG     TYPE STRING,
      TOTAL     TYPE VBRK-NETWR.

PARAMETERS CCODE  TYPE VBRK-BUKRS DEFAULT 3000 VALUE CHECK.
                  " the clause VALUE CHECK will check values
                  " in the primary table of this foreign key field
**********************************************************************
TOP-OF-PAGE.

WRITE :/5 STRNG, 129(3) SY-PAGNO. " STRNG - refer CONCATENATE statement in
                                  " START-OF-SELECTION
SKIP 1.
WRITE:/5(127) SY-ULINE.
WRITE:/5 TEXT-003,11 TEXT-004, 22 TEXT-005, 33 TEXT-006, 46 TEXT-007,
         83 TEXT-008, 126 TEXT-009.

WRITE:/6 TEXT-010, 35 TEXT-011.
WRITE:/5(127) SY-ULINE.

**********************************************************************
START-OF-SELECTION.

SELECT SINGLE * FROM T001 WHERE BUKRS = CCODE." fetches a single row, no
                                               " loop construct SELECT
                                               " ENDSELECT

CONCATENATE TEXT-001 CCODE '/' T001-BUTXT TEXT-002 T001-WAERS INTO STRNG.
```

```
SELECT VBELN FKDAT KUNNR NAME1 ORT01 NETWR KURRF FROM
  YCL_CH05_VBRKKNA INTO  " dumps filtered full data from
  TABLE BILL_DOCS_TAB    " view into the internal table
  WHERE BUKRS = CCODE.

*********************************************************************
LOOP AT BILL_DOCS_TAB INTO BILL_DOCS_TAB.

 BILL_DOCS_TAB-NETWR = BILL_DOCS_TAB-NETWR * BILL_DOCS_TAB-KURRF.

 WRITE:/5(5) SY-TABIX, BILL_DOCS_TAB-VBELN, BILL_DOCS_TAB-FKDAT,
             BILL_DOCS_TAB-KUNNR, BILL_DOCS_TAB-NAME1,
             BILL_DOCS_TAB-ORT01, (17) BILL_DOCS_TAB-NETWR.

 TOTAL = TOTAL + BILL_DOCS_TAB-NETWR.

ENDLOOP.
********************************

END-OF-SELECTION.
SKIP 1.

WRITE: /(17) TOTAL UNDER BILL_DOCS_TAB-NETWR. " the field TOTAL will
                                               " be output
                                               " UNDER NETWR.
```

The outputs will look like Figures 6-5 and 6-6.

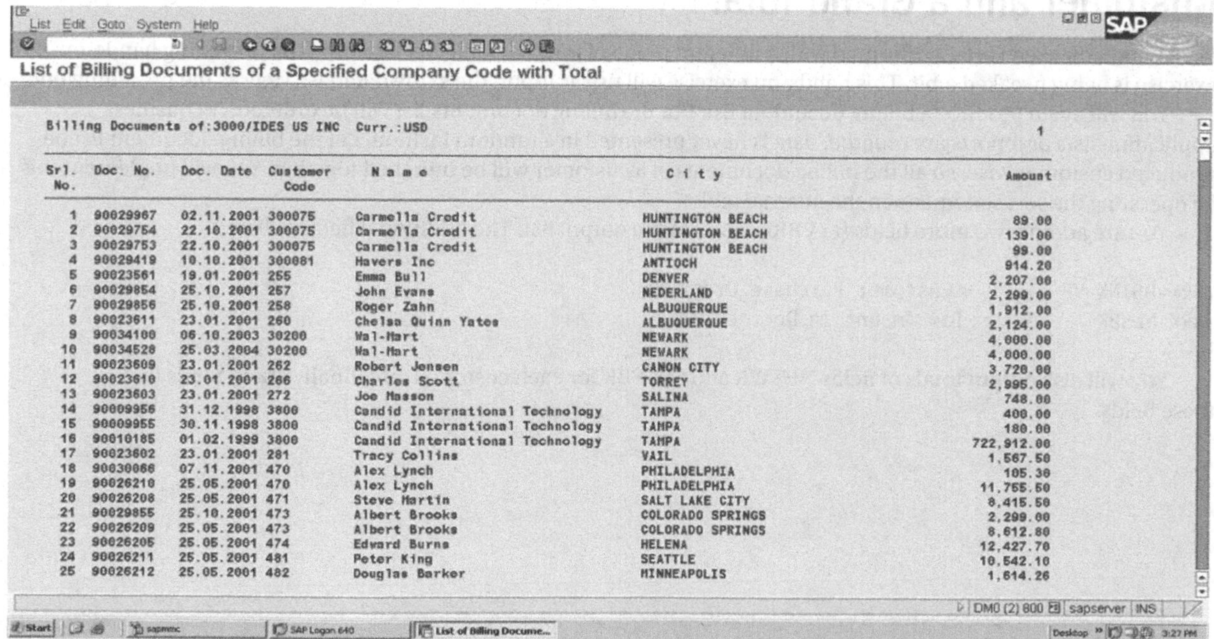

Srl. No.	Doc. No.	Doc. Date	Customer Code	N a m e	C i t y	Amount
1	90029967	02.11.2001	300075	Carmella Credit	HUNTINGTON BEACH	89.00
2	90029754	22.10.2001	300075	Carmella Credit	HUNTINGTON BEACH	139.00
3	90029753	22.10.2001	300075	Carmella Credit	HUNTINGTON BEACH	99.00
4	90029419	10.10.2001	300081	Havers Inc	ANTIOCH	914.20
5	90023561	19.01.2001	255	Emma Bull	DENVER	2,207.00
6	90029854	25.10.2001	257	John Evans	NEDERLAND	2,299.00
7	90029856	25.10.2001	258	Roger Zahn	ALBUQUERQUE	1,912.00
8	90023611	23.01.2001	260	Chelsa Quinn Yates	ALBUQUERQUE	2,124.00
9	90034100	06.10.2003	30200	Wal-Mart	NEWARK	4,000.00
10	90034528	25.03.2004	30200	Wal-Mart	NEWARK	4,000.00
11	90023609	23.01.2001	262	Robert Jensen	CANON CITY	3,720.00
12	90023610	23.01.2001	266	Charles Scott	TORREY	2,995.00
13	90023603	23.01.2001	272	Joe Masson	SALINA	748.00
14	90009956	31.12.1998	3800	Candid International Technology	TAMPA	400.00
15	90009955	30.11.1998	3800	Candid International Technology	TAMPA	180.00
16	90010185	01.02.1999	3800	Candid International Technology	TAMPA	722,912.00
17	90023602	23.01.2001	281	Tracy Collins	VAIL	1,567.50
18	90030066	07.11.2001	470	Alex Lynch	PHILADELPHIA	105.30
19	90026210	25.05.2001	470	Alex Lynch	PHILADELPHIA	11,765.50
20	90026208	25.05.2001	471	Steve Martin	SALT LAKE CITY	8,415.50
21	90029855	25.10.2001	473	Albert Brooks	COLORADO SPRINGS	2,299.00
22	90026209	25.05.2001	473	Albert Brooks	COLORADO SPRINGS	8,612.80
23	90026205	25.05.2001	474	Edward Burns	HELENA	12,427.70
24	90026211	25.05.2001	481	Peter King	SEATTLE	10,542.10
25	90026212	25.05.2001	482	Douglas Barker	MINNEAPOLIS	1,614.26

Figure 6-5. *Output of Program YCL_CH06_ITAB01*

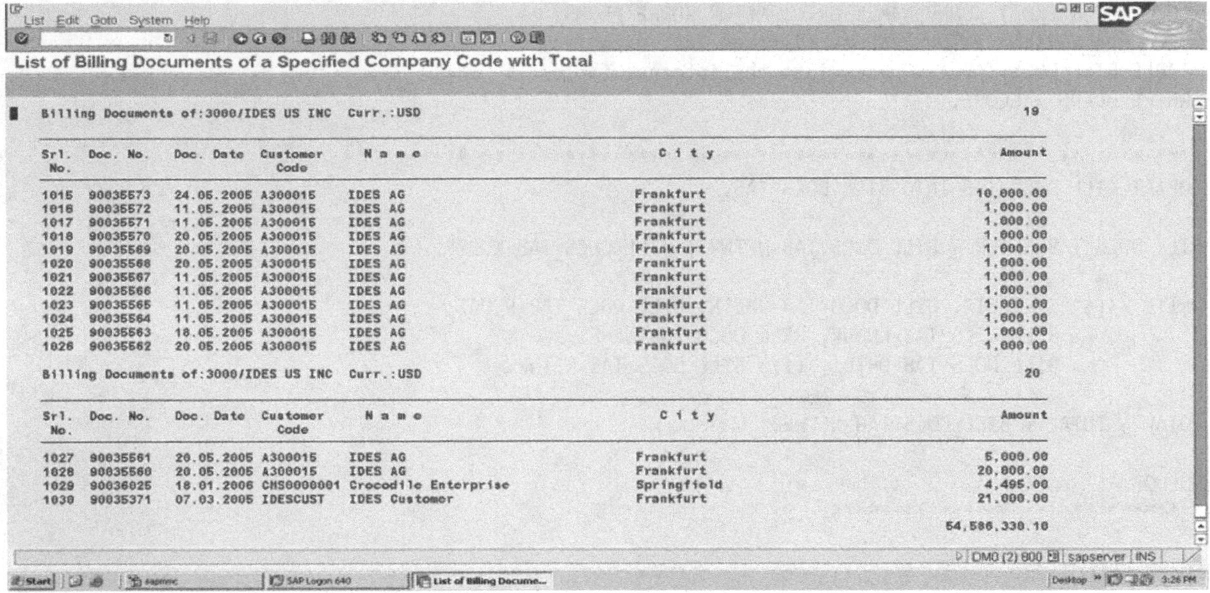

Figure 6-6. Output of Program YCL_CH06_ITAB01 - Grand Total

Hands-On Exercise: Customer Code Wise List of Billing Documents of a Specified Company Code with Totals for Every Customer and a Grand Total

Let a hands-on exercise be performed with a different mode of internal table declaration. The preceding hands-on exercise is being tweaked a bit. This hands-on exercise will use as input, the same database view as the preceding one.

You will again produce a billing document list. But the billing documents list will be ordered. All business application lists or reports are ordered: data is never presented in a random fashion. Let the billing document list be produced customer wise, so all the billing documents of a customer will be bunched together. You will implement this by operating the sort statement on the internal table.

You are adding two more fields (of VBRK table) to the output list. The additional fields will be:

```
VBRK-BSTNK_VF         Customer Purchase Order No
VBRK-MWSBK           Tax Amount in Doc. Currency
```

You will also output totals of fields NETWR and MWSBK for each customer, and finally grand totals for these fields.

You can either create a new database view with these additional fields incorporated or add these two fields to the existing database view YCL_CH05_VBRKKNA. Since you are building totals to output them, you will convert the billing document amounts (net value & tax) into the operating currency of the company code. A rough layout of your output:

```
List of Billing Documents of Company Code: XXXX/XXXXXXXXXXXXXXXXXXXXXXXXX Page: XX
                                 Currency: XXXXX

-------------------------------------------------------------------------------
Srl.  Doc.No.    Doc. Date   Customer Order No.              Amount    Tax Amount
No.
-------------------------------------------------------------------------------
Customer: XXXXXXXXXX/XXXXXXXXXXXXXXXXXXXXXXXXXXXXXXXXXXX

XXXXX XXXXXXXXXX XX/XX/XXXX  XXXXXXXXXXXXXXXXXXXX        XXXXXXXXXX.XX  XXXXXXXX.XX
...................
...................

                                     Total for Customer  XXXXXXXXXX.XX  XXXXXXXXX.XX

Customer: XXXXXXXXXX/XXXXXXXXXXXXXXXXXXXXXXXXXXXXXXXXXXX
............
............
```

Study this layout carefully. You have planned to have all the billing documents of a customer bunched in the output. So you need not output customer info in the regular output body as columns with column headings: the same values will repeat again and again. The customer information (KUNNR, NAME1) is planned to be output as a subheading. The data in the internal table is sorted in ascending order of the field KUNNR. You should build the logic in a way that when a customer changes, output the total for the previous customer, next output the code and name of the current customer; then the billing documents for the current customer will follow as the list body.

The serial number is not a running serial number; it is a serial number of a billing document for a customer. For every customer, it will commence from 1. Hence a variable CNT (type I) is declared. The variable CNT is incremented before the WRITE statement of a billing document and initialized before output for the next customer starts (SY-TABIX will not serve this present context).

The list body layout:

Table 6-2. Output Body Layout

Field Name	Table Name	Description	Column Positions
CNT	Program Field	Serial No.	005,009 (5)
			010
VBELN	VBRK	Billing Document No.	011,020 (10)
			021
FKDAT	VBRK	Billing Document Date	022,031 (10)
			032
BSTNK_VF	VBRK	Customer Purchase Order No.	033-067 (35)
			068
NETWR	VBRK	Billing Document Net Value (Converted to Company Code Currency)	069-085 (17)
			086
MWSBK	VBRK	Tax (Converted to Company Code Currency)	087-100 (14)

Create, perform syntax check and activate the program. Create and activate the text symbols. The source code to generate the output:

```
REPORT YCL_CH06_ITAB02 LINE-SIZE 105 LINE-COUNT 60
      NO STANDARD PAGE HEADING.

************************************************************************
* Customer Wise List of Billing Documents of a Specified Company Code **
************************************************************************
*******************************************************************
* declare internal table in 3.X mode:                            **
*                <itab> TYPE <database view name> OCCURS <n>.     **
*                                                                **
* declare structure <structure name> TYPE <database view name>.  **
*                                                                **
* PARAMETERS CCODE TYPE VBRK-BUKRS VALUE CHECK DEFAULT 3000      **
* to select company code                                         **
*                                                                **
* get BUTXT WAERS from T001 - SELECT SINGLE etc.                 **
*                                                                **
* load the internal table from the view YCL_CH05_VBRKKNA         **
* with SELECT * from YCL_CH05_VBRKKNA INTO TABLE <itab>          **
*       WHERE BUKRS = CCODE.                                     **
*                                                                **
* SORT <itab> BY KUNNR ASCENDING                                 **
*                                                                **
* set LOOP AT <itab> into <structure name>.                      **
*                                                                **
```

```
*       check for customer change. if change output totals for    **
*        previous customer, output current customer info          **
*                                                                 **
*       calculate amount in operating currency of chosen CCODE    **
*                                                                 **
*       WRITE...                                                  **
*                                                                 **
*       build customer totals, grand totals                       **
*                                                                 **
*      ENDLOOP.                                                   **
*                                                                 **
*  output customer total, grand total                             **
*                                                                 **
*******************************************************************
TABLES: T001.

DATA: BILL_DOCS_TAB  TYPE YCL_CH05_VBRKKNA OCCURS 5, " reference to view
      BILL_DOCS_STRU TYPE YCL_CH05_VBRKKNA, " reference to view
      CNT            TYPE I, "count of billing docs of a customer
      PREV_KUNNR     TYPE KNA1-KUNNR, " previous KUNNR
      CTOTAL         TYPE VBRK-NETWR, " customer net value total
      CTAX_TOTAL     TYPE VBRK-MWSBK, " customer tax total
      GTOTAL         TYPE VBRK-NETWR, " grand net value total
      GTAX_TOTAL     TYPE VBRK-MWSBK. " grand tax total

PARAMETERS CCODE  TYPE VBRK-BUKRS DEFAULT 3000 VALUE CHECK.
*******************************************************************
TOP-OF-PAGE.

WRITE :/5  TEXT-001, CCODE NO-GAP, '/' NO-GAP, T001-BUTXT,
        93  TEXT-003, 98(3) SY-PAGNO.
WRITE :/33 TEXT-002, T001-WAERS.
SKIP 1.
WRITE:/5(96) SY-ULINE.

WRITE:/5 TEXT-004,11 TEXT-005, 22 TEXT-006, 33 TEXT-007,
        79 TEXT-008, 91 TEXT-009.
WRITE:/6 TEXT-010, 34 TEXT-011.

WRITE:/5(96) SY-ULINE.

*******************************************************************
START-OF-SELECTION.

SELECT SINGLE * FROM T001 WHERE BUKRS = CCODE." fetches a single row, no
                                               " loop construct SELECT
                                               " ENDSELECT

SELECT * FROM
  YCL_CH05_VBRKKNA INTO                        " dumps filtered full data from
  TABLE BILL_DOCS_TAB                          " view into the internal table
  WHERE BUKRS = CCODE.
```

```
SORT BILL_DOCS_TAB BY KUNNR ASCENDING. " SORT table on the field KUNNR
                                       " in ASCENDING order
*****************************************************************
LOOP AT BILL_DOCS_TAB INTO BILL_DOCS_STRU.

 IF BILL_DOCS_STRU-KUNNR <> PREV_KUNNR .

  IF CNT > 1 AND SY-TABIX > 1.

   FORMAT INVERSE COLOR COL_GROUP. " customer total-different color
   WRITE: /(17) CTOTAL UNDER BILL_DOCS_STRU-NETWR,
          (15) CTAX_TOTAL UNDER BILL_DOCS_STRU-MWSBK.
   FORMAT RESET. " restore default colors
  ENDIF.

  IF SY-TABIX > 1.
   SKIP.
   CTOTAL = 0.
   CTAX_TOTAL = 0.
   CNT = 0.
  ENDIF.

  FORMAT INVERSE COLOR COL_POSITIVE. "customer info-different color
  WRITE:/5 TEXT-011, BILL_DOCS_STRU-KUNNR USING NO EDIT MASK,
           BILL_DOCS_STRU-NAME1.
  FORMAT RESET. " restore default colors

 ENDIF.

 BILL_DOCS_STRU-NETWR = BILL_DOCS_STRU-NETWR * BILL_DOCS_STRU-KURRF.
 BILL_DOCS_STRU-MWSBK = BILL_DOCS_STRU-MWSBK * BILL_DOCS_STRU-KURRF.

 CNT = CNT + 1.
 WRITE:/5(5) CNT, BILL_DOCS_STRU-VBELN, BILL_DOCS_STRU-FKDAT,
             BILL_DOCS_STRU-BSTNK_VF, (17) BILL_DOCS_STRU-NETWR,
             (15) BILL_DOCS_STRU-MWSBK.

 GTOTAL = GTOTAL + BILL_DOCS_STRU-NETWR.
 CTOTAL = CTOTAL + BILL_DOCS_STRU-NETWR.

 GTAX_TOTAL = GTAX_TOTAL + BILL_DOCS_STRU-MWSBK.
 CTAX_TOTAL = CTAX_TOTAL + BILL_DOCS_STRU-MWSBK.

 PREV_KUNNR = BILL_DOCS_STRU-KUNNR.

ENDLOOP.
********************************

END-OF-SELECTION.

IF CNT > 1.
```

```
 FORMAT INVERSE COLOR COL_GROUP. " customer total-different color
 WRITE: /(17) CTOTAL UNDER BILL_DOCS_STRU-NETWR,
         (15) CTAX_TOTAL UNDER BILL_DOCS_STRU-MWSBK.

ENDIF.

SKIP 1.

FORMAT INVERSE COLOR COL_TOTAL. " grand total-different color

WRITE: /(17) GTOTAL UNDER BILL_DOCS_STRU-NETWR,
        (15) GTAX_TOTAL UNDER BILL_DOCS_STRU-MWSBK.
```

- The customer info (BILLS_STRU-KUNNR, BILLS_STRU-NAME1) are output in a different color (COL_POSITIVE).
- The customer wise totals (CTOTAL, CTAX_TOTAL) are output in a different color (COL_GROUP).
- The grand totals (GTOTAL, GTAX_TOTAL) are output in a different color (COL_TOTAL).

For the rest of the info, you are using the default color, hence the FORMAT RESET statement.

If a customer has only one billing document, that is, CNT = 1, customer wise totals are not output. The rest of the logic should be okay! The output will appear like Figures 6-7 and 6-8.

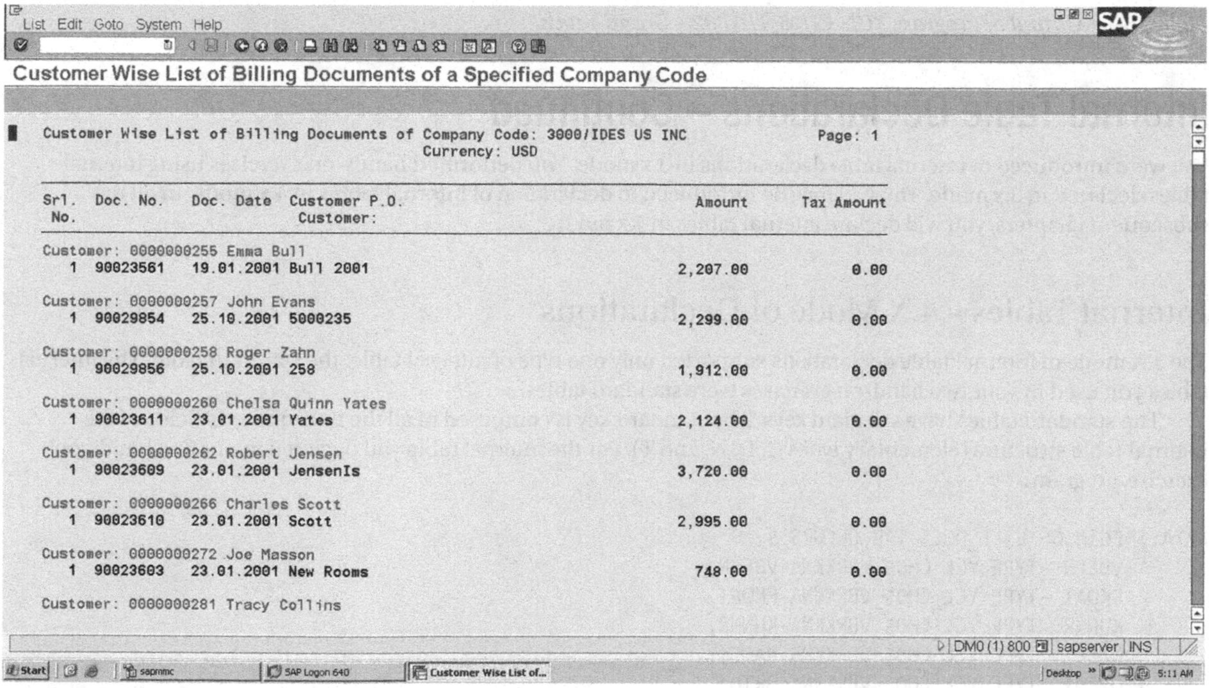

```
List  Edit  Goto  System  Help
Customer Wise List of Billing Documents of a Specified Company Code

 Customer Wise List of Billing Documents of Company Code: 3000/IDES US INC          Page: 1
                                         Currency: USD

 Srl.  Doc. No.   Doc. Date  Customer P.O.                     Amount       Tax Amount
 No.                         Customer:

 Customer: 0000000255 Emma Bull
    1  90023561   19.01.2001 Bull 2001                       2,207.00            0.00

 Customer: 0000000257 John Evans
    1  90029854   25.10.2001 5000235                         2,299.00            0.00

 Customer: 0000000258 Roger Zahn
    1  90029856   25.10.2001 258                             1,912.00            0.00

 Customer: 0000000260 Chelsa Quinn Yates
    1  90023611   23.01.2001 Yates                           2,124.00            0.00

 Customer: 0000000262 Robert Jensen
    1  90023609   23.01.2001 JensenIs                        3,720.00            0.00

 Customer: 0000000266 Charles Scott
    1  90023610   23.01.2001 Scott                           2,995.00            0.00

 Customer: 0000000272 Joe Masson
    1  90023603   23.01.2001 New Rooms                         748.00            0.00

 Customer: 0000000281 Tracy Collins
```

Figure 6-7. *Output of Program YCL_CH06_ITAB02*

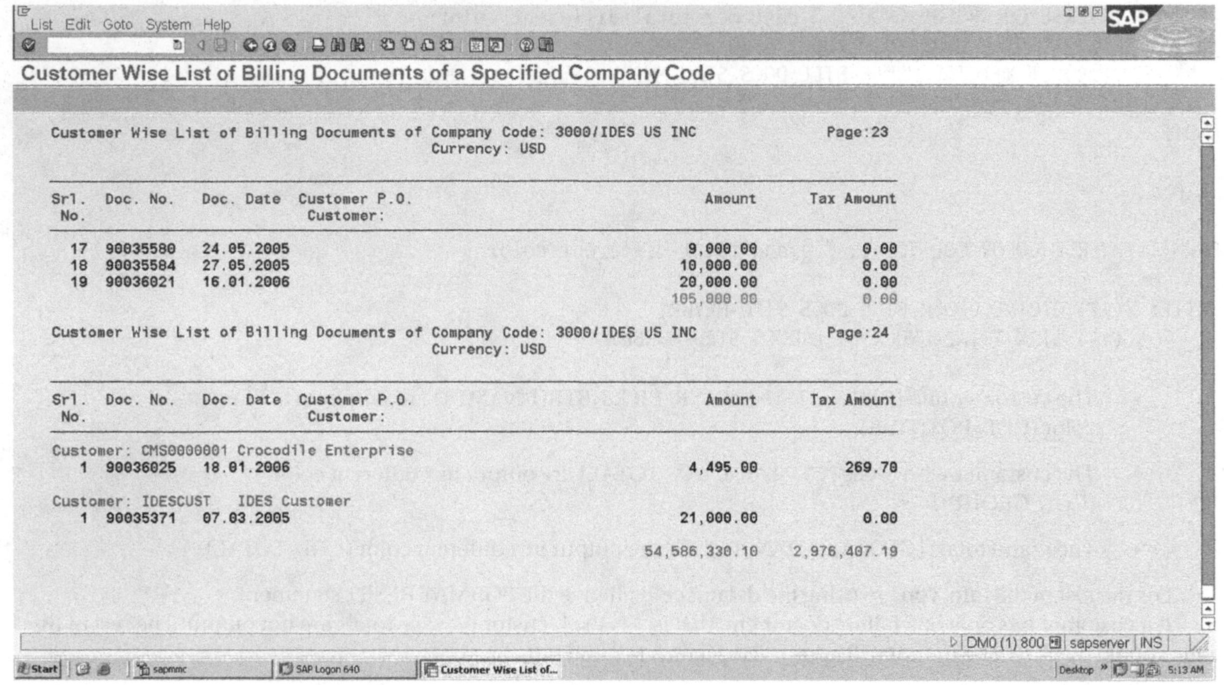

Figure 6-8. *Output of Program YCL_CH06_ITAB02 - Grand Totals*

Internal Table Declarations – Continued

You were introduced to internal table declarations in 3.x mode. You performed hands-on exercises using internal tables declared in 3.x mode. You will now be introduced to declaration of internal tables in 4.x mode. In all the subsequent chapters, you will declare internal tables in 4.x mode.

Internal Tables - 4.X Mode of Declarations

The 3.X mode of internal table declarations supported only one type of internal table: the standard table. The internal tables you used in your two hand-on exercises were standard tables.

The standard tables have standard keys. The standard key is composed of all the non-numeric fields of the internal table structure (elementary types C, D, N, and T). For the internal table you declared in our first hands-on exercise program:

```
DATA: BEGIN OF BILL_DOCS_TAB OCCURS 5,
       VBELN  TYPE YCL_CH05_VBRKKNA-VBELN,
       FKDAT  TYPE YCL_CH05_VBRKKNA-FKDAT,
       KUNNR  TYPE YCL_CH05_VBRKKNA-KUNNR,
       NAME1  TYPE YCL_CH05_VBRKKNA-NAME1,
       ORT01  TYPE YCL_CH05_VBRKKNA-ORT01,
       NETWR  TYPE YCL_CH05_VBRKKNA-NETWR,
       KURRF  TYPE YCL_CH05_VBRKKNA-KURRF,
      END OF BILL_DOCS_TAB,
```

The standard key of this internal table is VBELN, FKDAT, KUNNR, NAME1, and ORT01.

The 4.X mode of internal table declarations support the standard tables as well as two additional internal table types: the sorted tables and the hashed tables.

Internal Tables Features, Attributes

Key

A standard table can have the default/standard key (all fields of TYPES C, D, N, and T) or a defined key. The key fields of a defined key are specified with the table declaration. A standard table supports only a NON-UNIQUE defined key. Rows with duplicate key values can exist in standard tables.

Sorted and hashed tables can have only defined keys. The key fields are a mandatory part of table declaration for sorted and hashed tables.

A sorted table can be declared with UNIQUE KEY or with NON-UNIQUE KEY. If a sorted table has been declared with UNIQUE KEY, rows with duplicate key values cannot exist. If a sorted table is declared with NON-UNIQUE KEY, rows with duplicate key values can exist.

A hashed table can be declared only with UNIQUE KEY. Rows with duplicate key values cannot exist in the hashed internal table.

Search Method

There is an internal table statement

```
READ TABLE <internal table name> WITH TABLE KEY <k1> = <f1>
 ...INTO <structure name>.
```

This statement searches for a row on the basis of the key field values provided through <k1> = <f1>. If located, it fetches the row into the <structure name>.

In the standard tables, the searching for the row with the provided key field values is by default a linear search. The search will commence from the first row and will continue until a row is located with provided key field values or the search concludes with the last row without locating a row with the provided key field values. The access time in linear search is dependent on the number of rows in the internal table. For the standard tables, you can specify a binary search method with the READ statement, but it is your responsibility to ensure that the table is sorted in ascending order of key fields specified in the READ statement. If the internal table is not ordered, the system will not check and alert; it will provide erroneous results. The access time in binary search is logarithmically proportionally to the number of rows in the internal table.

In the sorted tables, the READ...statement uses the binary search method to locate a row with the provided key fields. The access time in binary search is logarithmically proportional to the number of rows in the internal table.

In hashed tables, the READ...statement uses a hashed algorithm method to locate a row with the provided key fields. The access time in hashed tables is independent of the number of rows in the internal table.

Sort

A standard table can sorted any number of times with the SORT statement.

You cannot perform SORT on a sorted table. When data is loaded into the sorted table with the SELECT statement or with the INSERT statement, the rows are maintained in the ascending order of the key fields automatically.

A hashed table can be sorted, but it does not make sense. You sort data when you want to process data sequentially or serially with the data appearing in ordered manner. The hashed table is conceived for random and frequent speedy access and not serial access.

Indexed Access: (SY-INDEX Operative)

With standard tables and sorted tables, you can access a row by providing the row number (indexed access is the fastest access). These tables together are called as indexed tables. For these tables, the system field SY-TABIX contains the row number operated upon or the number of rows processed, that is, the system field SY-TABIX is operative for these tables. A hashed table cannot be accessed through a row number. The system field SY-TABIX is inoperative for a hashed table and will contain a value zero after an operation on a hashed table.

The three internal table types - standard, sorted, and hashed - with their features is listed in Table 6-3.

- When totally serial or sequential processing is required, a standard table can be used.
- When the processing is part random and part sequential, a sorted table can be used.
- When processing a large amount of data with totally frequent random key access, a hashed table can be used.

Table 6-3. *Internal Table Types - Features and Attributes*

Table Type	Key	Search	Sort	SY-TABIX
Standard	Standard key as well as defined key Defined key can be only be NON-UNIQUE	By default linear search Binary search - optional user should ensure that table is in sorted order of search field/s Time for search dependent on number of entries	Can be sorted or resorted any number of times	Indexed table, row can be accessed with row no. SY-TABIX operative
Sorted	Defined key The standard key fields can be assigned to defined key Defined key can be UNIQUE & NON-UNIQUE	Binary search Time for search dependent on number of entries Logarithmically proportional to number of entries	Table is in the order of defined key Cannot be sorted	Indexed table, row can be accessed with row no. SY-TABIX operative
Hashed	Defined key The standard key fields can be assigned to defined key Defined key can be only UNIQUE	Hashed algorithm Search Time for search independent on number of entries	Can be resorted Sorting does not make sense	Non Indexed table, row cannot be accessed with row no. SY-TABIX inoperative

What follows are different ways of declaring internal tables in 4 x mode. The roman numerals signify the ways of declaring internal tables in 4.x mode.

4.X Mode: Declaring the Internal Table (and Structure as well) by Referring to a Local/Global Structured TYPE or Local/Global Structure

Global structure includes a database table or any type of view.

General Syntax:

```
DATA <internal table name> {TYPE|LIKE} {STANDARD|SORTED|HASHED} TABLE
 OF <structure name> WITH {UNIQUE|NON_UNIQUE} KEY <field1><field2>...
[INITIAL SIZE <n>] [WITH HEADER LINE].
```

INITIAL SIZE is equivalent to OCCURS of 3.X mode. The INITIAL SIZE clause is optional.

The WITH HEADER LINE has the same meaning as in 3.X mode, that is, an internal table and a structure of the same name get defined.

```
<structure name> is either
```

a. A structured TYPE declared locally with the TYPES keyword. The keyword TYPE not LIKE should be used when referring to it.

Examples:

```
* Internal tables declared by referring to
* a local structure TYPE

TYPES: BEGIN OF CUSTOMER_STRU_TYPE,
        KUNNR TYPE KNA1-KUNNR,
        NAME1 TYPE KNA1-NAME1,
END OF CUSTOMER_STRU_TYPE.

DATA: CUSTOMER_ST_TAB TYPE STANDARD TABLE OF CUSTOMER_STRU_TYPE.

DATA: CUSTOMER_SR_TAB TYPE SORTED TABLE OF CUSTOMER_STRU_TYPE
      WITH NON-UNIQUE KEY KUNNR INITIAL SIZE 5.

DATA: CUSTOMER_HS_TAB TYPE HASHED TABLE OF CUSTOMER_STRU_TYPE
      WITH UNIQUE KEY KUNNR INITIAL SIZE 5.
```

b. A structured TYPE declared in DDIC object Type Group. The keyword TYPE not LIKE should be used when referring to it.

Examples:

```
* Internal tables declared by referring to
* a DDIC structure TYPE in Type Group

TYPE-POOLS YCLG1.

DATA: CUSTOMER_ST_TAB TYPE STANDARD TABLE OF YCLG1_CUSTOMER_TYPE
WITH NON-UNIQUE KEY KUNNR.
```

```
DATA: CUSTOMER_SR_TAB TYPE SORTED TABLE OF YCLG1_CUSTOMER_TYPE
WITH UNIQUE KEY KUNNR.

DATA: CUSTOMER_HS_TAB TYPE SORTED TABLE OF YCLG1_CUSTOMER_TYPE
WITH UNIQUE KEY KUNNR WITH HEADER LINE.
```

A TYPE YCLG1_CUSTOMER_TYPE has been created in the Type Group YCLG1 as shown in Figure 6-9 (repeat of Figure 6-2).

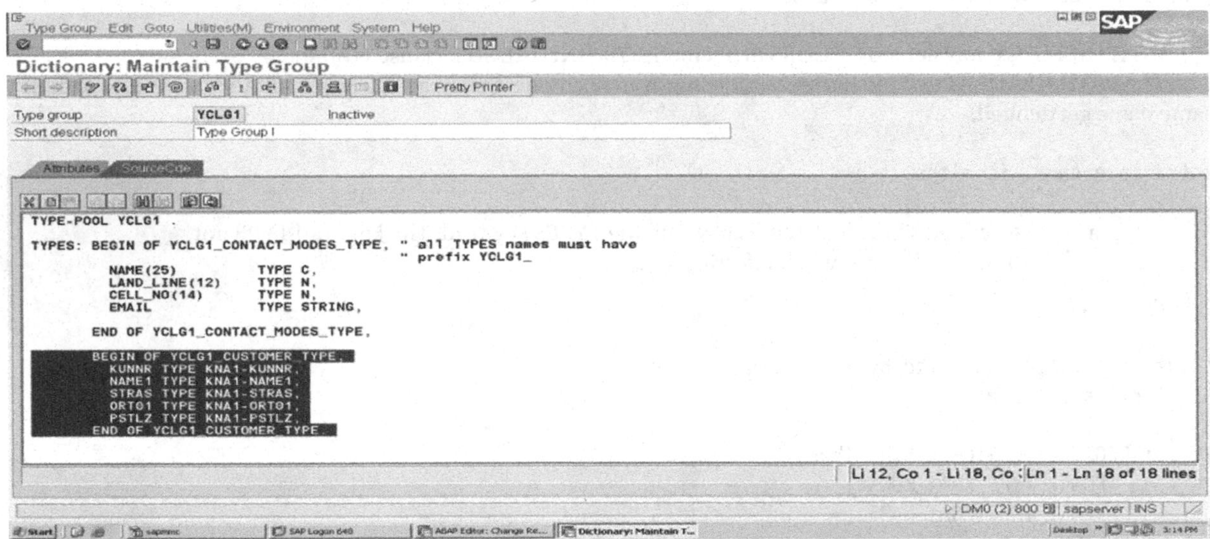

Figure 6-9. *TYPE YCLG1_CUSTOMER_TYPE in Type Group YCLG1 [Highlighted]*

c. A structure declared locally. The keyword LIKE not TYPE should be used when referring to it.

Example:

```
* Internal tables declared by referring to
* a local structure
DATA:  BEGIN OF CUSTOMER_STRU,
         KUNNR TYPE KNA1-KUNNR,
         NAME1 TYPE KNA1-NAME1,
       END OF CUSTOMER_STRU.

DATA: CUSTOMER_ST_TAB LIKE STANDARD TABLE OF CUSTOMER_STRU
WITH NON-UNIQUE KEY KUNNR." defined key for standard table

DATA: CUSTOMER_SR_TAB LIKE SORTED TABLE OF CUSTOMER_STRU WITH
NON-UNIQUE KEY KUNNR.

DATA: CUSTOMER_HS_TAB LIKE HASHED TABLE OF CUSTOMER_STRU WITH
UNIQUE KEY KUNNR.
```

d. A structured type declared in a DDIC data type or a database table or a view. The keyword TYPE or LIKE can be used when referring to it.

Examples:

```
* Internal table declared by referring to
* a DDIC table definition
DATA: CUSTOMER_TAB LIKE STANDARD TABLE OF KNA1.

* Internal tables declared by referring to
* a DDIC structure
DATA: CUSTOMER_SR_TAB TYPE SORTED TABLE OF YCL_CH06_CUST_STRU WITH
NON-UNIQUE KEY KUNNR.

* Internal table declared by referring to
* a DDIC view
DATA: CUSTOMER_HS_TAB TYPE HASHED TABLE OF YCL_CH05_VBRKKNA WITH
UNIQUE KEY KUNNR.
```

A DDIC type structure YCL_CH06_CUST_STRU is shown in Figure 6-10 (repeat of Figure 6-1).

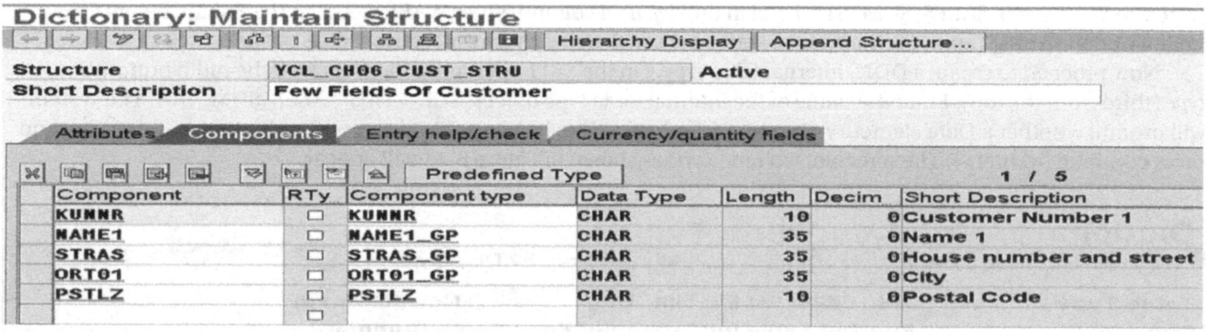

Dictionary: Maintain Structure

Hierarchy Display | Append Structure...

Structure: YCL_CH06_CUST_STRU Active
Short Description: Few Fields Of Customer

Attributes | Components | Entry help/check | Currency/quantity fields

Predefined Type 1 / 5

Component	RTy	Component type	Data Type	Length	Decim	Short Description
KUNNR	☐	KUNNR	CHAR	10	0	Customer Number 1
NAME1	☐	NAME1_GP	CHAR	35	0	Name 1
STRAS	☐	STRAS_GP	CHAR	35	0	House number and street
ORT01	☐	ORT01_GP	CHAR	35	0	City
PSTLZ	☐	PSTLZ	CHAR	10	0	Postal Code

Figure 6-10. *DDIC Structure YCL_CH06_CUST_STRU*

Create DDIC Internal Table Type

This is a digression from describing various modes of internal table declarations in 4.X mode, which will be resumed after the coverage of creation of the DDIC *Table type* (internal table type).

You can create a DDIC internal table type. You can then refer to it to declare internal tables in ABAP programs. Let a DDIC internal table type be created.

Before you create an internal table type, you need to have a DDIC structure that will be used in the DDIC internal table type. Let DDIC objects that you will use in your forthcoming hands-on exercises are created.

You are going to do a hands-on exercise of customer wise sales summary. Each customer's billing documents amounts are summed or accumulated and outputted. You will need the following fields to enable you to generate the customer wise sales summary.

```
====================================
Field           Table       Data
Name            of          Element
                Origin
=====================================
KUNNR           KNA1        KUNNR
NAME1           KNA1        NAME1_GP
ORT01           KNA1        ORT01_GP
NETWR           VBRK        NETWR
WAERK           VBRK        WAERK
KURRF           VBRK        KURRF
```

Earlier you created a DDIC structure YCL_CH06_CUST_STRU. In a like manner, you will create a DDIC structure YCL_CH06_SALES_SUM_STRU. You do not need the billing document currency code field WAERK. It is incorporated because for the DDIC Data Type CURR field NETWR and the structure definition insists on a corresponding DDIC Data Type CUKY field in the structure or elsewhere. Recall from Chapter 2, DDIC Data Types, the SAP supplied database table viewing. Enter all the six fields in the structure along with the data elements. For the field NETWR, (DDIC Data Type CURR), click on the fourth tab *Currency/quantity fields*. In the *Reference table* column, enter the name of your structure YCL_CH06_SALES_SUM_STRU and in the *Ref. field* column, enter WAERK. Assign the Enhancement Category (menu option Extras) *Cannot Be Enhanced*. Perform a consistency check and activate the structure.

Now proceed to create a DDIC internal table type. On the SE11 opening screen, click on the radio button *Data type* (third from the top). Enter the name of the internal table type object: YCL_CH06_SALES_SUM_TAB. The system will prompt whether a Data element / Structure / Table type is to be created? Click on the radio button Table type and press continue (<Enter>). The screen of tab *Line Type* as shown in Figure 6-11 will appear.

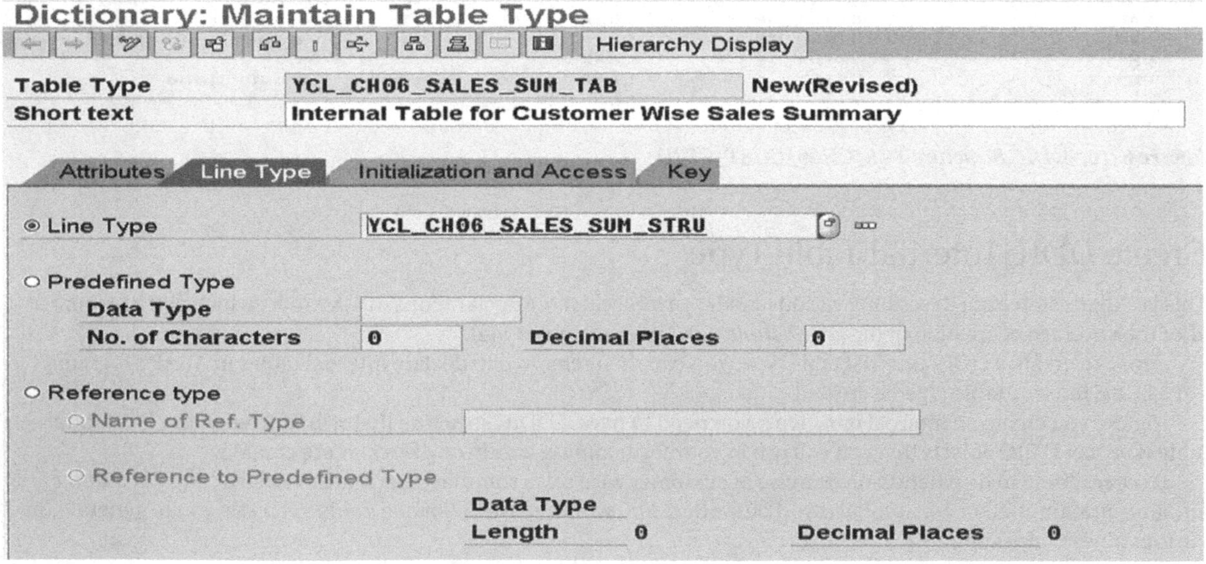

Figure 6-11. *Create Table Type YCL_CH06_SALES_SUM_TAB: Tab Line Type*

Enter the Short text. In the *Line Type* tab, three main radio button options appear:

1. Line Type: If you want your table type be structured type, enter the name of the structure here (it can be a DDIC structure, database structure, or view structure). Enter the DDIC structure created in the previous step. You can get a selection list by entering the pattern YCL_CH06* and pressing F4.
2. If you select the second radio button, you can enter one of the DDIC predefined Data Types: CHAR, NUMC, and DEC, etc. You are then defining an unstructured table type (what you call the simple array).
3. If you select the third radio button, you will enter the name of the reference type.

Next, click on the *Initialization and Access* tab. This tab will like that in Figure 6-12.

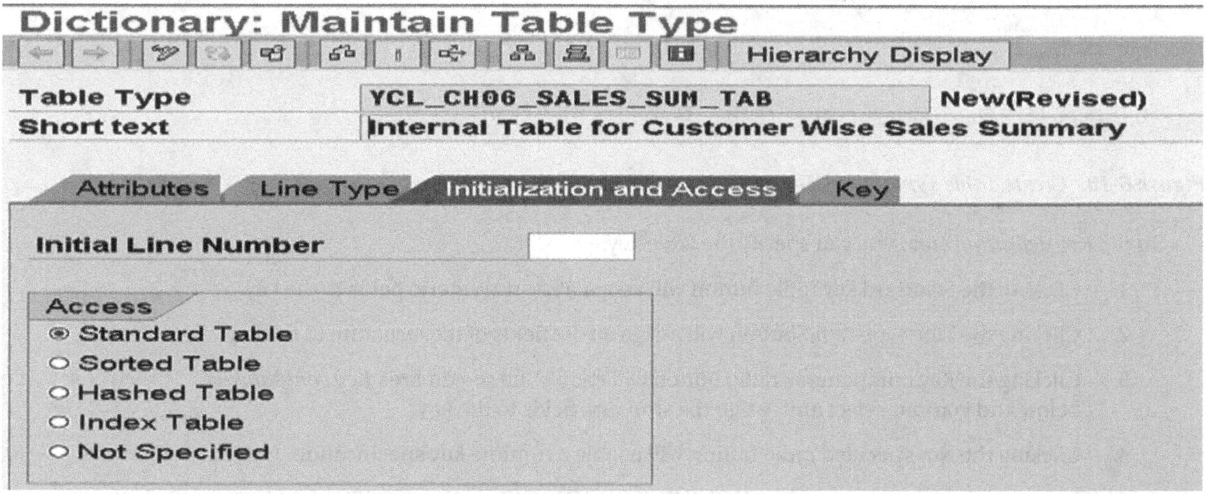

Figure 6-12. *Create Table Type YCL_CH06_SALES_SUM_TAB: Tab Initialization and Access*

In this tab, you select the table type: standard, sorted, or hashed. There are two more radio buttons: (i) Indexed Table and (ii) Not Specified. These types are generic. They are in the context of OOP. At runtime the table type can be decided. For the Indexed Table, you can make the table type at runtime either a standard or sorted. For the Not Specified, you could assign at runtime any of the table types: standard, sorted, or hashed.

The field *Initial Line Number* corresponds to the Initial Size clause when you declare an internal table in an ABAP program. It is optional.

Next, click on the tab key. A screen like the one shown in Figure 6-13 will appear.

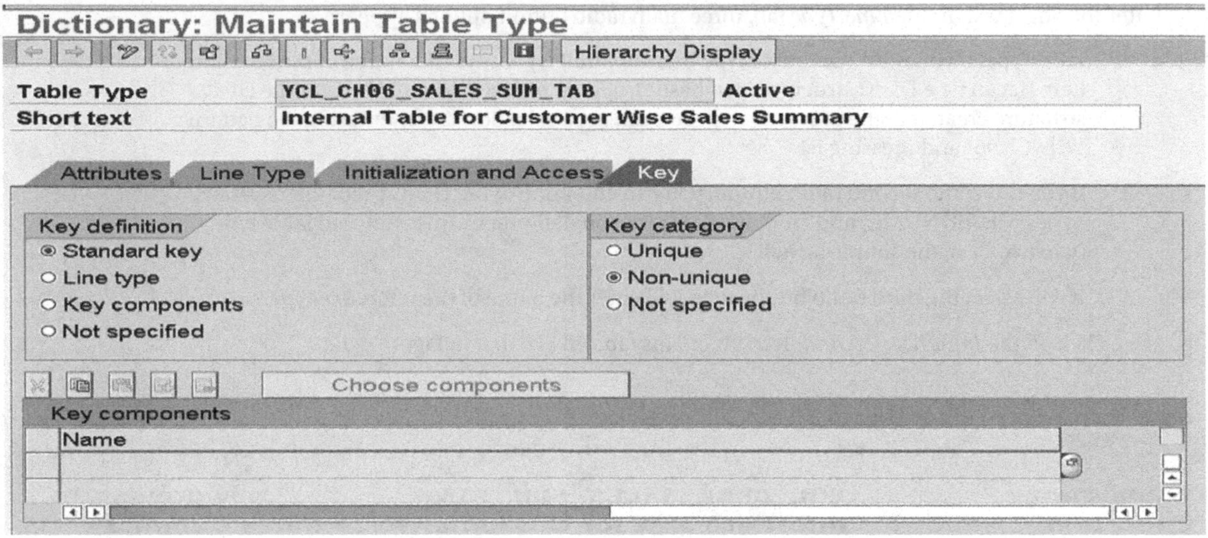

Figure 6-13. *Create Table Type YCL_CH06_SALES_SUM_TAB: Tab Key*

In the *Key definition* area, you can specify the table key:

1. Clicking the Standard key radio button will assign all non-numeric fields to the key.
2. Clicking the Line type radio button will assign all the fields of the structure to the key.
3. Clicking the Key components radio button will enable the screen area *Key components* below and you can select and assign the structure fields to the key.
4. Clicking the Not specified radio button will enable a runtime key specification.

In the *Key category* area, you can opt for UNIQUE, NON-UNIQUE, or Not specified *(the Not specified* selection specifies a key category at runtime).

Create a standard table with a standard key. Perform a consistency check and activate this DDIC table type definition.

Internal Tables – 4.X Mode of Declarations – Continued

4.X Mode: Declaring Internal Table by Referring to a DDIC Table Type

Only key word TYPE can be used.

Examples:

```
* Internal tables declared by referring to
* a DDIC table type - no HEADER LINE

DATA: SALES_SUM_TAB_ST_TAB1 TYPE YCL_CH06_SALES_SUM_TAB.

* Internal tables declared by referring to
* a DDIC table type WITH HEADER LINE

DATA: SALES_SUM_TAB_ST_TAB2 TYPE YCL_CH06_SALES_SUM_TAB
WITH HEADER LINE.
```

4.X Mode: Declaring Nonstructured Internal Tables (Simple Arrays)

The nonstructured internal tables can be declared by referring to an elementary data type (local/global) data object, (local/global) and data element similar to the 3.X mode.

Refer to examples of 3.X. You can declare standard, sorted, and hashed nonstructured internal tables.

Declaring a Structure by Referring to an Internal Table

Refer to examples of 3.X.

The internal tables will be featured in most of our forthcoming chapters' hands-on exercises. You will stick to declaring tables in 4.X mode only. You will also try to avoid the WITH HEADER LINE feature (where internal table and structure names are the same). This mode of declaration is not supported in the OOP environment.

To start with, you will do a couple of simple hands-on exercises with internal table declarations in 4.X mode.

Hands-On Exercise: Split a String, Get Output in Nonstructured Internal Table

In Chapter 4, you had used a SPLIT statement to split a string into its constituent words and each word returned in a separate variable. The issue was posed that the number of words in a string in the real world cannot be predetermined. The SPLIT statement used in Chapter 4 was not a practical feature. With internal tables, a variation of the SPLIT statement will get each word of a string in a separate row. So the issue of a predetermined number of words in a string is resolved.

The source program:

```
REPORT YCL_CH06_ITAB03 NO STANDARD PAGE HEADING.

*****************************************************************
* Internal Tables - Split a String & Get Words Into itab Rows **
*****************************************************************
*****************************************
* PARAMETERS - input string            **
*                                      **
* perform SPLIT statement, each word   **
* will be returned as a row in the     **
* unstructured internal table          **
*                                      **
* set LOOP AT...ENDLOOP to output      **
* rows of unstructured internal table  **
*****************************************

DATA: WORD(15)    TYPE C,
      WORDS_TAB   LIKE STANDARD TABLE OF WORD. "unstructured internal table

PARAMETERS: ISTRING(50)  TYPE C DEFAULT
   'ONCE UPON A TIME THERE LIVED A NERD'.
```

```
*************************************************************
START-OF-SELECTION.

SPLIT ISTRING AT ' ' INTO TABLE WORDS_TAB. "each word returned as a row

LOOP AT WORDS_TAB INTO WORD.

 WRITE:/5 WORD.

ENDLOOP.
```

The output will appear like that in Figure 6-14.

Internal Tables - Split a String & Get Words Into itab Rows

```
ONCE
UPON
A
TIME
THERE
LIVED
A
NERD
```

Figure 6-14. *Program YCL_CH06_ITAB03: Output*

SORT Statement

This is a statement to order rows of internal tables. You have already used a simple version of this statement in the hands-on exercise: *Customer Wise List of Billing Documents of a Specified Company Code.*

The statement can be used for standard and hashed tables. The syntax and different forms of this statement: *SORT <internal table name> [ASCENDING|DESCENDING] [AS TEXT] [STABLE].*

This form of the statement sorts the table in ascending (lowest values first and highest values last)/ descending (highest values first and lowest values last) order of defined key fields of the table. For the standard tables, if key fields are undefined, the sorting will be performed in the order of the standard key fields. If the order ASCENDING|DESCENDING is omitted, by default it will sort in ascending order. The sort fields in this form of sort statement are implicit. The ASCENDING|DESCENDING applies to all key fields. You do not have the option to specify ASCENDING|DESCENDING for each field separately.

The option [AS TEXT] is applicable to TYPE C fields. It is specified for alphabetic sorting. The codes used to store characters in bytes ASCII, EBCDIC, etc., were organized to store English alphabet letters. Other European languages such as German and French contain extra vowels (more than five). These extra vowels are not contained in the alphabetic range of the ASCII orEBCDIC codes. Ordinary sorting will go by the byte value. For example, the German alphabet has the vowel ö. (o with two dots on top), and the vowel ö in the German alphabet set occurs after the letter o. But in the ASCII or EBCDIC code, it occurs after z. To take care of this, SAP has provided the feature TEXT sort to generate true alphabetic order. A hands-on exercise demonstrates and elucidates this issue better. A hands-on exercise on TEXT sort follows the sort syntax explanations.

The option STABLE is relevant in the context of an internal table being sorted again and again on the same key fields. The option ensures that order of multiple key values is retained after every sort on the same key fields.

The second form of sort statement is:

```
SORT <internal table name> [STABLE] BY <field1> [ASCENDING|DESCENDING]
 [AS TEXT] <field2> [ASCENDING|DESCENDING] [AS TEXT].......
```

The fields on which sorting are to be performed are explicit. For each field, you have the option of ASCENDING|DESCENDING.

APPEND Statement

The APPEND statement can be used only for indexed tables, that is, standard and sorted. For sorted tables, it is not advisable to use the APPEND statement. With this statement, you can (i) transfer the contents of the structure as a new row in the internal table, (ii) create a new blank row in the internal table, or (iii) transfer rows from a source internal table to a destination internal table. In these three operations, the new rows are added at the end of the existing rows in the destination internal table.

Most of the time, you are using (i), so the APPEND statement is elaborated on here in this context. If the internal table is empty to start with, an APPEND statement will transfer the structure contents as the first row in the internal table. A second APPEND will transfer the structure contents as a second row in the internal table and so on. It can be used in a scenario such as where an internal table has to be filled row by row. This is unlike the way you have filled internal tables until now: multiple rows dumped from a database table or view into an internal table. A graphic representation of this form of APPEND statement is shown in Figure 6-15.

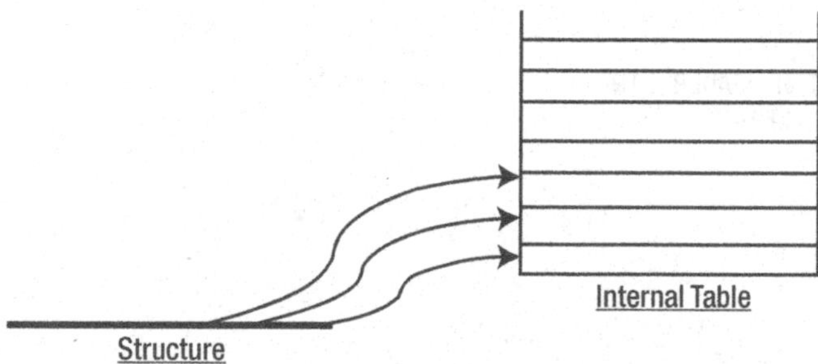

Figure 6-15. *Operation of APPEND Statement*

Hands-On Exercise: Internal Table Text Sort (Use APPEND to Populate Internal Table)

You will use the APPEND statement to fill an unstructured internal table with data having the additional vowels to add to English. You will assign literal values containing extra vowels to the elementary field and APPEND the value of elementary field to the internal table. This is one of the few times you are using literals in an ABAP program. You will perform the sort without the *AS TEXT* option and output from the internal table; next perform the sort with the *AS TEXT* option and output from the internal table and note the results.

The source program is:

```
REPORT YCL_CH06_ITAB04.

**************************************
* Internal Tables: APPEND, TEXT SORT **
**************************************
************************************************************
* declare simple/non-structured TYPE C internal table     **
* in 4.X mode                                             **
*                                                         **
* fill this table with text containing extra vowels       **
* through APPEND statement                                 **
*                                                         **
* output table rows - LOOP...ENDLOOP                      **
* output will appear in order in which rows were appended **
*                                                         **
* perform ordinary sort on the table                      **
* output will appear in order of byte values              **
*                                                         **
* perform text sort on the table                          **
* output will appear in true alphabetic order             **
************************************************************
TYPES: NAME_TYPE(25)  TYPE C.

DATA : NAMES TYPE STANDARD TABLE OF NAME_TYPE WITH HEADER LINE
        INITIAL SIZE 0. " unstructured internal table

NAMES = 'BÖLLINGER'.
APPEND NAMES TO NAMES. " adds a row at the end

NAMES = 'BOLLINGER'.
APPEND NAMES TO NAMES.

NAMES = 'BILLINGER'.
APPEND NAMES TO NAMES.

NAMES = 'BÏLLINGER'.
APPEND NAMES TO NAMES.

NAMES = 'BULLINGER'.
APPEND NAMES TO NAMES.

FORMAT INVERSE ON COLOR COL_TOTAL.
WRITE:/5 'Original Data:'.
LOOP AT NAMES.
WRITE:/5 NAMES.
ENDLOOP.
```

```
SORT NAMES.
SKIP.
FORMAT INVERSE ON COLOR COL_KEY.
WRITE:/5 'Ordinary Sort:'.
LOOP AT NAMES.
WRITE:/5 NAMES.
ENDLOOP.

SORT NAMES AS TEXT.
SKIP.
FORMAT INVERSE ON COLOR COL_POSITIVE.
WRITE:/5 'Text Sort:'.
LOOP AT NAMES.
WRITE:/5 NAMES.
ENDLOOP.
```

The output will appear like this:

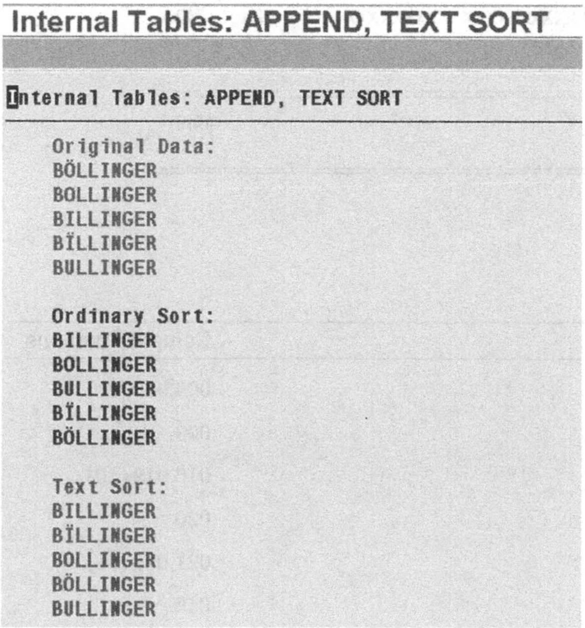

```
Internal Tables: APPEND, TEXT SORT

Internal Tables: APPEND, TEXT SORT

    Original Data:
    BÖLLINGER
    BOLLINGER
    BILLINGER
    BÏLLINGER
    BULLINGER

    Ordinary Sort:
    BILLINGER
    BOLLINGER
    BULLINGER
    BÏLLINGER
    BÖLLINGER

    Text Sort:
    BILLINGER
    BÏLLINGER
    BOLLINGER
    BÖLLINGER
    BULLINGER
```

Figure 6-16. *Program YCL_CH06_ITAB04: Output*

The ordinary sort is placing BÏLLINGER and BÖLLINGER at the end. The text sort is positioning BÏLLINGER after BILLINGER and BÖLLINGER after BOLLINGER.

Hands-On Exercise: Customer Wise Sales Summary of a Specified Company Code Using the COLLECT Internal Table Statement on a Standard Table

You will produce a customer wise sales summary. Let the output be ordered customer wise. In this output, if a customer has n number of billing documents, the amounts of this n number of billing documents are accumulated, and the total amount of the customer along with the customer code, name, and city will appear as one line in the output. Since you are adding amount figures, they need to be converted to a single currency: the operating currency of the company code. You will use the exchange rate field to convert the amount from document currency to the operating currency.

Summary output lists are a very common demand in enterprises.

Output

The rough layout of the customer wise sales summary will appear like this:

```
Customer Wise Sales Summary of Company Code: XXXX/XXXXXXXXXXXXXXXXXXXXXXXXX      Page: XXX
                                             Currency: XXXXX

==================================================================================
Srl. Customer    N a m e                      C i t Y                       Amount
No.  Code
==================================================================================
```

The output body layout:

Table 6-4. Output Body Layout

Field Name	Table Name	Description	Column Positions
SY-TABIX	System Field	Serial No.	005,008 (4)
			009
KUNNR	KNA1	Customer Code	010,019 (10)
			020
NAME1	KNA1	Name	021,055 (35)
			056
ORT01	KNA1	City	057-091 (35)
			092
NETWR	VBRK	Total of Converted Billing Document Net Value	093-109 (17)

Inputs

The input data for this output will be our database view YCL_CH05_VBRKKNA.

To declare the internal table in the ABAP program, you will refer to the DDIC table type YCL_CH06_SALES_SUM_TAB you created earlier in this chapter.

COLLECT Statement

You will be using the COLLECT statement to produce the summary. The COLLECT statement is a handy feature to consolidate or summarize data. With the COLLECT statement you can generate a one-level summary. You are summarizing data here based on the customer. If you were requiring a list for each customer of how much of material 'A' was sold and how much of material 'B' was sold - that is, a two-level summary output involving the customer and material, the COLLECT statement cannot be used.

An understanding of the COLLECT statement is crucial. The COLLECT statement works for all table types: standard, sorted, or hashed. In the current hands-on exercise, you are using a standard table. So for now, the discussion of the COLLECT statement is in the standard table context. Subsequently, there will be discussions of the COLLECT statement in the context of sorted and hashed tables.

The syntax of the COLLECT statement:

```
COLLECT <structure name> INTO <internal table name>.
```

COLLECT Statement Operation

Like in an APPEND statement, there is a transfer of data from a structure to an internal table, but in a peculiar way.

The COLLECT statement is a two-in-one statement. It operates on the basis of the standard key values. So the standard table on which you operate a COLLECT statement must not have a defined key or a defined key that is the same as the standard key. Recall that the standard key of an internal table consists of all the structure fields of type C, D, N, and T.

The COLLECT statement first checks whether the standard key value in the structure has any corresponding row in the table.

- If no row exists with the standard key values of the structure in the table, the structure data will go as a new row in the table; this is effectively an APPEND operation.
- If a row exists in the table of the standard key values in the structure, the numeric field values from the structure are added to the numeric field values in the corresponding row in the table. Numeric fields in the present context will mean type F, I, and P. The type N fields as part of standard key are not considered numeric fields.

An example will help elucidate this. Let there be an internal table with the following structure:

```
DATA: BEGIN OF EMP_STRU,
       DEPT_CODE(2)    TYPE C,
       EMP_CODE(4)     TYPE N,
       POINTS(3)       TYPE P DECIMALS 0,
      END OF EMP_STRU,EMP_TAB LIKE STANDARD TABLE OF EMP_STRU.
```

The standard key in this instance will be DEPT_CODE, EMP_CODE. Let values be assigned to the structure fields and the COLLECT statement be operated on the internal table.

```
EMP_STRU-DEPT_CODE = 'A1'.
EMP_STRU-EMP_CODE  = 1234.
EMP_STRU-POINTS    = 100.
COLLECT EMP_STRU INTO EMP_TAB. " this will operate as an APPEND
                               " first row A1 1234 100
```

```
EMP_STRU-POINTS    = 200.
COLLECT EMP_STRU INTO EMP_TAB.  " row with standard key values A1 1234
                                " already exists, 200 will be added
                                " to 100. first row: A1 1234 300

EMP_STRU-DEPT_CODE = 'A1'.
EMP_STRU-EMP_CODE  = 1236.
EMP_STRU-POINTS    = 400.
COLLECT EMP_STRU INTO EMP_TAB.  " this will operate as an APPEND
                                " second row : A1 1236 400
EMP_STRU-DEPT_CODE = 'B1'.
EMP+_STRU-EMP_CODE  = 1234.
EMP_STRU-POINTS    = 100.
COLLECT EMP_STRU INTO EMP_TAB.  " this will operate as an APPEND
                                " third row: B1 1234 100

EMP_STRU-DEPT_CODE = 'A1'.
EMP_STRU-EMP_CODE  = 1236.
EMP_STRU-POINTS    = 100.
COLLECT EMP_STRU INTO EMP_TAB.  " row with standard key vales A1 1236
                                " already exists, 100 will be added to 400
                                " second row : A1 1236 500
At the end of the above operations, the internal table will contain:

A1 1234 300
A1 1236 500
B1 1234 100
```

If you want to output the summary table at the end of COLLECT statements operation, you need to have a LOOP AT...WRITE...ENDLOOP.

An internal table with only the COLLECT statement operating on it in a loop construct (SELECT...ENDSELECT) will result at the end with unique standard key values, and the numeric fields of standard key values will be summarized.

How you frame the table structure standard key consisting of the non-numeric fields is critical. The summarization occurs on its basis.

Reverting to your hands-on exercise, your table structure should be:

```
KUNNR   Customer Code
NAME1   Name
ORT01   City
NETWR   Billing Document Net Value
KURRF   Exchange Rate
```

Your standard key will consist of KUNNR, NAME1, and ORT01 (non-numeric fields). You only need to summarize on the basis of customer code KUNNR, but you need NAME and ORT021 in your output. The addition of these two fields in the standard key does not affect the results in any way.

The two numeric fields NETWR and KURRF will be accumulated. You do not need to have KURRF accumulated. It makes no sense to total exchange rate. You need the KURRF of each row from the view (each unique value of the billing document) to convert the net billing document value NETWR from billing document currency to the operating currency of the company code. But you can't help it. The COLLECT statement accumulates all numeric fields. You have to ignore the accumulation of KURRF. The accumulation of KURRF might result in a numeric over flow. This overflow issue can be addressed as you will see.

You will input the company code for which a sales summary is required (PARAMETERS...). To build your customer wise sales summary internal table, you have to have a SELECT...ENDSELECT looping construct with your database view YCL_CH05_VBRKKNA. After each row is fetched from the database view, you must issue the COLLECT statement in the SELECT...ENDSELECT loop. At the end of the SELECT...ENDSELECT loop, your summarized table will be ready. You will sort the table on KUNNR, you will then use LOOP...WRITE...ENDLOOP...to output your sorted summary table. At the end of LOOP... ENDLOOP... you will output the grand total.

The source program to generate a customer wise sales summary of a specified company code using COLLECT statement on a standard table is:

```
REPORT YCL_CH06_ITAB05 LINE-SIZE 120 LINE-COUNT 60
       NO STANDARD PAGE HEADING.

*******************************************************
* Customer Wise Sales Summary of a company code using **
* COLLECT statement                                   **
*******************************************************
*********************************************************
* declare internal table by reference to DDIC table     **
* type. declare structure by reference to internal      **
* table                                                 **
*                                                       **
* PARAMETERS to input company code                      **
* SELECT SINGLE.. to fetch company code name(BUTXT)     **
* operating currency of company code WAERS              **
*                                                       **
* SELECT...ENDSELECT to fetch rows from database view   **
* multiply NETWR KURRF to convert NETWR to operating    **
* currency. initialize KURRF to 0 after multiplication  **
* to prevent KURRF accumulation overflow.               **
* issue COLLECT                                         **
*                                                       **
* at end of SELECT...ENDSELECT, summary table created   **
*                                                       **
* sort summary internal table by KUNNR                  **
*                                                       **
* set up LOOP...WRITE...ENDLOOP                         **
*                                                       **
* end of LOOP.. WRITE...ENDLOOP output grand total      **
*********************************************************

DATA: SALES_TAB  TYPE YCL_CH06_SALES_SUM_TAB, "key word TYPE only
      SALES_STRU LIKE LINE OF SALES_TAB,      " declare structure by
                                              " referring to internal
                                              " table


      TOTAL    TYPE VBRK-NETWR,
      BUTXT    TYPE T001-BUTXT,
      WAERS    TYPE T001-WAERS,
      BUTXTS   TYPE STRING.
```

```
*********************************************
PARAMETERS: CCODE TYPE VBRK-BUKRS DEFAULT 3000.
*********************************************

TOP-OF-PAGE.
WRITE:/5 TEXT-001, CCODE NO-GAP, '/' NO-GAP,  BUTXTS, 102 TEXT-003,
         107(3) SY-PAGNO.
WRITE:/40 TEXT-002, WAERS.
SKIP 1.
WRITE:/5(104) SY-ULINE.
WRITE:/5 TEXT-004, 11 TEXT-005, 23 TEXT-006, 60 TEXT-007, 91(17)
         TEXT-008 RIGHT-JUSTIFIED.
WRITE:/5 TEXT-009, 13 TEXT-010.
WRITE:/5(104) SY-ULINE.

*********************************************
START-OF-SELECTION.

SELECT SINGLE BUTXT WAERS FROM T001 INTO (BUTXT, WAERS) WHERE
       BUKRS = CCODE.

BUTXTS = BUTXT. "assignment to TYPE STRING drops trailing blanks

SELECT KUNNR NAME1 ORT01 NETWR KURRF FROM YCL_CH05_VBRKKNA INTO
  CORRESPONDING FIELDS OF SALES_STRU WHERE BUKRS = CCODE.

 SALES_STRU-NETWR =  SALES_STRU-NETWR * SALES_STRU-KURRF.
 SALES_STRU-KURRF = 0. "to prevent overflow
 COLLECT SALES_STRU INTO SALES_TAB.
ENDSELECT.

SORT SALES_TAB BY KUNNR.

LOOP AT SALES_TAB INTO SALES_STRU.
 WRITE :/5(4) SY-TABIX, SALES_STRU-KUNNR USING NO EDIT MASK,
  SALES_STRU-NAME1,SALES_STRU-ORT01, (17) SALES_STRU-NETWR.
 TOTAL = TOTAL + SALES_STRU-NETWR.
ENDLOOP.

SKIP 1.
WRITE :/(17) TOTAL UNDER SALES_STRU-NETWR.
```

The SELECT statement in the program is:

```
SELECT KUNNR NAME1 ORT01 NETWR KURRF FROM YCL_CH05_VBRKKNA
INTO CORRESPONDING FIELDS OF SALES_STRU WHERE BUKRS = CCODE.
```

You are using a variation of the SELECT statement with *CORRESPONDING FIELDS OF.* This variation is to be used whenever the source and destination are not identical. In your present situation, the database view (source) does not have the field currency code WAERK present in your destination structure. This is analogous to the statement MOVE-CORRESPONDING to be used when moving data from a source structure to a destination structure; the source and destination are not identical in terms of number of fields and/or ordering of the fields in the structures (Chapter 4).

The currency code DDIC Data Type *CUKY* field WERK had to be incorporated in your DDIC structure YCL_CH06_SALES_STRU to take care of the DDIC Data Type CURR field (NETWR) having a corresponding CUKY field.

The text symbols for the program are:

Program YCL_CH06_ITAB05 Active

Text symbols | Selection texts | List Headings

Sy	Text	dLen	mLen
001	Customer Wise Sales Summary of Company Code:	44	44
002	Currency:	9	9
003	Page:	5	5
004	Srl.	4	4
005	Customer	8	8
006	N a m e	7	7
007	C i t y	7	7
008	Amount	6	6
009	No.	3	3
010	Code	4	4
		0	

Figure 6-17. *Program YCL_CH06_ITAB05: Text Symbols*

The program output will be like this:

Customer Wise Sales Summary using COLLECT

```
Customer Wise Sales Summary of Company Code: 3000/IDES US INC                    Page: 1
                              Currency: USD

Srl.  Customer    N a m e                          C i t y                          Amount
No.    Code

  1  0000000255 Emma Bull                     DENVER                              2,207.00
  2  0000000257 John Evans                    NEDERLAND                           2,299.00
  3  0000000258 Roger Zahn                    ALBUQUERQUE                         1,912.00
  4  0000000260 Chelsa Quinn Yates            ALBUQUERQUE                         2,124.00
  5  0000000262 Robert Jensen                 CANON CITY                          3,720.00
  6  0000000266 Charles Scott                 TORREY                              2,995.00
  7  0000000272 Joe Masson                    SALINA                                748.00
  8  0000000281 Tracy Collins                 VAIL                                1,567.50
  9  0000000470 Alex Lynch                    PHILADELPHIA                       11,860.80
 10  0000000471 Steve Martin                  SALT LAKE CITY                      8,415.50
 11  0000000473 Albert Brooks                 COLORADO SPRINGS                   10,911.80
 12  0000000474 Edward Burns                  HELENA                             12,427.70
 13  0000000481 Peter King                    SEATTLE                            10,542.10
 14  0000000482 Douglas Barker                MINNEAPOLIS                         1,614.26
 15  0000000504 Janett Adams                  DENVER                              2,957.16
```

Figure 6-18. *Program YCL_CH06_ITAB05: Output*

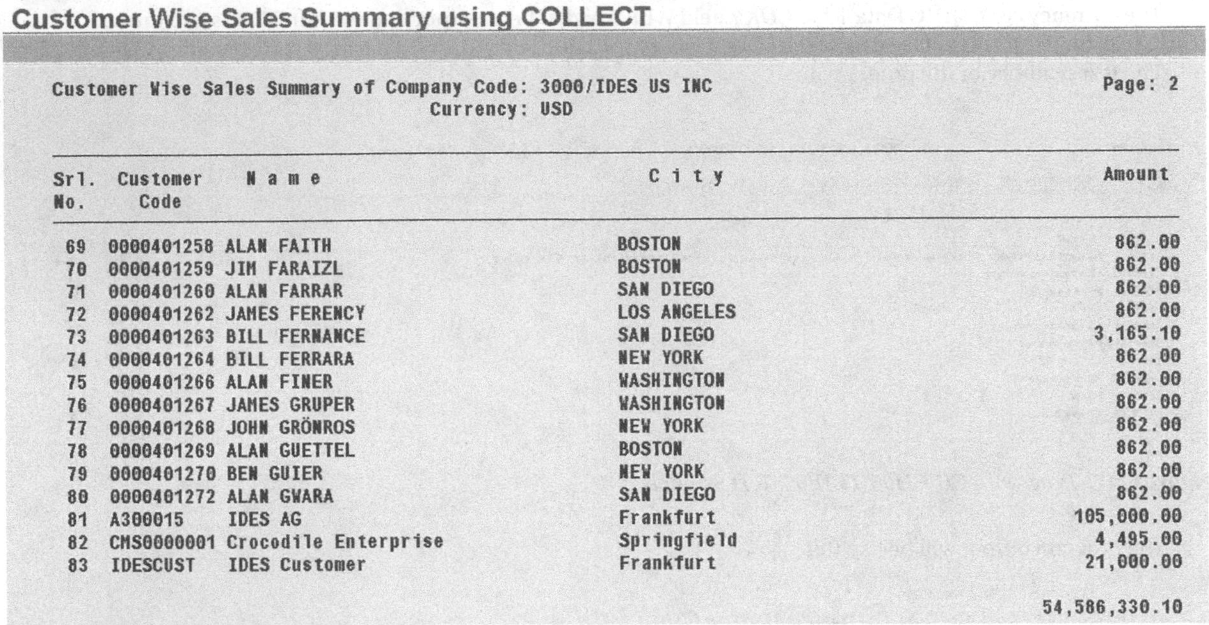

Customer Wise Sales Summary using COLLECT

Customer Wise Sales Summary of Company Code: 3000/IDES US INC   Page: 2
Currency: USD

Srl. No.	Customer Code	N a m e	C i t y	Amount
69	0000401258	ALAN FAITH	BOSTON	862.00
70	0000401259	JIM FARAIZL	BOSTON	862.00
71	0000401260	ALAN FARRAR	SAN DIEGO	862.00
72	0000401262	JAMES FERENCY	LOS ANGELES	862.00
73	0000401263	BILL FERNANCE	SAN DIEGO	3,165.10
74	0000401264	BILL FERRARA	NEW YORK	862.00
75	0000401266	ALAN FINER	WASHINGTON	862.00
76	0000401267	JAMES GRUPER	WASHINGTON	862.00
77	0000401268	JOHN GRÖNROS	NEW YORK	862.00
78	0000401269	ALAN GUETTEL	BOSTON	862.00
79	0000401270	BEN GUIER	NEW YORK	862.00
80	0000401272	ALAN GWARA	SAN DIEGO	862.00
81	A300015	IDES AG	Frankfurt	105,000.00
82	CMS0000001	Crocodile Enterprise	Springfield	4,495.00
83	IDESCUST	IDES Customer	Frankfurt	21,000.00
				54,586,330.10

Figure 6-19. *Program YCL_CH06_ITAB05: Total Output*

You have generated the customer wise sales summary for a specified company code as per your specifications. You employed the COLLECT statement on a standard table. The COLLECT statement operates on the basis of the standard key. The COLLECT statement is a two-in-one statement, APPEND and updating of numeric fields. You used a DDIC defined table type to declare the internal table.

Hands-On Exercise: Customer Wise Sales of a Specified Company Code Using COLLECT Internal Table Statement on a Sorted Table

Let this exercise be repeated with a sorted table. You will define the sorted internal table in the ABAP program itself unlike the previous exercise where you had defined the standard table in the DDIC. For this sorted table, you have to define the key. The defined key must have all the fields of the standard key, that is, fields of TYPE C, D, N, and T for the COLLECT statement to operate.

If the defined key has all the standard key fields, only then the COLLECT statement will be accepted at the source level. If your defined key is different from the standard key fields, a syntax error occurs during compilation.

In a sorted internal table, rows are always in the ascending order of key values. The operation of the COLLECT statement would ensure this. So you can say that the COLLECT statement for a sorted table is a two-in-one command: if the key values in the structure do not exist in the table, a row INSERT will occur (instead of APPEND in the case of standard table), and the row will be inserted at the appropriate position. If the structure key value exists, the numeric field values from the structure are added to the numeric fields of the corresponding row in the table.

You can copy the preceding exercise's ABAP program and make appropriate changes or code a new program. You can make a copy ABAP program with a different name from the SE38 opening screen. Enter the name of the source program to be copied, and click on the button on the application toolbar. The system will prompt for the name of the destination program (YCL_CH06_ITAB06). The copied program will be in an inactive state. You can rename programs from the SE38 opening screen by entering the name of the ABAP program and clicking on the button on the application toolbar.

Copy and activate the text symbols from the preceding exercise into the current one using transaction code SE32.

In the preceding exercise, you sorted the summary table generated. In the current exercise this is unnecessary as our table is a sorted table. The rest of the statements are the same as in the preceding exercise.

The source program is available in the source programs resource. Execute and tally the results with the results of YCL_CH06_ITAB05. The results should be identical.

Until now, you have filled an internal table with a SELECT statement using an APPEND statement and a COLLECT statement. You have retrieved rows from an internal table only with the LOOP...ENDLOOP construct: fetching one row at a time sequentially from the internal table into structure.

The APPEND statement, even though it can be used, hypothetically, for indexed tables, that is, standard and sorted tables, should be used on standard tables. In sorted tables, when you use an APPEND statement, the structure key field value should be greater than or greater than or equal to (depending on the defined key to be UNIQUE / NON-UNIQUE) the highest key value in the table. Recall that the APPEND statement adds the row at the very end. So if you try to APPEND to a sorted table, the row should be able to fit at the end. If this doesn't happen, a runtime error occurs. You can test this out as an exercise.

Hands-On Exercise: READ with Index (Retrieve a Row Given a Row Number)

The indexed tables (standard or sorted) allow you to retrieve data of any row from the table into a structure (READ with the index statement). You have to provide the row number. If the row number exists, the row will be fetched from the table into the structure; if the row number does not exist, this is an error condition. In the ABAP programming environment, you use a system field to ascertain the result of an operation. The system field is SY-SUBRC. If after an operation the system field contains a zero value, the operation is successful; otherwise it is a failure. The syntax of READ with Index is:

```
READ TABLE <internal table name>
    INDEX <Variable/literal>/<constant>
    INTO <structure name>
    [TRANSPORTING {<field1> [<field2>..]} | {ALL FIELDS} | {NO FIELDS}.
```

- <Variable/literal> - You can supply either a variable (the variable must contain a number) or a numeric literal.
- If the addition TRANSPORTING <field1><field2>...is used, you have the option to transfer selected fields from a table into the structure.
- If the addition TRANSPORTING NO FIELDS is used, the INTO <structure name> should be omitted. In this case, when the read operation is performed and the supplied row number exists, it will set the system field SY-TABIX to the row number value and set the system field SY-SUBRC to zero. If the supplied row does not exist, the system field SY-TABIX is set to zero and the system field SY-SUBRC is set to a non-zero value.
- If the addition TRANSPORTING ALL FIELDS is used, all the fields will be fetched from the table into the structure. By default all the fields are fetched from the table to the structure.

- If the row number provided exists, the system field SY-TABIX is set to the value of the row number, and the system field SY-SUBRC is set to zero.
- In your exercise program, you have declared a structure TABLES TCURT. The database table TCURT is a text table. It is containing the world's currency descriptions in all the languages supported by SAP. The TCURT structure:

```
Field Name      DDIC       Leng-  Description
                TYPE       th
=============================================
MANDT           CLNT       3      Client
SPRAS           LANG       1      Language Key
WAERS           CUKY       5      Currency Key
LTEXT           CHAR       40     Long Text
KTEXT           CHAR       15     Short text
```

- Referring to this structure, you have declared an internal table of type sorted. You are loading this internal table from the database table TCURT with only the currency descriptions of the logged in language: WHERE SPRAS = SY-LANGU.
- You are retrieving a row through the PARAMETERS variable ROW_NO. You have given the addition TRANSPORTING WAERS LTEXT. This will fetch data of only two fields WAERS and LTEXT. You are checking if SY-SUBRC = 0 (retrieval successful); then you output the currency code (WAERS), the long text (LTEXT), and the short text. (KTEXT) KTEXT will be output as blank/space as you are not retrieving this field from table into the structure. If SY-SUBRC is non-zero, you are highlighting ROW_NO as an invalid row number.

The Source program:

```
REPORT YCL_CH06_ITAB07.

**********************************
* Internal Table READ With Index **
**********************************
*****************************************
* declare TABLES TCURT. declare sorted  **
* table with TCURT structure key WAERS  **
*                                       **
* input record/row no. (PARAMETERS)     **
*                                       **
* load internal table from TCURT WHERE  **
* SPRAS = SY-LANGU                      **
*                                       **
* issue READ.. INDEX..                  **
* check SY-SUBRC & output               **
*****************************************

TABLES TCURT. " local structure having all fields
              " of database table TCURT

DATA: CURR_TAB TYPE SORTED TABLE OF TCURT WITH
       UNIQUE KEY WAERS.

***********************************************
```

```
PARAMETERS: REC_NO(4) TYPE N DEFAULT 75.

START-OF-SELECTION.

SELECT * FROM TCURT INTO TABLE CURR_TAB WHERE " *(star) justified. table
       SPRAS = SY-LANGU.                      " consists of few fields

READ TABLE CURR_TAB INTO TCURT INDEX REC_NO   " fetch only
     ."TRANSPORTING WAERS LTEXT.              " WAERS LTEXT

IF SY-SUBRC = 0.
 FORMAT INVERSE COLOR COL_POSITIVE.
 WRITE:/5(4) SY-TABIX, TCURT-WAERS, TCURT-LTEXT, TCURT-KTEXT.
ELSE.
 FORMAT INVERSE COLOR COL_NEGATIVE.
 WRITE:/5 'Row No.:', REC_NO, 'Invalid'.
ENDIF.
```

Comment the TRANSPORTING addition in the READ...statement and confirm that the value of field KTEXT is output.

Execute the program with a high value of REC_NO to trigger an invalid row condition.

The outputs will look like this:

```
Internal Table READ With Index

Internal Table READ With Index

   75  GBP  British Pound
```

Figure 6-20. *Program YCL_CH06_ITAB07: With REC_NO = 75 & TRANSPORTING WAERS LTEXT*

```
Internal Table READ With Index

Internal Table READ With Index

   Row No.: 0555 Invalid
```

Figure 6-21. *Program YCL_CH06_ITAB07: With REC_NO = 555*

```
Internal Table READ With Index

Internal Table READ With Index

   75  GBP  British Pound                          Pounds sterling
```

Figure 6-22. *Program YCL_CH06_ITAB07: With REC_NO = 75 & TRANSPORTING Option Commented*

Hands-On Exercise: READ...WITHKEY... (Retrieve a Row Given Key Field Values)

Fetch a row from the table into the structure corresponding to the supplied table key field values.

The syntax of READ...WITH KEY...statement is:

```
READ TABLE <internal table name>
  WITH KEY <key field1> = <data object1>
          [<key field2> = <data object2>..]
  [BINARY SEARCH}
INTO <structure name> [TRANSPORTING options].
```

The <data object1> can be variables, literals, and hypothetically constants.

The TRANSPORTING options are TRANSPORTING ALL FIELDS | TRANSPORTING NO FIELDS | TRANSPORTING <field1> [<field2]...

This statement works for all the three table types: standard, sorted, and hashed.

For the *sorted table*, a binary search method is used to locate a row of the supplied key field values. This is the way data from a sorted table is to be retrieved on a random basis.

For the *hashed table*, the hashed algorithm is used to locate a row of the supplied field values. This READ statement should be used to retrieve data from a hashed table when frequently accessing on random basis (key field values changing) from a very large number of entries.

For the *standard table*, a binary search method is used to locate a row of the supplied field values if the key phrase *BINARY SEARCH* is specified with the statement. It should be ensured that the table is in the ascending order of the key field values. If this additional phrase is not specified with the statement, the system will use the linear search method to locate a row with the supplied key field values.

You will repeat the exercise you did with 3.X declaration of internal tables: listing out the billing documents of a specified company code. In this hands-on exercise, you were loading an internal table with data from the database view (created with tables VBRK and KNA1). Subsequently you output from the internal table with the LOOP...WRITE... ENDLOOP statements.

In the present hands-on exercise, you will not use the view. You will load one internal table (standard - sequential/ serial processing) say, 'itab I' with data from the database table VBRK of a specified company code (WHERE BUKRS =...) You will choose the following fields from this database table:

```
VBELN   Billing Document Number
FKDAT   Billing Document Date
KUNAG   Customer Code
NETWR   Net Value in Document Currency
KURRF   Exchange Rate
```

You will load a second internal table (hashed - frequent random access) say, 'itab II' with data from the database table KNA1. You will choose the following fields from this database table:

```
KUNNR   Customer Code
NAME1   Name
ORT01   City
```

You need to output the following fields:

```
SRL_NO (internal data object/program variable)
VBELN
FKDAT
```

```
NAME1
ORT01
NETWR   this will be NETWR * KURRF
```

You will have the output in order of billing document number (i.e., VBELN).

You will set a LOOP...ENDLOOP with 'itab I.' You can output fields VBELN, FKDAT, KUNAG, and NETWR from this internal table. For the fields NAME1, ORT01, you will read the 'itab II' through READ...WITH KEY...Retrieving customer info NAME1, ORT01 with KUNAG of 'itab I.'

You can copy the earlier program into a new name or code the program from scratch. If you code the program from scratch, you can copy text symbols from the earlier program using the transaction code SE32 and activate.

This whole exercise is to demonstrate the frequent random access of an internal table (hashed) using READ... WITH KEY...Statement.

The source program to generate a List of Billing Documents of a specified company code using two internal tables: a standard table and a hashed table is:

```
REPORT YCL_CH06_ITAB08 LINE-SIZE 135 LINE-COUNT 60
       NO STANDARD PAGE HEADING.

****************************************************************
* List of Billing Docs of a Specified Company Code with Total **
* Using Two Internal Tables                                   **
****************************************************************
*****************************************************************
* declare 2 structures & internal tables:(1)loading data from VBRK**
* (2) loading data from KNA1                                     **
*                                                                **
* PARAMETERS CCODE TYPE VBRK-BUKRS VALUE CHECK DEFAULT 3000      **
* to select company code                                         **
*                                                                **
* get BUTXT WAERS from T001 - SELECT SINGLE etc.                 **
*                                                                **
* load internal table <iatb1> from the VBRK                      **
*  SELECT <fields> from VBRK INTO TABLE <itab1>                  **
*       WHERE BUKRS = CCODE.                                     **
*                                                                **
* load internal table <iatb2> from the KNA1                      **
*  SELECT <fields> from KNA1 INTO TABLE <itab2>.                 **
*                                                                **
*  set LOOP AT <itab> into <itab>.                               **
*       calculate amount in operating currency of chosen CCODE   **
*                                                                **
*       Retrieve NAME1, ORT01 from <itab2> by READ.. WITH KEY..  **
*        from second internal table <itan2>                      **
*       increment SRL_NO (serial no)                             **
*       WRITE...                                                 **
*       build total                                              **
*      ENDLOOP.                                                  **
*                                                                **
*  output total                                                  **
*                                                                **
*****************************************************************
TABLES: T001.
```

```
DATA: BEGIN OF BILL_DOCS_STRU,
       VBELN  TYPE VBRK-VBELN,
       FKDAT  TYPE VBRK-FKDAT,
       KUNAG  TYPE VBRK-KUNAG,
       NETWR  TYPE VBRK-NETWR,
       KURRF  TYPE VBRK-KURRF,
      END OF BILL_DOCS_STRU,

      BILL_DOCS_TAB LIKE STANDARD TABLE OF BILL_DOCS_STRU,

      BEGIN OF CUST_INFO_STRU,
       KUNNR  TYPE KNA1-KUNNR,
       NAME1  TYPE KNA1-NAME1,
       ORT01  TYPE KNA1-ORT01,
      END OF CUST_INFO_STRU,

      CUST_INFO_TAB LIKE HASHED TABLE OF CUST_INFO_STRU
        WITH UNIQUE KEY KUNNR,

      STRNG      TYPE STRING,
      SRL_NO     TYPE SY-TABIX,
      TOTAL      TYPE VBRK-NETWR.

PARAMETERS CCODE  TYPE VBRK-BUKRS DEFAULT 3000 VALUE CHECK.
**********************************************************************
TOP-OF-PAGE.

WRITE :/5 STRNG, 129(3) SY-PAGNO.

SKIP 1.
WRITE:/5(127) SY-ULINE.
WRITE:/5 TEXT-003,11 TEXT-004, 22 TEXT-005, 33 TEXT-006, 46 TEXT-007,
         83 TEXT-008, 126 TEXT-009.

WRITE:/6 TEXT-010, 35 TEXT-011.
WRITE:/5(127) SY-ULINE.

**********************************************************************
START-OF-SELECTION.

SELECT SINGLE * FROM T001 WHERE BUKRS = CCODE.

CONCATENATE TEXT-001 CCODE '/' T001-BUTXT TEXT-002 T001-WAERS INTO STRNG.

SELECT VBELN FKDAT KUNAG NETWR KURRF FROM
  VBRK INTO
  TABLE BILL_DOCS_TAB
  WHERE BUKRS = CCODE.
```

```
SELECT KUNNR NAME1 ORT01 FROM
  KNA1 INTO
  TABLE CUST_INFO_TAB.
**********************************************************************
SORT BILL_DOCS_TAB BY VBELN. "default is ASCENDING

LOOP AT BILL_DOCS_TAB INTO BILL_DOCS_STRU.

 BILL_DOCS_STRU-NETWR = BILL_DOCS_STRU-NETWR * BILL_DOCS_STRU-KURRF.

 READ TABLE CUST_INFO_TAB WITH KEY KUNNR = BILL_DOCS_STRU-KUNAG
   INTO CUST_INFO_STRU. " the READ operation will set SY-TABIX to zero

 SRL_NO = SRL_NO + 1.

 WRITE:/5(5) SRL_NO, BILL_DOCS_STRU-VBELN, BILL_DOCS_STRU-FKDAT,
             BILL_DOCS_STRU-KUNAG, CUST_INFO_STRU-NAME1,
             CUST_INFO_STRU-ORT01, (17) BILL_DOCS_STRU-NETWR.

 TOTAL = TOTAL + BILL_DOCS_STRU-NETWR.

ENDLOOP.
********************************

END-OF-SELECTION.
SKIP 1.

WRITE: /(17) TOTAL UNDER BILL_DOCS_STRU-NETWR.
```

Observe the fact that you cannot use the system field SY-TABIX for a serial number. When you are at the statement next to the LOOP AT...statement (LOOP AT is operating on a standard table/indexed table), the system field SY-TABIX will contain the fetched row number. But after the statement READ... WITH KEY...is executed (READ... WITH KEY...is operating on a hashed/non-indexed table), the system field SY-TABIX is set to zero. Recall that for a q hashed table, the system field SY-TABIX is inoperative.

You could have saved a SY-TABIX value in another declared variable before the READ...WITH KEY...statement and output this variable as a serial number. You cannot avoid a declared variable to output a serial number.

The output will be identical to the one generated by your earlier program YCL_CH06_ITAB01. The output will appear like this:

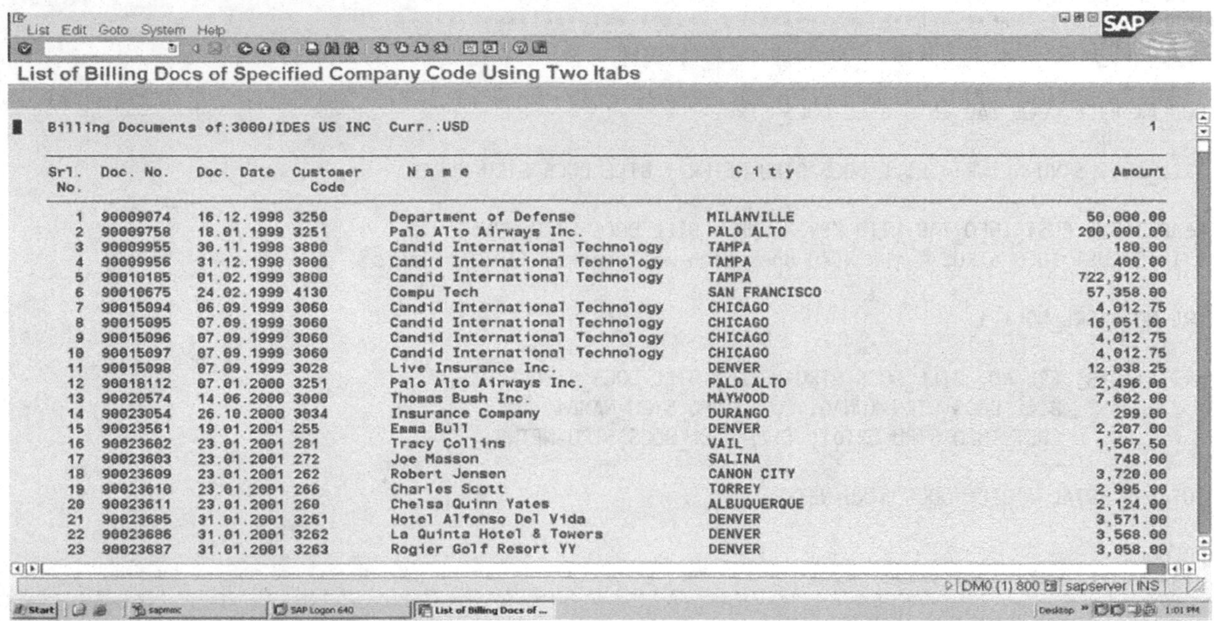

List of Billing Docs of Specified Company Code Using Two Itabs

Billing Documents of:3000/IDES US INC Curr.:USD 1

Srl. No.	Doc. No.	Doc. Date	Customer Code	N a m e	C i t y	Amount
1	90009074	16.12.1998	3250	Department of Defense	MILANVILLE	50,000.00
2	90009758	18.01.1999	3251	Palo Alto Airways Inc.	PALO ALTO	200,000.00
3	90009955	30.11.1998	3800	Candid International Technology	TAMPA	180.00
4	90009956	31.12.1998	3800	Candid International Technology	TAMPA	400.00
5	90010185	01.02.1999	3800	Candid International Technology	TAMPA	722,912.00
6	90010675	24.02.1999	4130	Compu Tech	SAN FRANCISCO	57,358.00
7	90015094	06.09.1999	3060	Candid International Technology	CHICAGO	4,012.75
8	90015095	07.09.1999	3060	Candid International Technology	CHICAGO	16,051.00
9	90015096	07.09.1999	3060	Candid International Technology	CHICAGO	4,012.75
10	90015097	07.09.1999	3060	Candid International Technology	CHICAGO	4,012.75
11	90015098	07.09.1999	3028	Live Insurance Inc.	DENVER	12,038.25
12	90018112	07.01.2000	3251	Palo Alto Airways Inc.	PALO ALTO	2,496.00
13	90020574	14.06.2000	3000	Thomas Bush Inc.	MAYWOOD	7,602.00
14	90023054	26.10.2000	3034	Insurance Company	DURANGO	299.00
15	90023561	19.01.2001	255	Emma Bull	DENVER	2,207.00
16	90023602	23.01.2001	281	Tracy Collins	VAIL	1,567.50
17	90023603	23.01.2001	272	Joe Masson	SALINA	748.00
18	90023609	23.01.2001	262	Robert Jensen	CANON CITY	3,720.00
19	90023610	23.01.2001	266	Charles Scott	TORREY	2,995.00
20	90023611	23.01.2001	260	Chelsa Quinn Yates	ALBUQUERQUE	2,124.00
21	90023685	31.01.2001	3261	Hotel Alfonso Del Vida	DENVER	3,571.00
22	90023686	31.01.2001	3262	La Quinta Hotel & Towers	DENVER	3,568.00
23	90023687	31.01.2001	3263	Rogier Golf Resort YY	DENVER	3,058.00

Figure 6-23. *Output of Program YCL_CH06_ITAB08*

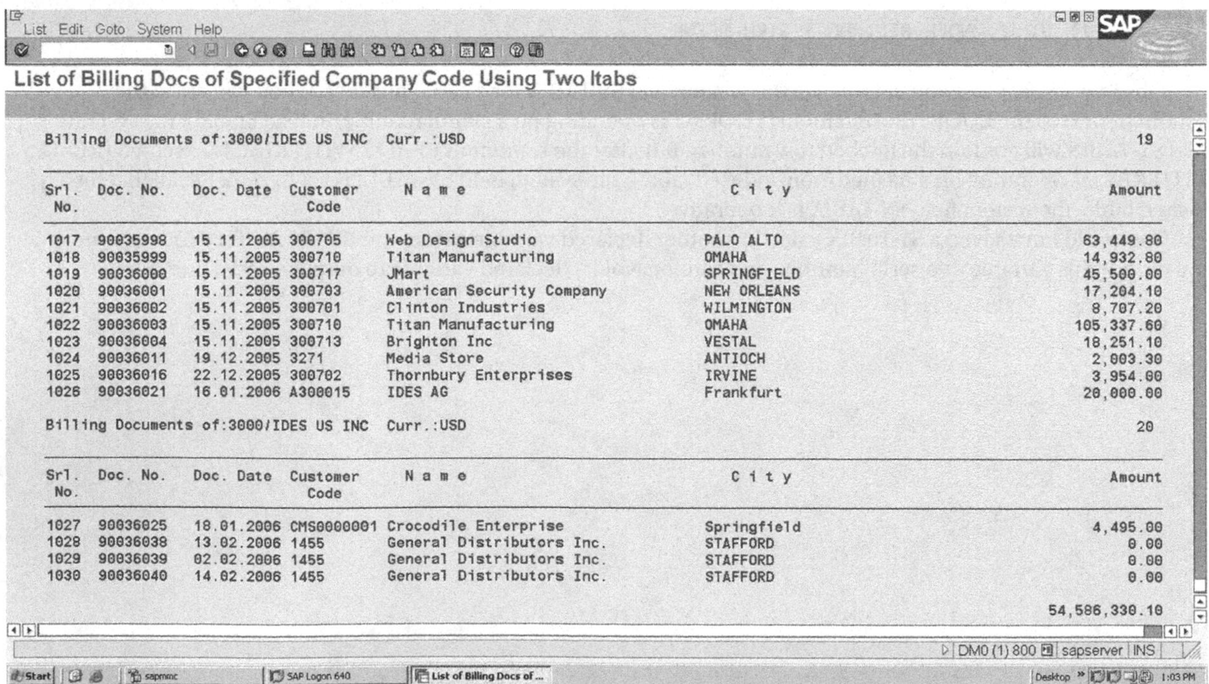

List of Billing Docs of Specified Company Code Using Two Itabs

Billing Documents of:3000/IDES US INC Curr.:USD 19

Srl. No.	Doc. No.	Doc. Date	Customer Code	N a m e	C i t y	Amount
1017	90035998	15.11.2005	300705	Web Design Studio	PALO ALTO	63,449.80
1018	90035999	15.11.2005	300710	Titan Manufacturing	OMAHA	14,932.80
1019	90036000	15.11.2005	300717	JMart	SPRINGFIELD	45,500.00
1020	90036001	15.11.2005	300703	American Security Company	NEW ORLEANS	17,204.10
1021	90036002	15.11.2005	300701	Clinton Industries	WILMINGTON	8,707.20
1022	90036003	15.11.2005	300710	Titan Manufacturing	OMAHA	105,337.60
1023	90036004	15.11.2005	300713	Brighton Inc	VESTAL	18,251.10
1024	90036011	19.12.2005	3271	Media Store	ANTIOCH	2,003.30
1025	90036016	22.12.2005	300702	Thornbury Enterprises	IRVINE	3,954.00
1026	90036021	16.01.2006	A300015	IDES AG	Frankfurt	20,000.00

Billing Documents of:3000/IDES US INC Curr.:USD 20

Srl. No.	Doc. No.	Doc. Date	Customer Code	N a m e	C i t y	Amount
1027	90036025	10.01.2006	CMS0000001	Crocodile Enterprise	Springfield	4,495.00
1028	90036038	13.02.2006	1455	General Distributors Inc.	STAFFORD	0.00
1029	90036039	02.02.2006	1455	General Distributors Inc.	STAFFORD	0.00
1030	90036040	14.02.2006	1455	General Distributors Inc.	STAFFORD	0.00
						54,586,330.10

Figure 6-24. *Output Of Program YCL_CH06_ITAB08 Grand Totals*

Hands-On Exercise: INSERT...INDEX... (Insert a Row at a Specified Row Position)

This statement can be used to insert a row at a specified row position and can be used for indexed tables, that is, standard and sorted tables, though for sorted tables, it is not very advisable. The sorted table rows have to be in the ascending order of the key fields. So in this form of INSERT statement, the row being inserted into a sorted table must fit in that row position as to maintain the ascending order key values.

The syntax of this statement is:

```
INSERT <structure name> INTO <internal table name>
  INDEX <index data object>
```

The data from the <structure name> will get inserted in the row position specified by <index data object>. The row existing in that row position and beyond, if any, are shifted one row position ahead. For instance, if there are 10 rows in a table, and you insert a row at row position 5, the row existing in 5th position prior to the INSERT statement will be shifted to the 6th row position and so on with the 10th row prior to the INSERT statement shifted to the 11th row position.

If the INSERT is successful, the system field SY-TABIX is set to the row number value of the inserted row; the system field SY-SUBRC is set to zero.

If the INSERT is a failure, the row insertion cannot take place because:

1. It is disrupting the ascending order state of the sorted table.
2. It is attempting to create duplicate key value rows in a sorted table with UNIQUE KEY.
3. The <index data object> LT 1.
4. The <index data object> GT current number of rows + 1. For instance, if a table is containing 10 rows, you can assign a maximum value of 11 to <index data object>. You cannot assign a value > 11. The system will not be able to insert a row in that position.

In this case of INSERT failure, the system field SY-TABIX is set to zero and the system field SY-SUBRC is set to non-zero.

A source program of a hands-on exercise with a standard table to highlight this feature:

```
REPORT YCL_CH06_ITAB09.

***************************************
* Internal Tables - INSERT.. INDEX.. **
***************************************
******************************************
* declare structure TCURT, internal table **
* of this structure                      **
*                                        **
* input INSERT row number PARAMETERS     **
*                                        **
* load internal table with data from     **
* database table TCURT for currency code **
* starting with 'I' - WHERE WAERS LIKE   **
* 'I%'.                                  **
*                                        **
```

```
* LOOP...ENDLOOP. output from internal    **
* table output: pre-insert                **
*                                         **
* INSERT TCURT INTO CURR_TAB index REC_NO **
*                                         **
* if SY-SUNRC = 0 LOOP..ENDLOOP output    **
* from internal table: post insert        **
* else                                    **
* output error                            **
*******************************************

TABLES TCURT. " currency description text table

DATA : CURR_TAB TYPE STANDARD TABLE OF TCURT.

PARAMETERS: REC_NO(2) TYPE N DEFAULT 5.

START-OF-SELECTION.
SELECT * FROM TCURT INTO TABLE CURR_TAB
        WHERE SPRAS = 'E' AND WAERS LIKE 'I%'. " currency codes starting
                                               " with I

WRITE: /5 'Pre-Insertion:'.

LOOP AT CURR_TAB INTO TCURT.
 WRITE: /5(2) SY-TABIX, TCURT-WAERS, TCURT-LTEXT.
ENDLOOP.

TCURT = SPACE. " initial structure TCURT

TCURT-WAERS = 'IJK'.
TCURT-LTEXT = 'DUMMY CURRENCY'.

INSERT TCURT INTO CURR_TAB INDEX REC_NO.

IF SY-SUBRC = 0.
 SKIP 1.
 WRITE: /5 'Post-Insertion:'.

 LOOP AT CURR_TAB INTO TCURT.
  WRITE: /5(2) SY-TABIX, TCURT-WAERS, TCURT-LTEXT.
 ENDLOOP.

ELSE.
 SKIP 1.
 FORMAT INVERSE COLOR COL_NEGATIVE.
 WRITE:/5 'Error Inserting Row No.', (2) REC_NO.

FORMAT RESET.
ENDIF.
```

The outputs of program YCL_CH06_ITAB09 will look like this:

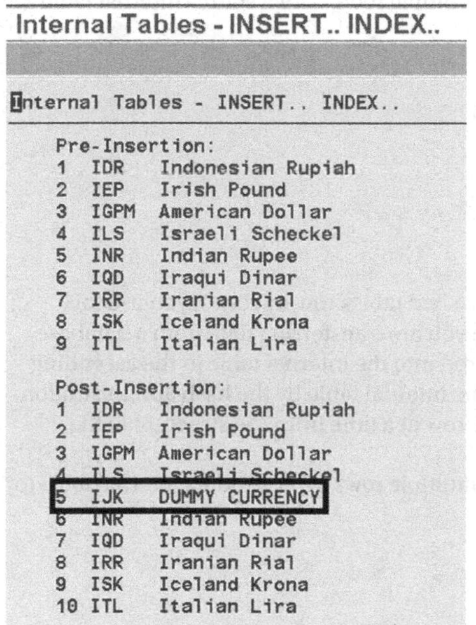

Figure 6-25. *Output Of Program YCL_CH06_ITAB09 Row INSERTED*

You inserted a row at row position 5. The row existing in this position prior to INSERT was INR Indian Rupee, and the following rows have been pushed ahead by one row.

In the next instance, you tried to INSERT a row at row position 11.

```
Internal Tables - INSERT.. INDEX..

Internal Tables - INSERT.. INDEX..

    Pre-Insertion:
    1  IDR   Indonesian Rupiah
    2  IEP   Irish Pound
    3  IGPM  American Dollar
    4  ILS   Israeli Scheckel
    5  INR   Indian Rupee
    6  IQD   Iraqui Dinar
    7  IRR   Iranian Rial
    8  ISK   Iceland Krona
    9  ITL   Italian Lira

    Error Inserting At Row No. 11
```

Figure 6-26. *Output of Program YCL_CH06_ITAB09 Row INSERT Error*

The number of rows existing prior to INSERT is 9. The last row position where you can successfully INSERT a row is 10. So this has resulted in an error condition.

There is a variation of this INSERT statement whereby you can insert multiple rows from a source internal table to a destination internal table.

Non-Index INSERT Statement

The statement Syntax is:

```
INSERT <structure name> INTO TABLE <internal table name>.
```

This form of INSERT statement is generally used to build sorted and hashed tables row by row. If you use this statement for a standard table, it operates as an APPEND statement. When you are transferring data from a database table to an internal table: In the case of the sorted tables, the rows are entered into the internal table in the ascending order of the key fields; In the case of hashed tables rows are inserted into the internal table by the hash administration according to its key values. The same principles apply when you insert one row at a time from the structure to the internal table of type sorted or hashed.

There is a variation of this INSERT statement whereby you can insert multiple rows from a source internal table to a destination internal table.

Delete Data from Internal Tables

Sometimes, you need to delete a row or rows from an internal table. You use the DELETE statement to do this.

DELETE Single Rows

The syntax to DELETE single rows is:

```
DELETE {TABLE <internal table name><key values>}|
       {<internal table name> [INDEX <data object>]}.
```

You can delete a row by supplying the key values - for sorted or hashed tables.

You can delete a row by supplying the index or row number - for indexed tables.

When a DELETE with index statement is located inside a LOOP...ENDLOOP construct, the INDEX specification is optional. Implicitly it will delete the currently fetched row.

DELETE Multiple Rows

The syntax for deleting multiple rows from an internal statement is:

```
DELETE <internal table name> [FROM <start index>] [TO <end index>
 [WHERE <condition>].
```

All the rows starting from <start index> and till <end index> satisfying the <condition> will be deleted.

Hands-On Exercise: Delete Adjacent Duplicates

Scenario

Suppose you want to have a list of customers with billing documents against them. This is just a simple list containing customer code, name, and city for customers with billing documents.

Recall the database view you created with the tables KNA1 and VBRK. This contains the information you want but not in the exact fashion. A customer having n number of billing documents will have n number of rows in this database view. In our output you want this n number of rows to be reduced to one row. You can reduce the n number of rows to one row with the statement DELETE ADJACENT DUPLICATES. This statement, on specification of fields, deletes all duplicates and retains one row for one value of the specified fields (equivalent in effect to SQL SELECT DISTINCT...). The prerequisite for this is that the internal table should be sorted in the ascending order of the fields on which you want to delete duplicates. The system will not check whether the table is in the sorted order.

As usual, you will provide for the output to be produced for a specified company code.

The syntax of this statement is:

```
DELETE ADJACENT DUPLICATES FROM <internal table name>
[COMPARING { <field1>  [<field2>...]} | {ALL FIELDS}].
```

Your output body layout is shown in Table 6-5.

Table 6-5. *Output Body Layout*

Field Name	Table Name	Description	Column Positions
SY-TABIX	System Field	Serial No.	005,008 (4)
			009
KUNNR	KNA1	Customer Code	010,019 (10)
			020
NAME1	KNA1	Name	021,055 (35)
			056
ORT01	KNA1	City	057-091 (35)

The source program:

```
REPORT YCL_CH06_ITAB10 LINE-SIZE 95 LINE-COUNT 60
       NO STANDARD PAGE HEADING.

*************************************************************************
* DELETE ADJACENT DUPLICATES - List of Customers With Billing Documents **
*************************************************************************
*************************************************
* declare structure and internal table        **
*                                              **
* input company code - PARAMETERS             **
*                                              **
* load internal table -SELECT etc.            **
*                                              **
```

```
* sort internal table BY KUNNR                     **
* DELETE ADJACENT DUPLICATES...COMPARING KUNNR     **
*                                                  **
* LOOP AT...WRITE..ENDLOOP.                        **
*****************************************************
DATA: BEGIN OF CUST_STRU,
       KUNNR TYPE  KNA1-KUNNR,
       NAME1 TYPE  KNA1-NAME1,
       ORT01 TYPE  KNA1-ORT01,
      END OF CUST_STRU,

      CUST_TAB LIKE STANDARD TABLE OF CUST_STRU,

      BUTXT    TYPE T001-BUTXT.
****************************************************
PARAMETERS CCODE TYPE VBRK-BUKRS DEFAULT 3000 VALUE CHECK.

TOP-OF-PAGE.

WRITE:/5 TEXT-001 NO-GAP, CCODE NO-GAP, '/' NO-GAP, BUTXT, 92(2) SY-PAGNO.
WRITE:/5(88) SY-ULINE.
WRITE:/5 TEXT-002, 11 TEXT-003, 22 TEXT-004, 58 TEXT-005.
WRITE:/6 TEXT-006, 13 TEXT-007.
WRITE:/5(88) SY-ULINE.

START-OF-SELECTION.

SELECT SINGLE BUTXT FROM T001 INTO (BUTXT) WHERE BUKRS = CCODE.

SELECT KUNNR NAME1 ORT01 FROM YCL_CH05_VBRKKNA
       INTO TABLE CUST_TAB
       WHERE BUKRS = CCODE.

SORT CUST_TAB BY KUNNR.

DELETE ADJACENT DUPLICATES FROM CUST_TAB COMPARING KUNNR.

*****************************************************************
LOOP AT CUST_TAB INTO CUST_STRU.

 WRITE:/5(4) SY-TABIX, CUST_STRU-KUNNR USING NO EDIT MASK,
             CUST_STRU-NAME1, CUST_STRU-ORT01.

ENDLOOP.
```

Create text symbols and activate. They will appear like Figure 6-27.

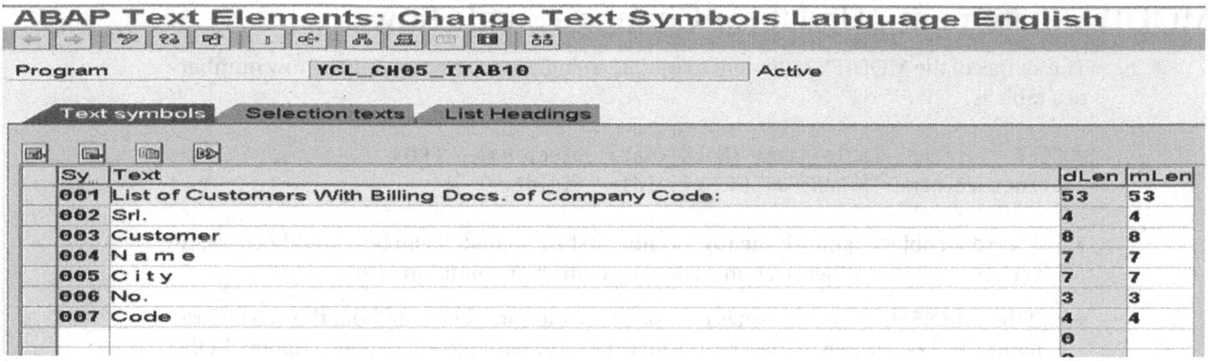

ABAP Text Elements: Change Text Symbols Language English

Program YCL_CH05_ITAB10 Active

Text symbols | Selection texts | List Headings

Sy	Text	dLen	mLen
001	List of Customers With Billing Docs. of Company Code:	53	53
002	Srl.	4	4
003	Customer	8	8
004	N a m e	7	7
005	C i t y	7	7
006	No.	3	3
007	Code	4	4
		0	

Figure 6-27. *Program YCL_CH06_ITAB10 - Text Symbols*

The output will appear like this:

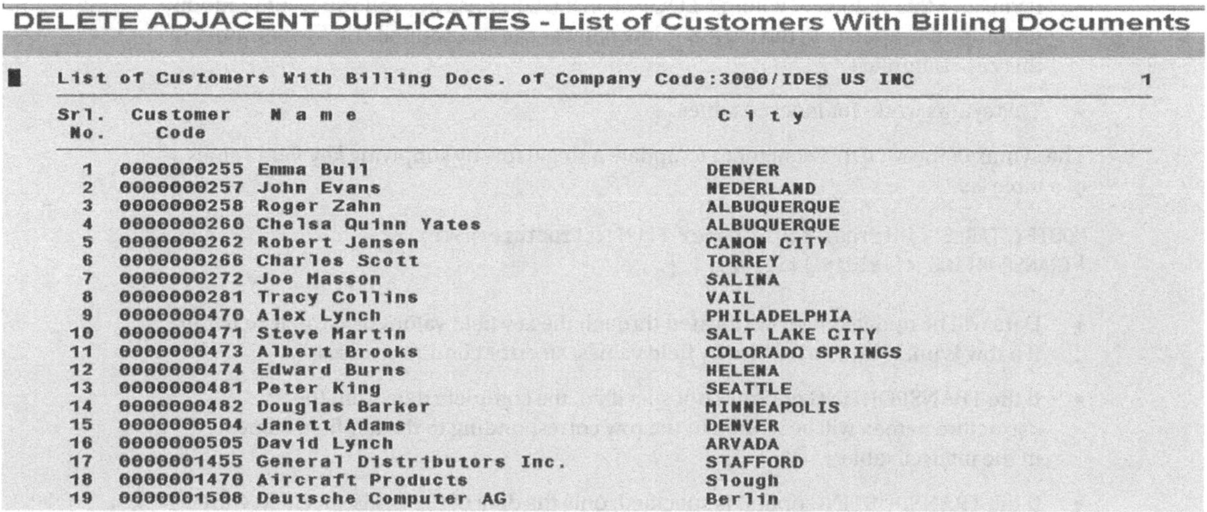

```
DELETE ADJACENT DUPLICATES - List of Customers With Billing Documents

List of Customers With Billing Docs. of Company Code:3000/IDES US INC          1

Srl.  Customer   N a m e                          C i t y
 No.    Code

  1  0000000255 Emma Bull                         DENVER
  2  0000000257 John Evans                        NEDERLAND
  3  0000000258 Roger Zahn                        ALBUQUERQUE
  4  0000000260 Chelsa Quinn Yates                ALBUQUERQUE
  5  0000000262 Robert Jensen                     CANON CITY
  6  0000000266 Charles Scott                     TORREY
  7  0000000272 Joe Masson                        SALINA
  8  0000000281 Tracy Collins                     VAIL
  9  0000000470 Alex Lynch                        PHILADELPHIA
 10  0000000471 Steve Martin                      SALT LAKE CITY
 11  0000000473 Albert Brooks                     COLORADO SPRINGS
 12  0000000474 Edward Burns                      HELENA
 13  0000000481 Peter King                        SEATTLE
 14  0000000482 Douglas Barker                    MINNEAPOLIS
 15  0000000504 Janett Adams                      DENVER
 16  0000000505 David Lynch                       ARVADA
 17  0000001455 General Distributors Inc.         STAFFORD
 18  0000001470 Aircraft Products                 Slough
 19  0000001508 Deutsche Computer AG              Berlin
```

Figure 6-28. *Program YCL_CH06_ITAB10 - Output*

MODIFY Statement – Update/Change Existing Rows in Internal Tables

You can update or change rows in internal tables with the MODIFY statement. You can update one or multiple rows with this statement.

MODIFY Statement – Update or Change a Single Row

a. The syntax of the MODIFY statement to update a single row by supplying the row number of a table is:

```
MODIFY <internal table name> INDEX <data object name> FROM
 <structure name> [TRANSPORTING <field1> [field2..] ].
```

- The <data object name> is the row number to be updated. It can be a literal / constant / variable. If this number is a nonexistent row, an error condition arises.
- If the TRANSPORTING option is not specified, the complete data from the <structure name> will be written to the row number specified with the <data object name> in the internal table.
- If the TRANSPORTING option is specified, only the data of the fields specified with TRANSPORTING are written to the row number specified with the <data object name> in the internal table.
- If you give this statement within a LOOP...ENDLOOP construct and you want to modify the current row fetched; the INDEX <data object> can be dropped. The row number in this case is implicit.
- This syntax works for indexed tables.

b. The syntax of the MODIFY statement to update a single row by supplying key field values of a table is:

```
MODIFY TABLE <internal table name> FROM <structure name>
[TRANSPORTING <field1> [field2..] ].
```

- Data will be updated for rows located through the key field values of <structure name>. If a row is not locatable for the key field values, an error condition arises.
- If the TRANSPORTING option is not specified, the complete data from the <structure name> will be written to the row corresponding to the key field values in the internal table.
- If the TRANSPORTING option is specified, only the data of the fields specified with TRANSPORTING are written to the row corresponding to the key field values in the internal table.

MODIFY Statement – Update or Change Multiple Rows

The syntax of the MODIFY statement to update or change multiple rows is:

```
MODIFY <internal table name> FROM <structure name>
 TRANSPORTING <field1> [field2>..]WHERE <condition>.
```

All the rows in the internal table fulfilling the <condition> will be updated.

Hands-On Exercise: MODIFY Single Row

As it was enumerated, single rows can be updated through (a) The INDEX, that is, supply the row number to the MODIFY statement and the supplied row number if it exists will be updated with the data from the structure; (b) Key field values. Assign the key fields of the structure with the appropriate values, issue the MODIFY statement and the MODIFY statement will locate the row corresponding the key field values of the structure and will update this row if it exists from the structure.

These two forms of the MODIFY statement have been used to update misspelled data loaded from the database table T005U into a sorted internal table. The T005U table contains texts of the states/provinces/regions of all the countries.

Refer to the comment lines of the source program for a detailed description of the exercise.

The source program is:

```
REPORT YCL_CH06_ITAB11.

*****************************************************
* Internal Tables - MODIFY statement on Sorted Table **
*                 (Single row)                      **
*****************************************************
*******************************************************
* table T005U is a text table. it contains the state/    **
* region/province texts of all countries. like for       **
* example it contains the texts of all the indian states **
* and union territories. the texts are in all the        **
* languages supported. the primary key fields of this    **
* table are                                              **
*          MANDT   client code                           **
*          SPRAS   language key code                     **
*          LAND1   country code                          **
*          BLAND   state/region/province code            **
*                                                        **
* the text field is BEZEI                                **
*                                                        **
* for india (LAND1 = 'IN'), language english (language   **
* key code SPRAS = 'E'), the state code '01': the state  **
* has been miss-spelt. it is 'Andra Pradesh' instead of  **
* being 'Andhra Pradesh' (letter h is missing in first   **
* word)                                                  **
*                                                        **
* similarly for BLAND = '26' the text is 'Andaman und    **
* Nico.In.' instead of 'Andaman and Nico.In.' ('and' has **
* miss-spelt as 'und'                                    **
*                                                        **
* you will load texts of indian states in english into a **
* sorted internal table from database table T005U.       **
* (WHERE SPRAS = 'E' AND LAND1 = 'IN')                   **
* this sorted table defined key will be MANDT, SPRAS,    **
* LAND1, BLAND                                           **
*                                                        **
```

```
* you will assign the structure text field:               **
* BEZEI = 'Andhra Pradesh'                                **
*                                                         **
* you will issue the MODIFY statement with INDEX 1 and    **
* TRANSPORTING BEZEI i.e. only update field BEZEI.        **
*                                                         **
* the system will locate the row in the internal          **
* sorted table thru the INDEX 1 (row number 1)            **
* it will update the field BEZEI from the value in the    **
* structure field into the BEZEI field in the located     **
* row.                                                    **
* this is MODIFY with INDEX                               **
*                                                         **
*                                                         **
* you will assign the structure primary key fields the    **
* values:                                                 **
* MANDT = 800, SPRAS = 'E', LAND1 = 'IN', BLAND = '26'    **
*                                                         **
* you will assign the structure text field:               **
* BEZEI = 'Andaman and Nico.In.                           **
*                                                         **
* you will issue the MODIFY statement with TRANSPORTING   **
* BEZEI i.e. only update field BEZEI.                     **
*                                                         **
* the system will locate the row in the internal          **
* sorted table thru the values in structure key fields    **
* it will update the field BEZEI from the value in the    **
* structure field into the BEZEI field in the located     **
* row.                                                    **
* this is MODIFY with key                                 **
*                                                         **
*                                                         **
* this is happening only in the internal table. no        **
* changes are occurring in the database table T005U       **
************************************************************
TABLES T005U.
DATA: STATES_TAB LIKE SORTED TABLE OF T005U WITH UNIQUE KEY
      MANDT SPRAS LAND1 BLAND.

START-OF-SELECTION.

SELECT * FROM T005U INTO TABLE STATES_TAB WHERE
         SPRAS = 'E' AND LAND1 = 'IN'.

WRITE:/5 'Pre MODIFY Output (Only States Starting With A)'.
SKIP.
LOOP AT STATES_TAB INTO T005U WHERE BEZEI CP 'A*'.
 WRITE:/5 T005U-BLAND, T005U-BEZEI.
ENDLOOP.
```

```
*T005U-MANDT = 800.
*T005U-SPRAS = 'E'.
*T005U-LAND1 = 'IN'.
*T005U-BLAND = '01'.
T005U-BEZEI  = 'Andhra Pradesh'.
MODIFY STATES_TAB FROM T005U INDEX 1 TRANSPORTING BEZEI.

T005U-MANDT = 800.
T005U-SPRAS = 'E'.
T005U-LAND1 = 'IN'.
T005U-BLAND = '26'.
T005U-BEZEI = 'Andaman and Nico.In.'.
MODIFY TABLE STATES_TAB FROM T005U TRANSPORTING BEZEI.

SKIP 3.
WRITE:/5 'Post MODIFY Output (Only States Starting With A)'.
SKIP.
LOOP AT STATES_TAB INTO T005U WHERE BEZEI CP 'A*'.
 WRITE:/5 T005U-BLAND, T005U-BEZEI.
ENDLOOP.
```

In the LOOP statement, you have given a WHERE condition. You want to filter out the field BEZEI values starting with 'A.' You have given the string comparison operator 'CP' (contains pattern). Refer to Chapter 4. It is equivalent to giving LIKE 'A%' in a SQL statement. The '*' (asterisk) is for pattern, just like '%' in a SQL statements.

The output will be like this:

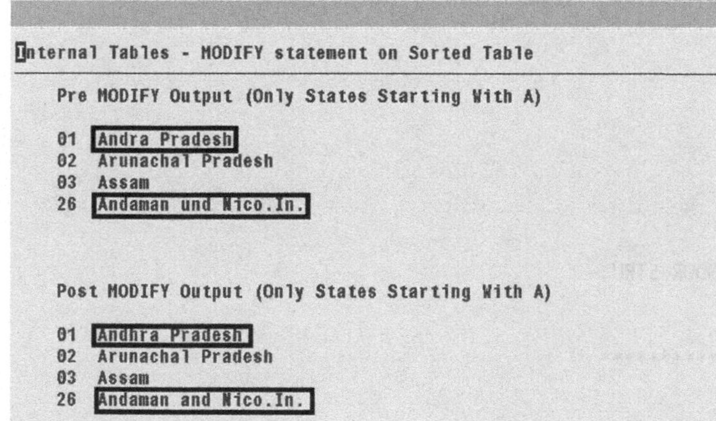

Figure 6-29. *Program YCL_CH06_ITAB11 - Output*

Hands-On Exercise: MODIFY Multiple Rows

As has been spelled out in II, you can update multiple rows with the MODIFY statement.

You are using the database table LFA1 – supplier/vendor primary table. It is on parallel lines of the customer primary table KNA1. You are loading a few fields of this table into an internal table. The field ANRED contains blanks for some rows. Where the value for ABRED is blank, you are replacing it with 'Messrs.' using the MODIFY statement. The internal table is output before MODIFY and after MODIFY.

The source program:

```
REPORT YCL_CH06_ITAB12 LINE-SIZE 110 LINE-COUNT 60
       NO STANDARD PAGE HEADING.

************************************************************
* Internal Tables - Update/Change (MODIFY) - Multiple Rows **
************************************************************
****************************************************************
* database table LFA1 is supplier/vendor primary table.       **
* the table has a field ANRED which contains the title for    **
* the enterprise like 'Company', 'Firma' etc.                 **
* (the same field is there in customer primary table KNA1)    **
*                                                             **
* Many of the rows have blank in this field ANRED             **
* you will load the fields LIFNR (supplier code), ANRED, NAME1,**
* ORT01 into an internal table. you will replace the blank    **
* ANRED values with 'Messrs.' with the MODIFY statement       **
* output the internal table before the MODIFY statement and   **
* after the MODIFY statement                                  **
****************************************************************

DATA: BEGIN OF VENDOR_STRU,
       LIFNR  TYPE LFA1-LIFNR,
       ANRED  TYPE LFA1-ANRED,
       NAME1  TYPE LFA1-NAME1,
       ORT01  TYPE LFA1-ORT01,
      END OF VENDOR_STRU,

      VENDOR_TAB LIKE STANDARD TABLE OF VENDOR_STRU,

      STRNG   TYPE STRING.
*****************************************************
TOP-OF-PAGE.
WRITE :/5 TEXT-001, STRNG, 104(3) SY-PAGNO.
WRITE:/5(102) SY-ULINE.
WRITE:/5 TEXT-002, 12 TEXT-003, 23 TEXT-004, 39 TEXT-005, 75 TEXT-006.
WRITE:/5 TEXT-007, 13 TEXT-008.
WRITE:/5(102) SY-ULINE.
*****************************************************
START-OF-SELECTION.

SELECT LIFNR ANRED NAME1 ORT01 FROM LFA1 INTO TABLE VENDOR_TAB
       UP TO 100 ROWS.
```

```
SORT VENDOR_TAB BY LIFNR.

STRNG = TEXT-009.
LOOP AT VENDOR_TAB INTO VENDOR_STRU.

 WRITE:/5(4) SY-TABIX, VENDOR_STRU-LIFNR USING NO EDIT MASK,
       VENDOR_STRU-ANRED, VENDOR_STRU-NAME1, VENDOR_STRU-ORT01.

ENDLOOP.

VENDOR_STRU-ANRED = 'Messrs.'.

MODIFY VENDOR_TAB FROM VENDOR_STRU TRANSPORTING ANRED
    WHERE ANRED = ' '.

STRNG = TEXT-010.

NEW-PAGE. "start post MODIFY on a new page

LOOP AT VENDOR_TAB INTO VENDOR_STRU.

 WRITE:/5(4) SY-TABIX, VENDOR_STRU-LIFNR USING NO EDIT MASK,
       VENDOR_STRU-ANRED, VENDOR_STRU-NAME1, VENDOR_STRU-ORT01.

ENDLOOP.
```

The text symbols:

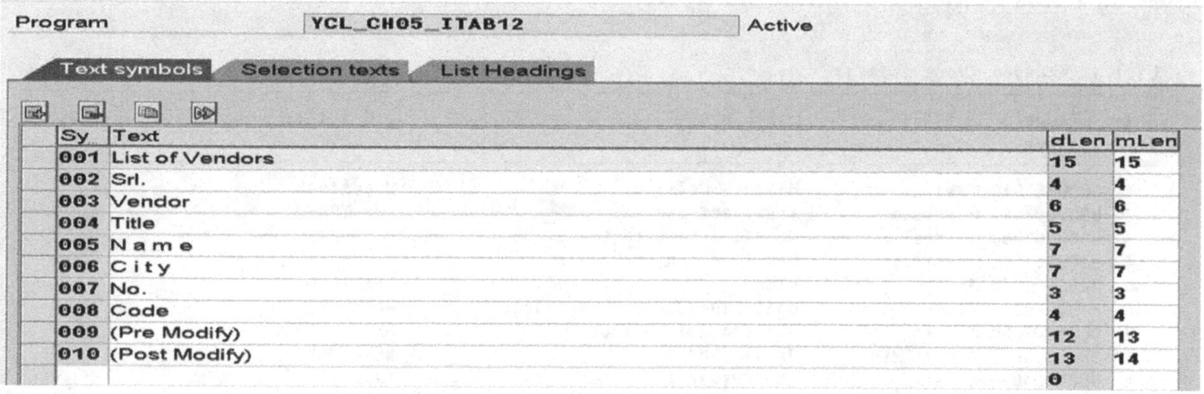

Program YCL_CH05_ITAB12 Active

Text symbols | Selection texts | List Headings

Sy	Text	dLen	mLen
001	List of Vendors	15	15
002	Srl.	4	4
003	Vendor	6	6
004	Title	5	5
005	N a m e	7	7
006	C i t y	7	7
007	No.	3	3
008	Code	4	4
009	(Pre Modify)	12	13
010	(Post Modify)	13	14
		0	

Figure 6-30. *Program YCL_CH06_ITAB12 – Text Symbols*

The output:

Internal Tables - MODIFY - Multiple Rows

List of Vendors (Pre Modify) 1

Srl. No.	Vendor Code	Title	N a m e	C i t y
1	0000003940		Mitch & Collins	Woodstock
2	0000003941		Transport Express	NEW YORK
3	0000003950		One Time Vendors L - P	
4	0000003960		One Time Vendors A - K	
5	0000003970		VISA	NEW YORK
6	0000003980		Main Line Cleaning Services	WAYNE
7	0000003990		Plastic Bottle Inc	SAINT LOUIS
8	0000003999		Jabil Vendor	NEW YORK
9	0000004000		Iron Power Inc.	Vancover
10	0000004010		Electric Engines	Montreal
11	0000004020		E-Tech Inc.	Whitehorse
12	0000004041	Company	Express Transport	NEW YORK
13	0000004042	Company	Reliable Trucking	PHILADELPHIA
14	0000004043	Company	Parcel Service Express	ATLANTA
15	0000004165	Company	Alexander Inc.	WESTON
16	0000004212		ALT's Autom. Release Vendor	DETROIT
17	0000004250	Company	Washington Realty Corporation	PHILADELPHIA
18	0000071600	Company	Family Court - Alberta	Calgary
19	0000071601	Company	Family Court - British Columbia	Vancouver

Figure 6-31. *Program YCL_CH06_ITAB12 – Output [Pre-MODIFY]*

Internal Tables - MODIFY - Multiple Rows

List of Vendors (Post Modify) 3

Srl. No.	Vendor Code	Title	N a m e	C i t y
1	0000003940	Messrs.	Mitch & Collins	Woodstock
2	0000003941	Messrs.	Transport Express	NEW YORK
3	0000003950	Messrs.	One Time Vendors L - P	
4	0000003960	Messrs.	One Time Vendors A - K	
5	0000003970	Messrs.	VISA	NEW YORK
6	0000003980	Messrs.	Main Line Cleaning Services	WAYNE
7	0000003990	Messrs.	Plastic Bottle Inc	SAINT LOUIS
8	0000003999	Messrs.	Jabil Vendor	NEW YORK
9	0000004000	Messrs.	Iron Power Inc.	Vancover
10	0000004010	Messrs.	Electric Engines	Montreal
11	0000004020	Messrs.	E-Tech Inc.	Whitehorse
12	0000004041	Company	Express Transport	NEW YORK
13	0000004042	Company	Reliable Trucking	PHILADELPHIA
14	0000004043	Company	Parcel Service Express	ATLANTA
15	0000004165	Company	Alexander Inc.	WESTON
16	0000004212	Messrs.	ALT's Autom. Release Vendor	DETROIT
17	0000004250	Company	Washington Realty Corporation	PHILADELPHIA
18	0000071600	Company	Family Court - Alberta	Calgary
19	0000071601	Company	Family Court - British Columbia	Vancouver

Figure 6-32. *Program YCL_CH06_ITAB12 – Output [Post-MODIFY]*

Hands-On Exercise: DESCRIBE TABLE Statement, Function: LINES( )

You can know the attributes of an internal table using the DESCRIBE TABLE statement. You can ascertain the number of rows in the internal table, the table type, the number given with the clause INITIAL SIZE. The syntax of the DESCRIBE TABLE is:

```
DESCRIBE TABLE <internal table name> [LINES <lines variable name]
[OCCURS <occurs variable name] [KIND <table kind variable name>].
```

- After the statement is issued, the system field SY-TFILL will contain the number of rows of the internal table on which the DESCRIBE TABLE statement was operated upon.
- If you want the number of rows of the internal table in your declared variable, you can use the optional LINES <lines variable name>.
- If you want the number specified with the INITIAL SIZE or OCCURS clause, you can give the optional addition OCCURS <occurs variable name>.
- If you want the internal table TYPE: standard, sorted, or hashed; you can give the optional addition KIND <table kind variable name>. This addition returns a one character internal table type: 'T' for standard, 'S' for sorted, or 'H' for hashed.

As an alternative to the DESCRIBE TABLE.. statement, a function is available to determine the number of rows in an internal table:

```
<no of rows variable> = LINES( internal table name ).
```

The function LINES(itab) is the preferred way of ascertaining the number of rows in an internal table over the statement DESCRIBE TABLE...LINES...

These features have been highlighted in the hands-on exercise program. For this hands-on exercise, a hashed table YCL_CH06_TCURT_TAB has been defined in the DDIC with line type TCURT and INITIAL SIZE 50, and UNIQUE KEY FIELDS: MANDT, SPRAS, and WAERS. This internal table is loaded from currency text database table TCURT.

```
The source program is:

REPORT YCL_CH06_ITAB13.

************************************
* Internal Tables - DESCRIBE TABLE **
* Function: <var> = LINES( itab ). **
************************************
************************************************
* DESCRIBE TABLE statement returns:          **
*                                            **
* (1) the internal table TYPE - H for hashed   **
*                       /KIND - S for sorted   **
*                             - T for standard **
*     the table TYPE is returned by using the  **
*     addition/clause KIND followed by the     **
*     variable name                            **
*                                              **
```

```
* (2) the number rows/lines in the internal     **
*     table. you can get this info              **
*     (a) in your defined variable by using     **
*         the addition/clause LINES followed    **
*         by your variable name                 **
*     (b) it is automatically loaded into the   **
*         system field SY-TFILL. another        **
*         DESCRIBE statement will overwrite     **
*         this system field                     **
*                                               **
* (3) INITIAL SIZE: returned by using the       **
*     addition/clause OCCURS followed by the    **
*     variable name                             **
*                                               **
* The number of rows/lines in the internal      **
* table are also determined by the function     **
* LINES( ). To get the number of rows/lines     **
* in your defined variable using this function **
* <variable> = LINES( <internal table name> ). **
*                                               **
*************************************************

DATA: INT_TABLE        TYPE YCL_CH06_TCURT_TAB,
                            "referring to DDIC table TYPE

      TABLE_TYP(1)     TYPE C,
      TABLE_LINES1     TYPE SY-TFILL, "SY-TFILL is TYPE I
      TABLE_LINES2     TYPE SY-TFILL,
      INIT_SIZE(2)     TYPE N.
**************************************************
START-OF-SELECTION.

SELECT * FROM TCURT INTO TABLE INT_TABLE.

DESCRIBE TABLE INT_TABLE LINES TABLE_LINES1
         KIND TABLE_TYP OCCURS INIT_SIZE.

TABLE_LINES2 = LINES( INT_TABLE ). "function to determine table lines

SKIP 5.
WRITE:/5 'TABLE TYPE ''H''/''S''/''T''    :', TABLE_TYP,
      /5 'TABLE ROWS/LINES-DESCRIBE       :', (4) TABLE_LINES1,
      /5 'TABLE ROW/LINES-LINES( )        :', (4) TABLE_LINES2,
      /5 'SY-TFILL                        :', (4) SY-TFILL,
      /5 'INITIAL SIZE                    :', INIT_SIZE.
```

The output:

```
Internal Tables - DESCRIBE TABLE

Internal Tables - DESCRIBE TABLE

    TABLE TYPE 'H'/'S'/'T'     : H
    TABLE ROWS/LINES-DESCRIBE : 4501
    TABLE ROW/LINES-LINES( )   : 4501
    SY-TFILL                   : 4501
    INITIAL SIZE               : 50
```

Figure 6-33. Program YCL_CH06_ITAB13 – Output

Hands-On Exercise: Produce Multilevel Summary Using Internal Table Control Level Processing

The internal table feature of control level processing facilitates easy production of multilevel summary lists. You had produced single level summary lists using the COLLECT statement in programs YCL_CH06_ITAB05 and YCL_CH06_ITAB06. Both the programs produced customer wise sales summary. There was one summarizing entity: the customer. You can produce single level summary outputs without the COLLECT statement. That would have entailed extra coding. Similarly, the control level processing helps cut down on coding.

Scenario

You require a two-level summary list involving the entities: customer and material. In technical terms, our fields of summarization are KUNNR and MATNR. The output should list the sale of different materials for each customer.

A very rough layout:

```
Customer Wise, Material Wise Sales:

Customer ABC
 Material AAA          12345.00
 Material BBB          34567.00
 Material CCC          56789.00
                                 103701.00

Customer DEF
Material BBB           23456.00
Material EEE           67890.00
                                  91346.00 195047.00
```

Observe that under each customer the sales total of each material for the customer is listed.

When all the materials for the customer are exhausted the total for the customer is output to the right of the totals for each material.

Similarly, when all the customers are exhausted, a grand total is output to the right of the totals for each customer.

An output would generally be proposed by the end use. A less rough output layout:

```
Customer Wise/Material Wise Sales of Company Code: XXXX/XXXXXXXXXXXXXXXXXXXXXXXXX
                                       Currency: XXXXX

----------------------------------------------------------------------------------
 Material Code  D e s c r i p t i o n                                       Amount
----------------------------------------------------------------------------------
Customer: XXXXXXXXXX/XXXXXXXXXXXXXXXXXXXXXXXXXXXXXXXXXXX

 XXXXXXXXXXXX XXXXXXXXXXXXXXXXXXXXXXXXXXXXXXXXXXXXXXXXXXX XXXXXXXXXXXXXXXXX
                                                                          XXXXXXXXXXXXXXXXX
```

In this layout, you have not been able to accommodate the grand total on the extreme right due to lack of horizontal space. So it is implicit.

Input Data Identification

You must identify the tables and fields required to produce this output. The table of the basic data always should be identified. You need material wise sales basic data. This is available in the billing document item database table VBRP. In the table the amount for each material or item is available as a separate row. The fields required by you in VBRP table are:

```
MATNR     Material Code length 18
NETWR     Net Value of Material/Item in Document Currency
```

Note that material code MATNR is 18 characters. The NETWR in VBRP should be distinguished from the NETWR of VBRK. In VBRP, this is the net value of each material. If in a billing document, 10 bolts are sold for $1000, NETWR of that row in VBRP will contain this. If in the same billing document there is one more material or item 5 nuts for $250, this will be another row in VBRP and the field NETWR in this row will contain $250. In the VBRK table (billing document header), the billing document row to which these materials or items belong, the NETWR field will contain a total of these two materials or items (i.e., 1000+250 = $1250. The document currency of this billing document was US Dollar denoted by USD. Note that in the data model, VBRK is the primary table and VBRP the secondary. They are related through the fields MANDT and VBELN.

Earlier, in your customer wise sales summary, you were using the NETWR of the table VBRK. You wanted a customer wise summary and were not bothered with individual materials/items.

Each billing document of a company code can have a different currency. Suppose the company code to which this billing document belongs has the operating currency as Indian Rupee denoted as INR. Then for your summary list purposes, you need to convert the amounts from USD to INR. Similarly for every amount, you need to convert the amounts from document currency to the company code currency. So you need the exchange rate. The exchange rate field KURRF is available in the table VBRK:

```
KURRF in table VBRK -    Exchange Rate
```

You need material descriptions. The material descriptions are maintained in multiple languages in the text table MAKT.

```
MAKTX in table MAKT - Material Description
```

You need a customer code and customer name. These are available in table KNA1:

```
KUNNR     Customer Code
NAME1     Customer Name
```

The table KNA1 cannot be linked to table VBRP directly. There are no common fields. They are to be linked through the table VBRK that contains customer code field KUNAG. You are accessing the field KURRF from VBRK.

So you need to retrieve data from four database tables:

```
VBRP  Billing Documents - Item
MAKT  Material Descriptions
VBRK  Billing Document - Header
KNA1  Customer Primary
```

You will create a database view consisting of these four tables and gather all the data in one DDIC object.

Your data model for the view is:

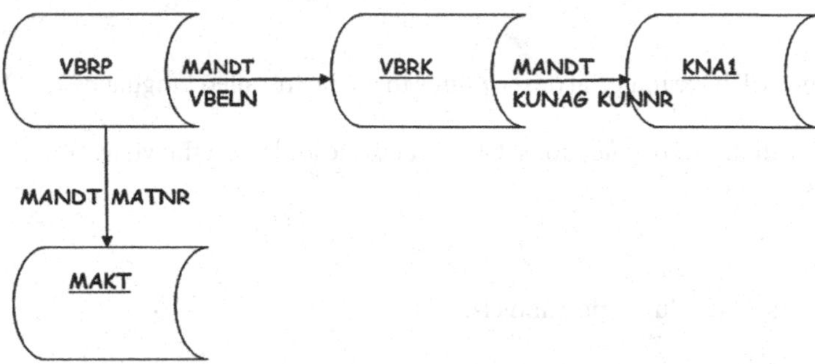

Figure 6-34. *Data Model - Database View YCL_CH06_CM_SALE*

Since the database view uses an inner join, positioning a table on the left or right does not matter. You are treating the table VBRP at the top of the hierarchy because it is containing the basic data.

Database View

The database view *table* column and *join conditions* columns will be like this:

```
KNA1
VBRK          VBRP        MANDT = MAKT    MANDT
MAKT          VBRP        MATNR = MAKT    MATNR
VBRP          VBRP        MANDT = VBRK    MANDT
              VBRP        VBELN = VBRK    VBELN
              VBRK        MANDT = KNA1    MANDT
              VBRK        KUNAG = KNA1    KUNNR
```

The database *view field list* will be like this:

```
MANDT    VBRP    MANDT
VBELN    VBRP    VBELN
POSNR    VBRP    POSNR
SPRAS    MAKT    SPRAS
KUNNR    KNA1    KUNNR
MATNR    VBRP    MATNR
NETWR    VBRP    NETWR
MAKTX    MAKT    MAKTX
BUKRS    VBRK    BUKRS
KURRF    VBRK    KURRF
WAERK    VBRK    WAERK
NAME1    KNA1    NAME1
```

The database view *selection conditions* should be like this:

```
MAKT    SPRAS    EQ    'E'
```

You need to have this condition, or else the view will have material descriptions in all the installed languages. You are filtering out the descriptions in English.

Create a database view YCL_CH06_CM_SALE with these specifications. Check, activate and audit the view.

Output Main Body Layout

The output body layout in terms of fields, table origins, and column positions is:

Table 6-6. *Customer, Material Wise Sales Summary of a Company Code: Output Layout*

Field Name	Table Name	Description	Column Positions
KUNNR	KNA1	Customer Code	005-014 (10)
			015
NAME1	KNA1	Name	016-050 (35)
MATNR	VBRP	Material Code	008-025 (18)
			026
MAKTX	MAKT	Material Description	027,066 (40)
			067
Total of (NETWR * KURRF)	VBRP VBRK	Total of Material Net Value – Material Wise Total in Company Code Currency	068,083 (16)
			084
Total of (NETWR * KURRF)	VBRP, VBRK	Total of Customer Net Value – Customer Wise Total in Company Code Currency	085,100 (16)
			101
Total of (NETWR * KURRF)	VBRP, VBRK	Grand Total of Net Value – Grand Total in Company Code Currency	102-117 (16)

Control Levels

The whole process of a multilevel summarization of data takes place within the LOOP...ENDLOOP.

There are the hierarchical control level statements corresponding or mapping to your summarization levels or fields. Like in your scenario, your summarization fields are KUNNR (customer code) and MATNR (material code). The control will jump to these control level statements depending on conditions arising with the processing of data. A control level statement block starts with the key word AT and ends or terminates with the key word ENDAT.

You should ensure that your table is sorted in the ascending order of summarization or control fields, that is, KUNNR or MATNR.

The control level statements are as follows:

- AT FIRST
- AT NEW <control field>
- AT END OF <control field>
- ON CHANGE <control field>
- AT LAST

With the LOOP...ENDLOOP, the control level statements will appear like this:

```
LOOP AT <internal table name> INTO <structure name>.

  AT FIRST.
   <statement block>.
  ENDAT

  AT NEW <first level of control field>.
   <statement block>.
  ENDAT.

  AT NEW <second level of control field>.
   <statement block>.
  ENDAT.

  ...... " more AT NEW controls if any
  ...... " more AT END OF controls if any

  AT END OF <second level of control field>.
   <statement block>.
  ENDAT.

  AT END OF <first level of control field>.
   <statement block>.
  ENDAT.

  AT LAST.
   <statement block>.
  ENDAT.

ENDLOOP.
```

The order or hierarchy of these control level statements is to be maintained as shown in the preceding pseudo code as a standard practice. You may not have any action to be taken for a particular control level and can omit it.

Note that for the AT NEW control levels, the order is the same as the summarization levels, that is, AT NEW <first level of control or summarization>, AT NEW <second level of control or summarization> and so on if there are more than two levels of summarization.

The order of AT END OF control levels is the reverse of the order of AT NEW control levels. Starting with AT END OF <second level of control or summarization>, next the AT END OF <first level of control or summarization>.

The control level AT FIRST is at the top and the control level AT LAST at the bottom.

The control level statements cannot be used in LOOP...ENDLOOP with WHERE and/or FROM and TO. Also, the table should not be modified during the LOOP...ENDLOOP.

AT FIRST: After the first row is fetched from the internal table (first pass of the loop), the control will jump to the control level AT FIRST. If you have some action to be performed for this control level, you need to put this control level else you can omit it. This applies to all control levels.

AT NEW: Every time a new value of <second level of control field> or <first level of control field> is fetched, control will jump to this control level.

In case of a new value of <first level of control field>, it first jumps to the control level of <first level of control field> followed by a jump to <second level of control field>.

In case where a new value of <second level of control field>, it only jumps to <second level of control field>.

AT END OF: Every time all the rows for a particular value of <second level of control field> or <first level of control field> have been fetched, control will jump to this control level.

In the case where all rows of a particular value of <first level of control field> have been fetched, it first jumps to the control level of <second level of control field> followed by a jump to <first level of control field>.

In the case where all rows of a particular value of <second level of control field> have been fetched, it only jumps to <second level of control field>.

ON CHANGE OF: This is similar to AT NEW control. Every time there is a change of value in the field, control will jump to this level. This is not specified in the LOOP ENDLOOP pseudo code.

AT LAST: When all the rows of the internal table have been fetched, before exiting the LOOP...ENDLOOP, control will jump to this control level.

To recapitulate, you need to use control levels within the LOOP...ENDLOOP to be able to take action for the situations triggering the control levels. There are the two essential prerequisites: (a) The control levels should be in the order given in the pseudo code as a standard practice; (b) The internal table should be sorted in the ascending order of the summarization or control fields. The discussion has been conducted for the sake of easy understanding, in terms of two control fields. It would apply to n number of control fields.

Mapping Application of Control Levels to Scenario

Now, let these control levels be mapped to your output layout:

Every time a new customer row is fetched, you need to output the customer info, that is, customer code and name. These are serial numbers 1 and 2 in Table 6-6. So you can use AT NEW KUNNR for this.

Consider the output of summary lines for each material sold to this customer. A material could be sold once, twice, or n number of times to a customer. These n number of rows of a material need to be summarized and a total is to be output along with a material code and material description. So you want control when all the rows for a particular material under a particular customer have been fetched. You can use the AT END OF MATNR control level. You output the material code, description, and total amount for a material, that is, serial numbers 3, 4, and 5 of Table 6-6.

When all the rows of a particular customer have been fetched, you need to output the total for the customer appearing to the right of material wise total. You can use the AT END OF KUNNR. This is serial number 6 of Table 6-6.

For your grand total, you can use the control level AT LAST. This is serial number 7 of Table 6-6.

SUM statement

The next issue is how the totals will be built and accumulated for the three instances: material wise, customer wise, and the grand total. Along with the control level feature the SUM statement is provided. The syntax of the SUM statement is:

```
SUM.
```

The SUM statement can only be given inside a LOOP...ENDLOOP construct. If there is a nesting of LOOP... ENDLOOP, the SUM statement is not accepted.

The SUM statement operates in the following way:

The SUM statement operates on types F, I, and P that are numeric fields.

It accumulates the numeric fields for all the rows fetched for a particular value of the control field if the SUM statement is given in the AT END OF...control block.

It accumulates the numeric fields for all the rows to be fetched for a particular value of the control field if the SUM statement is given in the AT NEW...control block.

The accumulated totals are placed in the numeric fields of the structure. You can use the accumulated control, numeric fields, and output it, etc.

To illustrate with an example, your internal table name is SALES_SUM_TAB and your work area/structure name is SALES_SUM_STRU. Suppose some of your data is as follows:

```
 MATNR   MAKTX  NETWR
---------------------------
1234        BOLT        50000
1234        BOLT        20000
1234        BOLT        70000
1234        BOLT        30000
1235        NUT         10000
...................

LOOP AT SALES_SUM_TAB INTO SALES_SUM_TRU.

  AT END OF MATNR.
   SUM.
  ENDAT.
ENDLOOP.
```

So, when the four rows of MATNR value equal to 1234 have been fetched, control will jump to the AT END OF MATNR. The SUM STATEMENT will be executed. After the execution of the SUM statement, the field SALES_SUM_STRU-NETWR will contain 170000. Now, all that is required is to output this field with MATNR and MAKTX.

A similar illustration can be given for the customer wise total and the grand total.

Extra Processing

You need to take care of two more issues.

I. The first issue is related to the field NETWR and the SUM statement. The SUM statement will total the NETWR values of individual rows. So the individual rows in the internal table must have the converted value of NETWR, that is, NETWR multiplied by KURRF, the exchange rate field. This will convert all the values of NETWR into one currency, the currency of the company code (or the operating currency). Otherwise you will end up adding Indian Rupee (INR) values to US Dollars (USD) values, a meaningless exercise. To incorporate these converted amounts into internal table individual rows, you will run a LOOP...ENDLOOP in which you fetch one row from the internal table into the structure and multiply the structure fields:

```
SALES_SUM_STRU-NETWR = SALES_SUM_STRU-NETWR * SALES_SUM_STRU-KURRF.
```

Write/update this converted amount from the structure to the internal table row using the MODIFY statement. The code will be like this:

```
LOOP AT SALES_SUM_TAB INTO SALES_SUM_STRU.

 SALES_SUM_STRU-NETWR = SALES_SUM_STRU-NETWR  * SALES_SUM_STRU-KURRF.

 MODIFY SALES_SUM_TAB FROM SALES_SUM_STRU INDEX SY-TABIX
TRANSPORTING NETWR.

ENDLOOP.
```

This will result in all the NETWR values in the internal table in converted form.

II. When there is a jump to the control levels, the non-numeric, non-control fields like NAME1 and MAKTX are filled with null (output as '*' asterisks). You need to output these fields. So these fields need to be appropriately saved as to enable you to output. This is being taken care of in the program.

The source code for customer, material wise sales summary:

```
REPORT YCL_CH06_ITAB14 LINE-SIZE 120 LINE-COUNT 60
       NO STANDARD PAGE HEADING.

*******************************************************
* Internal Tables Control Totals For Two Level Summary **
*******************************************************
**********************************************************
* declare table structure. ensure the control fields      **
* are in the beginning of structure. the order of these   **
* fields should be same as control order KUNNR MATNR      **
* declare table & other variables                         **
*                                                         **
* input company code - PARAMETERS                         **
*                                                         **
* load internal table with data from the view. set up     **
* LOOP...ENDLOOP. for each row convert amount NETWR       **
* to the operating currency of company code. make KURRF   **
* = 0 to prevent overflow. update in the table MODIFY etc.**
*                                                         **
* sort table on fields of control levels i.e. KUNNR MATNR **
*                                                         **
* set up LOOP...ENDLOOP.. set up control levels           **
* AT NEW KUNNR, AT END OF MATNR, AT END OF KUNNR, AT LAST **
* as per output format. output appropriate info in each   **
* these control levels as per output format               **
**********************************************************
```

```
DATA:  BEGIN OF SALES_SUM_STRU,
        KUNNR   TYPE KNA1-KUNNR, " I level of control
        MATNR   TYPE VBRP-MATNR, " II level of control
        NAME1   TYPE KNA1-NAME1,
        MAKTX   TYPE MAKT-MAKTX,
        NETWR   TYPE VBRP-NETWR,
        KURRF   TYPE VBRK-KURRF,
       END OF SALES_SUM_STRU,

       SALES_SUM_TAB LIKE STANDARD TABLE OF SALES_SUM_STRU,

        NAME1   TYPE KNA1-NAME1,
        MAKTX   TYPE MAKT-MAKTX,
        STR(50) TYPE C,
        BUTXT   TYPE T001-BUTXT,
        WAERS   TYPE T001-WAERS.
***************************************************************
PARAMETERS CMP_CD   TYPE VBRK-BUKRS VALUE CHECK DEFAULT 3000.

TOP-OF-PAGE.
WRITE:/5 TEXT-001, CMP_CD NO-GAP, '/' NO-GAP, BUTXT, 81(3) SY-PAGNO.
WRITE:/46 TEXT-002, WAERS.
SKIP 1.
WRITE:/5(79) SY-ULINE.
WRITE:/9 TEXT-003, 29 TEXT-004, 78 TEXT-005.
WRITE:/5(79) SY-ULINE.

***************************************************************
START-OF-SELECTION.

SELECT SINGLE BUTXT WAERS FROM T001 INTO (BUTXT, WAERS) WHERE
       BUKRS = CMP_CD.

SELECT KUNNR MATNR NAME1 MAKTX NETWR KURRF FROM
       YCL_CH06_CM_SALE
       INTO TABLE SALES_SUM_TAB WHERE BUKRS = CMP_CD.

** convert amount NETWR to company code currency
**********************************************
LOOP AT SALES_SUM_TAB INTO SALES_SUM_STRU.
 SALES_SUM_STRU-NETWR = SALES_SUM_STRU-NETWR * SALES_SUM_STRU-KURRF.
 SALES_SUM_STRU-KURRF = 0.
 MODIFY SALES_SUM_TAB FROM SALES_SUM_STRU.
ENDLOOP.

SORT SALES_SUM_TAB BY KUNNR MATNR. " sort in order of control levels
```

```
** loop to generate customer, material summary
**********************************************
LOOP AT SALES_SUM_TAB INTO SALES_SUM_STRU.

 NAME1 = SALES_SUM_STRU-NAME1.

 AT NEW KUNNR. " first row of new value of KUNNR fetched
  SKIP 1.
  FORMAT INVERSE ON COLOR COL_POSITIVE.
  CONCATENATE SALES_SUM_STRU-KUNNR NAME1 INTO STR SEPARATED BY '/'.
  WRITE:/5 TEXT-006, STR.
 ENDAT.

 MAKTX = SALES_SUM_STRU-MAKTX.

 AT END OF MATNR. " all rows of particular value of KUNNR & MATNR fetched
  SUM.
  FORMAT INVERSE ON COLOR COL_GROUP.
  WRITE:/8 SALES_SUM_STRU-MATNR USING NO EDIT MASK, MAKTX,
        (16) SALES_SUM_STRU-NETWR.
 ENDAT.

 AT END OF KUNNR. " all rows of particular value of KUNNR fetched
  SUM.
  FORMAT INVERSE ON COLOR COL_POSITIVE.
  WRITE:/85(16) SALES_SUM_STRU-NETWR.
 ENDAT.

 AT LAST. "all rows in internal table fetched
  SUM.
  FORMAT INVERSE ON COLOR COL_TOTAL.
  WRITE:/102(16) SALES_SUM_STRU-NETWR.
 ENDAT.

ENDLOOP.
```

The text symbols:

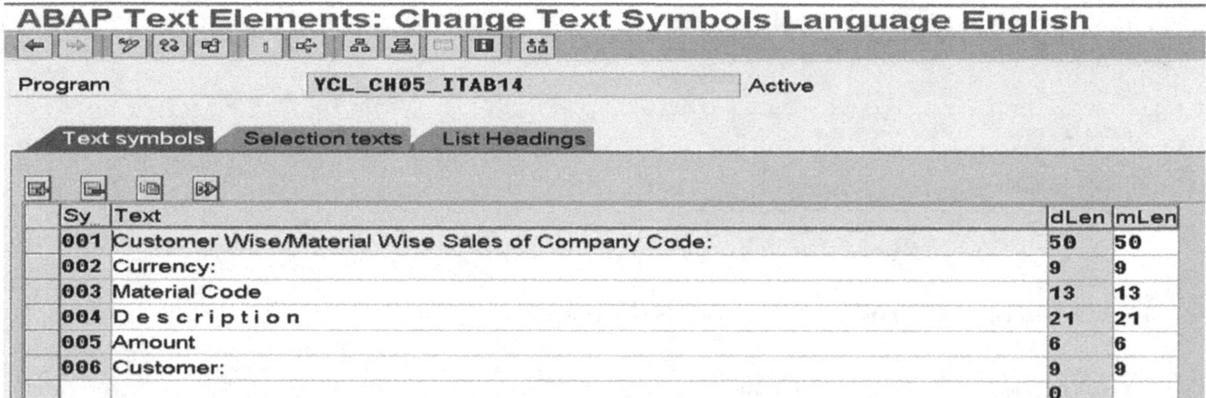

Sy	Text	dLen	mLen
001	Customer Wise/Material Wise Sales of Company Code:	50	50
002	Currency:	9	9
003	Material Code	13	13
004	D e s c r i p t i o n	21	21
005	Amount	6	6
006	Customer:	9	9
		0	

Figure 6-35. *Program YCL_CH06_ITAB14 – Text Symbols*

The outputs:

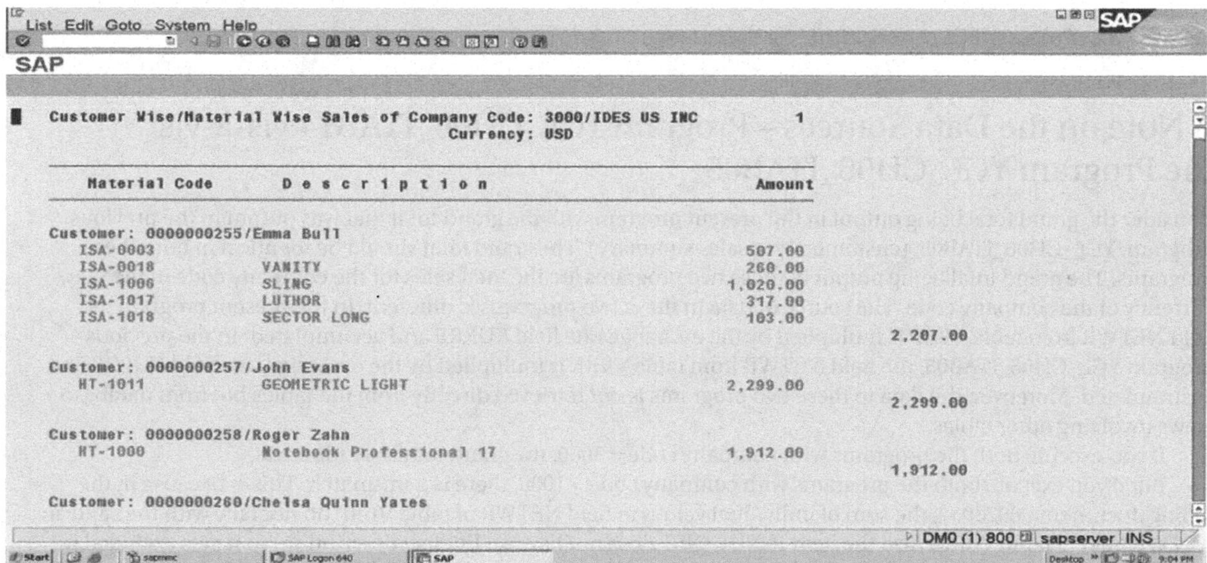

Figure 6-36. *Program YCL_CH06_ITAB14 – Output*

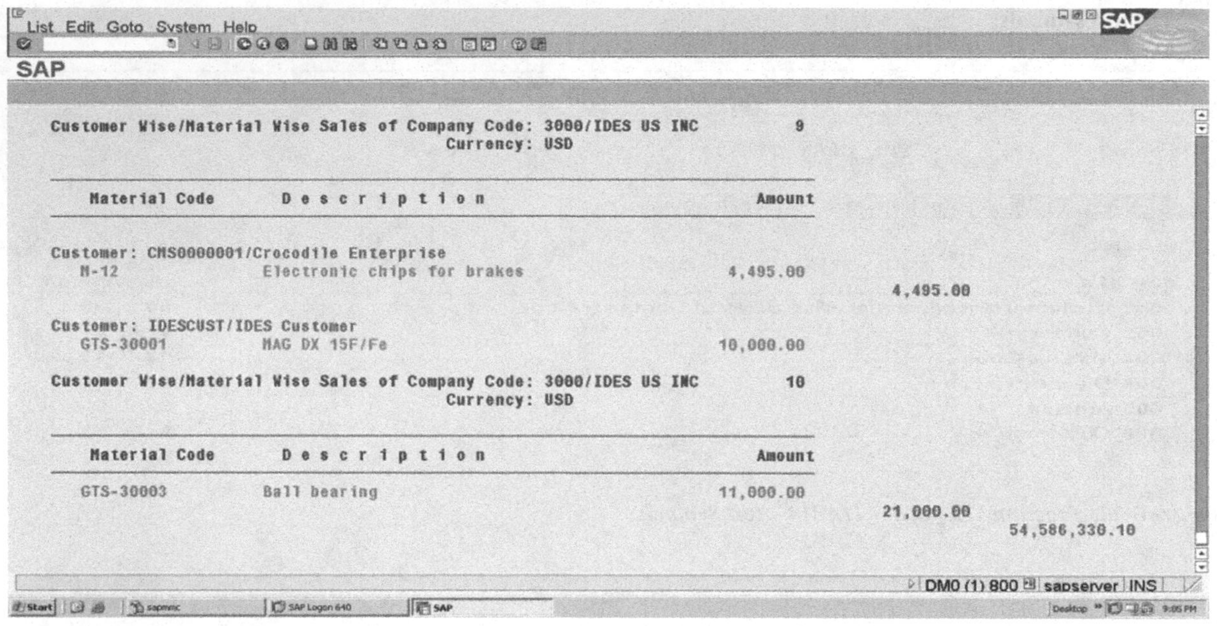

Figure 6-37. *Program YCL_CH06_ITAB14 - Output with Grand Total*

A Note on the Data Sources - Program YCL_CH06_ITAB14 vis-à-vis the Program YCL_CH06_ITAB05

Consider the grand total being output in the present program with the grand total that was output in the previous program, YCL_CH06_ITAB05, (customer wise sales summary). The grand total should be identical in both these programs. The grand total being output in these two programs are the total sales for the company code in the currency of the company code. The source of data in these two programs is different. In the present program the field NETWR from table VBRP is multiplied by the exchange rate field KURRF and accumulated. In the previous program YCL_CH06_ITAB05, the field NETWR from table VBRK is multiplied by the exchange rate field KURRF and accumulated. Moreover, the data in these two programs is not retrieved directly from the tables but from database views involving other tables.

If you execute both the programs with company code = 3000, the grand totals are identical.

But if you execute both the programs with company code = 1000, there is a mismatch. This is because in the billing document 90023037, the sum of individual values in field NETWR of table VBRP do not tally with the value in NETWR field of table VBRK. Also the item R-NET-INST does not have an English description, so it gets excluded in your database view.

For company code = 0001, there is no output with the current program (no data in the view for company code = 001). Whereas, if you execute the program YCL_CH06_ITAB05, there is output. This is because, for company code = 0001, all billing document items have a material number = Erste Hilfe. The material number = Erste Hilfe has no corresponding row in the tables MARA and MAKT (an orphan row), so it gets omitted in the database view.

These are problems related to the IDES server data.

In your database views, you are not involving the sales administration table VBUK. The billing documents tables VBRK and VBRP are not directly linked. These two tables are linked to each other through the table sales administration VBUk. In all the hand-on exercises in the book, you are linking these two tables directly for simplicity.

You are being made aware of the issues. In the present learning paradigm, you will not bother with these issues.

Hands-On Exercise: Initialize Internal Tables Rows or Complete Data

You can initialize internal tables, that is, delete all the rows with a single statement. There are three separate statements available to clear internal data. The three statements are:

Clear

The CLEAR statement can clear any data object, that is, elementary, structured, or internal table.

When the CLEAR statement is used on an elementary data object, the elementary data object is filled with the INITIAL value. The INITIAL value for type C is spaces; it is Unicode/ASCII/EBCDIC zeroes for type D, etc. Refer to Chapter 4 for INITIAL values of different predefined ABAP elementary types.

When the CLEAR statement is operated on a structured data object, each of the elementary data objects or fields in the structure are filled with the INITIAL values of the corresponding type.

When the CLEAR statement is operated on an internal table, all the rows in the internal table are deleted.

If an internal table exists with a header line and you want the CLEAR statement to operate on the internal table, you should add brackets - [].

When operating with the APPEND statement, it is a good programming practice to use the CLEAR statement after the APPEND statement as to ensure the old data that has not been overwritten is cleared.

Refresh

The REFRESH statement is exclusive to internal tables. It deletes all rows in the internal table.

Free

The FREE statement is exclusive to internal tables. It deletes all rows in the internal table and releases the memory as well.

The program YCL_CH06_ITAB15 demonstrates the three statements to clear internal tables of data.

The source program:

```
REPORT YCL_CH06_ITAB15.

********************************************************
* Internal Tables, Remove Data - CLEAR, REFRESH, FREE **
********************************************************
********************************************************
* declare three internal tables of structure TCURT    **
*                                                     **
* load the three internal tables with TCURT data      **
*                                                     **
* operate DESCRIBE TABLE on the three internal tables **
* determine number of rows. output the number of rows **
*                                                     **
* operate CLEAR, REFRESH, FREE statements on the      **
* internal tables.                                    **
*                                                     **
* operate DESCRIBE TABLE on the three internal tables **
* determine number of rows. output the number of rows **
********************************************************
```

```
DATA: CURR_TAB1   TYPE STANDARD TABLE OF TCURT WITH HEADER LINE,
      CURR_TAB2   TYPE STANDARD TABLE OF TCURT,
      CURR_TAB3   TYPE STANDARD TABLE OF TCURT WITH HEADER LINE.
****************************************************
START-OF-SELECTION.
SELECT * FROM TCURT INTO TABLE : CURR_TAB1,
                                 CURR_TAB2,
                                 CURR_TAB3.
************************************************
DESCRIBE TABLE CURR_TAB1.
WRITE:/5 'CURR_TAB1-PRE CLEAR STATUS  :', (4) SY-TFILL.

DESCRIBE TABLE CURR_TAB2.
WRITE:/5 'CURR_TAB2-PRE REFRESH STATUS:', (4) SY-TFILL.

DESCRIBE TABLE CURR_TAB3.
WRITE:/5 'CURR_TAB3-PRE FREE STATUS   :', (4) SY-TFILL.

SKIP 2.
CLEAR CURR_TAB1[]." to distinguish itab from structure of
                  " the same name
DESCRIBE TABLE CURR_TAB1.
WRITE:/5 'CURR_TAB1-POST CLEAR STATUS  :', (4) SY-TFILL.

REFRESH CURR_TAB2.
DESCRIBE TABLE CURR_TAB2.
WRITE:/5 'CURR_TAB2-POST REFRESH STATUS:', (4) SY-TFILL.

FREE CURR_TAB3.
DESCRIBE TABLE CURR_TAB3.
WRITE:/5 'CURR_TAB3-POST FREE STATUS   :', (4) SY-TFILL.
```

The output will look like this:

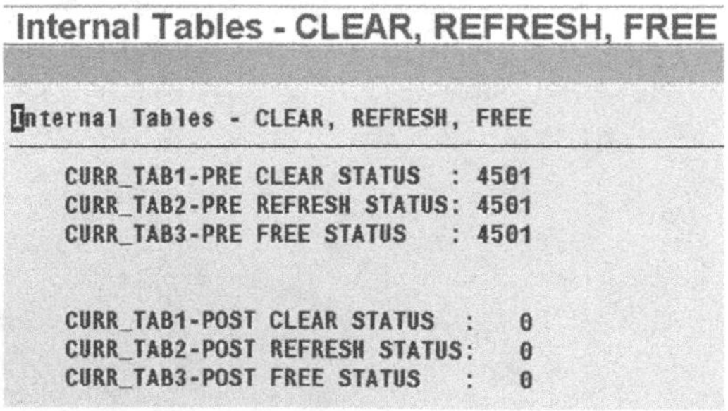

```
Internal Tables - CLEAR, REFRESH, FREE

Internal Tables - CLEAR, REFRESH, FREE

    CURR_TAB1-PRE CLEAR STATUS  : 4501
    CURR_TAB2-PRE REFRESH STATUS: 4501
    CURR_TAB3-PRE FREE STATUS   : 4501


    CURR_TAB1-POST CLEAR STATUS  :    0
    CURR_TAB2-POST REFRESH STATUS:    0
    CURR_TAB3-POST FREE STATUS   :    0
```

Figure 6-38. *Program YCL_CH06_ITAB15 - Output*

MOVE, Assign, Copy, Internal Tables

You can use internal tables as operands in the MOVE and assignment statements. When using the MOVE statement or making assignments, ensure that the source and destination internal tables have identical structures.

Conclusion

In the remaining chapters of this book, internal tables are invariably used. For better performance, the de facto way of processing retrieved data from database tables or views is through the internal tables.

Refer to the E-Resource program YCL_CH06_DATA_DEC_REFS. It summarizes the different references used to declare data in ABAP programs.

CHAPTER 7

Modularization

Introduction

In the ABAP environment, modularization involves the organization of programs into modular units, also known as logical blocks. The modularization should reduce redundancy and increase program readability even as you are creating it and subsequently during the maintenance cycle. Modularization also enables reusability of the same code again. ABAP, with its roots in procedure oriented technology, has made it necessary for developers to modularize: organize the programs relatively more than in the OOPS based languages, which have relatively more built-in modular features.

In addition to modularization, ABAP message maintenance and the MESSAGE... statement is also covered in the present chapter. The MESSAGE... statement is used to issue messages as well as raise error exceptions inside a function module. Function modules are part of modularization.

Recall from Chapter 4 about the structure of ABAP programs. The ABAP programs are made up of processing blocks. Two of the processing blocks are:

- The processing blocks called from outside the program and from the ABAP runtime environment (i.e., event blocks and dialog modules).
- Processing blocks called from ABAP programs:
    - Subroutines - Internal and external
    - Function modules (basically generic subroutines)
    - Methods

These processing blocks are called as the modularizing processing blocks. Event processing blocks have been already introduced. As more contexts arise, more events will be introduced. Dialog modules will be covered in Chapter 14 entitled 'Screen Programming.'

Apart from allowing the modularization with processing blocks, ABAP also facilitates modularization with source code through local macros and global include programs. The following will be discussed in this chapter:

- Modularization at Source Code Level
    - Local Macros
    - Global Include programs
- Modularization through processing blocks Called from ABAP programs
    - Internal subroutines
    - Function modules

External subroutines are essential only in one context (i.e., SAP Scripts). Function modules are the preferred option over external subroutines. Methods will be covered in Chapters 11, 12, and 13.

For now, the coverage will consist of:

- Macros
- Internal subroutines
- Include programs
- Function modules

Macros

This is the most rudimentary mode of modularization. A typical situation when a macro can be used is when in an ABAP program, a number of source lines or statements are being repeated. The repeated statements can be located at one place as a macro and invoked from multiple places. It is a case of reducing redundancy and avoiding the cluttering of too many statements. The ABAP compiler on encountering the macro will expand the macro, that is, replace its invocation with the statements contained in the macro definition.

A rough syntax of a macro definition is as follows:

```
DEFINE <macro name1>. "DEFINE is key word
<statements>
END-OF-DEFINITION. "END-OF-DEFINITION is key phrase
........
<macro name1> [<parameters 1> <parameters 2>..]. "Macro invocation
```

- It is necessary to define a macro first before invoking it.
- The <parameter 1>... etc. replace the place holders &1... in the ABAP statements contained in the macro definition. There can be a maximum of nine placeholders in a macro definition.
- You can invoke a macro within another macro, but not the same macro.
- You should be careful when using both macros and include programs, as there is no syntax check of include programs except the *top include*.

If you recall from Chapter 4, we had a program DESCRIBE FIELD... It offers you the scope of macro application. There are a lot of repetitive lines in that program. But before you apply macros to this program, let the internal subroutine be introduced, and you will then apply macros and subroutines to the Chapter 4 program DESCRIBE FIELD...

Subroutines

This discussion is confined to internal subroutines. When the word subroutine is used, internal is implicit.

Like macros, the subroutines also reduce redundancy and enhance program readability, but with some more advantages over the macros. The subroutines can accept all types of parameters unlike the macros, which accept only strings in the placeholders. The subroutines can also return values (output parameters). Error handling or *raising exception* is supported within the subroutines. The subroutines can also have local data. Like the macros, the subroutines have to be defined and then invoked or called.

Subroutine Definition

A rough syntax of a subroutine definition is:

```
FORM <subroutine name> USING <formal parameter 1>
  VALUE(<formal parameter 2>) TYPE <data object2>
  CHANGING <formal parameter 3> LIKE <data object 3>
  VALUE(<formal parameter 4>). "this is a single statement to define subroutine
   <statements block>
ENDFORM.
```

Deliberately, four parameters have been specified to make the explanation easy to understand. The parameter/s specified with the subroutine definition is the formal parameters.

- FORM is the keyword to define a subroutine. The keyword has to be followed by the name of the subroutine.
- Parameters can be passed by reference (the default), value, and value and result.
- If you use either of the keywords USING or CHANGING followed by the formal parameter, (without the key word *VALUE*), the parameter is passed by reference.
- If you use the keywords USING VALUE followed by the formal parameter enclosed in parentheses, then the parameter is passed by value.
- If you use the key words CHANGING VALUE followed by the formal parameter enclosed in parenthesis, then the parameter is passed by value and result.
- You can assign a type to a parameter by using the appropriate keyword TYPE or LIKE followed by either the predefined ABAP elementary types, C, D, F, I, N, P, T, X, STRING, and XSTRING) or a local type declared with the *TYPES* statement or a DDIC data type in the DDIC *type group* or a data object name (in most cases a DDIC data object) or a system field. You can also assign type to the formal parameters by referring to the ABAP *generic types*. A table of the ABAP generic types is to be found in the online documentation through the navigation: ABAP - By Theme ➤ Built-In Types and Data Objects and Functions ➤ Built-In Data Types ➤ Generic ABAP Types. When subroutine formal parameters are assigned types, then at compile time, the actual parameter type will be compared with the type specified for this formal parameter, and a mismatch will trigger a compatibility error condition.
- The keyword ENDFORM is to indicate the end of the subroutine.

In the syntax statement, you are passing <formal parameter 1> by reference, <formal parameter 2> by value, <formal parameter 3> by reference and <formal parameter 4> by value and result.

You have assigned type to the parameters <formal parameter 2> and <formal parameter 3>.

A subroutine cannot be located within a subroutine - no nesting.

A subroutine can call itself, and a subroutine can be recursive. Subroutines should be located at the end of an ABAP program.

You can also specify along with parameters, the exceptions in the subroutine. The parameters' specification along with the exceptions is called the subroutine *interface*. In Chapter 11, the class based exceptions will be elaborated, and class based exceptions raised inside subroutines will be illustrated.

Subroutine calling

A rough syntax of calling a subroutine:

```
PERFORM <subroutine name> USING     <actual parameter1> <actual parameter2>
                          CHANGING  <actual parameter3> <actual parameter4>.
```

PERFORM is the key word to call a subroutine. The control jumps to the first executable statement in the subroutine <subroutine name>. When *ENDFORM* is encountered, control jumps back to the statement following the *PERFORM* statement.

The keyword VALUE is specified only with the formal parameters in the subroutine definition. The keyword VALUE with the keyword USING is to indicate parameters are being passed by value. The keyword VALUE with the keyword CHANGING is to indicate parameters are being passed by value and result.

The order and number of the formal parameters must be identical to the actual parameters.

Subroutine Parameter Passing

By Reference

You are passing parameters by reference when you are using either of the keywords USING or CHANGING without the keyword VALUE. The key words USING or CHANGING can be used interchangeably. They serve the purpose of documentation. If you are changing the value of this parameter within the subroutine, use the keyword CHANGING; or else use the key word USING. The memory address of the data object is passed on to the formal parameter of the subroutine. The subroutine will directly operate on this data object passed as parameter by reference. If within the subroutine, the value of the formal parameter is changed, the value of actual parameter also changes because they are one and the same.

By Value

You are passing parameters by value when you use the keyword USING followed by the keyword VALUE and the formal parameter enclosed in parentheses. In this case, the subroutine creates a duplicate of the actual parameter within the subroutine as a local copy. Any changes made to the formal parameter are performed on the local copy, and the original or actual parameter remains unchanged.

By Value and Result

You are passing parameters by value and result when you use the keyword CHANGING followed by the keyword VALUE and the formal parameter enclosed within parentheses. When a parameter is passed in this manner, the subroutine again makes a duplicate local copy of the actual parameter. When the formal parameter is changed within the subroutine, the changes are performed on the local copy. If the subroutine exits in a normal way (not through an error exception), the values of the formal parameter or the duplicate copy is copied back to the original or actual parameter. If the subroutine exits through an error exception, the value of formal parameter is not copied to the original or actual parameter. Class based error exceptions are covered in Chapter 11; and the effect of value and result subroutine parameter is demonstrated in Chapter 11.

Subroutines – Internal Tables and Structures as Parameters

You can pass internal tables and structures like any other elementary type parameters by reference, value, and by value and result.

Internal Tables

When passing internal tables by value and value and result, you should bear in mind (a) the extra RAM to maintain a duplicate of internal table, and (b) that there is an operation of copying of internal tables (once in the case of passing by value and twice in the case of passing by value and result). This could have an effect on performance. The internal tables should preferably be passed by reference.

You must assign type to an internal table formal parameter as STANDARD TABLE, INDEX TABLE, ANY TABLE, SORTED TABLE, and HASHED TABLE. A hands-on exercise demonstrates the passing of an internal table as a subroutine parameter. You can pass a standard internal table by reference using the keyword TABLES in place of USING or CHANGING. But this notation is now considered obsolete.

Structures

When a structure is passed as a parameter and the components or fields of the structure are to be accessed in the subroutine, the structure formal parameter must be assigned a type by referring to an appropriate DDIC or program structure. When assigning a type to a structure parameter, you can use the keyword *STRUCTURE* instead of the keywords TYPE or LIKE. A hands-on exercise demonstrates the passing of structure parameter and accessing of structure fields inside the subroutine.

Subroutines – Local Data and Local Data Declarations

Data can be declared within a subroutine like you do with the keywords DATA, TABLES, and CONSTANTS. The data declared within a subroutine is local to the subroutine and can be accessed only within the subroutine. The data declared in a subroutine comes into existence only when the subroutine is entered but ceases to exist when the subroutine is exited. In this context, data declared within a subroutine is referred as local data vis-à-vis the data declared in the main program, which is referred to as program global data: data that can be referred anywhere within an ABAP program.

Subroutine – STATIC: Retain Local Variable Values

Sometimes when you are executing a subroutine a multiple number of times, you want the data declared within a subroutine to retain values. Normally, like it has been mentioned in the preceding item, every time you enter a subroutine, the data declared within the subroutine comes into existence and gets undefined on exiting the subroutine. So whatever values were assumed by the variables within the subroutine are lost when you next enter the subroutine again. If you want the values to be retained, declare the data using keyword STATIC instead of the keyword *DATA*.

Subroutine – LOCAL: Protect Global Data

Within a subroutine, if you declare data with the same name as data objects in the main program, the locally declared data objects will be operated upon within the subroutine. The local data objects will mask out the main program data objects of the same name. The subroutine local data objects (declared with keyword DATA) having the same name as the data objects in the main program might not have the same attributes (type, length, etc.).

You could enforce the subroutine local data objects having the same name as main program data objects to have the same attributes as the main program data objects by using the keyword *LOCAL* to declare such data objects. With the keyword *LOCAL*, the system will not allow the type, length, etc., to be specified. The type, length, etc., will be inherited from the main program data objects attributes of the same name. The following bit of ABAP code will elucidate this further:

```
TABLES: TCURT.
DATA: COUNT1  TYPE I VALUE 100,
      COUNT2  TYPE I VALUE 200,
      T005T   TYPE T005T.

TCURT-LTEXT = 'U.S. Dollar'.
PERFORM SRTN.
WRITE:/5 TCURT-LTEXT.
WRITE:/5(6) COUNT1, (6) COUNT2.
*************************************
FORM SRTN.
*TABLES TCURT. "erroneous, will give syntax error
LOCAL: TCURT,
       COUNT1. "type I in main program.

DATA: T005T  TYPE T005T,
      COUNT2 TYPE P. "type I in main program.

TCURT-LTEXT = 'DOLLAR'.
COUNT1      = 1000.
COUNT2      = 2000.
ENDFORM.
```

Subroutine - Reference to Main Program Global Data within a Subroutine

A subroutine can refer to any of the main program's data object (program global data objects). This makes the parameter passing a redundant exercise. In this case, there will be no encapsulation. Hence, to enforce encapsulation, all the references to the main program's data objects should be channeled through the subroutine's parameter interface.

Subroutine – Terminating or Exiting

You can use the EXIT statement to exit a subroutine. You used an EXIT statement to exit a loop in Chapter 4. You can also use the CHECK statement. If the CHECK statement condition is true, the statements following the CHECK statement are executed or else the subroutine is exited.

Hands-On Exercise: Modify Chapter 44 Program on DESCRIBE FIELD – Use Macro and Subroutine to Make It an Efficient Program

After the theoretical background and the syntax of macros and subroutines, let the features be applied to an ABAP program. In Chapter 4, you had a hands-on exercise using the DESCRIBE FIELD statement. In this program, you have a lot of repetitive, similar statements. The repetitiveness gives scope for locating the repetitive statements in macros or subroutines.

One awkward issue you were facing in this program was related to the determination of the length of a field. You wanted the length to be returned in characters (IN CHARACTER MODE) when the field type is C or D or N or T. You wanted the length to be returned in bytes (IN BYTE MODE) if the field type is other than C, D, N, and T. You were using an IF statement to check the field type and appropriately giving the addition: IN CHARACTER MODE or IN BYTE MODE in the DESCRIBE FIELD <field> LENGTH <length> statement. The compiler was doing its own checking of type and syntactically not accepting IN CHARACTER MODE if the field type is other than C, D, N, and T. You do not want this checking by the compiler, because you want your checking to take effect. You circumvented the problem by simply commenting the lines with the syntax error. You could do this because you already knew field types: NAME1 is type C; NETWR is type P, etc.

If you locate the DESCRIBE FIELD <field> LENGTH <length> statement inside a subroutine, the compiler is not performing any check of the field type and relating it to the addition IN CHARACTER MODE or IN BYTE MODE. The compiler is treating it as a runtime issue, not a compile time issue.

So, in the current hands-on exercise, you will locate the repetitive similar statements in a macro and locate a *DESCRIBE FIELD <field> LENGTH <length>* statement in a subroutine. But first, a segment of the original Chapter 4 program:

```
*******************************************************
* DESCRIBE FIELD: Determine Attributes of Data objects *
*******************************************************
DATA: NAME1          TYPE KNA1-NAME1, "DDIC table field
      FKDAT          TYPE VBRK-FKDAT, "DDIC table field
      NETWR          TYPE VBRK-NETWR, "DDIC table field
      .............
      TYP(1)         TYPE C,
      LEN            TYPE I,
      OLEN           TYPE I,
      DECI           TYPE I,
      COMPO          TYPE I.

************************************************************************
DESCRIBE FIELD NAME1 TYPE TYP.
IF TYP = 'C' OR TYP = 'D' OR TYP = 'N' OR TYP = 'T'.
 DESCRIBE FIELD NAME1 LENGTH LEN IN CHARACTER MODE.
ELSE.
 DESCRIBE FIELD NAME1 LENGTH LEN IN BYTE MODE.
ENDIF.
WRITE:/5 'KNA1-NAME1 TYPE & LENGTH                     :', TYP, (3) LEN.
************************************************************************
DESCRIBE FIELD FKDAT TYPE TYP.
IF TYP = 'C' OR TYP = 'D' OR TYP = 'N' OR TYP = 'T'.
 DESCRIBE FIELD FKDAT LENGTH LEN IN CHARACTER MODE.

ELSE.
 DESCRIBE FIELD FKDAT LENGTH LEN IN BYTE MODE.

ENDIF.

WRITE:/5 'VBRK-FKDAT TYPE & LENGTH                     :', TYP, (3) LEN.
************************************************************************
............
```

Repetitive

The statements:

```
DESCRIBE FIELD <field name> TYPE TYP...
If TYP = ...
    WRITE...
..........
```

are repetitive. They are marked in the source program listed above. So you can locate these repetitive lines in a macro. You will also create text symbols for the text literals in the WRITE statements. Each call or invocation to the macro will determine and output the attributes of one field. You will feed the macro with two parameters: the field name whose attributes are to be determined and the text symbol.

From within the macro you will call a subroutine to determine the field length. The subroutine will have three parameters (i.e., field whose length is to be determined), a variable in which length will be returned, and the field type to be used in the IF statement. The call to the subroutine is enabling you to overcome the awkward situation of compiler checking field type when you don't want it to be checked.

The program text symbols will look like Figure 7-1.

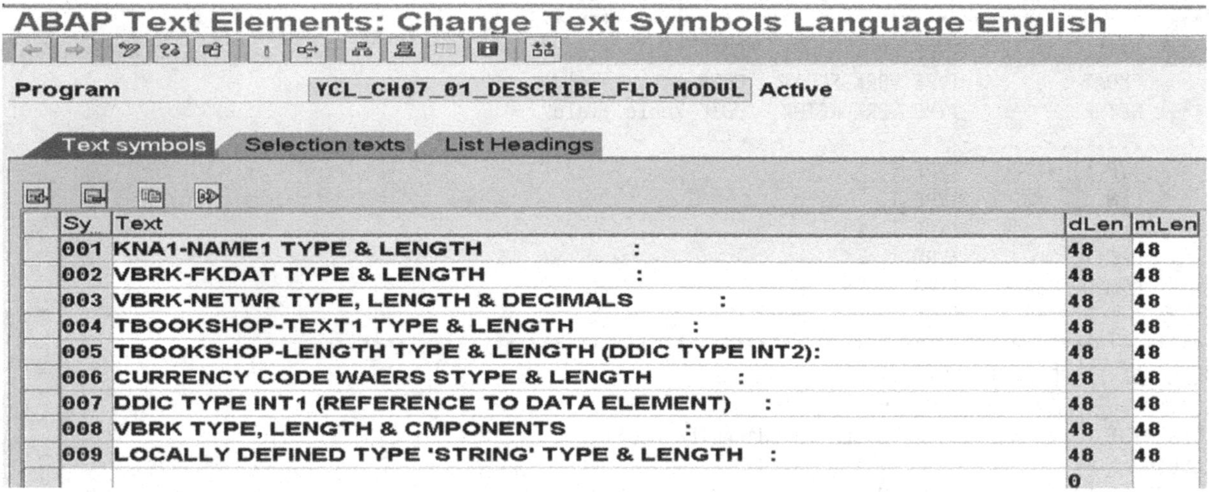

ABAP Text Elements: Change Text Symbols Language English

Program YCL_CH07_01_DESCRIBE_FLD_MODUL Active

Text symbols | Selection texts | List Headings

Sy	Text	dLen	mLen
001	KNA1-NAME1 TYPE & LENGTH :	48	48
002	VBRK-FKDAT TYPE & LENGTH :	48	48
003	VBRK-NETWR TYPE, LENGTH & DECIMALS :	48	48
004	TBOOKSHOP-TEXT1 TYPE & LENGTH :	48	48
005	TBOOKSHOP-LENGTH TYPE & LENGTH (DDIC TYPE INT2):	48	48
006	CURRENCY CODE WAERS STYPE & LENGTH :	48	48
007	DDIC TYPE INT1 (REFERENCE TO DATA ELEMENT) :	48	48
008	VBRK TYPE, LENGTH & CMPONENTS :	48	48
009	LOCALLY DEFINED TYPE 'STRING' TYPE & LENGTH :	48	48
		0	

Figure 7-1. *Program YCL_CH07_01_DESCRIBE_FLD_MODUL - Text Symbols*

Remember to remove the occurrence of single quotes twice in literals, if you are copying Chapter 4 literals to the text symbols.

The revised source program:

```
REPORT YCL_CH07_01_DESCRIBE_FLD_MODUL.

*******************************************************
* DESCRIBE FIELD: Determine Attributes of Data objects *
* Modularize Code. Usage of Macro & Subroutine         *
*******************************************************
```

```
**********************************************************************
* declare elementary data objects referring to DDIC table fields     **
* declare elementary data object referring to DDIC data element      **
* declare structure data object referring to DDIC table definition   **
* declare elementary TYPE STRING                                     **
*                                                                    **
* invoke macro which uses DESCRIBE FIELD to determine TYPE.          **
* from within the macro, PERFORM subroutine which uses DESCRIBE FIELD **
*                       to determine length.                         **
*                                                                    **
* from within the macro, output attributes TYPE, length              **
* (also no of decimals for TYPE P, no of components for structure)   **
*                                                                    **
**********************************************************************

DATA: NAME1          TYPE KNA1-NAME1, "DDIC table field
      FKDAT          TYPE VBRK-FKDAT, "DDIC table field
      NETWR          TYPE VBRK-NETWR, "DDIC table field
      TEXT1          TYPE TBOOKSHOP-TEXT1,  "DDIC table field
      LENGTH         TYPE TBOOKSHOP-LENGTH, "DDIC table field
      WAERS          TYPE WAERS, "reference to data element
      INT1           TYPE MCSAPINT1, "reference to data element
      VBRK           TYPE VBRK, "reference to table structure
      STRNG          TYPE STRING,

      TYP(1)         TYPE C,
      LEN            TYPE I,
      DECI           TYPE I,
      COMPO          TYPE I.

***********************************************
* macro to avoid repetition of similar lines **
* macro takes two parameters:                **
*                          &1 the field name **
*                          &2 text symbol id.**
***********************************************
DEFINE DESCRIBE_FLD. " macro definition

 DESCRIBE FIELD &1 TYPE TYP. " determine TYPE
 PERFORM GET_LENGTH USING &1 LEN TYP. " determine length

 IF TYP <> 'F' AND TYP <> 'P' AND TYP <> 'u' AND TYP <> 'v'.
  WRITE:/5 &2, TYP, (4) LEN.

 ELSEIF TYP = 'F' OR TYP = 'P'.
  DESCRIBE FIELD &1 DECIMALS DECI. " determine no of decimals
  WRITE:/5 &2, TYP, (4) LEN, (2) DECI.

 ELSEIF TYP = 'u' OR TYP = 'v'.
 DESCRIBE FIELD &1 TYPE TYP COMPONENTS COMPO. " determine no of fields
  WRITE:/5 &2, TYP, (4) LEN, (3) COMPO.
*  DESCRIBE FIELD &1 COMPONENTS COMPO.
```

```
ENDIF.
END-OF-DEFINITION.
*****************************************
START-OF-SELECTION.

DESCRIBE_FLD NAME1 TEXT-001. " macro calls

DESCRIBE_FLD FKDAT TEXT-002.

DESCRIBE_FLD NETWR TEXT-003.

DESCRIBE_FLD TEXT1 TEXT-004.

DESCRIBE_FLD LENGTH TEXT-005.

DESCRIBE_FLD WAERS TEXT-006.

DESCRIBE_FLD INT1 TEXT-007.

DESCRIBE_FLD VBRK TEXT-008.

DESCRIBE_FLD STRNG TEXT-009.

************************************************************
* subroutine to determine length. takes three parameters     **
* (1) field (FLD) whose length is to be determined - by value**
* (2) returning field length (LNGT) - by reference           **
* (3) field TYPE (TP) - by value                             **
*                                                            **
* returns length in characters for TYPES C, D, N, T          **
* returns length in bytes for TYPES other than C, D, N, T    **
************************************************************
FORM GET_LENGTH USING VALUE(FLD) LNGT VALUE(TP).

IF TP <> 'C' AND TP <> 'D' AND TP <> 'N' AND TP <> 'T'.

 DESCRIBE FIELD FLD LENGTH LNGT IN BYTE MODE.

ELSE.
 DESCRIBE FIELD FLD LENGTH LNGT IN CHARACTER MODE.

ENDIF.
ENDFORM.
```

You have incorporated the START-OF-SELECTION statement. In Chapter 4, the events were not introduced though alluded to. You had decided in Chapter 5 that every ABAP program will have an explicit START-OF-SELECTION statement.

The output will look like Figure 7-2.

```
DESCRIBE FIELD:  Modularized Code With Macro & Subroutine

DESCRIBE FIELD:  Modularized Code With Macro & Subroutine

    KNA1-NAME1 TYPE & LENGTH                            : C  35
    VBRK-FKDAT TYPE & LENGTH                            : D   8
    VBRK-NETWR TYPE, LENGTH & DECIMALS                  : P   8  2
    TBOOKSHOP-TEXT1 TYPE & LENGTH                       : C 2400
    TBOOKSHOP-LENGTH TYPE & LENGTH (DDIC TYPE INT2)     : s   2
    CURRENCY CODE WAERS STYPE & LENGTH                  : C   5
    DDIC TYPE INT1 (REFERENCE TO DATA ELEMENT)          : b   1
    VBRK TYPE, LENGTH & CMPONENTS                       : u 1156 97
    LOCALLY DEFINED TYPE 'STRING' TYPE & LENGTH         : g   8
```

Figure 7-2. *Program YCL_CH07_01_DESCRIBE_FLD_MODUL - Output*

Hands-On Exercise: Modify Chapter 44 Program on DESCRIBE FIELD – Use Subroutine Only

This is another version of the DESCRIBE FIELD program, this time using a subroutine only. Macros should be used only in the scenario of just text replacement. You have also shifted the variables TYP, LEN, DECI, and COMPO from the main program to the subroutine.

All three programs (of Chapter 4 and the two programs in the current chapter) produce identical results, but the code is progressively more efficient from the first program to the third.

The source program:

```
REPORT YCL_CH07_02_DESCRIBE_FLD_SROUT.

*******************************************************
* DESCRIBE FIELD: Determine Attributes of Data objects *
* Modularized Program - Usage of Subroutine            *
*******************************************************

**********************************************************************
* declare elementary data objects referring to DDIC table fields     **
* declare elementary data object referring to DDIC data element      **
* declare structure data object referring to DDIC table definition   **
* declare elementary TYPE STRING                                     **
*                                                                    **
* call subroutine to determine field attributes & output             **
*                                                                    **
**********************************************************************

DATA: NAME1          TYPE KNA1-NAME1, "DDIC table field
      FKDAT          TYPE VBRK-FKDAT, "DDIC table field
      NETWR          TYPE VBRK-NETWR, "DDIC table field
      TEXT1          TYPE TBOOKSHOP-TEXT1,  "DDIC table field
```

```
      LENGTH          TYPE TBOOKSHOP-LENGTH, "DDIC table field
      WAERS           TYPE WAERS, "reference to data element
      INT1            TYPE MCSAPINT1, "reference to data element
      VBRK            TYPE VBRK, "reference to table structure
      STRNG           TYPE STRING.

****************************************************************
START-OF-SELECTION.

PERFORM PROCESS USING NAME1 TEXT-001.

PERFORM PROCESS USING FKDAT TEXT-002.

PERFORM PROCESS USING NETWR TEXT-003.

PERFORM PROCESS USING TEXT1 TEXT-004.

PERFORM PROCESS USING LENGTH TEXT-005.

PERFORM PROCESS USING WAERS TEXT-006.

PERFORM PROCESS USING INT1 TEXT-007.

PERFORM PROCESS USING VBRK TEXT-008.

PERFORM PROCESS USING STRNG TEXT-009.

******************************************************************
* subroutine to process & output. takes two parameters         **
*                                                              **
* (1) field (FLD) whose attributes to be determined - by value **
* (2) text symbol id (TSYM) - by value                         **
*                                                              **
* variables TYP, LEN, DECI, COMPO shifted from main program to **
* the subroutine.                                              **
******************************************************************
FORM PROCESS USING VALUE(FLD) VALUE(TSYM).

DATA: TYP(1)          TYPE C,
      LEN             TYPE I,
      DECI            TYPE I,
      COMPO           TYPE I.


DESCRIBE FIELD FLD TYPE TYP. " determine TYPE
******************************************************
IF TYP <> 'C' AND TYP <> 'D' AND TYP <> 'N' AND TYP <> 'T'.

 DESCRIBE FIELD FLD LENGTH LEN IN BYTE MODE.
```

```
ELSE.
 DESCRIBE FIELD FLD LENGTH LEN IN CHARACTER MODE.

ENDIF.
*******************************************************
 IF TYP <> 'F' AND TYP <> 'P' AND TYP <> 'u' AND TYP <> 'v'.
  WRITE:/5 TSYM, TYP, (4) LEN.

 ELSEIF TYP = 'F' OR TYP = 'P'.
  DESCRIBE FIELD FLD DECIMALS DECI. " determine no of decimals
  WRITE:/5 TSYM, TYP, (4) LEN, (2) DECI.

 ELSEIF TYP = 'u' OR TYP = 'v'.
 DESCRIBE FIELD FLD TYPE TYP COMPONENTS COMPO. " determine no of fields
  WRITE:/5 TSYM, TYP, (4) LEN, (3) COMPO.
*  DESCRIBE FIELD &1 COMPONENTS COMPO. "syntactically not acceptable

ENDIF.

ENDFORM.
```

The main program consists here of just calls to the subroutines. A typical procedure oriented environment modular program would be just like this. Every other functionality is implemented by subroutines, with the main program just consisting of calls to the subroutines. Even no repetitive program lines consisting of exclusive logic and action are located in a subroutine.

The output of this program will look like this:

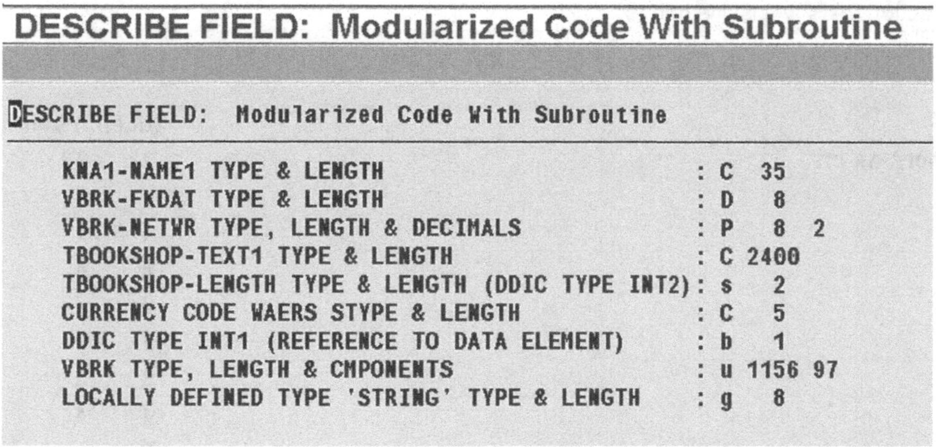

```
DESCRIBE FIELD: Modularized Code With Subroutine

DESCRIBE FIELD:  Modularized Code With Subroutine

    KNA1-NAME1 TYPE & LENGTH                        : C  35
    VBRK-FKDAT TYPE & LENGTH                        : D   8
    VBRK-NETWR TYPE, LENGTH & DECIMALS              : P   8  2
    TBOOKSHOP-TEXT1 TYPE & LENGTH                   : C 2400
    TBOOKSHOP-LENGTH TYPE & LENGTH (DDIC TYPE INT2) : s   2
    CURRENCY CODE WAERS STYPE & LENGTH              : C   5
    DDIC TYPE INT1 (REFERENCE TO DATA ELEMENT)      : b   1
    VBRK TYPE, LENGTH & CMPONENTS                   : u 1156 97
    LOCALLY DEFINED TYPE 'STRING' TYPE & LENGTH     : g   8
```

Figure 7-3. *Program YCL_CH07_02_DESCRIBE_FLD_SROUT - Output*

Hands-On Exercise: Subroutine with an Internal Table as Parameter

This hands-on exercise is to demonstrate a subroutine having an internal table as a parameter. You will load an internal table with data and call a subroutine in which you set up LOOP AT...WRITE ...ENDLOOP.

You can declare an internal table referring to a DDIC structure you created earlier: YCL_CH06_CUST_STRU in Chapter 6. You will fill this internal table with data from DDIC customer primary table KNA1. Then, you call a subroutine passing this internal table as a parameter by reference. Within the subroutine you will have the LOOP AT... WRITEENDLOOP. Let the following fields be output:

```
SY-TABIX        Serial No.          05-09
KUNNR           Customer code       11-20
NAME1           Name                22-56
ORT01           City                58-92
```

You will need within the subroutine a work area or structure to fetch one row at a time from the internal table. You will declare the structure within the subroutine referring to the DDIC structure YCL_CH06_CUST_STRU.

The text symbols for a nonstandard page heading are shown in Figure 7-4.

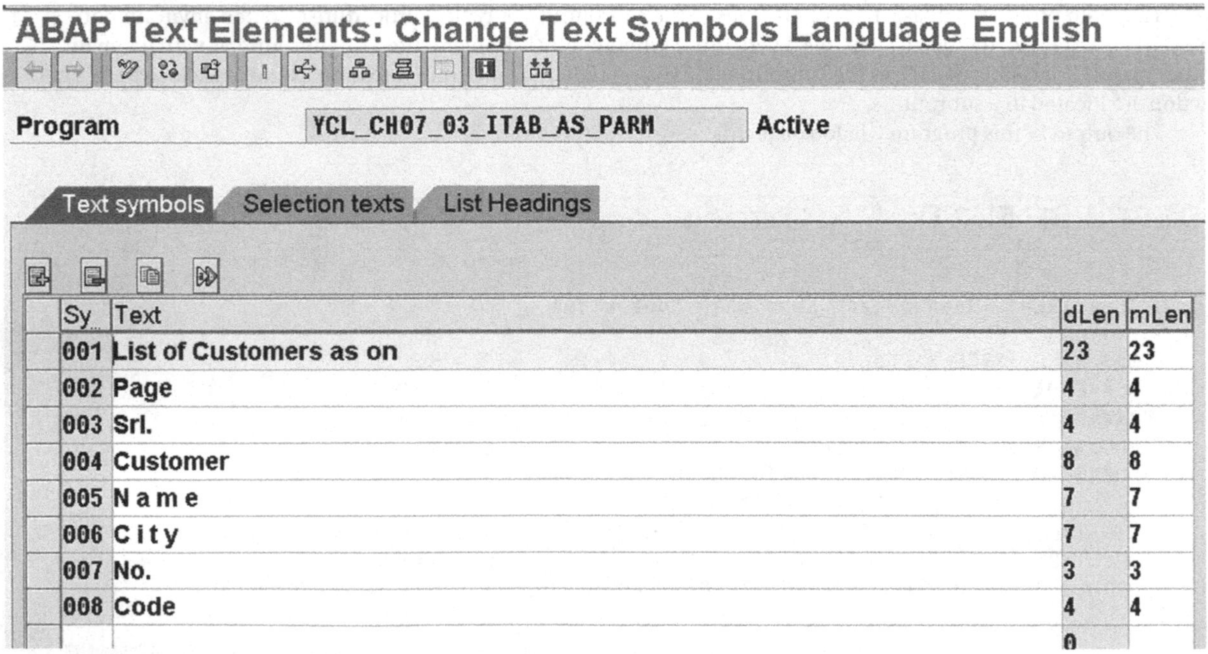

ABAP Text Elements: Change Text Symbols Language English

Program YCL_CH07_03_ITAB_AS_PARM Active

Text symbols | Selection texts | List Headings

Sy	Text	dLen	mLen
001	List of Customers as on	23	23
002	Page	4	4
003	Srl.	4	4
004	Customer	8	8
005	N a m e	7	7
006	C i t y	7	7
007	No.	3	3
008	Code	4	4
		0	

Figure 7-4. *Program YCL_CH07_03_ITAB_AS_PARM - Text Symbols*

The source program:

```
REPORT YCL_CH07_03_ITAB_AS_PARM LINE-SIZE 95 LINE-COUNT 60
         NO STANDARD PAGE HEADING.

************************************************
* Subroutine With Internal Table As Parameter **
* Simple Customer List                        **
************************************************

************************************************
* declare internal table                      **
*                                             **
* report heading                              **
* fill internal table from table KNA1         **
* PEFFORM <subroutine> using <internal table> **
*                                             **
* FORM <subroutine using <internal table>     **
* TYPE ANY TABLE.                             **
* LOOP AT...WRITE...ENDLOOP.                  **
* ENDFORM                                     **
************************************************

DATA: CUSTOMER_TAB TYPE SORTED TABLE OF YCL_CH05_CUST_STRU
                        WITH UNIQUE KEY KUNNR,
      DAT(10)      TYPE C.
***********************************************************
TOP-OF-PAGE.
WRITE:/5 TEXT-001, DAT, 81 TEXT-002, (3) SY-PAGNO.
WRITE:/5(83) SY-ULINE.
WRITE:/5 TEXT-003, 12 TEXT-004, 24 TEXT-005, 60 TEXT-006.
WRITE:/6 TEXT-007, 14 TEXT-008.
WRITE:/5(83) SY-ULINE.
***********************************************************
START-OF-SELECTION.

CONCATENATE SY-DATUM+6(2) SY-DATUM+4(2) SY-DATUM+0(4) INTO DAT
 SEPARATED BY '/'.

SELECT KUNNR NAME1 STRAS ORT01 PSTLZ FROM KNA1 INTO TABLE CUSTOMER_TAB.

PERFORM OUTPUT_LIST USING CUSTOMER_TAB.

***********************************************************
FORM OUTPUT_LIST USING CUST_TAB TYPE ANY TABLE. " internal table parameter
                                                " has to be assigned type

DATA CUST_STRU LIKE YCL_CH05_CUST_STRU. " subroutine local data
```

```
LOOP AT CUST_TAB INTO CUST_STRU.
 WRITE: /5(5) SY-TABIX, CUST_STRU-KUNNR USING NO EDIT MASK,
      CUST_STRU-NAME1, CUST_STRU-ORT01.
ENDLOOP.

ENDFORM.
```

The output is found in Figure 7-5.

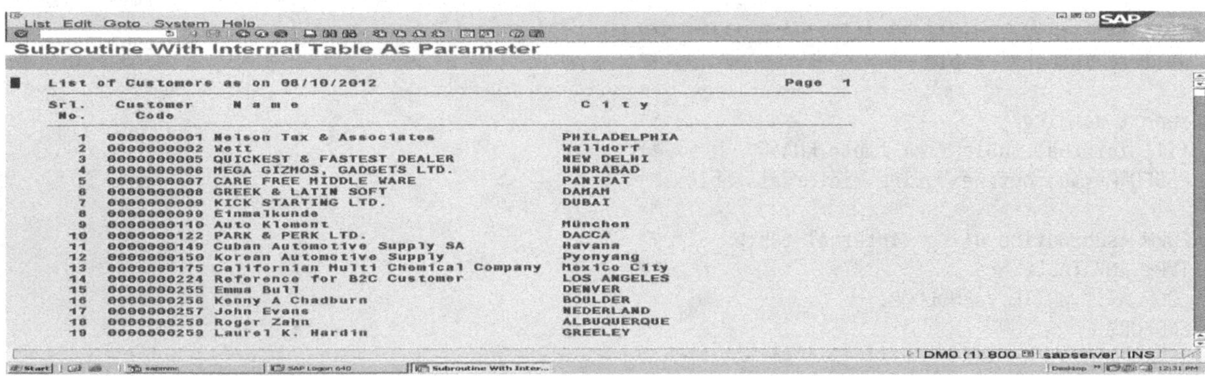

Figure 7-5. *Program YCL_CH07_03_ITAB_AS_PARM - Output*

Hands-On Exercise: Subroutine with a Structure as Parameter

The program YCL_CH07_03_ITAB_AS_PARM has been modified so that only the WRITE statement is executed inside the subroutine. LOOP AT...ENDLOOP is shifted to the main program. The subroutine is receiving the structure data. Since you want to access the individual fields of the structure, you have to assign a type to the formal structure parameter. The formal parameter is referring to the DDIC structure YCL_CH06_CUST_STRU, and the keyword STRUCTURE is used instead of TYPE or LIKE. This is a demonstrative program used to demonstrate the passing of a structure parameter.

The source:

```
REPORT YCL_CH07_04_STRU_AS_PARM LINE-SIZE 95 LINE-COUNT 60
        NO STANDARD PAGE HEADING.

************************************************
* Subroutine With Structure As Parameter      **
* Simple Customer List                        **
************************************************

************************************************
* declare internal table                      **
*                                             **
* report heading                              **
* fill internal table from table KNA1         **
* LOOP AT...PERFORM WRITER...ENDLOOP.         **
*                                             **
```

```
* FORM <subroutine using <structure>          **
* TYPE YCL_CH05_CUST_STRU.                    **
* WRITE...                                    **
* ENDFORM                                     **
***********************************************

DATA: CUSTOMER_TAB TYPE SORTED TABLE OF YCL_CH05_CUST_STRU
                        WITH UNIQUE KEY KUNNR WITH HEADER LINE,
      DAT(10)      TYPE C.

***********************************************************
TOP-OF-PAGE.
WRITE:/5 TEXT-001, DAT, 81 TEXT-002, (3) SY-PAGNO.
WRITE:/5(83) SY-ULINE.
WRITE:/5 TEXT-003, 12 TEXT-004, 24 TEXT-005, 60 TEXT-006.
WRITE:/6 TEXT-007, 14 TEXT-008.
WRITE:/5(83) SY-ULINE.
***********************************************************
START-OF-SELECTION.

CONCATENATE SY-DATUM+6(2) SY-DATUM+4(2) SY-DATUM+0(4) INTO DAT
 SEPARATED BY '/'.

SELECT KUNNR NAME1 STRAS ORT01 PSTLZ FROM KNA1 INTO TABLE CUSTOMER_TAB.

LOOP AT CUSTOMER_TAB INTO CUSTOMER_TAB.
 PERFORM WRITER USING CUSTOMER_TAB.
ENDLOOP.
***********************************************************
FORM WRITER USING CUST_STRU STRUCTURE " key word STRUCTURE
                  YCL_CH05_CUST_STRU. " structure parameter
                                      " has to be assigned type
                                      " for accessing fields

 WRITE: /5(5) SY-TABIX, CUST_STRU-KUNNR USING NO EDIT MASK,
       CUST_STRU-NAME1, CUST_STRU-ORT01.

ENDFORM.
```

The output will appear like Figure 7-6.

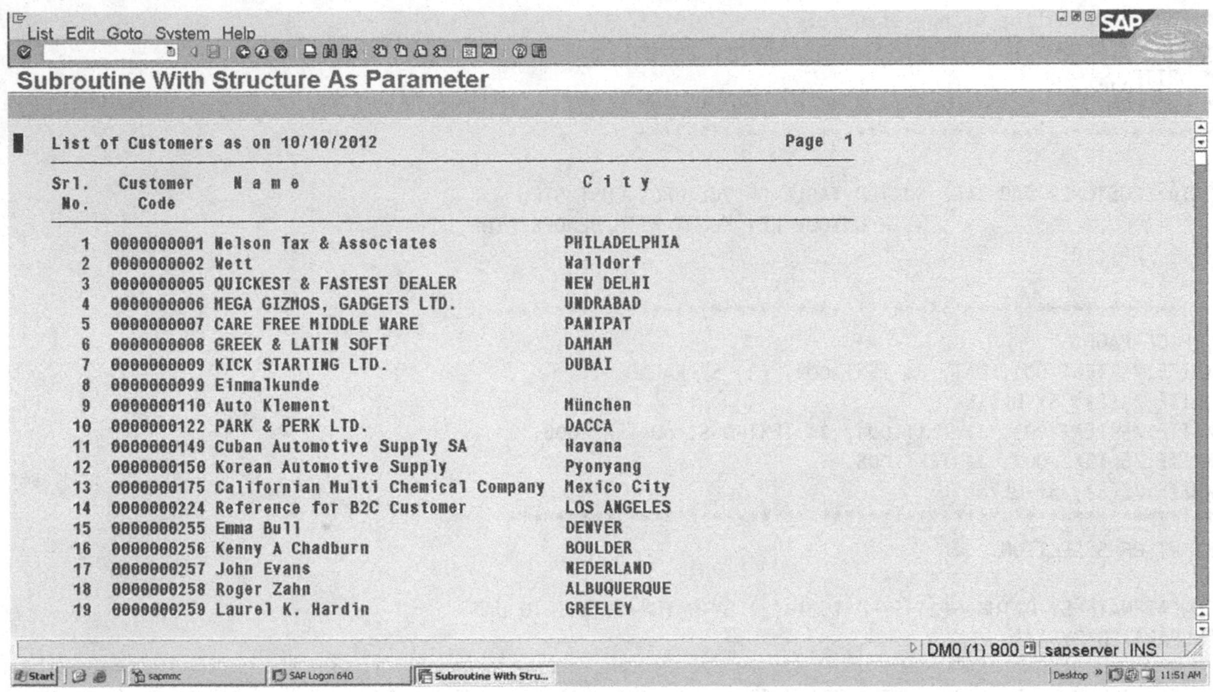

Figure 7-6. *Program YCL_CH07_03_STRU_AS_PARM - Output*

Hands-On Exercise: List of Icons in SAP GUI Environment – Fields Enclosed in Boxes Using Macro and Subroutine

The database table ICON contains the icons and their particulars (icon name, icon id, etc.). You will list these icons' particulars, enclosing each field in a box.

A macro is enclosing the output field in a box. The macro outputs one field at a time. The macro outputs a field with a SY-VLINE on the left and right side of it and SY-ULINE at the top and bottom. Only the first field being output on a line requires a SY-VLINE on the left. The subsequent fields already have a SY-VLINE on the left (the right side SY-VLINE of previous field serves as left side SY-VLINE of the next field). Similarly, the first line of the output requires an SY-ULINE at the top. Subsequent lines can use the bottom SY-ULINE of the previous line as their top SY-ULINE. These things are not taken care by the macro. There is an occurrence of overwriting. You can, as an exercise, eliminate the overwriting and refine the macro.

The macro is also imparting color to the output field through FORMAT statement. The FORMAT statement in the macro takes as macro parameters whether INVERSE is ON/OFF, INTENSIFIED is ON/OFF and color name (COL_KEY et al.). The other parameters of macro are field or text symbol and output width in columns.

The particulars of the icons appearing in SAP GUI environment are stored in the database table ICON. There are 13 fields in this table. You output only two fields in your list.

```
ID          Icon picture
ID+1(2)     Icon Code (second, third character of the field ID)
NAME        Icon Name
```

You output field ID twice and the full field once (this will output the icon picture) and next the second and third characters of the field ID (i.e., ID+1(2); this will output the icon code). All the icons are identified by two character codes as well as icon names. You have used icon names in Chapter 5. You used the *Type Group* ICON in the Chapter 5 program. The *Type Group* ICON contains all the SAP GUI icon definitions. You output icon pictures in the Chapter 5 program by referring to the icon name and using the key phrase AS ICON with the WRITE statement. You can also output the icon picture with the WRITE statement by giving the icon code enclosed within the character '@'. If you want to output the icon 'ICON_SYSTEM_SAVE,' the code for this icon is 2L and the field ID in the corresponding row in the table ICON contains @2L@. Similarly, the code for the icon 'ICON_CHECK' is 38. So the field ID in the corresponding row will contain @38@. The two programs given below will generate the same output.

You generate the list header in this program through a subroutine that is called conditionally and not through the TOP-OF-PAGE event. The mix of the TOP-OF-PAGE event and the macro did not generate correctly formatted output.

You are using two new system fields in this program:

```
SY-COLNO              Current Output Column Position
SY-LINNO              Current Line Number in a Page (Varies from 1 to SY-LINCT)
```

The source program:

```
REPORT YCL_CH07_05_OUTPUT_INBOX_MACRO NO STANDARD PAGE HEADING
   LINE-COUNT 60 LINE-SIZE 75.

*****************************************************************
* SAP Icon List-Use Macro To Impart Color & Enclose Output In Box **
* Use Subroutine to Output Report Header Instead of TOP-OF-PAGE   **
* Event                                                           **
*****************************************************************

***************************************************************
* retrieve data from the database table ICON. SELECT ENDSELECT **
* output ICON particulars i.e. ICON-NAME (icon name)          **
*                              ICON-ID   (icon id.)           **
*                            & ICON+1(2) (icon code)          **
*                                                             **
* use a macro to output icon particulars enclosed in box in   **
* specified color.                                            **
*                                                             **
* each time macro is invoked, one item of info (field) is     **
* output. each field is enclosed in a box: SY-VLINE on left & **
* right, SY-ULINE on top & bottom.                            **
*                                                             **
* the column pointer after output points to the column next to **
* the right side SY-VLINE.                                    **
* (system field SY-COLNO stores the current column number)    **
*                                                             **
* the row pointer points to the row between top & bottom      **
*  horizontal SY-ULINE.                                       **
* (system field SY-LINNO stores the current row)              **
*                                                             **
* color is through the FORMAT statement.                      **
*                                                             **
* macro takes 5 parameters(place holders &1, &2, &3, &4, &5) : **
*            (1) field name/text symbol id.                   **
```

```
*          (2) output width in column positions                **
*          (3) ON/OFF for INVERSE ON/OFF                       **
*          (4) ON/OFF for INTENSIFIED ON/OFF                   **
*          (5) color name (COL_KEY, COL_POSITIVE et al)        **
*                                                              **
* usage of 'SKIP TO..' & 'POSITION..' statements.              **
*                                                              **
* After each line, (all fields are output) two lines are       **
* skipped. column position is set to 5.                        **
****************************************************************

****************************************************************
* in the report heading, the page number (SY-PAGNO) is         **
* output as well as the column headings. the column headings   **
* are enclosed in boxes & output through the macro again.      **
* the report heading is not generated using the TOP-OF-PAGE    **
* event. it is generated using a subroutine. this subroutine   **
* is called either when CNT IS INITIAL OR CNTR >= 58.          **
* you are using the NEW-PAGE statement to start output on a new**
* page every time the report heading is to be output. this     **
* was happening automatically with TOP-OF-PAGE event.          **
*                                                              **
* you are not using the TOP-OF-PAGE event because the mix of   **
* TOP-OF-PAGE event & macro is not generating properly         **
* formatted output.                                            **
*                                                              **
****************************************************************


TABLES: ICON.
DATA:  COL       TYPE SY-COLNO,
       LIN       TYPE SY-LINNO,
       LENGTH    TYPE I,
       PG        TYPE SY-PAGNO,
       CNTR      TYPE I,
       CNT(6)    TYPE C.


**** OUTPUT IN A BOX MACRO ***
******************************


DEFINE WRITE_GRID.
 COL = SY-COLNO. LIN = SY-LINNO. " save current column & line/row no.

 FORMAT INVERSE &3 INTENSIFIED &4 COLOR &5.

 WRITE: '|' NO-GAP, (&2) &1 NO-GAP,
  '|' NO-GAP. " output field with left & right SY-VLINE

 LENGTH = SY-COLNO - COL. " derive length of horizontal line
```

```
 LIN = LIN - 1. SKIP TO LINE LIN. POSITION COL.

 ULINE AT COL(LENGTH). " top horizontal line

 LIN = LIN + 2. SKIP TO LINE LIN. POSITION COL.

 ULINE AT COL(LENGTH). " bottom horizontal line

 LIN = LIN - 1. COL = SY-COLNO - 2.

 SKIP TO LINE LIN. " set line & column no for next output
 POSITION COL.

END-OF-DEFINITION.

********************
********************
START-OF-SELECTION.

SELECT * FROM ICON ORDER BY NAME.
 IF CNTR >=58 OR CNT IS INITIAL. " value 58 arrived by trial & error
  PERFORM PHEAD.
 ENDIF.

 CNT = SY-DBCNT. " CNT TYPE C to suppress thousand separator/comma

 WRITE_GRID CNT 6 ON OFF COL_TOTAL. " output CNT column width 6
                                    " INVERSE ON INTENSIFIED OFF
                                    " COLOR COL_TOTAL
 WRITE_GRID ICON-NAME 35 ON OFF COL_KEY.

 WRITE_GRID ICON-ID 7 ON OFF COL_POSITIVE.

 WRITE_GRID ICON+1(2) 4 ON OFF COL_HEADING.

 SKIP 2. " one extra line for bottom horizontal line

 POSITION 5.

 CNTR = CNTR + 2. " increase line count by 2

ENDSELECT.

************* report header ******************
FORM PHEAD.

NEW-PAGE NO-HEADING.

PG = PG + 1.

WRITE 59(3)  PG.
```

```
SKIP 2. " make one row available for top horizontal line

POSITION 5. "all output is starting as usual from column 5

WRITE_GRID TEXT-001 6 ON OFF COL_TOTAL.

WRITE_GRID TEXT-002 35 ON OFF COL_KEY.

WRITE_GRID TEXT-003 7 ON OFF COL_POSITIVE.

WRITE_GRID TEXT-004 4 ON OFF COL_HEADING.

 SKIP 2.

 POSITION 5. " for next row column position 5

 CNTR = 4. " line count set to 4

ENDFORM.
```

The output will appear like Figures 7-7 and 7-8.

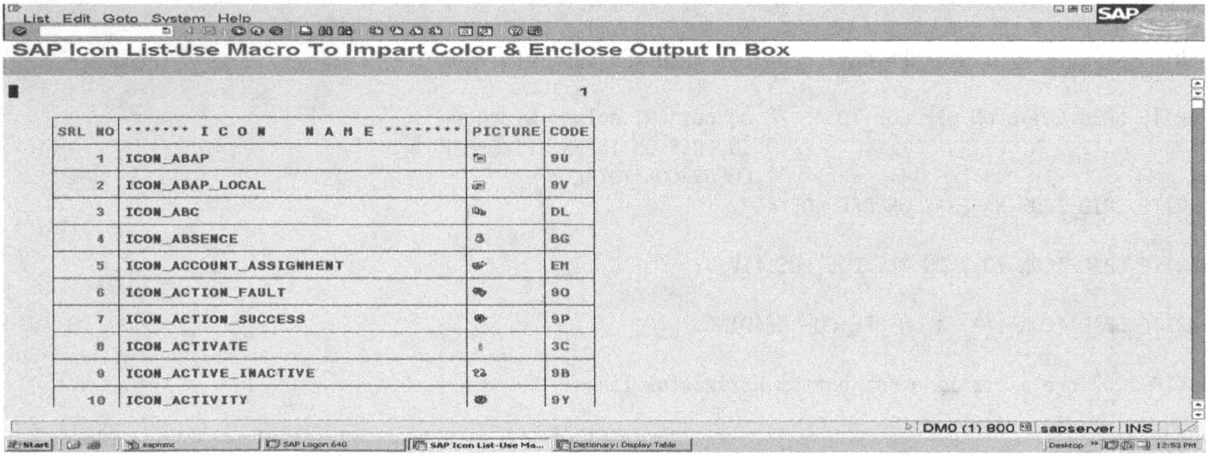

List Edit Goto System Help

SAP Icon List-Use Macro To Impart Color & Enclose Output In Box

SRL NO	******* I C O N N A M E ********	PICTURE	CODE
1	ICON_ABAP		9U
2	ICON_ABAP_LOCAL		9V
3	ICON_ABC		DL
4	ICON_ABSENCE		BG
5	ICON_ACCOUNT_ASSIGNMENT		EM
6	ICON_ACTION_FAULT		9O
7	ICON_ACTION_SUCCESS		9P
8	ICON_ACTIVATE		3C
9	ICON_ACTIVE_INACTIVE		9B
10	ICON_ACTIVITY		9Y

DMO (1) 800 sapserver INS

Figure 7-7. *Program YCL_CH07_05_OUTPUT_INBOX_MACRO -Output*

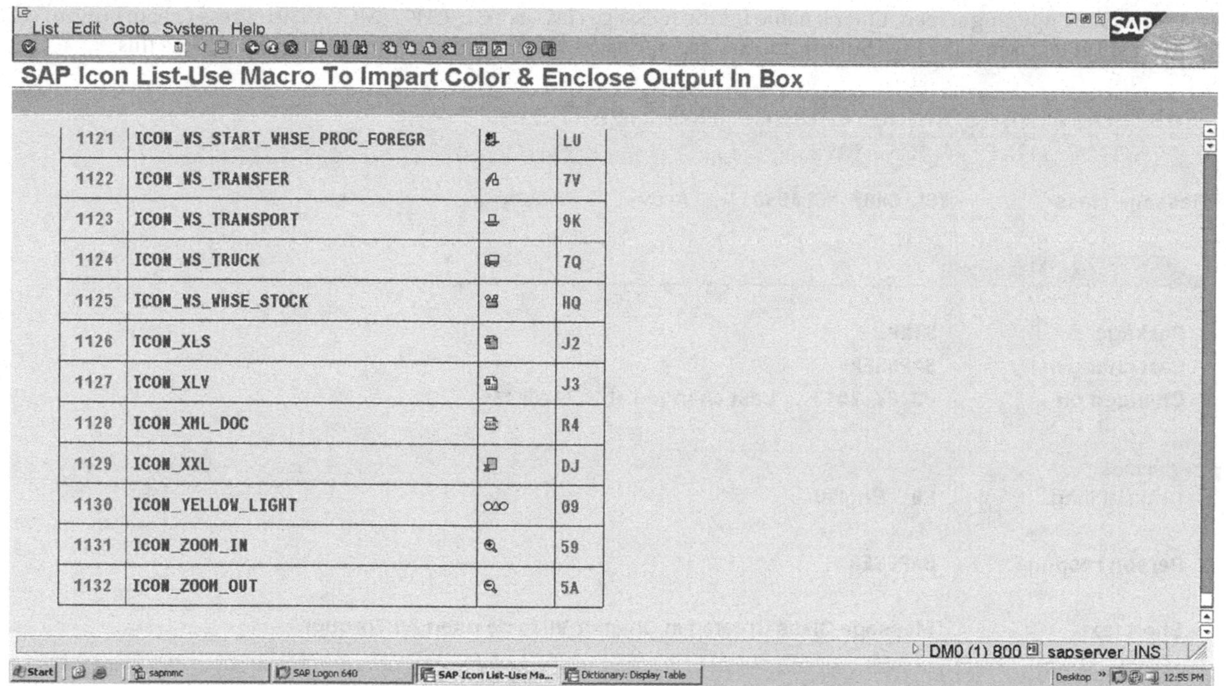

1121	ICON_WS_START_WHSE_PROC_FOREGR		LU
1122	ICON_WS_TRANSFER		7V
1123	ICON_WS_TRANSPORT		9K
1124	ICON_WS_TRUCK		7Q
1125	ICON_WS_WHSE_STOCK		HQ
1126	ICON_XLS		J2
1127	ICON_XLV		J3
1128	ICON_XML_DOC		R4
1129	ICON_XXL		DJ
1130	ICON_YELLOW_LIGHT		09
1131	ICON_ZOOM_IN		59
1132	ICON_ZOOM_OUT		5A

Figure 7-8. *Program YCL_CH07_05_OUTPUT_INBOX_MACRO - Output*

Messages Maintenance and Issuing in ABAP Workbench

Notifications and alerts have to be given to a user of a system for the basic man machine interaction. You have encountered these notifications when you were alerted about a syntax error in your ABAP program and when you activated an object in Workbench environment and so on. These notifications and alerts are designated as messages in the ABAP Workbench environment.

Message Text Maintenance

Message texts are maintained centrally in the ABAP Workbench environment. As usual, like in any other context of text maintenance, the message texts can be maintained in multiple languages. Messages can be issued in an ABAP program through the MESSAGE statement. There is a provision to pass runtime information to the MESSAGE statement through the concept of placeholders in message texts. This is similar to the placeholder facility in *List Heading* component of text elements of an ABAP program (&0...&9 in Chapter 5). There can be a maximum of four placeholders: &1, &2, &3, &4 for one message text.

Message texts are maintained through the transaction code SE91. The message texts are contained in an entity called message class or message id. A single message class can contain a maximum of one thousand message texts. The message texts in the message class are identified by message numbers, with the numbers running from 000 to 999. You can enter texts arbitrarily in any of these number slots. When a message is issued with the MESSAGE statement, the message class, message number, and the runtime information to sit in the placeholders if any, has to be given.

Go to SE91 opening screen. Enter a name for the message class as YCL_CH07_MCLASS01. Press Create button/ F5, enter short text, press the save button, and assign your usual $TMP package. The screen will look like this:

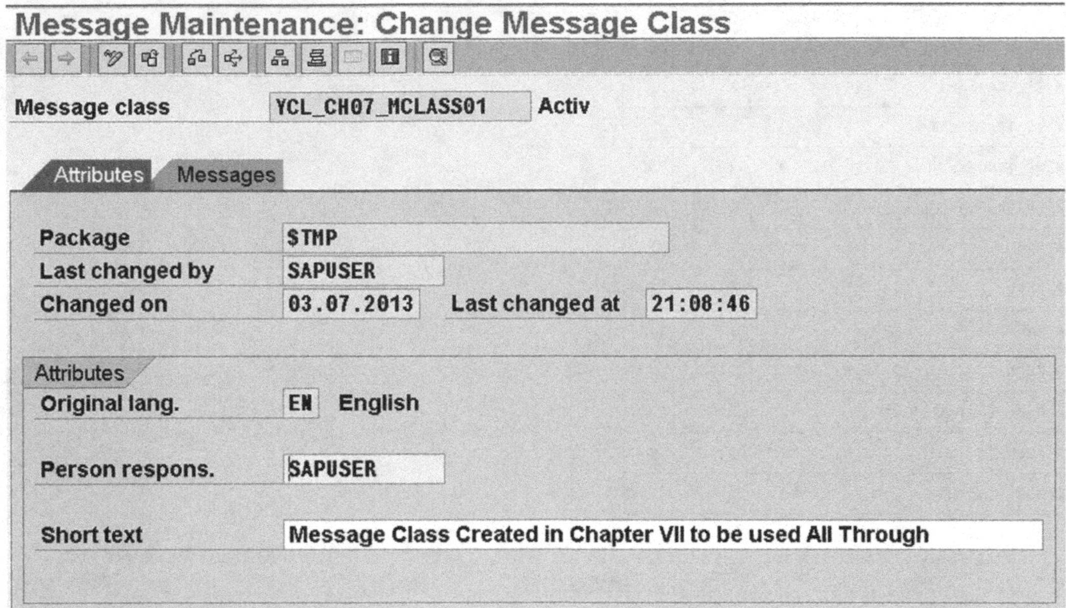

Figure 7-9. *Message Class Creation*

There is no explicit activation process for a message class. The saving is enough.

The naming conventions follow the naming conventions of any other ABAP Workbench object. The name space of message class is a maximum of 20 characters.

You are on the *Attributes* tab. Click on the *Messages* tab. The screen will look like this:

Figure 7-10. *Message Texts Screen*

You can enter the texts against the text identification numbers. The text entry can be a maximum of 73 characters. There are the usual buttons to handle multiple row screen entries: namely, select, cut, copy, paste, delete, etc. There are additional buttons to find, find, and replace. There is a check box on the right with the column heading *Self-explanatory* (Self-explanatory). If you disable this check box, you can create a long text for the message. When the normal text appears on message issuance and the user double-clicks on it, the long text of the message appears. In any case, you can create the long text for a message. If the check box *Self-explanatory* is enabled, a confirmatory dialog box will appear before the long text dialog box appears. If the check box *Self-explanatory* is disabled, no confirmatory dialog box will appear before the long text dialog box appears. The long text can be created by clicking the Long Text button on the application toolbar.

Message Issuance

Let there be a simple scenario for creation and issuance of a message:

Messages are issued with the MESSAGE statement.

In an ABAP program input customer code through PARAMETERS statement. You will check the validity of the customer code. If the customer is valid (should be available in the database table KNA1), you will issue a message that the input customer code is valid. If the customer code is invalid, you will issue a message that the input customer code is invalid. If the input customer is blank, issue a message that the input customer code is blank. So there will be three messages. The messages reporting validity or invalidity of customer code must have runtime information: the input customer code.

So, on the SE91 screen, in the message class YCL_CH07_MCLASS01, in the *Messages* tab, enter the messages 000, 001, 002 as shown in Figure 7-11.

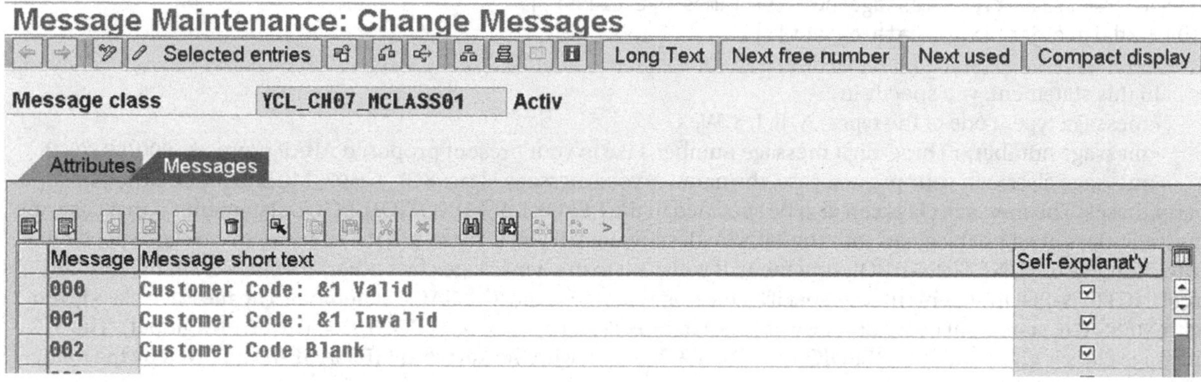

Figure 7-11. *Message Texts – Messages 000, 001, 002*

The placeholder &1 in messages 000, 001 will be replaced by the runtime information you will provide with the message issuing statement.

There are six types of messages. You can use any one of these message types depending on the context when issuing messages. Table 7-1 lists the message types with their meanings.

Table 7-1. *Message Types*

Message Type	Description
A	Abort. Issue of this Message Type Aborts the Program/Job
E	Error. Issue of this Message Type may Abort the Program/Job
I	Information. Appears as a dialog
S	Status
W	Warning. Issue of this Message Type may Abort the Program/Job
X	Exit. Issue of this Message Type Aborts the Program/Job with a Short Dump

The message type determines how the message appears and whether the program continues execution or aborts/terminates. In online documentation, you will find elaborate descriptions of how messages appear for each message type and whether the program continues or aborts in different contexts. For message types I and S, the program continues execution. For message types A and X, the program terminates.

Message Statement Syntaxes

Before you write an ABAP program, let the ABAP message issuing statement MESSAGE syntax be introduced. Two syntaxes are being introduced. When you do classes, more syntax will be introduced. The two syntaxes of a message statement:

Syntax 1

```
MESSAGE <message type><message number>[(<message class>)]
[WITH <data object1>...<data object4>].
```

In this statement, you specify in

<message type>: one of the types: A, E, I, S, W, X.

<message number>: Three-digit message number. Like in your present proposed ABAP program: 000/001/002.

<message class>: In your present case, the name of your message class: YCL_CH07_MCLASS01 enclosed in parentheses. The message class can also be specified in the REPORT or FUNCTION-POOL statement. In that case, the message class need not be given with the MESSAGE statement, if you want to use the same message class specified with REPORT or FUNCTION-POOL statement. If you want to use a message class other than the one in the REPORT or FUNCTION-POOL statement, you specify a message class with the MESSAGE statement. The message class given with MESSAGE statement overrides the one given in REPORT or FUNCTION-POOL (local overrides global). The message class is given with the REPORT or FUNCTION-POOL with the keyword MESSAGE-ID followed by the name of the message class.

WITH: You specify data object/s following the keyword WITH. This is optional but required if you want to pass runtime information to the message text placeholders. There is a maximum limit of four. In your case this could be the following:: WITH CUST_CD. CUST_CD will be your PARAMETERS variable name. So if you were issuing message for a valid customer, your message statement will be:

```
MESSAGE S001(YCL_CH07_MCLASS01) WITH CUST_CD.
```

Syntax 2

```
MESSAGE ID <message id data object> TYPE <message type data object>
NUMBER <message number data object> [WITH <data object1>..<data object4>].
```

This syntax offers the facility of having the message class, type, and number as variables. The earlier syntax hard-coded this information. So appropriate values can be put in the three variables: <message id data object>, <message type data object> and <message number data object> and the message issued with these variables.

There are seven system fields associated with the issuing of messages. These system fields are filled with values after the MESSAGE statement is executed: They are:

SY-MSGID: This is filled with the message class given with the message statement.

SY-MSGTY: This is filled with the message type given with the message statement.

SY-MSGNO: This is filled with the message number given with the message statement.

SY-MSGV1, SY-MSGV2, SY-MSGV3 and SY-MSGV4: Filled with values in the data objects specified after the key word WITH in MESSAGE statement. If less than four data objects are specified, these system fields will contain blanks.

Message Statement Additional Options

There are two more options you can specify with the two syntaxes of MESSAGE statement. They are:

[RAISING <exception name>]

This option can be specified only in a function module. Specifying this option does not result in issuing of a message. The system fields are filled with the values and the function module terminates. This option is used in the forthcoming topic *Function modules* of the present chapter.

[DISPLAY LIKE <message type>]

Sometimes, you want a message to look like an error message but do not want the program termination. This kind of a requirement can be handled through this option. So if a message has been issued as a status (S) message, you can use the option DISPLAY LIKE 'E' to give the appearance of error type 'E' message. The program will not be terminated. A hands-on exercise demonstrating message issuance follows.

Hands-On Exercise: Message Issuance

The source program:

```
*******************************
* Demonstrate Issuing Messages *
*******************************

DATA:  KUNNR TYPE KNA1-KUNNR.

PARAMETERS: CUST_CD TYPE KNA1-KUNNR.

****************************************
START-OF-SELECTION.

SELECT SINGLE KUNNR FROM KNA1 INTO KUNNR
  WHERE KUNNR = CUST_CD.

IF CUST_CD IS INITIAL.
 MESSAGE S002(YCL_CH07_MCLASS01) DISPLAY LIKE 'E'.

ELSEIF SY-SUBRC = 0.
 MESSAGE S000(YCL_CH07_MCLASS01) WITH CUST_CD.

ELSE.
 MESSAGE S001 WITH CUST_CD DISPLAY LIKE 'E'.

ENDIF.
```

The outputs for a valid, invalid, blank customer code - CUST_CD are shown:

***Figure 7-12.** Program YCL_CH07_11_ISSUE_MESSAGE - Output: Customer Code Valid*

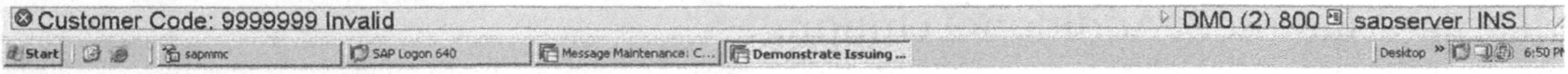

Figure 7-13. Program YCL_CH07_11_ISSUE_MESSAGE - Output: Customer Code Invalid

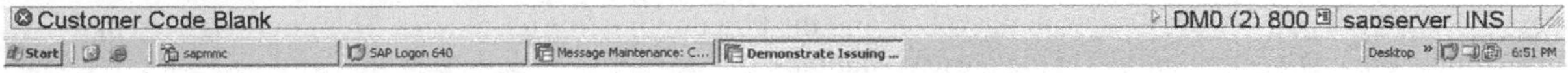

Figure 7-14. Program YCL_CH07_11_ISSUE_MESSAGE - Output: Customer Code Blank

Function Modules, INCLUDE Programs

Function Modules Introduction

The function modules can be viewed as generic or general purpose external subroutines. They can be called from multiple ABAP programs - reusability. They reside in a central library. They are contained in function groups (special ABAP programs): a function group can contain one or more function modules. If you call or invoke one function module in the group, all the function modules in that group are loaded into RAM. If you have a situation where you are calling more than one function module in an ABAP program frequently, then you can locate these function modules in a function group to improve performance. One other scenario where you will locate multiple function modules in a function group is when the function modules located in a function group share lot of common data and data objects. In this scenario, the common data can be located in the global area of the function group and shared by the function modules in a function group.

The function groups and function modules are maintained in the function builder. The transaction code to navigate to the function builder is SE37.

The function modules have an interface to define the input, output parameters, and the error exceptions. Error exceptions can be raised in function modules through the MESSAGE statement as well as through class based exceptions. In this chapter; the exceptions raised through a MESSAGE statement will be described and demonstrated. In Chapter 11, class based exceptions will be described and demonstrated in function modules.

There are more than 300,000 SAP supplied function modules, most of them used by SAP for its own internal purpose. A list of 50 odd function modules is given at the end of this chapter. Good enough for a beginner.

Examine or View an SAP Delivered Function Module: SPELL_AMOUNT

You will examine the SAP delivered function module SPELL_AMOUNT. This function module converts an amount figure into text or words. It takes four input parameters:

- An Amount Figure (DDIC Data Type CURR etc.) - Formal parameter name: AMOUNT
- A Language Code (the language in which to return the text - DDIC Data Type LANG) - Formal parameter name: LANUAGE
- A Currency Code (DDIC Data Type CUKY) - Formal parameter name: CURRENCY
- The Separator character or string between the words (by default a space) - Formal parameter name: FILLER

The function module output parameter is the amount figure converted into text in the language specified in input parameter.

A business document (check, billing document, etc.) in most countries must have the amount figure presented in text on the business document. The function module SPELL_AMOUNT is used to convert amount figure into text.

Let this function module be examined. Navigate to the function builder opening screen - transaction code SE37 - enter the name of the function module SPELL_AMOUNT. The screen will look like Figure 7-15.

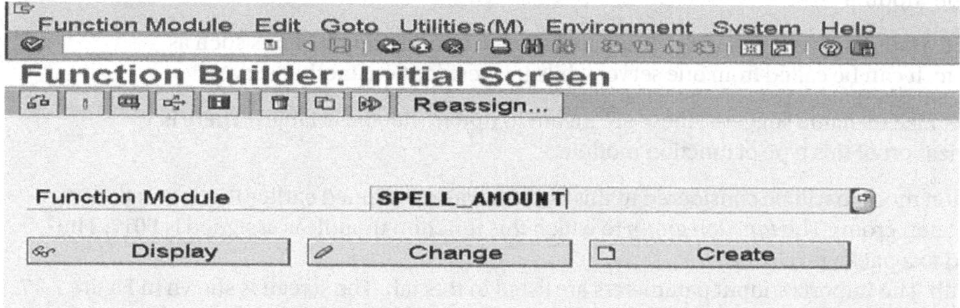

Figure 7-15. Function Builder Initial Screen - Examine Function Module SPELL_AMOUNT

Click on the Display button. The screen will show seven tabs: *Attributes, Import, Export, Changing, Tables, Exceptions,* and *Source code...* Click the *Attributes* tab. The screen in Figure 7-16 will appear.

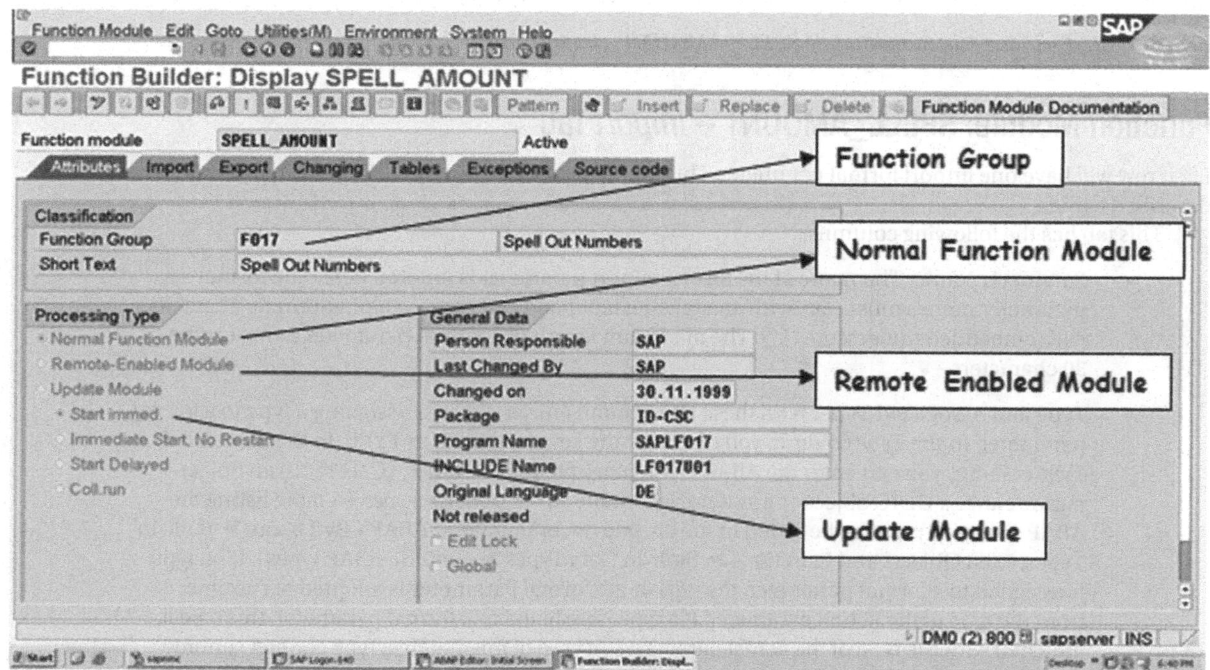

Figure 7-16. Examine Function Module SPELL_AMOUNT - Attributes Tab

Function Module: SPELL_AMOUNT – Attributes Tab

There are three types of function modules (three radio buttons):

- Normal Function Module
- Remote Enabled Module: This function module can be called in other applications such as Java, Dot Net, etc. It can be called from one server while it is resident on another server.
- Update Module: Like its name suggests, these are meant to update database tables. There is further categorization of this type of function module.

Only the normal function module will be considered in this book. It was mentioned earlier that a function module is assigned to a function group. The *function group* to which this function module is assigned is F017. The function module is assigned to a package ID-CSC.

Next, click the *Import* tab. The import or input parameters are listed in this tab. The screen is shown in Figure 7-17.

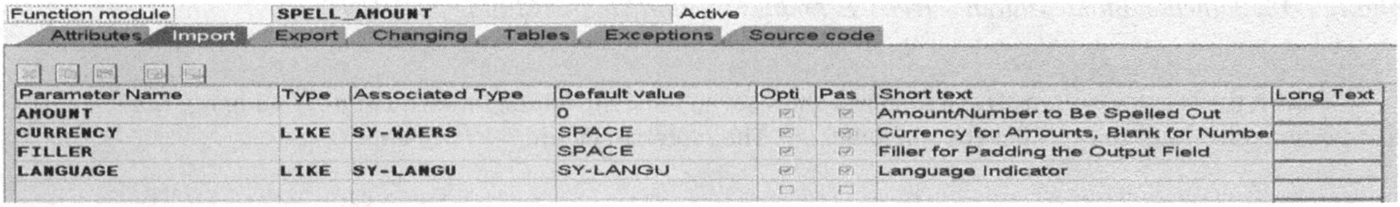

Function module SPELL_AMOUNT Active

Attributes Import Export Changing Tables Exceptions Source code

Parameter Name	Type	Associated Type	Default value	Opti	Pas	Short text	Long Text
AMOUNT			0	☑	☑	Amount/Number to Be Spelled Out	
CURRENCY	LIKE	SY-WAERS	SPACE	☑	☑	Currency for Amounts, Blank for Numbe	
FILLER			SPACE	☑	☑	Filler for Padding the Output Field	
LANGUAGE	LIKE	SY-LANGU	SY-LANGU	☑	☑	Language Indicator	
				☐	☐		

Figure 7-17. *Examine Function Module SPELL_AMOUNT - Import Tab*

Function Module: SPELL_AMOUNT – *Import* Tab

Each row will have one import formal parameter. This function module has four import formal parameters as described earlier.

This tab has the following columns:

- Parameter Name: The name of the formal import parameter is entered here. The formal parameter names must start with an alphabet letter and can contain alphanumeric characters with embedded underscores (_). The maximum length of a formal parameter name can be 30 characters.
- Type and Associated Type: With these two column entries, you are assigning a type to a formal parameter. In the *Type* column, you can enter the key word LIKE or TYPE. In the *Associated Type* column, you can enter the ABAP elementary predefined types, (C, D et al.) an object name: either a DDIC object or a system field or the ABAP *Generic Types*. (A table listing the ABAP *Generic Types* can be found in the on-line documentation: ABAP - By Theme ➤ Built-In Types, Data Objects and Functions ➤ Built-In Data Types ➤ Generic ABAP types). If no type is assigned to a formal parameter, the type of the formal parameter is adopted at runtime from the type of the actual parameter. If a type is assigned to a formal parameter, this type is matched with the type of the actual parameter. In case of mismatch, a type conflict runtime error is triggered.
- The parameter CURRENCY has been assigned the system field SY-WAERS. The system field SY-WAERS is of DDIC TYPE CUKY. The system field SY-WAERS is classified as obsolete in the SAP ABAP documents.

- Default value: Under this column, you can assign a default value to the formal parameter. If no value is received from the actual parameter, the function module will execute with this default value assigned to the import formal parameter.
- Optional (check box): You can indicate whether the import parameter is mandatory (check box disabled) or optional (check box enabled).
- Pass Value: If you enable this check box, the import parameter is received by value; or else it is received by reference (pass by value or pass by reference).
- Short text: A short description about the import parameter can be optionally entered under this column.
- Long Text: If you click on this button, the SAP environment *word processor* screen appears, where you can enter an elaborate description about the import parameter.

All the four import parameters in this function module: AMOUNT, CURRENCY, FILLER and LANGUAGE is optional, and all are received or passed by value.

Next, click the *Export* tab. Here the export or output parameters are listed. The screen will appear like Figure 7-18.

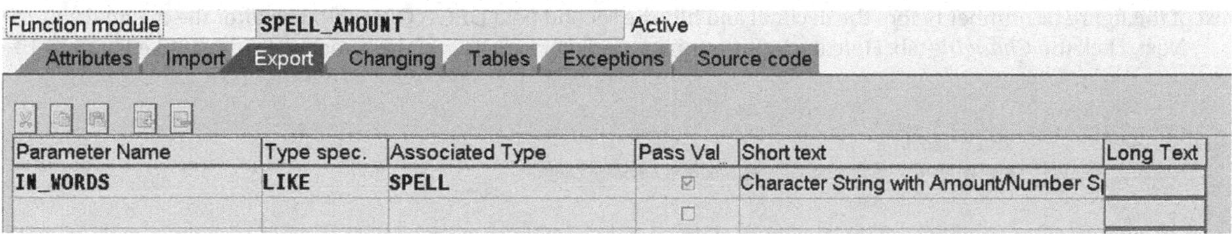

Figure 7-18. *Examine Function Module SPELL_AMOUNT - Export Tab*

Function Module: SPELL_AMOUNT – *Export* Tab

This tab has two columns less than the *Import* tab: the columns *Default value* and *Optional* are omitted. They are irrelevant to export parameters. If the check box *Pass Value* is enabled, the parameter is passed by *value and result* else parameter is passed by reference. The meaning of parameter passing by *value and result* is the same as in the context of subroutines. That is, when the function module is entered, a local copy of the parameters passed by *value and result* is made. All operations on the parameters by *value and result* are performed on the local copy. If the function module exits without an error exception, the local copies are copied back to the originals, if the function module exits through error exception, original values of parameters by *value and result* remain unchanged.

Other columns do not need explanation.

There is only one export parameter in this function module SPELL_AMOUNT. This is IN_WORDS. The parameter is being passed by value and result. It is assigned to a type, the DDIC structure SPELL. The DDIC structure SPELL has the following fields with particulars as in Table 7-2.

Table 7-2. *Examine Function Module SPELL_AMOUNT - Field Particulars of DDIC Structure: SPELL*

Field Name	Data Element	Data Type	Length	Description
NUMBER	IN_NUMBERS	NUMC	15	Whole digits of the amount converted
DECIMAL	IN_DECI	NUMC	03	Decimal places of the amount converted
CURRDEC	CURRDEC	INT1	03	Number of decimal places
WORD	IN_WORDS	CHAR	255	Amount in words - before decimal
DECWORD	DECWORD	CHAR	128	Amount in words - after decimal
DIG01	DZWORT	CHAR	07	Figure in words (units, tens, ...)
......	....	....	.....	....
DIG15	DZWORT	CHAR	07	Figure in words (units, tens, ...)

Out of the 20 fields in this structure, you will concern yourself with the two fields: WORD DDIC Data Type CHAR, length 255 and DECWORD DDIC Data Type CHAR, length 128. The function module fills the first field WORD with text of the figure or number before the decimal and fills the second field DECWORD with text after the decimal.

Next, click the *Changing* tab. Here the input-output parameters are listed. The screen will appear like Figure 7-19.

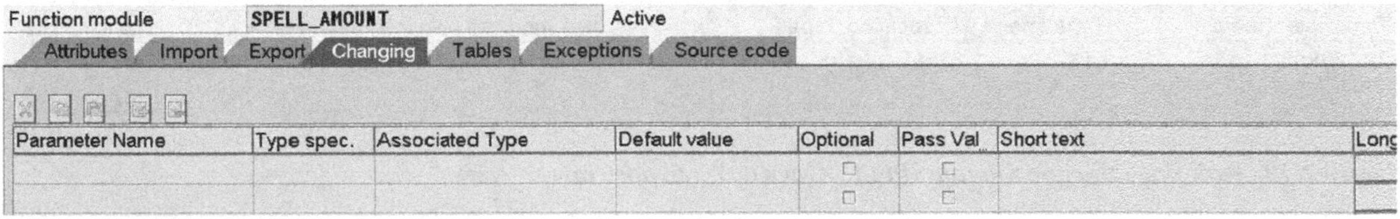

Figure 7-19. *Examine Function Module SPELL_AMOUNT - Changing Tab*

Function Module: SPELL_AMOUNT – *Changing* Tab

In this tab, you will enter parameters that are received, as well as send values (i.e., input-output parameters or changing parameters). This has the same number of columns as the import parameters. There is a column for default value. Enabling the *Pass Value* check box is to have the parameter passed by *value and result* else by reference.

There are no changing parameters for this particular function module.

Next, click the *Tables* tab. Here the internal table parameters are listed. The screen will appear like this:

Function Module: SPELL_AMOUNT – *Tables* Tab

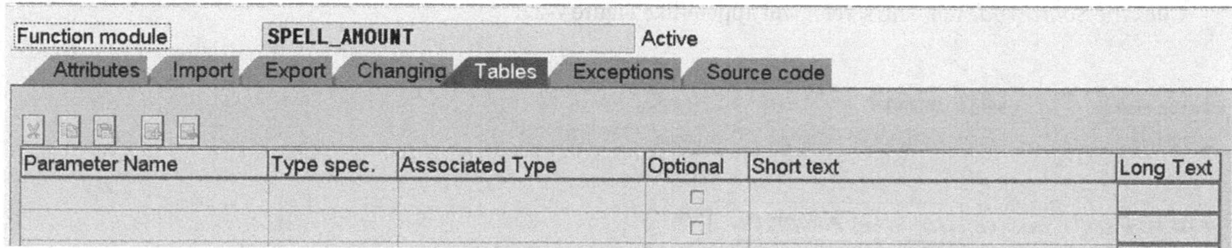

Figure 7-20. *Examine Function Module SPELL_AMOUNT - Tables Tab*

You can enter the internal table parameters in this tab. The internal tables can be passed through other tabs as well (import, export, changing). When you enter internal table parameters here, they are passed by reference (there is no *Pass Value* check box column). There is no *Default value* column.

When you pass internal tables through this tab, you will implicitly get a header line (a structure of the same name as the formal parameter name).

There are no internal table parameters for the function module.

Click the *Exceptions* tab. The screen will appear like Figure 7-21.

Exception	Short text	Long txt
NOT_FOUND	Argument Not Found in T015Z	
TOO_LARGE	Amount Too Large to Be Spelled Out	

Figure 7-21. *Examine Function Module SPELL_AMOUNT - Exceptions Tab*

Function Module: SPELL_AMOUNT – *Exceptions* Tab

As mentioned earlier, error exceptions can be raised in function modules through either the MESSAGE statement or the class based exceptions. When you develop and create a custom function module, you must anticipate the possible error conditions and provide exceptions for the possible errors.

The exception names must start with an alphabet letter and can contain alphanumeric characters with embedded underscores (_). The maximum length of an exception name can be 30 characters.

For the function module SPELL_AMOUNT, there are two exceptions listed:

- NOT_FOUND Argument Not Found in T015Z
- TOO LARGE Amount Too Large to Be Spelled Out

All of the numerical text used to convert figure or number into text is stored in the database table T015Z (see contents of table T015Z as an exercise). The first exception is related to not able to retrieve text for a particular argument or key value (the error seems to be a bit hypothetical).

The second exception is related to the maximum upper limit of the number submitted for conversion to text. The function module supports a maximum of fifteen (15) digits before the decimal. With 15 digits you can represent a figure of nine hundred ninety trillion... This is an astronomical figure in the context of the business and commercial world.

Click the *Source code* tab. The screen will appear like Figure 7-22.

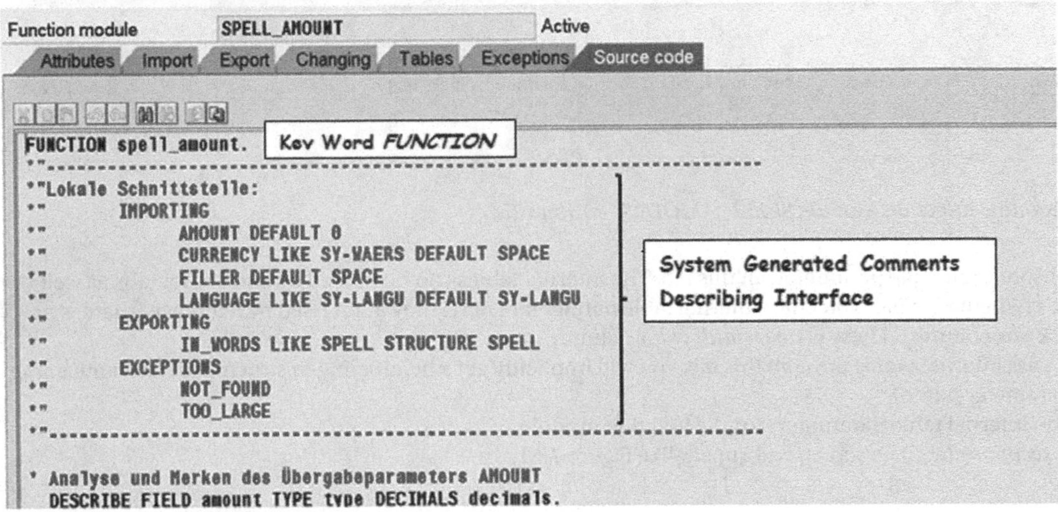

Figure 7-22. *Examine Function Module SPELL_AMOUNT - Source code Tab (Beginning of the function module)*

Function Module: SPELL_AMOUNT – *Source code* Tab

The first statement starts with the key word FUNCTION equivalent to the key word FORM for a subroutine. This keyword is followed by the name of the function module.

Following this, there are the system generated comment lines describing the function module interface, that is, the various parameters and the exceptions. If you change the function module interface, these comment lines are regenerated.

If you scroll down to the end of the function module, the screen will look like Figure 7-23.

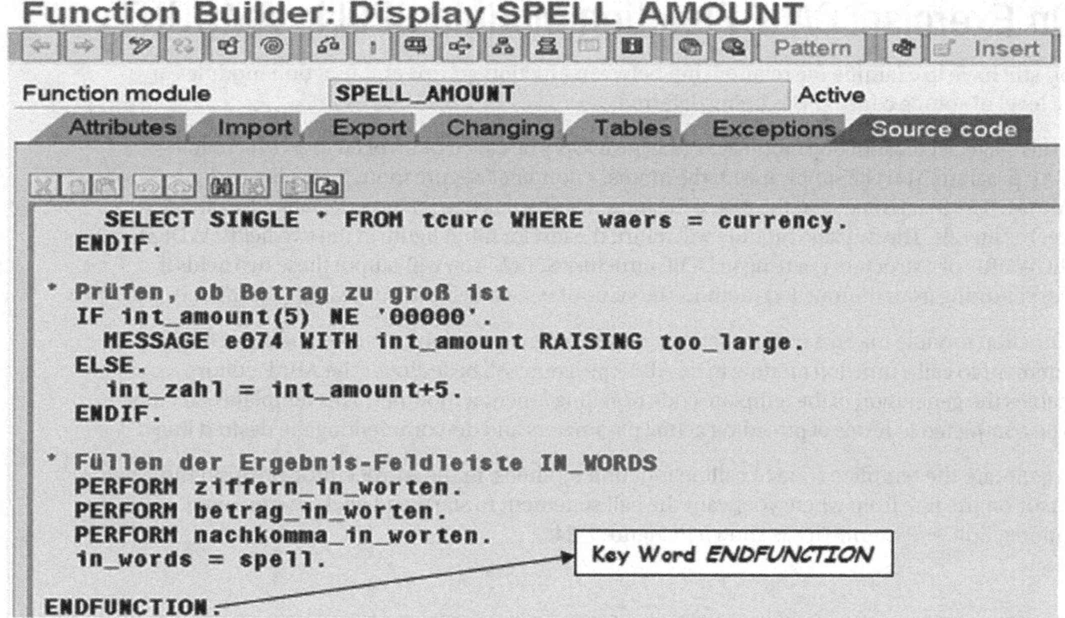

***Figure 7-23.** Examine Function Module SPELL_AMOUNT - Source code Tab (End of function module)*

The function module concludes with the keyword ENDFUNCTION equivalent to the keyword ENDFORM of subroutines.

All the function module statements have to be located between the keywords FUNCTION and ENDFUNCTION. You are not bothering about the implementation of logic in this function module. To use a function module, you don't have to do so. You generally treat the logic implemented in an SAP supplied function module as an encapsulated black box. You should understand what the function module takes and what it gives: that is, understand the parameters.

The raising of an exception in a function module with the MESSAGE statement has the following effect:

- The system fields: SY-MSGID, (message class/id.) SY-MSGNO, (message number) SY-MSGTY, (message type) SY-MSGV1, (first placeholder) SY-MSGV2, (second placeholder) SY-MSGV3 (third placeholder), and SY-MSGV4 (fourth placeholder) are filled with appropriate values from the MESSAGE statement. No message is issued at this stage.

- Further execution of the function module ceases. The function module is exited and control returns to the program or procedure from where the function module was called. The message may be issued in the program calling the function module using the system field values for message class, message type, message number, and the placeholders.

Hands-On Exercise: CALL Function Module SPELL_AMOUNT

- You still have to examine the relationship between function groups and function modules at the level of source code. This is being deferred.
- At this stage, let the function module: SPELL_AMOUNT be called or invoked in an executable ABAP program. You will supply it with the inputs: a number or figure input through a PARAMETERS statement and the rest of the input parameters (currency code, language, and filler) as literals. The function module will return the text for input figure in the two fields: WORD, DECWORD of a structure referring to DDIC structure SPELL. You will output these two fields if after returning from the function module, the value of system field SY-SUBRC = 0 (successful).
- A function module may have many parameters and error exceptions. Manual coding of the statement to call a function module in an ABAP program will be tedious. The ABAP editor enables the generation of the template code of calling function modules. This template code has to be completed in terms of providing actual parameters and de-commenting the desired lines.
- To generate the template code of calling function modules, in the ABAP editor, position the cursor on the line from where you want the call statement to start, and click on the menu options: Edit ➤ Pattern. This is shown in Figure 7-24.

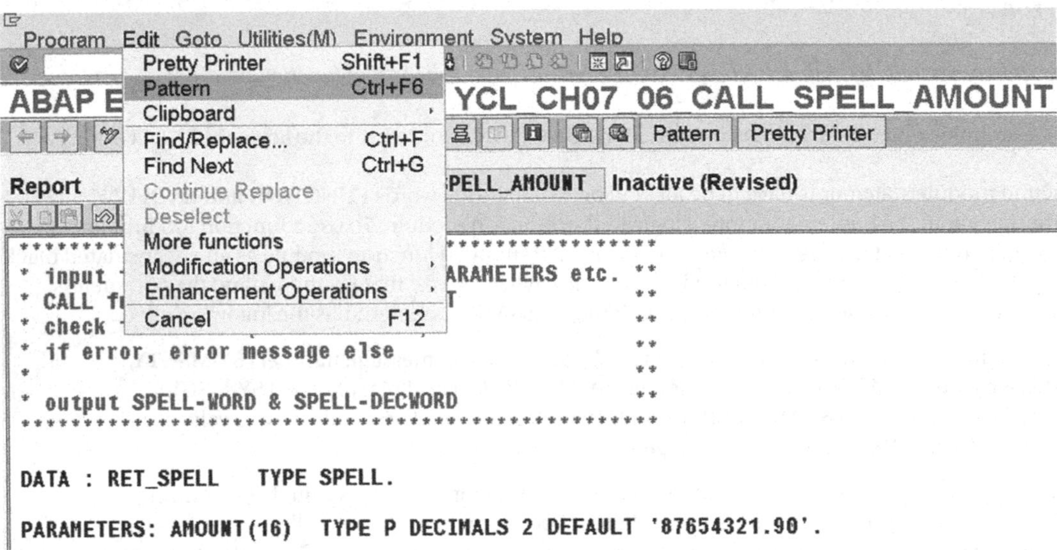

Figure 7-24. *Menu Options to Generate Template Code of Calling a Function Module*

On selecting this menu option, a dialog box will appear prompting for the statement for which template code is to be generated, etc., as shown in Figure 7-25:

YCL_CH07_06_CALL_SPELL_AMOUNT Inactive (Revised)

Ins. statement

◉ CALL FUNCTION SPELL_AMOUNT
○ ABAP Objects Patterns
○ MESSAGE ID Cat E Number
○ SELECT * FROM
○ PERFORM
○ AUTHORITY CHECK
○ WRITE
○ CASE for status
○ Structured Data Object
◉ with fields from structure
○ with TYPE for struct
○ CALL DIALOG
○ Other Pattern

***Figure 7-25.** Dialog Box to Generate ABAP Template Code for Different Statements*

As you observe in the dialog box, there is provision to generate template source code for different ABAP statements such as CALL FUNCTION, MESSAGE, SELECT * FROM et al. The autogeneration of template code works in case of CALL FUNCTION (calling a function module). In the case of other statements, less of the code is generated, and more code has to be entered manually.

You want the template code for calling a function module, so the first of the radio button (default) will do. Enter the name of the function module: SPELL_AMOUNT. You can make a selection from a list, and a search help is attached to this field (function key F4, etc.).

The generated template code, after pressing the continue key will be like Figure 7-26.

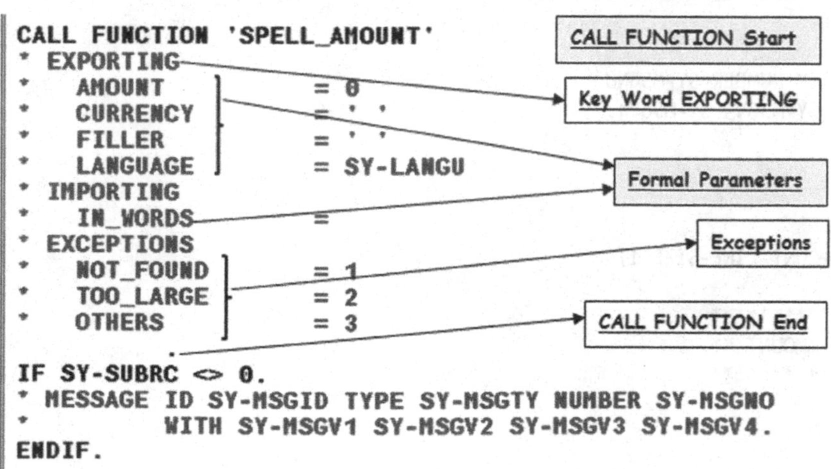

```
CALL FUNCTION 'SPELL_AMOUNT'
* EXPORTING
*   AMOUNT              = 0
*   CURRENCY            = ' '
*   FILLER              = ' '
*   LANGUAGE            = SY-LANGU
* IMPORTING
*   IN_WORDS            =
* EXCEPTIONS
*   NOT_FOUND           = 1
*   TOO_LARGE           = 2
*   OTHERS              = 3
          .
IF SY-SUBRC <> 0.
* MESSAGE ID SY-MSGID TYPE SY-MSGTY NUMBER SY-MSGNO
*         WITH SY-MSGV1 SY-MSGV2 SY-MSGV3 SY-MSGV4.
ENDIF.
```


***Figure 7-26.** Template Code Generated for Function Module SPELL_AMOUNT*

Observe that the statement starts with CALL FUNCTION... and ends with a period or full stop appearing in a separate line just above the IF SY-SUBRC... statement. This is a single ABAP statement running into multiple lines.

The keyword EXPORTING is for export parameters. The export parameters in the CALL... statement are the import parameters in the function module (calling program is sending and function module is receiving).

The keyword IMPORTING is for import parameters. The import parameters in the CALL... statement are the export parameters in the function module (calling program is receiving and the Function module is sending).

Following the keywords EXPORTING, IMPORTING (also CHANGING and TABLES) are name of the formal parameters (AMOUNT, CURRENCY, FILLER et al.) followed by the equal sign (=). On the right side of the equal sign, you should provide the actual parameter (the equal sign '=' should be followed by a space and the name of the formal parameter).

The function module exceptions are listed with values (NOT_FOUND = 1...). These are the values for the system field SY-SUBRC. You can modify these values if you want to.

The optional formal parameters with the exceptions are generated as comment lines. You need to de-comment these lines.

The message issuing statement MESSAGE ID... is also commented. This also should be de-commented. Recall that when an exception is raised in a function module, the system fields SY-MSGID, SY-MSGNO, SY-MSGTY, SY-MSGV1, SY-MSGV2, SY-MSGV3, and SY-MSGV4 are filled with the appropriate values. No message is issued, and the function module is exited.

The statements with the appropriate modifications will look like this:

```
CALL FUNCTION 'SPELL_AMOUNT' " CALL statement starts here

 EXPORTING
   AMOUNT              = AMOUNT   " amount figure
   CURRENCY            = 'USD'    " currency code
   FILLER              = ' '
   LANGUAGE            = SY-LANGU " language code
 IMPORTING
   IN_WORDS            = RET_SPELL
 EXCEPTIONS
   NOT_FOUND           = 1
   TOO_LARGE           = 2
   OTHERS              = 3
          .                         " CALL statement ends here

IF SY-SUBRC <> 0.
 MESSAGE ID SY-MSGID TYPE SY-MSGTY NUMBER SY-MSGNO
         WITH SY-MSGV1 SY-MSGV2 SY-MSGV3 SY-MSGV4.
ENDIF.
```

The complete source program:

```
REPORT YCL_CH07_06_CALL_SPELL_AMOUNT LINE-SIZE 170.

*****************************************
* CALLING Function Module SPELL_AMOUNT **
*****************************************
```

```
**************************************************
* input figure to be converted - PARAMETERS etc. **
* CALL function module SPELL_AMOUNT              **
* check for error (SY-SUBRC <> 0)                **
* if error, error message else                   **
*                                                **
* output SPELL-WORD & SPELL-DECWORD              **
**************************************************

DATA : RET_SPELL  TYPE SPELL.

PARAMETERS: AMOUNT(16)  TYPE P DECIMALS 2 DEFAULT '87654321.90'.

START-OF-SELECTION.

CALL FUNCTION 'SPELL_AMOUNT' " CALL statement starts here

 EXPORTING
   AMOUNT           = AMOUNT   " amount figure
   CURRENCY         = 'INR'    " currency code
   FILLER           = ' '
   LANGUAGE         = SY-LANGU " language code
 IMPORTING
   IN_WORDS         = RET_SPELL
 EXCEPTIONS
   NOT_FOUND        = 1
   TOO_LARGE        = 2
   OTHERS           = 3
         .                      " CALL statement ends here

IF SY-SUBRC <> 0.
 MESSAGE ID SY-MSGID TYPE SY-MSGTY NUMBER SY-MSGNO
        WITH SY-MSGV1 SY-MSGV2 SY-MSGV3 SY-MSGV4.
ELSE.

WRITE /5: RET_SPELL-WORD,
          RET_SPELL-DECWORD.
ENDIF.
```

You are checking for SY-SUBRC <> 0 (error condition), and if there is no error, the fields RET_SPELL-WORD and RET_SPELL-DECWORD are output. The output will look like Figure 7-27.

CALLING Function Module SPELL_AMOUNT

CALLING Function Module SPELL_AMOUNT

EIGHTY-SEVEN MILLION SIX HUNDRED FIFTY-FOUR THOUSAND THREE HUNDREDTWENTY-ONE
NINETY

Figure 7-27. *Program YCL_CH07_06_CALL_SPELL_AMOUNT - Output*

This was an illustration of how a function module can be called in an ABAP program.

Link, Relationship between Function Group & Function Module Source Code (Examine/View Function Module SPELL_AMOUNT – Continued)

The examination of the function module SPELL_AMOUNT will be resumed. There was a digression to demonstrate the calling of the function module SPELL_AMOUNT in an ABAP program.

From the attributes tab of the function module SPELL_AMOUNT, you know that the function group containing the function module SPELL_AMOUNT is F017 (refer to Figure 7-10). In the SE37 function builder opening screen, ensure the field *Function Module* is blank, and select menu options: Goto ➤ Function Groups ➤ Display Group like it is shown in Figure 7-28.

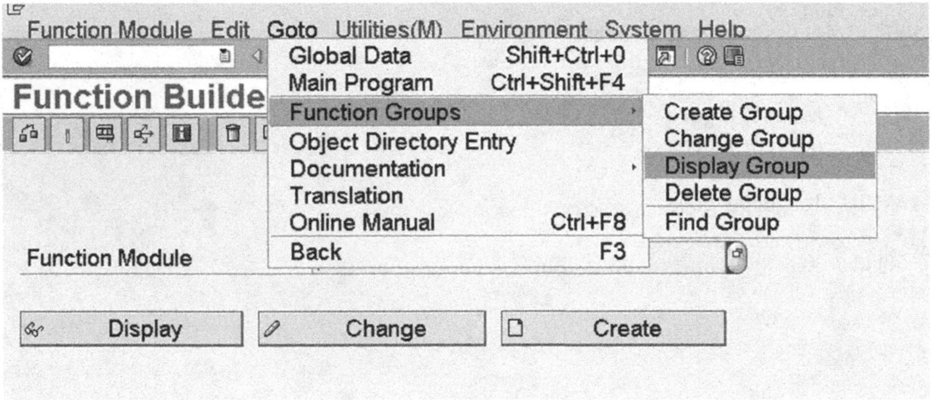

Figure 7-28. *Menu Options - Display Function Group*

This menu option selection will pop-up a dialog box for input of function group name like this:

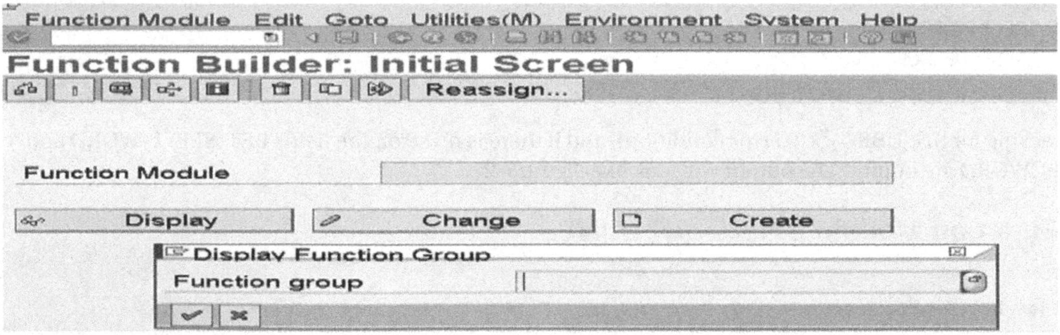

Figure 7-29. *Display Function Group - Enter Name*

Enter the name of the function group F017 and press the continue button. The screen in Figure 7-30 will appear.

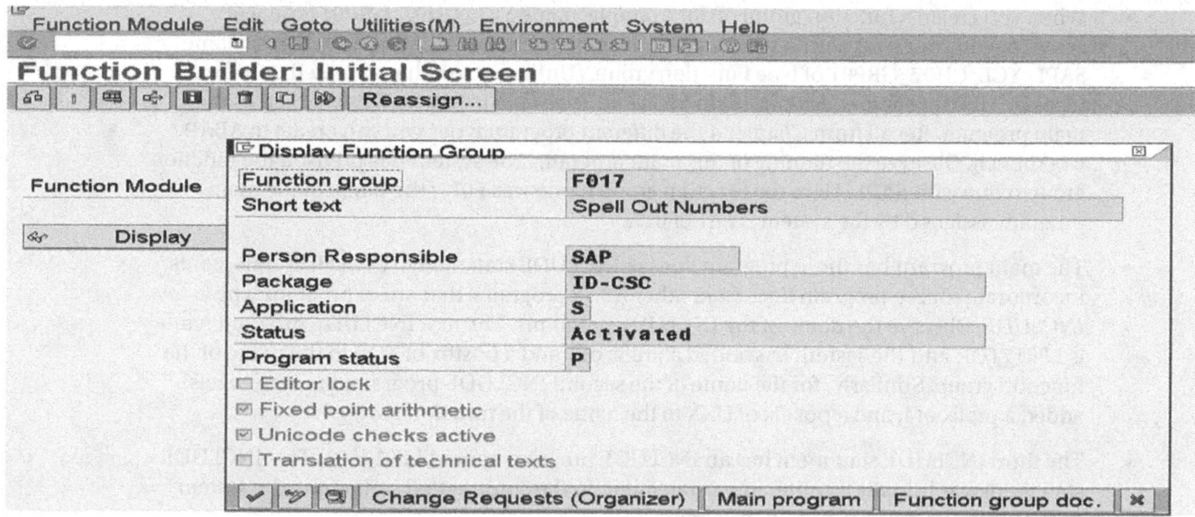

Figure 7-30. *Display Function Group F017*

Click on the *Main program* button. This will take you to

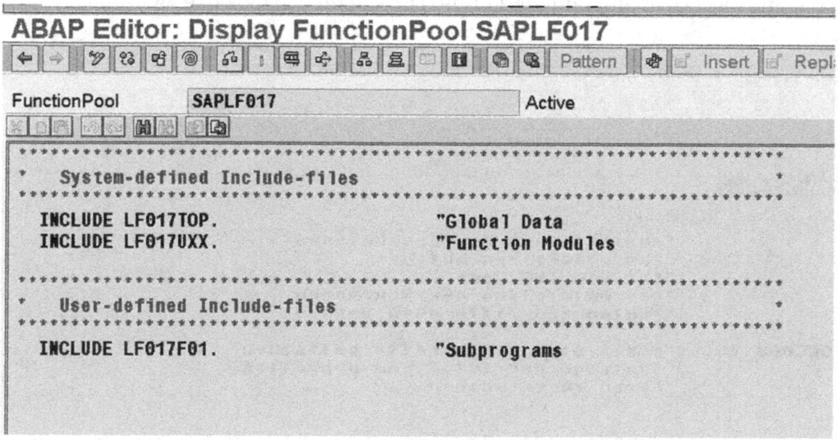

ABAP Editor: Display FunctionPool SAPLF017

Pattern Insert Repl

FunctionPool SAPLF017 Active

```
*******************************************************************
*   System-defined Include-files                                  *
*******************************************************************
  INCLUDE LF017TOP.                          "Global Data
  INCLUDE LF017UXX.                          "Function Modules

*******************************************************************
*   User-defined Include-files                                    *
*******************************************************************
  INCLUDE LF017F01.                          "Subprograms
```

Figure 7-31. *Function Group F017 – Main Program: SAPLF017*

- When you create a function group of, for example, name YCL_CH07_GRP01 (you will create one in your next hands-on exercise), the system creates an ABAP program of name SAPL_YCL_CH07_GRP01 of type Function group. (Until now, you have created only two types of ABAP programs: *Executable* in SE38 and *Type Pool* in SE11). This is called as the main program. Recall from Chapter 4 the different program types you can create in ABAP workbench. Observe the naming of this main program. The system has prefixed the function group name with SAPL. Here the function group name was F017; the name of the main program assigned by the system is SAPLF017.
- The main program has these program lines of INCLUDE statements. INCLUDE statements incorporate source program lines from other ABAP programs that are of program type *INCLUDE*. Observe the name of the INCLUDE programs. The first INCLUDE program name is LF017TOP, and the system has added a prefix of L and a postfix of TOP to the name of the function group. Similarly, for the name of the second INCLUDE program, the system has added a prefix of L and a postfix of UXX to the name of the function group.
- The third INCLUDE statement has an INCLUDE program named LF017F01. This INCLUDE statement was initially a commented statement. In the commented statement, the system proposes the name of INCLUDE programs.

Double-click on the statement:

```
INCLUDE LF017TOP.                        "Global Data
```

The double-click will navigate you to the INCLUDE program LF017TOP. The screen will look like Figure 7-32.

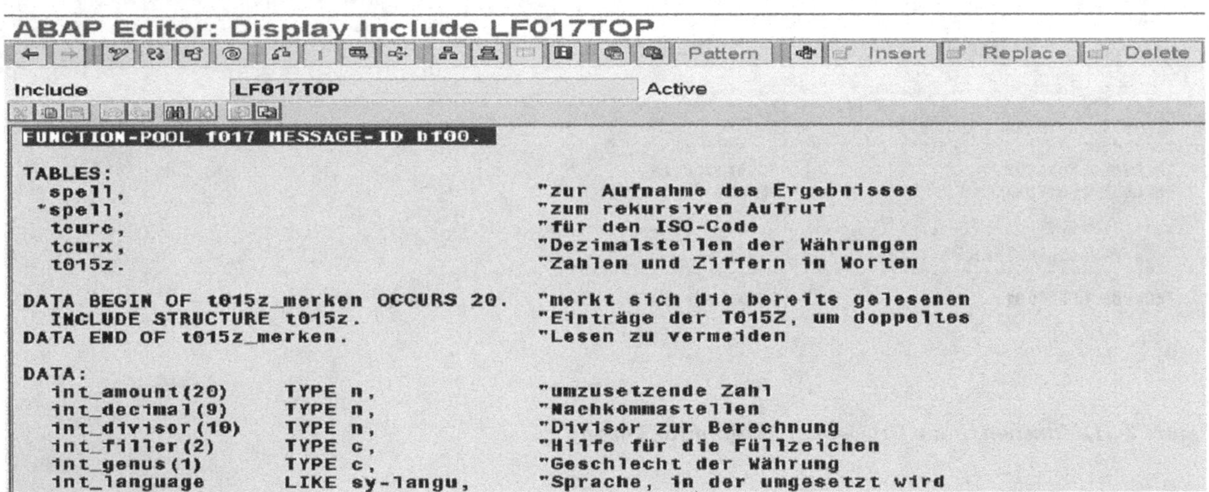

***Figure 7-32.** Function Group F017 – Include Program: LF017TOP*

- This first INCLUDE program of the function group F017 has the first statement FUNCTION-POOL F017. The key phrase FUNCTION-POOL is followed by the name of the function group F017. This is similar to REPORT <name of program> in the ABAP Executable programs.
- There are DATA, TABLES statements in this INCLUDE program. This INCLUDE program with the first statement FUNCTION POOL is a function group global declarative area. You declare data and types that can be shared and referred in all the function modules residing in this function group.

Go back to the previous screen with the INCLUDE statements, the screen of Figure 7-31. Now double-click on the INCLUDE statement:

```
INCLUDE LF017UXX.                          "Function Modules
```

The screen will be like this:

ABAP Editor: Display Include LF017UXX

Pattern Insert

Include LF017UXX Active

```
*******************************************************************
*   THIS FILE IS GENERATED BY THE FUNCTION LIBRARY.               *
*   NEVER CHANGE IT MANUALLY, PLEASE!                             *
*******************************************************************
INCLUDE LF017U01.    "SPELL_AMOUNT
```

Figure 7-33. *Function Group F017 – Include Program: LF017UXX*

In this INCLUDE program with postfix 'UXX' there will be as many INCLUDE statements as there are function modules in the function group. Initially, when only a function group has been created without any function modules, this would be empty. As the function group F017 contains only one function module SPELL_AMOUNT and there is only one INCLUDE statement:

```
INCLUDE LF017U01    "SPELL_AMOUNT.
```

Observe again the naming of INCLUDE program: Prefix L followed by the function group name, followed by the postfix U01. If there were more function modules, the second function module would have a postfix of U02 and so on. The developer can change these system generated names with attendant task of changing the source code wherever a reference is made to these names. So it better to stick to the names proposed and generated by the system.

If you now double-click on the line:

```
INCLUDE LF017U01    "SPELL_AMOUNT.
```

The system will navigate to the source lines of function module SPELL_AMOUNT. The screen will look like Figure 7-34: a repeat of Figure 7-22.

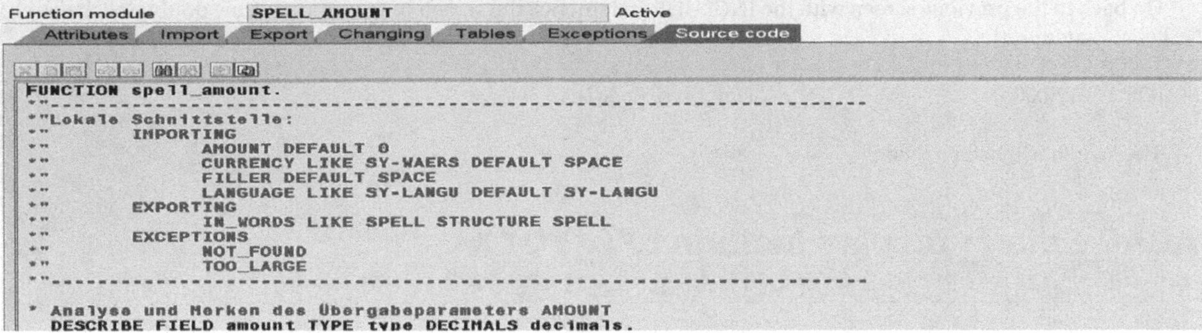

Figure 7-34. Function Group F017 – Include Program: LF017U01 (Source Lines of Function Module SPELL_AMOUNT)

This is the source of the function module SPELL_AMOUNT, with all the source lines enclosed between the keywords FUNCTION and ENDFUNCTION. It is a good idea to go through these source lines at a later date.

Now, go back to the screen of Figure 7-31 (press function key F3 twice). Double-click on the statement:

```
INCLUDE LF017F01.                    "Subprograms
```

The screen in Figure 7-35 will appear.

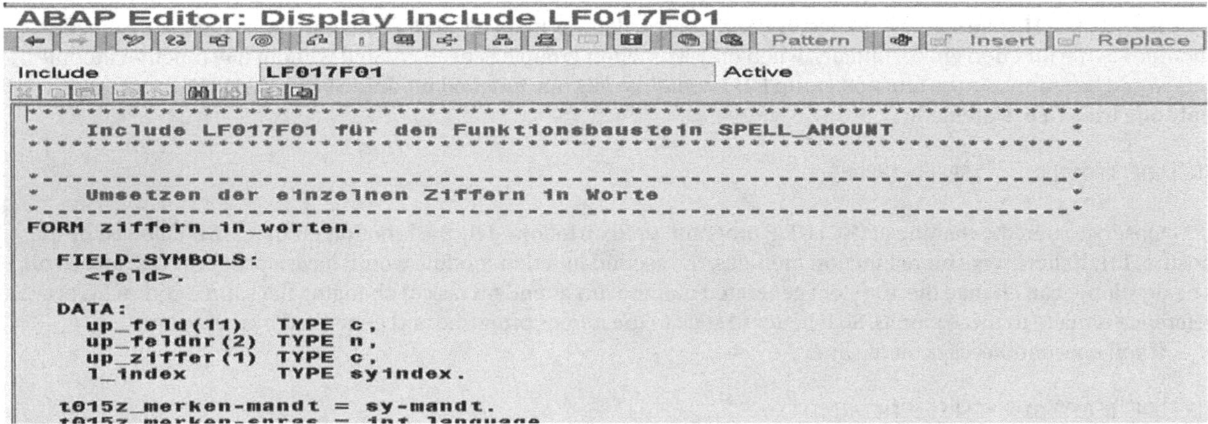

Figure 7-35. Function Group F017 – Include Program: LF017F01 (Subroutines Called From Function Modules in the Function Group)

This INCLUDE program contains the subroutines called from the different function modules of the function group. If there are no subroutines, this will be empty. If a subroutine is called from only one function module in the function group, it can be located after the ENDFUNCTION statement within the function module code. The better choice is to locate all the subroutines in this INCLUDE program.

In addition to these, a developer can always put additional INCLUDE statements in the main program with their corresponding INCLUDE programs. This is the link or relationship between the function group and the function modules source lines. It might take a while to get the hang of the structure or layout of these INCLUDES. Figure 7-36 sums up the links.

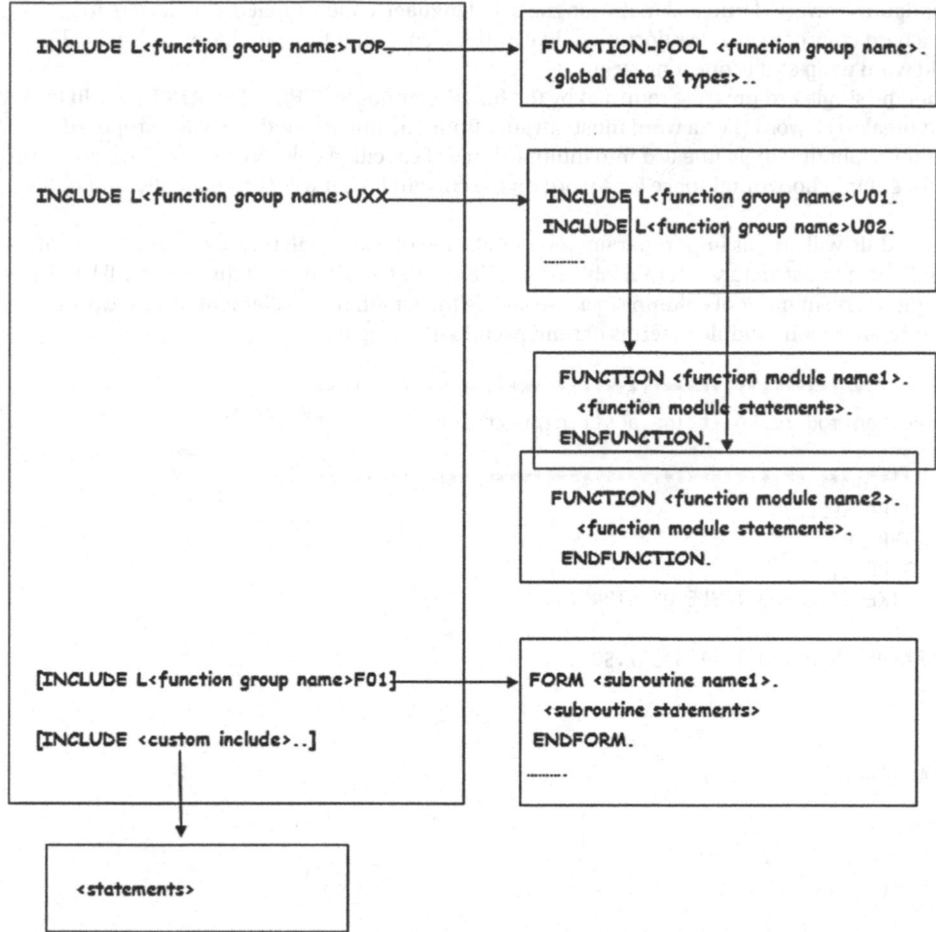

Figure 7-36. *Structure of a Function Group and the Relationship between the Programs*

Having examined the function module SPELL_AMOUNT in its entirety, the next stage is to create a function group of your own, locate a function module in this function group, and then call this custom created function module in an ABAP program.

Hands-On Exercise: Create a Function Module to Split a String without breaking a Word

The function module SPELL_AMOUNT takes:

An amount figure

A language code

A currency code

A filler string

and returns the amount figure converted into text in the language of language code supplied. If you were to output this returned text on a hard copy of a business document like a check, customer bill, purchase, etc. (typically on A4 size 8.5" x 11"), it could word wrap as it is one long string.

It would be desirable that the single text or string returned by the function module SPELL_AMOUNT be split into multiple lines of text without breaking a word (i.e., a word must not split from one line to another). Your proposed function module will do just this: split the single line text into multiple lines of specified column length without breaking a word, if there is not enough horizontal space for a word on the current line, it will automatically shift to the next line.

The proposed function module will take as import parameter a single line of text. It will return this single line of text into multiple lines loaded into a nonstructure internal table or simple array. The element of this array will be of ABAP type C of a specified length. The number of columns in a line will be the length of this element. If you express the program calling the proposed function module in terms of semi pseudo ABAP code:

```
************************************************************************
* Program Calling the function module splitting a string/text into       **
* multiple Lines                                                           **
************************************************************************
DATA: SPELL_RET           TYPE SPELL,
      TO_SPLIT_STR(300)   TYPE C,
      STRNG(35)           TYPE C,
      STRNG_TAB           LIKE STANDARD TABLE OF STRNG.

PARAMETERS: AMT  TYPE VBRK-NETWR DEFAULT '1234567.50'.

START-OF-SELECTION.

CALL FUNCTION 'SPELL_AMOUNT'
 EXPORTING
  AMOUNT    = AMT
  CURRENCY  = 'INR'
  FILLER    = ' '
  LANGUAGE  = SY-LANGU
IMPORTING
 IN_WORDS   = SPELL_RET
....

CONCATENATE SPELL_RET-WORD SPELL_RET-DECWORD INTO TO_SPLIT_STR
 SEPARATED BY ' '.

CALL <proposed function module>
 EXPORTING
  INPUT_STR = TO_SPLIT_STR
 TABLES
  STR_TAB   = STRNG_TAB
...
LOOP AT STRNG_TAB INTO STRNG.
 WRITE:/5 STRNG.
ENDLOOP.
```

So, you will have in the proposed function module:

- An IMPORT parameter of TYPE C or TYPE STRING. (will support both types)
- A TABLES parameter (nonstructure internal table)
- You will raise exceptions for the failure of following checks in the proposed function module:
    - You will check the type for the IMPORT parameter and raise an exception if IMPORT parameter type is not 'C' or 'STRING' (the DESCRIBE statement will return 'C' or 'g'). Refer to Table 4-7 of Chapter 4.
    - Your second formal parameter will be defined in the *TABLES* tab; and the system will automatically check the actual parameter type during compile time. If the actual parameter is not of type internal table, a syntax error will occur and the message will be issued in the calling program.
    - As mentioned earlier, when a function module has a *TABLES* parameter, the function module automatically creates a header line of the same name as the formal parameter name (in your case of nonstructure internal table, this will be an elementary data item). You will check the type for this header line and raise an exception if it is not type 'C'.

Proposed Function Module Interface:

- The proposed function module will have two parameters:

  (i) IMPORT – text to be split

  (ii) TABLES – to return the split text (without breaking a word)

- It will have two exceptions:

  (i) The IMPORT parameter is not of TYPE 'C' OR 'STRING'.

  (ii) The header line of *TABLES* parameter is not of TYPE 'C'.

Tasks to Create, CALL, and Test the Proposed Function Module

Having identified the proposed function module interface (parameters and exceptions), let the tasks be identified and carried out to create, call, and test the proposed function module.

- Create a function group, perform consistency check and activate.
- Create two message texts for the two exceptions in the already created message class YCL_CH07_MCLASS01 (transaction code SE91).
- Create the proposed function module; assign it to the function group created in the preceding step.
    - Enter parameters
    - Enter exceptions
    - Enter source
    - Do consistency check, activate the function module

- Create an ABAP program to call the function module. In this program, input the amount figure through the parameters statement.
  - Call the function module SPELL_AMOUNT
  - Check for SY-SUBRC error: if error exit, else continue
  - Call the proposed function module
  - Check for SY-SUBRC error
  - If no error, output the un-split and split string.

Create a Function Group

On the SE37 function builder opening screen, ensure a blank in the field *Function Module* and click on menu options Goto ➤ Function Groups ➤ Create Group.

This menu selection will pop up a dialog box prompting for the name of the function group and short text. Enter the name of the function group: YCL_CH07_GROUP01 and short text. The usual naming rules that apply to other Workbench objects apply to the function group as well. The name space for function group is 26 characters. Save. The system will prompt for a package. Assign as usual the $TMP package. The function group is created.

The function group created is not in active status. You need to activate the function group. So again click on menu options Goto ➤ Function Groups ➤ Change Group. The system will again prompt for the name of the function group to be changed. Enter the name. A screen as shown in Figure 7-37 will appear.

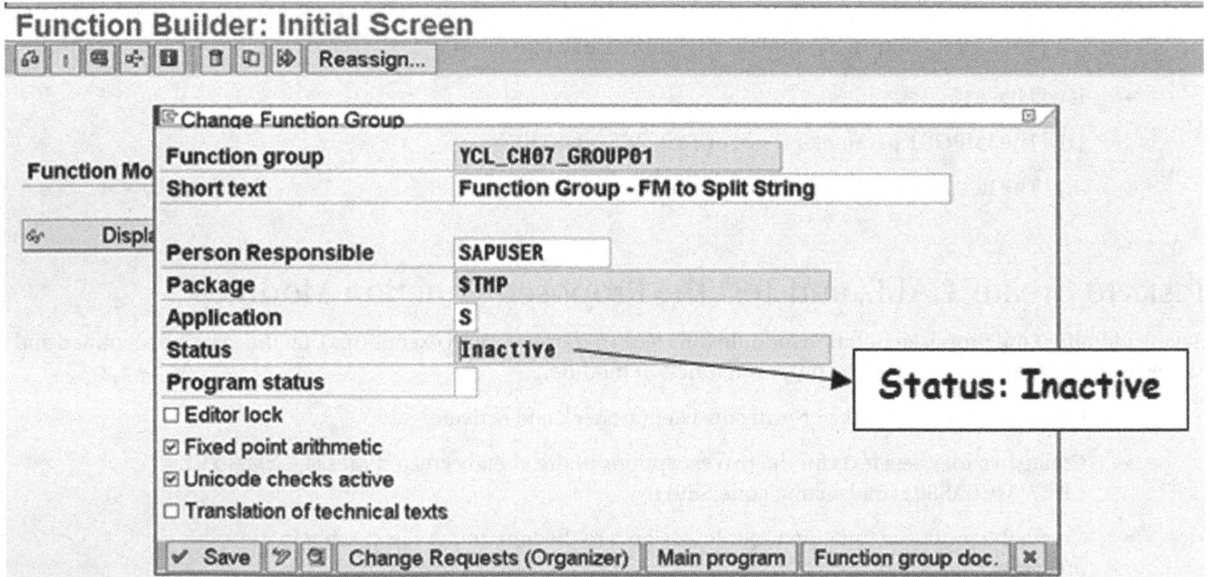

***Figure 7-37.** Function Group: YCL_CH07_GROUP01 Attributes*

Click on the *Main program* button. This will display the main program screen in Figure 7-38.

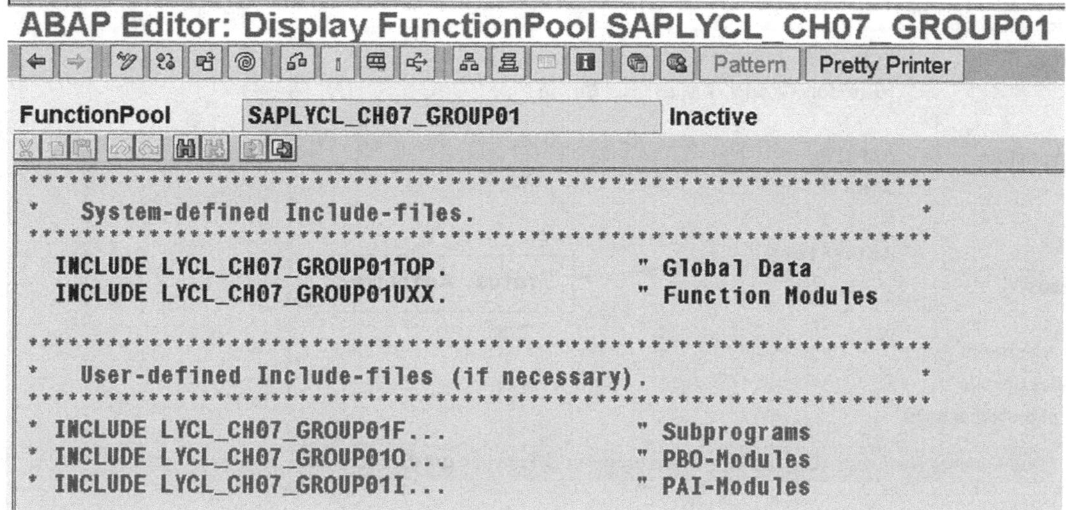

Figure 7-38. *Function Group: YCL_CH07_GROUP01 Main Program*

On this screen, click on the activate button or the key combination <Ctrl>+<F3>. The object activation list will appear:

Activate *Main Program* and *Global Data*

Ensure that both the main program (SAPLYCL_CH07_GROUP01) and global data program (LYCL_CH07_GROUP01TOP) are selected for activation like it is shown in Figure 7-39. After activation, go back (function key F3). This will take you back to the *Change Function Group* screen in Figure 7-40.

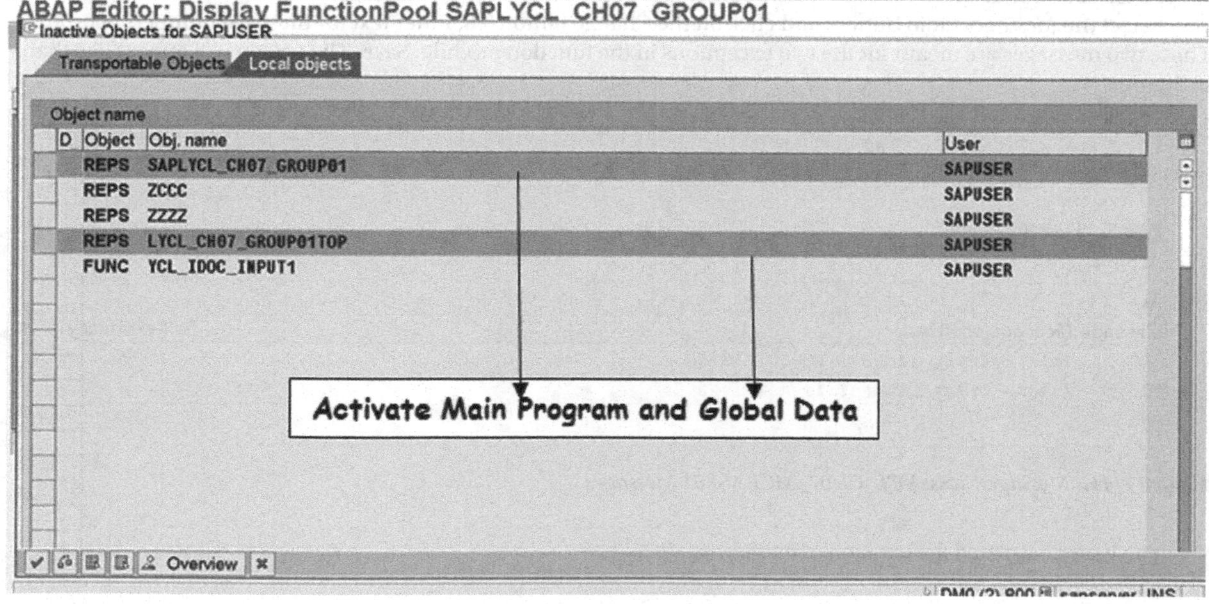

Figure 7-39. *Function Group: YCL_CH07_GROUP01 Activation*

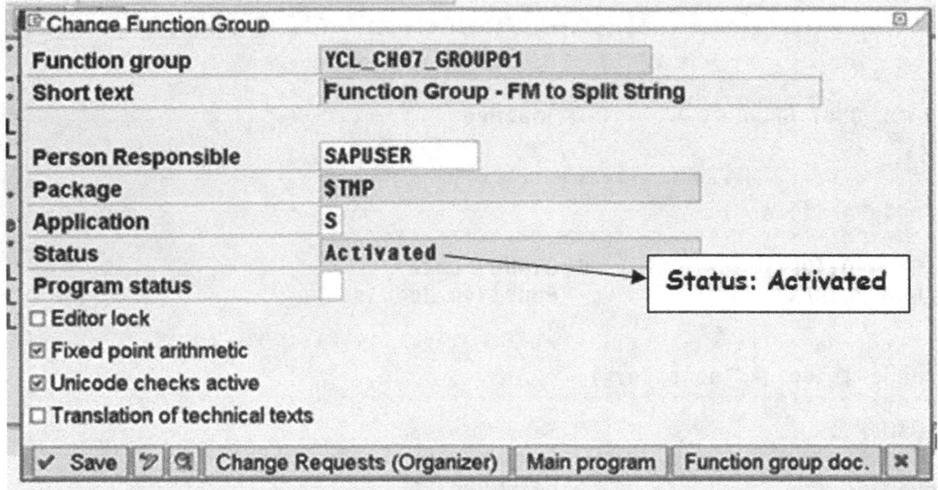

Figure 7-40. *Function Group: YCL_CH07_GROUP01 Activated*

Do not click on the Save button. This will create a new inactive version. Click on the cancel button to navigate back to the SE37 opening screen.

It is better to create function groups in the transaction code SE80. In the transaction code SE80, you do not have to go through a tedious procedure of activation. The function group is activated as it is created. You will use transaction code SE80 to create Workbench objects in Chapter 14.

Create Messages

Go to transaction code SE91. Enter the name of message class: YCL_CH07_MCLASS01.

Select the *Messages* radio button, and click on the Change button/F6. Enter text for message numbers 006, 007. These two messages are meant for the two exceptions in the function module. Save. The screen will appear like that in Figure 7-41.

Message class YCL_CH07_MCLASS01 Activ

Attributes Messages

Message	Message short text	Self-explanat'y
006	Import/Input is not Type C/STRING	☑
007	Return Array Element is not Type C	☑
008		☑

Figure 7-41. *Message Class: YCL_CH07_MCLASS01 Messages*

You have completed the creation of messages.

Create Function Module

On the transaction code SE37 opening screen, enter the name of the function module as: YCL_CH07_SPLIT_STRING. Click on the Create button/F5. The system will prompt for the function group and the short text. Enter the short text and function group name or assign a function group from the selection list. Press the Save button. The system pops up an information message (the main program and function pool do not start with Y/Z). The screen should look like Figure 7-42.

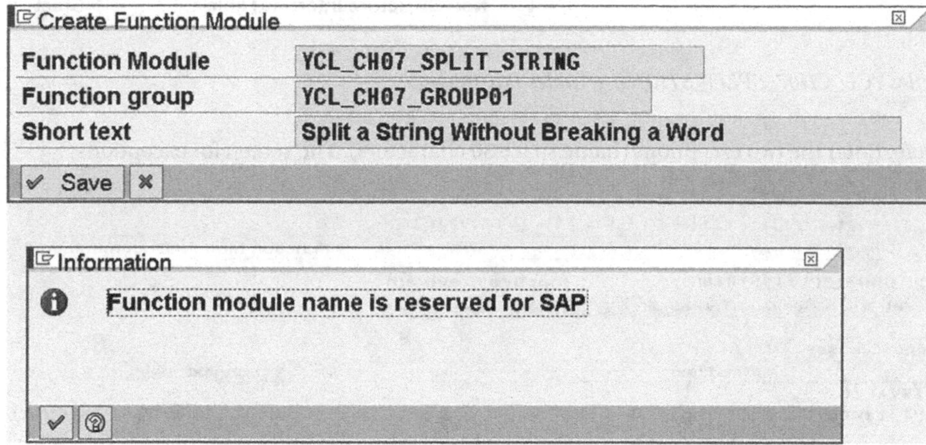

Figure 7-42. *Function Module: YCL_CH07_SPLIT_STRING - Assign Function Group*

Next click on the *Import* tab. Enter the import parameter (nspace: 30 characters). Click on the *Pass Value* check box to have the parameter passed by value. The screen will look like Figure 7-43.

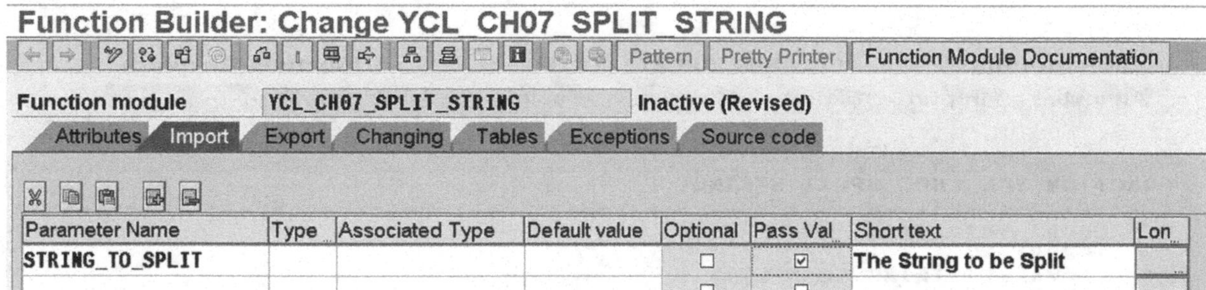

Figure 7-43. *Function Module: YCL_CH07_SPLIT_STRING - Import Parameter*

Click on the *Tables* tab. Enter the table parameter. The screen will be like Figure 7-44.

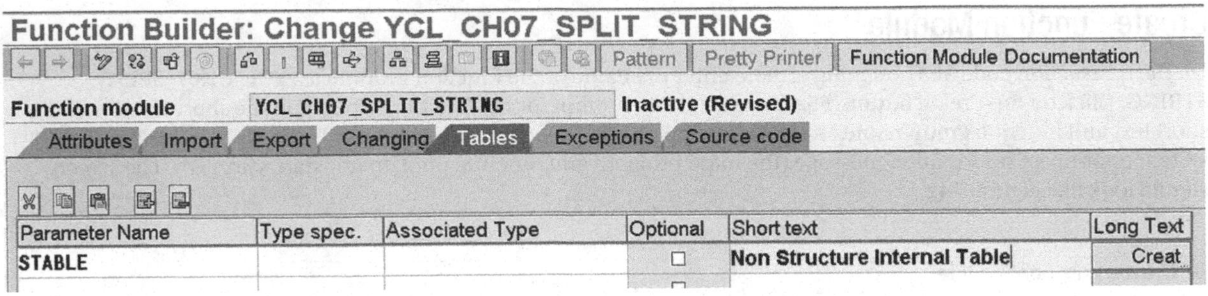

Function Builder: Change YCL_CH07_SPLIT_STRING

Parameter Name	Type spec.	Associated Type	Optional	Short text	Long Text
STABLE			☐	Non Structure Internal Table	Creat

Figure 7-44. *Function Module: YCL_CH07_SPLIT_STRING - Tables Parameter*

Click on the *exceptions* tab. Enter the two exceptions (name space 30 characters). The screen for exceptions:

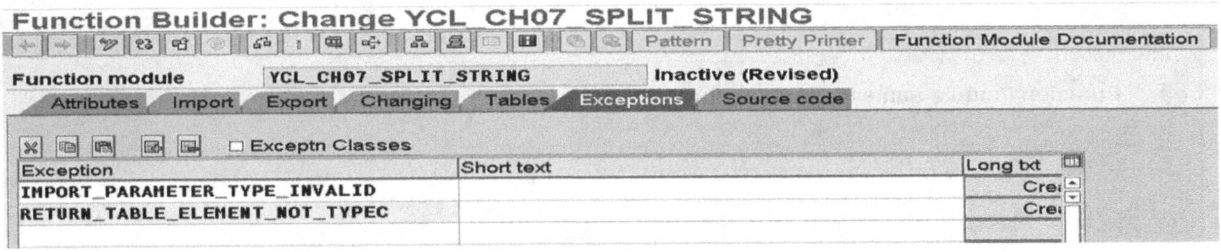

Function Builder: Change YCL_CH07_SPLIT_STRING

Exception	Short text	Long txt
IMPORT_PARAMETER_TYPE_INVALID		Cre
RETURN_TABLE_ELEMENT_NOT_TYPEC		Cre

Figure 7-45. *Function Module: YCL_CH07_SPLIT_STRING - Exceptions*

When you click on the *Source* tab, the system will generate the statements FUNCTION and ENDFUNCTION as well as the comments of the interface description (parameters and exceptions). All the functions of an ABAP editor are available here. This is shown in Figure 7-46.

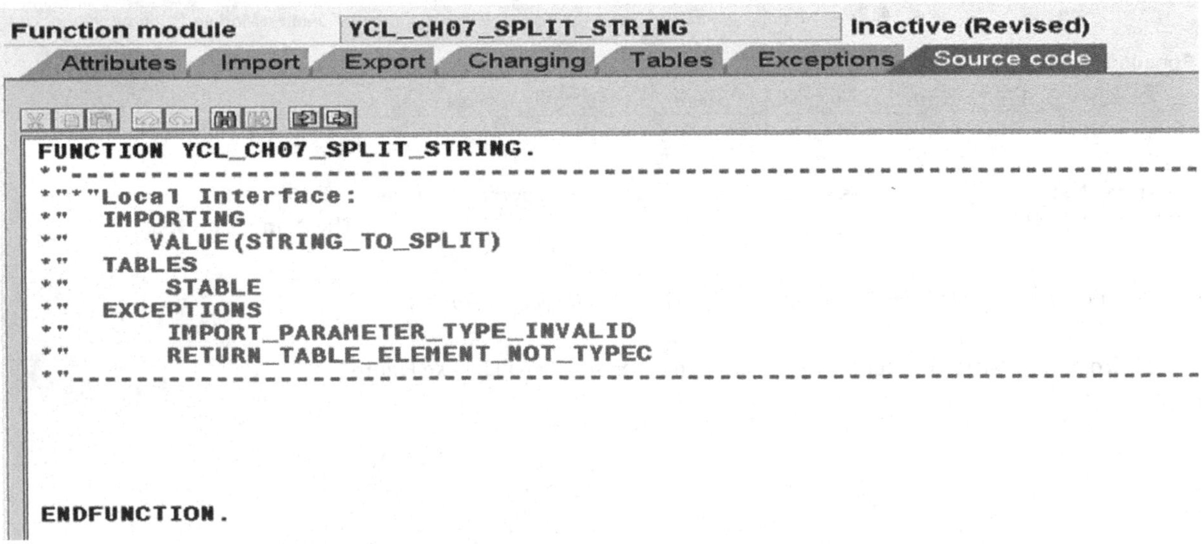

```
FUNCTION YCL_CH07_SPLIT_STRING.
*"----------------------------------------------------------------------
*"*"Local Interface:
*"  IMPORTING
*"     VALUE(STRING_TO_SPLIT)
*"  TABLES
*"      STABLE
*"  EXCEPTIONS
*"      IMPORT_PARAMETER_TYPE_INVALID
*"      RETURN_TABLE_ELEMENT_NOT_TYPEC
*"----------------------------------------------------------------------



ENDFUNCTION.
```

Figure 7-46. *Function Module: YCL_CH07_SPLIT_STRING - Initial Source Screen*

The source code of function module YCL_CH07_SPLIT_STRING is listed. The logic employed is elaborated in the comments at the beginning:

```
FUNCTION YCL_CH07_SPLIT_STRING.
*"----------------------------------------------------------------------
*"*"Local Interface:
*"  IMPORTING
*"     VALUE(STRING_TO_SPLIT)
*"  TABLES
*"      STABLE
*"  EXCEPTIONS
*"      IMPORT_PARAMETER_TYPE_INVALID
*"      RETURN_TABLE_ELEMENT_NOT_TYPEC
*"----------------------------------------------------------------------

**********************************************************
* note: the parameter STABLE is being passed as TABLES. **
* in your case it is expected to be an unstructured     **
* internal table. in function modules parameters passed **
* as TABLES implicitly generate a header line.          **
* so in your function module, there are two data objects**
* of the same name STABLE: (i) STABLE - unstructured    **
* internal table (ii) STABLE - elementary pre-defined   **
* TYPE C.                                               **
* you are referring to internal table as STABLE[] and   **
* elementary pre-defined TYPE as STABLE. Strictly       **
* speaking, this is not necessary/mandatory.            **
*                                                       **
* you are operating directly on the IMPORT parameter    **
* STRING_TO_SPLIT. this is being passed by value. so    **
* operations are on local copy. original remains intact **
**********************************************************

**********************************************************
* declare data.                                         **
*                                                       **
* check & RAISE exceptions                              **
*                                                       **
* REFRESH STABLE[] (remove existing rows)               **
*                                                       **
* determine length of element & assign to LEN, CLEN     **
* this is the max number of characters in each row of   **
* split string/text being returned                      **
* LEN after this assignment will remain constant        **
*                                                       **
* CLEN value reflects available characters in a row     **
* at any time. during start of row CLEN = LEN           **
*                                                       **
* the logic is: in a loop extract one word at a time    **
* from STRING_O_SPLIT (source) and concatenate/assign to**
* STABLE - elementary. (destination)                    **
*                                                       **
```

```
* if columns are available in STABLE - elementary,      **
* CONCATENATE the extracted word.                       **
*                                                       **
* if columns are not available to accommodate extracted **
* word, APPEND STABLE TO STABLE[]. assign word to       **
* STABLE - elementary.                                  **
*                                                       **
* continue this process till all the words are          **
* extracted and transferred to final destination i.e.   **
* unstructured internal table STABLE[]                  **
*                                                       **
* set up unconditional loop DO.                         **
* check if all words extracted from STRING_TO_SPLIT     **
* i.e. STRING_TO_SPLIT = ' ' if so EXIT loop.           **
*                                                       **
* you are extracting one word at a time from            **
* STRING_TO_SPLIT into WORD through SEARCH ' . .' i.e.  **
* search for embedded blank i.e. more than one word in  **
* the STRING_TO_SPLIT.                                  **
*                                                       **
* if this SEARCH is success/                            **
* SY-SUBRC = 0, SPLIT STRING_TO_SPLIT INTO WORD         **
* STRING_TO_SPLIT i.e. get the first word in WORD,      **
* residual text back in STRING_TO_SPLIT.                **
*                                                       **
* if SEARCH SY-SUBRC <> 0 i.e. only one last word in    **
* the STRING_TO_SPLIT. assign i.e.WORD = STRING_TO_SPLIT**
*                                                       **
* determine length of WORD and store in WLEN            **
*                                                       **
* check whether WLEN <= CLEN. if so CONCATENATE WORD to **
* STABLE.                                               **
*                                                       **
* if VLEN not <= CLEN, CONDENSE STABLE. APPPEND STABLE  **
* TO STABLE[]. STABLE = WORD. CLEN = LEN                **
*                                                       **
* adjust CLEN i.e. CLEN = CLEN - WLEN - 1               **
* ENDDO end loop                                        **
*                                                       **
* if STABLE <> ' ' APPEND STABLE TO STABLE[]            **
*                                                       **
*********************************************************
DATA: WORD       TYPE STRING, " store extracted word
      TYP(1)     TYPE C,      " store variable TYPE
      LEN        TYPE I,      " store length of string
      CLEN       TYPE I,      " store available characters/columns
      WLEN       TYPE I.      " store extracted word length
*************************************
DESCRIBE FIELD STRING_TO_SPLIT TYPE TYP.
```

```
IF TYP <> 'C' AND TYP <> 'g'.
 MESSAGE S006(YCL_CH06_MCLASS01) RAISING
  IMPORT_PARAMETER_TYPE_INVALID.
ENDIF.

DESCRIBE FIELD STABLE TYPE TYP. " STABLE reference to the elementary
                                " data item, STABLE[] reference to itab
IF TYP <> 'C' .
 MESSAGE S007(YCL_CH06_MCLASS01) RAISING
  RETURN_TABLE_ELEMENT_NOT_TYPEC.
ENDIF.

REFRESH STABLE[]. " clear internal table of existing rows

DESCRIBE FIELD STABLE LENGTH LEN IN CHARACTER MODE. " get length of element

CLEN   = LEN.

DO.

 IF STRING_TO_SPLIT IS INITIAL.
  EXIT.
 ENDIF.

 SEARCH STRING_TO_SPLIT FOR '. .'. " SEARCH for embedded blank

 IF SY-SUBRC <> 0. "last word in the text
  WORD    = STRING_TO_SPLIT.
  STRING_TO_SPLIT = ''.
 ELSE.
  SPLIT STRING_TO_SPLIT AT ' ' INTO WORD STRING_TO_SPLIT.
 ENDIF.

 WLEN = STRLEN( WORD ).

 IF SY-INDEX = 1.
  STABLE = WORD.
 ELSEIF WLEN <= CLEN.
  CONCATENATE STABLE WORD INTO STABLE SEPARATED BY ' '.
 ELSE.
  APPEND STABLE TO STABLE[].
  STABLE = WORD.
  CLEN = LEN.
 ENDIF.

 CLEN = CLEN - WLEN - 1.
ENDDO.

IF STABLE <> ' '.
 APPEND STABLE TO STABLE[].
ENDIF.

ENDFUNCTION.
```

The MESSAGE statement to raise exceptions is supported only inside a function module and method of a class. This form of MESSAGE statement is not acceptable in an executable ABAP program.

Create an ABAP Program to Call Function Module

The program calling the function module YCL_CH07_SPLIT_STRING is YCL_CH07_CALL_SPLIT_STRING. The source code of YCL_CH07_CALL_SPLIT_STRING:

```
REPORT YCL_CH07_07_CALL_SPLIT_STRING LINE-SIZE 150.

**************************************************
* Calling Function Module YCL_CH07_SPLIT_STRING **
**************************************************

***********************************************
* note on MESSAGE statement:-               **
*                                           **
* exceptions raised in function module has  **
* message type 'S' or status. if you raise  **
* exception with message type 'E' or error  **
* the program exits after return from       **
* function module, on issuing the message.  **
* you do not want the program to be exit,   **
* yet you want the message to appear like   **
* an error message. that is why you have    **
* added the phrase DISPLAY LIKE 'E' with the **
* message statement after return from       **
* function module 'YCL_CH07_SPLIT_STRING'.  **
***********************************************

***********************************************
* declare data.                             **
* input amount figure through PARAMETERS    **
*                                           **
* CALL FUBCTION 'SPELL_AMOUNT'..            **
* check SY-SUBRC etc.                       **
* CONCATENATE SPELL-WORD SPELL-DECWORD INTO **
* ISTR SEPARATED BY ' '                     **
*                                           **
* CALL FUNCTION 'YCL_CH07_SPLIT_STRING'...  **
* check SY-SUBRC etc.                       **
* output ISTR, STRGA (LOOP...ENDLOOP.)      **
***********************************************


DATA: STRG(40)   TYPE C,
      STRGA      LIKE STANDARD TABLE OF STRG,
      ISTR       TYPE STRING,
*      ISTRD(300) TYPE N,
      SPELL      TYPE SPELL.
**************************************************
```

```
PARAMETERS: AMT(7) TYPE P DECIMALS 2 DEFAULT
    '987654321.50'.

START-OF-SELECTION.

CALL FUNCTION 'SPELL_AMOUNT'
 EXPORTING
   AMOUNT          =  AMT
   CURRENCY        = 'INR'
   FILLER          = ' '
   LANGUAGE        = SY-LANGU
 IMPORTING
   IN_WORDS        = SPELL
 EXCEPTIONS
   NOT_FOUND       = 1
   TOO_LARGE       = 2
   OTHERS          = 3
          .
IF SY-SUBRC <> 0.
 MESSAGE ID SY-MSGID TYPE SY-MSGTY NUMBER SY-MSGNO
         WITH SY-MSGV1 SY-MSGV2 SY-MSGV3 SY-MSGV4.
 EXIT.
ENDIF.

CONCATENATE SPELL-WORD SPELL-DECWORD INTO ISTR
  SEPARATED BY ' '.

CALL FUNCTION 'YCL_CH07_SPLIT_STRING'
  EXPORTING
    STRING_TO_SPLIT                      = ISTR
*   STRING_TO_SPLIT                      = ISTRD
  TABLES
    STABLE                               = STRGA
 EXCEPTIONS
   IMPORT_PARAMETER_TYPE_INVALID       = 1
   RETURN_TABLE_ELEMENT_NOT_TYPEC      = 2
   OTHERS                              = 3
          .
IF SY-SUBRC <> 0.
 MESSAGE ID SY-MSGID TYPE SY-MSGTY NUMBER SY-MSGNO
         WITH SY-MSGV1 SY-MSGV2 SY-MSGV3 SY-MSGV4
         DISPLAY LIKE 'E'.
ELSE.

 WRITE:/5 ISTR.
 SKIP 2.
 LOOP AT STRGA INTO STRG.
  WRITE:/5 STRG .
 ENDLOOP.

ENDIF.
```

You will execute the calling program and thereby test that the function module is working.

Let the exceptional conditions be tested first. The first exception checks the type of input parameter: it should be either type C or STRING (DESCRIBE statement returns 'g' for type STRING). For this testing, you can de-comment the data declaration of variable ISTRD in the DATA statement. In the CALL FUNCTION YCL_CH07_SPLIT_STRING... statement, you can comment the line STRING_TO_SPLIT = ISTR and de-comment the STRING_TO_SPLIT = ISTRD. ISTRD is type N and will result in exception: IMPORT_PARAMETER_TYPE_INVALID. Execute the program. The PARAMETER statement prompt will appear on the screen, and press the execute button/F8. The screen with the error message on the status bar will appear like this:

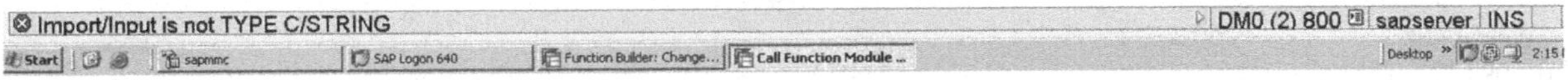
Import/Input is not TYPE C/STRING
DM0 (2) 800
sapserver
INS
Start
sapmmc
SAP Logon 640
Function Builder: Change...
Call Function Module ...
Desktop

Figure 7-47. *Program: YCL_CH07_CALL_SPLIT_STRING - Exception I*

The second exception checks for the return internal table element type to be C. Restore the source program to status prior to testing of first exception. Make the STRG some other type than C. Run the program. The second exception will be raised, and the screen with the error message on the status bar will appear like this:

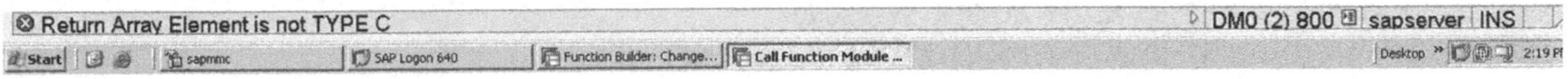
Return Array Element is not TYPE C
DM0 (2) 800
sapserver
INS
Start
sapmmc
SAP Logon 640
Function Builder: Change...
Call Function Module ...
Desktop

Figure 7-48. *Program: YCL_CH07_CALL_SPLIT_STRING - Exception II*

Restore the type of STRG to C. Execute the program. The default input of 987654321.50 had been changed to 7777777777.50. The output will appear like Figure 7-49.

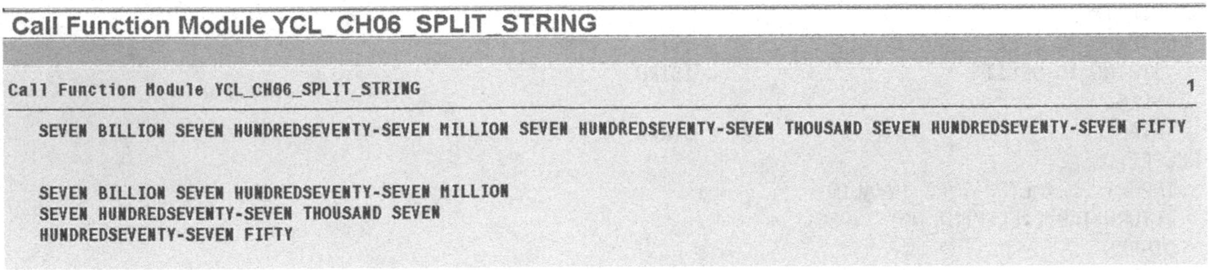
Call Function Module YCL_CH06_SPLIT_STRING
Call Function Module YCL_CH06_SPLIT_STRING
1
SEVEN BILLION SEVEN HUNDREDSEVENTY-SEVEN MILLION SEVEN HUNDREDSEVENTY-SEVEN THOUSAND SEVEN HUNDREDSEVENTY-SEVEN FIFTY
SEVEN BILLION SEVEN HUNDREDSEVENTY-SEVEN MILLION
SEVEN HUNDREDSEVENTY-SEVEN THOUSAND SEVEN
HUNDREDSEVENTY-SEVEN FIFTY

Figure 7-49. *Program: YCL_CH07_CALL_SPLIT_STRING - Output*

Reduce the length of STRG from its existing value of 50 to 40. Execute the program again. The output will appear like Figure 7-50.

```
Call Function Module YCL_CH06_SPLIT_STRING

Call Function Module YCL_CH06_SPLIT_STRING                                                                1

   SEVEN BILLION SEVEN HUNDREDSEVENTY-SEVEN MILLION SEVEN HUNDREDSEVENTY-SEVEN THOUSAND SEVEN HUNDREDSEVENTY-SEVEN FIFTY


   SEVEN BILLION SEVEN HUNDREDSEVENTY-SEVEN
   MILLION SEVEN HUNDREDSEVENTY-SEVEN
   THOUSAND SEVEN HUNDREDSEVENTY-SEVEN
   FIFTY
```

Figure 7-50. *Program: YCL_CH07_CALL_SPLIT_STRING - Output, Reduced Line Width*

With the reduced number of characters or columns in a line from 50 to 40, the output has extended from 3 lines in the first instance to 4 lines in the second instance.

So now you have created and tested your own function module, which is of some practical usage.

You could have created some DDIC objects and assigned a type to the function module parameters by reference to the DDIC objects. But that would not have given you scope for exception handling. In a practical scenario, assigning a type to function module parameters by reference to DDIC objects should be the desired procedure. Here, you have not done so, in order to use the exception handing feature.

Normally, a function module is not created directly. The functionality and logic of proposed function module is created in a normal, executable ABAP program. This program is tested thoroughly. It is then transferred and fitted into the function module. This is especially true of function modules requiring substantial data for testing.

The function module has its own testing environment. You can, as an exercise tryout testing this function module in SE37 test environment.

You have tested the function module by calling it in an executable ABAP program.

Special Function Modules - Conversion Routines

Conversion Routines Background

In the first hands-on exercise in Chapter 5 (WRITE statement...) while having the field KUNNR (customer code/ number) output from the table KNA1, you had an addition USING NO EDIT MASK. As an explanation, it had mentioned that this addition was to output KUNNR with leading zeroes: by default, the WRITE statement outputs KUNNR field with suppressed zeroes. It was also mentioned that in the SAP environment, the internal storage of data in database tables is different from the way it presented on the screen or printer.

So a numeric customer code (KUNNR) is stored in the database table with leading zeroes (a customer code can be alphanumeric as well). The field KUNNR is DDIC Data Type CHAR and length 10. When it is output, the zeroes are suppressed by default. The idea is to save the labor of entering the leading zeroes by the end user during input. An end user can just enter '1' for the customer '0000000001' on an input screen; and the system will automatically insert the leading zeroes for internal storage.

Conversion Routines Assignment

The behind-the-scenes action of inserting and suppressing zeroes is performed by the conversion routine function modules. The conversion routine function modules are attached to domains. If you open the screen for the domain KUNNR (field KUNNR in table KNA1 is assigned the data element KUNNR and data element KUNNR in turn is assigned the domain KUNNR), you will see in the *Output Characteristics* area of the *Definition* tab and the value 'ALPHA' entered in the field *Convers Routine*. This is shown in Figure 7-51.

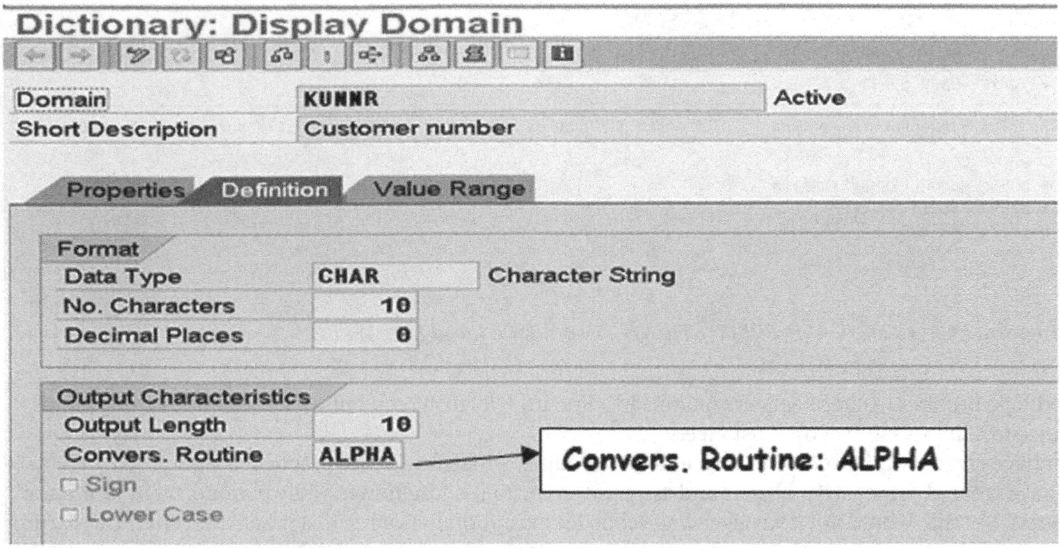

Figure 7-51. Domain: KUNNR - Convers. Routine ALPHA

Conversion Routine Attributes

The full name of the function modules are:

CONVERSION_EXIT_ALPHA_INPUT

CONVERSION_EXIT_ALPHA_OUTPUT

The conversion routine function modules exist in pairs: an input version and an output version. The conversion routine function modules have the prefix: CONVERSION_EXIT_ followed by the five-character identification (in your chosen context ALPHA) followed by the postfix of either INPUT or OUTPUT.

At the domain level, only the five-character identification is specified, and the prefix and postfix are implicit. In the case of ALPHA, the function module ending with input inserts zeroes and the one ending with output suppresses the zeroes. The ALPHA is also attached to the domain LIFNR (the domain associated with vendor code). Look this up, as well as just look up the function modules:

CONVERSION_EXIT_ALPHA_INPUT

CONVERSION_EXIT_ALPHA_OUTPUT

The conversion routine function modules have only two parameters: one import parameter named INPUT and one export parameter named OUTPUT. If you create your custom conversion routine function modules, you can define only two parameters: one import parameter named INPUT and one export parameter named OUTPUT.

If you are having a database table field with the same characteristics as KUNNR or LIFNR - TYPE CHAR, length 10, you want the same action to happen: automatic zero insertion/suppression. You can use the same domain or create a domain and assign ALPHA to the conversion routine field of the domain.

From what has been described, the conversion routine function modules are getting invoked behind the scenes. You can also call the conversion routine function modules explicitly like any other function module.

You used the addition USING NO EDIT MASK in the Chapter 5 WRITE statement to skip or bypass the execution of conversion routine CONVERSION_EXIT_ALPHA_OUTPUT, which gets executed by default. There is an addition which is the opposite of USING NO EDIT MASK i.e. USING EDIT MASK <conversion routine id>. Through this addition with the WRITE statement, you can have for the field the output version of the conversion routine executed. The syntax of the statement:

```
WRITE:/5 ......<field name> USING EDIT MASK '==<conversion routine id>...
```

A forthcoming hands-on exercise is demonstrating this.

You can also determine the conversion routine associated with a field with the DESCRIBE FIELD statement covered earlier in Chapter 4.

The exact syntax is: DESCRIBE FIELD <field name> EDIT MASK <edit mask name>.

If you execute the following lines:

```
DATA: KUNNR TYPE KUNNR,
      EMASK TYPE STRING.

DESCRIBE FIELD KUNNR EDIT MASK EMASK.
WRITE: /5 'Edit Mask of KUNNR:', EMASK.
```

It will output:

Edit Mask of KUNNR: ==ALPHA

The DESCRIBE statement returns the conversion routine name prefixed by '=='.

Conversion Routine – Hands-On Exercise: 1

In this program, there is an input of the field CUST_CD.

The input field is defined referring to the data element KUNNR. So you are assured of the conversion routine ALPHA in action for this field.

The user can enter a number: for example, 1 (just 1 without leading zeroes). After entering the number, press execute button/F8.

The statements following the event START-OF-SELECTION start getting executed. You are assigning the input field CUST_CD to another field: STRING10. The input field CUST_CD will contain internally 0000000001 as the conversion routine ALPHA (CONVERSION_EXIT_ALPHA_INPUT) will insert the leading zeroes. So the field STRING10 having been assigned to CUST_CD will also contain 0000000001.

The field STRING10 is declared as type C and length 10. Though the fields CUST_CD and STRING10 have the same characteristics of type C and length 10, STRING10 is not associated with domain KUNNR. So conversion routine ALPHA is not in action for the field STRING10.

You output both the fields CUST_CD and STRING10 twice.

CUST_CD is output without the addition USING NO EDIT MASK. This will output with leading zeroes suppressed as CONVERSION_EXIT_ALPHA_OUTPUT is executed through the association with domain KUNNR.

CUST_CD is output with the addition USING NO EDIT MASK. This will output with leading zeroes as execution of CONVERSION_EXIT_ALPHA_OUTPUT is bypassed.

STRING10 is output without the addition USING EDIT MASK. This will output with leading zeroes as STRING10 has no association with domain KUNNR.

STRING10 is output with the addition USING EDIT MASK. This will output with leading zeroes suppressed because the addition USING EDIT MASK will execute CONVERSION_EXIT_ALPHA_OUTPUT.

The source code, input, and output are shown under:

```
REPORT YCL_CH07_08_TEST_CONV_ROUT01.

DATA STRING10(10)  TYPE C.
**************************************************
* Function modules CONVERSION_EXIT_ALPHA_INPUT  **
*                  CONVERSION_EXIT_ALPHA_OUTPUT **
*                  in action                    **
**************************************************

********************************************************
* input: PARAMETERS: CUST_CD TYPE KUNNR               **
* assign CUST_CD to STRING10 (TYPE C length 10)       **
*                                                     **
* output CUST_CD,                                     **
*        CUST_CD USING NO EDIT MASK                   **
*        STRING10                                     **
*        STRING10 USING EDIT MASK                     **
********************************************************

PARAMETERS: CUST_CD  TYPE KUNNR.

START-OF-SELECTION.

STRING10 = CUST_CD.

WRITE: /5 'CUST_CD                          :', CUST_CD,
                                             "output without leading zeroes
       /5 'CUST_CD (USING NO EDIT MASK)     :', CUST_CD USING NO EDIT MASK.
                                             "output with leading zeroes
SKIP 2.

WRITE: /5 'STRING10                         :', STRING10,
                                             "output with leading zeroes
       /5 'STRING10 (USING EDIT MASK)       :', STRING10 USING
            EDIT MASK '==ALPHA'.
                                             "output without leading zeroes
```

Function modules CONVERSION_EXIT_ALPHA_INPUT/OUTPUT	
CUST_CD	1

Figure 7-52. *Program: YCL_CH07_08_TEST_CONV_EXIT01 – Input*

```
Function modules CONVERSION_EXIT_ALPHA_INPUT/OUTPUT

Function modules CONVERSION_EXIT_ALPHA_INPUT/OUTPUT

    CUST_CD                              : 1
    CUST_CD (USING NO EDIT MASK)         : 0000000001

    STRING10                             : 0000000001
    STRING10 (USING EDIT MASK)           : 1
```

Figure 7-53. *Program: YCL_CH07_08_TEST_CONV_EXIT01 - Output*

Conversion Routine – Hands-On Exercise: 2 and 3

In this hands-on exercise, you will create your own pair of conversion routines. They are:

```
CONVERSION_EXIT_ICOMA_INPUT
CONVERSION_EXIT_ICOMA_OUTPUT
```

The two function modules insert and suppress commas for numeric TYPE P fields. The internal storage of numeric fields has been described earlier. You have also been familiarized with the default output of numeric fields and the thousand separators or comma appearing after thousand, million, billion, etc. This is to make large numeric figures easily readable.

The conversion routine introduced above inserts a comma character as per the Indian business practice. In the Indian business practice, you have the first comma after thousand; a second comma after hundred thousand - called Lakh/Lac; and a third comma after ten million - called Crore. You are stopping at this. Since this is a demonstration, the function modules support a maximum figure of 99,99,99,999 (i.e., 99 crore, 99 lac, 99 thousand...).

You locate the two function modules CONVERSION_EXIT_ICOMA_INPUT and CONVERSION_EXIT_ICOMA_OUTPUT in the same function group (this is mandatory). The function group is YCL_CH07_GROUP02.

You will use two subroutines in the function group that are being called from an output conversion routine. You will locate some data in the global data area. This was not essential but done to demonstrate declaration and usage of data in the global data area.

The logic used might not be the best. The focus is on creation of conversion routine, locating data in the global data area, using subroutines in the function group, and deploying the conversion routines.

The various components of the function group YCL_CH07_GROUP02:

I. Main program-SAPLYCL_CH07_GROUP02

II. Global data area - LYCL_CH07_GROUP02TOP

III. Function modules - LYCL_CH07_GROUP02UXX

   LYCL_CH07_GROUP02U01

   LYCL_CH07_GROUP02U02

IV. Include program for subroutines

   LYCL_CH07_GROUP02F01

Copy the source program lines of global data definitions from the E-resource into the function group global data area - LYCL_CH07_GROUP02TOP. Activate the function group.

When you double-click on the include statement of LYCL_CH07_GROUP02F0, the system will alert that the program does not exist. Create the program? This message will appear on the status bar and not as a pop-up. Press the <Enter> key to create the include program. Copy the source lines of subroutines from the E-Resource into the include program LYCL_CH07_GROUP02F01. Activate the include program as well as the main program.

To invoke and demonstrate the function modules, the ABAP executable programs: YCL_CH07_09_TEST_CONV_ROUT02 and YCL_CH07_10_TEST_CONV_ROUT03 are coded. The source code of the function group, function modules and executable programs is available in the E-Resource. Copy the source lines from the E-Resource. Test the ABAP programs and the function modules.

INCLUDE Programs

Include programs have not been elaborated upon, for the reason that there is not much of conceptuality associated with them. But they are handy and, like macros, a modularization aid at source code level. They help uncluttering a program as well enable reusability. You can maintain include programs in SE38 or double-clicking on the program name of the INCLUDE statement. In SE38, in the program attributes, where you were assigning all the while program type as executable, you need to assign program type as Include for include programs. An include program cannot include itself.

There is no independent syntax check for include programs. The source lines in the include program undergo syntax checking only at the time of syntax check of the program where include program lines are included.

Function Modules Tidbits

On the function builder opening screen, you have the usual set of buttons available on any of the ABAP Workbench object maintenance screens and some more relevant to function modules and function groups such as:

- Check for consistency and activation buttons.
- Execute the button for execution of the function module in the function module test environment.
- Delete a function module button.
- Rename a function module button.

Deletion and renaming should be done with caution. The system checks for static calls to the function module and will disallow deletion or renaming if a function module is statically being called elsewhere. But there cannot be a check for dynamic calls. You have called function modules with the CALL statement, specifying the function module name as a literal (a static call). There is a variation of the CALL statement that accepts a variable containing the function module name (a dynamic call). The system cannot check such dynamic calls.

- Copy function module button.
- Reassign a function module to another function group.
- From the menu, you can navigate to the global data (program: L<function group name>TOP>) the program with the first statement as: FUNCTION-POOL, where you can declare global (global to the function group) types and data.
- From the menu, you can go to the main program (program: SAPL<function group name>). All the INCLUDE statements are in this main program.
- You can from the menu and navigate to the documentation if it is available. There is separate documentation for the function group and function modules.

Except for delete, rename, copy, and reassign, other options are available inside the function module editor screen as well.

List of a Few Function Modules

A few (50 odd) SAP Standard function modules are listed in Table 7-3. They are categorized under various heads. Some of these, you will be using in your hands-on exercise of forthcoming topics. The function modules names in italics can be tried out as exercises immediately before proceeding to the next chapter. Contrive scenarios to call these function modules. Go through the function module interface. You need not pass all optional parameters always.

Table 7-3. *List of a Few SAP Supplied Function Modules*

Function Module Name	Description
Pop-Up to Decide	
POPUP_TO_CONFIRM	A 2/3 Buttons dialog Pop-up
POPUP_TO_INFORM	A Pop-up to Inform
POPUP_TO_CONFIRM_DATA_LOSS	A Pop-up to Confirm Abort and Lose Data
Pop-Up to Select	
F4_CLOCK	A Pop-up to Select Time
F4_DATE	A Pop-up to Select Date
POPUP_TO_SELECT_MONTH	A Pop-up to Select Month
POPUP_TO_DECIDE_LIST	A Pop-up to Make Single/Multiple Selections
POPUP_WITH_TABLE_DISPLAY	A Pop-up Selection from an Internal Table, Returns Row Number Selected
FITRV_CALCULATOR	A Pop-Up Calculator
Conversion Routines	
CONVERSION_EXIT_ALPHA_INPUT CONVERSION_EXIT_ALPHA_OUTPUT	Suppress, Insert Leading Zeroes in Customer Code and Vendor Code (Data Type CHAR, Length 10)
CONVERSION_EXIT_MATN1_INPUT *CONVERSION_EXIT_MATN1_OUTPUT*	Suppress, Insert Leading Zeroes in Material Code (Data Type CHAR, Length 18)
Conversions	
ROUND_AMOUNT	Rounding Amount as per Company Code Currency
CURRENCY_CODE_SAP_TO_ISO	Convert Currency Code: SAP to ISO
CURRENCY_CODE_ISO_TO_SAP	Convert Currency Code: ISO to SAP
UNIT_OF_MEASURE_ISO_TO_SAP	Unit of Measure Code ISO to SAP
UNIT_OF_MEASURE_SAP_TO_ISO	Unit of Measure Code SAP to ISO
SPELL_AMOUNT	Convert Amount Figure into Text
SO_SPLIT_FILE_AND_PATH	Split the Full File Name to Drive, Directories, and File Name
CONVERT_ABAPSPOOLJOB_2_PDF	Convert Spool Output to PDF File

(continued)

Table 7-3. (*continued*)

Function Module Name	Description
Date & Time	
ADD_TIME_TO_DATE	Used in MM Module to Determine Date of Expiry from Shelf Life
HR_SGPBS_ADD_TIME_TO_DATE	Used in HR Module to determine End Date by Adding Days/Months/Years to a Date
COMPUTE_YEARS_BETWEEN_DATES	Years between Two Dates
DAYS_BETWEEN_TWO_DATES	Days Between Two Dates for Interest Calculation
MONTH_NAMES_GET	Get All the Month Names in an Internal Table in Specified Language
MONTH_PLUS_DETERMINE	Add/Subtract Months to Get Forward/Backward Date
WEEKDAY_GET	Get All the Week Days in an Internal Table in Specified Language
Strings	
STRING_CENTER	Center a String
STRING_MOVE_RIGHT	Move String Right
STRING_REVERSE	Reverse a String
Files	
GUI_DOWNLOAD	Download Internal Table to a File on Presentation Server
GUI_UPLOAD	Upload a File on Presentation Server into an Internal Table
F4_FILENAME	Displays a Dialog Box for File Selection from Presentation Server
TMP_GUI_BROWSE_FOR_FOLDER	Displays a Dialog Box for Folder Selection from Presentation Server
TMP_GUI_GET_FILE_EXIST	Check File Existence on Presentation Server
Lists	
SAPGUI_PROGRESS_INDICATOR	Progress Meter/Indicator for a Process
Miscellaneous	
CLOI_PUT_SIGN_IN_FRONT	Get the Sign on Left
RS_VARIANT_VALUES_TECH_DATA	Retrieve variant values
RS_VARIANT_EXISTS	Check variant existence
SAP_CONVERT_TO_XLS_FORMAT	Convert internal table data into Excel
RS_COPY_SELECTION_SETS	Copy variant from one program to another
MG_FIELDNAME_TEXT	Retrieve texts from data elements
ICON_CREATE	Transfer icon name and text to screen field
ALV	
REUSE_ALV_GRID_DISPLAY	Simple ALV grid type display (Three Dimensional)

(*continued*)

Table 7-3. (*continued*)

Function Module Name	Description
REUSE_ALV_LIST_DISPLAY	Simple ALV list type display (Two Dimensional)
REUSE_MINIALV_LIST_DISPLAY	ALV grid (no event support)
REUSE_ALV_FIELDCATALOG_MERGE	Create default field catalog (ALV using function modules)
LVC_FIELDCATALOG_MERGE	Create default field catalog (ALV using classes)
REUSE_ALV_COMMENTARY_WRITE	ALV output header at top of page
REUSE_ALV_EVENTS_GET	Get possible events of an ALV list
REUSE_ALV_BLOCK_LIST_APPEND	Append ALV list to a block
REUSE_ALV_BLOCK_LIST_DISPLAY	Output ALV Block
Random Numbers	
QF05_RANDOM	Random number generator
QF05_RANDOM_INTEGER	Random number generator - integer

Conclusion

In the forthcoming chapters, you will use a few of the SAP supplied function modules. You will not create any custom function modules, though. Going forward in this book, whenever the context warrants a subroutine and INCLUDE program, they will be created and used.

CHAPTER 8

Open SQL Data Retrieval

Introduction

SAP Open SQL is the de facto SQL used to operate database tables in ABAP programs. It was introduced in Chapter 5 on a preview basis. In Chapter 5, you wanted substantial output running into multiple pages. You resorted to retrieving large amounts of data available in a database table that could produce multiple page output. You used Open SQL to retrieve the data. You also used Open SQL data retrieval in Chapter 6 to load internal tables.

You have been exposed to some basic forms of the SELECT statement in these chapters. Similar to other SQL offerings, the SELECT statement is used in Open SQL to retrieve data from database tables and views. You can use the SQL of a specific database as well. Called *Native SQL* in SAP documentation terminology, it restricts you to running the program only on SAP systems with that specific database installed. In this chapter, you are learning only the SELECT statement (data retrieval) with its variants. The other data manipulation statements: INSERT, UPDATE, MODIFY, DELETE, etc., are covered in Chapter 14.

Figure 8-1 represents the processing of Open SQL vis-à-vis Native SQL statements by the ABAP interpreter and ABAP runtime database interface system.

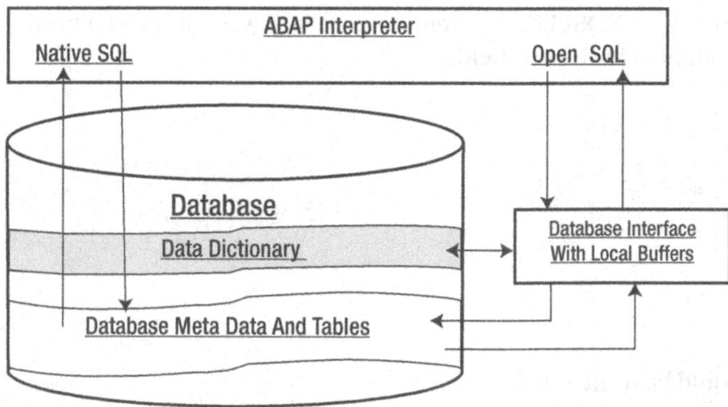

Figure 8-1. *Open SQL, Native SQL Data Manipulation Flow*

Let the processing of Open SQL statements by the ABAP runtime database interface system be traced. From the ABAP interpreter, the Open SQL statement is processed first by the database interface. It is determined whether the table definition exists in the DDIC. If a table definition exists in the DDIC, the Open SQL statements are translated to the SQL statements of the installed database. Other information is extracted from the DDIC table definition such as table maintenance, technical settings, domain and data element information, etc. The Open SQL translated statements are passed to the database metadata. And then the database metadata takes over.

After the Open SQL operation on the database, processing is via the database interface (filling buffers, etc.) and back to the ABAP interpreter.

As elaborated upon in Chapter 1, under the heading 'Client Code Perspectives', the Open SQL by default filters and operates only on row/s belonging to the client code into which the user is logged in for client dependent tables.

In Native SQL, the SQL statements are passed directly from the ABAP interpreter to the installed database's metadata and after the operation on the database, back to the ABAP interpreter. There is absolutely no reference to the DDIC.

In this chapter, you will go through the different variations of the Open SQL SELECT statement. The variations are these: the <result> specification, <source> specification, <destination> specification, WHERE <condition> specification, and the ORDER BY <sort> specification.

The Open SQL special features of runtime specifications of <result>, <source>, <destination>, WHERE <condition>, and ORDER BY <sort> are introduced.

The chapter also covers the ABAP FIELD-SYMBOLS. Some rudimentary applications of the FIELD-SYMBOLS are demonstrated. The FIELD-SYMBOLS are used to access and process rows of an internal table directly instead of fetching them into a structure and processing. The creation of runtime or dynamic data objects (OOPS) is introduced. FIELD-SYMBOLS are then used to access individual fields of a runtime created structured object.

Open SQL SELECT Statement

Instead of introducing you to a single comprehensive syntax of the SELECT statement, it is being introduced in pieces as different features and variants. After chapter completion, you can navigate to the online SAP documentation of the SELECT statement (press F1 on the keyword SELECT), and you will be able to relate to the single comprehensive syntax of the SELECT statement with its myriad options.

SELECT... ENDSELECT with WHERE Condition, ORDER BY and UP TO Clauses

The most basic form of the SELECT statement is the SELECT...ENDSELECT statement, where one row is fetched from the database table into a destination structure or destination of individual fields:

```
SELECT <result> FROM <source>
INTO [CORRESPONDING FIELDS OF] <destination>
[WHERE <condition>]
[ORDER BY <sort specification>]
[UP TO <no of rows> ROWS].
..................
ENDSELECT.
```

<result>: This can be '*' or individual fields. ('*' should be used judiciously).

<source>: This can be a database table or database view or projection view.

<destination>: This can be a structure or list of individual fields. The individual fields have to be enclosed in parentheses separated by commas, like: `(KUNNR, NAME1, ORT01)`. For a single field as destination, the parentheses can be omitted.

CORRESPONDING FIELDS OF: The addition of this phrase applies when the destination is a structure and when the source and destination are not identical in terms of the number of fields and/or their order. The data movement takes place field by field with the CORRESPONDING FIELDS OF usage.

<condition>: A condition can be simple or compound. In a compound condition, the simple conditions are conjoined by the logical operators AND and OR. The logical operator NOT is to be used judiciously for performance reasons.

The following condition operators are supported:

Table 8-1. *Condition Operators in Open SQL*

Operator	Description
EQ / =	Equal To
NE / <> / ><	Not Equal To
GT / >	Greater Than
GE / >=	Greater Than Or Equal To
LT / <	Less Than
LE / <=	Less Than Or Equal To
BETWEEN	Between Two Values (interval)
IN	In a Set Of Values
LIKE (%, _)	String Pattern Comparison

<sort specification>: You can get data sorted by fields in ascending/descending order like: ORDER BY ORT01 ASCENDING NAME1 DESCENDING.

If you do not specify the addition ASCENDING/DESCENDING, the default is ASCENDING.

<no of rows>: The loop will run <no of rows> times or it will fetch only <no of rows> rows. This variation is used at the testing stage.

The SELECT statement can also be nested but is not advisable. You can use one-level loop construct SELECT... ENDSELECT judiciously. You used it to build a summary internal table with the COLLECT statement. If the data is small, you can use it. In a client server environment, the suggested procedure is to load an internal table from the database table and set up row-by-row processing with the internal table looping construct.

The system field SY-DBCNT is set to the number of rows fetched or the pass number of the SELECT...ENDSELECT loop. The system field SY-SUBRC is set to zero if a row is fetched and is set to non-zero, if a row cannot be fetched.

SELECT SINGLE with/without WHERE condition

To retrieve a single row from a database table or database view or projection view, you use:

```
SELECT SINGLE <result>
FROM <source>
INTO [CORRESPONDING FIELDS OF] <destination>
[WHERE <condition>].
```

This is not a looping construct – no ENDSELECT. The meaning of <result>, <source>, <destination>, etc., are the same as explained in the preceding syntax. The statement will fetch the first row in the table or view fulfilling the WHERE condition if there is a WHERE condition, else it fetches the first row.

Though the WHERE condition is optional, in practical terms it could be mandatory.

If a row is fetched, the system field SY-SUBRC is set to zero or else to non-zero. The system field SY-DBCNT is set to 1 if SY-SUBRC = 0.

SELECT... INTO TABLE

To fetch data from a database table or database view or projection view into an internal table, you use the following syntax:

```
SELECT <result> FROM <source>
INTO [CORRESPONDING FIELDS OF] TABLE <itab>
[WHERE <condition>]
[ORDER BY <sort specification>]
[UP TO <no of rows> ROWS].
```

<itab> is the specification for the internal table; other clauses have the same meaning as in earlier syntaxes. There is no ENDSELECT statement; there is no repetitive, looping process, and data is fetched into the internal table at one go. This is the preferred way of data retrieval in the client server environment.

The system field SY-DBCNT is set to the number of rows fetched. The system field SY-SUBRC is set to zero if a row/rows is fetched, or else it is set to non-zero.

Hands-On Exercise – INTO TABLE... PACKAGE SIZE...

If the number of rows being fetched into an internal table is very high, there is a pressure on the application server of RAM usage. Then, instead of loading the internal table fully, it can be loaded partially in batches of a specified number of rows. The fetched rows are processed and the next batch of rows fetched into the internal table replacing the preceding batch. This process of fetching and processing goes on until all rows are processed. This is a looping process and hence the ENDSELECT statement. The syntax:

```
SELECT <result> FROM <source>
INTO [CORRESPONDING FIELDS OF] TABLE <itab>
PACKAGE SIZE <no of rows in batch> [WHERE <condition>]
[ORDER BY <sort specification>]
[UP TO <no of rows> ROWS].
........
ENDSELECT.
```

PACKAGE SIZE is the key phrase to provide the batch size in number of rows.

<no of rows in batch> can be literal or variable to specify the number of rows in the batch.

Other clauses carry the same meaning as in the earlier syntaxes.

As a hands-on to fetch, process data with this syntax, you output customer list, fetching the data in batches, batch size, or package size input through the PARAMETERS statement. The source program:

```
REPORT YCL_CH08_02_PSIZE_INTO_TAB NO STANDARD PAGE HEADING
      LINE-SIZE 95 LINE-COUNT 60.

********************************************************
* Fetch Data From Database Table In Batches INTO TABLE **
********************************************************

*****************************************************
* if no of rows/data is very large exerting pressure**
* on RAM usage, then in this scenario data can be   **
* fetched in batches of smaller size.               **
*                                                   **
```

```
* in the present scenario, you are fetching data in **
* batches of 1000 rows at a time. this batch size   **
* can be specified with the phrase PACKAGE SIZE & a **
* literal/variable.                                 **
*                                                   **
* every time batch of rows is fetched, existing data**
* in the internal table is overwritten/deleted.     **
*                                                   **
* at any instant only one batch of data/rows is     **
* existing in the internal table.                   **
*                                                   **
* you are using an INCLUDE program                  **
* YCL_CH08_01_INCLUDE_HEADING for non standard      **
* header. you are using this same INCLUDE program   **
* for the hands-on YCL_CH08_03_PSIZE_APPEND_TAB     **
******************************************************
******************************************************
* declare data. input PACKAGE SIZE thru PARAMETERS  **
* INCLUDE program for heading                       **
*                                                   **
* retrieve a batch of rows with SELECT...PACKAGE    **
* SIZE...etc.                                       **
* output retrieved batch LOOP AT...WRITE...ENDLOOP  **
* ENDSELECT.                                        **
******************************************************

DATA: CUSTOMER_TAB TYPE STANDARD TABLE OF YCL_CH05_CUST_STRU
                          WITH HEADER LINE,
       CNTR(3)      TYPE P DECIMALS 0,
       CDATE        TYPE STRING.

PARAMETERS: PKSZ(4)  TYPE N DEFAULT 1000.
********************************************
INCLUDE YCL_CH08_01_INCLUDE_HEADING. " INCLUDE program for heading

START-OF-SELECTION.

CONCATENATE SY-DATUM+6(2) SY-DATUM+4(2) SY-DATUM+0(4)
 INTO CDATE SEPARATED BY '/'.
**********************************************
SELECT KUNNR NAME1 STRAS ORT01 PSTLZ FROM KNA1 INTO
  TABLE CUSTOMER_TAB PACKAGE SIZE PKSZ.

 LOOP AT CUSTOMER_TAB. " output fetched batch
  CNTR = CNTR + 1.      " cannot use SY-TABIX for serial number

  WRITE:/5(5) CNTR, CUSTOMER_TAB-KUNNR USING NO EDIT MASK,
   CUSTOMER_TAB-NAME1, CUSTOMER_TAB-ORT01.
 ENDLOOP.
```

```
 SKIP 2. " gap between batches of data

ENDSELECT.
```

You are using INCLUDE program YCL_CH08_01_INCLUDE_HEADING to output the heading for the customer list. You are also using this same INCLUDE program to output the header for the next hands-on exercise: YCL_CH08_03_PSIZE_APPEND_TAB.

This INCLUDE program contains the TOP-OF-PAGE event along with the other code lines to output the header. Notice the position of the INCLUDE statement in the program YCL_CH08_03_PSIZE_INTO_TAB. Reusability - that is, modularization techniques, has been employed.

The source lines of INCLUDE program YCL_CH08_01_INCLUDE_HEADING:

```
****************************************************
* INCLUDE program for heading of customer list    **
* used by programs: - YCL_CH08_02..               **
*                     YCL_CH08_03..               **
****************************************************

TOP-OF-PAGE.

WRITE:/5 TEXT-001, CDATE, 92(3) SY-PAGNO.
WRITE:/5(89) SY-ULINE.
WRITE:/5 TEXT-002, 11 TEXT-003, 22 TEXT-004, 58 TEXT-005.
WRITE:/6 TEXT-006, 13 TEXT-007.
WRITE:/5(89) SY-ULINE.
******************************************************************
```

A screenshot of the text symbols is shown in Figure 8-2.

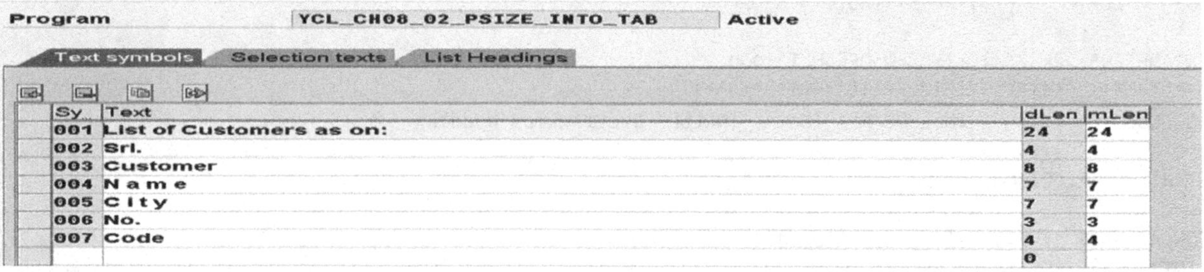

Program YCL_CH08_02_PSIZE_INTO_TAB Active

Text symbols | Selection texts | List Headings

Sy	Text	dLen	mLen
001	List of Customers as on:	24	24
002	Srl.	4	4
003	Customer	8	8
004	N a m e	7	7
005	C i t y	7	7
006	No.	3	3
007	Code	4	4
		0	

Figure 8-2. *Program: YCL_CH08_02_PSIZE_INTO_TAB - Text Symbol*

The output will be like Figure 8-3.

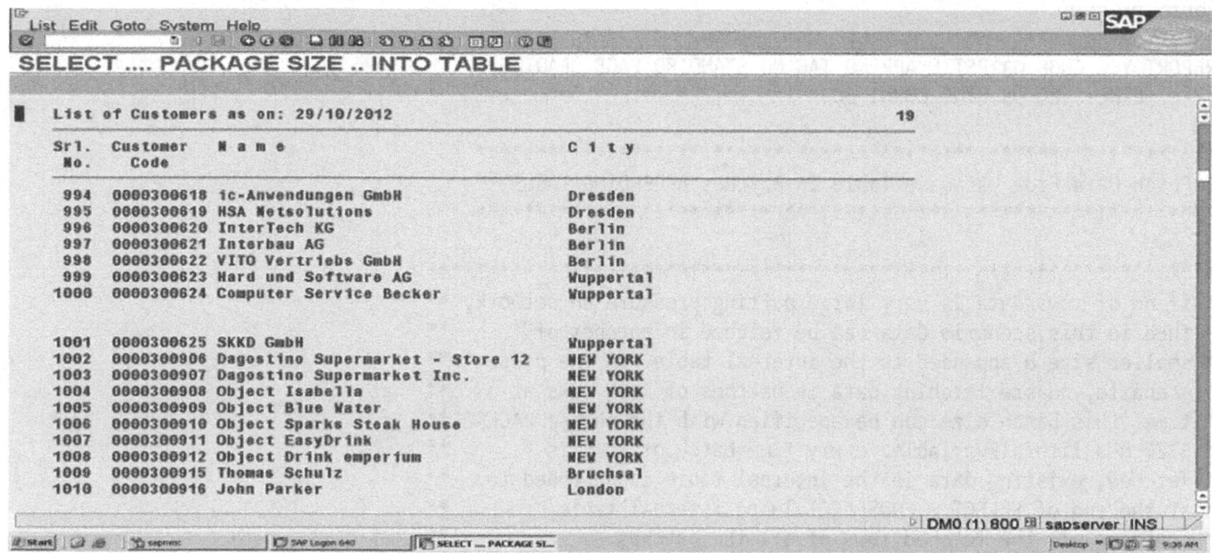

Figure 8-3. Program: YCL_CH08_02_PSIZE_INTO_TAB - Output

Hands-On Exercise – APPENDING TABLE… PACKAGE SIZE…

If the number of rows being fetched into an internal table is very high and clogging the network and database server and there no application server RAM issues, then, instead of loading the internal table fully at one go, it can be loaded in increments of batches of a specified number of rows. When the internal table has been fully loaded, it can be processed. The process of loading the internal table with an incremental number of rows is again a looping process and hence the ENDSELECT statement. The syntax:

```
SELECT <result> FROM <source>
APPENDING [CORRESPONDING FIELDS OF] TABLE <itab>
PACKAGE SIZE <no of rows in batch>
[WHERE <condition>]
[ORDER BY <sort specification>]
[UP TO <no of rows> ROWS].
........
ENDSELECT.
```

The only difference between the preceding syntax and the current one are the keywords: INTO and APPENDING. The preceding syntax was using INTO TABLE.

When the keyword INTO is used as in the preceding example, data was fetched in batches of a specified number of rows, and the current batch wiped or deleted the existing data in the internal table.

When the keyword APPENDING is used, data is fetched in batches of a specified number of rows, and the current batch is appended to the already existing data in the internal table in the case of a standard table. In case of sorted and hashed tables, the current batch of rows insert to the existing data in the internal table.

In all other situations, clauses remain the same for the two syntaxes.

As a hands-on exercise using this syntax to fetch in batches and build the internal table, then process the internal table, you output again the customer list, batch size, or package size input through the PARAMETERS statement. The source program:

```
REPORT YCL_CH08_03_PSIZE_APPEND_TAB NO STANDARD PAGE HEADING
      LINE-SIZE 95 LINE-COUNT 60.

**************************************************************
* Fetch Data From Database Table In Batches APPENDING TABLE **
**************************************************************

******************************************************************
* if no of rows/data is very large putting pressure on network, **
* then in this scenario data can be fetched in batches of       **
* smaller size & appended to the internal table. in the present **
* scenario,you are fetching data in batches of 1000 rows at a   **
* time. this batch size can be specified with the phrase PACKAGE**
* SIZE & a literal/variable. every time batch of rows is        **
* fetched, existing data in the internal table is appended to.  **
* at the end of SELECT...ENDSELECT loop, internal table         **
* contains all the fetched rows of all the batches.             **
******************************************************************
******************************************************
* declare data. input PACKAGE SIZE thru PARAMETERS  **
* INCLUDE program for heading                       **
*                                                   **
* retrieve a batch of rows with SELECT...PACKAGE    **
* SIZE...etc. append to existing data ENDSELECT.    **
*                                                   **
* output retrieved batch LOOP AT...WRITE...ENDLOOP  **
******************************************************

DATA: CUSTOMER_TAB TYPE STANDARD TABLE OF YCL_CH05_CUST_STRU
                        WITH HEADER LINE,
       CNTR(3)      TYPE P DECIMALS 0,
       CDATE        TYPE STRING.

PARAMETERS: PKSZ(4)  TYPE N DEFAULT 1000.
*********************************************
INCLUDE YCL_CH08_01_INCLUDE_HEADING. " heading

START-OF-SELECTION.

CONCATENATE SY-DATUM+6(2) SY-DATUM+4(2) SY-DATUM+0(4)
 INTO CDATE SEPARATED BY '/'.

SELECT KUNNR NAME1 STRAS ORT01 PSTLZ FROM KNA1 APPENDING
  TABLE CUSTOMER_TAB PACKAGE SIZE PKSZ.
```

```
ENDSELECT.
**********************************************************

LOOP AT CUSTOMER_TAB.

 WRITE:/5(5) SY-TABIX, CUSTOMER_TAB-KUNNR USING NO EDIT MASK,
   CUSTOMER_TAB-NAME1, CUSTOMER_TAB-ORT01.

 CNTR = SY-TABIX MOD PKSZ.

 IF CNTR = 0.
  SKIP 2. " gap between batches
 ENDIF.

ENDLOOP.
```

The output should look like Figure 8-4.

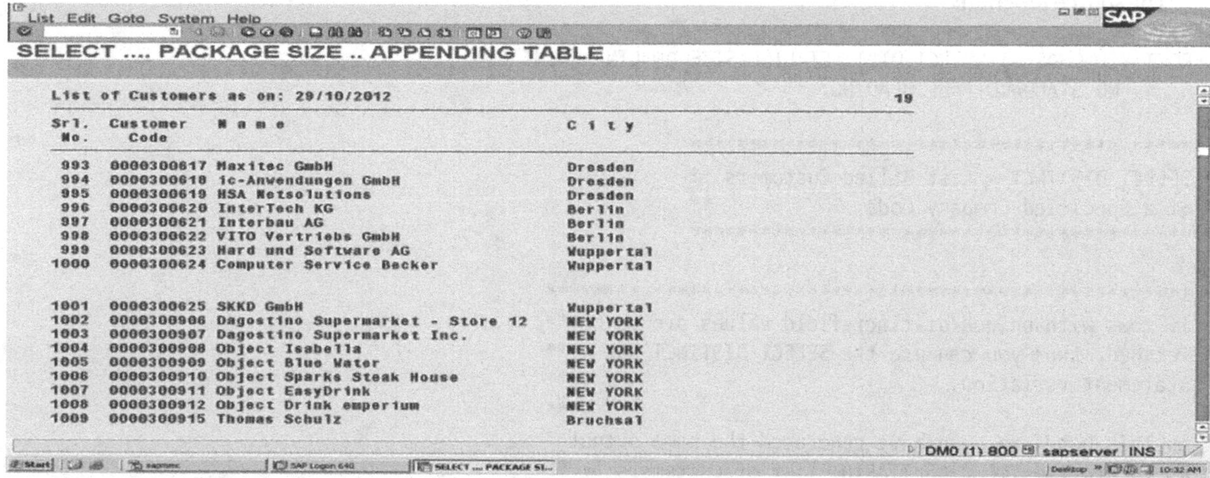

Figure 8-4. *Program: YCL_CH08_03_PSIZE_APPEND_TAB - Output*

Hands-On Exercise – SELECT DISTINCT…

To retrieve distinct or unique values for field/s, you use the Open SQL SELECT DISTINCT… statement.

The syntax:

```
SELECT DISTINCT <result> FROM <source>
{INTO|APPENDING}  [CORRESPONDING FIELDS OF] <destination>
[PACKAGE SIZE <no of rows in batch>]
[WHERE <where condition>]
[ORDER BY <sort specification>]
[UP TO <no of rows> ROWS].

 .........
[ENDSELECT].
```

Apart from DISTINCT, all the other clauses have been explained and have the same meaning as in earlier syntaxes. The ENDSELECT has been indicated as optional, depending on the <destination>. If the <destination> is a structure or individual fields, it will be a looping construct with ENDSELECT. If the destination is an internal table and PACKAGE SIZE is used, again it will be a looping construct with ENDSELECT. If the destination is an internal table without the addition of PACKAGE SIZE, then it is case of retrieving data at one go, and there will be no ENDSELECT.

As a hands-on exercise, you are repeating the Chapter 6 internal table hands-on exercise: YCL_CH06_ITAB10. This hands-on exercise listed out the customers with billing documents of a given company code. Your basic source of data was the table VBRK, and there were two issues you faced then: the table VBRK could contain multiple entries for a customer, and the table VBRK does not contain the customer name and city that you wanted in the output. You addressed these issues by creating a database view with tables VBRK and KNA1 (to incorporate the customer name and city) loading an internal table with data from this view and using the internal table statement DELETE ADJACENT DUPLICATES.... Before issuing the DELETE ADJACENT DUPLICATES... statement, the internal table was sorted in ascending order of the field KUNNR. (Internal table has to be sorted in ascending order of the fields for which duplicates are to be eliminated.) This statement deleted multiple entries in the internal table for a value of field KUNNR, reducing them to one row for every value of KUNNR.

For the current hands-on exercise, you are using the same database view of Chapter 6. You are using the SELECT DISTINCT... statement to fetch distinct values of fields KUNNR, NAME1, and ORT01.

Copy the text symbols from program YCL_CH06_ITAB10 (transaction code SE32, etc.) to output the header.

The source program:

```
REPORT YCL_CH08_04_SELECT_DISTINCT LINE-SIZE 95 LINE-COUNT 60
       NO STANDARD PAGE HEADING.

*******************************************
* SELECT DISTINCT - List Billed Customers **
* of a Specified Company Code           **
*******************************************

*****************************************************
* if rows with unique/distinct field values are to be **
* fetched, then you can use the SELECT DISTINCT SQL   **
* statement variation.                                **
*                                                     **
* in this hands-on, you have generated the same output**
* as in program YCL_CH06_ITAB10: list of customers    **
* with billing documents.                             **
*                                                     **
* a customer may have multiple billing documents.     **
* you were using the internal table statement         **
* DELETE ADJACENT DUPLICATES...to reduce multiple     **
* occurrences of a customer code value KUNNR to a     **
* single occurrence. your source data was a database  **
* view with tables KNA1 & VBRK.                       **
*                                                     **
* you are using the same view, using a SELECT DISTINCT**
* statement to generate a customer list with billing  **
* documents.                                          **
*****************************************************
*****************************************************
* declare data. input company code. retrieve company  **
* code name. (SELECT SINGLE etc.) for heading         **
*                                                     **
```

```
* use SELECT DISTINCT...to retrieve data from view      **
* into internal table. sort internal table. output      **
* from internal table: LOOP AT...ENDLOOP.               **
*********************************************************

TYPES: BEGIN OF CUSTOMERS_STRU_TYPE,
        KUNNR   TYPE KNA1-KUNNR,
        NAME1   TYPE KNA1-NAME1,
        ORT01   TYPE KNA1-ORT01,
       END OF CUSTOMERS_STRU_TYPE.


DATA: CUSTOMERS_TAB   TYPE STANDARD TABLE OF CUSTOMERS_STRU_TYPE,
      CUSTOMERS_STRU  TYPE CUSTOMERS_STRU_TYPE,
      BUTXT           TYPE T001-BUTXT.

PARAMETERS CCODE TYPE VBRK-BUKRS DEFAULT 3000 VALUE CHECK.
****************************************************************
TOP-OF-PAGE.

WRITE:/5 TEXT-001 NO-GAP, CCODE NO-GAP, '/' NO-GAP, BUTXT, 92(2) SY-PAGNO.
WRITE:/5(88) SY-ULINE.
WRITE:/5 TEXT-002, 11 TEXT-003, 22 TEXT-004, 58 TEXT-005.
WRITE:/6 TEXT-006, 13 TEXT-007.
WRITE:/5(88) SY-ULINE.
******************************************************************
START-OF-SELECTION.

SELECT SINGLE BUTXT FROM T001 INTO (BUTXT) WHERE BUKRS = CCODE.

SELECT DISTINCT KUNNR NAME1 ORT01 FROM YCL_CH05_VBRKKNA
       INTO TABLE CUSTOMERS_TAB
       WHERE BUKRS = CCODE.

SORT CUSTOMERS_TAB BY KUNNR.

LOOP AT CUSTOMERS_TAB INTO CUSTOMERS_STRU.

 WRITE:/5(4) SY-TABIX, CUSTOMERS_STRU-KUNNR USING NO EDIT MASK,
             CUSTOMERS_STRU-NAME1, CUSTOMERS_STRU-ORT01.

ENDLOOP.
```

The output will appear like Figure 8-5.

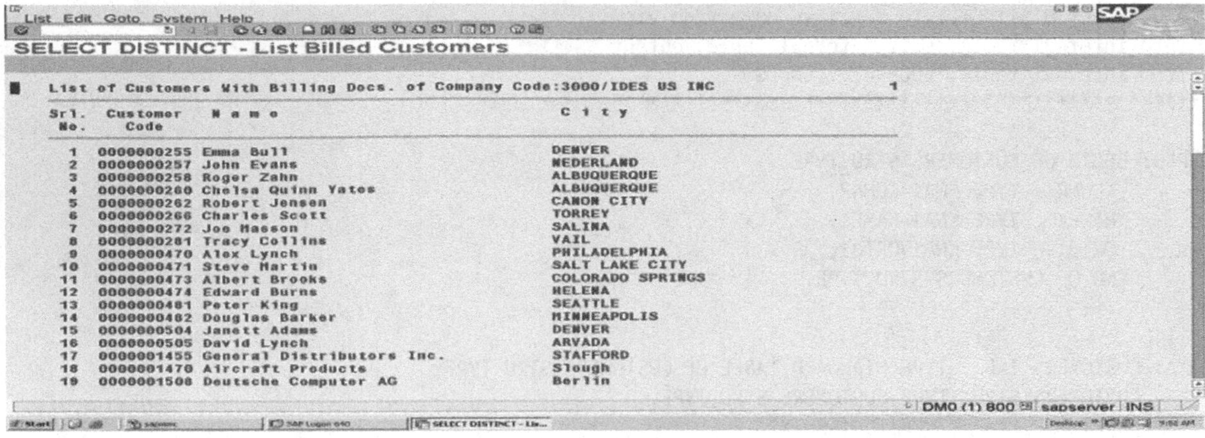

List of Customers With Billing Docs. of Company Code:3000/IDES US INC 1

Srl. No.	Customer Code	N a m e	C i t y
1	0000000255	Emma Bull	DENVER
2	0000000257	John Evans	NEDERLAND
3	0000000258	Roger Zahn	ALBUQUERQUE
4	0000000260	Chelsa Quinn Yates	ALBUQUERQUE
5	0000000262	Robert Jensen	CANON CITY
6	0000000266	Charles Scott	TORREY
7	0000000272	Joe Masson	SALINA
8	0000000281	Tracy Collins	VAIL
9	0000000470	Alex Lynch	PHILADELPHIA
10	0000000471	Steve Martin	SALT LAKE CITY
11	0000000473	Albert Brooks	COLORADO SPRINGS
12	0000000474	Edward Burns	HELENA
13	0000000481	Peter King	SEATTLE
14	0000000482	Douglas Barker	MINNEAPOLIS
15	0000000504	Janett Adams	DENVER
16	0000000505	David Lynch	ARVADA
17	0000001455	General Distributors Inc.	STAFFORD
18	0000001470	Aircraft Products	Slough
19	0000001508	Deutsche Computer AG	Berlin

Figure 8-5. *Program: YCL_CH08_04_SELECT_DISTINCT - Output*

Hands-On Exercise – Aggregate Functions

One-level summarized data can be produced by using aggregate functions of the Open SQL SELECT statement.

The Open SQL aggregate functions do not support expressions. You cannot write SUM(NETWR * KURRF) that is, the sum of the amount in document currency multiplied by the exchange rate). Practically speaking, the Open SQL aggregate feature cannot be used for amount summarizations. Alternatively, you can write to an intermediate database table, for the result of amount multiplied by the exchange rate and use this intermediate table in an Open SQL statement with aggregate functions for amount fields like NETWR.

The aggregate functions, though, can be used for quantity fields. You are assured that materials are sold in one specific unit of measure for a material code and purchased in another specific unit of measure for a material code for a plant.

The syntax:

```
SELECT <group by fields> <aggregate function>( [DISTINCT]<field> ) as <alias1> <aggregate function>
( [DISTINCT]<field> ) as <alias2>.........
{INTO|APPENDING} <destination>  [UP TO <no of rows.]
[WHERE <where condition>]
GROUP BY <group by fields>
[HAVING <having condition>]
[ORDER BY <sort specification>].
.........
[ENDSELECT].
```

<group by fields>: The summarizing fields.

<aggregate function>: The Open SQL supports the following aggregate functions:

SUM

Total for the <field>. This should be a numeric field. If the key word DISTINCT is used in the argument of the aggregate function, only distinct values are considered for aggregate operation.

COUNT

Number of rows for the <field>. COUNT(*) returns number of rows for the selection. COUNT(DISTINCT <field>) will return the number of rows for DISTINCT values of <field>.

MAX

Maximum value for the <field>. If the keyword DISTINCT is used in the argument of the aggregate function, only distinct values are considered for aggregate operation.

MIN

Minimum value for the <field>. If the key word DISTINCT is used in the argument of the aggregate function, only distinct values are considered for aggregate operation.

AVG

Average for the <field>. This should be a numeric field. If the keyword DISTINCT is used in the argument of the aggregate function, and only distinct values are considered for aggregate operation.

<alias1>: The aggregate values returned have to be loaded into a structure or table or individual fields. (INTO/APPENDING <destination>....) Through the <alias1>, <alias2>.., you are assigning names to the returned aggregate values to enable them to be loaded into the destination.

<having condition>: The conditions operating on aggregate functions.

The other clauses carry the same meaning as in earlier syntaxes. The ENDSELECT has been indicated as optional and will depend on the <destination> and presence/absence of the clause PACKAGE SIZE.

The current hand-on exercise is a summarization of material wise quantities sold. Your basic Source of data is the table VBRP (Billing Document - Items). For material descriptions, you need to access table MAKT. So you are using the view YCL_CH08_VBRP_MK created with the tables VBRP and MAKT. The output layout:

Table 8-2. *Program: YCL_CH08_05_AGGREGATE_FUNC - Output Layout*

Field	Description	Column Positions
SY-DBCNT	Serial Number	005-008 (4)
MATNR	Material Code	010-027(18)
MAKTX	Material Description	029-068(40)
VRKME	Unit of Measure	070-072(3)
COUNT(*)	Count of Sales	074-078(5)
SUM(FKIMG)	Sum of Quantity Sold	080-091(12)
MAX(FKIMG)	Maximum of Quantity Sold	093-104(12)
MIN(FKIMG)	Minimum of Quantity Sold	106-117(12)

The database view YCL_CH08_VBRP_MK will appear like Figures 8-6 to 8-8.

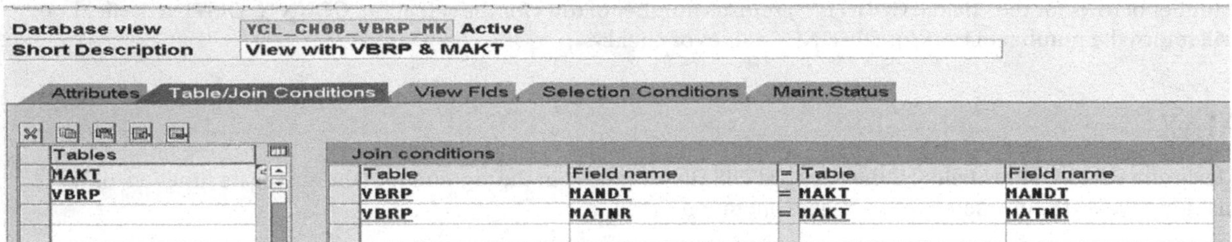

Figure 8-6. *Database View: YCL_CH08_VBRP_MK – Tables and Join Conditions*

Database view: YCL_CH08_VBRP_MK Active

Short Description: View with VBRP & MAKT

Attributes | Table/Join Conditions | View Flds | Selection Conditions | Maint.Status

Table fields

View field	Table	Field	Key	Data elem.	Mod	DTyp
MANDT	VBRP	MANDT	☑	MANDT	☐	CLNT
VBELN	VBRP	VBELN	☑	VBELN_VF	☐	CHAR
POSNR	VBRP	POSNR	☑	POSNR_VF	☐	NUMC
MATNR	MAKT	MATNR	☑	MATNR	☐	CHAR
SPRAS	MAKT	SPRAS	☑	SPRAS	☐	LANG
FKIMG	VBRP	FKIMG	☐	FKIMG	☐	QUAN
VRKME	VBRP	VRKME	☐	VRKME	☐	UNIT
MAKTX	MAKT	MAKTX	☐	MAKTX	☐	CHAR

Figure 8-7. *Database View: YCL_CH08_VBRP_MK – View Fields*

Database view: YCL_CH08_VBRP_MK Active

Short Description: View with VBRP & MAKT

Attributes | Table/Join Conditions | View Flds | Selection Conditions | Maint.Status

Table fields

Table	Field name	Operator	Comparison Value	AND/O
MAKT	SPRAS	EQ	'E'	

Figure 8-8. *Database View: YCL_CH08_VBRP_MK – Selection Conditions*

The source program:

```
REPORT YCL_CH08_05_AGGREGATE_FUNC NO STANDARD PAGE HEADING
       LINE-SIZE 120 LINE-COUNT 60.

**********************************************
* SELECT Statement with Aggregate Functions **
**********************************************
*************************************************************
* SELECT statement aggregate functions to get summarized    **
* data.                                                     **
*                                                           **
* a clarification:- the open sql aggregte functions do      **
* not support expressions. you cannot write                 **
```

```
* SUM( NETWR * KURRF ) i.e. sum of                        **
* (amount in document currency multiplied by exchange rate) **
*                                                         **
* practically speaking, the open sql aggregate feature    **
* cannot be used for amount summarization. unless you write **
* to an intermediate database table the result of amount  **
* multiplied by the exchange rate and use this intermediate **
* table in open sql statement with aggregate functions for **
* amount fields like NETWR.                               **
*                                                         **
* the aggregate functions though can be used for quantity **
* fields. because you are assured that quantities are mostly**
* sold in one specific unit of measure for a material code, **
* purchased in another specific unit of measure for a     **
* material code. (of specific organizational unit)        **
*                                                         **
* the current hand-on, is summarization of material wise  **
* quantities sold                                         **
* your basic Source of data is the table VBRP. for material **
* description, you need to access table MAKT. so you are  **
* usimg the view YCL_CH08_VBRP_MK created with the tables **
* VBRP, MAKT.                                             **
************************************************************
************************************************************
* declare data. code for heading.                         **
* use SELECT statement with aggregate functions SUM( ),   **
* MAX( ), MIN( ), COUNT( * ) to retrieve and store for a  **
* material code total quantity sold, maximum quantity sold **
* at a time, minimum sold at a time, number of times sold. **
* output the retrieved data. ENDSELECT.                   **
************************************************************

DATA: BEGIN OF SALES_STRU,
       MATNR    TYPE MATNR,
       MAKTX    TYPE MAKTX,
       VRKME    TYPE VRKME,
       CONT     TYPE I,
       TOTAL    TYPE FKIMG,
       MAX      TYPE FKIMG,
       MIN      TYPE FKIMG,
      END OF SALES_STRU.
*****************************************
TOP-OF-PAGE.
WRITE:/5 TEXT-001, 115(3) SY-PAGNO.
SKIP 1.
WRITE:/5(112) SY-ULINE.
WRITE:/5 TEXT-002, 10 TEXT-003, 30 TEXT-004,
        70 TEXT-005, 74 TEXT-006, 82 TEXT-007,
        96 TEXT-008, 109 TEXT-009.
```

```
WRITE:/6 TEXT-010.

WRITE:/5(112) SY-ULINE.

*******************************************
START-OF-SELECTION.

SELECT MATNR MAKTX VRKME COUNT( * ) AS CONT SUM( FKIMG ) AS TOTAL
      MAX( FKIMG ) AS MAX MIN( FKIMG ) AS MIN FROM YCL_CH08_VBRP_MK
      INTO SALES_STRU
      GROUP BY MATNR MAKTX VRKME HAVING SUM( FKIMG ) <> 0
      ORDER BY MATNR .

 WRITE:/5(4) SY-DBCNT, SALES_STRU-MATNR USING NO EDIT MASK,
   SALES_STRU-MAKTX, SALES_STRU-VRKME, (5) SALES_STRU-CONT,
   (12) SALES_STRU-TOTAL, (12) SALES_STRU-MAX, (12) SALES_STRU-MIN.

ENDSELECT.
```

The output will be like Figure 8-9.

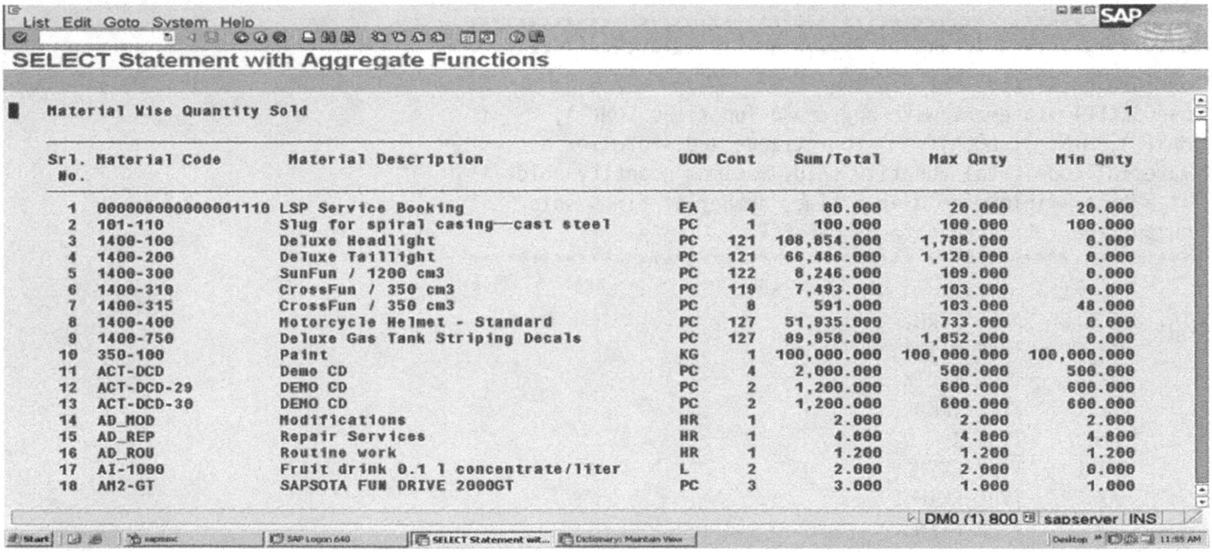

List Edit Goto System Help

SELECT Statement with Aggregate Functions

Material Wise Quantity Sold 1

Srl. No.	Material Code	Material Description	UOM	Cont	Sum/Total	Max Qnty	Min Qnty
1	000000000000001110	LSP Service Booking	EA	4	80.000	20.000	20.000
2	101-110	Slug for spiral casing—cast steel	PC	1	100.000	100.000	100.000
3	1400-100	Deluxe Headlight	PC	121	108,854.000	1,788.000	0.000
4	1400-200	Deluxe Taillight	PC	121	66,486.000	1,120.000	0.000
5	1400-300	SunFun / 1200 cm3	PC	122	8,246.000	109.000	0.000
6	1400-310	CrossFun / 350 cm3	PC	119	7,493.000	103.000	0.000
7	1400-315	CrossFun / 350 cm3	PC	8	591.000	103.000	48.000
8	1400-400	Motorcycle Helmet - Standard	PC	127	51,935.000	733.000	0.000
9	1400-750	Deluxe Gas Tank Striping Decals	PC	127	89,958.000	1,852.000	0.000
10	350-100	Paint	KG	1	100,000.000	100,000.000	100,000.000
11	ACT-DCD	Demo CD	PC	4	2,000.000	500.000	500.000
12	ACT-DCD-29	DEMO CD	PC	2	1,200.000	600.000	600.000
13	ACT-DCD-30	DEMO CD	PC	2	1,200.000	600.000	600.000
14	AD_MOD	Modifications	HR	1	2.000	2.000	2.000
15	AD_REP	Repair Services	HR	1	4.800	4.800	4.800
16	AD_ROU	Routine work	HR	1	1.200	1.200	1.200
17	AI-1000	Fruit drink 0.1 l concentrate/liter	L	2	2.000	2.000	0.000
18	AM2-GT	SAPSOTA FUN DRIVE 2000GT	PC	3	3.000	1.000	1.000

DM0 (1) 800 sapserver INS

Figure 8-9. *Program: YCL_CH08_05_AGGREGATE_FUNC - Output*

In this program, you have assigned the aggregates aliases (AS ...) and the Open SQL destination is a structure. You wanted the unit of measure field VRKME in the output. So you had to include it perforce in the GROUP BY fields.

You output this list for a specified company code. You will be producing this kind of lists plant wise (i.e., field WERKS). A plant within a company code will be producing specified products or product lines. You are not producing a report for a specified plant. In the training paradigm, you can be absolved of this.

In the E-Resource, there are two more variations of this program using aggregate functions of SELECT statement. They are:

YCL_CH08_06_AGGREGATE_FUNC_VR1

YCL_CH08_07_AGGREGATE_FUNC_VR2

In the first program YCL_CH08_06_AGGREGATE_FUNC_VR1, the destination in SELECT statement is specified as individual fields. No aliases are required, and so no aliases are assigned.

In the second program YCL_CH08_07_AGGREGATE_FUNC_VR2, the destination in SELECT statement is specified as an internal table with a PACKAGE SIZE addition, just to demonstrate that the addition PACKAGE SIZE can be used in an aggregate function SELECT statement. No aliases are required, and so no aliases are assigned.

All the three programs:

YCL_CH08_05_AGGREGATE_FUNC

YCL_CH08_06_AGGREGATE_FUNC_VR1

YCL_CH08_07_AGGREGATE_FUNC_VR2

Produce the same output.

SELECT Statement Using More Than One Table or View – Joins

You have used a single database table or database view in the SELECT statements until now. You can code SELECT statement using more than one table or can view it by employing the inner and left outer join.

The DDIC database views implement inner join. So instead of writing an Open SQL statement implementing inner join, a better option is to create a DDIC database view with the reusability advantage and avoidance of coding. This is true if you want only database tables to participate in the inner join. But if you want database views and projection views to participate in the inner join, you have to write a SELECT statement for inner join. In the DDIC database and projection views, the source of data can only be tables. Syntax: the syntax for joins given below is only for the join part of the SELECT statement. Other clauses such as destination and the WHERE condition, etc., are implicit.

The syntax for inner and left outer joins:

```
<source left> [AS <alias left>]
{ [INNER] JOIN } |{ LEFT [OUTER] JOIN }
{<source right> [AS <alias right>] ON <join condition}
```

INNER JOIN, JOIN is synonymous.

LEFT OUTER JOIN, LEFT JOIN is synonymous.

Since you are fetching and comparing fields from multiple sources, (tables and views), the fields have to be referred with source qualification in the SELECT statement. You will refer to field KUNNR as KNA1~KUNNR. You use the tilde character (~) to associate a field with its origin or source just like you were using the hyphen/dash (-) character to associate a field with a structure.

You can assign aliases to the source (tables and views). You should then refer to the sources by aliases only.

Join Operation: Firstly, a recapitulation of inner join and a bare definition of left outer join are in place.

Let there be a simple scenario with the very familiar tables. Let the SELECT inner and outer joins be implemented with fields from tables KNA1 and VBRK (customer primary and billing document header). The two tables are joined through foreign key relationship fields: MANDT, KUNNR from KNA1 and MANDT, and KUNAG from VBRK.

If you have inner join of these tables, a row must exist in both the tables for it to appear in the result. If you assume that there is no billing document without a valid customer code (no orphan rows), all the rows from the table VBRK will appear in the result. Or all the customers having billing documents will appear in the result, and a customer having multiple billing documents will have that many rows in the result. But customers having no billing documents will not appear in the result.

When you have left outer join of these tables, with the primary table KNA1 on the left side of the join, a row existing in either of the tables will appear in the result. If you assume that there is no billing document without a valid customer code (no orphan rows), all the rows from the table VBRK plus the customers having no billing documents will appear in the result. A customer having multiple billing documents will have that many rows in the result. For customers having no billing documents in the result, the fields from the table VBRK will contain INITIAL values (blanks, zeros, etc.).

You will use the same data sources for your two hands-on inner join and left outer join. You can then compare results.

Hands-On Exercise – Inner Join

The first of the hands-on exercise is on inner join. You are deliberately using a database view as the left source instead of the table KNA1 to demonstrate the usage of database view in join SELECT statement. The database view you created in Chapter 5 contains your frequently used fields from table KNA1 and country text - field LANDX from the table T005T. The view name is YCL_CH05_KNAT5T. The right source is the table VBRK.

You input the customer code in both of the hands-on exercises for inner join and left outer join. You are fetching customer codes less than or equal to this value. This is to limit the output as to be able to compare results of inner join and left outer join more easily.

The output layout:

***Table 8-3.** Program: YCL_CH08_09_INNER_JOIN - Output Layout*

Field Name	Description	Column Positions
SY=TABIX	Serial Number	005-009(5)
KUNNR	Customer Code	011-020(10)
NAME1	Customer Name	022-056(35)
LANDX	Country	058-072(15)
VBELN	Billing Document Number	074-083(10)
FKDAT	Billing Document Date	085-094(10)

You have the same output layout for the hands-on exercise of inner join and left outer join. So you have a common INCLUDE program to output the list headers.

INCLUDE program source code: (YCL_CH08_08_HEADER_JOINS)

```
***********************
TOP-OF-PAGE.
WRITE: /5 TEXT-001, TEXT-010, 93(3) SY-PAGNO.

WRITE:/5(90) SY-ULINE.
WRITE:/5 TEXT-002, 12 TEXT-003, 24 TEXT-004, 59 TEXT-005,
      74 TEXT-006, 85 TEXT-007.
WRITE:/6 TEXT-008, 13 TEXT-009.

WRITE:/5(90) SY-ULINE.
```

The main program source code:

```
REPORT YCL_CH08_09_INNER_JOIN NO STANDARD PAGE HEADING
       LINE-SIZE 100 LINE-COUNT 60.

*******************************************************
* INNER JOIN With Customer Primary Data & Billing Docs. **
*******************************************************

************************************
* declare TYPES, DATA              **
* input customer code - PARAMETERS **
*                                  **
* INCLUDE heading                  **
*                                  **
* SELECT statement using INNER JOIN **
* into internal table for customer **
* less than or equal to input      **
* customer                         **
*                                  **
* sort internal table on KUNNR     **
*                                  **
* output from internal table       **
************************************

TYPES: BEGIN OF CUST_BILLS_TYPE,
        KUNNR    TYPE KNA1-KUNNR,
        NAME1    TYPE KNA1-NAME1,
        LANDX    TYPE T005T-LANDX,
        VBELN    TYPE VBRK-VBELN,
        FKDAT    TYPE VBRK-FKDAT,
       END OF CUST_BILLS_TYPE.

DATA: CUST_BILLS TYPE STANDARD TABLE OF CUST_BILLS_TYPE
  WITH HEADER LINE.

PARAMETERS: CUST_CD TYPE VBRK-KUNAG VALUE CHECK
 DEFAULT '0000001000'.
**********************************************
INCLUDE YCL_CH08_08_HEADER_JOINS.

START-OF-SELECTION.

SELECT VW~KUNNR VW~NAME1 VW~LANDX TB~VBELN TB~FKDAT
       INTO CORRESPONDING FIELDS OF TABLE CUST_BILLS
       FROM ( YCL_CH05_KNAT5T AS VW
       INNER JOIN VBRK AS TB ON VW~MANDT = TB~MANDT
                            AND VW~KUNNR = TB~KUNAG )
       WHERE VW~KUNNR <= CUST_CD.

SORT CUST_BILLS BY KUNNR.
```

```
LOOP AT CUST_BILLS.
 WRITE:/5(5) SY-TABIX, CUST_BILLS-KUNNR USING NO EDIT MASK,
   CUST_BILLS-NAME1, CUST_BILLS-LANDX, CUST_BILLS-VBELN,
   CUST_BILLS-FKDAT.
ENDLOOP.
```

The text symbols for the heading are shown in Figure 8-10.

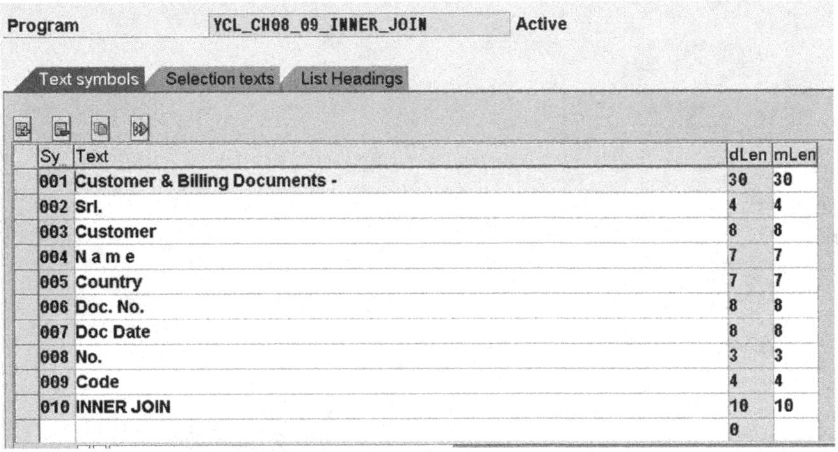

Program YCL_CH08_09_INNER_JOIN Active

Text symbols | Selection texts | List Headings

Sy	Text	dLen	mLen
001	Customer & Billing Documents -	30	30
002	Srl.	4	4
003	Customer	8	8
004	N a m e	7	7
005	Country	7	7
006	Doc. No.	8	8
007	Doc Date	8	8
008	No.	3	3
009	Code	4	4
010	INNER JOIN	10	10
		0	

Figure 8-10. *Program: YCL_CH08_09_INNER_JOIN – Text Symbols*

The output will appear like Figure 8-11.

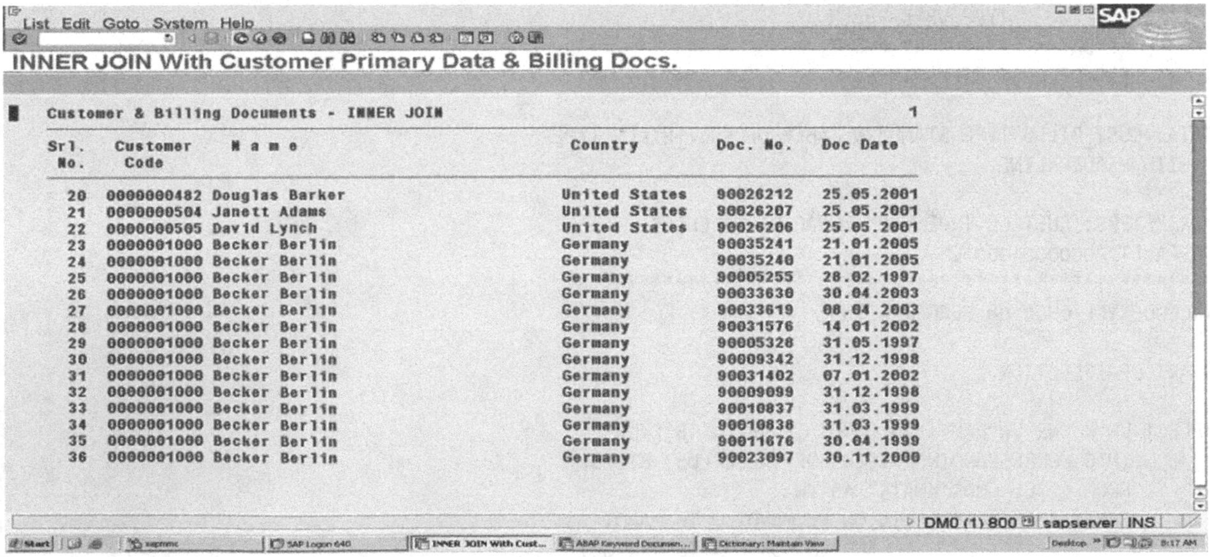

```
List  Edit  Goto  System  Help
INNER JOIN With Customer Primary Data & Billing Docs.

Customer & Billing Documents - INNER JOIN                                1

Srl.  Customer    N a m e                  Country        Doc. No.  Doc Date
No.    Code

  20  0000000482 Douglas Barker            United States  90026212  25.05.2001
  21  0000000504 Janett Adams              United States  90026207  25.05.2001
  22  0000000505 David Lynch               United States  90026206  25.05.2001
  23  0000001000 Becker Berlin             Germany        90035241  21.01.2005
  24  0000001000 Becker Berlin             Germany        90035240  21.01.2005
  25  0000001000 Becker Berlin             Germany        90005255  28.02.1997
  26  0000001000 Becker Berlin             Germany        90033630  30.04.2003
  27  0000001000 Becker Berlin             Germany        90033619  08.04.2003
  28  0000001000 Becker Berlin             Germany        90031576  14.01.2002
  29  0000001000 Becker Berlin             Germany        90005326  31.05.1997
  30  0000001000 Becker Berlin             Germany        90009342  31.12.1998
  31  0000001000 Becker Berlin             Germany        90031402  07.01.2002
  32  0000001000 Becker Berlin             Germany        90009099  31.12.1998
  33  0000001000 Becker Berlin             Germany        90010837  31.03.1999
  34  0000001000 Becker Berlin             Germany        90010836  31.03.1999
  35  0000001000 Becker Berlin             Germany        90011676  30.04.1999
  36  0000001000 Becker Berlin             Germany        90023097  30.11.2000

DMO (1) 800  sapserver  INS
```

Figure 8-11. *Program: YCL_CH08_09_INNER_JOIN – Output*

For KUNNR <= '0000001000', 36 rows have appeared in the output as shown in Figure 8-11.

Hands-On Exercise – Outer Join

You will use the same source of data as for the inner join: database view YCL_CH05_KNAT5T and database table VBRK. You will output the same fields, so the output layout of Table 8-3 can be adopted.

In the inner join program, you sorted the internal table before output. In the result of the outer join, the rows existing in both the sources will appear first followed by the rows in the left side source having no corresponding rows in the right side source (i.e., customers having billing documents first), followed by customers having no billing documents. In this hands-on exercise, you are not sorting the data generated by the outer join statement. So your output will, first, have all the rows with billing documents, followed by the rows having no billing documents. The fields VBELN and FKDAT in the rows having no billing documents will contain INITIAL values. This is reflected in the output.

The source code:

```
REPORT YCL_CH08_10_OUTER_JOIN NO STANDARD PAGE HEADING
       LINE-SIZE 100 LINE-COUNT 60.

*********************************************************
* OUTER JOIN With Customer Primary Data & Billing Docs. **
*********************************************************

*************************************
* declare TYPES, DATA              **
* input customer code - PARAMETERS **
*                                  **
* INCLUDE heading                  **
*                                  **
* SELECT statement using OUTER JOIN **
* into internal table for customer **
* less than or equal to input      **
* customer                         **
*                                  **
* sort internal table on KUNNR     **
*                                  **
* output from internal table       **
*************************************

TYPES: BEGIN OF CUST_BILLS_TYPE,
        KUNNR    TYPE KNA1-KUNNR,
        NAME1    TYPE KNA1-NAME1,
        LANDX    TYPE T005T-LANDX,
        VBELN    TYPE VBRK-VBELN,
        FKDAT    TYPE VBRK-FKDAT,
       END OF CUST_BILLS_TYPE.

DATA: CUST_BILLS TYPE STANDARD TABLE OF CUST_BILLS_TYPE
                     WITH HEADER LINE.

PARAMETERS: CUST_CD TYPE VBRK-KUNAG VALUE CHECK
 DEFAULT '0000001000'.
************************************************
```

```
INCLUDE YCL_CH08_08_HEADER_JOINS.

START-OF-SELECTION.

SELECT VW~KUNNR VW~NAME1 VW~LANDX TB~VBELN TB~FKDAT
       INTO CORRESPONDING FIELDS OF TABLE CUST_BILLS
       FROM ( YCL_CH05_KNAT5T AS VW
       LEFT OUTER JOIN VBRK AS TB ON VW~MANDT = TB~MANDT
                           AND VW~KUNNR = TB~KUNAG )
       WHERE VW~KUNNR <= CUST_CD.

*SORT CUST_BILLS BY KUNNR.

LOOP AT CUST_BILLS.
 WRITE:/5(5) SY-TABIX, CUST_BILLS-KUNNR USING NO EDIT MASK,
   CUST_BILLS-NAME1, CUST_BILLS-LANDX, CUST_BILLS-VBELN,
   CUST_BILLS-FKDAT.
ENDLOOP.
```

The text symbols:

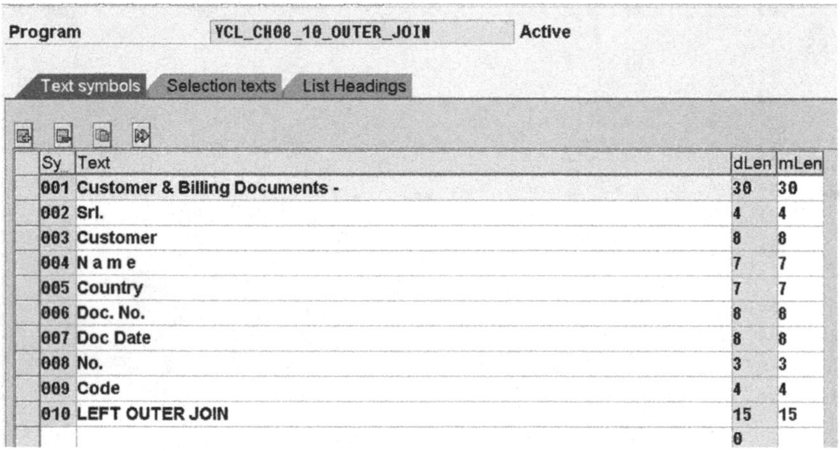

Program YCL_CH08_10_OUTER_JOIN Active

Text symbols | Selection texts | List Headings

Sy	Text	dLen	mLen
001	Customer & Billing Documents -	30	30
002	Srl.	4	4
003	Customer	8	8
004	N a m e	7	7
005	Country	7	7
006	Doc. No.	8	8
007	Doc Date	8	8
008	No.	3	3
009	Code	4	4
010	LEFT OUTER JOIN	15	15
		0	

Figure 8-12. *Program: YCL_CH08_10_OUTER_JOIN – Text Symbols*

The output will appear like Figure 8-13.

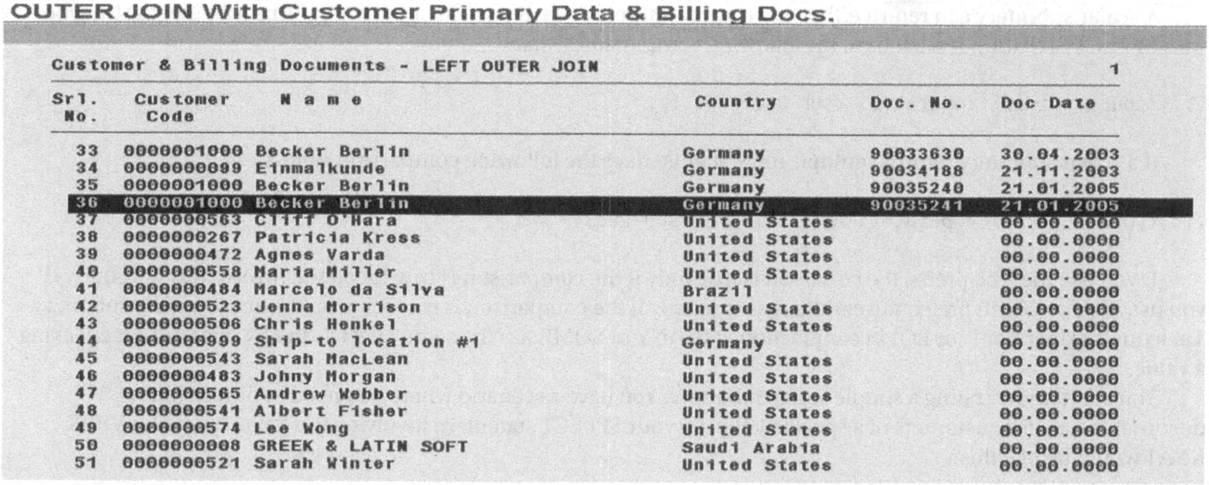

```
OUTER JOIN With Customer Primary Data & Billing Docs.

Customer & Billing Documents - LEFT OUTER JOIN                                        1
Srl.  Customer    N a m e                      Country         Doc. No.   Doc Date
No.    Code

 33  0000001000 Becker Berlin                  Germany         90033630   30.04.2003
 34  0000000099 Einmalkunde                    Germany         90034188   21.11.2003
 35  0000001000 Becker Berlin                  Germany         90035240   21.01.2005
 36  0000001000 Becker Berlin                  Germany         90035241   21.01.2005
 37  0000000563 Cliff O'Hara                   United States              00.00.0000
 38  0000000267 Patricia Kress                 United States              00.00.0000
 39  0000000472 Agnes Varda                    United States              00.00.0000
 40  0000000558 Maria Miller                   United States              00.00.0000
 41  0000000484 Marcelo da Silva               Brazil                     00.00.0000
 42  0000000523 Jenna Morrison                 United States              00.00.0000
 43  0000000506 Chris Henkel                   United States              00.00.0000
 44  0000000999 Ship-to location #1            Germany                    00.00.0000
 45  0000000543 Sarah MacLean                  United States              00.00.0000
 46  0000000483 Johny Morgan                   United States              00.00.0000
 47  0000000565 Andrew Webber                  United States              00.00.0000
 48  0000000541 Albert Fisher                  United States              00.00.0000
 49  0000000574 Lee Wong                       United States              00.00.0000
 50  0000000008 GREEK & LATIN SOFT             Saudi Arabia               00.00.0000
 51  0000000521 Sarah Winter                   United States              00.00.0000
```

Figure 8-13. *Program: YCL_CH08_10_OUTER_JOIN - Output*

The row highlighted in black (serial number 36) is the last row that has a row existing in the left side source as well as the right side source. From the next row onward until the end (serial no 112), rows of the left side source do not have any corresponding rows in the right side source. The fields VBELN and FKDAT have INITIAL values reflected in the output in Figures 8-13 and 8-14.

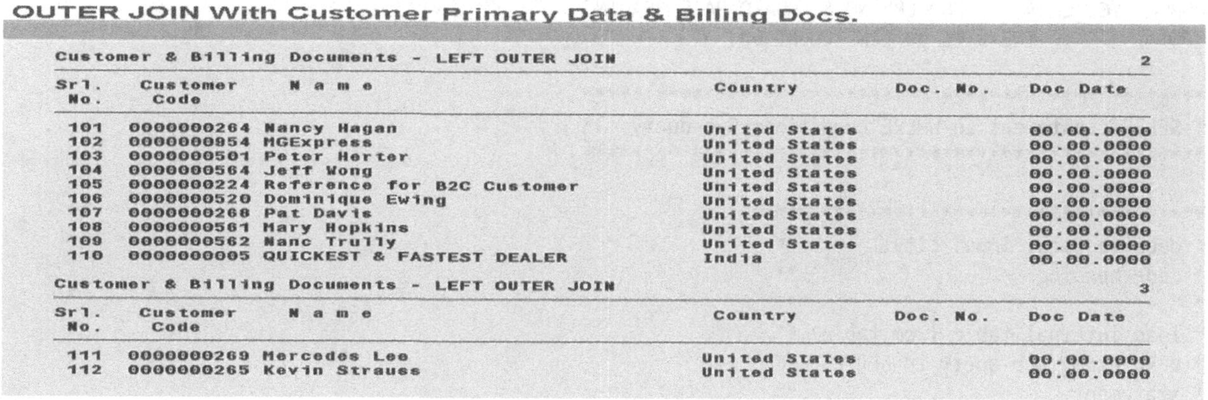

```
OUTER JOIN With Customer Primary Data & Billing Docs.

Customer & Billing Documents - LEFT OUTER JOIN                                        2
Srl.  Customer    N a m e                      Country         Doc. No.   Doc Date
No.    Code

101  0000000264 Nancy Hagan                    United States              00.00.0000
102  0000000954 MGExpress                      United States              00.00.0000
103  0000000501 Peter Herter                   United States              00.00.0000
104  0000000564 Jeff Wong                      United States              00.00.0000
105  0000000224 Reference for B2C Customer     United States              00.00.0000
106  0000000520 Dominique Ewing                United States              00.00.0000
107  0000000268 Pat Davis                      United States              00.00.0000
108  0000000561 Mary Hopkins                   United States              00.00.0000
109  0000000562 Nanc Trully                    United States              00.00.0000
110  0000000005 QUICKEST & FASTEST DEALER      India                      00.00.0000
Customer & Billing Documents - LEFT OUTER JOIN                                        3
Srl.  Customer    N a m e                      Country         Doc. No.   Doc Date
No.    Code

111  0000000269 Mercedes Lee                   United States              00.00.0000
112  0000000265 Kevin Strauss                  United States              00.00.0000
```

Figure 8-14. *Program: YCL_CH08_10_OUTER_JOIN - End of Output*

Hands-On Exercise – Subquery

You can specify a SELECT statement in the WHERE and HAVING clauses (SELECT within a SELECT), called subqueries.

The subquery cannot have INTO and ORDER BY clauses. You can nest subqueries. The subquery cannot be given in the ON <condition> of join clause. Subqueries can be scalar or non-scalar. Scalar subqueries will have only one field or aggregate function in the subquery SELECT statement.

A scalar subquery can return either one row or multiple rows. If a scalar subquery returns a single row (maybe with SELECT SINGLE), it must have the following comparison *syntax*:

```
... <source field> <operator> <sub-query> ...
```

If a scalar subquery returns multiple rows, it must have the following comparison syntax:

```
... <source field> <operator> ALL|ANY|SOME <sub-query> ...
```

If you use the ALL prefix, the condition is true only if the comparison is true for all the rows in the subquery. If you use ANY or SOME prefix, the condition is true only if the comparison is true for at least one row of the subquery. The equality operator (=or EQ) in conjunction with ANY or SOME has the same effect as the IN operator for checking a value.

You are demonstrating a simple scalar subquery. You have a scenario where you need to output billing documents data for customers of a specified city. So your SELECT statement involving the database tables VBRK, KNA1 would be like this:

```
SELECT VBELN FKDAT KUNAG WAERK NETWR FROM VBRK
INTO TABLE BILLS_TAB
WHERE KUNAG IN ( SELECT KUNNR FROM KNA1 WHERE ORT01 = 'Berlin'  ).
```

This will return all billing document rows from VBRK for customer codes having ORT01 value = 'Berlin' in the table KNA1.

The program source code:

```
REPORT YCL_CH08_11_SUBQUERY NO STANDARD PAGE HEADING
             LINE-SIZE 90 LINE-COUNT 60.

*****************************************************
* SELECT statement in WHERE condition: Sub-query   **
*****************************************************

************************************
* declare data. input city.       **
* code heading                    **
*                                 **
* load internal table from table  **
* VBRK using sub-query in SELECT  **
* statement.                      **
*                                 **
* sort internal table by VBELN    **
* output from internal table      **
************************************

DATA: BEGIN OF BILL_STRU,

       VBELN   TYPE VBRK-VBELN,
       FKDAT   TYPE VBRK-FKDAT,
       KUNAG   TYPE VBRK-KUNAG,
       WAERK   TYPE VBRK-WAERK,
       NETWR   TYPE VBRK-NETWR,
      END OF BILL_STRU,
```

```
      BILL_TAB LIKE STANDARD TABLE OF BILL_STRU.

PARAMETERS: ORT01 TYPE ORT01_GP LOWER CASE " reference to data element
            DEFAULT 'Berlin'.
*****************************************************************
* try: Frankfurt, Hamburg, Bonn, San Francisco, NEW YORK etc. **
* note the case sensitivity of field ORT01                    **
*****************************************************************
TOP-OF-PAGE.

WRITE: /5 TEXT-001, ORT01, 66(3) SY-PAGNO.
SKIP.
WRITE:/5(63) SY-ULINE.
WRITE:/5 TEXT-002, 11 TEXT-003, 22 TEXT-004, 33 TEXT-005,
       56 TEXT-006, 64 TEXT-007.
WRITE:/6 TEXT-008, 34 TEXT-009.
WRITE:/5(63) SY-ULINE.
*****************************************************************

START-OF-SELECTION.

SELECT VBELN FKDAT KUNAG WAERK NETWR FROM VBRK INTO TABLE BILL_TAB
  WHERE KUNAG IN ( SELECT KUNNR FROM KNA1  WHERE ORT01 = ORT01 ).

SORT BILL_TAB BY VBELN.

LOOP AT BILL_TAB INTO BILL_STRU.
 WRITE:/5(4) SY-TABIX, BILL_STRU-VBELN, BILL_STRU-FKDAT,
            BILL_STRU-KUNAG USING NO EDIT MASK,
            BILL_STRU-NETWR, BILL_STRU-WAERK.
ENDLOOP.
```

The text symbols used in the header are shown in Figure 8-15.

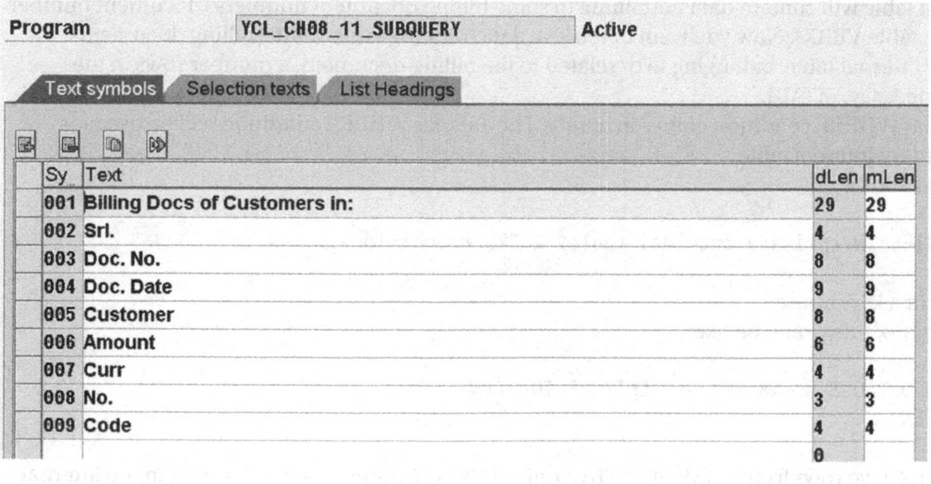

Program YCL_CH08_11_SUBQUERY Active

Text symbols | Selection texts | List Headings

Sy	Text	dLen	mLen
001	Billing Docs of Customers in:	29	29
002	Srl.	4	4
003	Doc. No.	8	8
004	Doc. Date	9	9
005	Customer	8	8
006	Amount	6	6
007	Curr	4	4
008	No.	3	3
009	Code	4	4
		0	

Figure 8-15. *Program: YCL_CH08_11_SUBQUERY - Text Symbols*

The Output is shown in Figure 8-16.

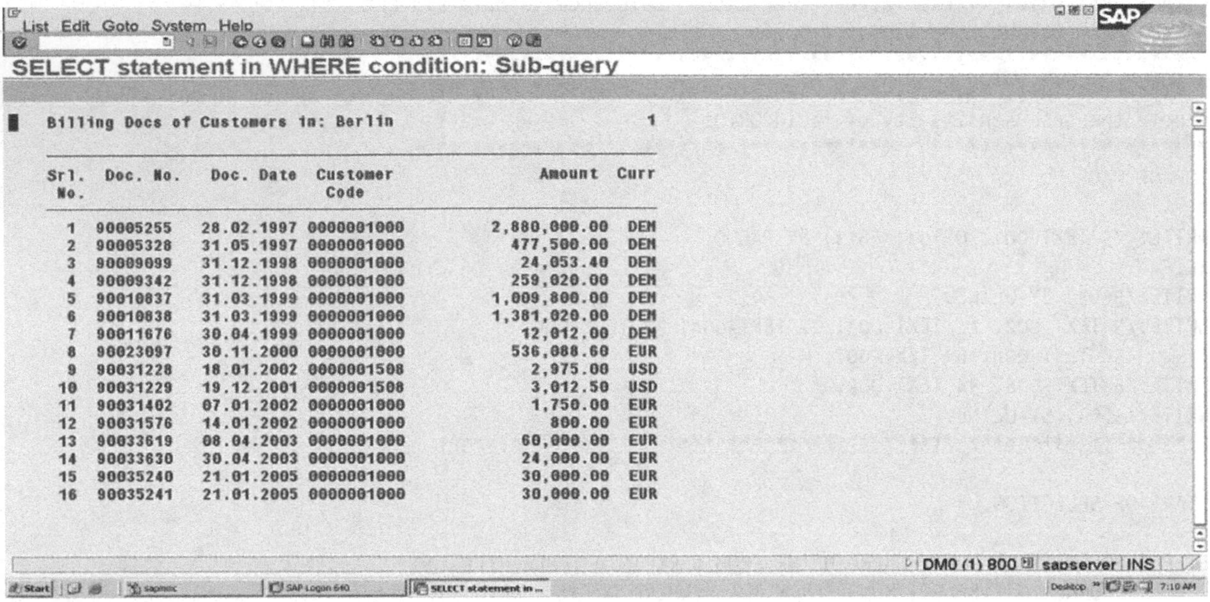

```
List  Edit  Goto  System  Help

SELECT statement in WHERE condition: Sub-query

Billing Docs of Customers in: Berlin                          1
---------------------------------------------------------------------
Srl.  Doc. No.    Doc. Date  Customer                  Amount  Curr
No.                          Code
---------------------------------------------------------------------
   1  90005255   28.02.1997 0000001000          2,880,000.00  DEM
   2  90005328   31.05.1997 0000001000            477,500.00  DEM
   3  90009099   31.12.1998 0000001000             24,053.40  DEM
   4  90009342   31.12.1998 0000001000            259,020.00  DEM
   5  90010837   31.03.1999 0000001000          1,009,800.00  DEM
   6  90010838   31.03.1999 0000001000          1,381,020.00  DEM
   7  90011676   30.04.1999 0000001000             12,012.00  DEM
   8  90023097   30.11.2000 0000001000            536,088.60  EUR
   9  90031228   18.01.2002 0000001508              2,975.00  USD
  10  90031229   19.12.2001 0000001508              3,012.50  USD
  11  90031402   07.01.2002 0000001000              1,750.00  EUR
  12  90031576   14.01.2002 0000001000                800.00  EUR
  13  90033619   08.04.2003 0000001000             60,000.00  EUR
  14  90033630   30.04.2003 0000001000             24,000.00  EUR
  15  90035240   21.01.2005 0000001000             30,000.00  EUR
  16  90035241   21.01.2005 0000001000             30,000.00  EUR

DMO (1) 800  sapserver  INS
```

Figure 8-16. *Program: YCL_CH08_11_SUBQUERY - Output*

Tabular WHERE Condition

Consider the scenario: you have two internal tables, one designated as primary and the second one designated as secondary. Into the primary internal table, you have retrieved data from a database table or view. Now you want to retrieve into the secondary internal table only the data that is related to the data in the primary internal table.

Let this scenario be in terms of specific database tables. Suppose you have retrieved into the primary internal table (named, say, PITAB) data from the database table VBRK (billing documents - header) for specific customer codes. The primary internal table will contain data pertaining to some billing document numbers (document number is part of the primary key in table VBRK). Now you want to retrieve data from the table VBRP (billing documents - items) into the secondary internal table, belonging to or related to the billing document, a number rows in the primary internal table (named, say, SITAB).

This is where the tabular WHERE condition comes in handy. The Tabular WHERE condition will be used for retrieving data of the secondary internal table.

The syntax for a tabular condition:

```
SELECT ... FOR ALL ENTRIES IN <primary internal table> WHERE <condition>...
```

FOR ALL ENTRIES IN in a key phrase.

In your described scenario, this would be like:

```
SELECT ... FROM VBRP INTO TABLE SITAB FOR ALL ENTRIES IN PITAB
WHERE VBELN = PITAB-VBELN.
```

The semantics of this: retrieve rows from VBRP into SITAB only of VBELN values that are residing in the internal table PITAB.

The program source code:

```
REPORT YCL_CH08_12_TABULAR_CONDITION.

****************************
* Tabular WHERE Condition **
****************************
*******************************************************
* try this with customer codes: 473, 401081         **
*                                                    **
* the following billing documents will be loaded    **
* into primary internal table PITAB                  **
*                                                    **
* customer code    billing document no.              **
* (KUNAG)           (VBELN)                          **
*                                                    **
* 473                 0090026209                     **
* 473                 0090029855                     **
*                                                    **
* 401081              0090032165                     **
*                                                    **
*                                                    **
* corresponding to these three billing documents     **
* the following materials/items will be loaded into  **
* secondary internal table SITAB                     **
*                                                    **
* billing document no.     material code             **
*  (VBELN)                   (MATNR)                 **
*                                                    **
* 0090026209                HT-1011                  **
* 0090026209                HT-1010                  **
*                                                    **
* 0090029855                HT-1011                  **
*                                                    **
* 0090032165                HT-1040                  **
*                                                    **
*                                                    **
*******************************************************
*******************************************************
* declare data. prompt input for two customers       **
*                                                    **
* load primary internal table with billing documents **
* of the input customers                             **
*                                                    **
* load the secondary internal table with materials/  **
* items belonging to the billing documents in the    **
* primary internal table with the tabular WHERE      **
* condition                                          **
*                                                    **
* output from primary, secondary internal tables     **
*******************************************************
```

```
DATA: BEGIN OF PITAB_STRU,
       VBELN   TYPE VBELN_VF,
       FKDAT   TYPE FKDAT,
       KUNAG   TYPE KUNAG,
       NETWR   TYPE NETWR,
       WAERK   TYPE WAERK,
      END OF PITAB_STRU,
      PITAB LIKE STANDARD TABLE OF PITAB_STRU,
      BEGIN OF SITAB_STRU,
       VBELN   TYPE VBELN_VF,
       MATNR   TYPE MATNR,
       NETWR   TYPE NETWR,
      END OF SITAB_STRU,
      SITAB LIKE STANDARD TABLE OF SITAB_STRU.
**********************************************************
PARAMETERS: CUST_CD1  TYPE VBRK-KUNAG VALUE CHECK
            DEFAULT '473',
            CUST_CD2  TYPE VBRK-KUNAG VALUE CHECK
            DEFAULT '401081'.

*SELECT-OPTIONS CUST_CDS FOR PITAB_STRU-KUNAG.
************************************************************
START-OF-SELECTION.

SELECT VBELN FKDAT KUNAG NETWR WAERK FROM VBRK
 INTO TABLE PITAB WHERE KUNAG IN (CUST_CD1, CUST_CD2). " IN CUST_CDS

SELECT VBELN MATNR NETWR FROM VBRP
 INTO TABLE SITAB FOR ALL ENTRIES IN PITAB
 WHERE VBELN = PITAB-VBELN. " tabular condition

LOOP AT PITAB INTO PITAB_STRU.
 WRITE:/5(4) SY-TABIX, PITAB_STRU-KUNAG, PITAB_STRU-VBELN.
ENDLOOP.

SKIP 2.

LOOP AT SITAB INTO SITAB_STRU.
 WRITE:/5(4) SY-TABIX, SITAB_STRU-VBELN, SITAB_STRU-MATNR.
ENDLOOP.
```

You have used the IN operator in the first SELECT statement. You could have used
WHERE KUNAG = CUST_CD1 OR KUNAG = CUST_CD2.

To enable an easy demonstration, a small amount of data has been identified and selected (i.e., two customers having few billing documents): two billing documents for the first customer and one for the second, a total of three billing documents (see the program comments).

The billing documents identified have few items: one billing document having two items and two other billing documents having a single item – a total of four items.

You can check this data for tables VBRK and VBRP in the data browser SE16 transaction code. You can execute the program with other customer codes and verify results.

The output is shown in Figure 8-17.

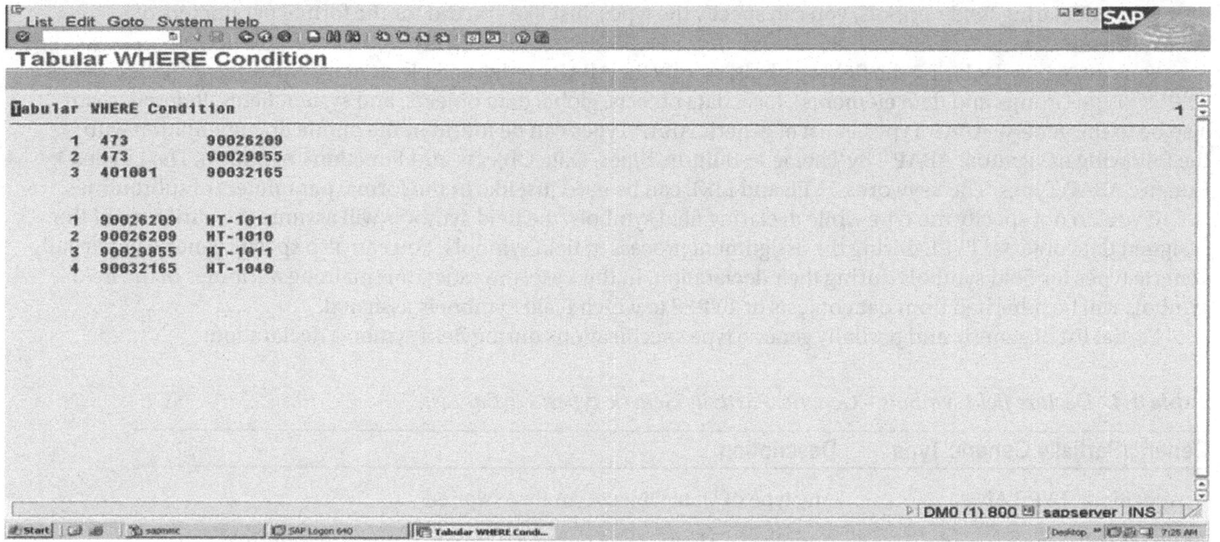

Figure 8-17. *Program: YCL_CH08_12_TABULAR_CONDITION - Output*

ABAP FIELD-SYMBOLS

The ABAP FIELD-SYMBOLS, which will be referred as field symbols, is a digression from the coverage of SELECT statement variants. The field symbols enable dynamic access of data objects. The field symbols have been part of the ABAP procedure oriented language. RTTS - Run Time TYPE Services, a feature of ABAP OOP, enables creation of runtime data objects or the dynamic data objects that are unlike the static data objects you were declaring with keywords DATA, TABLES, etc. The combination of runtime data objects and field symbols take Open SQL data retrieval to a different level as you will see in the forthcoming hands-on exercises.

Until now you were accessing data objects in a static manner by using the name of the data objects or fields. The field symbols and ABAP OOP data references enable you to access data objects whose name, attributes (TYPE, length, etc.) you know only at runtime.

The field symbols can be assigned to data objects. They serve as a kind of symbolic name for the data objects assigned to them. When you use field symbols, the system works with the contents of the data object and not with the contents of the field symbols.

ABAP OOP data references point to the data objects. To access the contents of a data object to which ABAP OOP data reference is pointing, you must dereference it.

Field Symbol Declarations

The field symbols have to be declared before they are assigned to data objects. The field symbols are declared in the following way:

```
FIELD-SYMBOLS: <FSYBOL1>, <FS>, <FSTRU>.
```

The FIELD-SYMBOLS is a keyword just like DATA, TYPES, etc. The name of field symbols starts with the less than (<) character and ends with the greater than (>) character. The name space of field symbols is a maximum of 30 characters including the enclosing characters: <>. The usual naming conventions apply: name (after '<') has to start with an alphabet, and the rest of the characters can be alphanumeric with embedded underscores (_).

While declaring field symbols, you can specify the types, just like you did for the formal parameters of subroutines.

You can, while declaring the field symbols, specify the ABAP predefined elementary types, local TYPES, global TYPES (Type Groups and data elements), local data objects, global data objects, and system fields. Reference can also be to the generic ABAP Types. A list of generic ABAP Types can be found in the online documentation with the following navigation: ABAP - By Theme ➤ Built-In Types, Data Objects and Functions ➤ Built-In Data Types ➤ Generic ABAP Types. The keywords TYPE and LIKE can be used just like in the formal parameters of subroutines.

If you do not specify the type while declaring field symbols, the field symbols will assume the attributes of the assigned data objects/TYPE during the assignment process to field symbols. You can also specify generic or partially generic types for field symbols during their declaration. In this case, the exact or remaining attributes of the field symbols will be inherited from data objects or TYPES to which Field Symbol is assigned.

Partial list of generic and partially generic type specifications during field symbols declaration:

Table 8-4. *Declare field symbols - Generic, Partially Generic types: Partial List*

Generic/Partially Generic Type	Description
Unspecified/ TYPE ANY	Any type of Data Object Can Be Assigned
TYPE C, N, P, X	Any One of Them. The Length, Decimals If Any Are Inherited From the Assigned Data Object
TYPE TABLE	Standard Internal Table Can Be Assigned
TYPE STANDARD TABLE	
TYPE ANY TABLE	Standard Table or Sorted Table or Indexed Table or Hashed Table Can Be Assigned
TYPE INDEX TABLE	Standard Table or Sorted Table Can Be Assigned
TYPE SORTED TABLE	Sorted Table Can Be Assigned
TYPE HASHED TABLE	Hashed Table Can Be Assigned

Field symbols declarations using generic or partially generic TYPES:

```
FIELD-SYMBOLS: <ANY1>       TYPE ANY,
               <ANY2>,
               <ELEM1>      TYPE C,
               <ELEM2>      TYPE P,
               <STABL>      TYPE TABLE,
               <ATABL>      TYPE ANY TABLE,
               <STAB>       TYPE SORTED TABLE.
```

List of fully specified TYPE during Field Symbols Declaration:

Table 8-5. *Declare field symbols – Specify types fully*

Fully Specified TYPE	Description
TYPE D, F, I, T	Any One of Them
TYPE <type>	Declaration In ABAP Program With TYPES DDIC Type Group DDIC Data Element Other DDIC Global Data Objects: Table, Structure, Table/Structure Field
TYPE <data object>	Internal, External, System, Special Data Object
TYPE REF TO	Reference Variable, Referring To Class/Interface
TYPE /LIKE LINE OF	Structure Of Internal Table

Field symbols declaration using fully specified TYPES:

```
DATA: NAME(25)        TYPE C,
      CURR_TAB        TYPE STANDARD TABLE OF TCURT.

PARAMETERS DAY(9)     TYPE C.

FIELD-SYMBOLS:  <DATE>          TYPE D,
                <INT4>          TYPE I,
                <TYP1>          TYPE KUNNR,
                <TYP2>          TYPE VBRK-NETWR,
                <DOBJ1>         LIKE NAME,
                <DOBJ2>         LIKE DAY,
                <TLINE>         LIKE LINE OF CURR_TAB.
```

Field Symbol Static Assignments

You can assign or reassign a field symbol to data objects. If the field symbol specified type does not match with the assigned data object type, a syntax error or runtime error is triggered, depending on the assignment being done to a static or dynamic data object.

If the assignment is successful, the system field SY-SUBRC is set to zero or else to non-zero.

Field symbol declarations, assignments:

```
DATA: CURR_TAB TYPE STANDARD TABLE OF TCURT
               WITH HEADER LINE.

FIELD-SYMBOLS:  <ITAB>      TYPE ANY TABLE,
                <TLINE>     LIKE LINE OF CURR_TAB,
                <FIELD>.
```

```
ASSIGN: CURR_TAB[]        TO <ITAB>,
        CURR_TAB          TO <TLINE>,
        CURR_TAB-LTEXT    TO <FIELD>
```

ASSIGN is the keyword to assign data objects to Field Symbols.

Following the keyword *ASSIGN*, you specify the name of the data object to be assigned and the keyword *TO* be followed by the name of the field symbol to which you want to assign the data object.

In these code lines:

When you use <ITAB> or CURR_TAB[], you are accessing the same data object and the internal table CURR_TAB.

When you use <TLINE> or CURR_TAB, you are accessing the same structure data object CURR_TAB.

When you use <FIELD> or <TLINE>-LTEXT or CURR_TAB-LTEXT, you are accessing the same data object as the field LTEXT of structure CURR_TAB.

You can use the offsets and lengths in case of TYPES C, D, N, and T.

You can also assign one field symbol to another.

In this example, the structure CURR_TAB declared with the keyword DATA is a static data object. If your structure data object is not static (i.e., you do not know it till runtime), you can access its fields or components with another variation of the ASSIGN statement.

```
ASSIGN COMPONENT <component number> OF STRUCTURE <structure name>
 TO <field symbol name>.
```

<component number> is the sequence number of the field in the structure. It can be either literal/variable.

<structure name> is the name of the structure or name of another Field Symbol assigned to a structure.

<field symbol name> is the field symbol to which assignment is being made.

In your preceding example, if you had written:

```
ASSIGN COMPONENT 4 OF STRUCTURE CURR_TAB TO <FIELD>.
```

It is equivalent to:

```
ASSIGN: CURR_TAB-LTEXT TO <FIELD>
```

The fourth field of structure CURR_TAB is LTEXT.

These are static assignments. The data object to which assignments are made is predetermined.

Field Symbol Hands-On Exercise

Let the field symbols be applied in a hands-on exercise. Until now, in the context of internal tables, you were always retrieving a row of data from the internal table into a work area or header line (i.e., a structure and operating on the contents of the structure like output, etc.). With the help of field symbols you can directly operate on the row in the internal table without fetching it into a structure. The definition of a separate structure is uncalled for. Consider the code lines:

```
DATA: CURR_TAB TYPE STANDARD TABLE OF TCURT.
FIELD-SYMBOLS: <ROW_POINTER> LIKE LINE OF CURR_TAB.
SELECT * FROM TCURT INTO TABLE CURR_TAB WHERE SPRAS = SY-LANGU.

LOOP AT CURR_TAB ASSIGNING <ROW_POINTER>.
 WRITE:/5(4) SY-TABIX, <ROW_POINTER>-WAERS, <ROW_POINTER>-LTEXT.
ENDLOOP.
```

The LOOP...ENDLOOP construct is different from the ones you were using. In this construct, you are not fetching a row from the internal table into the structure for each pass of the loop (there is no work area/header line declared). Rather, the field symbol <ROW_POINTER> is accessing the contents of internal table's first row directly during the first pass of the loop, the contents of the second row during the second pass of the loop, and so on until all the rows have been accessed. It is like during each pass of the loop, the corresponding row is the work area.

If you are processing very large volume of data with a LOOP...ENDLOOP construct, this is the preferred way of doing it. It saves the overhead of moving data from the internal table into structure, resulting in reduced execution time.

A hands-on using this notation of LOOP...ENDLOOP will be performed using the data from the customer primary table KNA1.

You will code two programs to provide a comparison of execution times. The two programs are identical except for the LOOP...ENDLOOP construct. The first program YCL_CH08_13_CUST_LIST_WITHSTRU generates a customer list with a LOOP AT...INTO...notation. The second program YCL_CH08_14_CUST_LIST_WOUTSTRU generates a customer list with a LOOP AT ASSIGNING... notation.

A statement GET RUN TIME... is used to get the execution time in micro seconds in both the programs. The statement is elaborated in the comment lines of the programs. The first program is not listed here, as its code is obvious. It is available in E-Resource. The second program YCL_CH08_14_CUST_LIST_WOUTSTRU is listed here:

```
REPORT YCL_CH08_14_CUST_LIST_WOUTSTRU LINE-SIZE 140 LINE-COUNT 60
        NO STANDARD PAGE HEADING.

*************************************************************
* List Customers - Use Field Symbol To Access Row Directly **
* No Work Area/Header Line                                 **
*************************************************************

****************************************************
* the GET RUN TIME statement is used to ascertain **
* the execution time for a program block in micro **
* seconds. the first time it is executed, it      **
* assigns zero to the specified variable. from    **
* the second and subsequent occurrences, it loads **
* /assigns cumulative elapsed time in micro       **
* seconds.                                        **
*                                                 **
* so you can determine the execution time of a    **
* program block by subtracting the value assigned **
* at the beginning of programming block from the  **
* value assigned at the end of the programming    **
* block (difference)                              **
****************************************************

DATA: TIME_ELAPSED  TYPE I VALUE 100,
      DATE_CHR(10)  TYPE C.
DATA: CUSTOMERS_TAB LIKE STANDARD TABLE OF
       YCL_CH05_CUST_STRU.

FIELD-SYMBOLS: <FS1> LIKE LINE OF CUSTOMERS_TAB.
               " specifying TYPE/LIKE to static data object
**************************************************
TOP-OF-PAGE.
```

```
WRITE:/5 TEXT-001, DATE_CHR, 130 TEXT-002, 137(3) SY-PAGNO.
SKIP 1.
WRITE:/5(135) SY-ULINE.
WRITE:/6 TEXT-003, 12 TEXT-004, 23 TEXT-005, 60 TEXT-006, 96
 TEXT-007, 130 TEXT-008.
WRITE:/6 TEXT-009, 13 TEXT-010, 131 TEXT-010.
WRITE:/5(135) SY-ULINE.
************************************************
START-OF-SELECTION.

GET RUN TIME FIELD TIME_ELAPSED.

CONCATENATE SY-DATUM+6(2) SY-DATUM+4(2) SY-DATUM+0(4) INTO DATE_CHR
   SEPARATED BY '/'.

SELECT KUNNR NAME1 STRAS ORT01 PSTLZ FROM KNA1
   INTO TABLE CUSTOMERS_TAB.

SORT CUSTOMERS_TAB BY KUNNR.

LOOP AT CUSTOMERS_TAB ASSIGNING <FS1>.
         " <FS1> addresses/accesses first row, second row & so on

 WRITE:/5(5) SY-TABIX, <FS1>-KUNNR USING NO EDIT MASK,
         <FS1>-NAME1, <FS1>-STRAS, " structure components/fields are
         <FS1>-ORT01, <FS1>-PSTLZ. " addressable because <FS1> TYPE to static data object
ENDLOOP.

GET RUN TIME FIELD TIME_ELAPSED.

SKIP 2.
WRITE:/5 'Time elapsed:', (7) TIME_ELAPSED.
```

The text symbols are shown in Figure 8-18.

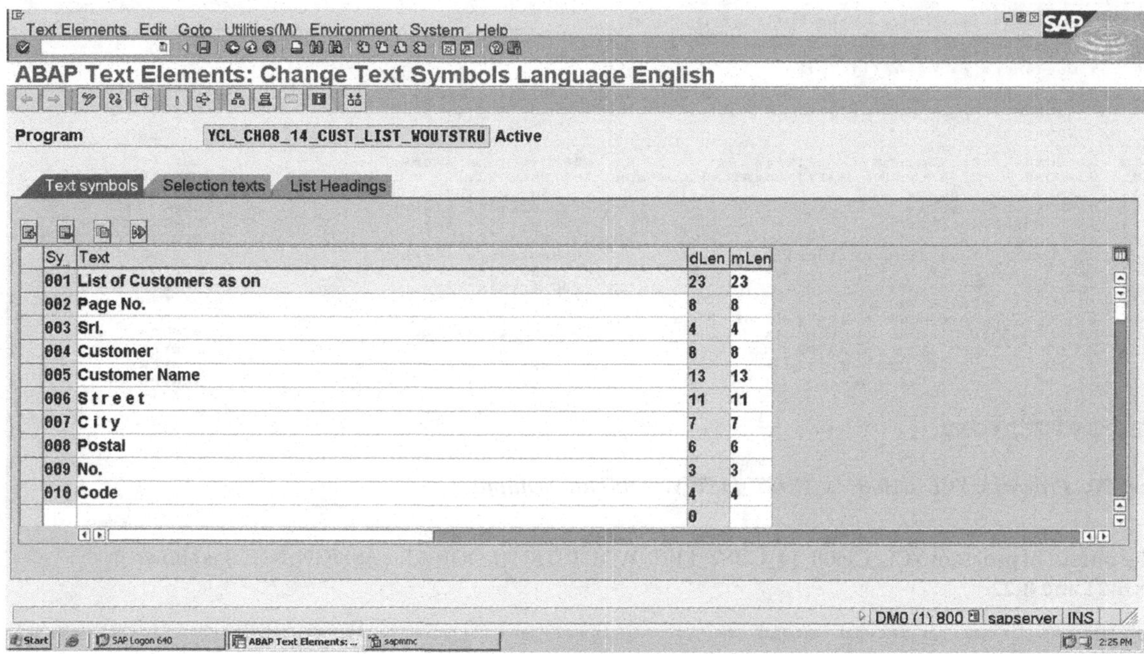

Figure 8-18. *Program: YCL_CH08_14_CUST_LIST_WOUTSTRU - Text Symbols*

The output of program YCL_CH08_13_CUST_LIST_WITHSTRU (LOOP AT... INTO...) is shown in Figures 8-19 and 8-20.

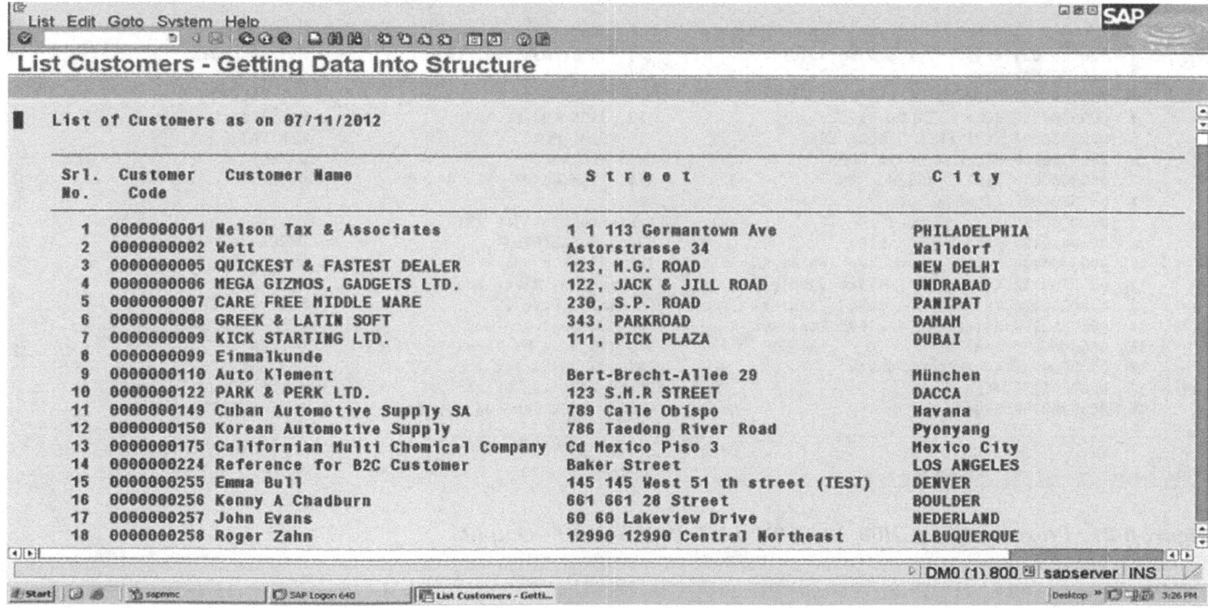

Figure 8-19. *Program: YCL_CH08_13_CUST_LIST_WITHSTRU - Output*

List Customers - Getting Data Into Structure

List of Customers as on 07/11/2012

Srl. No.	Customer Code	Customer Name	Street	City
7615	US-CUS3	Customer Site - Three	656 Michigan Avenue	LOS ANGELES
7616	US-CUS9	Californian Multi Chemical Company	100 Chem Way	IRVINE
7617	US-NEUMANS	Neumans	e. Fourth Blain Blvd	TEMPE
7618	US-RISKWAY	Riskway	9487 Western Highway	RENO
7619	US-SUPMART	Supermart	1234 Main Street	FLAGSTAFF
7620	US-TARGE	Targe	One Targe Lane	PHOENIX
7621	US-TOYS	Toys International	40 Montgomry Street	PAWTUCKET
7622	VIPER	VIPER	411 Camille Circle	San Jose
7623	VMI-00	Priced Less	1100 Archrer Ave	GREENSBORO
7624	VMI-99	Value Mart	605 Broadway	RALEIGH
7625	W-1200	Anonymous Factory Sales (Plant 1200		
7626	XI_BPM	BPM Auto Spare Parts	8 1 133 W Park Ave.	DENVER
7627	XI_BPM_2	BPM Auto Spare Parts	8 1 133 New Ave.	DENVER
7628	XI_EDI	XI EDI Demo Customer	3 1 133 W Park Ave.	DENVER
7629	XI_RNET	Rnet Customer	2 1 133 W Park Ave.	DENVER

Time elapsed: 744768

Figure 8-20. *Program: YCL_CH08_13_CUST_LIST_WITHSTRU - Output*

The output of program YCL_CH08_14_CUST_LIST_WOUTSTRU (LOOP AT... ASSIGNING...) is shown in Figures 8-21 and 8-22.

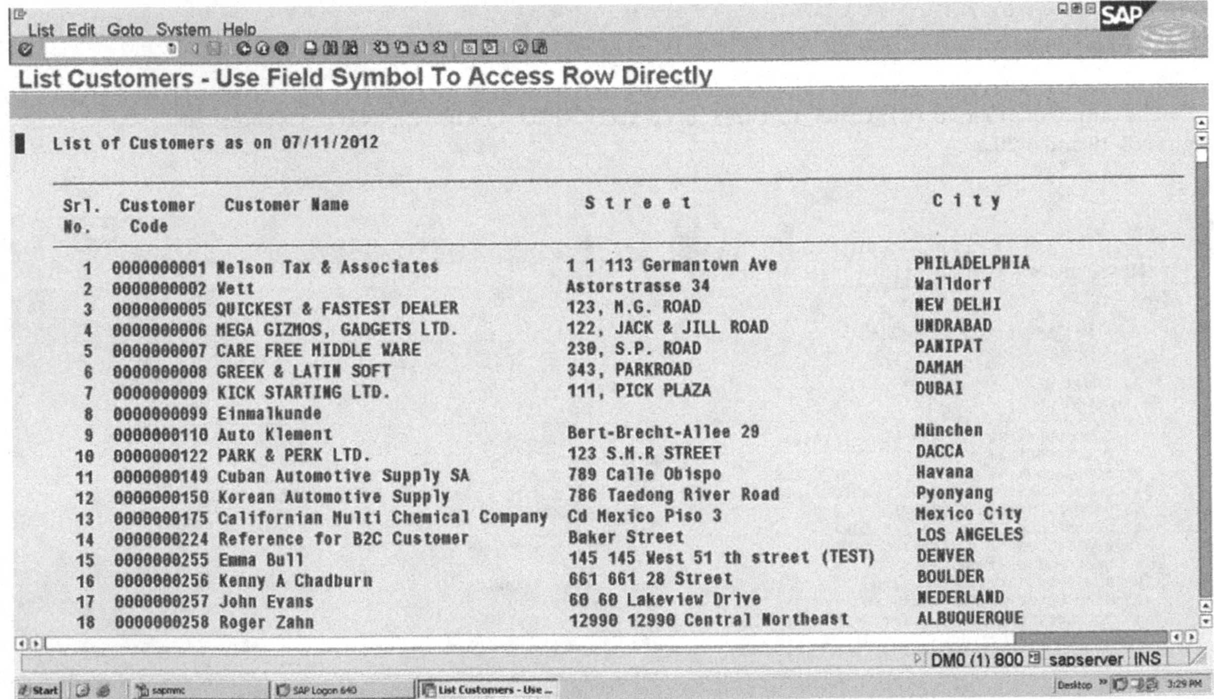

List Customers - Use Field Symbol To Access Row Directly

List of Customers as on 07/11/2012

Srl. No.	Customer Code	Customer Name	Street	City
1	0000000001	Nelson Tax & Associates	1 1 113 Germantown Ave	PHILADELPHIA
2	0000000002	Wett	Astorstrasse 34	Walldorf
3	0000000005	QUICKEST & FASTEST DEALER	123, M.G. ROAD	NEW DELHI
4	0000000006	MEGA GIZMOS, GADGETS LTD.	122, JACK & JILL ROAD	UNDRABAD
5	0000000007	CARE FREE MIDDLE WARE	230, S.P. ROAD	PANIPAT
6	0000000008	GREEK & LATIN SOFT	343, PARKROAD	DAMAN
7	0000000009	KICK STARTING LTD.	111, PICK PLAZA	DUBAI
8	0000000099	Einmalkunde		
9	0000000110	Auto Klement	Bert-Brecht-Allee 29	München
10	0000000122	PARK & PERK LTD.	123 S.M.R STREET	DACCA
11	0000000149	Cuban Automotive Supply SA	789 Calle Obispo	Havana
12	0000000150	Korean Automotive Supply	786 Taedong River Road	Pyonyang
13	0000000175	Californian Multi Chemical Company	Cd Mexico Piso 3	Mexico City
14	0000000224	Reference for B2C Customer	Baker Street	LOS ANGELES
15	0000000255	Emma Bull	145 145 West 51 th street (TEST)	DENVER
16	0000000256	Kenny A Chadburn	661 661 28 Street	BOULDER
17	0000000257	John Evans	60 60 Lakeview Drive	NEDERLAND
18	0000000258	Roger Zahn	12990 12990 Central Northeast	ALBUQUERQUE

Figure 8-21. *Program: YCL_CH08_14_CUST_LIST_WOUTSTRU - Output*

```
List Customers - Use Field Symbol To Access Row Directly

List of Customers as on 07/11/2012

Srl.  Customer    Customer Name                         S t r e e t              C i t y
No.    Code

7615  US-CUS3     Customer Site - Three                 656 Michigan Avenue      LOS ANGELES
7616  US-CUS9     Californian Multi Chemical Company    100 Chem Way             IRVINE
7617  US-NEUMANS  Neumans                               e. Fourth Blain Blvd     TEMPE
7618  US-RISKWAY  Riskway                               9487 Western Highway     RENO
7619  US-SUPMART  Supermart                             1234 Main Street         FLAGSTAFF
7620  US-TARGE    Targe                                 One Targe Lane           PHOENIX
7621  US-TOYS     Toys International                    40 Montgomry Street      PAWTUCKET
7622  VIPER       VIPER                                 411 Camille Circle       San Jose
7623  VMI-00      Priced Less                           1100 Archrer Ave         GREENSBORO
7624  VMI-99      Value Mart                            605 Broadway             RALEIGH
7625  W-1200      Anonymous Factory Sales (Plant 1200
7626  XI_BPM      BPM Auto Spare Parts                  8 1 133 W Park Ave.      DENVER
7627  XI_BPM_2    BPM Auto Spare Parts                  8 1 133 New Ave.         DENVER
7628  XI_EDI      XI EDI Demo Customer                  3 1 133 W Park Ave.      DENVER
7629  XI_RNET     Rnet Customer                         2 1 133 W Park Ave.      DENVER

Time elapsed: 73.130
```

Figure 8-22. *Program: YCL_CH08_14_CUST_LIST_WOUTSTRU - Output*

The syntax and notation of the AGGIGNING <field symbol> can be used in the internal tables' READ statements. You can directly access a row through the READ statement with an ASSIGNING notation. You can also directly assign values to fields of a row to which the Field Symbol is pointing, thus avoiding the MODIFY statement you used earlier to alter the contents of internal table rows. The use of the MODIFY statement involves transfer of data from the table into the structure and then from the structure to the table. With the ASSIGNING notation, these transfers can be avoided. These features are demonstrated in the programs: YCL_CH08_15_READ_KEY_ASSIGN, YCL_CH08_16_READ_INDEX_ASSIGN, and YCL_CH08_17_CHANGE_WOUT_MODIFY. These programs are not listed here, but you can find them in the E-Resource.

Field Symbol Dynamic Assignments, UNASSIGN, Check If Assigned

You can decide at runtime, what data object is to be assigned to a field symbol. This is called dynamic assignment. The syntax for dynamic assignment:

```
ASSIGN: (<variable name>) TO <Field Symbol>.
```

<variable name> will contain the name of the runtime field to which you want to assign the <Field Symbol>. The <variable name> has to be enclosed in parentheses. You cannot use offsets and length with dynamic assignments.

You can unassign a Field Symbol. The syntax:

```
UNASSIGN: <Field Symbol>.
```

You can check in the IF condition statement whether a field symbol is assigned or not:

```
IF <Field Symbol> IS ASSIGNED.
```

You can refer to this topic in the PDF document **ABAP Programming (BC-ABA)**.
You will see the power of Field Symbols in the current and forthcoming Chapters 10, 12, and 13.
A switch back to the main topic: Open SQL SELECT statement variants.

Specify the <source> In Open SQL SELECT Statement at Runtime

The Open SQL SELECT statement allows the <source> (i.e., the database table/view) from which data is to be retrieved to be specified at runtime.

Associated with the runtime specification of the source and the <destination> (following the keywords: INTO/APPENDING, etc.), not known until runtime cannot be declared/defined statically with DATA and TABLES statements. The <destination> data object (structure/internal table) needs to be created dynamically at runtime.

Create Dynamic Data Objects

The ABAP OOP feature (run time type services) RTTS provides for the creation of runtime data objects.. RTTS will be covered in more detail in Chapter 11 entitled 'ABAP OOP,' but here's a short introduction so that you can see how it's used in the Open SQL SELECT statement. To create a runtime data object using RTTS:

- You have to declare a reference variable using the keyword DATA like this:

  ```
  DATA: RF_VAR TYPE REF TO DATA.
  ```

  RF_VAR is the name of the ABAP reference variable following the naming conventions of any other ABAP variable.
  TYPE REF TO DATA is a key phrase, indicating that this reference variable will point to the runtime data object to be created.

- Using the declared reference variable, you have to create the runtime data object:

  ```
  CREATE DATA RF_VAR {TYPE/LIKE} <referred object>.
  ```

  <referred object> can be any local/DDIC TYPES or any of the local/DDIC data objects.

For example, if you want to create a dynamic data object the same as the DDIC table structure KNA1, you should be writing:

```
CREATE DATA RF_VAR TYPE KNA1.
```

But again you are hard-coding. This will create only a data object like the table structure KNA1, not any other. Hence, you have to use another variation of the statement CREATE DATA... The code will be like this:

```
DATA: RF_VAR TYPE REF TO DATA.
PARAMETERS: OBJ_NAME(50) TYPE C DEFAULT 'KNA1'.
START-OF-SELECTION.
CREATE DATA RF_VAR TYPE (OBJ_NAME).
```

This will create a runtime data object of the TYPE whose name is contained in the variable OBJ_NAME (input through the PARAMETERS statement). Whatever object name you enter in the input variable OBJ_NAME, the CREATE DATA... statement will create a data object of that TYPE. The reference variable points to this data object, not to the contents of the data object. You need to access the contents. One way doing this – that is, to get access to contents is to dereference the reference variable RF_VAR and assign it to a field symbol. The code to do this will be like this:

```
DATA: RF_VAR TYPE REF TO DATA.

FIELD-SYMBOLS: <DOBJ>.

PARAMETERS: OBJ_NAME(50) TYPE C DEFAULT 'KNA1'.
START-OF-SELECTION.
CREATE DATA RF_VAR TYPE (OBJ_NAME).

ASSIGN RF_VAR->* TO <DOBJ>.
```

The ->* is to dereference.

Run Time <source> Specification in SELECT Statement – Hands-on

Having been introduced to the bare essentials of the creation of dynamic data objects, let a hands-an exercise be performed.

In the ABAP program, let the database table or view name from which the data is to be retrieved be input through the PARAMETERS statement. Using this input, you will create two dynamic data objects: (a) a structure, and (b) an internal table.

You will load data from the database table or view into the internal table.

You will use LOOP...ENDLOOP construct to retrieve data from the internal table into a structure. As you do not know the field names, you will use the ASSIGN COMPONENT variation of the ASSIGN field symbol statement to access individual fields. You will output the first five fields.

The source program:

```
REPORT YCL_CH08_18_SRCE_AT_RUN_TIME LINE-SIZE 150
       NO STANDARD PAGE HEADING.

*****************************************************
* <source> In SELECT At Runtime, Dynamic Data Objects *
*****************************************************

**********************************************
* from which database table/view to retrieve   **
* data is decided at run time.                 **
*                                              **
* the runtime database table name is input     **
* through PARAMETERS statement. (TABLE_NM)     **
*                                              **
* when you are retrieving data from a database **
* table/view into an internal table, the       **
* internal table must have a structure which   **
* can accommodate the retrieved fields. (all   **
* fields of database table/view for now)       **
*                                              **
```

```
* when you are retrieving data, one row at a    **
* time from the internal table into a structure**
* you do not know the structure's attributes    **
* in terms of fields/components till runtime    **
*                                               **
* so you are creating a dynamic structure data **
* object using the table/view name input.       **
* the way to create dynamic structure data      **
* object is:                                    **
* (a) declare using DATA statement a reference **
*     variable like:                            **
*     DATA STRU_REF  TYPE REF TO DATA.          **
* (b) create dynamic structure data object by  **
*     referring to the input table/view name    **
*     like:                                     **
*     CREATE DATA STRU_REF TYPE (TABLE_NM).     **
*                                               **
* this will create a structure data object      **
* having the same fields as the table/view      **
* input in TABLE_NM. if for Instance, KNA1      **
* was input, the CREATE DATA STRU_REF TYPE      **
* (TABLE_NM). will create a structure data      **
* object having all the fields of table         **
* structure KNA1. the reference variable        **
* STRU_REF will point to the structure data     **
* object.                                       **
*                                               **
* to be able to refer/point to the data         **
* you need to de-reference the reference        **
* variable STRU_REF. you are dereferencing and **
* assigning to a Field Symbol <FS_STRU> like    **
* ASSIGN STRU_REF->* TO <FS_STRU>.              **
*                                               **
* you are creating a dynamic internal table     **
* data object using the table/view name input. **
* the way to create dynamic internal table      **
* data object is:                               **
* (a) declare using DATA statement a reference **
*     variable like:                            **
*     DATA ITAB_REF  TYPE REF TO DATA.          **
* (b) create dynamic internal table data object**
*     by referring to the input table/view      **
*     name like:                                **
*     CREATE DATA ITAB_REF TYPE STANDARD TABLE **
*     OF (TABLE_NM).                            **
*                                               **
* this will create a internal table data object**
* having the same fields as the table/view      **
* input in TABLE_NM. if for instance, KNA1      **
* was input, the CREATE DATA ITAB_REF TYPE      **
* STANDARD TABLE OF (TABLE_NM). will create an **
```

```
* internal table data object having all the     **
* fields of table structure KNA1. the reference**
* variable ITAB_REF will point to the internal **
* table data object.                           **
*                                              **
* to be able to refer/point to the data in the **
* internal table, you need to dereference the  **
* reference variable ITAB_REF. you are         **
* dereferencing and assigning to a Field Symbol**
* <FS_ITAB> like:                              **
* ASSIGN ITAB_REF->* TO <FS_ITAB>.             **
*                                              **
* to access the individual fields of structure **
* you are using the Field Symbol assignment    **
* statement form:                              **
*     ASSIGN COMPONENT <component number> OF   **
*     <structure name> TO <field symbol name>. **
*                                              **
* the individual fields accessed in this way   **
* are output.                                  **
*                                              **
* the concept of creating dynamic data objects **
* is being introduced in a preview manner. it  **
* is covered with in the regular course in     **
* Chapter 10.                                  **
************************************************

************************************************
* input the table/view name from which data to **
* be retrieved                                 **
*                                              **
* create a dynamic structure data object of    **
* type same as the inputted table/view.        **
* deference and assign to Field Symbol         **
*                                              **
* create a dynamic internal table data object  **
* whose structure type is same as the inputted **
* table/view.                                  **
* deference and assign To another Field Symbol **
*                                              **
* use the SELECT statement variation with      **
* runtime <source> to fetch data into dynamic  **
* internal table data object                   **
*                                              **
* set up LOOP...ENDLOOP                        **
*                                              **
* assign individual fields of structure data   **
* object to another Field Symbol & output      **
*                                              **
* LOOP...ENDLOOP will run through till all     **
* rows fetched & outputted                     **
************************************************
```

```
DATA: STRU_REF TYPE REF TO DATA, " reference variable for structure
      ITAB_REF TYPE REF TO DATA. " reference variable for internal table

FIELD-SYMBOLS: <FS_STRU>, " Field Symbol for table/view structure
               <FS_ITAB> TYPE TABLE, " Field Symbol for internal table
               <FS_FLD>.  " Field Symbol for individual fields

PARAMETERS TABLE_NM  TYPE DD03L-TABNAME DEFAULT 'T001' VALUE CHECK.

*******************************************************************
START-OF-SELECTION.

CREATE DATA STRU_REF TYPE (TABLE_NM). " creation of run time structure

ASSIGN STRU_REF->* TO <FS_STRU>. " dereference and assign to Field Symbol

CREATE DATA ITAB_REF TYPE STANDARD TABLE OF (TABLE_NM). " creation of run time internal table

ASSIGN ITAB_REF->* TO <FS_ITAB>. " dereference and assign to Field Symbol

SELECT * FROM (TABLE_NM) INTO TABLE <FS_ITAB>. " source at run time

LOOP AT <FS_ITAB> INTO <FS_STRU>.
 DO 6 TIMES.
  IF SY-INDEX = 1. " bypass the presumed client code (first) field
   CONTINUE.
  ENDIF.
  ASSIGN COMPONENT SY-INDEX OF STRUCTURE <FS_STRU> TO <FS_FLD>.
   " Field Symbol <FS_FLD> being assigned & re-assigned
  IF SY-INDEX = 2.
   WRITE:/5 <FS_FLD>. " new line for the first outputted field
  ELSE.
   WRITE: <FS_FLD>.
  ENDIF.
 ENDDO.
ENDLOOP.
```

The output for the input value T001 will look like Figure 8-23.
You can try this for a few other tables.

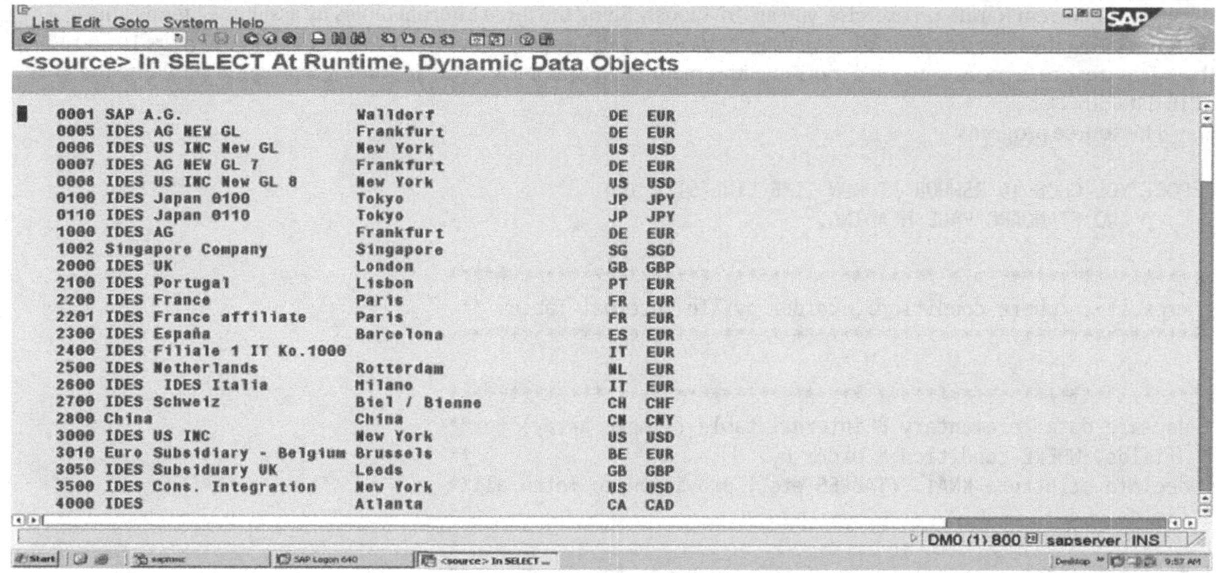

Figure 8-23. Program: YCL_CH08_18_SRCE_AT_RUN_TIME - Output

You have seen the power of SELECT statement, field symbols and dynamic data objects in combination in this program.

In Chapter 10 entitled 'Interactive Lists,' you will incorporate further functionality into this program. The program on input of database table or view name will first display all the fields of the table or view structure with check boxes for the user to select/de-select fields. Once the fields are selected, the program will retrieve data only for the selected fields and output the selected fields with column headings, etc.

Specify in the Open SQL SELECT Statement Run Time <result>, <where condition>, and <order by>

```
SELECT (<result>) FROM <source>
INTO <destination>
WHERE (<where condition>)
ORDER BY (<order by>).
```

Mark the *<result>*, *<where condition>* and *<order by>* enclosed in parentheses.

With this syntax:

You can load an internal table with the name of the fields *<result>* for which you want data to be retrieved.

You can load another internal table with the WHERE condition *<where condition>* to be applied to the SELECT statement. Part of the WHERE condition can be in the internal table *<where condition>*, part can be hard-coded and the two conjoined by the logical operators AND and OR if required.

You can load a third internal table with the name of the fields *<order by>* for which you want the data to be sorted.

When you are supplying the *<result>*, *<where condition>* and *<order by>* in internal tables, you have the facility to effectively build these on a runtime basis.

You can supply any one of these, any two of these, or all of these in internal tables.

The Open SQL system concatenates the individual rows of each of these internal tables into one string.

In your current hands-on exercise, you are frivolously filling the three internal tables by assigning literals and demonstrating the features of *<result>*, *<where condition>*, and *<order by>* in internal tables. But in Chapters 10 and 13, these features are demonstrated in a more effective manner. In Chapter 13, you are coding a program similar to the SE16 data browser.

The source program:

```
REPORT YCL_CH08_19_RSWHOR_AT_RUN_TIME LINE-SIZE 140
       NO STANDARD PAGE HEADING.

*************************************************************
* <result>, <where condition>, <order by> In Internal Tables **
*************************************************************

*************************************************************
* declare data: elementary & internal table (simple array) for**
*  fields, WHERE condition & order by.                       **
* declare structure KNA1. (TABLES etc.) provision to fetch all**
* fields.                                                    **
*                                                            **
* fill the first internal table with field names for which   **
* data to be retrieved.                                      **
* fill the second internal table with the WHERE condition    **
* fill the third internal table with order by field names with**
* order by option: ASCENDING/DESCENDING.                     **
*                                                            **
* SELECT...WRITE...ENDSELECT statements with the usage of the **
* three internal tables                                      **
*************************************************************

TABLES: KNA1.

DATA: FIELD(15)   TYPE C,
      FIELDS_TAB  LIKE STANDARD TABLE OF FIELD, " for <result> in internal table
      CONDT(50)   TYPE C,
      CONDTS_TAB  LIKE STANDARD TABLE OF CONDT, " for <where condition> in internal table
      ORDER(30)   TYPE C,
      ORDER_TAB   LIKE STANDARD TABLE OF ORDER. " for <order by> in internal table
*****************************************************
START-OF-SELECTION.

FIELD  = 'KUNNR'.
APPEND FIELD TO FIELDS_TAB.

FIELD  = 'NAME1'.
APPEND FIELD TO FIELDS_TAB.

*FIELD  = 'STRAS'. " de-comment these lines & try out
*APPEND FIELD TO FIELDS_TAB.

FIELD  = 'ORT01'.
APPEND FIELD TO FIELDS_TAB.
```

```
CONDT = 'NAME1 LIKE ''A%'' OR '.
APPEND CONDT TO CONDTS_TAB.

CONDT = 'NAME1 LIKE ''C%'' OR '.
APPEND CONDT TO CONDTS_TAB.

CONDT = 'NAME1 LIKE ''S%'''.
APPEND CONDT TO CONDTS_TAB.

ORDER = 'ORT01 DESCENDING'.
APPEND ORDER TO ORDER_TAB.

ORDER = 'NAME1 ASCENDING'.
APPEND ORDER TO ORDER_TAB.

****************************************
SELECT (FIELDS_TAB) FROM KNA1
     INTO CORRESPONDING FIELDS OF KNA1
     WHERE (CONDTS_TAB)
     ORDER BY (ORDER_TAB).

 WRITE:/5(5) SY-DBCNT, KNA1-ORT01, KNA1-NAME1, KNA1-KUNNR USING NO EDIT MASK,
        KNA1-STRAS.
ENDSELECT.
```

The output will appear like Figure 8-24.

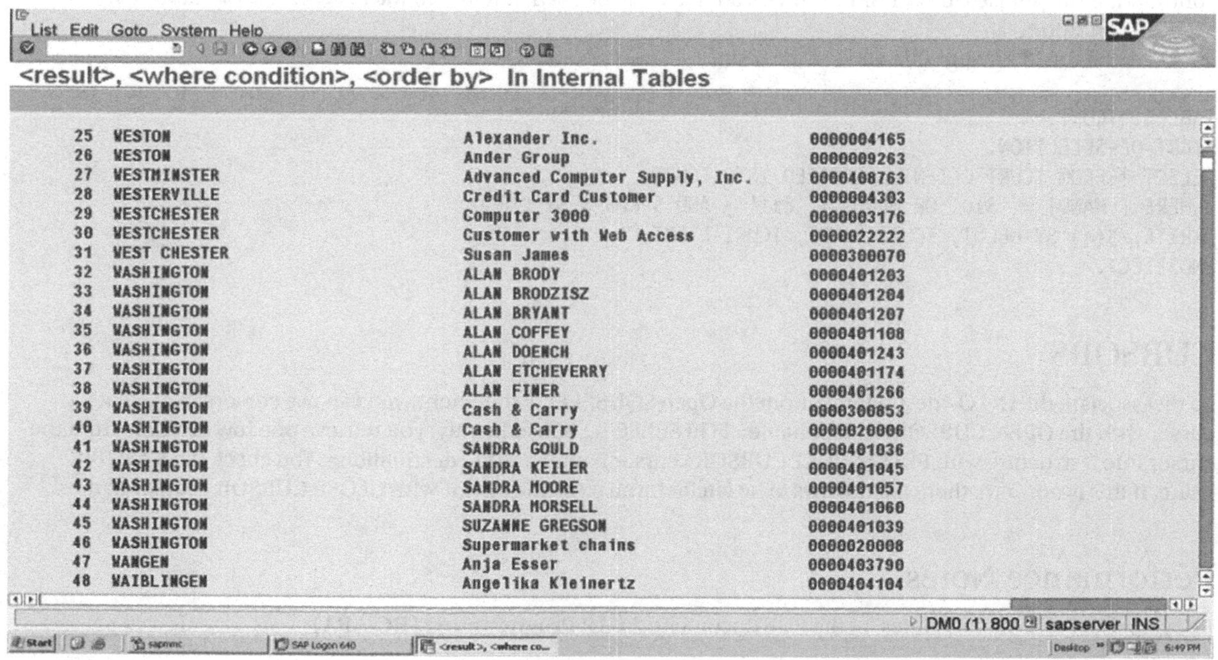

Figure 8-24. *Program: YCL_CH08_19_RSWHOR_AT_RUN_TIME - Output*

If you scroll to the right, the field STRAS will appear blank, because you are not retrieving data for it. De-comment the lines to append a row for the field STRAS. Executing the program after de-commenting the lines will make the output for field STRAS appear.

Similarly, a SELECT statement with aggregate functions can have the <group by fields> and <having condition> entered in an internal table and specified (i.e., run time <group by fields> and <having condition>).

BYPASSING BUFFER, CLIENT SPECIFIED, CURSORS

BYPASSING BUFFER

To circumvent the buffer, fetch data directly from the database table or view, or you can use the BYPASSING BUFFER phrase in the Open SQL SELECT statement:

```
SELECT ... FROM <source>
BYPASSING BUFFER..
```

CLIENT SPECIFIED

It was emphasized earlier that OPEN SQL by default retrieves only data belonging to the user's logged-in client. If you want to retrieve data other than the one belonging to the logged-in client, you can use the phrase CLIENT SPECIFIED in the Open SQL SELECT statement:

```
SELECT ... FROM <source>
CLIENT SPECIFIED..
```

By default, the Open SQL SELECT statement does not allow the client code field MANDT in the WHERE condition. If the phrase CLIENT SPECIFIED is added in the SELECT statement, the field MANDT is allowed in the WHERE condition.

Execute the following code and see the result:

```
TABLES: TCURT.
START-OF-SELECTION.
SELECT * FROM TCURT CLIENT SPECIFIED INTO TCURT
 WHERE ( MANDT = '810' OR MANDT = '811' ) AND SPRAS = SY-LANGU.
 WRITE:/5(4) SY-DBCNT, TCURT-MANDT, TCURT-LTEXT.
ENDSELECT.
```

CURSORS

To disassociate the INTO <destination> from the Open SQL SELECT statement, you can use cursors. You create a cursor with the OPEN CURSOR <cursor name> FOR SELECT... Subsequently, you retrieve one row at a time from the cursor into a structure with FETCH NEXT CURSOR <cursor name> INTO <destination>. You check the SY-SUBRC value. If this is not zero, there are no rows to be fetched. You close the cursor with CLOSE CURSOR <cursor name>.

Performance Notes

Read up the 'Performance Notes' of the PDF document: **ABAP Programming (BC-ABA)**.

A Brief on ABAP Debugger

A program debugger is part of any developmental platform. When programs do not execute as per specifications, errors or bugs have to be located and identified. The identified bugs have to be fixed. The debuggers help in locating and identifying the bugs. The program bugs relate to program flow and variables not assuming values as planned. So the debuggers must have the facility to trace program flow and interrogate variable values at different stages of program execution, even at the level of single statement execution.

Break Points, Watch Points, and Executing Programs in Debugging Mode

The ABAP debugger provides for break points and watch points during program execution. Program halts occur because of the break points and/or watch points. A break point can be set on any executable ABAP statement (dynamic break points). A break point can also be set with a special ABAP statement: BREAK-POINT (static break points). When the program executes and reaches the statement where a break point has been set or reaches the special ABAP statement 'BREAK-POINT,' a program halt occurs. The watch points, like the break points, generate halts in program execution. The watch point halts are determined by values of watch point variables. The watch points are set by associating a watch point with a variable and specifying the value/range of a watch point variable. When a watch point variable assumes a value/range set for the watch point variable, a halt occurs in the program execution. When a program halt occurs, generated by a break point or a watch point, the ABAP debugger pop ups a dialog box. This dialog box will be called the debugger dialog box. The ABAP debugger dialog box is a full screen dialog box. In the debugger dialog box, the developer can interrogate data object values, change data object values, set further break points, reset existing break points, view memory allocation of data objects including the internal tables, and set and reset watch points, etc.

Apart from the break points and watch points generating program halts and popping up the debugger dialog box, you can execute an ABAP program in a debugging mode instead of the normal mode.

Dynamic break points can be set and reset before the commencement of program execution and also during program execution during the halts. Watch points cannot be set and reset before the commencement of program execution. Watch points can be set and reset only during program halts (i.e., when debugging, the dialog box pops up).

Debugger Types

In the ABAP workbench, two debugger types are available: the *classical debugger* and the *new debugger.* You can set which debugger type you want to use either from the ABAP editor opening screen or the ABAP program editor screen. The menu path to set the debugger: Utilities ➤ Settings. In the settings dialog box, ensure that you have selected the *ABAP Editor* tab and the *Debugging* tab. The screen for setting the debugger is shown in Figure 8-25.

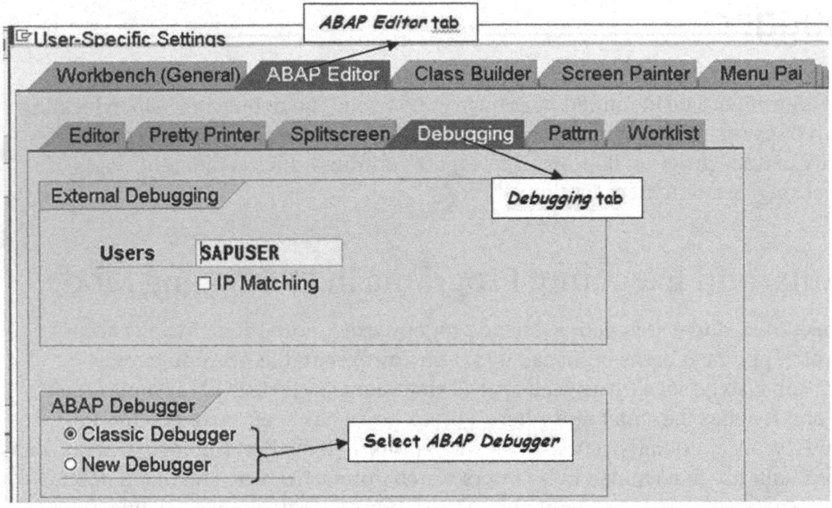

Figure 8-25. *Select ABAP Debugger*

The *new debugger* is an advanced version of the older *classical debugger*.

One of the basic and obvious differences between the *classical debugger* and the *new debugger* is the appearance of a debugger dialog box during program halts. With the *new debugger*, the debugger dialog box appears in a new external session (extra external session); whereas with the *classical debugger*, the debugger dialog box appearing during program execution halt is in the same external session in which the program is being executed and debugged. Apart from this, there are a host of other differences between the *new debugger* and the *classical debugger*. The *new debugger* is to suitable for use in advanced programming involving many levels of procedure and method calls.

This brief on an ABAP debugger is confined to coverage of only the classical debugger.

Break Point Types

There are two types of break points: static and dynamic.

The static break points can be set with the special ABAP statement: BREAK-POINT. When the program execution reaches this statement, the debugger dialog pops up, enabling the developer to interrogate data object values, set new dynamic break points, reset existing dynamic break points, set watch points, reset existing watch points, and control subsequent program halts, etc. The static break point statements should be deleted or commented before the program is released to the end user.

There are two types of dynamic break points: internal and external. If you want program halts to occur in external procedures like external subroutines, function modules, and methods of global classes being called by your main program, you set external break points in the external subroutines, function modules, and methods of global classes. The external break points expire or get reset after a time period (time out) set by the basis administrator.

The internal break points are set in the main program you are testing. The internal break points get reset when the user logs off. The internal break points can be set only for activated programs.

The dynamic break points can be set by positioning the cursor on a program executable line and clicking on the internal/external break point button on the application toolbar.

The static break points are rarely used in ABAP programs. They are used in environments where there is no facility for dynamic break points – like, for example, the 'Smart Forms' (not covered in this book). In the present coverage and demonstrations, you will only use dynamic break points. So the terms 'dynamic break point' and 'break point' are synonymous in the present discussion.

Execute Programs in Debugging Mode

You can execute a program in debugging mode by selecting the following menu option on the ABAP editor opening screen: Program ➤ Execute ➤ Debugging. You can also execute an ABAP program in debugging mode from inside the ABAP editor with the menu option: Program ➤ Test ➤ Debugging.

With this brief introduction and description of break points and watch points, further debugging features will be explained through hands-on exercises.

At any given time, for a logged-in user, you can have a maximum of 30 dynamic (internal + external) break points and a maximum of 10 watch points.

Hands-On Exercise I - ABAP Debugger

Let the ABAP source program YCL_CH05_05_CUST_:LIST04 of Chapter 5 be debugged. A dynamic (internal) break point is set on the statement: `FLAG = 'X'` as shown in Figure 8-26.

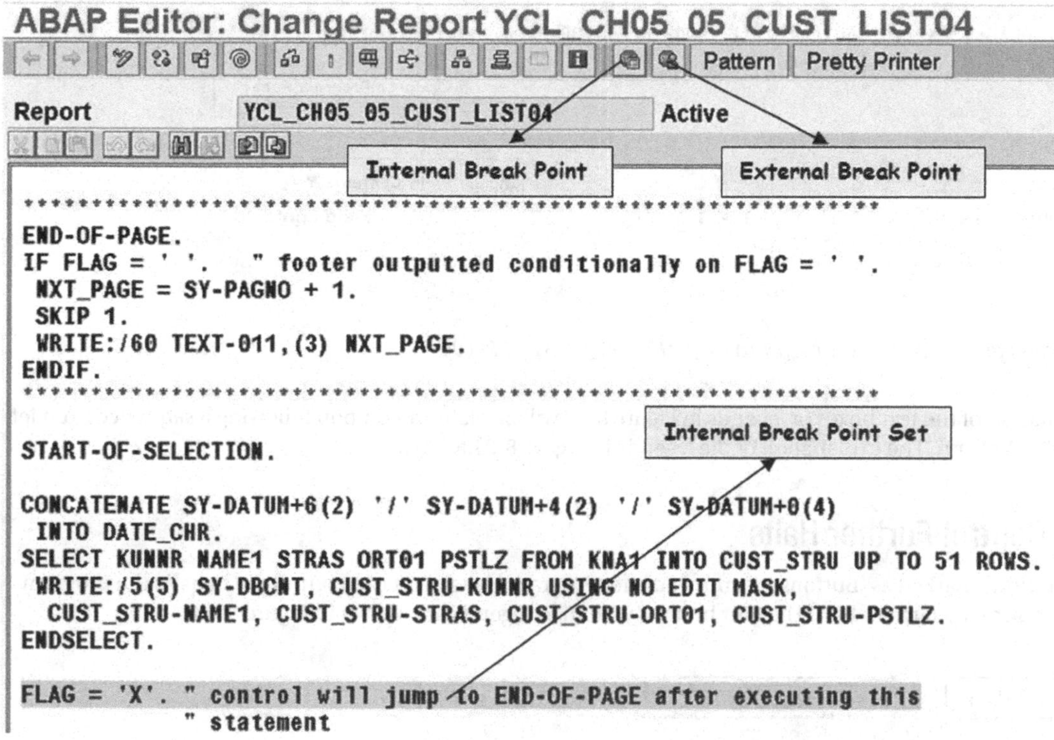


```
*****************************************************************
END-OF-PAGE.
IF FLAG = ' '.    " footer outputted conditionally on FLAG = ' '.
 NXT_PAGE = SY-PAGNO + 1.
 SKIP 1.
 WRITE:/60 TEXT-011,(3) NXT_PAGE.
ENDIF.
*****************************************************************

START-OF-SELECTION.

CONCATENATE SY-DATUM+6(2) '/' SY-DATUM+4(2) '/' SY-DATUM+0(4)
 INTO DATE_CHR.
SELECT KUNNR NAME1 STRAS ORT01 PSTLZ FROM KNA1 INTO CUST_STRU UP TO 51 ROWS.
 WRITE:/5(5) SY-DBCNT, CUST_STRU-KUNNR USING NO EDIT MASK,
  CUST_STRU-NAME1, CUST_STRU-STRAS, CUST_STRU-ORT01, CUST_STRU-PSTLZ.
ENDSELECT.

FLAG = 'X'. " control will jump to END-OF-PAGE after executing this
            " statement
```

Figure 8-26. *Program YCL_CH05_CUST_:LIST04 - Set Internal Break Point*

In this program, you listed the customer data with a nonstandard header and footer. You output one line of footer as 'Continued on XX.' The footer should not appear on last page of the list. The footer was appearing on the last page if the rows output were a multiple of lines output in the list body. A solution to this problem was proposed, which was based on the flow/sequence of execution of program lines. It was maintained that the event END-OF-PAGE for the last page was triggered after execution of program lines following the ENDSELECT statement. You can verify this program flow using the debugger.

As shown in Figure 8-26, a break point is set on the statement FLAG = 'X' following the statement ENDSELECT. With a default color setting, an ABAP program statement with a break point set appears in a yellow background. When the program is executed, the break point on the statement FLAG = 'X' will trigger a halt, and the debugger dialog box will pop up as shown in Figure 8-27.

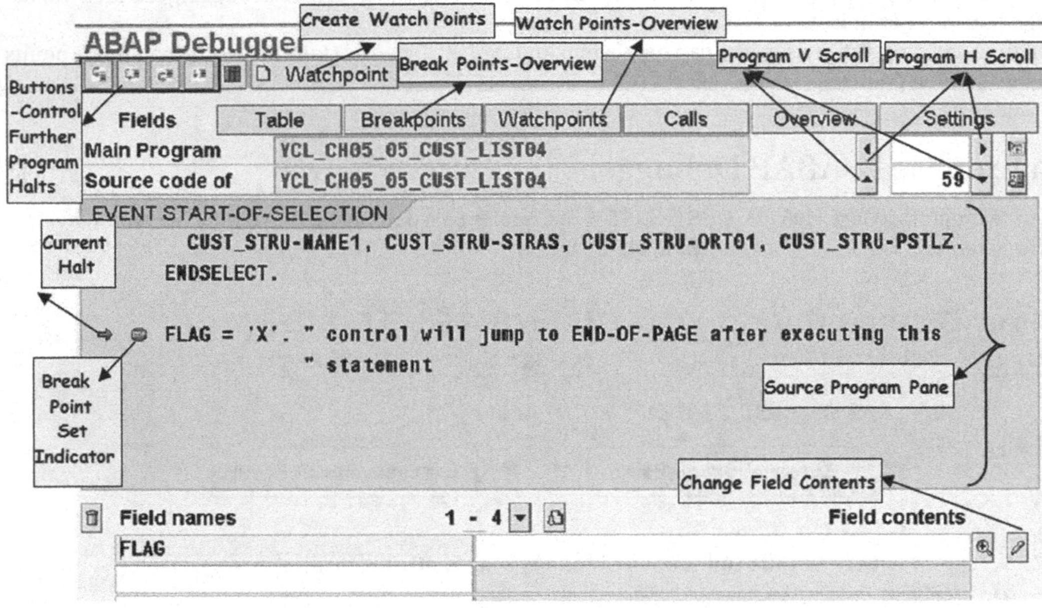

Figure 8-27. *Debugger Dialog Box, Program YCL_CH05_05_CUST_:LIST04*

The explanation of the text boxes or legends in Figure 8-27 will be elaborated upon following a sequence from left to right and top to bottom. The explanation of the legends in Figure 8-27 follows.

Buttons to Control Further Halts

With the four buttons marked as 'Buttons - Control Further Program Halts', you can control the halts as the program executes further from the current halt. The four buttons with their legends are shown in Figure 8-28.

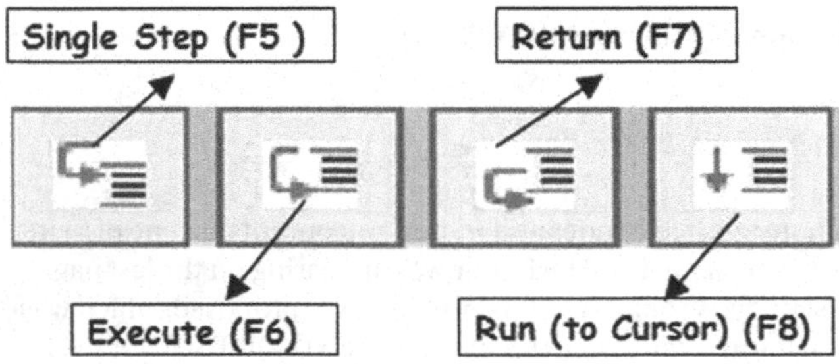

Figure 8-28. *Debugger Dialog Box: Buttons for 'Control Further Program Halts'*

The left-most button with the legend 'Single Step (F5)' enables you to execute the program statement by statement (i.e., halt will occur on each statement). If a procedure (external subroutine or function module or method) is called, the halts occur at every statement of the called procedure as well. This button should be used as the last resort, as in the extreme case when you want to debug every statement.

The second button from the left with the legend 'Execute (F6)' also enables you to execute the program statement by statement but differs from the execution when using the first button. A procedure call (external subroutine or function module or method) is considered a single statement. If there are no break points or watch points in the called procedure, then, when you click on this button when a halt has occurred on a statement calling the procedure, the next halt occurs on the statement following the statement calling the procedure.

If your current halt is inside a procedure (external subroutine or function module or method), there are no further break points or watch points in this procedure, and clicking on the third button from the left with the legend 'Return (F7)' will trigger the next halt at a statement following the statement calling the procedure. This is shown graphically in Figure 8-29.

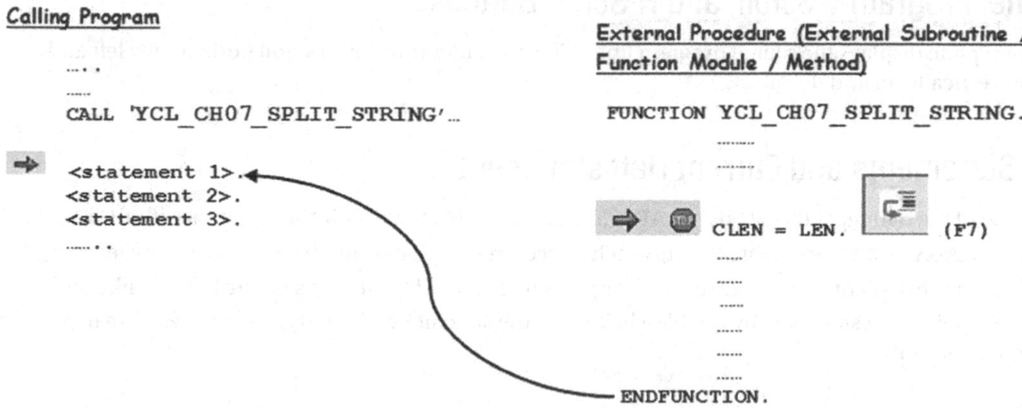

Figure 8-29. *Operation of 'Control Further Program Halts' Button: 'Return (F7)'*

Clicking the button on the extreme right with the legend 'Run (To Cursor) (F8)' will execute the program and trigger program halts based only on break points and watch points encountered.

Button to Create Watch Point

Clicking on this button will pop up the watch point creation dialog box. In the watch point creation dialog box, you can specify the watch point data object (variable) and the value/range of watch point variable. The watch point creation is demonstrated in the subsequent hands-on exercise.

Buttons – Display Field (Contents) and Table (Internal Table Contents)

The first of the two buttons is used to display and change elementary data object contents. The second of the two buttons is used to display and change internal table contents. You can also insert and append rows to internal tables. You can delete rows from internal tables. You can change contents of rows of internal tables. The debugger dialog box showing internal table contents is covered in the subsequent hands-on exercise.

To view structure contents, select the following menu path in the debugger dialog box: Go to ➤ Display data object ➤ structure field. The system will prompt for structure name. When you enter the structure name, the structure is displayed field wise, each field in one row. Structure contents cannot be changed directly. To change structure data, you have to access individual fields of the structure. If the structure contains only elementary types: C, D, N, and T, the structure can be displayed as one field.

In Figure 8-27, the field 'FLAG' is entered and its value is displayed. You can enter any elementary data object or a system field and its value will be displayed. By default, four system fields values are displayed at the bottom of the debugger dialog box.

Buttons – Break Points and Watch Points Overview

These two buttons pop up the break points and watch points overview dialog boxes.

Program Pane, Program V Scroll, and H Scroll Buttons

The source program pane displays the source program lines. There are four buttons to scroll horizontally left and right, and to scroll vertically up and down.

Break Point Statements and Current Halt statement

In the program pane of the debugger dialog box, an ABAP statement with a break point set appears with the icon on the left side and an ABAP statement where the current halt occurred appears with the icon on the left side. An ABAP statement with a break point and the current halt appears with both of these icons on the left side like this: . You can reset a break point on a statement by double-clicking on the statement. Similarly, you can set a break point by double-clicking on the statement.

Change Field Contents Button

At the bottom right, there is a button to confirm the change of contents of a field.

Following the Program Flow

In Figure 8-27, the program has halted at the statement `FLAG = 'X'`. The value of the variable FLAG is blank at this stage.

In the source program pane, scroll up and set a break point at the statement `IF FLAG = ' '` following the event statement: END-OF-PAGE. A break point can be set by positioning the cursor on the statement and selecting the menu option: Break Points ➤ Create/Delete. A break point on a statement can be set or reset by double-clicking on the statement.

Next, click on the 'Run' (function key F8) button. The debugger dialog box will appear for the break point set at the statement `IF FLAG = ' '`. The value of the variable FLAG is now 'X'. This is shown in Figure 8-30.

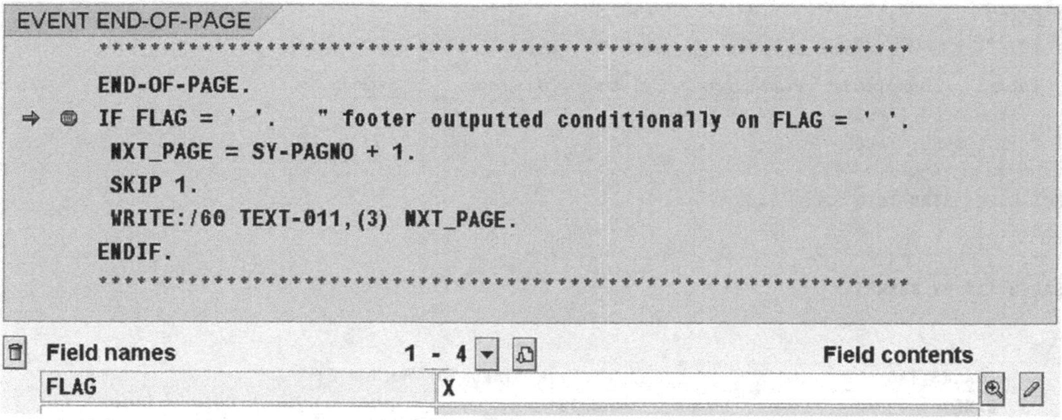

```
EVENT END-OF-PAGE
     ****************************************************************
     END-OF-PAGE.
⇒ ●  IF FLAG = ' '.    " footer outputted conditionally on FLAG = ' '.
      NXT_PAGE = SY-PAGNO + 1.
      SKIP 1.
      WRITE:/60 TEXT-011,(3) NXT_PAGE.
     ENDIF.
     ****************************************************************

Field names                    1 - 4          Field contents
FLAG                           X
```

Figure 8-30. *Break Point halt at statement:* `IF FLAG = ' '`

The program flow is as per the claims made in Chapter 5, and the program lines following the ENDSELECT statement get executed before the END-OF-PAGE event gets triggered for the last page of the list.

The next hands-on exercise will demonstrate the display of internal table content and watch points.

Hands-on Exercise II - ABAP Debugger

Let the ABAP source program YCL_CH06_ITAB05 of Chapter 6 be debugged. In this program, you listed customer wise sales summary of a specific company code. You used the internal table COLLECT statement to generate the sales summary. A dynamic (internal) break point is set on the statement: `SORT SALES_TAB BY KUNNR`. Execute the program with company code '3000'. When the program is executed with this dynamic break point, the program comes to a halt and pops up the debugger dialog box as shown in Figure 8-31.

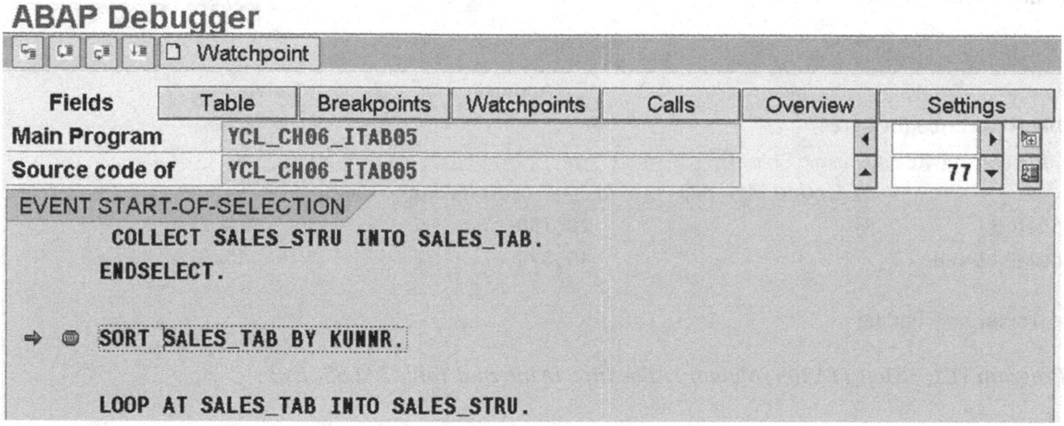

```
ABAP Debugger
Watchpoint
Fields | Table | Breakpoints | Watchpoints | Calls | Overview | Settings
Main Program     YCL_CH06_ITAB05
Source code of   YCL_CH06_ITAB05                          77
EVENT START-OF-SELECTION
      COLLECT SALES_STRU INTO SALES_TAB.
     ENDSELECT.

⇒ ●  SORT SALES_TAB BY KUNNR.

     LOOP AT SALES_TAB INTO SALES_STRU.
```

Figure 8-31. *Internal Break Point in Program YCL_CH06_ITAB05*

If you click on the Table button, the debugger dialog box will prompt for the internal table name. Enter the internal table name as SALES_TAB. You can view the contents of the internal table SALES_TAB as shown in Figure 8-32.

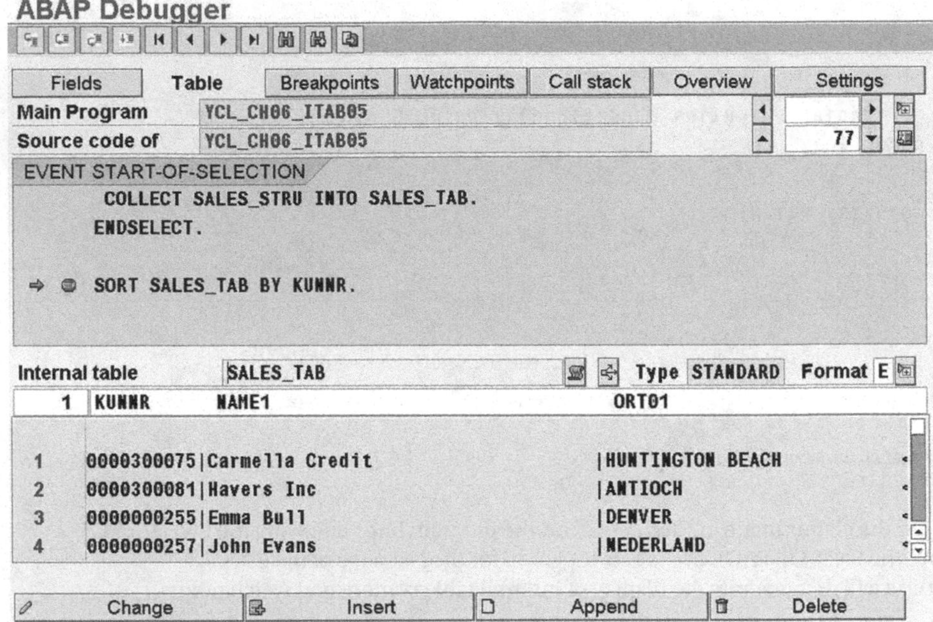

Figure 8-32. *Program YCL_CH06_ITAB05: Internal Table SALES_TAB Contents*

As shown in Figure 8-32, you can change row contents, insert rows, append rows, and delete rows in the internal table with buttons provided at the bottom of the debugger dialog box.

If you want the memory allocation information for the internal tables, select the menu option: Settings ➤ Memory Display On/Off. This menu option toggles for appearance or disappearance of the memory allocation of data objects. The memory allocations appear at the bottom of the ABAP debugger screen. Figure 8-33 shows the memory allocation for the internal table SALES_TAB.

Change | Insert | Append | Delete

Length of Table Reference (in Bytes) 88

Memory Consumption in Bytes (Dynamic Share)

	Bound Memory	Referenced Memory
Memory Allocated	20,760	20,760
Memory Actually Used	15,376	15,376

Memory use display switched on

Figure 8-33. *Program YCL_CH06_ITAB05 -Memory Allocation of Internal Table SALES_TAB*

Let a watch point be created. When you click the button to display internal table contents, the application tool bar changes and the button to create watch points disappears. So to create a watch point, make the following menu selection: Break Points ➤ Create watchpoint. When you make this menu selection, the following dialog appears:

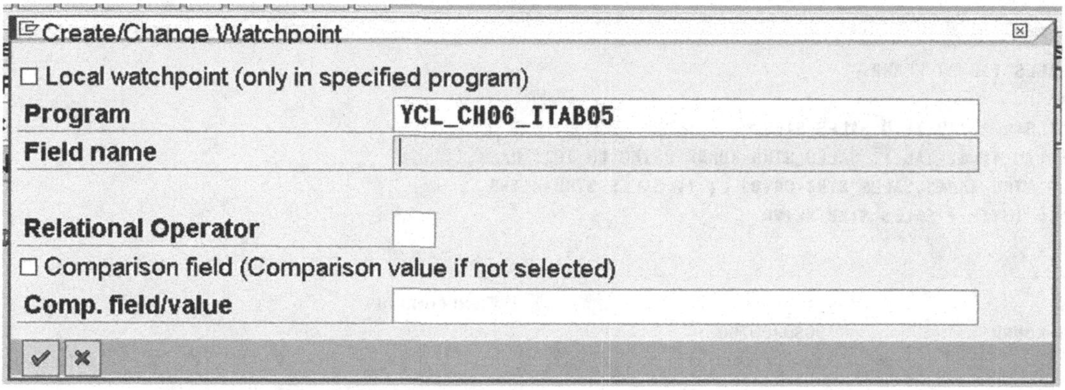

Create/Change Watchpoint
☐ Local watchpoint (only in specified program)
Program YCL_CH06_ITAB05
Field name
Relational Operator
☐ Comparison field (Comparison value if not selected)
Comp. field/value

Figure 8-34. *Dialog Box to Create a Watch Point*

In the watch point dialog box, you enter the watch point field name or watch point variable for which you want to establish a watch point in the field 'Field name'. You enter the watch point relation operator in the field 'Relational Operator'. The relational operators accepted are <, <=, =, <>, >=, and >. The mnemonic equivalents of these arithmetical relational operators are also accepted. A selection list (F4) is available. You can compare the watch point variable either with another variable or a literal. If you are comparing the watch point variable with another variable, (comparison variable), enable the check box with the legend 'Comparison field...' If you are comparing the watch point variable with a literal, then ensure this check box is disabled. Enter the comparison variable or literal in the field 'Comp. field/value'.

Let a watch point be created for the variable 'SALES_STRU-NETWR'. So enter this variable as the watch point variable. Select the relational operator as 'GE' (>=). Let the watch point variable be compared with a literal. Enter the value 4000000 (four million) in the field 'Comp. field value'. What you desire is that whenever the watch point variable 'SALES_STRU-NETWR' is greater than or equal to four million, a halt must occur. Figure 8-35 shows the watch point dialog box with the entered values.

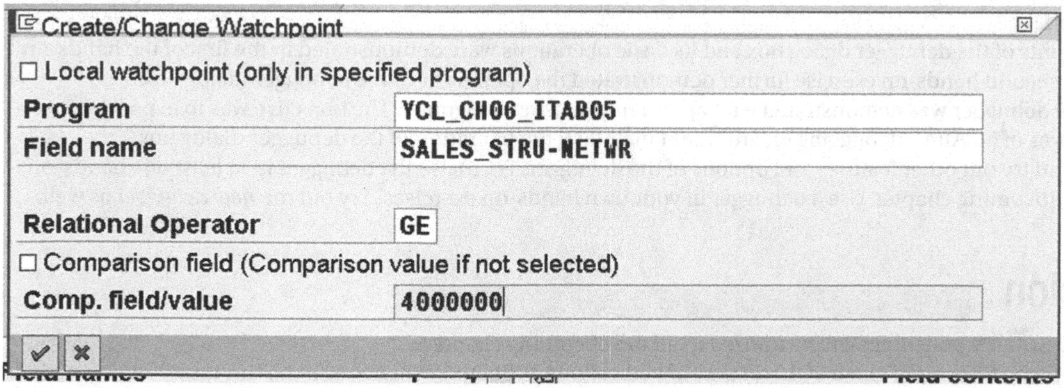

Create/Change Watchpoint
☐ Local watchpoint (only in specified program)
Program YCL_CH06_ITAB05
Field name SALES_STRU-NETWR
Relational Operator GE
☐ Comparison field (Comparison value if not selected)
Comp. field/value 4000000

Figure 8-35. *Watch Point Dialog Box with Entered Values*

Click on the continue button of the watch point creation dialog box. A watch point creation message will appear on the status bar. Click on the 'Run (To Cursor) (F8)' button. A halt will occur every time the value of the watch point variable >= 4,000,000. In this program, the first time the watch point halt occurs for the customer code SALES_STRU-KUNNR = '0000300700'. The value of system field SY-TABIX is 46. This is shown in Figure 8-36.

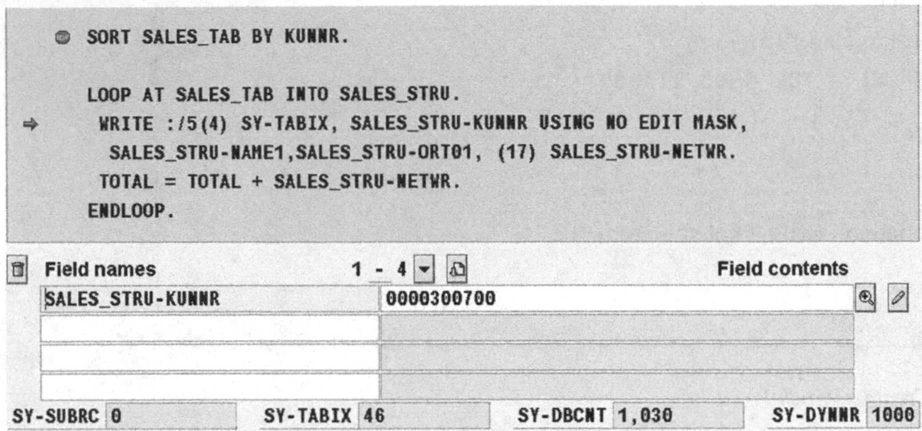

Figure 8-36. *Watch Point Halt for SALES_STRU-KUNNR = '0000300700'*

In a like manner, five more halts will occur when the watch point variable SALES_STRU-NETWR >= 4000000. The corresponding values of the field SALES_STRU-KUNNR for the five halts are '0000300701', '0000300703', '0000300704', '0000300705', and '0000300719'. The corresponding values of the system field SY-TABIX for the five halts are 47, 48, 50, 51, and 60.

This was a demonstration of viewing an internal table contents, viewing memory allocation of an internal table, and the setting up of a watch point.

Conclusion - ABAP Debugger

This brief on the ABAP debugger introduced you to the debugger types and setting a debugger type. It introduced you to the break points, types of break points, and watch points. You learned how to execute an ABAP program in debugging mode.

The elements of the debugger dialog box and its basic operations were demonstrated in the first of the hands-on exercises. The second hands-on exercise further demonstrated the operations of the debugger dialog box.

The ABAP debugger was demonstrated with apparently bug-free programs. The objective was to expose you to the basic features of an ABAP debugging environment including the operation of the debugger dialog box.

Explore and try out other features and options of the debugger. Try to use the debugger in at least one hands-on exercise of an upcoming chapter. Use a debugger in your own hands-on exercises. Try out the *new debugger* as well.

Conclusion

The Open SQL SELECT statement will be utilized in all the upcoming chapters.

The threesome features of Open SQL run time specifications, FIELD-SYMBOLS, and the run time creation of data objects is carried forward and developed in Chapters 10 and 13 into advanced sophisticated applications.

You were also introduced in this chapter to the ABAP debugger.

CHAPTER 9

SELECTION-SCREENS

ABAP programs that are generating outputs or reports use selection screens for simple inputs. For full-fledged, multiple screen data input and data capturing, the ABAP Workbench provides a screen painter with drag and drop and all the other facilities associated with creating input screens and programs in a graphical environment.

You have used some forms of the selection screen statement PARAMETERS in your hands-on exercises. You used it in the program demonstrating the COLLECT statement to input the company code for which the customer wise sales summary report was to be generated.

In enterprise environments, the output to be generated will, for the most part, be of filtered data: of specified company codes, plant codes, etc. The basis of filtering data is to be decided at runtime. So the appropriate values for data filtration are input through the selection screen.

The PARAMETERS statement enabled input of single values. The ABAP selection screen provides for multiple, complex inputs through the SELECT-OPTIONS statement to be covered later in this chapter.

The PARAMETERS and SELECT-OPTIONS variables belong to the category of special data objects. In Chapter 4, ABAP program data objects were categorized as the following:

Internal data objects (through declarative statements: DATA, TABLES, and CONSTANTS, etc.)

External data objects (references to DDIC tables, structures, table or structure fields, internal tables, and data elements)

Special data objects (selection screen PARAMETERS and SELECT-OPTIONS variables)

System data objects (the SY- series variables: SY-DATUM, SY-MANDT..., etc.)

The selection screen does not provide for positioning of screen elements through drag-and drop-facility. With the selection screen, you have to write ABAP code to create and position screen elements. The ABAP runtime system automatically generates the screens from the selection screen code.

In the ABAP Workbench environment, screens are numbered from 1-9999 for identification. The selection screens can be standard with a preassigned screen number 1000. The selection screens can be user defined with the screen number assigned during the selection screen definition. With the user defined selection screens, they need to be called after the definition.

With an executable ABAP program, you can have one standard selection screen (screen number 1000) and any number of user defined selection screens. With module pool programs and function modules, you can have only user defined selection screens.

You can create the following screen elements on the selection screens:

- Labels or texts
- Text boxes or input fields
- Radio buttons
- Check boxes
- Multiple complex selections (SELECT-OPTIONS)
- Push buttons

- Blank lines
- Blocks
- Horizontal lines
- Subscreens
- Tab strip controls

In the hands-on exercises in this chapter, the major screen elements are going to be covered. The screen elements subscreens and tab strip controls will be covered in Chapter 14.

The selection screen will be covered in two separate stages: (a) the layout - how to create position screen elements on the selection screen, and (b) the selection screen events and other subtopics.

All selection screen statements start with one of the key phrases:

1. SELECTION-SCREEN
2. PARAMETERS
3. SELECT-OPTIONS

Recapitulation – PARAMETERS Statement

Before a hands-on exercise, let the features of PARAMETERS statement that you have used until now be recapitulated formally. The syntax of PARAMETERS statement:

```
PARAMETERS: <variable name> {TYPE | LIKE}
<ABAP elementary TYPE or reference to local or global TYPE or local or global data object>
LOWER CASE
DEFAULT <default value>
VALUE CHECK
MATCHCODE OBJECT <search help name>.
```

<variable name> - Can be a maximum of eight characters, must start with an alphabet letter, and the rest can be alphanumeric with embedded underscores (_).

{TYPE | LIKE} - You can use the keyword TYPE/LIKE. Refer to 'Summary of Data Declaration by Reference to Other Data Objects, Types' available in the E-Resource of Chapter 6.

<ABAP elementary predefined TYPES> - TYPES C, D, I, N, P, T, X, STRING. TYPE 'F' and TYPE XSTRING are not supported.

<reference to local or global TYPES> -Reference can be to locally declared types with the keyword TYPES. Or it can be a reference to a DDIC data element or a DDIC TYPE GROUP.

<reference to local or global data object> - Reference can be to a locally declared data object or it can be a reference to a DDIC data object.

LOWER CASE - Case sensitivity for TYPE C and TYPE STRING (by default, case insensitive).

DEFAULT <default value> - To assign an initial or starting value to the input field.

VALUE CHECK - To have the entered value checked against values in a check table. The PARAMETERS variable should be declared by reference to a foreign key field in a secondary table.

MATCHCODE OBJECT <search help name> - Attach a search help.

There are some more clauses or additions available with the PARAMETERS statement. They will be covered as contexts arise.

By convention, the selection screen statements are located in an ABAP program after the data declarations. An ABAP program should have the program's global data declared in the very beginning followed by the selection screen statements.

By convention, the selection screen events follow the selection screen statements. When an ABAP program is executed, the selection screen statements get executed with input prompts that appear. When the execute button/F8 is pressed on the selection screen, the non-selection screen statements get executed. The program after the end of execution of non-selection screen statements returns to the selection screen input prompt.

You can check this out executing the ABAP program with the COLLECT statement (YCL_CH06_ITAB05). Initially the system prompts for the company code. Input of a valid company code and pressing the execute button/F8 generates the sales summary list or report for the input company code. Pressing the back button/F3 on the list takes you back to the selection screen prompting you for the company code.

Selection Screen: Layout and Positioning of Screen Elements

Instead of covering each of the selection screen elements creation and positioning in isolation, a hands-on exercise will be undertaken; and the creation and positioning of selection screen elements will be introduced in the context of the hands-on exercise.

Your exercise is to reproduce in appearance and looks the ABAP Editor opening screen using the selection screen statements.

A screenshot of the SE38 ABAP Editor opening screen is shown in Figure 9-1.

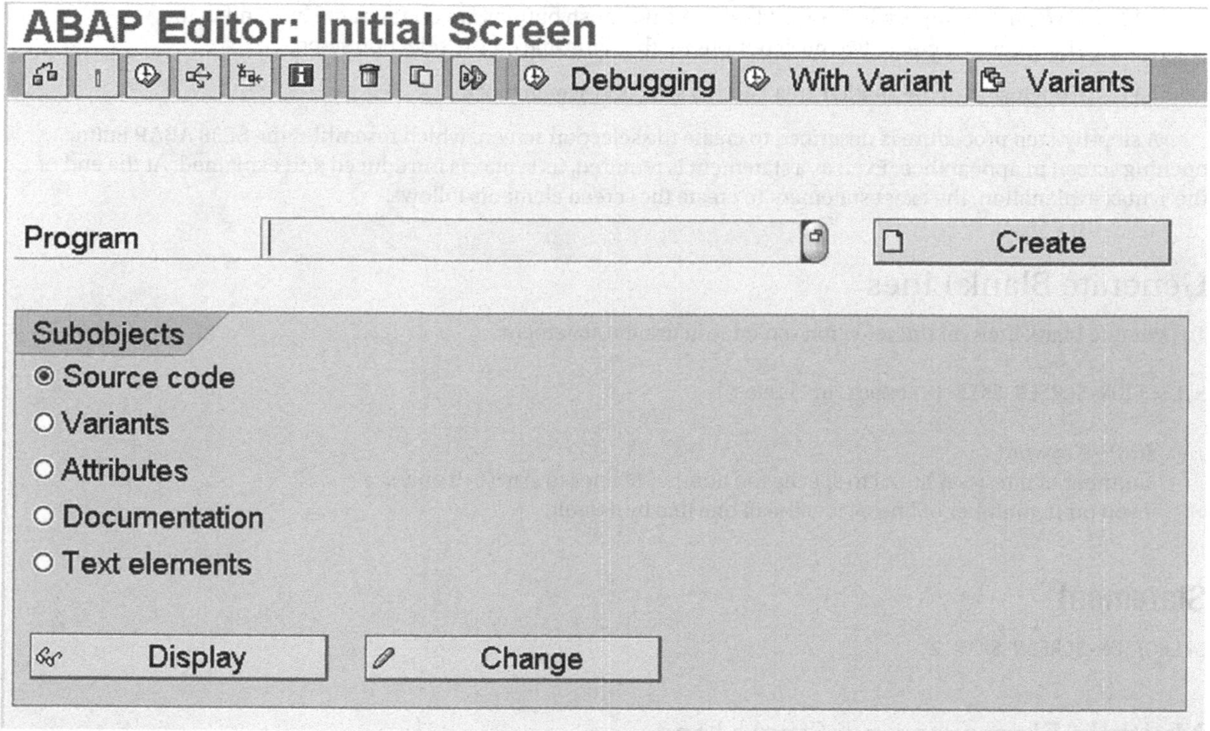

Figure 9-1. *SE38 ABAP Editor Opening Screen*

The selection screen that you are going to produce will resemble the SE38 ABAP Editor opening screen only in terms of look and appearance - not the functionality.

The SE38 ABAP Editor opening screen layout consists and involves the following:

1. A gap of two lines at the top - generates blank lines on the selection screen
2. A label, an input field, and a push button on a single line - place multiple selection screen elements on a single line
3. Create a label or text (Program) on the Selection Screen
4. Create an input field for entering the program name or accepting it from a selection list (search help, F4, etc.) on the selection screen
5. Create a push button with an icon and text on the selection screen
6. A gap of one line - generates a blank line on selection screen
7. Commencement of a shaded area with a title ('Subobjects') extending to a little more than half the width of the screen - begins a selection screen block
8. Within the shaded area are five radio buttons. Each radio button with its label or text appears in one line. - creates five radio buttons (one in each line) with labels on the select screen
9. A gap of one line after the five radio buttons. - generate a blank line on selection screen
10. Two push buttons with icon and text. The two push buttons are on the same line and in the shaded area - create two push buttons on the same line on the selection screen
11. Conclusion of the shaded area - ends a selection screen block

A step-by-step procedure is described to create the selection screen, which resembles the SE38 ABAP Editor opening screen in appearance. Even as a statement is required, its syntax is introduced and explained. At the end of the syntax explanation, the exact statement to create the screen elements follows.

Generate Blank Lines

To generate blank lines on the selection screen, you use the statement:

```
SELECTION-SCREEN SKIP [<number of lines>].
```

SKIP - Keyword.
<number of lines> - A literal to specify the number of lines to skip (0-9 only).
If you omit <number of lines>, it will skip one line by default.

Statement

```
SELECTION-SCREEN SKIP 2.
```

Multiple Elements on a Single Line

By default, each screen element on the selection screen occupies one full line. To position multiple screen elements in the same line on the selection screen, you use the statements:

```
SELECTION-SCREEN BEGIN OF LINE.
..........
SELECTION-SCREEN END OF LINE.
```

You locate the statements to create the three screen elements: that is, a label or text, an input field, and a push button on the same selection screen line between the following:

Statements

```
SELECTION SCREEN BEGIN OF LINE. & SELECTION-SCREEN END OF LINE.
```

Create Label or Text

To create label or text on the selection screen, you use the statement:

```
SELECTION-SCREEN COMMENT [/]<col position>(<width in columns/characters>) { <text symbol id> |
<comment id> }.
```

COMMENT - Keyword.

[/] - (Optional) to start the label or text on a new line.

<col position> - The starting column position from where to start the label or text. It can be a literal in the range 1-83.

(<width in columns/characters>) - The width of the label or text in characters. It can be a literal in the range 1-83.

{ <text symbol id> | <comment id> } - You can either give a <text symbol id.> or a <comment id.>. The <comment id.> can be a maximum of eight characters, starting with an alphabet, and the rest alphanumeric with embedded underscores (_).

The <comment id.> must be assigned text at an appropriate event: INITIALIZATION, AT SELECTION-SCREEN OUTPUT.

Statement

```
SELECTION-SCREEN COMMENT 1(15) TEXT-001.
```

The text symbol TEXT-001 will contain: 'Program'.

Input Field

To input value in a field, you use the familiar PARAMETERS statement.

```
PARAMETERS <variable name> MATCHCODE OBJECT <search help>
VISIBLE LENGTH <visible columns>
```

You are using an additional clause VISIBLE LENGTH. The length of field TRDIRT-NAME is 40 characters. In the SE38 screen, you are able to view only 30 characters of a program name. The name space of an ABAP program name is 30 characters. The name space of SAP delivered program names can be 40 characters. Hence in the SE38 screen, after 30 columns, there is horizontal scrolling (check this out). Through the clause VISIBLE LENGTH, you can reduce visible columns of any selection screen element.

Statement

```
PARAMETERS PROGRAM TYPE TRDIRT-NAME
                   MATCHCODE.OBJECT YCL_CH09_TRDIRT
                   VISIBLE LENGTH 30.
```

The SE38 screen functionality has been created using the full-fledged screen programming features of the ABAP Workbench. When you press F4 in the program field of ABAP Editor opening screen, there is no search help operating: there is a complex code that presents the user with a very sophisticated dialog box. You can't be doing this with your limited first formal exposure to a selection screen.

So you are creating a simple search help using the table TRDIRT. This table contains only three fields: the ABAP program name, language code, and the title or short text that you enter on the attributes screen of program creation. A screenshot of the search help YCL_CH09_TRDIRT is shown in Figure 9-2.

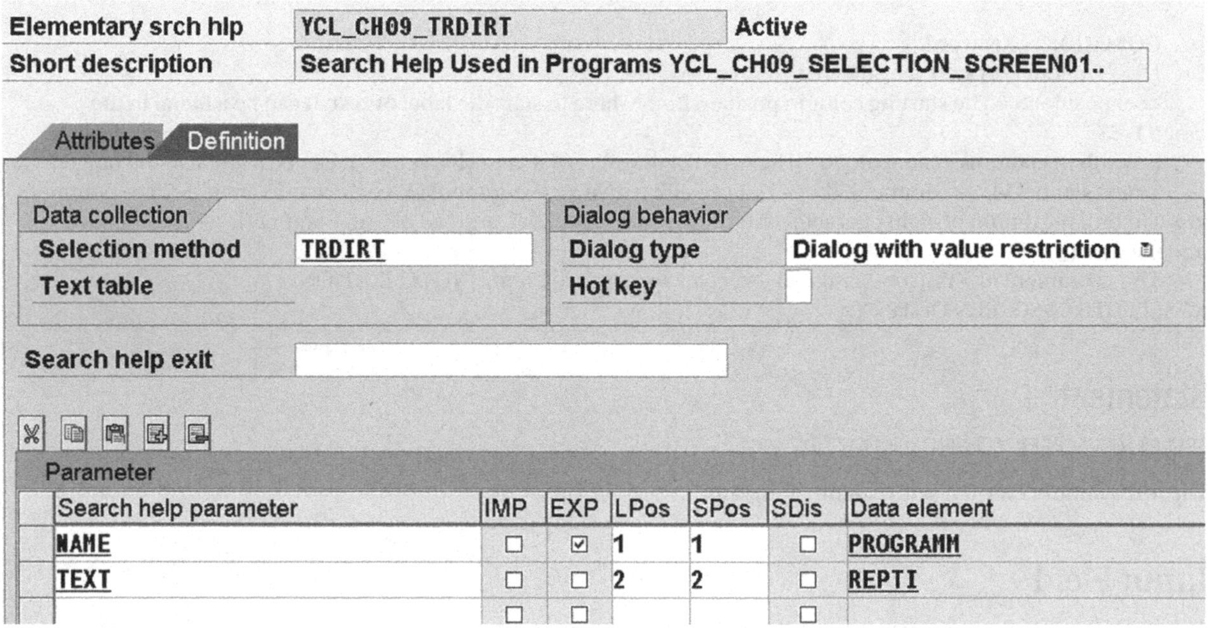

Elementary srch hlp: YCL_CH09_TRDIRT Active
Short description: Search Help Used in Programs YCL_CH09_SELECTION_SCREEN01..

Attributes | Definition

Data collection
Selection method: TRDIRT
Text table:

Dialog behavior
Dialog type: Dialog with value restriction
Hot key:

Search help exit:

Parameter

Search help parameter	IMP	EXP	LPos	SPos	SDis	Data element
NAME	☐	☑	1	1	☐	PROGRAMM
TEXT	☐	☐	2	2	☐	REPTI
	☐	☐			☐	

Figure 9-2. *Search Help: YCL_CH09_TRDIRT*

Create a Push Button with Icon and Text

A push button is created and located on the Selection Screen with the statement:

```
SELECTION-SCREEN PUSHBUTTON [/]<col position>
(<width in columns/characters>)
{ <text symbol id> | <push button name> }
USER-COMMAND <user command>.
```

PUSHBUTTON - Keyword.
[/] - (Optional) to position the push button on a new line.
<col position> - Is starting column from where to position the push button. It can be a literal in the range 1-83.
(<width in columns/characters>) - The width of the push button in characters. It can be a literal in the range 1-83.

{ <text symbol id> | <push button name>} - You can either give a <text symbol id.> or a <push button name>. The <push button name> can be a maximum of eight characters, starting with a letter of the alphabet, and the rest alphanumeric with embedded underscores (_).

The <push button name> must be assigned text at an appropriate event: INITIALIZATION, AT SELECTION-SCREEN OUTPUT.

USER-COMMAND <user command> -

A push button mandatorily should be assigned a <user-command>. It is through this <user-command> that you will know in the program which push button was pressed and take the appropriate action. The <user command> can start with special characters such as * _ = etc., but it is a good convention to start them with an alphabet letter and stick to alphanumeric combinations with embedded underscores (_). The <user-command> can be a maximum of 20 characters. The system field SY-UCOMM is loaded with assigned <user-command> when the push button is pressed. The event AT SELECTION-SCREEN is triggered when a user clicks on a push button. Which push button is pressed is ascertained by interrogating the contents of the system field SY-UCOMM in the event AT SELECTION-SCREEN. Caution: the <user command> is case insensitive. Synonymous terms for USER-COMMAND: function code and fcode.

Statement

```
SELECTION-SCREEN PUSHBUTTON 53(15) TEXT-002

                    USER-COMMAND CREAT.
```

The text symbol TEXT-002 will contain '@0Y@ Create'.

Your aim is to put the icon picture and text on the push button face. The contents of text symbol id. TEXT-002 could be like '@0Y@ Create'. If you want the create icon followed by the text 'Create' in the push button, you have to enclose the icon code 0Y with the character '@' followed by the text 'Create'.

For a list of icon codes and names, execute the Chapter 7 program: YCL_CH07_05_OUTPUT_INBOX_MACRO. You can locate the 'Create' icon in the list by pressing <Ctrl> F and entering 'create' in the dialog box. The find result will list out all icons names containing the string 'create'. You can select the appropriate icon and look up the icon code for the icon. Whenever the icon code is enclosed in the character '@' and presented on screen, it will automatically output an icon picture or image.

There is another elaborate way of placing an icon picture and text on a Selection Screen push button. This involves the usage of function module: ICON_CREATE demonstrated in program: YCL_CH09_SELECTION_SCREEN01VR. The function module takes as one of the inputs the icon name and does the same thing, gets the icon code, and encloses it like @<icon code>@ The function module also returns the 'info text' or 'tool tip'. The program: YCL_CH09_SELECTION_SCREEN01VR is not listed here. But it is available in the E-Resource. Upload it, peruse its code, and try it out.

Generate a blank line through the already covered statement

Statement: SELECTION-SCREEN SKIP.

Selection Screen Block, BEGIN OF BLOCK

Create a shaded area with a title: 'Subobjects'. This can be produced with the selection screen element: block. The syntax for creating a selection screen block:

```
SELECTION-SCREEN BEGIN OF BLOCK <name of block>
[TITLE { <text symbol id.> | <title name> } ]
[WITH FRAME]
[NO INTERVALS].
...........
SELECTION-SCREEN END OF BLOCK <name of block>.
```

BEGIN OF BLOCK - Key phrase to commence a block.

<name of block> - A block name can be a maximum of 20 characters, should start with a letter of the alphabet, but the rest can be alphanumeric with embedded underscores (_).

TITLE - Keyword.

{ <text symbol id> | <title name> } - You can either give a <text symbol id.> or a <title name>. The <title name> can be a maximum of eight characters, starting with an alphabet letter, with the rest being alphanumeric with embedded underscores (_).

WITH FRAME - Key phrase. If you provide this optional key phrase, the shading effect is created.

NO INTERVALS - Key phrase. This has relevance only if you have specified the key phrase *WITH FRAME*. If you provide this optional key phrase, the shading will extend to half the width of the screen. If you omit this key phrase, shading will extend to the end of the screen.

END OF BLOCK - Key phrase to end a block.

You locate all the selection screen elements within a block by enclosing the selection screen elements' creation statements within SELECTION-SCREEN BEGIN OF BLOCK...& SELECTION-SCREEN ENDOF BLOCK.

You can nest blocks (i.e., blocks within blocks). The nesting can be up to five levels.

Statements:

```
    SELECTION-SCREEN BEGIN OF BLOCK BL1
 WITH FRAME TITLE TEXT-003 NO INTERVALS.
..............
SELECTION-SCREEN END OF BLOCK BL1.
```

The text symbol TEXT-003 will contain 'Subobjects'.

Selection screen radio buttons

Create radio buttons with labels or texts. As each radio button with its corresponding label or text has to be positioned in a single line, you have to enclose the label or text and radio button creation statements within `SELECTION-SCREEN BEGIN OF LINE` and `SELECTION-SCREEN END OF LINE`.

To create a radio button on a selection screen, you use a variation of the PARAMETERS statement:

```
PARAMETERS: <variable name> RADIOBUTTON
GROUP <radio button group name> [USER-COMMAND <user command>].
```

PARAMETERS: - Keyword.

<variable name> - Maximum of eight characters, must start with a letter of the alphabet, but the rest can be alphanumeric with embedded underscores. (_)

RADIOBUTTON GROUP - Key phrase.

<radio button group name> - A radio button has to be assigned to a radio button group. A radio button group must consist of a minimum of two radio buttons. Within a radio button group, if you click/enable one, all others in the group get disabled. The TYPE and length of radio button variables is 'C' and 1. If a radio button is enabled, it assumes the value 'X' and when disabled assumes a value blank or ' '. A radio button group name can be a maximum of four characters. Other rules applicable to user defined ABAP variables apply to the radio button group name.

By default, the first radio button in the group is enabled when the selection screen appears. If you want other than the first radio button in a group to be enabled initially when the selection screen appears, you can do this by assigning a DEFAULT 'X' to the radio button variable you want as enabled initially.

USER-COMMAND - Key phrase.

<user command> - Same as described in the context of push button.

You can assign a <user command> to a radio button group. This is optional. If you assign a <user command> to a radio button group, clicking on any of the radio buttons in the group will trigger the events AT SELECTION-SCREEN,

AT SELECTION-SCREEN ON RADIOBUTTON GROUP <radio button group name>, etc. To assign a <user command> to a radio button group, use the clause USER-COMMAND *<user command>* for the first radio button in the group only.

Statements:

```
SELECTION-SCREEN BEGIN OF BLOCK BL1
  WITH FRAME TITLE TEXT-003 NO INTERVALS.

 SELECTION-SCREEN BEGIN OF LINE.
  PARAMETERS SRCE RADIOBUTTON GROUP GRP. " radio button Source
  SELECTION-SCREEN COMMENT 2(20) TEXT-004.
 SELECTION-SCREEN END OF LINE.

 SELECTION-SCREEN BEGIN OF LINE.
  PARAMETERS VARA RADIOBUTTON GROUP GRP. " radio button Variants
  SELECTION-SCREEN COMMENT 2(20) TEXT-005.
 SELECTION-SCREEN END OF LINE.

…………………….

SELECTION-SCREEN END OF BLOCK BL1.
```

The text symbols TEXT-004 will contain 'Source' and TEXT-005 will contain 'Variants'. In a like manner you will code for the remaining three radio buttons.

Two Push Buttons on a Line

At the last, you have to create two push buttons ('Display', 'Change') on a single line. So you have to enclose the push button creation statements within SELECTION-SCREEN BEGIN OF LINE. & SELECTION-SCREEN END OF LINE.

Statements:

```
SELECTION-SCREEN BEGIN OF LINE.

 SELECTION-SCREEN PUSHBUTTON 1(15) TEXT-009
 USER-COMMAND DISPL.

 SELECTION-SCREEN PUSHBUTTON 19(15) TEXT-010
 USER-COMMAND CHANG.

SELECTION-SCREEN END OF LINE.
```

Generate a blank line through the already covered statement

Statement: `SELECTION-SCREEN SKIP.`

END OF BLOCK

The shaded area - block - has to be concluded with this statement:

Statement: SELECTION-SCREEN END OF BLOCK.

AT SELECTION-SCREEN event

In the program, you have triggered the selection screen event AT SELECTION-SCREEN. This event is triggered when user interacts with the selection screen, such as when:

- The <Enter> key is pressed.
- A selection screen push button is clicked.
- A selection screen radio button is clicked and the optional USER-COMMAND clause was used for this radio button group.
- A selection screen check box is clicked and the optional USER-COMMAND clause was used for this check box.
- Application toolbar or standard toolbar button is clicked, and a menu selection is made.

You have imparted a very limited functionality to this program through this AT SELECTION-SCREEN event.

You are checking which of the selection screen push button ('Create', 'Display', or 'Change') is pressed and issuing a message to this effect with the MESSAGE statement. You are determining which of the push buttons is pressed by checking the contents of the system field SY-UCOMM against the USER-COMMAND string assigned to each of the three push buttons. Please keep in mind that the system field SY-UCOMM is case insensitive. Do not assign lower case USER-COMMAND strings. They will be converted to upper case.

The complete source program:

```
REPORT YCL_CH09_SELECTION_SCREEN01
   MESSAGE-ID YCL_CH07_MCLASS01.

****************************************************
* SLECTION-SCREEN - Create SE38 Look Alike Screen **
* Put Icon & Text On SLECTION-SCREEN Push Buttons **
* Without Usage Of Function Module 'ICON_CREATE'  **
****************************************************

*******************************************************
* generate 2 blank lines:                           **
* SELECTION-SCREEN SKIP 2.                          **
*                                                   **
* three elements on the same line:                  **
*       (1) a label 'Program' for field             **
*       (2) a field (of type text box)              **
*           to input the program name               **
*       (3) a 'Create' push button                  **
*                                                   **
* SELECTION-SCREEN BEGIN OF LINE.                   **
* SELECTION-SCREEN COMMENT 1(20) TEXT-001.          **
* PARAMETERS PROGRAM TYPE TRDIRT-NAME MATCHCODE OBJECT **
*   ...... VISIBLE LENGTH 30.                       **
* SELECTION-SCREEN PUSHBUTTON 53(15) TEXT-002       **
```

```
* USER-COMMAND CREAT.                                  **
* SELECTION-SCREEN END OF LINE.                        **
*                                                      **
* a gap of one line i.e.                               **
* SELECTION-SCREEN SKIP 1.                             **
*                                                      **
* START block with title 'Subobjects' & shaded effect **
* extending to half the screen width:                  **
*                                                      **
* SELECTION-SCREEN BEGIN OF BLOCK BL1 WITH FRAME       **
* TITLE TEXT-003 NO INTERVALS.                         **
*                                                      **
* five radio buttons. each radio button with           **
* label on the same line:                              **
*                                                      **
* SELECTION-SCREEN BEGIN OF LINE.                      **
* PARAMETERS: SRCE RADIOBUTTON GROUP GRP.              **
* SELECTION-SCREEN COMMENT 2(20) TEXT-004.             **
* SELECTION-SCREEN END OF LINE.                        **
* ........                                             **
* ........                                             **
* a gap of one line after 5 radio buttons i.e.         **
* SELECTION-SCREEN SKIP 1.                             **
*                                                      **
* two push buttons ('Display' & 'Change') on same line **
*                                                      **
* SELECTION-SCREEN BEGIN OF LINE.                      **
* SELECTION-SCREEN PUSHBUTTON 1(15) TEXT-009...        **
* .....                                                **
* ......                                               **
* SELECTION-SCREEN END OF LINE.                        **
*                                                      **
* SELECTION-SCREEN END OF BLOCK BL1                    **
*                                                      **
********************************************************

SELECTION-SCREEN SKIP 2. " 2 blank lines at top

SELECTION-SCREEN BEGIN OF LINE.
  SELECTION-SCREEN COMMENT 1(15) TEXT-001. " label 'Program'

  PARAMETERS PROGRAM TYPE TRDIRT-NAME MATCHCODE OBJECT
    YCL_CH09_TRDIRT VISIBLE LENGTH 30. " input program name

  SELECTION-SCREEN PUSHBUTTON 53(15) TEXT-002
    USER-COMMAND CREAT. " push button 'Create'
SELECTION-SCREEN END OF LINE.

SELECTION-SCREEN SKIP 1. " a blank line

SELECTION-SCREEN BEGIN OF BLOCK BL1 WITH FRAME TITLE
 TEXT-003 NO INTERVALS. " block BL1 commencement
```

```
  SELECTION-SCREEN BEGIN OF LINE.
    PARAMETERS SRCE RADIOBUTTON GROUP GRP. " radio button Source
    SELECTION-SCREEN COMMENT 2(20) TEXT-004.
  SELECTION-SCREEN END OF LINE.

  SELECTION-SCREEN BEGIN OF LINE.
    PARAMETERS VARA RADIOBUTTON GROUP GRP. " radio button Variants
    SELECTION-SCREEN COMMENT 2(20) TEXT-005.
  SELECTION-SCREEN END OF LINE.

  SELECTION-SCREEN BEGIN OF LINE.
    PARAMETERS ATTR RADIOBUTTON GROUP GRP. " radio button Attributes
    SELECTION-SCREEN COMMENT 2(20) TEXT-006.
  SELECTION-SCREEN END OF LINE.

  SELECTION-SCREEN BEGIN OF LINE.
    PARAMETERS DOCU RADIOBUTTON GROUP GRP. " radio button Documentation
    SELECTION-SCREEN COMMENT 2(20) TEXT-007.
  SELECTION-SCREEN END OF LINE.

  SELECTION-SCREEN BEGIN OF LINE.
    PARAMETERS TXEL RADIOBUTTON GROUP GRP. " radio button Text elements
    SELECTION-SCREEN COMMENT 2(20) TEXT-008.
  SELECTION-SCREEN END OF LINE.

  SELECTION-SCREEN  SKIP 1. " a blank line

  SELECTION-SCREEN BEGIN OF LINE.

    SELECTION-SCREEN PUSHBUTTON 01(15) TEXT-009 " @10@ Display
     USER-COMMAND DISPL. " push button 'Display'
    SELECTION-SCREEN PUSHBUTTON 19(15) TEXT-010 " @0Z@ Change
     USER-COMMAND CHANG. " push button 'Change'

  SELECTION-SCREEN END OF LINE.

SELECTION-SCREEN END OF BLOCK BL1.

*********************************************************
AT SELECTION-SCREEN. " triggered when user interacts with
                    " the Selection-Screen
CASE SY-UCOMM.
 WHEN 'CREAT'.
 MESSAGE I011 WITH 'Create'.
 WHEN 'DISPL'.
 MESSAGE I011 WITH 'Display'.
 WHEN 'CHANG'.
 MESSAGE I011 WITH 'Change'.
ENDCASE.
```

The text symbols screen is shown in Figure 9-3.

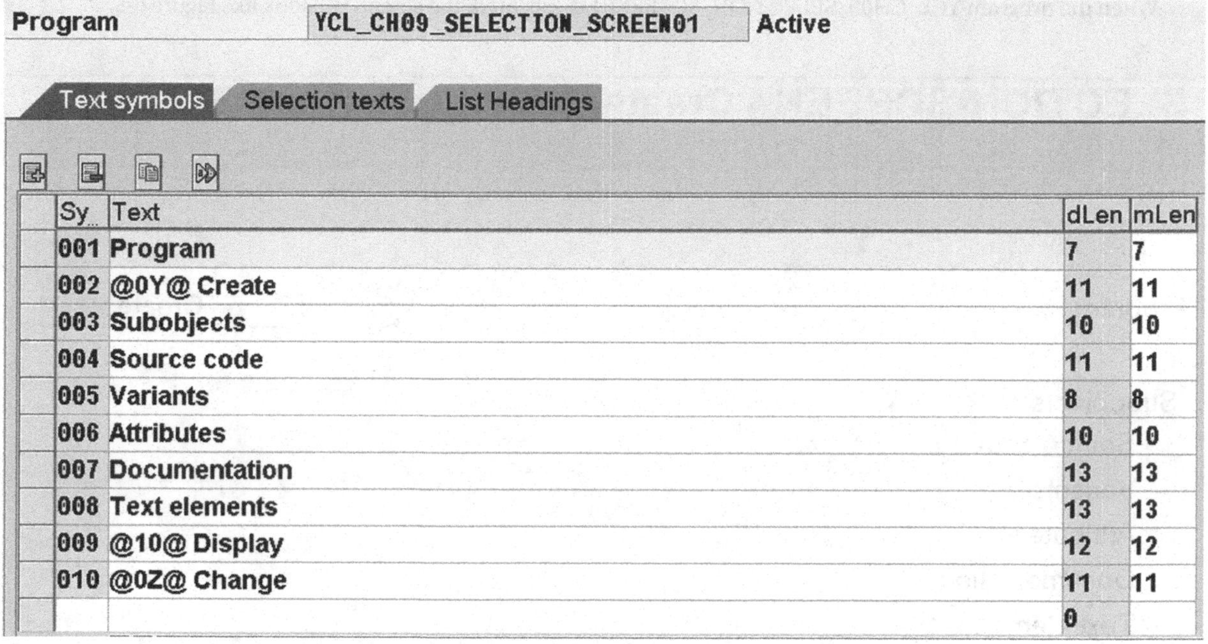

Program YCL_CH09_SELECTION_SCREEN01 Active

Text symbols | Selection texts | List Headings

Sy	Text	dLen	mLen
001	Program	7	7
002	@0Y@ Create	11	11
003	Subobjects	10	10
004	Source code	11	11
005	Variants	8	8
006	Attributes	10	10
007	Documentation	13	13
008	Text elements	13	13
009	@10@ Display	12	12
010	@0Z@ Change	11	11
		0	

Figure 9-3. *Program: YCL_CH09_SELECTION_SCREEN01 - Text Symbols*

You have used the message class created in Chapter 7. You are using a single message (message number 011) to take care of the three situations with a place holder. The place holder is receiving the button pressed info. A screen shot of SE91 messages is shown in Figure 9-4.

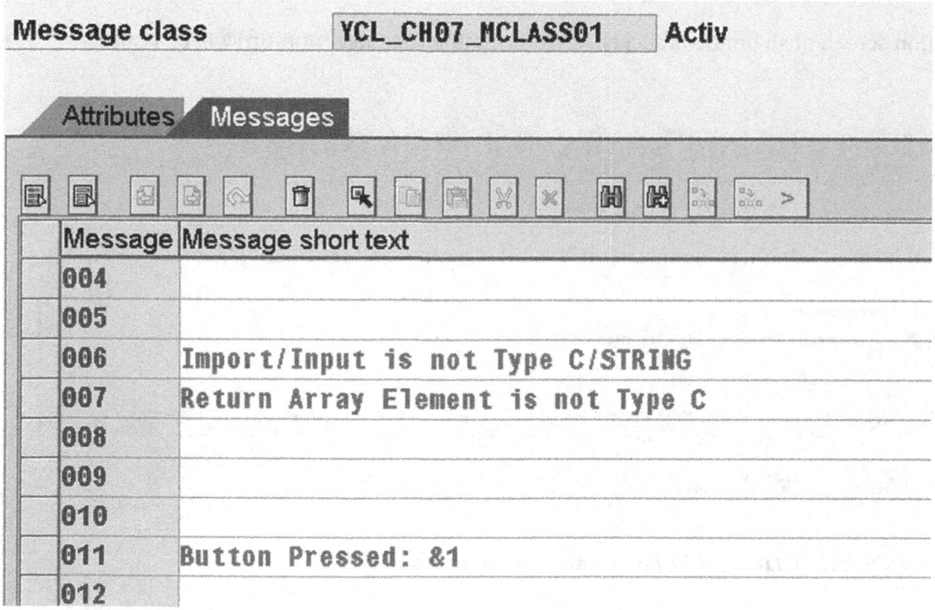

Message class YCL_CH07_MCLASS01 Activ

Attributes | Messages

Message	Message short text
004	
005	
006	Import/Input is not Type C/STRING
007	Return Array Element is not Type C
008	
009	
010	
011	Button Pressed: &1
012	

Figure 9-4. *Message Class: YCL_CH07_MCLASS01 - Messages*

When the program YCL_CH09_SELECTION_SCREEN01 is executed, the screen will look like Figure 9-5.

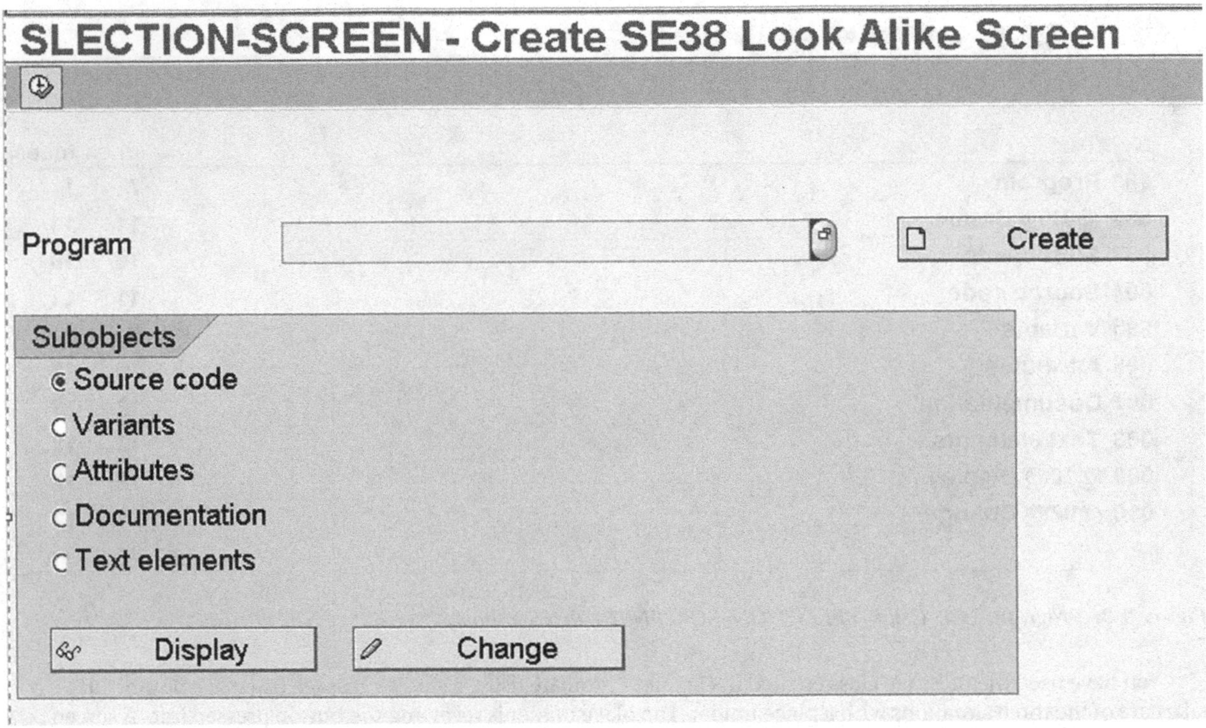

Figure 9-5. *Program: YCL_CH09_SELECTION_SCREEN01 - Reproduced SE38 Screen*

When one of the selection screen push button is clicked, an information message (pop-up) will be issued like Figure 9-6.

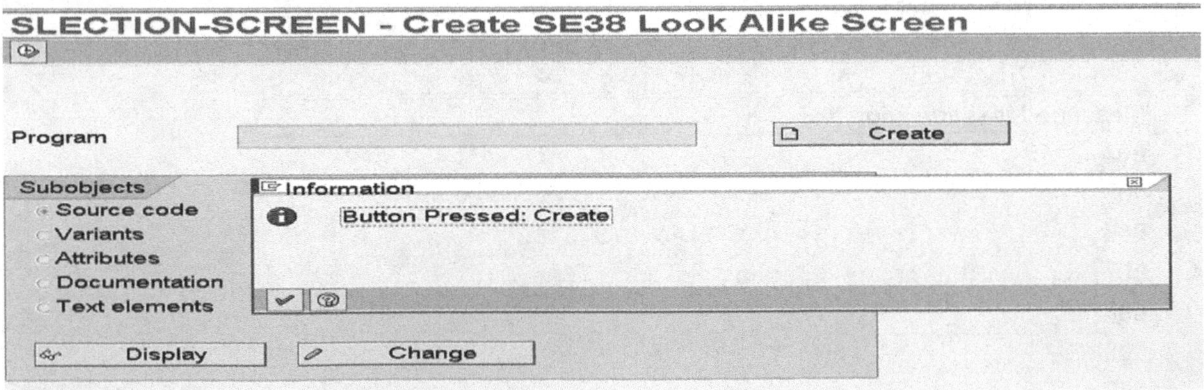

Figure 9-6. *Program: YCL_CH09_SELECTION_SCREEN01 - Message on Button Click*

When F4 is pressed on the field 'PROGRAM' with a pattern YCL_CH07* entered in the filter dialog box, the search help selection list will appear like Figure 9-7.

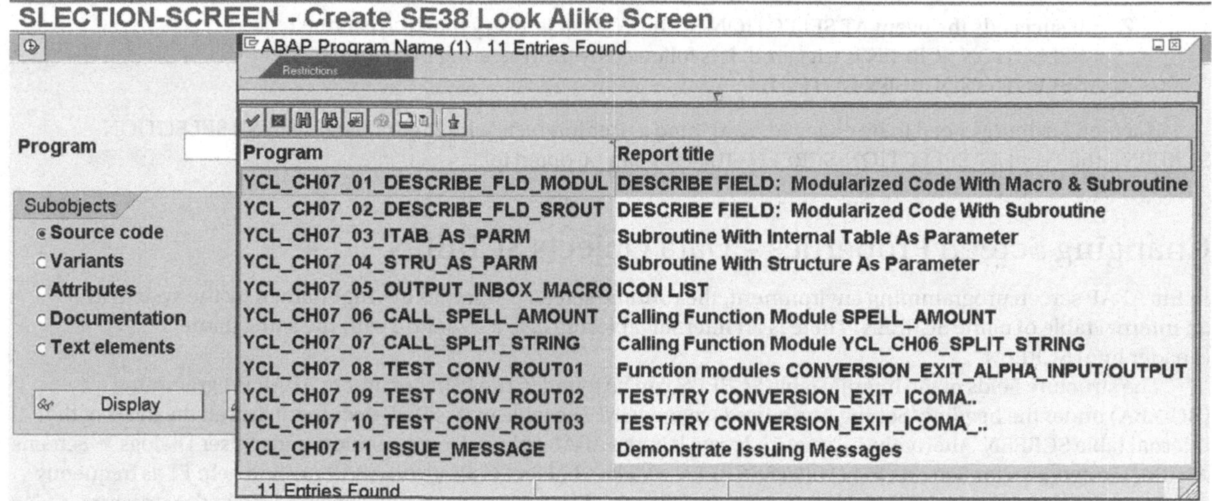

Figure 9-7. *Program: YCL_CH09_SELECTION_SCREEN01 - Selection List on Field 'PROGRAM'*

The original ABAP Editor opening screen has been created using the screen painter, etc., where you have a larger degree of control than when creating screens through selection screen statements. That is why the width of the shaded area (block frame) might differ in the output of your program from the original of which you have tried to create a replica. For most part, the screen of your program resembles the SE38 ABAP Editor opening screen.

Try to re-create some of the other ABAP Workbench screens: SE11, SE91, SE32, etc., to get proficient in laying the selection screen elements.

Take care not to overlap screen elements. If screen elements are overlapped, the ABAP runtime will be unable to generate a screen and will result in a dump if you are executing an inactive version of the program. If you have overlapping screen elements and are activating the program, the ABAP runtime will alert with 'error when generating selection screen..'.

A selection screen must have a minimum of one input element for it to appear. A selection screen consisting only of label or text, (COMMENT) blocks will not appear.

Event INITIALIZATION, Selection Screen Event – AT SELECTION-SCREEN OUTPUT

Changing Screen Properties - Events

In screen programming environments; a common, basic requirement is changing the properties of screen elements at runtime. This could involve enabling/disabling a field for input or making a field appear/disappear, etc. In the selection screen environment, the properties can only be changed through the events: AT SELECTION-SCREEN OUTPUT or INITIALIZATION.

The event INITIALIZATION is not a selection screen event. It is triggered only once when the user presses the execute button, etc. If screen attributes need to be changed only once before the screen appears to the user for the first time, the INITIALIZATION event can be opted for.

The event AT SELECTION-SCREEN OUTPUT is triggered on two occasions:

1. Before the selection screen appears to the user for the first time. Between the user pressing the execute button and the appearance of the screen. After the INITIALIZATION event.
2. It succeeds the event AT SELECTION-SCREEN. That is, every time the event AT SELECTION SCREEN is triggered, it is followed by the triggering of the event AT SELECTION-SCREEN OUTPUT.

If screen attributes need to be changed every time a user interacts with the screen (event AT SELECTION-SCREEN), the event AT SELECTION-SCREEN OUTPUT can be opted for.

Changing Screen Properties - Data Objects SCREEN

In the ABAP screen programming environment, the runtime screen properties are maintained by the system in an internal table of name SCREEN. There is an internal table and also a structure with the same name: (header line) SCREEN.

The structure fields of the internal table SCREEN can be found in the PDF document ABAP Programming (BC-ABA) under the heading 'Setting Attributes Dynamically.' The table in this PDF document lists all the fields of the internal table SCREEN. Alternatively, you can locate it in the ABAP online documentation under User Dialogs ➤ Screens ➤ ABAP Statements for Screens ➤ LOOP AT SCREEN. (Make a habit of visiting the ABAP on-line help F1 as frequently as you can.) This internal table will contain one row for each of the screen elements. The first field in the structure 'NAME' contains the screen element name as identifier, and the rest of the 14 (very few compared to other platforms) fields are the various attributes of a screen element. Here, a partial list of these fields of structure SCREEN is reproduced:

Table 9-1. *Few Fields of Internal Table Structure SCREEN*

Field Name	Type, Length	Description
NAME	C, 30	Name of the screen element. Like when you created a PARAMETER variable of name 'PROGRAM,' this name of the screen element/variable will be stored in this field.
GROUP1	C, 3	Modification Group I (will be explained subsequently in this chapter).
INPUT	C, 1	Whether the screen field is enabled / disabled for input. A flag variable: assumes 1/0 values. By default is set to 1.
OUTPUT	C, 1	Whether the screen field is displayed or not. A flag variable: assumes 1/0 values. By default is set to 1.
INVISIBLE	C, 1	Whether the screen field is invisible / visible. A flag variable: assumes 1/0 values. By default is set to 0.
ACTIVE	C, 1	Whether the screen field is active or not. A flag variable: assumes 1/0 values. By default is set to 1.

Changing Screen Properties - Operations on Data Objects SCREEN

You can perform limited operations on these system maintained data objects SCREEN. You can:

1. Set up LOOP AT SCREEN...ENDLOOP.
2. Assign values to the different fields of the structure SCREEN. Assigning values to the field SCREEN-NAME is not advisable.
3. Perform MODIFY (update internal table) statement on the internal table SCREEN.

Apart from these, you cannot perform any other operations on the internal table SCREEN. You cannot perform READ, INSERT, APPEND, DELETE, CLEAR, REFRESH, FREE, etc. You cannot have LOOP AT ASSIGNING...ENDLOOP.

The permitted operations on the internal table SCREEN are sufficient to be able to change the attributes of screen elements.

Let a very simple exercise be performed to demonstrate the event AT SELECTION-SCREEN OUTPUT along with the manipulation of the internal table SCREEN to change properties of screen elements.

In the PDF document ABAP Programming (BC-ABA), under the heading 'Setting Attributes Dynamically,' there is a table listing out the screen behavior for different values of the screen attribute fields ACTIVE, INPUT, OUTPUT, INVISIBLE. By default the fields ACTIVE, INPUT, OUTPUT are set to 1 and INVISIBLE is set to 0. If all the four fields ACTIVE, INPUT, OUTPUT, INVISIBLE are set to 1, the field assumes the password mode and entered values are invisible.

So in an ABAP program with a single input field, let the event INITIALIZATION be triggered. In this event for the input field screen element, let the field attribute INVISIBLE be set to 1 and use the MODIFY statement to alter the internal table row. This should set the input field to password mode.

The source program:

```
REPORT YCL_CH09_SELECTION_SCREEN02.

*****************************************************
* Demo INITIALIZATION event, LOOP AT SCREEN Etc. **
* to change screen element properties          **
*****************************************************

SELECTION-SCREEN SKIP 5.

SELECTION-SCREEN BEGIN OF LINE.
SELECTION-SCREEN COMMENT 1(12) COMMENT1. "label
PARAMETERS: PASS_WRD(10) TYPE C. " input field
SELECTION-SCREEN END OF LINE.

*********************************************
INITIALIZATION.
COMMENT1 = 'Pass word:'(001). " this notation means use text symbol
                              " TEXT-001 if it exists. if it does not
                              " exist, use the literal text
LOOP AT SCREEN.

 IF SCREEN-NAME = 'PASS_WRD'. " there are two screen elements
                              " COMMENT1 & PASS_WRD. we are interested
                              " to change properties of PASS_WRD only
  SCREEN-INVISIBLE = '1'.
  MODIFY SCREEN.
 ENDIF.

ENDLOOP.
```

A new notation has been used for assignment of text to COMMENT1:

```
COMMENT1 = 'Pass word:'(001).
```

(See the code in the INITIALIZATION event)

This notation means, use the text of text symbol id. TEXT-001 if it exists. If the text symbol id. does not exist, use the literal text. It ensures that a text is always assigned to an element.

When you execute this program, the screen will look like Figure 9-8.

Demo INITIALIZATION event, LOOP AT SCREEN Etc.

Pass word: ***********

Figure 9-8. *Program: YCL_CH09_SELECTION_SCREEN02 - Screen*

This was a demonstration of the event INITIALIZATION.

When you are on the selection screen of this code, if you press <Enter> key, the 'INVISIBLE' property of the screen element 'PASS_WRD' gets set to 0 and the entered valued in the field become visible. The 'INVISIBLE' property has to be set to 1 in the event AT SELECTION-SCREEN OUTPUT to ensure the entered values in the field 'PASS_WRD' remains invisible. This is implemented in the program YCL_CH09_SELECTION_SCREEN02_VR. The program is not listed here but is available in the E-Resource.

Changing Screen Properties Using Event AT SELECTION-SCREEN OUTPUT (A Simple Payment Mode Scenario)

A demonstration of changing the screen attributes using the event AT SELECTION-SCREEN OUTPUT with a scenario:

Scenario

You want to represent a mode of payment on the selection screen. The mode of payments can be either by (a) Cash, (b) Check, or (c) Credit Card. This can be represented on the screen by three radio buttons with labels like Figure 9-9.

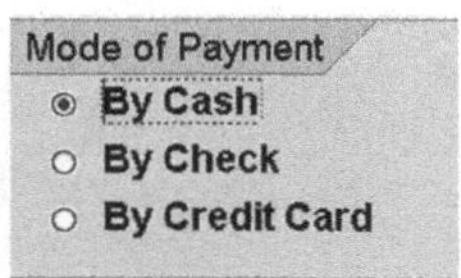

Figure 9-9. *A Screen for Mode of Payment*

If the mode of payment is by check, you want a further input field for the check number. The check number input field should be enabled for input only if the radio button corresponding to the mode of payment by check is enabled. If the mode of payment by check radio button is disabled, the input field for check number should be disabled.

Similarly, if the mode of payment is by credit card, you want a further input field for the credit card number. The credit card number input field should be enabled for input only if the radio button corresponding to the mode of payment by credit card is enabled. If the mode of payment by credit card radio button is disabled, the input field for credit card number should be disabled.

If the mode of payment is by cash, both the input fields check number and credit card number should be disabled for input.

Since you want the selection screen to interact when radio buttons are clicked, you should use the optional reserved phrase USER-COMMAND and assign <user command> to the radio button group.

The screen could look like Figure 9-10.

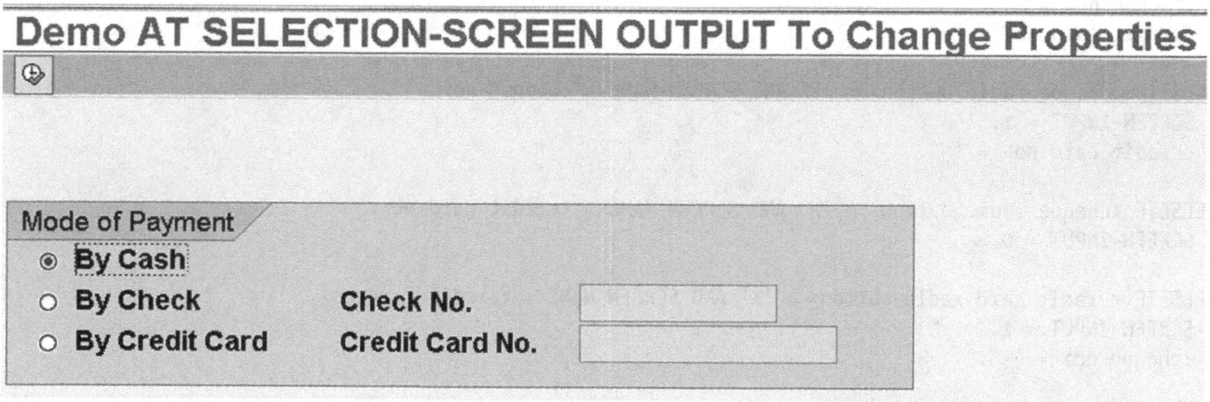

Figure 9-10. *Mode of Payment, Proposed Screen*

The properties should be changed in the event AT SELECTION-SCREEN OUTPUT. This is because properties need to be changed every time a user interacts with the selection screen by clicking on one of the radio buttons. The event INITIALIZATION will not help.

Since the radio button group has been assigned <user command>, clicking one of them in the group will trigger the event AT SELECTION-SCREEN. You don't want to have any action/code for this event. This event is succeeded by the event AT SELECTION-SCREEN OUTPUT. You need to manipulate the properties of the selection screen elements in this event. In effect, this is a manipulation of the internal table SCREEN with LOOP AT SCREEN.... and MODIFY statements.

We are interested in changing the properties of only two selection screen elements: the check number and the credit card number. You have to enable/disable these elements depending on the values of the three radio buttons corresponding to cash, check, and credit card. The enabling/disabling of input is carried by assigning values 1/0 to the field INPUT of the internal table SCREEN.

If the cash radio button is enabled, both the fields check number and credit card number should be disabled for input.

If the check radio button is enabled, the field check number should be enabled for input and the field credit card number should be disabled for input.

If the credit card radio button is enabled, the field credit card number should be enabled for input and the field check number should be disabled for input.

Your pseudo code in the selection screen event at SELECTION-SCREEN OUTPUT should look like:

```
LOOP AT SCREEN.

IF SCREEN-NAME <> <cheque no> AND SCREEN-NAME <> <credit card no>.
 CONTINUE. " properties of <cheque no>, <credit card no> only to be changed
ENDIF.

IF <cash radio button> = 'X'.  " <cash radio button> enabled
 SCREEN-INPUT = 0.
 <cheque no> = ' '.
 <credit card no> = ' '.

ELSEIF <cheque radio button> = 'X' AND SCREEN-NAME = <cheque no>.
 SCREEN-INPUT = 1.
 <credit card no> = ' '.

ELSEIF <cheque radio button> = 'X' AND SCREEN-NAME = <credit card no>.
 SCREEN-INPUT = 0.

ELSEIF <credit card radio button> = 'X' AND SCREEN-NAME = <credit card no>.
 SCREEN-INPUT = 1.
 <cheque no> = ' '.

ELSEIF <credit card radio button> = 'X' AND SCREEN-NAME = <cheque no>.
 SCREEN-INPUT = 0.
ENDIF.
   MODIFY SCREEN.

ENDLOOP.
```

You are already familiar with selection screen layout statements, so there will be no explanations of the layout statements here. You have located all the elements within a selection screen block to enhance the screen appearance.

You have assigned explicitly DEFAULT 'X' to the cash radio button variable 'CASH_RB.' In SAP R/3 earlier versions, if you do not do so, the initial appearance of selection screen is not proper. At the time the event AT SELECTION-SCREEN OUTPUT is triggered for the first time, before the screen appears to the user for the first time, the values of all the radio buttons are indeterminate if no explicit DEFAULT has been assigned. The implicit DEFAULT 'X' is assigned only after the event AT SELECTION-SCREEN OUTPUT. To ensure that the radio buttons do not have indeterminate values at the time of first triggering of the event AT SELECTION-SCREEN OUTPUT, you have added the DEFAULT 'X' clause for cash radio button variable 'CASH_RB.'

The source code:

```
REPORT YCL_CH09_SELECTION_SCREEN03.

**********************************************************
* Demo AT SELECTION-SCREEN OUTPUT To Change Properties **
* Of Screen Elements                                   **
**********************************************************


SELECTION-SCREEN SKIP 2.
```

```
SELECTION-SCREEN BEGIN OF BLOCK BLK1 WITH FRAME TITLE
 TEXT-001 NO INTERVALS.

SELECTION-SCREEN BEGIN OF LINE.

PARAMETERS CASH_RB RADIOBUTTON GROUP MOP DEFAULT 'X'
 USER-COMMAND RBCLICK.

 SELECTION-SCREEN COMMENT 3(20) TEXT-002.

SELECTION-SCREEN END OF LINE.

SELECTION-SCREEN BEGIN OF LINE.

 PARAMETERS CHEQ_RB RADIOBUTTON GROUP MOP.
 SELECTION-SCREEN COMMENT 3(15) TEXT-003.
 SELECTION-SCREEN COMMENT 20(15) TEXT-004.
 PARAMETERS CHQNO(12) TYPE C.

SELECTION-SCREEN END OF LINE.

SELECTION-SCREEN BEGIN OF LINE.

 PARAMETERS CCRD RADIOBUTTON GROUP MOP.
 SELECTION-SCREEN COMMENT 3(15) TEXT-005.
 SELECTION-SCREEN COMMENT 20(15) TEXT-006.
 PARAMETERS CCRDNO(16) TYPE C.

SELECTION-SCREEN END OF LINE.

SELECTION-SCREEN END OF BLOCK BLK1.
*****************************************************

AT SELECTION-SCREEN OUTPUT.

LOOP AT SCREEN.

 IF SCREEN-NAME <> 'CHQNO' AND SCREEN-NAME <> 'CCRDNO'.
  CONTINUE.   " changing properties of only 'CHQNO' & 'CCRDNO'
 ENDIF.

 IF CASH_RB = 'X' .
   SCREEN-INPUT = 0.
   MOVE ' ' TO CCRDNO.
   MOVE ' ' TO CHQNO.

 ELSEIF SCREEN-NAME = 'CHQNO' AND CHEQ_RB = 'X'.
   SCREEN-INPUT = 1.
   MOVE ' ' TO CCRDNO.
```

```
 ELSEIF  SCREEN-NAME = 'CHQNO' AND CHEQ_RB = ' '.
   SCREEN-INPUT = 0.

 ELSEIF SCREEN-NAME = 'CCRDNO' AND CCRD = 'X'.
   SCREEN-INPUT = 1.
   MOVE ' ' TO CHQNO.

 ELSEIF SCREEN-NAME = 'CCRDNO' AND CCRD = ' '.
   SCREEN-INPUT = 0.

 ENDIF.

 MODIFY SCREEN.

ENDLOOP.
```

The text symbol screen is shown in Figure 9-11.

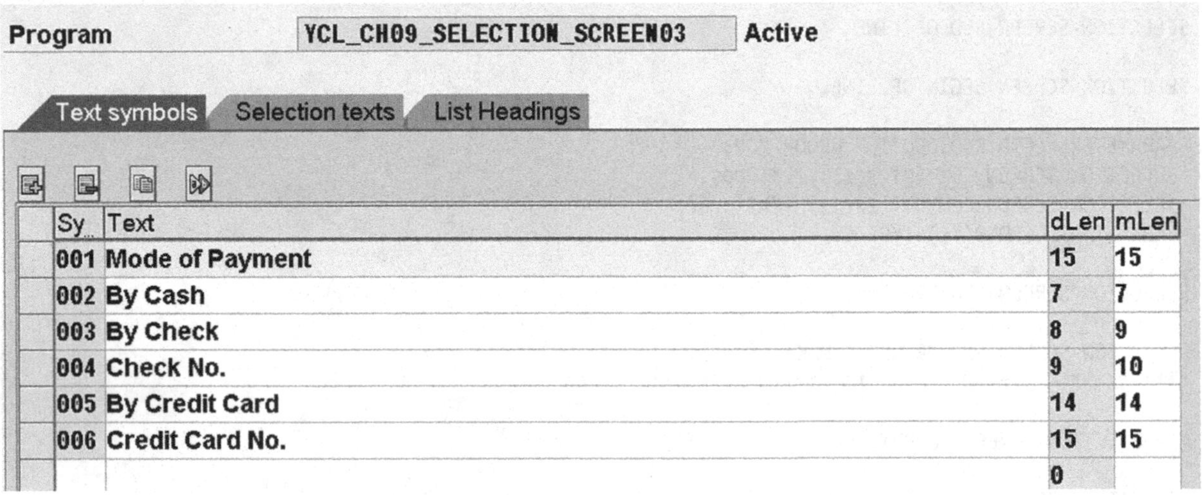

Program YCL_CH09_SELECTION_SCREEN03 Active

Text symbols | Selection texts | List Headings

Sy...	Text	dLen	mLen
001	Mode of Payment	15	15
002	By Cash	7	7
003	By Check	8	9
004	Check No.	9	10
005	By Credit Card	14	14
006	Credit Card No.	15	15
		0	

***Figure 9-11.** Program: YCL_CH09_SELECTION_SCREEN03 – Text Symbols*

When the check/credit card radio buttons are enabled in turn, the screens will look like Figure 9-12 and 9-13.

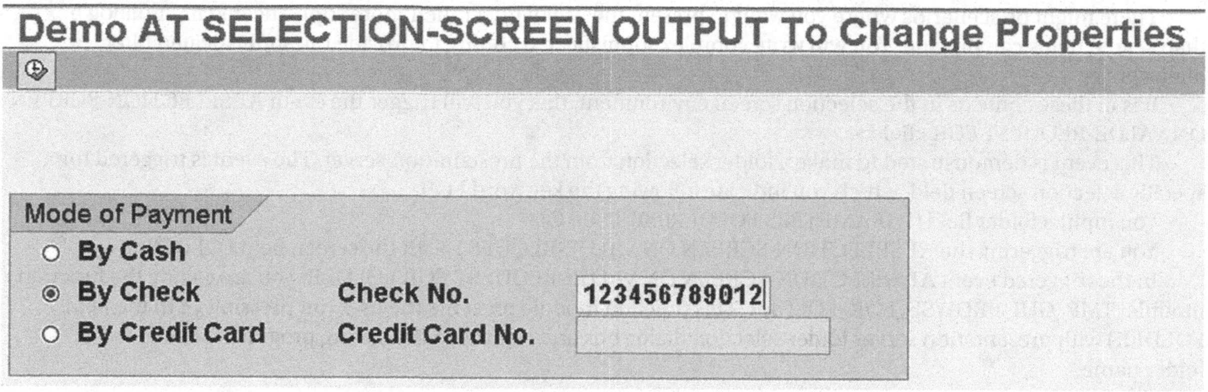

Demo AT SELECTION-SCREEN OUTPUT To Change Properties

Mode of Payment

- By Cash
- By Check   Check No. 123456789012
- By Credit Card   Credit Card No.

Figure 9-12. Program: YCL_CH09_SELECTION_SCREEN03 - Radio Button Check Enabled

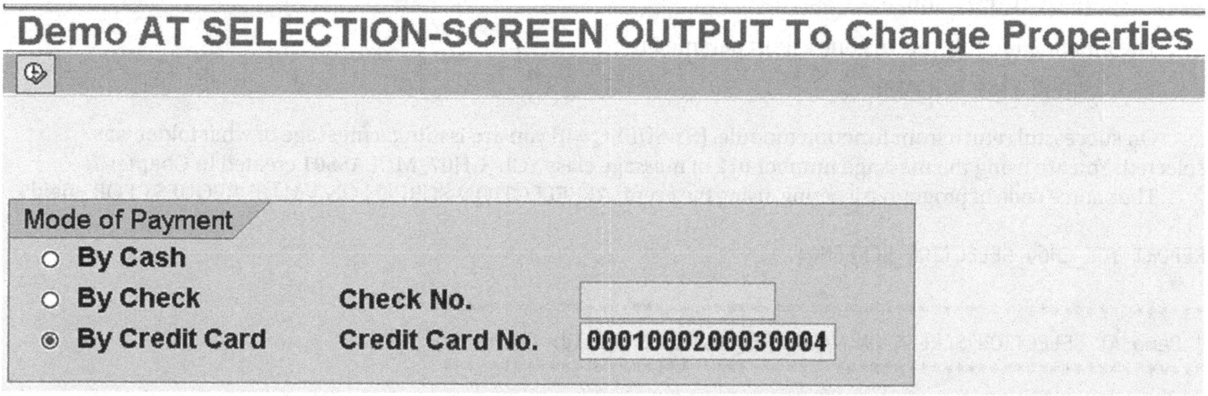

Demo AT SELECTION-SCREEN OUTPUT To Change Properties

Mode of Payment

- By Cash
- By Check   Check No.
- By Credit Card   Credit Card No. 0001000200030004

Figure 9-13. Program: YCL_CH09_SELECTION_SCREEN03 - Radio Button Credit Card Enabled

This concludes the demonstration of the selection screen event AT SELECTION-SCREEN OUTPUT.

Selection Screen Event – AT SELECTION-SCREEN ON VALUE-REQUEST FOR <field>

Whenever you wanted to provide the user, for a screen field, the facility of making a selection from a pop-up list instead of manually entering a value for the field, you have attached search help to the field (MATCHCODE OBJECT etc.). Often, when you are declaring screen fields by referring to DDIC table fields, search helps have been inherited from the original DDIC fields (KNA1-KUNNR is one such instance). You are able to provide a pop-up selection list by creating fixed values in the DDIC domain. (An option you should exercise only if these values are few: maximum of 25–30, and these values do not change over time, so there is no necessity for maintenance of these values.)

You must remember that search helps derive their list data from the SAP database: tables and views. The DDIC domain fixed values are also part of the SAP database. If you want to present the user with a list whose data is not derived from the SAP database, obviously the search helps will not be relevant. An example of presenting the user with non-SAP database data: present the user with a dialog box for making a selection of a folder on presentation server.

There might be scenarios where you want to present the user with a much more sophisticated filter dialog box than search helps can provide. You will write complex sophisticated coding to provide the sophisticated filter dialog boxes.

It is in these contexts in the selection screen environment, that you will trigger the event AT SELECTION-SCREEN ON VALUE-REQUEST FOR <field>.

This event is demonstrated to make a folder selection from the presentation server. The event is triggered for a specific selection screen field, which you indicate following the key word FOR.

You input a folder field (PARAMETERS FOLDER(50) TYPE C).

You are triggering the AT SELECTION-SCREEN ON VALUE-REQUEST FOR the screen field FOLDER.

In the triggered event AT SELECTION-SCREEN ON VALUE-REQUEST FOR FOLDER, you are calling the function module: TMP_GUI_BROWSE_FOR_FOLDER. This function module presents the user (on pressing F4 in the field FOLDER) with presentation server folder selection dialog box and returns to the calling program the selected folder name.

The function module accepts two optional import parameters:

WINDOW_TITLE

INITIAL_FOLDER

The function module returns one export parameter:

SELECTED_FOLDER.

On successful return from function module, (SY-SUBRC = 0) you are issuing a message of what folder was selected. You are using the message number 012 of message class YCL_CH07_MCLASS01 created in Chapter 7.

The source code of program triggering, using the event: AT SELECTION-SCREEN ON VALUE-REQUEST FOR <field>.

```
REPORT YCL_CH09_SELECTION_SCREEN04.

****************************************************************
* Demo AT SELECTION-SCREEN ON VALUE-REQUEST FOR <field> Event **
****************************************************************

SELECTION-SCREEN BEGIN OF BLOCK BL1 WITH FRAME TITLE
  TEXT-001.

SELECTION-SCREEN SKIP 2.
PARAMETERS FOLDER(50)  TYPE C.

SELECTION-SCREEN SKIP 2.
SELECTION-SCREEN END OF BLOCK BL1.
************************************************
AT SELECTION-SCREEN ON VALUE-REQUEST FOR FOLDER.

CALL FUNCTION 'TMP_GUI_BROWSE_FOR_FOLDER'
 EXPORTING
   WINDOW_TITLE           = 'Select Folder'
*    INITIAL_FOLDER         =
 IMPORTING
   SELECTED_FOLDER        = FOLDER
 EXCEPTIONS
   CNTL_ERROR             = 1
   OTHERS                 = 2
          .
```

```
IF SY-SUBRC <> 0.
 MESSAGE ID SY-MSGID TYPE SY-MSGTY NUMBER SY-MSGNO
        WITH SY-MSGV1 SY-MSGV2 SY-MSGV3 SY-MSGV4.
ELSE.
 MESSAGE S012(YCL_CH07_MCLASS01) WITH FOLDER.

ENDIF.
***********************************
```

The initial selection screen will look like Figure 9-14.

Figure 9-14. *Program: YCL_CH09_SELECTION_SCREEN04 – Initial Selection Screen*

On pressing F4 in the selection screen field 'FOLDER,' the screen will appear like Figure 9-15.

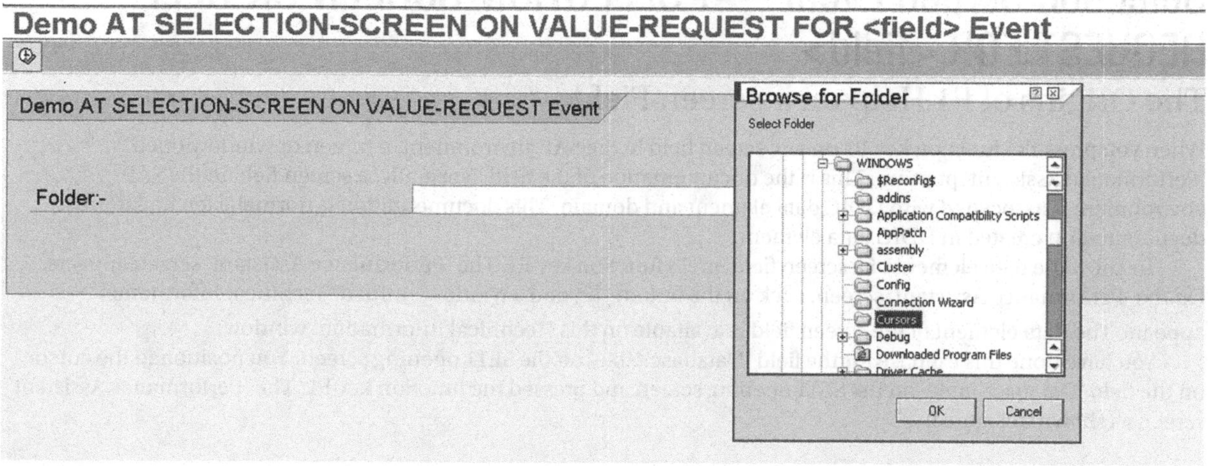

Figure 9-15. *Program: YCL_CH09_SELECTION_SCREEN04 – F4 on Field 'FOLDER'*

After making a folder selection, the screen will look like Figure 9-16.

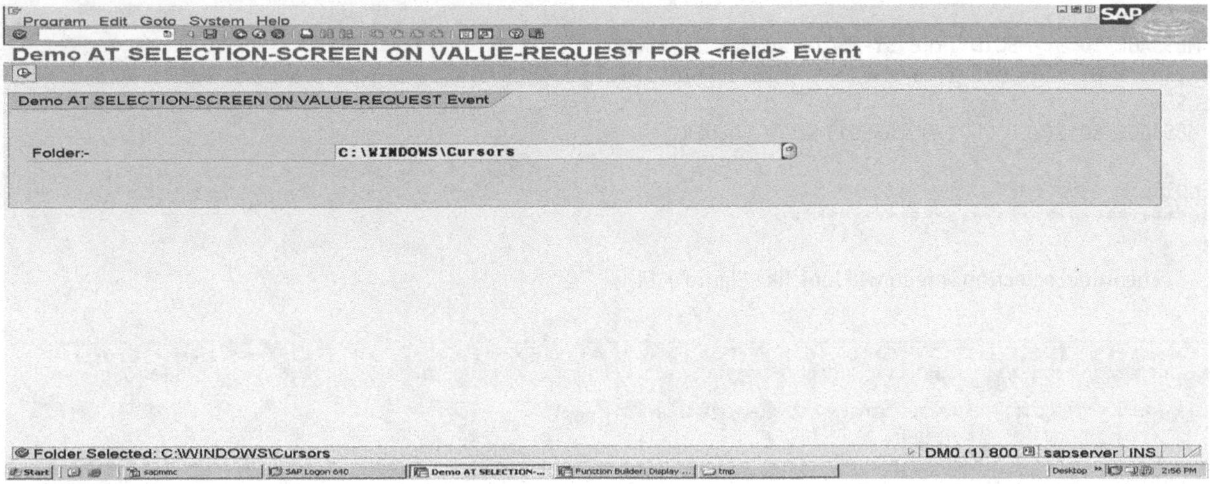

Figure 9-16. Program: YCL_CH09_SELECTION_SCREEN04 - Folder Selection

This was a demonstration of the SELECTION-SCREEN event: AT SELECTION-SCREEN OUTPUT.

Selection Screen Event – AT SELECTION-SCREEN ON HELP REQUEST FOR <field>

The Origins of F1 Help on a Screen Field

When you press the function key F1 on any screen field in the SAP environment, a screen or window titled 'Performance Assistant' pops up. This is the documentation of the field. Normally, a screen field in the SAP environment is associated with DDIC data element and domain. This documentation is normally fetched from the documentation created in DDIC data element.

To know the data element of a screen field, press function key F1. The 'Performance Assistant' screen appears. On the 'Performance Assistant' screen, click on the button , and a window entitled 'Technical Information' appears. The data element of the screen field is available on this 'Technical Information' window.

You have done this exercise for the field 'Database table' on the SE11 opening screen. You positioned the cursor on the field 'Database table' on the SE11 opening screen and pressed the function key F1. The 'Performance Assistant' screen as shown in Figure 9-17.

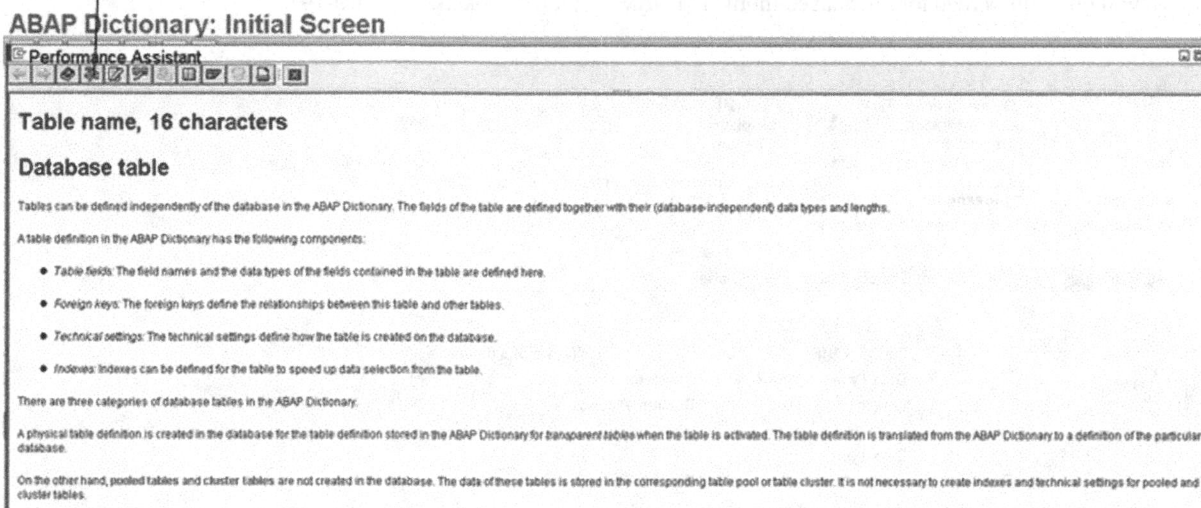

Technical Information
ABAP Dictionary: Initial Screen
Performance Assistant
Table name, 16 characters
Database table
Tables can be defined independently of the database in the ABAP Dictionary. The fields of the table are defined together with their (database-independent) data types and lengths.
A table definition in the ABAP Dictionary has the following components:
Table fields: The field names and the data types of the fields contained in the table are defined here.
Foreign keys: The foreign keys define the relationships between this table and other tables.
Technical settings: The technical settings define how the table is created on the database.
Indexes: Indexes can be defined for the table to speed up data selection from the table.
There are three categories of database tables in the ABAP Dictionary.
A physical table definition is created in the database for the table definition stored in the ABAP Dictionary for transparent tables when the table is activated. The table definition is translated from the ABAP Dictionary to a definition of the particular database.
On the other hand, pooled tables and cluster tables are not created in the database. The data of these tables is stored in the corresponding table pool or table cluster. It is not necessary to create indexes and technical settings for pooled and cluster tables.

***Figure 9-17.** Screen 'Performance Assistant' On Pressing F1 on Field Database Table of SE11 Opening Screen*

Clicking the button on the screen will make 'Technical Information' window appear as shown in Figure 9-18.

Data Element: TABNAME16

Technical Information

Screen Data

Program Name	SAPMSRD0
Screen number	0102

GUI Data

Program Name	SAPMSRD0
Status	MAIN_NEW

Field Data

Table Name	RSRD1
Field Name	TBMA_VAL
Data Element	TABNAME16
DE Supplement	0
Parameter ID	DTB

Field Description for Batch Input

Screen Field	RSRD1-TBMA_VAL

Navigate

***Figure 9-18.** Technical Information of Field Database Table of SE11 Opening Screen*

The data element for the field 'Database table' on the SE11 opening screen is 'TABNAME16' highlighted in Figure 9-18.

If you open the screen for the data element 'TABNAME16,' it will look like Figure 9-19.

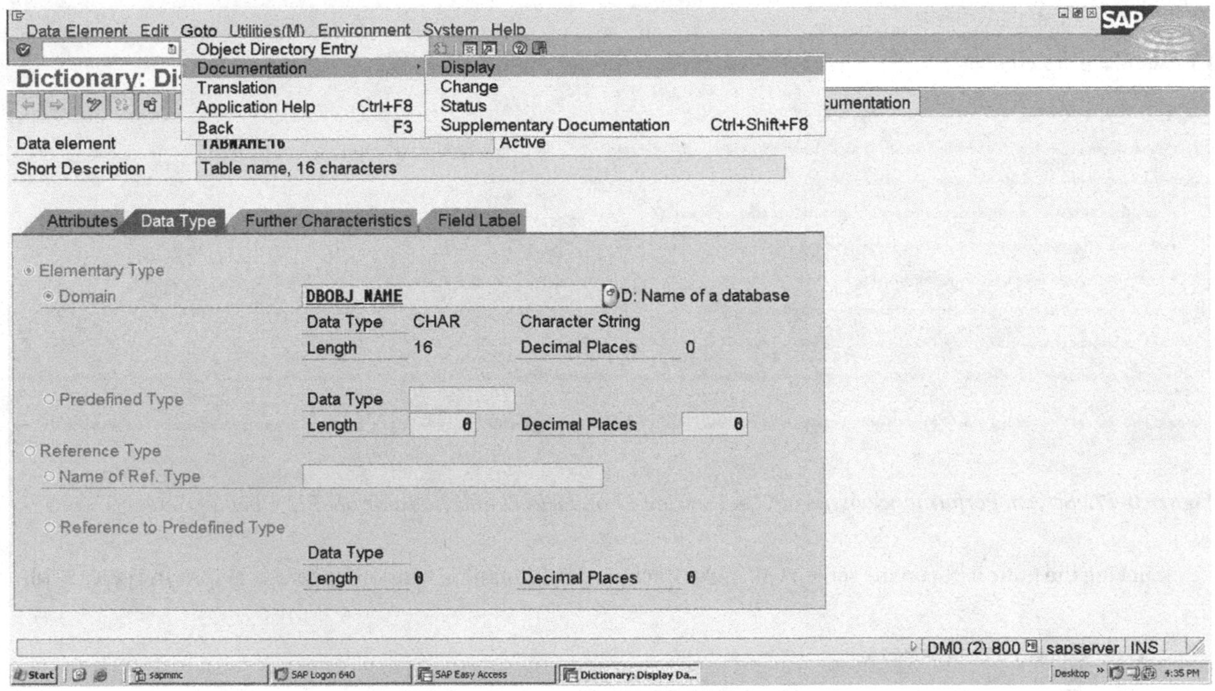

__Figure 9-19.__ Data Element: 'TABNAME16' – Goto ➤ Documentation

On the data element screen, if you select the menu option: Goto ➤ Documentation ➤ Display as shown in Figure 9-19, you will have the same screen as in Figure 9-17, the screen that appeared when you pressed function key F1 on the field 'Database table' of the SE11 opening screen. In the data element, there is provision to create documentation. This documentation appears by default when the user presses the function key F1 on a screen field assigned to the data element.

Situation for the Event: AT SELECTION-SCREEN ON HELP REQUEST FOR <field>

You will trigger the event AT SELECTION-SCRREN ON HELP REQUEST FOR <field> for a specific selection screen field, where you do not want the default documentation created in data element associated with the screen field to be displayed. You want some alternative text to be displayed. You will fetch the text from its origin and create the requisite coding to display the custom text when the user presses the function key F1 on the specified selection screen field.

There is no hands-on exercise for this event. The basic concept has been described here.

Selection Screen Event – AT SELECTION-SCREEN ON <field>

You can validate a selection screen field and report error of invalid field value by triggering the event AT SELECTION SCREEN On <field name>. When reporting the error, the selection screen disables all the fields for input except the field with the invalid value. If validation is being performed on more than one selection screen field, the physical order of fields on the selection screen will determine the order of error reporting. At this time, error for only one field will be reported. On correction of the value of error field, error of subsequent field/s, if any, will be reported.

This is being demonstrated with the program YCL_CH09_SELECTION-SCREEN05.

In this program, the selection screen has three fields: NAME1, KUNNR, and ORT01 in this order (through the PARAMETERS statement). You are triggering the event AT SELECTION-SCREEN on <field name> for the fields KUNNR and ORT01. You are checking for INITIAL value in these fields and issuing error message (message type 'E').

The system will issue error message if KUNNR contains INITIAL value. The field KUNNR will be enabled for input, and the other two fields NAME1 and ORT01 are disabled for input.

On entering a value in the field KUNNR, with INITIAL value in the field ORT01, the event AT SELECTION-SCREEN ON ORT01 will be triggered. An error message will be issued, the field ORT01 will be enabled for input, and other fields NAME1 and KUNNR will be disabled for input.

The source program:

```
REPORT YCL_CH09_SELECTION_SCREEN05.

*********************************************
* Demo AT SELECTION-SCREEN ON <field name> **
*********************************************

*******************************************************************
* you are triggering the event AT SELECTION-SCREEN ON <field name>**
* for two fields: (1) KUNNR (2) ORT01. the event for ORT01 is     **
* positioned first and then event for KUNNR. this positioning of  **
* events is immaterial. since KUNNR is positioned on the selection**
* first, the event AT SELECTION-SCREEN ON KUNNR will be triggered **
* first followed by the event AT SELECTION-SCREEN ON ORT01        **
*                                                                 **
* which ever validating first field triggers error will be        **
* reported. on correction of this field's error, error of         **
* subsequent field if any will be reported. at any time only      **
* one field's error will be reported                              **
*******************************************************************

PARAMETERS: NAME1 TYPE KNA1-NAME1,
            KUNNR TYPE KNA1-KUNNR,
            ORT01 TYPE KNA1-ORT01.
*****************************************
AT SELECTION-SCREEN ON ORT01.

IF ORT01 IS INITIAL.
 MESSAGE E013(YCL_CH07_MCLASS01).
ENDIF.
*****************************************
AT SELECTION-SCREEN ON KUNNR.

IF KUNNR IS INITIAL.
 MESSAGE E013(YCL_CH07_MCLASS01).
ENDIF.
```

With INITIAL value in field KUNNR, pressing the <Enter> key will have the screen look like Figure 9-20.

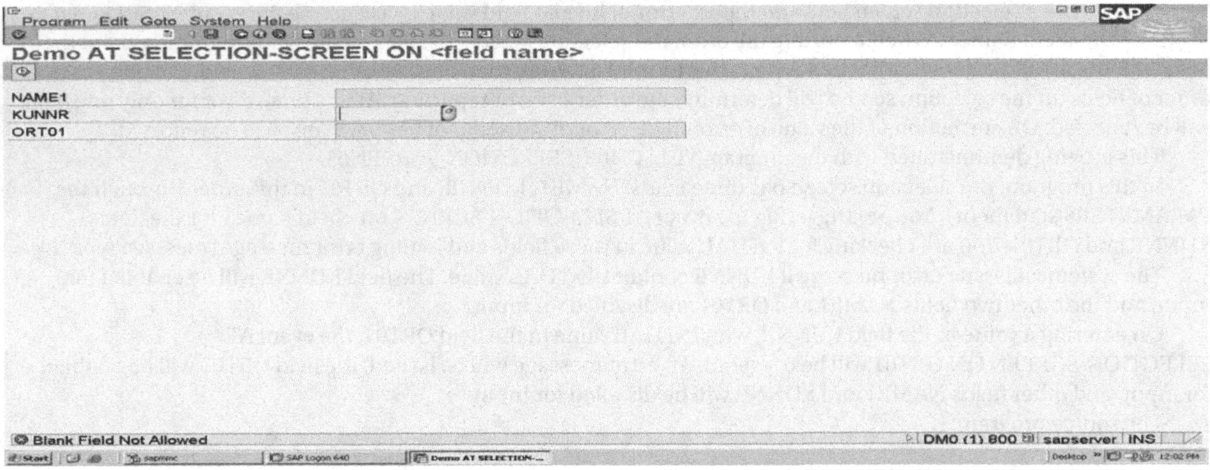

Figure 9-20. *Program: YCL_CH09_SELECTION_SCREEN05 - Field KUNNR Blank*

With a non-blank value the field KUNNR and INITIAL value in field ORT01, pressing the <Enter> key will have the screen look like Figure 9-21.

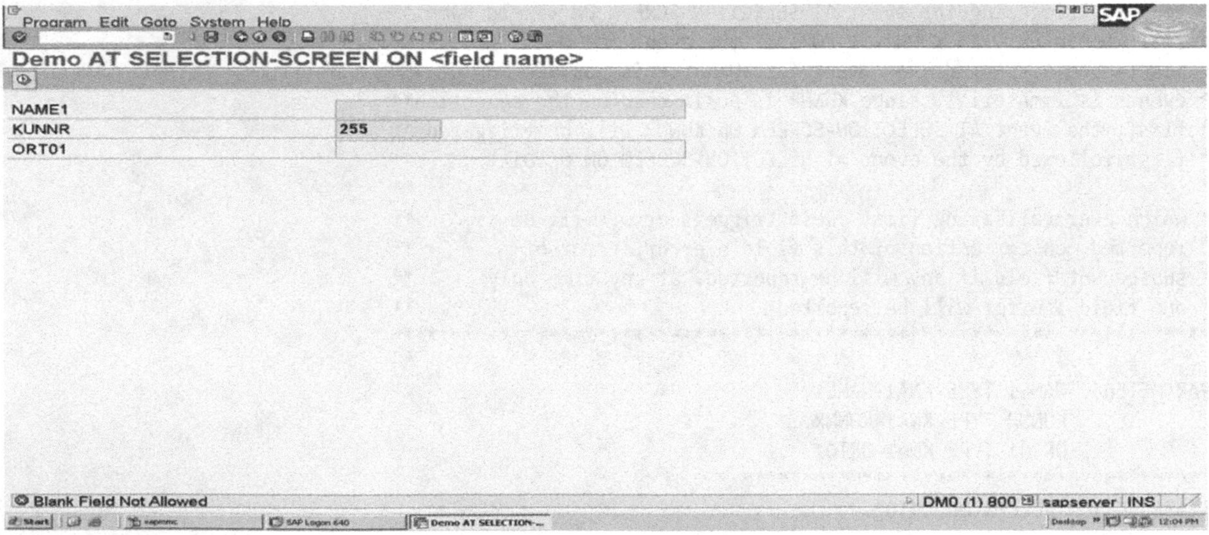

Figure 9-21. *Program: YCL_CH09_SELECTION_SCREEN05 - Field ORT01 Blank*

This program is contrived to demonstrate the event AT SELECTION-SCREEN on <field name>. There is a simpler way to check for blank fields. You can use the addition clause OBLIGATORY with the PARAMETERS statement. (It is obligatory or mandatory to enter values in the fields having the addition clause OBLIGATORY.) The system will check for INITIAL values in the fields and report INITIAL value error. The syntax:

```
PARAMETERS <field name> {TYPE | LIKE} {<ABAP elementary TYPE> |
<TYPE or data object>} OBLIGATORY.
```

Example: `PARAMETERS KUNNR TYPE KUNNR OBLIGATORY.`

But this check by the ABAP runtime system will not disable other fields for input after the error. And if you want custom message to be issued, you will opt for the triggering of event AT SELECTION-SCREEN ON <field name>. Moreover, you confined yourselves to validating the fields not containing INITIAL values. Validation would in real life consist of checking against a set of values (in a check table, etc.) and more. In the present program, the objective was to highlighted in a simple way: the event AT SELECTION-SCREEN ON <field name>.

The program YCL_CH09_SELECTION_SCREEN05VR demonstrates the addition OBLIGATORY. The program is not listed here but can be found in the E-Resource.

An obligatory or mandatory field in the SAP environment is signified by ☑ .

Selection Screen Event – AT SELECTION-SCREEN ON BLOCK <block name>

If on the selection screen, you want validation to apply on multiple fields, you can locate these fields in a block and trigger the event AT SELECTION-SCREEN ON BLOCK <block name>.

Consider the customer info database table KNB1. This table stores the company code of customers. If you look up the primary key fields of this table, they are 'MANDT', 'KUNNR', and 'BUKRS'. The same customer code can exist for multiple company codes.

If you want to validate the existence of field values in the table KNB1, you have to provide the values of the two primary key fields: 'KUNNR' and 'BUKRS' (the field 'MANDT' value is implicitly the value of the logged-in client).

The hands-on exercise is doing exactly this. On the selection screen, you have the two fields 'KUNNR' and 'BUKRS' located inside the block 'BLK1'. You are triggering the event AT SELECTION-SCREEN ON BLOCK BLK1. In this event, you are using the SELECT SINGLE... statement to ascertain whether the combination of the two field values entered on the selection screen exists in the database table KNB1. In case the combination of selection screen field values do not exist in the database table KNB1, (SY-SUBRC <> 0), you are issuing an error message. This will enable only the two fields inside the block 'BLK1' for input; all other fields outside the block on the selection screen are disabled for input.

You are referring to the DDIC structure fields: 'RF02D-KUNNR' and 'RF02D-BUKRS' when defining the selection screen fields 'KUNNR' and 'BUKRS'. The search help 'DEBI' is attached to the structure field: 'RF02D-KUNNR'. (Recall the collective search help DEBI you reviewed in Chapter 3.) The definition of selection screen fields by reference to the structure 'RF02D' fields is enabling you to have a selection pop-up list on the selection screen field 'KUNNR'. It is also enabling the export of multiple fields ['KUNNR' and 'BUKRS' for collective search help tab 'Customers (by company code)'] from the search help to the selection screen fields. For some reason the field 'KUNNR' in the structure 'RF02D' is DDIC TYPE CHAR and length 16, whereas in the database tables KNA1 and KNB1, the field 'KUNNR' is DDIC TYPE CHAR and length 10. This is being taken care before the SELECT statement is issued in the event AT SELECTION-SCREEN ON BLOCK BLK1.

The source program:

```
REPORT YCL_CH09_SELECTION_SCREEN06.

***************************************************
* Demo AT SELECTION-SCREEN ON BLOCK <block name> **
***************************************************
DATA: KEY_KUNNR   TYPE KUNNR.

PARAMETERS: NAME1 TYPE KNA1-NAME1.

SELECTION-SCREEN BEGIN OF BLOCK BLK1 WITH FRAME.

PARAMETERS: KUNNR TYPE  RF02D-KUNNR, " combination of these two fields
            BUKRS TYPE  RF02D-BUKRS. " checked for in the table KNB1

SELECTION-SCREEN END OF BLOCK BLK1.

SELECTION-SCREEN BEGIN OF BLOCK BLK2 WITH FRAME.

PARAMETERS: STRAS TYPE KNA1-STRAS,
            ORT01 TYPE KNA1-ORT01.

SELECTION-SCREEN END OF BLOCK BLK2.

*****************************************
AT SELECTION-SCREEN ON BLOCK BLK1.

 KEY_KUNNR = KUNNR+6(10). " adjust for KUNNR length being 16

  SELECT SINGLE KUNNR BUKRS FROM KNB1 INTO (KUNNR, BUKRS)
     WHERE KUNNR = KEY_KUNNR AND BUKRS = BUKRS.

  IF SY-SUBRC <> 0.
    MESSAGE E014(YCL_CH07_MCLASS01) WITH KUNNR BUKRS.
  ENDIF.
```

When the user presses F4 on the field 'KUNNR,' the screen will appear like Figure 9-22.

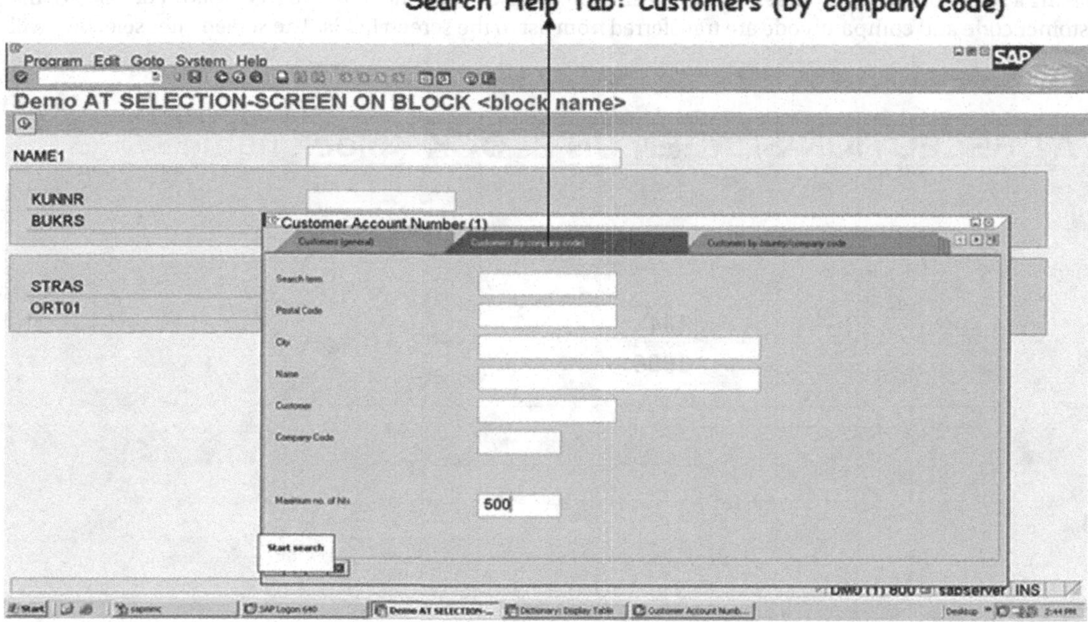

Figure 9-22. Program: YCL_CH09_SELECTION_SCREEN06 – F4 on Field KUNNR

On pressing <Enter> key on this dialog box, the screen will appear like Figure 9-23.

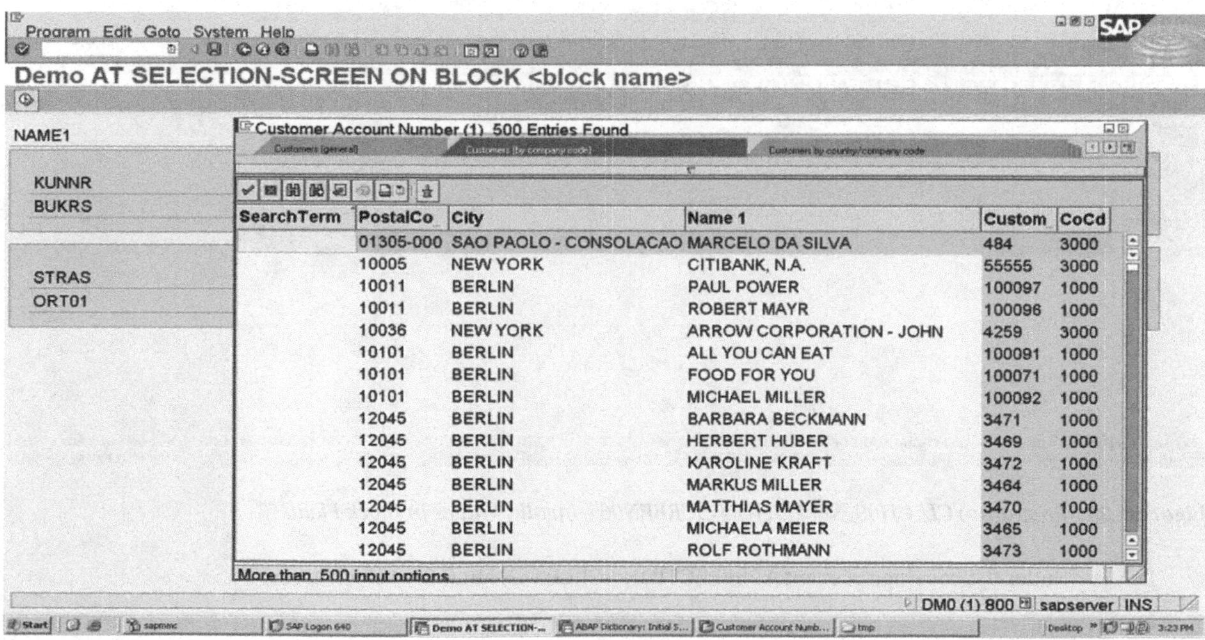

Figure 9-23. Program: YCL_CH09_SELECTION_SCREEN06 – F4 Customer List

After making a selection, (the very first highlighted entry in the list - customer code 484, company code 3000), the values of customer code and company code are transferred from list to the screen fields. The screen after selection will look like Figure 9-24.

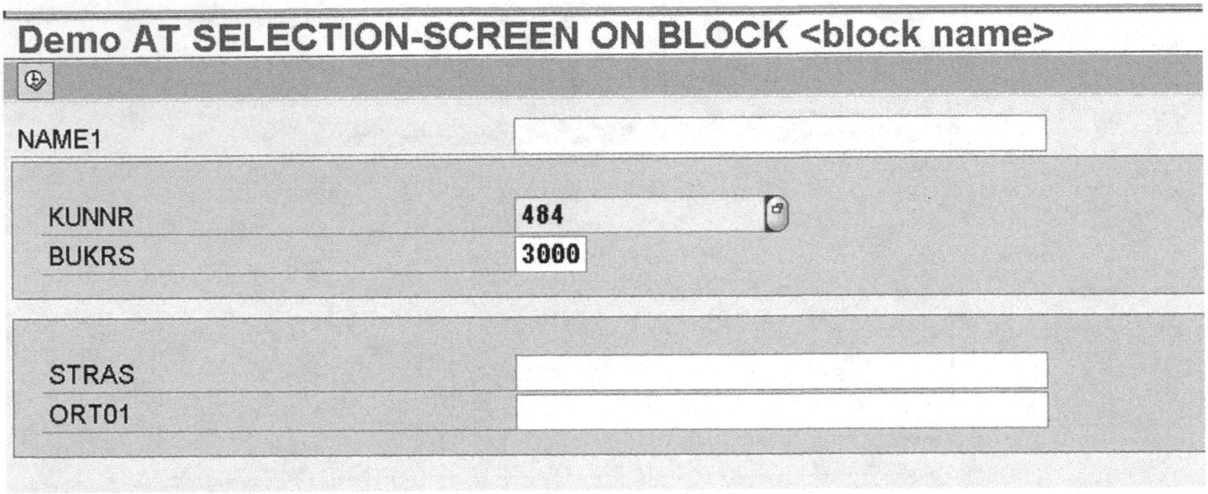

Demo AT SELECTION-SCREEN ON BLOCK <block name>

NAME1

KUNNR 484

BUKRS 3000

STRAS

ORT01

Figure 9-24. *Program: YCL_CH09_SELECTION_SCREEN06 - Selection Screen after Making Selection from List*

If you deliberately change the selection screen field values as to be invalid and press <enter> key, the event AT SELECTION-SCREEN ON BLOCK BLK1 is triggered, and the values do not exist in the database table KNB1 - the error message is issued and only the fields within the block 'BLK1' are enabled for input. The screen will look like Figure 9-25.

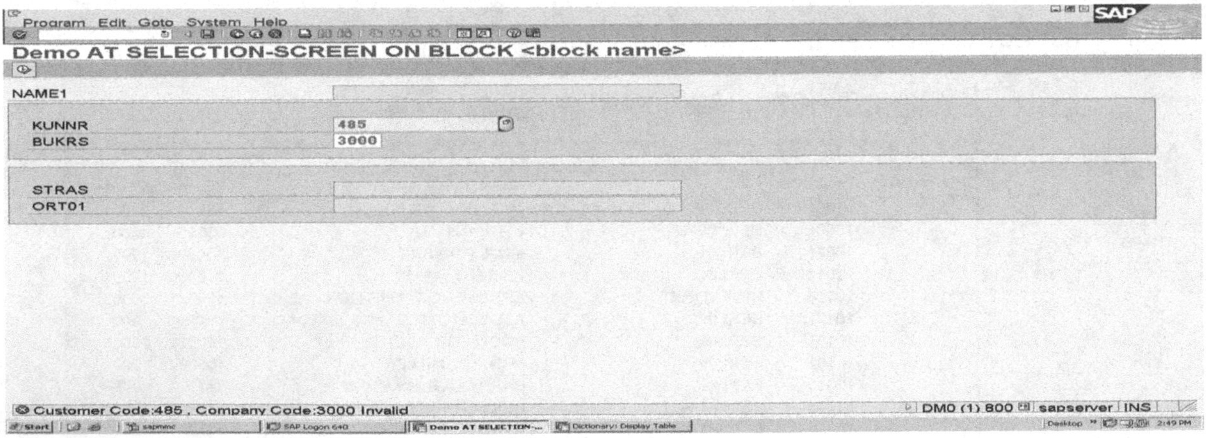

Program Edit Goto System Help

Demo AT SELECTION-SCREEN ON BLOCK <block name>

NAME1

KUNNR 485

BUKRS 3000

STRAS

ORT01

Customer Code:485 , Company Code:3000 Invalid

Figure 9-25. *Program: YCL_CH09_SELECTION_SCREEN06 - Invalid Values in Block Fields*

This concludes the coverage of event AT SELECTION-SCREEN ON BLOCK <block name>.

SELECTION-SCREEN Complex and Multiple Selections – SELECT-OPTIONS

The PARAMETERS statement enables a user to enter single values. On the basis of this single value, you can in the SELECT statement use the operators EQ, NE, GT, LT, GE, and LE (or their equivalent mathematical operators) to filter out data. Of course you can have multiple PARAMETERS input prompt statements/variables that you can use to filter data with SELECT statement.

With the selection screen statement: SELECT-OPTIONS, a user can make complex multiple value selections for a variable.

SELECT-OPTIONS - Syntax

The syntax of the SELECT-OPTIONS statement

```
SELECT-OPTIONS <variable name> FOR
 { <local data object> | (<data object>) }
 [OBLIGATORY]
 [VISIBLE LENGTH]
 [NO INTERVALS]
 [NO-EXTENSION]
 [DEFAULT <default value>]
 [LOWER CASE]
 [MATCHCODE OBJECT <search help name>]
 [<more addition clauses>]...
```

SELECT-OPTIONS - Key phrase.

<variable name> - A variable name can be maximum of eight characters, has to start with an alphabet letter, but the rest can be alphanumeric with embedded underscores (_).

FOR - Keyword.

<local data object> - A field or an elementary data object defined in the ABAP program.

<data object> - A field or an elementary data object in ABAP program (TYPE: C/STRING) that has been assigned the name of a global/DDIC field like 'LFA1-LIFNR.' This <data object> is to be enclosed in parentheses as part of the syntax.

The addition clauses OBLIGATORY, VISIBLE LENGTH, DEFAULT, LOWER CASE, MATCHCODE OBJECT <search help name> have been introduced in the context of the PARAMETERS statement and carry the same meaning here except DEFAULT has some more additions or options here and will be explained in subsequent TEXT.

The additions NO INTERVALS, NO-EXTENSION will be explained, along with <more addition clauses>...

Let the SELECT-OPTIONS be elaborated with a simple example:

SELECT-OPTIONS - Data objects

Consider the following code:

```
DATA: KUNNR TYPE KUNNR.

SELECT-OPTIONS: CUST_CD1 FOR KUNNR.
```

When a selection screen statement SELECT-OPTIONS is made in the manner as in the preceding code lines, the system internally creates two data objects of the same name 'CUST_CD1':

1. CUST_CD1 - a structure.
2. CUST_CD1 - an internal table - called the selection table.

The structure 'CUST_CD1' contains the following four fields with their TYPES and lengths:

```
SIGN(1)      TYPE C, " this field can take two values:-
                     " 'I' for include
                     " 'E' for exclude

OPTION(2)    TYPE C, " this field can take the following values:-
                     " 'EQ','NE','GT','GE','LT','LE','CP','NP' & 'BT','NB'

LOW          LIKE KUNNR,
HIGH         LIKE KUNNR.
```

1. The first field 'SIGN' of structure 'CUST_CD1' is TYPE C and length 1. It can assume only two values: 'I' for inclusion of values, 'E' for exclusion of values.
2. The second field 'OPTION' of structure 'CUST_CD1' is TYPE C, length 2. It can assume a value from either one of the two sets of values depending on whether the fourth field 'HIGH' has INITIAL value or NON-INITIAL value.

If the field 'HIGH' has INITIAL value, the second field 'OPTION' can assume one of the following values:

EQ	Equal To
NE	Not Equal To
GT	Greater Than
LT	Less Than
GE	Greater Than or Equal To
LE	Less Than or Equal To
CP	Contains Pattern
NP	Does Not Contain Pattern

If the field 'HIGH' has NON-INITIAL value, the second field 'OPTION' can assume one of the following values:

BT	Between
NB	Not Between

3. The third field 'LOW' of structure 'CUST_CD1' derives it attributes from the field or data object specified after the keyword 'FOR.' In the present example, you have specified the ABAP program field/data object 'KUNNR' The ABAP field 'KUNNR' has been declared referring to the DDIC data element 'KUNNR.' Hence, the field 'LOW' of structure 'CUST_CD1' has all the attributes of the data element 'KUNNR' including the attached search help 'C_KUNNR' (refer to data element 'KUNNR,' tab: 'Further Characteristics').
4. Like the third field 'LOW,' the fourth field 'HIGH' of structure 'CUST_CD1' derives its attributes from the field or data object specified after the key word 'FOR.'

If for a row in the selection table 'CUST_CD1,' the fields 'LOW' and 'HIGH' have values, it serves as a range of value selection: the 'LOW' field having the start value of the range, the 'HIGH' field having the end value of the range. In this case, the field 'HIGH' must contain value greater than or equal to the value in the field 'LOW.'

If for a row in the selection table 'CUST_CD1,' the field 'LOW' has a value and the field 'HIGH' has INITIAL value, this serves as a single value selection.

Having described the data object aspect of the selection screen statement: SELECT-OPTIONS, let the selection screen input prompts and the associated dialog boxes aspect be described next.

SELECT-OPTIONS – Screens, Prompts And Dialog Boxes

When the simple code lines introduced in the preceding head: SELECT_OPTIONS - Data Objects is executed, a screen appears as in Figure 9-26.

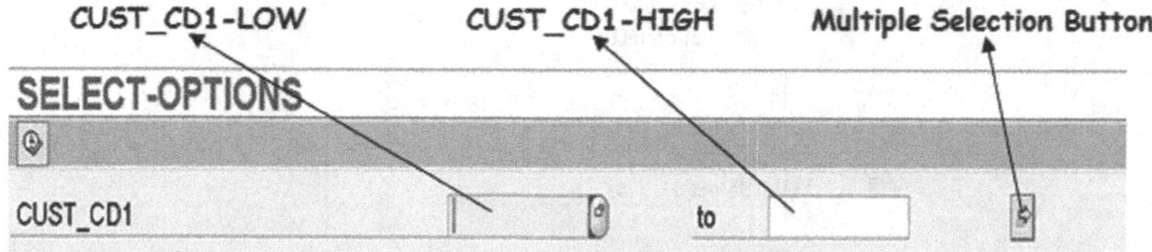

Figure 9-26. SELECT-OPTIONS: CUST_CD1 - Opening Screen

The screen has input prompts for the fields 'LOW' and 'HIGH'. On the extreme right it has the 'Multiple selection' button. Clicking on this 'Multiple selection' button, the dialog box as in Figure 9-27 will appear.

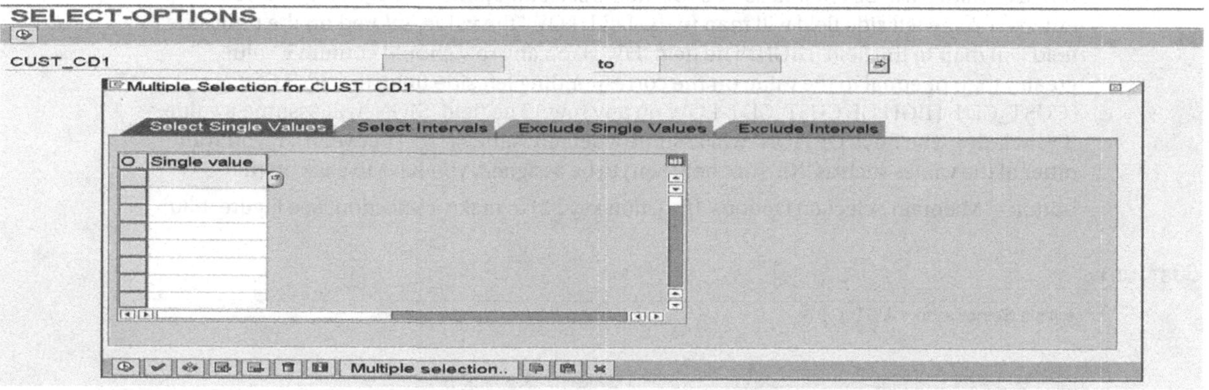

Figure 9-27. SELECT-OPTIONS: CUST_CD1 - Multiple Selection Dialog Box, 'Select Single Values' tab

Tabs: The multiple selection dialog box has four tabs:

1. 'Select Single Values': If you enter values (one value in each row), each value will be entered as one row in the selection table CUST_CD1. The value will map to the field 'LOW'. The field 'HIGH' will contain INITIAL value. The field 'SIGN' will assume a value 'I' (Include). The field 'OPTION' will assume a default value of 'EQ'. If you want other of the values such as 'NE', 'GT', 'LT', 'GE', or 'LE' to be assigned, you have to click on the button - 'Maintain Select Options' (function key F2) to make a selection. You can use the operators CP, NP (contains pattern, etc.) if you end a row value with '*' or '+'. See Figure 9-28.

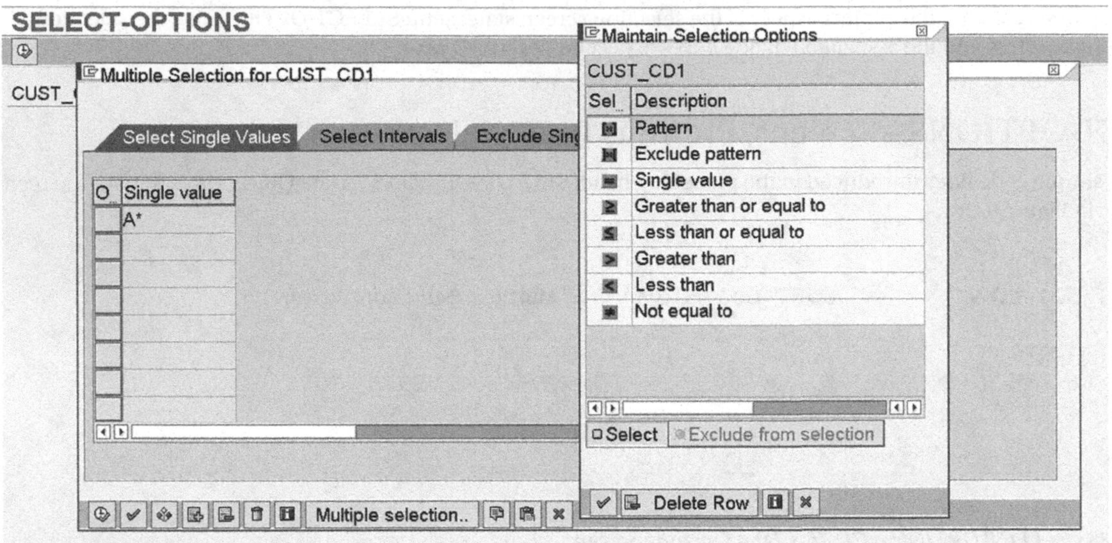

Figure 9-28. *SELECT-OPTIONS: CUST_CD1 – 'Select Single Values' tab, 'Maintain Select Options' Dialog Box*

2. 'Select Intervals': If you click on this tab, you can enter range of values (Figure 9-29). Each range of values will be entered as one row in the selection table CUST_CD1. The value entered on the left side field will map to the field 'LOW', the value entered on the right side field will map to the field 'HIGH'. The field 'HIGH' on any row should contain a value greater than or equal to the value on the corresponding left side field: that is, 'LOW'. (CUST_CD1-HIGH GE CUST_CD1-LOW on any row.) The field 'SIGN' will assume a value 'I' (Include). The field 'OPTION' will assume a default value of 'BT (Between). If you want other of the values such as 'NB' (not between) to be assigned, you have to click on the button – 'Maintain Selection Options' (function key F2) to make a selection. See Figure 9-30.

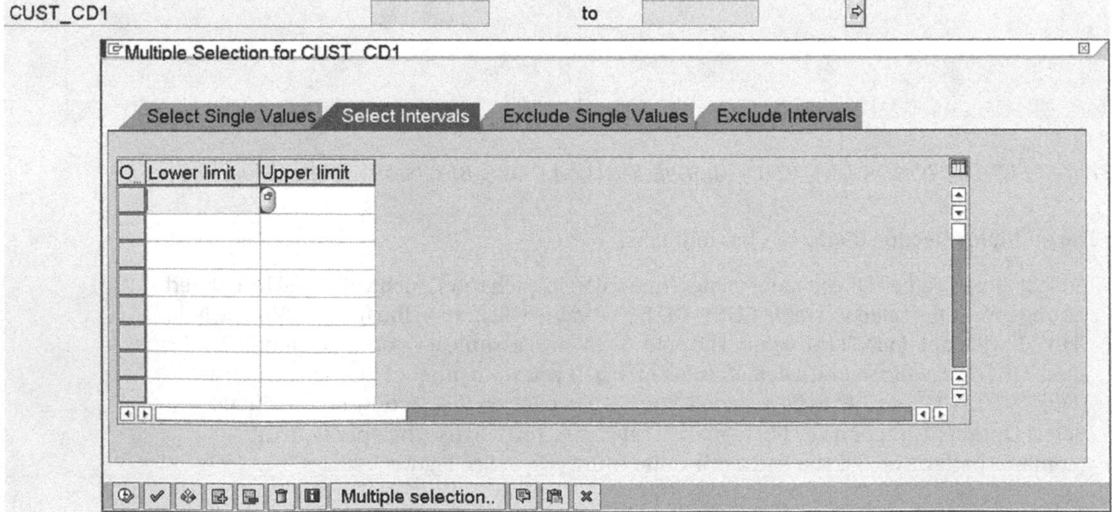

Figure 9-29. *SELECT-OPTIONS: CUST_CD1 – Multiple Selection Dialog Box, tab 'Select Intervals'*

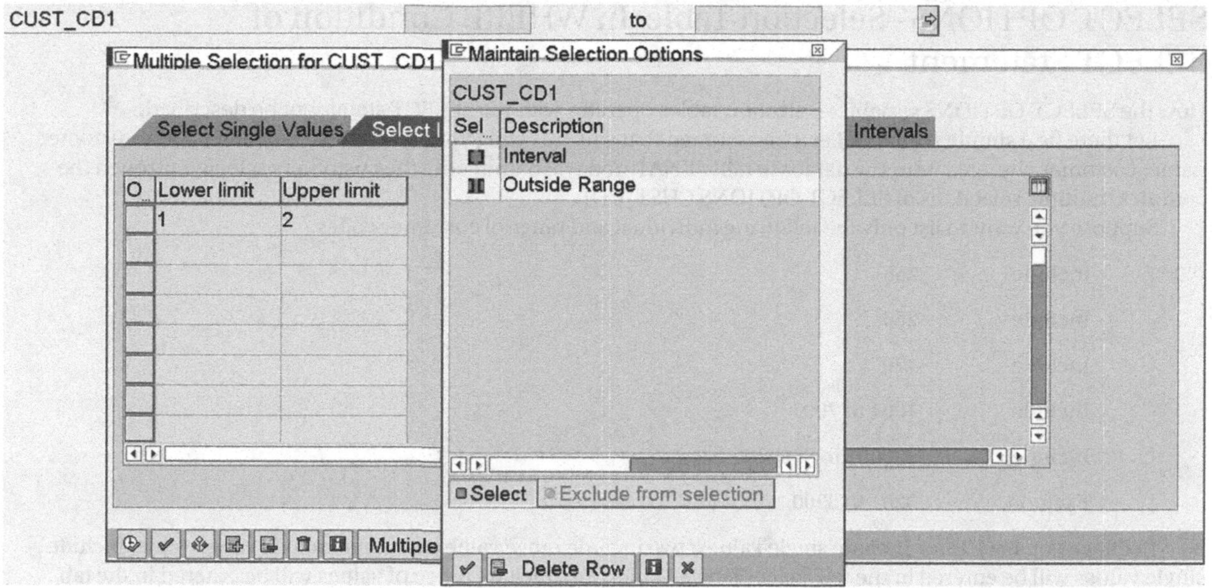

***Figure 9-30.** SELECT-OPTIONS: CUST_CD1 – tab 'Select Intervals,' 'Maintain Select Options' Dialog Box*

3. And 4. are similar to 1. and 2., respectively, except that the field 'SIGN' will take a value of 'E' (Exclude). For the first two tabs the field 'SIGN' will have value 'I' and for the last two tabs the field 'SIGN' will have value 'E.'

Buttons at the Bottom of the Dialog Box: A brief on the buttons at the bottom of the multiple selection dialog box:

Accept entered values, close the multiple selection dialog box, and go back to selection screen.

Check or validate entered values (values are validated. HIGH LOW, etc.)

Maintain Select Options. You can select an operator from a list (EQ, NE...).

Insert/Delete rows.

Delete all values.

Help.

Multiple selection.. Clicking on the button will bring up the value selection/filter dialog box of a search help, if any.

Import values from a text file on presentation server.

Paste from clipboard.

Cancel, close the multiple selection dialog box.

This is about the SELECT-OPTIONS input prompts and dialog boxes.

SELECT-OPTIONS -Selection Table In WHERE Condition of SELECT Statement

How the SELECT-OPTIONS variable - selection tables operates with the SELECT statement be described.

Let there be a simple scenario. Let it be assumed that you are listing your customers: customer code, customer name, customer city, etc., from the database table KNA1. You will output only the customers selected through the complex multiple selections of SELECT-OPTIONS CUST_CD1.

Suppose you want to list only the following individual and range of customer codes:

Include	255
Include	260
Include	470
Include	1001 to 7000
Include	300001 to 399999
Exclude	3201 to 3300

In effect, you have three include single values; two include range values and one exclude range value. Include single values will be entered in the tab 'Select Single Values,' and include range of values will be entered in the tab 'Select Intervals.' The exclude range value will be entered in the tab 'Exclude Intervals.' The three tabs of the multiple selection dialog box with the entered values will appear like Figure 9-31, 9-32, and 9-33.

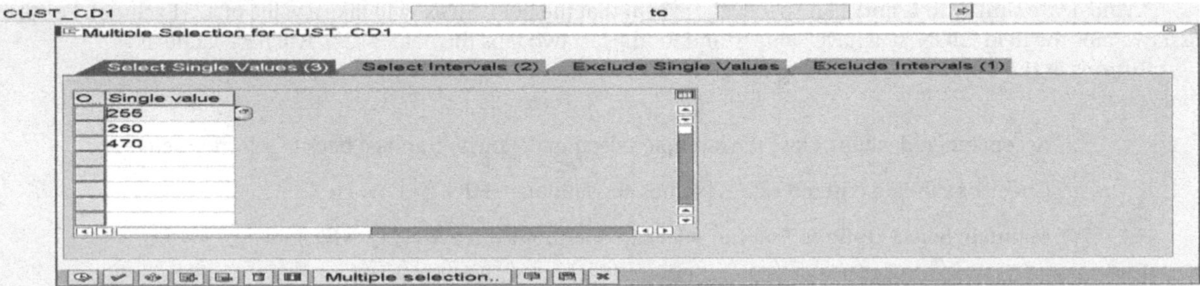

Figure 9-31. *SELECT-OPTIONS: CUST_CD1 - Entered Include Single Values*

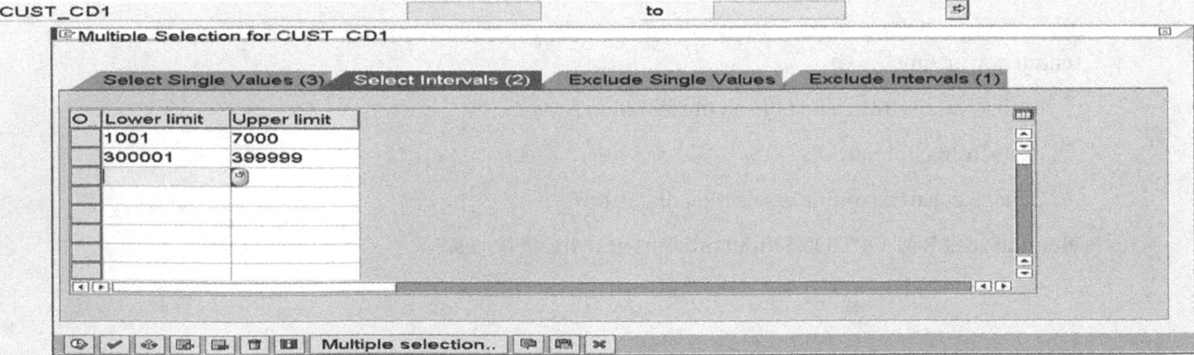

Figure 9-32. *SELECT-OPTIONS: CUST_CD1 - Entered Include Range of Values*

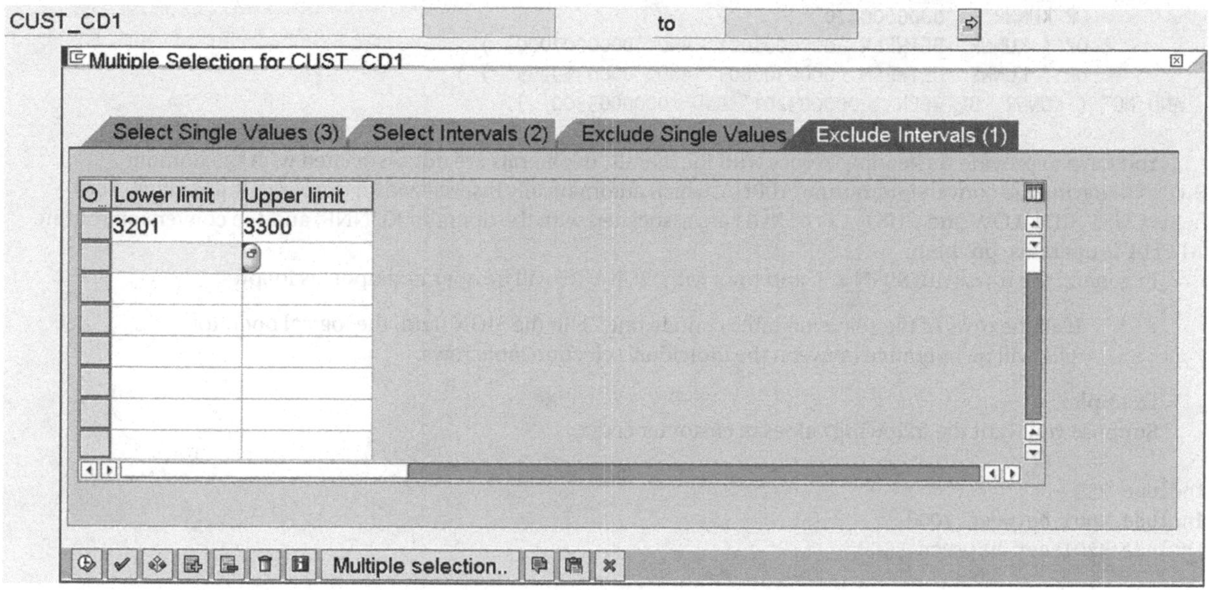

Figure 9-33. *SELECT-OPTIONS: CUST_CD1 – Entered Exclude Range of Values*

There will a total of six rows in the selection table CUST_CD1 with following field values:

Table 9-2. *Contents of Selection Table CUST_CD1 as Per Entries in Figures 9-31, 9-32, and 9-33*

SIGN	OPTION	LOW	HIGH
I	EQ	255	
I	EQ	260	
I	EQ	470	
I	BT	1001	7000
I	BT	300001	399999
E	BT	3201	3300

The Open SQL SELECT statement to filter out customer codes with the SELECT-OPTIONS selection table using the 'IN' operator will be:

```
SELECT <result> from KNA1 INTO <destination itab>
 WHERE KUNNR IN CUST_CD1.
```

This Open SQL statement implicitly operates the 'OR' logic between the individual CUST_CD1 row contents with SIGN = 'I'. The Open SQL statement operates the 'AND NOT' logic between the individual row contents with SIGN = 'E'. For your set of values, it is equivalent to writing:

```
SELECT <result> from KNA1 INTO TABLE <destination itab>
  WHERE  ( KUNNR = '0000000255'
           OR KUNNR = '0000000260'
```

```
        OR KUNNR = '0000000470'
        OR ( KUNNR  BETWEEN '0000001001' AND '0000007000' )
        OR ( KUNNR  BETWEEN '0000300001' AND '0000399999' ) )
  AND NOT ( KUNNR  BETWEEN '0000003201' AND '0000003300' ).
```

You have to provide the leading zeroes with the literals; the literals are not associated with the domain 'KUNNR' having the conversion routine 'ALPHA,' which automatically inserts leading zeroes to input fields. The fields CUST_CD1-LOW and CUST_CD1-HIGH are associated with the domain 'KUNNR,' and the conversion routine 'ALPHA' is operative on them.

In general the rows with SIGN = 'I' and rows with SIGN = 'E' will be operated upon as follows:

1. If all the rows of the selection table contain only 'I' in the SIGN field, the logical operator 'OR' will be operative between the individual selection table rows.

Example:
Suppose you want the following values of customer codes:

```
Include 255
Include 4001 between 7000
Include 3201 not between 3300
```

For this set of values, it is equivalent to writing:

```
SELECT <result> from KNA1 INTO TABLE <destination itab>
WHERE
KUNNR = '0000000255' OR ( KUNNR BETWEEN '0000004001' AND '0000007000' )
 OR ( KUNNR NOT BETWEEN '0000003201' AND '0000003300' ).
```

2. If all the rows of the selection table contain only 'E' in the SIGN field, the logical operator 'AND NOT' will be operative between the individual selection table rows and the logical operator 'NOT' will operate on the first row.

Example:
Suppose you want the following values of customer codes to be output:

```
Exclude 1000
Exclude 1001 between 7000
```

For this set of values, it is equivalent to writing:

```
SELECT <result> from KNA1 INTO TABLE <destination itab>
WHERE
NOT KUNNR = '0000001000'
AND NOT ( KUNNR BETWEEN '0000001001' AND '0000007000' ).
```

3. If the rows of the selection table contain 'I' and 'E' in the SIGN field, the logical operator 'OR' will be operative between the rows with SIGN = 'I,' the logical operator 'AND NOT' between the rows with SIGN = 'E' and the logical operator 'AND NOT' will operate between the rows with SIGN = 'I' and the rows with SIGN = 'E.'

Example:

Suppose you want the following values of customer codes to be output:

```
Include 255
Include 1001 between 7000
Exclude 3001 between 4000
```

For this set of values, it is equivalent to writing:

```
SELECT <result> from KNA1 INTO TABLE <destination itab>
WHERE
( KUNNR = '0000000255' OR KUNNR BETWEEN '0000001001' AND '0000007000' )
AND NOT ( KUNNR BETWEEN '0000003001' AND '0000004000' ).
```

The program YCL_CH09_SELECTION_SCREEN07 is not being listed here. It is available in E-Resource. You can try out the various SELECT-OPTIONS values with the SELECT statement with selection table in the WHERE condition with the IN operator. You can compare this with the equivalent SELECT statements with logical operators and literals values.

The program YCL_CH09_SELECTION_SCREEN08 is listed. It is a modified version of the Chapter 6 program YCL_CH06_ITAB05. You were summarizing the sales data customer wise for a specified company code input through the PARAMETERS statement. You were using the COLLECT statement to generate summarized data. In the present program you have added the SELECT-OPTIONS statement for customer code, so that you can report the summarized customer wise sales for a specified company code for specified customers. You can copy the text symbols (used in the non-standard header) from the program YCL_CH06_ITAB05 using transaction code SE32.

At the very beginning of the list, you will output the contents of the selection table. It serves as a record, as to the generated report based on what values in the selection table.

The source:

```
REPORT YCL_CH09_SELECTION_SCREEN08 NO STANDARD PAGE HEADING
          LINE-SIZE 120 LINE-COUNT 60.

**************************************************
* Demo SELECT-OPTIONS: Customer Sales Summary   **
**************************************************

DATA: SALES_TAB  TYPE YCL_CH06_SALES_SUM_TAB,
      SALES_STRU LIKE LINE OF SALES_TAB,
      TOTAL      TYPE VBRK-NETWR,
      BUTXT      TYPE T001-BUTXT,
      WAERS      TYPE T001-WAERS,
      BUTXTS     TYPE STRING.

PARAMETERS: CCODE TYPE VBRK-BUKRS DEFAULT 3000 VALUE CHECK.

SELECT-OPTIONS CUST_CD1 FOR SALES_STRU-KUNNR.
                                              " data object/field after key word
                                              " FOR has to be a local data object
```

```
******************************************
TOP-OF-PAGE.
WRITE:/5 TEXT-001, CCODE NO-GAP, '/' NO-GAP,  BUTXTS, 102 TEXT-003,
        107(3) SY-PAGNO.
WRITE:/40 TEXT-002, WAERS.
SKIP 1.
WRITE:/5(104) SY-ULINE.
WRITE:/5 TEXT-004, 11 TEXT-005, 23 TEXT-006, 60 TEXT-007, 91(17)
        TEXT-008 RIGHT-JUSTIFIED.
WRITE:/5 TEXT-009, 13 TEXT-010.
WRITE:/5(104) SY-ULINE.

********************************************
START-OF-SELECTION.

SELECT SINGLE BUTXT WAERS FROM T001 INTO (BUTXT, WAERS) WHERE
       BUKRS = CCODE.

BUTXTS = BUTXT.

SELECT KUNNR NAME1 ORT01 NETWR KURRF FROM YCL_CH05_VBRKKNA INTO
  CORRESPONDING FIELDS OF SALES_STRU

  WHERE BUKRS = CCODE
        AND KUNNR IN CUST_CD1. " IN operator with SELECT-OPTIONS
                               " variable

 SALES_STRU-NETWR =  SALES_STRU-NETWR * SALES_STRU-KURRF.
 SALES_STRU-KURRF = 0. "to prevent overflow
 COLLECT SALES_STRU INTO SALES_TAB.
ENDSELECT.

SORT SALES_TAB BY KUNNR.

LOOP AT CUST_CD1.

 WRITE:/5(2) SY-TABIX, CUST_CD1-SIGN, CUST_CD1-OPTION, CUST_CD1-LOW,
  CUST_CD1-HIGH.

ENDLOOP.

SKIP 4. " a gap of 4 lines between CUST_CD1 data &
        " customer data.

LOOP AT SALES_TAB INTO SALES_STRU.

 WRITE :/5(4) SY-TABIX, SALES_STRU-KUNNR USING NO EDIT MASK,
  SALES_STRU-NAME1,SALES_STRU-ORT01, (17) SALES_STRU-NETWR.
 TOTAL = TOTAL + SALES_STRU-NETWR.

ENDLOOP.

SKIP 1.
WRITE :/(17) TOTAL UNDER SALES_STRU-NETWR.
```

The output will look like Figures 9-34 and 9-35.

```
Contents of Selection Table CUST_CD1

Demo SELECT-OPTIONS: Customer Sales Summary

Customer Wise Sales Summary of Company Code: 3000/IDES US INC                        Page: 1
                                   Currency: USD

Srl. Customer    N a m e                          C i t y                            Amount
No.    Code

1  I EQ 250
2  I EQ 255
3  I EQ 470
4  I BT 1001       7000
5  I BT 300001     399999

  1  0000000255 Emma Bull                         DENVER                           2,207.00
  2  0000000470 Alex Lynch                        PHILADELPHIA                    11,860.80
  3  0000001455 General Distributors Inc.         STAFFORD                             0.00
  4  0000001470 Aircraft Products                 Slough                          11,000.00
  5  0000001508 Deutsche Computer AG              Berlin                           5,987.50
  6  0000003000 Thomas Bush Inc.                  MAYWOOD                          7,602.00
  7  0000003001 Industrial Supplies Inc.          VIRGINIA BEACH                   4,320.00
  8  0000003028 Live Insurance Inc.               DENVER                          12,038.25
```

Figure 9-34. *Program: YCL_CH09_SELECTION_SCREEN08 – Output*

```
Demo SELECT-OPTIONS: Customer Sales Summary

Customer Wise Sales Summary of Company Code: 3000/IDES US INC                        Page: 1
                                   Currency: USD

Srl. Customer    N a m e                          C i t y                            Amount
No.    Code

 39  0000300713 Brighton Inc                      VESTAL                       2,785,285.30
 40  0000300715 Sunburst Inc                      STUART                       1,062,936.00
 41  0000300716 Matrax                            AUGUSTA                        996,115.00
 42  0000300717 JMart                             SPRINGFIELD                  1,344,350.00
 43  0000300718 Innovative Systems, Inc.          CARSON CITY                  1,153,532.80
 44  0000300719 Hall Manufacturing                EVERETT                     12,313,262.00
Customer Wise Sales Summary of Company Code: 3000/IDES US INC                        Page: 2
                                   Currency: USD

Srl. Customer    N a m e                          C i t y                            Amount
No.    Code

 45  0000301090 Townsend Company                  LAWRENCEVILLE                    2,350.00

                                                                              54,362,420.98
```

Figure 9-35. *Program: YCL_CH09_SELECTION_SCREEN08 – Output With Total*

The three aspects of the SELECT-OPTIONS were described: the internally created data objects, (selection table and structure) the screen prompts and dialog boxes and the use of the SELECT-OPTIONS variable in the SELECT statement with the 'IN' operator to filter data. The SELECT-OPTIONS data object provides a sophisticated means of filtering data based on runtime values. This concludes the coverage of the SELECT-OPTIONS.

ABAP Program Variants

An ABAP program may have a number of SELECT-OPTIONS variables as well as a number of PARAMETERS variables to enter values and filter out data based on these values for output. The multiple selection values of SELECT-OPTIONS variables as well as the single values of PARAMETERS variables may be fixed. That is, the same set of values is being used again and again (every week or every month...). In this situation, it could be a good idea to be able to save and retrieve these values being used again and again.

The variants feature of ABAP program enables you to do this. You can save any number of set of values for the SELECT-OPTIONS and PARAMETERS variables. You can retrieve any of the stored set of values before executing a program.

You can store a set of SELECT-OPTIONS and PARAMETERS values under a variant name. The name space of a variant is a maximum of 14 characters. A variant name can contain special characters except '&' and '%.' But it is better to stick to the convention of starting a variant name with an alphabet letter, and the rest of the characters as alphanumeric with embedded underscores. (_)

The variants like the text elements, etc., do not have an independent existence. They are attached to a program and are part of an ABAP program.

You can create variants from the ABAP editor opening screen. It is assumed that you have already created the source code. Enter the ABAP source program name in the program field, select the radio button 'Variants,' and click on the change button. You are now creating variants for the program YCL_CH09_SELECTION_SCREEN07. The selection screen of this program consists of a single SELECT-OPTIONS variable 'CUST_CD1' referring to a local data object 'KUNNR,' which, in turn, is referring to the data element 'KUNNR.' The variant maintenance screen will look like Figure 9-36.

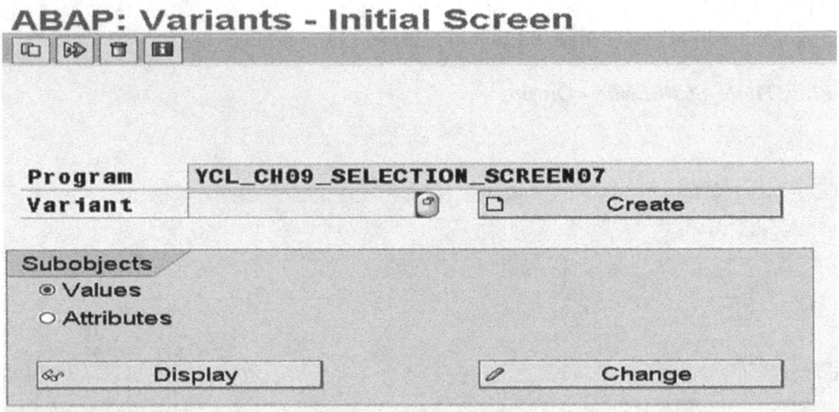

Figure 9-36. *Program: YCL_CH09_SELECTION_SCREEN07 - Maintain Variants*

Enter a variant name 'VAR1,' and click on the Create button. (If variants already exist, you can select from a selection list: F4, etc.). The familiar SELECT-OPTIONS prompt will appear with 'Multiple Selection' button on the extreme right. Click on the 'Multiple Selection' button. Enter the values in the tabs: 'Select Single Values,' 'Select Intervals,' 'Exclude Single Values,' 'and Exclude Intervals.' You entered the following values for the selection table 'CUST_CD1':

Select Single Values:
250
260
470

Select Intervals
1001 to 7000
300001 to 399999

Exclude Single Values
1031

Exclude Intervals
3201 to 3300
4001 to 4500

Click on the copy button (first button from the left) of the multiple selection dialog box. The screen after returning from the multiple selection dialog box will look like Figure 9-37.

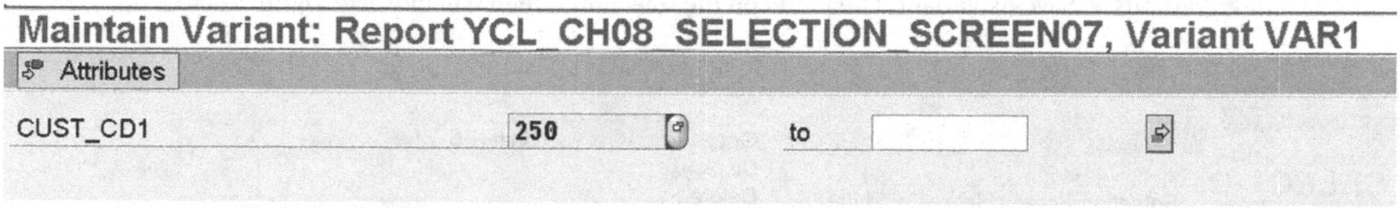

Figure 9-37. *Program: YCL_CH09_SELECTION_SCREEN07 - Create Variant: After Entry of Values*

There is only one prompt variable: 'CUST_CD1'; if more SELECT-OPTIONS and PARAMETERS statements were given in the program, more prompts will appear on the selection screen. You can enter values for as many selection screen variables as you want.

The multiple selection screen has been skipped now as you are already familiar with it, being exposed to it in the previous topic:' SELECTION-SCREEN Complex and Multiple Selections: SELECT-OPTIONS.'

You can optionally enter attributes for the variants by clicking on the attributes button on the application toolbar. The variants attributes screen will be like Figure 9-38.

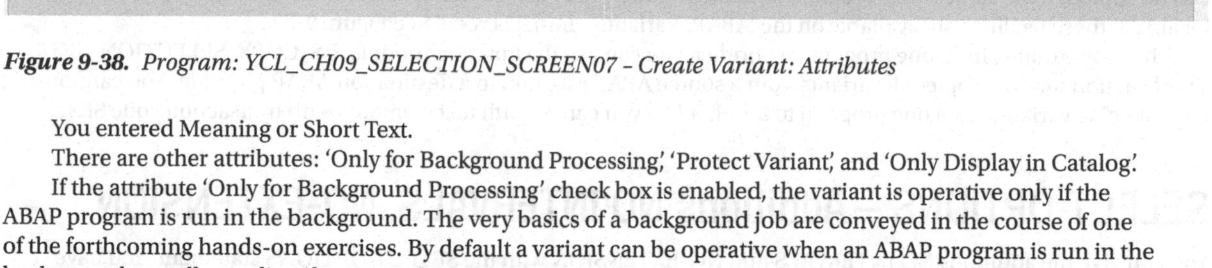

Figure 9-38. *Program: YCL_CH09_SELECTION_SCREEN07 - Create Variant: Attributes*

You entered Meaning or Short Text.

There are other attributes: 'Only for Background Processing,' 'Protect Variant,' and 'Only Display in Catalog.'

If the attribute 'Only for Background Processing' check box is enabled, the variant is operative only if the ABAP program is run in the background. The very basics of a background job are conveyed in the course of one of the forthcoming hands-on exercises. By default a variant can be operative when an ABAP program is run in the background as well as online/foreground mode.

If you enable the check box for the attribute 'Protect Variant,' only the user who created it can change the variant.

If you enable the check box 'Only Display in Catalog,' the variant is inoperative. It will appear only in the list/catalog of the ABAP program's variants. To view the list/catalog of an ABAP program's variants, in the ABAP: Variants – Initial Screen (Figure 9-36), select the menu option: Variants ➤ Catalog. You can make a catalogued, inoperative variant operative by disabling this check box.

These attributes are the attributes of all the variables/objects of a variant. In your program YCL_CH09_SELECTION_SCREEN07, you have a single selection screen variable, CUST_CD1. In the other program YCL_CH09_SELECTION_SCREEN08, you have two selection screen variables, CCODE and CUSTCD1. There can any number of selection screen variables. The set of values stored as a variant will cover all selection screen variables. There are attributes pertaining to each selection screen variable. You can see this in Figure 9-38 under 'Objects for selection screen.' These attributes of individual selection screen variables are not discussed.

Variants can be created in one other way. When you execute the program, the selection screen prompts will appear. You can enter the values. Single values are entered for PARAMETERS statement/s, and single and/or multiple values are entered for SELECT-OPTIONS statement/s. After entering all the desired values, you can click on the menu option: Goto ➤ Variants ➤ Save As Variant. The menu on the selection screen will look like Figure 9-39.

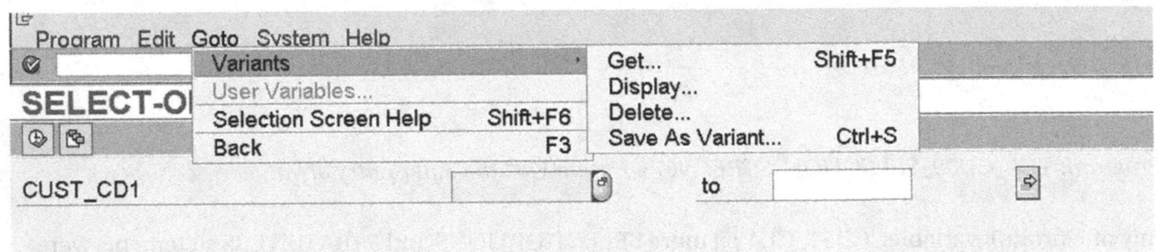

Figure 9-39. *Variant Creation after Selection Screen Variables Entry*

The clicking on the menu option Goto ➤ Variants ➤ Save As Variant will bring up the variant attributes screen. You can enter the name of the variant and optional Meaning/Short Text and save. The entered values will be saved under this variant name.

If variants exist for an ABAP program and the program is executed, the selection screen prompts will appear. On the application toolbar, the get variant button will appear. If an ABAP program has no variants, this button will not appear on the application toolbar. You can retrieve a variant (have the saved values loaded into the selection screen variables) by clicking on this button. The variants of the program will be listed. You can make a variant selection from the list.

The options 'Get,' 'Display,' and 'Delete' under the main menu option 'Goto' are in a disabled state if variants do not exist for an ABAP program, and in an enabled state for an ABAP program having variants.

Variants can be deleted, modified, and saved under the same or another name. They can also be renamed. They can be copied in the same ABAP program to another name. They can be transported. (Package should not be '$TMP'/local.) All these facilities are available on the 'ABAP: Variants - Initial Screen.' See Figure 9-36.

To copy variants from one program to another, you can use the function module: RS_COPY_SELECTION_SETS. This function module copies all variants from a source ABAP program to a destination ABAP program. You cannot copy specific variants from one program to another like you can do with text elements with transaction code SE32.

SELECT-OPTIONS – Additions NO INTERVALS, NO-EXTENSION

You can give the additions NO INTERVALS and NO-EXTENSION with the SELECT-OPTIONS statement. You have seen the effect of the phrase NO INTERVALS along with the addition WITH FRAME in the context of a block on the selection screen. It created a shaded area that extended only to half the screen width with the addition NO-INTERVALS.

In the following hands-on exercise, you observe the effect of the NO INTERVALS in the context of the SELECT-OPTIONS statement. With this addition on the selection screen, only the 'LOW' field will appear. The 'HIGH' field will not appear on the selection screen. The multiple selection button appears on the extreme right. Multiple selections are available. See Figure 9-40.

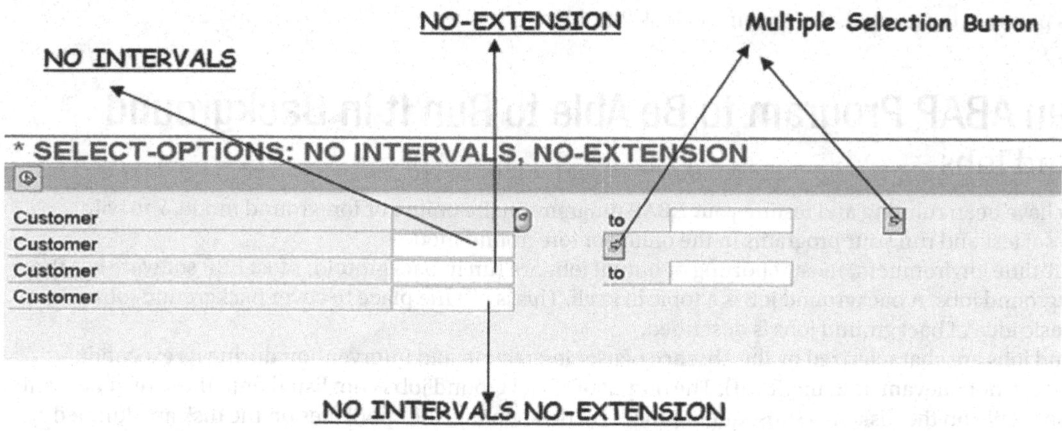

Figure 9-40. Program: YCL_CH09_SELECTION_SCREEN09 - NO INTERVALS, NO-EXTENSION

With the addition NO-EXTENSION to the SELECT-OPTIONS statement, the multiple selection button disappears, and multiple selections are not available. You can then enter either a single value or one range of values.

With the additions NO INTERVALS and NO-EXTENSION, the 'HIGH' field will not appear on the selection screen, and the multiple selection button disappears. You can enter only one single value.

In the following ABAP source program, four SELECT-OPTIONS statements have been issued:

1. SELECT-OPTIONS statement without any additional clause
2. SELECT-OPTIONS statement with the addition clause NO INTERVALS
3. SELECT-OPTIONS statement with the addition clause NO-EXTENSION
4. SELECT-OPTIONS statement with addition clauses NO INTERVALS and NO-EXTENSION

Until now you have issued a SELECT-OPTIONS statement by reference to an ABAP local data object (a variable name following the keyword 'FOR') In the following ABAP program, you have issued a SELECT-OPTIONS statement by reference to a DDIC table field. The name of the DDIC table field (KNA1-KUNNR) has been stored in a local data object. (STRNG) When issuing the SELECT-OPTIONS statement, this local data object containing the DDIC table field name is given within parenthesis (a variable name following the key word 'FOR'). This is the way to issue a SELECT-OPTIONS statement referring to DDIC table/structure field.

The source program:

```
REPORT YCL_CH09_SELECTION_SCREEN09.

*************************************************
* SELECT-OPTIONS: NO INTERVALS, NO-EXTENSION    **
* SELECT-OPTIONS Declaration By Reference To    **
* DDIC Field Stored In An Internal Data Object **
*************************************************

DATA: STRNG TYPE STRING VALUE 'KNA1-KUNNR'.

SELECT-OPTIONS: CUST_CD1  FOR (STRNG), " reference to DDIC field/not local field
                CUST_CD2  FOR (STRNG) NO INTERVALS,
                CUST_CD3  FOR (STRNG) NO-EXTENSION,
                CUST_CD4  FOR (STRNG) NO INTERVALS NO-EXTENSION.
```

When this program is executed, the screen will look like this:

Coding an ABAP Program to Be Able to Run It in Background

Background Jobs

Until now, you have been running and testing your ABAP programs in the online or foreground mode. You will continue to do so: test and run your programs in the online or foreground mode.

In SAP real-time environment, most reporting or output jobs are run in background. Most ERP software has the feature of background jobs. A background job is a topic in itself. This is not the place to cover background jobs as a topic. A very basic idea of background jobs is described.

Background jobs are characterized by the absence of user interaction and intervention during its execution (response times are not relevant and uncritical). The output of a background job is not listed onto the screen but sent to the printer spool file on the disk. In a subsequent process of de-spooling, the spool files on the disk are dumped onto the printers attached to application servers.

There are many other facilities in background jobs. One specific facility is the ability to schedule jobs. Scheduling can be on the basis of specific date and time. Background jobs can also be scheduled on a periodical basis, triggering every first working day of a week, month, etc.

A New Version of the Program YCL_CH09_SELECTION_SCREEN08 Enabling it to Run in the Background

Scenario:

Let it be assumed that a new version of your program YCL_CH09_SELECTION_SCREEN08 (customer wise sales summary for a specified company code and specific customer codes input through PARAMETERS and SELECT-OPTIONS statements) needs to be run in the background. The first requirement of a background job is the absence of user interaction. You cannot have the input prompts waiting for the end user to input values (i.e., no PARAMETERS, SELECT-OPTIONS statements). The new version of program YCL_CH09_SELECTION_SCREEN08 should not have any selection screen. But, it should still have the facility to filter data of a specific company code and specific customer codes (filter and selection values).

The program has to be fed the filter, selection values some other way than through a selection screen. Recall the data object aspect of the SELECT-OPTIONS statement (i.e., the selection table with its four fields: SIGN, OPTION, LOW, and HIGH).

Declaring an Internal Table Having Structure of Selection Table

In your new version of the program YCL_CH09_SELECTION_SCREEN08, you can have an internal table declared with a data declarative statement having the structure like the selection table. You can have this internal table having the structure of a selection table filled with the requisite filter values from the variant of another ABAP program. You can then use this internal table with the 'IN' operator in the SELECT statement to filter data. The rest of the new version of program can remain the same as the original YCL_CH09_SELECTION_SCREEN08.

You can declare an internal table having the structure of selection table for the DDIC field 'KNA1-KUNNR' in the following manner:

```
TYPES: BEGIN OF SEL_TABLE_TP,
         SIGN(1)    TYPE C,
         OPTION(2)  TYPE C,
         LOW        TYPE KNA1-KUNNR,
         HIGH       TYPE KNA1-KUNNR,
       END OF SEL_TABLE_TP.
DATA: CUST_CD TYPE STANDARD TABLE OF SEL_TABLE_TP
       WITH HEADER LINE.
```

ABAP language provides for declaration of internal table having structure of selection table in a simpler way with the following syntax:

```
DATA: <itab name> TYPE | LIKE RANGE OF <field> [WITH HEADER LINE].
```

<itab name> - Name of the internal table data object

RANGE OF – Key phrase to declare an internal table having structure of selection table

<field> - Any local/global elementary data object, any elementary field declared locally with TYPES statement or in global Type Groups. The attributes of the fields 'LOW' and 'HIGH' are derived from this <field>.

So, the preceding declaration is simplified to:

```
DATA: CUST_CD TYPE RANGE OF KNA1-KUNNR WITH HEADER LINE.
```

Filling the internal table having the structure of selection table with required filter values

Let an ABAP program you want to run in the background (new version of program: YCL_CH09_SELECTION_SCREEN08) be designated as 'Program A.' This 'Program A' needs to retrieve variant values from another ABAP program and load the variant values into the internal table with the structure of the selection table. Let this ABAP program with variants be designated as 'Program B.' The 'Program B' has the selection screen with the PARAMETERS and SELECT-OPTIONS statement. You will maintain variants in 'Program B' running in online/foreground mode. The variants in 'Program B' can modified before 'Program A' is submitted for execution or triggered in the background. Using a function module you can retrieve the variant values of 'Program B' and load them into the internal table having structure of selection table in 'Program A.'

The function module to retrieve variants is RS_VARIANT_VALUES_TECH_DATA. It takes two import parameters: the name of the ABAP program and the name of the variant. It returns variant values in an internal table having a structure like the DDIC structure RSPARMS. The DDIC structure RSPARMS has the following fields:

Table 9-3. DDIC Structure RSPARMS Fields

Field Name	Data Type & Length	Description
SELNAME	CHAR / 8	Name of the SELECTION-SCREEN data object / variable: i.e., PARAMETERS / SELECT-OPTIONS variable name
KIND	CHAR / 1	Kind of SELECTION-SCREEN variable: 'S' for SELECT-OPTIONS 'P' for PARAMETERS
SIGN	CHAR / 1	'I' for include, 'E' for exclude
OPTION	CHAR / 2	'EQ', 'NE', 'GT', 'LT', 'GE', 'LE', 'CP', 'NP', 'BT', 'NB'
LOW	CHAR / 45	Start value of range
HIGH	CHAR / 45	End value of range

After the function module RS_VARIANT_VALUES_TECH_DATA has retrieved the variant values into an internal table of structure RSPARMS, you can set up LOOP...ENDLOOP of this internal table and build your selection table like an internal table.

The variant storage system stores the values in the fields 'LOW' and 'HIGH' without the leading zeroes. You are inserting leading zeroes using the conversion routine CONVERSION_EXIT_ALPHA_INPUT (can be used for variables of length 10 only).

Program that can be run in background

In your case you have chosen the ABAP program YCL_CH09_SELECTION-SCREEN08 as 'Program B' (the program where variant values are to be retrieved). Your 'Program A' is YCL_CH09_SELECTION_SCREEN10 (the program that can be run in the background).

The 'Program A' source:

```
REPORT  YCL_CH09_SELECTION_SCREEN10 NO STANDARD PAGE HEADING
          LINE-SIZE 120 LINE-COUNT 60.

******************************************************
* Use F.M. RS_VARIANT_VALUES_TECH_DATA To Retrieve  **
* Variant Values Into Internal Data Object          **
* Use Internal Data Object In SELECT Statement To   **
* Filter Data.                                      **
* Program Submit-able IN BACKGROUND                 **
******************************************************

*******************************************************
* I. declare selection table like data object without  **
*    using selection screen statement SELECT-OPTIONS   **
*                                                      **
* you can declare an internal table data object like   **
* the selection table - internal table having the      **
* four fields: SIGN, OPTION, LOW, HIGH using the       **
* DATA statement with the key phrase RANGE OF..        **
*                                                      **
```

```
* DATA: CUST_CD TYPE RANGE OF KNA1-KUNNR.                **
*                                                        **
*                                                        **
* II. retrieve variant values into internal table        **
*                                                        **
* the variants are stored in the DDIC structure form     **
* RSPARAMS. the fields with TYPES, lengths of DDIC       **
* structure RSPARAMS:                                    **
*                                                        **
* SELNAME(8) TYPE C selection screen variable name       **
* KIND(1)    TYPE C 'S' for SELECT-OPTIONS variable      **
*                   'P' for PARAMETERS variable          **
* SIGN(1)    TYPE C                                      **
* OPTION(2)  TYPE C                                      **
* LOW(45)    TYPE C                                      **
* HIGH(45)   TYPE C                                      **
*                                                        **
* this is the way the variant data is stored. (source)  **
* it is retrieved into the program declared internal     **
* table VAR_VALUES using the function module:            **
* RS_VARIANT_VALUES_TECH_DATA. this function module      **
* takes two import parameters i.e. program name and      **
* variant name. it returns the variant values in the     **
* internal table of structure RSPARAMS.                  **
*                                                        **
* your import parameters to the function module:         **
* program name: YCL_CH08_SELECTION_SCREEN08              **
* variant name: VARIANT_I                                **
*                                                        **
* the variant values will be retrieved for two           **
* selection screen variables defined/declared in         **
* program YCL_CH09_SELECTION_SCREEN08:                   **
* (1) CCODE:    thru PARAMETERS for company code         **
* (2) CUST_CD1: thru SELECT-OPTIONS for customer code    **
*                                                        **
* III. transfer variant values from internal table       **
*      VAR_VALUES into selection table CUST_CD declared**
*      with TYPE RANGE OF.. etc. and CCODE.              **
*                                                        **
* setup LOOP AT VAR_VALUES.                              **
*                                                        **
*  check VAR_VALUES-SELNAME = 'CUST_CD1' and             **
*  VAR_VALUES-KIND = 'S'                                 **
*                                                        **
*   then use MOVE-CORRESPONDING to move data from        **
*   structure VAR_VALUES to structure CUST_CD.           **
*   variant values are not saved/stored with leading     **
*   zeroes. use conversion exit routine                  **
*   'CONVERSION_EXIT_ALPHA_INPUT' to insert leading      **
*   zeroes to CUST_CD-LOW, CUST_CD-HIGH fields.          **
*   APPEND to selection table like internal table        **
*   CUST_CD.                                             **
```

```
*                                                    **
*  check if VAR_VALUES-SELNAME = 'CCODE' and         **
*   KIND = 'P' then CCODE = VAR_VALUES-LOW.          **
*                                                    **
* ENDLOOP.                                           **
*                                                    **
*                                                    **
* IV. use the variables CCODE and CUST_CD in the     **
*     SELECT statement to filter data as per variant **
*     values                                         **
*                                                    **
* rest of program same as YCL_CH09_SELECTION_SCREEN08 **
*******************************************************

DATA: SALES_TAB  TYPE YCL_CH06_SALES_SUM_TAB,
      SALES_STRU LIKE LINE OF SALES_TAB,
      TOTAL      TYPE VBRK-NETWR,
      BUTXT      TYPE T001-BUTXT,
      WAERS      TYPE T001-WAERS,
      BUTXTS     TYPE STRING,
      CCODE      TYPE VBRK-BUKRS,

      CUST_CD    TYPE RANGE OF KNA1-KUNNR WITH HEADER LINE,
                   "create internal table of stru SIGN, OPTION, LOW, HIGH

      VAR_VALUES    TYPE STANDARD TABLE OF RSPARAMS WITH HEADER LINE.
                    " function module formal parameter VARIANT_VALUES
                    " is TYPE RSPARAMS
****************************************************************************
TOP-OF-PAGE.
WRITE:/5 TEXT-001, CCODE NO-GAP, '/' NO-GAP,  BUTXTS, 102 TEXT-003,
         107(3) SY-PAGNO.
WRITE:/40 TEXT-002, WAERS.
SKIP 1.
WRITE:/5(104) SY-ULINE.
WRITE:/5 TEXT-004, 11 TEXT-005, 23 TEXT-006, 60 TEXT-007, 91(17)
         TEXT-008 RIGHT-JUSTIFIED.
WRITE:/5 TEXT-009, 13 TEXT-010.
WRITE:/5(104) SY-ULINE.
****************************************************************************
START-OF-SELECTION.

CALL FUNCTION 'RS_VARIANT_VALUES_TECH_DATA'
  EXPORTING
    REPORT                      = 'YCL_CH09_SELECTION_SCREEN08'
    VARIANT                     = 'VARIANT_I'
*   SEL_TEXT                    = ' '
*   MOVE_OR_WRITE               = 'W'
*   SORTED                      = ' '
*   EXECUTE_DIRECT              =
* IMPORTING
```

```
*   TECHN_DATA                     =
  TABLES
    VARIANT_VALUES                 = VAR_VALUES[]
*   VARIANT_TEXT                   =
 EXCEPTIONS
   VARIANT_NON_EXISTENT          = 1
   VARIANT_OBSOLETE              = 2
   OTHERS                        = 3
          .
IF SY-SUBRC <> 0.
 MESSAGE ID SY-MSGID TYPE SY-MSGTY NUMBER SY-MSGNO WITH SY-MSGV1 SY-MSGV2
  SY-MSGV3 SY-MSGV4.
 EXIT.
ENDIF.
*************************
LOOP AT VAR_VALUES.
 IF VAR_VALUES-SELNAME = 'CUST_CD1' AND VAR_VALUES-KIND = 'S'.
                                      " = 'S' - SELECT-OPTIONS variable

   MOVE-CORRESPONDING VAR_VALUES TO CUST_CD. " MOVE to selection table stru

   CALL FUNCTION 'CONVERSION_EXIT_ALPHA_INPUT' " insert leading zeroes into
                                               " CUST_CD-LOW
     EXPORTING
       INPUT          = CUST_CD-LOW
     IMPORTING
       OUTPUT          = CUST_CD-LOW
          .

   CALL FUNCTION 'CONVERSION_EXIT_ALPHA_INPUT' " insert leading zeroes into
                                               " CUST_CD-HIGH
     EXPORTING
       INPUT          = CUST_CD-HIGH
     IMPORTING
       OUTPUT          = CUST_CD-HIGH
        .

   APPEND CUST_CD.

 ELSEIF VAR_VALUES-SELNAME = 'CCODE' AND VAR_VALUES-KIND = 'P'.
                                        " = 'P' - PARAMETERS variable

   CCODE = VAR_VALUES-LOW.
 ENDIF.

ENDLOOP.
***********************************

SELECT SINGLE BUTXT WAERS FROM T001 INTO (BUTXT, WAERS) WHERE
       BUKRS = CCODE.

BUTXTS = BUTXT.
```

```
SELECT KUNNR NAME1 ORT01 NETWR KURRF FROM YCL_CH05_VBRKKNA INTO
  CORRESPONDING FIELDS OF SALES_STRU

  WHERE BUKRS = CCODE
        AND KUNNR IN CUST_CD . " IN operator with selection table
                               " type variable

 SALES_STRU-NETWR =  SALES_STRU-NETWR * SALES_STRU-KURRF.
 SALES_STRU-KURRF = 0. "to prevent overflow
 COLLECT SALES_STRU INTO SALES_TAB.

ENDSELECT.

SORT SALES_TAB BY KUNNR.

LOOP AT CUST_CD. " output selection table

 WRITE:/5(2) SY-TABIX, CUST_CD-SIGN, CUST_CD-OPTION, CUST_CD-LOW,
  CUST_CD-HIGH.

ENDLOOP.

SKIP 4. " a gap of 4 lines between CUST_CD data &
        " customer data.

LOOP AT SALES_TAB INTO SALES_STRU.

 WRITE :/5(4) SY-TABIX, SALES_STRU-KUNNR USING NO EDIT MASK,
  SALES_STRU-NAME1,SALES_STRU-ORT01, (17) SALES_STRU-NETWR.
 TOTAL = TOTAL + SALES_STRU-NETWR.

ENDLOOP.

SKIP 1.
WRITE :/(17) TOTAL UNDER SALES_STRU-NETWR.
```

You are executing the program in the o-line/foreground mode only to demonstrate the results (list on screen). The output will appear like Figure 9-41 and 9-42.

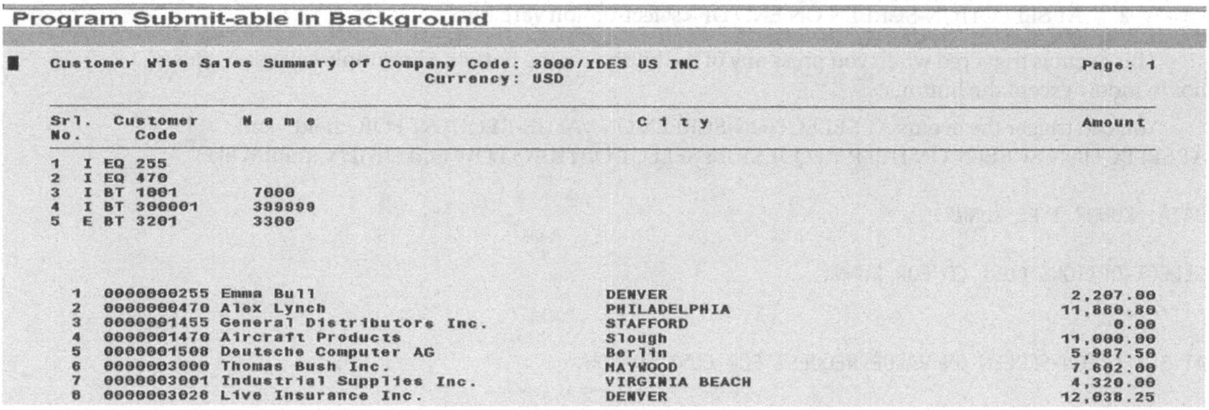

```
Program Submit-able In Background

Customer Wise Sales Summary of Company Code: 3000/IDES US INC                     Page: 1
                               Currency: USD
------------------------------------------------------------------------------------------
Srl.  Customer    N a m e                         C i t y                         Amount
No.     Code
------------------------------------------------------------------------------------------
1  I EQ 255
2  I EQ 470
3  I BT 1001       7000
4  I BT 300001     399999
5  E BT 3201       3300

   1 0000000255 Emma Bull                        DENVER                           2,207.00
   2 0000000470 Alex Lynch                       PHILADELPHIA                    11,860.80
   3 0000001455 General Distributors Inc.        STAFFORD                             0.00
   4 0000001470 Aircraft Products                Slough                          11,000.00
   5 0000001508 Deutsche Computer AG             Berlin                           5,987.50
   6 0000003000 Thomas Bush Inc.                 MAYWOOD                          7,602.00
   7 0000003001 Industrial Supplies Inc.         VIRGINIA BEACH                   4,320.00
   8 0000003028 Live Insurance Inc.              DENVER                          12,038.25
```

Figure 9-41. *Program: YCL_CH09_SELECTION_SCREEN10 – Output*

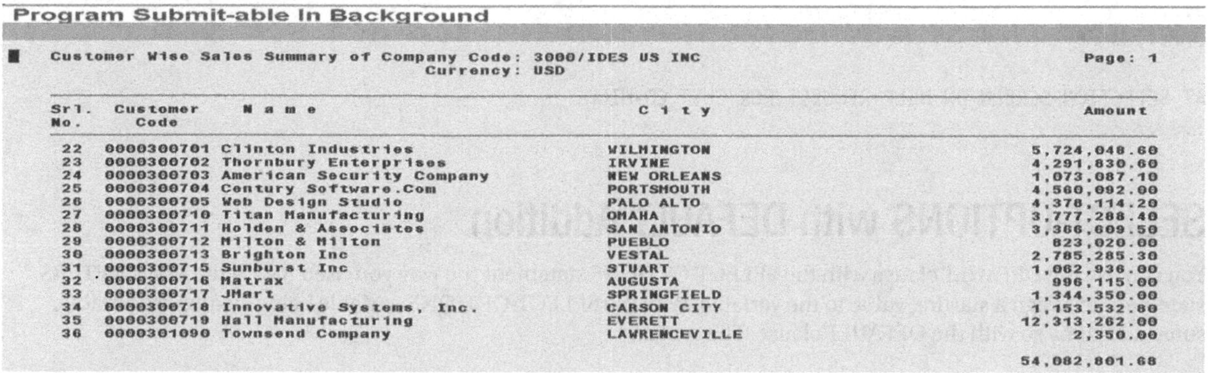

```
Program Submit-able In Background

Customer Wise Sales Summary of Company Code: 3000/IDES US INC                     Page: 1
                               Currency: USD
------------------------------------------------------------------------------------------
Srl.  Customer    N a m e                         C i t y                         Amount
No.     Code
------------------------------------------------------------------------------------------
  22 0000300701 Clinton Industries               WILMINGTON                   5,724,048.60
  23 0000300702 Thornbury Enterprises            IRVINE                       4,291,830.60
  24 0000300703 American Security Company        NEW ORLEANS                  1,073,087.10
  25 0000300704 Century Software.Com             PORTSMOUTH                   4,560,092.00
  26 0000300705 Web Design Studio                PALO ALTO                    4,378,114.20
  27 0000300710 Titan Manufacturing              OMAHA                        3,777,288.40
  28 0000300711 Holden & Associates              SAN ANTONIO                  3,366,609.50
  29 0000300712 Milton & Milton                  PUEBLO                         823,020.00
  30 0000300713 Brighton Inc                     VESTAL                       2,785,285.30
  31 0000300715 Sunburst Inc                     STUART                       1,062,936.00
  32 0000300716 Matrax                           AUGUSTA                        996,115.00
  33 0000300717 JMart                            SPRINGFIELD                  1,344,350.00
  34 0000300718 Innovative Systems, Inc.         CARSON CITY                  1,153,532.80
  35 0000300719 Hall Manufacturing               EVERETT                     12,313,262.00
  36 0000301090 Townsend Company                 LAWRENCEVILLE                    2,350.00

                                                                             54,082,801.68
```

Figure 9-42. *Program: YCL_CH09_SELECTION_SCREEN10 – Output*

The output is identical to the output of program YCL_CH09_SELECTION_SCREEN08, but this program having no selection screen can be run in the background.

SELECT-OPTIONS - Miscellanea

SELECT-OPTIONS Events

There are two events related to SELECT-OPTIONS statement:

1. AT SELECTION-SCREEN ON <select-option variable>

This is of the same category as the AT SELECTION-SCREEN ON <parameters variable> in some aspects because of the SELECT-OPTIONS variable being complex. It is triggered in the following contexts:

- When the <Enter> key, execute button/F8 etc. (screen processing is over) is pressed on the selection screen.
- When the multiple selection button is pressed on the selection screen.
- If values have been entered in multiple selection dialog box/window, this event is triggered for all buttons except for the following buttons:

2. AT SELECTION-SCREEN ON END OF <select-option variable>

This event is triggered when you press any of the buttons at the bottom of multiple selection dialog box/window except the buttons: 🗑 ✖

You can trigger the events AT SELECTION-SCREEN ON VALUE-REQUEST FOR <field> and AT SELECTION-SCREEN ON HELP-REQUEST for SELECT-OPTIONS LOW and HIGH variables like:

```
DATA: KUNNR TYPE KUNNR.

SELECT-OPTIONS CUST_CD FOR KUNNR.
........

AT SELECTION-SCREEN ON VALUE-REQUEST FOR CUST_CD-LOW.
......
.......

AT SELECTION-SCREEN ON VALUE-REQUEST FOR CUST_CD-HIGH.
.....
......

AT SELECTION-SCREEN ON HELP-REQUEST FOR CUST_CD-HIGH.
.....
```

SELECT-OPTIONS with DEFAULT Addition

You can use the DEFAULT clause with the SELECT-OPTIONS statement the way you used it with the PARAMETERS statement to assign a starting value to the variable. With the SELECT-OPTIONS variable being a complex variable, some additions go with the DEFAULT clause. The syntax:

```
SELECT-OPTIONS <variable> FOR <field> DEFAULT  <low value>
 [TO <high value>] [SIGN <sign value>] [OPTION <option value>].
```

<sign value> - Can be either I or E (should not be enclosed within single quotes)
By default, <sign value> will assume I value
<option value> - Can be EQ, NE, GT, LT, GE, LE, BT, NB, CP, NP
(Should not be enclosed within single quotes)
By default, <option value> will assume value EQ if there is no <high value>
By default, <option value> will assume value BT if there is a <high value>
Example:

```
DATA: KUNNR TYPE KUNNR.

SELECT-OPTIONS CUST_CD FOR KUNNR DEFAULT 1 TO 1000 SIGN E OPTION BT.
```

SELECT-OPTIONS Other Additions

The following additions you used with PARAMETERS statement also apply to SELECT-OPTIONS statement.

- OBLIGATORY (mandatory input)
- VISIBLE LENGTH <length in columns> (reduce the visible length of screen element)
- LOWER CASE (input with case sensitivity)
- MATCHCODE OBJECT <search help name> (attach search help)
- NO-DISPLAY (makes element disappear, sets property INVISIBLE = 1. Can be reset in the AT SELECTION-SCREEN OUTPUT event: i.e., set property SCREEN-INVISIBLE = 0)

Selection Texts

When you issue PARAMETERS / SELECT-OPTIONS statements without COMMENTS, without locating any other screen elements on the same line, the ABAP runtime system uses the name of the selection screen variable as a label or text.

Example:

```
PARAMETERS: CUST_CD TYPE KNA1-KUNNR.
```

The selection screen for this statement:

Figure 9-43. Variable Name as Label or Text

If you issue PARAMETERS / SELECT-OPTIONS statements without COMMENTS and locate other screen elements on the same line, the ABAP runtime system assigns blank label or text.

Example:

```
SELECTION-SCREEN BEGIN OF LINE.

PARAMETERS: CUST_CD1 TYPE KNA1-KUNNR.
SELECTION-SCREEN PUSHBUTTON 25(15) BUTTON1 USER-COMMAND ABC.

SELECTION-SCREEN END OF LINE.
*********************************
INITIALIZATION.
BUTTON1 = 'Button I'.
```

The selection screen for the statements is shown in Figure 9-44.

Figure 9-44. Blank Label or Text

There is another way of assigning label or text to the PARAMETERS / SELECT-OPTIONS variables. This is through the 'Selection texts' component of ABAP program 'Text elements'. You have already used two of the 'Text elements' components: 'List Heading' (standard headers) and the 'Text symbols'.

For each PARAMETERS / SELECT-OPTIONS statement, the 'Selection texts' creates a row/entry with a blank label.

Consider the source lines of the program YCL_CH09_SELECTION_SCREEN11:

```
REPORT YCL_CH09_SELECTION_SCREEN11.

********************
* Selection Texts **
********************

PARAMETERS: CUST_CD1 TYPE KNA1-KUNNR. " name of variable will appear
                                      " as label by default
SELECTION-SCREEN SKIP 2.

SELECTION-SCREEN BEGIN OF LINE.

PARAMETERS: CUST_CD2 TYPE KNA1-KUNNR. " blank label by default

SELECTION-SCREEN END OF LINE.

SELECTION-SCREEN SKIP 2.

PARAMETERS: CUST_CD3 TYPE KNA1-KUNNR. " label from selection text
                                      " selection text from data element
                                      " label
```

In this program, when you open the 'Selection texts' tab of text element screen, the screen will appear like Figure 9-45.

Enter Selection Texts for Variables

Program YCL_CH09_SELECTION_SCREEN11 Inactive

Text symbols | Selection texts | List Headings

Enable Check Box to Fetch Data Element Text

Name	Text	Dictionary ref.
CUST_CD1	?...	☐
CUST_CD2	?...	☐
CUST_CD3	?...	☐

Figure 9-45. *Program YCL_CH09_SELECTIONSCREEN11 - Selection texts Screen: Initially*

You can enter selection texts for variables. The selection texts entered for the variables will appear as label or text on the selection screen. If you enable check box on the extreme right and save, it will fetch text from the data element associated with the field. (In your present program, the data element is 'KUNNR'.) It fetches the 'Medium' field label. Recall that in the data element, field labels are 'Short', 'Medium', 'Long', and 'Heading'.

The screen with the 'Medium' field label text fetched from data element will look like Figure 9-46.

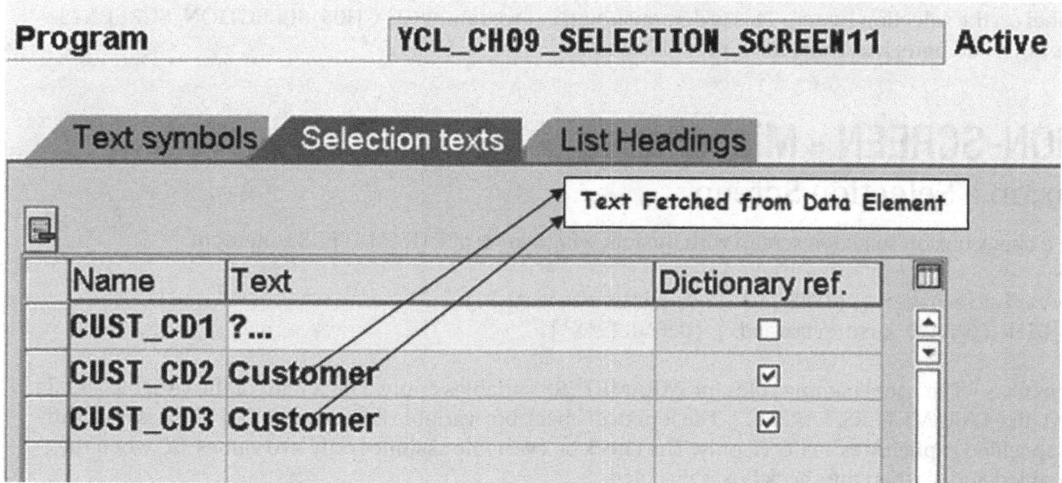

Figure 9-46. *Program YCL_CH09_SELECTION_SCREEN11 - Selection texts Screen: Labels or Texts from Data Element*

The selection screen of the program YCL_CH09_SELECTION_SCREEN11 now will be like 9-47.

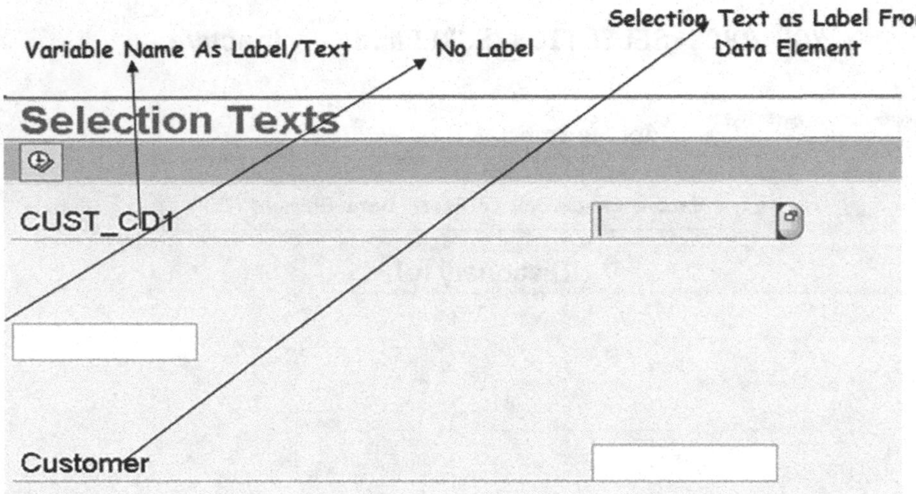

Figure 9-47. *Program: YCL_CH09_SELECTION_SCREEN11 - Selection Screen*

When using selection texts, you must remember that you cannot control/format the line (SELECTION-SCREEN BEGIN OF LINE, etc.).

There is a function module: MG_FIELDNAME_TEXT

retrieves the short, medium, long, and heading texts from data element. The function module has two import parameters: DDIC table/structure name and field name. The function module returns texts in the logged-in language. It also returns short text of the data element. You can retrieve the data element texts for DDIC fields in this manner and use it as label on the selection screen. This is demonstrated in program: YCL_CH09_SELECTION_SCREEN13. The program is not listed here. It is available in the E-Resource.

SELECTION-SCREEN - Miscellanea

Check Box on a Selection Screen

You can locate a check box on selection screen with the following syntax of PARAMETERS statement:

```
PARAMETERS: <variable name> [ {TYPE C | TYPE <data element>} ]
AS CHECKBOX [USER-COMMAND <user command>] [DEFAULT 'X'].
```

<variable name> - The usual naming rules for PARAMETERS variables apply. The length of the variable should not be specified [like PARAMETERS: VAR(2)...]. The length of check box variable is fixed as 1. The TYPE is implicitly 'C' and can be specified explicitly as TYPE 'C' only. The check box variable assumes only two values: 'X' when the check box is enabled and ' ' when the check box is disabled.

<data element> - This data element should have been assigned a domain where the 'Data Type' is 'CHAR' and length is 1. Further in the fixed values of this domain, there can be two rows of values: 'X' and ' '.

AS CHECKBOX - Key phrase to define a check box. This key phrase can be omitted when you are referring to a data element that has been assigned a domain where the 'Data Type' is 'CHAR' and length is 1. Further in the fixed values of this domain, there should be two rows of values: 'X' and ' '.

The USER-COMMAND <user command> - Like in the case of the radio buttons, this can be optionally specified. When IT is specified, clicking on the check box will trigger the events AT SELECTION-SCREEN and AT SELECTION-SCREEN ON <field>, etc.

The rest of the terms carry the same meaning as explained in earlier syntax descriptions of the PARAMETERS statement.

An example:

```
PARAMETERS: VL_ONOFF TYPE RUNSIMUL, " reference to data element assigned
                                    "to domain: Data Type CHAR, length 1
                                    " fixed values: two rows: 'X' & ' '
                                    " domain:'CHCKBX'

            IN_ONOFF TYPE RUNSIMUL NO-DISPLAY, " can use NO-DISPLAY
                                               " addition when referring
                                               " to data element
            BL_ONOFF TYPE C AS CHECKBOX DEFAULT 'X',
            GR_ONOFF AS CHECKBOX,
            YL_ONOFF TYPE CHAR1 AS CHECKBOX. " reference to data element
                                             " assigned to domain: Data
                                             " Type CHAR, length 1 but no
                                             " fixed values.
```

Horizontal Line on a Selection Screen

You can draw a horizontal line on selection screen with the following syntax:

```
SELECTION-SCREEN ULINE [/]<col position>(<width in columns/characters>).
```

ULINE - Keyword to draw a horizontal line on a selection screen
Other terms are obvious and were explained earlier.
Example:

```
SELECTION-SCREEN ULINE /5(15).
```

Addition MODIF ID with Selection Screen Elements

The addition MODIF ID can be used with most of the selection screen elements covered:

- COMMENT (For Labels or Texts)
- Text Boxes/Input Fields (PARAMETERS statement)
- Radio Buttons (PARAMETERS statement)
- Check Boxes (PARAMETERS statement)
- Multiple Complex Selections (SELECT-OPTIONS statement)
- Push Buttons
- Horizontal Lines

Example for the addition MODIF ID:

```
PARAMETERS: CHQNO(12)   TYPE C MODIF ID GP1,
            CCRDNO(16)  TYPE C MODIF ID GP1.
```

The addition MODIF ID is being explained in the context of this chapter's program YCL_CH09_SELECTION_SCREEN03. In this program you used the event AT SELECTION-SCREEN OUTPUT to change screen properties.

MODIF ID is a key phrase. It is to be followed by a three-character string like the one you have given in the example above 'GP1.' In this example, basically, you are assigning selection screen elements 'CHQNO' and 'CCRDNO' (check number and credit card number) to a group with identification 'GP1.' In this manner, you can assign two or more screen elements to a group. You can have any number of group identifications assigned to various selection screen elements.

In the current chapter, while dealing with the events INITIALIZATION, and AT SELECTION-SCREEN OUTPUT, you were introduced to the structure of system maintained internal table SCREEN. The second field in this structure is GROUP1 TYPE 'C,' length 3. Refer to Table 9-1.

The MODIF ID is a three-character string (group identifications) assigned to the selection screen elements and will be stored in the field GROUP1 for the selection screen elements with MODIF ID addition.

Inside LOOP AT SCREEN...ENDLOOP you had the statement:

```
IF SCREEN-NAME <> 'CHQNO' AND SCREEN-NAME <> 'CCRDNO'.
  CONTINUE.   " changing properties of only 'CHQNO' & 'CCRDNO'
ENDIF.
```

You wanted to change the properties of only 'CHQNO' and 'CCRDNO.' You wanted to bypass all other rows (in the internal table SCREEN) corresponding to selection screen elements other than 'CHQNO' and 'CCRDNO.'

As you have assigned both the selection screen elements 'CHQNO' and 'CCRDNO' to 'GP1,' you can simplify the above IF statement to:

```
IF SCREEN-GROUP1 <> 'GP1'.
  CONTINUE.   " changing properties of only 'CHQNO' & 'CCRDNO'
ENDIF.
```

When you have a long string of logical operators 'AND' and 'OR' being used inside the execution of the LOOP AT SCREEN...ENDLOOP construct, you can assign the selection screen elements to groups and simplify your code, avoiding the logical operators.

This is the purpose and function of the addition MODIF ID.

Event AT SELECTION SCREEN ON EXIT-COMMAND

When you press on the system toolbar any of the buttons: (Back), (Exit), or (Cancel), this event is triggered. Clean-up operations can be performed in this event.

Define and Call User Defined SELECTION-SCREEN

The selection screens you have created and used until now are the standard selection screens. The ABAP runtime system generates screen number 1000 for the standard selection screens. In addition to this standard selection screen, you can have user defined selection screens.

The user defined selection screens need to be defined and then called. The syntax for user defined selection screens:

```
SELECTION-SCREEN BEGIN OF SCREEN <screen number>
 [TITLE <title>] [AS WINDOW].
 ...
 ......
SELECTION-SCREEN END OF SCREEN <screen number>.
```

SELECTION-SCREEN BEGIN OF SCREEN – Key phrase to start selection screen Definition

<screen number> - Any number 1-9999 excluding 1000 reserved for standard selection screen

TITLE – Keyword

<title> – You can specify either a text symbol id with the prefix 'TEXT-' like TEXT-001 or a name (name can be maximum of eight characters long, starting with an alphabetic character, and the rest of characters can be alphanumeric with embedded underscores (_). The name should be assigned text in an INITIALIZATION / AT SELECTION-SCREEN OUTPUT event. This will appear as a window title. If no <title> is specified, the program title/ short text will appear as a window title.

AS WINDOW – This addition will make the selection screen a modal window.

SELECTION-SCREEN END OF SCREEN - Key phrase to end selection screen Definition

All the selection screen statements to create the elements: PARAMETERS, SELECT-OPTIONS, SELECTION-SCREEN... for the user defined selection screen must be enclosed within the SELECTION-SCREEN BEGIN OF SCREEN... and the SELECTION-SCREEN END OF SCREEN... statements.

After the definition of user defined selection screens, they need to be called. The syntax for calling a user defined selection screen:

```
CALL SELECTION-SCREEN <screen number>
[ STARTING AT <start column number> <start line number>
[ENDING AT <end column number> <end line number>] ]
[USING SELECTION-SET <variant name>].
```

CALL SELECTION-SCREEN – Key phrase to call user defined selection screen

<screen number> – The selection screen number defined earlier

STARTING AT – Key phrase to indicate the starting coordinates of the user defined selection screen in terms of column and row number

<start column number> – Starting column number

<start row number> – Starting row number

ENDING AT – Key phrase to indicate the ending coordinates of the user defined selection screen in terms of column and row number

<end column number> – Ending column number

<end row number> – Ending row number

USING SELECTION-SET – Key phrase to load variant values into selection screen variables

<variant name> - Variant name. The Variant must exist in the same program

A hands-on exercise program YCL_CH09_SELECTION_SCREEN12 demonstrates the definition and calling of a user defined selection screen. In this program, some random variant values have been created for the SELECT-OPTIONS (customers) and PARAMETERS (company code) under the name 'VAR1.'

The source program:

```
REPORT YCL_CH09_SELECTION_SCREEN12.

**********************************
* User Defined SELECTION-SCREEN **
**********************************
```

```
DATA: KUNNR TYPE KUNNR.

SELECTION-SCREEN BEGIN OF SCREEN 500.

SELECT-OPTIONS CUST_CD FOR KUNNR.
SELECTION-SCREEN SKIP 2.
PARAMETERS: CCODE TYPE T001-BUKRS DEFAULT 1000.

SELECTION-SCREEN END OF SCREEN 500.

CALL SELECTION-SCREEN 500 STARTING AT 5 1
     ENDING AT 85 15 USING SELECTION-SET 'VAR1'.
                    " start row & column, end row & column
```

The selection screen displayed as a modal window will look like Figure 9-48.

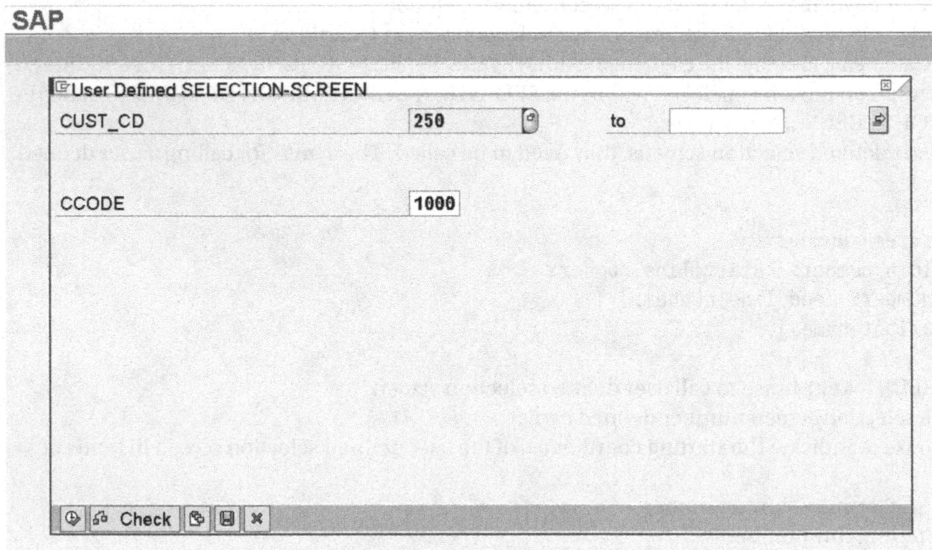

Figure 9-48. *Program: YCL_CH09_SELECTION_SCREEN12 - Selection Screen*

When multiple selection screens are used in a program, you can determine the current selection screen by interrogating the contents of the system field SY-DYNNR. The system field SY-DYNNR contains the current screen number.

With the definition, calling of user defined selection screen; the chapter on SELECTION-SCREEN is being concluded.

Conclusion

The selection screens will be part of report programs (programs producing outputs) executed in foreground mode to make data selections. The selection screens will be used indirectly to provide selections through variants of report programs executed in background mode. The use of a selection screen to provide selections through variants was demonstrated in the program YCL_CH09_SELECTION_SCREEN10. The selection screens can be deployed for simple inputs.

CHAPTER 10

Interactive Lists

Multiple Lists Generation by an ABAP Program

Through the feature of 'I=interactive lists', an ABAP program can generate multiple lists or reports. Frequently, in an enterprise, reporting requires the data to be presented initially in a summarized form, and as an option, levels of detail of selected summarized data should be available. Let's look at this in terms of a simple business scenario. Recall the customer sales summary list of a specified company code, generated in Chapter 6, using the COLLECT statement. In this list, you totaled the converted individual billing document amounts of a customer and output this totaled/summarized amount as one line. A customer can have n number of billing documents, and the sum total of the n number of billing documents converted amounts was output as a single line. Let this customer sales summary be called the first list. Now, suppose the end user wants the following on this first list as an option: for any selected customer, the billing documents of the selected customer to be listed as a second list (I level detail). Then, again, the end user wants as an option on the second list, for a selected billing document, all the items or materials of the selected billing document to be output as a third list (II level detail). At any time one of the lists will be displayed. A diagrammatic representation of these three lists appears in Figure 10-1.

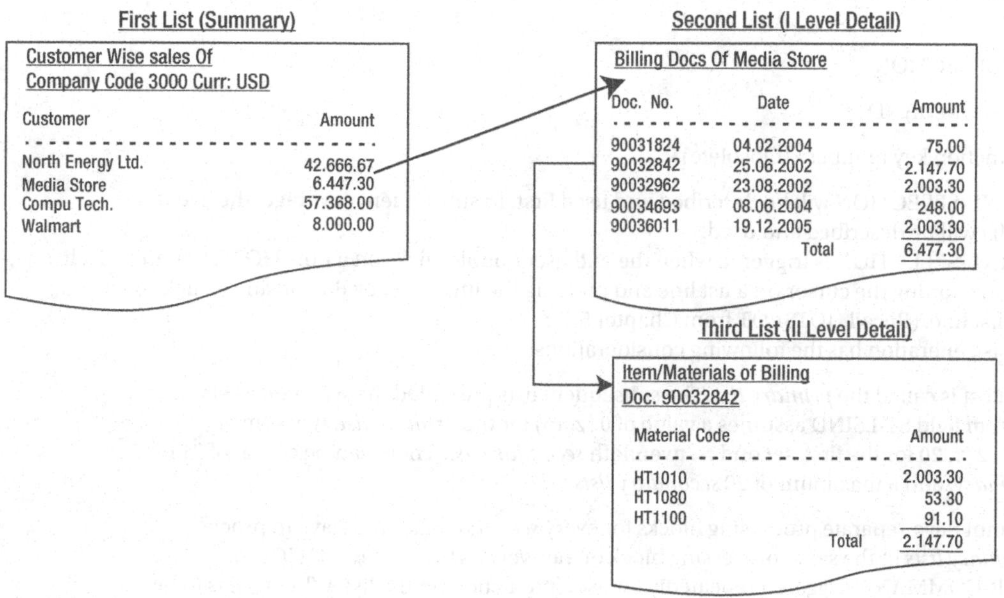

Figure 10-1. *Summary & Detailed Lists*

In Figure 10-1, the first list is the same as the one generated by the program YCL_CH06_ITAB05, that is, for a specific company code (say 3000), the total sales of each customer in the currency of the company code.

When the end user double clicks on any customer (or positions the cursor on a customer and presses the function key F2), for example, for customer 'Media Store', a second list will appear, (I Level Detail) listing out all the billing documents of the customer 'Media Store'. There are five billing documents listed for the customer 'Media Store'. The total derived and output at the end, $6,447.30, will be equal to the amount in the preceding list line on which the end user double clicked.

Similarly, in the second list, when an end user double clicks on a billing document, say, billing document number '90032842', a third list will appear, (II Level Detail) listing out all the items in the billing document '90032842'. There are three items in the billing document '90032842': HT1010, HT1080, and HT1100 with their respective individual amounts. The total derived and output at the end, $2,147.70 will be equal to the amount in the preceding list line on which the end user double clicked. It is to be ensured that all the amounts are in the one and same currency, the currency of the company code '3000': USD ($).

At any time only one list will be active. If you are on the third list, you can navigate to the previous second list by pressing on the standard toolbar, the 'Back' button or pressing the function key F3. And if you are on the second list, you can navigate to the previous first list by pressing on the standard toolbar, the 'Back' button or pressing the function key F3. When you are navigating forward from one list level to the next higher list level, the ABAP runtime system saves the previous list before generating a new list. When you are navigating back from one list level to the previous lower list level, the system releases or deletes the list from where you are navigating back.

Navigating back to the first list, the end user can double click on another customer to get details for that customer and so on. Details lists are always for one specific selected item (customer, billing document).

These multiple lists are called interactive lists, as they enable end-user interaction.

Such business requirements are common and frequent, where a summarized list is produced with the option to produce details of any one selected item in the summary at a time, not detailed reporting of all the data.

Interactive Lists: Events and Considerations

Let's take a look at this in more detail. This generation of interactive lists is enabled through the two (the third is obsolete) list events:

AT LINE-SELECTION

AT USER-COMMAND

AT PF<function key number> (Obsolete)

The event AT LINE-SELECTION will be described and used first. In subsequent coverage, the event AT USER-COMMAND will be described and used.

The event AT LINE-SELECTION is triggered when the end user double clicks on a non-HOTSPOT area of a list line - equivalent to positioning the cursor on a list line and pressing the function key F2 - or single clicks on a HOTSPOT area of a list line. (Recall HOTSPOT from Chapter 5.)

The multiple lists generation has the following considerations:

- The first list is called the *primary list.* The subsequent lists are called the *secondary* lists. The system field SY-LSIND assumes a value of 0 (zero) for the *primary list.* It assumes values 1, 2 ... 20 for the first, second ... twentieth *secondary list.* There can be a total of 21 lists, one *primary*, and a maximum of 20 *secondary lists.*

- You cannot have separate processing blocks for every *secondary list.* You have to process all *secondary lists* in the same processing block of the event: AT LINE-SELECTION or AT USER-COMMAND triggered repeatedly on user interaction on the list. Which list is to be processed can be determined by interrogating the value of the system field SY-LSIND in the processing block of the event.

- Preferably, in one ABAP program, use one of the two events: either the AT LINE-SELECTION or the AT USER-COMMAND.
- The headers for the *secondary lists* cannot be produced through the text element component *List Headings* (standard header) or the event TOP-OF-PAGE. The headers for *secondary lists* will have to be produced using the event TOP-OF-PAGE DURING LINE-SELECTION.
- The footers for the *secondary lists* can be produced through the event END-OF-PAGE, which you used earlier in Chapter 5.
- The interactive lists requiring user interaction can be run only in online or foreground mode and cannot be run in the background mode of processing.
- The first list is also referred as a *basic list*, the further lists as *detail lists*. In this book, the first list is being referred to as the *primary list*, and the subsequent lists as *secondary lists*.

Hands-on Exercise to Highlight Event AT LINE-SELECTION and the Operation of the System Field SY-LSIND

In this hands-on exercise, a single line is output in the event START-OF-SELECTION. A literal is output along with the system field SY-LSIND. This will constitute the *primary list*. Single clicking (HOTSPOT) on this list will trigger the event AT LINE-SELECTION. A literal is output with the system field SY-LSIND. This will constitute the *secondary lists*. Double clicking on the first *secondary list* will trigger the event AT LINE-SELECTION again, and the same literal with the incremented value of the system field SY-LSIND will be output. Double clicking again and again on the *secondary list* will produce the same output with the system field SY-LSIND incremented every time. Double clicking on the twentieth *secondary list* will result in a dump error because a maximum of only 20 *secondary lists* are supported.

Every time you click the 'Back' button of the standard toolbar on the *secondary list*, it will navigate to the previous list if any.

The Source:

```
REPORT YCL_CH10_ILISTS01.

*************************************************
* Inter Active Lists - Demo Maximum Of 21 lists **
*************************************************
*************************************************
* single click (because of HOTSPOT) on primary  **
* list will trigger event AT LINE-SELECTION and **
* output the first secondary list.              **
* subsequent double clickings will trigger      **
* the event AT LINE-SELECTION and output the    **
* respective secondary list. every clicking     **
* increments the system field SY-LSIND          **
*                                               **
* you are changing the color of each secondary  **
* list by incrementing the variable COLOUR. when**
* all colour codes are exhausted i.e. COLOUR = 7**
* you are initializing the variable COLOUR = 1  **
*                                               **
```

```
* the system field SY-LSIND is zero for the      **
* primary list, 1,2...20 for a maximum of 20     **
* secondary lists. if you double click on 20th   **
* secondary list, it will result in dump error   **
**************************************************
DATA: COLOUR  TYPE I VALUE 1.

START-OF-SELECTION.

WRITE:/5 'This is a Primary List. List No.:' HOTSPOT, (2) SY-LSIND .

******************************************
AT LINE-SELECTION.

FORMAT INVERSE ON COLOR = COLOUR.
WRITE:/10 'This is a Secondary List. List No.:', (2) SY-LSIND.
IF COLOUR = 7.
 COLOUR = 1.
ELSE.
  COLOUR = COLOUR + 1.
ENDIF.
```

The *Primary list* output will look like Figure 10-2.

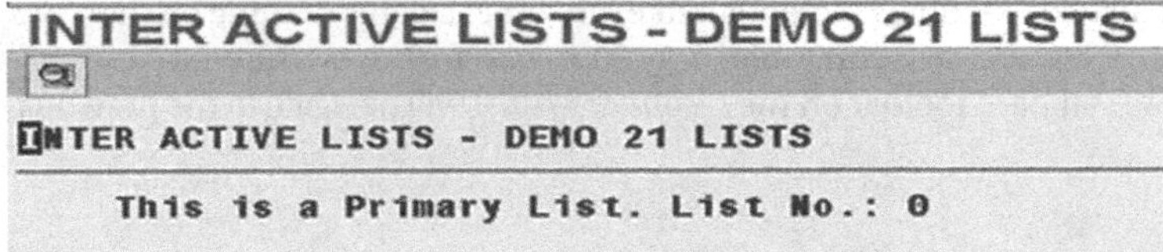

Figure 10-2. *Program YCL_CH10_ILISTS01 – Primary List*

The first *secondary list* output will look like Figure 10-3.

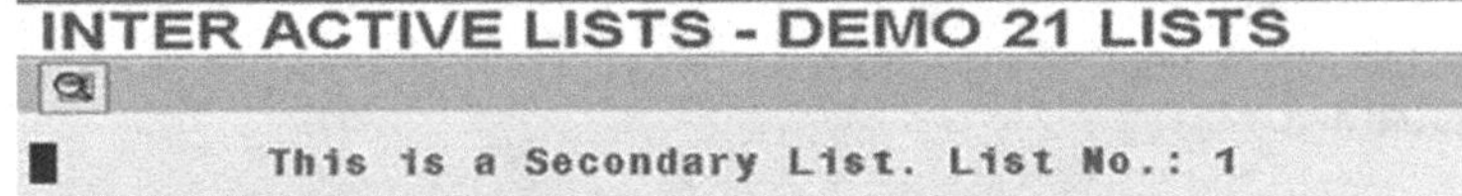

Figure 10-3. *Program YCL_CH10_ILISTS01 – First Secondary List*

The Twentieth *secondary list* output will look like Figure 10-4.

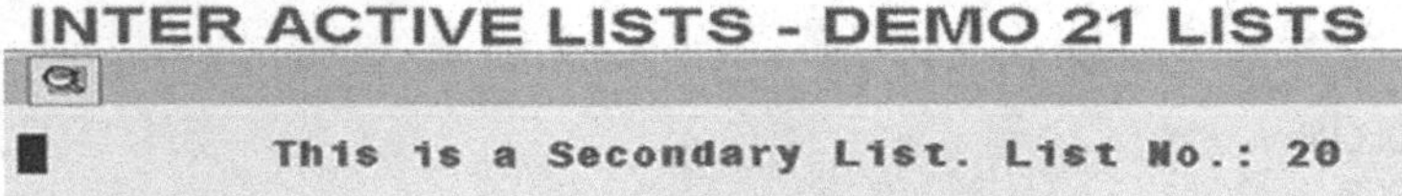

Figure 10-4. *Program YCL_CH10_ILISTS01 – Twentieth Secondary List*

This was a demonstration of the generation of a *primary list* and 20 *secondary lists.*

Hands-on Exercise: Produce Two Level Sales Report Using the AT LINE-SELECTION Event (1 Primary and 1 Secondary)

This hands-on exercise will produce a customer wise sales summary of a specified company code as the *primary list* (one line, one customer). This list is same as the output of the Chapter 6 program YCL_CH06_ITAB05. You can copy lines from this program into the current program YCL_CH10_ILISTS02 and test out this part.

The layout of the primary list body is shown in Table 10-1.

Table 10-1. *Customer Wise Sales - Output Body Layout*

Field Name	Table Name	Description	Column Positions
SY-TABIX	System Field	Serial No	005,008 (4)
			009
KUNNR	KNA1	Customer Code	010,019 (10)
			020
NAME1	KNA1	Name	021,055 (35)
			056
ORT01	KNA1	City	057-091 (35)
			092
NETWR	VBRK	Total of Converted Billing Document Net Value	093-109 (17)

When the end user double clicks on a line, you will list out all the billing documents of the customer on that line. This will constitute your *secondary list*. You will stop at this in this current exercise. There will be one *primary list* and one *secondary list*. You will generate the *secondary list* using the event AT-LINE-SELECTION. A rough layout of *secondary list* is shown in Figure 10-5.

```
List of Bills for
XXXXXXXXXXXXXXXXXX/XXXXXXXXXXXXXXXXXXXXXXXXXXXXXXXXXXXXXXXXXXXXXXXXXXXXXXXXXXXX
-----------------------------------------------------------------------------
Srl.    Doc.   No.        Doc. Date          Doc.                Amount
No.                                          Curr.
-----------------------------------------------------------------------------

XXXXXXXXXXXXXXXXX                                           - KUNNR
XXXXXXXXXXXXXXXXXXXXXXXXXXXXXXXXXXXXXXXXXXXXXXXXXXXXXXXXXX           - NAME1
```

Figure 10-5. *The Body Layout of the Secondary List*

Table 10-2. *Billing Docs of a Customer Output Body Layout*

Field Name	Table Name	Description	Column Positions
SY-TABIX	System Field	Serial No.	005,008 4)
			009
VBELN	VBRK	Billing Doc. Number	010,019 (10)
			020
FKDAT	VBRK	Billing Doc. Date	021,030 (10)
			031
WAERK	VBRK	Billing Doc. Currency	032-036 (5)
			037
NETWR	VBRK	Converted Billing Document Net Value (Amount)	038-052 (15)

In a subsequent hands-on exercise, you will extend this to a second *secondary list* as described in the opening section of this chapter 'Multiple Lists Generation by an ABAP Program', Figure 10-1, etc.

To generate the *secondary list*, you have to know the customer code on which an end user double clicked on the *primary list*. On the basis of customer code, you will be retrieving data of billing documents to be output in the *secondary list*. There are a few methods that enable the extraction of information of a *primary list* or any previous list in the processing block of event AT LINE-SELECTION for the current list. One of these methods will be described now, and the other methods will be described in the subsequent hands-on exercises.

The system field SY-LISEL contains, after double clicking on a line (on any of the lists), the contents of the clicked line as it was output on the screen. To know on which customer the end user double clicked, you need to extract the customer code information (or any other field value on the clicked line) from this system field SY-LISEL.

To generate the *secondary list*, you have to perform the following coding tasks:

Data Declarations

- Declare an internal table and structure to store smf process data to be output for a *secondary list*.
- Declare data to store the customer code and name to appear in the heading of the *secondary list*. The customer code is also used in the WHERE condition of SELECT statement to retrieve data for the *secondary list*.
- Declare data to build and output the total amount in the *secondary list*.

Coding in the Event Block AT LINE-SELECTION

- Ensure that the system field SY-LSIND does not exceed value 1. If it exceeds 1, assign it the value 1. You are supporting with this program one *primary* and one *secondary list*. If the end user double clicks on the *secondary list*, nothing must happen and no further interactivity.
- Extract customer code and name from the system field SY-LISEL into the declared variables.
- Load internal table from database table VBRK for extracted customer code and entered company code (Data for the *secondary list*).

- Initialize total field for *secondary list*. It could contain a value from previous processing.
- Set up LOOP AT ... ENDLOOP ... to output *secondary list* and build *secondary list* total.
- Write code for the header of the *secondary list* using the event TOP-OF-PAGE DURING LINE-SELECTION. (Event TOP-OF-PAGE cannot be used for *secondary lists.*)
- Output the *secondary list* total at the end of LOOP AT ... ENDLOOP.

It was mentioned that the system field SY-LISEL contains the complete line on which clicking was done as it was output on the screen (i.e., amount fields will contain commas, and the field 'KUNNR' will contain leading zeroes if the clause USING NO EDIT MASK was used to output the field, etc.).

So, if you want to extract the value of output 'KUNNR' field and store it in the field 'KUNNR' declared with DATA statement, you will be doing the following:

$$KUNNR = SY - LISEL + 9(10).$$

Refer to the output layout of primary list in Table 10-1. The 'KUNNR' field in the primary list is output in columns 10-19. The starting column is 10 (i.e., offset 9). The length of output is 10. Hence the expression SY – LISEL + 9(10). You have output the 'KUNNR' field with leading zeroes in the *primary list.* So there is no necessity of inserting leading zeroes to the field before using it in the WHERE condition of the SELECT statement for retrieving data for the *secondary list.*

Similarly, the customer name field is extracted from the system field SY-LISEL and stored in the declared field 'NAME1':

$$NAME1 = SY - LISEL + 20(35).$$

The extracted customer code and name are being used in the heading of the *secondary list.*

The DDIC Data Type of system field SY-LISEL is CHAR and length 255.

The source program:

```
REPORT YCL_CH10_ILISTS02 NO STANDARD PAGE HEADING
       LINE-COUNT 60.

*********************************************************
* Customer Wise Sales Summary & 1 Level Detail. Click  **
* On a Customer To List Billing Docs of That Customer  **
*********************************************************

*************************************************
* Primary list same as the output of program   **
* YCL_CH06_ITAB05. Copy those lines.           **
*                                              **
* declare internal table, structure to store   **
* Data to be output for secondary list.        **
* declare data to store customer code, name to **
* appear in the heading of secondary list      **
* declare data to total amount to be output in **
* secondary list.                              **
*                                              **
* in the event block AT LINE-SELECTION:-       **
* 1.ensure that the system field SY-LSIND Does **
*   not exceed 1.                              **
*                                              **
```

```
* 2. extract customer code & name on which     **
*    clicking was done                         **
*                                              **
* 3. load internal table from database table   **
*    VBRK for extracted customer code and      **
*    company code input                        **
*                                              **
* 4. initialize total field for secondary list **
*                                              **
* 5. set up LOOP AT...ENDLOOP to output        **
*    secondary list and build secondary list   **
*    total.                                    **
*                                              **
* 6. code for the secondary list heading using **
*    event TOP-OF-PAGE DURING LINE-SELECTION   **
*                                              **
* 7. end of loop, output secondary list total  **
************************************************

DATA: SALES_TAB  TYPE YCL_CH06_SALES_SUM_TAB,
      SALES_STRU LIKE LINE OF SALES_TAB,

      BEGIN OF BILLS_STRU,
       VBELN    TYPE VBRK-VBELN,
       FKDAT    TYPE VBRK-FKDAT,
       WAERK    TYPE VBRK-WAERK,
       KURRF    TYPE VBRK-KURRF,
       NETWR    TYPE VBRK-NETWR,
      END OF BILLS_STRU,
      BILLS_TAB LIKE STANDARD TABLE OF BILLS_STRU,

      KUNNR    TYPE KNA1-KUNNR,
      NAME1    TYPE KNA1-NAME1,
      TOTAL    TYPE VBRK-NETWR,
      TOTAL1   TYPE VBRK-NETWR,
      BUTXT    TYPE T001-BUTXT,
      WAERS    TYPE T001-WAERS,
      BUTXTS   TYPE STRING.
**********************************************
PARAMETERS: CCODE TYPE VBRK-BUKRS VALUE CHECK
            DEFAULT 3000.
**********************************************

TOP-OF-PAGE.

WRITE:/5 TEXT-001, CCODE NO-GAP, '/' NO-GAP,  BUTXTS,
         102 TEXT-003, 107(3) SY-PAGNO.
WRITE:/40 TEXT-002, WAERS.
SKIP 1.
WRITE:/5(104) SY-ULINE.
```

```
WRITE:/5 TEXT-004, 11 TEXT-005, 23 TEXT-006, 60 TEXT-007, 91(17)
         TEXT-008 RIGHT-JUSTIFIED.
WRITE:/5 TEXT-009, 13 TEXT-010.
WRITE:/5(104) SY-ULINE.

*********************************************
START-OF-SELECTION.

SELECT SINGLE BUTXT WAERS FROM T001 INTO (BUTXT, WAERS) WHERE
       BUKRS = CCODE.

BUTXTS = BUTXT. "assignment to TYPE STRING drops trailing blanks

SELECT KUNNR NAME1 ORT01 NETWR KURRF FROM YCL_CH05_VBRKKNA INTO
  CORRESPONDING FIELDS OF SALES_STRU WHERE BUKRS = CCODE.

 SALES_STRU-NETWR =  SALES_STRU-NETWR * SALES_STRU-KURRF.
 SALES_STRU-KURRF = 0. "to prevent overflow
 COLLECT SALES_STRU INTO SALES_TAB.
ENDSELECT.

SORT SALES_TAB BY KUNNR.

LOOP AT SALES_TAB INTO SALES_STRU.
 WRITE :/5(4) SY-TABIX, SALES_STRU-KUNNR USING NO EDIT MASK,
  SALES_STRU-NAME1,SALES_STRU-ORT01, (17) SALES_STRU-NETWR.
 TOTAL = TOTAL + SALES_STRU-NETWR.
ENDLOOP.

SKIP 1.
WRITE :/(17) TOTAL UNDER SALES_STRU-NETWR.
*******************************************************************
*******************************************************************
AT LINE-SELECTION.

IF SY-LSIND > 1. " ensure SY-LSIND does not exceed 1
 SY-LSIND = 1.
ELSE.
 TOTAL1 = 0.
 KUNNR = SY-LISEL+9(10).  " extract customer code
 NAME1 = SY-LISEL+20(35). " extract customer name

 SELECT VBELN FKDAT WAERK KURRF NETWR FROM VBRK INTO TABLE BILLS_TAB
   WHERE KUNAG = KUNNR AND BUKRS = CCODE.

 LOOP AT BILLS_TAB INTO BILLS_STRU.
  BILLS_STRU-NETWR = BILLS_STRU-NETWR * BILLS_STRU-KURRF.
  TOTAL1 = TOTAL1 + BILLS_STRU-NETWR.
  WRITE:/5(4) SY-TABIX, BILLS_STRU-VBELN, BILLS_STRU-FKDAT,
   BILLS_STRU-WAERK, (15) BILLS_STRU-NETWR.
 ENDLOOP.
```

```
 SKIP 1.
 WRITE:/38(15) TOTAL1.
ENDIF.
********************************************************************
********************************************************************
TOP-OF-PAGE DURING LINE-SELECTION. " event for secondary list headers

WRITE:/5 TEXT-011, 44 TEXT-003, 49(3) SY-PAGNO.
WRITE:/5 KUNNR USING NO EDIT MASK NO-GAP, '/' NO-GAP, NAME1.
WRITE:/5(48) SY-ULINE.
WRITE:/5 TEXT-004, 10 TEXT-012, 21 TEXT-013, 32 TEXT-014, 46 TEXT-008.
WRITE:/6 TEXT-009, 32 TEXT-015.
WRITE:/5(48) SY-ULINE.
********************************************************************
```

The text symbols used in the lists' headers are shown in Figure 10-6.

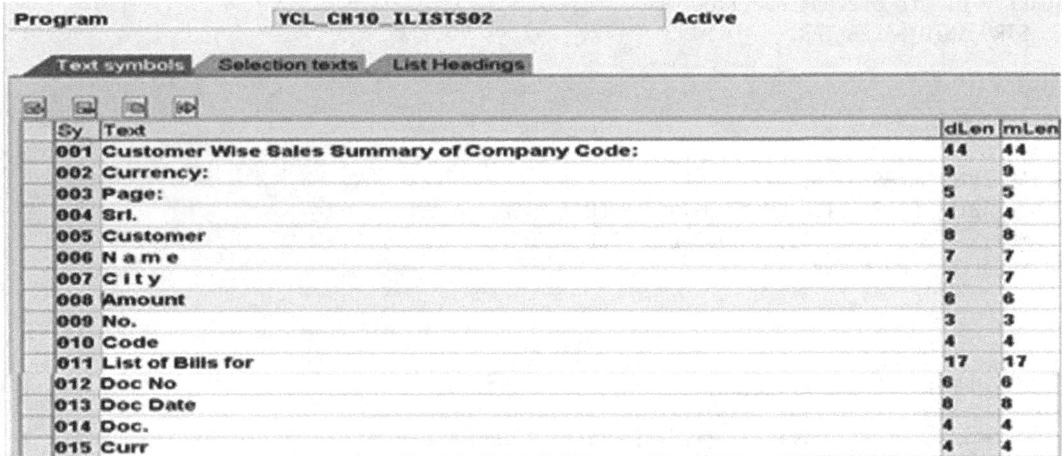

Program YCL_CH10_ILISTS02 Active

Text symbols | Selection texts | List Headings

Sy	Text	dLen	mLen
001	Customer Wise Sales Summary of Company Code:	44	44
002	Currency:	9	9
003	Page:	5	5
004	Srl.	4	4
005	Customer	8	8
006	N a m e	7	7
007	C i t y	7	7
008	Amount	6	6
009	No.	3	3
010	Code	4	4
011	List of Bills for	17	17
012	Doc No	6	6
013	Doc Date	8	8
014	Doc.	4	4
015	Curr	4	4

Figure 10-6. *Program YCL_CH10_ILISTS02 - Text Symbols*

The *primary list* - Customer Wise Sales of a Specified Company Code - will look like Figure 10-7.

```
INTERACTIVE LISTS -2 LEVEL

Customer Wise Sales Summary of Company Code: 3000/IDES US INC                Page: 1
                               Currency: USD

Srl.  Customer   N a m e                                  C i t y                       Amount
No.     Code

 23  0000003034 Insurance Company                         DURANGO                       299.00
 24  0000003060 Candid International Technology           CHICAGO                    20,089.25
 25  0000003221 Andyna and Dynana Laboratories, Inc       MONSEY                      6,153.60
 26  0000003250 Department of Defense                     MILANVILLE                 50,000.00
 27  0000003251 Palo Alto Airways Inc.                    PALO ALTO                 202,496.00
 28  0000003261 Hotel Alfonso Del Vida                    DENVER                      3,571.00
 29  0000003262 La Quinta Hotel & Towers                  DENVER                      3,560.00
 30  0000003263 Rogier Golf Resort YY                     DENVER                      3,058.00
 31  0000003271 Media Store                               ANTIOCH                     6,477.30
 32  0000003272 ADCOM COMPUTER                            SEATTLE                     2,147.70
 33  0000003273 ALPHA Center                              MINNEAPOLIS                 2,147.70
 34  0000003800 Candid International Technology           TAMPA                     723,492.00
 35  0000004000 North Energy Ltd                          Calgary                    42,666.67
 36  0000004130 Compu Tech                                SAN FRANCISCO              57,358.00
 37  0000006000 RIWA Headquarters                         LOS ANGELES                 2,251.76
 38  0000006002 RIWA Regional Storage Trenton             TRENTON                    78,780.00
 39  0000006006 RIWA Regional Warehouse Denver            DENVER                    152,712.00
 40  0000030200 Wal-Mart                                  NEWARK                      8,000.00
 41  0000300000 Havers  Inc.                              ANTIOCH                     4,133.00
 42  0000300075 Carmella Credit                           HUNTINGTON BEACH              327.00
 43  0000300081 Havers Inc                                ANTIOCH                       914.20
 44  0000300286 Dynamic Industries                        EVERETT                   300,000.00
```

Figure 10-7. *Program YCL_CH10_ILISTS02 - Primary List*

Double click on the customer code '0000003271' ('Media Store', Srl. No. 31). The explanation of multiple lists in the opening section of this chapter (Figure 10-1) used this customer 'Media Store'. Using the same customer makes the perusal easier.

The *secondary list* will be like Figure 10-8.

```
INTERACTIVE LISTS -2 LEVEL

List of Bills for                                   Page: 1
0000003271/Media Store

Srl. Doc No       Doc Date     Doc.                 Amount
 No.                           Curr

   1 90031824     04.02.2002   USD                   75.00
   2 90032841     25.06.2002   USD                2,147.70
   3 90032962     23.08.2002   USD                2,003.30
   4 90034693     08.06.2004   USD                  248.00
   5 90036011     19.12.2005   USD                2,003.30

                                                  6,477.30
```

Figure 10-8. *Program YCL_CH10_ILISTS02 - Secondary List*

The five billing documents of customer '0000003271' are output in the secondary list.

In the IDES server, the billing documents data is for multiple years: 2002, 2004, and 2005. So, multiple years' data was output. In a real-life situation, output or reporting will be for specific time periods: month/quarter/financial year. You are not reporting for a specific period, you are reporting using the full data. In the current learning paradigm, this is okay.

This is the end of the hands-on exercise of two level lists. You will extend this two level interactive list to a three level interactive list in the next hands-on exercise.

Hands-on Exercise: Produce Three Level Sales Report Using the AT LINE-SELECTION Event (1 Primary and 2 Secondary)

You will extend the two level interactive lists to a three level interactive list in the current hands-on exercise. When the end user clicks on a billing document in the first *secondary list,* you will list all the items of the billing document clicked upon.

The program will generate one *primary list* and two *secondary lists*: *secondary list* I and *secondary list* II.

The *primary list* will be customer wise sales summary for a specified company code. (Already generated earlier, code lines can be copied.)

The *secondary list* I will be the billing documents of a customer line double clicked upon. (Already generated earlier, code lines can be copied.)

The *secondary list* II will be the items of a billing document line double clicked upon. (New code lines to be created and other required modifications to be done.)

Layout:

```
Items/Materials of Billing Doc. XXXXXXXXXXX                                Page: XXX
------------------------------------------------------------------------------------
Srl.    Material Code                          Quantity        UOM            Amount
No.
------------------------------------------------------------------------------------

XXXXXXXXXXXXXXX                    - VBELN
```

Figure 10-9. *The Body Layout of the Secondary List II*

Table 10-3. *Items/Materials of a Billing Doc. Output Body Layout*

Field Name	Table Name	Description	Column Positions
SY-TABIX	System Field	Serial No.	005,008 (4) 009
MATNR	VBRP	Material Code	010,027 (18) 028
FKIMG	VBRP	Billed Quantity	029,040 (12) 041
VRKME	VBRP	Unit of Measure (Sales)	042-046 (5) 047
NETWR	VBRP	Converted Item Net Value (Amount)	048-062 (15)

Information Passing: From One List to Another – the HIDE Statement

If you have to retrieve the items of the billing document clicked upon, you have to know the billing document number clicked upon (i.e., the value of the variable 'VBELN'). You can retrieve it the way you did in the previous hands-on exercise from the system field SY-LISEL.

The HIDE statement is being introduced in this hands-on exercise. The HIDE statement will be used to retrieve the data of the line clicked upon a list.

The statement 'HIDE' is misleading. There is nothing being hidden as such. With the HIDE statement, data objects are being saved and retrieved. The HIDE statement is a means of saving and retrieving data object values. In the current exercise, the code lines to output the *secondary list* I:

```
LOOP AT BILLS_TAB INTO BILLS_STRU.
  .....
  WRITE:/5(4) SY-TABIX, BILLS_STRU-VBELN, BILLS_STRU-FKDAT,
   BILLS_STRU-WAERK, (15) BILLS_STRU-NETWR.

   HIDE: BILLS_STRU-KURRF, BILLS_STRU-VBELN.
ENDLOOP.
```

The HIDE statement will save or store the names and values of the data objects or variables specified, that is, BILLS_STRU-KURRF, BILLS_STRU-VBELN in the hide area for every list line in a kind of table form. If there are 100 output lines in the list, the HIDE statement will store 100 values of the variables. Each value of each variable is associated with the line number of the most recent output. When a list line is double clicked, the saved values of data objects or variables corresponding to the clicked line will be fetched into the variables.

In the present context, when an end user double clicks on a billing document, the system will fetch the corresponding billing document number and exchange rate from the saved or hide area and load them into the variables BILLS_STRU-VBELN and BILLS_STRU-KURRF. You can then use the retrieved values in these variables in your *secondary list* II. You will use BILLS_STRU-VBELN in the WHERE condition of the SELECT statement to retrieve items for the billing document number contained in BILLS_STRU-VBELN. You will use the exchange rate value in the field BILLS_STRU-KURRF to derive the amount in the currency of the company code from the amount in the currency of the billing document.

A demonstrative example of the HIDE statement:

```
START-OF-SELECTION.

 DO 5 TIMES.
  WRITE:/5 'Primary List. Line No.:', SY-INDEX.
  HIDE SY-INDEX.
ENDDO.

AT LINE-SELECTION.
WRITE:/5 'Secondary List. Clicked Line No.:', SY-INDEX.
```

The *primary list* output will be:

```
Line No.: 1
Line No.: 2
Line No.: 3
Line No.: 4
Line No.: 5
```

If you double click on the fourth line, the secondary list will be:

```
Secondary List. Clicked Line No.: 4
```

Whichever of the five lines you double click on the *primary list*, the *secondary list* will output that line number with the literal 'Secondary List. Clicked Line No::'. The value of system field SY-INDEX saved through the HIDE SY-INDEX statement is being retrieved and placed into SY-INDEX by double clicking on a line of the *primary list*.

It is important where you locate your HIDE statement. Since the saving and retrieval is based on list line, it is preferable that you have the HIDE statement right next to the WRITE statement if you are using a single WRITE statement to output a line (as you are doing in your *secondary list* I). If you are using multiple WRITE statements to output one line, the HIDE statement should follow the last WRITE statement used to output a line.

A demonstrative code to show how an inapt positioning of HIDE statement will lead to erroneous results:

```
START-OF-SELECTION.

 DO 5 TIMES.
  HIDE SY-INDEX.
  WRITE:/5 'Primary List. Line No.:', SY-INDEX.
ENDDO.

AT LINE-SELECTION.
WRITE:/5 'Secondary List. Clicked Line No.:', SY-INDEX.
```

You have placed the HIDE statement before the WRITE statement. The SY-INDEX value will be saved and retrieved as follows:

The first time the HIDE SY-INDEX statement is encountered; there is no prior output line, or no corresponding list line, so no saving of SY-INDEX = 1.

When the statement: HIDE SY-INDEX is encountered in the second pass of the loop, that is, SY-INDEX = 2, the only output line is ' Line No.: 1'. So the first line of the *primary list* gets associated or linked to the SY-INDEX value 2. On the same pattern, the output line 'Line No.: 2' of the *primary list* gets associated or linked to the SY-INDEX value 3. And the output line ' Line No.: 4' of the *primary list* gets associated or linked to the SY-INDEX value 5. The last line of the *primary list* ' Line No.: 5' is not associated with any value of SY-INDEX. After the output of this line, no HIDE statement is encountered and the loop exits.

When you double click on the first line of the *primary list* 'Line No.: 1', you get the following output:

```
Secondary List: Clicked Line No.: 2
```

This was because the first line of the primary list was associated with the SY-INDEX value 2.

The data objects you can save and retrieve through the HIDE statement can be elementary or flat structures.

Create the Text in Text Symbols for the Header of a Secondary List II

To generate the secondary list II, you have to perform the following coding tasks:

Data Declarations

- Declare an internal table and structure to store, and process data to be output for *secondary list* II.
- Declare data to build, and output total amount in *secondary list* II.

Coding in LOOP ... ENDLOOP of Secondary List I

```
HIDE: BILLS_STRU-KURRF, BILLS_STRU-VBELN.
```

Coding in the Event Block AT LINE-SELECTION

- You have now two *secondary lists*. The value of the system field SY-LSIND should not exceed 2. If the end user double clicks on the *secondary list* II, there should be no further interaction.
- Both the *secondary list* will be in the event AT LINE-SELECTION. So you have to check the value of system field SY-LSIND to produce a specific *secondary list* - CASE ... ENDCASE statements, etc.
- Initialize the total for *secondary list* II; it might contain a value from previous processing.
- Load data into the internal table from database table VBRP to produce the secondary list II. The WHERE condition: VBELN = BILLS_STRU-VBELN.
- Set up LOOP ... ENDLOOP ... to produce the body of secondary list II and build total. Refer to layout tables whenever coding for the body of a list. Output the built total at the end of LOOP AT ... ENDLOOP process.

Coding For the Secondary List II Header

In the event: TOP-OF-PAGE DURING LINE-SELECTION, you have to check the value of the system field SY-LSIND and code for the appropriate *secondary list* header.

Coding for Improvements, Sophistication

- **No Data Check:** When there is no data to be listed, you should not output anything like a heading, etc. You must issue a message and alert the end user. This is what you are doing for all the three lists (i.e., one primary and two *secondary lists*). Strictly speaking, in your present context, you will have data for the *secondary list* I. Your source of data for the *primary list* is a database view that has gathered data of customers having billing documents. So the scenario of customers having no bills does not arise with the view data you are using. But you are checking the no data condition for the *secondary list* I also. (Redundant.) You can test the no data condition for a primary list with company code values 2000, 4000, 5000, etc., In a real-life scenario, the no data condition will be incorporated in every listing or reporting program.
- **Produce lists only when double clicking on valid data:** In the output generated by the program YCL_CH10_ILISTS02, if the user double clicks on the report area, other than in the body of the report-like report heading or column headings, the AT LINE-SELECTION event will be triggered, and an erroneous *secondary list* will be generated.

For example, if the user double clicks on the *primary list* heading, the system field SY-LISEL will be filled up with the contents of the clicked line, that is, 'Customer Wise Sales Summary of Company Code ...' You are extracting the 10-19 columns/bytes of this system field SY-LISEL into the variable 'KUNNR' as customer code: KUNNR = SY-LISEL+9(10). In this case, you will have the value 'Wise Sales' in the field 'KUNNR'. This is not a valid customer code. No data will be fetched from the database table 'VBRK'. You will not have any output in the body of the *secondary list.* Though there is nothing wrong happening, this is an awkward situation. You overcome this awkward situation in the current program. You can ensure that only when the user double clicks on any of the fields of the list body, interaction and further list generation occurs.

If the user double clicks on any area of the list other than the fields of the list body, there should be no interaction. The Fields in the list body of the *primary list* are:

(i)

SY-TABIX

SALES_STRU-KUNNR

SALES_STRU-NAME1

SALES_STRU-ORT01

SALES_STRU-NETWR

The fields in the list body of *secondary list I* are:

(ii)

SY-TABIX

BILLS_STRU-VBELN

BILLS_STRU-FKDAT

BILLS_STRU-WAERK

BILLS_STRU-NETWR

You have to determine before the generation of *secondary list* I that double clicking occurred on any of the fields listed under (i). And determine before the generation of *secondary list* II that double clicking occurred on any of the fields listed under (ii). You use the GET CURSOR … ABAP statement to determine the field on which an end user double clicked. A simple syntax of the GET CURSOR statement:

```
GET CURSOR FIELD <data object>.
GET CURSOR FIELD - Key phrase
<data object> - A character type variable: TYPE C or STRING.
```

The name of the list field double clicked upon is returned in the <data object>. If there is no field like the blank column being implicitly generated between adjoining data objects output on the same line, the GET CURSOR statement will return blank. That is why, in the current program, if the end user double clicks on the blank column between adjoining fields of the list body, there is no interaction and generation of a further list.

After the GET CURSOR … statement, you are using the IF statement to determine the field double clicked upon. If the field name is not as per your fields listed in (i) and (ii), you are decrementing the system field SY-LSIND by 1 and exiting the processing block. Double clicking incremented the system field SY-LSIND, as you want to stay put on the current list with no interaction, you have to restore to the system field the value of the list on which the user double clicked.

Variations of the GET CURSOR … statement can obtain field values from any page and line. So the statement can be used to exchange information from the lower level lists to a higher level list. So you can use GET CURSOR … statement in lieu of the system field SY-LISEL, HIDE … statement if you want.

You can look up these variations of the GET CURSOR … in the online documentation or the documents under ABAP Programming (BC-ABA).

When using the event AT LINE-SELECTION, the control of the system field SY-LSIND is critical and has to be taken care of in the coding.

The source code:

```
REPORT YCL_CH10_ILISTS03 NO STANDARD PAGE HEADING
        LINE-COUNT 60.

****************************************************************
* Customer Wise Sales Summary & 2 Level Detail.              **
* 1. Click On A Customer To List Billing Docs Of That Customer **
* 2. Click On A Billing Doc To List items Of That Billing Doc. **
****************************************************************

************************************************
* primary list same as the output of program   **
* YCL_CH06_ITAB05. copy those lines.           **
*                                              **
* secondary list I same as the output of       **
* program YCL_CH10_ILISTS02. copy those lines. **
*                                              **
* to pass info from secondary list I to II, use**
* the HIDE statement after the WRITE statement **
* in secondary list I like:                    **
* HIDE: BILLS_STRU-VBELN, BILLS_STRU-KURRF.     **
*                                              **
* declare internal table, structure to store   **
* data to be output for secondary list. II     **
* declare data to total amount to be output    **
* in secondary list II.                        **
*                                              **
* in the event block AT LINE-SELECTION:-       **
* 1.ensure that the system field SY-LSIND Does **
*   not exceed 2. chech value of SY_LSIND and  **
*   code for appropriate secondary lists       **
*                                              **
* 2. load internal table from database table   **
*    VBRP for value in BILLS_STRU-VBELN        **
*                                              **
* 3. initialize total field for secondary      **
*    list II                                   **
*                                              **
* 4. set up LOOP AT...ENDLOOP to output        **
*    secondary list II and build secondary     **
*    list II total.                            **
*                                              **
* 5. code for the secondary list II heading    **
*    using event TOP-OF-PAGE DURING            **
*    LINE-SELECTION                            **
*                                              **
* 6. end of loop, output secondary list II     **
*    total                                     **
*                                              **
```

```
* 7. check for no data condition in primary    **
*    list, issue message for no data           **
*    you have done no data check for secondary **
*    lists I & II though not necessary         **
*                                              **
* 8. use GET CURSOR statement to determine     **
*    user double clicked on a valid output     **
*    field on the primary and secondary list I,**
*    generate subsequent lists only if double  **
*    click on valid fields                     **
************************************************

DATA: SALES_TAB  TYPE YCL_CH06_SALES_SUM_TAB,
      SALES_STRU LIKE LINE OF SALES_TAB,

      BEGIN OF BILLS_STRU,
       VBELN    TYPE VBRK-VBELN,
       FKDAT    TYPE VBRK-FKDAT,
       WAERK    TYPE VBRK-WAERK,
       KURRF    TYPE VBRK-KURRF,
       NETWR    TYPE VBRK-NETWR,
      END OF BILLS_STRU,
      BILLS_TAB LIKE STANDARD TABLE OF BILLS_STRU,

      BEGIN OF BILL_ITEMS_STRU,
       MATNR    TYPE VBRP-MATNR, " material code
       FKIMG    TYPE VBRP-FKIMG, " quantity
       VRKME    TYPE VBRP-VRKME, " unit of measure
       NETWR    TYPE VBRP-NETWR, " amount for item
      END OF BILL_ITEMS_STRU,
      BILL_ITEMS_TAB LIKE STANDARD TABLE OF BILL_ITEMS_STRU,

      KUNNR    TYPE KNA1-KUNNR,
      NAME1    TYPE KNA1-NAME1,
      TOTAL    TYPE VBRK-NETWR,
      TOTAL1   TYPE VBRK-NETWR,
      TOTAL2   TYPE VBRK-NETWR,
      FNAME    TYPE STRING, " to store field name in GET CURSOR

      BUTXT    TYPE T001-BUTXT,
      WAERS    TYPE T001-WAERS,
      BUTXTS   TYPE STRING.
**********************************************
PARAMETERS: CCODE TYPE VBRK-BUKRS VALUE CHECK
            DEFAULT 3000.
**********************************************

TOP-OF-PAGE.

WRITE:/5 TEXT-001, CCODE NO-GAP, '/' NO-GAP,  BUTXTS,
         102 TEXT-003, 107(3) SY-PAGNO.
WRITE:/40 TEXT-002, WAERS.
```

```
SKIP 1.
WRITE:/5(104) SY-ULINE.
WRITE:/5 TEXT-004, 11 TEXT-005, 23 TEXT-006, 60 TEXT-007, 91(17)
         TEXT-008 RIGHT-JUSTIFIED.
WRITE:/5 TEXT-009, 13 TEXT-010.
WRITE:/5(104) SY-ULINE.

**********************************************
START-OF-SELECTION.

SELECT SINGLE BUTXT WAERS FROM T001 INTO (BUTXT, WAERS) WHERE
       BUKRS = CCODE.

BUTXTS = BUTXT. "assignment to TYPE STRING drops trailing blanks

SELECT KUNNR NAME1 ORT01 NETWR KURRF FROM YCL_CH05_VBRKKNA INTO
  CORRESPONDING FIELDS OF SALES_STRU WHERE BUKRS = CCODE.

 SALES_STRU-NETWR =  SALES_STRU-NETWR * SALES_STRU-KURRF.
 SALES_STRU-KURRF = 0. "to prevent overflow
 COLLECT SALES_STRU INTO SALES_TAB.
ENDSELECT.

IF SY-DBCNT > 0.

 SORT SALES_TAB BY KUNNR.

 LOOP AT SALES_TAB INTO SALES_STRU.
  WRITE :/5(4) SY-TABIX, SALES_STRU-KUNNR USING NO EDIT MASK,
   SALES_STRU-NAME1,SALES_STRU-ORT01, (17) SALES_STRU-NETWR.
  TOTAL = TOTAL + SALES_STRU-NETWR.
 ENDLOOP.

 SKIP 1.
 WRITE :/(17) TOTAL UNDER SALES_STRU-NETWR.
ELSE.
 MESSAGE S021(YCL_CH07_MCLASS01) WITH " no data for the company code
  'Primary List' DISPLAY LIKE 'W'.
ENDIF.
*****************************************************************
*****************************************************************
AT LINE-SELECTION.

IF SY-LSIND > 2. " ensure SY-LSIND does not exceed 2
 SY-LSIND = 2.

ELSE.
 CASE SY-LSIND.

 WHEN 1.
```

```
  GET CURSOR FIELD FNAME. "check for cursor on a field
  IF FNAME <> 'SY-TABIX' AND FNAME <> 'SALES_STRU-KUNNR' AND
    FNAME <> 'SALES_STRU-NAME1' AND FNAME <> 'SALES_STRU-NETWR'.

   SY-LSIND = SY-LSIND - 1.
   EXIT.
  ENDIF.

  TOTAL1 = 0.
  KUNNR = SY-LISEL+9(10).  " extract customer code
  NAME1 = SY-LISEL+20(35). " extract customer name

  SELECT VBELN FKDAT WAERK KURRF NETWR FROM VBRK INTO TABLE BILLS_TAB
   WHERE KUNAG = KUNNR AND BUKRS = CCODE.

  IF SY-DBCNT = 0.
   MESSAGE S021(YCL_CH07_MCLASS01) WITH 'Secondary List I' DISPLAY LIKE 'W'.
   SY-LSIND = 0.
   EXIT.
  ENDIF.
  LOOP AT BILLS_TAB INTO BILLS_STRU.

   BILLS_STRU-NETWR = BILLS_STRU-NETWR * BILLS_STRU-KURRF.
   TOTAL1 = TOTAL1 + BILLS_STRU-NETWR.
   WRITE:/5(4) SY-TABIX, BILLS_STRU-VBELN, BILLS_STRU-FKDAT,
   BILLS_STRU-WAERK, (15) BILLS_STRU-NETWR.

   HIDE: BILLS_STRU-KURRF, BILLS_STRU-VBELN.

  ENDLOOP.

  SKIP 1.
  WRITE:/38(15) TOTAL1.

************************************
 WHEN 2.

  GET CURSOR FIELD FNAME. "check for cursor on a field
  IF FNAME <> 'SY-TABIX' AND FNAME <> 'BILLS_STRU-VBELN' AND
    FNAME <> 'BILLS_STRU-FKDAT' AND FNAME <> 'BILLS_STRU-WAERK'
    AND FNAME <> 'BILLS_STRU-NETWR'.

   SY-LSIND = SY-LSIND - 1.
   EXIT.
  ENDIF.

  TOTAL2 = 0.
```

```
  SELECT MATNR FKIMG VRKME NETWR FROM VBRP INTO TABLE BILL_ITEMS_TAB
   WHERE VBELN = BILLS_STRU-VBELN.

  IF SY-DBCNT = 0.
   MESSAGE S021(YCL_CH07_MCLASS01) WITH 'Secondary List II' DISPLAY LIKE 'W'.
   SY-LSIND = 1.
   EXIT.
  ENDIF.

  LOOP AT BILL_ITEMS_TAB INTO BILL_ITEMS_STRU.

   BILL_ITEMS_STRU-NETWR = BILL_ITEMS_STRU-NETWR * BILLS_STRU-KURRF.
   TOTAL2 = TOTAL2 + BILL_ITEMS_STRU-NETWR.
   WRITE:/5(4) SY-TABIX, BILL_ITEMS_STRU-MATNR, (12) BILL_ITEMS_STRU-FKIMG,
   BILL_ITEMS_STRU-VRKME, (15) BILL_ITEMS_STRU-NETWR.
  ENDLOOP.

  SKIP 1.
  WRITE:/46(15) TOTAL2.

 ENDCASE.

 ENDIF.
*******************************************************************
*******************************************************************
TOP-OF-PAGE DURING LINE-SELECTION. " event for secondary list headers

CASE SY-LSIND.

 WHEN 1.

  WRITE:/5 TEXT-011, 44 TEXT-003, 49(3) SY-PAGNO.
  WRITE:/5 KUNNR USING NO EDIT MASK NO-GAP, '/' NO-GAP, NAME1.
  WRITE:/5(48) SY-ULINE.
  WRITE:/5 TEXT-004, 10 TEXT-012, 21 TEXT-013, 32 TEXT-014,
    46 TEXT-008.
  WRITE:/6 TEXT-009, 32 TEXT-015.
  WRITE:/5(48) SY-ULINE.

 WHEN 2.

  WRITE:/5 TEXT-016, BILLS_STRU-VBELN, 53 TEXT-003, 59(3) SY-PAGNO.
  WRITE:/5(56) SY-ULINE.
  WRITE:/5 TEXT-004, 11 TEXT-017, 32 TEXT-018, 42 TEXT-019, 55 TEXT-008.
  WRITE:/6 TEXT-009.
  WRITE:/5(56) SY-ULINE.

ENDCASE.
*******************************************************************
```

A partial list of Text symbols is listed in Figure 10-10.

Program YCL_CH10_ILISTS03 Active

Text symbols | Selection texts | List Headings

Sy	Text	dLen	mLen
012	Doc No	6	6
013	Doc Date	8	8
014	Doc.	4	4
015	Curr	4	4
016	Items/Materials Of Billing Doc.	31	31
017	Material Code	13	13
018	Quantity	8	8
019	UOM	3	3

Figure 10-10. Program YCL_CH10_ILISTS03 – Text Symbols

Figure 10-11 shows the no data condition.

INTERACTIVE LISTS - 3 LEVEL

CCODE 2000

No Data For Primary List

Figure 10-11. Program YCL_CH10_ILISTS03 – No Data Condition

The primary list will look like Figure 10-12.

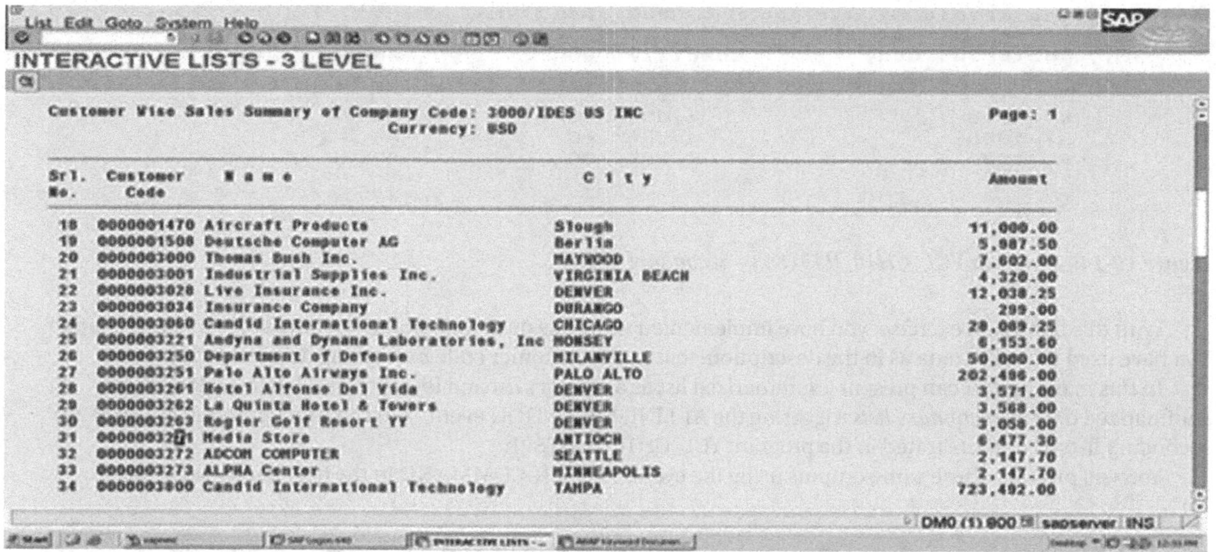

List Edit Goto System Help

INTERACTIVE LISTS - 3 LEVEL

Customer Wise Sales Summary of Company Code: 3000/IDES US INC   Page: 1
Currency: USD

Srl. No.	Customer Code	Name	City	Amount
18	0000001470	Aircraft Products	Slough	11,000.00
19	0000001508	Deutsche Computer AG	Berlin	5,987.50
20	0000003000	Thomas Bush Inc.	MAYWOOD	7,602.00
21	0000003001	Industrial Supplies Inc.	VIRGINIA BEACH	4,320.00
22	0000003028	Live Insurance Inc.	DENVER	12,038.25
23	0000003034	Insurance Company	DURANGO	299.00
24	0000003060	Candid International Technology	CHICAGO	28,089.25
25	0000003221	Amdyna and Dynana Laboratories, Inc	MONSEY	6,153.60
26	0000003250	Department of Defense	MILANVILLE	50,000.00
27	0000003251	Palo Alto Airways Inc.	PALO ALTO	202,496.00
28	0000003261	Hotel Alfonso Del Vida	DENVER	3,571.00
29	0000003262	La Quinta Hotel & Towers	DENVER	3,568.00
30	0000003263	Regier Golf Resort YY	DENVER	3,058.00
31	0000003271	Media Store	ANTIOCH	6,477.30
32	0000003272	ADCOM COMPUTER	SEATTLE	2,147.70
33	0000003273	ALPHA Center	MINNEAPOLIS	2,147.70
34	0000003800	Candid International Technology	TAMPA	723,492.00

DM0 (1) 800 sapserver INS

***Figure 10-12.** Program YCL_CH10_ILISTS03 – Primary List*

The secondary list I will look like Figure 10-13.

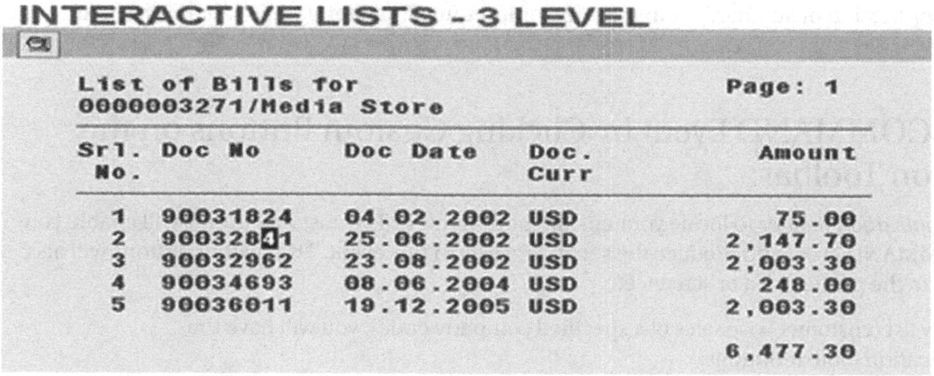

INTERACTIVE LISTS - 3 LEVEL

List of Bills for   Page: 1
0000003271/Media Store

Srl. No.	Doc No	Doc Date	Doc. Curr	Amount
1	90031824	04.02.2002	USD	75.00
2	90032841	25.06.2002	USD	2,147.70
3	90032962	23.08.2002	USD	2,003.30
4	90034693	08.06.2004	USD	248.00
5	90036011	19.12.2005	USD	2,003.30
				6,477.30

***Figure 10-13.** Program YCL_CH10_ILISTS03 – Secondary List I*

The secondary list II will look like Figure 10-14.

```
INTERACTIVE LISTS - 3 LEVEL

   Items/Materials Of Billing Doc. 90032841              Page:   1

   Srl.  Material Code              Quantity  UOM          Amount
    No.

     1   HT-1010                       1.000  PC         2,003.30
     2   HT-1080                       1.000  PC            53.30
     3   HT-1100                       1.000  PC            91.10

                                                         2,147.70
```

Figure 10-14. *Program YCL_CH10_ILISTS03 - Secondary List II*

With this hands-on exercise, you have implemented what was described in the opening section of this chapter. You have used the same data as in the description, that is, the customer code and billing document number.

In this manner, you can present a summarized list as a *primary list* and levels of detail of the selected summarized data as *secondary lists* triggering the AT LINE-SELECTION event. You can produce a maximum of 20 secondary lists as demonstrated in the program YCL_CH10_ILISTS01.

You will produce these same outputs using the event AT USER-COMMAND in the next hands-on exercise.

Hands-on Exercise: Produce Three Level Sales Reports Using the AT USER-COMMAND Event (1 Primary and 2 Secondary)

You will produce the same outputs as of previous program YCL_CH10_ILISTS03 using or triggering the event AT USER-COMMAND instead of the event AT LINE-SELECTION. The event AT USER-COMMAND is triggered when the end user clicks on an application or standard toolbar button or its equivalent menu option or an assigned *function key*.

Trigger AT USER-COMMAND Event by Clicking Custom Buttons on the Custom Application Toolbar:

You will create your own *application toolbar* to locate your custom buttons on it. The custom buttons will enable you to trigger the AT USER-COMMAND event and produce the secondary lists in this event. The custom buttons will also enable the navigation back to the previous list or screen, etc.

1. In your primary list (customer wise sales of a specified company code), you will have the following application toolbar buttons:

The 'Exit' button is used to leave the primary list and return to the PARAMETERS Selection Screen prompting for a company code.

The 'Detail I' button is to produce the first level detail: billing documents of a customer.

2. In your secondary list I (billing documents of a specified customer), you will have the following *application toolbar* buttons:

The 'Back' button is used to leave the secondary list I and navigate back to the primary list.

The 'Detail II' button is used to produce the second level detail: the items/materials of a specified billing document.

3. In your secondary list II (the items/materials of a specified billing document), you will have the following *application toolbar* button:

⇐ Back

The 'Back' button is used to leave the secondary list II and navigate back to the secondary list I.

You may copy the previous hands-on exercise program YCL_CH10_ILISTS03 to the current program YCL_CH10_ILISTS04 and carry out the requisite modifications. All the declarations and logic of the previous program can be used. The program needs to be modified for some extra text symbols, some extra declarations, setting of a custom *application toolbar* for the lists, and triggering the AT USER-COMMAND event instead of the AT LINE-SELECTION.

Create a Custom Application Toolbar in the Menu Painter

The custom *application toolbars* called 'GUI Statuses' or 'Statuses' can be maintained in transaction code SE41 – Menu Painter.

A 'Status' is an ensemble of *application toolbar* buttons with its equivalent menu options, function keys, and *context menus*. For an *application toolbar*, an end user must have the choice of using the buttons on the *application toolbar* or the menu options or *function keys* or *context menu* options. It constitutes a good user interface. A 'Status' can be positioned on a *Normal Screen* or on a *Dialogue Box Screen*. A 'Status' can be a '*context menu*'. (Mouse right click.) For now, in the current chapter, you will create a 'Status' for the *Normal Screen* and *Dialogue Box Screen*; *context menus* will be covered in Chapter 11.

You can also create in the SE41 transaction – menu painter, the 'Title Lists'. With the 'Title Lists', you can assign windows or dialogue box screens 'titles'. By default, when you execute an ABAP program, the short text of the program appears as the window title. You can override this by creating titles in 'Title Lists' in the menu painter and set these titles on the windows or dialogue box screens in an ABAP program.

A 'Status'/'Title List' is identified with or attached to an ABAP program. It has no independent existence. The multiple 'Statuses' and 'Title Lists' created for an ABAP program, together, are called an 'Interface'.

A program can use more than one 'Status' (i.e., more than one ensemble of buttons, etc., and *context menus*). A program can use more than one 'Title List'. The program YCL_CH10_ILISTS04 will be using two 'Statuses' for your three lists. (One *primary* and two *secondary lists*.) As shown in items I, II, and III above, you have three sets of buttons, one for each list. The third set (only one button) is a subset of the second set. Hence, you will manage with two 'Statuses'.

A 'Status' other than the *Context Menu* consists of *Menu Bar*, *Application Toolbar* and *Function Keys*. Figure 10-15 shows the 'Interface', 'Status', and its constituents.

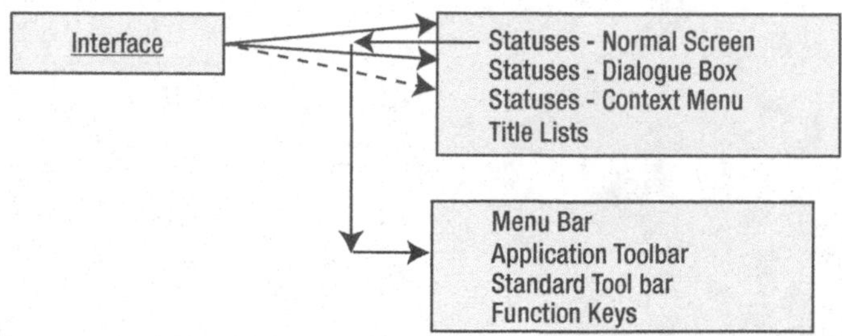

Figure 10-15. *Interface, Status, Etc*

Let two statuses be created with the menu painter.

Creation of statuses in the menu painter is the first part of this process. This is described in the following pages. The created status has to be used in the ABAP program. The appropriate statuses must appear in appropriate lists. To use a status or make it appear in a list, you use the ABAP statement SET PF-STATUS ... described subsequently.

Status for Primary List

Create a status for the primary list consisting of the 'Exit', 'Detail I' buttons.

Navigate to the Menu Painter screen - transaction code SE41. Enter the name of the ABAP program: YCL_CH10_ILISTS04. Ensure the radio button 'Status' is enabled. Enter the name of the status: it must start with a letter. The rest can be alphanumeric with embedded underscores (_). You need not start with 'Y'/'Z'. The maximum namespace is 20 characters. We have named the first status 'STAT1'. The screen will look like Figure 10-16.

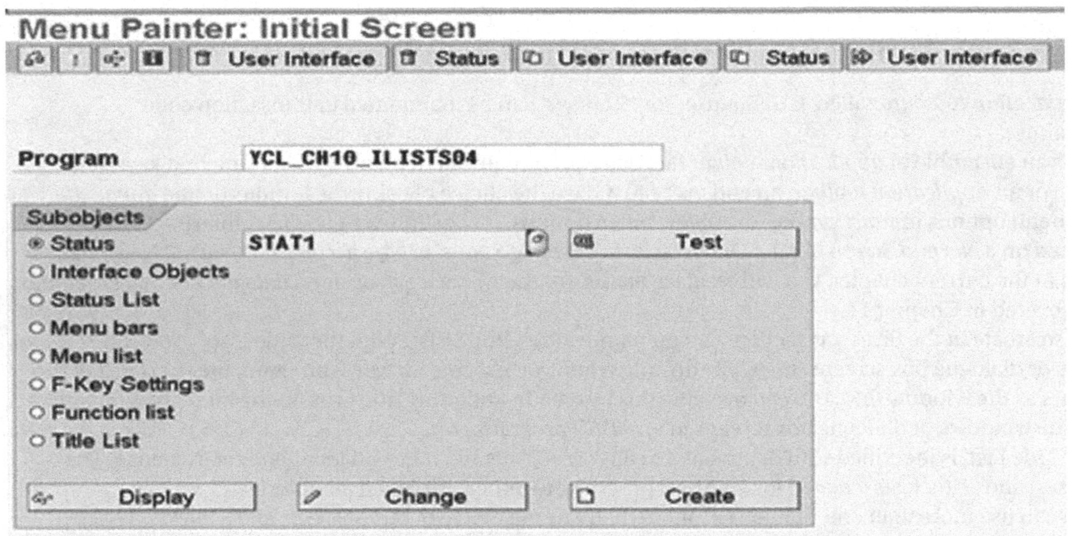

Figure 10-16. *Program YCL_CH10_ILISTS04, Create Status 'STAT1': Opening Screen*

Click the create button or press function key F5. A pop-up dialogue box appears and will look like Figure 10-17.

Create Status
Program YCL_CH10_ILISTS04
Status STAT1
Status Attributes
Short Text For Primary List
Status type
Normal Screen
Dialog Box
Context Menu

Figure 10-17. *Create Status 'STAT1': Short Text, Status Type*

You are creating a status for a normal screen. (The normal screen is the default option.) Enter the short text and click on the continue button. The screen will be like Figure 10-18.

Expandable Nodes (Menu Bar, Application Toolbar & Function Keys)
Maintain Status STAT1 of Interface YCL_CH10_ILISTS04
Function Code
Delete subobject
User Interface
YCL_CH10_ILISTS04
Inactive(revised)
Menu Bar
For Primary List
Application Toolbar
For Primary List
Function Keys
For Primary List

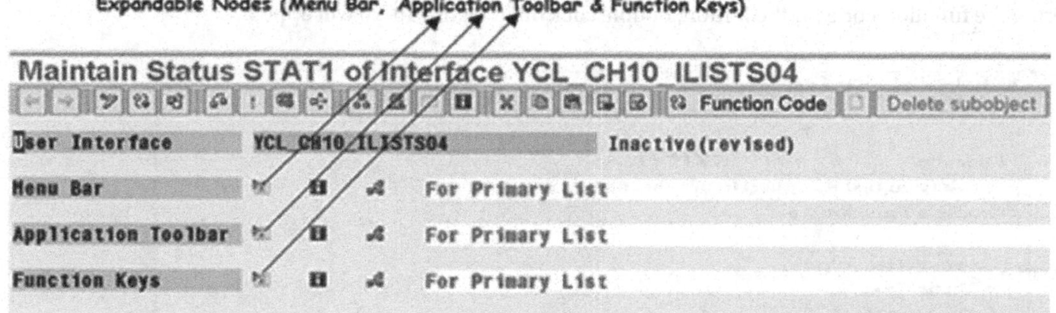

Figure 10-18. *Create Status 'STAT1'*

There are three expandable nodes: *Menu Bar*, *Application Toolbar*, and *Function Keys*. Click on the node of the *Application Toolbar*. The entries to be made in each of these three nodes are described under steps (1), (2), and (3).

Application Toolbar (Second Node)

When you expand the *Application Toolbar* node, the screen will look like Figure 10-19:

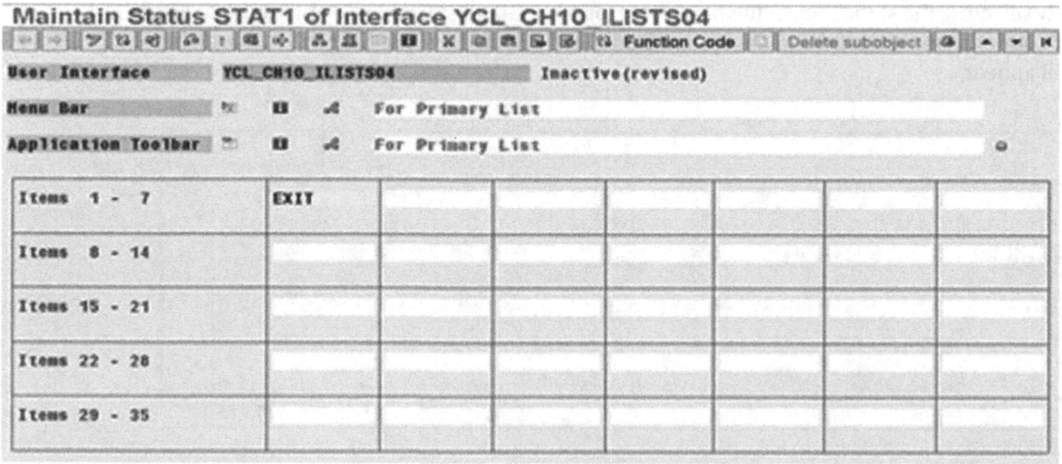

Maintain Status STAT1 of Interface YCL_CH10_ILISTS04
Function Code
Delete subobject
User Interface
YCL_CH10_ILISTS04
Inactive(revised)
Menu Bar
For Primary List
Application Toolbar
For Primary List
Items 1 - 7
EXIT
Items 8 - 14
Items 15 - 21
Items 22 - 28
Items 29 - 35

Figure 10-19. *Create Status 'STAT1': Application Toolbar Bar*

There is a provision for creation of a maximum of 35 buttons on the *application toolbar*. An *application toolbar* button can have either an icon or text or both. There is only one row of buttons available, that is, the *application toolbar* does not extend to multiple rows.

On this screen, you should enter the function codes for the buttons you intend to place on the *application toolbar*. The meaning of the function code is the same as was explained in the context of function codes for push buttons on Selection Screens. The function code can be a string of maximum 20 characters. It can have special characters. But it is better to stick to the convention of starting it with a letter, with the rest alphanumeric with embedded underscores (_). The function code is case insensitive. If you enter it in lower case, it will be converted to upper case. The function code of a button will be loaded into the system field SY-UCOMM when the corresponding button is pressed on the *application toolbar*.

You entered function code 'EXIT' for your exit button as shown in Figure 10-19.

After entering the function code for the button, double click on it. Figure 10-20 will appear.

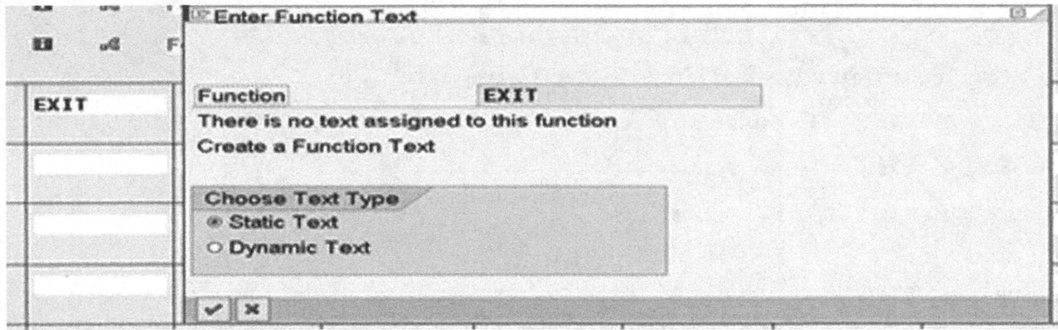

Figure 10-20. *Create Status 'STAT1': Application Toolbar Bar – Text Type*

The system is prompting you for the text type: whether static or dynamic. If runtime text is to be provided, you should opt for the dynamic text. (Text at run time).

Whatever text is created in the menu painter environment viz. icon text, *menu bar* text, menu item text, etc., can be maintained (like in other text environments) in multiple languages. The menu path to maintain multiple language texts is: Goto ➤ Translation etc.

You are now selecting the static text. In the next status for secondary list I, you will opt for the dynamic test. In this way, both options are covered. With the option 'Static Text' selected, on pressing the continue button Figure 10-21 will appear.

Figure 10-21. *Create Status 'STAT1': Application Toolbar Bar – Entry of Button Texts*

The first field to be entered in the dialogue box is *Function Text*. This text is mandatory. This text appears as menu text in the *menu bar* items or the *context menu*. If you do not enter the icon name field and/or the icon text field, the function text will also appear on the button. It can be a maximum of forty characters. We entered in the function text field: 'Exit'.

The second field to be entered is *Icon name*. You can choose from a list. (Function key F4, etc.) You have chosen the icon ICON-PDIR_BACK/  . This field is optional.

The third field to be entered is *Info.text*. The text entered in this field appears as a tool tip (i.e., when the mouse is positioned on the button, this text appears). It can be a maximum of sixty characters. If you do not enter the Info.text field, the function text will be used as Info.text. We have entered in the Info.text field: 'Exit Lists'.

The screen with three fields entered will be like Figure 10-22.

Enter Function Text

EXIT

Function code EXIT

Function text Exit

Icon name ICON_PDIR_BACK

Info. text Exit List

Figure 10-22. *Create Status 'STAT1': Application Toolbar Bar - Entered Button Texts*

Press the continue button after the entry of button texts, etc. The system prompts for the assignment of a *function key* to the button. *Function key* assignment is mandatory. You cannot assign the reserved function keys in the context. (F1, F3, F4) We have assigned 'Shift-F9' as shown in Figure 10-23.

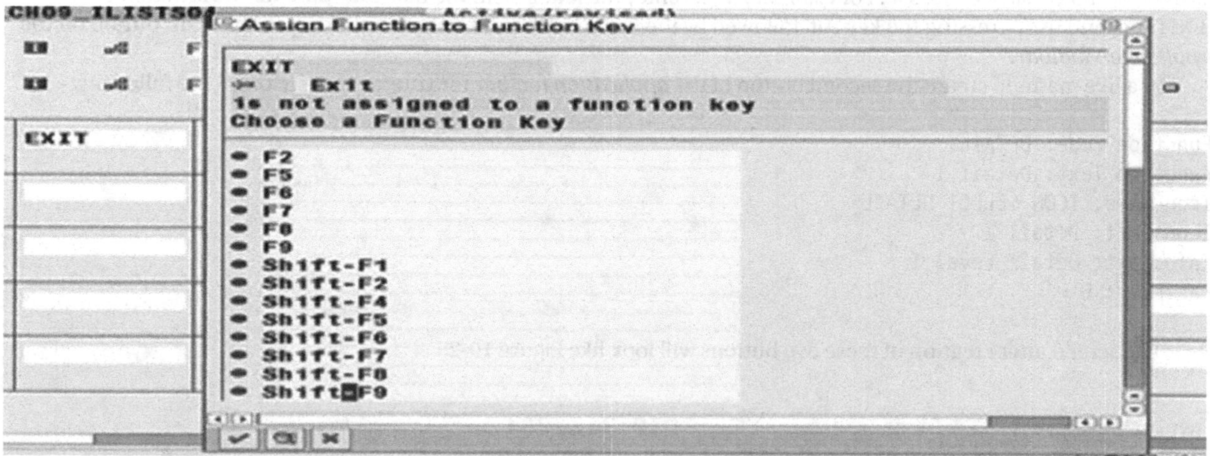

Figure 10-23. *Create Status 'STAT1': Application Toolbar Bar - Function Key Assignment*

After the *function key* assignment, pressing the continue button will pop up the function attributes screen shown in Figure 10-24.

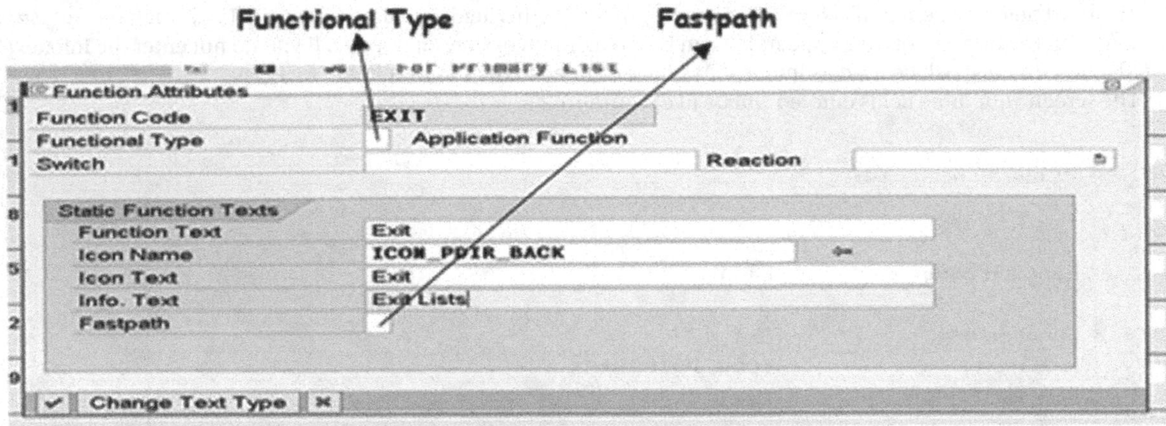

Figure 10-24. *Create Status 'STAT1': Application Toolbar Bar – Function Attributes*

We have entered in the icon text field 'Exit' as shown in Figure 10-24.

In the function attributes screen, the field: *Functional Type*, will be explained in Chapter 14. You are using in this chapter, the *Functional Type* value 'Normal Application Function', which is the default having the value blank / ' 'code. A selection list is available (i.e., function key F4, etc).

In the field *Fastpath*, you can enter a character. This will enable the end user to operate exclusively with the keys and without the usage of mouse. For example, if you enter the letter 'X' in the field *Fast path* for the function code 'EXIT' the end user pressing the key 'Alt' followed by the key 'X' will be the same as clicking on the 'Exit' button on the *application toolbar*.

In a like manner, create the second button of the *application toolbar* for your primary list with the following:

```
Function Code: DETAIL1
Function Text: Detail I
Icon Name: ICON_SELECT_DETAIL
Icon Text: Detail I
Info.Text: Detail Level I
Fastpath: D
```

The screen after creation of these two buttons will look like Figure 10-25.

Maintain Status STAT1 of Interface YCL_CH10_ILISTS04

Function Code   Delete subobject

User Interface   YCL_CH10_ILISTS04   Inactive(revised)

Menu Bar   For Primary List

Application Toolbar   For Primary List

Items 1 - 7	EXIT Exit	DETAIL1 Detail				
Items 8 - 14						

Figure 10-25. *Create Status 'STAT1': Application Toolbar Bar Buttons*

Function Keys (Third Node)

Collapse the *Application Toolbar* node and expand the *Function Keys* node. Under this node, you can view the *function key* assignments made and the *function keys* available for assignments. You can reassign *function keys*, if needed. Scroll down, if *function key* assignments are not visible.

You can also view the standard toolbar. By default, when you create a status, the buttons: on standard toolbar are disabled. If you want one or more of them enabled, you can assign function codes to them. We have assigned the function code 'BACK' to the button . This is shown in Figure 10-26.

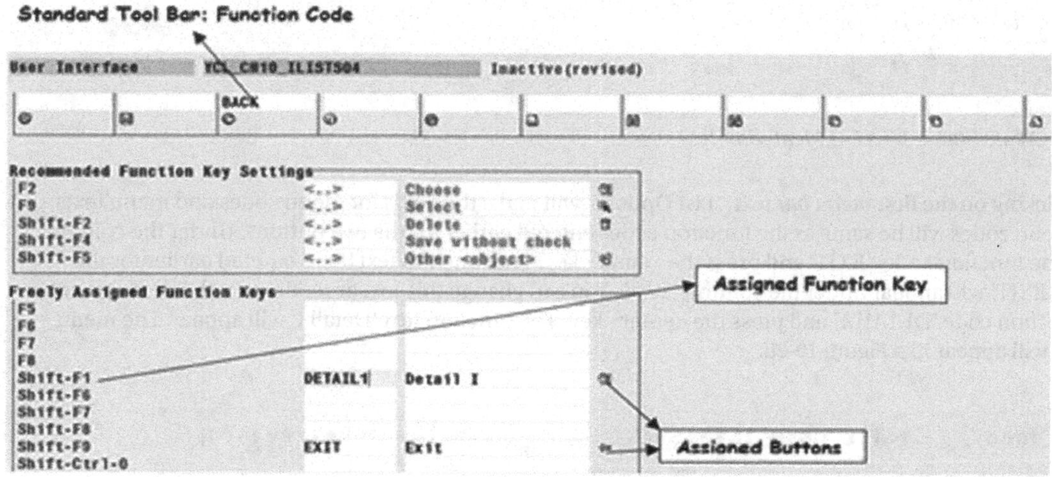

Figure 10-26. *Create Status 'STAT1': Function Key Assignments, Standard Toolbar*

The button will be operational with your status.

Next, you can enter values into the *Menu Bar* and its subobjects. This is not mandatory. If you do not enter values, the menu options will not appear. But a good user interface must have *application toolbar* buttons and its equivalent menu options.

Menu Bar (First Node)

Clicking on the *Menu Bar* node will expand it. The screen with *menu bars* will appear. You will create one *menu bar*. So enter the text in the first *menu bar* as 'List Options' as shown in Figure 10-27.

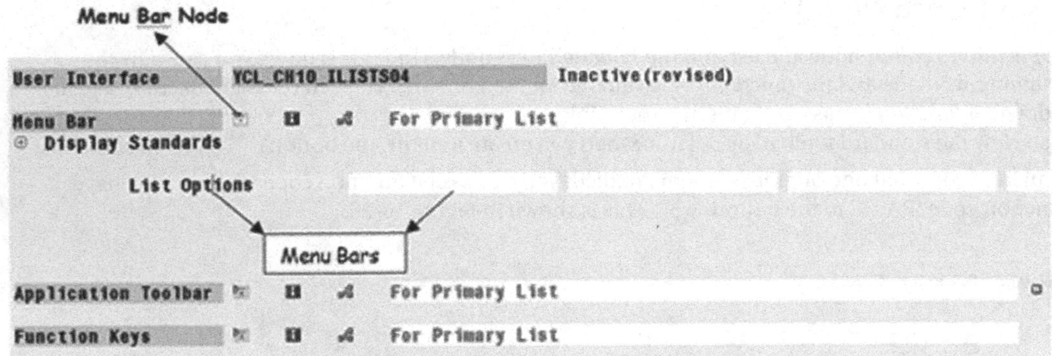

Figure 10-27. *Create Status 'STAT1': Menu Bar Text*

Double clicking on the first *menu bar* text: 'List Options' will make the fields for menu codes and menu texts appear. The menu codes will be same as the function codes entered earlier for the two buttons. Under the column 'Code', enter the function code: 'EXIT' and press the <enter> key. The function text 'Exit' entered earlier for the function code 'EXIT' will appear under the column 'Text'. You can change this text or retain it. In the next row enter the second function code 'DETAIL1' and press the <enter> key. The function text 'Detail I' will appear. The menu codes and text will appear like Figure 10-28.

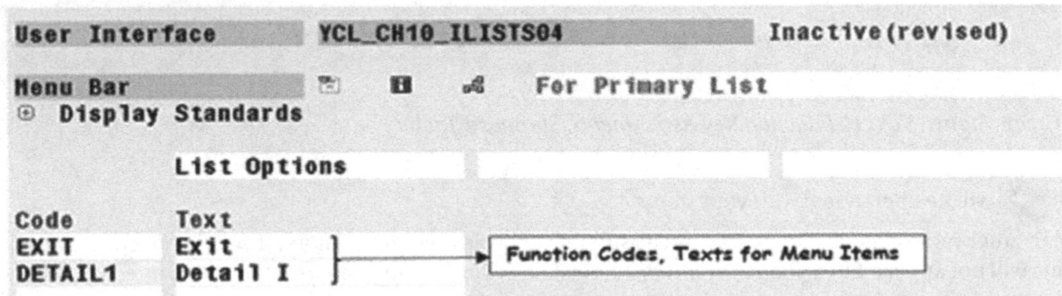

Figure 10-28. *Create Status 'STAT1': Menu Codes, Texts*

You have completed the process of creating a status 'STAT1'. You can save the status. Check the syntax by clicking the button /Ctrl+F2. Activate the status by clicking the button /Ctrl+F3. As has been stated earlier, the status 'STAT1' will appear on the primary list. The activated status 'STAT1' screen will be like Figure 10-29.

Maintain Status STAT1 of Interface YCL_CH10_ILISTS04

Function Code

User Interface YCL_CH10_ILISTS04 Active

Menu Bar For Primary List

Application Toolbar For Primary List

Function Keys For Primary List

Figure 10-29. *Status 'STAT1' Activated*

Status for Secondary List I

Let a status be created to appear for the secondary list I consisting of the 'Back' and 'Detail II' buttons like the following.

You will name this status 'STAT2'.

The 'Back' button will have the following values:

```
Function Code: BACK
Function Text: Back
Icon Name: ICON_PDIR_BACK
Icon Text: Back
Info.Text: Back
```

The 'Detail II' button will have the following values:

```
Function Code: DETAIL2
Function Text: Detail II
Icon Name: ICON_SELECT_DETAIL
Icon Text: Detail II
Info.Text: Detail II
```

Earlier, when creating the status 'STAT1', you used 'Static Text'. Let the 'Dynamic Text' be used in creating the status 'STAT2'.

In the 'Dynamic Text' feature, the text can be provided through (a) ABAP program fields of a prespecified DDIC structure or (b) database table fields. In the present hands-on exercise, dynamic texts are being provided through ABAP program fields of DDIC structure SMP_DYNTXT with the fields in Table 10-4.

Table 10-4. *Menu Painter - DDIC Structure for Passing Dynamic Texts*

Field Name	TYPE/Length	Description
TEXT	CHAR/40	Function Text
ICON_ID	CHAR/4	Icon Code Enclosed in @
ICON_TEXT	CHAR/40	Icon Text
QUICKINFO	CHAR/60	Info.Text
PATH	CHAR/1	Fastpath

Referring to the DDIC structure SMP_DYNTXT, you have to declare as many structures as the number of buttons and *menu bars* to which you want to provide dynamic texts. In the status 'STATUS2', you have two buttons and one *menu bar*. Let dynamic texts be provided to both these buttons and the *menu bar*. Your ABAP program will contain the following declarations:

```
DATA:.....
       .....
        BACK_TXT TYPE SMP_DYNTXT, " text for BACK button
        DTL2_TXT TYPE SMP_DYNTXT, " text for DETAIL2 button
        MNU_BAR2 TYPE SMP_DYNTXT, " text for meznu bar
```

These structure fields are to be assigned appropriate values before the *application toolbar* for the secondary list I appears. You will maintain the text values in text symbols. They can be maintained in other ways such as in a database text table. The aim is to provide multi-language support for text maintenance. The code lines for the assignment of values will be as follows:

```
BACK_TXT-TEXT       = TEXT-020.
BACK_TXT-ICON_ID    = '@CF@'. " code for icon ICON_PDIR_BACK
BACK_TXT-ICON_TEXT  = TEXT-020.
BACK_TXT-QUICKINFO  = TEXT-020.

DTL2_TXT-TEXT       = TEXT-021.
DTL2_TXT-ICON_ID    = '@16@'. " code for icon ICON_SELECT_DETAIL
DTL2_TXT-ICON_TEXT  = TEXT-021.
DTL2_TXT-QUICKINFO  = TEXT-021.

MNU_BAR2-TEXT       = TEXT-022.
```

A screenshot of the text symbols used in these statements:

020	Back	4	4
021	Detail II	9	9
022	List Options	12	12

Figure 10-30. *Status 'STAT2': Text Symbols Used in Dynamic Texts*

For simplicity, you have used the same text symbol TEXT-020 for *Function Text, Icon Text,* and *Info.Text* of 'Back' button. And the same text symbol TEXT-021 for *Function Text, Icon Text,* and *Info.Text* of 'Detail II' button.

To create status 'STAT2', navigate to the menu painter, and enter the name of the program as YCL_CH10_ILISTS04 and the name of status as 'STAT2' in the respective fields; click on create button/function key F5. You are creating status for a normal screen, the default radio button in the pop-up dialogue box; enter the short text and click the continue button.

Click on the *Application Toolbar* node. Enter the function code 'BACK' for your first button. Double click on this function code. The dialogue box prompting for the static or dynamic text option appears. Select the dynamic text option and click on the continue button. Figure 10-31 will appear.

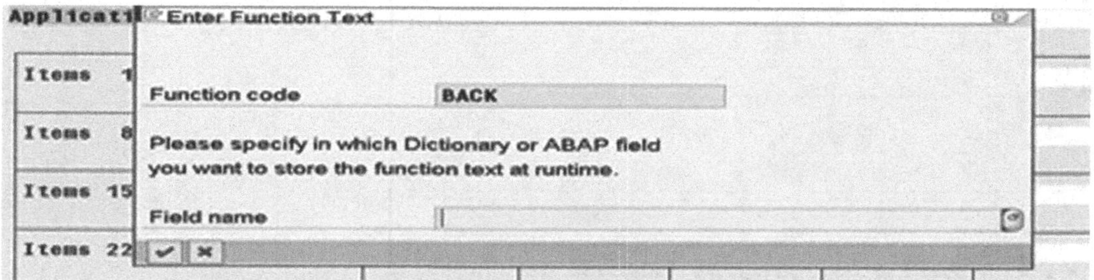

Figure 10-31. *Create Status 'STAT2': Field Name for Dynamic Text - 'Back' Button*

Press function key F4 for a list. This will present the dialogue box in Figure 10-32.

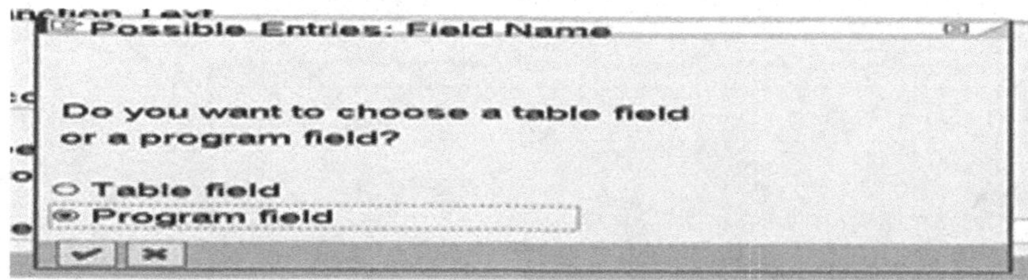

Figure 10-32. *Create Status 'STAT2': Field Name for Dynamic Text - 'Back' Button*

If you had declared the structure for function texts with the keyword TABLES in the ABAP program, you could use the first radio button option: 'Table field'. You have stored text values in different structure fields of declared structures with the key word DATA, (BACK_TXT, DTL2_TXT, etc.) so you will use the second radio button option: 'Program field' in the dialogue box shown in Figure 10-32. Clicking the continue button will pop up the list of fields declared in the ABAP program as a selection list shown in Figure 10-33.

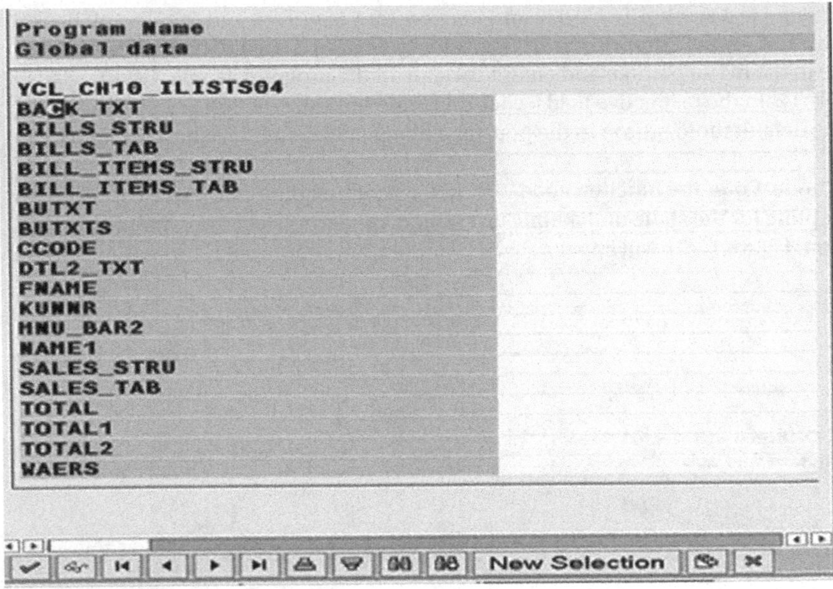

Figure 10-33. Create Status 'STAT2': Select Field Name for 'Back' Button

Make the selection of field 'BACK_TXT' as shown in Figure 10-33. After selection and return from the selection list, the screen will look like Figure 10-34.

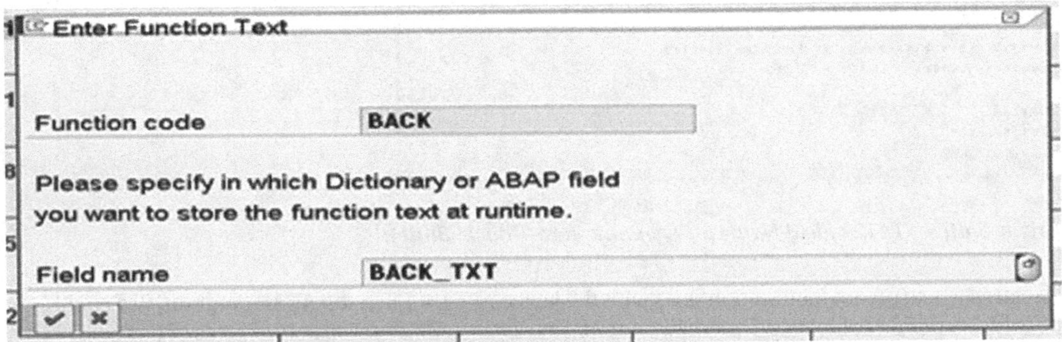

Figure 10-34. Create Status 'STAT2': Selection of Field Name for 'Back' Button

Pressing the continue button will show the dialogue box for *function key* assignment in Figure 10-35.

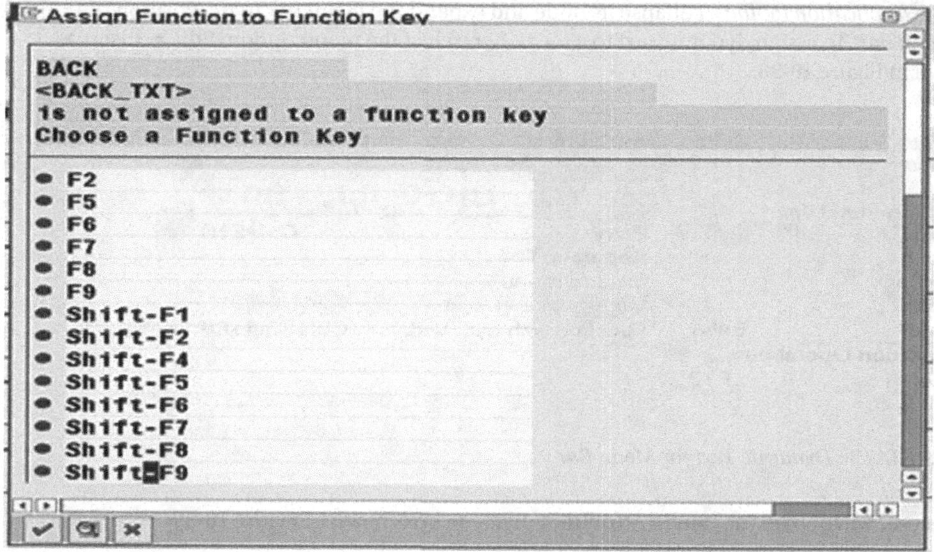

Figure 10-35. *Create Status 'STAT2': Function Key Assignment for 'Back' Button*

After the *function key* assignment, the dialogue box for entry of function attributes (function type, etc.) is prompted as in Figure 10-36.

Function Attributes
Function Code BACK
Functional Type Application Function
Switch Reaction
Dynamic Function Texts
Field Name BACK_TXT
Change Text Type

Figure 10-36. *Create Status 'STAT2': Function Attributes for 'Back' Button*

Clicking on the continue button will take you to the screen with the three nodes: *Menu Bar, Application Toolbar,* and *Function Keys.*

In a similar fashion, create the second button of your application toolbar: 'Detail II'. After the creation of the two buttons the screen will be like this:

Application Toolbar For Secondary List I

Items 1 - 7	BACK <BACK_TXT>	DETAIL2 <DTL2_TXT>	

Figure 10-37. *Create Status 'STAT2': Application Toolbar Buttons*

Having finished with the *application toolbar*, collapse its node and expand the *menu bar* node. Position the cursor on the empty first *menu bar*. To assign dynamic text to a *menu bar*, select the menu option: Edit ➤ Insert ➤ Menu with dyn.text as shown in Figure 10-38.

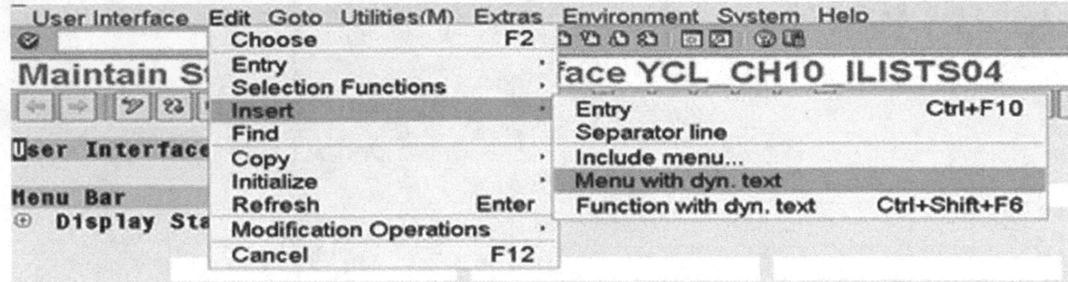

Figure 10-38. *Create Status 'STAT2': Dynamic Text for Menu Bar*

Making this menu selection will pop up the 'Menu Attributes' dialogue box shown in Figure 10-39.

Menu Attributes

Program	YCL_CH10_ILISTS04
Short Documentation	Menu Bar for Secondary List I
Possible Uses	up to 2 casc. menus
Switch	Reaction

Dynamic Text

Field Name	MNU_BAR2

Figure 10-39. *Create Status 'STAT2': 'Menu Attributes' Dialogue Box*

Pressing the function key F4 in the field 'Field Name' will again first prompt for 'Table field' or 'Program field'. Selecting the 'Program field' radio button and clicking the continue button will pop up the selection list of the program fields. Select the program field MNU_BAR2 from the list. Figure 10-40 shows the screen after the program field selection. Clicking the continue button will take you to the screen with the nodes.

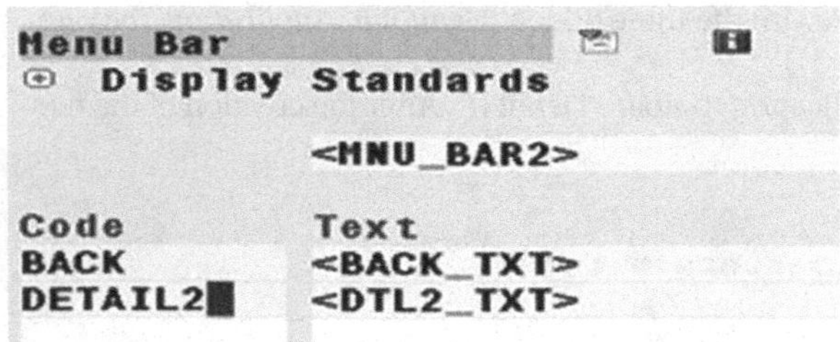

Figure 10-40. *Create Status 'STAT2': Menu Bar Text, Menu Codes, and Function Texts*

Double click on the *menu bar* with the text '<MNU_BAR2>'. The function code, text fields, will appear. Enter the function codes for the two buttons: 'BACK' and 'DETAIL2'. Pressing the <enter> key after keying the function code will automatically fetch the function texts. The codes and texts for the menu items will appear like this:

This is the end of status 'STAT2' creation. Check and activate the status. The activated status screen is shown in Figure 10-41.

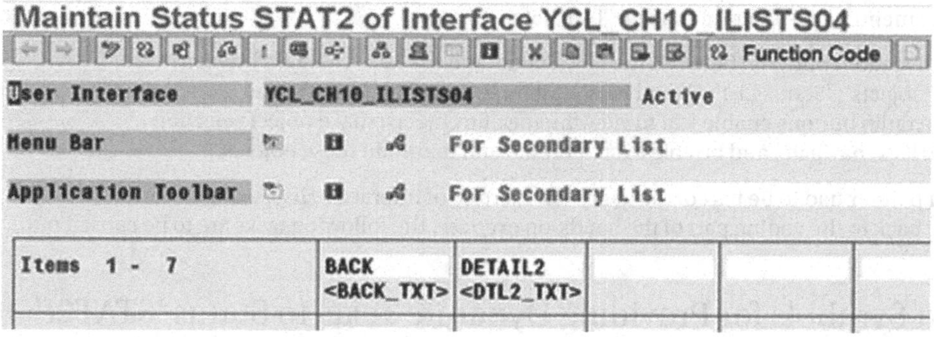

Figure 10-41. *Activated Status 'STAT2'*

You have completed the task of creating two statuses: 'STAT1', and 'STAT2'. These will serve your three lists: 1 primary, two secondary. The secondary list II has only one 'Back' button, which is a subset of the status 'STAT2'.

More of Menu Painter

Function codes and function texts are shared between different statuses, between *application toolbar*, menu items, and *context menus*. By default, whatever options are on the *application toolbar* are available in the *context menu*. If something other than these default entries is required in the *context menu*, you have to tweak things at runtime. The runtime manipulation of the *context menu* is covered in Chapter 11.

There are a lot more facilities and features in the menu painter. Here is a list of some of these features:

- Maintain Status Screen
    - Cut, copy, and paste functions for subobjects of status.
    - Delete / , Insert / functions for subobjects of status. (Delete button/s, insert button/s between existing buttons.)
    - Activate/deactivate a function code Function Code.
    - Attributes of objects/subobjects: interface, status, function, etc. Menu path - Goto ➤ Attributes.
    - Test Status .
- Menu Painter: Initial Screen
    - Delete User Interface. (Will delete the entire interface with all the statuses, titles, etc.)
    - Delete Status. (Will delete a specific status.)
    - Copy User Interface. (Will copy the entire interface with all the statuses, titles, etc. from one ABAP program to another. The destination ABAP program must exist.)

- Copy status. (Will copy the specific status from one ABAP program to another. The destination ABAP program must exist.)
- Create title: enable the 'Title List' radio button (at the bottom) click on the create button.
- Copy, delete, and rename titles: enable the 'Title List' radio button, (at the bottom) click on the change button, etc.
- Test status: menu path - User Interface ➤ Test Status.
- There are five radio buttons (between the first 'Status' and the last 'Title List') such as 'Interface Objects', 'Status List', 'Menu bars', 'Menu list', 'F-Key Settings' and 'Function list'. These radio buttons enable you to view the specific objects; make object selection from these lists; navigate; and be able to create, edit, and maintain these objects.

This coverage of menu painter had to be part of the hands-on exercise of interactive lists using the event AT USER-COMMAND. Getting back to the coding part of the hands-on exercise, the following tasks are to be carried out:

Create Text in Text Symbols for Providing Dynamic Texts to Status 'STAT2f'

For this exercise, refer to Figure 10-30.

Coding Tasks:

To generate the primary list and two secondary lists using the event AT USER-COMMAND, you have to perform the following code modification tasks to the program YCL_CH10_ILISTS03:

Data Declarations:

- Declare structures to provide dynamic texts to status 'STAT2' referring to DDIC structure 'SMP_DYNTXT' for two buttons and one *menu bar.*

```
BACK_TXT TYPE SMP_DYNTXT, "text for BACK button
DTL2_TXT TYPE SMP_DYNTXT, "text for DETAIL2 button
MNU_BAR2 TYPE SMP_DYNTXT. "text for menu bar
```

Assign Text Symbols To Dynamic Text Structure Fields: Coding at the Beginning of the Event START-OF-SELECTION

```
BACK_TXT-TEXT      = TEXT-020.
BACK_TXT-ICON_ID   = '@CF@'.
BACK_TXT-ICON_TEXT = TEXT-020.
BACK_TXT-QUICKINFO = TEXT-020.

DTL2_TXT-TEXT      = TEXT-021.
DTL2_TXT-ICON_ID   = '@16@'.
DTL2_TXT-ICON_TEXT = TEXT-021.
DTL2_TXT-QUICKINFO = TEXT-021.

MNU_BAR2-TEXT = TEXT-022.
```

SET PF-STATUS

The statement to place your custom status (*application toolbar*, menu, etc., created in menu painter) is SET PF-STATUS. The syntax of the SET PF-STATUS statement is:

```
SET PF-STATUS <status name>  [OF PROGRAM <program name> ]
 [EXCLUDING  <function code/s>]  [IMMEDIATELY].
SET PF-STATUS - Key phrase
<status name> - Name/identification of the status
OF PROGRAM - Key phrase
```

<program name> - Name of the program. This needs to be given only if the status is created for a program other than where the SET PF-STATUS statement is located. That is, you can use a status of another program.

```
EXCLUDING - Key word
```

<function code/s> - The function code/s of a button/s to be excluded. If a single button is to be excluded, the function code of the button can be specified as a literal or an elementary data item of TPPE C or STRING to which the function code to be excluded is assigned. If multiple buttons are to be excluded, the function codes of these buttons to be excluded have to be stored in an internal table and this internal table specified with the keyword EXCLUDING.

IMMEDIATELY – By default, the SET PF-STATUS ... sets the status to current list, the list represented by the value of system field SY-LSIND. If the key word 'IMMEDIATELY' is used, the SET PF-STATUS ... sets the status to the list represented by the value of system field SY-LISTI. The system field SY-LISTI contains the value of the list number that last triggered the event AT LINE-SELECTION or AT USER-COMMAND.

The SET PF-STATUS statement is located before the generation of each of your lists: 1 primary, 2 secondary. The statement is located before the LOOP AT ... END LOOP construct of each list.

The statement `SET PF-STATUS SPACE` restores the default list *application toolbar*.

Primary List:

```
SET PF-STATUS 'STAT1'.
```

Secondary List I:

```
SET PF-STATUS 'STAT2'.
```

Secondary List II:

```
SET PF-STATUS 'STAT2' EXCLUDING 'DETAIL2'.
      " to exclude Detail II button
```

Code Changes or Modifications in the Event Block AT USER-COMMAND

You have to modify the source code in the secondary list event block as you are triggering the AT USER-COMMAND event instead of the AT LINE-SELECTION event in the earlier hands-on exercise.

- You need not bother about controlling the maximum value of the system field SY-LSIND depending on the number of lists being supported now. You controlled the maximum value of the system field SY-LSIND while triggering the event AT LINE-SELECTION in the previous hands-on exercise YCL_CH10_ILISTS03. Every time, the end user double clicked on a line, the event AT LINE-SELECTION was triggered incrementing the system field SY-LSIND by one. You are not triggering the event AT LINE-SELECTION. The list interacts on pressing the toolbar buttons. As you have not provided any button on the *application toolbar* to go beyond the last list, the system field SY-LSIND will not assume values to generate lists beyond the secondary list II.

- You are using the CASE ... ENDCASE construct to interrogate the system field SY-UCOMM (function code) and produce the appropriate list.
- When exiting the primary list - WHEN 'EXIT', you have used the statement: `LEAVE SCREEN`. This statement will, in the ABAP environment, take the end user back to the previous screen in your context; the Selection Screen prompting for the company code. Alternatively, you can also use the back button of the standard toolbar that you enabled for 'STAT1' and 'STAT2'.

  In the previous hands-on exercise, you did not have your own toolbar, the back button of the standard toolbar was enabled by default, and you were using it to navigate from the primary list to Selection Screen and from secondary lists to previous lists.
- You have provided your own button to navigate to the previous list in addition to the standard toolbar back button. The process of navigating to a previous list using your own button should be clearly understood. You are managing it by manipulating the value of the system field SY-LSIND. Suppose the end user is on the secondary list I. (SY-LSIND = 1) the end user wants to navigate to the primary list. (SY-LSIND should be 0) When the end user presses the *application toolbar* button [⇐ Back], the event AT USER-COMMAND is triggered, and the value of the system field SY-LSIND will get incremented from its present value 1 to 2. (Every time the AT USER-COMMAND is triggered, the system field SY-LSIND get incremented by 1.) You want to navigate to the primary list; the value of system field SY-LSIND should be 0. That is why the system field SY-LSIND is being decremented by 2. The same inductive logic you can apply to navigating from secondary list II to *secondary list me*. You are using the same button [⇐ Back] in both of the lists - secondary list I and secondary list II - to navigate to previous lists.

Apart from the above enumerated modifications, all the other code lines of the current program YCL_CH10_ILISTS04 are identical to the previous program YCL_CH10_ILISTS03. That is why the full list of this program is not provided here. It is available, though, in the E-Resource.

The outputs of the program YCL_CH10_ILISTS04 are shown in Figures 10-42 to 10-44.

List Options System Help

INTERACTIVE LISTS - 3 LEVEL

⇐ Exit | Detail I

Customer Wise Sales Summary of Company Code: 3000/IDES US INC — Page: 1

Currency: USD

Srl. No.	Customer Code	Name	City	Amount
30	0000003263	Rogier Golf Resort YY	DENVER	3,058.00
31	0000003271	Media Store	ANTIOCH	6,477.30
32	0000003272	ADCOM COMPUTER	SEATTLE	2,147.70
33	0000003273	ALPHA Center	MINNEAPOLIS	2,147.70
34	0000003800	Candid International Technology	TAMPA	723,492.00
35	0000004000	North Energy Ltd	Calgary	42,666.67
36	0000004130	Compu Tech	SAN FRANCISCO	57,358.00
37	0000006000	RIVA Headquarters	LOS ANGELES	2,251.76
38	0000006002	RIVA Regional Storage Trenton	TRENTON	78,780.00
39	0000006006	RIVA Regional Warehouse Denver	DENVER	152,712.00
40	0000030200	Wal-Mart	NEWARK	8,000.00
41	0000300000	Havers Inc.	ANTIOCH	4,133.00
42	0000300075	Carmella Credit	HUNTINGTON BEACH	327.00
43	0000300081	Havers Inc	ANTIOCH	914.20
44	0000300286	Dynamic Industries	EVERETT	300,000.00
45	0000300325	Antipolis	ANTIOCH	22,320.00
46	0000300700	Builders Depot	Eveleth	4,986,654.75

DM0 (2) 800 sapserver INS

Figure 10-42. *Program YCL_CH10_ILISTS04: Primary List*

List Options System Help

INTERACTIVE LISTS - 3 LEVEL

Back | Detail II

List of Bills for 0000003271/Media Store — Page: 1

Srl. No.	Doc No	Doc Date	Doc. Curr	Amount
1	90031824	04.02.2002	USD	75.00
2	90032841	25.06.2002	USD	2,147.70
3	90032962	23.08.2002	USD	2,003.30
4	90034693	08.06.2004	USD	248.00
5	90036011	19.12.2005	USD	2,003.30
				6,477.30

Figure 10-43. Program YCL_CH10_ILISTS04: Secondary List I

List Options System Help

INTERACTIVE LISTS - 3 LEVEL

Back

Items/Materials Of Billing Doc. 90032841 — Page: 1

Srl. No.	Material Code	Quantity	UOM	Amount
1	HT-1010	1.000	PC	2,003.30
2	HT-1080	1.000	PC	53.30
3	HT-1100	1.000	PC	91.10
				2,147.70

Figure 10-44. Program YCL_CH10_ILISTS04: Secondary List II

This discussion was about production of three level lists: one primary and two secondary. The lists were produced triggering the event AT USER-COMMAND. You used the HIDE ... statement. The hands-on exercise involved the creation of custom statuses and their deployment. The custom statuses were created using the menu painter. So the menu painter was introduced in this chapter.

Hands-on Exercise: Output Data of Runtime Specified Fields of a Runtime Specified Database Table or View with Column Heading from Corresponding Data Elements

Lists or Outputs

The program in this hands-on exercise is a generic program to list values from specific fields of any database table or view. The database tables can be transparent, pooled, or clustered. The views can be database views or projection views (i.e., views you can use in the SELECT ... statement).

The program will take as input a database table or view. Name (PARAMETERS statement, etc.). The input is being checked for its validity. If the database table or view name is invalid, an alert message is issued.

The fields of the input database table or view are retrieved from the database metadata table DD03L and listed (primary list) with checkboxes so that the end user can select fields to be output. After the field selections are made, by pressing the button ✔ Output on the *application toolbar*, the selected fields' data from the input database table or view are retrieved and output with the column headings (the Secondary list). The column headings of the fields are fetched from the corresponding data elements. If no fields are selected and the button ✔ Output is pressed, an alert message is issued.

On the *application toolbar*, (Figure 10-46) there are two other buttons: to select all the fields and to deselect all the fields. There is, of course, the usual 'Exit' button.

The output appears in ascending order of the primary key fields.

If the database table or view is a text table (with DDIC Data Type LANG field as part of primary key), the data is retrieved only for the logged-in language.

To sum up, you will first produce a primary list of the fields of an input table or view along with checkboxes to enable the end user to make field selections. You will then produce a secondary list (triggering the event AT USER-COMMAND) consisting of data for the selected fields of the input table or view. The secondary list of the selected field's data will have column headings. These column headings are fetched from the corresponding data elements of the selected fields. It should be clear what you are setting out to implement. The input and the outputs should be like Figure 10-45 to Figure 10-47.

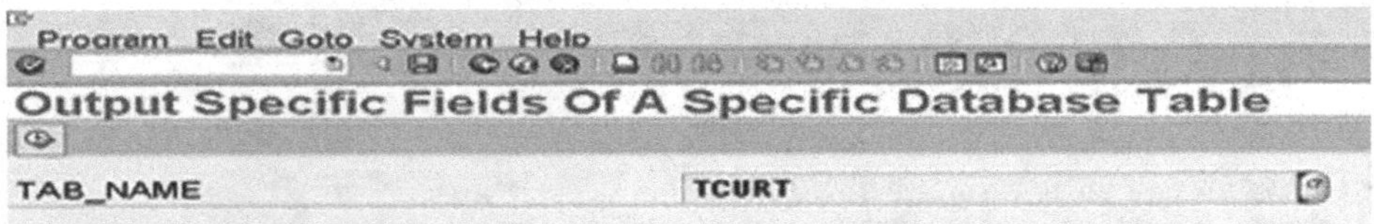

Figure 10-45. *Output Specific Fields of a Database Table or View Name- Input*

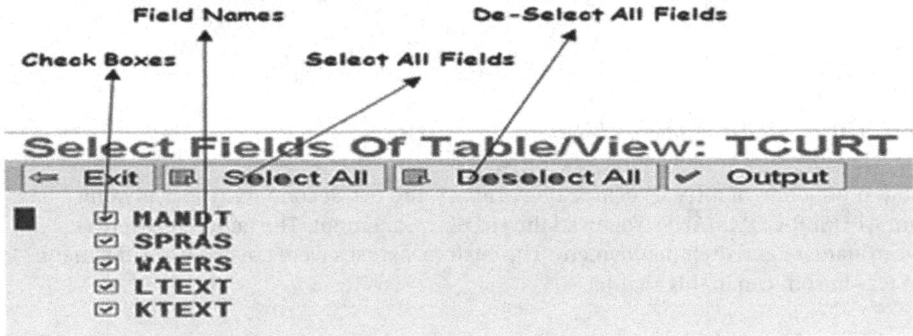

Figure 10-46. *Output Specific Fields of a Database Table or View - Make Field Selections*

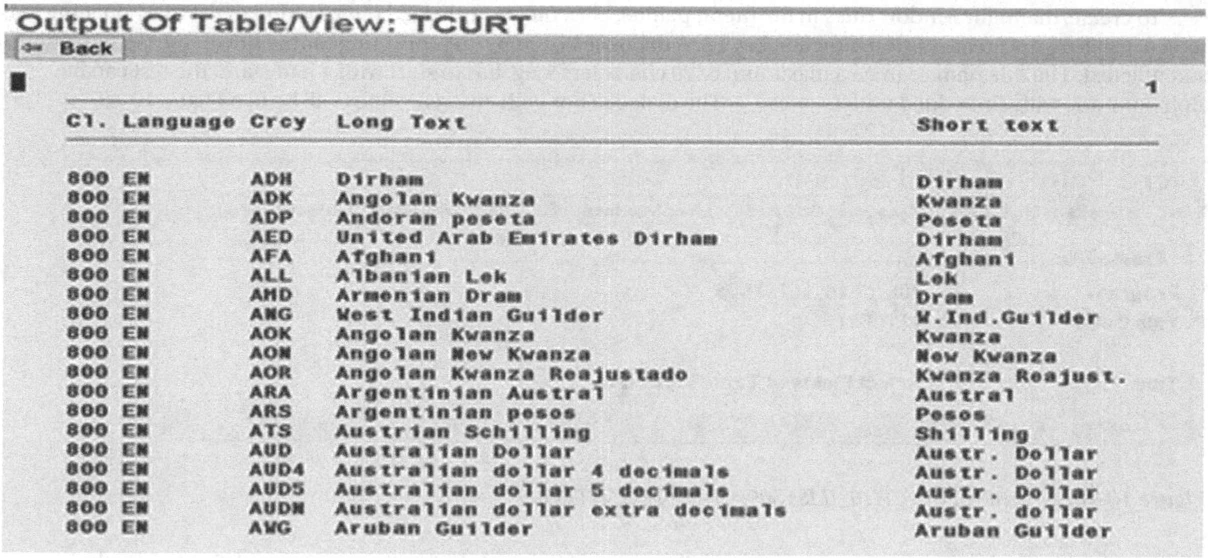

Output Of Table/View: TCURT

Back

1

Cl.	Language	Crcy	Long Text	Short text
800	EN	ADH	Dirham	Dirham
800	EN	ADK	Angolan Kwanza	Kwanza
800	EN	ADP	Andoran peseta	Peseta
800	EN	AED	United Arab Emirates Dirham	Dirham
800	EN	AFA	Afghani	Afghani
800	EN	ALL	Albanian Lek	Lek
800	EN	AMD	Armenian Dram	Dram
800	EN	ANG	West Indian Guilder	W.Ind.Guilder
800	EN	AOK	Angolan Kwanza	Kwanza
800	EN	AON	Angolan New Kwanza	New Kwanza
800	EN	AOR	Angolan Kwanza Reajustado	Kwanza Reajust.
800	EN	ARA	Argentinian Austral	Austral
800	EN	ARS	Argentinian pesos	Pesos
800	EN	ATS	Austrian Schilling	Shilling
800	EN	AUD	Australian Dollar	Austr. Dollar
800	EN	AUD4	Australian dollar 4 decimals	Austr. Dollar
800	EN	AUD5	Australian dollar 5 decimals	Austr. Dollar
800	EN	AUDN	Australian dollar extra decimals	Austr. dollar
800	EN	AWG	Aruban Guilder	Aruban Guilder

Figure 10-47. Output Specific Fields Data of a Database Table or View – Output

Program Features, Considerations

- The validity of an input database table/view is implemented using the AT SELECTION-SCREEN event and the database metadata table DD02L.
- The detailed process of creating statuses in the menu painter need not be repeated here. The program is using two statuses: 'STAT1', 'STAT2' each for the primary and secondary list respectively. The statuses can be created as per the buttons appearing in Figures 10-46 and 10-47. You have used only static text.
- You are using window titles: 'TITLE01', 'TITLE02' for the primary and secondary lists. The window titles can be created in the menu painter. Recall that the window titles are part of the user interface in the menu painter. Subsequently, window titles can set for a screen or window with the statement:

```
SET TITLEBAR <title bar name> [WITH <var11> [<var2>]...[<var9>]].
```

The optional WITH addition enables variable or runtime information to be incorporated in a title. The variables provided with the addition 'WITH' will replace the placeholders in title text. There can be a maximum of nine placeholders.

If you do not create and set a window title, the short text from the ABAP program attributes appears as the window title by default.

You will have window titles for each of the lists: primary and secondary. The window titles for primary and secondary lists are:

```
'Select Fields of Table/View: <Table/View Name>'
'Output of Table/View: <Table/View Name>'
```

To create/maintain window titles in the menu painter, click on the 'Title List' radio button of the SE41 opening screen. Click on the create button/function key F5. A dialogue box pops up prompting for the title name ('Title Code') and title text. The title name can be a maximum of 20 characters long, has to start with a letter, and the rest can be alphanumeric with embedded underscores (_). The dialogue box with entered values will be like Figure 10-48.

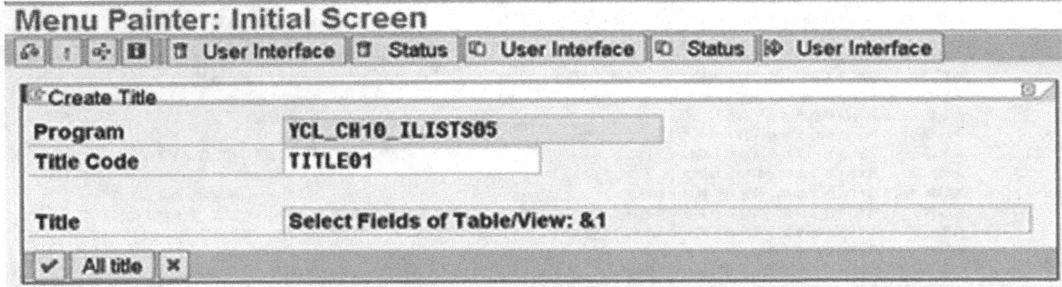

Figure 10-48. *Program YCL_CH10_ILISTS05: Create Title 'TITLE01'*

If you click on the continue button, the title will be created but the interface is not activated. So click on the 'All title' (second) button. The screen will appear like Figure 10-49.

User Interface YCL_CH10_ILISTS05 Inactive

Title Number	Title
TITLE01	Select Fields of Table/View: &1

Figure 10-49. *Program YCL_CH10_ILISTS05: Created, Inactive Title 'TITLE01'*

Activate the interface by pressing the ctrl-F3 keys or the activate button. After activation, the screen will look like Figure 10-50.

User Interface YCL_CH10_ILISTS05 Active

Title Number	Title
TITLE01	Select Fields of Table/View: &1

Figure 10-50. *Program YCL_CH10_ILISTS05: Created, Activated Title 'TITLE01'*

In a similar manner create the 'TITLE02'. On the screen shown in Figure 10-50, there are buttons to create, delete copy, and rename titles.

Titles can be maintained in multiple languages (such as text symbols, messages, etc.) in the menu painter.

- The 'Select All', 'Deselect All' buttons in the primary list enables the end user to select or deselect all fields. The checkbox values are changed for all the lines or fields using the ABAP statement: MODIFY LINE … being introduced in this program. With this statement, you can alter the contents of lists but not the value of the variables output in the lists. The MODIFY LINE … statement you have used (inside LOOP AT … ENDLOOP) for enabling or disabling all checkboxes of the list:

  ```
  MODIFY LINE SY-TABIX FIELD VALUE FIELDS_STRU-CBOX FROM 'X'
      FIELDS_STRU-FIELDNAME FROM FIELDS_STRU-FIELDNAME.
  ```

  Within the LOOP AT … ENDLOOP the value of SY-TABIX will assume values 1, 2 … You are modifying each output line of primary list in the event AT USER-COMMAND (i.e., the list number contained in system field SY-LISTI) until all output lines have been modified. With the MODIFY LINE … statement, the output checkbox variable 'FIELDS_STRU-CBOX' in each line is changed to 'X' or enabled for every pass of the loop. For disabling all check box values of all lines, the FROM 'X' in the above statement would be FROM ' '.

  The full syntax of the MODIFY LINE … statement can referred to in the online documentation. There is a provision for modifying or altering lines from any of the pages of any of the preceding lists.

- Which of the listed database table or view fields have enabled check boxes is determined using the ABAP statement: READ LINE … being introduced in this program. With this statement, you can read a complete output line and/or the individual variable values in the output line. In your present context, you want to read the value of checkbox output with each database table or view field variable on each line.

  To read the values of the checkboxes on each line of output, we have set up a DO … ENDDO loop. Inside the loop the following statement reads the value of check box on each line:

  ```
  READ LINE SY-INDEX FIELD VALUE FIELDS_STRU-CBOX INTO CK_BOX
  ```

  Inside the loop, the system field SY-INDEX will assume values 1,2 … You are reading each output line of the primary list that triggered the event AT USER-COMMAND (i.e., the list number contained in system field SY-LISTI) until all output lines have been read. With the READ LINE … statement, the output variable 'FIELDS_STRU-CBOX' in each line is fetched into the CK_BOX for every pass of the loop. Thus you are able to ascertain whether a field is enabled for it to be output in the subsequent secondary list. You are assuming that the first field name of the table or view with the checkbox variable 'FIELDS_STRU-CBOX' in the primary list is on the first line on the screen. This is ensured by giving the addition NO STANDARD PAGE HEADING in the REPORT statement and not having any standard header for the primary list.

  The full syntax of the READ LINE … statement can be referred in the online documentation. There is a provision for reading lines from any of the pages/lines of any of the preceding lists. The system field SY-LISEL and the fields specified with the HIDE … statement are affected.

  The READ LINE … statement can be used to exchange information from the lower level lists to a higher level list. So you can use this statement in lieu of the system field SY-LISEL, HIDE … GET CURSOR … statements if you want.

- The retrieval of data of runtime specified fields from a database table or view specified at runtime is implemented using the special form of the Open SQL SELECT statement, dynamic/run time creation of data objects and field symbols. (Internal table: SFIELDS_TAB)

- The ordering of the output data in ascending order of primary key fields is implemented using the runtime ORDER BY feature of the Open SQL SELECT statement. (Internal Table: ORDER_BY_TAB)
- Retrieval of data only of the logged-in language for text tables or views is implemented using the runtime WHERE condition feature of the Open SQL SELECT statement. (Internal Table: CONDS_TAB)
- The column headings of the output fields are fetched from the corresponding data elements using the function module: MG_FIELDNAME_TEXT. This function module takes two input parameters such as database table/view/structure name and field name. It returns the short, medium, long, and heading (field or column heading) field labels from the data element assigned to the field in the database table/view/structure.
- The LINE-SIZE (maximum width of a line in terms of number of columns) is set as per the total width of all fields or columns. The width of a field or column is determined on the basis of the output length of the field (derived with the `DESCRIBE FIELD. OUTPUT-LENGTH...` statement) and the length of the column heading retrieved from the data element. The higher of these two values is adopted as the width of the field for output. An example of this: the width of language code in any text table is output in two columns, ('EN', 'DE' etc.) the column heading for language code is 'Language' (i.e. eight columns). Hence the output width of language code field is adopted as eight. The LINE-SIZE for secondary lists can be set with the NEW-PAGE ... statement. The NEW-PAGE ... statement accepts variable values for LINE-SIZE as well as LINE-COUNT. The LINE-SIZE for the primary list can be set only with the REPORT ... statement, the REPORT ... statement can only accept literals for LINE-SIZE, LINE-COUNT. Before the LINE-SIZE is set, its value (based on the total width of all fields to be output including the gap or single space between two fields) is checked. If it exceeds 1023, an alert message is issued.
- You are using a LINE-COUNT of 60 for your secondary list. You are setting the LINE- COUNT along with the LINE-SIZE in the statement NEW-PAGE.
- To output the secondary list body, you are using two WRITE ... statements: one to output the first field or column of a row, this should start on a new line. The other WRITE ... statement is to output fields or columns other than the first field or column. These fields or columns are to be output on the same line. You are using WRITE AT ... notation instead of the WRITE .... This is necessary, if you are specifying the output width, column positions as variables instead of literals.
- The column heading of numeric variables (TYPE I, P, etc.) is output RIGHT-JUSTIFIED.
- The messages used in program - message numbers 022, 023, 024 of message id./class YCL_CH10_MCLASS01 are listed in Figure 10-51.

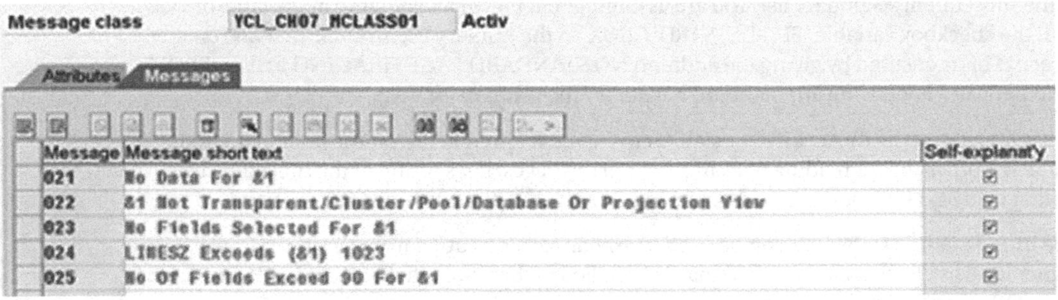

Message class YCL_CH07_MCLASS01 Activ

Attributes | Messages

Message	Message short text	Self-explanat'y
021	No Data For &1	☑
022	&1 Not Transparent/Cluster/Pool/Database Or Projection View	☑
023	No Fields Selected For &1	☑
024	LINESZ Exceeds (&1) 1023	☑
025	No Of Fields Exceed 90 For &1	☑

Figure 10-51. *Program YCL_CH10_ILISTS05: Messages Used*

- Other small tweaks and logics have been used in the program. You should peruse and resolve.

The source:

```
REPORT YCL_CH10_ILISTS05 NO STANDARD PAGE HEADING.

*************************************************************
* Output Specific Fields Of A Specific Database Table/View **
*************************************************************

DATA: BEGIN OF FIELDS_STRU,
       FIELDNAME TYPE DD03L-FIELDNAME," field name
       POSITION  TYPE DD03L-POSITION, " field position in stru 1, 2..
                                      " line no. & field position map
                                      " one-to-one. helps in accessing
                                      " a field with line no.
       INTTYPE   TYPE DD03L-INTTYPE,  " ABAP TYPE: C,D,F,I,N,P etc.
       DATATYPE  TYPE DD03L-DATATYPE, " DDIC TYPE: CHAR, NUMC etc.
       KEYFLAG   TYPE DD03L-KEYFLAG,  " flag for primary key field
       CBOX(1)   TYPE C,              " field enabled/disabled check box
       OBLEN     TYPE I,              " width of output
      END OF FIELDS_STRU,

      BEGIN OF SFIELDS_STRU,
       FIELDNAME TYPE DD03L-FIELDNAME,
      END OF SFIELDS_STRU,

      BEGIN OF ORDERBY_STRU,
       FIELDNAME TYPE DD03L-FIELDNAME,
      END OF ORDERBY_STRU,

      BEGIN OF OHEAD_STRU,
       FIELDNAME TYPE DD03L-FIELDNAME,
       OLEN      TYPE I, " width of output
       OTEXT     TYPE STRING,
       INTTYPE   TYPE DD03L-INTTYPE,
      END OF OHEAD_STRU,

      FIELDS_TAB  LIKE STANDARD TABLE OF FIELDS_STRU, " all fields of
                                                      " selected table

      SFIELDS_TAB LIKE STANDARD TABLE OF SFIELDS_STRU," selected fields of
                                                      " selected table. used
                                                      " in SELECT statement

      ORDERBY_TAB LIKE STANDARD TABLE OF ORDERBY_STRU,  " primary key fields
                                                        " (in sort)
      CONDS_TAB   TYPE STRING OCCURS 0 WITH HEADER LINE, " condition for
                                                         " text tables
      OHEAD_TAB   LIKE STANDARD TABLE OF OHEAD_STRU,     " texts for
                                                         " column headings
```

```
      CTR         TYPE I, " outputted field number
      LINSZ       TYPE I, " LINE-SIZE
      LCNT        TYPE I, " temporary
      PAGE(3)     TYPE C,
      CK_BOX(1)   TYPE C, " READ..FIELDS_STRU-CBOX INTO..
      TABCLASS    TYPE DD02L-TABCLASS, " destination field from table DD02L
      DSTRU       TYPE REF TO DATA.    " ref. variable of structure object

FIELD-SYMBOLS: <DSTRU>, " field symbol to access structure
               <FLD>.   " field symbol to access field

***********SELECTION-SCREEN***************************
PARAMETERS: TAB_NAME  TYPE DD03L-TABNAME VALUE CHECK.

AT SELECTION-SCREEN.

SELECT SINGLE TABCLASS FROM DD02L INTO TABCLASS WHERE TABNAME = TAB_NAME.

IF TABCLASS <> 'TRANSP' AND TABCLASS <> 'CLUSTER' AND
  TABCLASS <> 'POOL' AND TABCLASS <> 'VIEW'.
 MESSAGE E022(YCL_CH07_MCLASS01) WITH TAB_NAME.
ENDIF.

************************************************************
************************************************************

START-OF-SELECTION.

SELECT FIELDNAME POSITION INTTYPE DATATYPE KEYFLAG FROM DD03L
 INTO CORRESPONDING FIELDS OF TABLE FIELDS_TAB
 WHERE TABNAME = TAB_NAME AND FIELDNAME NOT LIKE '.%' AND
  FIELDNAME NOT LIKE '/%'.

SORT FIELDS_TAB BY POSITION.

SET PF-STATUS 'STAT1'.
SET TITLEBAR 'TITLE01' WITH TAB_NAME.

*********primary list - list of fields *********************

LOOP AT FIELDS_TAB INTO FIELDS_STRU.
 WRITE:/5 FIELDS_STRU-CBOX AS CHECKBOX, FIELDS_STRU-FIELDNAME.
ENDLOOP.

**************************
* AT USER-COMMAND event **
**************************

AT USER-COMMAND.

CASE SY-UCOMM.
```

```
 WHEN 'EXIT'.
 LEAVE SCREEN.

 WHEN 'BACK'.
  SY-LSIND = SY-LSIND - 2.

****************select all*************
 WHEN 'SALL'.

 LOOP AT FIELDS_TAB INTO FIELDS_STRU .
  MODIFY LINE SY-TABIX FIELD VALUE FIELDS_STRU-CBOX FROM 'X'
    FIELDS_STRU-FIELDNAME FROM FIELDS_STRU-FIELDNAME.
 ENDLOOP.

 SY-LSIND = 0.

***************de-select all************
 WHEN 'DSALL'.

  LOOP AT FIELDS_TAB INTO FIELDS_STRU .
   MODIFY LINE SY-TABIX FIELD VALUE FIELDS_STRU-CBOX FROM ' '
    FIELDS_STRU-FIELDNAME FROM FIELDS_STRU-FIELDNAME.
 ENDLOOP.

 SY-LSIND = 0.

*****************output**************
 WHEN 'DDATA'.
 REFRESH: SFIELDS_TAB, ORDERBY_TAB, OHEAD_TAB, CONDS_TAB.
              " initialize internal tables
 LINSZ = 0.
 CREATE DATA DSTRU TYPE (TAB_NAME).
 ASSIGN DSTRU->* TO <DSTRU>.

******determine selected fields, build internal tables******
 DO.
  READ LINE SY-INDEX FIELD VALUE FIELDS_STRU-CBOX INTO CK_BOX.
  IF SY-SUBRC <> 0. " no more lines in the list
   EXIT.
  ENDIF.
  IF CK_BOX = 'X'.
   READ TABLE FIELDS_TAB INTO FIELDS_STRU INDEX SY-INDEX.
   FIELDS_STRU-CBOX = CK_BOX.
   SFIELDS_STRU-FIELDNAME = FIELDS_STRU-FIELDNAME.
   APPEND SFIELDS_STRU TO SFIELDS_TAB.

   ASSIGN COMPONENT SY-INDEX OF STRUCTURE <DSTRU> TO <FLD>.

   PERFORM FILL_OHEAD_TAB TABLES OHEAD_TAB USING TAB_NAME
     FIELDS_STRU <FLD>.
```

```
   MODIFY FIELDS_TAB FROM FIELDS_STRU INDEX SY-INDEX.

   IF FIELDS_STRU-KEYFLAG = 'X'.
    ORDERBY_STRU-FIELDNAME = FIELDS_STRU-FIELDNAME.
    APPEND ORDERBY_STRU TO ORDERBY_TAB.
   ENDIF.

   IF FIELDS_STRU-DATATYPE = 'LANG' AND FIELDS_STRU-KEYFLAG = 'X'.
    CONCATENATE FIELDS_STRU-FIELDNAME '= SY-LANGU' INTO
     CONDS_TAB SEPARATED BY ' '.
    APPEND CONDS_TAB TO CONDS_TAB.
   ENDIF.

  ELSE.

   READ TABLE FIELDS_TAB INTO FIELDS_STRU INDEX SY-INDEX.
   FIELDS_STRU-CBOX = CK_BOX.
   MODIFY FIELDS_TAB FROM FIELDS_STRU INDEX SY-INDEX.

   IF FIELDS_STRU-KEYFLAG = 'X'.
    ORDERBY_STRU-FIELDNAME = FIELDS_STRU-FIELDNAME.
    APPEND ORDERBY_STRU TO ORDERBY_TAB.
   ENDIF.

  IF FIELDS_STRU-DATATYPE = 'LANG' AND FIELDS_STRU-KEYFLAG = 'X'.
    CONCATENATE FIELDS_STRU-FIELDNAME '= SY-LANGU' INTO
     CONDS_TAB SEPARATED BY ' '.
    APPEND CONDS_TAB TO CONDS_TAB.
   ENDIF.

  ENDIF.
 ENDDO.

 DESCRIBE TABLE SFIELDS_TAB.

 IF SY-TFILL = 0. " no fields selected
  MESSAGE S023(YCL_CH07_MCLASS01) WITH
  TAB_NAME DISPLAY LIKE 'W'.
  SY-LSIND = SY-LSIND - 1.
  EXIT.
 ENDIF.

 LINSZ = LINSZ + 3.

 IF LINSZ > 1023. " SY-LINSZ CANNOT EXCEED 1023.
  MESSAGE S024(YCL_CH07_MCLASS01) WITH
  LINSZ DISPLAY LIKE 'W'.
  SY-LSIND = SY-LSIND - 1.
  EXIT.

 ENDIF.
```

```
 CREATE DATA DSTRU TYPE (TAB_NAME).
 ASSIGN DSTRU->* TO <DSTRU>.
 SET PF-STATUS 'STAT2'.

 NEW-PAGE  LINE-SIZE LINSZ LINE-COUNT 60. " LINSZ as per total width
                                          " of all outputted columns

 SET TITLEBAR 'TITLE02' WITH TAB_NAME.

*************retrieve data & output**********************
 SELECT (SFIELDS_TAB) FROM (TAB_NAME) INTO CORRESPONDING FIELDS OF
  <DSTRU> WHERE (CONDS_TAB) ORDER BY (ORDERBY_TAB).
  CTR = 0.
  DO.
   ASSIGN COMPONENT SY-INDEX OF STRUCTURE <DSTRU> TO <FLD>.
   IF SY-SUBRC <> 0.
    EXIT.
   ENDIF.
   READ TABLE FIELDS_TAB INTO FIELDS_STRU INDEX SY-INDEX.
   IF FIELDS_STRU-CBOX <> 'X'.
    CONTINUE.
   ENDIF.
   CTR = CTR + 1.
   IF CTR = 1.
    WRITE AT :/5(FIELDS_STRU-OBLEN) <FLD>.
   ELSE.
    WRITE AT :(FIELDS_STRU-OBLEN) <FLD>.
   ENDIF.
  ENDDO.

 ENDSELECT.

ENDCASE.

*********************************************************
* heading using event TOP-OF-PAGE DURING LINE-SELECTION **
*********************************************************
TOP-OF-PAGE DURING LINE-SELECTION.

 LCNT = LINSZ - 2.
 PAGE = SY-PAGNO.
 WRITE AT /LCNT PAGE RIGHT-JUSTIFIED.

 LCNT = LINSZ - 4.

 WRITE AT /5(LCNT) SY-ULINE.

 LOOP AT OHEAD_TAB INTO OHEAD_STRU.
```

```
  IF SY-TABIX = 1.
   IF OHEAD_STRU-INTTYPE = 'F' OR OHEAD_STRU-INTTYPE = 'I'
    OR OHEAD_STRU-INTTYPE = 'P'.
    WRITE AT /5(OHEAD_STRU-OLEN) OHEAD_STRU-OTEXT RIGHT-JUSTIFIED.
   ELSE.
    WRITE AT /5(OHEAD_STRU-OLEN) OHEAD_STRU-OTEXT.
   ENDIF.
  ELSE.
   IF OHEAD_STRU-INTTYPE = 'F' OR OHEAD_STRU-INTTYPE = 'I'
    OR OHEAD_STRU-INTTYPE = 'P'.
    WRITE AT (OHEAD_STRU-OLEN) OHEAD_STRU-OTEXT RIGHT-JUSTIFIED.
   ELSE.
    WRITE AT (OHEAD_STRU-OLEN) OHEAD_STRU-OTEXT.
   ENDIF.
  ENDIF.
 ENDLOOP.

 WRITE AT /5(LCNT) SY-ULINE.
 SKIP 1.

****************************************
* Get Column Heading Texts,           **
* build column heading internal table **
****************************************

FORM  FILL_OHEAD_TAB
       TABLES
        OTAB LIKE OHEAD_TAB

       USING
        VALUE(TNAME)
        FSTRU LIKE FIELDS_STRU VALUE(FLD).

 DATA: LNGT     TYPE I,
       OSTRU    LIKE LINE OF OTAB.

 CALL FUNCTION 'MG_FIELDNAME_TEXT'
  EXPORTING
    TABNAME        = TNAME
    FIELDNAME      = FSTRU-FIELDNAME
 IMPORTING
   REPTEXT         = OSTRU-OTEXT.

 OSTRU-FIELDNAME = FSTRU-FIELDNAME.
 OSTRU-INTTYPE   = FSTRU-INTTYPE.

 DESCRIBE FIELD FLD OUTPUT-LENGTH OSTRU-OLEN.
```

```
  LNGT = STRLEN( OSTRU-OTEXT ).

  IF LNGT > OSTRU-OLEN.
   OSTRU-OLEN = LNGT.
  ENDIF.

  FSTRU-OBLEN = OSTRU-OLEN.
  APPEND OSTRU TO OTAB.
  LINSZ = LINSZ + OSTRU-OLEN + 1.

ENDFORM.
**********************************
```

This was a generic program to output data of runtime specified fields of a data source - table or view- that is also specified at runtime. You have used a range of tools and features to implement your lists' generation in the program. You have used two SAP metadata database tables: DD02L and DD03l.

The advanced concepts Field Symbols, dynamic (run time) data objects, introduced in Chapter 8 entitled 'Open SQL Data Retrieval' are used to good effect in this exercise. The special features of Open SQL SELECT statement specifying source, destination, ORDER BY and WHERE conditions at runtime have been demonstrated.

Two new list features MODIFY LINE ... and READ LINE ... are also used in the program.

This concludes the hands-on exercise.

Hands-on Exercise: Demonstration of SET USER-COMMAND and Lists in Dialogue Boxes

A concluding hands-on-exercise of this chapter, the program YCL-CH09_ILISTS06 demonstrates the features of lists in dialogue boxes or windows and the statement SET USER-COMMAND. You can locate lists in dialogue boxes instead of the normal full screen. Until now, you have located all your lists in a normal full screen, which is by default. By locating lists in dialogue boxes, you could have the end user viewing more than one list at a time. But only the secondary lists can be located in dialogue boxes. The primary list has to be necessarily located in the normal full screen.

If you want to locate secondary lists in dialogue boxes, simply precede the list generation with the WINDOW ... statement. The syntax of the WINDOW ... statement:

```
WINDOW STARTING AT <start column> <start row>
  [ ENDING AT <end column> <end row> ].
```

If the 'ENDING AT ...' is omitted, the dialogue box will spread to the end of the screen at the bottom.

If the status is set (SET PF-STATUS ...) the *application toolbar* appears at the bottom of the dialogue box. If no status is set, the system default *application toolbar* appears at the bottom of the dialogue box. The dialogue boxes do not have menu or standard toolbar. You can set the dialogue box/window title by the SET TITLEBAR ... statement.

The SET USER-COMMAND ... statement triggers list events: AT USER-COMMAND, AT LINE-SELECTION without any buttons pressed or double clicking performed. The syntax of SET USER-COMMAND ...:

```
SET USER-COMMAND <function code>.
```

If the function code is the predefined function code 'PICK' (function key F2) the AT LINE-SELECTION event is triggered. Refer to the document ABAP Programming (BC-ABA) on page 861 for a list of predefined function codes. If the function code is user defined, the AT USER-COMMAND event is triggered.

This hands-on exercise is producing effectively two lists:

- The customer wise sales summary of a specified company code;
- Billing documents of a selected customer.

The program is using the AT USER-COMMAND event. Both the lists are appearing in dialogue boxes. So both these lists are secondary lists. Your primary list is just one line of output: WRITE: 'DUMMY'. You are preceding this statement with the SET USE-COMMAND 'ABCD' triggering the AT USER-COMMAND and paving the way for the appearance of your first secondary list: customer wise sales summary of a specified company code. This way the primary list is bypassed and not appearing on the screen. You have an 'EXIT' button on this first secondary list as part of the status. On pressing of this button on the *application toolbar* of your first secondary list, the LEAVE SCREEN statement will be executed, thus navigating back to the Selection Screen statement prompting for company code. In this manner, the primary list is being bypassed on forward and backward navigation. The primary list remains behind the scenes not making any appearance.

You have the 'DETAIL' button on the first secondary list, which will take you to the second secondary list - billing documents of a selected customer - this is appearing in an adjoining dialogue box/window. Though the first secondary list is visible with the appearance of second secondary list in the adjoining window, you cannot operate on the first secondary list when the second secondary list has been produced in terms of clicking on its *application toolbar* buttons, etc. On the second secondary list, you have not set any status. So the system default buttons appear on the *application toolbar* at the bottom of the second secondary list. Clicking on the Cancel ✖ button on the second secondary list will take you to the first secondary list.

You can create a status 'STAT1' for the first secondary list consisting of the two buttons 'EXIT' and 'DETAIL' with their respective icons. Remember, when creating the status 'STAT1', that it is for a dialogue box - not for a normal screen.

There could be a demand from a capricious end user: to output all the lists in dialogue boxes!

Fewer fields are output in both the secondary lists only so that screen shot captures all fields of the two lists.

The output screens will look like Figures 10-52 and 10-53.

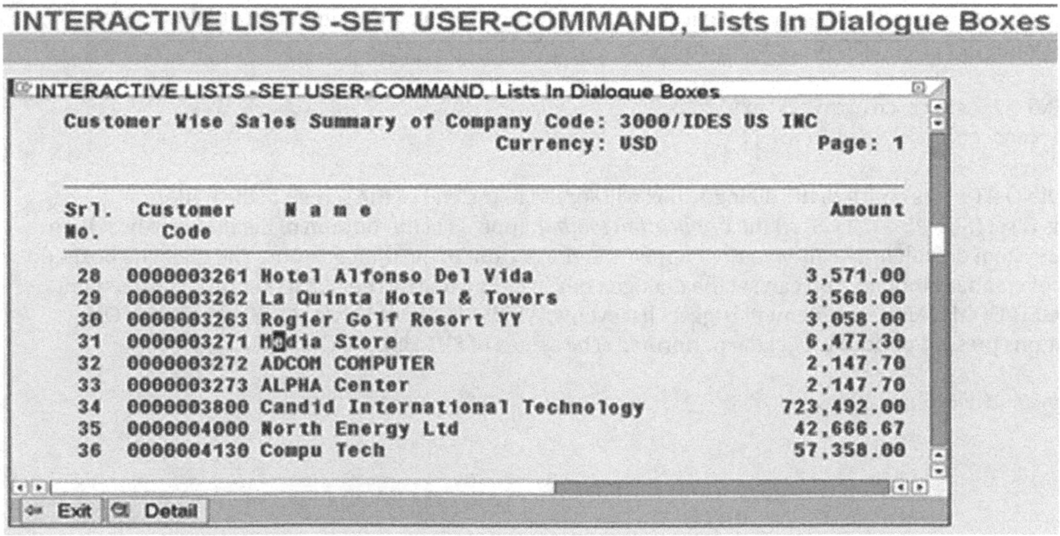

Figure 10-52. *Program YCL_CH10_ILISTS06: Secondary List I*

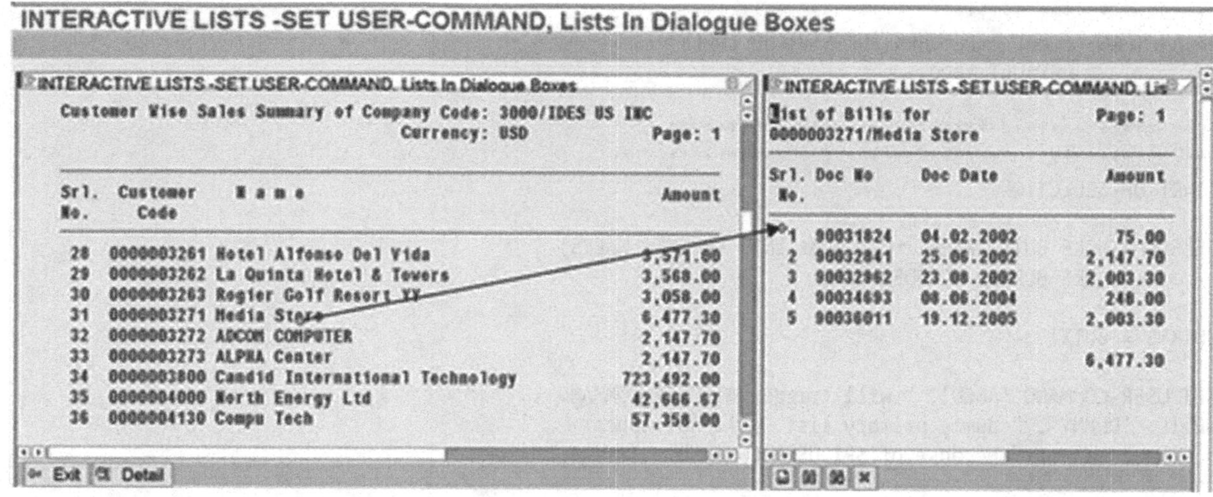

Figure 10-53. *Program YCL_CH10_ILISTS06: Secondary Lists I & II*

The source:

```
REPORT YCL_CH10_ILISTS06 NO STANDARD PAGE HEADING
        LINE-COUNT 60.

************************************************
* INTERACTIVE LISTS - SET USER-COMMAND,       **
*                     Lists In Dialogue Boxes **
************************************************

DATA: SALES_TAB  TYPE YCL_CH06_SALES_SUM_TAB,
      SALES_STRU LIKE LINE OF SALES_TAB,

      BEGIN OF BILLS_STRU,
       VBELN     TYPE VBRK-VBELN,
       FKDAT     TYPE VBRK-FKDAT,
       WAERK     TYPE VBRK-WAERK,
       KURRF     TYPE VBRK-KURRF,
       NETWR     TYPE VBRK-NETWR,
      END OF BILLS_STRU,
      BILLS_TAB LIKE STANDARD TABLE OF BILLS_STRU,

      KUNNR     TYPE KNA1-KUNNR,
      NAME1     TYPE KNA1-NAME1,
      TOTAL     TYPE VBRK-NETWR,
      TOTAL1    TYPE VBRK-NETWR,
      BUTXT     TYPE T001-BUTXT,
      WAERS     TYPE T001-WAERS,
      BUTXTS    TYPE STRING.
```

```
*********************************************
PARAMETERS: CCODE TYPE VBRK-BUKRS VALUE CHECK
            DEFAULT 3000.

*********************************************
*********************************************
START-OF-SELECTION.

SELECT SINGLE BUTXT WAERS FROM T001 INTO (BUTXT, WAERS)
        WHERE BUKRS = CCODE.

BUTXTS = BUTXT.

SET USER-COMMAND 'ABCD'. " will trigger AT USER-COMMAND
WRITE: 'DUMMY'. " dummy primary list. will not appear
                " because of SET USER-COMMAND

********************************************************
********************************************************
AT USER-COMMAND.

IF SY-UCOMM = 'EXIT'. " EXIT button on secondary i
 LEAVE SCREEN.
ENDIF.

 CASE SY-LSIND.

 WHEN 1.

  TOTAL = 0.

  SELECT KUNNR NAME1 ORT01 NETWR KURRF FROM YCL_CH05_VBRKKNA INTO
    CORRESPONDING FIELDS OF SALES_STRU WHERE BUKRS = CCODE.

   SALES_STRU-NETWR =  SALES_STRU-NETWR * SALES_STRU-KURRF.
   SALES_STRU-KURRF = 0. "to prevent overflow
   COLLECT SALES_STRU INTO SALES_TAB.
  ENDSELECT.

  DESCRIBE TABLE SALES_TAB.

  IF SY-TFILL > 0.

   SORT SALES_TAB BY KUNNR.

   WINDOW STARTING AT 1 1 ENDING AT 73 13. " WINDOW statement start column
                                           " start row end column end row
```

```
   SET PF-STATUS 'STAT1'.
   LOOP AT SALES_TAB INTO SALES_STRU.
    WRITE :/5(4) SY-TABIX, SALES_STRU-KUNNR USING NO EDIT MASK,
     SALES_STRU-NAME1, (17) SALES_STRU-NETWR.
    TOTAL = TOTAL + SALES_STRU-NETWR.
   ENDLOOP.

   SKIP 1.
   WRITE :/(17) TOTAL UNDER SALES_STRU-NETWR.
  ELSE.
   MESSAGE S021(YCL_CH07_MCLASS01) WITH " no data for the company code
    'Customer Summary' DISPLAY LIKE 'W'.
   LEAVE SCREEN.
  ENDIF.

 WHEN 2.

  TOTAL1 = 0.
  KUNNR = SY-LISEL+9(10).  " extract customer code
  NAME1 = SY-LISEL+20(35). " extract customer name

  SELECT VBELN FKDAT WAERK KURRF NETWR FROM VBRK
    INTO TABLE BILLS_TAB
    WHERE KUNAG = KUNNR AND BUKRS = CCODE.

  DESCRIBE TABLE BILLS_TAB.

  IF SY-TFILL > 0.

   WINDOW STARTING AT 78 1 ENDING AT 120 13.

   SET PF-STATUS ' '.

   LOOP AT BILLS_TAB INTO BILLS_STRU.
    BILLS_STRU-NETWR = BILLS_STRU-NETWR * BILLS_STRU-KURRF.
    TOTAL1 = TOTAL1 + BILLS_STRU-NETWR.
    WRITE:/1(4) SY-TABIX, BILLS_STRU-VBELN, BILLS_STRU-FKDAT,
     (15) BILLS_STRU-NETWR.
   ENDLOOP.

   SKIP 1.
   WRITE:/28(15) TOTAL1.

  ELSE.
    MESSAGE W021(YCL_CH07_MCLASS01) WITH " no data for the company code
    'Bills Of A Customer' DISPLAY LIKE 'I'.

   SY-LSIND = 1.

  ENDIF.
 ENDCASE.
```

```
************************************
************************************
TOP-OF-PAGE DURING LINE-SELECTION.

CASE SY-LSIND.

 WHEN 1.

  WRITE:/5 TEXT-001, CCODE NO-GAP, '/' NO-GAP,  BUTXTS.
  WRITE:/40 TEXT-002, WAERS, 66 TEXT-003, 71(3) SY-PAGNO..
  SKIP 1.
  WRITE:/5(68) SY-ULINE.
  WRITE:/5 TEXT-004, 11 TEXT-005, 23 TEXT-006, 56(17)
          TEXT-008 RIGHT-JUSTIFIED.
  WRITE:/5 TEXT-009, 13 TEXT-010.
  WRITE:/5(68) SY-ULINE.

 WHEN 2.

  WRITE:/1 TEXT-011, 35 TEXT-003, 40(3) SY-PAGNO.
  WRITE:/1 KUNNR USING NO EDIT MASK NO-GAP, '/' NO-GAP, NAME1.
  WRITE:/1(42) SY-ULINE.
  WRITE:/1 TEXT-004, 06 TEXT-012, 17 TEXT-013,  36 TEXT-008.
  WRITE:/2 TEXT-009 .
  WRITE:/1(42) SY-ULINE.

ENDCASE.
*****************************************************************
```

Interactive Lists Tid Bits

Features of Interactive Lists Not Covered:

- System fields associated with interactive lists not used by you: SY-LILLI, SY-CUROW, SY-CUCOL, SY-CPAGE, SY-STARO, and SY-STACO.
- DESCRIBE LIST..: With this statement, you can ascertain the number of pages, number of lines, LINE-SIZE, LINE-COUNT, etc., of a list.
- ABAP statements to scroll in lists.
- Positioning on lists – SET CURSOR: Position the cursor on a page, line, and/or field of a list.
- MODIFY LIST FORMAT ...: To modify or alter the output format of fields in lists after its generation.

Conclusion

In this chapter, we generated multiple lists in an ABAP program. This facility of generating multiple lists can be deployed in situations where you want to provide summary information to the end user and detailed information of specific summary information through end-user actions. These lists are called *interactive lists*. We used the list events AT LINE-SELECTION and AT USER-COMMAND to generate the *interactive lists*.

When generating *interactive lists* using the event AT USER-COMMAND, you were introduced to creating custom *user interfaces* in the menu painter using the transaction code SE41. The custom *user interfaces* consisted of statuses, title lists, etc. You further learned to position the statuses, titles, etc., created in the custom *user interface* on a list.

Next, we coded a generic program. The generic program outputs data of runtime specified fields from a runtime specified database table. The generic program uses the *interactive lists feature* and special constructs of open SQL, field symbols, and *dynamic data objects*. The *dynamic data objects* are introduced on a preview basis in this chapter. The *dynamic data objects* will be formally introduced in Chapter 11 entitled 'ABAP OOP'.

The chapter concluded with *interactive lists* located inside dialogue boxes. We produced *interactive lists* in this chapter using the WRITE statement. In Chapters 12 and 13, we will produce *interactive lists* using ALV classes.

CHAPTER 11

ABAP OOP

Introduction

The incorporation of object orientation into the formerly procedure-oriented ABAP language is an extension of the original. With the OOP extension in an ABAP program, you can work with or without the constructs of OOP.

This chapter proceeds on the premise that readers have an awareness of the fundamentals of object-oriented programming: classes and interfaces; instances or objects; and the components of classes such as attributes, methods, and events. Readers know about encapsulation, inheritance, polymorphism, and visibility. And readers understand instance attributes, instance methods, and instance events; class attributes, class methods, and class events; and special methods, event handler methods, etc.

In the ABAP environment, you can define and implement classes locally in an ABAP program. You can use these classes only in the program where you have located them, analogous to the internal subroutines. You can define and implement classes globally in the class builder - transaction code SE24. These classes can be used in multiple ABAP programs (reusable) analogous to the function module library.

The scope of this chapter and of Chapters 12 and 13 is to enable you to use SAP supplied built-in classes, especially the built-in classes pertaining to the generation of class based lists or reports (ALV reports.) These built-in classes have events that you will trigger. The triggering entails execution of methods - event handler methods - in your own defined classes. Since these event handler methods are specific to a scenario or context (not generic for the most part), it makes sense to locate the classes containing the event handler methods in the ABAP program itself (local classes). You can locate these event handler methods, if you so desire, in your own created global classes. This chapter exposes you to the process of creating and maintaining global classes (i.e., the class builder) - transaction code SE24.

In this chapter, you will learn to create and maintain global class based exceptions and deploy these global class based exceptions for error conditions in your programs, procedures, etc. You will also learn how to create and deploy context menus that involve usage of a class.

Terminology Clarification: The term 'data objects,' which you have been using since Chapter 2, will continue to carry the same meaning. By data objects we mean (a) Whatever you declare in an ABAP program with reserved words: DATA, TABLES, CONSTANTS, along with the literals; these constitute the internal data objects. (b) The DDIC tables, views, and structures; the fields of DDIC tables, views, and structures; the data elements; the DDIC internal table definitions (table types) - these constitute the external data objects. (c) The system fields constitute system data objects. (d) The PARAMETERS variables and the SELECT-OPTIONS variables - these constitute the special data objects.

You refer to the components of DDIC such as table definitions, data elements, and domains, etc., as DDIC objects. The word 'object' is used here not in the context of OOP.

Local Class Syntaxes: Definition, Implementation, Declaration of Methods, Calling Methods

First, there will be coverage of local classes and the connected syntaxes. The essentials of syntaxes are described. For detailed syntaxes, you can refer to the online documentation.

Class Definition:

The syntax of a local class definition:

```
CLASS <class name> DEFINITION.

PUBLIC SECTION.
TYPE-POOLS:....
TYPES:.....
COMSTANTS:.....
DATA:....
CLASS-DATA:.....
METHODS: <method1> ...
CLASS-METHODS <class method1>...
EVENTS:...
CLASS-EVENTS.....
INTERFACES..

PROTECTED SECTION.
........
.....
PRIVATE SECTION.
......
.......
ENDCLASS.
```

An explanation of the different terms of the syntax follows.

Visibility of Components

PUBLIC SECTION: The components declared in this section are accessible to all the users of the class; to other methods of the class; and inherited classes, if any.

PROTECTED SECTION: The components declared in this section are accessible to methods of the class and inherited classes, if any.

PRIVATE SECTION: The components declared in this section are accessible only in methods of the class.

The prefix `'CLASS'` is used to declare static components.

Syntactically, all of the above are optional. Practically, a class could contain attributes (DATA and/or CLASS-DATA), methods (METHODS and/or CLASS-METHODS), and events (EVENTS and/or CLASS-EVENTS) in one or more of the three sections: PUBLIC, PROTECTED, and PRIVATE. The class could contain other statements: TYPES, CONSTANTS, etc., as mentioned in the syntax above.

Declaration of Methods

In the class or interface definition, methods are declared using the following syntax:

```
METHODS <method name>

  [IMPORTING <ip1> TYPE <type> [OPTIONAL|DEFAULT <default value>].....]
  [EXPORTING <ep1> TYPE <type> [OPTIONAL|DEFAULT <default value>].....]
  [CHANGING <cp1> TYPE <type> [OPTIONAL|DEFAULT <default value>].....]
  [RETURNING <rp> TYPE <type> [OPTIONAL|DEFAULT <default value>]]

       [{RAISING|EXCEPTIONS} exc1 exc2 ...].
```

Parameters:

The sole RETURNING parameter is for the functional methods. The functional method can have any number of IMPORTING parameters and one RETURNING parameter. A functional method will not have any EXPORTING and CHANGING parameters.

An event handler method will have only IMPORTING parameter. A 'CONSTRUCTOR' method will have only IMPORTING parameter. For the rest of methods, there can be any number of IMPORTING, EXPORTING, CHANGING parameters. The parameters can be passed by the following:

- Reference: REFERENCE(<ip1>) or <ip1>
- Value: VALUE(<ip1>)

If EXPORTING, CHANGING, or RETURNING parameters are specified such as VALUE(<ep1>), VALUE(<cp1>), and VALUE(<rp>), the parameters are passed by value and result.

Parameter TYPES:

All the parameters have to be assigned TYPES. The TYPES assigned will be matched with the respective TYPES of actual parameters, and a mismatch will result in an error. The TYPES that can be assigned:

- Generic ABAP Types – Refer to the table in the online documentation with the following path:

  ABAP - By Theme ➤ Built-In Types, Data Objects and Functions ➤ Built-In Data Types ➤ Generic ABAP Types

- Locally declared, DDIC TYPES including data elements, DDIC data objects, and system fields.

The OPTIONAL clause is to indicate that the parameter is optional, not mandatory. The DEFAULT clause is to indicate a default value. Either of the OPTIONAL or DEFAULT clauses can be specified. If the DEFAULT clause is given, the parameter is optional.

Exceptions:

The key word 'RAISING' is to be used for class based exceptions and the key word 'EXCEPTIONS' used for the error conditions with the MESSAGE statement (non-class based). The parameters along with the exceptions are called the *signatures* of the methods.

Having covered class definition syntax, we proceed to the syntax of class implementation.

Class Implementation

The syntax of a local class implementation:

```
CLASS <class name> IMPLEMENTATION.

METHOD <method1>.
  .....
  .....
ENDMETHOD.
METHOD: <method2>.
  .....
  .....
ENDMETHOD.
......
.....
ENDCLASS.
```

Calling Methods, Referring to Attributes

To use a class as an object - to create an instance of a class - you have to first declare a reference variable with the DATA statement referring to the class:

```
DATA: CREF TYPE REF TO <class name>.
```

You create an instance of a class with the create statement (executes the CONSTRUCTOR method):

```
CREATE OBJECT CREF [IMPORTING <importing parameters>].
```

With this statement, the reference variable CREF contains a reference to an instance of the class.
The syntax for calling an instance method (similar to calling a function module):

```
CALL METHOD CREF-><method name>
 [IMPORTING <ifp1> = <iap1>... ]
 [EXPORTING <efp1> = <eap1>... ]
 [CHANGING <cfp1> = <cap1>... ]

 [EXCEPTIONS
  <exception1> = 1
 ....]
 .
```

where
<.fp.> - formal parameters
<.ap.> - actual parameters

To refer to an attribute of an instance of a class:

```
CREF-><attribute name>
```

A static method will be called with the following syntax:

```
CALL METHOD <class name>=><method name>
 [IMPORTING <ifp1> = <iap1>... ]
 [EXPORTING <efp1> = <eap1>... ]
 [CHANGING <cfp1> = <cap1>... ]

[EXCEPTIONS
 <exception1> = 1
....]
.
```

To refer to a static attribute of a class:

```
<class name>=><static attribute name>
```

-> For referring to an instance attribute, instance method, etc.
=> For referring to a static attribute, static method, etc.

Interface Declaration

The features of interface and inheritance are used to implement polymorphism. The syntax of an interface declaration is as follows:

```
INTERFACE <interface name>.
......
ENDINTERFACE.
```

You can define the same components in an interface as in a class (i.e., attributes, methods, events, etc.). There is no concept of visibility in the interface. The components of an interface belong to the public section of the classes where the interface is implemented. To implement an interface in a class, you have to include the interface:

```
CLASS <class name> DEFINITION.
PUBLIC SECTION.
.....
INTERFACES: <interface name>..
.....
```

In a class with an included interface, the interface components can be referred to as <interface name>~ <component name>.

Interface methods will be implemented by more than one class, and they will be implemented differently in different classes.

You can declare reference variables with references to interfaces:

```
DATA: IF_REF TYPE REF TO <interface name>.
```

Having been introduced to the essentials of the class syntax, you will now perform hands-on exercises.

Hands-on Exercise: Define and Implement a Simple Local Class

(Method to Concatenate a Text Array into a String)

This hands-on exercise is to expose you to basic syntaxes rather than implement intricate functionalities. The hands-on exercise class has a single method. This method takes an import parameter, an internal table (elementary text array), and concatenates the individual rows into one string, which is a returning parameter.

The exercise might seem a bit trivial, but the objective is to get the hang of the syntax.

You load the text array in the program with the name of the months from the database text table 'T247.' You could have loaded any text into the text array.

The program code:

```
REPORT YCL_CH11_01_BEAD_STRINGS_LCLAS.

**************************************
* Local Class With One Method:      **
* Concatenate rows Of An Array      **
**************************************

CLASS OWN_LOCAL_CLASS DEFINITION DEFERRED.
                           " class not defined yet

DATA:  CL_REF      TYPE REF TO OWN_LOCAL_CLASS,
       RESULT      TYPE STRING,
       STRING_TABL TYPE STRING_TABLE WITH HEADER LINE.
                     " DDIC TABLE TYPE (array of TYPE STRING)

**************** class definition ************************
CLASS OWN_LOCAL_CLASS DEFINITION.

*************************************************
* class contains one method: BEAD_STRINGS      **
*                                              **
* the method takes two import parameters:      **
* (1) an array of DDIC TYPE STRING_TABLE whose **
*     line is TYPE STRING                      **
* (2) separator character between the words of **
*     concatenated string. DEFAULT is ' '      **
*                                              **
* concatenates all the rows of the array &     **
* returns a single string of TYPE STRING       **
*                                              **
* the method has one exception. checks for no  **
* data in the array STR_TAB - NO_DATA          **
*                                              **
* this is a functional method. can be used in  **
* expressions though not in WRITE statement.   **
* the WRITE statement does not support functions**
* in its usage                                 **
*************************************************
```

```
 PUBLIC SECTION.

 METHODS BEAD_STRINGS IMPORTING
                       VALUE(STR_TAB)   TYPE STRING_TABLE
                       VALUE(SEPARATOR) TYPE C DEFAULT ' '

                      RETURNING
                       VALUE(STRNG)     TYPE STRING

                      EXCEPTIONS NO_DATA.
PRIVATE SECTION.
 DATA: STR            TYPE STRING.

ENDCLASS.


**************** class implementation ********************

CLASS OWN_LOCAL_CLASS IMPLEMENTATION.

METHOD BEAD_STRINGS.

 DESCRIBE TABLE STR_TAB..

 IF SY-TFILL = 0.
  MESSAGE S035(YCL_CH07_MCLASS01) RAISING
   NO_DATA.
 ENDIF.

 LOOP AT STR_TAB INTO STR.
   IF SY-TABIX > 1.
     CONCATENATE STRNG STR INTO STRNG SEPARATED
      BY SEPARATOR.
   ELSE.
     STRNG = STR.
   ENDIF.
 ENDLOOP.

ENDMETHOD.

ENDCLASS.
****************************************************

START-OF-SELECTION.

SELECT LTX FROM T247 INTO STRING_TABL
  WHERE SPRAS = SY-LANGU.

 APPEND STRING_TABL.
ENDSELECT.
```

```
CREATE OBJECT CL_REF.

**CALL METHOD CL_REF->BEAD_STRINGS
** EXPORTING
**  STR_TAB   = STRING_TABL[]
**  SEPARATOR = '-'
** RECEIVING
** STRNG = RESULT.
**

RESULT = CL_REF->BEAD_STRINGS( STR_TAB   = STRING_TABL[]
                               SEPARATOR = '-' ).
IF SY-SUBRC <> 0.

 MESSAGE ID SY-MSGID TYPE SY-MSGTY NUMBER SY-MSGNO
         WITH SY-MSGV1 SY-MSGV2 SY-MSGV3 SY-MSGV4
         DISPLAY LIKE 'E'.
ELSE.

 WRITE:/5 RESULT.
ENDIF.
```

A function method can be used in an expression (like you are doing in the program) or can be invoked with the CALL METHOD... statement. You can comment the expression and de-comment the CALL METHOD... statement in the program and see the results.

The program output will look like Figure 11-1.

Local Class With One Method: Concatenate Rows Of An Array

Local Class With One Method: Concatenate Rows Of An Array

January-February-March-April-May-June-July-August-September-October-November-December

Figure 11-1. *Program: YCL_CH11_01_BEAD_STRINGS_LCLAS - Output*

This was an example of a simple method in a locally defined and implemented class.

Hands-on Exercise: Define and Implement a Simple Global Class

(Method to Concatenate a Text Array into a String)

You will implement a method of concatenating rows of a text array in a global class so that you are exposed to the process of creating (i.e., defining and implementing a global class).

To maintain global classes, execute the transaction code SE24 to navigate to the class builder. Enter the name of the class as YCL_CH11_CL_STRING_OPERATIONS. (The class name must start with 'Y'/'Z' and have a maximum name space of thirty characters.) Press the create button or the function key F5. Figure 11-2 will appear.

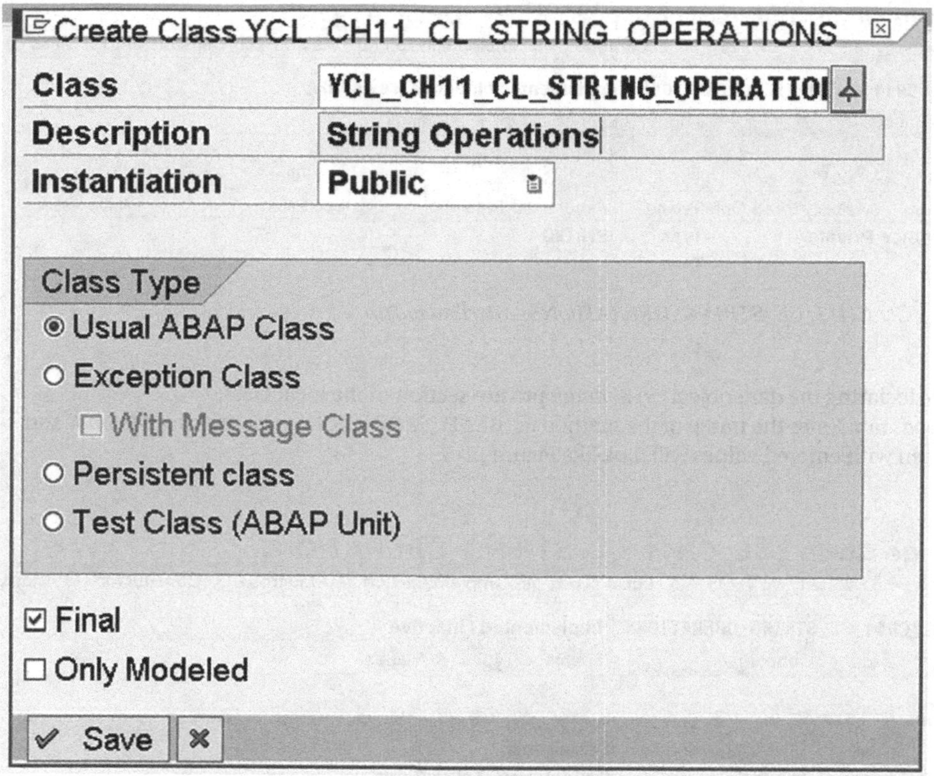

Create Class YCL_CH11_CL_STRING_OPERATIONS

Class	YCL_CH11_CL_STRING_OPERATIOI
Description	String Operations
Instantiation	Public

Class Type

◉ Usual ABAP Class
○ Exception Class
☐ With Message Class
○ Persistent class
○ Test Class (ABAP Unit)

☑ Final
☐ Only Modeled

✔ Save ✖

Figure 11-2. Global Class: YCL_CH11_CL_STRING_OPERATIONS - Initial Screen

Enter the description. Accept the defaults for other fields. Click the Save button. The system will prompt for a package ($TMP). After the package is assigned, Figure 11-3 will appear.

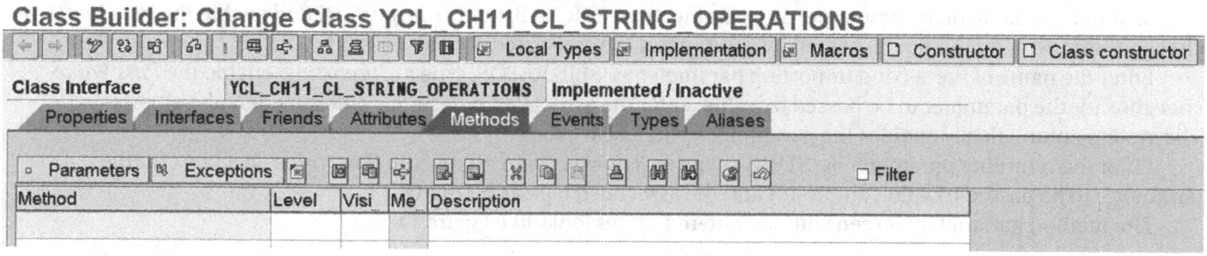

Class Builder: Change Class YCL_CH11_CL_STRING_OPERATIONS

Local Types | Implementation | Macros | Constructor | Class constructor

Class Interface YCL_CH11_CL_STRING_OPERATIONS Implemented / Inactive

Properties | Interfaces | Friends | Attributes | Methods | Events | Types | Aliases

Parameters | Exceptions | ☐ Filter

Method	Level	Visi	Me	Description

Figure 11-3. Global Class: YCL_ch11_CL_STRING_OPERATIONS - Methods Tab

There are eight tabs; the system by default takes you to the *Methods* tab. The information in the *Properties* tab, like in any other ABAP workbench object, is maintained by the system (user, date created, package, etc.).

Corresponding to the data object you declared in the private section of the local class, you need to create an attribute in the private section in the global class. So, click on the *Attributes* tab. Enter the name of the attribute as 'STR,' the level as *Instance Attribute* (other options are *Static Attribute* and *Constant*); visibility as *Private*, and the associated type as 'STRING.' The screen with the entered values will look like Figure 11-4.

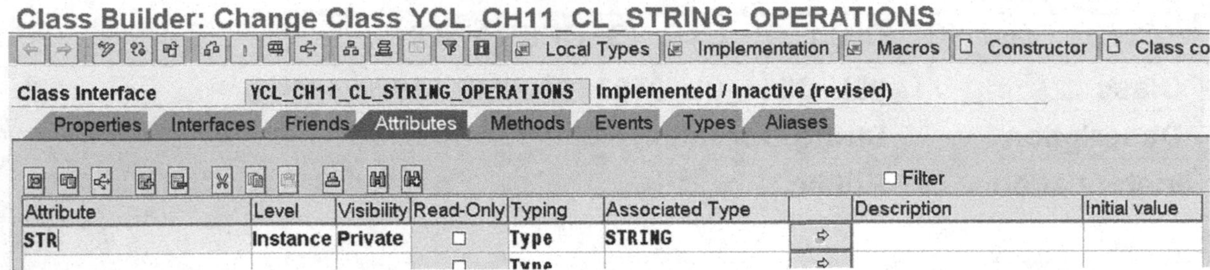

Figure 11-4. *Global Class: YCL_CH11_CL_STRING_OPERATIONS - Attributes Tab*

This was equivalent to declaring the data object 'STR' in the private section of the local class.

Now click on the *Methods* tab. Enter the name of the method as 'BEAD_STRINGS', level as *Instance Method*, and visibility as *Public*. The screen with entered values will look like Figure 11-5.

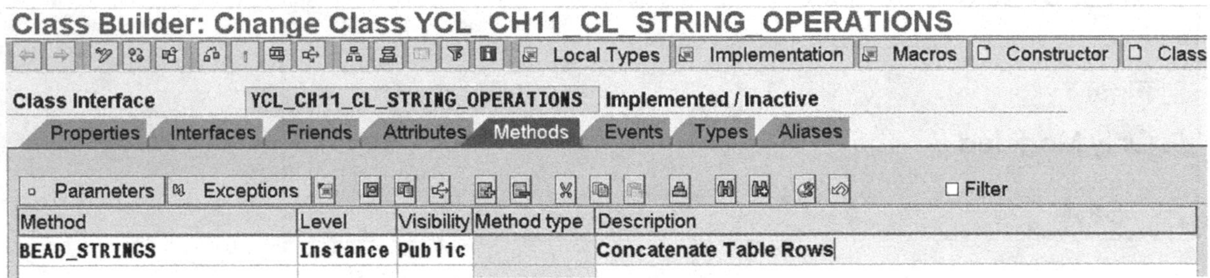

Figure 11-5. *Global Class: YCL_CH11_CL_STRING_OPERATIONS - Methods Tab*

Next, you need to enter the method parameters. So click on the parameters button. The method 'BEAD_STRINGS' has two importing parameters and one returning parameter.

So enter the name of the first importing parameter as 'STR_TAB', type as *Importing*, and enable the *Pass Value* checkbox for the parameter to be passed by value; enter the associated type as 'STRING_TABLE'.

Enter the name of the second importing parameter as 'SEPARATOR', type as *Importing*; enable the *Pass Value* checkbox for the parameter to be passed by value; enter the associated type as 'C'; enter the default value as ' '. The system automatically enables the parameter optional checkbox.

Enter the returning parameter as 'STRNG', type as *Returning*, and enable the *Pass Value* checkbox for the parameter to be passed by value and result and the associated type as 'STRING'.

The method parameters screen with the entered values looks like Figure 11-6.

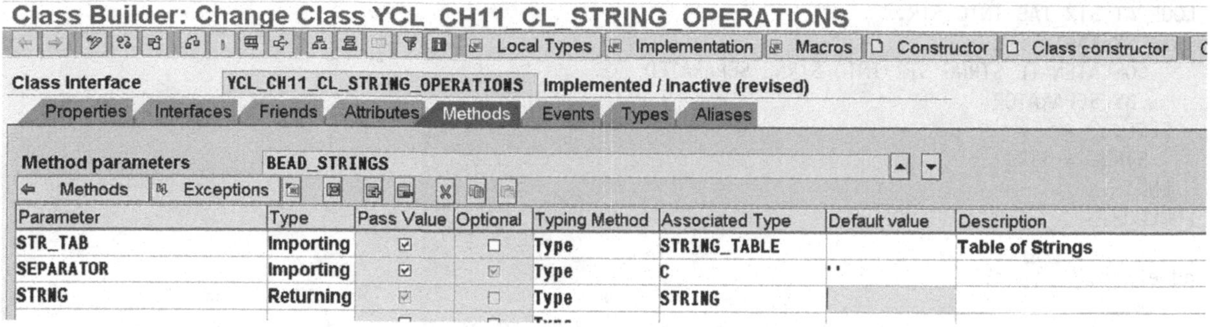

Class Builder: Change Class YCL_CH11_CL_STRING_OPERATIONS

Class Interface YCL_CH11_CL_STRING_OPERATIONS Implemented / Inactive (revised)

Properties | Interfaces | Friends | Attributes | Methods | Events | Types | Aliases

Method parameters BEAD_STRINGS

Parameter	Type	Pass Value	Optional	Typing Method	Associated Type	Default value	Description
STR_TAB	Importing	☑	☐	Type	STRING_TABLE		Table of Strings
SEPARATOR	Importing	☑	☑	Type	C	' '	
STRNG	Returning	☑	☐	Type	STRING		

Figure 11-6. *Method: BEAD_STRINGS – Method Parameters*

You need to enter the exceptions. Click the *Exceptions* tab. The screen with the exception 'NO_DATA' entered will look like Figure 11-7.

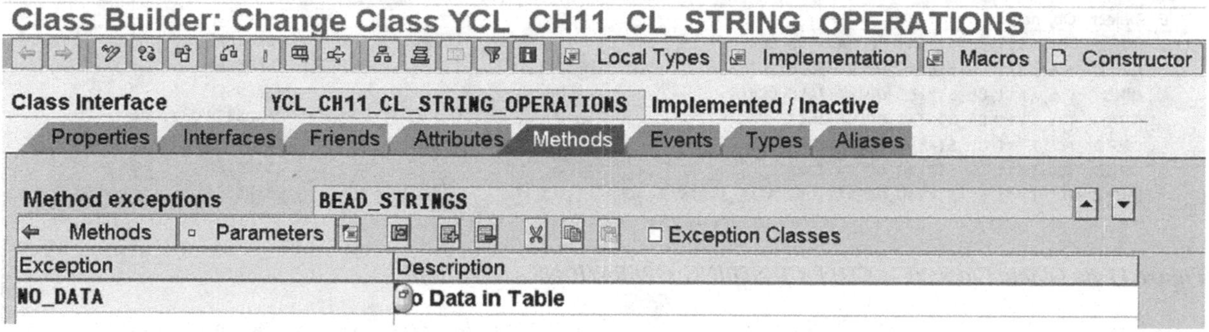

Class Builder: Change Class YCL_CH11_CL_STRING_OPERATIONS

Class Interface YCL_CH11_CL_STRING_OPERATIONS Implemented / Inactive

Properties | Interfaces | Friends | Attributes | Methods | Events | Types | Aliases

Method exceptions BEAD_STRINGS

Exception	Description
NO_DATA	No Data in Table

Figure 11-7. *Method: BEAD_STRINGS – Method Exceptions*

Click on the *Methods* button to return to the methods screen. You have to enter the program code for the method. So double click on the method name. The screen will prompt for saving. Click the Save button. The screen then will present the template for the method:

```
method BEAD_STRINGS.
endmethod.
```

Copy the lines from the local class method between the lines method... and end method.

```
method BEAD_STRINGS.

DESCRIBE TABLE STR_TAB..

 IF SY-TFILL = 0.
  MESSAGE S035(YCL_CH07_MCLASS01) RAISING
   NO_DATA.
 ENDIF.
```

```
 LOOP AT STR_TAB INTO STR.
   IF SY-TABIX > 1.
     CONCATENATE STRNG STR INTO STRNG SEPARATED
      BY SEPARATOR.
   ELSE.
     STRNG = STR.
   ENDIF.
 ENDLOOP.

endmethod.
```

Perform a syntax check of the program code. Go back to the method screen. Check for consistency. Activate the class. The class activation involves multiple components, and the screen will look like Figure 11-8.

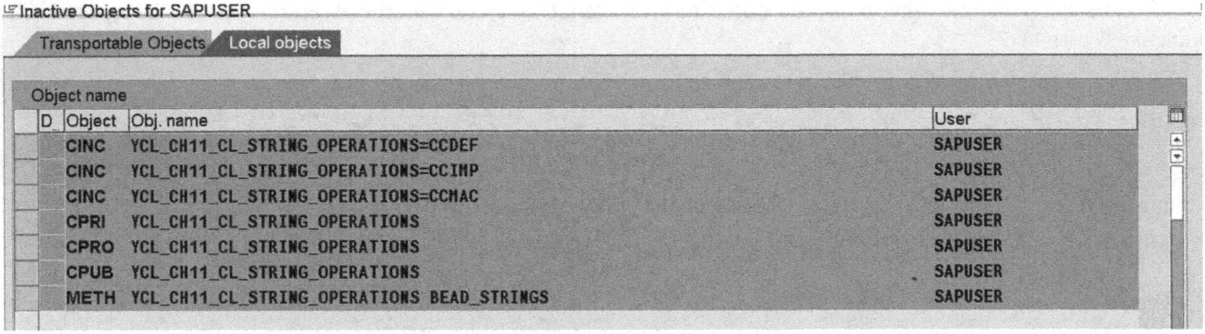

Inactive Objects for SAPUSER

Transportable Objects | Local objects

Object name

D	Object	Obj. name	User
	CINC	YCL_CH11_CL_STRING_OPERATIONS=CCDEF	SAPUSER
	CINC	YCL_CH11_CL_STRING_OPERATIONS=CCIMP	SAPUSER
	CINC	YCL_CH11_CL_STRING_OPERATIONS=CCMAC	SAPUSER
	CPRI	YCL_CH11_CL_STRING_OPERATIONS	SAPUSER
	CPRO	YCL_CH11_CL_STRING_OPERATIONS	SAPUSER
	CPUB	YCL_CH11_CL_STRING_OPERATIONS	SAPUSER
	METH	YCL_CH11_CL_STRING_OPERATIONS BEAD_STRINGS	SAPUSER

Figure 11-8. *Global Class: YCL_CH11_CL_STRING_OPERATIONS – Activation*

The class is ready for use. The ABAP program code where the method BEAD_STRINGS of this class is being used:

```
REPORT YCL_CH11_02_BEAD_STRINGS_GCLAS.

*********************************************
* Use Method BEAD_STRINGS in Global Class: **
* YCL_CH10_CL_STRING_OPERATIONS            **
*********************************************

DATA: CL_REF       TYPE REF TO YCL_CH11_CL_STRING_OPERATIONS,
      RESULT       TYPE STRING,
      STRING_TABL TYPE STRING_TABLE.


START-OF-SELECTION.

SELECT LTX FROM T247 INTO TABLE STRING_TABL
  WHERE SPRAS = SY-LANGU.

CREATE OBJECT CL_REF.
```

```
*CALL METHOD CL_REF->BEAD_STRINGS
*  EXPORTING
*    STR_TAB   = STRING_TAB
*    SEPARATOR = '-'
*  RECEIVING
*    STRNG     = RESULT
*  EXCEPTIONS
*    NO_DATA   = 1
*    others    = 2
*        .
*IF SY-SUBRC <> 0.
* MESSAGE ID SY-MSGID TYPE SY-MSGTY NUMBER SY-MSGNO
*            WITH SY-MSGV1 SY-MSGV2 SY-MSGV3 SY-MSGV4.
*ENDIF.


RESULT = CL_REF->BEAD_STRINGS( STR_TAB   = STRING_TABL[]
                               SEPARATOR = '-' ).
IF SY-SUBRC <> 0.

 MESSAGE ID SY-MSGID TYPE SY-MSGTY NUMBER SY-MSGNO
         WITH SY-MSGV1 SY-MSGV2 SY-MSGV3 SY-MSGV4
         DISPLAY LIKE 'E'.
ELSE.

 WRITE:/5 RESULT.
ENDIF.
```

The output is the same as that obtained with the local class (Figure 11-9).

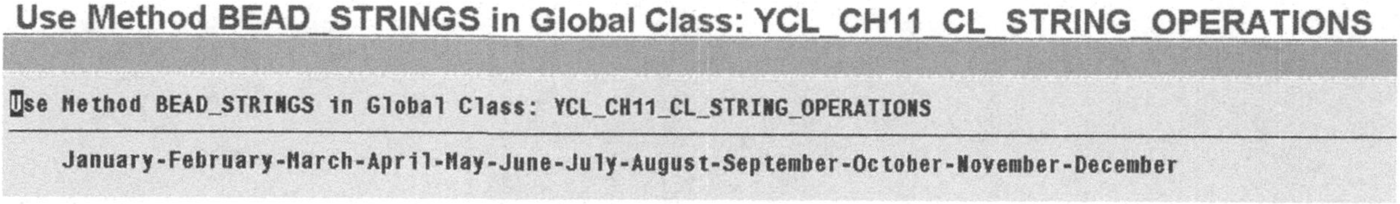

Use Method BEAD_STRINGS in Global Class: YCL_CH11_CL_STRING_OPERATIONS

Use Method BEAD_STRINGS in Global Class: YCL_CH11_CL_STRING_OPERATIONS

January-February-March-April-May-June-July-August-September-October-November-December

Figure 11-9. *Program: YCL_CH11_02_BEAD_STRINGS_GCLAS - Output*

You were generating the program code for calling a function module in Chapter 7 entitled 'Modularization' (inside the ABAP editor, the menu option: Edit ➤ Pattern etc.). The same facility can be availed to generate program code for calling a method. The screen when you choose, inside the ABAP editor, the menu option Edit ➤ Pattern is shown in Figure 11-10.

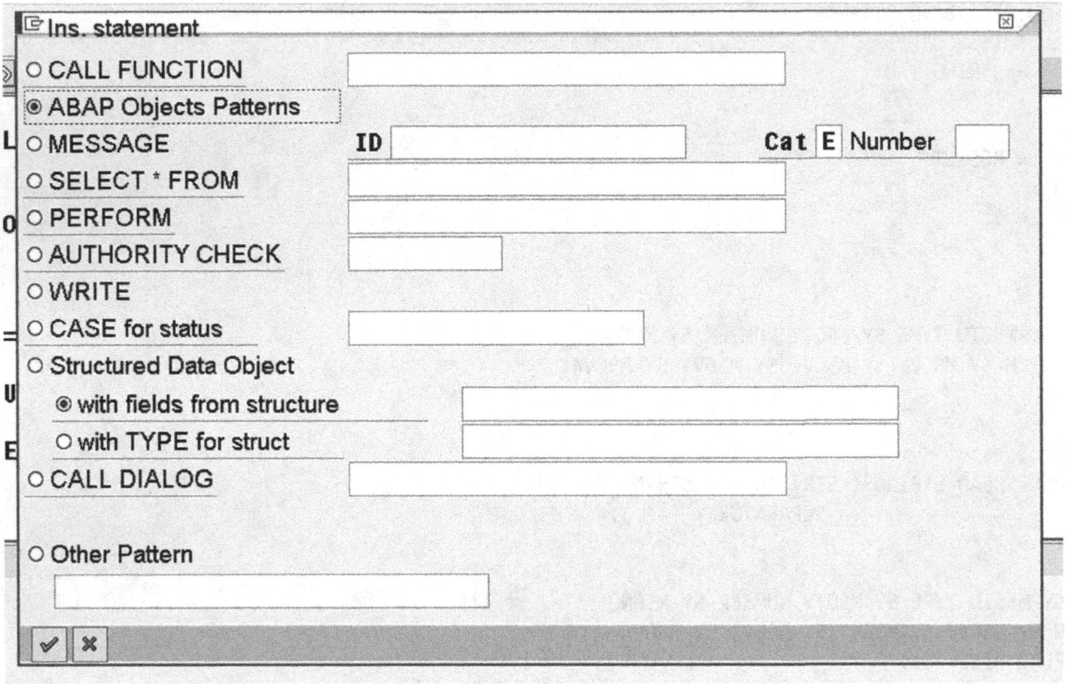

Figure 11-10. *Generate Code - ABAP Editor Option: Edit ➤ Pattern*

Click on the second radio button ABAP Objects Patterns. Press the continue button/<enter key>. The screen with the entered values will appear like Figure 11-11.

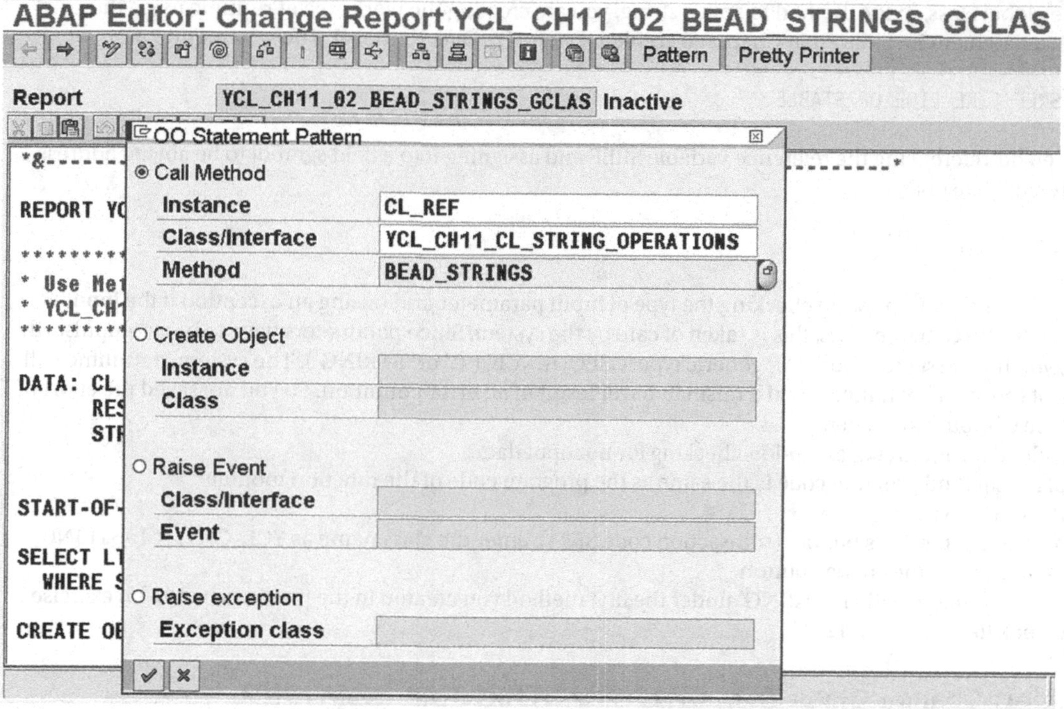

ABAP Editor: Change Report YCL_CH11_02_BEAD_STRINGS_GCLAS

Pattern Pretty Printer

Report YCL_CH11_02_BEAD_STRINGS_GCLAS Inactive

OO Statement Pattern

◉ Call Method
Instance: CL_REF
Class/Interface: YCL_CH11_CL_STRING_OPERATIONS
Method: BEAD_STRINGS

○ Create Object
Instance
Class

○ Raise Event
Class/Interface
Event

○ Raise exception
Exception class

Figure 11-11. *Generate Code – For Calling a Method*

You entered the name of the reference variable (instance or object), the global class name, and selected the method of the class from the selection list.

In this dialogue box, you can generate program code for CREARE OBJECT..., RAISE EVENT..., and RAISE EXCEPTION statements by selection of respective radio buttons.

You created a global class in the class builder and declared and implemented a method in this global class. Then you invoked the method from an executable ABAP program.

Hands-on Exercise: Global Class (Method to Split a String without Breaking a Word)

In Chapter 7, entitled 'Modularization,' you created a function module that split a string into multiple strings of specified length in characters without breaking a word. The name of this function module was YCL_CH07_SPLIT_STRING. You will now implement the same functionality in a method using the global class you created in the previous exercise.

The function modules accept the type *TABLES* parameter. This type of parameter is not available for methods of a class (only *IMPORTING, EXPORTING, CHANGING,* and *RETURNING*). With a *TABLES* parameter in a function module, you were implicitly getting a work area of the same name (HEADER LINE) as the formal 'TABLES' parameter name. In the present context, the work area is expected to be an elementary TYPE 'C' data object. You need the work area to determine the length in characters of the output string as well needing it in the APPEND statement.

Within the global class, in the method to split a string, you are creating the work area at runtime using the CREATE DATA... statement introduced in Chapter 8 entitled 'Open SQL Data Retrieval.' The statement:

```
CREATE DATA SREF LIKE LINE OF STABLE.
```

You are then de-referencing the reference variable SREF and assigning it to a field symbol to be able to address the runtime created data object:

```
ASSIGN SREF->* TO <WA>.
```

In the function module, you were checking the type of input parameter and raising an exception if the input type is not 'C' or 'STRING.' In the class, this is taken of care by the system. Since parameters have to be a compulsorily assigned type, you have assigned the ABAP generic type 'CSEQUENCE' ('C' or' STRING'). The system at runtime will check the type of the actual parameter, and a mismatch will result in an error condition. So you are saved the effort of checking the type of input parameter.

You have added an additional exception checking for no input data.

The rest of the method program code is the same as the program code of the function module YCL_CH07_SPLIT_STRING.

You can navigate to the class builder (transaction code SE24); enter the class name as YCL_CH11_CL_STRING_OPERATIONS and click on the change button.

Enter the method name 'SPLIT_STRING' under the first method you created in the previous hands-on exercise. The screen will look like Figure 11-12.

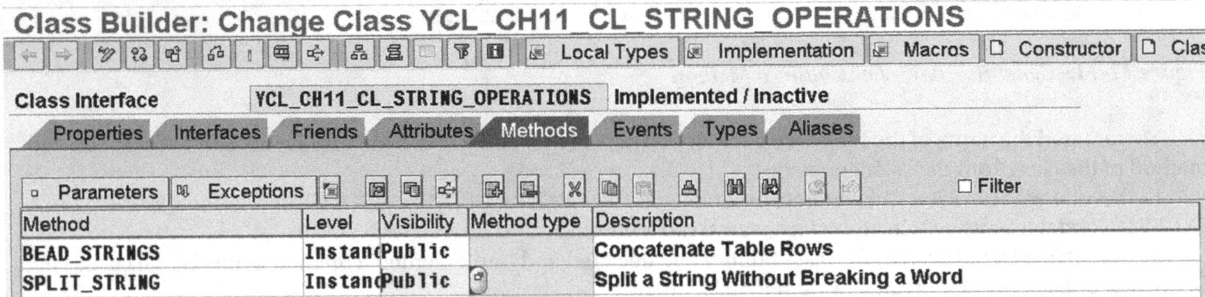

Figure 11-12. Class: YCL_CH11_CL_STRING_OPERATIONS – Method 'SPLIT_STRING'

Position the cursor on the second row (i.e., method 'SPLIT_STRING'). Click on the Parameters button. The screen after entry of the parameters will look like Figure 11-13.

Class Builder: Change Class YCL_CH11_CL_STRING_OPERATIONS

Local Types | Implementation | Macros | Constructor | Class constructor

Class Interface: YCL_CH11_CL_STRING_OPERATIONS Implemented / Inactive

Properties | Interfaces | Friends | Attributes | Methods | Events | Types | Aliases

Method parameters: SPLIT_STRING

Methods | Exceptions

Parameter	Type	Pass Value	Optional	Typing M	Associated Type	Default value	Description
STRING_TO_SPLIT	Importing	☑	☐	Type	CSEQUENCE		String to Split
STABLE	Exporting	☑	☐	Type	STANDARD TABLE		Table to Return Split String

Figure 11-13. Method SPLIT_STRING: Parameters

Click on the Exceptions button. The screen after entry of Exceptions will look like Figure 11-14.

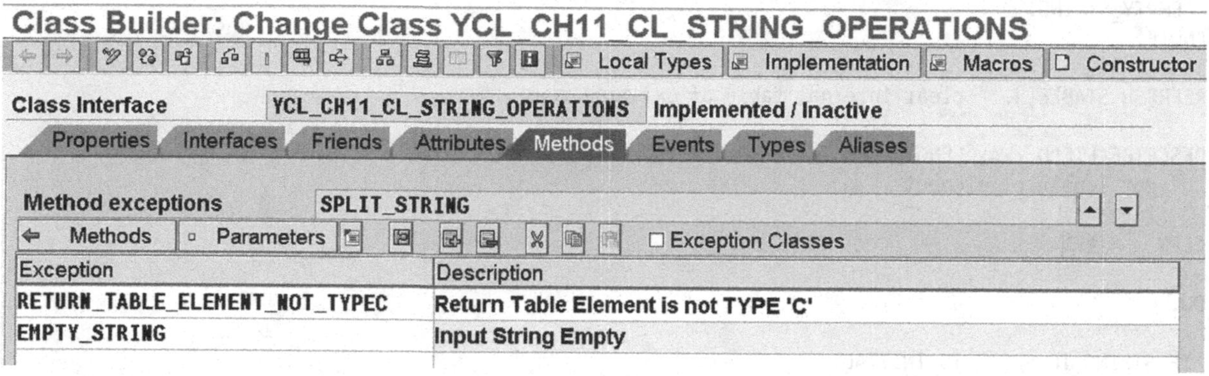

Class Builder: Change Class YCL_CH11_CL_STRING_OPERATIONS

Local Types | Implementation | Macros | Constructor

Class Interface YCL_CH11_CL_STRING_OPERATIONS Implemented / Inactive

Properties | Interfaces | Friends | Attributes | Methods | Events | Types | Aliases

Method exceptions SPLIT_STRING

Methods | Parameters | Exception Classes

Exception	Description
RETURN_TABLE_ELEMENT_NOT_TYPEC	Return Table Element is not TYPE 'C'
EMPTY_STRING	Input String Empty

Figure 11-14. *Method SPLIT_STRING: Exceptions*

Click on the Method button. Then double click on the method 'SPLIT_STRING'. The screen will present the method template in Figure 11-15.

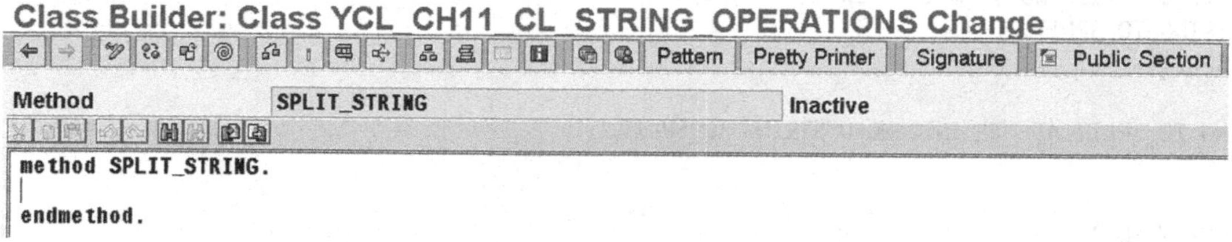

Class Builder: Class YCL_CH11_CL_STRING_OPERATIONS Change

Pattern | Pretty Printer | Signature | Public Section

Method SPLIT_STRING Inactive

```
method SPLIT_STRING.

endmethod.
```

Figure 11-15. *Method SPLIT_STRING: Method Template*

The program code of the method:

```
method SPLIT_STRING.

DATA: WORD       TYPE STRING, " store extracted word
      TYP(1)     TYPE C,      " store variable TYPE
      LEN        TYPE I,      " store length of string
      CLEN       TYPE I,      " store available characters/columns
      WLEN       TYPE I,      " store extracted word length
      SREF       TYPE REF TO DATA. " ref variable for line of STABLE

FIELD-SYMBOLS: <WA> TYPE ANY. " field symbol to address line of STABLE
***********************************
CREATE DATA SREF LIKE LINE OF STABLE.
ASSIGN SREF->* TO <WA>.
DESCRIBE FIELD <WA> TYPE TYP. " <WA> reference to the elementary
                              " data item i.e. line of STABLE
IF TYP <> 'C' .
 MESSAGE S007(YCL_CH07_MCLASS01) RAISING
  RETURN_TABLE_ELEMENT_NOT_TYPEC.
ENDIF.
```

```
IF STRING_TO_SPLIT  IS INITIAL.
 MESSAGE S035(YCL_CH07_MCLASS01) RAISING
  EMPTY_STRING.
ENDIF.

REFRESH STABLE[]. " clear internal table of existing rows

DESCRIBE FIELD <WA> LENGTH LEN IN CHARACTER MODE.
  " get length of element

CLEN   = LEN.

DO.

 IF STRING_TO_SPLIT IS INITIAL.
  EXIT.
 ENDIF.

 SEARCH STRING_TO_SPLIT FOR '. .'. " SEARCH for embedded blank

 IF SY-SUBRC <> 0. "last word in the text
  WORD   = STRING_TO_SPLIT.
  STRING_TO_SPLIT = ''.
 ELSE.
  SPLIT STRING_TO_SPLIT AT ' ' INTO WORD STRING_TO_SPLIT.
 ENDIF.

 WLEN = STRLEN( WORD ).

 IF SY-INDEX = 1.
  <WA> = WORD.
 ELSEIF WLEN <= CLEN.
  CONCATENATE <WA> WORD INTO <WA> SEPARATED BY ' '.
 ELSE.
  APPEND <WA> TO STABLE[].
  <WA> = WORD.
  CLEN = LEN.
 ENDIF.

 CLEN = CLEN - WLEN - 1.
ENDDO.

IF <WA> <> ' '.
 APPEND <WA> TO STABLE[].
ENDIF.
endmethod.
```

You have declared data inside the method. This is local to the method. In the previous method 'BEAD_STRINGS,' you were using an attribute 'STR' declared in the 'PRIVATE' section of the class. You could have as well declared this inside the class. The idea was to create an attribute. An attribute in the 'PRIVATE' section of a class can be accessed by the entire class, and data declared within a method can be accessed only within that method.

Save, perform a consistency check, and reactivate the class YCL_CH11_STRING_OPERATIONS again. The activating screen is shown in Figure 11-16.

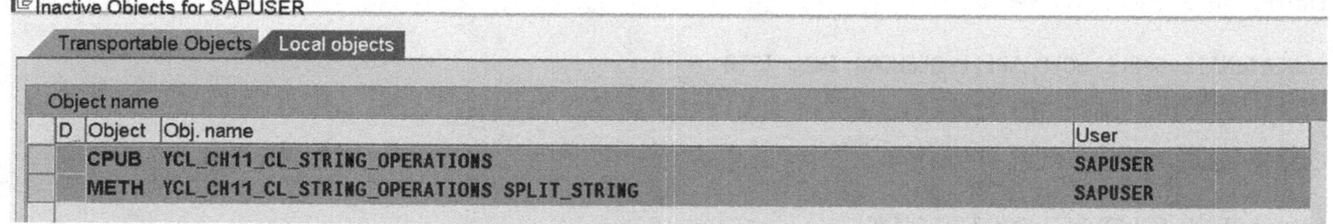

Figure 11-16. *Class: YCL_CH11_CL_STRING_OPERATIONS - Reactivation*

The source program using this method is, first, calling the function module SPELL_AMOUNT, which is converting the input figure or amount into one line of text. Next, you are calling the method 'SPLIT_STRING' to split the one line of text into multiple lines.

The source:

```
REPORT YCL_CH11_03_SPLIT_STRING_GCLAS.

***************************************
* Call Method SPLIT_STRING In Class:   **
* YCL_CH11_CL_STRING_OPERATIONS        **
***************************************

DATA: STRG(30)  TYPE C,
      STRGA     LIKE STANDARD TABLE OF STRG,
      ISTR      TYPE STRING,
      SPELL     TYPE SPELL,
      SPLIT_REF TYPE REF TO YCL_CH11_CL_STRING_OPERATIONS.
*****************************************************

PARAMETERS: AMT(7) TYPE P DECIMALS 2 DEFAULT
    '987654321.50'.

START-OF-SELECTION.

CALL FUNCTION 'SPELL_AMOUNT'
 EXPORTING
   AMOUNT           =  AMT
   CURRENCY         = 'INR'
   FILLER           = ' '
   LANGUAGE         = SY-LANGU
 IMPORTING
   IN_WORDS         = SPELL
 EXCEPTIONS
   NOT_FOUND        = 1
   TOO_LARGE        = 2
   OTHERS           = 3
          .
```

```
IF SY-SUBRC <> 0.
 MESSAGE ID SY-MSGID TYPE SY-MSGTY NUMBER SY-MSGNO
         WITH SY-MSGV1 SY-MSGV2 SY-MSGV3 SY-MSGV4.
ENDIF.

CONCATENATE SPELL-WORD SPELL-DECWORD INTO ISTR
  SEPARATED BY ' '.

CREATE OBJECT SPLIT_REF.

CALL METHOD SPLIT_REF->SPLIT_STRING
  EXPORTING
    STRING_TO_SPLIT                = ISTR
  IMPORTING
    STABLE                         = STRGA
  EXCEPTIONS
    RETURN_TABLE_ELEMENT_NOT_TYPEC = 1
    EMPTY_STRING                   = 2
    others                         = 3
        .
IF SY-SUBRC <> 0.
 MESSAGE ID SY-MSGID TYPE SY-MSGTY NUMBER SY-MSGNO
            WITH SY-MSGV1 SY-MSGV2 SY-MSGV3 SY-MSGV4
            DISPLAY LIKE 'E'.

ELSE.

 LOOP AT STRGA INTO STRG.
  WRITE:/5 STRG.
 ENDLOOP.

ENDIF.
```

The input and output screens will be like those in Figures 11-17 and 11-18.

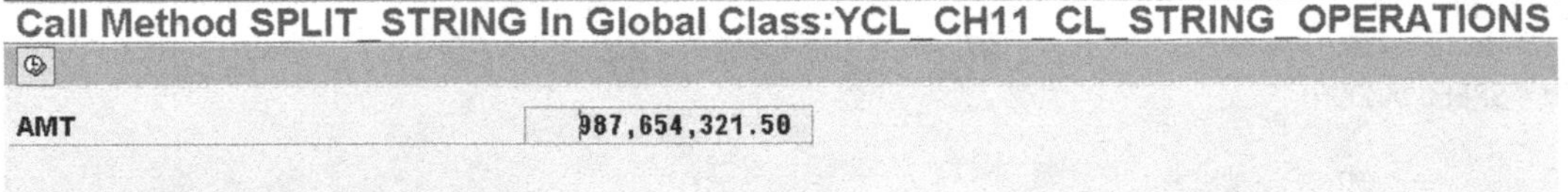

Figure 11-17. *Program: YCL_CH11_03_SPLIT_STRING_GCLAS - Input*

Call Method SPLIT_STRING In Global Class:YCL_CH11_CL_STRING_OPERATIONS

```
Call Method SPLIT_STRING In Global Class:YCL_CH11_CL_STRING_OPERATIONS

    Input Number: 987,654,321.50

    NINE HUNDREDEIGHTY-SEVEN
    MILLION SIX HUNDRED FIFTY-FOUR
    THOUSAND THREE
    HUNDREDTWENTY-ONE FIFTY
```

Figure 11-18. *Program: YCL_CH11_03_SPLIT_STRING_GCLAS - Output*

You located another method in an existing global class created in the preceding hands-on exercise. The method splits a line of string into multiple lines without breaking a word. The method implements functionality implemented earlier with a function module in Chapter 7.

Hands-on Exercise: Define Local Interface, Implement Interface Method in Local Classes (Method to Fetch Business Partner Name & Address)

Scenario

Customers and vendors/suppliers are business partners. Given the code of the business partner, fetching the name and address of customers involves retrieving data from the database table KNA1, and fetching this same information of vendors involves retrieving data from the database table LFA1.

A local interface has been defined in which a method is declared. This method has an importing parameter as the business partner code and exporting parameters as the name and address of the business partner.

Two different local classes implement this method. One class retrieves name and address data from the database table KNA1, and the other class retrieves name and address data from the database table LFA1.

This could have been achieved with simple conditional statements without an interface and classes. The idea is to illustrate the usage of interface and its basic syntaxes as they exist in ABAP.

The source code:

```
REPORT YCL_CH10_04_LOCAL_IF_CLASS.

*****************************************************
* Demo local INTERFACE (polymorphism) and syntaxes **
*****************************************************

***********************************************************
* on the SELECTION-SCREEN input:                        **
* (1) business partner/partner type: customer or vendor **
* (2) customer/vendor code                              **
*                                                       **
* using the feature of INTERFACE declared method and this**
* method implemented in two different classes, the      **
* address of customer/vendor is retrieved and output    **
*                                                       **
```

```
* same method in different classes gets different info   **
*                                                         **
* the method GET_ADDRESS in class GET_CUST_ADDR retrieves**
* the customer address from database table KNA1           **
*                                                         **
* the method GET_ADDRESS in class GET_VEND_ADDR retrieves**
* the vendor address from database table LFA1             **
*                                                         **
* the name, address fields: NAME1 STRAS ORT01 PSTLZ are  **
* common/same in database tables KNA1 & LFA1              **
*                                                         **
* exception raised using MESSAGE statement. subsequently **
* class based exception is covered                        **
**********************************************************

TYPES: TYP_BPCODE(10)  TYPE C. " business partner code TYPE

CLASS: GET_CUST_ADDR DEFINITION DEFERRED, " CLASS yet to be defined
       GET_VEND_ADDR DEFINITION DEFERRED. " ditto

INTERFACE: IF_GET_PARTNER_ADDR DEFERRED.
              " INTERFACE yet to be declared

DATA: CUST_ADDR        TYPE REF TO GET_CUST_ADDR,
                              " customer address

      VEND_ADDR        TYPE REF TO GET_VEND_ADDR,
                              " vendor address

      IF_PARTNER_ADDR TYPE REF TO IF_GET_PARTNER_ADDR,

      PARTNER_TP(1)    TYPE C VALUE 'C',
      BPCODE           TYPE TYP_BPCODE,
      NAME1            TYPE NAME1_GP,
      STRAS            TYPE STRAS_GP,
      ORT01            TYPE ORT01_GP,
      PSTLZ            TYPE PSTLZ.

******************** INTERFACE ************************

INTERFACE IF_GET_PARTNER_ADDR.
   "convention: start interface names with IF_

  METHODS: GET_ADDRESS IMPORTING  VALUE(BPCODE) TYPE TYP_BPCODE
                       EXPORTING  PNAME         TYPE NAME1_GP
                                  PSTREET       TYPE STRAS_GP
                                  PCITY         TYPE ORT01_GP
                                  PPIN          TYPE PSTLZ
                       EXCEPTIONS INVALID_CODE.
```

```
ENDINTERFACE.

****** class definition, implementation for customer info ******

CLASS GET_CUST_ADDR DEFINITION. "custmer address

 PUBLIC SECTION.
  INTERFACES IF_GET_PARTNER_ADDR.
            "interfaces used by class specified

 PRIVATE SECTION.
   DATA:  KNA1            TYPE KNA1.

ENDCLASS.

CLASS GET_CUST_ADDR IMPLEMENTATION.

 METHOD IF_GET_PARTNER_ADDR~GET_ADDRESS.
  "qualifying interface method in this way with ~ (tilde)

  SELECT SINGLE * FROM KNA1 INTO KNA1 WHERE KUNNR = BPCODE.

  IF SY-SUBRC <> 0.
   MESSAGE S036(YCL_CH07_MCLASS01) RAISING
    INVALID_CODE WITH BPCODE.
  ENDIF.

  PNAME    = KNA1-NAME1.
  PSTREET  = KNA1-STRAS.
  PCITY    = KNA1-ORT01.
  PPIN     = KNA1-PSTLZ.
 ENDMETHOD.

ENDCLASS.

****** class definition, implementation for vendor info ******

CLASS GET_VEND_ADDR DEFINITION.

 PUBLIC SECTION.
  INTERFACES IF_GET_PARTNER_ADDR.
            "interfaces used by class specified like this

 PRIVATE SECTION.
  DATA:  LFA1 TYPE LFA1.

ENDCLASS.

CLASS GET_VEND_ADDR IMPLEMENTATION.

 METHOD IF_GET_PARTNER_ADDR~GET_ADDRESS.
  "qualifying interface method in this way with ~ (tilde)
```

```
  SELECT SINGLE * FROM LFA1 INTO LFA1 WHERE LIFNR = BPCODE.

  IF SY-SUBRC <> 0.
   MESSAGE S037(YCL_CH07_MCLASS01) RAISING
    INVALID_CODE WITH BPCODE.
  ENDIF.

  PNAME    = LFA1-NAME1.
  PSTREET  = LFA1-STRAS.
  PCITY    = LFA1-ORT01.
  PPIN     = LFA1-PSTLZ.
 ENDMETHOD.

ENDCLASS.

********************
* SELECTION-SCREEN **
********************

SELECTION-SCREEN SKIP 1.

SELECTION-SCREEN BEGIN OF BLOCK BL1 WITH FRAME TITLE
  COM1 NO INTERVALS.

SELECTION-SCREEN SKIP 1.

  SELECTION-SCREEN BEGIN OF LINE.
   PARAMETERS: CUST RADIOBUTTON GROUP GR1 USER-COMMAND
    PART_TYPE DEFAULT 'X'.
   SELECTION-SCREEN COMMENT 3(15) COM2.

   PARAMETERS: VEND RADIOBUTTON GROUP GR1.
   SELECTION-SCREEN COMMENT 21(15) COM3.
  SELECTION-SCREEN END OF LINE.

  SELECTION-SCREEN SKIP 1.

  SELECTION-SCREEN BEGIN OF LINE.
   SELECTION-SCREEN COMMENT 1(14) COM4 FOR FIELD CUST_CD
     MODIF ID CG1.
   PARAMETERS: CUST_CD LIKE KNA1-KUNNR MODIF ID CG1.
  SELECTION-SCREEN END OF LINE.

  SELECTION-SCREEN BEGIN OF LINE.
   SELECTION-SCREEN COMMENT 1(14) COM5 MODIF ID CG2
     FOR FIELD VEND_CD.
   PARAMETERS:  VEND_CD LIKE LFA1-LIFNR VALUE CHECK
     MODIF ID CG2.
  SELECTION-SCREEN END OF LINE.

 SELECTION-SCREEN SKIP 1.
```

```
SELECTION-SCREEN END OF BLOCK BL1.

*********************************
INITIALIZATION.
COM1 = '----- Select Business Partner Type -----'(001).
COM4 = 'Customer Code:'(004).
COM5 = 'Vendor Code:'(005).
COM2 = 'Customer'(002).
COM3 = 'Vendor'(003).

********************************************
********************************************
AT SELECTION-SCREEN OUTPUT.
IF CUST = 'X'.
 PARTNER_TP = 'C'.
ELSE.
 PARTNER_TP = 'V'.
ENDIF.

LOOP AT SCREEN .
 IF SCREEN-GROUP1 <> 'CG1' AND SCREEN-GROUP1 <> 'CG2'.
  CONTINUE.
 ENDIF.

 IF ( SCREEN-GROUP1 = 'CG1' AND PARTNER_TP = 'C' ) OR
    ( SCREEN-GROUP1 = 'CG2' AND PARTNER_TP = 'V' ).

  SCREEN-INPUT     = 1.
  SCREEN-ACTIVE    = 1.
  SCREEN-INVISIBLE = 0.

 ELSEIF ( SCREEN-GROUP1 = 'CG1' AND PARTNER_TP <> 'C' ) OR
        ( SCREEN-GROUP1 = 'CG2' AND PARTNER_TP <> 'V' ).

  SCREEN-INPUT     = 0.
  SCREEN-ACTIVE    = 0.
  SCREEN-INVISIBLE = 1.
 ENDIF.

 MODIFY SCREEN.

ENDLOOP.

**************** main processing **************

START-OF-SELECTION.

CREATE OBJECT CUST_ADDR.

CREATE OBJECT VEND_ADDR.
```

```
IF CUST = 'X'.

 BPCODE = CUST_CD.
  IF_PARTNER_ADDR = CUST_ADDR. " UP/WIDE CASTING

ELSE.

 BPCODE = VEND_CD.
 IF_PARTNER_ADDR = VEND_ADDR. " UP/WIDE CASTING
ENDIF.
********************

CALL METHOD IF_PARTNER_ADDR->GET_ADDRESS
  EXPORTING
              BPCODE    = BPCODE
  IMPORTING
              PNAME     = NAME1
              PSTREET   = STRAS
              PCITY     = ORT01
              PPIN      = PSTLZ
              EXCEPTIONS INVALID_CODE = 4.

IF SY-SUBRC <> 0.

 MESSAGE ID SY-MSGID TYPE SY-MSGTY NUMBER SY-MSGNO
         WITH SY-MSGV1 SY-MSGV2 SY-MSGV3 SY-MSGV4
         DISPLAY LIKE 'E'.

ELSE.

 WRITE /5: BPCODE USING NO EDIT MASK,
           NAME1, STRAS, ORT01, PSTLZ.
ENDIF.
**********************************************
```

The text symbol screen is shown in Figure 11-19.

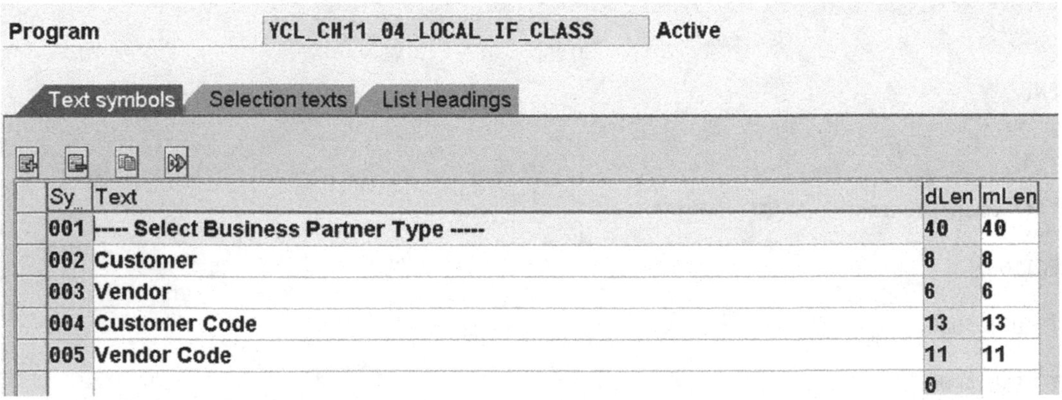

Program YCL_CH11_04_LOCAL_IF_CLASS Active

Text symbols | Selection texts | List Headings

Sy	Text	dLen	mLen
001	----- Select Business Partner Type -----	40	40
002	Customer	8	8
003	Vendor	6	6
004	Customer Code	13	13
005	Vendor Code	11	11
		0	

Figure 11-19. *Program: YCL_CH11_04_LOCAL_IF_CLASS – Text Symbols*

The customer input screen is shown in Figure 11-20.

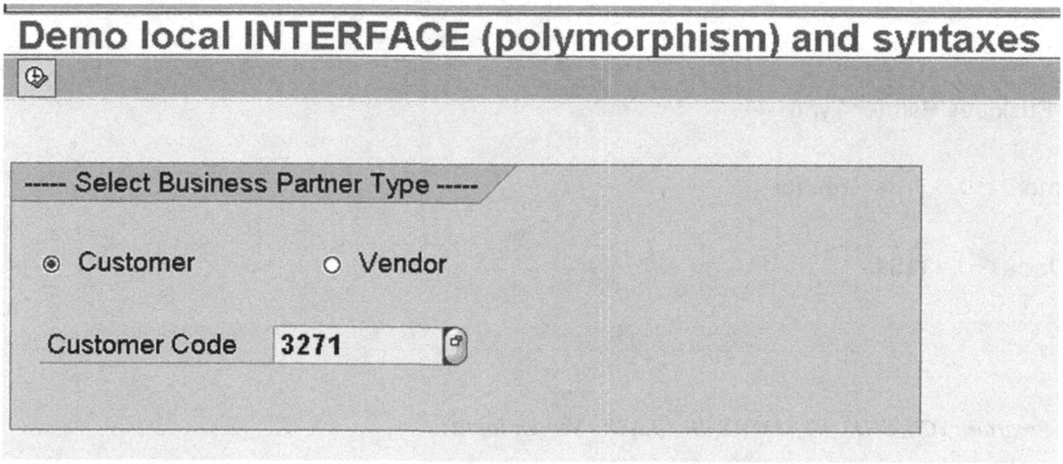

Demo local INTERFACE (polymorphism) and syntaxes

----- Select Business Partner Type -----

◉ Customer ○ Vendor

Customer Code 3271

Figure 11-20. *Program: YCL_CH11_04_LOCAL_IF_CLASS - Customer Input*

The customer output screen:

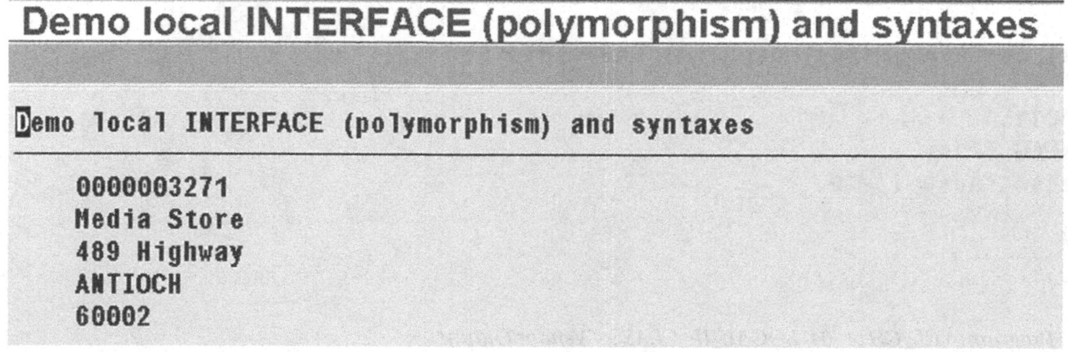

Figure 11-21. *Program: YCL_CH11_04_LOCAL_IF_CLASS - Customer Output*

The vendor input screen:

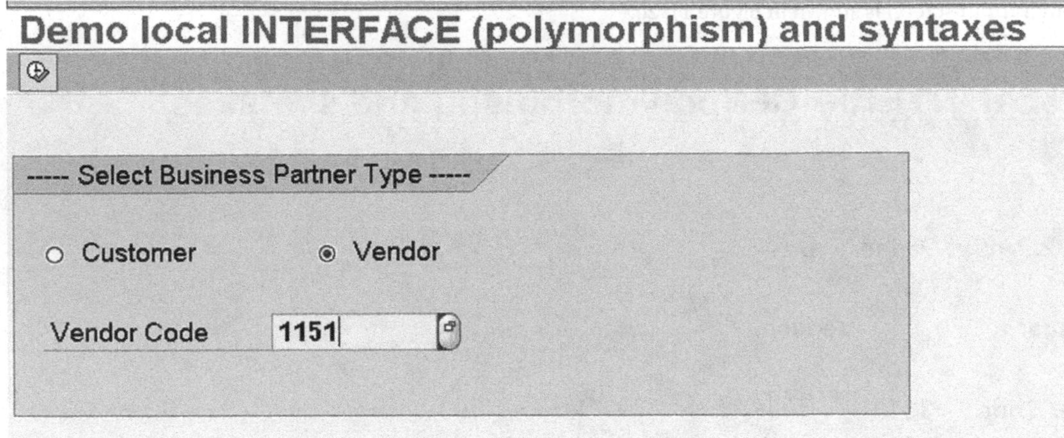

Figure 11-22. *Program: YCL_CH11_04_LOCAL_IF_CLASS – Vendor Input*

The vendor output screen:

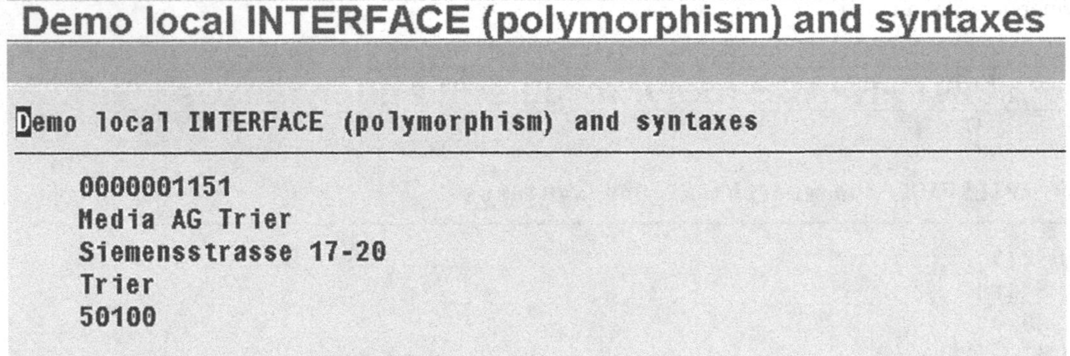

Figure 11-23. *Program: YCL_CH11_04_LOCAL_IF_CLASS – Vendor Output*

The screen for an error condition:

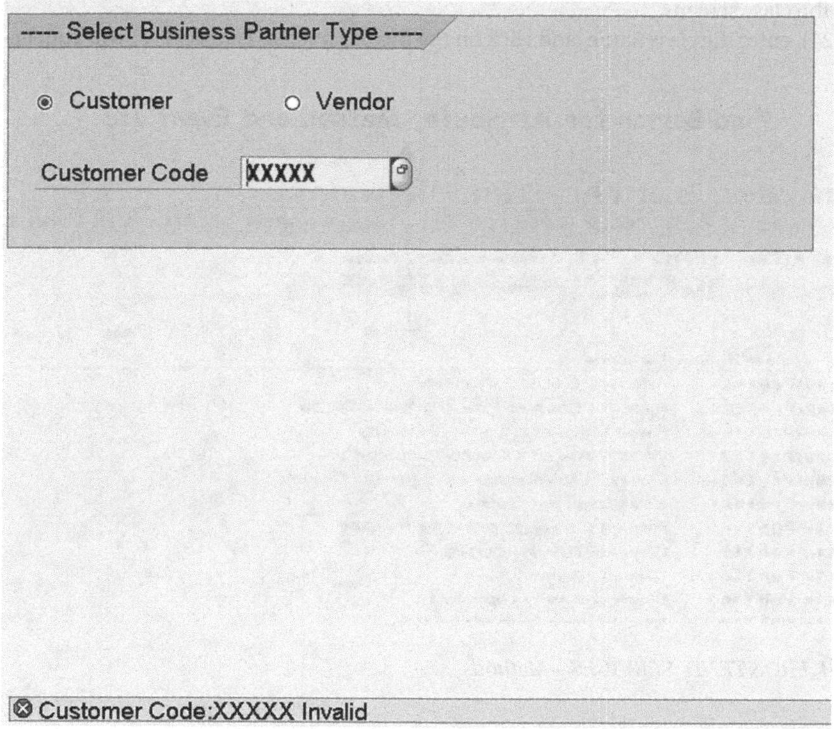

Figure 11-24. *Program: YCL_CH11_04_LOCAL_IF_CLASS - Input Error Condition*

This was an illustration of generalization (business partner) and specialization (business partner: customers, and business partner: vendors). Polymorphism was implemented using interfaces. A similar illustration of polymorphism using inheritance is implemented in the program YCL_CH11_04A_LOCAL_INH_CLASS. The program is not listed here. It is available in the E-Resource.

Hands-on Exercise: Use Methods of SAP Delivered Class 'CL_GUI_FRONTEND_SERVICES'

Tour of Class CL_GUI_FRONTEND_SERVICES

The built-in class CL_GUI_FRONTEND_SERVICES offers functionalities-methods associated with the presentation server or the front end.

You will use the following methods of this class in the current exercise:

- FILE_OPEN_DIALOG - This method enables a selection of an operating system file located on the presentation server. The method presents a dialogue box with the folders/files list to enable an end user to make file selections. There is a provision to make single or multiple file selection.
- FILE_EXIST - This method checks for the existence of a given file on the presentation server. This is a function method, and it takes the file name as an input parameter and returns a value 'X' if the file exists and blank if the file is nonexistent.
- GUI_DOWNLOAD - This method downloads the data of an internal table to a file on the presentation server. The main input parameters are the file name and file type (ASCII/BINARY), etc. If a file already exists, there is provision to overwrite/append to the existing file.

Let these methods be viewed in the class screens.

Navigate to the class builder (SE24), enter the class name, and click on the display button. Figure 11-25 will appear.

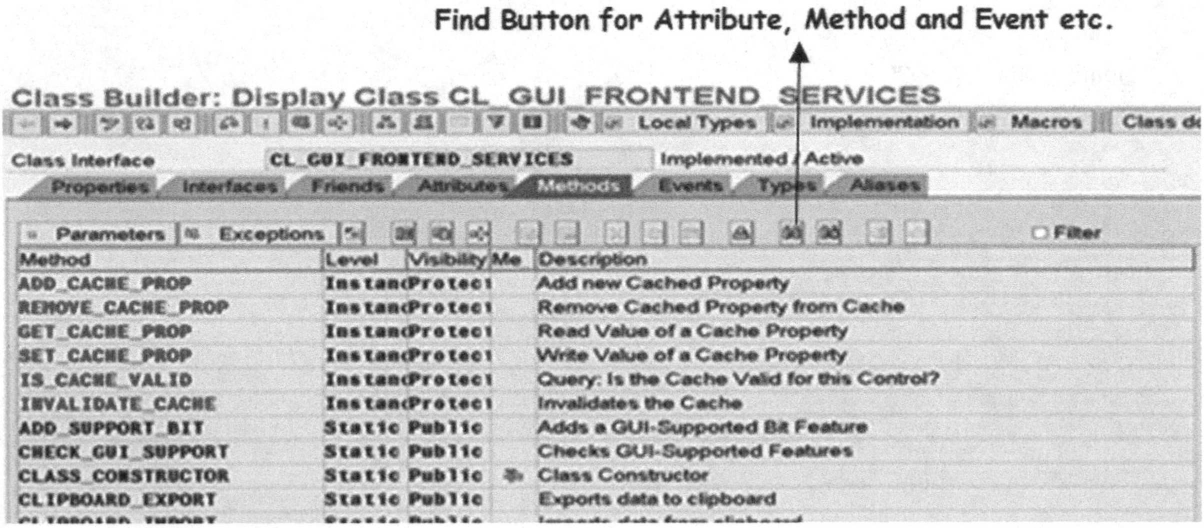

Figure 11-25. *Built-in Class: CL_GUI_FRONTEND_SERVICES – Methods*

Initial methods are appearing in blue, and they are the inherited methods of the super class: CL_GUI_OBJECT (click on the *Properties* tab and confirm this). You can use only the methods, attributes, and events with visibility *Public.*

Ensure you are on the *Methods* tab. Click on the find method/item button (the button with the arrow mark in Figure 11-25). Enter 'FILE_OPEN_DIALOG' in the find dialogue box and press continue button. The cursor will position on the method: FILE_OPEN_DIALOG, and the screen will appear like Figure 11-26.

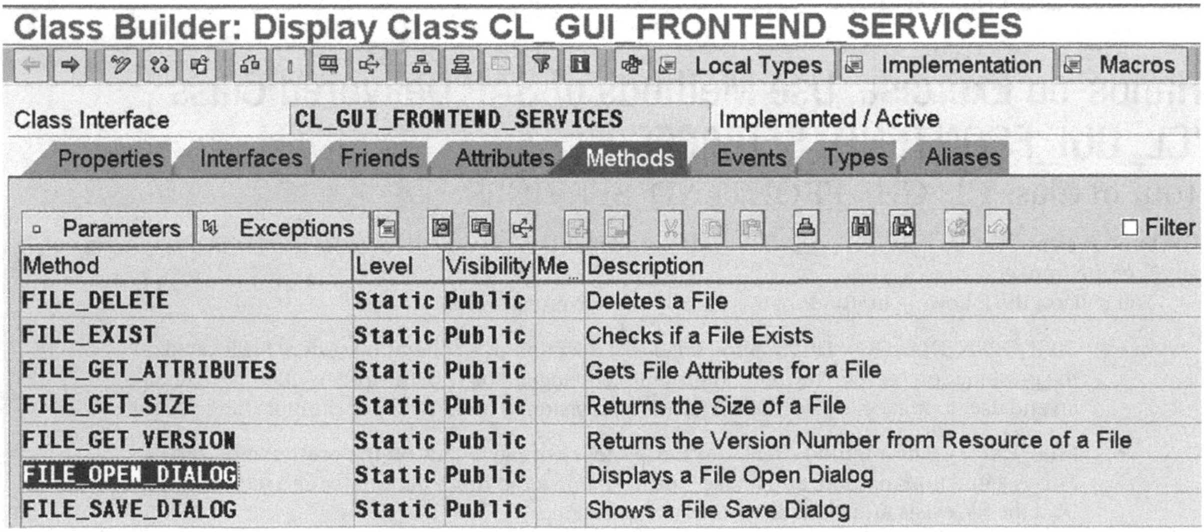

Figure 11-26. *Class:CL_GUI_FRONTEND_SERVISES – Method FILE_OPEN_DIALOG*

When you click on the parameters, you can view the parameters of this method. The screen for the parameters of method FILE_OPEN_DIALOG will look like Figure 11-27.

Class Builder: Display Class CL_GUI_FRONTEND_SERVICES

Local Types | Implementation | Macros | Class documentation

Class Interface CL_GUI_FRONTEND_SERVICES Implemented / Active

Properties | Interfaces | Friends | Attributes | Methods | Events | Types | Aliases

Method parameters FILE_OPEN_DIALOG

Methods | Exceptions

Parameter	Type	Pa	Op	Typing M	Associated Type	Default value	Description
WINDOW_TITLE	Importin	☑	☑	Type	STRING		Title Of File Open Dialog
DEFAULT_EXTENSION	Importin	☑	☑	Type	STRING		Default Extension
DEFAULT_FILENAME	Importin	☑	☑	Type	STRING		Default File Name
FILE_FILTER	Importin	☑	☑	Type	STRING		File Extension Filter String
WITH_ENCODING	Importin	☑	☑	Type	ABAP_BOOL		File Encoding
INITIAL_DIRECTORY	Importin	☑	☑	Type	STRING		Initial Directory
MULTISELECTION	Importin	☑	☑	Type	ABAP_BOOL		Multiple selections poss.
FILE_TABLE	Changin	☐	☐	Type	FILETABLE		Table Holding Selected Files
RC	Changin	☐	☐	Type	I		Return Code, Number of Files or -1 If Error Occurre
USER_ACTION	Changin	☐	☑	Type	I		User Action (See Class Constants ACTION_OK, AC
FILE_ENCODING	Changin	☐	☑	Type	ABAP_ENCODING		

Figure 11-27. *Class: CL_GUI_FRONTEND_SERVISES - Parameters of Method FILE_OPEN_DIALOG*

Navigate back to the *Methods* tab. Ensure that you vertically scrolled to the top, so that search for a method starts at the beginning. Click on the find button (under the tabs). Enter the method name 'FILE_EXIST' in the dialogue box, and press continue. The cursor will position on the method FILE_EXIST as shown in Figure 11-28.

Class Builder: Display Class CL_GUI_FRONTEND_SERVICES

Local Types | Implementation | Macros | Class documentation

Class Interface CL_GUI_FRONTEND_SERVICES Implemented / Active

Properties | Interfaces | Friends | Attributes | Methods | Events | Types | Aliases

Parameters | Exceptions ☐ Filter

Method	Level	Visi	Me	Description
FILE_EXIST	Static	Publi		Checks if a File Exists
FILE_GET_ATTRIBUTES	Static	Publi		Gets File Attributes for a File
FILE_GET_SIZE	Static	Publi		Returns the Size of a File

Figure 11-28. *Class: CL_GUI_FRONTEND_SERVISES - Method FILE_EXIST*

When you click on the parameters, you can view the parameters of this method. The screen for the parameters of method FILE_EXIST is shown in Figure 11-29.

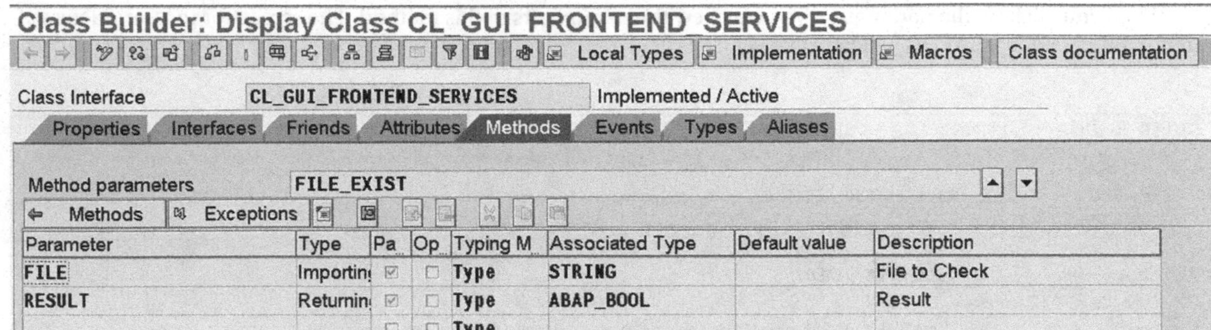

Figure 11-29. *Class: CL_GUI_FRONTEND_SERVISES - Parameters of Method FILE_EXIST*

A similar exercise can be done for location and viewing of the method GUI_DOWNLOAD. The screens for the method and its parameters are shown in Figures 11-30 and 11-31.

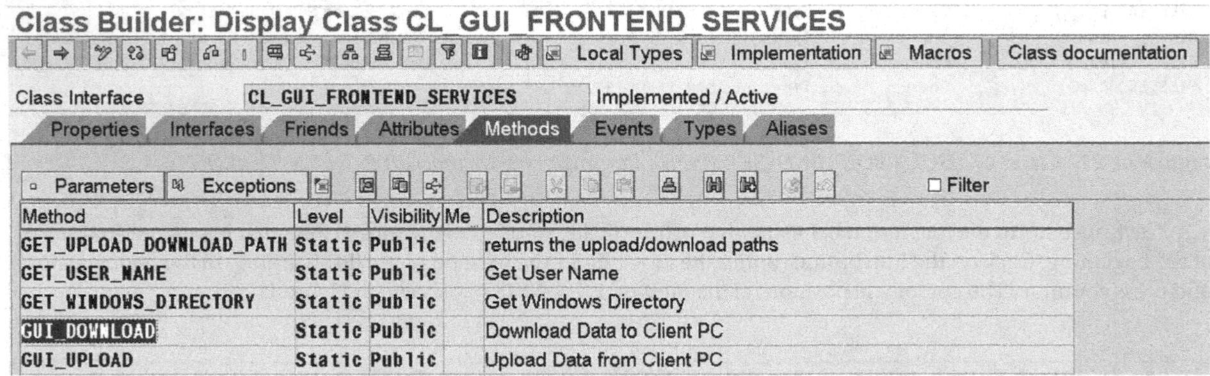

Figure 11-30. *Class: CL_GUI_FRONTEND_SERVISES - Method GUI_DOWNLOAD*

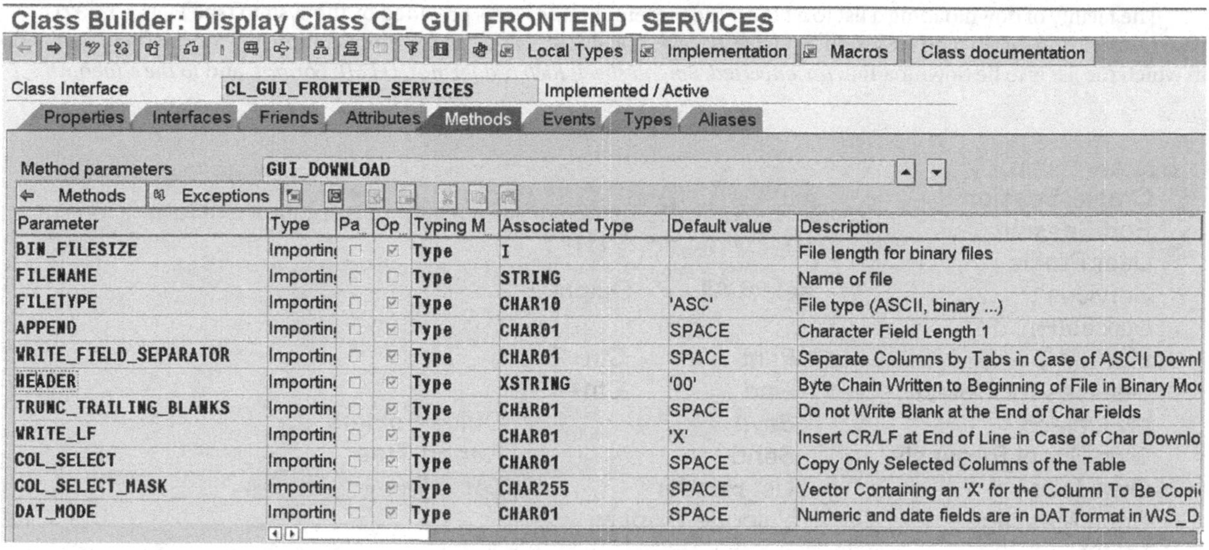

Class Builder: Display Class CL_GUI_FRONTEND_SERVICES

Local Types | Implementation | Macros | Class documentation

Class Interface CL_GUI_FRONTEND_SERVICES Implemented / Active

Properties | Interfaces | Friends | Attributes | Methods | Events | Types | Aliases

Method parameters GUI_DOWNLOAD

Methods | Exceptions

Parameter	Type	Pa	Op	Typing M	Associated Type	Default value	Description
BIN_FILESIZE	Importin	☐	☑	Type	I		File length for binary files
FILENAME	Importin	☐	☐	Type	STRING		Name of file
FILETYPE	Importin	☐	☑	Type	CHAR10	'ASC'	File type (ASCII, binary ...)
APPEND	Importin	☐	☑	Type	CHAR01	SPACE	Character Field Length 1
WRITE_FIELD_SEPARATOR	Importin	☐	☑	Type	CHAR01	SPACE	Separate Columns by Tabs in Case of ASCII Downl
HEADER	Importin	☐	☑	Type	XSTRING	'00'	Byte Chain Written to Beginning of File in Binary Mo
TRUNC_TRAILING_BLANKS	Importin	☐	☑	Type	CHAR01	SPACE	Do not Write Blank at the End of Char Fields
WRITE_LF	Importin	☐	☑	Type	CHAR01	'X'	Insert CR/LF at End of Line in Case of Char Downlo
COL_SELECT	Importin	☐	☑	Type	CHAR01	SPACE	Copy Only Selected Columns of the Table
COL_SELECT_MASK	Importin	☐	☑	Type	CHAR255	SPACE	Vector Containing an 'X' for the Column To Be Copi
DAT_MODE	Importin	☐	☑	Type	CHAR01	SPACE	Numeric and date fields are in DAT format in WS_D

Figure 11-31. *Class: CL_GUI_FRONTEND_SERVISES - Parameters of Method GUI_DOWNLOAD*

All of the three methods: FILE_OPEN_DIALOG, FILE_EXIST, and GUI_DOWNLOAD are static methods.

Exercise and ABAP Program Specifications

The functionalities of the Chapter 10 program YCL_CH10_ILISTS05 are being extended. To recapitulate, this program was taking a database table/view as input and listing out the fields of the input database table/view with checkboxes against the fields for making field selections. The program was retrieving the data of the selected fields from the database table/view to output. The program was using the features of runtime data objects, field symbols, and Open SQL special constructs and interactive lists.

You will add a button to the application toolbar of the output list of the selected fields of an input database table/view (first secondary list). Clicking on this button will download the list to a file on the presentation server in HTML format (in the event AT USER-COMMAND).

In the process of downloading the list to a file on the presentation server, you will be invoking the three methods of the built-in class: CL_GUI_FRONTEND_SERVICES.

When the additional button on the application toolbar is clicked, you will first present the user with a Selection Screen prompting for the file name. The event AT SELECTION-SCREEN ON VALUE-REQUEST... is triggered for this prompt to enable the user to make a selection of an existing file on the presentation server. You are using the method FILE_OPEN_DIALOG to present a file selection dialogue box in the event AT SELECTION-SCREEN ON VALUE-REQUEST.... The user can, of course, make a manual entry for the file name.

After the entry of the file name, when the user presses the execute button/function key F8, you will check for the existence of the file using the method FILE_EXIST. If a file is existent, you are popping a dialogue box for confirmation of file overwriting using the function module POPUP_TO_CONFIRM.

If the file exists and overwriting is confirmed or the downloading file is nonexistent, the list (first secondary list) is converted to HTML format using the function module: WWW_LIST_TO_HTML. This function module takes as input the list number (0, 1 ...) and returns the HTML formatted list into an internal table.

This internal table containing the list in HTML format is downloaded to the presentation server file using the method GUI_DOWNLOAD.

If the file exists and overwriting is not confirmed, a message is issued and the system remains on the first secondary list.

The facility of downloading a list to a file on the presentation server is provided by the system (see Figure 11-32). From any list, the menu path is System ➤ List ➤ Save ➤ Local File. The system prompts for the file format (Figure 11-33) in which the list is to be downloaded: *unconverted, Spread sheet, Rich text format, HTML Format,* and *to the clipboard.*

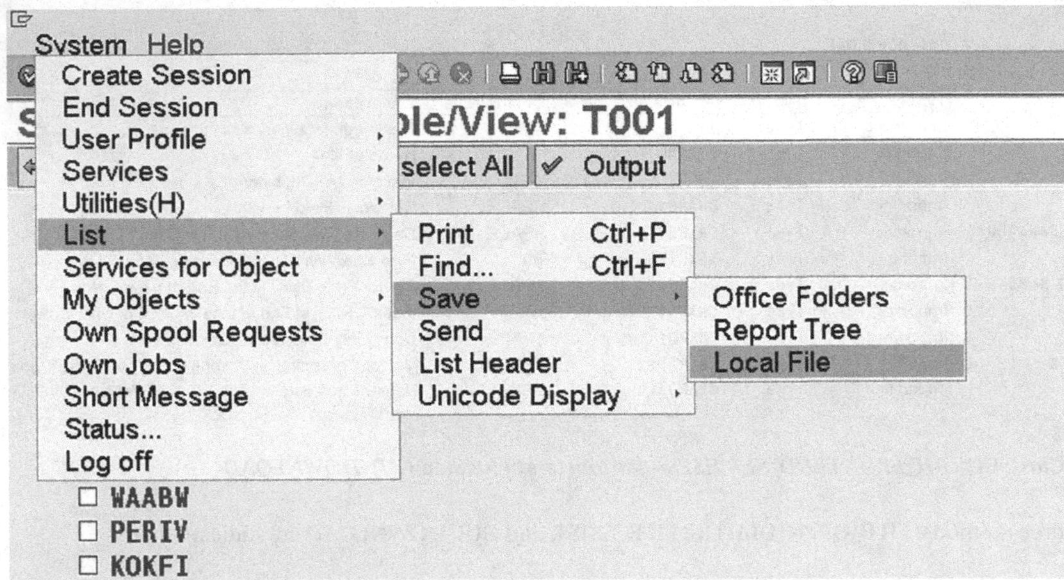

Figure 11-32. *Menu Path for Saving/Downloading a List to a Presentation Server File*

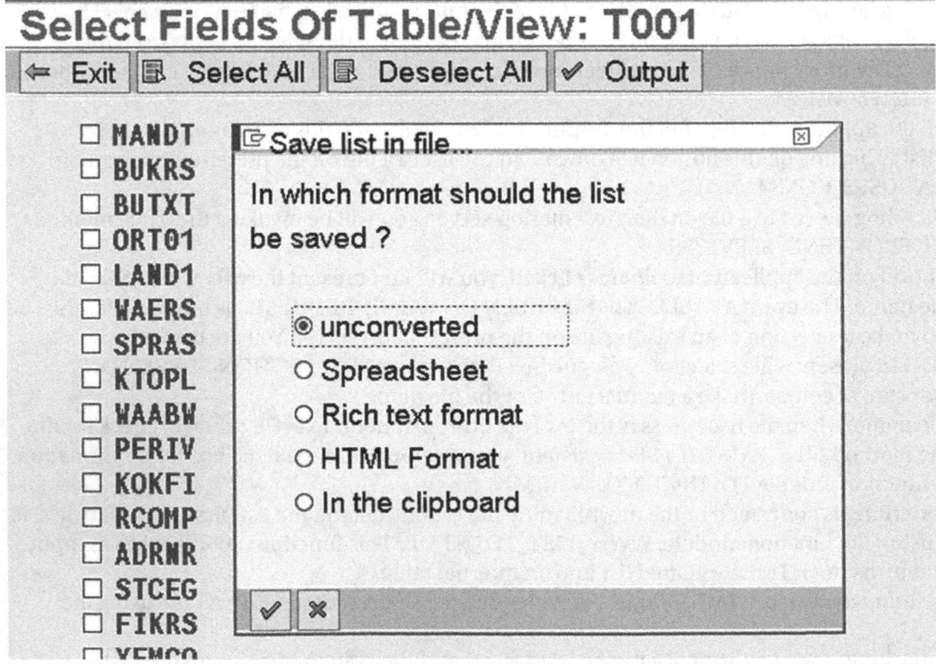

Figure 11-33. *File Format Selection for Saving/Downloading a List to a Presentation Server File*

The idea of providing the facility already available in the system through custom program coding would seem inane and redundant. The objective here is to demonstrate the use of the methods of the class CL_GUI_FRONTEND_SERVICES.

The changes made to the original program YCL_CH10_ILISTS05' are marked in the current program.

The source code:

```
REPORT YCL_CH11_05_USE_GCLASS_FES NO STANDARD PAGE HEADING.

*********************************************************
* Use Methods FILE_OPEN_DIALOG, FILE_EXIST, GUI_DOWNLOAD **
* of Class CL_GUI_FRONTEND_SERVICES to Download First   **
* Secondary List in HTML Format to a File on the        **
* Presentation Server/Front-end                         **
*********************************************************

DATA: BEGIN OF FIELDS_STRU,
       FIELDNAME TYPE DD03L-FIELDNAME," field name
       POSITION  TYPE DD03L-POSITION, " field position in stru 1, 2..
                                      " line no. & field position map
                                      " one-to-one. helps in accessing
                                      " a field with line no.
       INTTYPE   TYPE DD03L-INTTYPE,  " ABAP TYPE: C,D,F,I,N,P etc.
       DATATYPE  TYPE DD03L-DATATYPE, " DDIC TYPE: CHAR, NUMC etc.
       KEYFLAG   TYPE DD03L-KEYFLAG,  " flag for primary key field
       CBOX(1)   TYPE C,              " field enabled/disabled check box
       OBLEN     TYPE I,              " width of output
      END OF FIELDS_STRU,

      BEGIN OF SFIELDS_STRU,
       FIELDNAME TYPE DD03L-FIELDNAME,
      END OF SFIELDS_STRU,

      BEGIN OF ORDERBY_STRU,
       FIELDNAME TYPE DD03L-FIELDNAME,
      END OF ORDERBY_STRU,

      BEGIN OF OHEAD_STRU,
       FIELDNAME TYPE DD03L-FIELDNAME,
       OLEN      TYPE I, " width of output
       OTEXT     TYPE STRING,
       INTTYPE   TYPE DD03L-INTTYPE,
      END OF OHEAD_STRU,

      FIELDS_TAB  LIKE STANDARD TABLE OF FIELDS_STRU, " all fields of
                                                      " selected table

      SFIELDS_TAB LIKE STANDARD TABLE OF SFIELDS_STRU," selected fields of
                                                      " selected table. used
                                                      " in SELECT statement

      ORDERBY_TAB LIKE STANDARD TABLE OF ORDERBY_STRU,  " primary key fields
                                                        " (in sort)
```

```
      CONDS_TAB   TYPE STRING OCCURS 0 WITH HEADER LINE, " condition for
                                                         " text tables
      OHEAD_TAB   LIKE STANDARD TABLE OF OHEAD_STRU,     " texts for
                                                         " column headings
      CTR        TYPE I, " outputted field number
      LINSZ      TYPE I, " LINE-SIZE
      LCNT       TYPE I, " temporary
      PAGE(3)    TYPE C,
      CK_BOX(1)  TYPE C, " READ..FIELDS_STRU-CBOX INTO..
      TABCLASS   TYPE DD02L-TABCLASS, " destination field from table DD02L
      DSTRU      TYPE REF TO DATA,    " ref. variable of structure object

* addition in this program  start *
***********************************
      STR_TAB     TYPE FILETABLE WITH HEADER LINE, " return selected file
      HTML_TAB    TYPE STANDARD TABLE OF W3HTML, "HTML formatted list
      CNT         TYPE I, " no of files selected in file open dialog
      ANS(1)      TYPE C, " return value of popup dialogue box
      CANCEL(1)   TYPE C. " cancel download

* addition in this program end *
********************************

FIELD-SYMBOLS: <DSTRU>, " field symbol to access structure
               <FLD>.   " field symbol to access field

***********SELECTION-SCREEN**************************
PARAMETERS: TAB_NAME  TYPE DD03L-TABNAME VALUE CHECK.

AT SELECTION-SCREEN.

  SELECT SINGLE TABCLASS FROM DD02L INTO TABCLASS WHERE TABNAME = TAB_NAME.

  IF TABCLASS <> 'TRANSP' AND TABCLASS <> 'CLUSTER' AND
    TABCLASS <> 'POOL' AND TABCLASS <> 'VIEW'.
   MESSAGE E022(YCL_CH07_MCLASS01) WITH TAB_NAME.
  ENDIF.
************************************************************
************************************************************

START-OF-SELECTION.

SELECT FIELDNAME POSITION INTTYPE DATATYPE KEYFLAG FROM DD03L
 INTO CORRESPONDING FIELDS OF TABLE FIELDS_TAB
 WHERE TABNAME = TAB_NAME AND FIELDNAME NOT LIKE '.%' AND
  FIELDNAME NOT LIKE '/%'.

SORT FIELDS_TAB BY POSITION.
```

```
SET PF-STATUS 'STAT1'.
SET TITLEBAR 'TITLE01' WITH TAB_NAME.

*********primary list - list of fields **********************

LOOP AT FIELDS_TAB INTO FIELDS_STRU.
 WRITE:/5 FIELDS_STRU-CBOX AS CHECKBOX, FIELDS_STRU-FIELDNAME.
ENDLOOP.

**************************
* AT USER-COMMAND event **
**************************

AT USER-COMMAND.

CASE SY-UCOMM.

 WHEN 'EXIT'.
 LEAVE SCREEN.

 WHEN 'BACK'.
  SY-LSIND = SY-LSIND - 2.

*****************select all**************
 WHEN 'SALL'.

 LOOP AT FIELDS_TAB INTO FIELDS_STRU .
  MODIFY LINE SY-TABIX FIELD VALUE FIELDS_STRU-CBOX FROM 'X'
    FIELDS_STRU-FIELDNAME FROM FIELDS_STRU-FIELDNAME.
 ENDLOOP.

 SY-LSIND = 0.

****************de-select all*************
 WHEN 'DSALL'.

  LOOP AT FIELDS_TAB INTO FIELDS_STRU .
   MODIFY LINE SY-TABIX FIELD VALUE FIELDS_STRU-CBOX FROM ' '
    FIELDS_STRU-FIELDNAME FROM FIELDS_STRU-FIELDNAME.
 ENDLOOP.

 SY-LSIND = 0.

*******************output***************
 WHEN 'DDATA'.
 REFRESH: SFIELDS_TAB, ORDERBY_TAB, OHEAD_TAB, CONDS_TAB.
               " initialize internal tables
 LINSZ = 0.
 CREATE DATA DSTRU TYPE (TAB_NAME).
 ASSIGN DSTRU->* TO <DSTRU>.
```

```
******determine selected fields, build internal tables******
 DO.
  READ LINE SY-INDEX FIELD VALUE FIELDS_STRU-CBOX INTO CK_BOX.
  IF SY-SUBRC <> 0. " no more lines in the list
   EXIT.
  ENDIF.
  IF CK_BOX = 'X'.
   READ TABLE FIELDS_TAB INTO FIELDS_STRU INDEX SY-INDEX.
   FIELDS_STRU-CBOX = CK_BOX.
   SFIELDS_STRU-FIELDNAME = FIELDS_STRU-FIELDNAME.
   APPEND SFIELDS_STRU TO SFIELDS_TAB.


   ASSIGN COMPONENT SY-INDEX OF STRUCTURE <DSTRU> TO <FLD>.

   PERFORM FILL_OHEAD_TAB TABLES OHEAD_TAB USING TAB_NAME
     FIELDS_STRU <FLD>.

   MODIFY FIELDS_TAB FROM FIELDS_STRU INDEX SY-INDEX.

   IF FIELDS_STRU-KEYFLAG = 'X'.
    ORDERBY_STRU-FIELDNAME = FIELDS_STRU-FIELDNAME.
    APPEND ORDERBY_STRU TO ORDERBY_TAB.
   ENDIF.

   IF FIELDS_STRU-DATATYPE = 'LANG' AND FIELDS_STRU-KEYFLAG = 'X'.
    CONCATENATE FIELDS_STRU-FIELDNAME '= SY-LANGU' INTO
     CONDS_TAB SEPARATED BY ' '.
    APPEND CONDS_TAB TO CONDS_TAB.
   ENDIF.

  ELSE.

   READ TABLE FIELDS_TAB INTO FIELDS_STRU INDEX SY-INDEX.
   FIELDS_STRU-CBOX = CK_BOX.
   MODIFY FIELDS_TAB FROM FIELDS_STRU INDEX SY-INDEX.

   IF FIELDS_STRU-KEYFLAG = 'X'.
    ORDERBY_STRU-FIELDNAME = FIELDS_STRU-FIELDNAME.
    APPEND ORDERBY_STRU TO ORDERBY_TAB.
   ENDIF.

  IF FIELDS_STRU-DATATYPE = 'LANG' AND FIELDS_STRU-KEYFLAG = 'X'.
    CONCATENATE FIELDS_STRU-FIELDNAME '= SY-LANGU' INTO
     CONDS_TAB SEPARATED BY ' '.
    APPEND CONDS_TAB TO CONDS_TAB.
   ENDIF.

  ENDIF.
 ENDDO.
```

```
DESCRIBE TABLE SFIELDS_TAB.

IF SY-TFILL = 0. " no fields selected
 MESSAGE S023(YCL_CH07_MCLASS01) WITH
 TAB_NAME DISPLAY LIKE 'W'.
 SY-LSIND = SY-LSIND - 1.
 EXIT.
ENDIF.

LINSZ = LINSZ + 3.

IF LINSZ > 1023. " SY-LINSZ CANNOT EXCEED 1023.
 MESSAGE S024(YCL_CH07_MCLASS01) WITH
 LINSZ DISPLAY LIKE 'W'.
 SY-LSIND = SY-LSIND - 1.
 EXIT.

ENDIF.

CREATE DATA DSTRU TYPE (TAB_NAME).
ASSIGN DSTRU->* TO <DSTRU>.
SET PF-STATUS 'STAT2'.

NEW-PAGE  LINE-SIZE LINSZ LINE-COUNT 60. " LINSZ as per total width
                                         " of all outputted columns

SET TITLEBAR 'TITLE02' WITH TAB_NAME.

**************retrieve data & output***********************

SELECT (SFIELDS_TAB) FROM (TAB_NAME) INTO CORRESPONDING FIELDS OF
 <DSTRU> WHERE (CONDS_TAB) ORDER BY (ORDERBY_TAB).
 CTR = 0.
 DO.
  ASSIGN COMPONENT SY-INDEX OF STRUCTURE <DSTRU> TO <FLD>.
  IF SY-SUBRC <> 0.
   EXIT.
  ENDIF.
  READ TABLE FIELDS_TAB INTO FIELDS_STRU INDEX SY-INDEX.
  IF FIELDS_STRU-CBOX <> 'X'.
   CONTINUE.
  ENDIF.
  CTR = CTR + 1.
  IF CTR = 1.
   WRITE AT :/5(FIELDS_STRU-OBLEN) <FLD>.
  ELSE.
   WRITE AT :(FIELDS_STRU-OBLEN) <FLD>.
  ENDIF.
 ENDDO.

ENDSELECT.
```

```
* addition in this program  start *
***********************************

*********download HTML**********
 WHEN 'DOWNH'.

   SY-LSIND = SY-LSIND - 1.

   SELECTION-SCREEN BEGIN OF SCREEN 2000.
   PARAMETERS FILE TYPE STRING.
   SELECTION-SCREEN END OF SCREEN 2000.
   CALL SELECTION-SCREEN 2000  STARTING AT 3 2 ENDING AT 90 7.

*********************************************************
  IF CANCEL = 'C'. " cancel download
   CANCEL = ' '.

  ELSE.
   ANS = ' '.
   IF CL_GUI_FRONTEND_SERVICES=>FILE_EXIST( FILE = FILE ) = 'X'.

    CALL FUNCTION 'POPUP_TO_CONFIRM'
      EXPORTING
        TEXT_QUESTION                = 'Confirm Overwriting'(001)
        TEXT_BUTTON_1                = 'Yes'(002)
        TEXT_BUTTON_2                = 'No'(003)
        DEFAULT_BUTTON               = '2'
        DISPLAY_CANCEL_BUTTON        = ' '
        START_COLUMN                 = 25
        START_ROW                    = 6
      IMPORTING
        ANSWER                       = ANS
          .

   ENDIF.

*********************************************************
   IF ANS <> '2'.

    CALL FUNCTION 'WWW_LIST_TO_HTML'
     EXPORTING
       LIST_INDEX       = 1
     TABLES
       HTML             = HTML_TAB[].

    CALL METHOD CL_GUI_FRONTEND_SERVICES=>GUI_DOWNLOAD
      EXPORTING
        FILENAME                    = FILE "'D:\TMP\EEE.HTM'
        FILETYPE                    = 'BIN'
        WRITE_LF                    = 'X'
*       CONFIRM_OVERWRITE           = 'X'
      CHANGING
```

```
        DATA_TAB                    = HTML_TAB[]
        .
      IF SY-SUBRC <> 0.
       MESSAGE ID SY-MSGID TYPE SY-MSGTY NUMBER SY-MSGNO
              WITH SY-MSGV1 SY-MSGV2 SY-MSGV3 SY-MSGV4.
      ENDIF.
     ELSE.
      MESSAGE S038(YCL_CH07_MCLASS01)
       WITH FILE. " Overwriting Existing File:&1 Cancelled

     ENDIF.
   ENDIF.
  ENDCASE.

******************************************************
AT SELECTION-SCREEN ON EXIT-COMMAND.

CANCEL = 'C'. " for cancel download
******************************************************
AT SELECTION-SCREEN ON VALUE-REQUEST FOR FILE.

CALL METHOD CL_GUI_FRONTEND_SERVICES=>FILE_OPEN_DIALOG
  EXPORTING
*     WINDOW_TITLE            =
      MULTISELECTION          = ' '
  CHANGING
    FILE_TABLE              = STR_TAB[]
    RC                      = CNT
  EXCEPTIONS
    FILE_OPEN_DIALOG_FAILED = 1
    CNTL_ERROR              = 2
    ERROR_NO_GUI            = 3
    NOT_SUPPORTED_BY_GUI    = 4
    others                  = 5
        .
IF SY-SUBRC <> 0.
 MESSAGE ID SY-MSGID TYPE SY-MSGTY NUMBER SY-MSGNO
            WITH SY-MSGV1 SY-MSGV2 SY-MSGV3 SY-MSGV4.
ELSE.

 READ TABLE STR_TAB INDEX 1.
 IF STR_TAB IS NOT INITIAL.
  FILE = STR_TAB.
 ENDIF.

ENDIF.

* addition in this program end *
********************************
```

```
**********************************************************
* heading using event TOP-OF-PAGE DURING LINE-SELECTION **
**********************************************************
TOP-OF-PAGE DURING LINE-SELECTION.

 LCNT = LINSZ - 2.
 PAGE = SY-PAGNO.
 WRITE AT /LCNT PAGE RIGHT-JUSTIFIED.

 LCNT = LINSZ - 4.

 WRITE AT /5(LCNT) SY-ULINE.

 LOOP AT OHEAD_TAB INTO OHEAD_STRU.

  IF SY-TABIX = 1.
   IF OHEAD_STRU-INTTYPE = 'F' OR OHEAD_STRU-INTTYPE = 'I'
    OR OHEAD_STRU-INTTYPE = 'P'.
    WRITE AT /5(OHEAD_STRU-OLEN) OHEAD_STRU-OTEXT RIGHT-JUSTIFIED.
   ELSE.
    WRITE AT /5(OHEAD_STRU-OLEN) OHEAD_STRU-OTEXT.
   ENDIF.
  ELSE.
   IF OHEAD_STRU-INTTYPE = 'F' OR OHEAD_STRU-INTTYPE = 'I'
    OR OHEAD_STRU-INTTYPE = 'P'.
    WRITE AT (OHEAD_STRU-OLEN) OHEAD_STRU-OTEXT RIGHT-JUSTIFIED.
   ELSE.
    WRITE AT (OHEAD_STRU-OLEN) OHEAD_STRU-OTEXT.
   ENDIF.
  ENDIF.
 ENDLOOP.

 WRITE AT /5(LCNT) SY-ULINE.
 SKIP 1.

****************************************
* Get Column Heading Texts,           **
* build column heading internal table **
****************************************

FORM  FILL_OHEAD_TAB
       TABLES
        OTAB LIKE OHEAD_TAB

       USING
        VALUE(TNAME)
        FSTRU LIKE FIELDS_STRU VALUE(FLD) .

 DATA: LNGT     TYPE I,
       OSTRU    LIKE LINE OF OTAB.
```

```
CALL FUNCTION 'MG_FIELDNAME_TEXT'
 EXPORTING
   TABNAME          = TNAME
   FIELDNAME        = FSTRU-FIELDNAME
IMPORTING
  REPTEXT          = OSTRU-OTEXT
         .

OSTRU-FIELDNAME = FSTRU-FIELDNAME.
OSTRU-INTTYPE   = FSTRU-INTTYPE.

DESCRIBE FIELD FLD OUTPUT-LENGTH OSTRU-OLEN.

LNGT = STRLEN( OSTRU-OTEXT ).

IF LNGT > OSTRU-OLEN.
 OSTRU-OLEN = LNGT.
ENDIF.

FSTRU-OBLEN = OSTRU-OLEN.
APPEND OSTRU TO OTAB.
LINSZ = LINSZ + OSTRU-OLEN + 1.

ENDFORM.
***********************************
```

The Input screen will like that in Figure 11-34.

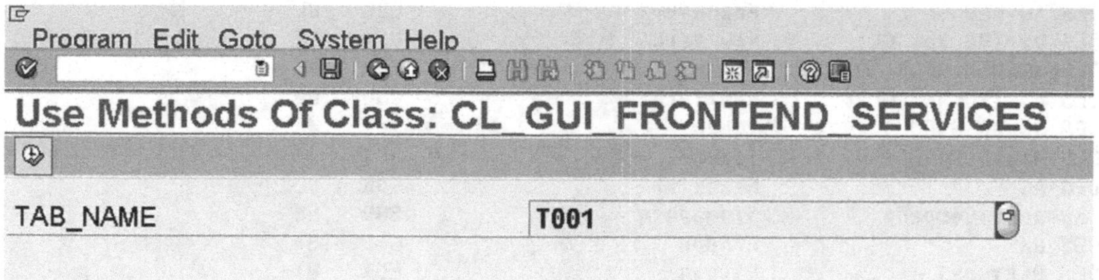

Figure 11-34. *Program YCL_CH11_05_USE_GCLASS_FES: Input*

The field list with field selections is shown in Figure 11-35.

Select Fields Of Table/View: T001

Exit | Select All | Deselect All | Output

- ☐ MANDT
- ☑ BUKRS
- ☑ BUTXT
- ☑ ORT01
- ☐ LAND1
- ☑ WAERS
- ☑ SPRAS
- ☐ KTOPL

Figure 11-35. *Program YCL_CH11_05_USE_GCLASS_FES: Selected Fields*

The output screen is shown in Figure 11-36.

Output Of Table/View: T001

Back | Download HTML

1

CoCd	Company Name	City	Crcy	Language
0001	SAP A.G.	Walldorf	EUR	DE
0005	IDES AG NEW GL	Frankfurt	EUR	DE
0006	IDES US INC New GL	New York	USD	EN
0007	IDES AG NEW GL 7	Frankfurt	EUR	DE
0008	IDES US INC New GL 8	New York	USD	EN
0100	IDES Japan 0100	Tokyo	JPY	JA
0110	IDES Japan 0110	Tokyo	JPY	JA
1000	IDES AG	Frankfurt	EUR	DE
1002	Singapore Company	Singapore	SGD	EN
2000	IDES UK	London	GBP	EN
2100	IDES Portugal	Lisbon	EUR	PT
2200	IDES France	Paris	EUR	FR
2201	IDES France affiliate	Paris	EUR	FR
2300	IDES España	Barcelona	EUR	ES
2400	IDES Filiale 1 IT Ko.1000		EUR	DE
2500	IDES Netherlands	Rotterdam	EUR	NL
2600	IDES IDES Italia	Milano	EUR	IT

Figure 11-36. *Program YCL_CH11_05_USE_GCLASS_FES: Output*

Clicking on the 'Download HTML' button will pop up the dialogue box in Figure 11-37.

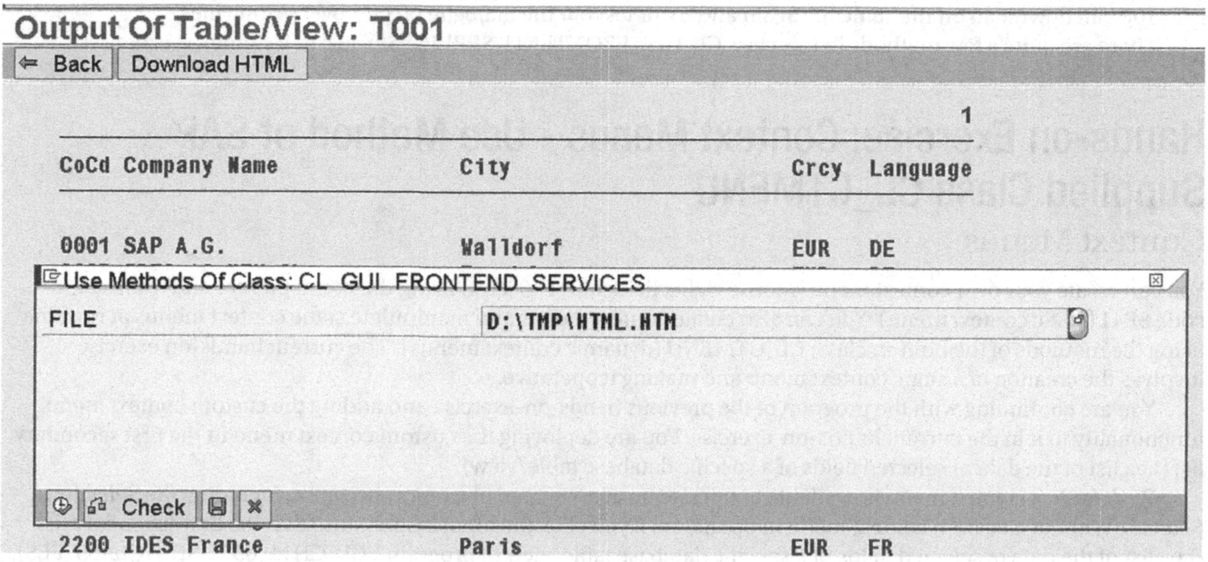

```
Output Of Table/View: T001
Back | Download HTML
                                                                     1
CoCd Company Name                  City                   Crcy  Language

0001 SAP A.G.                      Walldorf               EUR   DE
Use Methods Of Class: CL_GUI_FRONTEND_SERVICES
FILE                 D:\TMP\HTML.HTM
Check
2200 IDES France                   Paris                  EUR   FR
```

Figure 11-37. *Program YCL_CH11_05_USE_GCLASS_FES: Download in HTML Format*

Enter the file name or select an existing file (Function key F4, etc.). Press F8/Execute.

After the downloading process is over, the system displays a message with the number of bytes transferred:

```
2700 IDES Schweiz                  Biel / Bienne          CHF   DE
2800 China                         China                  CNY   ZH
156,060 Bytes Transferred
```

Figure 11-38. *Program YCL_CH11_05_USE_GCLASS_FES: Download System Alert*

When you open the downloaded HTML file in a web browser, it will look like Figure 11-39.

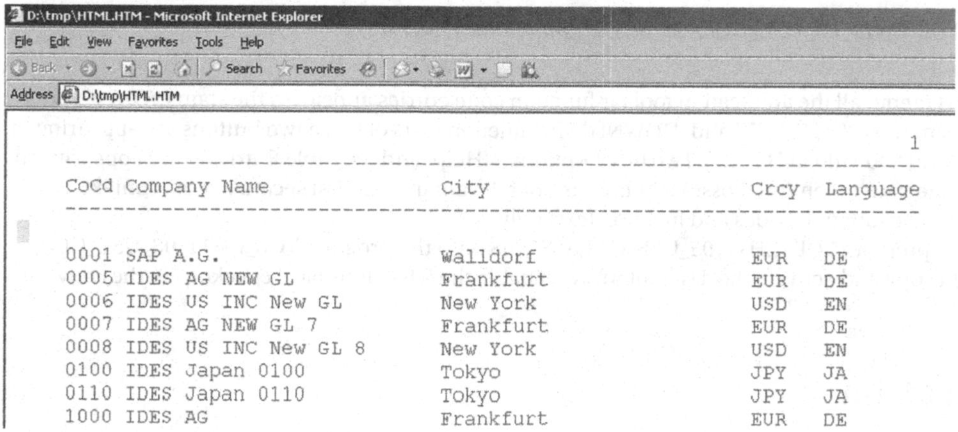

```
D:\tmp\HTML.HTM - Microsoft Internet Explorer
File  Edit  View  Favorites  Tools  Help
Address  D:\tmp\HTML.HTM
                                                                     1
--------------------------------------------------------------------------
CoCd Company Name                  City                   Crcy  Language
--------------------------------------------------------------------------

0001 SAP A.G.                      Walldorf               EUR   DE
0005 IDES AG NEW GL                Frankfurt              EUR   DE
0006 IDES US INC New GL            New York               USD   EN
0007 IDES AG NEW GL 7              Frankfurt              EUR   DE
0008 IDES US INC New GL 8          New York               USD   EN
0100 IDES Japan 0100               Tokyo                  JPY   JA
0110 IDES Japan 0110               Tokyo                  JPY   JA
1000 IDES AG                       Frankfurt              EUR   DE
```

Figure 11-39. *Program YCL_CH11_05_USE_GCLASS_FES: Contents of Downloaded File*

You can download on the same file again and try or test out the dialogue box for overwriting files.

There are quite a few methods in this class CL_GUI_FRONTEND_SERVICES. You can try them as exercises.

Hands-on Exercise: Context Menus - Use Method of SAP Supplied Class CL_CTMENU

Context Menus

You can create your own context menu (mouse right click/shift+F10 keys) using the menu painter and transaction code SE41 (static context menu). You can also create context menus and manipulate static context menus at runtime using the methods of the built-in class: CL_CTMENU (dynamic context menus). The current hands-on exercise involves the creation of a static context menu and making it operative.

You are continuing with the program of the previous hands-on-exercise and adding the custom context menu functionality to it in the current hands-on-exercise. You are deploying the custom context menu in the first secondary list (i.e., list of the data of selected fields of a specific database table/view).

By default, a context menu is available to operate on every screen of a report program, including the Selection Screens. Without a custom context menu in operation, if you click the mouse right button on the first secondary list (i.e., list of the data of selected fields of a specific database table/view of program YCL_CH11_05_ USE_GCLASS_FES), the menu options available are as shown in Figure 11-40.

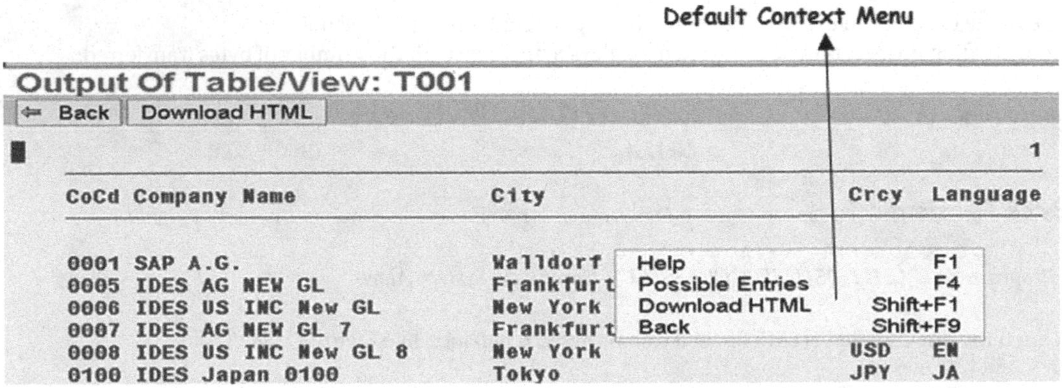

Default Context Menu

Output Of Table/View: T001

⇐ Back | Download HTML

CoCd	Company Name	City	Crcy	Language
0001	SAP A.G.	Walldorf		
0005	IDES AG NEW GL	Frankfurt		
0006	IDES US INC New GL	New York		
0007	IDES AG NEW GL 7	Frankfurt		
0008	IDES US INC New GL 8	New York	USD	EN
0100	IDES Japan 0100	Tokyo	JPY	JA

Help	F1
Possible Entries	F4
Download HTML	Shift+F1
Back	Shift+F9

Figure 11-40. *Program YCL_CH11_05_USE_GCLASS_FES: Default Context Menu*

In this default context menu, all the application toolbar function code entries appear. In the status 'STAT2,' you had incorporated two functions codes: 'BACK' and 'DOWNH.' The function texts of these two buttons are appearing in the context menu ('Back' and 'Download HTML'). Two other options – 'Help' and 'Possible Entries' – are appearing in the context menu. The context menu option 'Possible Entries' is not relevant in your first secondary list context.

Context menu options use function codes and function texts only.

If you are Copying the program YCL_CH11_05_USE_GCLASS_FES onto the program YCL_CH11_06_USE_CL_CTMENU, ensure that you copy and activate the 'User interface.' (Enable the 'User interface' checkbox in the copy dialogue box.)

Create a Context Menu

You will create a custom static context menu with the two function codes 'BACK' and 'DOWNH' with their corresponding function texts 'Back' and 'Download HTML.'

To create a context menu, navigate to the menu painter with the transaction code SE41. Enter the name of the program as YCL_CH10_06_USE_CL_CTMENU. Activate the interface.

Next, enter the context menu status name as 'STAT3.' Click on the create button/function key F5. The screen prompt for status type: Normal Screen, Dialogue Box, or Context Menu will appear. Enter the short text, select the Context Menu radio button, and press the continue button as shown in Figure 11-41.

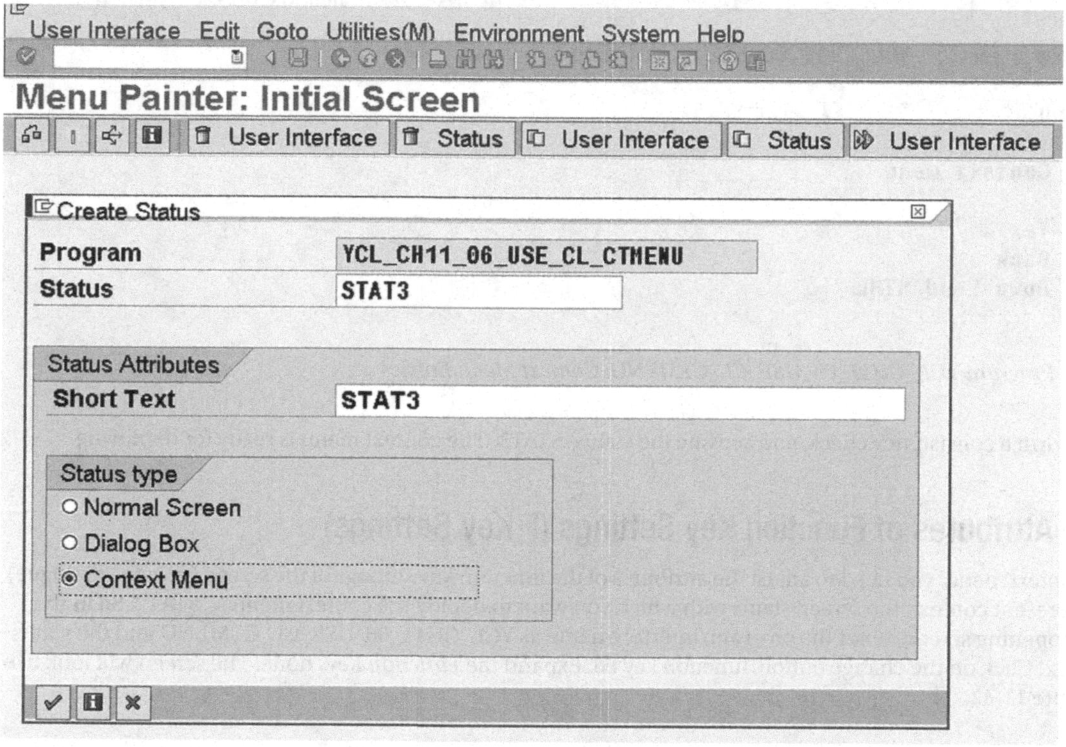

Figure 11-41. *Program YCL_CH11_06_USE_CL_CTMENU: Create Context Menu*

A screen will appear with the 'Context menu' bar. Double click on this bar. Figure 11-42 will appear.

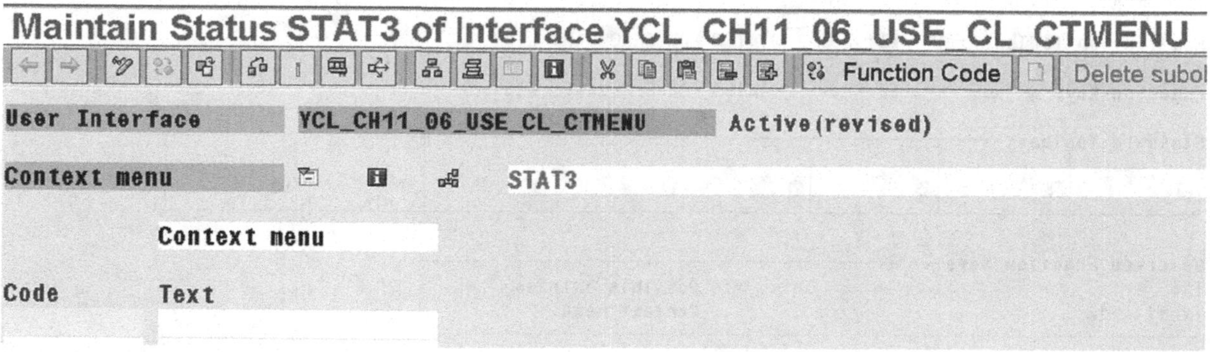

Figure 11-42. *Program YCL_CH11_06_USE_CL_CTMENU: Create Context Menu*

As decided earlier, you will enter the two function codes 'BACK' and 'DOWNH' under the column 'Code.' Pressing the <enter> key after entering the function code will fetch the respective function texts. The screen after the entry of the function codes will look like the one in Figure 11-43.

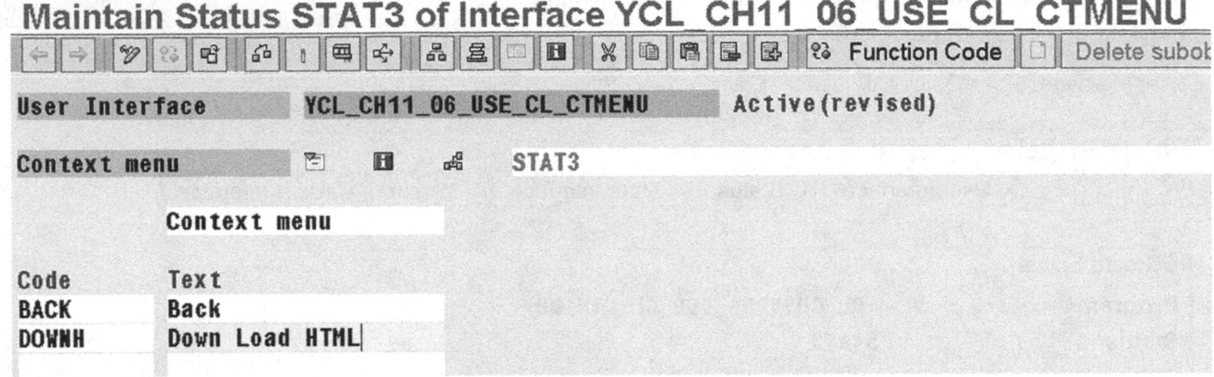

Figure 11-43. *Program YCL_CH11_06_USE_CL_CTMENU: Context Menu Entries*

Save, perform a consistency check, and activate the status 'STAT3.' The context menu is ready for deploying.

Adjust the Attributes of Function Key Settings (F Key Settings)

To deploy a context menu, you need to adjust the attributes of the function key settings of the screen (normal/dialogue) status. In the present context, the screen status with which you want to deploy the context menu is 'STAT2.' So in the menu painter opening screen, enter the program/interface name as YCL_CH11_06_USE_CL_CTMENU and the status name as 'STAT2.' Click on the change button/function key F6. Expand the *Function Keys* node. The screen will look like the one in Figure 11-42.

Maintain Status STAT2 of Interface YCL_CH11_06_USE_CL_CTMENU

Function Code | Delete subobject

User Interface YCL_CH11_06_USE_CL_CTMENU Active

Menu Bar STATUS FOR SECONDARY LIST

Application Toolbar STATUS FOR SECONDARY LIST

Function Keys STATUS FOR SECONDARY LIST

Standard Toolbar

Reserved Function Keys

F4 <..> Possible entries

Shift-F10 <..> Context menu

Figure 11-44. *Program YCL_CH11_06_USE_CL_CTMENU: Status 'STAT2'*

At the bottom of the screen, there is the *Reserved Function Keys* area. In this area, position the cursor in the field next to 'Shift+F10' and prior to *Context menu*. Next, select the following menu path: Goto ➤ Attributes ➤ F key setting as shown in Figure 11-45.

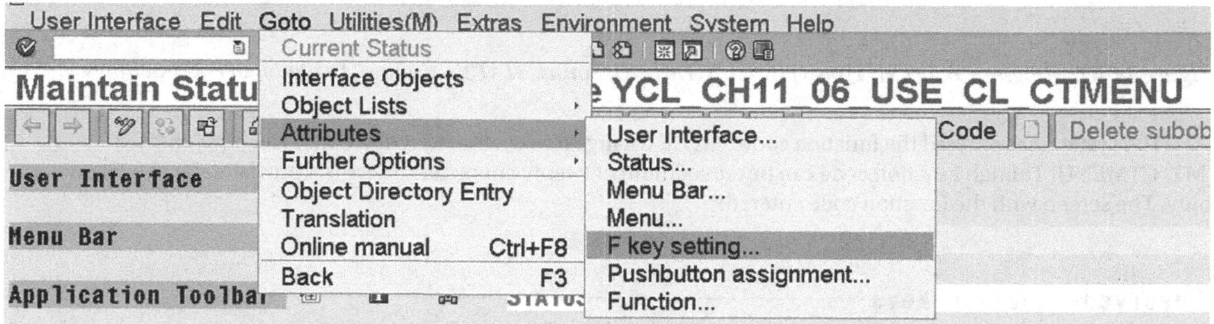

Figure 11-45. Program YCL_CH11_06_USE_CL_CTMENU: Status 'STAT2' – Change Attributes of F Key Settings

Choosing the menu path will pop up the dialogue box in Figure 11-46.

User Interface YCL_CH11_06_USE_CL_CTMENU Active(revised)

F Key Setting Attributes

Program YCL_CH11_06_USE_CL_CTMENU

Name STATUS FOR SECONDARY LIST

Type of Key Assignment

◉ Screen

○ Dialog box

☑ Function keys for standard function handling in lists

☑ List with Context Menu

Figure 11-46. Program YCL_CH11_06_USE_CL_CTMENU: Status 'STAT2' – Change Attributes of F Key Settings

In this dialogue box, enable the check box 'List with Context Menu' and press the continue button. This will take you back to the function key settings node as shown in Figure 11-47.

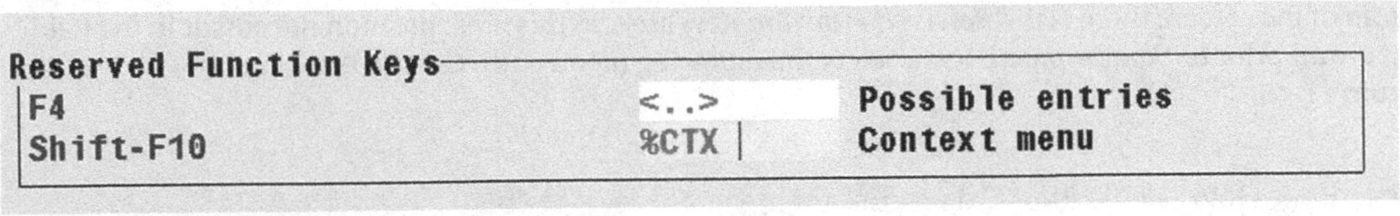

Reserved Function Keys		
F4	<..>	Possible entries
Shift-F10	%CTX	Context menu

Figure 11-47. *Program YCL_CH11_06_USE_CL_CTMENU: Status 'STAT2' – Change Attributes of F Key Settings*

The system has entered the function code '%CTX'. Change it to custom function code. You have entered 'MY_CTMENU'. Though function code can be a maximum of twenty characters, there is a provision for ten characters only. The screen with the function code entered:

Reserved Function Keys		
F4	<..>	Possible entries
Shift-F10	MY_CTMENU	Context menu

Figure 11-48. *Program YCL_CH11_06_USE_CL_CTMENU: Status 'STAT2' – Change Attributes of F Key Settings*

Save and perform a consistency check and activate the status 'STAT2'.

This changing of attributes of function key settings is to indicate the deployment of custom context menu instead of the default context menu.

You have to write program code for the call back subroutine 'ON_CTMENU_REQUEST'. Every time a user clicks on the mouse's right button or presses shift+F10, control will jump to this subroutine, and program code in this subroutine will be executed.

Built-in Class CL_CTMENU – Method LOAD_GUI_STATUS

The built-in class CL_CTMENU has methods to load static context menus, manipulate them at runtime, and build a whole context menu at runtime. You will be using the static method LOAD_GUI_STATUS to deploy your static context menu 'STAT3' created in the menu painter. Figure 11-49 is a screenshot of the built-in class CL_CTMENU with the method LOAD_GUI_STATUS selected.

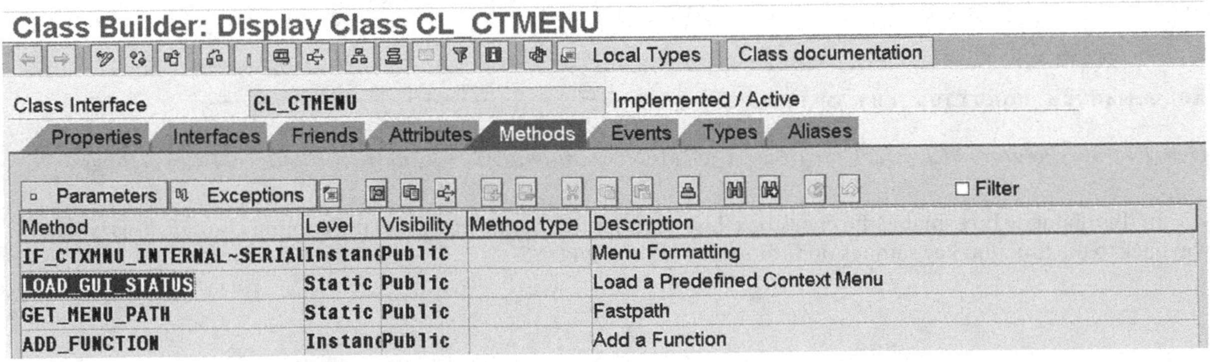

Class Builder: Display Class CL_CTMENU

Local Types | Class documentation

Class Interface CL_CTMENU Implemented / Active

Properties | Interfaces | Friends | Attributes | Methods | Events | Types | Aliases

Parameters | Exceptions | Filter

Method	Level	Visibility	Method type	Description
IF_CTXMNU_INTERNAL~SERIAL	Instanc	Public		Menu Formatting
LOAD_GUI_STATUS	Static	Public		Load a Predefined Context Menu
GET_MENU_PATH	Static	Public		Fastpath
ADD_FUNCTION	Instanc	Public		Add a Function

Figure 11-49. *Class CL_CTMENU: Method LOAD_GUI_STATUS*

Figure 11-50 shows the parameters of the method LOAD_GUI_STATUS.

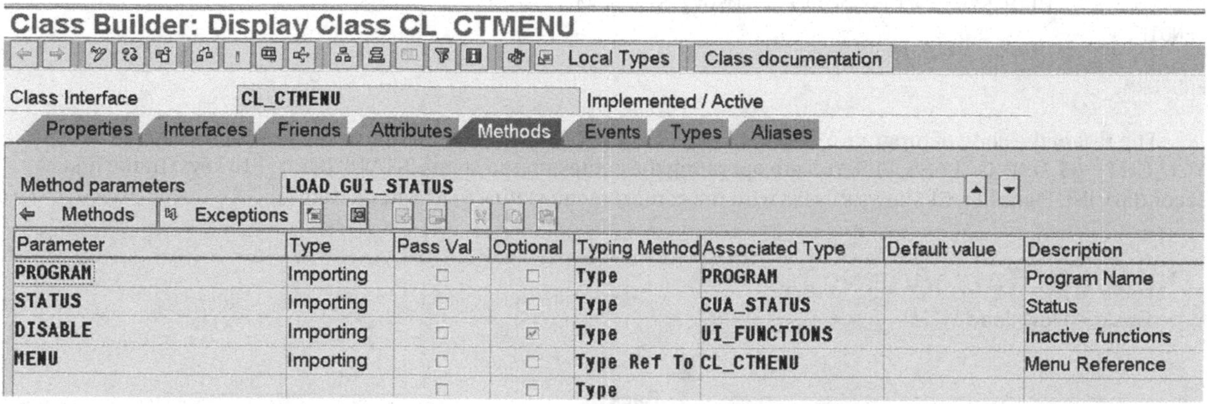

Class Builder: Display Class CL_CTMENU

Local Types | Class documentation

Class Interface CL_CTMENU Implemented / Active

Properties | Interfaces | Friends | Attributes | Methods | Events | Types | Aliases

Method parameters LOAD_GUI_STATUS

Methods | Exceptions

Parameter	Type	Pass Val	Optional	Typing Method	Associated Type	Default value	Description
PROGRAM	Importing	☐	☐	Type	PROGRAM		Program Name
STATUS	Importing	☐	☐	Type	CUA_STATUS		Status
DISABLE	Importing	☐	☑	Type	UI_FUNCTIONS		Inactive functions
MENU	Importing	☐	☐	Type Ref To	CL_CTMENU		Menu Reference
		☐	☐	Type			

***Figure 11-50.** Class CL_CTMENU: Parameters of Method LOAD_GUI_STATUS*

The method has four importing parameters. The first two importing parameters are the name of the program and the name of the context menu. The optional third importing parameter provides the function codes to be disabled, if any. The fourth importing parameter 'MENU' must be a reference variable referring to the built-in class CL_CTMENU.

Call Back Subroutine ON_CTMENU_REQEST

Every time the user clicks on the mouse's right button, the control jumps to the call back subroutine 'N_CTMENU_REQUEST (i.e., the subroutine is executed). The subroutine takes one importing parameter: MENU. This parameter should be typed as the class CL_CTMENU (i.e., TYPE REF TO CL_CTMENU).

The call back subroutine receives the reference to the instance the class created. Using this formal parameter reference variable, you can use the instance methods, etc., of the built-in class CL_CT_MENU within the call back subroutine.

You have to locate all the code of loading, manipulating static context menu statuses, and building runtime context menus in the call back subroutine.

In the present scenario you need to load a static context menu status. You are using the static method LOAD_GUI_STATUS, already described to deploy the context menu status 'STAT3'.

The program code for the call back subroutine ON_CTMENU_REQUEST:

```
***************************************
* call back routine for context menu **
***************************************
FORM ON_CTMENU_REQUEST USING CT_MENU TYPE REF TO CL_CTMENU.

 CALL METHOD CL_CTMENU=>LOAD_GUI_STATUS
   EXPORTING
     PROGRAM    = 'YCL_CH11_06_USE_CL_CTMENU' " program name
     STATUS     = 'STAT3' " context menu status name
     MENU       = CT_MENU  " first/only formal parameter
   EXCEPTIONS
     READ_ERROR = 1
     others     = 2
       .
```

```
 IF SY-SUBRC <> 0.
  MESSAGE ID SY-MSGID TYPE SY-MSGTY NUMBER SY-MSGNO
           WITH SY-MSGV1 SY-MSGV2 SY-MSGV3 SY-MSGV4.
 ENDIF.

ENDFORM.
```

The rest of the code of program YCL_CH11_06_USE_CL_CTMENU is the same as the previous program YCL_CH11_05_USE_GCLASS_FES. You are operating the context menu status 'STAT3' (shift+F10 keys) in the first secondary list. Figure 11-51 shows this list with the context menu status 'STAT3 in operation'.

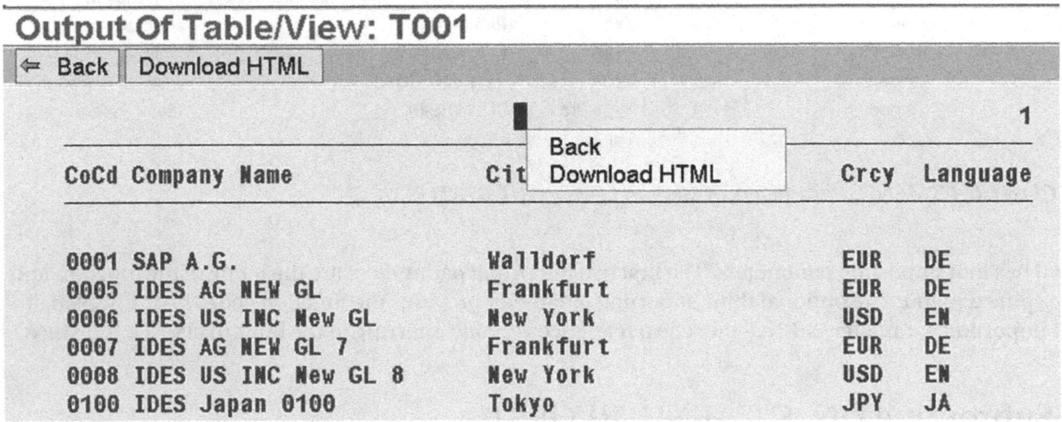

```
Output Of Table/View: T001
⇐ Back | Download HTML

                                                                 1
                                            Back
CoCd Company Name                        Cit Download HTML   Crcy  Language

0001 SAP A.G.                            Walldorf            EUR   DE
0005 IDES AG NEW GL                      Frankfurt           EUR   DE
0006 IDES US INC New GL                  New York            USD   EN
0007 IDES AG NEW GL 7                    Frankfurt           EUR   DE
0008 IDES US INC New GL 8                New York            USD   EN
0100 IDES Japan 0100                     Tokyo               JPY   JA
```

Figure 11-51. *Program YCL_CH11_06_USE_CL_CTMENU: Custom Context Menu*

The program YCL_CH11_06_USE_CL_CTMENU has been copied to another program YCL_CH11_07_USE_CL_CTMENU_V1 (copied with interface and the interface activated).

In the call back subroutine of this program, the instance method CLEAR is used to initialize the context menu. With the execution of this method, no context menu (custom or default) will be operative. The clearing operation is followed by the execution of instance method ADD FUNCTION, which can add function codes and texts to a runtime context menu. In the call back subroutine of this program we are adding just one function code and function text (ADD_FUNCTION) corresponding to the application toolbar 'Back' button. This is a demonstration of building a runtime context menu.

You can find the programs YCL_CH11_06_USE_CL_CTMENU and YCL_CH11_07_USE_CL_CTMENU_V1 in the E-Resource. This concludes the context menu coverage.

Class Based Exceptions in ABAP

You have raised exceptions in function modules (Chapter 7) and methods of classes (this chapter) using a variation of the MESSAGE... statement. The text for these messages is created and maintained in transaction code 'SE91' and stored in database table 'T100'.

You can raise exceptions using existing or custom-created exception classes. The class based exceptions are more flexible, comprehensive, and powerful. You will create a custom exception class and use it to raise exceptions in an ABAP report program, an internal subroutine, a function module, and a method in a class.

There are built-in exception classes relating to database operations, arithmetic operations, RFC operations et al. If your exception raising requirements are fulfilled by these, you may as well use them. All the built-in exception classes have names starting with 'CX_SY'.

You create an exception class in the class builder (transaction code SE24). While creating a custom exception class, you assign it one of the three built-in exception classes as a super class.

Create a Custom Exception Class (OTR Texts)

The following three super classes are used to create custom exception classes:

- CX_NO_CHECK:-

When using this as a super class for your custom exception class, you do not declare the exceptions with procedure (subroutine, function module, method) interface. They are implicitly declared and propagated.

- CX_STATIC_CHECK:

When you create a custom exception subclass of this class, exceptions raised in a procedure (subroutine, function module, method) with the RAISE... statement are either declared in the interface of the procedure or handled with the CATCH... statement. There is a compile time check for this.

- CX_DYNAMIC_CHECK

With subclasses of this class, exceptions raised in a procedure (subroutine, function module, method) are declared in the interface of the procedure. This is not checked at compile time, but at the time of its propagation.

Based on your scenario criterion, you choose one of the three built-in exception class as a super class. These classes contain the interface to maintain message texts, attributes, and the required methods to retrieve the error/message text, etc. These three classes are, in turn, subclasses of the super class CX_ROOT.

For your hands-on exercise, you are assigning the exception class CX_STATIC_CHECK as a super class to your custom exception class YCX_YCL_CH11_EXCEPTIONS1.

Create Exception Class – Opening Screen

Navigate to the class builder. The name of a custom exception class must start with either 'YCX' or 'ZCX.' Enter a name for the exception class: YCX_YCL_CH11_EXCEPTIONS1.

Click the create button/function key F5. Figure 11-52 will appear.

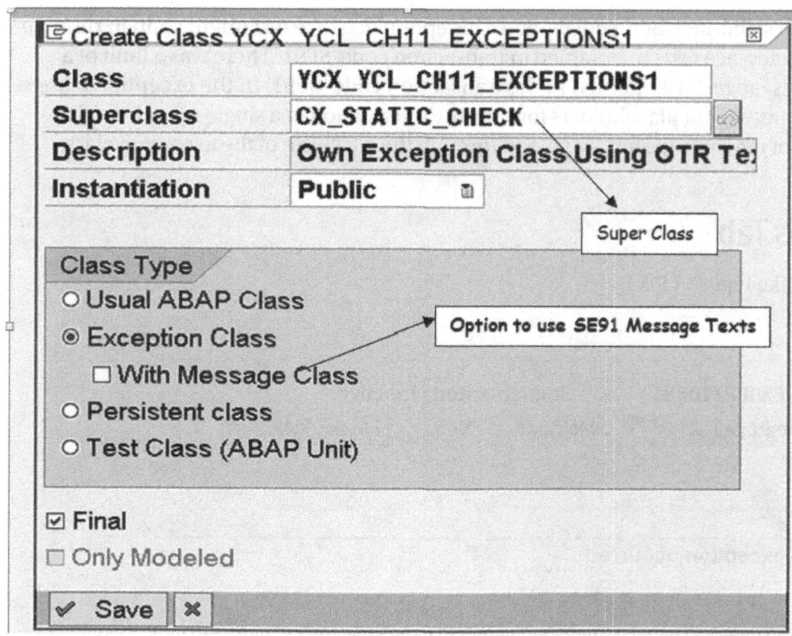

Figure 11-52. *Create Exeption Class YCX_YCL_CH11_EXCEPTIONS1*

The radio button of *Exception Class* is enabled. You have assigned the super class CX_STATIC_CHECK. If you enable the checkbox: *With Message Class*; you can use the message texts maintained in transaction code 'SE91' (database table T100). If you do not enable this checkbox, you can create/maintain the texts within the exception class. This is OTR (Online Text Repository) text. Within an exception class, you can use either one of these: 'SE91' maintained texts or the OTR texts. In the present exception class, you will use the OTR texts.

Click the save button. The system will prompt for a package.

Create Exception Class – *Attributes* Tab

After the package assignment, the screen in Figure 11-53 will appear.

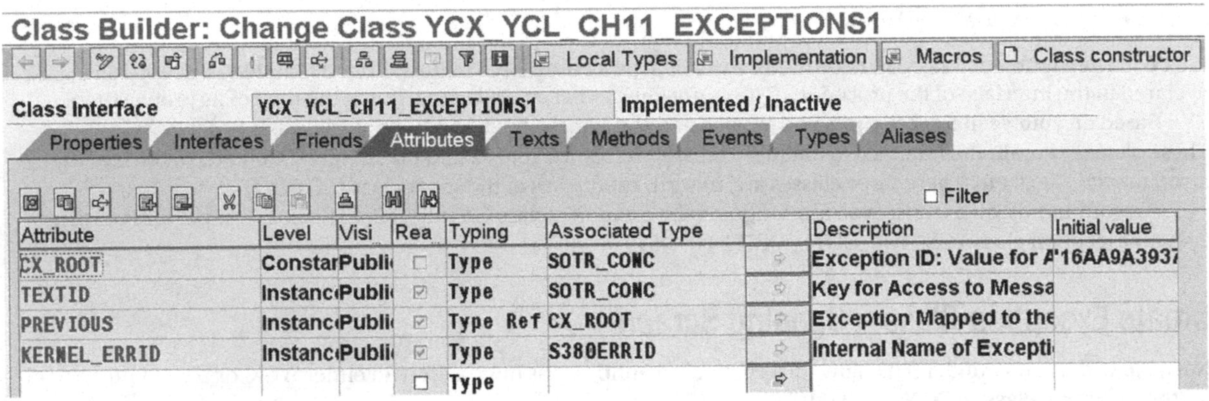

Figure 11-53. *Exception Class YCX_YCL_CH11_EXCEPTIONS1: Attributes Tab*

You can create and maintain attributes: static, instance, constants. An exception message text might contain runtime information. Recall the placeholders in the message texts maintained in transaction code 'SE91.' There was a limit of a maximum of four placeholders of one message text maintained in the transaction code 'SE91.' In the exception classes using the OTR texts, there is no limit on the number of placeholders for runtime information in a single exception Id or text Id. The runtime information to be part of the message texts is passed through the attributes of the exception class.

Create Exception Class – *Texts* Tab

Click on the *text* tab. The screen will look like Figure 11-54.

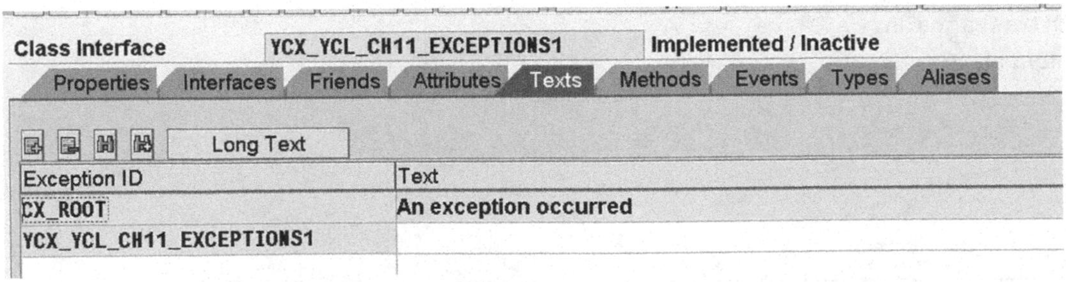

Figure 11-54. *Exception Class YCX_YCL_CH11_EXCEPTIONS1: Texts Tab*

Under the column *Exception ID*, you can enter the exception text identifiers. (*Exception Id* and *Text Id* are synonymous.) The name space for these text identifiers is a maximum of thirty characters. Stick to the first character as alphabet and the rest as alphanumeric with embedded underscores (_) convention. Under the column *Text*, you can enter the text. There is an option to enter long text. (Button *Long Text* over the column *Exception ID*.)

The runtime information in the message text is indicated by enclosing the exception class's attribute names within ampersands (&).

For example, if you are reporting an invalid customer code, you can create an attribute of name 'KUNNR' and assign it the data element type 'KUNNR.' Within the message text, you will embed the following 'Customer Code: &KUNNR& Invalid.' Before issuing the message, you will assign or set the attribute 'KUNNR,' the invalid customer code you are reporting as error. You can embed any number of attributes in a message text (i.e., there is no limit to the runtime information in an OTR message text). The attributes embedded in message texts must be defined in the exception class.

Create Exception Class – *Methods* Tab

Now, click on the Methods tab. The screen will look like Figure 11-55.

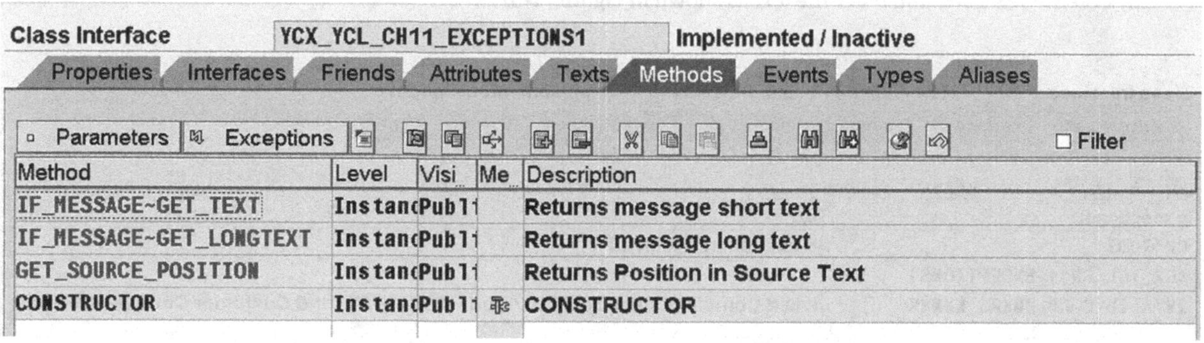

Class Interface YCX_YCL_CH11_EXCEPTIONS1 Implemented / Inactive

Properties | Interfaces | Friends | Attributes | Texts | Methods | Events | Types | Aliases

Parameters | Exceptions | Filter

Method	Level	Visi	Me	Description
IF_MESSAGE~GET_TEXT	Instanc	Publi		Returns message short text
IF_MESSAGE~GET_LONGTEXT	Instanc	Publi		Returns message long text
GET_SOURCE_POSITION	Instanc	Publi		Returns Position in Source Text
CONSTRUCTOR	Instanc	Publi		CONSTRUCTOR

Figure 11-55. *Exception Class YCX_YCL_CH11_EXCEPTIONS1: Methods Tab*

The methods IF_MESSAGE~GET_TEXT and IF_MESSAGE~GET_LONGTEXT will be used to retrieve the respective texts.

Use Your Own Exception Class in the Event AT SELECTION-SCREEN of an ABAP Program

Error Scenario: Let there be a scenario of raising an exception in an ABAP program. Let two fields 'BUKRS' (company code) and 'KUNNR' (customer code) input through the PARAMETERS... statement.

You will check for the presence of the combination of the values of these two input fields in the database table KNB1 (SELECT SINGLE...). If the combination of values entered is not available in the database table KNB1, issue message, etc., you will report the erroneous values of the company code and customer code as runtime information with the message.

Create Attributes and Texts for Error Scenario: Let the requisite attributes and text be created in your exception class for handling this scenario.

You will need two attributes for the two runtime information to be reported. Open the exception class YCX_YCL_CH11_EXCEPTIONS1 in change/edit mode. Get to the *Attributes* tab. Enter the two attributes as shown in Figure 11-56.

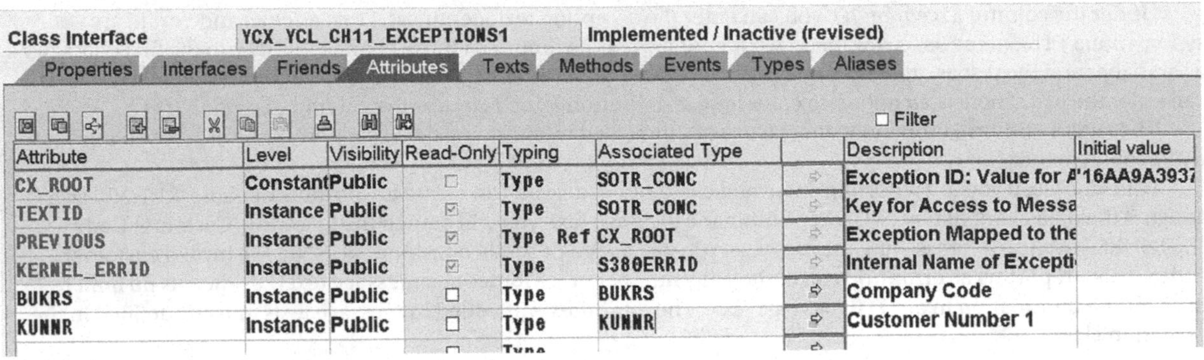

Class Interface YCX_YCL_CH11_EXCEPTIONS1 Implemented / Inactive (revised)

Properties | Interfaces | Friends | Attributes | Texts | Methods | Events | Types | Aliases

☐ Filter

Attribute	Level	Visibility	Read-Only	Typing	Associated Type		Description	Initial value
CX_ROOT	Constant	Public	☐	Type	SOTR_CONC	⇨	Exception ID: Value for A	'16AA9A3937
TEXTID	Instance	Public	☑	Type	SOTR_CONC	⇨	Key for Access to Messa	
PREVIOUS	Instance	Public	☑	Type Ref	CX_ROOT	⇨	Exception Mapped to the	
KERNEL_ERRID	Instance	Public	☑	Type	S380ERRID	⇨	Internal Name of Excepti	
BUKRS	Instance	Public	☐	Type	BUKRS	⇨	Company Code	
KUNNR	Instance	Public	☐	Type	KUNNR	⇨	Customer Number 1	

Figure 11-56. *Class YCX_YCL_CH11_EXCEPTIONS1: Attributes –'BUKRS' & 'KUNNR'*

The *attributes* 'BUKRS' and 'KUNNR' have been assigned the TYPES 'BUKRS' and 'KUNNR' (data elements), respectively.

Click on the *Texts* tab, and enter the text as shown in Figure 11-57.

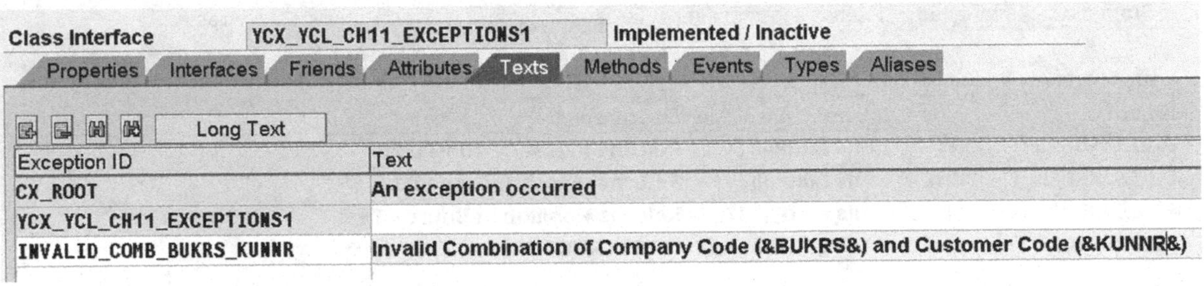

Class Interface YCX_YCL_CH11_EXCEPTIONS1 Implemented / Inactive

Properties | Interfaces | Friends | Attributes | Texts | Methods | Events | Types | Aliases

Long Text

Exception ID	Text
CX_ROOT	An exception occurred
YCX_YCL_CH11_EXCEPTIONS1	
INVALID_COMB_BUKRS_KUNNR	Invalid Combination of Company Code (&BUKRS&) and Customer Code (&KUNNR&)

Figure 11-57. *Class YCX_YCL_CH11_EXCEPTIONS1: Exception ID –INVALID_COMB_BUKRS_KUNNR*

Save and activate the class. The activation screen will look like Figure 11-58.

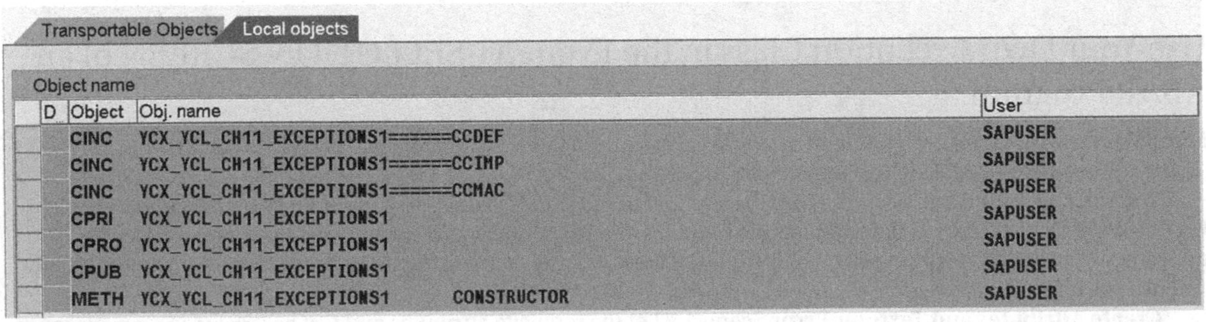

Transportable Objects | Local objects

Object name

D	Object	Obj. name		User
	CINC	YCX_YCL_CH11_EXCEPTIONS1======CCDEF		SAPUSER
	CINC	YCX_YCL_CH11_EXCEPTIONS1======CCIMP		SAPUSER
	CINC	YCX_YCL_CH11_EXCEPTIONS1======CCMAC		SAPUSER
	CPRI	YCX_YCL_CH11_EXCEPTIONS1		SAPUSER
	CPRO	YCX_YCL_CH11_EXCEPTIONS1		SAPUSER
	CPUB	YCX_YCL_CH11_EXCEPTIONS1		SAPUSER
	METH	YCX_YCL_CH11_EXCEPTIONS1	CONSTRUCTOR	SAPUSER

Figure 11-58. *Class YCX_YCL_CH11_EXCEPTIONS1: Activation*

RAISE... Statement Syntax: An exception raising statement (using the class based exceptions) has the following syntax:

```
RAISE EXCEPTION TYPE <exception name> EXPORTING
   TEXTID = <exception name>=><Exception ID name>
   [<attribute name1> = <run time value1>.. ].
```

The RAISE... statement should be included within the TRY & ENDTRY statement block. In your present program, you will be issuing the SELECT SINGLE... statement to attempt to retrieve the row corresponding to the input values of 'BUKRS' and 'KUNNR.' Following the SELECT SINGLE... statement, you will check the value of the system field SY-SUBRC and raise an exception if its value is non-zero.

Your code segment will be like this:

```
TRY.
  SELECT SINGLE <result> FROM KNB1 INTO <destination>
    WHERE BUKRS = BUKRS AND KUNNR = KEY_KUNNR.

  IF SY-SUBRC <> 0.
     RAISE EXCEPTION TYPE YCX_YCL_CH11_EXCEPTIONS1
      EXPORTING
       TEXTID = YCX_YCL_CH11_EXCEPTIONS1=>INVALID_COMB_BUKRS_KUNNR
       BUKRS  = BUKRS
       KUNNR = KUNNR_KEY.
  ENDIF.
........
ENDTRY.
```

In a procedure (i.e., a subroutine/function module/method), this will be the end of the error-raising process. If the RAISE... statement is executed, the procedure is exited, the error condition is propagated or transmitted to the calling program and will be handled, and then reported in the calling program or propagated further.

In your current program, after trapping the error, you will have to report the error as well. So you have a CATCH... statement block for handling and reporting. You will get a reference to your exception class in a reference variable with the CATCH... statement. With this reference variable, you will retrieve the error message text and report the error with a message statement.

For detailed explanation of TRYENDTRY and CATCH... statement blocks, refer to the online documentation.

Source Program:

```
REPORT YCL_CH11_08_TEST_CBE_ABAP_PG.

**************************************************
* Demo Class Based Exception Outside A Procedure **
**************************************************

DATA: KEY_KUNNR    TYPE KUNNR,
      ER_REF       TYPE REF TO YCX_YCL_CH11_EXCEPTIONS1,
      ETEXT        TYPE STRING.
******************************************************
SELECTION-SCREEN SKIP 4.

SELECTION-SCREEN BEGIN OF BLOCK BLK1 WITH FRAME NO INTERVALS.
```

```
PARAMETERS: KUNNR TYPE  RF02D-KUNNR, " combination of these two fields
            BUKRS TYPE  RF02D-BUKRS. " checked for in the table KNB1

SELECTION-SCREEN END OF BLOCK BLK1.

****************************************
AT SELECTION-SCREEN ON BLOCK BLK1.

IF KUNNR CO '0123456789'   " check all numeric
  KEY_KUNNR = KUNNR+6(10). " adjust for KUNNR length being 16
                           " in structure RF02D of all numeric data
 ELSE.
  KEY_KUNNR = KUNNR.       " non numeric data
 ENDIF.

 TRY.

  SELECT SINGLE KUNNR BUKRS FROM KNB1 INTO (KUNNR, BUKRS)
     WHERE KUNNR = KEY_KUNNR AND BUKRS = BUKRS.

  IF SY-SUBRC <> 0.
   RAISE EXCEPTION TYPE YCX_YCL_CH11_EXCEPTIONS1 EXPORTING
   TEXTID = YCX_YCL_CH11_EXCEPTIONS1=>INVALID_COMB_BUKRS_KUNNR
   BUKRS  = BUKRS KUNNR = KEY_KUNNR.

  ENDIF.

  CATCH YCX_YCL_CH11_EXCEPTIONS1 INTO ER_REF.
  ETEXT = ER_REF->IF_MESSAGE~GET_TEXT( ).
  MESSAGE ETEXT TYPE 'E'.

ENDTRY.

****************************************
START-OF-SELECTION.

WRITE:/5 'Valid Combination:', BUKRS, KEY_KUNNR.
```

The combination of KUNNR = 486 and BUKRS = 3000 is invalid. The input of these values results in an exception. The screen reporting the error will look like Figure 11-59.

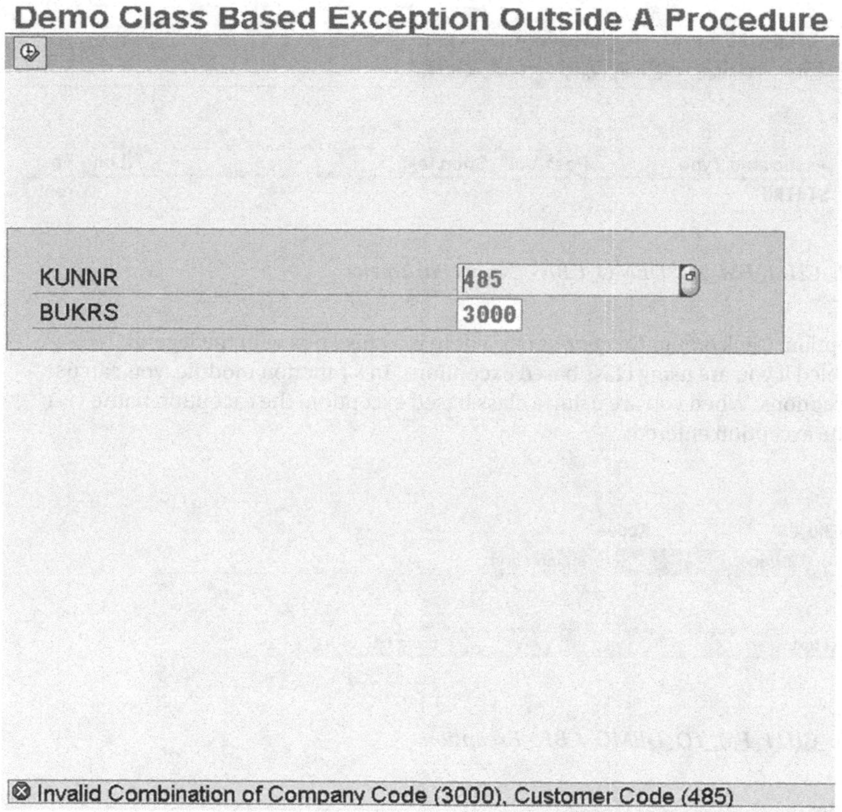

Demo Class Based Exception Outside A Procedure

KUNNR	485
BUKRS	3000

Invalid Combination of Company Code (3000), Customer Code (485)

Figure 11-59. Program: CL_CH11_08_TEST_CBE_ABAP_PG Error Condition

Use a Custom Class Based Exception in the Function Module

Error Scenario: You had created a method 'BEAD_STRINGS' in the custom class YCL_CH11_CL_STRING_OPERATIONS. You implemented this same logic in a function module. In the method of this class, you were raising an exception using the MESSAGE... statement variation (non-classed based exception) if input internal table or textual array was empty. In the function module, you will raise an exception using your exception class YCX_YCL_CH11_EXCEPTION1.

Navigate to the function builder (transaction code: SE37), create a new function group YCL_CH11_TO_DEMO_CBE, and activate it. Create a new function module YCL_CH11_FM_TO_DEMO_CBE. It accepts the text array as 'TABLEs' parameter, returning a concatenated sting of individual rows of the text array separated by a space.

The parameters are as follows:

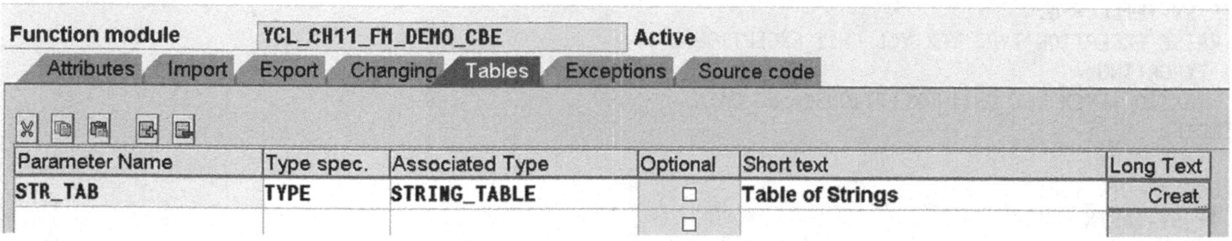

Function module YCL_CH11_FM_DEMO_CBE Active

Attributes | Import | Export | Changing | Tables | Exceptions | Source code

Parameter Name	Type spec.	Associated Type	Optional	Short text	Long Text
STR_TAB	TYPE	STRING_TABLE	☐	Table of Strings	Creat
			☐		

Figure 11-60. Function Module: YCL_CH11_FM_TO_DEMO_CBE - Tables Parameter

Function module YCL_CH11_FM_DEMO_CBE Active

Attributes Import Export Changing Tables Exceptions Source code

Parameter Name	Type spec.	Associated Type	Pass Val	Short text	Long Text
RETURN_STR	TYPE	STRING	☐		Creat

Figure 11-61. *Function Module: YCL_CH11_FM_TO_DEMO_CBE - Export Parameter*

You are using a class based exception. Click on the *Exceptions* tab. There is a checkbox with the legend *Exception Classes*. This has to be enabled if you are using class based exceptions. In a function module, you can use either non-classed or class based exceptions. When you are using a class based exception, the exception name you enter should exist. The screen with the exception entered:

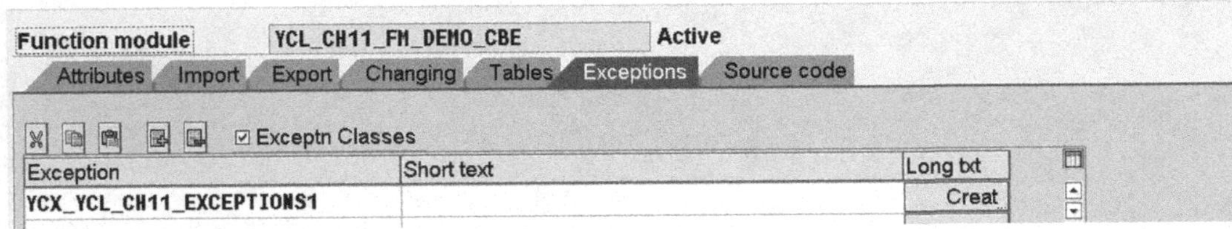

Figure 11-62. *Function Module: YCL_CH11_FM_TO_DEMO_CBE - Exception*

The function module source code:

```
FUNCTION YCL_CH11_FM_DEMO_CBE.
*"----------------------------------------------------------------------
*"*"Local Interface:
*"  EXPORTING
*"     VALUE(RETURN_STR) TYPE  STRING
*"  TABLES
*"      STR_TAB TYPE  STRING_TABLE
*"  RAISING
*"      YCX_YCL_CH11_EXCEPTIONS1
*"----------------------------------------------------------------------

DESCRIBE TABLE STR_TAB.

IF SY-TFILL = 0.
 RAISE EXCEPTION TYPE YCX_YCL_CH11_EXCEPTIONS1
  EXPORTING
  TEXTID = YCX_YCL_CH11_EXCEPTIONS1=>NO_DATA.
ENDIF.

LOOP AT STR_TAB.
 IF SY-TABIX = 1.
  RETURN_STR = STR_TAB.
```

```
  ELSE.
   CONCATENATE RETURN_STR STR_TAB INTO RETURN_STR
    SEPARATED BY ' '.
  ENDIF.
 ENDLOOP.

 ENDFUNCTION.
```

In the ABAP program calling this function module, it contains an option to load the array (or not) because your main interest is in testing the exception, and not so much the concatenation process.

The source program calling the function module:

```
REPORT YCL_CH11_09_TEST_CBE_IN_FM.

*************************************************
* Demo Class Based Exception in Function Module **
*************************************************

DATA: TABA     TYPE STRING_TABLE,
      RESULT   TYPE STRING,
      EXCPT    TYPE REF TO YCX_YCL_CH11_EXCEPTIONS1,
      ERR_TEXT TYPE STRING.

PARAMETERS: LOAD_DAT(1)  TYPE C DEFAULT 'X'.

START-OF-SELECTION.

IF LOAD_DAT = 'X'.
 SELECT LTX FROM T247 INTO TABLE TABA WHERE SPRAS = SY-LANGU.
ENDIF.

TRY.

CALL FUNCTION 'YCL_CH11_FM_DEMO_CBE'
 IMPORTING
   RETURN_STR                      = RESULT
  TABLES
    STR_TAB                        = TABA
          .

WRITE:/5 'Result:', RESULT. " all non-error statements

CATCH YCX_YCL_CH11_EXCEPTIONS1 INTO EXCPT.

ERR_TEXT = EXCPT->IF_MESSAGE~GET_TEXT( ).

MESSAGE ERR_TEXT TYPE 'S' DISPLAY LIKE 'E'.

ENDTRY.
```

Testing with LOAD_DAT = '   ' will trigger the exception. The screen with an error message will look like Figure 11-63.

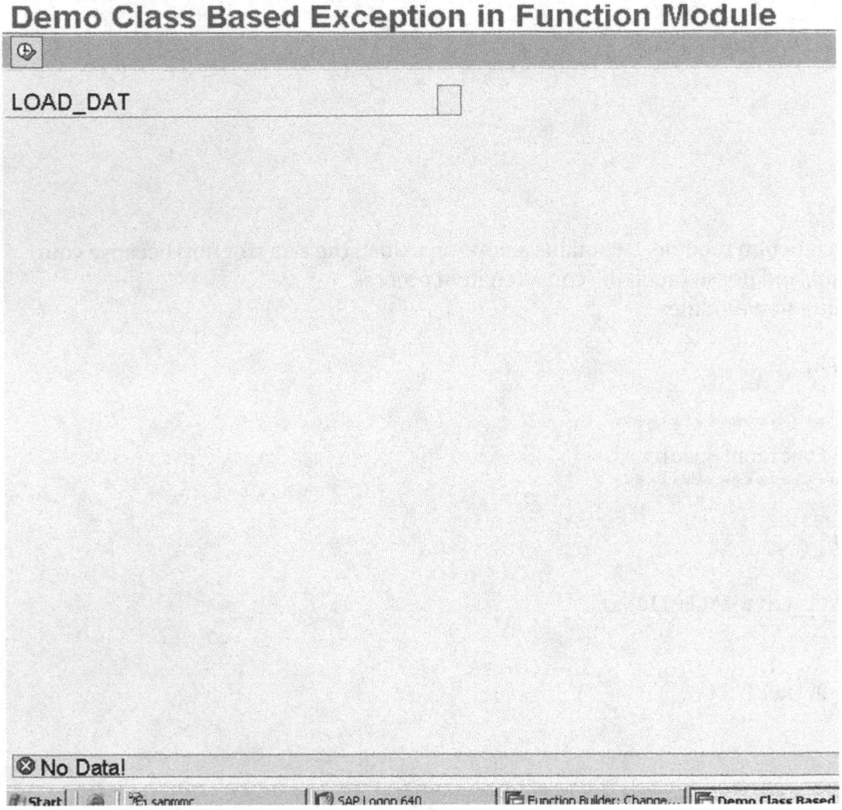

Figure 11-63. Program: YCL_CH11_09_TEST_CBE_IN_FM - Exception

This is the end of the demonstration of class based exception in a function module.

In a similar way, you can use class based exceptions inside methods of classes. Within a class, you can either use class based exceptions or non-class based exceptions.

You created your exception class YCX_YCL_CH11_EXCEPTIONS1 with OTR text. Let another exception class YCX_YCL_CH11_EXCEPTIONS2 be created that will take texts that are maintained in the transaction code SE91.

Create a Custom Exception Class (Message Class Text)

Navigate to the class builder opening screen (transaction code: SE24), enter the class name as YCX_YCL_CH11_ EXCEPTIONS2, and press create button/function key F5. In the opening dialogue box, enable the checkbox with the legend 'With Message Class' as shown in Figure 11-64.

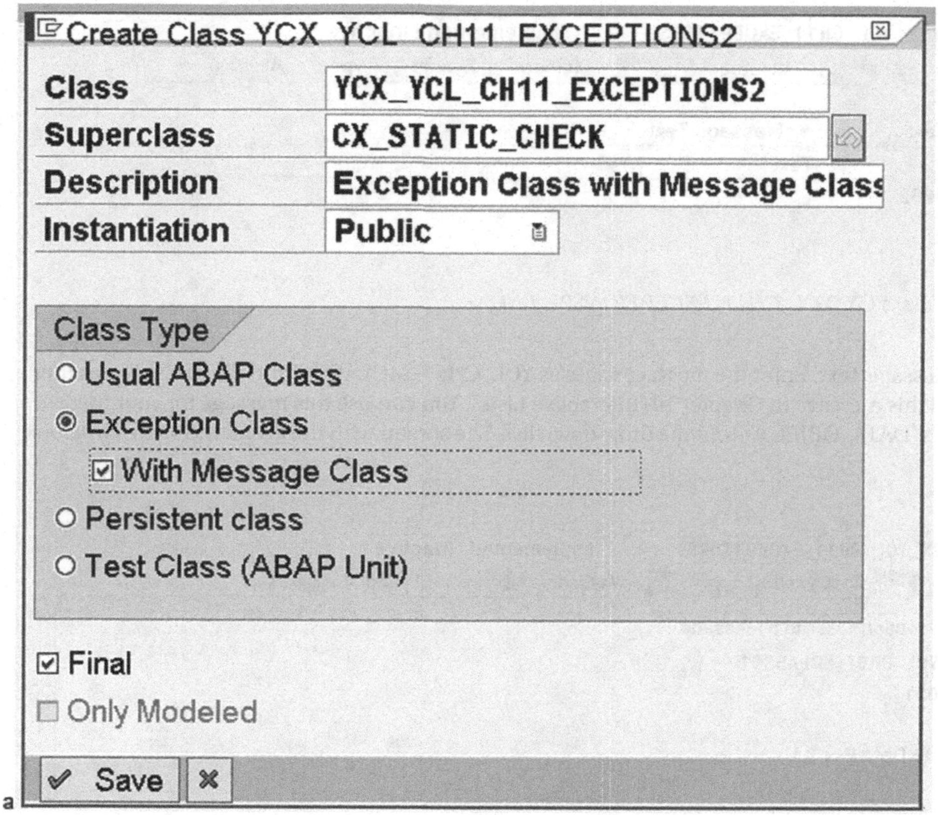

Figure 11-64. Exception Class: YCX_YCL_CH11_EXCEPTIONS2

Click the save button. The attribute screen is presented. You can enter attributes and fetch SE91 texts.

Use a Custom Exception Class in a Subroutine

Error Scenario: You will have a subroutine concatenating the rows of a text array - same as what you implemented in the function module of the preceding example. You will raise an exception if an input internal table or text array is empty. In the subroutine, you will raise an exception using your exception class YCX_YCL_CH11_EXCEPTIONS2.

You will display in the error message the name of the data object (i.e., the name of the text table as runtime information). You are doing this so as to have, at the least, one runtime information in your message. You will pass the runtime information through an attribute.

Attributes & Text in the Exception Class: To pass the runtime information of data object name, create an attribute 'DATA_OBJECT' as 'Instance', 'Public', and type as 'STRING' in the exception class YCX_YCL_CH11_EXCEPTIONS2.

Click on the *Texts* tab. Enter a name for the text ('Exception ID') as 'REPORT_NO_DATA'. The screen will look like this:

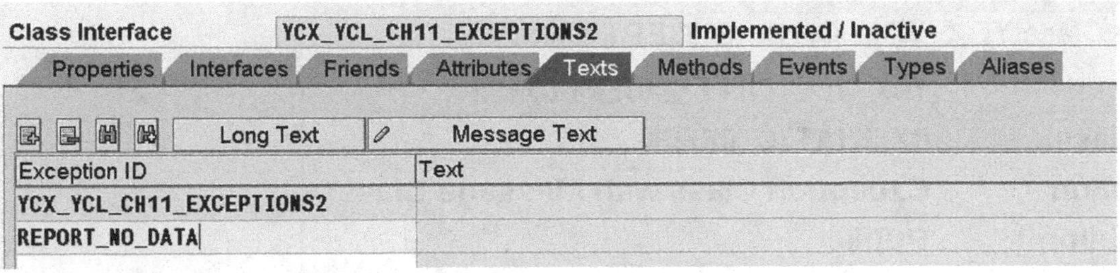

Figure 11-65. Exception Class: YCX_YCL_CH11_EXCEPTIONS2 - Text

Click on the button 'Message Text'. Enter the message Class as YCL_CH07_MCLASS01 and the message number as 21. You created and used this message in Chapter 10 (Interactive Lists). You can use this message for your present purposes. Select 'Attrib. 1' as 'DATA_OBJECT' from the drop-down list. The screen with these entered values will look like Figure 11-66.

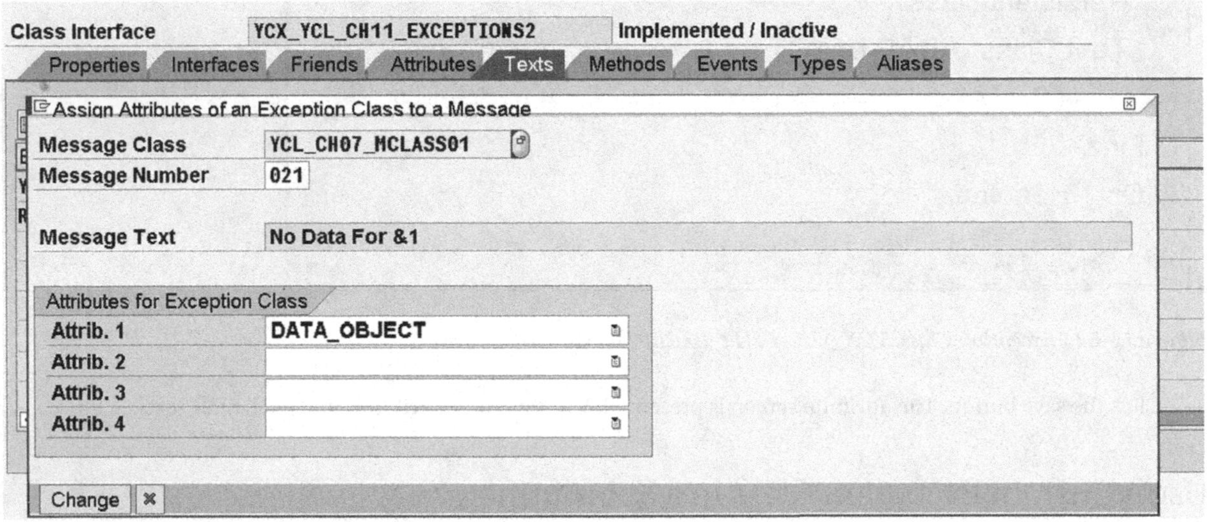

Figure 11-66. Exception Class: YCX_YCL_CH11_EXCEPTIONS2 - Text from Message Class

Press on the Change/continue button. The screen after return to *Texts* tab will look like Figure 11-67.

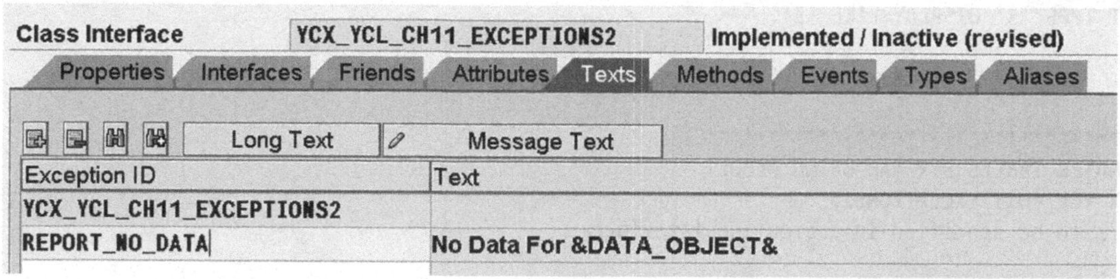

Class Interface YCX_YCL_CH11_EXCEPTIONS2 Implemented / Inactive (revised)

Properties Interfaces Friends Attributes Texts Methods Events Types Aliases

Long Text | Message Text

Exception ID	Text
YCX_YCL_CH11_EXCEPTIONS2	
REPORT_NO_DATA	No Data For &DATA_OBJECT&

Figure 11-67. *Exception Class: YCX_YCL_CH11_EXCEPTIONS2 - Text from Message Class*

Save, perform a consistency check, and activate the class.

The class is used to raise an exception in the subroutine concatenating the rows of a text table. The exception is being raised if the text table is empty. The source program:

```
REPORT YCL_CH11_10_TEST_CBE_IN_SUBR.

*********************************************
* Test Class Based Exception In Subroutine **
*********************************************
DATA: TABA    TYPE STRING_TABLE,
      RESULT  TYPE STRING,
      ERR_REF TYPE REF TO YCX_YCL_CH11_EXCEPTIONS2,
      ETEXT   TYPE STRING.

*********************************************
PARAMETERS: LOAD_DAT(1)   TYPE C DEFAULT 'X'.

*********************************************
START-OF-SELECTION.

IF LOAD_DAT = 'X'.

 SELECT LTX FROM T247 INTO TABLE TABA
   WHERE SPRAS = SY-LANGU.
ENDIF.

TRY.

PERFORM CONCATENATER TABLES TABA USING RESULT.

WRITE:/5 RESULT. " non-error process

CATCH YCX_YCL_CH11_EXCEPTIONS2 INTO ERR_REF.
ETEXT = ERR_REF->IF_MESSAGE~GET_TEXT( ).

REPLACE ALL OCCURRENCES OF '&' IN ETEXT WITH ''.
  " removing the ampersands from message class text
```

```
MESSAGE ETEXT TYPE 'S' DISPLAY LIKE 'E'.

ENDTRY.

*********************************************
FORM CONCATENATER TABLES STR_TAB USING RESULT
  RAISING YCX_YCL_CH11_EXCEPTIONS2.
 " exception/s to be specified in subroutine interface

DATA: STR TYPE  LINE OF STRING_TABLE.

 DESCRIBE TABLE STR_TAB.

 IF SY-TFILL = 0.
  RAISE EXCEPTION TYPE YCX_YCL_CH11_EXCEPTIONS2
   EXPORTING
   TEXTID = YCX_YCL_CH11_EXCEPTIONS2=>REPORT_NO_DATA
   DATA_OBJECT = 'TABA'.
  ENDIF.

  LOOP AT STR_TAB INTO STR.
   IF SY-TABIX = 1.
    RESULT = STR.
   ELSE.
    CONCATENATE RESULT STR INTO RESULT SEPARATED BY ' '.
   ENDIF.
  ENDLOOP.
ENDFORM.
```

Execute the program with LOAD_DAT equal to blank to simulate the error condition. The screen of the error condition will look like Figure 11-68.

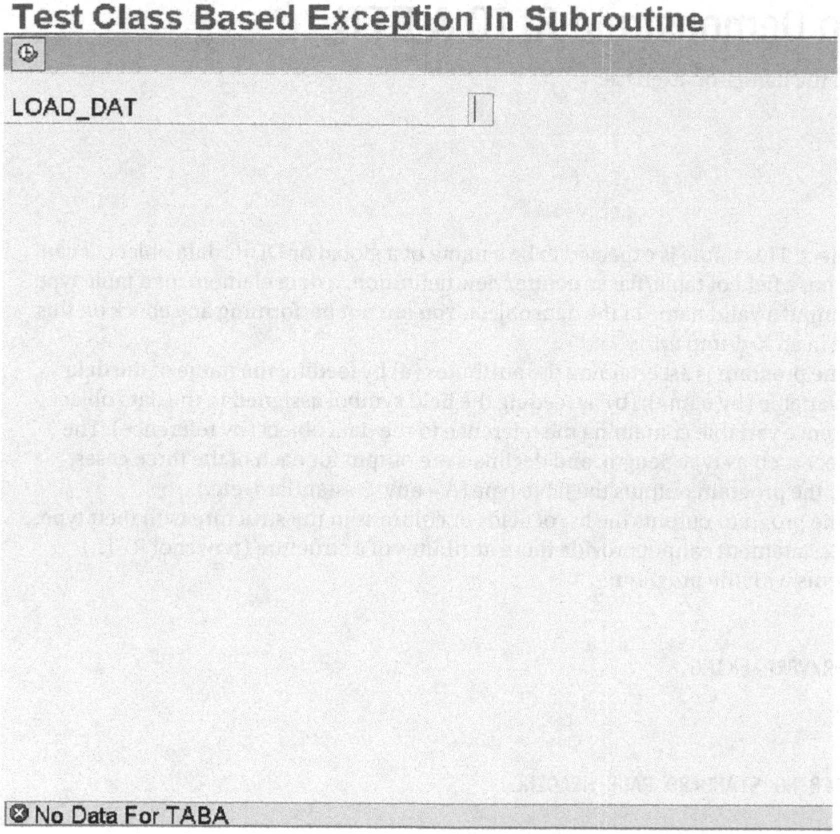

Test Class Based Exception In Subroutine

LOAD_DAT

No Data For TABA

Figure 11-68. Program: YCL_CH11_10_TEST_CBE_IN_SUBR - Error Message

You demonstrated the class based exceptions in an executable ABAP program, in a function module, and in a subroutine. The coverage of class based exceptions is over.

A Brief on the ABAP RTTS (Runtime Type Services)

The RTTS enables the creation of runtime data objects and the determination of attributes of data objects. It has two components: (1) the RTTC (runtime type creation) and (2) the RTTI (runtime type identification). The RTTC enables the creation of runtime data objects. And it enables the determination of attributes of data objects.

You have already used RTTC in Chapter 8 (Field Symbols) where you created a runtime data object using the statement CREATE DATA.... You created a runtime structure based on the input database table/view. Similarly you can create runtime elementary data objects, runtime structure data objects, and runtime internal table data objects.

You use the RTTI to ascertain the attributes of data objects instead of using the procedure statements: DESCRIBE FIELD..., DESCRIBE TABLE..., etc., although ascertaining the number of rows in an internal table at any given point of time is not possible with RTTI. This can be easily achieved by using the DESCRIBE TABLE... statement or the function LINES(<itab>).

A hierarchy of the RTTS classes and their brief descriptions can be found in the online documentation: ABAP System Classes and interfaces ➤ RTTS - Runtime Type Services.

Hands-on Exercise to Demonstrate RTTC & RTTI

You are using the following classes in the hands-on exercise:

```
CL_ABAP_TYPE_DESCR
CL_ABAP_TABLE_DESCR
CL_ABAP_STRUCT_DESCR
```

You input the name of a data object. This name is expected to be a name of a global or DDIC data object. It can be a table/flat structure/view definition, a field of table/flat structure/view definition, a data element, or a table type (an internal table type). Take care to input a valid name of the data object. You are not performing any check on this name. An erroneous name will result in an X-dump error.

For an elementary data object, the program is ascertaining the attributes (a) by feeding the name of the data object contained in 'PARAMETERS' variable (by name); (b) by feeding the field symbol assigned to the data object (by data); and (c) by feeding the reference variable containing the reference to the data object (by reference). The attributes of the elementary data object such as type, length, and decimals are output for each of the three cases.

For an internal table data object, the program outputs the table type (A - any, S -standard, etc.).

For a flat structure data object, the program outputs the list of fields or columns in the structure with their types, lengths, and decimals. A DESCRIBE... statement cannot provide these attributes of a structure (power of RTTI.)

You can try out the following inputs with the program:

```
KNA1/LFA1/T001/VBRK/VBRP
KNA1-NAME!/T001-BUTXT/VBRK-NETWR/VBRP-FKIMG
```

The source program:

```
REPORT YCL_CH11_11_ABAP_TYPEDESCR NO STANDARD PAGE HEADING.

*****************************************************************
* Use CL_ABAP_TYPEDESCR to Determine TYPE, Length, Decimals etc.**
* Use CL_ABAP_STRUCTDESCR to Determine structure components     **
* Use CL_ABAP_TABLEDESCR to Determine Internal Table Attributes **
*****************************************************************

TYPE-POOLS ABAP.

DATA: ABAP_REF  TYPE REF TO CL_ABAP_TYPEDESCR,
      STRU_REF  TYPE REF TO CL_ABAP_STRUCTDESCR,
      TAB_REF   TYPE REF TO CL_ABAP_TABLEDESCR,
      DREF      TYPE REF TO DATA,
      ABAP_TYPE TYPE ABAP_BOOL,
      FWA       TYPE LINE OF ABAP_COMPDESCR_TAB,
      STR_TAB   TYPE STRING_TABLE.

FIELD-SYMBOLS: <FS1>.
*****************************************************
PARAMETERS: DATA_IT(30) TYPE C
  DEFAULT 'VBRP-NETWR'.
*****************************************************
START-OF-SELECTION.
```

```
CREATE DATA DREF TYPE (DATA_IT). " RTTC - dynamic creation of
                                 " elementary data object
ASSIGN DREF->* TO <FS1>. "de-referencing

*********elementary: by data*********
ABAP_REF = CL_ABAP_TYPEDESCR=>DESCRIBE_BY_DATA( <FS1> ).
" RTTI - call static method, get reference/instance getting created

IF ABAP_REF->KIND = 'E'.

    " elementary - not structure, internal table type

 WRITE: /5 'METHOD:DESCRIBE_BY_DATA'.
 WRITE: /5 'TYPE          :', (1) ABAP_REF->TYPE_KIND, "attribute
        /5 'LENGTH        :', (4) ABAP_REF->LENGTH LEFT-JUSTIFIED, "attribute
        /5 'DECIMALS      :', (2) ABAP_REF->DECIMALS LEFT-JUSTIFIED. "attribute

 ABAP_TYPE = ABAP_REF->IS_DDIC_TYPE( ).
 WRITE:/5 'IS DDIC TYPE:', ABAP_TYPE.

********elementary: by name**************
 ABAP_REF = CL_ABAP_TYPEDESCR=>DESCRIBE_BY_NAME( DATA_IT ).
 " RTTI - call static method, get reference/instance getting created

 SKIP 2.
 WRITE: /5 'METHOD:DESCRIBE_BY_NAME'.
 WRITE: /5 'TYPE          :', (1) ABAP_REF->TYPE_KIND, "attribute
        /5 'LENGTH        :', (4) ABAP_REF->LENGTH LEFT-JUSTIFIED, "attribute
        /5 'DECIMALS      :', (2) ABAP_REF->DECIMALS LEFT-JUSTIFIED. "attribute

 ABAP_TYPE = ABAP_REF->IS_DDIC_TYPE( ).
 WRITE:/5 'IS DDIC TYPE:', ABAP_TYPE.

*******elementary: by data reference***************
 ABAP_REF = CL_ABAP_TYPEDESCR=>DESCRIBE_BY_DATA_REF( DREF ).
 " RTTI - call static method, get reference/instance getting created

 SKIP 2.
 WRITE: /5 'METHOD:DESCRIBE_BY_DATA_REF '.
 WRITE: /5 'TYPE          :', (1) ABAP_REF->TYPE_KIND, "attribute
        /5 'LENGTH        :', (4) ABAP_REF->LENGTH LEFT-JUSTIFIED, "attribute
        /5 'DECIMALS      :', (2) ABAP_REF->DECIMALS LEFT-JUSTIFIED. "attribute

 ABAP_TYPE = ABAP_REF->IS_DDIC_TYPE( ).
 SKIP 1.
 WRITE:/5 'IS DDIC TYPE:', ABAP_TYPE.

************flat structure: by data****************
ELSEIF ABAP_REF->TYPE_KIND = 'u'. "structure

 ABAP_REF = CL_ABAP_STRUCTDESCR=>DESCRIBE_BY_DATA( <FS1> ).
```

```
 STRU_REF ?= ABAP_REF. " down/narrow casting with ?= operator

 LOOP AT STRU_REF->COMPONENTS INTO FWA.
  WRITE:/5(4) SY-TABIX, FWA-NAME, FWA-TYPE_KIND, FWA-LENGTH,
    FWA-DECIMALS.
 ENDLOOP.

ELSEIF ABAP_REF->TYPE_KIND = 'h'. " internal table

************internal table: by data***************
 ABAP_REF = CL_ABAP_TABLEDESCR=>DESCRIBE_BY_DATA( <FS1> ).
 TAB_REF ?= ABAP_REF. " down/narrow casting with ?= operator
 WRITE: /5 'METHOD:DESCRIBE_BY_DATA_REF '.
 WRITE: /5 'TABLE KIND  :', (1) TAB_REF->TABLE_KIND, "attribute
        /5 'KEY DEFINED :', (4) TAB_REF->KEY_DEFKIND, "attribute
        /5 'UNIQUE KEY  :', (2) TAB_REF->HAS_UNIQUE_KEY. "attribute

ENDIF.
```

The output of lengths for character-oriented TYPES ('C,' 'D,' et al.) will be equivalent to the lengths derived with the DESCRIBE FIELD... statement using the 'IN BYTE MODE' variation. You can view the outputs. The input and the outputs for a sample data object are in the following screenshots:

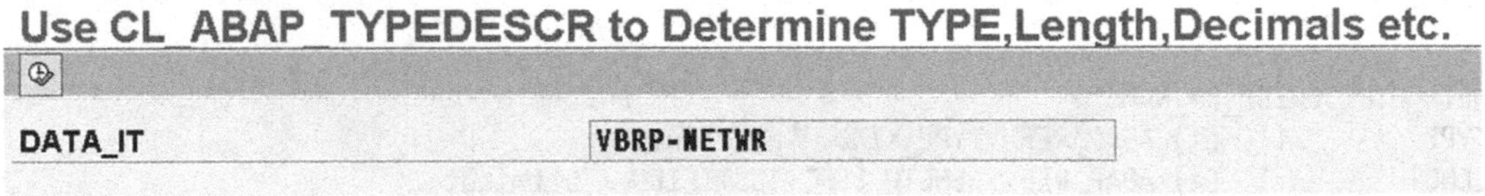

Use CL_ABAP_TYPEDESCR to Determine TYPE,Length,Decimals etc.

DATA_IT	VBRP-NETWR

Figure 11-69. *Program: YCL_CH11_11_ABAP_TYPEDESCR – Input*

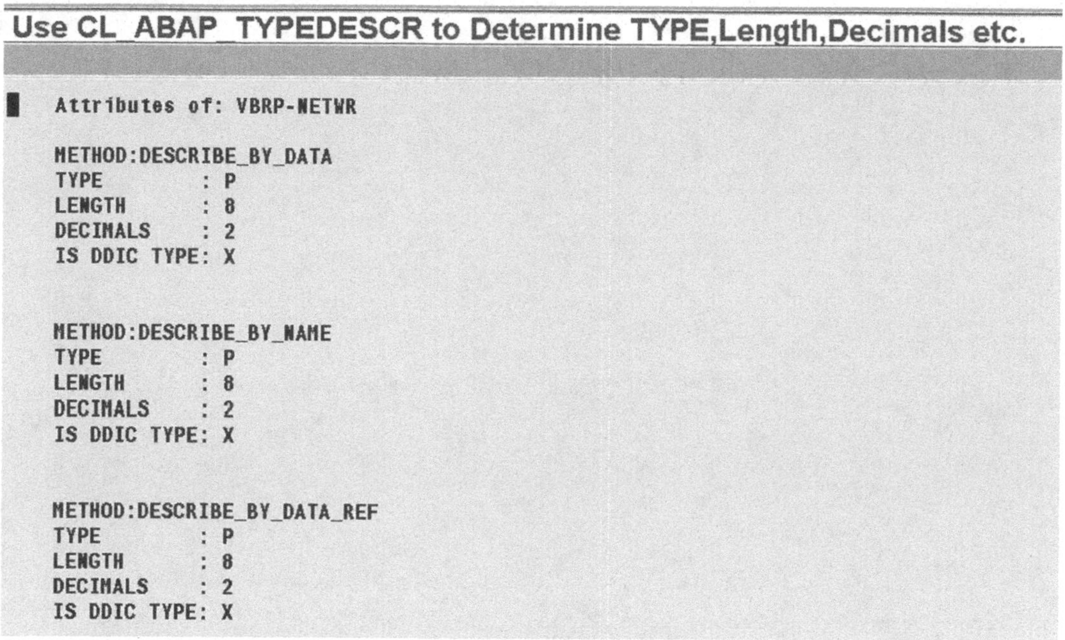

```
Use CL_ABAP_TYPEDESCR to Determine TYPE,Length,Decimals etc.

Attributes of: VBRP-NETWR

METHOD:DESCRIBE_BY_DATA
TYPE        : P
LENGTH      : 8
DECIMALS    : 2
IS DDIC TYPE: X

METHOD:DESCRIBE_BY_NAME
TYPE        : P
LENGTH      : 8
DECIMALS    : 2
IS DDIC TYPE: X

METHOD:DESCRIBE_BY_DATA_REF
TYPE        : P
LENGTH      : 8
DECIMALS    : 2
IS DDIC TYPE: X
```

Figure 11-70. *Program: YCL_CH11_11_ABAP_TYPEDESCR - Outputs*

Conclusion

In this chapter, you were introduced to the syntaxes of class definitions and implementations. You defined and implemented a local class. And you created a global class and used methods of this global class.

You defined a method in a local interface and implemented the interface method in local classes - an illustration of polymorphism using an interface. There is another program in the source program resource illustrating polymorphism using inheritance.

You used methods of the built-in class CL_GUI_FRONTEND_SERVICES to enhance functionalities of a previously performed hands-on exercise that listed data of runtime-specified fields of a database table/view. The database table/view was also specified at runtime. As a further enhancement of functionality, you created a custom context menu that you deployed in this program using the built-in class CL_CTMENU.

You created two custom exception classes using the built-in exception class CX_STATIC_CHECK. In one of these classes, you used OTR texts, while in the other you used texts maintained in transaction code SE91. You used these custom exception classes to handle error conditions in an executable ABAP program, a function module, and an internal subroutine. The chapter concluded with an overview of RTTS.

The class concepts will be carried forward to the next two chapters (i.e., 12 and 13) to produce lists or outputs using the built-in classes.

CHAPTER 12

ABAP List Viewer Outputs—Part 1

In all of the preceding eight chapters (Chapter 4 to Chapter 11), you produced output by using the `WRITE` statement. You have learned about the features of the `WRITE` statement, including interactive lists. But the output generated by the `WRITE` statement is static. The end user cannot manipulate that output any further.

In contrast, the output generated by the ABAP List Viewer (ALV) can be manipulated by end users. The ALV-generated output, called an *ALV report* (or sometimes called an *ALV grid report*), is class based. In this chapter and the next, you will use two ALV report classes: `CL_GUI_ALV_GRID` and `CL_SALV_TABLE`.

The end user can manipulate ALV reports in the following ways:

- Reorder or shuffle the field positions of ALV reports.
- Omit or drop fields from ALV reports.
- Reorder, or sort and re-sort ALV reports.
- Filter data by using `SELECT-OPTIONS` for any field in the ALV reports.
- Generate totals and subtotals for numeric fields. The end user can obtain other aggregate values of fields such as count, maximum, minimum, and average (only for numeric fields).
- Group fields.
- Generate graphs from ALV reports.
- Freeze fields.
- Perform ABC analysis.
- Save and maintain layouts of ALV reports.

You will gain a better understanding of these listed features as you perform hands-on exercises in this chapter.

The ALV reports, like the output from `WRITE` statements, can be downloaded to files on the presentation server in various file formats such as text, rich text, Excel spreadsheet, HTML, and XML. The ALV reports, like the output from `WRITE` statements, can be downloaded to the reporting tree and SAP office folder. The ALV reports also can be dispatched to a print spool.

ALV Output Architecture

A brief consideration of ALV architecture is required before you get to the nitty-gritty of ALV classes and their application.

Generating ALV reports by using the built-in classes (especially the class `CL_GUI_ALV_GRID`) requires screen programming. You will learn the details of screen programming in Chapter 14. But you will get a preview in this chapter in order to understand ALV report generation.

First, you will use the built-in class CL_GUI_ALV_GRID to generate ALV reports. These reports have to be located inside container classes, and these container classes have to be positioned on screens. As mentioned in Chapter 9, screens in the ABAP development environment are identified by four-digit numbers. As you may recall, the default selection screen is identified as screen number 1000. During the declaration of user-defined selection screens, you specified a number to define them (SELECTION-SCREEN BEGIN OF SCREEN...).

Some of the built-in container classes are as follows:

- CL_GUI_CUSTOM_CONTAINER
- CL_GUI_DIALOGBOX_CONTAINER
- CL_GUI_SPLIT_CONTAINER
- CL_GUI_DOCKING_CONTAINER

You will use the container class CL_GUI_CUSTOM_CONTAINER to locate your ALV report, which will use the class CL_GUI_ALV_GRID.

The container class CL_GUI_CUSTOM_CONTAINER has to be placed inside a custom control. A *custom control* is a screen element that can be dragged from the *Element palette* of the Screen Painter Layout Editor and dropped on the screen surface. A *custom control* is a reserved physical area on the screen, which allows runtime objects to be located inside it.

So, to start, you will have a custom control, which is a reserved physical area on the screen. In this custom control, you will locate an instance of the built-in class CL_GUI_CUSTOM_CONTAINER. Inside the instance of the class CL_GUI_CUSTOM_CONTAINER, you will locate an instance of the built-in class CL_GUI_ALV_GRID. Finally, you have to populate this instance of the built-in class CL_GUI_ALV_GRID with data from an internal table by using the instance method SET_TABLE_FOR_FIRST_DISPLAY. This layering is represented in Figure 12-1.

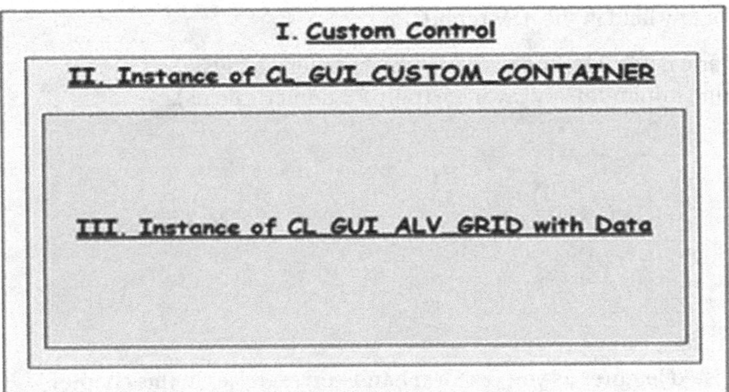

Figure 12-1. *Architecture of ALV report using class CL_GUI_ALV_GRID*

Normally, screen programming is employed to input data. But in the case of ALV reports, screen programming is being employed to output data.

Screen Programming Basics

The main constituent of screen programming is the Screen Painter. You access the ABAP Screen Painter by using the transaction code SE51. Screens do not exist independent of ABAP programs; they are attached to ABAP programs (just as statuses are attached in the Menu Painter). To create, display, or change a screen, you must enter an ABAP program and a screen number on the opening screen of the Screen Painter. The Screen Painter has the following components:

- Attributes
- Layout Editor
- Element List
- Flow Logic

Attributes

In the Attributes section, you have to specify the following:

- Short description of the screen
- Screen type (normal screen, subscreen, modal dialog box, or selection screen)
- Settings
- Other attributes

These are attributes of the overall screen, which are different from attributes of particular screen elements. Other information (for example, the date the screen was last changed) is maintained by the system.

Figure 12-2 shows the Screen Painter's Attributes tab.

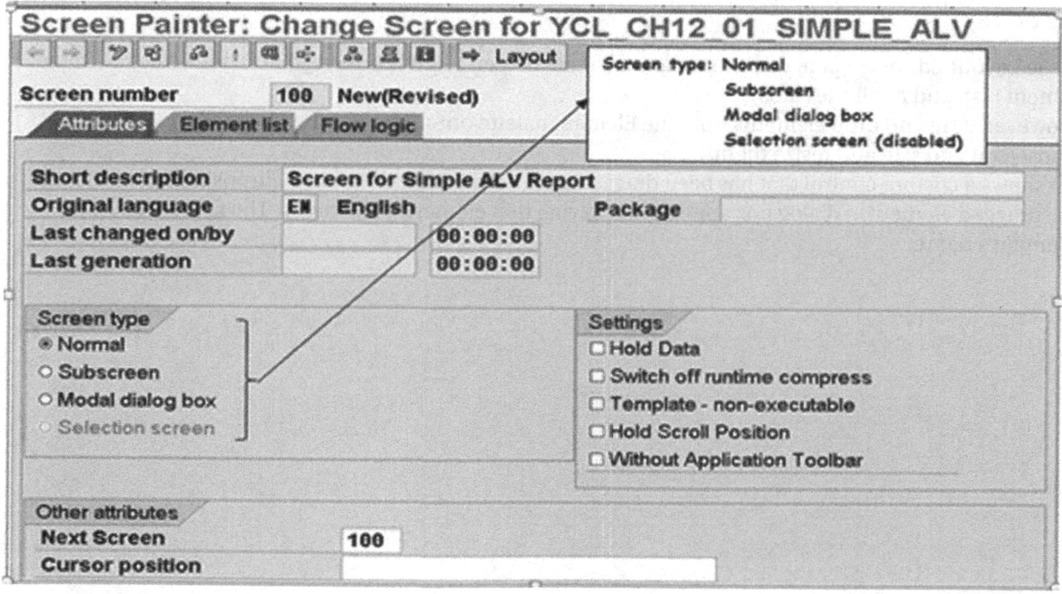

Figure 12-2. *Using the Screen Painter to set screen attributes*

Layout Editor

Screen layout is maintained with a graphical or nongraphical Layout Editor. In this chapter and the next, only the graphical editor is used.

You open the Layout Editor by clicking the ⇨ Layout button on the application toolbar of the Screen Painter. Figure 12-3 shows the Layout Editor with a blank screen.

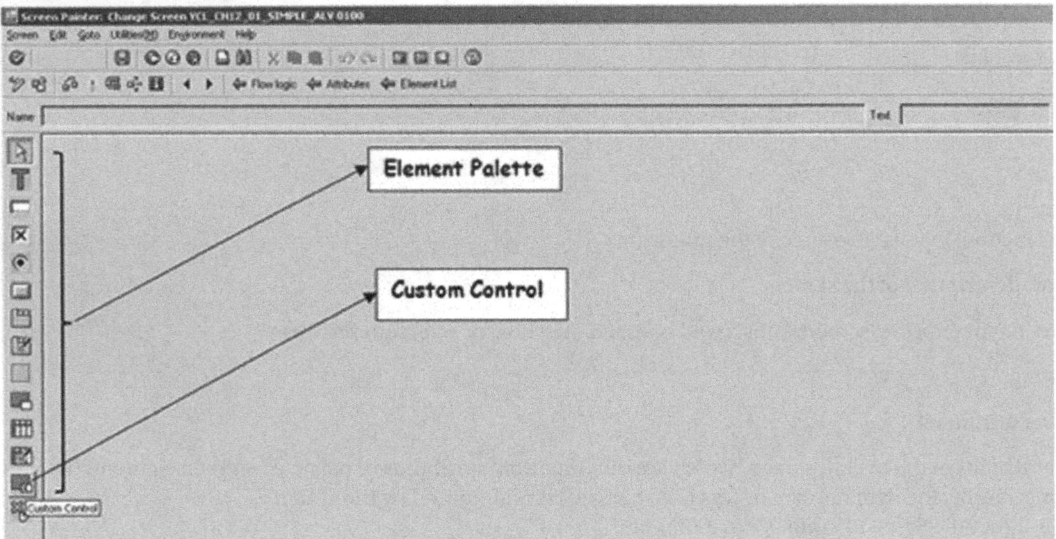

Figure 12-3. *The Screen Painter's Layout Editor*

As long as the Layout Editor is open, you cannot use the main Screen Painter screen (that is, the screen with the Flow Logic, Element List, and Attributes tabs).

You can, however, drag and drop elements from the Element palette onto the screen surface, and you can position them onscreen and size and resize them.

Figure 12-4 shows a custom control that has been dragged and dropped for illustrative purposes. If you double-click the dragged element, a dialog box appears, displaying that element's attributes. The first attribute indicates the element's name.

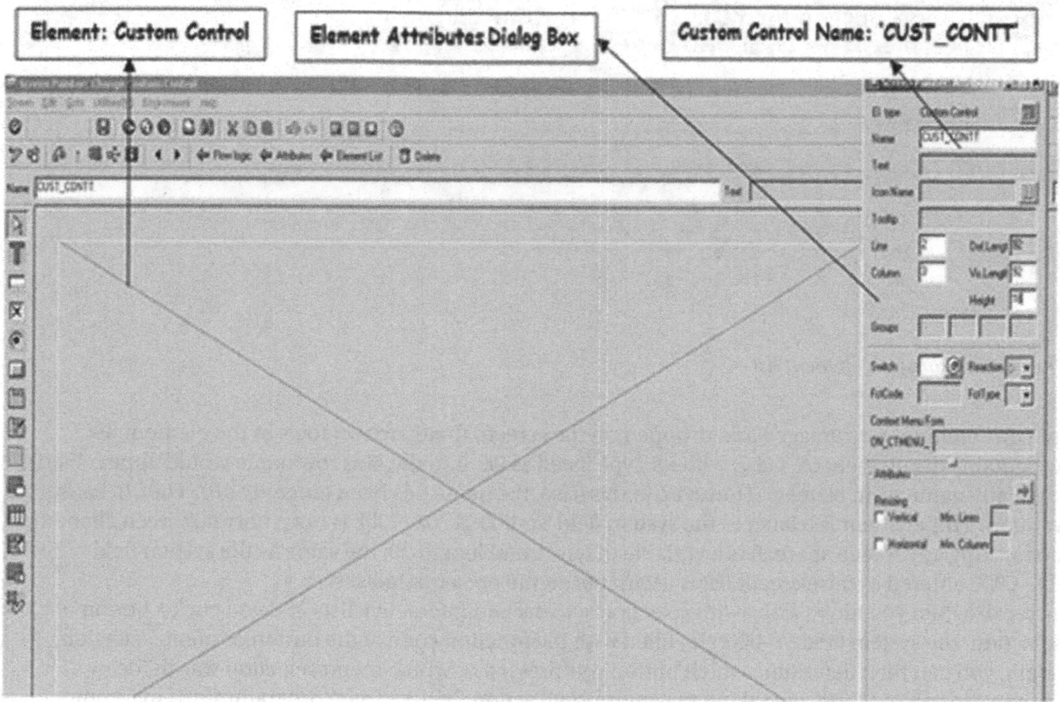

Figure 12-4. Positioning and sizing a custom control in the Layout Editor

Element List

After saving your work in the Layout Editor and then closing it, you return to the Screen Painter You can then click the Element List tab to see a nongraphical representation of the screen. All the elements that you positioned onscreen in the Layout Editor now appear as a list, along with their properties. In our example, the custom control element `CUST_CONTT` appears as the first entry in the element list. The various columns indicate the attributes of that element. For instance, the Type column specifies the type of element (in this case, the type is `CCtrl`, indicating *custom control*).

Line and Col specify the starting position of the element in terms of the row and column. In this example, the entries 2 and 3 represent the second row and third column, respectively. In the ABAP screen environment, you work with rows and columns and not with physical dimensions such as millimeters, centimeters, or inches.

The Deflg entry (82, in this example) indicates the element's defined length in columns. Vislg indicates visible length in columns (82). Height indicates the element's height, in terms of rows (18).

In this example, entries for other element attributes are blank. Figure 12-5 shows the element list.

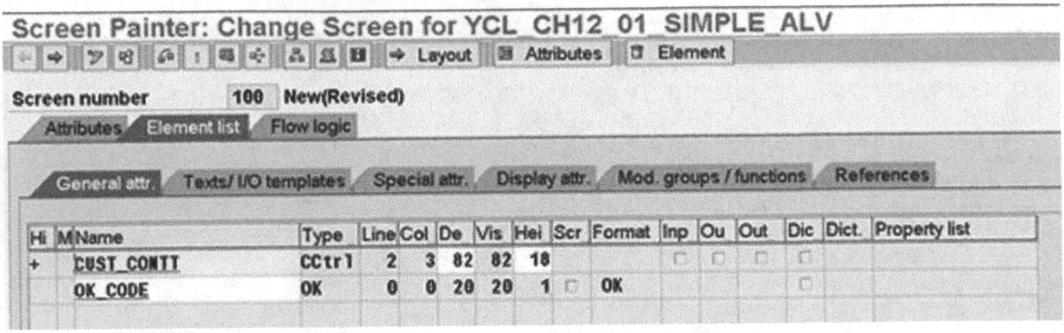

Figure 12-5. *The Screen Painter's element list*

Though only one element was dragged and dropped on the screen, there are two rows in the element list. The second row contains the element OK_CODE, with its Type listed as OK. Initially, this row name would appear blank, and you can assign any name to an element. However, in this case, the name has been entered as OK_CODE because that is the convention. This element is related to the system field SY-UCOMM. OK_CODE is not a normal screen element, in that it does not occupy any screen space. It is a variable of type C and length 20, the same as the system field SY-UCOMM. The OK_CODE entered in the element list is a variable on the presentation server.

As you may recall, when you are working with selection screens and interactive lists and you click a button or make a menu selection, the system field SY-UCOMM is filled with the function code of the button or menu selection. Within the program, you can then determine which button was pressed or which menu selection was made by interrogating the contents of SY-UCOMM and taking the appropriate action. In the screen programming environment (and especially in a multiple-screen programming environment), the convention is to not use the system field SY-UCOMM directly. Instead, the runtime system of the screen processor automatically transfers the contents of the system field SY-UCOMM into the variable you enter in the element list entry as an element of type OK. Corresponding to the OK_CODE variable on the presentation server side, there should be an OK_CODE variable on the application server side (that is, the ABAP program to which the screen is attached). So you need to declare in that ABAP program a variable that is identical in name and of the type OK, as specified in the element list. By convention, this is OK_CODE. In the PAI event, the contents of OK_CODE of the element list (presentation server) are transferred to the field OK_CODE declared in the program (application server). Data transfers to and from the presentation server to the application server are described in Chapter 14.

Flow Logic

In the screen programming environment, there are two main events: PROCESS AFTER INPUT (PAI) and PROCESS BEFORE OUTPUT (PBO). These events can be viewed as analogous to the selection screen events AT SELECTION-SCREEN and AT SELECTION-SCREEN OUTPUT.

Recall that the following actions trigger the selection screen event AT SELECTION-SCREEN:

- Pressing the Enter key
- Clicking a selection screen push button
- Clicking a selection screen radio button (with a USER-COMMAND clause for the radio button group)
- Clicking a selection screen check box with a USER-COMMAND clause
- Clicking a button on the application toolbar or standard toolbar, or making a menu selection

The PAI event is also triggered under identical circumstances.

The selection screen event `AT SELECTION-SCREEN OUTPUT` is triggered in two situations:

- Once, before the selection screen appears to the user for the first time—between the user pressing the execute button and the appearance of the screen, following the event `INITIALIZATION`
- Following the event `AT SELECTION-SCREEN`

The `PBO` event is triggered in an identical manner. `PBO` is triggered in two situations:

- Once, before the screen appears to the user for the first time.
- Every time the `PAI` event is triggered, it is followed by the triggering of the event `PBO`.

You can change the elements' attributes or properties in the `PBO` event by manipulating the internal table `SCREEN`, in which the system maintains the attributes of the screen elements (`LOOP AT SCREEN`, and so forth). The Flow Logic area of the Screen Painter supports only a few of the standard ABAP statements and some special statements of its own. The Flow Logic tab is shown in Figure 12-6.

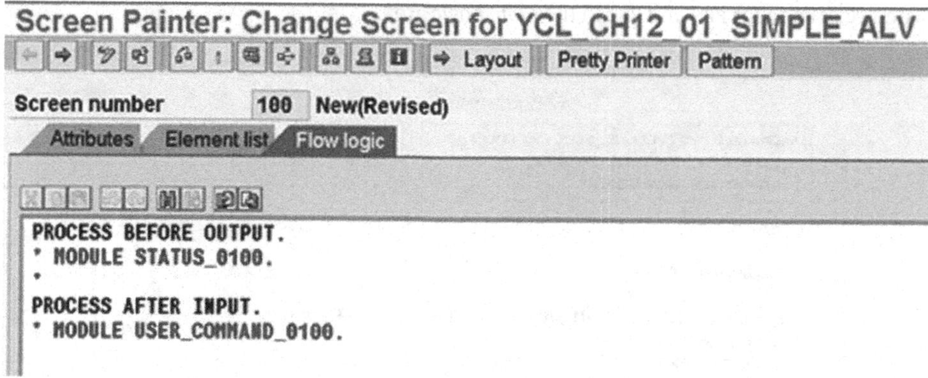

***Figure 12-6.** Screen Painter's Flow Logic tab*

In the Flow Logic area, the first two lines contain the key phrase `PROCESS BEFORE OUTPUT` (`PBO`) followed by a comment. Next, the key phrase `PROCESS AFTER INPUT` (`PAI`), followed by a commented line, appear as the bottom two lines.

Whenever the `PBO` event is triggered, control jumps to the statement following the key phrase `PROCESS BEFORE OUTPUT`. In the `PBO` event, you would, for example, like to change some properties of some elements (that is, execute the code for it). This is done through the ABAP statement `MODULE`. The `MODULE` statement of flow logic is not accepted in the normal ABAP program. It is acceptable only in the Flow Logic area of the Screen Painter. It operates in a manner similar to a subroutine invocation (`PERFORM`), except that there is no parameter or interface concept. The syntax of a simple `MODULE` statement is as follows:

```
MODULE <module name>.
```

Such a statement will make the control jump to a statement following the statement `MODULE <module name> OUTPUT` in the main ABAP program or an include program. The `MODULE <module name> OUTPUT` statement in an ABAP program is similar to the subroutine `FORM` statement. Just as a subroutine is exited with an `ENDFORM` statement, a `MODULE <module name> OUTPUT` statement in an ABAP program is exited with an `ENDMODULE` statement. Any code to be executed must be located between the statements `MODULE <module name> OUTPUT` and `ENDMODULE`.

To sum up, the MODULE <module name> statement is like a PERFORM statement and is allowed only in the Flow Logic area of the Screen Painter. The statement makes the control jump to the module located in an ABAP program, executes the code lines between MODULE <module name> OUTPUT and ENDMODULE statements in the ABAP program, and then returns.

Similarly, when the PAI event is triggered, control jumps to the statement following the key phrase PROCESS AFTER INPUT. In the PAI event, you check the contents of the system field SY-UCOMM (that is, the variable OK_CODE). A basic function you will perform is exiting the program, as shown here:

```
CASE OK_CODE.
 WHEN 'EXIT'.
  LEAVE PROGRAM.
...
ENDCASE.
```

Again, this is implemented through the MODULE <module name> statement in PAI of the Flow Logic area. In the ABAP program, you locate the preceding statements between the statements MODULE <module name> INPUT and ENDMODULE.

Figure 12-7 shows the structure of code for PBO and PAI in the *Flow Logic* area.

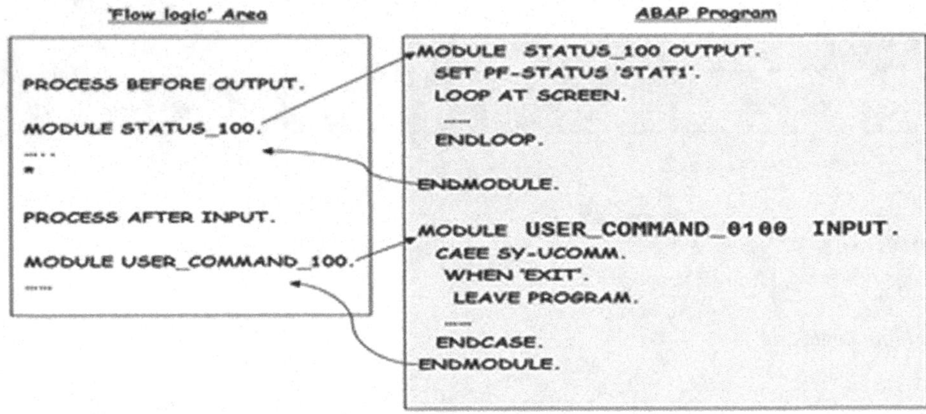

Figure 12-7. *PBO and PAI modules*

The module statements following the key phrase PROCESS BEFORE OUTPUT are called *PBO modules*, and the module statements following the key phrase PROCESS AFTER INPUT are called *PAI modules*.

You can execute any number of PBO and PAI modules with the statements MODULE <module name>, depending on your requirements.

Now that you've had a brief introduction to screen programming, you're ready to continue with this chapter's main topic of ALV output.

The Classes CL_GUI_CUSTOM_CONTAINER and CL_GUI_ALV_GRID

You will be using the CL_GUI_CUSTOM_CONTAINER and CL_GUI_ALV_GRID classes in the hands-on-exercises later in this chapter. So let's view the relevant methods and parameters of these methods in the Class Builder.

CL_GUI_CUSTOM_CONTAINER

Later in this chapter, you will use an instance of the CL_GUI_CUSTOM_CONTAINER class to locate your ALV report. You will not be using any other method of this class other than CONSTRUCTOR to create an instance of this class.

Follow these steps to [do what?]:

1. Navigate to the Class Builder opening screen (via transaction code SE24).
2. Enter the name of the class, CL_GUI_CUSTOM_CONTAINER.
3. Click the display button or press the function key F7. The screen in Figure 12-8 appears.

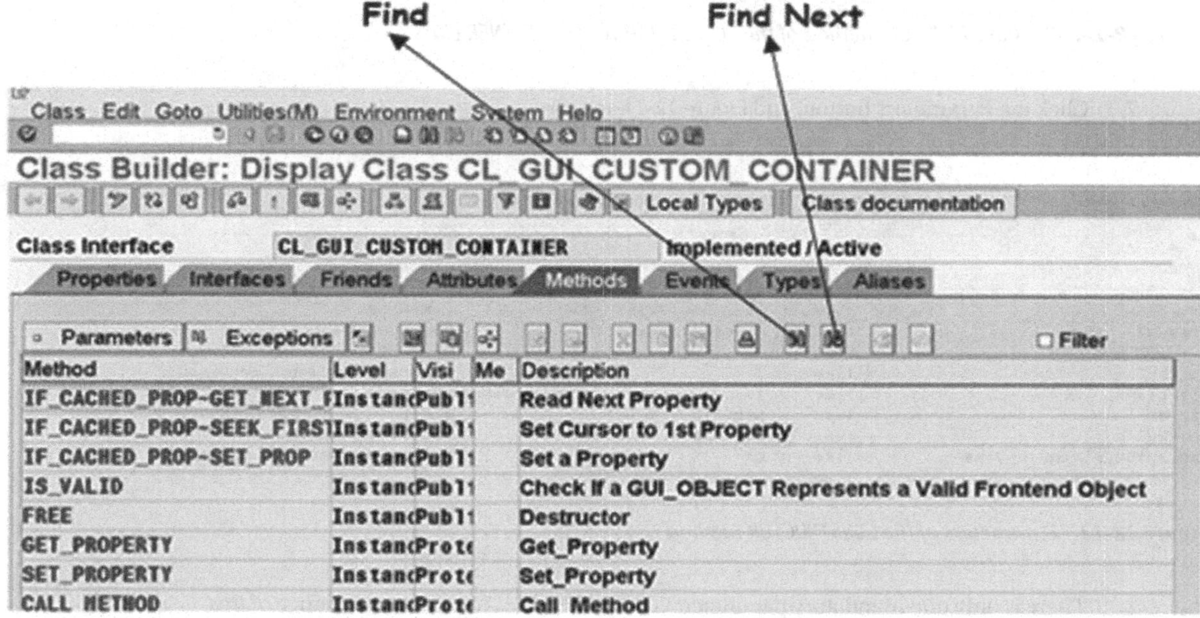

Figure 12-8. *The class CL_GUI_CUSTOM_CONTAINER*

4. You have to locate the CONSTRUCTOR method in the class, so click the Find button, as shown in Figure 12-8. A pop-up dialog box appears, prompting you for the Find string.
5. Enter the word CONSTRUCTOR, as shown in Figure 12-9.

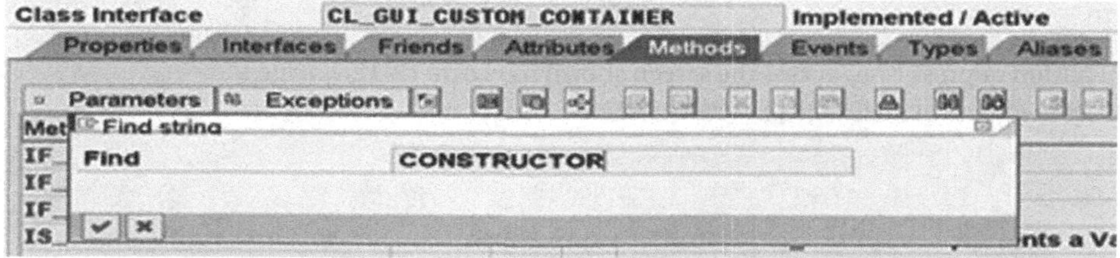

Figure 12-9. *Finding a method of the class CL_GUI_CUSTOM_CONTAINER*

6. If it does not locate the CONSTRUCTOR method, but stops at a location where the string CONSTRUCTOR is occurring, click the Find Next button until the CONSTRUCTOR method is located. When the method is located, the screen will look like Figure 12-10.

Figure 12-10. The CONSTRUCTOR method of the CL_GUI_CUSTOM_CONTAINER class

7. Click the Parameters button, and Figure 12-11 appears.

Class Interface CL_GUI_CUSTOM_CONTAINER Implemented / Active

Properties | Interfaces | Friends | Attributes | Methods | Events | Types | Aliases

Method parameters CONSTRUCTOR

Methods | Exceptions

Parameter	Pa	Op	Typing M	Associated Type	Default value	Description
PARENT			Type Ref	CL_GUI_CONTAINER		Parent container
CONTAINER_NAME			Type	C		Name of the Screen CustCtrl N
STYLE			Type	I		Windows Style Attributes Appli
LIFETIME			Type	I	lifetime_default	Lifetime
REPID			Type	SYREPID		Screen to Which this Containe
DYNNR			Type	SYDYNNR		Report To Which this Containe
NO_AUTODEF_PROGID_DYNNR			Type	C		Don't Autodefined Progid and
			Type			

Figure 12-11. Parameters of the CONSTRUCTOR method

8. There is only one mandatory parameter: CONTAINER_NAME. To create an instance of this class, CL_GUI_CUSTOM_CONTAINER, you need to provide the name of a custom control for this parameter. The instance will be placed in the custom control specified.

   That is all there is to the class CL_GUI_CUSTOM_CONTAINER.

CL_GUI_ALV_GRID

You need to look up two methods of this class: CONSTRUCTOR and SET_TABLE_FOR_FIRST_DISPLAY. Follow these steps:

9. Navigate to the Class Builder opening screen and enter the name of the class: CL_GUI_ALV_GRID.

10. Click the display button or press F7 to access the screen shown in Figure 12-12. Locate the CONSTRUCTOR method, as described for the preceding class.

Class Interface CL_GUI_ALV_GRID Implemented / Active

Properties Interfaces Friends Attributes Methods Events Types Aliases

Parameters Exceptions

Method	Level	Visi	Me	Description
CONSTRUCTOR	Instanc	Publi		Generates and Links ALV Control
FCODE_BOUNCER	Instanc	Publi		Internal, Temporary, Do not Use!

Figure 12-12. Locating the CONSTRUCTOR *method of the* CL_GUI_ALV_GRID *class*

11. Click the Parameters button to display the parameters of the CONSTRUCTOR method, shown in Figure 12-13.

Class Builder: Display Class CL_GUI_ALV_GRID

Local Types Implementation Macros Class doc

Class Interface CL_GUI_ALV_GRID Implemented / Active

Properties Interfaces Friends Attributes Methods Events Types Aliases

Method parameters CONSTRUCTOR

Methods Exceptions

Parameter	Pa	Op	Typing M	Associated Type	Default value	Description
I_SHELLSTYLE			Type	I	0	Control Style
I_LIFETIME			Type	I		Lifetime
I_PARENT			Type Ref	CL_GUI_CONTAINER		Parent Container
I_APPL_EVENTS			Type	CHAR01	space	Register Events as Application
I_PARENTDBG			Type Ref	CL_GUI_CONTAINER		Internal, Do not Use
I_APPLOGPARENT			Type Ref	CL_GUI_CONTAINER		Container for Application Log
I_GRAPHICSPARENT			Type Ref	CL_GUI_CONTAINER		Container for Graphics
I_NAME			Type	STRING		Name
I_FCAT_COMPLETE			Type	SAP_BOOL	SPACE	Boolean Variable (X=True, Spa
			Type			

Figure 12-13. Parameters of the CONSTRUCTOR *method*

Only one parameter, I_PARENT, is mandatory. The object reference variable of the instance of CL_GUI_CUSTOM_CONTAINER is to be provided to this I_PARENT parameter.

12. Click the Methods button to return to the methods list. Scroll to the top of the list to find the method SET_TABLE_FOR_FIRST_DISPLAY. This method will be used to populate the instance of the class CL_GUI_ALV_GRID with data from an internal table. Figure 12-14 shows the location of the method.

Class Interface CL_GUI_ALV_GRID Implemented / Active

Properties Interfaces Friends Attributes Methods Events Types Aliases

Parameters Exceptions Filter

Method	Level	Visi	Me	Description
SET_SELECTED_CELLS_ID	Instanc	Publi		Set Cell Selections
SET_SELECTED_COLUMNS	Instanc	Publi		Set Column Selections
SET_SELECTED_ROWS	Instanc	Publi		Set Selected Rows
SET_SORT_CRITERIA	Instanc	Publi		Set Sort Criteria
SET_TABLE_FOR_FIRST_DISPLAY	Instanc	Publi		Formatted Output Table is Sent to Control
SET_TOOLBAR_INTERACTIVE	Instanc	Publi		Set Toolbar Status

Figure 12-14. Locating the method SET_TABLE_FOR_FIRST_DISPLAY

13. Click the Parameters button, and the screen shown in Figure 12-15 appears.

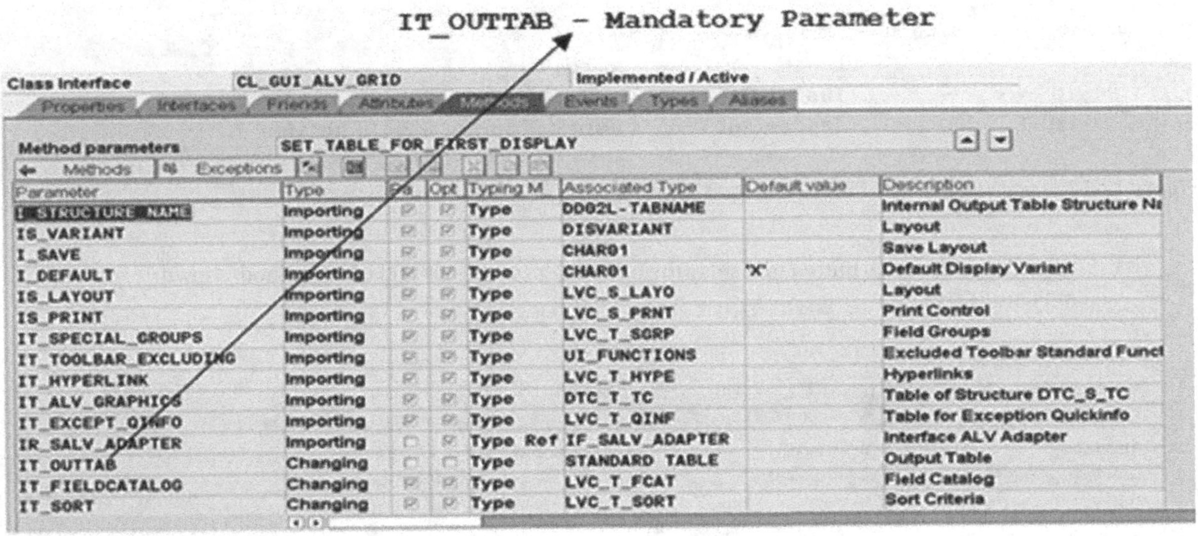

IT_OUTTAB - Mandatory Parameter

Class Interface CL_GUI_ALV_GRID Implemented / Active

Properties Interfaces Friends Attributes Methods Events Types Aliases

Method parameters SET_TABLE_FOR_FIRST_DISPLAY

Parameter	Type	Pa	Opt	Typing M	Associated Type	Default value	Description
I_STRUCTURE_NAME	Importing			Type	DD02L-TABNAME		Internal Output Table Structure Na
IS_VARIANT	Importing			Type	DISVARIANT		Layout
I_SAVE	Importing			Type	CHAR01		Save Layout
I_DEFAULT	Importing			Type	CHAR01	'X'	Default Display Variant
IS_LAYOUT	Importing			Type	LVC_S_LAYO		Layout
IS_PRINT	Importing			Type	LVC_S_PRNT		Print Control
IT_SPECIAL_GROUPS	Importing			Type	LVC_T_SGRP		Field Groups
IT_TOOLBAR_EXCLUDING	Importing			Type	UI_FUNCTIONS		Excluded Toolbar Standard Funct
IT_HYPERLINK	Importing			Type	LVC_T_HYPE		Hyperlinks
IT_ALV_GRAPHICS	Importing			Type	DTC_T_TC		Table of Structure DTC_S_TC
IT_EXCEPT_QINFO	Importing			Type	LVC_T_QINF		Table for Exception Quickinfo
IR_SALV_ADAPTER	Importing			Type Ref	IF_SALV_ADAPTER		Interface ALV Adapter
IT_OUTTAB	Changing			Type	STANDARD TABLE		Output Table
IT_FIELDCATALOG	Changing			Type	LVC_T_FCAT		Field Catalog
IT_SORT	Changing			Type	LVC_T_SORT		Sort Criteria

Figure 12-15. *Parameters of the method SET_TABLE_FOR_FIRST_DISPLAY*

This method has one mandatory parameter, IT_OUTTAB (a changing parameter), for providing the data to be output through an internal table.

For the output to appear, the method, at the least, requires one more parameter. It could be either the importing parameter I_STRUCTURE_NAME or the changing parameter IT_FIELDCATALOG.

If you provide the importing parameter I_STRUCTURE_NAME, you cannot manipulate the output field properties in the program. If you provide the changing parameter IT_FIELDCATALOG, you can manipulate them.

For the first hands-on exercise later in this chapter, you will provide the importing parameter I_STRUCTURE_NAME. The value provided to this importing parameter is commonly a DDIC structure. The output will be as per the fields in the DDIC structure and not as per the fields in the structure of the internal table provided to the changing parameter IT_OUTTAB. Ideally, these structures should be identical. The fields in the DDIC structure may be less than the fields in the structure of the internal table provided to the changing parameter IT_OUTTAB. The field titles, output lengths, and so forth, are derived (picked up) from data elements and domains associated with the fields of the DDIC structure.

You will provide the changing parameter FIELD_CATALOG in the subsequent hands-on exercises. This parameter enables you to control the output field attributes in the program. When you perform the hands-on exercise providing the changing parameter FIELD_CATALOG, there will be more detailed coverage.

You will use four more parameters of the method SET_TABLE_FOR_FIRST_DISPLAY in the following hands-on exercises.

ALV Miscellaneous Topics

You will be using the class CL_GUI_ALV_GRID all through this chapter and the class CL_SALV_TABLE in the next chapter to produce ALV output.

An internal table passed to the formal parameter IT_OUTTAB is a changing parameter. Though the ALV is an output, you can change the displayed data on the screen, which will change the data in the underlying internal table passed to IT_OUTTAB. An ALV can act as output as well as input if you are using the class CL_GUI_ALV_GRID. If you are using the class CL_SALV_TABLE, you cannot use the ALV to input.

The field catalog parameter is also a changing parameter; as an ALV output layout can be changed, the field catalog will change.

The input aspect of ALV when using the class CL_GUI_ALV_GRID is not covered. The drag-and-drop aspects of ALV are not covered. The selection aspects (selection of ALV rows, columns, and cells) are also not covered. These are less frequently used features of ALV.

More details about ALV documentation are presented in the resource section of this book.

The ALV output generated by the class CL_GUI_ALV_GRID has a three-dimensional visual effect and is often referred to as an *ALV grid*. Loosely, ALV output is referred to as an ALV grid. When you use the class CL_SALV_TABLE, there is an option to generate full-screen ALV output with two-dimensional visual effects, which is referred to as an *ALV list* or *ALV classical list*.

Hands-on Exercise: Customer-wise Sales Summary of a Specified Company Code as ALV Output: Use Class CL_GUI_ALV_GRID

Parameters for the method SET_TABLE_FOR_FIRST_DISPLAY:

Importing parameter: I_STRUCTURE_NAME

Changing parameter: IT_OUTTAB

In this exercise, you will do the following:

1. Decide the initial output layout and input (database view).
2. Perform all the developmental tasks to create various objects i.e. DDIC structure, menu painter interface, ABAP program, screen etc.
3. Execute the program to produce the output.
4. Change the ALV output layout in various ways as an end user will.
5. Perform ABC analysis and produce graphics from the ALV output.

Initial Output Layout

This is the same report that you generated in Chapter 6 and extended in subsequent chapters. You will now generate it by using the ALV class CL_GUI_ALV_GRID. You must locate an instance of this ALV class in an instance of the container class CL_GUI_CUSTOM_CONTAINER. The instance of this container class has to be placed in a custom control on the screen. This architecture was described earlier, in Figure 12-1.

Table 12-1 indicates the fields to appear in the report and their originating tables.

Table 12-1. Fields to Appear in the ALV Report

Field	Table	Description
KUNNR	KNA1	Customer code
NAME1	KNA1	Customer name
ORT01	KNA1	City
NETWR	VBRK	Total of converted NETWR for the customer

You used the database view YCL_CH05_VBRKKNA to retrieve data. You used the COLLECT statement to generate customer-wise summarized data in an internal table. With this internal table of summarized data, you set up a LOOP...ENDLOOP construct to output with the WRITE statement. This last stage of LOOP...ENDLOOP has to change. Now you want to output the summarized internal table data as an ALV report. A rough layout of the proposed ALV report is shown in Figure 12-16.

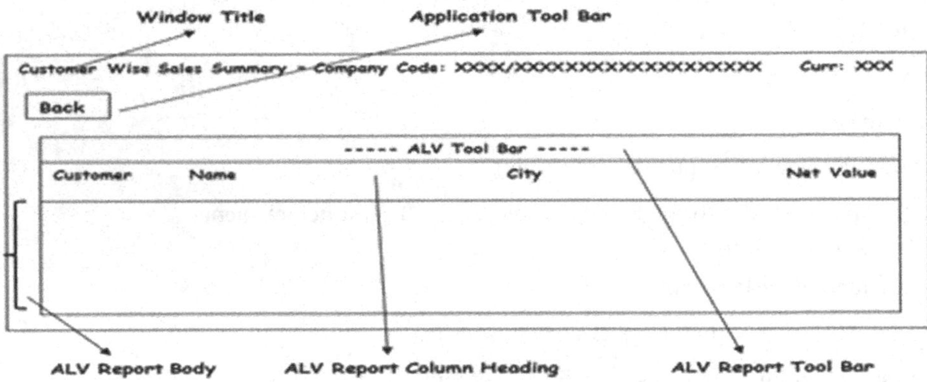

Figure 12-16. Rough layout of customer-wise sales of specified company code as an ALV report

The program will accept the company code for which a customer-wise sales summary is to be generated through the selection screen PARAMETERS statement.

The window title of the output will carry the company code, company code text, and currency. You will impart the window title through the Titles feature of the Menu Painter. The page header and footer for the ALV output are not covered.

You will place a single button on the application toolbar for navigating from the ALV output back to the selection screen and prompting for the company code for which the customer sales summary is to be output. You will create a status in the Menu Painter.

The ALV output will have its own toolbar, distinct from the standard and application toolbars. The ALV output toolbar enables the manipulation of the ALV output.

The field or column headings will automatically output, based on the Heading text from the field- or column-associated data element.

Performing Tasks for ALV Output

You have to perform the following tasks to generate ALV output:

1. Create a new DDIC structure consisting only of fields that will appear in the ALV output.

If you have a DDIC data type CURR field in the structure of the internal table that you will pass to the changing formal parameter IT_OUTTAB of the method SET_TABLE_FOR_FIRST_DISPLAY, it will insist that a DDIC data type CUKY field be specified. In your scenario, you are converting individual billing document amounts in different currencies to a single currency of the company code for which the sales summary is being generated. The currency code has to appear in the window title, not in the report body. Besides, in the ALV output, when you generate totals and subtotals, the ALV system automatically generates currency-wise totals and subtotals. To avoid these issues, the field NETWR should not be DDIC data type CURR in the structure. So you copy the data element NETWR into YCL_CH12_NETWR, to which you have assigned the preexisting domain DEC15_2, which is of DDIC data type DEC and length 15,2. You copied from data element NETWR to get the texts.

Figure 12-17 shows the activated DDIC structure YCL_CH12_SALES_SUM_STRU.

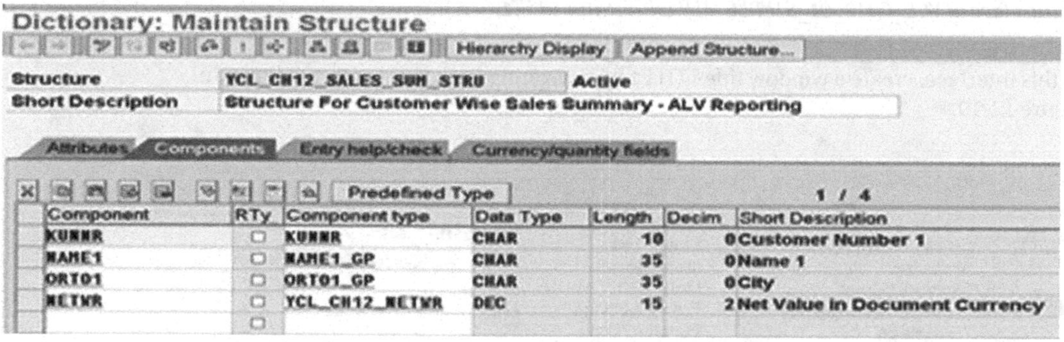

Figure 12-17. *DDIC structure YCL_CH12_SALES_SUM_STRU*

This structure consists only of fields appearing in the output (that is, KUNNR, NAME1, ORT01, and NETWR).

2. Create an ABAP program YCL_CH12_01_SIMPLE_ALV, into which you can copy lines from your Chapter 6 program YCL_CH06_ITAB05, excluding the lines starting from LOOP AT SALES_TAB INTO SALES_STRU. Save the ABAP program.

3. In the Menu Painter (SE41), create a status STAT1 with just one Back button, as shown in Figure 12-18.

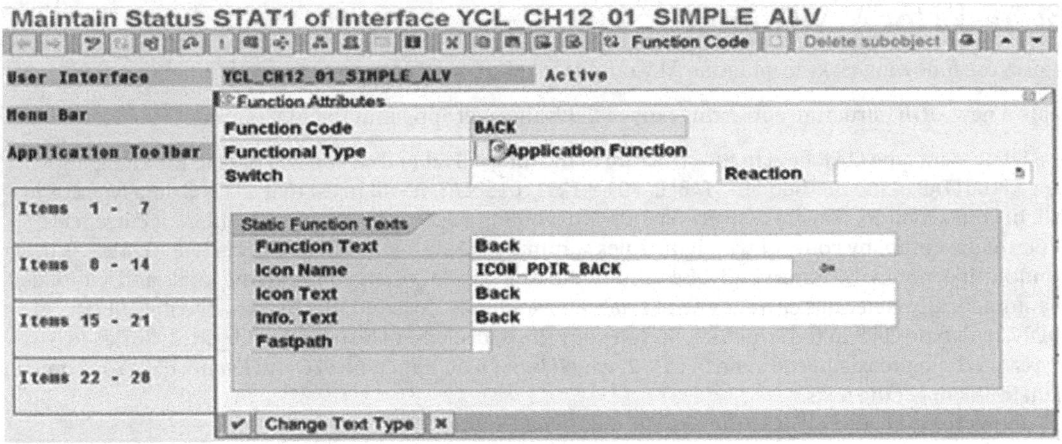

Figure 12-18. *Interface of YCL_CH12_01_SIMPLE_ALV with status STAT1*

4. In this interface, create a window title `TITLE1` by navigating from the status, as shown in Figure 12-19.

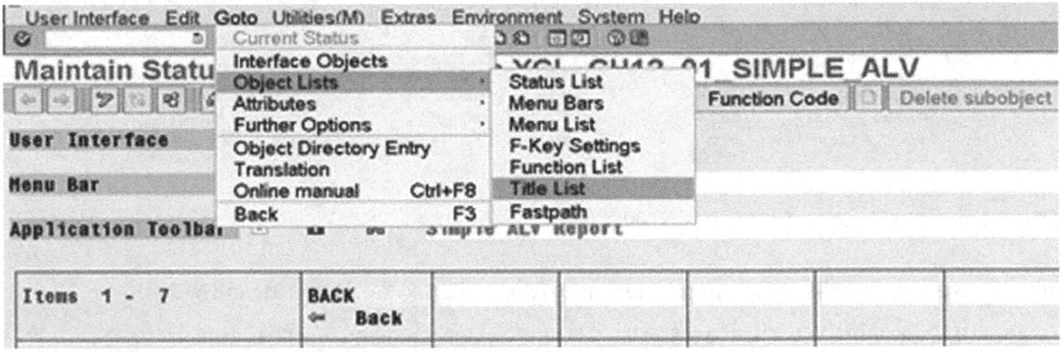

Figure 12-19. *Navigating to the title list*

The screen shown in Figure 12-20 appears.

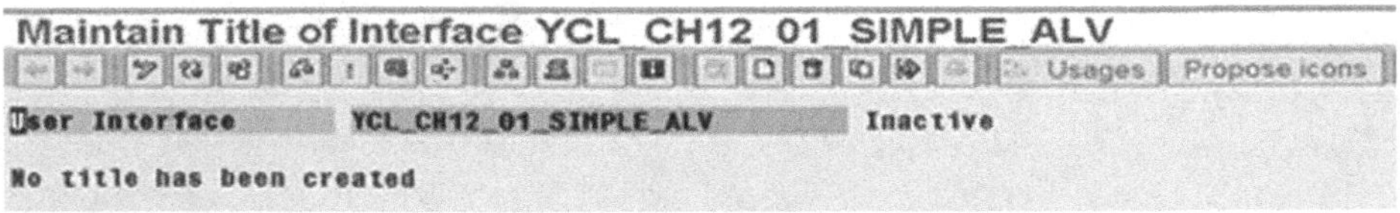

Figure 12-20. *The title list for the interface YCL_CH12_01_SIMPLE_ALV*

5. Click the Create button. Enter the name of the title as `TITLE1`. Enter the text as `Customer Wise Sales Summary - Company Code: &1/&2 Curr: &3`. Save, perform a consistency check, and activate the interface. The screen will look like that in Figure 12-21.

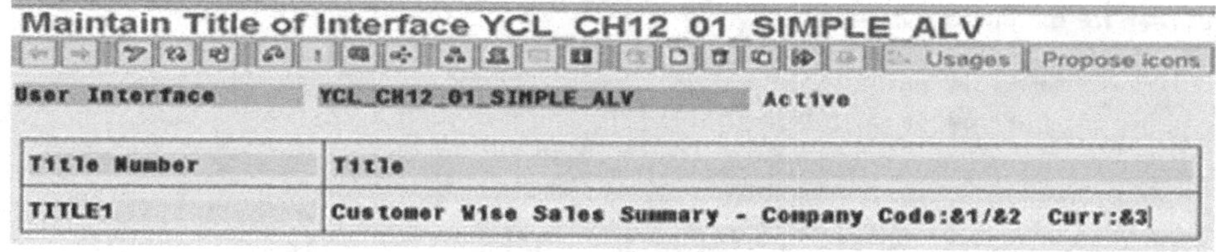

Figure 12-21. *Adding TITLE1 to the title list*

6. You need two reference variables to refer to an instance of the custom container and an instance of the ALV grid, respectively. You also need to declare the `OK_CODE` variable. In your ABAP program, make the following data declarations:

```
DATA:
       ......
       OK_CODE    TYPE SY-UCOMM,
       CCONTR     TYPE REF TO CL_GUI_CUSTOM_CONTAINER,
       ALV_GRID   TYPE REF TO CL_GUI_ALV_GRID.
```

7. You have to create a screen, place a custom control on the screen, create PBO and PAI modules, and so forth. Navigate to the Screen Painter (via transaction code SE51). Enter the program name as `YCL_CH12_01_SIMPLE_ALV` and the screen number as 100, as shown in Figure 12-22.

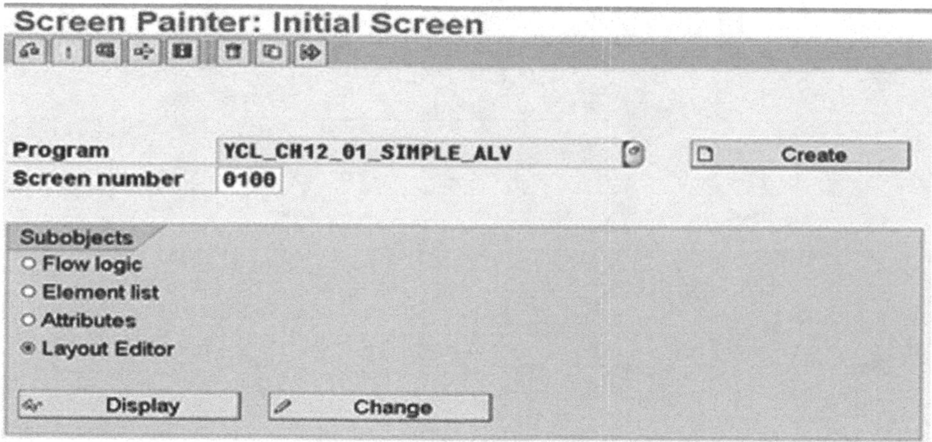

Figure 12-22. *Creating program YCL_CH12_01_SIMPLE_ALV on screen 100*

8. Click the Create button or press F5. In the screen attributes, enter a short description, as shown in Figure 12-23.

Screen Painter: Change Screen for YCL_CH12_01_SIMPLE_ALV

Layout

Screen number	100	New(Revised)	

Attributes | Element list | Flow logic

Short description	Screen for Simple ALV Report		
Original language	EN English	Package	
Last changed on/by		00:00:00	
Last generation		00:00:00	

Screen type
- Normal
- Subscreen
- Modal dialog box
- Selection screen

Settings
- Hold Data
- Switch off runtime compress
- Template - non-executable
- Hold Scroll Position
- Without Application Toolbar

Other attributes

Next Screen	100
Cursor position	

Figure 12-23. Adding screen attributes

9. Click the Layout button. Drag the custom control element from the Element palette. The screen looks like Figure 12-24.

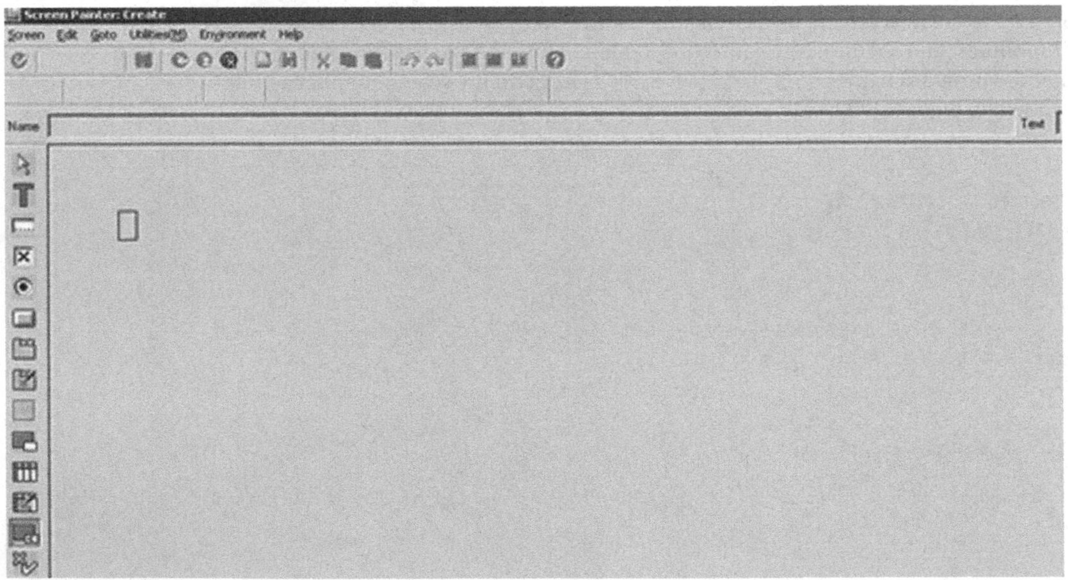

Figure 12-24. Dragging and dropping a custom control

10. Stretch and size the custom control, and then double-click it to access the Element Attributes dialog box. Enter the name of the custom control as CUST_CONTT. Save your work. The screen looks like Figure 12-25.

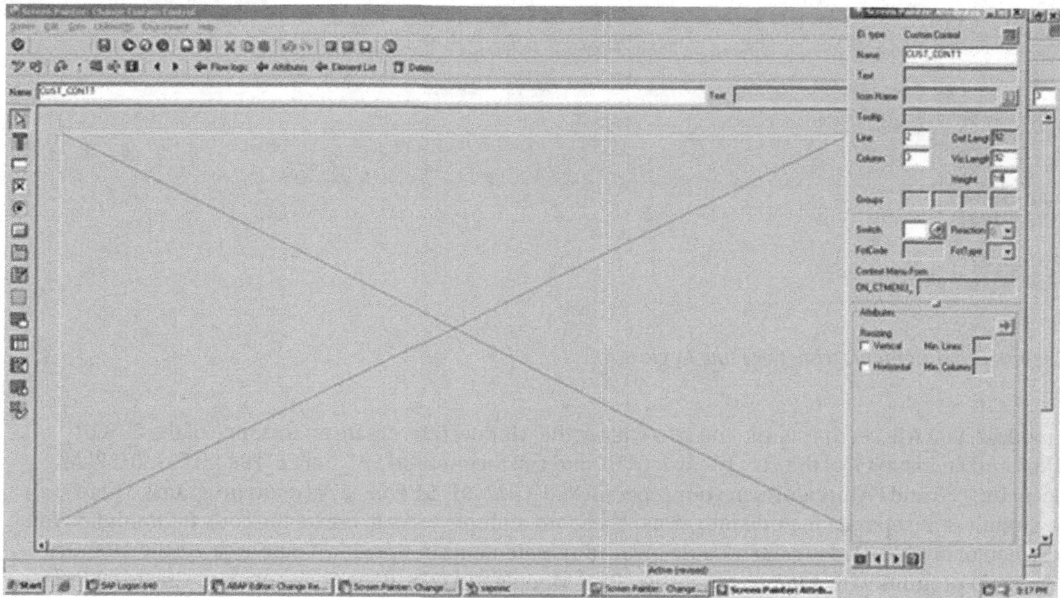

***Figure 12-25.** Naming the custom control in the Element Attributes dialog box*

11. Close the Layout Editor. Click the Element List tab. Enter OK_CODE in the row with type OK. The screen in Figure 12-26 appears.

Screen Painter: Change Screen for YCL_CH12_01_SIMPLE_ALV

Layout | Attributes | Element

Screen number 100 New(Revised)

Attributes | Element list | Flow logic

General attr. | Texts/ I/O templates | Special attr. | Display attr. | Mod. groups / functions | References

Hi	M	Name	Type	Line	Col	De	Vis	Hei	Scr	Format	Inp	Ou	Out	Dic	Dict.	Property list
+		CUST_CONTT	CCtrl	2	3	82	82	18								
		OK_CODE	OK	0	0	20	20	1		OK						

***Figure 12-26.** Adding to the element list*

12. Click the Flow Logic tab. You have to create the PBO and PAI modules. Remove the comments of the PBO and PAI module-invoking statements. You can retain the module names proposed by the system or change and specify your own. In this example, accept the proposed names (that is, STATUS_0100 and USER_COMMAND_0100). The Flow Logic tab after removing comments for the module-invoking statements is shown in Figure 12-27.

```
PROCESS BEFORE OUTPUT.
 MODULE STATUS_0100.
*
PROCESS AFTER INPUT.
 MODULE USER_COMMAND_0100.
```

Figure 12-27. Removing statements from the Flow Logic tab

In the PBO module, you will set the status. You also will set the window title, create an instance of the CL_GUI_CUSTOM_CONTAINER and an instance of the CL_GUI_ALV_GRID, and call the method SET_TABLE_FOR_FIRST_DISPLAY.

You will locate the PBO and PAI modules in your program YCL_CH12_01_SIMPLE_ALV (main program). There is an option to locate module/s in separate include programs. There are multiple ways to create the code for modules. You will adopt the method of double-clicking the module invocation statements in the Flow Logic area. As the modules do not exist, the system prompts with a message such as "PBO Module STATUS_0100 does not exist. Create Object?" Click the Yes button. The system then prompts further, whether to locate the module in the main program or an include program. Opt for the module to be located in the main program (YCL_CH12_01_SIMPLE_ALV). You should ensure that this program is not open in edit or change mode.

Double-click the PBO module-invoking statement MODULE STATUS_0100. The successive screens are shown in Figure 12-28 and Figure 12-29.

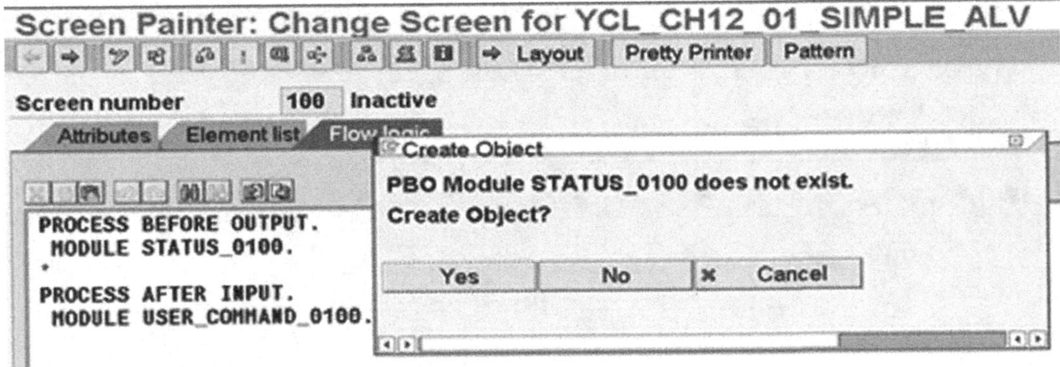

Figure 12-28. Creating the PBO module

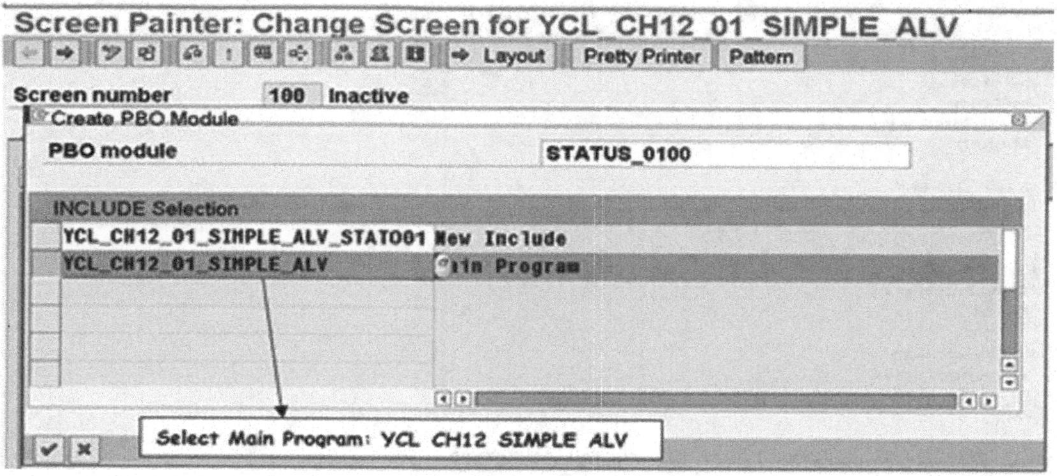

Figure 12-29. *Locating the module in the main program*

You have to locate your code between the lines `MODULE STATUS_0100 OUTPUT` and `ENDMODULE`, as shown in Figure 12-30.

```
*&---------------------------------------------------------------------*
*&      Module  STATUS_0100  OUTPUT
*&---------------------------------------------------------------------*
*       text
*----------------------------------------------------------------------*
MODULE STATUS_0100 OUTPUT.
*  SET PF-STATUS 'xxxxxxxx'.
*  SET TITLEBAR 'xxx'.

ENDMODULE.                 " STATUS_0100  OUTPUT
```

Figure 12-30. *Changing the module code*

Remove the comments from the two lines, and change them as follows:

```
SET PF-STATUS 'STAT1'.
SET TITLEBAR 'TITLE1' WITH CCODE BUTXT WAERS.
```

Next, you have to create an instance of the class `CL_GUI_CUSTOMER_CONTAINER`. You could use the Pattern button to generate template code for creating an instance. Figure 12-31 shows the dialog box with entered values for generating template code to create an instance of a global class.

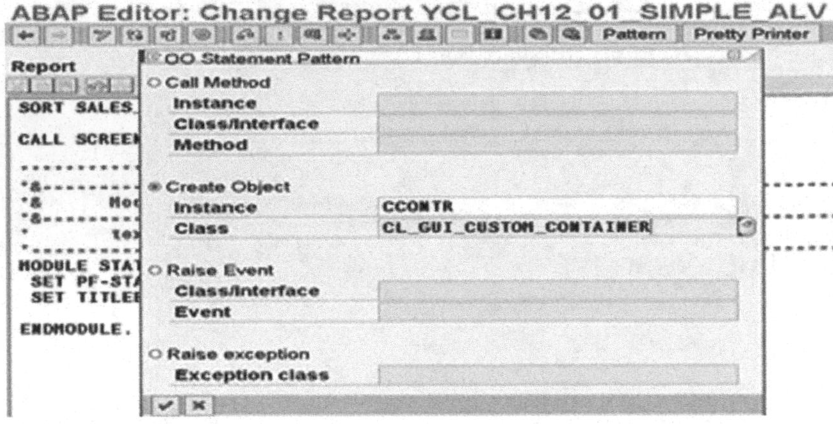

Figure 12-31. *Creating an instance of the class* `CL_GUI_CUSTOM_CONTAINER`

The generated, refined code (all lines for optional parameters deleted) is as follows:

```
CREATE OBJECT CCONTR
   EXPORTING
     CONTAINER_NAME              = 'CUST_CONTT'
   EXCEPTIONS
     CNTL_ERROR                  = 1
     CNTL_SYSTEM_ERROR           = 2
     CREATE_ERROR                = 3
     LIFETIME_ERROR              = 4
     LIFETIME_DYNPRO_DYNPRO_LINK = 5
     others                      = 6
     .
 IF SY-SUBRC <> 0.
  MESSAGE ID SY-MSGID TYPE SY-MSGTY NUMBER SY-MSGNO
             WITH SY-MSGV1 SY-MSGV2 SY-MSGV3 SY-MSGV4.
 ENDIF.
```

Similarly, to create an instance of the class `CL_GUI_ALV_GRID`, use the values shown in Figure 12-32.

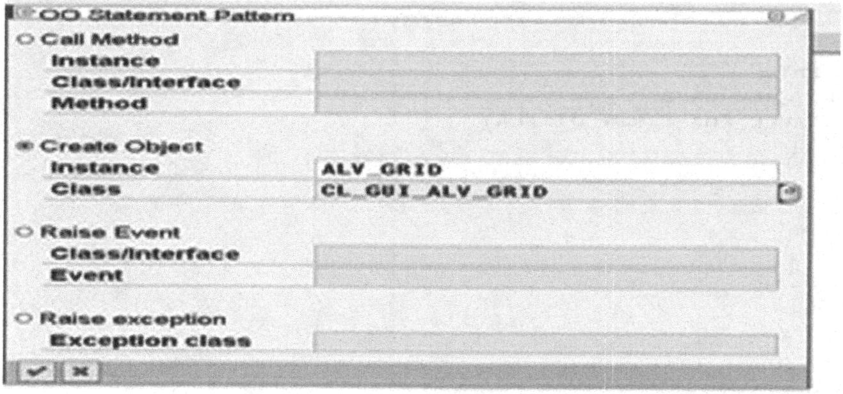

Figure 12-32. *Creating an instance of the class* `CL_GUI_ALV_GRID`

The generated, refined code (all lines for optional parameters deleted) is as follows:

```
CREATE OBJECT ALV_GRID
   EXPORTING
     I_PARENT            = CCONTR
   EXCEPTIONS
     ERROR_CNTL_CREATE = 1
     ERROR_CNTL_INIT   = 2
     ERROR_CNTL_LINK   = 3
     ERROR_DP_CREATE   = 4
     others            = 5
     .
 IF SY-SUBRC <> 0.
  MESSAGE ID SY-MSGID TYPE SY-MSGTY NUMBER SY-MSGNO
             WITH SY-MSGV1 SY-MSGV2 SY-MSGV3 SY-MSGV4.
 ENDIF.
```

To call the instance method `SET_TABLE_FOR_FIRST_DISPLAY`, set the values shown in Figure 12-33.

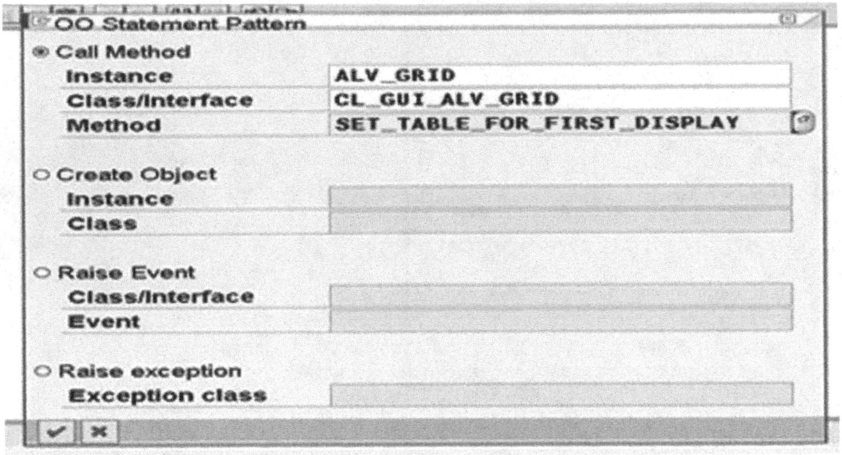

Figure 12-33. *Calling the method SET_TABLE_FOR_FIRST_DISPLAY*

The generated, refined code (all lines for optional parameters deleted) is as follows:

```
CALL METHOD ALV_GRID->SET_TABLE_FOR_FIRST_DISPLAY
   EXPORTING
     I_STRUCTURE_NAME               = 'YCL_CH12_SALES_SUM_STRU'
   CHANGING
     IT_OUTTAB                      = SALES_TAB
   EXCEPTIONS
     INVALID_PARAMETER_COMBINATION = 1
     PROGRAM_ERROR                  = 2
     TOO_MANY_LINES                 = 3
     others                         = 4
          .
 IF SY-SUBRC <> 0.
  MESSAGE ID SY-MSGID TYPE SY-MSGTY NUMBER SY-MSGNO
             WITH SY-MSGV1 SY-MSGV2 SY-MSGV3 SY-MSGV4.
 ENDIF.
```

Your coding in the PBO module is over. To summarize, you set up the status, set the window title, created an instance of the custom container, created an instance of ALV grid, called the instance method SET_TABLE_FOR_FIRST_DISPLAY, saved the program, and clicked the Back button to return to the Screen Painter's Flow Logic area.

You have to create a PAI module. Double-click the PAI module-invoking statement, MODULE USER_COMMAND_0100. The system will prompt with a message such as "PAI Module USER_COMMAND_0100 does not exist. Create Object?" Click the Yes button. The system then prompts further, whether to locate the module in the main program or an include program. Opt for the module to be located in main program. As you are locating the modules in the program YCL_CH12_01_SIMPLE_ALV (the main program), you should ensure that this program is not open in edit or change mode.

The successive screens look like Figure 12-34 and Figure 12-35.

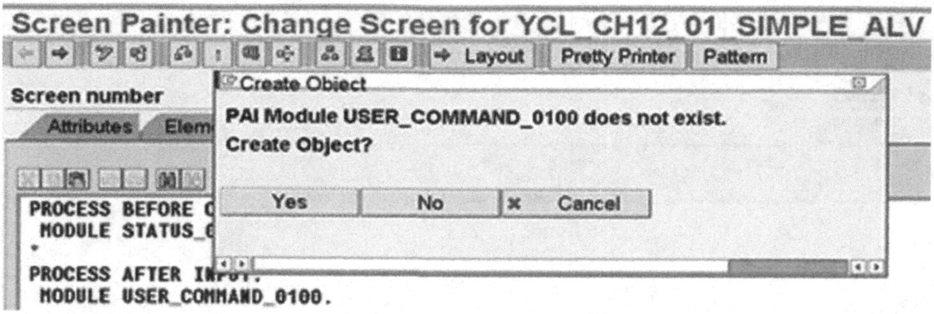

Figure 12-34. *Creating the PAI module*

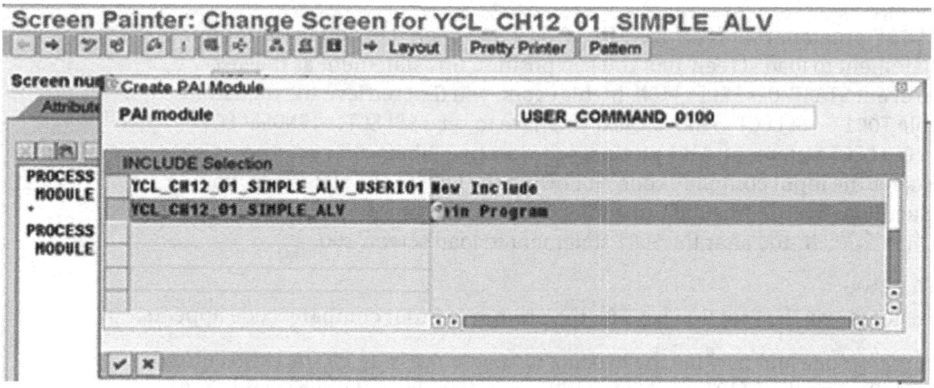

Figure 12-35. *Locating the PAI module in the main screen*

Enter the following code in the PAI module:

```
*&---------------------------------------------------------------------*
*&      Module  USER_COMMAND_0100  INPUT
*&---------------------------------------------------------------------*
*       text
*----------------------------------------------------------------------*
MODULE USER_COMMAND_0100 INPUT.

IF OK_CODE = 'BACK'.
 SET SCREEN 0.
 LEAVE SCREEN.
ENDIF.

ENDMODULE.                 " USER_COMMAND_0100  INPUT
```

The statements SET SCREEN 0 and LEAVE SCREEN will make the program exit screen 100 and display the prompt for company code. Save the program and then return to the Screen Painter by clicking the Back button. You have completed all tasks in the Screen Painter. Perform a consistency check and activate screen 100 in the Screen Painter. The screen after activation should look like Figure 12-36.

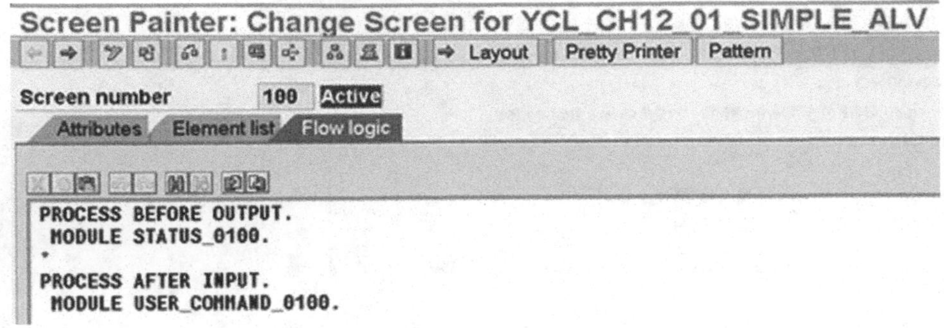

Figure 12-36. *The activated screen 100*

13. Go back to the ABAP program `YCL_CH12_01_SIMPLE_ALV` and open it in edit mode. You need to add a statement to load screen 100. You can position this statement as the last statement in the event `START-OF-SELECTION`. In this event, you first retrieve the data from the database table `T001 - SELECT SINGLE`. Next you have to set a `SELECT...ENDSELECT` construct with a `COLLECT` statement. This produces the internal table with customer-wise summarized data for the input company code. Following the `ENDSELECT` statement, you code the `SORT` statement to order the data customer code-wise ascending. You are coding the statement `CALL SCREEN 100` after the `SORT` statement to load screen 100.

The program flow is as follows:
When the program is executed (via the function key F8), the prompt to input company code appears.

1. Entering the company code and clicking the Execute button or pressing F8 starts execution of the statements following the `START-OF-SELECTION` event. Data from database table `T001` is retrieved. The customer-wise summarized sales internal table is created. The internal table is sorted on `KUNNR` ascending. The statement `CALL SCREEN 100` is executed.

2. The `CALL SCREEN 100` statement triggers the `PBO` event. The module `STATUS_0100` is executed. An instance of the customer container is created; an instance of the ALV grid is created. The method `SET_TABLE_FOR_FIRST_DISPLAY` populates the instance of the ALV grid with the customer-wise summarized sales data of the internal table, and the ALV output appears on the screen.

3. Clicking the Back button on the application toolbar triggers `PAI`, and the `PAI` module `USER_COMMAND_0100` executes. The code in the `PAI` module brings you back to the company code prompt.

The entire code of the program `YCL_CH12_01_SIMPLE_ALV` is available in the source code resource. The output looks like that in Figure 12-37.

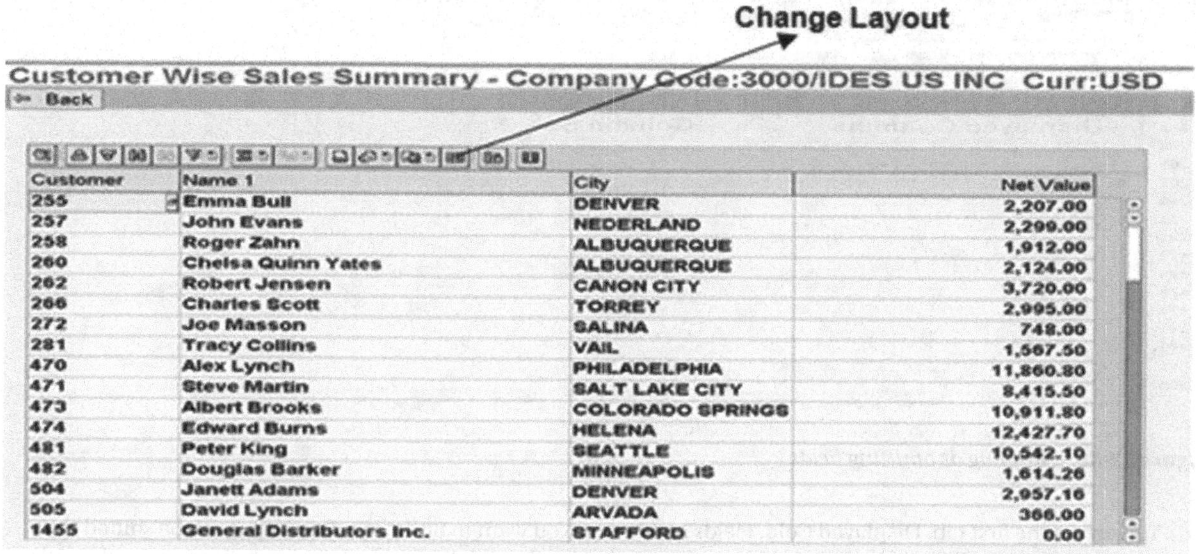

Change Layout

Customer Wise Sales Summary - Company Code:3000/IDES US INC Curr:USD

Back

Customer	Name 1	City	Net Value
255	Emma Bull	DENVER	2,207.00
257	John Evans	NEDERLAND	2,299.00
258	Roger Zahn	ALBUQUERQUE	1,912.00
260	Chelsa Quinn Yates	ALBUQUERQUE	2,124.00
262	Robert Jensen	CANON CITY	3,720.00
266	Charles Scott	TORREY	2,995.00
272	Joe Masson	SALINA	748.00
281	Tracy Collins	VAIL	1,567.50
470	Alex Lynch	PHILADELPHIA	11,860.80
471	Steve Martin	SALT LAKE CITY	8,415.50
473	Albert Brooks	COLORADO SPRINGS	10,911.80
474	Edward Burns	HELENA	12,427.70
481	Peter King	SEATTLE	10,542.10
482	Douglas Barker	MINNEAPOLIS	1,614.26
504	Janett Adams	DENVER	2,957.16
505	David Lynch	ARVADA	366.00
1455	General Distributors Inc.	STAFFORD	0.00

Figure 12-37. *Output of the program YCL_CH12_01_SIMPLE_ALV*

Clicking the buttons of the ALV output toolbar does not trigger the PAI event. Clicking the ALV output toolbar button triggers the class event USER_COMMAND. In complex programming, there could be a conflict between the PAI event and the events triggered by classes. The Control Frame Work (CFW) provides guidelines to resolve these conflicts.

The way you have configured this program, the PBO event is triggered only once after the Execute button is clicked or the F8 key is pressed on the selection screen and before the screen number 100 appears with the ALV report. When the ALV report appears, you have only one button on the application toolbar, which when clicked will take you back to the selection screen.

Changing Layout

Click the Change Layout button on the ALV toolbar (the third button from the right). A dialog box with five tabs appears, as shown in Figure 12-38.

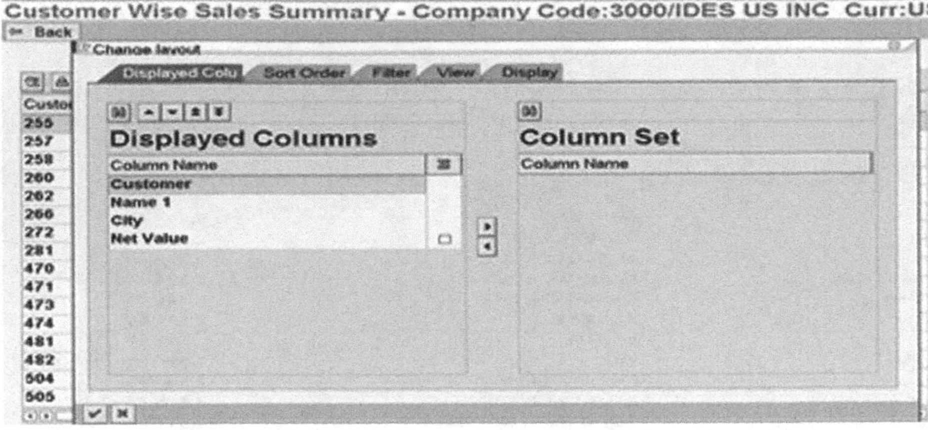

Figure 12-38. Shuffling or omitting fields

You are on the first tab, Displayed Colu. Fields or columns you want to omit from the output can be shifted from the left side to the right side. By shifting fields or columns to the right and then to the left, you can rearrange the order of the fields or columns in the output. Figure 12-39 shows this shuffling completed.

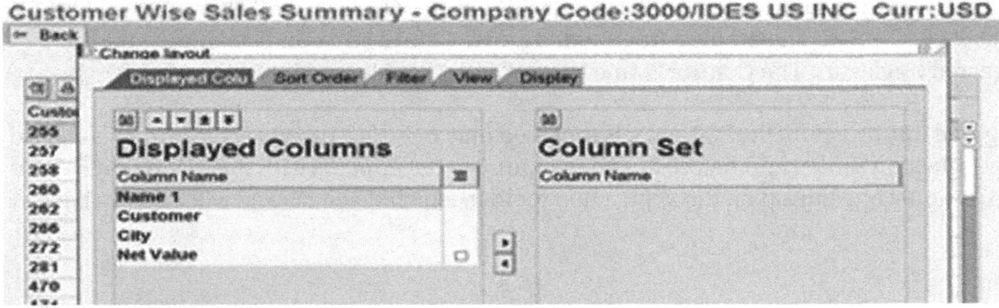

Figure 12-39. Shuffled fields

Figure 12-40 shows the ALV output with the fields shuffled.

Customer Wise Sales Summary - Company Code:3000/IDES US INC Curr:USD

Back

Name 1	Customer	City	Net Value
Emma Bull	255	DENVER	2,207.00
John Evans	257	NEDERLAND	2,299.00
Roger Zahn	258	ALBUQUERQUE	1,912.00
Chelsa Quinn Yates	260	ALBUQUERQUE	2,124.00
Robert Jensen	262	CANON CITY	3,720.00
Charles Scott	266	TORREY	2,995.00
Joe Masson	272	SALINA	748.00
Tracy Collins	281	VAIL	1,567.50
Alex Lynch	470	PHILADELPHIA	11,860.80

Figure 12-40. *Output with shuffled fields*

Click the Change Layout button again. Then click the Sort Order tab. The fields you want to sort on should be shifted from right to left. If you want the output to appear name-wise ascending, you shift the NAME1 field from right to left and enable the radio button for ascending order. By default, the descending radio button is enabled. Figure 12-41 shows the Sort Order tab.

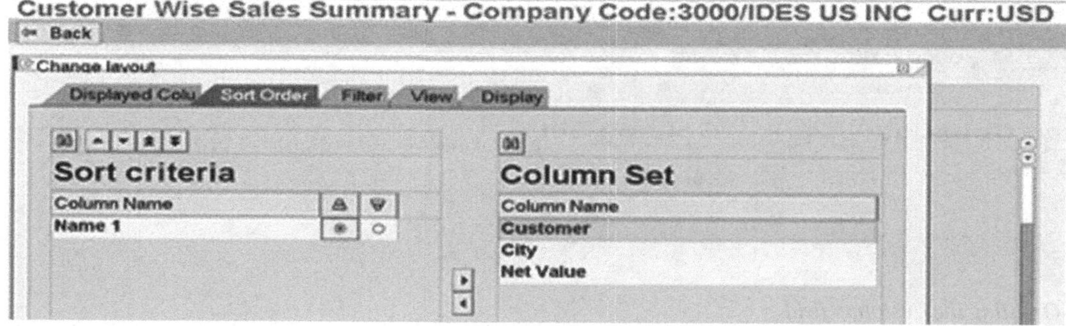

Figure 12-41. *Setting up the sort criteria*

Figure 12-42 shows the output with the sort setting.

Customer Wise Sales Summary - Company Code:3000/IDES US INC Curr:USD

Back

Name 1	Customer	City	Net Value
ADCOM COMPUTER	3272	SEATTLE	2,147.70
Aircraft Products	1470	Slough	11,000.00
ALAN FAITH	401258	BOSTON	862.00
ALAN FARRAR	401260	SAN DIEGO	862.00
ALAN FINER	401266	WASHINGTON	862.00
ALAN GUETTEL	401269	BOSTON	862.00
ALAN GWARA	401272	SAN DIEGO	862.00
Albert Brooks	473	COLORADO SPRINGS	10,911.80
Alex Lynch	470	PHILADELPHIA	11,860.80
ALPHA Center	3273	MINNEAPOLIS	2,147.70
American Security Company	300703	NEW ORLEANS	1,073,087.10
Andyna and Dynana Laboratories, Inc	3221	MONSEY	6,153.60
Antipolis	300325	ANTIOCH	22,320.00
BEN GUIER	401270	NEW YORK	862.00

Figure 12-42. *Ouput of program YCL_CH12_01_SIMPLE_ALV with fields shuffled and sort set up*

The sorting has been performed on the NAME1 contents translated to uppercase. Hence Aircraft Products appears before ALAN FAITH. That is how it is. If you use the Change Layout dialog box to set the sorting of fields, the sorting for text fields is being performed on the text translated to uppercase. But if you select a field (single-field sorting) and the sort buttons, the sorting is as per character (non-Unicode: ASCII) code order. An anomaly!

Click the Change Layout button again. Omit the field Customer (customer code or KUNNR). Figure 12-43 shows the omitted field.

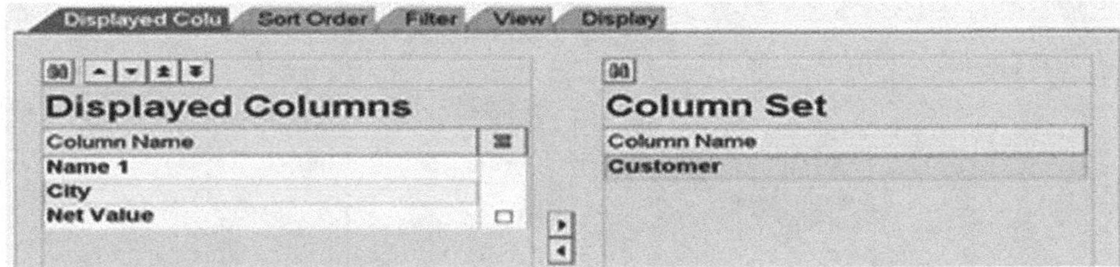

Figure 12-43. *Omitting the Customer field*

Figure 12-44 shows the output as per the settings.

Customer Wise Sales Summary - Company Code:3000/IDES US INC Curr:USD

Back

Name 1	City	Net Value
ADCOM COMPUTER	SEATTLE	2,147.70
Aircraft Products	Slough	11,000.00
ALAN FAITH	BOSTON	862.00
ALAN FARRAR	SAN DIEGO	862.00
ALAN FINER	WASHINGTON	862.00
ALAN GUETTEL	BOSTON	862.00
ALAN GWARA	SAN DIEGO	862.00

Figure 12-44. *Output of program* `YCL_CH12_01_SIMPLE_ALV`*, with fields Shuffled, sorted, and the Customer field omitted*

Change the original layout (the layout prevailing when you click the Execute button on the selection screen) per the following specifications:

- Field order:
  - City (`ORT01`)
  - Customer (`KUNNR`)
  - Name 1 (`NAME1`)
  - Net Value (`NETWR`)
- Total: Net Value
  - Sorting:
  - Sort: City (Ascending)
  - Group: City (Subtotals)
- Filter fields/columns:
  - Filter values for city: A*, B*, C*, M*, S*, T* (cities starting with A, B, C, M, S, and T)
  - Net Value: >= 500

Figures 12-45 through 12-50 depict the steps for carrying out these layout changes.

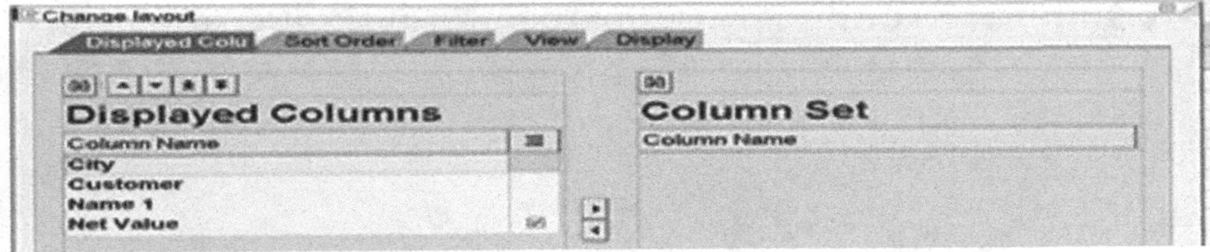

Figure 12-45. Changing layout of fields

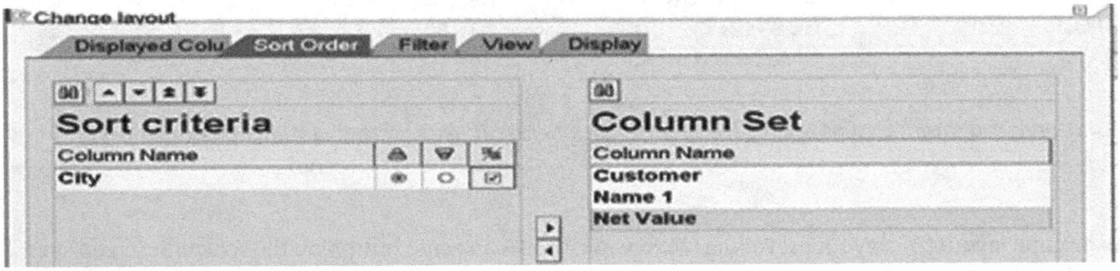

Figure 12-46. Setting sort criteria

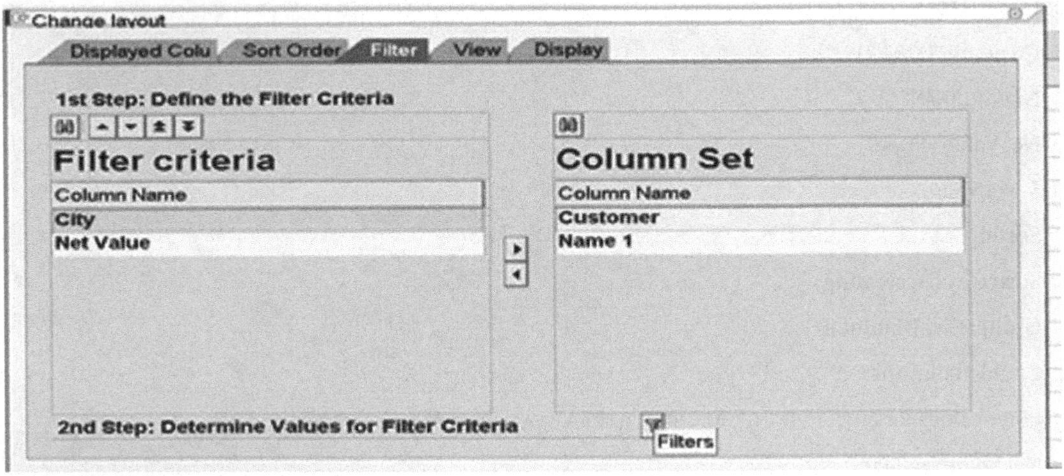

Figure 12-47. Filtering the fields

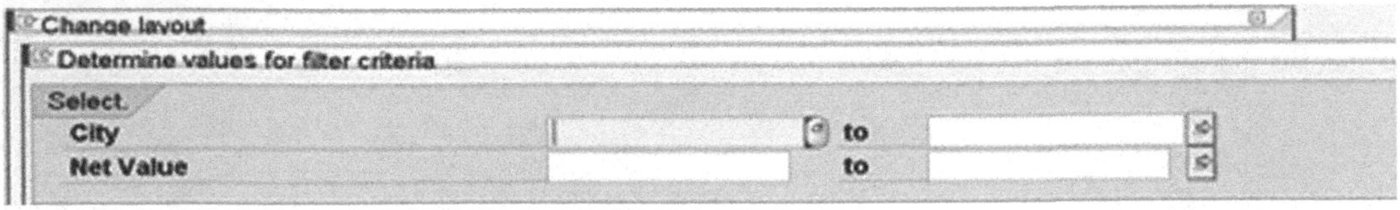

Figure 12-48. Program YCL_CH12_01_SIMPLE_ALV: Change Layout – Filter Fields SELECT-OPTIONS

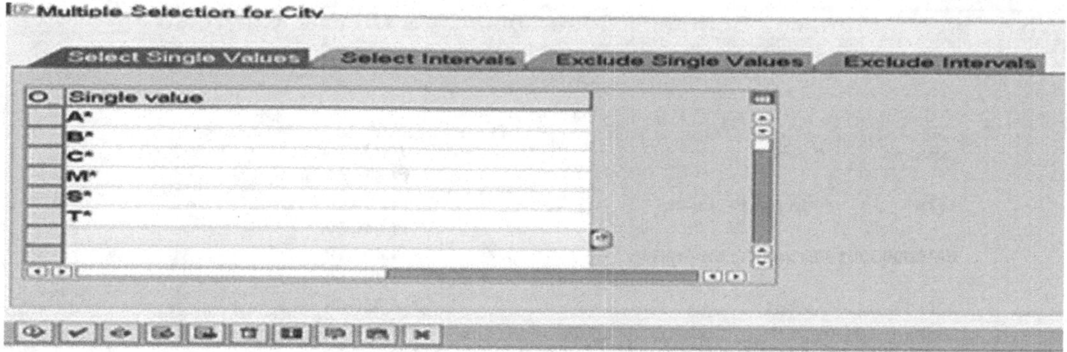

Figure 12-49. *Setting city values*

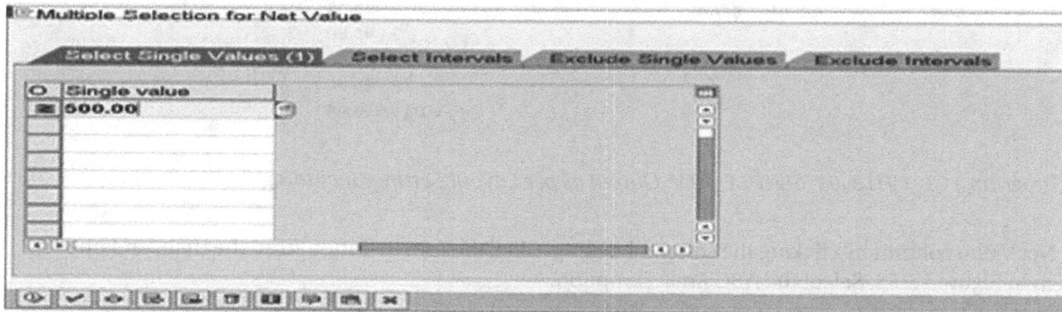

Figure 12-50. *Setting net value*

The output of the preceding steps as per the layout settings is shown in Figure 12-51 and Figure 12-52. Observe that the subtotals for each city and the grand total appear as separate rows.

Customer Wise Sales Summary - Company Code:3000/IDES US INC Curr:USD

City	Customer	Name 1	Net Value
ALBUQUERQUE	258	Roger Zahn	1,912.00
	260	Chelsa Quinn Yates	2,124.00
ALBUQUERQUE			4,036.00
ANTIOCH	3271	Media Store	6,477.30
	300000	Havers Inc.	4,133.00
	300081	Havers Inc	914.20
	300325	Antipolis	22,320.00
ANTIOCH			33,844.50
AUGUSTA	300716	Matrax	996,115.00
AUGUSTA			996,115.00
Berlin	1508	Deutsche Computer AG	5,987.50
Berlin			5,987.50
BOSTON	401258	ALAN FAITH	862.00
	401259	JIM FARAIZL	862.00
	401269	ALAN GUETTEL	862.00
BOSTON			2,586.00
Calgary	4000	North Energy Ltd	42,666.67

Figure 12-51. *Resulting output for program* YCL_CH12_01_SIMPLE_ALV

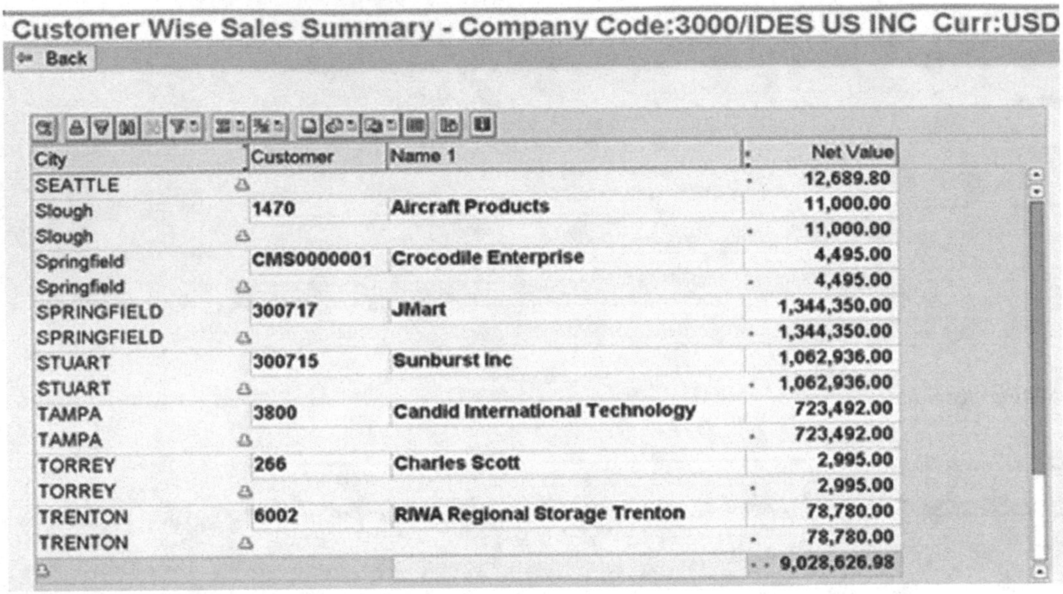

Customer Wise Sales Summary - Company Code:3000/IDES US INC Curr:USD

Back

City	Customer	Name 1	Net Value
SEATTLE			12,689.80
Slough	1470	Aircraft Products	11,000.00
Slough			11,000.00
Springfield	CMS0000001	Crocodile Enterprise	4,495.00
Springfield			4,495.00
SPRINGFIELD	300717	JMart	1,344,350.00
SPRINGFIELD			1,344,350.00
STUART	300715	Sunburst Inc	1,062,936.00
STUART			1,062,936.00
TAMPA	3800	Candid International Technology	723,492.00
TAMPA			723,492.00
TORREY	266	Charles Scott	2,995.00
TORREY			2,995.00
TRENTON	6002	RIWA Regional Storage Trenton	78,780.00
TRENTON			78,780.00
			9,028,626.98

Figure 12-52. Program YCL_CH12_01_SIMPLE_ALV: Output as per Layout Settings including the Total

Select the Net Value column by clicking the column heading. Click the fourth button from the right, and options appear, as shown in Figure 12-53. Select the ABC Analysis option.

Customer Wise Sales Summary - Company Code:3000/IDES US INC Curr:USD

Back

Spreadsheet
Word processing
Local File
Send
Office
ABC Analys.
XML Export
HTML download
Copy URL to Clipboard

City	Customer	Net Value
ALBUQUERQUE	258	1,912.00
	260	2,124.00
ALBUQUERQUE		4,036.00
ANTIOCH	3271	6,477.30
	300000	4,133.00
	300081	914.20
	300325	22,320.00

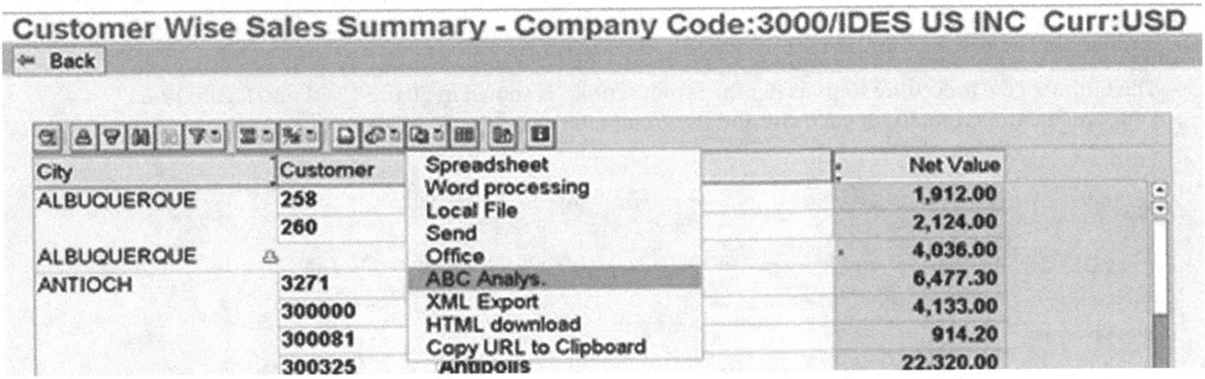

Figure 12-53. Selecting the ABC Analysis option

The ABC Analysis screen appears. You are going to do ABC analysis based on the customer. Accept the Analysis Type as Key Figure Percentage (the default). For the A Segment option, type in 80%. Set the B Segment option to 15%, and C Segment to 5%. You are indicating that the customers contributing 80% of total sales are A, the customers contributing the next 15% of total sales are B, and the customers contributing to the residual 5% of total sales are C.

The ABC analysis list appears below these settings, as shown in Figure 12-54. The customers appear in descending order of sales (field `NETWR`)—that is, the customer having the highest sales appears first, and the customer having the lowest sales appears last. You can observe that 5 customers out of a total of 36 contribute to 80% of total sales (that is, customers categorized as A), 1 customer contributes to the next 15% of total sales (the customer categorized as B), and 30-odd customers contribute to next 5% of total sales (customers categorized as C).

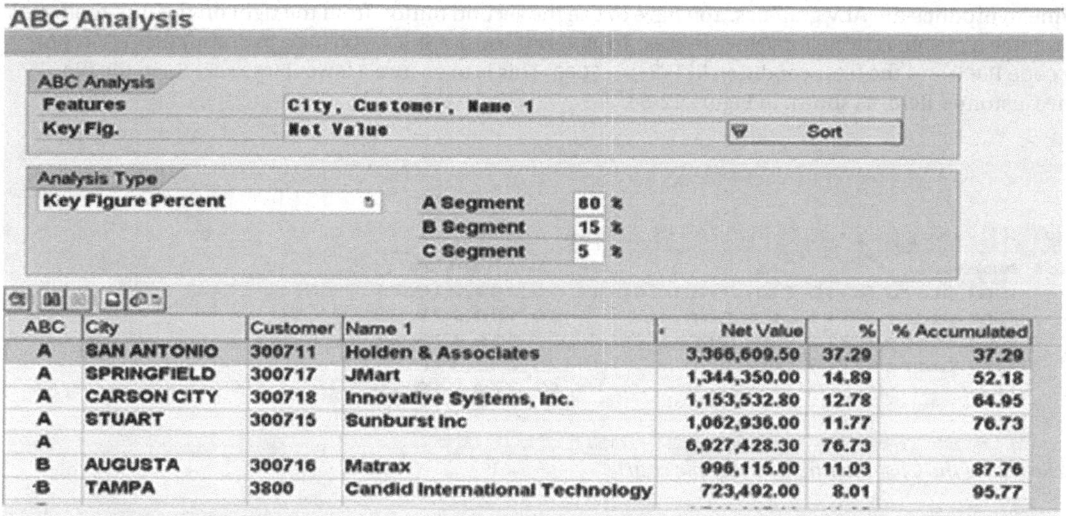

ABC Analysis

ABC Analysis

Features	City, Customer, Name 1
Key Fig.	Net Value

Sort

Analysis Type

Key Figure Percent

A Segment	80 %
B Segment	15 %
C Segment	5 %

ABC	City	Customer	Name 1	Net Value	%	% Accumulated
A	SAN ANTONIO	300711	Holden & Associates	3,366,609.50	37.29	37.29
A	SPRINGFIELD	300717	JMart	1,344,350.00	14.89	52.18
A	CARSON CITY	300718	Innovative Systems, Inc.	1,153,532.80	12.78	64.95
A	STUART	300715	Sunburst Inc	1,062,936.00	11.77	76.73
A				6,927,428.30	76.73	
B	AUGUSTA	300716	Matrax	996,115.00	11.03	87.76
B	TAMPA	3800	Candid International Technology	723,492.00	8.01	95.77

Figure 12-54. ABC analysis

The ABC analysis is employed typically in inventory or material cost control, when this phenomenon occurs that a few number of materials contribute to a large proportion of the total inventory or material cost. Controlling these few costly materials would substantially contribute to overall inventory cost control.

If you click the List button, a full-screen list of the ABC analysis appears, as shown in Figure 12-55 (with a two-dimensional visual effect).

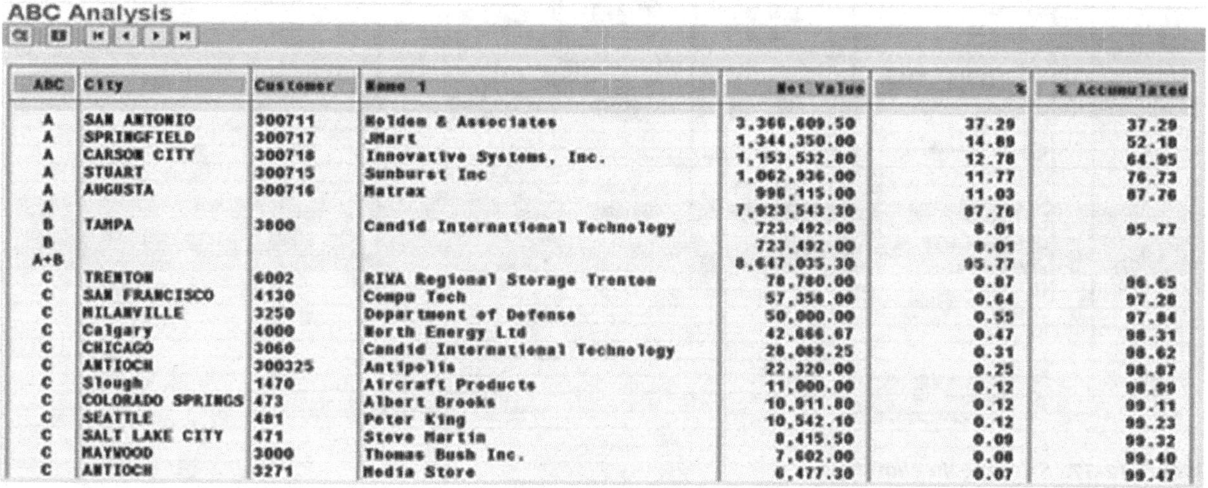

ABC Analysis

ABC	City	Customer	Name 1	Net Value	%	% Accumulated
A	SAN ANTONIO	300711	Holden & Associates	3,366,609.50	37.29	37.29
A	SPRINGFIELD	300717	JMart	1,344,350.00	14.89	52.18
A	CARSON CITY	300718	Innovative Systems, Inc.	1,153,532.80	12.78	64.95
A	STUART	300715	Sunburst Inc	1,062,936.00	11.77	76.73
A	AUGUSTA	300716	Matrax	996,115.00	11.03	87.76
A				7,923,543.30	87.76	
B	TAMPA	3800	Candid International Technology	723,492.00	8.01	95.77
B				723,492.00	8.01	
A+B				8,647,035.30	95.77	
C	TRENTON	6002	RIWA Regional Storage Trenton	78,780.00	0.87	96.65
C	SAN FRANCISCO	4130	Compu Tech	57,358.00	0.64	97.28
C	MILANVILLE	3250	Department of Defense	50,000.00	0.55	97.84
C	Calgary	4000	North Energy Ltd	42,666.67	0.47	98.31
C	CHICAGO	3060	Candid International Technology	28,089.25	0.31	98.62
C	ANTIOCH	300325	Antipolis	22,320.00	0.25	98.87
C	Slough	1470	Aircraft Products	11,000.00	0.12	98.99
C	COLORADO SPRINGS	473	Albert Brooks	10,911.80	0.12	99.11
C	SEATTLE	481	Peter King	10,542.10	0.12	99.23
C	SALT LAKE CITY	471	Steve Martin	8,415.50	0.09	99.32
C	MAYWOOD	3000	Thomas Bush Inc.	7,602.00	0.08	99.40
C	ANTIOCH	3271	Media Store	6,477.30	0.07	99.47

Figure 12-55. The full-screen ABC analysis list

Now it's time to produce the ALV graphics. You have to use the second button from the right on the ALV toolbar.

You will produce a pie chart of customer-wise sales. To generate the graphics, you have to output the ALV report with company code R300 and the filter condition `NETWR >= 5000`. This is to ensure a fewer large sectors in the pie chart. Select the Customer field, as shown in Figure 12-56.

Back

Customer	Name 1	City		Net Value
R310	GM Store R310	San Francisco		5,208,249.35
R311	GM Store R311	Los Angeles		10,180,223.23
R312	GM Store R312	San Diego		859,475.33
R313	GM Store R313	Oakland		1,051,410.28
			•	17,299,358.19

Figure 12-56. Selecting the Customer field for the pie chart

Click the Graphics button. Then click the right mouse button (or Shift+F10) to select the Chart Type option, as shown in Figure 12-57.

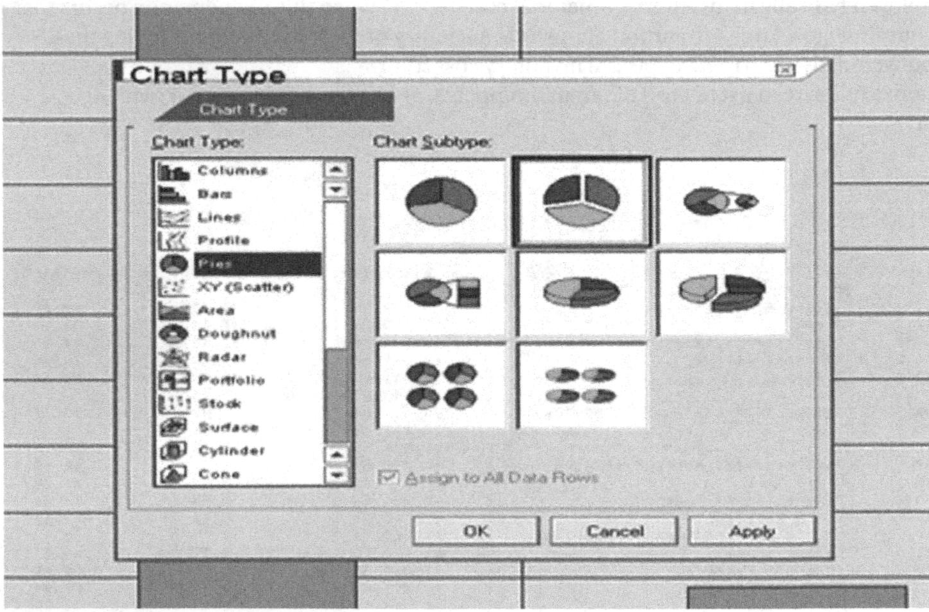

Figure 12-57. Selecting the chart type

Figure 12-58 shows the pie chart of customer-wise sales for the company code R300 and the filter setting of net value >= 5000.

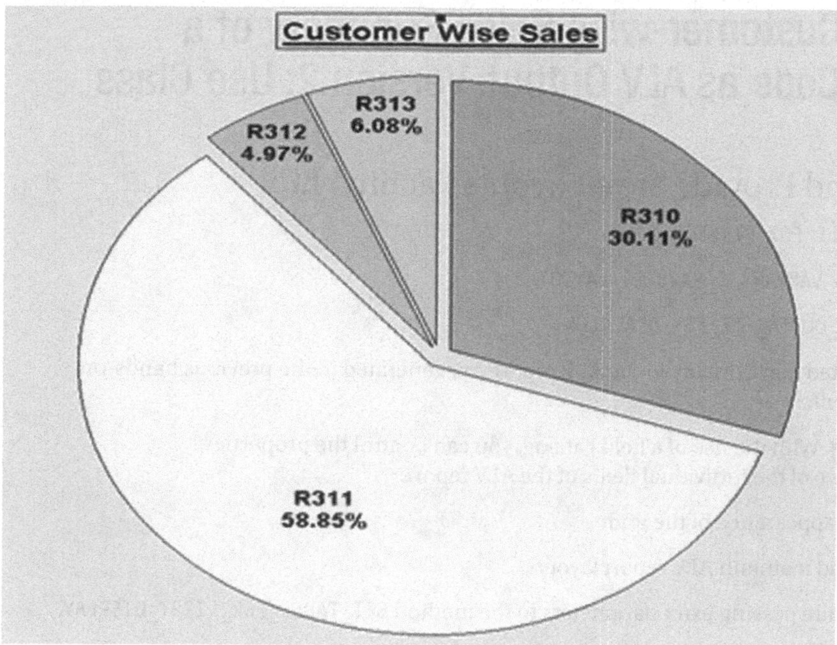

Figure 12-58. Pie chart of customer-wise sales

Graph options have been used to give a title to the chart and to have the customer codes with the sales percentages inside the pie chart sectors.

You can try out the various check box options in the display tab of the Change Layout ALV toolbar button. You can try the option Optimize Columns. This will automatically adjust the ALV field output width to the maximum width of output data. In other words, if the length of field NAME1 is 35 characters, but the maximum NAME1 content from the output data is only 30 characters, the field NAME1 will adjust to 30 characters.

If you have an Excel spreadsheet template, you can display ALV output in an Excel spreadsheet from the View tab by clicking the Change Layout ALV toolbar button.

You can try other ALV toolbar buttons and observe the results.

This was a demonstration of a simple ALV output, showing how end users can manipulate the output in various ways, similar to the way you can in an Excel spreadsheet. In this exercise, you changed the ALV output layout a number of times. But you could not save the layouts. In the next hands-on exercise, you will add more sophistication to the ALV output.

Hands-on Exercise: Customer-wise Sales Summary of a Specified Company Code as ALV Output, Version 2: Use Class CL_GUI_ALV_GRID

Use the Field Catalog and Provide Save Layouts Facility, Etc.

Parameters for the method: SET_TABLE_FOR_FIRST_DISPLAY:

Importing parameters: IS_VARIANT, I_SAVE, IS_LAYOUT

Changing parameters: IT_OUTTAB, IT_FIELDCATALOG

You will create more-sophisticated functionality in the ALV report you generated in the previous hands-on exercise by adding three enhancements:

- The use of a field catalog. With the use of a field catalog, you can control the properties, formatting, or appearance of the individual fields of the ALV report.
- Control over the overall appearance of the grid.
- The capability to save and maintain ALV report layouts.

These three enhancements require passing extra parameters to the method SET_TABLE_FOR_FIRST_DISPLAY.

Creating a Field Catalog

When using the method SET_TABLE_FOR_FIRST_DISPLAY of the class CL_GUI_ALV_GRID, you can give either one of the parameters:

- I_STRUCTURE_NAME
- IT_FIELDCATALOG

You have worked with the I_STRUCTURE_NAME parameter. The method automatically fetched the heading text from the associated data element of the field, the output length, the format from the associated domain of the field, and so forth. The customer code field KUNNR was output with the leading zeros suppressed (that is, the ALPHA conversion routine was referred to in the domain of the field and is getting executed by default). If you want to suppress the execution of the conversion routine ALPHA (as you were doing with the WRITE statement USING NO EDIT MASK), you had no means of doing it in the preceding hands-on exercise. This is where the field catalog can be used. Through the field catalog, you can control the appearance of each field appearing in the ALV report.

The field catalog is an internal table, containing one row for each field of the ALV report. The different fields of the field catalog structure constitute the different properties of the ALV report field.

The field catalog DDIC internal table type definition is LVC_T_FCAT, and the DDIC structure of this internal table is LVC_S_FCAT.

There are 96 fields in the field catalog structure LVC_S_FCAT. The third field in this structure is 'FIELDNAME, containing the name of the ALV report field. Table 12-2 provides a partial list of the fields of field catalog structure LVC_S_FCAT.

Table 12-2. A Few Fields of Field Catalog DDIC Structure LVC_S_FCAT

Field Name	Description
FIELDNAME	Name of the ALV output field (example: KUNNR).
TABNAME	Name of the ALV output field structure (example: SALES_STRU).
CURRENCY	Currency code.
QUANTITY	Unit-of-measure code.
JUST	Output justification (L—left, R—right, and C—centered).
LZERO	Output leading zeros for numeric fields.
NO_SIGN	Suppress sign.
NO_ZERO	Suppress output of zero.
NO_CONVEXT	Value = X, suppress execution of conversion exit routine. Value = space, execute conversion exit routine.
EDIT_MASK	Edit mask including conversion exit routine to be executed.
EMPHASIZE	Color control of output fields.
FIX_COLUMN	Freeze column.
NO_SUM	Disable totaling of the field (numeric fields).
NO_OUT	Omit output of this field.
TECH	Value = X, field is technical. The DDIC data type CLNT (client) is treated as a technical field. Technical fields by default do not output. They do not appear in the field list of Change Layout dialog boxes. If you want them to be output, set the value to ' '.
OUTPUTLEN	Output length.
CONVEXIT	Name of conversion exit routine.
HOTSPOT	Make the field hot spot.
COL_OPT	Column width optimization.
REF_FIELD	Name of the DDIC field to which this field is referring.
REF_TABLE	Name of the DDIC table structure/structure to which this field is referring is residing.

A detailed description of all the field catalog fields can be found in the manual *ALV Grid Control (BC-SRV-ALV)*, from page 129 onward.

You can directly manipulate the field catalog and then pass the manipulated field catalog internal table to the method SET_TABLE_FOR_FIRST_DISPLAY, and the ALV output will appear as per the field catalog entries for the different fields output by the ALV.

A field catalog internal table can be built from scratch, assigning all the myriad fields values and then appending rows. But it is seldom done this way. Normally, the function module LVC_FIELDCATALOG_MERGE is invoked to generate an initial default field catalog. This function module takes a DDIC structure as an importing parameter and returns a field catalog in an internal table of DDIC type LVC_T_FCAT. In the preceding exercise, you passed a structure directly to the method SET_TABLE_FOR_FIRST_DISPLAY. The method generated a field catalog internally to which you had no access, over which you had no control, and ALV output appeared with the default formatting. In this exercise, you will call the function module LVC_FIELDCATALOG_MERGE. You will pass to this function module the same structure that you passed to the method SET_TABLE_FOR_FIRST_DISPLAY (that is, YCL_CH12_SALES_SUM_STRU in the preceding exercise). The function module will generate and return a default field catalog in the internal table. You will manipulate this internal table and pass it to the method SET_TABLE_FOR_FIRST_DISPLAY as the formal changing parameter IT_FIELDCATALOG.

In this exercise, you will do the following:

- Impart different colors to different fields of ALV output (by using the field catalog column name EMPHASIZE).
- Suppress the execution of the conversion exit routine ALPHA for the field KUNNR (by assigning the value X to the field catalog column name NO_CONVEXT, and assigning the value SPACE to CONVEXIT).
- Optimize all column widths (by assigning the value X to the field catalog column name COL_OPT).

The field catalog field EMPHASIZE that is used to impart color to the ALV output columns is of type C and length 4. The colors you can impart are the same as in the WRITE statement, with the same color codes. You can have color in either the background (Inverse Off) or foreground (Inverse On). Color in the background can be sharp (Intensified On) or faint (Intensified Off).

The color field EMPHASIZE operates as follows:

- The first character has to be C.
- The second character signifies the color code (0-7).
- The third character signifies Intensified On/Off (that is, a value of 0 is Intensified Off, and a value of 1 is Intensified On). Intensified On works for background colors only.
- The fourth character signifies Inverse On/Off (that is, a value of 0 is Inverse Off, and a value of 1 is Inverse On).

You will define a color counter to contain the color code starting from 1, and increment it for every output field (KUNNR, NAME1, ORT01, and NETWR). You will output in background color with Intensified Off. So your field EMPHASIZE must assume the values C100, C200, C300, and C400.

The code related to the field catalog manipulation follows.

Data declarations:

```
DATA: FCAT       TYPE LVC_T_FCAT " field catalogue
                  WITH HEADER LINE,

      CLR(1)     TYPE N VALUE 1, " for color code
```

Code before calling the method SET_TABLE_FOR_FIRST_DISPLAY:

```
CALL FUNCTION 'LVC_FIELDCATALOG_MERGE'
  EXPORTING
     I_STRUCTURE_NAME           = 'YCL_CH12_SALES_SUM_STRU'
   CHANGING
     CT_FIELDCAT                = FCAT[]
  EXCEPTIONS
    INCONSISTENT_INTERFACE      = 1
    PROGRAM_ERROR               = 2
    OTHERS                      = 3
        .
```

```
IF SY-SUBRC <> 0.
 MESSAGE ID SY-MSGID TYPE SY-MSGTY NUMBER SY-MSGNO
        WITH SY-MSGV1 SY-MSGV2 SY-MSGV3 SY-MSGV4.
ENDIF.

LOOP AT FCAT.
 CLR = CLR + 1. " color codes 1 2 3 4
 CONCATENATE 'C' CLR '00' INTO FCAT-EMPHASIZE.

 FCAT-COL_OPT = 'X'. " column width optimization

 IF FCAT-FIELDNAME = 'KUNNR'. " output leading zeroes
  FCAT-NO_CONVEXT = 'X'.
  FCAT-CONVEXIT = ' '.
 ENDIF.
 MODIFY FCAT.
ENDLOOP.
```

Controlling Overall Appearance of ALV Output

You can establish control of the overall appearance of the ALV output by filling in appropriate fields of the structure referring to the DDIC structure LVC_S_LAYO. The structure is to be passed to the formal exporting parameter IS_LAYOUT. Table 12-3 provides a partial list of fields of this DDIC structure LVC_S_LAYO.

Table 12-3. *A Few Fields of the DDIC Structure LVC_S_LAYO*

Field Name	Description
CWIDTH_OPT	Optimize all column widths. (Optimization at the output level is distinct from optimization at the field level in the field catalog.)
GRID_TITLE	A title for the grid. In enlarged font, maximum of 70 columns.
NO_HEADERS	Hide field or column headers.
NO_HGRIDLN	Hide horizontal grid lines.
NO_VGRIDLN	Hide vertical grid lines.
NO_TOOLBAR	Hide ALV toolbar.
ZEBRA	Alternating color for fields.

You can find a full list with explanations starting on page 157 of the manual *ALV Grid Control (BC-SRV-ALV)*. You are using the field GRID_TITLE of this structure to output an ALV report with a title.

The source code related to the control of grid appearance follows.

Data declaration:

```
LAYOUT     TYPE LVC_S_LAYO, " overall grid appearance
```

Code before calling the method SET_TABLE_FOR_FIRST_DISPLAY:

```
CONCATENATE TEXT-001 CCODE '/' BUTXT '--'
   TEXT-002 INTO LAYOUT-GRID_TITLE.
```

The values of the text symbols are as follows:

```
[TEXT-001: 'Sales Summary-Company Code:'
 TEXT-002: 'Curr.']
```

Save and Manage ALV Output Layouts

For saving and managing ALV output layouts, you need to pass values to two formal exporting parameters, IS_VARIANT and I_SAVE, of the method SET_TABLE_FOR_FIRST_DISPLAY. The formal parameter IS_VARIANT is typed to the DDIC structure DISVARIANT. You need only to assign the name of the ABAP program to the field REPORT of this structure. The formal parameter I_SAVE (ABAP type C and length 1) is assigned values as follows:

- I_SAVE = U: User-defined layouts can be saved.
- I_SAVE = X: Global layouts can be saved.
- I_SAVE = A: User-defined and global layouts can be saved.
- I_SAVE = ‘ ’: Layouts cannot be saved. (This is the default.)

The source code related to providing the capability to save and retrieve layouts includes the following.
Data declaration:

```
DVARIANT   TYPE DISVARIANT. " for saving layouts
```

Code before calling the method SET_TABLE_FOR_FIRST_DISPLAY:

```
DVARIANT-REPORT = 'YCL_CH12_02_ALV_FCAT_ETC'.
```

Calling method SET_TABLE_FOR_FIRST_DISPLAY **with additional parameters:**

```
CALL METHOD ALV_GRID->SET_TABLE_FOR_FIRST_DISPLAY
   EXPORTING
     IS_VARIANT                    = DVARIANT " change, save layouts
     I_SAVE                        = 'U' " change, save layouts
     IS_LAYOUT                     = LAYOUT " change, save layouts
*      I_STRUCTURE_NAME              = 'YCL_CH12_SALES_SUM_STRU'
   CHANGING
     IT_OUTTAB                     = SALES_TAB
     IT_FIELDCATALOG               = FCAT[]  " field catalogue
   EXCEPTIONS
     INVALID_PARAMETER_COMBINATION = 1
     PROGRAM_ERROR                 = 2
     TOO_MANY_LINES                = 3
     others                        = 4
        .
```

The program is YCL_CH12_02_ALV_FCAT_ETC, and the full code can be found in the source code resource. The output appears as shown in Figure 12-59.

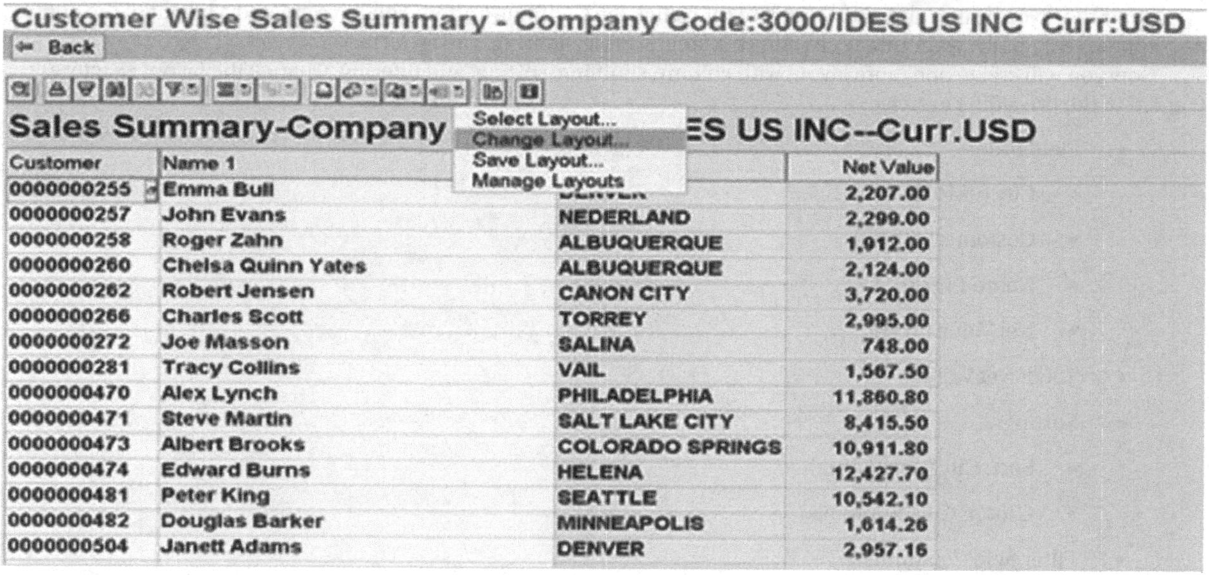

Figure 12-59. Output of the program YCL_CH12_02_ALV_FCAT_ETC

In the output:

- Fields are output in different colors.
- Customer code is output with leading zeros.
- Column widths are optimized.
- A title appears in the ALV grid.

When you click the third button from the right (earlier, the Change Layout button) on the ALV toolbar, a menu appears with Select Layout, Change Layout, Save Layout, and Manage Layouts options.

Select the Save Layout option. The screen shown in Figure 12-60 appears.

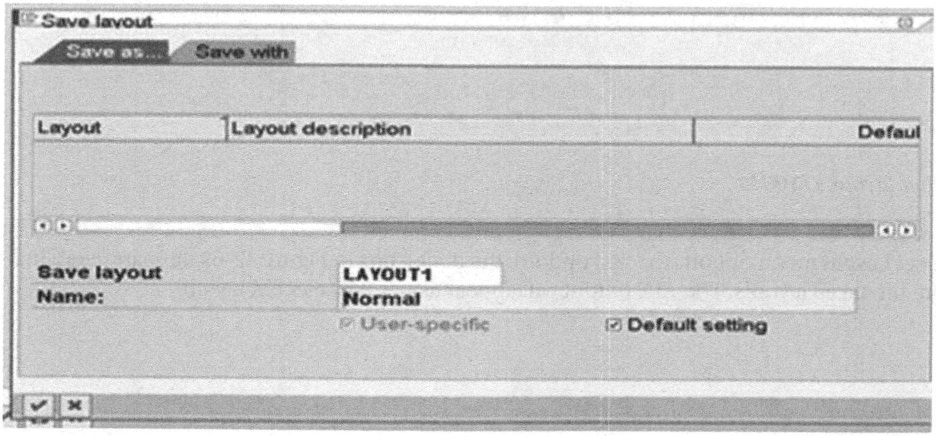

Figure 12-60. Saving the layout for YCL_CH12_02_ALV_FCAT_ETC

Enter the layout name and short text, and then click the Continue button. You have created a layout of the output as it appears originally, without any column shuffling, sorting, filtering, and so forth.

Now you will create one more layout with column shuffling, sorting, and filtering. Change the layout exactly as you did in the preceding exercise:

- Field order:
    - City (ORT01)
    - Customer (KUNNR)
    - Name 1 (NAME1)
    - Net Value (NETWR)
- Total: Net Value
- Sorting:
    - Sort: City (Ascending)
    - Group: City (Subtotals)
- Filter fields/columns:
    - Filter values for city: A*, B*, C*, M*, S*, T* (cities starting with A, B, C, M, S, and T)
    - Net Value: >= 500

Save this layout, as shown in Figure 12-61.

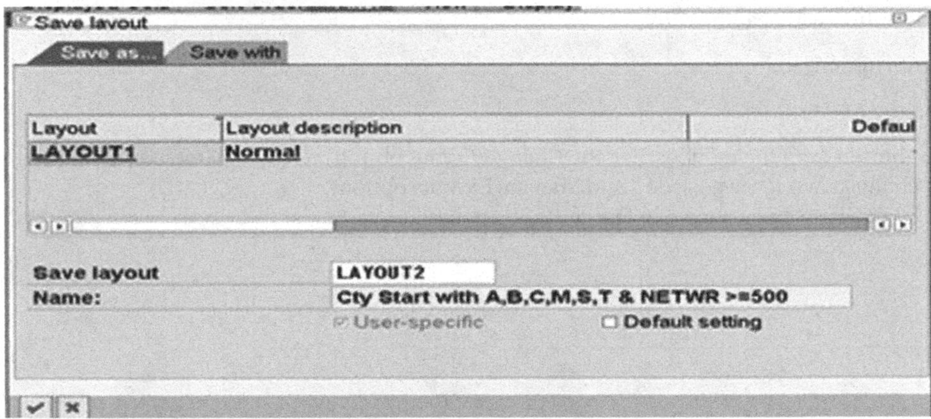

***Figure 12-61.** Saving another layout, LAYOUT2*

When you click the Select Layout menu option (the first option), the dialog box in Figure 12-62 appears, enabling you to make a selection from the saved layouts. The ALV output will appear as per the selected layout.

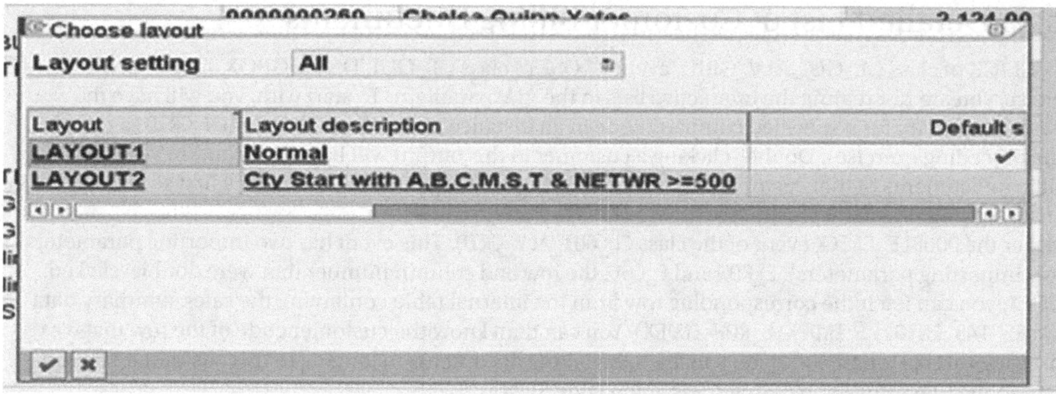

Figure 12-62. *Choosing a layout*

After saving layouts, if you choose a saved layout or load the program with a default layout, the customer code is output without the leading zeros. This happens even though you suppressed the execution of the ALPHA routine when manipulating the field catalog initially. You will fix this problem in the next hands-on exercise.

You can click the Maintain Layouts menu option to set a default layout, delete layouts, and so forth.

Hands-on Exercise: Customer-wise Sales Summary and Detail of a Specified Company Code as ALV Output: Use Class CL_GUI_ALV_GRID

- Trigger CL_GUI_ALV_GRID Events: TOOLBAR, USER_COMMAND, AFTER_USER_COMMAND, DOUBLE_CLICK, and CL_GUI_DIALOGBOX_CONTAINER Event: CLOSE

You will start this exercise with the customer-wise sales summary of a specific company code as ALV output. You will impart additional functionalities and features to this initial ALV output by triggering events of classes.

In this exercise, you are going to do the following:

- Generate a detailed list of customer billing documents by double-clicking a line of the customer-wise sales summary of a specific company code.
- Place a custom button on the ALV toolbar and make it operational.
- Output a serial number and then adjust it based on a change in the ALV layout (that is, regenerate the serial number every time a change occurs in the ALV layout). Recall the system fields SY-DBCNT or SY-TABIX you were using most of the time to output the serial number via the WRITE statement. The output of the serial number is being implemented for the first ALV output only. The serial number in the ALV output has to be dynamic because the ALV output can be manipulated. Regenerating the serial number again and again every time the ALV output is changed makes the issue complex.

Generating a Detailed List of Customer Billing Documents

Event DOUBLE_CLICK of class CL_GUI_ALV_GRID, event CLOSE of class CL_GUI_DIALOGBOX_CONTAINER

In this exercise, you are re-creating the interactive lists in the ALV paradigm. To start with, you will have the customer-wise sales summary for a specified company code in an instance of the class CL_GUI_ALV_GRID (a carry forward from the preceding exercise). Double-clicking a customer in this output will beget a second ALV output, listing all the billing documents of that customer. You were referring to this second ALV list as the first secondary list in the interactive lists paradigm.

You will trigger the DOUBLE_CLICK event of the class CL_GUI_ALV_GRID. This event has two importing parameters (events have only importing parameters): E_ROW and E_COL, the row and column number that were double-clicked. Using E_ROW-INDEX, you can fetch the corresponding row from the internal table containing the sales summary data (READ TABLE SALES_TAB INTO... INDEX E_ROW-INDEX). You can than know the customer code of the row that was double-clicked. Using this customer code, you can fetch the billing documents belonging to this customer. You can look up this event in the Class Builder by using transaction code SE24.

You will need a second instance of the class CL_GUI_ALV_GRID, in which you will output the billing documents of a specific customer. You will locate this second instance of the class CL_GUI_ALV_GRID in a dialog box container CL_GUI_DIALOGBOX_CONTAINER instead of the CL_GUI_CUSTOM_CONTAINER. The dialog box container, unlike a custom container, is not placed inside a custom control. It can be located anywhere on the screen by specifying the screen coordinates and the size at runtime. So you have to create an instance of this class CL_GUI_DIALOGBOX_CONTAINER; then create a second instance of the class CL_GUI_ALV_GRID, call the method SET_TABLE_FOR_FIRST_DISPLAY for this second instance, and pass it the data of billing documents of the specific customer. This is represented in Figure 12-63.

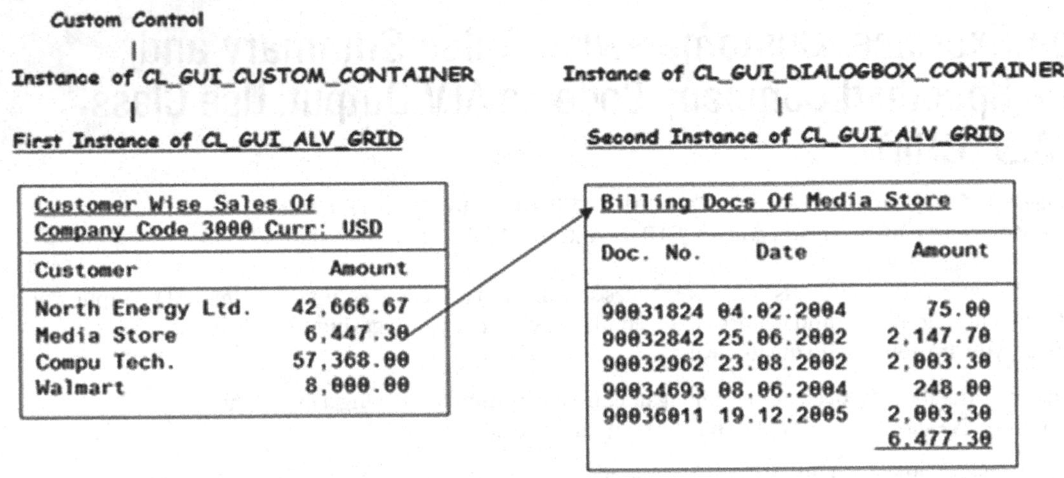

Figure 12-63. *Interactive reports in the ALV paradigm*

With an event of a class, when you trigger the event, a method in a class is executed. When you trigger the event DOUBLE_CLICK for the first instance of the class CL_GUI_ALV_GRID, you want to create an instance of the class CL_GUI_DIALOGBOX_CONTAINER, create a second instance of the class CL_GUI_ALV_GRID, create a default field catalog, manipulate this default field catalog, and execute the method SET_TABLE_FOR_FIRST_DISPLAY for the second instance of the class CL_GUI_ALV_GRID. All this code for the preceding described processes will have to reside in a method of a class. So, you will define and implement a local class, in which you will locate the method to be executed when you double-click a line of the customer-wise sales summary of a specific company code.

The methods that are executed when events of classes are triggered are called the *event handler methods* or *handler methods*. Even as your second ALV output is presented on the screen, you must ensure that the first ALV output is disabled. For this, you are using the ENABLE method of the class CL_GUI_ALV_GRID. When calling this method, you have to pass an exporting parameter. When this parameter has a value X, the ALV output is enabled, and when this parameter has a value ' ', the ALV output is disabled. When an instance of the ALV output is disabled, it is inaccessible to clicking and other actions.

When you are on the second ALV output located in the dialog box container, you would like to have the capability to close that container and navigate back to the first ALV output. The closing of the dialog box container is implemented through the event CLOSE of the class CL_GUI_DIALOGBOX_CONTAINER. You will trigger this event; locate the method to be executed when this event is triggered in the same local class you are using to locate the method to be executed for the event: DOUBLE_CLICK of the class CL_GUI_ALV_GRID. In fact, you are going to locate all the methods to be executed when various events are triggered in this same local class—that is, all the event handler methods in this program are being located in the local class named LCLASS.

In the method to be executed when event CLOSE is triggered for the class CL_GUI_DIA:OGBOX_CONTAINER, you are going to use the destructor method FREE to close the dialog box container and its embedded second instance of CL_GUI_ALV_GRID.

The event handler methods, when they are declared in the class (class definition) are related to the event and the class. This is one part of co-relating an event handler method. The second part of co-relating an event handler method is the registration of the event handler method. In the registration of the event handler method, the method is related to the instance of the class.

For example, in this program, you have two instances of class CL_GUI_ALV_GRID. The first instance outputs the customer-wise sales summary of a specific company. On double-clicking a line of this ALV output, you are creating a second instance of the class and generating the billing documents of the double-clicked customer. In the current exercise, you are supporting the DOUBLE_CLICK event of class CL_GUI_ALV_GRID only for the first instance, not the second instance. If double-clicking is done on the billing documents of a customer, nothing should happen; the event handler method in the local class for double-click should not get executed. This is managed through the concept of the registration of the event. You will register the DOUBLE_CLICK event handler method only for the first instance of the class CL_GUI_ALV_GRID.

The apt place of registration of an event handler method is just after creation of the instance of the class to which you are co-relating the event handler method. For example:

```
CREATE OBJECT ALV_GRID1 EXPORTING...
SET HANDLER LREF->DB_CLICK FOR ALV_GRID1.
```

Peruse the source code with its **comments.**

The extra code is required to implement the handler methods for events DOUBLE_CLICK of class CL_GUI_ALV_GRID and CLOSE of class CL_GUI_DIALOGBOX_CONTAINER.

Code in the declaration part:

```
CLASS LCLASS DEFINITION DEFERRED.

DATA: LREF         TYPE REF TO LCLASS,
......
```

Code for the local class:

```
***** class definition *****

CLASS LCLASS DEFINITION.

PUBLIC SECTION.

METHODS: DB_CLICK FOR EVENT DOUBLE_CLICK OF CL_GUI_ALV_GRID
          IMPORTING E_ROW,
```

```
        CLOSE_DBOX FOR EVENT CLOSE OF CL_GUI_DIALOGBOX_CONTAINER,
....

PRIVATE SECTION.

DATA: BILLS_STRU    TYPE YCL_CH12_BILLS_STRU,
      BILLS_TAB     TYPE STANDARD TABLE OF YCL_CH12_BILLS_STRU,
      DCONT         TYPE REF TO CL_GUI_DIALOGBOX_CONTAINER,
      ALV_GRID2     TYPE REF TO CL_GUI_ALV_GRID,
      CAPTON(70)    TYPE C,
      FCAT2         TYPE LVC_T_FCAT,
      FSTRU         TYPE LVC_S_FCAT,
......

ENDCLASS.

***** class implementation *****

CLASS LCLASS IMPLEMENTATION.

****** DB_CLICK *****

METHOD DB_CLICK.

CHECK E_ROW-ROWTYPE IS INITIAL. " double clicking is on a customer
                                " line, not subtotal/total line

 READ TABLE SALES_TAB INTO SALES_STRU INDEX E_ROW-INDEX.

 SELECT VBELN FKDAT WAERK KURRF NETWR FROM VBRK
  INTO TABLE BILLS_TAB WHERE KUNAG = SALES_STRU-KUNNR
  AND BUKRS = CCODE.

 LOOP AT BILLS_TAB INTO BILLS_STRU.
  BILLS_STRU-NETWR = BILLS_STRU-NETWR * BILLS_STRU-KURRF.
  MODIFY BILLS_TAB FROM BILLS_STRU.
 ENDLOOP.

 CALL FUNCTION 'LVC_FIELDCATALOG_MERGE'
  EXPORTING
    I_STRUCTURE_NAME               = 'YCL_CH12_BILLS_STRU'
   CHANGING
     CT_FIELDCAT                   = FCAT2
  EXCEPTIONS
    INCONSISTENT_INTERFACE         = 1
    PROGRAM_ERROR                  = 2
    OTHERS                         = 3
           .
 IF SY-SUBRC <> 0.
   MESSAGE ID SY-MSGID TYPE SY-MSGTY NUMBER SY-MSGNO
         WITH SY-MSGV1 SY-MSGV2 SY-MSGV3 SY-MSGV4.
 ENDIF.
```

```
 LOOP AT FCAT2 INTO FSTRU.
  FSTRU-COL_OPT = 'X'.
  IF FSTRU-FIELDNAME = 'KURRF'.
   FSTRU-NO_SUM = 'X'. " no sum for KURRF
  ENDIF.
  MODIFY FCAT2 FROM FSTRU.
 ENDLOOP.

 CONCATENATE TEXT-001 SALES_STRU-KUNNR '/' SALES_STRU-NAME1 INTO CAPTON.

 CREATE OBJECT DCONT
   EXPORTING
     WIDTH                       = 420 " dimension is points
     HEIGHT                      = 200 " " a point = 1/72 of inch
     TOP                         = 35
     LEFT                        = 550
     CAPTION                     = CAPTON
   EXCEPTIONS
     CNTL_ERROR                  = 1
     CNTL_SYSTEM_ERROR           = 2
     CREATE_ERROR                = 3
     LIFETIME_ERROR              = 4
     LIFETIME_DYNPRO_DYNPRO_LINK = 5
     EVENT_ALREADY_REGISTERED    = 6
     ERROR_REGIST_EVENT          = 7
     others                      = 8
     .
 IF SY-SUBRC <> 0.
  MESSAGE ID SY-MSGID TYPE SY-MSGTY NUMBER SY-MSGNO
          WITH SY-MSGV1 SY-MSGV2 SY-MSGV3 SY-MSGV4.
 ENDIF.

 SET HANDLER LREF->CLOSE_DBOX FOR DCONT.
  " registration of 'CLOSE_DBOX' handler method for instance DCONT

 CREATE OBJECT ALV_GRID2
   EXPORTING
    I_PARENT  = DCONT.

 CALL METHOD ALV_GRID2->SET_TABLE_FOR_FIRST_DISPLAY
   CHANGING
     IT_OUTTAB                     = BILLS_TAB
     IT_FIELDCATALOG               = FCAT2.

 CALL METHOD ALV_GRID1->SET_ENABLE
  EXPORTING
  ENABLE = ' '.
ENDMETHOD.
```

```
**********************

METHOD CLOSE_DBOX.

 CALL METHOD DCONT->FREE( ).

 CALL METHOD ALV_GRID1->SET_ENABLE
   EXPORTING
    ENABLE = 'X'.

ENDMETHOD.
***********************
```

DDIC structure YCL_CH12_BILLS_STRU has been created with the fields VBELN, FKDAT, WAERS, KURRF, and NETWR. The value of the text symbol is as follows:

```
[TEXT-001: 'Bills of Customer:' ]
```

Code for registration of handler method DB_CLICK for instance ALV_GRID1:

```
CREATE OBJECT ALV_GRID1.....
.....
CREATE OBJECT LREF.
***** registration of handler methods ****
 SET HANDLER LREF->DB_CLICK FOR ALV_GRID1.
......
```

This code enables the generation of the detailed second ALV output: billing documents of a customer. It enables closing of this second output and navigating back to the first ALV output: the customer-wise sales summary of a specific company code.

To ensure that double-clicking a subtotal or total line does not generate the detailed ALV report, you check the contents of the importing parameter E_ROW-ROWTYPE. If its value is blank or an initial value, double-clicking has been done on a regular row. Otherwise, double-clicking has been done on a subtotal or total row.

Placing a Custom Button on the ALV Toolbar and Making It Operative

Events TOOLBAR and USER_COMMAND of class CL_GUI_ALV_GRID

In this part of the exercise, you will incorporate a custom button on the ALV toolbar and then react to the clicking of that button. You will do this by shifting the Back button from the application toolbar (used in this chapter's preceding hands-on exercises) to the ALV toolbar. Then you do not have to code in the PAI event.

Having a custom button on the ALV toolbar requires two main steps:

- Locating the custom button on the ALV toolbar
- Making the custom button operational

You incorporate a custom button on the ALV toolbar by using the event TOOLBAR of the ALV class CL_GUI_ALV_GRID. This event is triggered each time the toolbar of the control (ALV grid) needs to be regenerated. It is also triggered by the method SET_TOOLBAR_INTERACTIVE of the class CL_GU_ALV_GRID.

The event TOOLBAR has two importing parameters (E_OBJECT of type CL_ALV_EVENT_TOOLBAR_SET and E_INTERACTIVE). You will use the first importing parameter, E_OBJECT. If you look up the TOOLBAR event of the class CL_GUI_ALV_GRID in the Class Builder, and then look up the class CL_ALV_EVENT_TOOLBAR_SET and click the attributes of that class, the DDIC table has an attribute MT_TOOLBAR of type TTB_BUTTON. The structure of the DDIC table (internal table) type is STB_BUTTON. You have to fill in the four fields (FUNCTION, ICON, QUICKINFO, and TEXT) of the structure STB_BUTTON and then append these button particulars to the internal table E_OBJECT->MT_TOOLBAR for your button to appear on the ALV toolbar. You can create a gap between buttons by assigning the field BUTN_TYPE of structure STB_BUTTON a value of 3 and appending it to the internal table E_OBJECT->MT_TOOLBAR. You also can create menu and menu entries. Refer to the single values of the domain TB_BTYPE associated with the field BUTN_TYPE of structure STB_BUTTON. You are placing the extra custom button only on first instance of the class CL_GUI_ALV_GRID.

You can use the event USER_COMMAND to execute actions following the clicking of ALV toolbar buttons. You have to locate the same program code that was in the PAI event of this chapter's preceding exercises in the event handler method of the event USER_COMMAND. Again, you want this method to be executed for the first instance of the class CL_GUI_ALV_GRID, not the second instance. The event USER_COMMAND has one importing parameter, E_UCOMM, containing the function code of the button pressed.

The extra code required to implement the handler methods for the events TOOLBAR and USER_COMMAND follows. Peruse the code with its comments.

Source code in the local class:

```
PUBLIC SECTION.
......

METHODS: TOOL_BAR FOR EVENT TOOLBAR OF CL_GUI_ALV_GRID
            IMPORTING E_OBJECT E_INTERACTIVE,


          GO_BACK FOR EVENT USER_COMMAND OF CL_GUI_ALV_GRID
            IMPORTING E_UCOMM.
.........

PRIVATE SECTION.

DATA: TOOL_STRU     TYPE STB_BUTTON, " stru for ALV tool bar
...

METHOD TOOL_BAR.

 CLEAR TOOL_STRU.
 TOOL_STRU-BUTN_TYPE = 3.
  " create gap - last existing button & own button

 APPEND TOOL_STRU TO E_OBJECT->MT_TOOLBAR.
 CLEAR TOOL_STRU.

 TOOL_STRU-FUNCTION    = 'BACK'. " function code
 TOOL_STRU-ICON        = '@CF@'. " icon code
 TOOL_STRU-QUICKINFO   = 'Back'(002). " button tool tip
 TOOL_STRU-TEXT        = 'Back'(002). " button text

 APPEND TOOL_STRU TO E_OBJECT->MT_TOOLBAR.

ENDMETHOD.
```

```
************************
METHOD GO_BACK.
 IF E_UCOMM = 'BACK'.

  SET SCREEN 0. " these two statements return
  LEAVE SCREEN. " control to PARAMETERS prompt

 ENDIF.
ENDMETHOD.
****************************
```

The values of text symbols:

```
[TEXT-002: 'Back']
```

Code for registration of handler methods `TOOL_BAR AND GO_BACK` **for instance** `ALV_GRID1`**:**

```
CREATE OBJECT ALV_GRID1.....
.....
CREATE OBJECT LREF.
......

SET HANDLER LREF->TOOL_BAR FOR ALV_GRID1.
SET HANDLER LREF->GO_BACK FOR ALV_GRID1.
```

Outputting a Serial Number and Adjusting It with the Change in ALV Layout

Event AFTER_USER_COMMAND of class CL_GUI_ALV_GRID

You are using the DDIC structure YCL_CH12_SALES_SUM_STRU1 to generate the default field catalog for the first instance ALV grid. It is a modified version of the DDIC structure YCL_CH12_SALES_SUM_STRU you used for your earlier ALV exercises. It contains the additional field SRL_NO as the first field of the structure.

The field SRL_NO (serial number) appearing in your ALV output has to be adjusted—regenerated every time the user changes the output layout by either omitting rows or including previously omitted rows (that is, a change in filter settings and/or every time the data is reordered via a change in sort settings).

In your previous exercise, you did not re-sort the customer-wise sales summary internal table in the program. The filter and sort settings were applied to the copy of the summarized sales data internal table on the presentation server. Now you need to re-sort the summarized sales data internal table in the program (application server) to be able to regenerate the serial numbers.

You can regenerate the serial numbers in an event handler method of event AFTER_USER_COMMAND. This event is triggered after the end user selects a function on the ALV toolbar and this function has been executed.

In case a default layout is operating (that is, a default layout has been set), when the ALV output is being produced for the first time via the Execute/F8 button on the selection screen prompting for company code, the serial numbers have to be generated as per filter and sort settings in the default layout. For the serial numbers to be generated correctly for the default layout, you execute the event handler method for the event AFTER_USER_COMMAND explicitly, just after calling the method SET_TABLE_FOR_FIRST_DISPLAY.

The filter and sort settings are maintained at the presentation server level. So you have to retrieve these settings with the methods GET_FILTER_CRITERIA and GET_SORT_CRITERIA. These methods retrieve and return the presentation server filter and sort settings to the program in the specific format of internal tables. There is another method, GET_FILTERED_ENTRIES. This method returns in a hashed internal table, the row numbers of filtered-out data. In the present exercise, you will use this method to retrieve the filtered-out or omitted rows returned in terms of row numbers in a hashed internal table.

The row numbers returned in a hashed internal table are the row numbers of the summarized sales data internal table as it existed before new sort criterion was applied. Referring to this hashed internal table, you can mark the rows in the summarized sales data internal table for which a serial number is to be generated. (For omitted row numbers, no serial number is to be generated.)

The sort criterion is returned in an internal table whose structure (DDIC type LVC_S_SORT) is as follows:

> SPOS: Indicates the sort sequence. If the field is first in the sort sequence, the value = 1; if it is second, the value = 2.
>
> FIELDNAME: Indicates the field name
>
> UP: Value = X if ascending
>
> DOWN: Value = X if descending

You need to sort the summarized sales data internal table as per new sort criterion to be able to generate the new serial numbers.

An internal table can be sorted by providing the sort specifications in an internal table similar to the runtime sort specification you provide in a SELECT statement. The syntax for this is as follows:

```
SORT <internal table> BY (<internal table with sort specifications>).
```

The `<internal table with sort specifications>` has the DDIC structure type ABAP_SORTORDER with the following fields:

```
NAME     Field name
DESCENDING = 'X', if descending
ASTEXT     = 'X', if text sort
```

So you have to convert the sort criterion internal table returned as DDIC structure type LVC_S_SORT into an internal table of DDIC structure type ABAP_SORTORDER.

To sum up, you have to perform the following to have serial numbers regenerated as per altered filter and/or sort settings in the event handler method of AFTER_USER_COMMAND:

- Reset/initialize serial numbers in the summarized sales data internal table.
- Retrieve the filtered-out or omitted rows at the presentation server/front-end.
- Using this information of filtered-out rows, mark in the summarized sales data internal table, the rows for which serial numbers are to be generated.
- Retrieve the sort settings.
- Convert the sort settings.
- Sort the summarized sales data internal table with the converted sort settings.
- Generate the serial numbers for the marked rows of the sorted summarized sales data internal table.

Whenever you are selecting saved layouts or operating the default layout, the field catalog at the front end or presentation server is not in sync with the back-end field catalog. (The suppression of leading zeros occurring in customer code output, and so forth.) To rectify this, you do the following:

- Retrieve the front-end or presentation server field catalog.
- Manipulate this field catalog for the appearance of leading zeros in the customer code. Suppress the totaling of field SRL_NO (serial number). Determine the maximum widths of the fields NAME1 and ORT01. Set the output lengths of these fields (field catalog field OUTPUTLEN) to the determined widths.
- Set the ALV output front-end field catalog with the manipulated field catalog.

You make the leading zeros appear in the customer code by using the function module CONVERSION_EXIT_ALZSN_OUTPUT in the field EDIT_MASK of the field catalog. You assign this field the value ==ALZSN. Note that the function module CONVERSION_EXIT_ALPHA_OUTPUT suppresses zeros in the output.

To make function module CONVERSION_EXIT_ALZSN_OUTPUT operative, you have to insert a row in the database table ADLZSN with the following code snippet:

```
TABLES ADLZSN.
ADLZSN-SETON = 'X'.
INSERT ADLZSN.
```

The optimizing of column widths with the field catalog field COL_WIDTH set to value X is not working with the initial loading of the ALV output with a default layout, especially with the fields NAME1 and ORT01. That is why you are determining the maximum widths for these fields while generating the serial numbers, by assigning the field catalog field OUTPUTLEN with determined widths.

The method should be executed only if there is change in the sort and filter settings. But for now, you are executing this method on operation of any of the ALV toolbar options. In the next version of this program using the ALV class CL_SALV_TABLE, you will implement this.

The extra code required to implement the handler method for event AFTER_USER_COMMAND (to regenerate serial number, and so forth) follows.

Peruse the source code with its comments.

Source code in the declaration part:

```
" internal table for sort run time spec
       SORT_TAB  TYPE LVC_T_SORT WITH HEADER LINE, " ALV sort entries
BYS        TYPE ABAP_SORTORDER_TAB WITH HEADER LINE.
```

Source code in the local class:

```
METHODS:
 .........
ADJUST_SRL_NO FOR EVENT AFTER_USER_COMMAND OF CL_GUI_ALV_GRID
            IMPORTING E_UCOMM E_SAVED E_NOT_PROCESSED.

PRIVATE SECTION.
DATA:
........
NAME1_LEN     TYPE I, " max length NAME1
ORT01_LEN     TYPE I, " max length ORT01
TFCAT         TYPE LVC_T_FCAT,
FL_ENTS       TYPE LVC_T_FIDX, " rows filtered out
INDEX         TYPE YCL_CH12_SRL_NO. " to generate serial no.
```

```
METHOD ADJUST_SRL_NO.
 REFRESH: FL_ENTS, SORT_TAB, BYS.
 ALV_GRID1->REFRESH_TABLE_DISPLAY( ).
***** rows to be filtered out *****
 CALL METHOD ALV_GRID1->GET_FILTERED_ENTRIES
   IMPORTING
     ET_FILTERED_ENTRIES = FL_ENTS
     .
***** rows to be filtered out over *****

 CALL METHOD ALV_GRID1->GET_SORT_CRITERIA
   IMPORTING
     ET_SORT = SORT_TAB[].

***** convert sort specs *****

 SORT SORT_TAB BY SPOS. " sort in order of sort sequence
 LOOP AT SORT_TAB INTO SORT_TAB.
  BYS-NAME = SORT_TAB-FIELDNAME.
  IF SORT_TAB-DOWN IS NOT INITIAL.
   BYS-DESCENDING = 'X'.
  ELSE.
   BYS-DESCENDING = ' '.

  ENDIF.
  APPEND BYS TO BYS.
 ENDLOOP.
***** convert sort specs over *****

***** mark rows for which serial numbers to be generated *****
** rows for which serial numbers to be generated assigned non-zero **

 INDEX = 0.

 CLEAR SALES_STRU-SRL_NO.
 MODIFY SALES_TAB FROM SALES_STRU TRANSPORTING SRL_NO
  WHERE SRL_NO <> 0.

 LOOP AT SALES_TAB INTO SALES_STRU.

  READ TABLE FL_ENTS FROM SY-TABIX TRANSPORTING NO FIELDS.
  IF SY-SUBRC = 0. " if row is in to-be-filtered-out internal
   CONTINUE.       " table, bypass for serial number generation
  ENDIF.
  INDEX = INDEX + 1.
  SALES_STRU-SRL_NO = INDEX.
  MODIFY SALES_TAB FROM SALES_STRU TRANSPORTING SRL_NO.
 ENDLOOP.
```

```
 SORT SALES_TAB BY (BYS). " BYS contains run time sort specs

 INDEX = 0.

*****  generate serial numbers **
 NAME1_LEN = 0.
 ORT01_LEN = 0.

 LOOP AT SALES_TAB INTO SALES_STRU.

  IF SALES_STRU-SRL_NO = 0.
   CONTINUE.
  ENDIF.
  INDEX = INDEX + 1.
  SALES_STRU-SRL_NO = INDEX.
  MODIFY SALES_TAB FROM SALES_STRU.

  " obtaining the maximum width of output: NAME1 & ORT01

  IF STRLEN( SALES_STRU-NAME1 ) > NAME1_LEN.
   NAME1_LEN = STRLEN( SALES_STRU-NAME1 ).
  ENDIF.

  IF STRLEN( SALES_STRU-ORT01 ) > ORT01_LEN.
   ORT01_LEN = STRLEN( SALES_STRU-ORT01 ).
  ENDIF.

 ENDLOOP.

***** adjust front-end field catalogue *****

                ALV_GRID1->GET_FRONTEND_FIELDCATALOG(
                IMPORTING ET_FIELDCATALOG = TFCAT ).
" get/retrieve front-end field catalogue
 LOOP AT TFCAT INTO FSTRU.

CASE FSTRU-FIELDNAME.

WHEN 'KUNNR'.

FSTRU-EDIT_MASK = '==ALZSN'.
FSTRU-CONVEXIT  = ' '.
FSTRU-NO_CONVEXT  = 'X'.
FSTRU-COL_OPT = 'X'.

WHEN  'NAME1'.
FSTRU-OUTPUTLEN = NAME1_LEN.
WHEN  'ORT01'.
FSTRU-OUTPUTLEN = ORT01_LEN.
WHEN OTHERS.
FSTRU-COL_OPT = 'X'.
ENDCASE.
```

```
  IF FSTRU-FIELDNAME = 'SRL_NO'.
   FSTRU-NO_SUM = 'X'.  " no totaling for serial nos.
  ENDIF.

  MODIFY TFCAT FROM FSTRU.

 ENDLOOP.

 ALV_GRID1->SET_FRONTEND_FIELDCATALOG( IT_FIELDCATALOG = TFCAT[] ).
" set front-end field catalogue

ENDMETHOD.
```

Source code for registration of handler method `ADJUST_SRL_NO` **for instance** `ALV_GRID1`**:**

```
SET HANDLER LREF->ADJUST_SRL_NO FOR ALV_GRID1.
.....
LREF->ADJUST_SRL_NO( ).
ALV_GRID1->REFRESH_TABLE_DISPLAY( ).
```

The program is `YCL_CH12_03_ALV_EVENTS`**, and the full code can be found in source code resource.** The output appears as shown in Figure 12-64.

Customer Wise Sales Summary - Company Code:3000/IDES US INC Curr:USD

Back

Srl No.	Customer	Name 1	City	Net Value
1	0000000255	Emma Bull	DENVER	2,207.00
2	0000000257	John Evans	NEDERLAND	2,299.00
3	0000000258	Roger Zahn	ALBUQUERQUE	1,912.00
4	0000000260	Chelsa Quinn Yates	ALBUQUERQUE	2,124.00
5	0000000262	Robert Jensen	CANON CITY	3,720.00
6	0000000266	Charles Scott	TORREY	2,995.00
7	0000000272	Joe Masson	SALINA	748.00
8	0000000281	Tracy Collins	VAIL	1,567.50
9	0000000470	Alex Lynch	PHILADELPHIA	11,860.80
10	0000000471	Steve Martin	SALT LAKE CITY	8,415.50
11	0000000473	Albert Brooks	COLORADO SPRINGS	10,911.80
12	0000000474	Edward Burns	HELENA	12,427.70
13	0000000481	Peter King	SEATTLE	10,542.10
14	0000000482	Douglas Barker	MINNEAPOLIS	1,614.26

Figure 12-64. *Output of program YCL_CH12_03_ALV_EVENTS*

In the output:

- The serial numbers appear.
- The Back button appears on the ALV toolbar.

Change the layout. In the changed layout, the order of fields is `SRL_NO`, `NAME1`, `KUNNR`, `ORT01`, and `NETWR`. Make the sort setting as `NAME1` ascending. The serial numbers have been regenerated for the changed layout. The output for this changed layout looks like Figure 12-65.

Customer Wise Sales Summary - Company Code:3000/IDES US INC Curr:USD

Srl No.	Name 1	Customer	City	Net Value
1	ADCOM COMPUTER	0000003272	SEATTLE	2,147.70
2	ALAN FAITH	0000401258	BOSTON	862.00
3	ALAN FARRAR	0000401260	SAN DIEGO	862.00
4	ALAN FINER	0000401266	WASHINGTON	862.00
5	ALAN GUETTEL	0000401269	BOSTON	862.00
6	ALAN GWARA	0000401272	SAN DIEGO	862.00
7	ALPHA Center	0000003273	MINNEAPOLIS	2,147.70
8	Aircraft Products	0000001470	Slough	11,000.00
9	Albert Brooks	0000000473	COLORADO SPRINGS	10,911.80
10	Alex Lynch	0000000470	PHILADELPHIA	11,860.80
11	American Security Company	0000300703	NEW ORLEANS	1,073,087.10
12	Andyna and Dynana Laboratories, Inc	0000003221	MONSEY	6,153.60
13	Antipolis	0000300325	ANTIOCH	22,320.00
14	BEN GUIER	0000401270	NEW YORK	862.00

Figure 12-65. *Output showing the changed layout of* YCL_CH12_03_ALV_EVENTS

Load the original layout with none of the filter and sort settings, and the data appearing in order of customer code. Scroll down to the customer code 0000003271 (serial number 31). Double-click this customer line. This produces the detailed ALV output, which looks like Figure 12-66.

Customer Wise Sales Summary - Company Code:3000/IDES US INC Curr:USD

Srl No.	Customer	Name 1	City	Net Value
27	0000003251	Palo Alto Airways Inc.	PALO ALTO	202,496.00
28	0000003261	Hotel Alfonso Del Vida	DENVER	3,571.00
29	0000003262	La Quinta Hotel & Towers	DENVER	3,568.00
30	0000003263	Rogier Golf Resort YY	DENVER	3,058.00
31	0000003271	Media Store	ANTIOCH	6,477.30
32	0000003272	ADCOM COMPUTER	SEATTLE	2,147.70
33	0000003273	ALPHA Center	MINNEAPOLIS	2,147.70
34	0000003800	Candid International Technology	TAMPA	723,492.00
35	0000004000	North Energy Ltd	Calgary	42,666.67
36	0000004130	Compu Tech	SAN FRANCISCO	57,358.00
37	0000006000	RIWA Headquarters	LOS ANGELES	2,251.76
38	0000006002	RIWA Regional Storage Trenton	TRENTON	78,780.00
39	0000006006	RIWA Regional Warehouse Denver	DENVER	152,712.00
40	0000030200	Wal-Mart	NEWARK	8,000.00

Bills of Customer:0000003271/Media Store

SD Doc.	Billing Date	Curr.	ExchRt	Net Value
90031824	04.02.2002	USD	1.000...	75.00
90032841	25.06.2002	USD	1.000...	2,147.70
90032962	23.08.2002	USD	1.000...	2,003.30
90034693	08.06.2004	USD	1.000...	248.00
90036011	19.12.2005	USD	1.000...	2,003.30
				6,477.30

Figure 12-66. *Summary and detail output*

The billing documents of a specified customer appear as detailed ALV output in the second instance of the ALV grid, in a dialog box container. You can operate the Close option of the dialog box container and test the execution of the event handler method. You can click the Back button on the ALV toolbar of the first instance of the ALV grid and test the event handler method.

As in the preceding exercise, create and save a few layouts. One of these is `LAYOUT2`, the same layout used in the preceding exercise. This layout is as follows:

- Field order:
    - Srl. No. (`SRL_NO`)
    - City (`ORT01`)
    - Customer (`KUNNR`)
    - Name 1 (`NAME1`)
    - Net Value (`NETWR`)
- Total: Net Value
- Sorting
    - Sort: City (Ascending)
    - Group: City (Subtotals)
- Filter fields/columns
    - Filter values for city: A*, B*, C*, M*, S*, T* (cities starting with A, B, C, M, S, and T)
    - Net Value: >= 500

For this layout, the output appears as shown in Figure 12-67 and Figure 12-68.

Srl No.	City	Customer	Name 1	Net Value
1	ALBUQUERQUE	0000000258	Rogèr Zahn	1,912.00
2		0000000260	Chelsa Quinn Yates	2,124.00
	ALBUQUERQUE			4,036.00
3	ANTIOCH	0000003271	Media Store	6,477.30
4		0000300000	Havers Inc.	4,133.00
5		0000300081	Havers Inc	914.20
6		0000300325	Antipolis	22,320.00
	ANTIOCH			33,844.50
7	AUGUSTA	0000300716	Matrax	996,115.00
	AUGUSTA			996,115.00
11	Berlin	0000001508	Deutsche Computer AG	5,987.50
	Berlin			5,987.50
8	BOSTON	0000401269	ALAN GUETTEL	862.00
9		0000401259	JIM FARAIZL	862.00

Figure 12-67. *Output with subtotals*

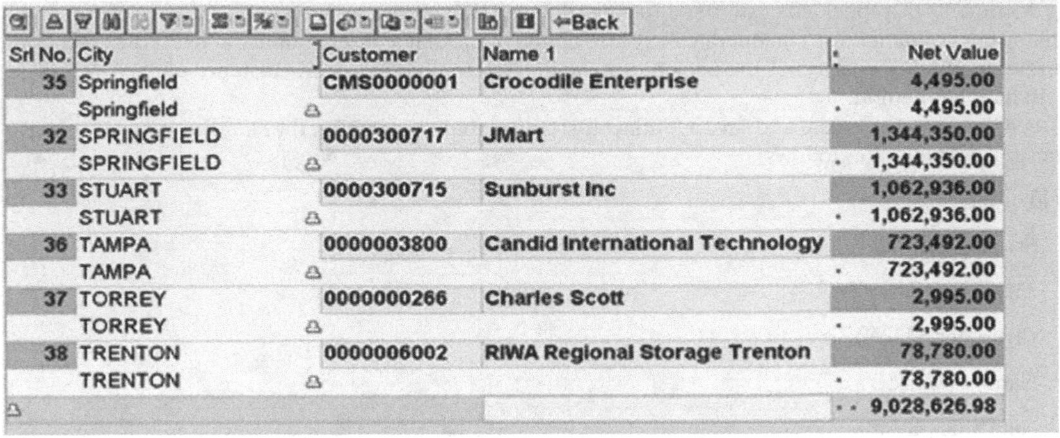

Srl No.	City	Customer	Name 1	Net Value
35	Springfield	CMS0000001	Crocodile Enterprise	4,495.00
	Springfield			• 4,495.00
32	SPRINGFIELD	0000300717	JMart	1,344,350.00
	SPRINGFIELD			• 1,344,350.00
33	STUART	0000300715	Sunburst Inc	1,062,936.00
	STUART			• 1,062,936.00
36	TAMPA	0000003800	Candid International Technology	723,492.00
	TAMPA			• 723,492.00
37	TORREY	0000000266	Charles Scott	2,995.00
	TORREY			• 2,995.00
38	TRENTON	0000006002	RIWA Regional Storage Trenton	78,780.00
	TRENTON			• 78,780.00
				•• 9,028,626.98

Figure 12-68. *Program YCL_CH12_03_ALV_EVENTS: Output with Subtotals*

The output has tested the event handler methods of events DOUBLE_CLICK, CLOSE, and AFTER_USER_COMMAND. The appearance of the Back button on the ALV toolbar and its operation has tested the event handler methods of events TOOLBAR and USER_COMMAND. The power of events has been demonstrated in this exercise.

Conclusion

You have created ALV output by using the built-in class CL_GUI_ALV_GRID. You have manipulated this output as an end user would—for instance, shuffling fields, omitting fields, sorting, filtering, performing ABC analysis, and [verb here] graphics. You have controlled the ALV output field attributes and the overall appearance of the grid, and you have enabled saving and managing of ALV layouts. You triggered events to add sophistication and enhance the functionality of the ALV output.

In the next chapter, you will use a more modern built-in class, CL_SALV_TABLE, and implement the same functionalities you implemented when using the built-in class CL_GUI_ALV_GRID.

CHAPTER 13

ABAP List Viewer Output—Part 2

In this chapter, you will continue the generation of ALV output that you started in the preceding chapter. Whatever ALV features you implemented by using the class CL_GUI_ALV_GRID will be implemented again in this chapter by using the class CL_SALV_TABLE.

This chapter also presents two data browser programs: the first program uses the class CL_GUI_ALV_GRID, and the second program uses the class CL_SALV_TABLE. These data browsers are like the transaction code SE16 data browser. On the opening screen, you input a table or view name. The fields of that table or view are displayed with check boxes, enabling you to select or deselect them. After field selection, you click the Output button on the application toolbar to output the selected fields' data in an ALV.

ALV Output Using the Class CL_SALV_TABLE

You have used various features of the class CL_GUI_ALV_GRID to produce ALV output. In this section, you'll learn about the deployment of the ALV class CL_SALV_TABLE.

You must have observed that the class CL_GUI_ALV_GRID is a mixture of class and procedure orientation. For instance, the way you were using the field catalog internal table does not comply with the idea of encapsulation. What data object the class is using should not be apparent to the user of the class. If that user wants to set the properties of a subobject or component of a class, it should be in terms of GET and SET statements and not in terms of directly accessing the data object used by the class and manipulating the data object as you were doing in the context of field catalog manipulation.

Main ALV class: CL_SALV_TABLE

The class CL_SALV_TABLE is more class- or OOPS-oriented than the class CL_GUI_ALV_GRID, which, as I've pointed out, is a mixture of class and procedure orientation. With the class CL_SALV_TABLE, you have the option to either locate the ALV output in a container or have the output occupy the full screen without using a container.

If you opt for ALV output without a container and occupying the full screen, you don't have to do any screen programming. You don't have to create a screen, give the statement CALL SCREEN, or provide PBO and PAI coding. That makes things relatively simple.

To generate ALV output with the class CL_SALV_TABLE, you use the static method FACTORY and the instance method DISPLAY.

FACTORY has the following parameters:

LIST_DISPLAY (importing): The parameter is relevant only when ALV output is not in a container (that is, full-screen output). The parameter can assume the value X or blank. When the value X is passed to it, the output displays as a so-called classical list with a two-dimensional visual effect. When the default value ' ' is passed, the output has a grid or three-dimensional visual effect. You cannot pass this parameter the value X if the ALV output is to be located inside a container. If X is passed and the ALV output is located inside a container, a runtime error results.

R_CONTAINER (importing): This reference variable points to the instance of a container class. You use this parameter if you are locating ALV output inside a container.

CONTAINER_NAME (importing): This is the container name as given in the Attributes dialog box for the screen element. You use this parameter if you are locating ALV output inside a container. You should provide one of the two parameters: either R_CONTAINER or CONTAINER_NAME.

R_SALV_TABLE (exporting): This reference variable is declared with type ref to the same class, CL_SALV_TABLE. The FACTORY method creates an instance of the class with the passed variable. The execution of the CONSTRUCTOR method CREATE OBJECT is unnecessary.

T_TABLE (changing): This internal table contains the data to be output.

After executing the FACTORY method, you have to execute the DISPLAY method to create the ALV output. The following source code illustrates the syntax:

```
DATA: CURRENCY_TAB TYPE STANDARD TABLE OF TCURT,
      ALV_GRID     TYPE REF TO CL_SALV_TABLE.

START-OF-SELECTION.

SELECT * FROM TCURT INTO TABLE CURRENCY_TAB WHERE SPRAS = SY-LANGU.

CALL METHOD CL_SALV_TABLE=>FACTORY
    EXPORTING
      LIST_DISPLAY      = 'X'
    IMPORTING
      R_SALV_TABLE      = ALV_GRID
    CHANGING
      T_TABLE           = CURRENCY_TAB.

ALV_GRID->DISPLAY( ).
```

You can test this source code.

This outputs the classical ALV list (full screen) with a two-dimensional visual effect. You don't have to create a screen and provide the associated screen programming. If you omit the LIST_DISPLAY parameter or pass as LIST_DISPLAY = ' ', the output will have a three-dimensional visual effect (grid). For full-screen ALV output not in a container, the ALV toolbar replaces the application toolbar.

Subobjects of the Class CL_SALV_TABLE

You need the program to have more capabilities, so you can do the following: change the properties of the fields or columns that are output (equivalent to the field catalog capabilities), control the overall appearance of the output (for example, the grid title), and enable the end user to save and retrieve the ALV layouts.

And finally, you would like to trigger events to modify the default ALV toolbar, to create interactive lists (via the DOUBLE_CLICK event), and to provide a serial number in the ALV output that you should be able to generate dynamically as the end user changes layouts or loads saved layouts. In short, whatever you did with the ALV output when using the class CL_GUI_ALV_GRID, you should be able to do when using the class CL_SALV_TABLE.

To provide these capabilities with the class CL_SALV_TABLE, you will use GET subobjects and SET subobjects statements.

For example, the preceding code snippet to output ALV by default does not provide the full set of default buttons on the ALV toolbar. To provide the full set, you have to get the subobject FUNCTIONS of the ALV object by using the GET_FUNCTIONS method of the main class CL_SALV_TABLE. The method GET_FUNCTIONS will return a reference to the instance of the subobject FUNCTIONS. Using this reference variable (refer to the parameters of the method GET_FUNCTIONS of the class CL_SALV_TABLE in SE24), you will execute the method SET_ALL to place a full set of default buttons on the ALV toolbar. The extra source code to place the full set of default buttons on the ALV toolbar follows.

Data declaration:

```
DATA: FUNCTIONS     TYPE REF TO CL_SALV_FUNCTIONS_LIST.
....
```

Source code before the ALV_GRID->DISPLAY( ) **statement:**

```
FUNCTIONS = ALV_GRID->GET_FUNCTIONS( ).
FUNCTIONS->SET_ALL( VALUE = 'X' ).
```

You can add buttons to the ALV toolbar by using the ADD_FUNCTION method. You also can enable and delete buttons. Refer to the method list of the classes CL_SALV_FUNCTIONS_LIST, CL_SALV_FUNCTIONS, CL_SALV_FUNCTION, and CL_SALV_FUNCTIONAL_SETTINGS.

In a similar manner, if you want to manipulate the properties of the ALV output fields or columns, you have to get the appropriate subobjects and set their properties. If you want to impart green color in an intensified background to the field or column LTEXT, for example, you use the following source code:

Data declaration:

```
DATA:    COLUMNS       TYPE REF TO CL_SALV_COLUMNS_TABLE,
         COLUMN        TYPE REF TO CL_SALV_COLUMN_TABLE,
         COL_STRU      TYPE LVC_S_COLO. " DDIC structure
```

Source code before the ALV_GRID->DISPLAY( ) **statement:**

```
COLUMNS =  ALV_GRID->GET_COLUMNS( ).
COLUMN ?=  COLUMNS->GET_COLUMN( COLUMNNAME = 'LTEXT' ).
COL_STRU-COL = 5. " color code
COL_STRU-INT = 1. " intensified on
COL_STRU-INV = 0. " inverse off

COLUMN->SET_COLOR( VALUE = COL_STRU ).
```

The method GET_COLUMNS gets instances of all the fields or columns of the ALV output. The method GET_COLUMN gets an instance of a specified field or column. The method SET_COLOR sets the color of the specific field or column.

Some property settings operate on all fields or columns, and others operate on a single field or column. If you want all the field or column widths optimized, you use COLUMNS->SET_OPTIMIZE(VALUE = 'X').

In this way with subobjects, you can have filter settings, sort settings, aggregations, selections, events, and so forth. Table 13-1 lists classes used to access subobjects of the main class CL_SALV_TABLE.

Table 13-1. *Classes Used to Access Subobjects of CL_SALV_TABLE*

Serial Number	Class Name
1	CL_SALV_AGGREGATIONS
2	CL_SALV_AGGREGATION
3	CL_SALV_COLUMNS_TABLE
4	CL_SALV_COLUMN_TABLE
5	CL_SALV_EVENTS_TABLE
6	CL_SALV_FUNCTIONS_LIST
7	CL_SALV_FILTERS
8	CL_SALV_FILTER
9	CL_SALV_LAYOUT
10	CL_SALV_SELECTIONS
11	CL_SALV_SELOPT
12	CL_SALV_SORTS
13	CL_SALV_SORT

You should spend some time familiarizing yourself with the class CL_SALV_TABLE and its associated classes and subclasses. The upcoming exercises further illustrate the use of CL_SALV_TABLE.

Hands-on Exercise: Customer-wise Sales Summary of a Specified Company Code as ALV Output: Use Class CL_SALV_TABLE

Change Field or Column Properties Provide for Save Layouts Facility, Etc.

This hands-on exercise is equivalent to the prior program, YCL_CH12_02_ALV_FCAT_ETC that used the class CL_GUI_ALV_GRID. In this program, YCL_CH13_01_USE_CL_SALV_TABLE, you control the output field properties, set up aggregation for the NETWR field, control the overall appearance of the ALV output, and provide for the saving of layouts.

You will locate an instance of the ALV class CL_SALV_TABLE inside an instance of the container class CL_GUI_CUSTOM_CONTAINER. You will place the instance of the container class CL_GUI_CUSTOM_CONTAINER in a custom control. This part of the architecture is identical to the one you were using for the ALV class CL_GUI_ALV_GRID.

You can copy the screen, status, and title from the earlier program, YCL_CH12_02_ALV_FCAT_ETC.

As stated earlier, the field catalog concept in the class CL_GUI_ALV_GRID is implemented in the class CL_SALV_TABLE with methods GET_COLUMNS, GET_COLUMN, and SET_COLUMN.

The class-based error handling after calling the class method FACTORY is through TRY...ENDTRY and the CATCH block. The error reporting is done inside a static method of a local class.

This error reporting uses the method GET_MESSAGE, which returns the values of the system fields SY-MSGID, SY-MSGNO, SY-MSGV1, SY-MSGV2, SY-MSGV3, and SY-MSGV4 into the corresponding fields of a locally declared structure referring to the DDIC structure BAL_S_MSG. You then issue the message by using the fields of this structure. The message could be fetched and issued in the CATCH block itself. You will use a class method in a local class for this task.

You will use an internal table with the DDIC structure YCL_CH06_SALES_SUM_STRU (having the KURRF field) for loading the data, fetching row by row, and calculating the amount. But you will use an internal table with the DDIC structure YCL_CH12_SALES_SUM_STRU (not having the KURRF field) to generate the final data to be passed to the FACTORY method. This is because the FACTORY method by default outputs all the fields of the internal table passed to it. You do not want the Exchange Rate field (KURRF) to be output.

The following source program, which includes elaborate comments, should clarify the new methods and features used in the program:

```
REPORT YCL_CH13_01_USE_CL_SALV_TABLE.

**********************************************************
* ALV Report WITH class CL_SALV_TABLE:                  **
* For a Specific Company Code: Customer Wise Sales Summary**
**********************************************************

******************************************************************
* you can copy screen 100, status 'STAT1' and title 'TITLE1' from **
* program 'YCL_CH12_02_ALV_FCAT_ETC'                             **
*                                                                **
* declarations:-                                                 **
* ==============                                                 **
* local class definition deferred                                **
*                                                                **
* global data                                                    **
* -----------                                                    **
* 1,2. internal table, stru for customer wise sales summary      **
*      (this contains the field KURRF to convert amounts. this is **
*       used to generate the customer wise sales summary)        **
* 3.   internal table customer wise sales summary                **
*      (this does not contain the field KURRF. passed as parameter**
*       to the 'FACTORY' method)                                 **
* 4. reference variable - instance of 'CL_SALV_TABLE'            **
* 5.                      instance of 'CL_GUI_CUSTOM_CONTAINER'  **
* 6.                      instance of 'CX_SALV_MSG' exception    **
* 7.                      instance of 'CL_SALV_FUNCTIONS_LIST'   **
* 8.                      instance of 'CL_SALV_COLUMNS_TABLE'    **
* 9.                      instance of 'CL_SALV_COLUMN_TABLE'     **
* 10.                     instance of 'CL_SALV_AGGREGATIONS'     **
* 11.                     instance of 'CL_SALV_AGGREGATION'      **
* 12.                     instance of 'CL_SALV_LAYOUT'           **
* 13. layout key equivalent to DISVARIANT in 'CL_GUI_ALV_GRID'   **
* 14. structure to pass color specification to column            **
* 15. OK_CODE                                                    **
* 16. company code description - from T001                       **
* 17. currency code of company code - from T001                  **
*                                                                **
```

```
* local class for exception reporting of 'CL_SALV_TABLE'          **
* definition & implementation                                     **
*                                                                 **
* PARAMETERS prompt for company code                              **
*                                                                 **
* START-OF-SELECTION                                              **
* ==================                                              **
* retrieve single row from T001                                   **
* set up SELECT.. COLLECT.. ENDSELECT for generating summary       **
* sort customer wise sales summary internal table by KUNNR        **
* CALL SCREEN 100.                                                **
*                                                                 **
* PBO code                                                        **
* ========                                                        **
* set pf status, set title                                        **
* create instance of custom container                             **
* call 'FACTORY' method                                           **
*                                                                 **
* <ALV instance>->GET_COLUNNS.                                    **
* set column properties - KUNNR: EDIT_MASK..                      **
* set column properties - all columns for color                   **
*                                                                 **
* <ALV instance>->GET_AGGREGATIONS. set aggregation for NETWR     **
*                                                                 **
* <ALV instance>->GET_FUNCTIONS. set for all functions            **
* set for functions - ..LAYOUT_CHANGE, ..LAYOUT_MAINTAIN and      **
*                     ..LAYOUT_SAVE                               **
*                                                                 **
* <ALV instance>->GET_LAYOUT. set for layout                      **
*                                                                 **
* <ALV instance>->DISPLAY( ).                                     **
*                                                                 **
* PAI code                                                        **
* ========                                                        **
* check OK_CODE = 'BACK', if so SET SCREEN 0. LEAVE SCREEN.       **
*                                                                 **
*******************************************************************

CLASS LCLASS DEFINITION DEFERRED.

DATA:
      SALES_TAB  TYPE STANDARD TABLE OF " data - summary
            YCL_CH12_SALES_SUM_STRU WITH HEADER LINE,
      SALES_STRU TYPE LINE OF YCL_CH06_SALES_SUM_TAB,

      ALV_GRID   TYPE REF TO CL_SALV_TABLE,
      CCONT      TYPE REF TO CL_GUI_CUSTOM_CONTAINER,
      ERROR      TYPE REF TO CX_SALV_MSG, " SALV exception
      FUNCTIONS  TYPE REF TO CL_SALV_FUNCTIONS_LIST, " functions
      COLUMNS    TYPE REF TO CL_SALV_COLUMNS_TABLE, " get columns
      COLUMN     TYPE REF TO CL_SALV_COLUMN_TABLE,  " get column
```

```
      AGGS       TYPE REF TO CL_SALV_AGGREGATIONS, " get aggregations
      AGG        TYPE REF TO CL_SALV_AGGREGATION,  " get aggregation
      LAYOUT_REF TYPE REF TO CL_SALV_LAYOUT, " for layout management

      LAYOUT_KEY TYPE SALV_S_LAYOUT_KEY, " for layout management
      COL_STRU   TYPE LVC_S_COLO, " for color

      OK_CODE    TYPE SY-UCOMM,
      BUTXT      TYPE T001-BUTXT,
      WAERS      TYPE T001-WAERS.

*********************************************
PARAMETERS: CCODE TYPE VBRK-BUKRS DEFAULT 3000.

***********************************************
***********************************************
CLASS LCLASS DEFINITION.
 PUBLIC SECTION.
 CLASS-METHODS:

  SALV_ERROR_MSG
   IMPORTING
    ERROR TYPE REF TO CX_SALV_MSG.

ENDCLASS.

CLASS LCLASS IMPLEMENTATION.

 METHOD SALV_ERROR_MSG.  " report error in ALV
  DATA: MESSAG TYPE BAL_S_MSG,
        TYPE   TYPE C VALUE 'E' .

  MESSAG = ERROR->GET_MESSAGE( ).

  MESSAGE ID MESSAG-MSGID
  TYPE TYPE "TYPE MESSAG-MSGTY
  NUMBER MESSAG-MSGNO
  WITH MESSAG-MSGV1
       MESSAG-MSGV2
       MESSAG-MSGV3
       MESSAG-MSGV4.

 ENDMETHOD.

ENDCLASS.

***********************************************
```

```
**************************************************

START-OF-SELECTION.

SELECT SINGLE BUTXT WAERS FROM T001 INTO (BUTXT, WAERS) WHERE
       BUKRS = CCODE.

SELECT KUNNR NAME1 ORT01 NETWR KURRF FROM YCL_CH05_VBRKKNA INTO
  CORRESPONDING FIELDS OF SALES_STRU WHERE BUKRS = CCODE.

 SALES_STRU-NETWR =  SALES_STRU-NETWR * SALES_STRU-KURRF.
 SALES_STRU-KURRF = 0. "to prevent overflow

 MOVE-CORRESPONDING SALES_STRU TO SALES_TAB.
 COLLECT SALES_TAB INTO SALES_TAB.

ENDSELECT.

SORT SALES_TAB BY KUNNR.

CALL SCREEN 100.

*********************************************
*&---------------------------------------------------------------------*
*&      Module  STATUS_0100  OUTPUT
*&---------------------------------------------------------------------*
MODULE STATUS_0100 OUTPUT.

SET PF-STATUS 'STAT1'.

SET TITLEBAR 'TITLE1' WITH CCODE BUTXT WAERS.

CREATE OBJECT CCONT
  EXPORTING
    CONTAINER_NAME              = 'CONT'.

***** call static method FACTORY *****
TRY.

  CALL METHOD CL_SALV_TABLE=>FACTORY
   EXPORTING
    R_CONTAINER        = CCONT " reference to container
*    LIST_DISPLAY      = ' '    " ' ' else run time error
   IMPORTING
    R_SALV_TABLE       = ALV_GRID  " get instance
   CHANGING
    T_TABLE            = SALES_TAB[]. " data
```

```
   CATCH CX_SALV_MSG INTO ERROR.
   CALL METHOD LCLASS=>SALV_ERROR_MSG
    EXPORTING
     ERROR = ERROR.

 ENDTRY.

******* optimize column width********

 COLUMNS = ALV_GRID->GET_COLUMNS( ).
 COLUMNS->SET_OPTIMIZE( VALUE = 'X' ).

**** color to columns

 COLUMN ?= COLUMNS->GET_COLUMN( COLUMNNAME = 'KUNNR').
 COLUMN->SET_EDIT_MASK( VALUE = ' ' ).

 COL_STRU-COL = 1.
 COLUMN->SET_COLOR( VALUE = COL_STRU ).

 COLUMN ?= COLUMNS->GET_COLUMN( COLUMNNAME = 'NAME1').
 COL_STRU-COL = 2.
 COLUMN->SET_COLOR( VALUE = COL_STRU ).
 COLUMN->SET_LOWERCASE( ).

 COLUMN ?= COLUMNS->GET_COLUMN( COLUMNNAME = 'ORT01').
 COL_STRU-COL = 3.
 COLUMN->SET_COLOR( VALUE = COL_STRU ).
 COLUMN->SET_LOWERCASE( ).

 COLUMN ?= COLUMNS->GET_COLUMN( COLUMNNAME = 'NETWR').
 COL_STRU-COL = 4.
 COLUMN->SET_COLOR( VALUE = COL_STRU ).

**** aggregation setting for NETWR *****

 AGGS = ALV_GRID->GET_AGGREGATIONS( ).

 AGG = AGGS->ADD_AGGREGATION( COLUMNNAME = 'NETWR' AGGREGATION = 1 ).

************ enable all(full) default functions *********

FUNCTIONS = ALV_GRID->GET_FUNCTIONS( ).
*FUNCTIONS->SET_DEFAULT( ).
FUNCTIONS->SET_ALL( ). "DEFAULT( ).

***** set more functions *****

FUNCTIONS->SET_LAYOUT_CHANGE( 'X' ).
FUNCTIONS->SET_LAYOUT_MAINTAIN( 'X' ).
FUNCTIONS->SET_LAYOUT_SAVE( 'X' ).
```

```
***** for save, maintain layouts *****

LAYOUT_REF = ALV_GRID->GET_LAYOUT( ).
LAYOUT_KEY-REPORT = 'YCL_CH13_01_USE_CL_SALV_TABLE'.

LAYOUT_REF->SET_KEY( LAYOUT_KEY ).
LAYOUT_REF->SET_SAVE_RESTRICTION( '1' ).
  " equivalent to the I_SAVE parameter in
  " the method SET_TABLE_FOR_FIRST_DISPLAY

*
 ALV_GRID->DISPLAY( ).

ENDMODULE.                    " STATUS_0100 OUTPUT

*&---------------------------------------------------------------------*
*&      Module  USER_COMMAND_0100  INPUT
*&---------------------------------------------------------------------*

MODULE USER_COMMAND_0100 INPUT.
IF OK_CODE = 'BACK'.
 SET SCREEN 0.
 LEAVE SCREEN.
ENDIF.
ENDMODULE.                    " USER_COMMAND_0100 INPUT
```

Figure 13-1 and 13-2 show the initial output.

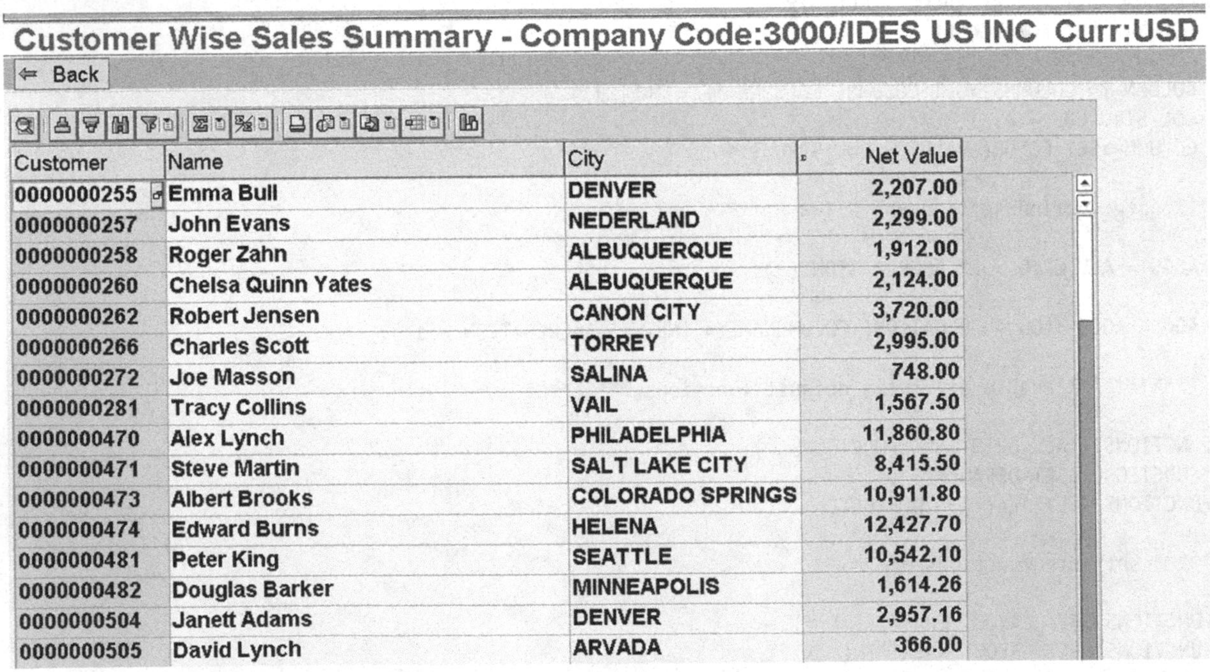

Customer Wise Sales Summary - Company Code:3000/IDES US INC Curr:USD

⇐ Back

Customer	Name	City	Net Value
0000000255	Emma Bull	DENVER	2,207.00
0000000257	John Evans	NEDERLAND	2,299.00
0000000258	Roger Zahn	ALBUQUERQUE	1,912.00
0000000260	Chelsa Quinn Yates	ALBUQUERQUE	2,124.00
0000000262	Robert Jensen	CANON CITY	3,720.00
0000000266	Charles Scott	TORREY	2,995.00
0000000272	Joe Masson	SALINA	748.00
0000000281	Tracy Collins	VAIL	1,567.50
0000000470	Alex Lynch	PHILADELPHIA	11,860.80
0000000471	Steve Martin	SALT LAKE CITY	8,415.50
0000000473	Albert Brooks	COLORADO SPRINGS	10,911.80
0000000474	Edward Burns	HELENA	12,427.70
0000000481	Peter King	SEATTLE	10,542.10
0000000482	Douglas Barker	MINNEAPOLIS	1,614.26
0000000504	Janett Adams	DENVER	2,957.16
0000000505	David Lynch	ARVADA	366.00

***Figure 13-1.** Initial output of the program YCL_CH13_01_USE_CL_SALV_TABLE*

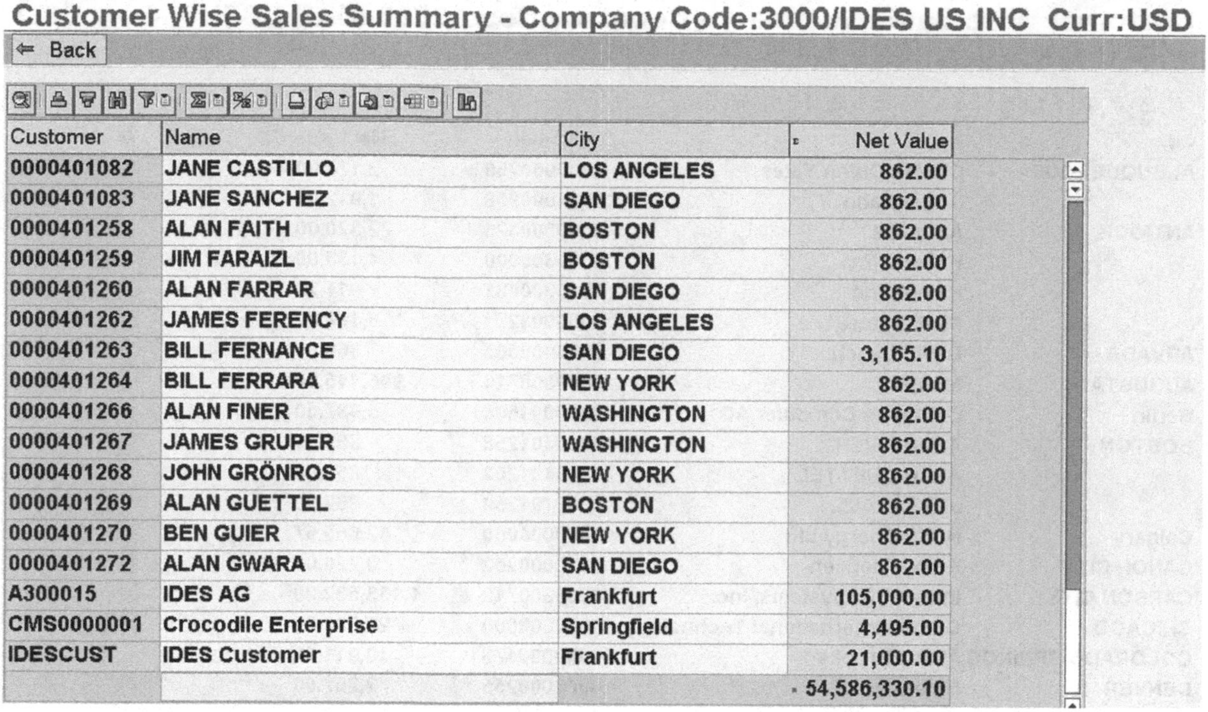

Customer Wise Sales Summary - Company Code:3000/IDES US INC Curr:USD

Customer	Name	City	Net Value
0000401082	JANE CASTILLO	LOS ANGELES	862.00
0000401083	JANE SANCHEZ	SAN DIEGO	862.00
0000401258	ALAN FAITH	BOSTON	862.00
0000401259	JIM FARAIZL	BOSTON	862.00
0000401260	ALAN FARRAR	SAN DIEGO	862.00
0000401262	JAMES FERENCY	LOS ANGELES	862.00
0000401263	BILL FERNANCE	SAN DIEGO	3,165.10
0000401264	BILL FERRARA	NEW YORK	862.00
0000401266	ALAN FINER	WASHINGTON	862.00
0000401267	JAMES GRUPER	WASHINGTON	862.00
0000401268	JOHN GRÖNROS	NEW YORK	862.00
0000401269	ALAN GUETTEL	BOSTON	862.00
0000401270	BEN GUIER	NEW YORK	862.00
0000401272	ALAN GWARA	SAN DIEGO	862.00
A300015	IDES AG	Frankfurt	105,000.00
CMS0000001	Crocodile Enterprise	Springfield	4,495.00
IDESCUST	IDES Customer	Frankfurt	21,000.00
			· 54,586,330.10

Figure 13-2. *Output of* `YCL_CH13_01_USE_CL_SALV_TABLE`

Change the layout in the following manner:

- Field/column order:
  - City (`ORT01`)
  - Name (`NAME1`)
  - Customer (`KUNNR`)
  - Net Value (`NETWR`)
- Sort order:
  - City (`ORT01`), Ascending
  - Name (`NAME1`), Ascending

Figure 13-3 shows the output after making these changes in the layout.

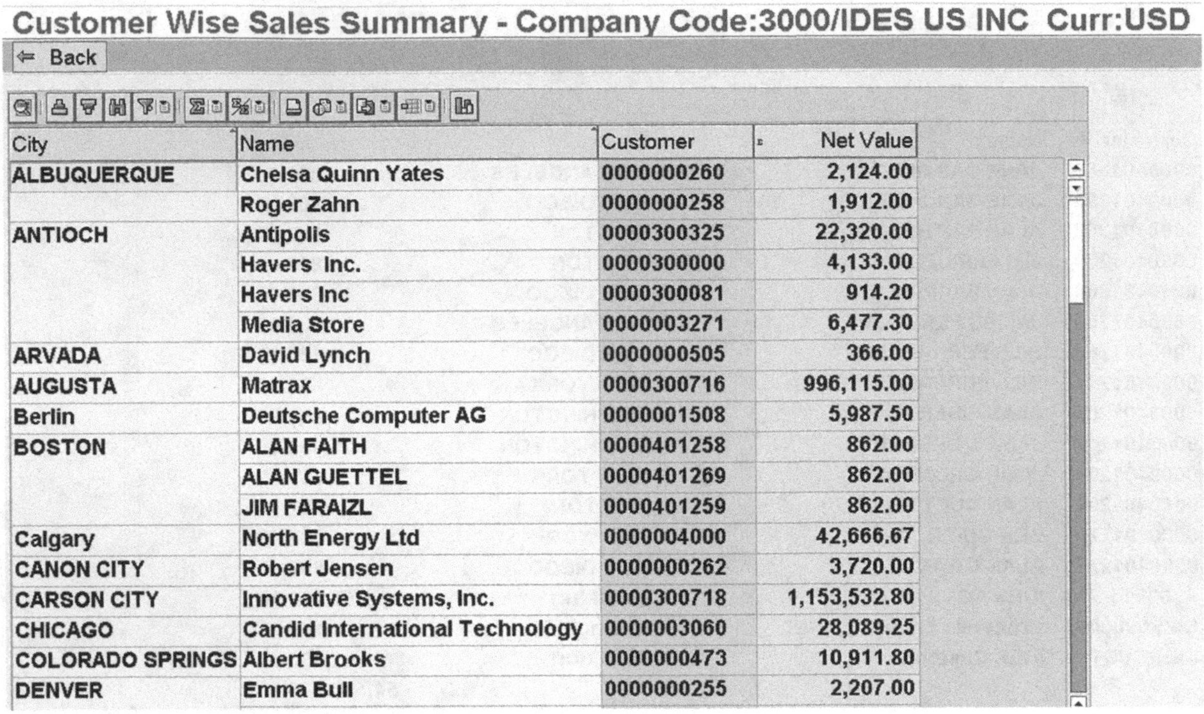

Customer Wise Sales Summary - Company Code:3000/IDES US INC Curr:USD

Back

City	Name	Customer	Net Value
ALBUQUERQUE	Chelsa Quinn Yates	0000000260	2,124.00
	Roger Zahn	0000000258	1,912.00
ANTIOCH	Antipolis	0000300325	22,320.00
	Havers Inc.	0000300000	4,133.00
	Havers Inc	0000300081	914.20
	Media Store	0000003271	6,477.30
ARVADA	David Lynch	0000000505	366.00
AUGUSTA	Matrax	0000300716	996,115.00
Berlin	Deutsche Computer AG	0000001508	5,987.50
BOSTON	ALAN FAITH	0000401258	862.00
	ALAN GUETTEL	0000401269	862.00
	JIM FARAIZL	0000401259	862.00
Calgary	North Energy Ltd	0000004000	42,666.67
CANON CITY	Robert Jensen	0000000262	3,720.00
CARSON CITY	Innovative Systems, Inc.	0000300718	1,153,532.80
CHICAGO	Candid International Technology	0000003060	28,089.25
COLORADO SPRINGS	Albert Brooks	0000000473	10,911.80
DENVER	Emma Bull	0000000255	2,207.00

Figure 13-3. *Output after changes in layout*

This class is sorting text data on the text data that is translated or converted to uppercase.

You can save and retrieve layouts as you did for ALV output when using the class CL_GUI_ALV_GRID. You can generate graphics and perform ABC analysis as well.

Hands-on Exercise: Customer-wise Sales Summary and Detail of a Specified Company Code as ALV Output: Use Class CL_SALV_TABLE

Trigger CL_SALV_TABLE Events: USER_COMMAND, AFTER_USER_COMMAND, DOUBLE_CLICK AND

CL_GUI_DIALOGBOX_CONTAINER Event: CLOSE

In this exercise, program YCL_CH13_02_SALV_EVENTS using the ALV class CL_SALV_TABLE. You will implement all the features that you implemented earlier for YCL_CH12_03_ALV_EVENTS (which used the class CL_GUI_ALV_GRID and demonstrated events). In this exercise, events are being demonstrated. Because this is a parallel of the earlier exercise and an extension of the preceding exercise, only the additional features incorporated in this program are described.

Events DOUBLE_CLICK, CLOSE, Put Buttons on ALV Toolbar and USER_COMMAND

Event DOUBLE_CLICK: The handling of event DOUBLE_CLICK, which you trigger for the first instance of the ALV class here, is similar to the way you handled this event when using the class CL_GUI_ALV_GRID. The differences are described here. The importing parameter ROW in the present class does not have a component through which you can determine whether the double-clicked row is a regular row or a total or subtotal row. The importing parameter E_ROW of the event DOUBLE_CLICK in the class CL_GUI_ALV_GRID had a component ROWTYPE. When ROWTYPE contains an initial value, you know that a regular row was double-clicked, not a total or subtotal row. In the present usage of class CL_SALV_TABLE, the method GET_SELECTIONS returns an instance reference to the class CL_SALV_SELECTIONS. This class has a method, GET_CURRENT_CELL, which returns values in the DDIC structure SALV_S_CELL. This structure has a field ROW, which contains the row number for regular rows, as well as negative values for subtotal or total rows. You will check that the values of the field ROW are greater than zero in order to execute lines in the handler method of the event DOUBLE_CLICK. When you double-click a subtotal or total line, nothing should happen. Only when you double-click a regular row (containing customer code, name, amount, and so forth) should the billing documents of the customer be output in the second instance of the ALV grid.

When you are on the second instance of ALV output in a dialog box container, you want the first instance of the ALV output disabled. You did this by using the ENABLE instance method of the class CL_GUI_ALV_GRID in the previous exercise program YCL_CH12_03_ALV_EVENTS. You passed an export parameter ' ' to the ENABLE method. There is no ENABLE method available in the class CL_SALV_TABLE. So you will use the ENABLE instance method of the container class CL_GUI_CUSTOM_CONTAINER to disable the first ALV output when you have produced the second ALV output. You will pass an export parameter ' ' to the ENABLE method of the class CL_GUI_CUSTOM_CONTAINER.

Event CLOSE: The CLOSE event for the dialog box container is identical to the earlier exercises and needs no elaboration here—except that you use the ENABLE method of the container class CL_GUI_CUSTOM_CONTAINER, as the ALV grid class CL_SALV_TABLE does not have a similar method. After execution of the ENABLE method with an export parameter X; you will be able to operate the first ALV output again after closing the second ALV output.

Place Buttons on ALV Toolbar: With the present class CL_SALV_TABLE, you do not need to trigger an event to place your custom buttons on the ALV toolbar. When using the class CL_GUI_ALV_GRID, you needed to trigger the event TOOLBAR to place your custom buttons. In this exercise, you will use the method ADD_FUNCTION of class CL_SALV_FUNCTIONS_LIST to do the same. The ADD_FUNCTION method can be executed before executing the DISPLAY method. You will place a custom button on the ALV toolbar with function code BACK to navigate back to the selection screen.

Event USER_COMMAND: In the class CL_GUI_ALV_GRID, you used the event USER_COMMAND to react to your own positioned buttons on the ALV toolbar. You used this event to react to the pressing of the BACK button to navigate back to the selection screen. What you were doing in the PAI event for reacting to button on the application toolbar in the last exercise has been shifted to the event handler method of event USER_COMMAND of the first instance of ALV output.

Event AFTER_USER_COMMAND: You will use the AFTER_USER_COMMAND event to adjust the serial number field upon change of layout or loading of layout. When using the class CL_GUI_ALV_GRID, the method GET_FILTERED_ENTRIES retrieved the filtered-out (omitted) rows at the front end. The availability of these filtered-out rows saved you the task of retrieving filter settings; you retrieved only the sort settings. A similar method is not available in the present class CL_SALV_TABLE. Therefore, you must retrieve filter settings for the variables, and convert the filter settings to range values for the variables (internal table of SIGN, OPTION, LOW, and HIGH fields). You declare the range variables (for example, KUNNR_SO) with the HEADER LINE clause in the program global area. They could have been declared in the PRIVATE SECTION of the local class. In this case, the clause HEADER LINE would not have been used, and separately named structures would have been declared and used.

Using the range values of the variables, you build another customer-wise sales summary internal table containing only the data as per the filter settings. When building this second internal table, the range values of fields KUNNR, NAME1, and ORT01 are applied in the SELECT statements WHERE condition when retrieving data from the database view. The range values of the field NETWR are applied in an IF statement when generating the serial number. This is because the range condition for NETWR has to be applied to the total, and not to individual rows retrieved from the database view. This second customer-wise sales summary internal table is generated in the event handler method of the event AFTER_USER_COMMAND. Using this second internal table as a reference, you are generating the serial number field in your original internal table of the customer-wise sales summary. You have omitted the NAME1 and ORT01 fields in the structure of the second internal table of customer wise sales summary.

The event should be executed only if the user has done one of the following:

- Changed the layout
- Selected a layout
- Opened and operated the Filter dialog box
- Opened and operated the Sort Ascending dialog box
- Opened and operated the Sort Descending dialog box

This is what you are doing with a CHECK statement at the beginning of the method.

Registration of Handler Methods of Class CL_SALV_TABLE:

When using the ALV class CL_SALV_TABLE for event handler method registration, you have to first execute the GET_EVENT method of the main class CL_SALV_TABLE. This method returns an instance reference to the class CL_SALV_EVENTS_TABLE. In the SET statement, instead of specifying the instance of the class after the key word FOR, you specify the reference variable specified in the GET_EVENT method. For example:

```
DATA: EVENT_REF  TYPE REF TO CL_SALV_EVENTS_TABLE,
      LCLASS_REF TYPE REF TO LCLASS,
.......

CALL METHOD CL_SALV_TABLE=>FACTORY
   EXPORTING
      R_CONTAINER        = CCONT
      LIST_DISPLAY       = '' " else run time error
   IMPORTING
      R_SALV_TABLE       = ALV_GRID1
   CHANGING
      T_TABLE            = SALES_TAB[].
.........

EVENT_REF = ALV_GRID1->GET_EVENT( ).

CREATE OBJECT LCLASS_REF.

SET HANDLER LCLASS_REF->DB_CLICK FOR EVENT_REF.
...
```

The program is YCL_CH13_02_SALV_EVENTS, and the full source code can be found in the source code resource. When this program is checked for syntax, it issues a warning message:

The exception CX_SALV_NOT_FOUND is neither caught nor is it declared in the RAISING clause of "DB_CLICK".

This warning arises because the TRY...ENDTRY block with the CATCH statement is inside the method DB_CLICK. The method DB_CLICK is an event handler method. You cannot specify the RAISING clause in the signature of this method.

You can ignore this warning, activate the program, and execute it. But if you are fastidious and want to eliminate this message, you can locate all the source code relating to invocation of the class method FACTORY inside a subroutine and specify the RAISING clause in the subroutine interface.

Figure 13-4 shows the output.

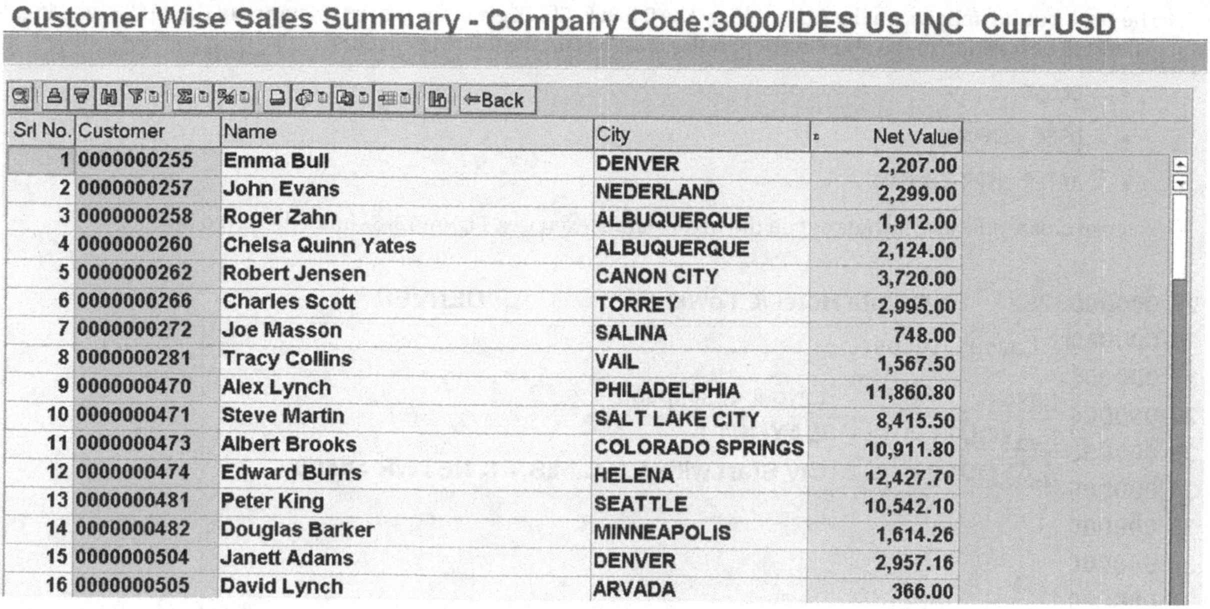

Customer Wise Sales Summary - Company Code:3000/IDES US INC Curr:USD

⇐Back

Srl No.	Customer	Name	City	Net Value
1	0000000255	Emma Bull	DENVER	2,207.00
2	0000000257	John Evans	NEDERLAND	2,299.00
3	0000000258	Roger Zahn	ALBUQUERQUE	1,912.00
4	0000000260	Chelsa Quinn Yates	ALBUQUERQUE	2,124.00
5	0000000262	Robert Jensen	CANON CITY	3,720.00
6	0000000266	Charles Scott	TORREY	2,995.00
7	0000000272	Joe Masson	SALINA	748.00
8	0000000281	Tracy Collins	VAIL	1,567.50
9	0000000470	Alex Lynch	PHILADELPHIA	11,860.80
10	0000000471	Steve Martin	SALT LAKE CITY	8,415.50
11	0000000473	Albert Brooks	COLORADO SPRINGS	10,911.80
12	0000000474	Edward Burns	HELENA	12,427.70
13	0000000481	Peter King	SEATTLE	10,542.10
14	0000000482	Douglas Barker	MINNEAPOLIS	1,614.26
15	0000000504	Janett Adams	DENVER	2,957.16
16	0000000505	David Lynch	ARVADA	366.00

Figure 13-4. *Output of YCL_CH13_02_SALV_EVENTS*

Scroll down to serial number 31, customer code 3271. Double-click this customer, and the detailed ALV output appears, as shown in Figure 13-5.

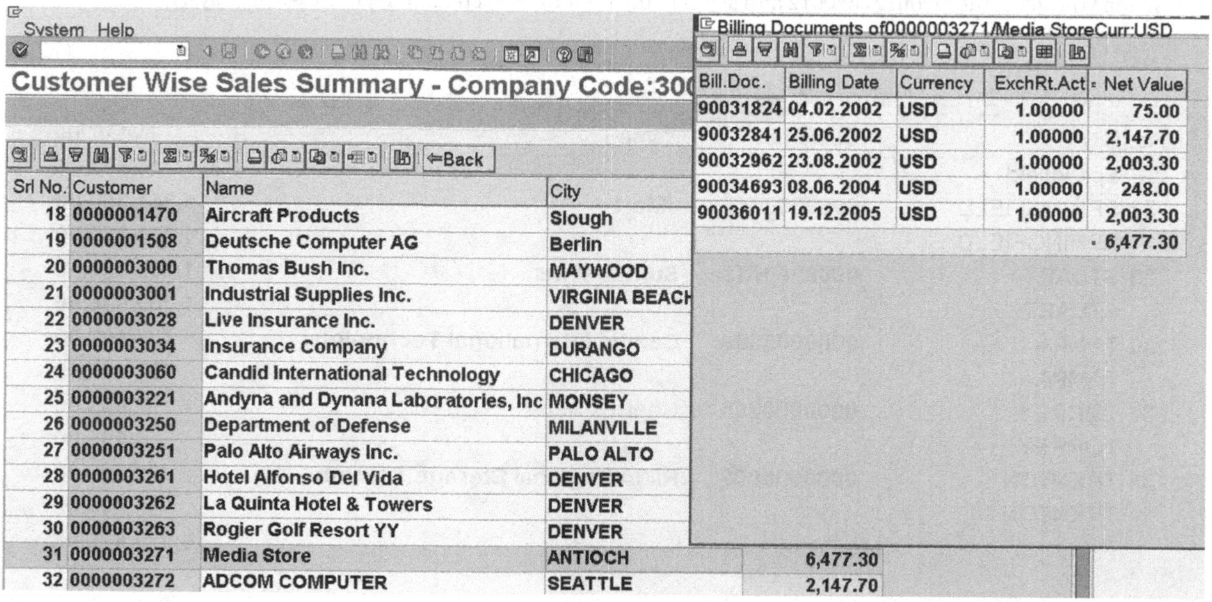

System Help

Customer Wise Sales Summary - Company Code:30

⇐Back

Srl No.	Customer	Name	City	Net Value
18	0000001470	Aircraft Products	Slough	
19	0000001508	Deutsche Computer AG	Berlin	
20	0000003000	Thomas Bush Inc.	MAYWOOD	
21	0000003001	Industrial Supplies Inc.	VIRGINIA BEACH	
22	0000003028	Live Insurance Inc.	DENVER	
23	0000003034	Insurance Company	DURANGO	
24	0000003060	Candid International Technology	CHICAGO	
25	0000003221	Andyna and Dynana Laboratories, Inc	MONSEY	
26	0000003250	Department of Defense	MILANVILLE	
27	0000003251	Palo Alto Airways Inc.	PALO ALTO	
28	0000003261	Hotel Alfonso Del Vida	DENVER	
29	0000003262	La Quinta Hotel & Towers	DENVER	
30	0000003263	Rogier Golf Resort YY	DENVER	
31	0000003271	Media Store	ANTIOCH	6,477.30
32	0000003272	ADCOM COMPUTER	SEATTLE	2,147.70

Billing Documents of0000003271/Media StoreCurr:USD

Bill.Doc.	Billing Date	Currency	ExchRt.Act	Net Value
90031824	04.02.2002	USD	1.00000	75.00
90032841	25.06.2002	USD	1.00000	2,147.70
90032962	23.08.2002	USD	1.00000	2,003.30
90034693	08.06.2004	USD	1.00000	248.00
90036011	19.12.2005	USD	1.00000	2,003.30
				· 6,477.30

Figure 13-5. *The customer's summary and detailed output*

The Back button appears on the ALV toolbar. The DOUBLE_CLICK event for the first instance of the ALV is working. You can test the execution of the other event handler methods for the following events:

- CLOSE
- USER_COMMAND
- AFTER_USER_COMMAND

You can create and save layouts as you did in the earlier exercises. Figure 13-6 shows the saved layouts.

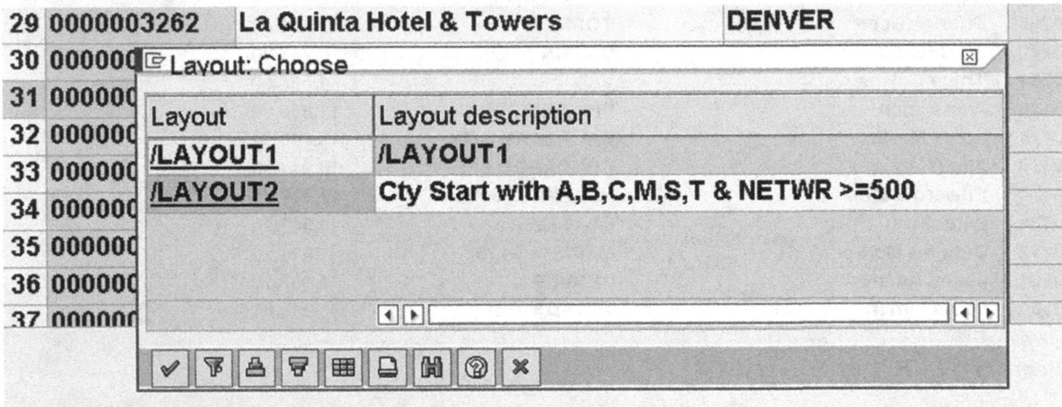

Figure 13-6. *Saved layouts for YCL_CH13_02_SALV_EVENTS*

When you select the layout /LAYOUT2 and scroll to the bottom, the screen in Figure 13-7 displays.

⇐Back

Srl No.	City	Customer	Name	Net Value
	Springfield			4,495.00
32	SPRINGFIELD	0000300717	JMart	1,344,350.00
	SPRINGFIELD			1,344,350.00
33	STUART	0000300715	Sunburst Inc	1,062,936.00
	STUART			1,062,936.00
36	TAMPA	0000003800	Candid International Technology	723,492.00
	TAMPA			723,492.00
37	TORREY	0000000266	Charles Scott	2,995.00
	TORREY			2,995.00
38	TRENTON	0000006002	RIWA Regional Storage Trenton	78,780.00
	TRENTON			78,780.00
				9,028,626.98

Figure 13-7. *Output for the layout /LAYOUT2*

So, you have used the class CL_SALV_TABLE and triggered the events DOUBLE_CLICK, USER_COMMAND, and AFTER_USER_COMMAND to generate a detailed second ALV report, react to your positioned ALV toolbar button, and adjust the serial number field in the first ALV report to be regenerated every time an ALV layout change occurs.

You have been able to produce almost identical output with the programs YCL_CH12_03_ALV_EVENTS and YCL_CH13_02_SALV_EVENTS by using the classes CL_GUI_ALV_GRID and CL_SALV_TABLE, respectively.

A Note on Problems with the Class CL_SALV_TABLE

There are a couple of significant issues you need to know about when using the class CL_SALV_TABLE. We will discuss those here.

Problem with Multiple Fields Sort

If you set the layout for multiple field sorting in the Change Layout dialog box—for example, City (ORT01) and Name1 (NAME1), this creates a problem. When you set sort settings in this manner, you want the data to be sorted alphabetically by city and within that city, by customer name: first, all the customer names starting with A, B, C.., in Atlanta; next, all the customer names starting with A, B, C... in Berlin, and so on. In the sort settings, City is the major field, and Name1 is the minor field.

But at the presentation server level, the order reverses every time you open the Change Layout dialog box. When the sort settings are retrieved in the event handler method AF_FN generates serial numbers, it fetches the settings properly, but at the front end it reverses the order every time you open the Change Layout dialog box. This has been tackled with a bit of tweaked code. It is working okay except when you enter the Change Layout dialog box and use the Cancel button. For saving and loading layouts, it works okay.

Methods of Class CL_SALV_SELOPT

In doing this exercise, while converting the filter values into range values, you had to use the methods GET_HIGH, GET_LOW, GET_OPTION, and GET_SIGN of the class CL_SALV_SELOPT (referring to the method AF_FN in the source program). There were problems with the methods GET_HIGH, GET_LOW, and GET_OPTION on our system, not running the latest patches.

Navigate to SE24 - Class Builder, enter the class name CL_SALV_SELOPT, and click the display button. Double-click any method to see its source code.

These methods have just one line of assignment statement. For example, for GET_SIGN (which is okay), the statements are as follows:

```
method get_sign.
  value = me->sign.
endmethod.
```

Here are the statements for GET_OPTION:

```
method get_option.
  me->option = value.
endmethod.
```

This is obviously erroneous, as the assignment is reversed. The assignment should have been as follows:

```
value = me->option.
```

A similar error has been committed for the two other methods, GET_HIGH and GET_LOW. We have managed to correct this erroneous situation by using the implicit enhancement option, by inserting source code before the SAP source code for the methods. Figure 13-8 clarifies this.

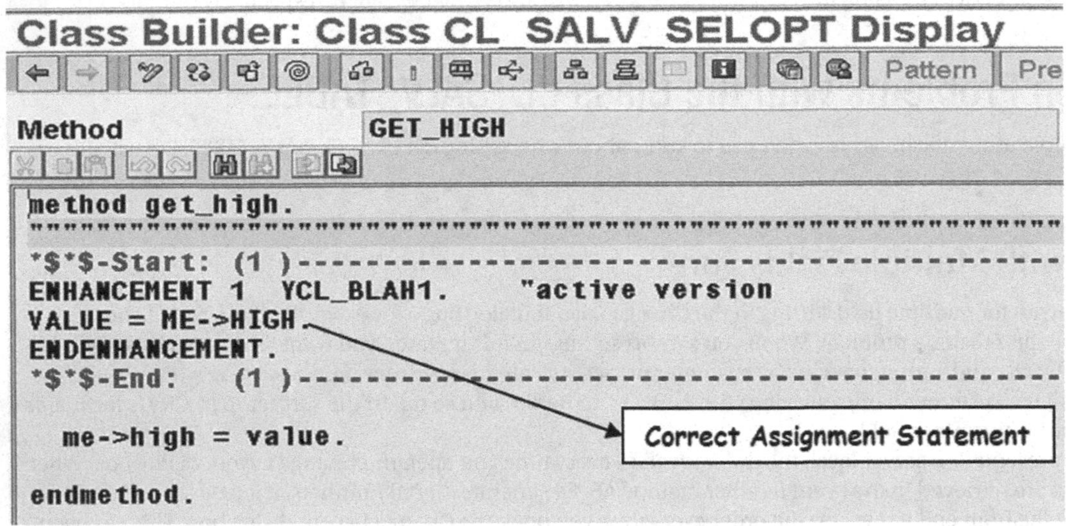

Figure 13-8. *Enhancement code for the method GET_HIGH*

We have also done such an enhancement for the two other methods, GET_HIGH and GET_LOW.

If you are facing this problem, we hope you manage it with these enhancements.

Create Data Browsers Using the Classes CL_GUI_ALV_GRID and CL_SALV_TABLE

As you may recall from Chapter 10, YCL_CH10_ILISTS05 is a generic program that accepts a database table or view through a PARAMETERS statement. This program lists all the fields of the input database table (or view) along with check boxes that enable field selections. After making field selections, you press the Output button on the application toolbar to retrieve data for the selected fields from the database table or view and output it by employing the WRITE statement. This program uses the features of dynamic creation of data objects, field symbols, and special constructs of the Open SQL SELECT statement. Data was retrieved row by row (SELECT... ENDSELECT) into a dynamically created structure and output from that structure. Field symbols were employed to address the dynamically created structure and the fields of the structure.

The next two hands-on exercises are variations of this Chapter 10 program. Instead of using the WRITE statement to output, you will output data as ALV reports. The two programs resemble the transaction code SE16 data browser.

Hands-on Exercise: Output Specific Selected Fields of a Specific Database Table or View in ALV: Use Class CL_GUI_ALV_GRID

The current YCL_CH13_03_ANY_TABLE_ALV uses the class CL_GUI_ALV_GRID to output data.

As the method SET_TABLE_FOR_FIRST_DISPLAY of class CL_GUI_ALV_GRID accepts data to populate the ALV from an internal table, you will have to create a dynamic internal table, load this internal table with the data, and pass it to the changing parameter IT_OUTTAB of the method SET_TABLE_FOR_FIRST_DISPLAY.

You have to have a screen with a custom control and an OK_CODE field in the element list.

In the AT USER_COMMAND area, when the fields are selected (there are buttons on the application toolbar to select or deselect all the listed fields) and you click the Output button, the statement LEAVE TO SCREEN 100 is coded. This loads screen 100 and triggers the PBO event for that screen. You are switching from list mode (displayed as a field list with check boxes output from the WRITE statement) to screen mode.

In the PBO module, you set a status, set a title, create an internal table dynamically, load data from the database table or view into the dynamically created internal table, create an instance of custom container, and create an instance of an ALV grid. You will generate a default field catalog by using the database table or view with the function module LVC_FIELDCATALOG_MERGE. You will retain in the field catalog, only the rows of the selected fields, deleting the rows of unselected fields. Finally, you will call the method SET_TABLE_FOR_FIRST_DISPLAY.

In the PAI module, you will check for the function code of the Back button and if so, you will call the destructor method for the custom container, ALV grid. You will have to switch from screen mode to list mode to return to the list of fields of a database table or view. You are using the statement LEAVE TO LIST-PROCESSING to make this switch. This is for navigating back to the list of fields with check boxes.

That is all. The extra program source code follows.

Copy the interface from the program YCL_CH10_ILISTS05 and activate it.

Peruse the source code with its comments.

Source code in declaration part:

```
DATA:
.....
****** extra code *****
  FCAT     TYPE LVC_T_FCAT WITH HEADER LINE, " internal table-field ctlg.
  ITAB     TYPE REF TO DATA,                 " reference variable-itab
  CONT     TYPE REF TO CL_GUI_CUSTOM_CONTAINER,
                                             " reference variable-c cont.
  ALV_GRID TYPE REF TO CL_GUI_ALV_GRID,      " reference variable-ALV grid
  OK_CODE  TYPE SY-UCOMM, " OK CODE
  INDX     TYPE I.        " to access internal table row

FIELD-SYMBOLS:
         ...........
              <iTAB> TYPE ANY TABLE.  " field symbol to access itab
Code in event AT USER-COMMAND:
AT USER-COMMAND.
.............
***** switch from list to screen mode, load screen 100 *****
  LEAVE TO SCREEN 100.
```

Source code in PBO **module:**

```
MODULE STATUS_0100 OUTPUT.

***** retrieve data & load internal table *****

 CREATE DATA ITAB TYPE STANDARD TABLE OF (TAB_NAME).
 ASSIGN ITAB->* TO <ITAB>.

 SELECT (SFIELDS_TAB) FROM (TAB_NAME) INTO CORRESPONDING FIELDS OF
  TABLE <ITAB> WHERE (CONDS_TAB) ORDER BY (ORDERBY_TAB).

***** create default field catalog *****
 CALL FUNCTION 'LVC_FIELDCATALOG_MERGE'
  EXPORTING
    I_STRUCTURE_NAME                 = TAB_NAME
   CHANGING
     CT_FIELDCAT                     = FCAT[]
  EXCEPTIONS
    INCONSISTENT_INTERFACE           = 1
    PROGRAM_ERROR                    = 2
    OTHERS                           = 3
          .
 IF SY-SUBRC <> 0.
  MESSAGE ID SY-MSGID TYPE SY-MSGTY NUMBER SY-MSGNO
         WITH SY-MSGV1 SY-MSGV2 SY-MSGV3 SY-MSGV4.
 ENDIF.

***** mark rows of unselected fields *****

 LOOP AT FCAT INTO FCAT.
  INDX = SY-TABIX.
  READ TABLE FIELDS_TAB INTO FIELDS_STRU INDEX INDX.
  IF FIELDS_STRU-CBOX = 'X'.
   FCAT-COL_OPT = 'X'.
   FCAT-TECH = ' '.
   MODIFY FCAT.
   CONTINUE.
  ENDIF.
  FCAT-FIELDNAME = ' '.
  MODIFY FCAT.
 ENDLOOP.

 DELETE FCAT WHERE FIELDNAME = ' '. " delete rows of unselected fields

***** set pf status, title *****

 SET PF-STATUS 'STAT_SCR'.
 SET TITLEBAR 'TITLE02' WITH TAB_NAME.
```

```
**** create instances of custom container, ALV grid ****

 CREATE OBJECT CONT
   EXPORTING
     CONTAINER_NAME              = 'CCONT'
   EXCEPTIONS
     CNTL_ERROR                  = 1
     CNTL_SYSTEM_ERROR           = 2
     CREATE_ERROR                = 3
     LIFETIME_ERROR              = 4
     LIFETIME_DYNPRO_DYNPRO_LINK = 5
     others                      = 6
     .
 IF SY-SUBRC <> 0.
  MESSAGE ID SY-MSGID TYPE SY-MSGTY NUMBER SY-MSGNO
             WITH SY-MSGV1 SY-MSGV2 SY-MSGV3 SY-MSGV4.
 ENDIF.

 CREATE OBJECT ALV_GRID
   EXPORTING
     I_PARENT          = CONT
   EXCEPTIONS
     ERROR_CNTL_CREATE = 1
     ERROR_CNTL_INIT   = 2
     ERROR_CNTL_LINK   = 3
     ERROR_DP_CREATE   = 4
     others            = 5
     .
 IF SY-SUBRC <> 0.
  MESSAGE ID SY-MSGID TYPE SY-MSGTY NUMBER SY-MSGNO
             WITH SY-MSGV1 SY-MSGV2 SY-MSGV3 SY-MSGV4.
 ENDIF.

***** call method SET_TABLE_FOR_FIRST_DISPLAY *****

CALL METHOD ALV_GRID->SET_TABLE_FOR_FIRST_DISPLAY
   CHANGING
      IT_OUTTAB                     = <ITAB>
      IT_FIELDCATALOG               = FCAT[]

   EXCEPTIONS
     INVALID_PARAMETER_COMBINATION = 1
     PROGRAM_ERROR                 = 2
     TOO_MANY_LINES                = 3
     others                        = 4
        .
 IF SY-SUBRC <> 0.
  MESSAGE ID SY-MSGID TYPE SY-MSGTY NUMBER SY-MSGNO
             WITH SY-MSGV1 SY-MSGV2 SY-MSGV3 SY-MSGV4.
 ENDIF.

 OK_CODE = ' '.
ENDMODULE.                    " STATUS_0100  OUTPUT
```

Source code in PAI module:

```
MODULE USER_COMMAND_0100 INPUT.

 IF OK_CODE = 'BACK'.  " check ok code

  CALL METHOD ALV_GRID->FREE. " destructor method
  CALL METHOD CONT->FREE.     " destructor method

***** release ram - ref variables & internal tables used in PBO *****

  FREE CONT.
  FREE ALV_GRID.
  FREE FCAT.
  FREE ITAB.

  PERFORM LISTER.
  LEAVE TO LIST-PROCESSING. " get back to WRITE output mode

 ENDIF.
ENDMODULE.
```

The entire source code of the program YCL_CH13_03_ANY_TABLE_ALV is available in the source code resource. Figures 13-9 through 13-14 show the inputs and respective outputs.

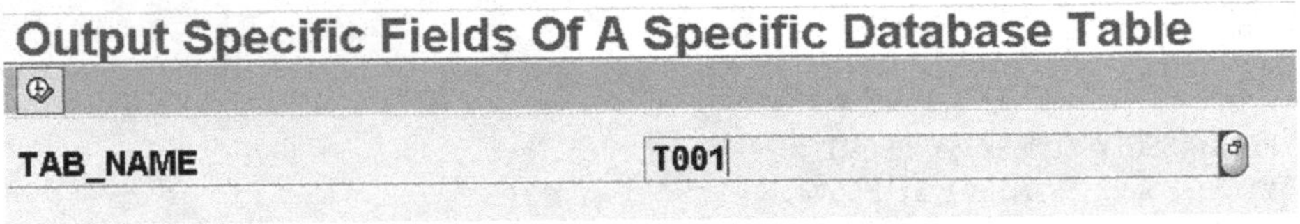

Output Specific Fields Of A Specific Database Table

TAB_NAME	T001

Figure 13-9. Input of T001

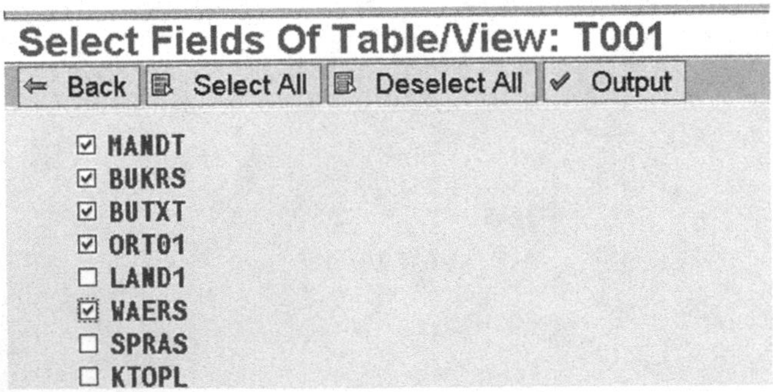

Select Fields Of Table/View: T001

Back | Select All | Deselect All | Output

- ☑ MANDT
- ☑ BUKRS
- ☑ BUTXT
- ☑ ORT01
- ☐ LAND1
- ☑ WAERS
- ☐ SPRAS
- ☐ KTOPL

Figure 13-10. Selecting fields for table T001

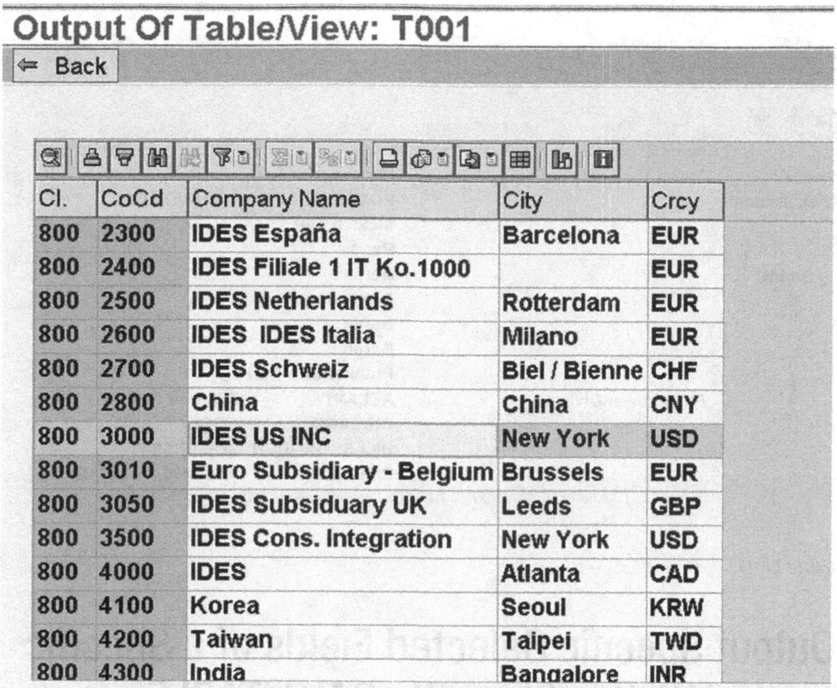

Output Of Table/View: T001

Back

Cl.	CoCd	Company Name	City	Crcy
800	2300	IDES España	Barcelona	EUR
800	2400	IDES Filiale 1 IT Ko.1000		EUR
800	2500	IDES Netherlands	Rotterdam	EUR
800	2600	IDES IDES Italia	Milano	EUR
800	2700	IDES Schweiz	Biel / Bienne	CHF
800	2800	China	China	CNY
800	3000	IDES US INC	New York	USD
800	3010	Euro Subsidiary - Belgium	Brussels	EUR
800	3050	IDES Subsiduary UK	Leeds	GBP
800	3500	IDES Cons. Integration	New York	USD
800	4000	IDES	Atlanta	CAD
800	4100	Korea	Seoul	KRW
800	4200	Taiwan	Taipei	TWD
800	4300	India	Bangalore	INR

Figure 13-11. Output of selected fields of table T001

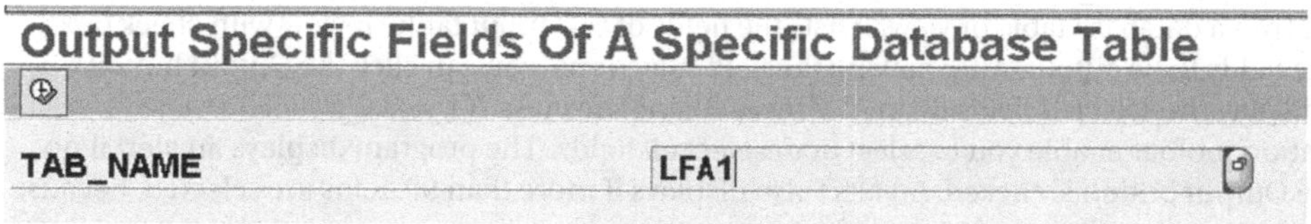

Output Specific Fields Of A Specific Database Table

TAB_NAME	LFA1

Figure 13-12. Input of LFA1

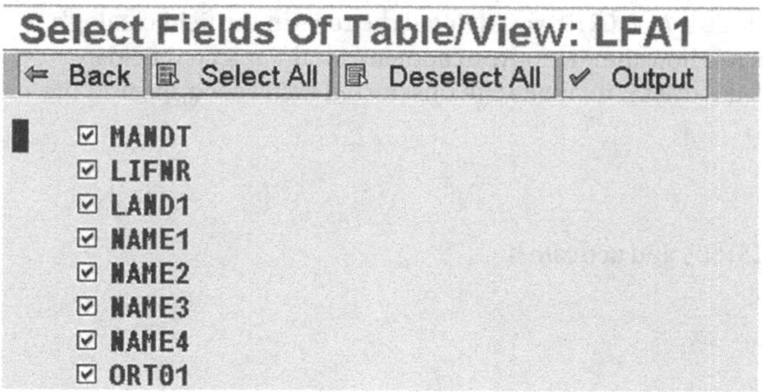

Select Fields Of Table/View: LFA1

Back | Select All | Deselect All | Output

- ☑ MANDT
- ☑ LIFNR
- ☑ LAND1
- ☑ NAME1
- ☑ NAME2
- ☑ NAME3
- ☑ NAME4
- ☑ ORT01

Figure 13-13. Selecting all fields of table LFA1

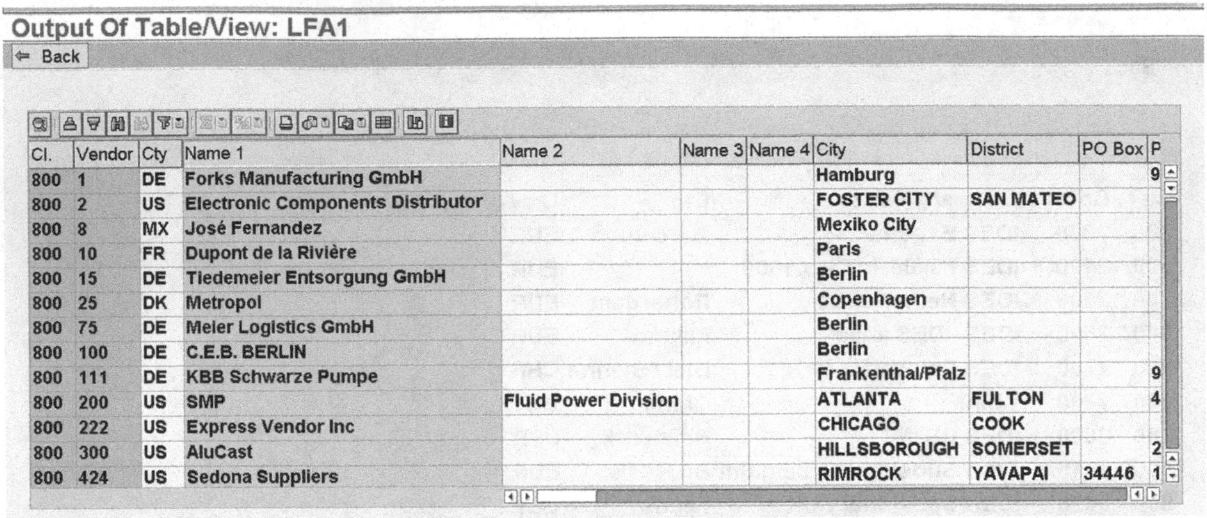

Output Of Table/View: LFA1

⇐ Back

Cl.	Vendor	Cty	Name 1	Name 2	Name 3	Name 4	City	District	PO Box	P
800	1	DE	Forks Manufacturing GmbH				Hamburg			9
800	2	US	Electronic Components Distributor				FOSTER CITY	SAN MATEO		
800	8	MX	José Fernandez				Mexiko City			
800	10	FR	Dupont de la Rivière				Paris			
800	15	DE	Tiedemeier Entsorgung GmbH				Berlin			
800	25	DK	Metropol				Copenhagen			
800	75	DE	Meier Logistics GmbH				Berlin			
800	100	DE	C.E.B. BERLIN				Berlin			
800	111	DE	KBB Schwarze Pumpe				Frankenthal/Pfalz			9
800	200	US	SMP	Fluid Power Division			ATLANTA	FULTON		4
800	222	US	Express Vendor Inc				CHICAGO	COOK		
800	300	US	AluCast				HILLSBOROUGH	SOMERSET		2
800	424	US	Sedona Suppliers				RIMROCK	YAVAPAI	34446	1

Figure 13-14. *Output of all fields of table* LFA1

Hands-on Exercise: Output Specific Selected Fields of a Specific Database Table or View in ALV: Use Class CL_SALV_TABLE

The program in this exercise—YCL_CH13_04_ANY_TABLE_SALV—is a variation of the program CL_CH13_03_ANY_TABLE_ALV. Instead of using the ALV class CL_GUI_ALV_GRID, it uses the ALV class CL_SALV_TABLE.

The program takes as input a database table or view. It lists the fields of this input table or view with check boxes that enable you to select the fields to be output. After making the field selections, you can click the Output button on the application toolbar to display the selected fields as an ALV report using the class YCL_SALV_TABLE.

Buttons on the application toolbar enable you to select or deselect all fields. The program displays an alert if no fields are selected when the Output button is clicked. An alert also displays if more than 90 fields are selected, because the class YCL_SALV_TABLE supports a maximum of 90 fields for output.

You do not locate the instance of the YCL_SALV_TABLE in a container. The ALV output in this exercise is full screen, with a two-dimensional visual effect (the classical ALV list). You do not have to create a screen; you do not have to code for the PBO and PAI modules.

In the version of this program using the ALV class CL_GUI_ALV_GRID, you deleted the rows in the field catalog's internal table corresponding to the unselected fields. That is how the ALV output appears for the selected fields. A similar capability is not available in the ALV class CL_SALV_TABLE. To make the unselected fields not appear in the output, you must set them as TECHNICAL:

```
COLUMN->SET_TECHNICAL( VALUE = 'X' )
```

Copy the interface from the program YCL_CH10_ILISTS05 and activate it.

The extra source code in declarations:

```
DATA:
.........
        ITAB        TYPE REF TO DATA,
        ALV_GRID    TYPE REF TO CL_SALV_TABLE,
        COLUMNS     TYPE REF TO CL_SALV_COLUMNS_TABLE,
        COLUMN      TYPE REF TO CL_SALV_COLUMN,
```

```
       LAYOUT_REF TYPE REF TO CL_SALV_LAYOUT, " for layout management
       LAYOUT_KEY TYPE SALV_S_LAYOUT_KEY, " for layout management

       FUNCTIONS  TYPE REF TO CL_SALV_FUNCTIONS_LIST.

FIELD-SYMBOLS: ........
               <iTAB> TYPE ANY TABLE. " field symbol to access itab
```

The changed source code in the AT USER_COMMAND event area, the new source code using the class CL_SALV_TABLE:

```
IF SY-TFILL > 90. " no of fields selected > 90
  MESSAGE S025(YCL_CH07_MCLASS01) WITH
  TAB_NAME DISPLAY LIKE 'W'.
  SY-LSIND = SY-LSIND - 1.
  EXIT.
 ENDIF.

****** no pf status, as ALV tool bar replaces application tool bar

 SET TITLEBAR 'TITLE02' WITH TAB_NAME.

**************retrieve data & output***********************

 CREATE DATA ITAB TYPE STANDARD TABLE OF (TAB_NAME).
 ASSIGN ITAB->* TO <ITAB>.
 SELECT (SFIELDS_TAB) FROM (TAB_NAME) INTO CORRESPONDING FIELDS OF
  TABLE <ITAB> WHERE (CONDS_TAB) ORDER BY (ORDERBY_TAB).

 CALL METHOD CL_SALV_TABLE=>FACTORY
   EXPORTING
     LIST_DISPLAY   = IF_SALV_C_BOOL_SAP=>TRUE
*    R_CONTAINER    =
*    CONTAINER_NAME =
   IMPORTING
     R_SALV_TABLE   = ALV_GRID
   CHANGING
     T_TABLE        = <ITAB>
    .

 COLUMNS = ALV_GRID->GET_COLUMNS( ).

 LOOP AT FIELDS_TAB INTO FIELDS_STRU.
  IF FIELDS_STRU-CBOX = 'X'.
   CONTINUE.
  ENDIF.
```

```
***** make unselected columns technical columns *****

  COLUMN = COLUMNS->GET_COLUMN(COLUMNNAME = FIELDS_STRU-FIELDNAME).
  COLUMN->SET_TECHNICAL(VALUE = 'X').
 ENDLOOP.

 LAYOUT_REF = ALV_GRID->GET_LAYOUT( ).
 LAYOUT_KEY-REPORT = 'YCL_CH13_04_ANY_TABLE_SALV'.

 LAYOUT_REF->SET_KEY( LAYOUT_KEY ).
 LAYOUT_REF->SET_SAVE_RESTRICTION( '2' ).

 FUNCTIONS = ALV_GRID->GET_FUNCTIONS( ).
 FUNCTIONS->SET_ALL( ). "DEFAULT( ).
 FUNCTIONS->SET_LAYOUT_CHANGE( 'X' ).
 FUNCTIONS->SET_LAYOUT_MAINTAIN( 'X' ).
 FUNCTIONS->SET_LAYOUT_SAVE( 'X' ).

 COLUMNS->SET_OPTIMIZE( VALUE = 'X' ).

 ALV_GRID->DISPLAY( ).

 FREE ITAB.
```

The complete source code of the program YCL_CH13_04_ANY_TABLE_SALV is available in the source code resource. Figure 13-15 through Figure 13-18 show the input and corresponding output.

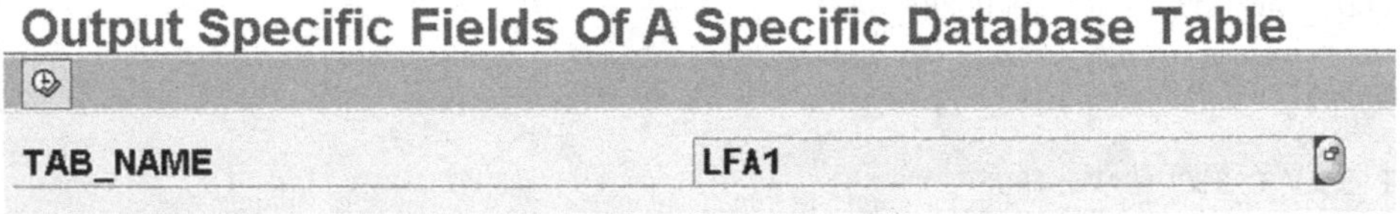

Output Specific Fields Of A Specific Database Table

TAB_NAME	LFA1

Figure 13-15. *Input*

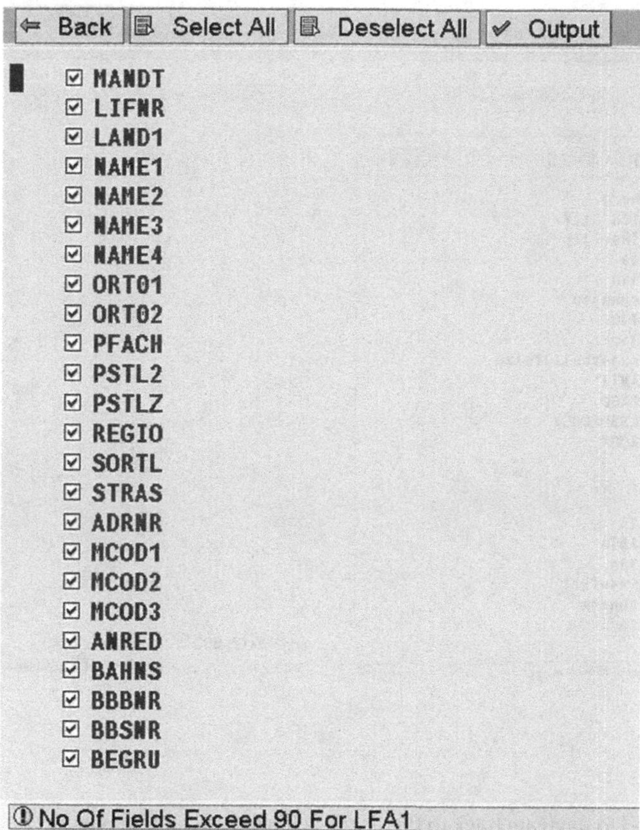

Figure 13-16. *Error indicating the number of fields is greater than 90*

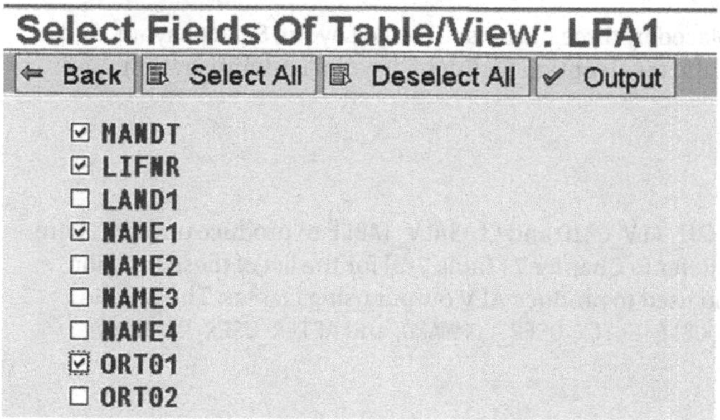

Select Fields Of Table/View: LFA1

Back | Select All | Deselect All | Output

☑ MANDT
☑ LIFNR
☐ LAND1
☑ NAME1
☐ NAME2
☐ NAME3
☐ NAME4
☑ ORT01
☐ ORT02

Figure 13-17. *Selecting fields*

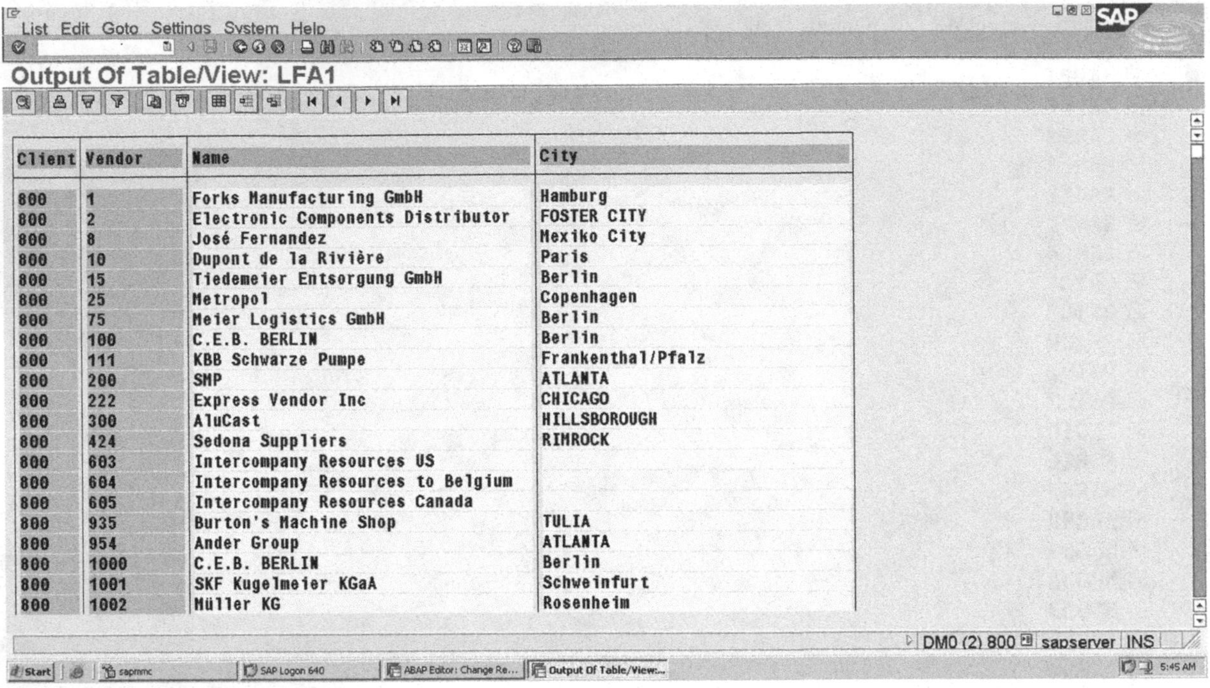

Client	Vendor	Name	City
800	1	Forks Manufacturing GmbH	Hamburg
800	2	Electronic Components Distributor	FOSTER CITY
800	8	José Fernandez	Mexiko City
800	10	Dupont de la Rivière	Paris
800	15	Tiedemeier Entsorgung GmbH	Berlin
800	25	Metropol	Copenhagen
800	75	Meier Logistics GmbH	Berlin
800	100	C.E.B. BERLIN	Berlin
800	111	KBB Schwarze Pumpe	Frankenthal/Pfalz
800	200	SMP	ATLANTA
800	222	Express Vendor Inc	CHICAGO
800	300	AluCast	HILLSBOROUGH
800	424	Sedona Suppliers	RIMROCK
800	603	Intercompany Resources US	
800	604	Intercompany Resources to Belgium	
800	605	Intercompany Resources Canada	
800	935	Burton's Machine Shop	TULIA
800	954	Ander Group	ATLANTA
800	1000	C.E.B. BERLIN	Berlin
800	1001	SKF Kugelmeier KGaA	Schweinfurt
800	1002	Müller KG	Rosenheim

Figure 13-18. *Output of the selected fields*

The ALV toolbar replaces the application toolbar.

The Back button of the standard toolbar can be used to navigate back to the list of fields for the table or view.

With a classical ALV list, you don't have the capability to sort and filter in the Change Layout dialog box. You can only shuffle or omit columns in the dialog box. You can perform filtering with the Filter button; clicking it pops up a dialog box. You can sort with the Sort button. If you want to apply multiple field sorting, don't select any column when clicking the Sort button. The Sort dialog box will pop up.

The Single Layout button with menu options is replaced by three buttons: Change Layout, Select Layout, and Save Layout. The Maintain Layout button is replaced by the menu option Settings ä Layout ä Administration.

Conclusion

You have used the major features of the ALV classes `CL_GUI_ALV_GRID` and `CL_SALV_TABLE` to produce output. There are function modules available to produce ALV output. Refer to Chapter 7 (Table 7-3) for the list of these function modules. You should try out a few with the scenarios you used to produce ALV output using classes. The function modules do not provide for interactive events such as `DOUBLE_CLICK`, `USER_COMMAND`, and `AFTER_USER_COMMAND`.

CHAPTER 14

Screen Programming

Basics of Screen Painter

You were introduced to the very basics of screen programming in Chapter 12 entitled 'ALV (ABAP List Viewer Outputs - Part 1'). Screen programming is for input of data. Inputs could involve multiple screens and complex screen elements (custom controls, tab strip controls, table controls and so on are complex screen elements. This chapter will recapitulate coverage of screen programming we covered earlier and add to it.

The core of screen programming is the screen painter. (Transaction code SE51). Screens are attached to programs and are identified by four-digit numbers. Screens consist of:

- **Attributes.** (Like any other workbench objects).
- **Flow Logic.** On triggering of screen events, to execute a limited repertoire of ABAP statements, most of these statements are permitted only in the *flow logic* area, notably the module invoking statement `MODULE <module name>`. The module invoking statements jump to the respective module (similar to jumping to a subroutine to execute normal ABAP code and return). Refer to the topic 'Screen Flow Logic' in the manual ABAP Programming (BC-ABA) for a full list of *flow logic* statements.
- **The Element List.** This is a non-graphical representation of the screen elements with their attributes.
- **The Layout Editor.** You can drag, drop, position, size, and statically adjust attributes of screen elements in the layout editor. The screen element palette is shown in Figure 14-1.

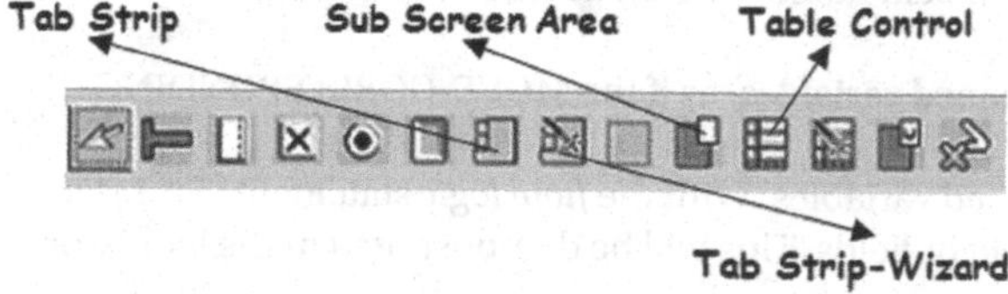

Figure 14-1. *Layout Editor - Screen ElementPalette*

Though it is shown horizontally in Figure 14-1, it is laid out vertically in the layout editor.

- **Main events.** Two main events have already been described, including PROCESS BEFORE OUTPUT, PBO, and PROCESS AFTER INPUT (PAI). The PBO event is triggered in two situations: (i) just before the screen appears to the user for the first time, and (ii) if it succeeds the PAI event. The PAI event is a reaction to a user interaction such as a user pressing a button, a user making a menu selection, or a user pressing the <Enter> key, etc.

By default the PBO event succeeds the PAI event. But if an error condition (invalid input) arises during a PAI event, the PBO event is suspended until the error condition is rectified.

There are two more events: PROCESS ON VALUE-REQUEST (POV) and PROCESS ON HELP-REQUEST (POH), analogous to the Selection Screen events AT SELECTION-SCREEN ON VALUE-REQUEST and AT SELECTION-SCREEN ON HELP-REQUEST, respectively.

- **Data transfer.** There is a continual exchange or transfer of data between the application servers and the presentation servers. The ABAP programs get executed on the application server; that is, all the data objects/variables declared with DATA and TABLES statements are allocated memory on the application servers. These declared variables, allocated memory on the application server, will be called as ABAP variables. Whatever variables you locate and position on the screen in the screen painter get defined on the presentation servers when the program executes. The variables positioned on screen will be called as screen variables. There is a transfer of values between ABAP variables and screen variables during the PBO and PAI events for identically named variables.

During the PBO event, data or values are transferred from the ABAP variables to the screen variables for identically named variables.

During the PAI event, it is the reverse (i.e. data or values are transferred from the screen variables to the ABAP variables for identically named variables). This is shown graphically in Figure 14-2.

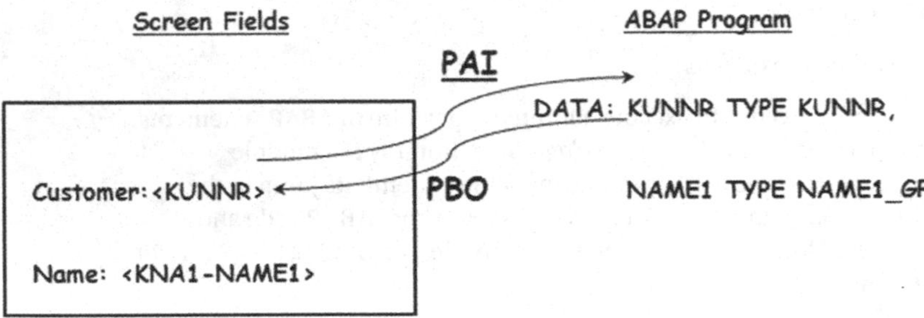

***Figure 14-2.** Transfer of Data during PBO and PAI Events*

The screen field names are 'KUNNR' and 'KNA1-NAME1'. The ABAP variables names are 'KUNNR' and 'NAME1'.

Therefore, data will get transferred between the screen field 'KUNNR' and ABAP variable 'KUNNR' only. (Screen field name and ABAP variable name being identical). The screen field name 'KNA1-NAME1' is not identical to the ABAP variable name 'NAME1'.

As stated earlier, this transfer occurs only for identically named variables, as if the MOVE-CORRESPONDING... statement is in operation.

By default the flow of data will occur for all identically named variables. With the *flow logic* statements FIELD and CHAIN... ENDCHAIN, the flow can be restricted to specific field or fields. This will be demonstrated in the hands-on exercises.

Hands-on Exercise. Operate on the Data of a Copy of Table 'T005T'

Data to Be Operated Upon

You will create an ABAP program and related objects to operate on the data of a copy of the SAP delivered text table T005T. The text table T005T stores the country-related texts. The table T005T has the fields shown in Table 14-1.

Table 14-1. *Fields in Table T005T*

Field Name	DDIC Type, Length	Description
MANDT	CLNT/3	Client Code
SPRAS	LANG/1	Language Code
LAND1	CHAR/3	Country Code
LANDX	CAHR/15	Country Text
NATIO	CHAR/15	Nationality Text
LANDX50	CHAR/50	Country Text, 50 Characters
NATIO50	CHAR/50	Nationality Text, 50 Characters
PRO_SPREGT	CHAR/50	Super Region Text

Through an ABAP program, you will be able to:

- Display the data of a specified language and country code.
- Change/edit the data of a specified language and country code.
- Add a new row in the table. (New language country codes with the related texts).
- Delete a row of a specified language and country code.

You are making a copy of the table structure T005T into the structure YCL_CH14_T005T. The table T005T is a text table and its primary table is T005. The new table YCL_CH14_T005T will also inherit T005 as its primary table. But you will make the new table YCL_CH14_T005T independent of the primary table T005 by deleting the foreign key relationship of the field 'LAND1'. After deleting the foreign key relationship of field 'LAND1' in the table structure YCL_CH14_T005T, you will activate the new table structure. With the foreign key relationship for the field 'LAND1' deleted, you will be able to insert/add new countries in the new table YCL_CH14_T005T as it is independent of the table T005.

You will copy rows from the table T005T into the table YCL_CH14_T005T for rows corresponding to the logged in language. (An arbitrary decision). The code for copying data from T005T into YCL_CH14_T005T.

```
TABLES T005T.
SELECT * FROM T005T WHERE SPRAS = SY-LANGU.
 INSERT INTO YCL_CH14_T005T VALUES T005T.
ENDSELECT.

WRITE./5 'Rows Transferred.', (4  SY-DBCNT.
```

Screens

You will have two screens for this exercise to demonstrate the navigation between the screens. The first screen will have just the primary key fields 'SPRAS' and 'LAND1' to be input. Based on the input values and operation to be performed, you will navigate to the second screen, which will have all the seven table fields. (Excluding the 'MANDT' field). You will provide for navigation from the second screen back to the first screen.

The first screen must have application tool bar buttons to carry out operations of display, change, create, and delete. And the application tool bar must contain a button to exit or quit the program.

A rough layout of the first screen is shown in Figure 14-3.

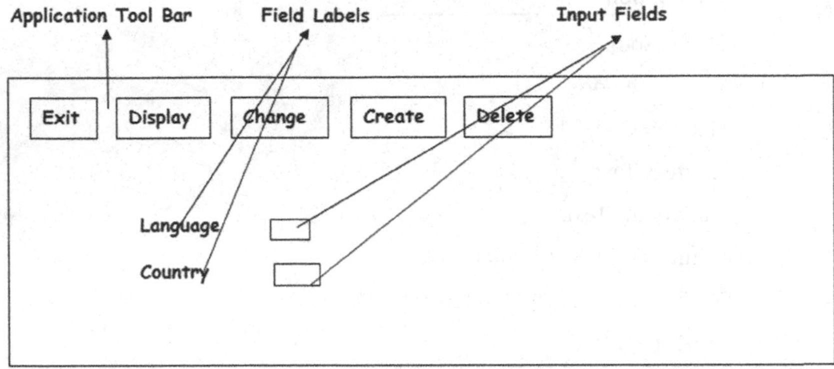

Figure 14-3. *Operate Data of YCL_CH14_T005T - First Screen*

You will designate the first screen as screen number 500.
On pressing the exit button, it will quit the program.
The following will apply for the display, change, and delete buttons.

> If invalid values are input for the language code and country code, an error condition is created and reported. This is the case when the language and country code combination input do not exist in the table YCL_CH14_T005T. The PBO is not triggered because of the error condition.

The following will apply for the create button:

> Invalid input values for language and country codes will create an error condition that is reported. This is the case when language and country code combination input for creation already exist in the table. The PBO is not triggered because of the error condition.

The inputs of language and country codes are validated together as a combination. This is implemented with the FIELD and CHAIN…ENDCHAIN statements in the *flow logic* area of the screen number 500. This will be elaborated upon when you code the PAI module of the first screen or screen number 500.

Once the inputs of language and country codes are valid, you are navigating to the second screen designated as screen number 550. You are navigating to the second screen for the three operations: display, change, and create.

When the delete button is pressed, a confirmation dialog box will appear. The delete operation does not involve navigation to the second screen.

A rough layout of the second screen or screen number 550 is shown in Figure 14-4.

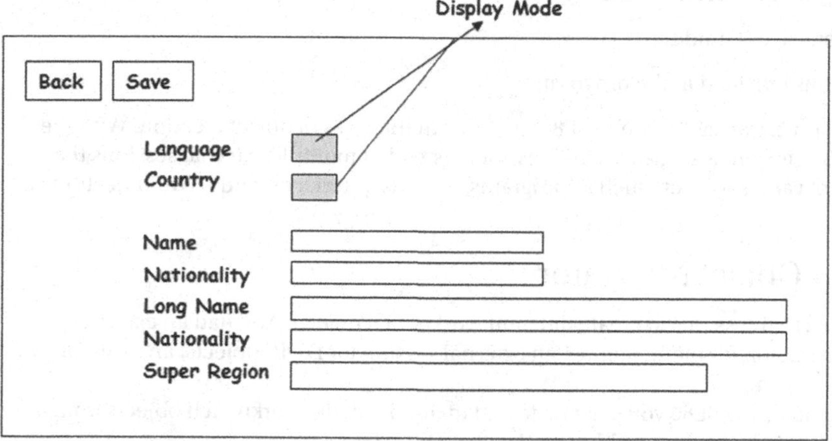

Figure 14-4. *Operate Data of YCL_CH14_T005T - Second Screen*

The second screen, screen number 550 will have the following attributes as per the operations being carried out:

- If the display button had been pressed on the opening screen, all the fields on the second screen will be in display mode. The application tool bar will contain only the back button to navigate to the first screen (i.e., screen number 500).
- If the change button had been pressed on the opening screen, the key fields - language and country codes - will be in display mode and the rest of the fields will be in change mode. The application tool bar will contain two buttons. The back button to navigate to first screen (i.e., screen number 500 and the save button to save the changes in the text fields to the database table).
- If the create button had been pressed on the opening screen, the key fields - language and country codes - will be in display mode and the rest of the fields will have initial values and will be ready for input. The application tool bar will contain two buttons: the back button to navigate to the first screen/screen number 500 and the save button to save the creation of new language and country data.

After navigating to the second screen, before the screen appears to the user, you need to change the properties of the input fields as per operations.

The application tool bar on the second screen needs to be adjusted as per the operations. The save button must not appear when the display button is pressed on the first screen.

The preceding descriptions would make it amply clear what you are setting out to do.

The following are Object Creation and Test Tasks to be carried out to Operate on the Data of Table YCL_CH14_T005T.

1. Create an ABAP program that will be the main program.
2. Create screen number 500, its layout, *element, list* and *flow logic* with the PBO module.
3. Create the status and title bar for screen number 500.
4. Create the screen number 500 PAI module.
5. Create a search help to be attached to the field 'LAND1' of the table YCL_CH14_T005T. The user can make a selection of a language country code combination from this list.

6. Create screen number 550: its layout, *element list,* and *flow logic* with the PBO module.
7. Create the status and title bar for screen number 550.
8. Create the screen number 550 PAI module.
9. Test the different operations provided in the program.

You are using the object navigator (i.e. transaction code SE80) to perform the tasks of object creation. With the object navigator, you can create all objects from a single external session, instead of multiple external sessions that you employed until now for creation of various objects such as programs, screens, interfaces, and DDIC objects et al.

Transaction Code SE80 – Object Navigator

Until now, you were using separate external sessions to create different workbench objects. You had an external session for screen painter, an external session for menu painter, an external session for DDIC objects, an external session for ABAP source program, and so on.

With the object navigator transaction code SE80 you can create and maintain all the workbench objects from a single session. You can view all the related objects in the object navigator.

You will carry out the developmental tasks of the current exercise in the object navigator. So, enter /NSE80 in the command box and navigate to the object navigator. The object navigator screen will look like Figure 14-5.

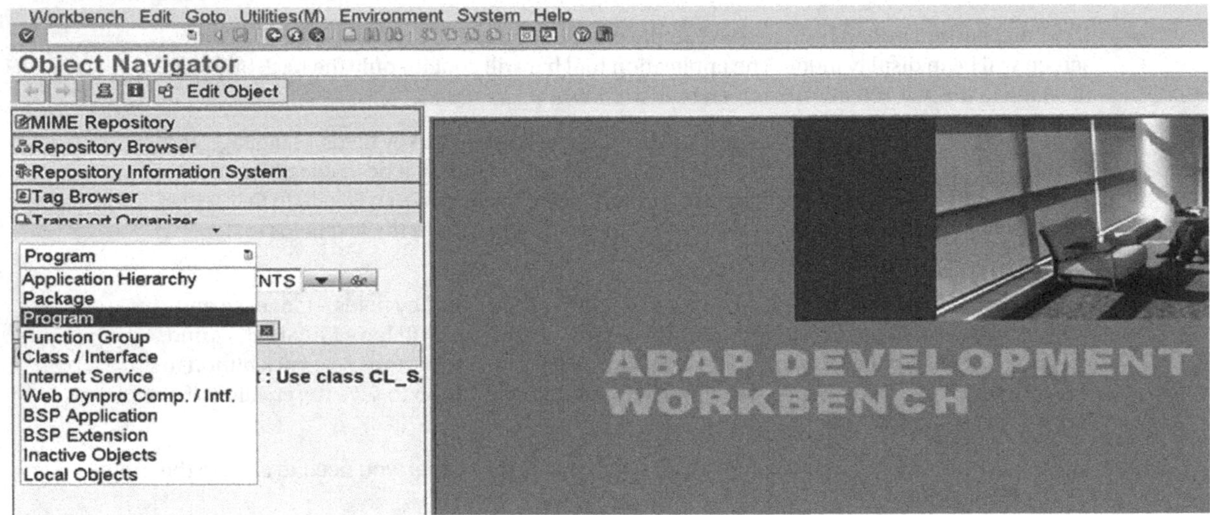

Figure 14-5. *Object Navigator Screen*

1. **ABAP program.** As you want to start off by first creating a program, select the option 'Program' from the drop-down list as shown in Figure 14-5. Right under the field where you entered the 'Program' option, enter the name of the new ABAP program: YCL_CH14_01_YCL_CH14_T005TDATA. Press <Enter>. The following prompt will appear, indicating that the program does not exist and asks if you want to create the new program.

Figure 14-6. *Object Navigator. Create New Program*

The system appears with another prompt so that you can decide whether to create a top include. A top include is an include program containing global data declarations, and a convention SAP follows in its programs. You do not want a top include, so ensure the check box for top include is disabled. The screen will look like Figure 14-7.

Figure 14-7. *Object Navigator. Create New Program - Top Include Option*

Next, the program attributes screen will appear as shown in Figure 14-8.

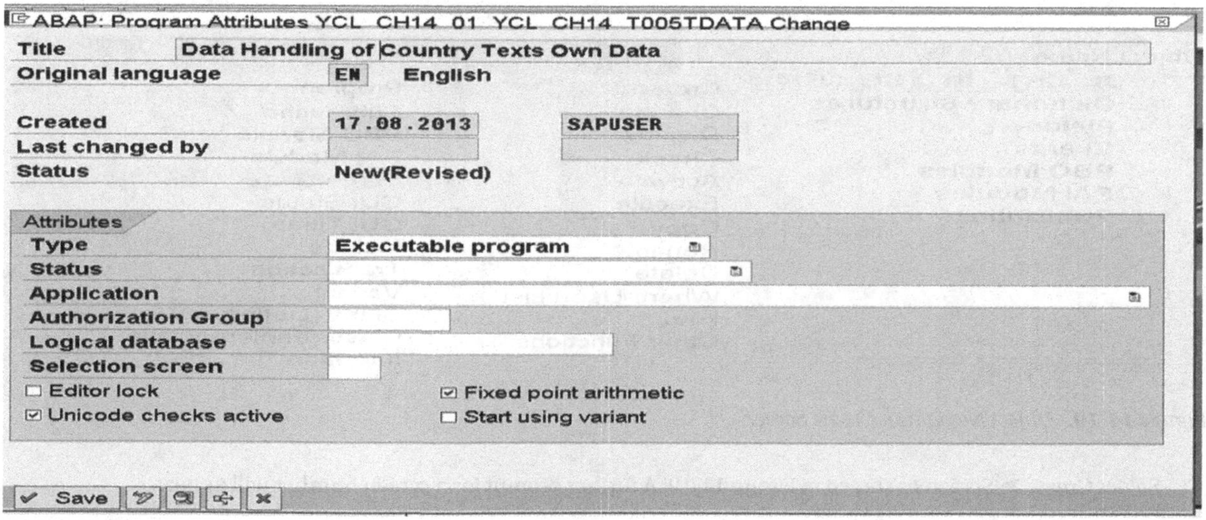

Figure 14-8. *Object Navigator. Create New Program – Program Attributes*

The ABAP source will appear like in Figure 14-9.

Button to Toggle - Full or Partial Screen

ABAP Editor: Change Report YCL_CH14_01_YCL_CH14_T005TDATA

```
*&---------------------------------------------------------------------*
*& Report  YCL_CH14_01_YCL_CH14_T005TDATA
*&
*&---------------------------------------------------------------------*
*&
*&
*&---------------------------------------------------------------------*

REPORT YCL_CH14_01_YCL_CH14_T005TDATA.
```

Figure 14-9. *Object Navigator. Create New Program – Program Source*

As indicated, there is a button to operate with a full screen or a partial screen for the object navigator on the left. You enter the following code.

```
TABLES. YCL_CH14_T005T.
DATA.   OK_CODE    TYPE SY-UCOMM.
START-OF-SELECTION.
CALL SCREEN 500.
```

More source code lines will be added when you create PBO and PAI modules.

2. **Screen number 500 - layout, *element list, flow logic,* and PBO module.** You want to start creating screen painter objects. To do this, select or click on the program name, click on the mouse's right button, and the context menu shown in Figure 14-10 will appear.

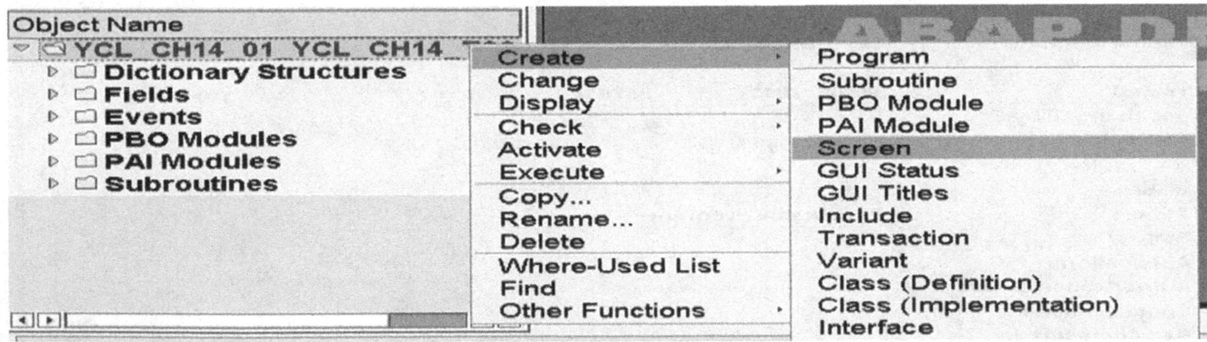

Figure 14-10. *Object Navigator. Create Screen*

Select Create ➤ Screen as shown in Figure 14-10. A further prompt for a screen number will appear.

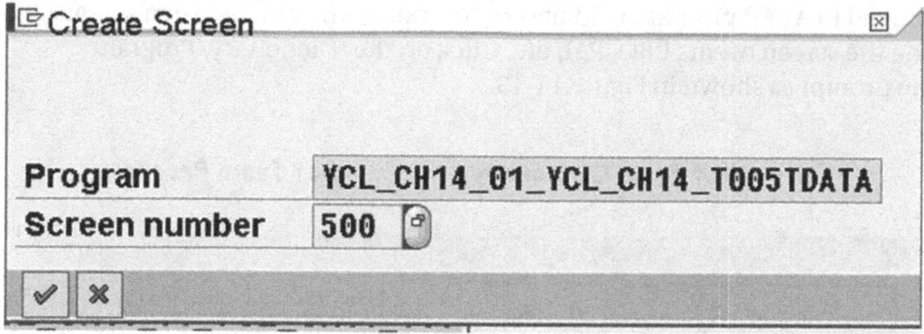

Figure 14-11. *Object Navigator. Create Screen – Prompt for Screen Number*

Entering the screen number as 500 and pressing the continue button will bring up the attribute screen. Enter short text on the attribute screen and bring up the layout editor as shown in Figure 14-12.

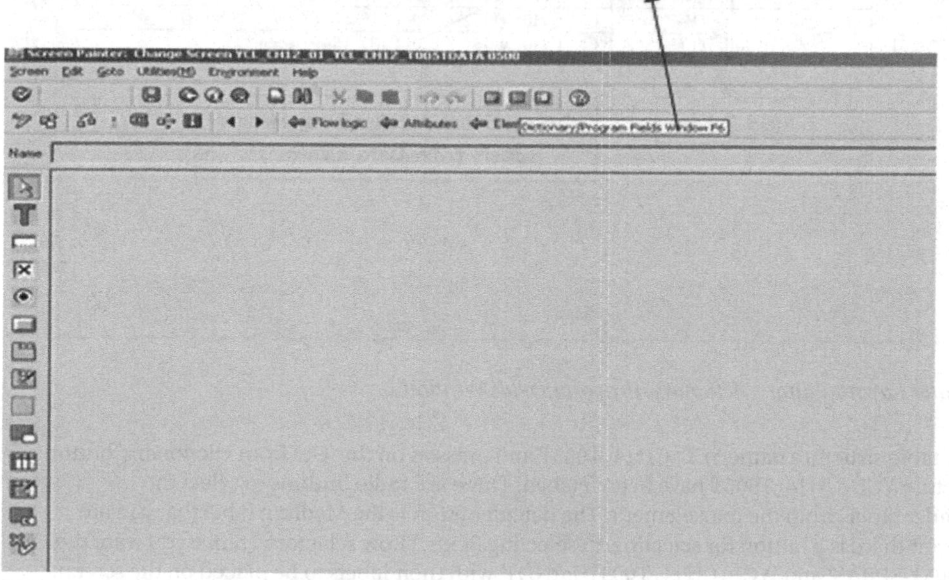

Figure 14-12. *Object Navigator. Create Screen – Layout Editor*

You want to place the two fields YCL_CH14_T005T-SPRAS and YCL_CH14_T005T- LAND1 of the table structure YCL_CH14_T005T on the screen with the respective field labels. The preferred way to do it is to use functionality of the third button from the right of the application toll bar as shown in Figure 14-12. This button enables you to place fields of DDIC structures or program structures on the screen. In the case of DDIC structure, it will automatically fetch and position the related field labels from the assigned data elements. In the case of program structure, you have to manually enter the labels. The preferred way is to get the fields from DDIC structures. This is what you will do in the present context. Since, mostly, you will be positioning screen fields by fetching them from the DDIC structure, the name of the screen fields will carry the structure name, hyphen, and the field name. If you desire that the ABAP program fields have the identical field names as the screen field names, the easy way to do it is to declare the structure in the ABAP program with the key word TABLES. This is what has been done here and this is a convention.

This ensures that screen field names are identical to ABAP program field names for transfer of data between screen variables and ABAP program variables during the screen events PBO, PAI, etc. Click on the 'Dictionary/Program Fields Window' button. This will bring up the prompt as shown in Figure 14-13.

Structure/Field Name
Get from Dictionary
Get from Program

Screen Painter: Dict./Program Fields

Table/Field Name: YCL_CH14_T005T [Get from Dictionary] [Get from Program]

Switch: Reaction: D RFC Destination:

Table Name	Field Name	Description	I/O Field		None	Short	Medium	Long	Header	Text	Copy as Text	ChkB	RadB
YCL_CH14_T00	MANDT		CLNT	3		10	15	20	3	Client			
YCL_CH14_T00	SPRAS		LANG	2		10	15	20	10	Language			
YCL_CH14_T00	LAND1		CHAR	3		10	12	20	3	Country			
YCL_CH14_T00	LANDX		CHAR	15		10	15	20	18	Name			
YCL_CH14_T00	NATIO		CHAR	15		10	15	20	15	Nationality			
YCL_CH14_T00	LANDX50		CHAR	50		10	16	20	20	Long name			
YCL_CH14_T00	NATIO50		CHAR	50		10	15	20	15	Nationality			
YCL_CH14_T00	PRQ_SPREGT		CHAR	30		10	15	20	30	Super region			

Field Names
Field Types
Option: Short/Medium/Long/Header Labels from Data Elements

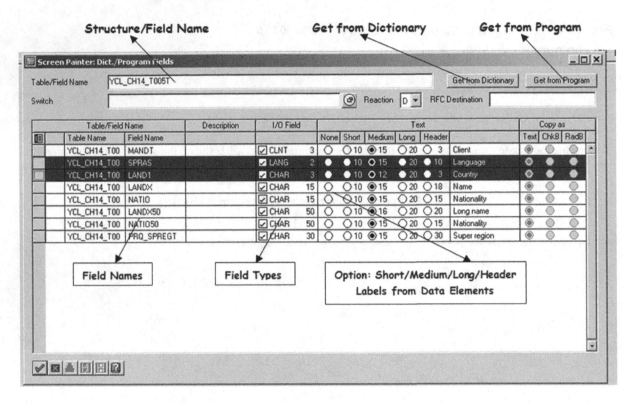

Figure 14-13. *Screen Painter Layout Editor. Dictionary/Program Fields Window*

You have entered the table structure name YCL_CH14_T005T and pressed on the 'Get from Dictionary' button. All the fields of table structure YCL_CH14_T005T have been fetched. There are radio buttons to select the Short/Medium/Long/Header labels from the data element. The default option is the Medium label that you are accepting. At the extreme left there is a button for selecting/deselecting fields. (Row selectors). Since you want the two fields 'YCL_CH14_T005T-SPRAS' and 'YCL_CH14_T005T-LAND1' with their labels to be placed on the screen, you have selected these two fields. Next, press the continue button. The screen will appear like in Figure 14-14.

Figure 14-14. *Screen Painter Layout Editor. Getting Dictionary Fields on Screen*

Position the fields with their labels at the desired position by releasing the left mouse button. All the screen elements would have been selected. Click on the blank area of the screen to deselect the fields and labels. The screen will look like the one in Figure 14-15.

Figure 14-15. *Screen Painter Layout Editor. Placing Dictionary Fields on Screen*

Save and close the screen. You will be back on the screen painter screen with the *Attribute, Element List,* and *Flow Logic* tabs. Click on the tab *Element List*, and enter the 'OK_CODE' in the *element list*. Save and navigate back to the object navigator. You will create the PBO module, interface, and PAI module from the object navigator. You will create the PBO module now. Select the program name, and click on the mouse right button to get the context menu as shown in Figure 14-16.

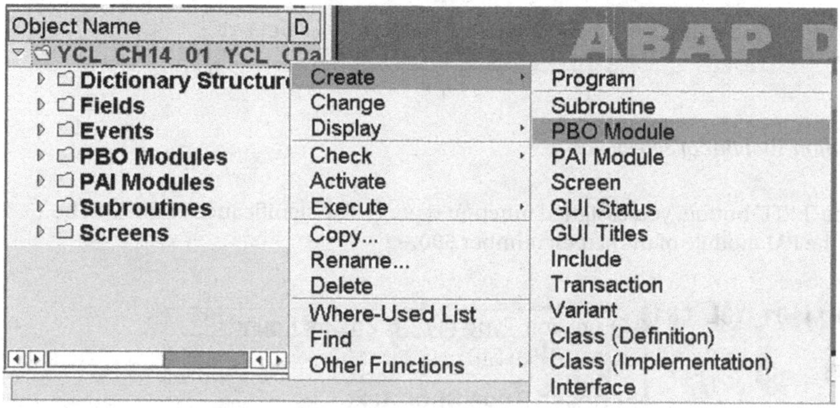

Figure 14-16. *Create the PBO Module*

The PBO in the *flow Logic will be*: MODULE STATUS_500.

Create the PBO module in the main program YCL_CH14_01_YCL_CH14_T005TDATA. The PBO module will be like the following one.

```
MODULE STATUS_0500 OUTPUT.
 SET PF-STATUS 'STAT1'.
 SET TITLEBAR 'TITLE01'.
 OK_CODE = ' '.
ENDMODULE.
```

Save and navigate back to the object navigator.

3. **Screen number 500 - status and title bar.** You have to create the status 'STAT1.' So again, select the program name, click on the mouse right button, and make the context menu selection as shown in Figure 14-17.

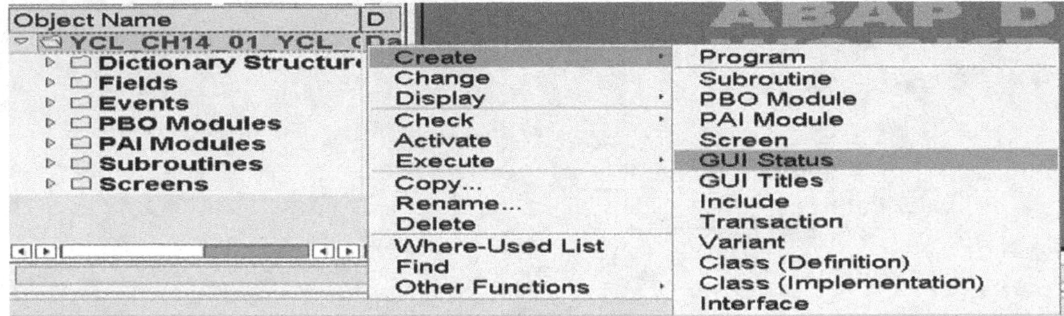

Figure 14-17. *Create Status*

Create the five buttons in status 'STAT1' as per the rough layout of screen number 500 in Figure 14-3. The status 'STAT1' application tool bar will look similar to Figure 14-18.

Application Toolbar STAT FOR YCL_CH12_T005T DATA

Items 1 - 7	EXIT Exit	DISPLAY Displa	CHANGE Change	CREATE Create	DELETE Delete	
Items 8 - 14						

Figure 14-18. *Status 'STAT1.' Application Tool Bar of Screen 500*

In the application tool bar, for the 'EXIT' button, you assigned function type 'E.' The significance of this will be explained during the elaboration on the PAI module of the screen number 500.

User Interface YCL_CH14_01_YCL_CH1

Menu Bar

Applicati

Function Attributes

Function Code EXIT

Functional Type

Switch

Static Function Texts

Function Type (1) 6 Entries Found

Function Type	Short text
E	Exit Command (MODULE
S	System Function
T	Call a Transaction
	Normal Application Func
P	Local GUI Functions
H	Internal Use

Figure 14-19. *Status 'STAT1.' 'EXIT' Button – Assigning Function Type 'E'*

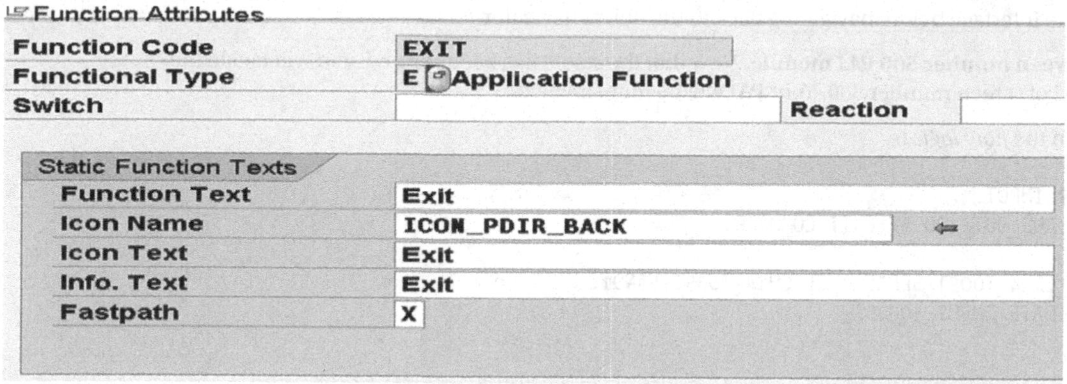

Function Attributes			
Function Code	EXIT		
Functional Type	E Application Function		
Switch		Reaction	

Static Function Texts	
Function Text	Exit
Icon Name	ICON_PDIR_BACK
Icon Text	Exit
Info. Text	Exit
Fastpath	X

Figure 14-20. *Status 'STAT1.' 'EXIT' Button – Assigned Function Type 'E'*

Save and return to object navigator.

You have to create the title bar 'TITLE01.' Select the program name, click on the mouse right button, and make the context menu selection as shown in Figure 14-21.

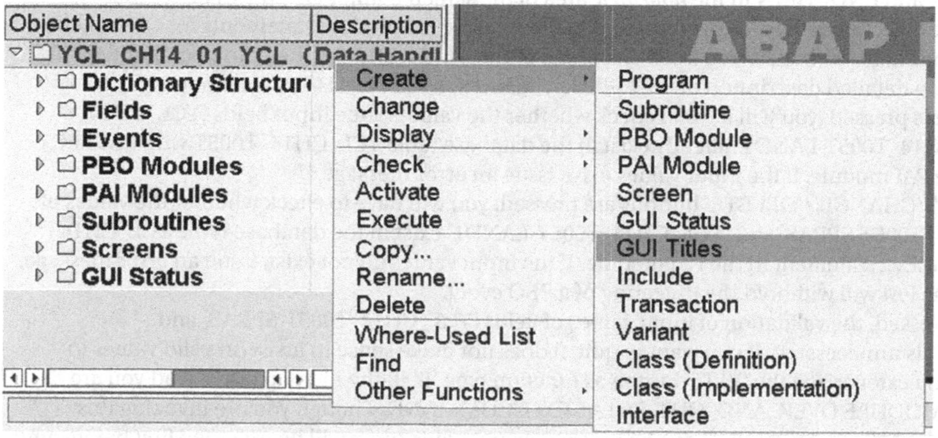

Figure 14-21. *Create Title Bar*

Create a title bar as shown in Figure 14-22.

User Interface YCL_CH14_01_YCL_CH14_T005TDATA Active

Title Number	Title
TITLE01	Table YCL_CH14_T005T Data

Figure 14-22. *Title Bar Created – Screen 500*

Activate the interface before navigating back to the object navigator.

4. **Screen number 500 PAI module.** Now that the status has been created, you will tackle the PAI of screen number 500. Your PAI will be more involved.

Your PAI in the *flow logic* is:

```
PROCESS AFTER INPUT.
 MODULE OVER_AND_OUT_500 AT EXIT-COMMAND.
 CHAIN.
  FIELD. YCL_CH14_T005T-SPRAS, YCL_CH14_T005T-LAND1.
  MODULE VALIDATE_INPUT_500.
 ENDCHAIN.

MODULE MAIN_PAI_500.
```

The PAI will be triggered by pressing one of the buttons on the application tool bar: 'EXIT,' 'DISPLAY,' 'CHANGE,' 'CREATE,' and 'DELETE.' (Reference to the buttons is by their function codes). The discussion on the 'EXIT' button is deferred for now. When any button other than the 'EXIT' is pressed, you will have to first validate the combination of the fields 'YCL_CH14_T005T-SPRAS' and 'YCL_CH14_T005T-LAND1.' The validation is carried out in the module VALIDATE_INPUT_500.

The statements CHAIN and ENDCHAIN in the *flow logic* area of the screen painter are equivalent to the declaration of a block in the Selection Screen environment. When executing the module statements for a chain, the values of only the field in the chain are transferred from the screen to the ABAP variables. Refer to document ABAP Programming (BC-ABA) for a detailed description of the FIELD..., CHAIN, and ENDCHAIN statements.

If the 'CREATE' button is pressed, you will have to check whether the values of the input fields 'YCL_CH14_T005T-SPRAS' and 'YCL_CH14_T005T-LAND1' already exist in the database table YCL_CH14_T005T with a SELECT SINGLE... statement in the PAI module. If the input values exist, issue an error message.

If any of the 'DISPLAY'/'CHANGE'/'DELETE' buttons are pressed, you will have to check whether the values of the input fields 'YCL_CH14_T005T-SPRAS' and 'YCL_CH14_T005T-LAND1' exist in the database table YCL_CH14_T005T with a SELECT SINGLE... statement in the PAI module. If the input values do not exist, issue an error message.

An error message in the PAI will withhold the triggering of a PBO event.

If the EXIT button is pressed, the validation of input values of fields 'YCL_CH14_T005T-SPRAS' and 'YCL_CH14_T005T-LAND1' is unnecessary. If you want to quit, it does not make sense to insist on valid values to be input. For this reason, you categorized the 'EXIT' button as function type 'E' in the menu painter. And you are executing the PAI module MODULE OVER_AND_OUT_500 AT EXIT-COMMAND. Though you are invoking this module in the *flow logic* area as the first module, it can be invoked in any order, but it will be executed first before any checks and validations. It will transfer only the 'OK_CODE' value from the screen variable to the ABAP variable. The values of other variables are not transferred. A module ending with the phrase AT EXIT-COMMAND will be executed for button(s) assigned the function type 'E' only.

When the values of input fields 'YCL_CH14_T005T-SPRAS' and 'YCL_CH14_T005T-LAND1' are found valid vis-à-vis the operational button pressed, the values should exist for the display/change/delete operations, and the values should not exist for the create operation when you execute the module MAIN_PAI_500.

In this module, you are saving the 'OK_CODE' contents into another variable 'SAVE_OK_CODE,' initializing the exclude button internal table. If a display/change/create button is pressed, you are navigating to screen number 550 with the statement LEAVE TO SCREEN 550. In the case of the create button being pressed, you are initializing the five fields: 'YCL_CH14_T005T-LANDX,' 'YCL_CH14_T005T-NATIO,' 'YCL_CH14_T005T-LANDX50,' 'YCL_CH14_T005T-NATIO50,' and 'YCL_CH14_T005T-PRQ_SPREGT.' These fields must appear blank for input when creating a new country text.

If the display button is pressed, you are appending the exclude button internal table with the function code of the save button. You do not want the save button to appear on the application tool bar of screen 550 when the screen 550 is in display mode.

If the delete button is pressed, you are issuing a pop-up dialog box for confirmation to delete country text row. If the deletion is confirmed in the pop-up dialog box, you are deleting the row and confirming the deletion with a message else issuing delete aborted message. You are using the open SQL statement DELETE YCL_CH14_T005T (i.e., DELETE <table structure name>).

5. **Search help for attachment to field 'LAND1' of table structureYCL_CH14_T005T.** You have to create a search help and a DDIC object. In the object navigator, from the drop-down list where you selected 'Program', select now Local Objects'. Select 'Dictionary', and invoke the context menu by clicking on the mouse right button as shown in Figure 14-23.

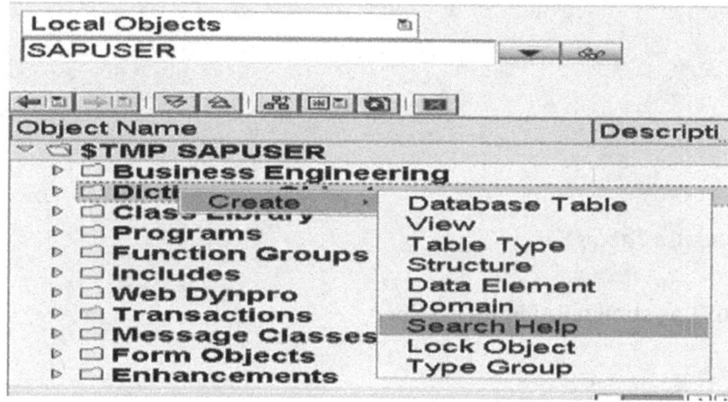

Figure 14-23. *Object Navigator. Create DDIC Search Help*

The system will prompt for the name of the search help and search help type (i.e., elementary or collective). Accept the default search help type (elementary), and enter the name of the search help as YCL_CH14_OWN_CNTRY_TEXTS_SH, and press the continue button. The search help with entered values will look similar to Figure 14-24.

Elementary srch hlp YCL_CH14_OWN_CNTRY_TEXTS_SH Active
Short description Search Help for field LAND1 of Structure YCL_CH14_T005T

Attributes Definition

Data collection
Selection method YCL_CH14_T005T
Text table

Dialog behavior
Dialog type Dialog with value restriction
Hot key

Search help exit

Parameter

Search help parameter	IMP	EXP	LPos	SPos	SDis	Data element	Mo	Default va
SPRAS	☐	☑	1	1	☐	SPRAS	☐	
LAND1	☐	☑	2	2	☐	LAND1	☐	
LANDX	☐	☐	3	3	☐	LANDX	☐	

Figure 14-24. *Search Help. YCL_CH14_OWN_CNTRY_TEXTS_SH*

Save and activate the search help and navigate back to the object navigator. You have to attach this search help to the field 'LAND1' of table structure YCL_CH14_T005T. Expand the 'Dictionary' node and the 'Database Tables' subnode in the object navigator as shown in Figure 14-25.

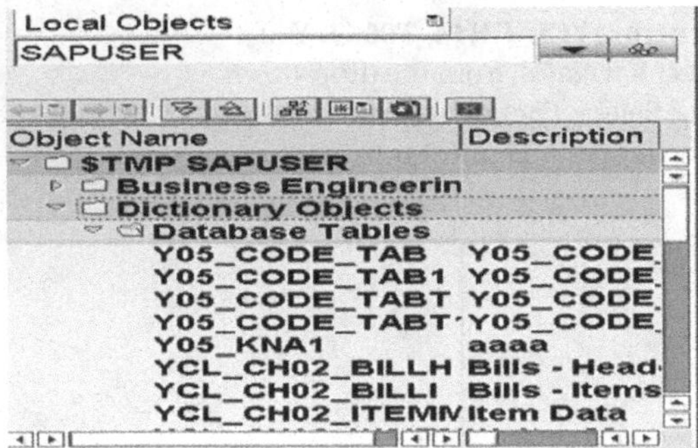

Figure 14-25. *Object Navigator. Dictionary Objects - Database Tables*

Scroll, and locate the database table YCL_CH14_T005T as shown in Figure 14-26.

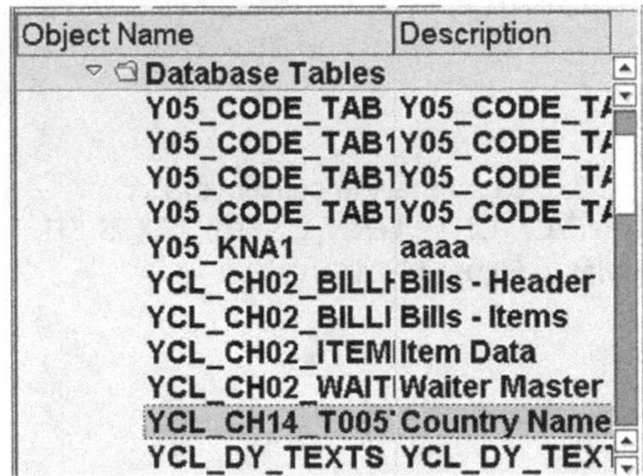

Figure 14-26. *Object Navigator. DDIC Database Table -YCL_CH14_T006T*

When you have the database table structure in change mode, position the cursor on the field 'LAND1' and click on the 'Srch Help' button. Enter the search help name YCL_CH14_OWN_CNTRY_TEXTS_SH in the dialog box and press the continue key. The search help proposal will appear as shown in Figure 14-27.

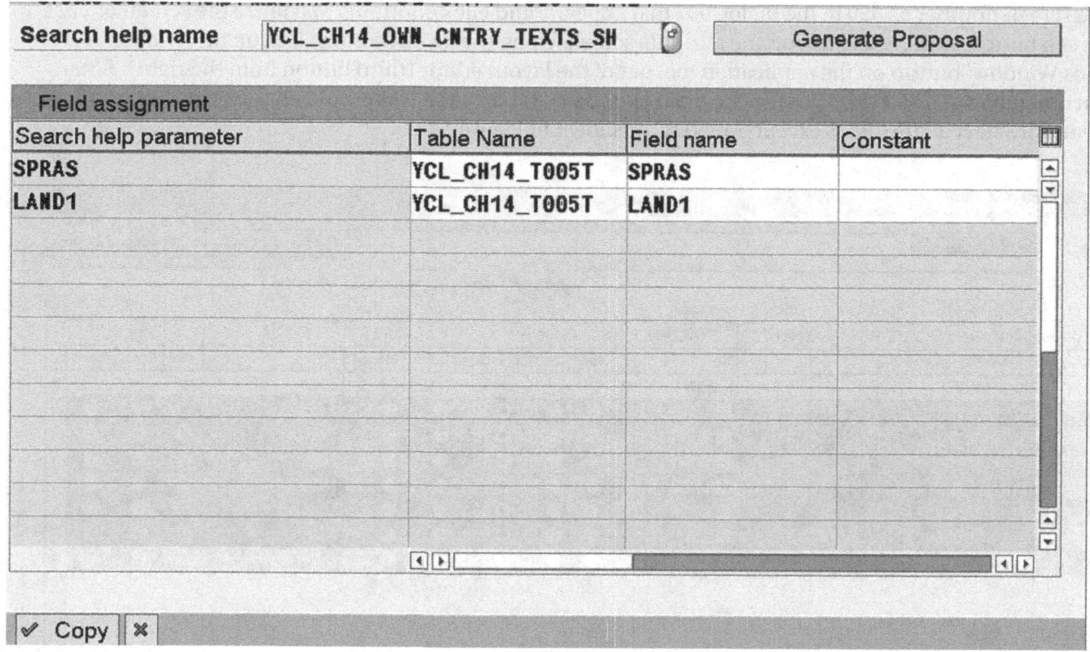

Figure 14-27. *Attach Search Help. YCL_CH14_OWN_CNTRY_TEXTS_SH*

Click on the copy button, save, and activate the database table YCL_CH14_T005T and return to the object navigator.

6. **Screen number 550 – layout, *element list* and *flow logic* PBO module.** You have to switch back to the program. Hence, select 'Program' from the drop-down list, and enter the program name as YCL_CH14_01_YCL_CH14_T005TDATA if it is not appearing as the default. Press the <Enter> key after the entry of the program name. You have the creation of screen number 550 as the next task.

Select/click on the program, and invoke the context menu as shown in Figure 14-28.

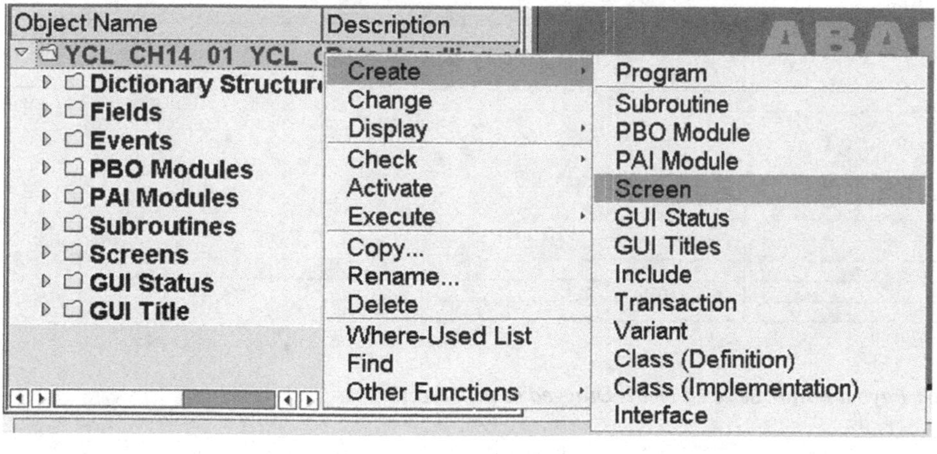

Figure 14-28. *Object Navigator. Create Screen 550*

Enter the screen number as 550 in the dialog box that appears, and click continue. Maximize the screen or click on the full screen button. Enter short text on the attribute screen. Open the layout editor. Click on the 'Dictionary/Program Fields Window' button on the application tool bar of the layout editor (third button from the right). Enter the table structure name YCL_CH14_T005T in the dialog box field 'Table/Field Name', and click on the 'Get from Dictionary' button. Select all the fields except 'MANDT' as shown in Figure 14-29.

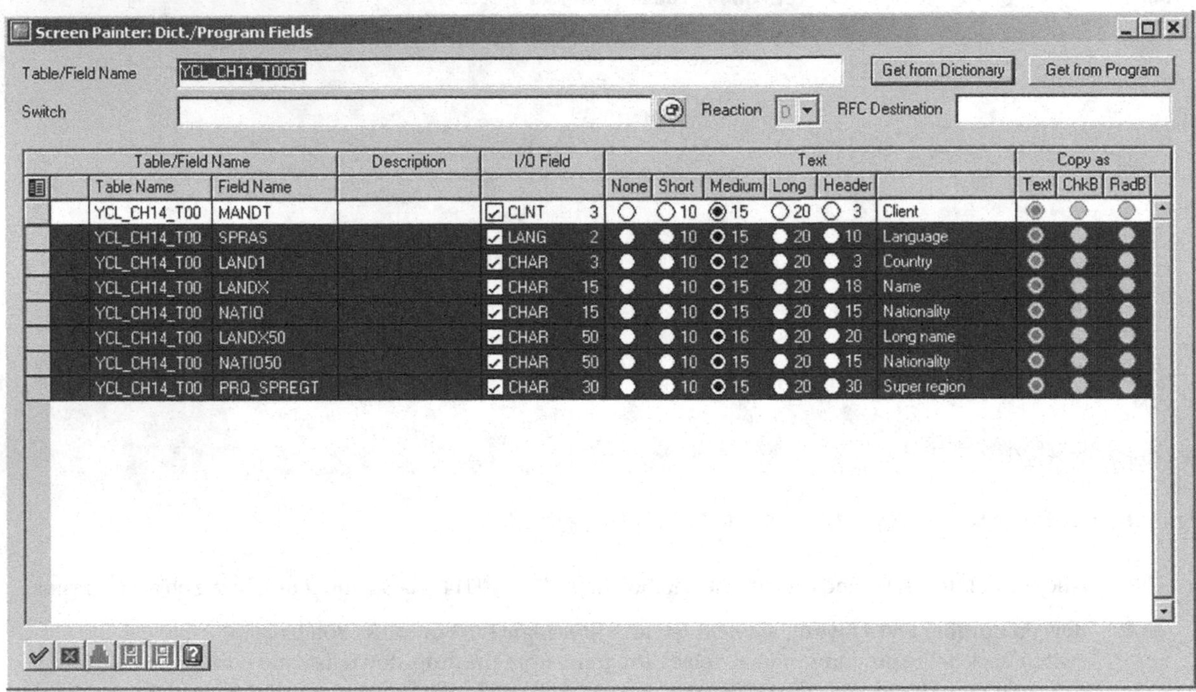

Figure 14-29. *Screen Painter Layout Editor. Dictionary/Program Fields Window*

The selected fields, when dragged onto the screen before releasing the mouse button, will look like in Figure 14-30.

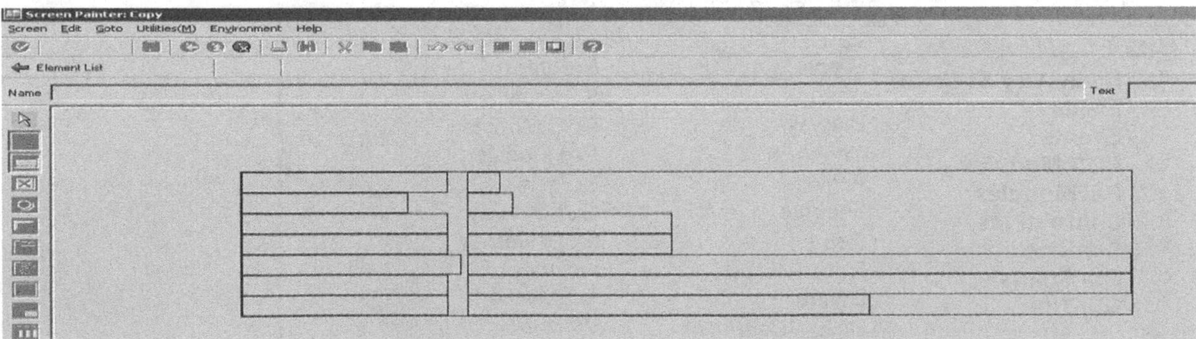

Figure 14-30. *Screen Painter Layout Editor. Selected Fields Dragged to the Screen*

Fetch the dialog box for screen element attributes for each of the input fields, and disable the 'Input Field' checkbox in the tab *Program*. All the input fields are in display mode to start with. The screen will look like the one in Figure 14-31.

Figure 14-31. *Screen Painter Layout Editor. Selected Fields Dragged, Dropped and Set to Display*

Save and close the layout editor screen. Select the '*element list*' tab, and enter the 'OK_CODE' field. Save and select the *flow logic* tab.

You will create the PBO module for screen 550 now. Invoke the context menu as described earlier. Get the template of the PBO module in the main program YCL_CH14_YCL_CH14_T005tDATA. In this PBO module, set the status and title bar for screen 550. In the screen number 550, the properties of the five fields

YCL_CH14_T005T-LANDX

YCL_CH14_T005T-NATIO

YCL_CH14_T005T-LANDX50

YCL_CH14_T005T-NATIO50

YCL_CH14_T005T-PRQ_SPREGT

are to be adjusted as per the button pressed on the application toolbar of screen 500. If 'DISPLAY' button is pressed on screen 500, all the fields on screen 550 have to appear in display mode. If the button pressed on screen 500 is either 'CHANGE' or 'CREATE,' all the five fields on screen 550 have to appear in input mode. The two primary key fields– YCL_CH14_T005T-SPRAS and YCL_CH14_T005T-LAND1 – on screen 550 are to appear in display mode only for all operations. The properties of the five listed fields on screen 550 are adjusted as per the button pressed on screen 500 inside a subroutine, which is being invoked in the PBO module of screen 550. While setting status on screen 550, the 'SAVE' button is to be excluded when the operation is 'DISPLAY.' This is being taken care of by checking contents of 'SAVE_OK_CODE' variable, etc. Here is the PBO module code:

```
MODULE STATUS_0550 OUTPUT.
 SET PF-STATUS 'STAT2' EXCLUDING EXCLUD_FC_TAB[].
 SET TITLEBAR 'TITLE02' WITH 'Table YCL_CH14_T005T'(001  STRNG.
 PERFORM CHANGE_SCR_550_PROP. " adjust screen properties
ENDMODULE.                      " STATUS_0550  OUTPUT
```

7. **Screen number 550 – status and title bar.** Create the status and title bar for screen 550 from the object navigator as described earlier. The status will look like Figure 14-32.

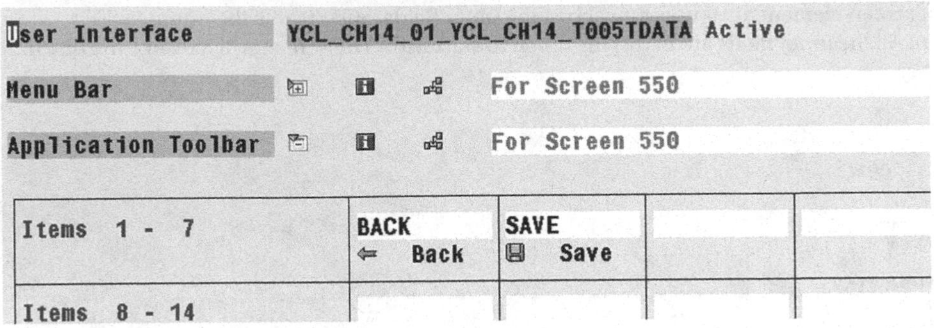

User Interface	YCL_CH14_01_YCL_CH14_T005TDATA Active			
Menu Bar	For Screen 550			
Application Toolbar	For Screen 550			
Items 1 - 7	BACK ⇐ Back	SAVE Save		
Items 8 - 14				

Figure 14-32. *Status 'STAT2.' Application Toolbar of Screen 550*

The title bar will look like Figure 14-33.

User Interface YCL_CH14_01_YCL_CH14_T005TDATA Active

Title Number	Title
TITLE01	Table YCL_CH14_T005T Data
TITLE02	&1 &2

Figure 14-33. *Title Bar 'TITLE02.' Screen 550*

8. **Screen number 550 – PAI module.** Your PAI in the *flow logic* is the following:

```
PROCESS AFTER INPUT.
 CHAIN.
  FIELD. YCL_CH14_T005T-LANDX, YCL_CH14_T005T-NATIO,
         YCL_CH14_T005T-LANDX50, YCL_CH14_T005T-NATIO50,
         YCL_CH14_T005T-PRQ_SPREGT.

  MODULE SET_CHANGE_550 ON CHAIN-REQUEST.

 ENDCHAIN.

 MODULE USER_COMMAND_0550.
```

The module SET_CHANGE_550 is executed when the PAI is triggered and only if any of the fields included in the CHAIN…ENDCHAIN has changed value. In this module, you are setting the variable DATA_CHG_550 to 'X.' Refer to the document ABAP Programming (BC-ABA) for a detailed description of these statements.

When the 'BACK' button is pressed, you are checking the value of variable DATA_CHG_550. If its value is equal to 'X,' you are producing a pop-up dialog box with a message to confirm whether to abort the changed data. You are navigating back to the screen number 500 with the LEAVE TO SCREEN 500 statement.

When the 'SAVE' button is pressed, you are issuing the open SQL statement MODIFY YCL_CH14_T005T. The open SQL statement MODIFY…is a two-in-one statement. Depending on the context, it operates as an INSERT statement or an UPDATE statement. The MODIFY…statement checks whether the primary key values in the fields of the ABAP structure variables exist in the database table. If the values exist in the database table, the MODIFY... statement operates as an UPDATE statement, updating an existing row. If the values do not exist in the database table, the MODIFY... statement operates as an INSERT statement, inserting a new row with values from the ABAP structure.

So you have been saved the effort to code for checking whether 'CHANGE'/'CREATE' button was pressed on screen 500 and issue separate UPDATE/INSERT statements appropriately.

There are variations of the open SQL statement MODIFY.... You can refer to the online help for this.

The full source code:

```
REPORT YCL_CH14_01_YCL_CH14_T005TDATA.

************************************
* Country Texts Custom Table - Data **
************************************

TABLES. YCL_CH14_T005T.

DATA.   OK_CODE         TYPE SY-UCOMM,
        SAVE_OK_CODE    TYPE SY-UCOMM, " save OK_CODE to process in
                                       " screen 550
        STRNG           TYPE STRING,
        ANSWER(1        TYPE C,     " delete confirmation. 1 yes 2 no

        EXCLUD_FC_TAB   TYPE STANDARD TABLE OF SY-UCOMM " exclude
                           WITH HEADER LINE,            " buttons table

        DATA_CHG_550(1  TYPE C. " data changed indicator

********************************
START-OF-SELECTION.

CALL SCREEN 500.

*&---------------------------------------------------------------------*
*&      Module  STATUS_0500  OUTPUT
*&---------------------------------------------------------------------*
*       text
*----------------------------------------------------------------------*

***** PBO screen 500 *****

MODULE STATUS_0500 OUTPUT.
 SET PF-STATUS 'STAT1'.
 SET TITLEBAR 'TITLE01'.
 OK_CODE = ' '.
ENDMODULE.                      " STATUS_0500  OUTPUT

*&---------------------------------------------------------------------*
*&      Module  VALIDATE_INPUT_500  INPUT
*&---------------------------------------------------------------------*
*       text
*----------------------------------------------------------------------*
```

```
***** PAI fields validation screen 500 *****

MODULE VALIDATE_INPUT_500 INPUT.

 SELECT SINGLE * FROM YCL_CH14_T005T WHERE
  SPRAS = YCL_CH14_T005T-SPRAS AND
  LAND1 = YCL_CH14_T005T-LAND1.

IF OK_CODE = 'CREATE' AND SY-SUBRC = 0.

 MESSAGE E041(YCL_CH07_MCLASS01  WITH
  YCL_CH14_T005T-SPRAS YCL_CH14_T005T-LAND1.
 " Language Code.&1 Country Code &2 Already Exists

ELSEIF OK_CODE <> 'CREATE' AND SY-SUBRC <> 0.

MESSAGE E042(YCL_CH07_MCLASS01  WITH
  YCL_CH14_T005T-SPRAS YCL_CH14_T005T-LAND1.
 " Language Code.&1 Country Code &2 Do Not Exist

ENDIF.

ENDMODULE.                 " VALIDATE_INPUT_500  INPUT

*&---------------------------------------------------------------------*
*&      Module  OVER_AND_OUT_500  INPUT
*&---------------------------------------------------------------------*
*       text
*----------------------------------------------------------------------*

***** PAI ON-EXIT screen 500 *****

MODULE OVER_AND_OUT_500 INPUT.

IF OK_CODE = 'EXIT'.
 LEAVE PROGRAM.
ENDIF.

ENDMODULE.                 " OVER_AND_OUT_500  INPUT

*&---------------------------------------------------------------------*
*&      Module  MAIN_PAI_500  INPUT
*&---------------------------------------------------------------------*
*       text
*----------------------------------------------------------------------*

***** PAI (main  screen 500 *****

MODULE MAIN_PAI_500 INPUT.

SAVE_OK_CODE = OK_CODE. " save OK_CODE for processing in screen 550
```

```
REFRESH EXCLUD_FC_TAB.  " initialize internal table for exclude buttons

DATA_CHG_550 = ' '.     " initialize indicator for changed data on screen 550

**************************
CASE OK_CODE.

 WHEN 'DISPLAY'.
 EXCLUD_FC_TAB = 'SAVE'. " exclude save button when display
 APPEND EXCLUD_FC_TAB.
 STRNG = 'Display'(002 .
 LEAVE TO SCREEN 550.

**************************
 WHEN 'CHANGE'.
 STRNG = 'Change'(003 .
 LEAVE TO SCREEN 550.

**************************
 WHEN 'CREATE'.
 CLEAR YCL_CH14_T005T-LANDX. " initialize five fields when create
 CLEAR YCL_CH14_T005T-NATIO.
 CLEAR YCL_CH14_T005T-LANDX50.
 CLEAR YCL_CH14_T005T-NATIO50.
 CLEAR YCL_CH14_T005T-PRQ_SPREGT.
 STRNG = 'Create'(004 .
 LEAVE TO SCREEN 550.

**************************
 WHEN 'DELETE'.
  PERFORM DELETE_SR USING ANSWER YCL_CH14_T005T. " delete confirmation

  IF ANSWER = 1.
   DELETE YCL_CH14_T005T.
   MESSAGE S044(YCL_CH07_MCLASS01  WITH
     YCL_CH14_T005T-SPRAS YCL_CH14_T005T-LAND1
      DISPLAY LIKE 'W'.
   " Language Code.&1 Country Code &2 Deleted!
  ELSE.

  MESSAGE S045(YCL_CH07_MCLASS01 .
   " Deletion Aborted

  ENDIF.

**************************
ENDCASE.
```

```
ENDMODULE.                 " MAIN_PAI_500  INPUT

*&---------------------------------------------------------------------*
*&      Module  STATUS_0550  OUTPUT
*&---------------------------------------------------------------------*
*       text
*----------------------------------------------------------------------*

***** PBO screen 550 *****

MODULE STATUS_0550 OUTPUT.

 SET PF-STATUS 'STAT2' EXCLUDING EXCLUD_FC_TAB[].
 SET TITLEBAR 'TITLE02' WITH 'Table YCL_CH14_T005T'(001  STRNG.
 PERFORM CHANGE_SCR_550_PROP. " adjust screen properties

ENDMODULE.                 " STATUS_0550  OUTPUT

*&---------------------------------------------------------------------*
*&      Module  USER_COMMAND_0550  INPUT
*&---------------------------------------------------------------------*
*       text
*----------------------------------------------------------------------*

***** PAI screen 550 *****

MODULE USER_COMMAND_0550 INPUT.

CASE OK_CODE.

 WHEN 'BACK'.
 IF DATA_CHG_550 = 'X'.
  PERFORM ABORT_SR USING ANSWER YCL_CH14_T005T. " save data pop-up
  IF ANSWER = 1.
   LEAVE TO SCREEN 500.
  ENDIF.
 ELSE.
  LEAVE TO SCREEN 500.
 ENDIF.

WHEN 'SAVE'.
 MODIFY YCL_CH14_T005T.
 DATA_CHG_550 = ' '.
 MESSAGE S043(YCL_CH07_MCLASS01  WITH
   YCL_CH14_T005T-SPRAS YCL_CH14_T005T-LAND1.
  " Language Code.&1 Country Code &2 Saved!

ENDCASE.
```

```
ENDMODULE.                   " USER_COMMAND_0550  INPUT

*&---------------------------------------------------------------------*
*&      Module  SET_CHANGE_550  INPUT
*&---------------------------------------------------------------------*
*       text
*----------------------------------------------------------------------*

***** PAI (change in data  screen 550 *****

MODULE SET_CHANGE_550 INPUT.

 DATA_CHG_550 = 'X'.

ENDMODULE.                   " SET_CHANGE_550  INPUT

************************************************************
***** sub routine to change screen 550 properties  *****

FORM CHANGE_SCR_550_PROP.

LOOP AT SCREEN.
 CASE SAVE_OK_CODE.

 WHEN 'CHANGE'.
  IF SCREEN-GROUP1 = 'DIS'.
   SCREEN-INPUT = 0.
  ELSE.
   SCREEN-INPUT = 1.
  ENDIF.

 WHEN 'DISPLAY'.
   SCREEN-INPUT = 0.

  WHEN 'CREATE'.
  IF SCREEN-GROUP1 = 'DIS'.
   SCREEN-INPUT = 0.
  ELSE.
   SCREEN-INPUT = 1.
  ENDIF.

 ENDCASE.
 MODIFY SCREEN.
ENDLOOP.
```

```
ENDFORM.
***********************

***** sub routine - delete confirmation *****

FORM DELETE_SR USING ANSWR STRU TYPE YCL_CH14_T005T.

DATA. TXT     TYPE STRING.

CONCATENATE
 'Confirm Deletion of Language Code'(005  STRU-SPRAS
  'Country Code'(006  STRU-LAND1
            INTO TXT SEPARATED BY ' '.

CALL FUNCTION 'POPUP_TO_CONFIRM'
  EXPORTING
    TITLEBAR                    = 'Confirm Deletion'(008
    TEXT_QUESTION               = TXT
    TEXT_BUTTON_1               = 'Yes, Delete'(009
    TEXT_BUTTON_2               = 'No To Delete'(010
    DEFAULT_BUTTON              = '2'
    DISPLAY_CANCEL_BUTTON       = ' '
    START_COLUMN                = 40
    START_ROW                   = 2
 IMPORTING
    ANSWER                      = ANSWR
          .

ENDFORM.

*******************************************************************
***** sub routine - abort changes in screen 550 confirmation *****

FORM ABORT_SR USING ANSWR STRU TYPE YCL_CH14_T005T.

DATA. TXT     TYPE STRING.

CONCATENATE
 'Abort Changes of Language Code'(011  STRU-SPRAS
 'Country Code'(006  STRU-LAND1
            INTO TXT SEPARATED BY ' '.

CALL FUNCTION 'POPUP_TO_CONFIRM'
  EXPORTING
    TITLEBAR                    = 'Abort Changes'(012
    TEXT_QUESTION               = TXT
    TEXT_BUTTON_1               = 'Yes, Abort'(013
    TEXT_BUTTON_2               = 'Do Not Abort'(014
    DEFAULT_BUTTON              = '2'
    DISPLAY_CANCEL_BUTTON       = ' '
    START_COLUMN                = 60
    START_ROW                   = 2
 IMPORTING
    ANSWER                      = ANSWR
          .

ENDFORM.
```

The program with its components, etc., will appear in the object navigator like in Figure 14-34.

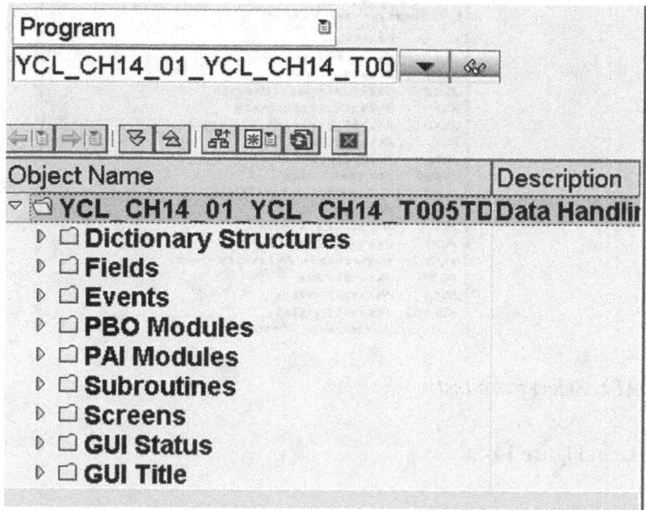

Figure 14-34. *Program with Components in Object Navigator*

In the ABAP program, the notation of specifying a literal with the text symbols has been used. ['Display' (002, etc]. This notation was introduced in Chapter 9. You can create text symbol ids: 001, 002, 003, 004, 005, 006, 008,009, 010, 011, 012, 013, and 014 (there is no text symbol id 007) by double clicking on the text symbol ids: 001, 002, etc., in the statements. You also need to create message text numbers 041, 042, 043, 044, and 045:

```
041      Language Code.&1 Country Code &2 Already Exists
042      Language Code.&1 Country Code &2 Do Not Exist
043      Language Code.&1 Country Code &2 Saved!
044      Language Code.&1 Country Code &2 Deleted!
045      Deletion Aborted
```

These message texts are to be created in message class/id YCL_CH07_MCLASS01.

It now remains for us to carry out the testing of all proposed operations on the data of table YCL_CH14_T005T.

Test Operations

Select the program, and toggle to full screen in the object navigator. Execute the program. Press function key F4 on the field 'Country'. The search help list will appear like in Figure 14-35.

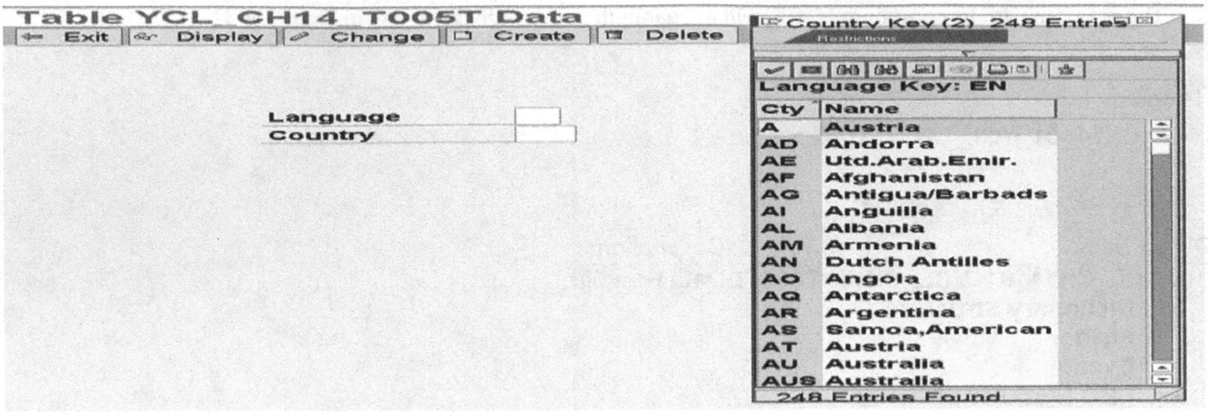

Figure 14-35. *Program YCL_CH14_YCL_CH14_T005TDATA. Select from List*

The screen after selection from the list will appear like in Figure 14-36.

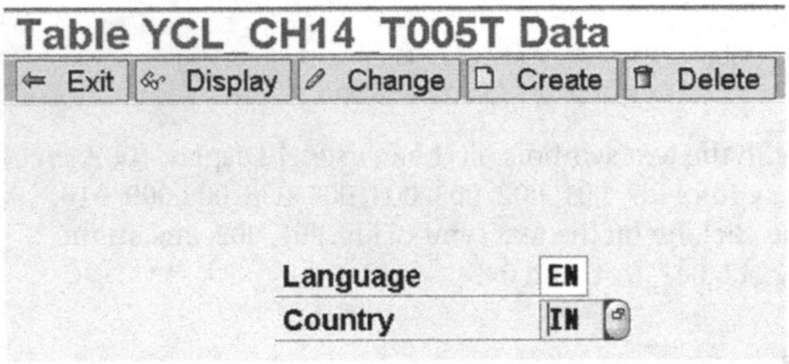

Figure 14-36. *Program YCL_CH14_YCL_CH14_T005TDATA. Screen after Selection*

Press the 'Display' button to display the values of all the fields for the primary key values 'EN' and 'IN'. The screen as appear like in Figure 14-37.

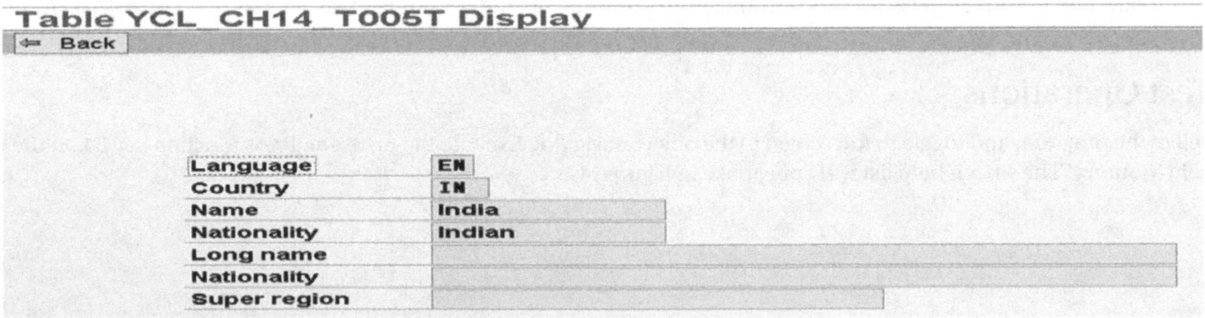

Figure 14-37. *Program YCL_CH14_YCL_CH14_T005TDATA. Display Data*

You have entered the second screen in display mode and that is why the 'Save' button on the application tool bar is excluded.

Press the back button to return to the first screen. On the first screen, press the 'Change' button for the same primary key field values: 'EN' and 'IN'. Enter a value in the field 'Super region', which is presently blank, and the screen will look like Figure 14-38.

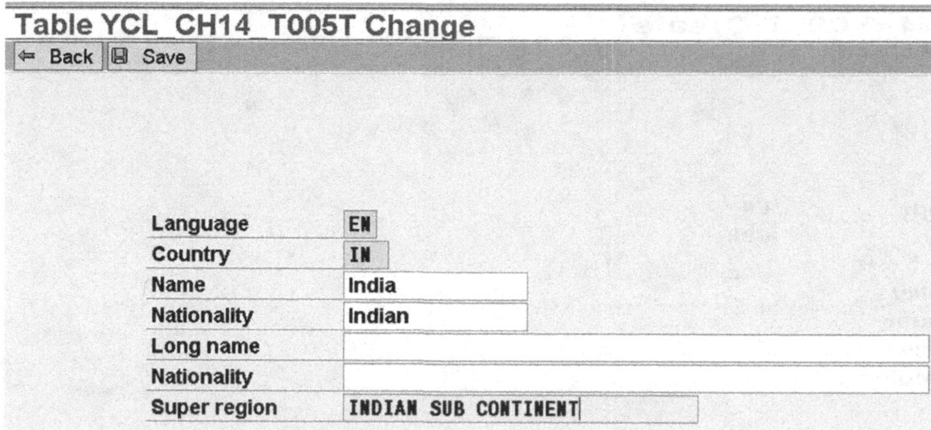

Figure 14-38. *Program YCL_CH14_YCL_CH14_T005TDATA. Change Data*

You have entered the second screen in change mode; that is why the 'Save' button on the application tool bar is appearing. After entering the value in the field 'Super region', press the 'Save' button. The screen after pressing the 'Save' Button will appear like Figure 14-39.

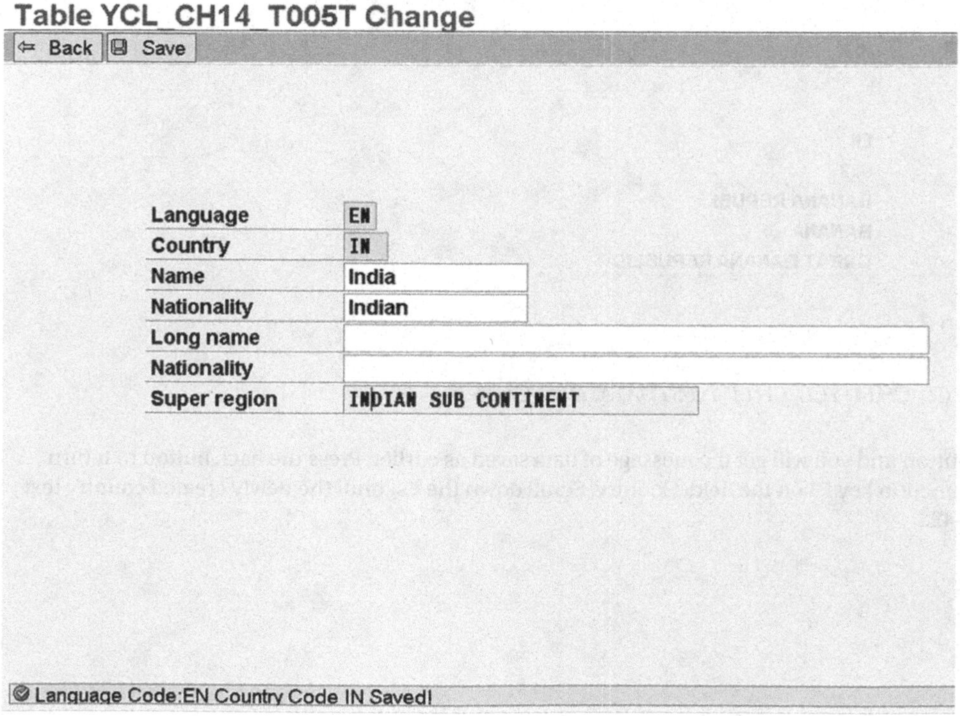

Table YCL_CH14_T005T Change

Back Save

Language EN
Country IN
Name India
Nationality Indian
Long name
Nationality
Super region INDIAN SUB CONTINENT

Language Code:EN Country Code IN Saved!

Figure 14-39. *Program YCL_CH14_YCL_CH14_T005TDATA. Data Changed, Saved*

Press the 'Back' button. On the opening screen, enter values 'EN,' 'GBR' in the opening screen fields. Press the 'Create' button. The second screen will contain blanks in all the input text fields waiting for input. The screen will appear like in Figure 14-40.

Table YCL_CH14_T005T Create

Back | Save

Language	EN
Country	GBR
Name	
Nationality	
Long name	
Nationality	
Super region	

Figure 14-40. *Program YCL_CH14_YCL_CH14_T005TDATA. Create Data*

The screen after entering values will appear like in Figure 14-41.

Table YCL_CH14_T005T Create

Back | Save

Language	EN
Country	GBR
Name	BANANA REPUBLI
Nationality	BANANA
Long name	GREAT BANANA REPUBLIC
Nationality	
Super region	

Figure 14-41. *Program YCL_CH14_YCL_CH14_T005TDATA. Data Created*

Press on the 'Save' button and you will get the message of data saved as earlier. Press the back button to return to the first screen. Press function key F4 on the field 'Country.' Scroll down the list until the newly created country text appears like in Figure 14-42.

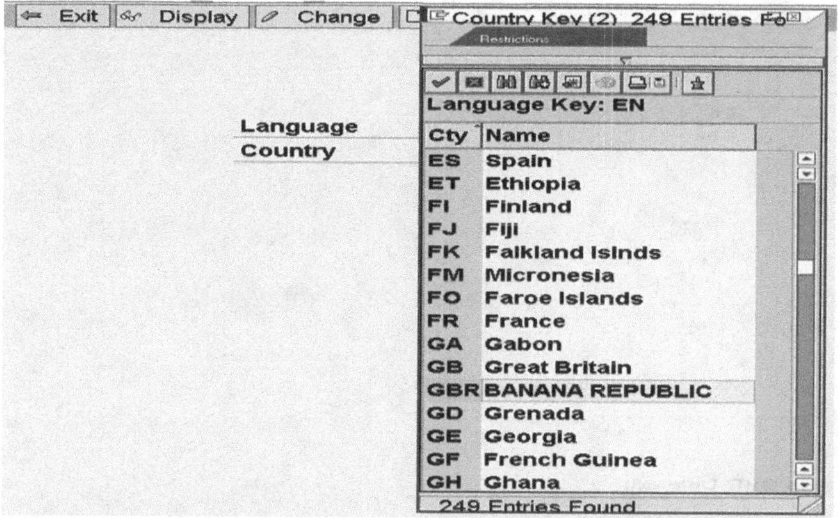

Figure 14-42. *Program YCL_CH14_YCL_CH14_T005TDATA. List after New Data*

Let this country text be deleted. Select from list/enter values 'EN' and 'GBR'. Press the delete button. A pop-up dialog box for delete confirmation will appear like in Figure 14-43.

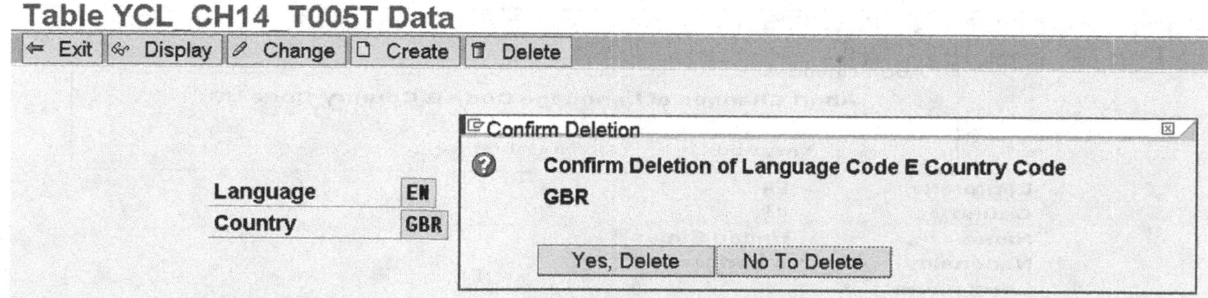

Figure 14-43. *Program YCL_CH14_YCL_CH14_T005TDATA. Confirm Delete*

You can confirm or abort the deletion. Confirm the deletion. The deletion alert message will appear like in Figure 14-44.

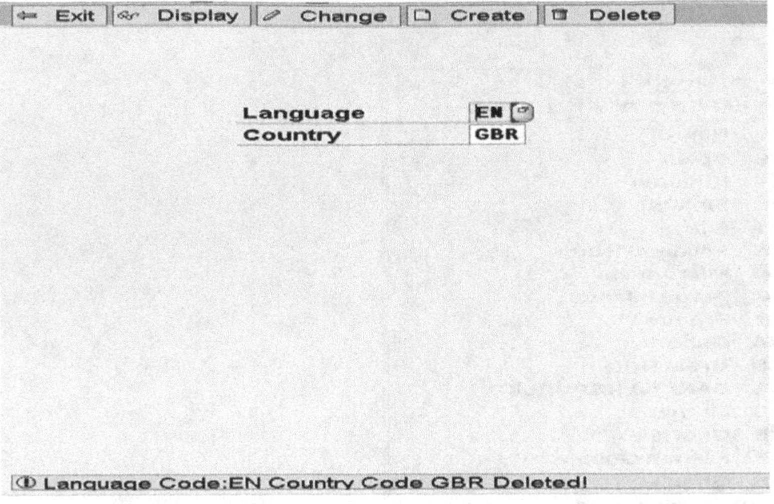

Figure 14-44. *Program YCL_CH14_YCL_CH14_T005TDATA. Row Deleted*

Enter values 'EN', 'US' in the 'Language' and 'Country' fields respectively. Press the change button to navigate to the second screen. On the second screen, enter some value in the field – say, 'Super region'. Now press the back button without saving. The abort changes pop-up alert will appear as shown in Figure 14-45.

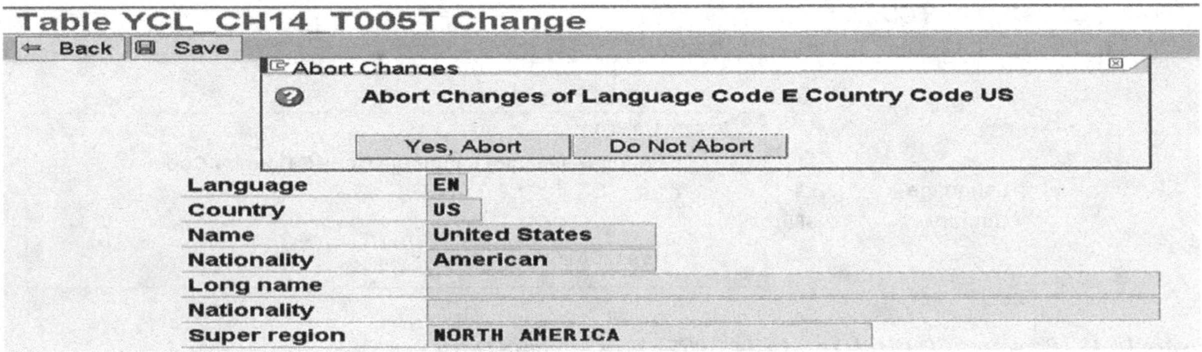

Figure 14-45. *Program YCL_CH14_YCL_CH14_T005TDATA. Confirming Abort Changes*

You have tested all the specifications that the program was set out to fulfill.

Recapitulation. A recapitulation of the hands-on exercise.

- The hands-on exercise performs all the operations needed to maintain data in a table.
- The hands-on exercise has the look and feel of a SAP data creation of common entities: customers, vendors, materials et al. Accept primary key data on the opening screen and further data on subsequent screens.
- You have been introduced to the object navigator, which enables the maintenance of all workbench objects from a single point in a single external session.

- In the layout editor of the screen painter, you were introduced to the procedure of placing fields of the DDIC structure on the screen with labels from their respective data elements. This is the frequently used mode of placing fields on the screen.
- You were introduced to two open SQL statements: DELETE... and MODIFY....
- You were introduced to the variations of the module invoking statements in the *flow logic* area. The concept of conditional execution of a module has been introduced. Like: MODULE SET_CHANGE_550 ON CHAIN-REQUEST. The module SET_CHANGE_550 gets executed only if the screen has been modified.
- You have used the combination of type 'E' button with the module ending with the phrase AT EXIT-COMMAND. This was used to skip input validation when quitting a program.

This concludes the hands-on exercise of maintaining a database table data with a screen program.

Hands-on Exercise. Demonstrate Search Help Import Parameters, Screen Event PROCESS ON VALUE-REQUEST – POV, etc

The feature of import parameters in DDIC objects search help can be better demonstrated in a screen programming environment.

There are business scenarios where you enter value/s in field/s on the screen. A search help attached to some other field will filter out data based on the value/s entered in earlier fields. The search help then imports field value/s from the screen.

Scenario

Let a specific scenario be considered. Suppose you have a screen with the following fields:

LIFNR	Vendor Code
.....	
BUKRS	Company Code
.....	
EBELN	Purchasing Document

You attach a search help to the field 'EBELN'. (Purchasing document). When you press function key F4 on the 'EBELN' field, you would like the list of purchasing documents to be filtered on the basis of values in the two other fields 'LIFNR' and 'BUKRS' (i.e., purchasing documents belonging to a specific combination of values of vendor code and company code). You will implement this with import parameters of the search help. The search help attached to the field 'EBELN' should have two importing parameters: 'LIFNR' and 'BUKRS'.

Each imported parameter can be in display mode; that is, the user cannot change the imported value in the restrictive dialog box and can be in edit mode (i.e., the user can change the imported value in the restrictive dialog box). A default value can also be assigned to the import parameter.

All this will work, provided all the participating fields (the fields of the present scenario): 'LIFNR', 'BUKRS', and 'EBELN' belong to the same structure as one entity.

Scenario Implementation

Let the described scenario be implemented with an exercise involving screen programming. You are not performing any other task (like fetching data from a database table, etc.) other than demonstrating the import parameter feature of search help.

Let there be a DDIC structure with the following fields:

LIFNR	Vendor Code
NAME1	Vendor Name
STRAS	Street
ORT01	City
BUKRS	Company Code
EBELN	Purchasing Document
BEDAT	Purchasing Document Date
WAERS	Document Currency

You have some extra fields just to make it feel like a real-life scenario.

The DDIC structure YCL_CH14_VENDOR_PD_STRU will look like Figure 14-46.

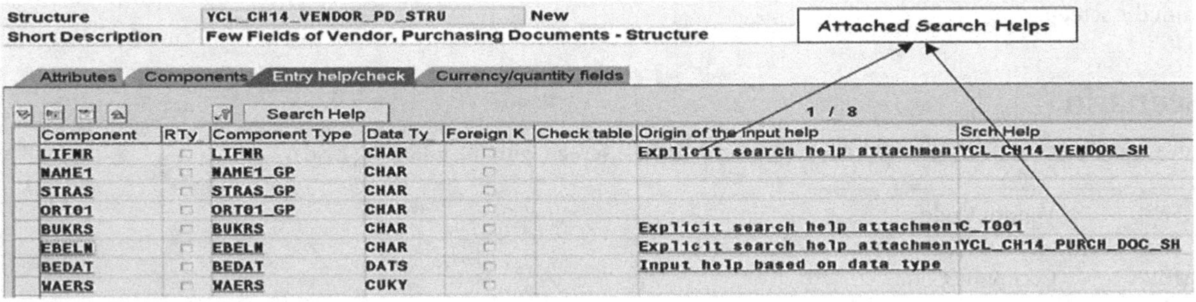

Structure YCL_CH14_VENDOR_PD_STRU New
Short Description Few Fields of Vendor, Purchasing Documents - Structure

Attached Search Helps

Attributes | Components | Entry help/check | Currency/quantity fields

Search Help 1 / 8

Component	RTy	Component Type	Data Ty	Foreign K	Check table	Origin of the input help	Srch Help
LIFNR		LIFNR	CHAR			Explicit search help attachmen	YCL_CH14_VENDOR_SH
NAME1		NAME1_GP	CHAR				
STRAS		STRAS_GP	CHAR				
ORT01		ORT01_GP	CHAR				
BUKRS		BUKRS	CHAR			Explicit search help attachmen	C_T001
EBELN		EBELN	CHAR			Explicit search help attachmen	YCL_CH14_PURCH_DOC_SH
BEDAT		BEDAT	DATS			Input help based on data type	
WAERS		WAERS	CUKY				

Figure 14-46. *DDIC Structure. YCL_CH14_VENDOR_PD_STRU*

This structure will be used to position fields on the screen.

As indicated in Figure 14-46, search helps are attached to the fields 'LIFNR' and 'EBELN'. The search help attached to the field 'EBELN' (YCL_CH14_PURCH_DOC_SH) is meant for demonstration. You have attached your own search help to the field 'LIFNR' to enable the transfer of name and city to the screen fields 'NAME1' and 'ORT01' upon selection of vendor from the selection list of the search help. This search help is YCL_CH14_VENDOR_SH. The default search help 'KRED' would not have performed this.

A screen shot of search help YCL_CH14_VENDOR_SH is shown in Figure 14-47.

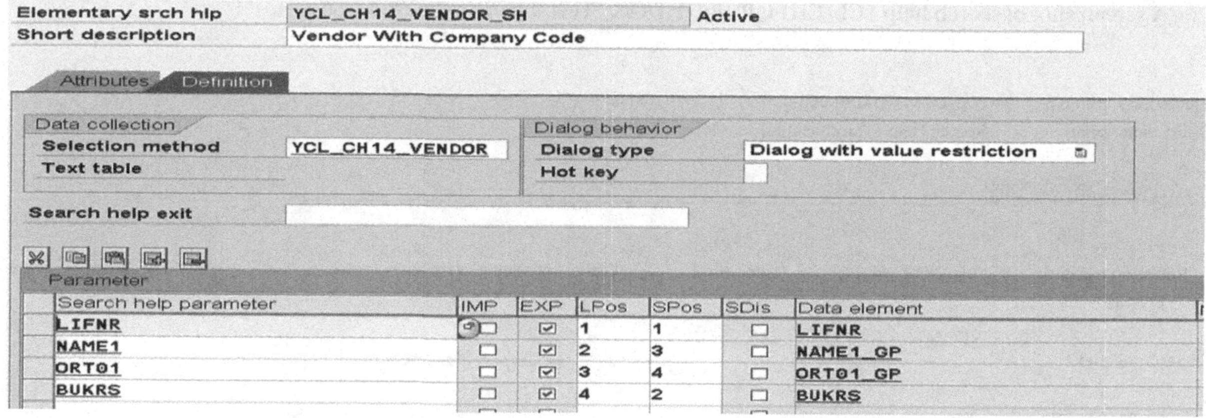

Figure 14-47. DDIC Search Help. YCL_CH14_VENDOR_SH

Screen shots of the database view YCL_CH14_vendor used by the search help YCL_CH14_VENDOR_SH is shown in Figures 14-48 and 14-49.

Database view: YCL_CH14_VENDOR Active
Short Description: View For Search Help

Attributes | Table/Join Conditions | View Flds | Selection Conditions | Maint.Status

Tables
T001
LFB1
LFA1

Join conditions

Table	Field name	=	Table	Field name
LFA1	MANDT	=	LFB1	MANDT
LFA1	LIFNR	=	LFB1	LIFNR
LFB1	MANDT	=	T001	MANDT
LFB1	BUKRS	=	T001	BUKRS

Figure 14-48. Database View YCL_CH14_VENDOR- Tables & Join Conditions

Database view: YCL_CH14_VENDOR Active
Short Description: View For Search Help

Attributes | Table/Join Conditions | View Flds | Selection Conditions | Maint.Status

Table fields

View field	Table	Field	Key	Data elem.	Mod	DTyp	Length
MANDT	LFA1	MANDT	☑	MANDT	☐	CLNT	3
LIFNR	LFA1	LIFNR	☑	LIFNR	☐	CHAR	10
BUKRS	LFB1	BUKRS	☑	BUKRS	☐	CHAR	4
NAME1	LFA1	NAME1	☐	NAME1_GP	☐	CHAR	35
ORT01	LFA1	ORT01	☐	ORT01_GP	☐	CHAR	35
BUTXT	T001	BUTXT	☐	BUTXT	☐	CHAR	25

Figure 14-49. Database View YCL_CH14_VENDOR- Fields

A screen shot of search help YCL_CH14_PURCH_DOC_SH is shown in Figure 14-50.

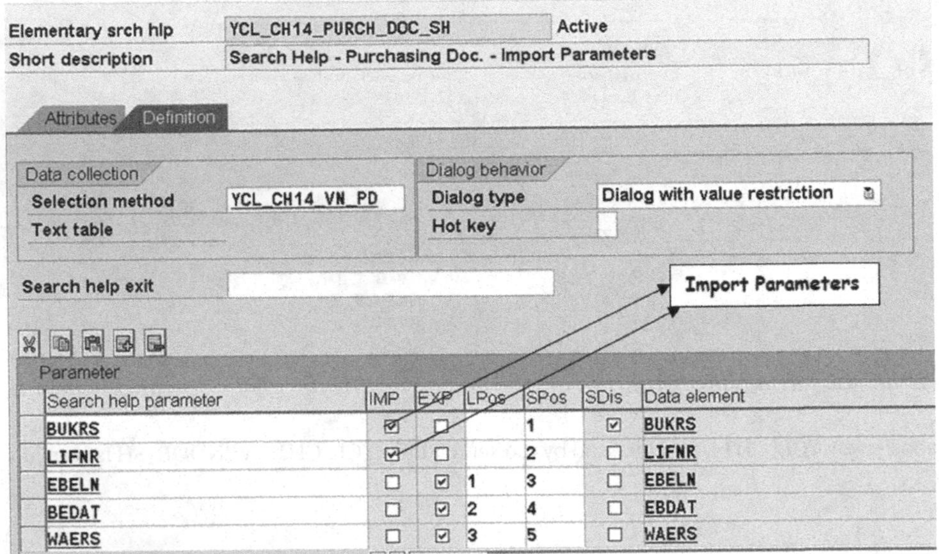

Figure 14-50. *DDIC Search Help. YCL_CH14_PURCH_DOC_SH*

The search help YCL_CH14_PURCH_DOC_SH uses the database view YCL_CH14_VN_PD. Screen shots of the view YCL_CH14_VN_PD is shown in Figures 14-51 and 14-52.

Database view YCL_CH14_VN_PD Active
Short Description View To Be Used In Search Help

Attributes | Table/Join Conditions | View Flds | Selection Conditions | Maint.Status

Tables
EKKO
LFB1
LFA1

Join conditions

Table	Field name	=	Table	Field name
LFA1	MANDT	=	LFB1	MANDT
LFA1	LIFNR	=	LFB1	LIFNR
LFB1	MANDT	=	EKKO	MANDT
LFB1	LIFNR	=	EKKO	LIFNR
LFB1	BUKRS	=	EKKO	BUKRS

Figure 14-51. *DDIC View. YCL_CH14_VN_PD – Tables & Join Conditions*

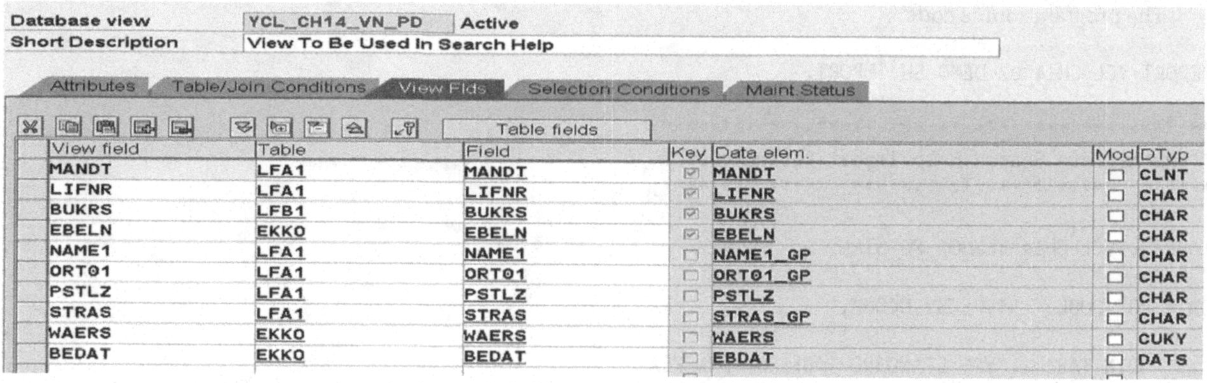
Database view
YCL_CH14_VN_PD
Active
Short Description
View To Be Used In Search Help
Attributes
Table/Join Conditions
View Flds
Selection Conditions
Maint.Status
Table fields

View field	Table	Field	Key	Data elem.	Mod	DTyp
MANDT	LFA1	MANDT	☑	MANDT	☐	CLNT
LIFNR	LFA1	LIFNR	☑	LIFNR	☐	CHAR
BUKRS	LFB1	BUKRS	☑	BUKRS	☐	CHAR
EBELN	EKKO	EBELN	☑	EBELN	☐	CHAR
NAME1	LFA1	NAME1	☐	NAME1_GP	☐	CHAR
ORT01	LFA1	ORT01	☐	ORT01_GP	☐	CHAR
PSTLZ	LFA1	PSTLZ	☐	PSTLZ	☐	CHAR
STRAS	LFA1	STRAS	☐	STRAS_GP	☐	CHAR
WAERS	EKKO	WAERS	☐	WAERS	☐	CUKY
BEDAT	EKKO	BEDAT	☐	EBDAT	☐	DATS

Figure 14-52. *DDIC View. YCL_CH14_VN_PD - Fields*

Create an ABAP program YCL_CH14_02_DEMO_SH_IMPORT
Place the fields of structure YCL_CH14_VENDOR_PD_STRU on the screen as shown in Figure 14-53.

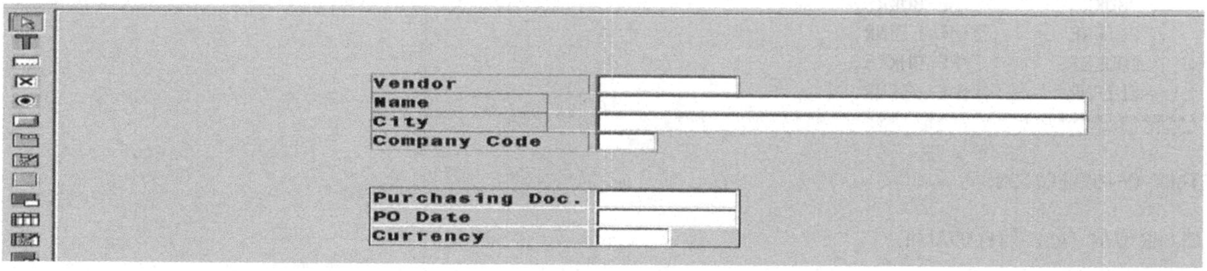
Vendor
Name
City
Company Code
Purchasing Doc.
PO Date
Currency

Figure 14-53. *Program YCL_CH14_02_DEMO_SH_IMPORT - Screen Layout*

The *flow logic* code:

```
PROCESS BEFORE OUTPUT.
 MODULE STATUS_0200.
*
PROCESS AFTER INPUT.
 MODULE USER_COMMAND_0200.

 PROCESS ON VALUE-REQUEST.
  FIELD YCL_CH14_VENDOR_PD_STRU-LIFNR MODULE POV_LIFNR.
```

The program source code:

```
REPORT YCL_CH14_02_DEMO_SH_IMPORT.

**********************************************
* Demonstrate Search Help Import Parameters **
**********************************************

TABLES. YCL_CH14_VENDOR_PD_STRU.

DATA. OK_CODE    TYPE SY-UCOMM,

      DYN_TAB1   TYPE STANDARD TABLE OF DYNPREAD
                  WITH HEADER LINE, " to output LIFNR BUKRS NAME1 ORT01

      DYN_TAB2   TYPE STANDARD TABLE OF DYNPREAD
                  WITH HEADER LINE. " to output blank EBELN BEDAT WAERS

DATA. RTAB         TYPE STANDARD TABLE OF DDSHRETVAL WITH HEADER LINE,
      PBUKRS       TYPE BUKRS,
      PLIFNR       TYPE LIFNR,
      CBUKRS       TYPE BUKRS,
      CLIFNR       TYPE LIFNR.
*****************************************************************

START-OF-SELECTION.

 CLEAR DYN_TAB2-FIELDVALUE.

 DYN_TAB2-FIELDNAME = 'YCL_CH14_VENDOR_PD_STRU-EBELN'.
 APPEND DYN_TAB2.

 DYN_TAB2-FIELDNAME = 'YCL_CH14_VENDOR_PD_STRU-BEDAT'.
 APPEND DYN_TAB2.

 DYN_TAB2-FIELDNAME = 'YCL_CH14_VENDOR_PD_STRU-WAERS'.
 APPEND DYN_TAB2.

 CALL SCREEN 200.
*&---------------------------------------------------------------------*
*&      Module  STATUS_0200  OUTPUT
*&---------------------------------------------------------------------*
*       text
*----------------------------------------------------------------------*
MODULE STATUS_0200 OUTPUT.

 SET PF-STATUS 'STAT1'.
```

```
ENDMODULE.                    " STATUS_0200  OUTPUT
*&---------------------------------------------------------------------*
*&      Module  USER_COMMAND_0200  INPUT
*&---------------------------------------------------------------------*
*       text
*----------------------------------------------------------------------*
MODULE USER_COMMAND_0200 INPUT.
IF OK_CODE = 'EXIT'.
 LEAVE PROGRAM.
ENDIF.
ENDMODULE.                    " USER_COMMAND_0200  INPUT
*&---------------------------------------------------------------------*
*&      Module  POV_LIFNR  INPUT
*&---------------------------------------------------------------------*
*       text
*----------------------------------------------------------------------*
MODULE POV_LIFNR INPUT.

 CALL FUNCTION 'F4IF_FIELD_VALUE_REQUEST'
   EXPORTING
     TABNAME = 'YCL_CH14_VENDOR_PD_STRU'
     FIELDNAME = 'LIFNR'
     DYNPPROG = 'YCL_CH14_02_DEMO_SH_IMPORT'
     DYNPNR = '0200'
     DYNPROFIELD = 'LIFNR'
   TABLES
     RETURN_TAB = RTAB.

 REFRESH DYN_TAB1.

 IF LINES( RTAB  > 0.

  READ TABLE RTAB WITH KEY FIELDNAME = 'BUKRS'.
  CBUKRS = RTAB-FIELDVAL.

  READ TABLE RTAB WITH KEY FIELDNAME = 'LIFNR'.
  CLIFNR = RTAB-FIELDVAL.

  LOOP AT RTAB.

   CONCATENATE 'YCL_CH14_VENDOR_PD_STRU-' RTAB-FIELDNAME
    INTO DYN_TAB1-FIELDNAME.
   DYN_TAB1-FIELDVALUE = RTAB-FIELDVAL.
   APPEND DYN_TAB1.

  ENDLOOP.

  IF CBUKRS <> PBUKRS OR CLIFNR <> PLIFNR.
   APPEND LINES OF DYN_TAB2[] TO DYN_TAB1.
  ENDIF.
```

```
 CALL FUNCTION 'DYNP_VALUES_UPDATE'
  EXPORTING
    DYNAME                        = 'YCL_CH14_02_DEMO_SH_IMPORT'
    DYNUMB                        = '0200'
  TABLES
    DYNPFIELDS                    = DYN_TAB1[]
          .

 PBUKRS = CBUKRS .
 PLIFNR = CLIFNR.
ENDIF.

ENDMODULE.                    " POV_LIFNR  INPUT
```

The detailed steps of each object creation have been skipped; the steps have been described several times.

You are triggering the event PROCESS ON VALUE-REQUEST (POV for short) for the field YCL_CH14_T005T-LIFNR. (See the *flow logic* code above). This event is equivalent to the Selection Screen event AT SELECTION-SCREEN ON VALUE-REQUEST. The event is triggered when the user presses the function key F4 on the field for which you are triggering the event, and an ABAP developer can put custom code for a filter dialog box, selection list, etc., instead of using search help. In the present context, you are triggering the event not for a custom coded selection list, etc., but to get the control and custom code for some other purpose than just producing the selection list, etc.

You want to initialize the bottom three fields: 'EBELN', 'BEDAT', and 'WAERS' every time there is a change in the values of two of the above fields 'LIFNR' and 'BUKRS'. This makes sense and produces a sophisticated effect. The invocation of the function module F4IF_FIELD_VALUE_REQUEST invokes the search help attached to the field provided as a parameter to this function module. So ultimately you are using the search help. But you are getting the control to locate the code that serves your purpose of initializing the bottom three fields on change of value of 'LIFNR' and 'BUKRS' fields. And simultaneously, the POV event is being demonstrated practically.

The parameters provided in this program to the function module F4IF_FIELD_VALUE_REQUEST are self-obvious except for the TABLES parameter RETURN_TAB.

If you do not provide this parameter, the program code in the event module gets executed first, regardless of the position of the program code, then the search help dialog boxes appears. After selection from the search help selection list, the values are returned to the respective screen fields.

If you provide this parameter RETURN_TAB, the program code located after the CALL F4IF_FIELD_VALUE_REQUEST statement in the event module does not get executed first. The search help dialog boxes appear first. After selection from the search help selection list, the values are returned not to the screen fields but in the internal table specified with formal TABLES parameter RETURN_TAB. The program code located after the CALL F4IF_FIELD_VALUE_REQUEST gets executed next. The returned values from the search help can then be copied to the screen fields using the function module DYNP_VALUES_UPDATE. This is what you are doing; you wanted control after the return of values from search help.

Let the program be tested. Switch to full screen mode in the object navigator.

Select the program and execute. Press function key F4 on the vendor field. Enter values in the restrictive dialog box as shown in Figure 14-54.

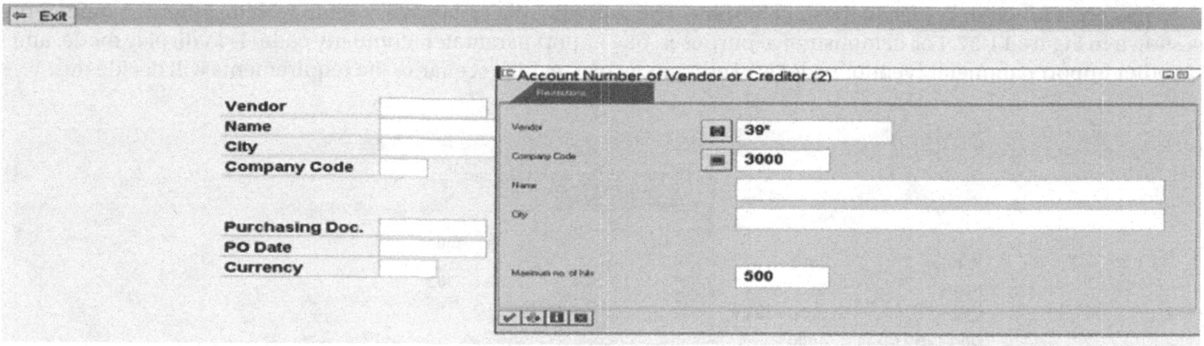

Figure 14-54. Program YCL_CH14_02_DEMO_SH_IMPORT – F4 on 'LIFNR'

Only the vendor codes starting with '39' and company code equal to '3000' will appear in the list as shown in Figure 14-55.

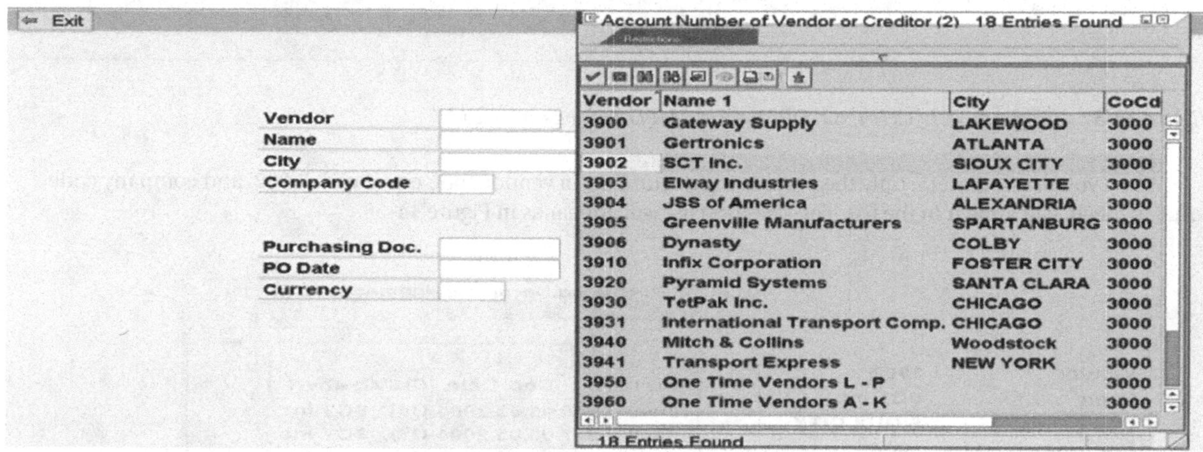

Figure 14-55. Program YCL_CH14_02_DEMO_SH_IMPORT – F4 List on 'LIFNR'

Make a selection on the list as shown in Figure 14-56.

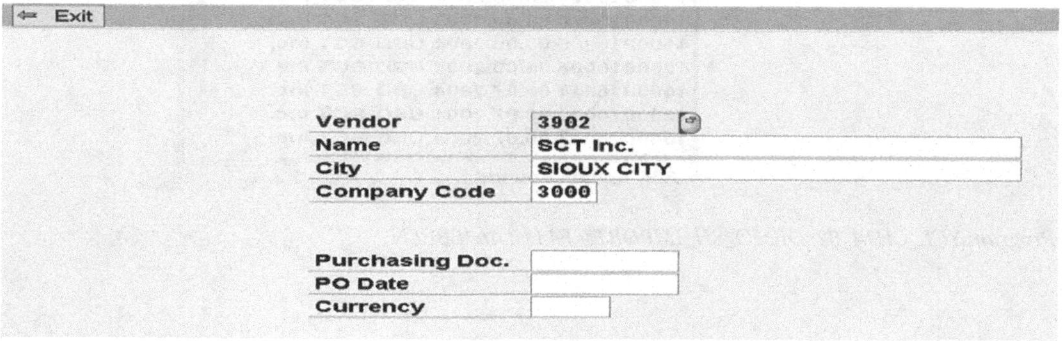

Figure 14-56. Program YCL_CH14_02_DEMO_SH_IMPORT – Vendor Selection

Now press function key F4 on the field 'EBELN'. The restrictive dialog box will pop up with the import parameters as shown in Figure 14-57. For demonstrative purposes, one import parameter (company code) is in display mode, and the other import parameter (vendor code) is in edit mode. In a real-life scenario, the requirements will decide this.

Exit
Purchasing Document Number (2)
Vendor
3902
Name
SCT Inc.
City
SIOUX CITY
Company Code
3000
Purchasing Doc.
PO Date
Currency
3000
3902
500

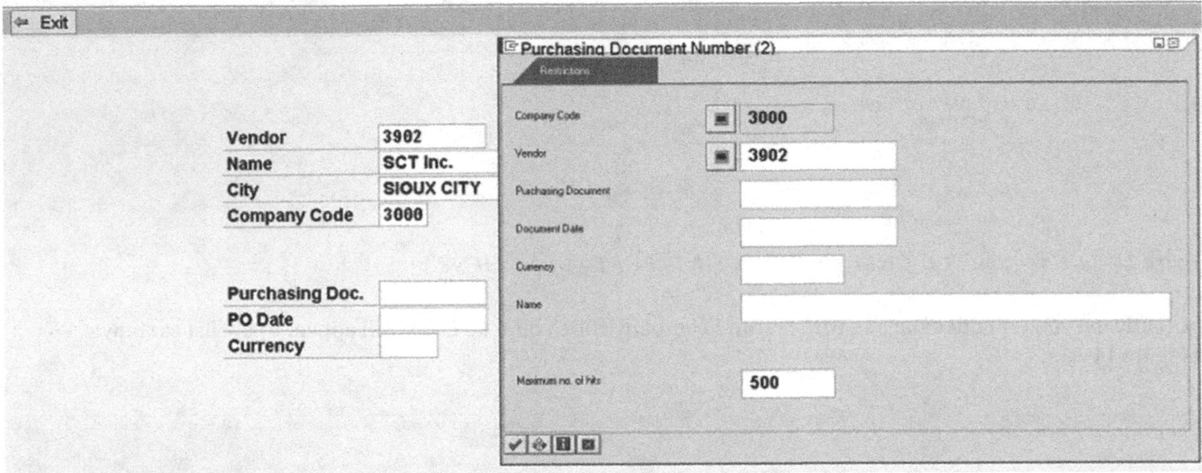

Figure 14-57. *Program YCL_CH14_02_DEMO_SH_IMPORT - F4 on 'EBELN'*

When you press <Enter>, only the purchasing documents of vendor code equal with '3902' and company code equal to '3000' will appear in the list. The selection list will appear as in Figure 14-58.

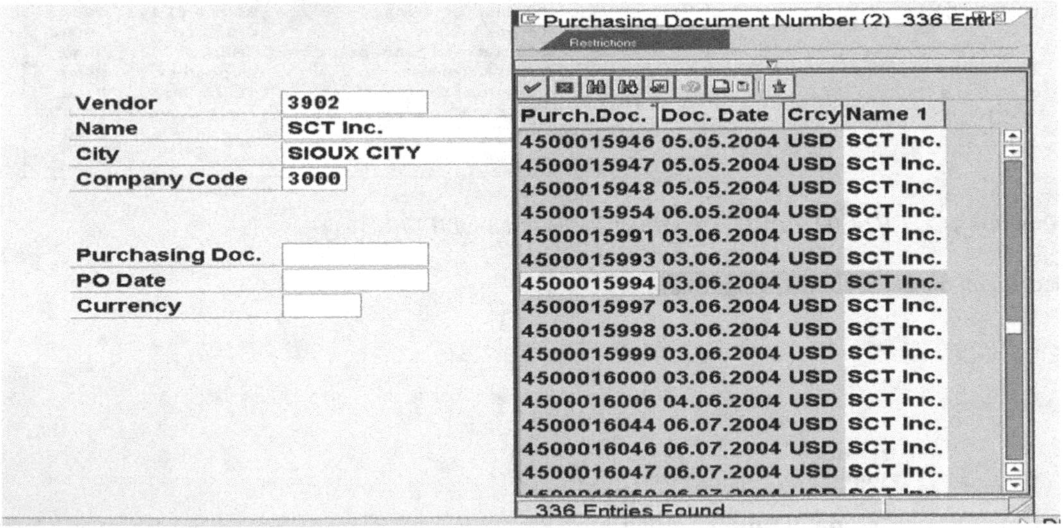

Purchasing Document Number (2) 336 Entri
Vendor
3902
Name
SCT Inc.
City
SIOUX CITY
Company Code
3000
Purchasing Doc.
PO Date
Currency
Purch.Doc. Doc. Date Crcy Name 1
4500015946 05.05.2004 USD SCT Inc.
4500015947 05.05.2004 USD SCT Inc.
4500015948 05.05.2004 USD SCT Inc.
4500015954 06.05.2004 USD SCT Inc.
4500015991 03.06.2004 USD SCT Inc.
4500015993 03.06.2004 USD SCT Inc.
4500015994 03.06.2004 USD SCT Inc.
4500015997 03.06.2004 USD SCT Inc.
4500015998 03.06.2004 USD SCT Inc.
4500015999 03.06.2004 USD SCT Inc.
4500016000 03.06.2004 USD SCT Inc.
4500016006 04.06.2004 USD SCT Inc.
4500016044 06.07.2004 USD SCT Inc.
4500016046 06.07.2004 USD SCT Inc.
4500016047 06.07.2004 USD SCT Inc.
336 Entries Found

Figure 14-58. *Program YCL_CH14_02_DEMO_SH_IMPORT - F4 List on 'EBELN'*

After making a selection of a purchasing document from the list, the screen will look like the one in Figure 14-59.

Vendor	3902
Name	SCT Inc.
City	SIOUX CITY
Company Code	3000
Purchasing Doc.	4500015994
PO Date	03.06.2004
Currency	USD

Figure 14-59. *Program YCL_CH14_02_DEMO_SH_IMPORT - Vendor Code, Company Code & Purchasing Doc. Selection*

Try with the values vendor code pattern '90*' and company code equal to '1000'. on the restrictive dialog box. Select the vendor code '90210' from the filtered vendor list, etc.

You can verify the initialization of the bottom three fields: 'EBELN', 'BEDAT', and 'WAERS' on change of values fields 'LIFNR' and/or 'BUKRS'.

A Qualification. The program is not coded to take care of normal PAI triggering apart from the 'EXIT' button. If the user presses the <Enter> key, you are not processing it in terms of validating the data, etc. The program assumes that you will not manually enter values in the fields of vendor and company code and that values will be fetched through a selection from the search help selection list. The program is only to demonstrate the import parameter feature of search help and the POV event.

Hands-on Exercise. Simulate Tab Strip Element Using Sub Screen Area, Sub Screens and Application Tool Bar Buttons

Tab Strip Element/Control

The tab strip element or tab strip control is a very common element in any Graphic User Interface (GUI). It enables the same area of screen to contain related information or options. A commonplace example of tab strip is in the MS Word software document maintenance screen as shown in Figure 14-60.

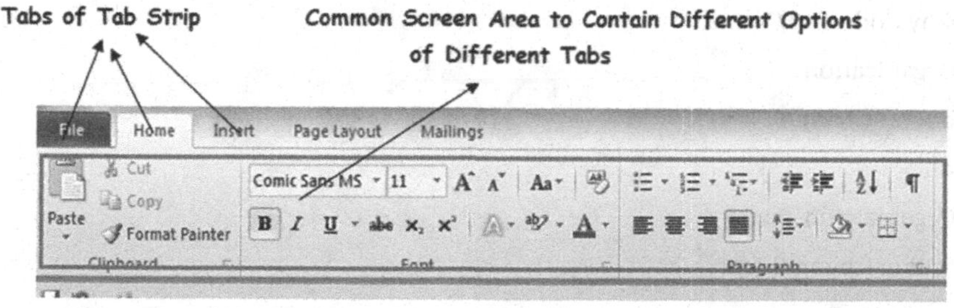

Figure 14-60. *Example of Tab Strip - Word Document Screen*

You will create an ABAP Screen program and related objects to illustrate the simulation of a tab strip control.

Scenario

Let a tab strip control be simulated with two buttons on the application toolbar and the same can be extended to any number of buttons. Let there be a scenario. The customer information can be categorized. You have used part of one category of customer information (i.e., address or contact). You will consider the following fields as customer contact information (table, field, field descriptions).

You will have one more category of customer information: organizational. A customer is associated with different organizational units. You have already been exposed to one prime organizational unit: the company code. You are being introduced to three more organizational units with which a customer is associated from the perspective of the functional module 'Sales & distribution.' These organizational units are:

- Sales Organization
- Distribution Channel
- Division

The three together is called a sales group.

You will consider the following fields as customer organizational information.

There are eight database tables containing the contact and organizational information (Tables 14-2 and 14-3).

Table 14-2. *Fields - Customer Contact Info*

Table	Field	Description
KNA1	STRAS	Street
KNA1	ORT01	City
KNA1	PSTLZ	Postal Code
T005T	LANDX	Country Text
KNA1	TELF1	Telephone No.
KNA1	TELFX	Telefax No.

Table 14-3. *Fields - Customer Organizational Info*

Table	Field	Description
KNB1	BUKRS	Company Code
T001	BUTXT	Company Code Text/Name
KNVV	VKORG	Sales Organization
KNVV	VTWEG	Distribution Channel
KNVV	SPART	Division
TVKOT	VTEXT	Sales Organization Text
TVTWT	VTEXT	Distribution Channel Text
TSPAT	VTEXT	Division Text

You can gather all the information - contact and organizational - in one database view using the eight database tables: KNA1, KNB1, T001, T005T, KNVV, TVKOT, TVTWT, and TSPAT.

If you try to implement this with a single database view, it runs into problems. On our system (the author's), a database view with more than twenty lines of join conditions is having problems. So, to reduce the lines of join conditions, the database table T005T is being excluded from the database view. A data model/ER diagram constituting the remaining seven database tables is shown in Figure 14-61.

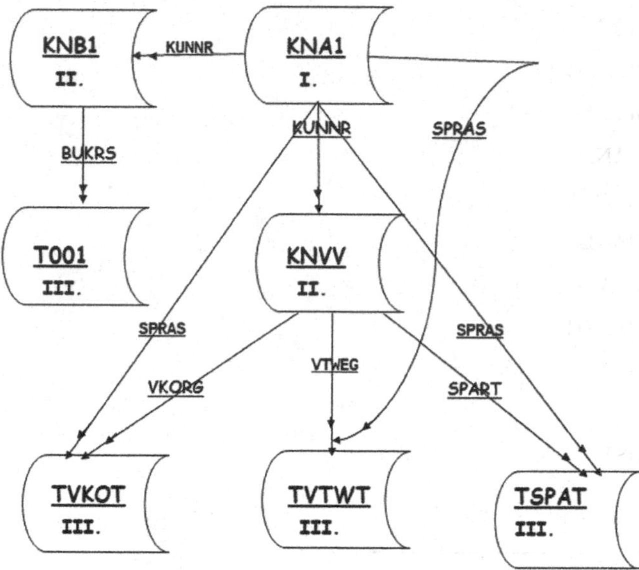

Figure 14-61. *ER diagram for a Database View of Contact and Organizational Info*

Data for the Scenario

You will create a database view for the data model in Figure 14-61. You will access the data in database table T005T separately (outside the view).

It is a good idea to look up the structures and relationships of the database tables: KNB1, KNVV, TVKOT, TVTWT, and TSPAT. Please do so as an additional exercise.

The database view is YCL_CH14_CUST_VW. The database tables and join conditions of the view are listed.

Table 14-4. *View YCL_CH14_CUST_VW - Tables & Join Conditions*

Tables	Table	Field name	Table	Field name
TSPAT	KNA1	MANDT	KNB1	MANDT
TVTWT	KNA1	KUNNR	KNB1	KUNNR
TVKOT	KNA1	MANDT	KNVV	MANDT
T001	KNA1	KUNNR	KNVV	KUNNR
KNVV	KNB1	MANDT	T001	MANDT
KNB1	KNB1	BUKRS	T001	BUKRS

(continued)

Table 14-4. *(continued)*

Tables	Table	Field name	Table	Field name
KNA1	KNA1	MANDT	TVKOT	MANDT
	KNA1	SPRAS	TVKOT	SPRAS
	KNA1	MANDT	TVTWT	MANDT
	KNA1	SPRAS	TVTWT	SPRAS
	KNA1	MANDT	TSPAT	MANDT
	KNA1	SPRAS	TSPAT	SPRAS
	KNVV	MANDT	TVKOT	MANDT
	KNVV	VKORG	TVKOT	VKORG
	KNVV	MANDT	TVTWT	MANDT
	KNVV	VTWEG	TVTWT	VTWEG
	KNVV	MANDT	TSPAT	MANDT
	KNVV	SPART	TSPAT	SPART

The list of fields in the database view YCL_CH14_CUST_VW.

Table 14-5. *View YCL_CH14_CUST_VW - View Fields*

View field	Table	Field	Primary Key/Remarks
MANDT	KNA1	MANDT	X
KUNNR	KNA1	KUNNR	X
BUKRS	KNB1	BUKRS	X
VKORG	KNVV	VKORG	X
VTWEG	KNVV	VTWEG	X
SPART	KNVV	SPART	X
SPRAS1	TVKOT	SPRAS	X
SPRAS2	TVTWT	SPRAS	X
SPRAS3	TSPAT	SPRAS	X
NAME1	KNA1	NAME1	
STRAS	KNA1	STRAS	
ORT01	KNA1	ORT01	
PSTLZ	KNA1	PSTLZ	
TELF1	KNA1	TELF1	
TELFX	KNA1	TELFX	

(continued)

Table 14-5. *(continued)*

View field	Table	Field	Primary Key/Remarks
LAND1	KNA1	LAND1	For Connect to T005T outside of view
BUTXT	T001	BUTXT	
VTEXT1	TVKOT	VTEXT	
VTEXT2	TVTWT	VTEXT	
VTEXT3	TSPAT	VTEXT	

A customer is associated with a language: a language with which to communicate with a customer. It is represented by the field 'SPRAS' of DDIC type 'LANG' in the structure of database table KNA1. You are retrieving the text of the sales organization,('VKORG'), distribution channel,('VTWEG'), and division,('SPART'), in the language of the customer. Hence the join conditions between the database table KNA1 and the database text tables: TVKOT, TVTWT, and TSPAT. The field name for the texts in the three database text tables TVKOT, TVTWT, and TSPAT is the same (i.e., 'VTEXT'). In the view, with the purpose of assigning unique field names, you have assigned the names 'VTEXT1' 'VTEXT2,' and 'VTEXT3' respectively. Similar is the case when incorporating the field 'SPRAS' from these three database text tables into the view ('SPRAS1,' 'SPRAS2,' and 'SPRAS3').

A customer can exist for more than one company code; that is, there can be more than one row for a value of 'KUNNR' in the database table KNB1. (The primary key of KNB1 is 'KUNNR' and 'BUKRS'). Also, a customer can be assigned to more than one sales group. (Combination of sales organization, distribution channel, and division). In other words, multiple rows of a value of 'KUNNR' can exist in the database table KNVV. (The primary key of database table KNVV is 'KUNNR,' 'VKORG,' 'VTWEG,' and 'SPART'). For these reasons, the number of rows getting generated in the view YCL_CH14_CUST_VW is over fifty thousand. The number of rows in the database table KNA1 is over seven thousand.

Having explicitly defined your data source, let the scenario description of simulating a tab strip to display related information on the same screen area be resumed.

Screen, Sub Screens Layout

In the screen painter layout editor, there is a screen element *Subscreen Area* in the *element palette*. A *Subscreen Area* is a reserved physical screen area into which you can load sub screens at runtime. The screens that you created in all your previous exercises were normal screens. Normal screens can be loaded with the CALL SCREEN... statement. You can create in screen painter sub screens by choosing the *Subscreen* radio button in the screen attributes instead of the *Normal* radio button, which is the default and what you have been using until now.

The sub screens can be loaded into the *Subscreen Area* at runtime through the statement CALL SUBSCREEN... in the *flow logic* area of the screen painter. With the statement CALL SUBSCREEN..., you specify the program name and the sub screen number. Sub screen numbers are screen identifiers just like the normal screen identifiers - a four-digit number.

So you will create a normal screen in which you will place two fields: customer code and customer name. You will place a '*Subscreen Area'* element under these two fields on this normal screen.

You will create a first sub screen on which you will place the fields related to the customer's contact information. \ ('STRAS,' 'ORT01' et al.).

You will create a second sub screen on which you will place the fields related to the customer's organizational information ('BUKRS,' 'BUTXT,' 'VKORG,' 'VTEXT1' et al.).

You will position two buttons (in addition to the other buttons) on the *application toolbar*. You will designate the first of these two buttons as the contact info button and the second of these two buttons as the organizational info button.

On pressing the contact info button, you will load the sub screen containing the customer contact info fields into the *Subscreen Area*. On pressing the organizational info button, you will load the sub screen containing the customer organizational info fields into the *Subscreen Area*.

In this manner the same screen area is being used to display either the customer's contact info or the customer's organizational info.

In the present exercise, you are simulating the tab strip operations with buttons on the *application toolbar* to induct you into the concepts of *Subscreen Area* and sub screens. The tab strip control is available as a screen element. The tab strip control element is implemented using the *Subscreen Area* and sub screens. In the next exercise, you will use the tab strip control.

A rough screen layout of the normal screen is shown. The normal screen will contain the two fields 'KUNNR' and 'NAME1' along with the *Subscreen Area* into which you load sub screens at runtime. This is shown in Figure 14-62.

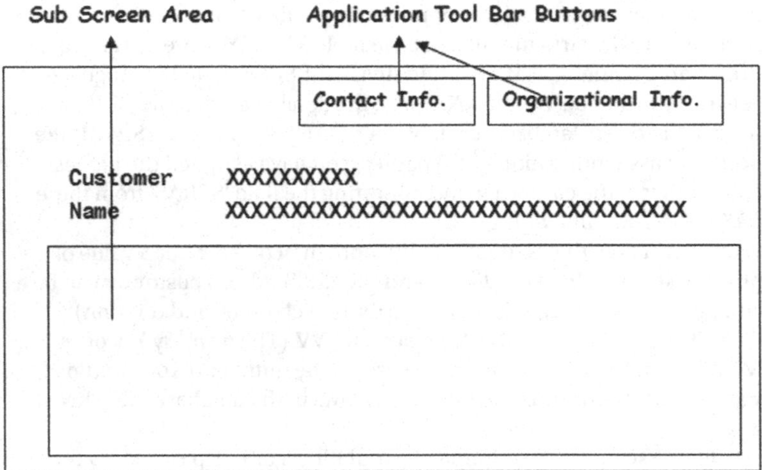

***Figure 14-62.** Rough Layout. Main Screen for Customer Info with Subscreen Area*

A rough layout of the sub screen containing the customer contact info fields is shown in Figure 14-63.

```
Street      XXXXXXXXXXXXXXXXXXXXXXXXXXXXXXXXXXX
City        XXXXXXXXXXXXXXXXXXXXXXXXXXXXXXXXXXX
Postal Code XXXXXXXXXX
Name        XXXXXXXXXXXXXXXXXXXXXXXXXXXXXXXXXXX
Telephone   XXXXXXXXXXXXXXXX
Fax Number  XXXXXXXXXXXXXXXXXXXXXXXXXXXXXXX
```

***Figure 14-63.** Rough Layout. Sub Screen for Customer Contact Info*

A rough layout of the sub screen containing the customer organizational info fields is shown in Figure 14-64.

```
Company Code    XXXX
Company Name    XXXXXXXXXXXXXXXXXXXXXXXXX
Sales Org.      XXX
Name            XXXXXXXXXXXXXXXXXXXX
Distr. Channel  XX
Name            XXXXXXXXXXXXXXXXXXXX
Division        XX
Name            XXXXXXXXXXXXXXXXXXXX
```

Figure 14-64. *Rough Layout. Sub Screen for Customer Organizational Info*

Program and Other Objects

You will create an ABAP program YCL_CH14_03_SIMULATE_TABSTRIP.

Create a normal screen (Screen Number 100). Position the two fields 'KUNNR' and 'NAME1' from the database view YCL_CH14_CUST_VW on the screen. Place the screen element *Subscreen Area* on the screen and name it as 'SAREA'. (The element *Subscreen Area* in the *element palette* is fifth from the bottom). The screen after placement of *Subscreen Area* will look like that in Figure 14-65.

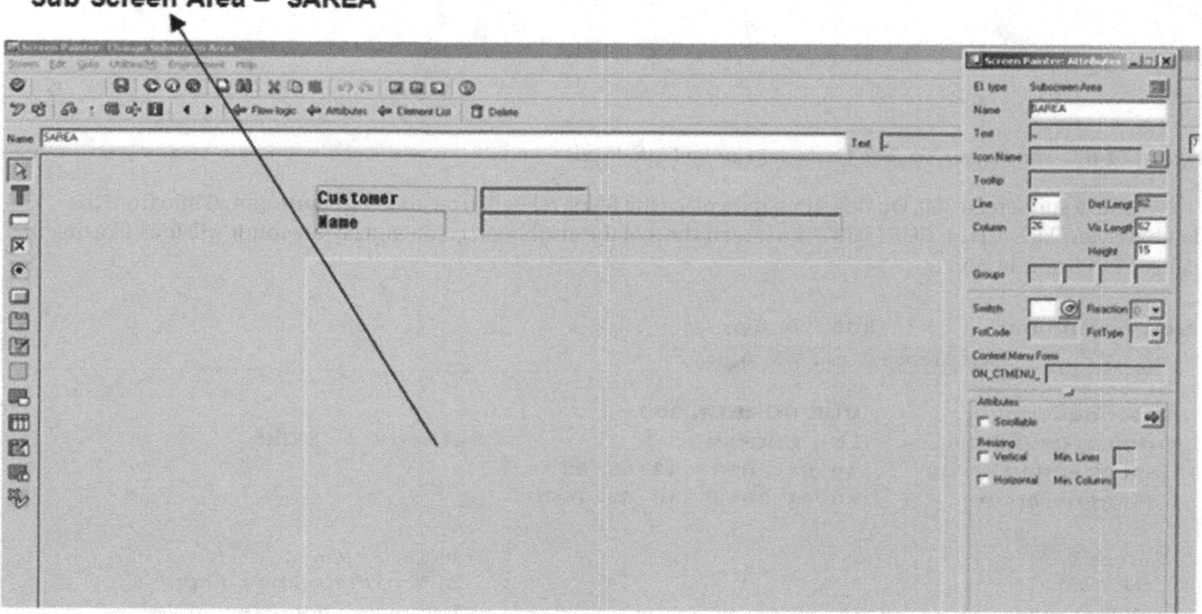

Figure 14-65. *Screen No. 100. Two Fields and Subscreen Area*

In the *Element list* tab, enter the OK_CODE.

Create a sub screen 200. On this sub screen place the fields related to customer contact info from the database view YCL_CH14_CUST_VW. The screen shots of the attributes screen and layout editor will look like that in Figures 14-66 and 14-67.

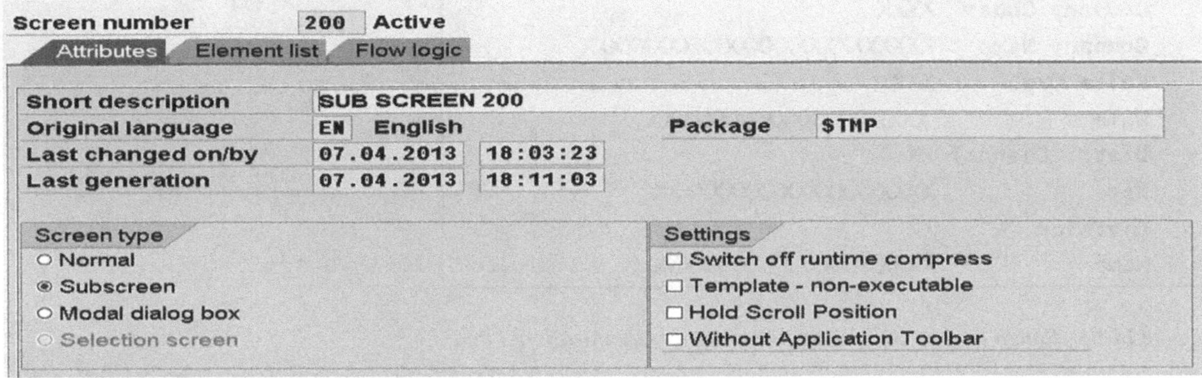

Figure 14-66. *Sub Screen No. 200. Attributes*

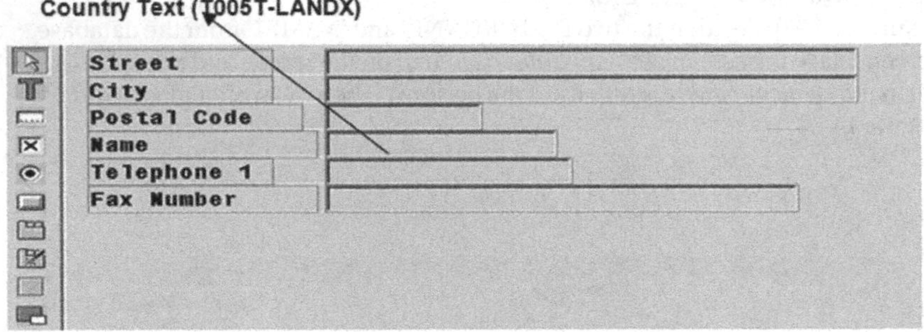

Figure 14-67. *Sub Screen No. 200. Customer Contact Info Fields*

Create a sub screen 300. On this sub screen place the fields related to customer organizational info from the database view YCL_CH14_CUST_VW. The screen shots of the attributes screen and layout editor will look like that in Figures 14-68 and 14-69.

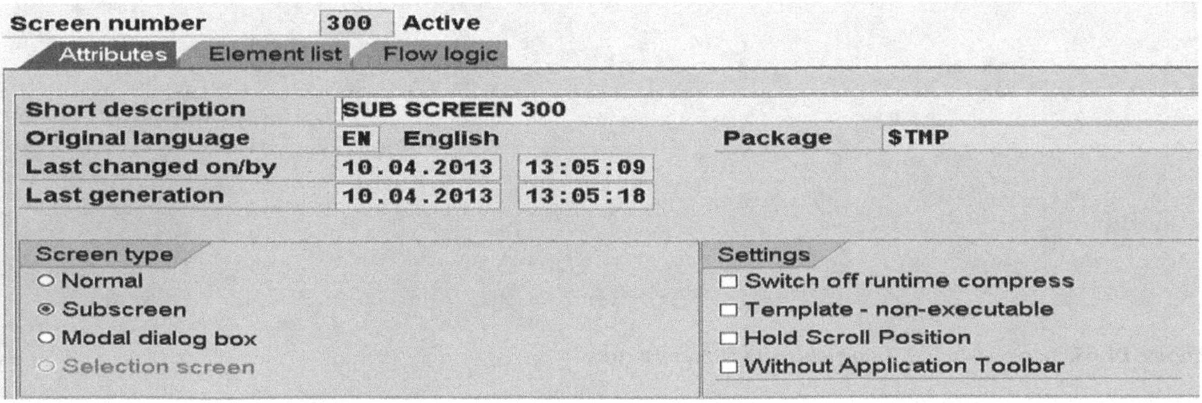

Figure 14-68. *Sub Screen No. 300. Attributes*

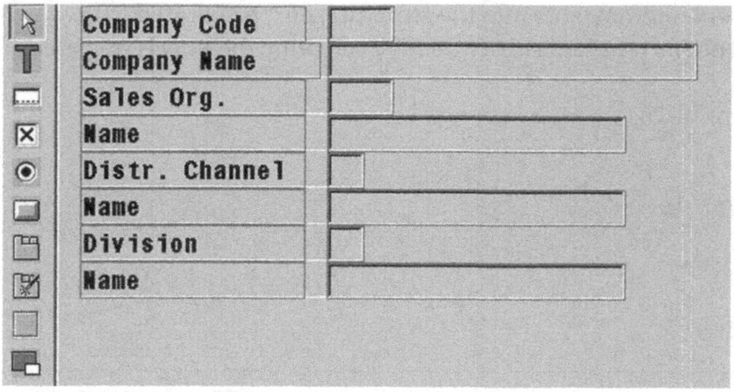

Figure 14-69. *Sub Screen No. 300. Customer Organizational Info Fields*

You are not bothering to enter 'OK_CODE' in the *Element list* tab for the sub screens. Since you are not handling or editing data in the *Subscreen Area,* you are not triggering any PAI and consequently PBO events for the sub screens. There are no PBO and PAI modules for the sub screens.

Set all the fields on the normal screen and sub screens in display mode.

The PAI and PBO events will be triggered for the main, normal screen (Screen Number 100).

The *flow logic* for the normal screen number 100:

```
PROCESS BEFORE OUTPUT.
MODULE STATUS_0100.
CALL SUBSCREEN SAREA INCLUDING PROG SCRN.
*
PROCESS AFTER INPUT.
MODULE USER_COMMAND_0100.
```

The statement CALL SUBSCREEN SAREA INCLUDING PROG SCRN will load a sub screen number contained in the variable 'SCRN' into the *Subscreen* Area 'SAREA.' The program name has to be supplied to the CALL SUBSCREEN... statement. You are supplying this through the variable 'PROG.' When the contact info button on the application tool bar is pressed, in the PAI module, you are assigning the sub screen number 200 to the variable 'SCRN.' And when the organizational info button is pressed, in the PAI module, you are assigning the sub screen number 300 to the variable 'SCRN.' As per these assignments, the appropriate sub screen number is loaded into the *Subscreen Area* through the statement CALL SUBSCREEN... in the PBO *flow logic* area of the screen painter.

In the ABAP program, you are loading two internal tables with the data from the database view YCL_CH14_CUST_VW and the database table T005T respectively. You have as usual declared structures using the keyword TABLES like TABLES. YCL_CH14_CUST_VW, T005T. You placed the screen variables on the normal screen and sub screens using the same structures of the database view and database table.

When the program is executed, you are first loading the first internal table ('MAIN_TAB,' standard) from the database view YCL_CH14_CUST_VW. You are loading the second internal table (T005T_TAB, sorted) from the database table T005T. You are sorting the first internal table on 'KUNNR'. You are then loading the screen number 100 with CALL SCREEN 100. This will trigger the PBO event and execute the PBO module. In PBO module, you are setting status ('STAT1') You are retrieving the first row from internal table 'MAIN_TAB' into the structure YCL_CH14_CUST_VW. You are fetching the corresponding 'LANDX' field value from the internal table 'T005T_TAB.' (Random access of sorted table). Initially when declaring the data, you are assigning the sub screen number 200 (customer contact info) to the variable 'SCRN.' The values from the fields of structure YCL_CH14_CUST_VW and the 'LANDX' field from the structure T005T will get transferred to corresponding screen variables. The customer contact info of the first row from the internal tables fetched into the structures YCL_CH14_CUST_VW and T005T will be displayed on the screen on execution of the program.

The setting of the status and fetching of the first row of internal table into the structure, etc., is required to be done only once when the program is executed and need not be repeated subsequently every time the PBO is triggered. You are managing this with the variable 'ONCE'.

A screen shot of the status 'STAT1' is shown in Figure 14-70.

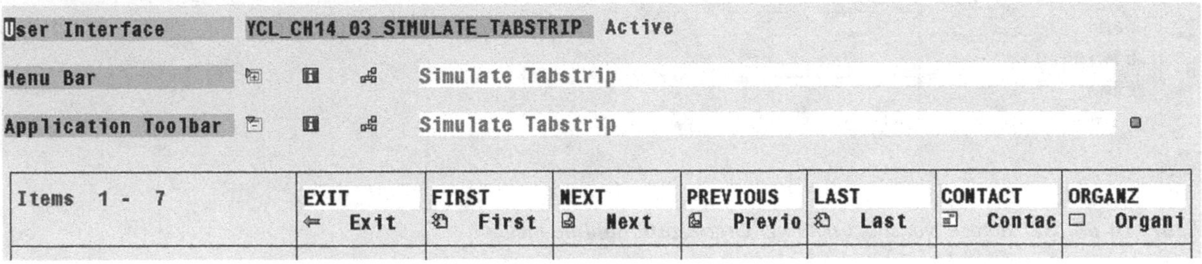

User Interface YCL_CH14_03_SIMULATE_TABSTRIP Active

Menu Bar Simulate Tabstrip

Application Toolbar Simulate Tabstrip

Items 1 - 7	EXIT	FIRST	NEXT	PREVIOUS	LAST	CONTACT	ORGANZ
	Exit	First	Next	Previo	Last	Contac	Organi

Figure 14-70. Status 'STAT1'

In addition to the 'EXIT', 'CONTACT', and 'ORGANZ' buttons, there are four additional buttons: 'FIRST', 'NEXT', 'PREVIOUS', and 'LAST'. The four buttons are for data navigation.

When the 'FIRST' button is pressed, data from the first row of 'MAIN_TAB' and the corresponding 'LANDX' from 'T005T_TAB' is fetched and displayed. When the 'NEXT' button is pressed, data from the next row, if any, is fetched and displayed. When the 'PREVIOUS' button is pressed, data of the previous row, if any, is fetched and displayed. When the 'LAST' button is pressed, data of the last row is fetched and displayed.

For the internal table 'MAIN_TAB', you are maintaining the total number of rows. ('NO_OF_ROWS'). You are also maintaining, for this table, the number of the current row being displayed ('CURRENT_RW'). In the PAI module, you are carrying out the task of navigating to the appropriate row by incrementing and decrementing the current row, etc.

The data navigation part has been added through the application toolbar buttons, just to put some additional meaningful functionality to the tab strip simulation demonstrative program.

The source program:

```
REPORT YCL_CH14_03_SIMULATE_TABSTRIP.

*******************************************************
* Simulate Tab Strip - Sub Screen Area & Sub Screens **
*******************************************************

TABLES. YCL_CH14_CUST_VW, T005T.

DATA. OK_CODE     TYPE SY-UCOMM,
      MAIN_TAB    TYPE STANDARD TABLE OF YCL_CH14_CUST_VW,
      T005T_TAB   TYPE SORTED TABLE OF T005T WITH
                       UNIQUE KEY SPRAS LAND1,
      ONCE(1      TYPE C,
      CURRENT_RW  TYPE SY-TABIX,
      NO_OF_ROWS  TYPE SY-TABIX,
      PROG        TYPE SY-REPID VALUE 'YCL_CH14_03_SIMULATE_TABSTRIP',
      SCRN        TYPE SY-DYNNR VALUE '0200'.
```

```
******************************************************************
START-OF-SELECTION.

SELECT * FROM YCL_CH14_CUST_VW INTO TABLE MAIN_TAB.
NO_OF_ROWS = SY-DBCNT.

SORT MAIN_TAB BY KUNNR.

SELECT * FROM T005T INTO TABLE T005T_TAB.

CALL SCREEN 100.
*&---------------------------------------------------------------------*
*&      Module  STATUS_0100  OUTPUT
*&---------------------------------------------------------------------*
*       text
*----------------------------------------------------------------------*
MODULE STATUS_0100 OUTPUT.

IF ONCE = ' '.
 ONCE = 'X'.
 SET PF-STATUS 'STAT1'.
 CURRENT_RW = 1.
 PERFORM READ_TABLE.

ENDIF.

ENDMODULE.                 " STATUS_0100  OUTPUT
*&---------------------------------------------------------------------*
*&      Module  USER_COMMAND_0100  INPUT
*&---------------------------------------------------------------------*
*   text
*----------------------------------------------------------------------*
MODULE USER_COMMAND_0100 INPUT.

CASE OK_CODE.

 WHEN 'EXIT'.
  LEAVE PROGRAM.

 WHEN 'FIRST'.
  CURRENT_RW = 1.
  PERFORM READ_TABLE.

 WHEN 'NEXT'.
  IF CURRENT_RW < NO_OF_ROWS.
   CURRENT_RW = CURRENT_RW + 1.
   PERFORM READ_TABLE.
  ENDIF.
```

```
 WHEN 'PREVIOUS'.
  IF CURRENT_RW > 1.
   CURRENT_RW = CURRENT_RW - 1.
   PERFORM READ_TABLE.
  ENDIF.

 WHEN 'LAST'.
   CURRENT_RW = NO_OF_ROWS.
   PERFORM READ_TABLE.

 WHEN 'CONTACT'.
  SCRN = '0200'.

 WHEN 'ORGANZ'.
  SCRN = '0300'.

ENDCASE.

ENDMODULE.                  " USER_COMMAND_0100  INPUT

*********************************************************
FORM READ_TABLE.

  READ TABLE MAIN_TAB INTO YCL_CH14_CUST_VW INDEX CURRENT_RW.
  READ TABLE T005T_TAB INTO T005T WITH KEY
     SPRAS = YCL_CH14_CUST_VW-SPRAS2 LAND1 = YCL_CH14_CUST_VW-LAND1.

ENDFORM.
```

The subroutine READ_TABLE is referring to global data objects (internal tables and structures directly). Not good programming! It has been done for expediency. In a real-life development environment, you must supply the parameters to pass the internal tables and structures.

The program, when executed, displaying screens for contact info and organizational info, will look like Figures 14-71 and 14-72.

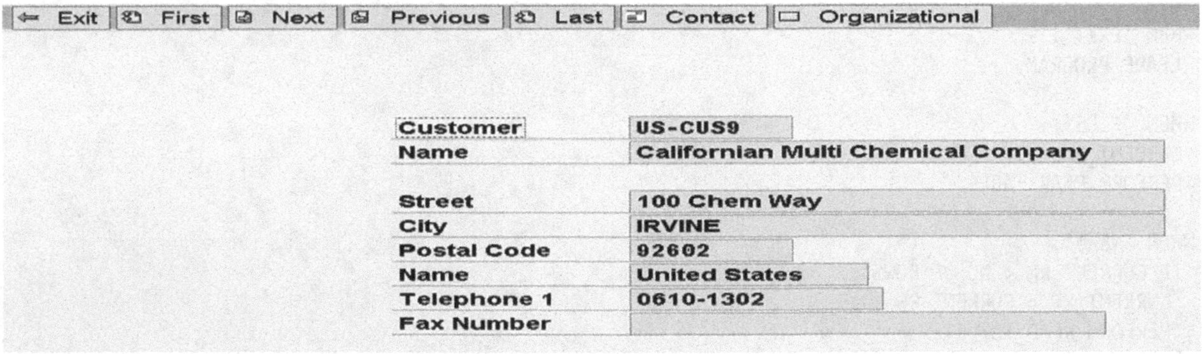

***Figure 14-71.** Program YCL_CH14_03_SIMULATE_TABSTRIP. Contact Info*

Exit | First | Next | Previous | Last | Contact | Organizational

Customer	US-CUS9
Name	Californian Multi Chemical Company
Company Code	3000
Company Name	IDES US INC
Sales Org.	3000
Name	USA Philadelphia
Distr. Channel	10
Name	Final customer sales
Division	00
Name	Cross-division

Figure 14-72. *Program YCL_CH14_03_SIMULATE_TABSTRIP. Organizational Info*

To display the row shown here, navigate to the last row and click on the 'Previous' button a few times.

You should try out all the navigational buttons. This was a simulation of the tab strip element using *Subscreen Area,* sub screens, and application toolbar buttons.

Hands-on Exercise. Tab Strip Element

You will perform the same exercise as the previous one, but with the tab strip screen element. You will omit the application toolbar buttons 'CONTACT' and 'ORGANZ.' The buttons to choose a particular tab will appear as part of the tab strip element.

You are using the same data sources: database view YCL_CH14_CUST_VW and database table T005T. You are loading data from these sources into internal tables and processing them the same way as in the previous exercise.

You create an ABAP program YCL_CH14_04_TABSTRIP. Copy the appropriate required lines from the previous program.

In the screen painter environment, on the normal screen (screen number 500), position the two fields YCL_CH14_CUST_VW-KUNNR and YCL_CH14_CUST_VW-NAME1. Then drag and drop the tab strip element on the normal screen from the *element palette.* (The tab strip element is the seventh element from the top or the eighth element from the bottom in the *element palette*). Assign a name to the tab strip element (CUST_INFO); insert tabs into the tab strip element; (minimum or default of two) and assign texts, icons, and function codes to each of the two tabs. Assign the following to the first tab:

Name. 'CONTACT'

Text. 'Contact'

Icon. 'ICON_ADDRESS'

Function code. 'CONTACT'

Assign the following to the second tab:

Name. 'ORGANZ'

Text. 'Organizational'

Icon. 'ICON_NEW_ORG_UNIT'

Function code. 'ORGANZ'

Select all the tabs. (Keep the 'Ctrl' key pressed and click on tabs successively to select all tabs). With all the tabs selected, drag and drop the *Subscreen Area* element into the tabs. Assign the *Subscreen Area* a name of 'SAREA'.

The screen shots of Figures 14-73, 14-74, and 14-75 show these elements and their attributes.

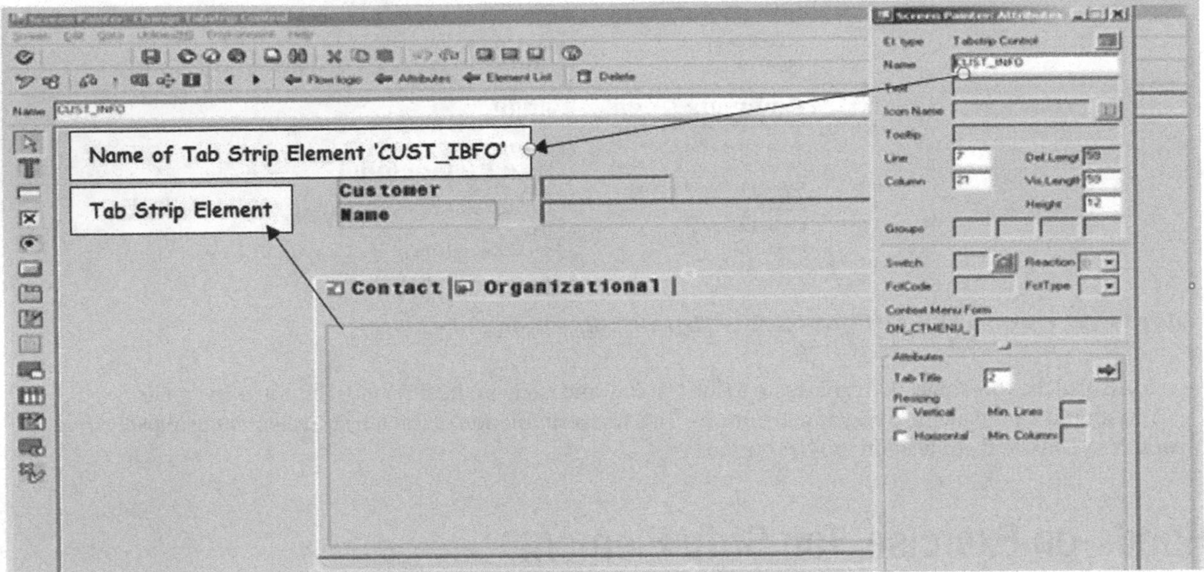

Figure 14-73. *Screen number 500. Tab Strip Element*

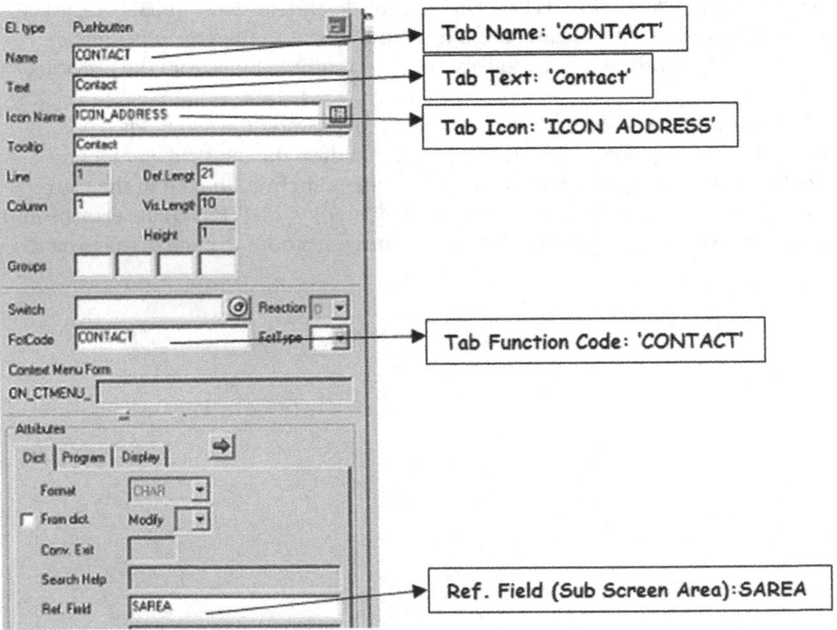

Figure 14-74. *Screen number 500. Tab 'CONTACT'*

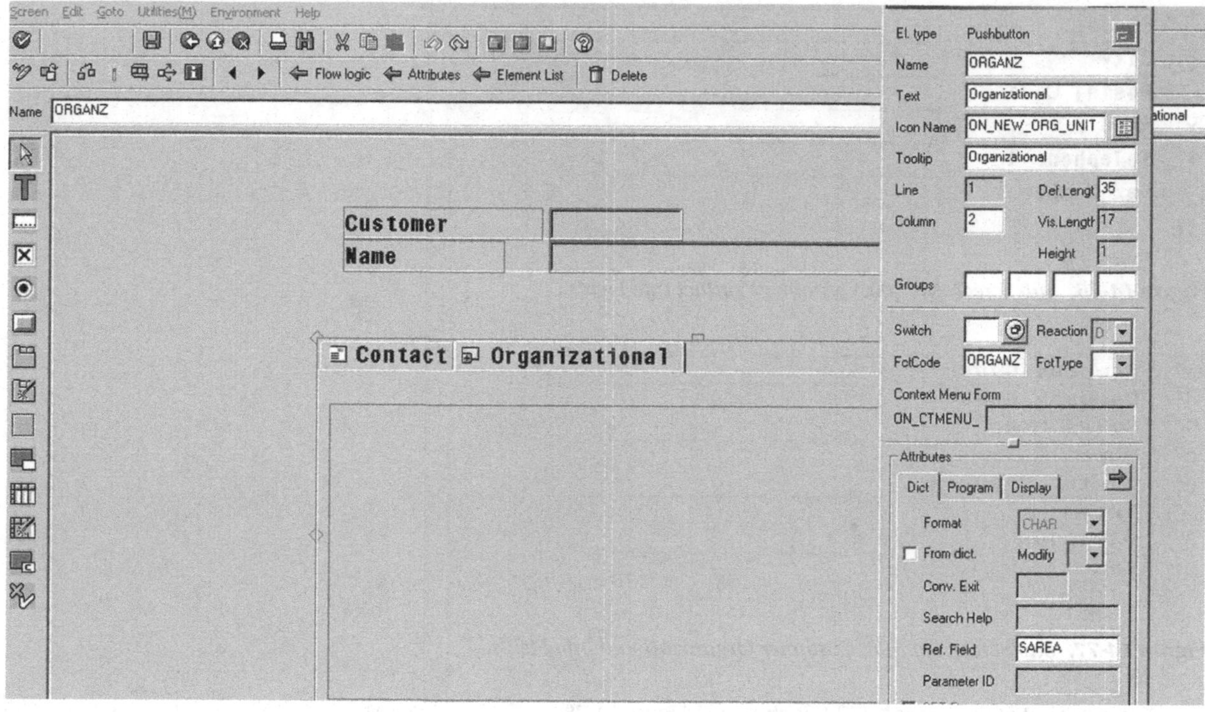

Figure 14-75. Screen number 500. Tab 'ORGANZ'

Instead of selecting all tabs and then dragging and dropping *Subscreen Area* into the tabs, you can assign the *Subscreen Area* name to each of the tabs in the attribute 'Ref. Field' as shown in Figure 14-74.

Create the 'OK_CODE' in the *Element list* tab of the normal screen 500. The *flow logic* of normal screen number 500 is similar to that of the previous program.

```
PROCESS BEFORE OUTPUT.
 MODULE STATUS_0500.
 CALL SUBSCREEN SAREA INCLUDING PROG SCRN.
*
PROCESS AFTER INPUT.
 MODULE USER_COMMAND_0500.
```

You can copy the sub screen numbers 200 and 300 of the previous exercise for the present program into screen numbers 600 and 700 respectively. On screen number 600, you have the customer contact fields; and on the screen number 700, you have the customer organizational fields. The layout of sub screen numbers 600 and 700 is shown in Figures 14-76 and 14-77.

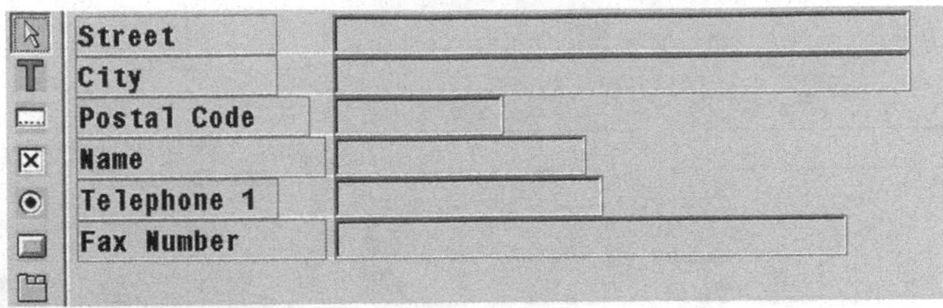

Figure 14-76. Sub Screen No. 600. Customer Contact Info Fields

Company Code
Company Name
Sales Org.
Name
Distr. Channel
Name
Division
Name

Figure 14-77. Sub Screen No. 700. Customer Organizational Info Fields

A screen shot of the status 'STAT1' is shown in Figure 14-78.

User Interface YCL_CH14_04_TABSTRIP Active
Menu Bar Simulate Tabstrip
Application Toolbar Simulate Tabstrip

Items 1 - 7	EXIT	FIRST	NEXT	PREVIOUS	LAST
	Exit	First	Next	Previo	Last

Figure 14-78. Status 'STAT1'

This is a copy of the status of the previous program, with the last two buttons deleted.

The source program is the same as in the previous exercise except that you have to indicate to the system which of the tabs in the tab strip element is currently active.

To indicate to the system which of the tabs in the tab strip element is currently active, you declare a structure with the key word 'CONTROLS':

```
CONTROLS. <name of tab strip element> TYPE TABSTRIP.
```

This statement defines a structure of the same name as tab strip element name. (In the present case 'CUST_INFO'). You are concerned with only one field of this structure (i.e., 'ACTIVETAB'). You have to assign the function code of the tab to this field to indicate the tab you want to be active (Displayed).

In the ABAP program, you will have a declaration along with your global data declarations and the statement:

```
CONTROLS. CUST_INFO TYPE TABSTRIP.
```

In the PAI code segment, where you are assigning the sub screen number to the variable 'SCRN,' you should also assign the function code of the tab to the field 'CUST_INFO-ACTIVETAB' in the following manner:

```
..........
WHEN 'CONTACT'.
 SCRN = 600.
 CUST_INFO-ACTIVETAB = 'CONTACT'.

WHEN 'ORGANZ'.
 SCRN = 700.
 CUST_INFO-ACTIVETAB = 'ORGANZ'.
......
```

The source code of program YCL_CH14_04_TABSTRIP:

```
REPORT YCL_CH14_04_TABSTRIP.

***************************
* Demo Control Tab Strip **
***************************

CONTROLS. CUST_INFO TYPE TABSTRIP.

TABLES. YCL_CH14_CUST_VW, T005T.

DATA. OK_CODE     TYPE SY-UCOMM,
      MAIN_TAB    TYPE STANDARD TABLE OF YCL_CH14_CUST_VW,

      T005T_TAB   TYPE SORTED TABLE OF T005T WITH
                       UNIQUE KEY SPRAS LAND1,
      ONCE(1      TYPE C,
      CURRENT_RW  TYPE SY-TABIX,
      NO_OF_ROWS  TYPE SY-TABIX,
      PROG        TYPE SY-REPID VALUE 'YCL_CH14_04_TABSTRIP',
      SCRN        TYPE SY-DYNNR VALUE '0600'.

******************************************************************
START-OF-SELECTION.

SELECT * FROM YCL_CH14_CUST_VW INTO TABLE MAIN_TAB.
NO_OF_ROWS = SY-DBCNT.

SORT MAIN_TAB BY KUNNR.

SELECT * FROM T005T INTO TABLE T005T_TAB.
```

```
CALL SCREEN 500.

*&---------------------------------------------------------------------*
*&      Module  STATUS_0500  OUTPUT
*&---------------------------------------------------------------------*
*       text
*----------------------------------------------------------------------*

MODULE STATUS_0500 OUTPUT.

IF ONCE = ' '.

 ONCE = 'X'.
 SET PF-STATUS 'STAT1'.
 CURRENT_RW = 1.
 PERFORM READ_TABLE.

ENDIF.

ENDMODULE.                    " STATUS_0500  OUTPUT

*&---------------------------------------------------------------------*
*&      Module  USER_COMMAND_0500  INPUT
*&---------------------------------------------------------------------*
*       text
*----------------------------------------------------------------------*
MODULE USER_COMMAND_0500 INPUT.

CASE OK_CODE.

 WHEN 'EXIT'.
  LEAVE PROGRAM.

 WHEN 'FIRST'.
  CURRENT_RW = 1.
  PERFORM READ_TABLE.

 WHEN 'NEXT'.
  IF CURRENT_RW < NO_OF_ROWS.
   CURRENT_RW = CURRENT_RW + 1.
   PERFORM READ_TABLE.
  ENDIF.

 WHEN 'PREVIOUS'.
  IF CURRENT_RW > 1.
   CURRENT_RW = CURRENT_RW - 1.
   PERFORM READ_TABLE.
  ENDIF.
```

```
 WHEN 'LAST'.
   CURRENT_RW = NO_OF_ROWS.
   PERFORM READ_TABLE.

 WHEN 'CONTACT'.
  SCRN = '0600'.
  CUST_INFO-ACTIVETAB = 'CONTACT'.
 WHEN 'ORGANZ'.
  SCRN = '0700'.
  CUST_INFO-ACTIVETAB = 'ORGANZ'.

ENDCASE.

ENDMODULE.                    " USER_COMMAND_0100  INPUT

*******************************************************

FORM READ_TABLE.

  READ TABLE MAIN_TAB INTO YCL_CH14_CUST_VW INDEX CURRENT_RW.
  READ TABLE T005T_TAB INTO T005T WITH KEY
     SPRAS = YCL_CH14_CUST_VW-SPRAS2 LAND1 = YCL_CH14_CUST_VW-LAND1.

ENDFORM.
```

When the program is executed, the screens will look like Figures 14-79 and 14-80.

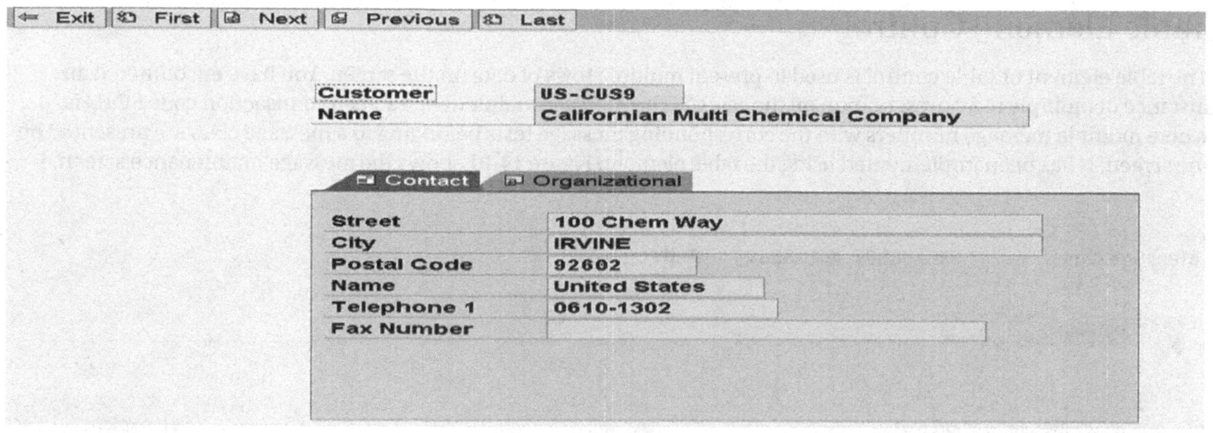

Figure 14-79. *Program YCL_CH14_04_TABSTRIP. Contact Info*

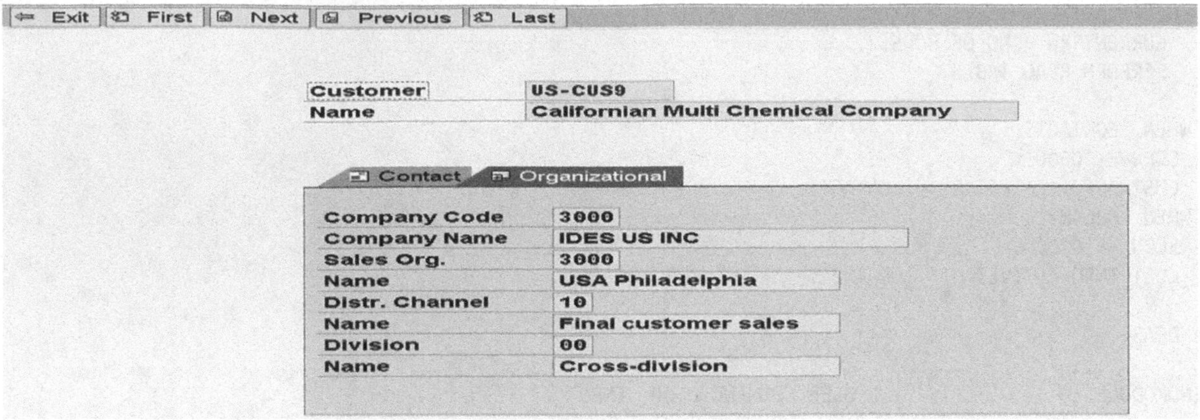

Figure 14-80. *Program YCL_CH14_04_TABSTRIP. Organizational Info*

You can test the navigation buttons. This concludes the hands-on exercise of the tab strip.

In the present hands-on exercise, in the layout editor, you have positioned the tab strip element without using a wizard. In the *element palette* of the screen painter, you have an option to position the tab strip element without using a wizard, and you also have with using a wizard. When you position a tab strip using a wizard, you are saved of writing the code related to the tab strip including the code to load sub screens in the *flow logic*. You can try, as an additional hands-on exercise, the following: place the tab strip element using the wizard.

Hands-on Exercise. Use Table Element

Table Element/Control

The table element or table control is used to present multiple rows of data on the screen. You have encountered an instance of multiple rows presentation on the screen. The message maintenance screen (transaction code SE91) is where multiple message numbers with the corresponding message texts belonging to a message class are presented on the screen. It has been implemented using the table element. Figure 14-81 shows the message maintenance screen.

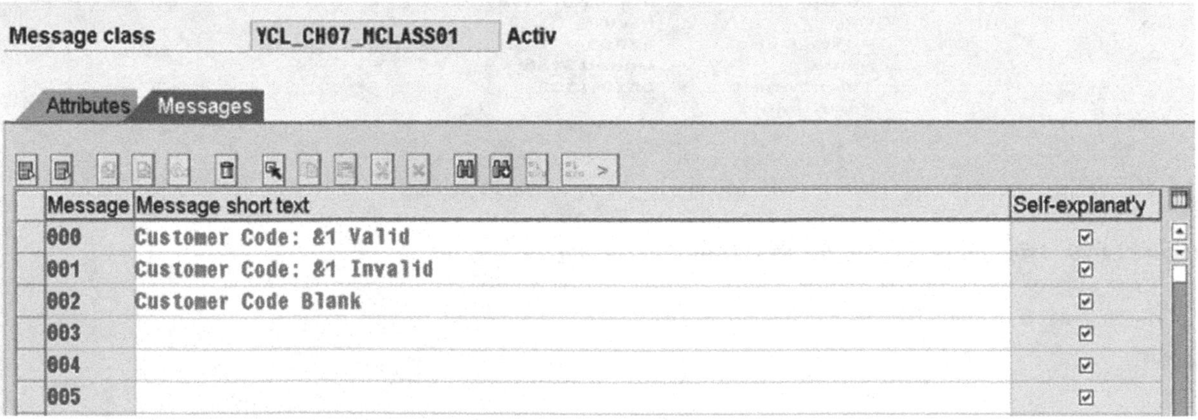

Figure 14-81. *Message Maintenance. Multiple Row Data with Table Control*

If you want to present, at one time, the data of one business document (billing document, purchasing document, etc). having a header and item information on a screen, you will have to locate the multiple item information rows belonging to one business document in a table element. A table element, like other screen elements, will occupy a physical area. Multiple rows of data are loaded into the table element. Depending on the height of the table element, a certain number of rows are visible at any time. If the number of loaded rows are greater than the number of rows visible at a time, the scroll down as well as the scroll up facility is available.

The transfer of data of the fields of multiple rows from the screen to ABAP variables and the other way around are handled through a special form of LOOP...ENDLOOP statements in the *flow logic* area of the screen painter.

Scenario

Let the billing document data be presented along with the related data: customer name & address and material descriptions on the screen. At one time, the data related to one specific billing document will be presented on the screen. You will place the header & related data on the normal area of the screen and place the item and related data inside a table element. A rough layout of the screen is shown in Figure 14-82.

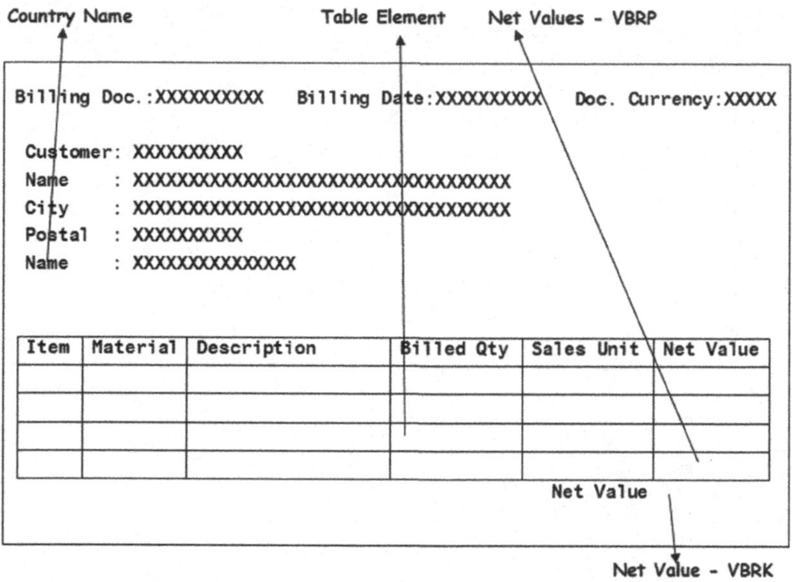

Figure 14-82. *Billing Document & Related Data. Rough Screen Layout*

Scenario Implementation

Data. Let the tables retrieve data for the screen layout of Figure 14-82. The following tables will have to be used to retrieve the data:

VBRK	Billing documents - header
KNA1	Customer primary
T005T	Country texts
VBRP	Billing documents – items
MAKT	Material description texts

Create two database views: the first view containing fields related to header information and the second view containing fields related to item information.

The particulars of database view containing fields related to header -YCL_CH14_KNVB.

View Tables and Join conditions.

Table 14-6. *View YCL_CH14_KNVB – Tables & Join Conditions*

Tables	Table	Field name	Table	Field name
T005T	KNA1	MANDT	VBRK	MANDT
VBRK	KNA1	KUNNR	VBRK	KUNAG
KNA1	KNA1	MANDT	T005T	MANDT
	KNA1	LAND1	T005T	LAND1

View Fields.

Table 14-7. *View YCL_CH14_KNVB – View Fields*

View field	Table	Field	Key
MANDT	KNA1	MANDT	X
KUNNR	KNA1	KUNNR	X
VBELN	VBRK	VBELN	X
SPRAS	T005T	SPRAS	X
LAND1	KNA1	LAND1	X
NAME1	KNA1	NAME1	
ORT01	KNA1	ORT01	
PSTLZ	KNA1	PSTLZ	
STRAS	KNA1	STRAS	
WAERK	VBRK	WAERK	
FKDAT	VBRK	FKDAT	
KURRF	VBRK	KURRF	
NETWR	VBRK	NETWR	
BUKRS	VBRK	BUKRS	
LANDX	T005T	LANDX	

View SELECT Condition.

T005T	SPRAS	EQ	'E'

The particulars of the database view containing fields related to items -YCL_CH14_VBP_MKT.

View Tables and Join conditions.

Table 14-8. *View YCL_CH14_VBP_MKT - Tables & Join Conditions*

Tables	Table	Fieldname	Table	Field name
MAKT	VBRP	MANDT	MAKT	MANDT
VBRP	VBRP	MATNR	MAKT	MATNR

View Fields.

Table 14-9. *View YCL_CH14_VBP_MKT - View Fields*

View field	Table	Field	Key
MANDT	VBRP	MANDT	X
VBELN	VBRP	VBELN	X
POSNR	VBRP	POSNR	X
SPRAS	MAKT	SPRAS	X
FKIMG	VBRP	FKIMG	
VRKME	VBRP	VRKME	
NETWR	VBRP	NETWR	
MATNR	VBRP	MATNR	
MAKTX	MAKT	MAKTX	

View SELECT Condition.

MAKT	SPRAS	EQ	'E'

You are arbitrarily fetching the text in language code 'E' (English from the country and material text tables).

Create an ABAP program YCH_CH14_05_TABLE_CTRL. In this program, declare structures for the two views with the TABLES statement. Also declare internal tables for these two structures.

Screens

Create a normal screen, screen number 300. On the layout editor, click the third button from the right of the application toolbar to select fields from the DDIC object. Enter the database view name as YCL_CH14_KNVB in the dialog box, click on the 'Get from Dictionary' button, and select the fields 'VBELN,' 'FKDAT,' 'WAERK,' 'KUNNR,' 'NAME1,' 'ORT01,' and 'LANDX.' Click on the continue button to place on the screen number 300, the fields from the database view containing fields related to header information as per the rough screen layout of Figure 14-82. The screen after placement of the header fields will look like Figure 14-83.

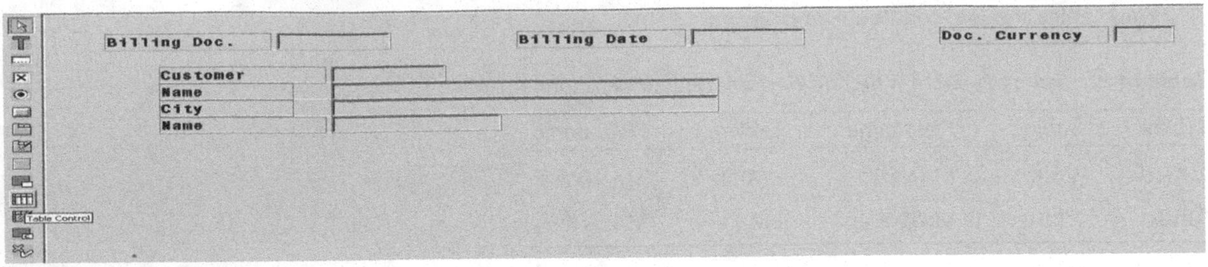

Figure 14-83. *Screen Number 300. Placement of Fields related to Header*

Drag and drop the table element, the third element from the bottom in the *element palette*. You can drag and drop the fourth element from the bottom in *element palette*. This also creates a table element using a wizard. Creating a table element with a wizard will save the writing of code. For now, you are creating a table element without using a wizard.

In the attributes screen of the table element, assign a name 'ITEMS' to the table element. Enable the check boxes for horizontal and vertical dividers (i.e., each field will appear as a cell as in an Excel spreadsheet). You are retaining the default options of other attributes: row selection, column selection and resizing by an end user, etc. The attributes screen of the table element 'ITEMS' is shown in Figure 14-84.

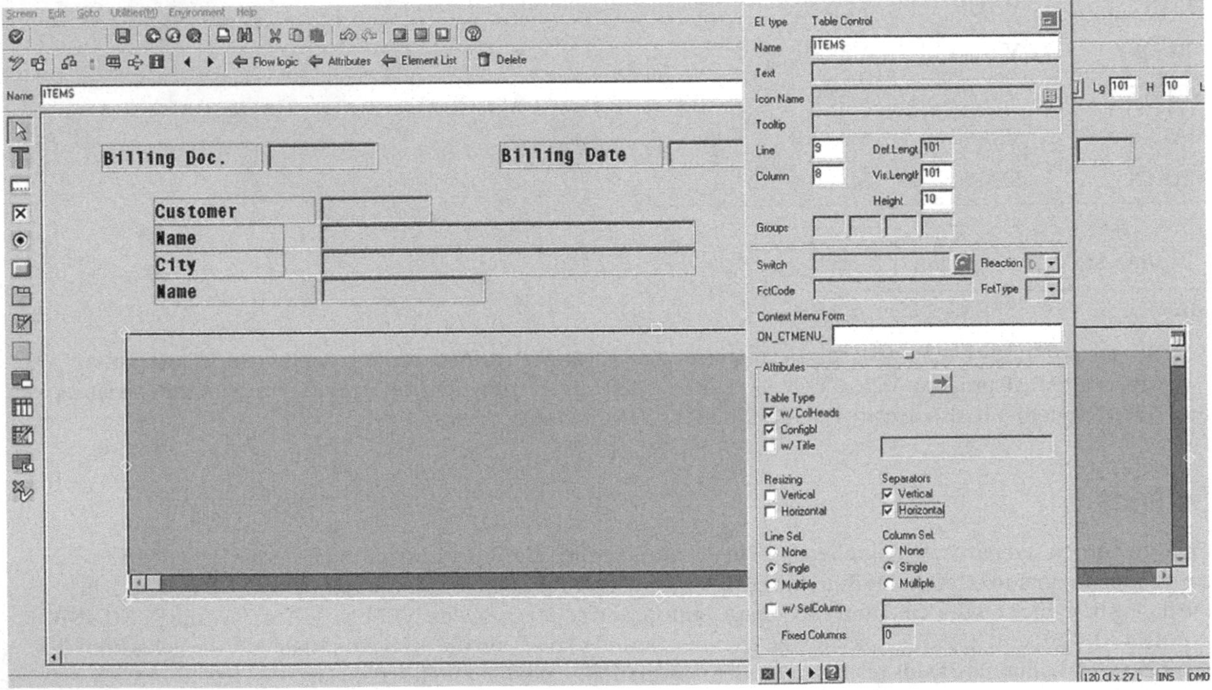

Figure 14-84. *Screen Number 300. Placement of Table Element*

The next step is to place fields inside the table element. Again, open the dialog box for field selection. (The third button from the right of the application toll bar, etc). Enter the view name as YCL_CH14_VBP_MKT for fields related to item information. Select the fields 'VBELN', 'POSNR', 'FKIMG', 'VRKME', 'NETWR' (sourced from database table 'VBRP'), and 'MAKTX', sourced from database table 'MAKT'. The screen after the field selections will look like Figure 14-85.

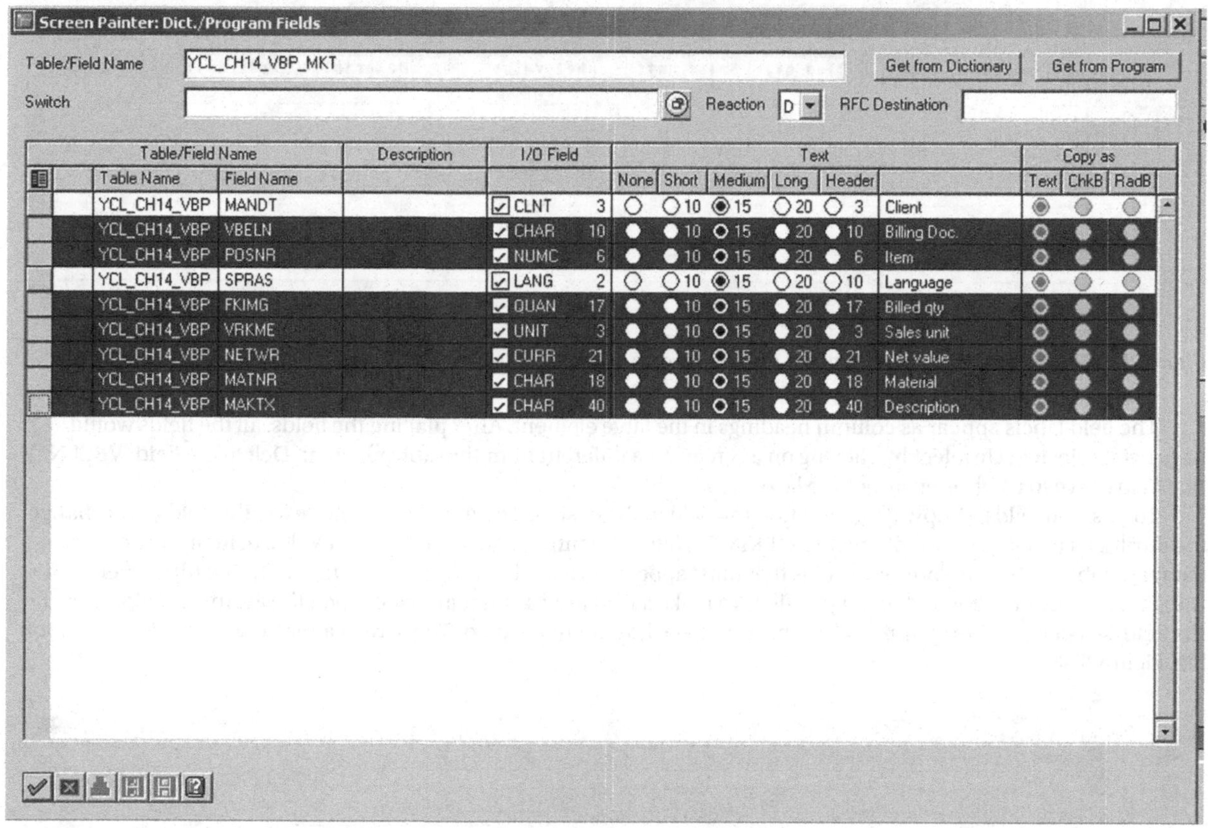

Figure 14-85. *Screen Number 300. Selection of Fields Related to Items*

You do not need the field 'VBELN' as per the layout. You included it just to demonstrate that fields and labels can be deleted after their placement in the table element. The screen after the fields are placed in the table element will look like Figure 14-86.

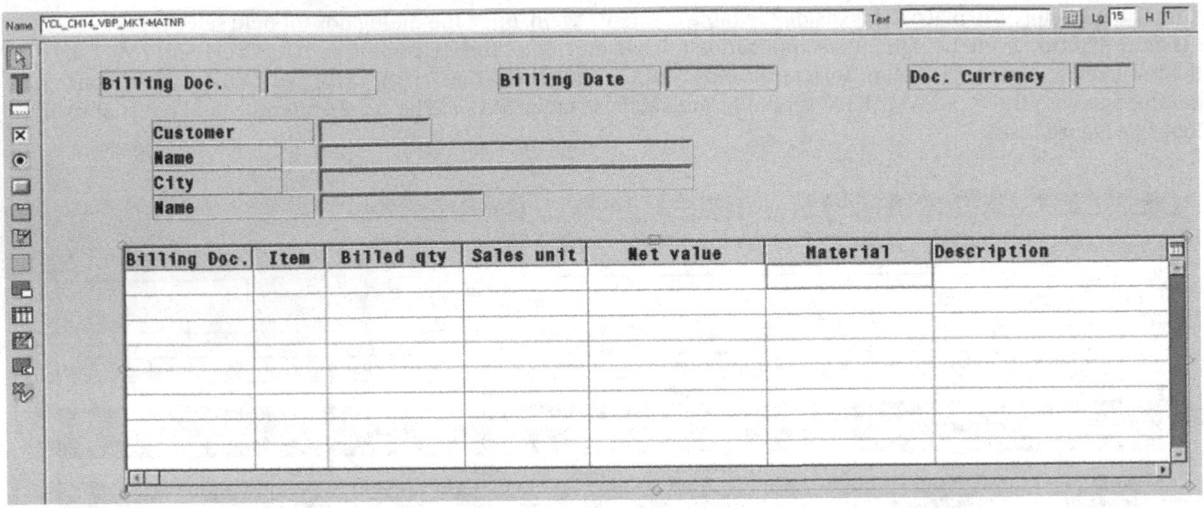

Figure 14-86. Screen Number 300. Initial Placement of Fields Related to Items

The field labels appear as column headings in the table element. After placing the fields, all the fields would have been selected. Unselect by clicking on a screen area different from the table element. Delete the field 'VBELN'. The fields have to be ordered as per the layout.

To position fields, simply drag and drop the field in the desired position. Order and resize the fields, and change the attributes to display. Two of the fields 'FKIMG' (Billed Quantity) and 'NETWR' (Net Value of item) sourced from database table 'VBRP' are numeric fields that must appear as right aligned or right justified. By default, all fields on the screen appear left aligned or left justified. To make a field appear right justified, open the attribute dialog box of the field, select the tab *Program*, and enable the check box 'Right justified'. The screen after these operations will look like Figure 14-87.

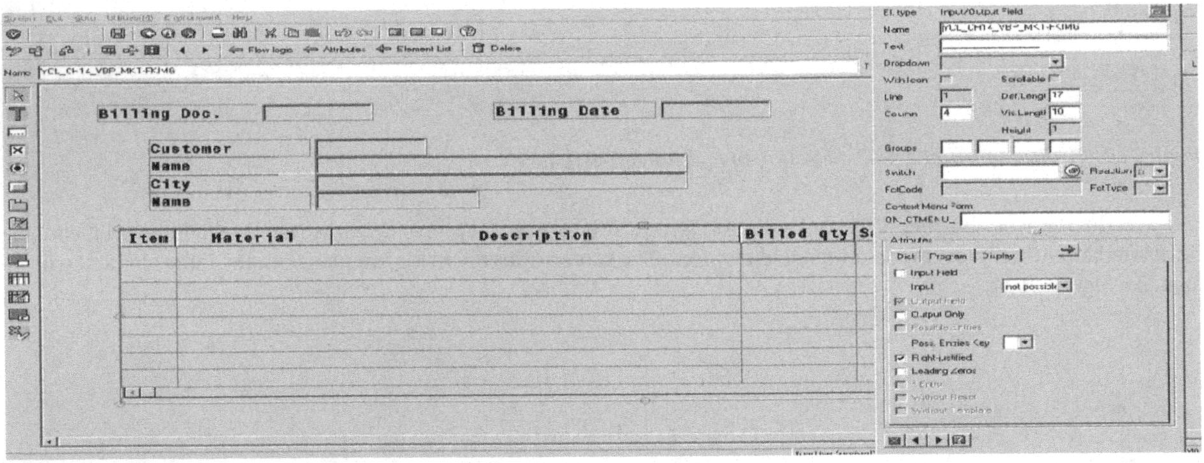

Figure 14-87. Screen Number 300. Final Placement of Fields Related to Items

Lastly, you have to place the fields 'NETWR' (sourced from the database table 'VBRK,' net value of billing document) at the bottom of the screen. Placing this field and the screen after field placement will look like Figure 14-88.

Billing Doc.		Billing Date		Doc. Currency	
Customer					
Name					
City					
Name					

Item	Material	Description	Billed qty	Sales unit	Net value

Net Value

Figure 14-88. *Screen Number 300. Final Placement of All Fields*

Save the screen, and close the layout editor. In the *element list*, enter the 'OK_CODE' field. In the *flow logic* area, de-comment the module statements. Create the PBO and PAI modules along the now familiar pattern. For the table element, you enter the following code in the *flow logic* area:

```
PROCESS BEFORE OUTPUT.
MODULE STATUS_0300.

LOOP AT BILLSI_TAB INTO YCL_CH14_VBP_MKT WITH CONTROL ITEMS.

ENDLOOP.
*
PROCESS AFTER INPUT.
MODULE USER_COMMAND_0300.

LOOP AT BILLSI_TAB.

ENDLOOP.
```

The LOOP... ENDLOOP statements in the PBO event, in the present context, transfer the data from the internal table to the work area (ABAP variables) into the screen variables in the table element.

The LOOP... ENDLOOP statements in the PAI event, in the present context, transfer the data from the screen variables in the table element into the internal table (ABAP variables).

The syntax of the LOOP ... ENDLOOP statement in the PBO event is different from that in the PAI event.

The step looping process (LOOP... ENDLOOP in *flow logic* area) can be perused in the document ABAP Programming (BC-ABA).

Interface

Create a status 'STAT1' in the interface YCL_CH14_05_TABLE_CTRL as shown in Figure 14-89.

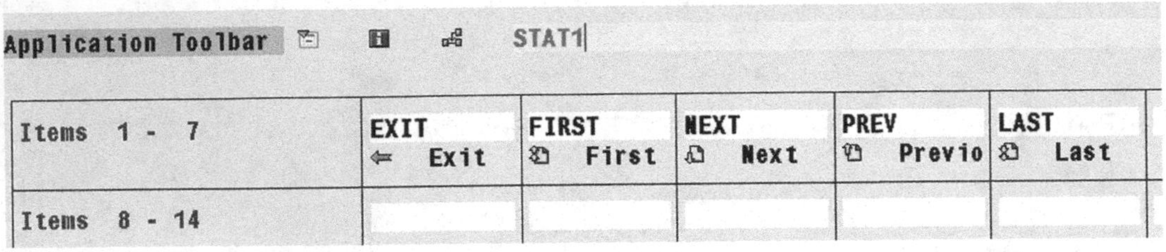

Application Toolbar STAT1

Items 1 - 7	EXIT Exit	FIRST First	NEXT Next	PREV Previo	LAST Last
Items 8 - 14					

Figure 14-89. *Interface. YCL_CH14_05_TABLE_CTRL – Status 'STAT1'*

Program. The Source Program

```
REPORT YCH_CH14_05_TABLE_CTRL.

*******************************
* Demonstrate Table Control  **
*******************************

CONTROLS.ITEMS TYPE TABLEVIEW USING SCREEN 300.

TABLES. YCL_CH14_KNVB, YCL_CH14_VBP_MKT.

DATA. BILLSH_TAB  TYPE STANDARD TABLE OF YCL_CH14_KNVB,
      BILLSI_TAB  TYPE STANDARD TABLE OF YCL_CH14_VBP_MKT,
      OK_CODE     TYPE SY-UCOMM,
      NO_ROWS     TYPE SY-TABIX,
      CUR_ROW     TYPE SY-TABIX,
      ONCE(1      TYPE C.
***************************************************

START-OF-SELECTION.
CALL SCREEN 300.

*&---------------------------------------------------------------------*
*&      Module  STATUS_0300  OUTPUT
*&---------------------------------------------------------------------*
*       text
*----------------------------------------------------------------------*
MODULE STATUS_0300 OUTPUT.

IF ONCE = ' '.

 ONCE = 'X'.
 SET PF-STATUS 'STAT1'.
```

```
 SELECT * FROM YCL_CH14_KNVB INTO TABLE BILLSH_TAB UP TO 100 ROWS
   WHERE VBELN >= '0090023219' .

 NO_ROWS = SY-DBCNT.
 SORT BILLSH_TAB BY VBELN.
 CUR_ROW = 1.
 PERFORM READ_ITEMS.

ENDIF.

OK_CODE = ' '.

ENDMODULE.                    " STATUS_0300  OUTPUT

*&---------------------------------------------------------------------*
*&      Module  USER_COMMAND_0300  INPUT
*&---------------------------------------------------------------------*
*       text
*----------------------------------------------------------------------*

MODULE USER_COMMAND_0300 INPUT.

CASE OK_CODE.

 WHEN 'EXIT'.
  LEAVE PROGRAM.

 WHEN 'FIRST'.
 CUR_ROW = 1.
 PERFORM READ_ITEMS.

 WHEN 'NEXT'.
 IF CUR_ROW < NO_ROWS.
  CUR_ROW = CUR_ROW + 1.
  PERFORM READ_ITEMS.
 ENDIF.

 WHEN 'PREV'.
 IF CUR_ROW > 1.
  CUR_ROW = CUR_ROW - 1.
  PERFORM READ_ITEMS.
 ENDIF.

 WHEN 'LAST'.
 IF CUR_ROW < NO_ROWS.
  CUR_ROW = NO_ROWS.
  PERFORM READ_ITEMS.

ENDIF.

ENDCASE.

ENDMODULE.                    " USER_COMMAND_0300  INPUT
```

```
**********************************************
FORM READ_ITEMS.

 READ TABLE BILLSH_TAB INTO YCL_CH14_KNVB INDEX CUR_ROW.

 SELECT * FROM YCL_CH14_VBP_MKT INTO TABLE BILLSI_TAB WHERE
   VBELN = YCL_CH14_KNVB-VBELN.

 ITEMS-LINES = SY-DBCNT.

ENDFORM.
```

The screen on program execution will look like the one in Figure 14-90.

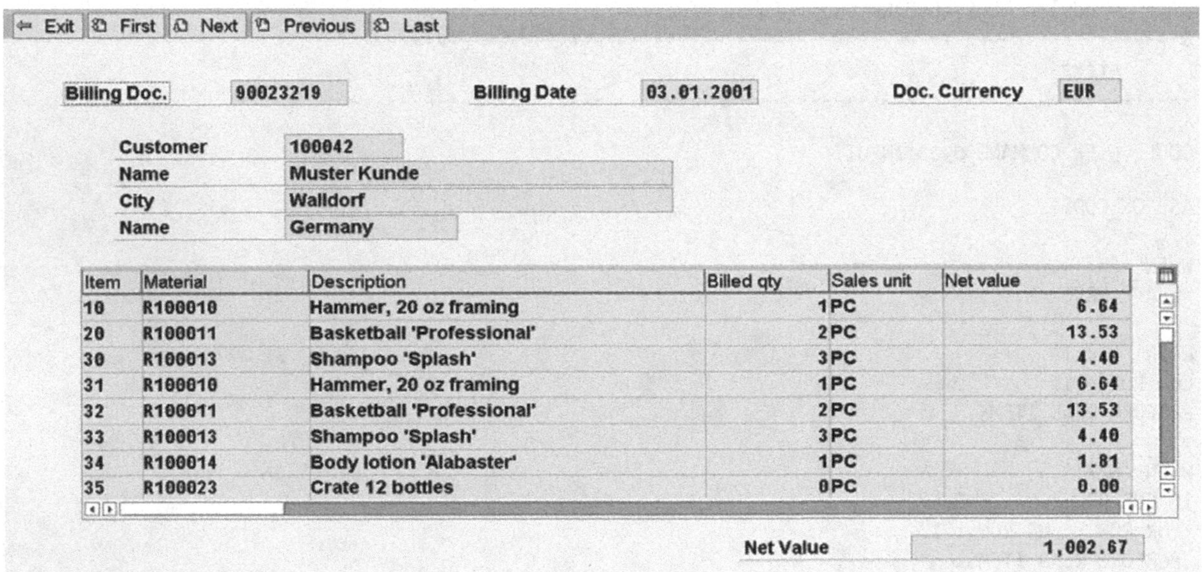

Figure 14-90. *Program YCL_CH14_05_TABLE_CTRL. Execution*

Deliberately, the first row fetched and loaded into the internal table BILLH_TAB corresponds to billing document number 0090023219. (WHERE VBELN >= '0090023219'). This billing document has the maximum number of items of all the billing documents in the table VBRK (fifty-three). It serves the purpose of providing the scope for demonstrating the vertical scrolling in the table control.

This was a demonstration of table control. It enables presentation of multiple rows of data. Data navigation facility is provided as in the hands-on exercises on the tab strip control. All the data on the screen for this hands-on exercise was in display mode. If you want to operate on the table control data; or insert, delete, and change rows, it involves complex screen programming beyond the scope of this book.

Miscellanea

Create Custom Transaction Code

You can create custom transaction codes. The ABAP programs created by developers of an implementation team are not executed by the end users - people who operate the SAP software - the way you have been testing and executing them by navigating to transaction SE38, entering the program name, and clicking the execution button. Instead, you will create custom transaction codes and assign the ABAP programs to these custom transaction codes. The end users will employ these custom transaction codes to execute the ABAP programs delivered by the implementation team developers.

To create a custom transaction code, use the transaction code SE93 to navigate to the screen for maintaining custom transaction codes.

Let a custom transaction code be created with the program you created for demonstrating the table control (i.e., YCL_CH14_05_TABLE_CTRL). So on the custom transaction code maintenance screen, enter the transaction code YCL_CH14_TC01. The screen will look like Figure 14-91.

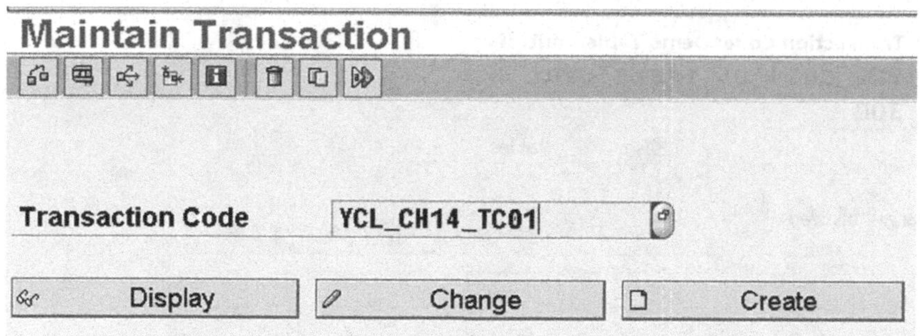

Figure 14-91. *Transaction Maintenance - SE93 Screen*

A custom transaction code must start with 'Y'/'Z' and can contain alphanumeric characters with embedded underscores (_, a maximum name space of twenty characters). Click on the create button. The transaction attribute dialog will appear like the one in Figure 14-92.

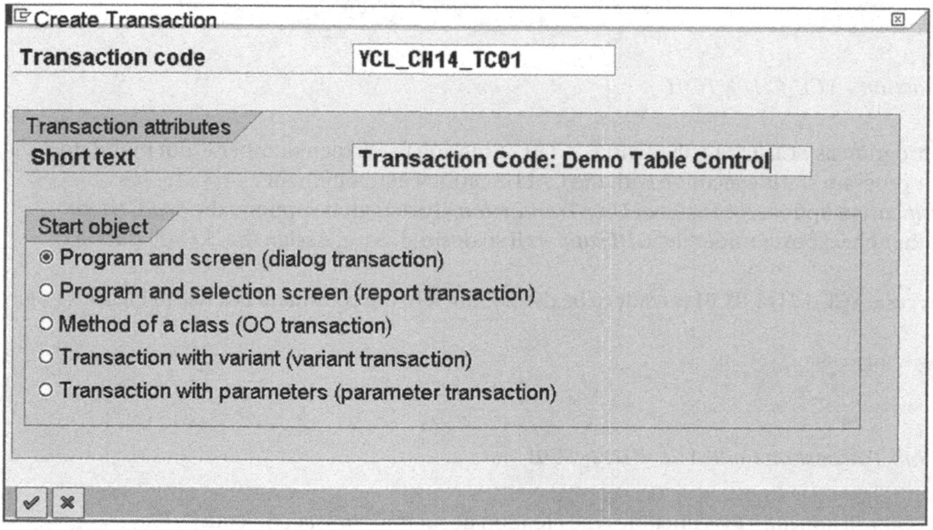

Figure 14-92. *Create Transaction - Transaction Attributes*

Enter a short bit of text. The five radio buttons specify the start object. The first three are self-explanatory.

For *Transaction with variant,* you can create a variation (a kind of version of an existing transaction code including the SAP delivered transaction codes). In these variants, you can set attributes of screen fields (like hiding preset values of screen fields and even hide entire screens).

For *Transaction with parameter,* you can pre-assign values to the fields on the opening screen.

In the present context, you are creating a transaction code for a screen/dialog program. Hence the first or the default radio button is to be enabled. Click on the continue button. The screen will appear like Figure 14-93.

Change Dialog Transaction

Transaction code YCL_CH14_TC01
Package $TMP

Transaction text Transaction Code: Demo Table Control
Program YCL_CH14_05_TABLE_CTRL
Screen number 300
Authorization object Values

☑ Maintenance of standard transaction variant allowed

Classification
Transaction classification
◉ Professional User Transaction
○ Easy Web Transaction Service
☐ Pervasive enabled

GUI support
☐ SAPGUI for HTML
☐ SAPGUI for Java
☑ SAPGUI for Windows

Figure 14-93. *Create Transaction – YCL_CH14_TC01*

Enter the name of the program as YCL_CH14_05_TABLE_CTRL. Entering the screen number is not mandatory in your present context as your program starts execution with the CALL SCREEN 300 statement.

Select the default *Classification* option. *Professional User Transaction.* By default it supports the *SAPGUI for Windows.* You can enable other checkboxes under the *GUI support* if so desired. Save. Assign the '$TMP' package when prompted.

The custom transaction code YCL_CH14_TC01 is ready to be used. Enter it in the command box like in Figure 14-94.

Figure 14-94. *Execute Custom Transaction Code. YCL_CH14_TC01*

The screen of Figure 14-90 will appear. This concludes the creation of custom transaction code.

A Brief Overview of DDIC Lock Objects

You have been exposed to a few of the SAP functional module database tables of the functional module 'Sales and Distribution' - SD. For instance, the customer entity data is located in more than one database table: KNA1, KNB1..., and the KN series of tables. The billing document data is located in two tables: VBRK and VBRP. Similarly, database tables of the functional module are located in 'Material Management'- MM. The vendor entity data is located in more than one database table: LFA1, LFB1..., and the LF series. The purchasing document data is located in two tables: EKKO and EKPO.

Most of the SAP functional module data is located in multiple tables.

When an end user is editing the data of a specific customer - for example, customer code equal to 'X001' - the row/s of this customer code 'X001' in all the customer database tables need to be locked to all other end users other than the end user who is editing the data. This is to ensure data integrity.

All database software provides locking mechanisms for maintaining data integrity. But the database software locking mechanisms operate on a single database table and cannot serve that purpose in a SAP environment where most entity data is located in multiple tables.

To take care of this requirement of simultaneously locking rows in multiple tables, SAP offers its own locking mechanism through the DDIC lock objects. All lock object names, including custom lock object names, must start with the letter 'E.'

A screen shot of the *Table*s tab of the SAP lock object 'EXKNA1' used for customer data is shown in Figure 14-95.

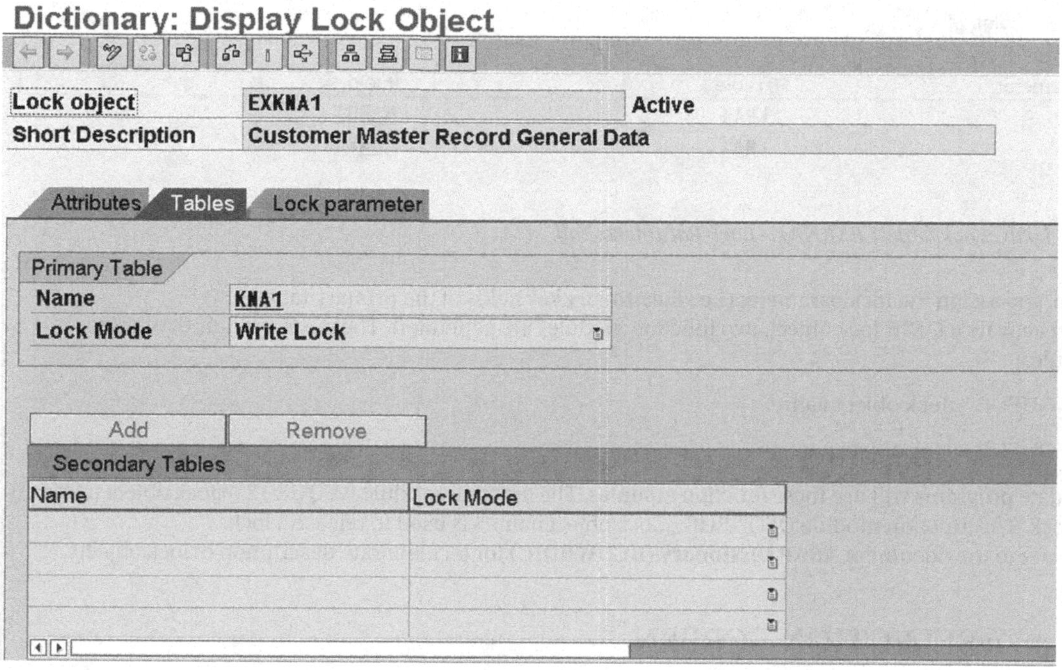

Dictionary: Display Lock Object

Lock object	EXKNA1	Active
Short Description	Customer Master Record General Data	

Attributes | Tables | Lock parameter

Primary Table

Name	KNA1
Lock Mode	Write Lock

Add | Remove

Secondary Tables

Name	Lock Mode

Figure 14-95. *DDIC Lock Object EXKNA1 - Tables Tab*

A lock object consists of a primary table. The lock object 'EXKNA1' has KNA1 as the primary table. You can explicitly assign secondary tables to the lock object. (At the bottom of the screen of the *Tables* tab). If the secondary tables are not explicitly assigned, there is implicit assignment through foreign key relationships of the primary table with other tables.

The implicit assignment of secondary tables through foreign key relationships is with restrictions. To give a rough example, if an end user is editing specific customer data, the row corresponding to this customer must be locked in all the tables containing customer data not any other tables like sales orders or billing document data. The sales orders and billing documents also have a foreign key relationship with customer data.

One prime rule of implicit assignment of secondary tables is that the foreign key fields in the secondary tables must also be primary key fields in the secondary tables.

Consider the tables KNA1 and KNB1. They are related through the field 'KUNNR'. The field 'KUNNR' is a primary key field in the primary table KNA1. It is a foreign key field in the table KNB1 as well as a primary key field. Hence the table KNB1 qualifies as an implicit secondary table in the lock object EXKNA.

Consider the tables KNA1 and VBRK. They are related through the field 'KUNNR and 'KUNAG'. The field 'KUNNR' is a primary key field in the primary table KNA1. The field 'KUNAG' is a foreign key field in the table VBRK and not a primary key field. Hence the table VBRK does not qualify as an implicit secondary table in the lock object EXKNA.

You can assign lock mode as *Exclusive, Shared,* or *Exclusive but cumulative.*

A screen shot of *Lock parameter* tab of the same SAP lock object 'EXKNA1' used for customer data is shown in Figure 14-96.

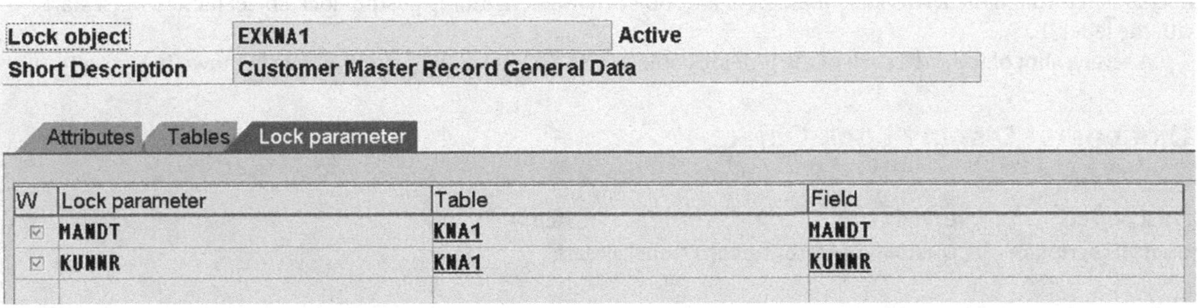

Lock object EXKNA1 Active
Short Description Customer Master Record General Data

Attributes | Tables | Lock parameter

W	Lock parameter	Table	Field
☑	MANDT	KNA1	MANDT
☑	KUNNR	KNA1	KUNNR

Figure 14-96. *DDIC Lock Object EXKNA1 – Lock Parameter Tab*

In this tab, you assign the lock parameter (i.e., the primary key fields of the primary table).

When you activate a DDIC lock object, two function modules are generated. These are the names of these function modules:

ENQUEUE _<lock object name>

DEQUEUE_<lock object name>

ABAP update programs will use these function modules. The function module ENQUEUE _<lock object name> is used to set a lock. The function module DEQUEUE _<lock object name> is used to release a lock.

You can refer to the document **ABAP Dictionary (BCDWBDIC)** for an elaborate description of lock objects.

Tab Strip on a SELECTION-SCREEN

You can place tab strip on selection screens. The location of tab strip on selection screen involves declaration of

1. Sub screens with BEGIN OFSCREEN... END OF SCREEN statements.
2. Tabbed Block with BEGIN OF TABBED... END OF BLOCK...

The following source program with the comments will make this clearer.

```
REPORT YCL_CH14_06_TABSTRIP_SL_SCREEN.

*********************************
* Tab Strip in SELECTION-SCREEN **
*********************************

********************************************
* SELECTION-SCREEN SUBSCREENS declarations **
********************************************
SELECTION-SCREEN BEGIN OF SCREEN 100 AS SUBSCREEN
                 NO INTERVALS.

PARAMETERS. KUNNR TYPE KUNNR,
            VKORG TYPE VKORG,
            VTEXT TYPE VTEXT.

SELECTION-SCREEN END OF SCREEN 100.

SELECTION-SCREEN BEGIN OF SCREEN 200 AS SUBSCREEN
                 NO INTERVALS.

PARAMETERS. LIFNR TYPE LIFNR,
            EKORG TYPE EKORG,
            EKOTX TYPE EKOTX.

SELECTION-SCREEN END OF SCREEN 200.

************************************************************
SELECTION-SCREEN. BEGIN OF BLOCK BLOCK1 WITH FRAME TITLE TL01
                  NO INTERVALS,

                 SKIP,
************************************************************
* TABBED BLOCK - special type of SELECTION-SCREEN BLOCK     **
* TABBED BLOCKS accept only SELECTION-SCREEN TAB statements **
* inside them to create tab strip tabs                      **
************************************************************
                 BEGIN OF TABBED BLOCK PART_TAB FOR 3 LINES
                  NO INTERVALS,

                 TAB (18 CUST_BT USER-COMMAND CUSTOMER
                                 DEFAULT SCREEN 100,

                 TAB (18 VEND_BT USER-COMMAND VENDOR
                                 DEFAULT SCREEN 200,

                 END OF BLOCK PART_TAB,
                 END OF BLOCK BLOCK1.
```

```
**************************************************************
INITIALIZATION.
  TL01    = 'Business Partner'(001 .
  CUST_BT = '@AO@ Customer'(002 .
  VEND_BT = '@AD@ Vendor'(003 .
```

Selection texts are created fetching the labels from the data elements. When the program is executed, the screen will look like Figure 14-97.

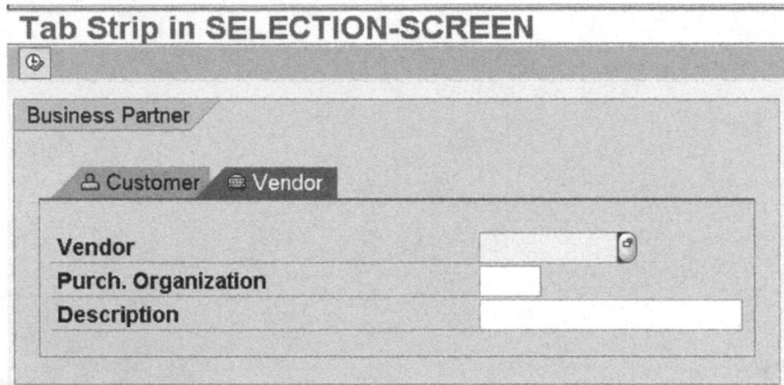

Figure 14-97. *Tab Strip in SELECTION-SCREEN*

Maintenance Views and Table Maintenance Dialogs

Overview. Maintenance Views, Table Maintenance Generator, and Table Maintenance Dialogs

Maintenance Views. You have been exposed to three DDIC types of views: database views, projection views, and help views. You can create one more type of view in DDIC: the maintenance view. Maintenance view can only be used in *table maintenance dialogs. Table maintenance dialog*s are mostly to be used for maintaining data in custom or user-defined database tables. Maintaining data in custom or user-defined database tables means creation, change, deletion, and display of data in these database tables.

You can create a maintenance view either with one or multiple database tables. In case of a maintenance view consisting of multiple database tables, these tables must be linked with foreign key relationships. When you create a maintenance view with multiple databases, the system automatically enters the table join conditions. You cannot modify or manually enter the join conditions like you were doing when creating database views. The rows in the maintenance view using multiple database tables is based on inner join like it is with database views.

To be able to insert, edit, and delete data in the underlying tables of a maintenance view, the following prerequisites should be fulfilled:

1. In each of the participating database tables of the maintenance view, in the tab 'Delivery and Maintenance', in the item 'Data Browser/Table View Maint.', the option 'Display/Maintenance Allowed' should have been assigned.

2. In the maintenance view, in the tab 'Maint. Status', the radio button 'read, change, delete and insert' (default) should have been selected.

There are constraints of cardinality when creating a maintenance view with multiple database tables. You can create a maintenance view with multiple database tables only when the cardinality between these tables is either N.1 or N.C. (Refer to Chapter 2 for cardinality). This constraint is operative when you use the maintenance view in a *table maintenance dialog* to create/edit/delete entries in all underlying tables of the maintenance view. If you employ a *table maintenance dialog* using a maintenance view with multiple database tables to create/edit/delete entries only in a single underlying database table at the bottom of the hierarchy of the maintenance view, you need not be bound by this cardinality constraint.

Table Maintenance Dialogs Using Maintenance Views and Table Maintenance Generator

When you created and activated custom database tables in Chapter 2, a default *table maintenance dialog* was created enabling you to insert, edit, delete, and display data in the database table: that is, perform data operations on the database tables. You used transaction code SE11 or SE16 to perform data operations on the database tables.

The process that generates the *table maintenance dialog* using the maintenance views is called the *table maintenance generator*.

Table maintenance dialogs using maintenance views offers some advantages and additional features over the default *table maintenance dialogs* generated when database tables are activated.

The additional advantages and features of *table maintenance dialog* using maintenance view over the default maintenance dialog are as follows.

- The maintenance dialog using maintenance view can be for multiple database tables subject to the cardinality constraints.
- The maintenance dialog using maintenance view can be assigned an authorization group enabling access by specific user group: that is, an extra security facility. With the authorization group and authorization object, access can be restricted to the level of any workbench object. The authorization group and authorization object is not in the scope of this book.

With the maintenance dialog box assigned an authorization group and an authorization object, it will operate in the following manner.

An end user envisaged to operate on the data of underlying table/s of a maintenance view will not have access to the transactions codes SE11 and SE16. They will be given access to transaction code SM30. In the transaction code SM30, you can access and operate only tables for which *table maintenance dialog* exists. With transaction code SM30, an end user can only access and operate data of specific database tables for which *table maintenance dialog* exists and has been authorized access to these through the authorization group and authorization object.

- The maintenance dialog using maintenance view can be modified and customized.

Once a maintenance view is created, a *table maintenance dialog* can be generated using this maintenance view screen or the transaction code SE54 by the *table maintenance generator*.

The *table maintenance generator* automatically generates a function group, function module/s, interfaces, and screens of a *table maintenance dialog*. This generated *table maintenance dialog* can then be used to maintain data in the database table/s of the maintenance view.

A *table maintenance dialog* generated using a maintenance view has option to operate the maintenance dialog with either one screen or with two screens.

When you choose the option of a maintenance dialog with two screens, the first screen presents an overview of existing maintenance view data (multiple row display displaying data of the first four fields). This is called the overview screen. To operate on existing rows, the rows to be operated upon have to be selected through the row selectors in the overview screen and control then shifts to a second screen. To create new rows, you click on the create button on the application tool bar and the control shifts to the second screen.

The second screen is to insert/edit/delete/display individual rows. This screen is called the single screen and presents one row at a time of the maintenance view. To get a feel of two screens *table maintenance dialog*, see the contents of SAP delivered maintenance view V_T001 using transaction code SE16 or SM30.

In a *table maintenance dialog* with a single screen, data from the maintenance view is presented in multiple row form with field headings and can be operated upon on the same screen. To get a feel of single screen *table maintenance dialog*, see the contents of SAP delivered maintenance view V_KNA1_CORE using transaction code SE16 or SM30.

When generating the table maintenance dialog, the table maintenance generator prompts for the function group. It is a good practice to input a nonexistent function group name. When you input a nonexistent function group name, the table maintenance generator creates a function group with that name and also generates function modules. All programming including screen related programming (PBO and PAI modules, etc.), are located in the code of the function group and the function modules. You can incorporate and execute your custom PBO and PAI modules and subroutines. The custom PBO and PAI modules will be invoked from the flow logic area of the screens. The subroutines are coded for events. There are more than thirty events supported in the maintenance dialog. The screen layouts can be changed in terms of repositioning, resizing, and changing the properties of screen elements.

Now that an overview has been provided of table maintenance views and *table maintenance dialog*, you can proceed to hands-on exercises.

Hands-on Exercise. Create and Operate Table Maintenance Dialog for the Custom Database Table YCL_CH02_BILLI

Scenario

Using a *table maintenance dialog*, you want to be able to insert, edit, delete, and display data for the database table YCL_CH02_BILLI. This table was created in Chapter 2 as part of your hands-on exercise on domains, data elements, and tables. You operated the data of this table using the default *table maintenance dialog* in Chapter 2. This table consists of items of bills. To recapitulate, the table consists of the following fields:

BILL_NO	Bill Number
SRL_NO	Serial Number
ITEM_CODE	Item Code
QNTY	Quantity
RATE	Rate (Selling Price)
AMOUNT	Amount for the Item

You had attached a search help to the field 'ITEM_CODE' of this table in Chapter 3. The search help had the table YCL_CH02_ITEMM as its source of data. The attached search help enabled a selection list to appear on pressing function key F4 in this field when entering data through the default *table maintenance dialog*. The selection list displayed the following fields: 'ITEM_CODE', 'ITEM_DESC' (Item Description), and 'RATE'. On making a selection in the selection list, the values of fields 'ITEM_CODE' and 'RATE' were returned to the screen fields.

You will create a maintenance view with the tables YCL_CH02_BILLI and YCL_CH02_ITEMM related through the field 'ITEM_CODE'. These two tables do not have N.1 cardinality. Since you will operate (insert/edit/delete) data of one table only (i.e., YCL_CH02_BILLI), this does not matter. The objective of including the table YCL_CH02_ITEMM is to display the 'ITEM_DESC' (item description) field alongside the item code ('ITEM_CODE') field when a row is presented. You will generate a *table maintenance dialog* using the maintenance view.

The participating fields with their originating tables in the maintenance view are shown in Table 14-10.

Table 14-10.

Field Name	Table Name	Description
BILL_NO	YCL_CH02_BILLI	Bill Number
SRL_NO	YCL_CH02_BILLI	Serial Number
ITEM_CODE	YCL_CH02_BILLI	Item Code
ITEM_DESC	YCL_CH02_ITEMM	Item Description
QNTY	YCL_CH02_BILLI	Quantity
RATE	YCL_CH02_BILLI	Rate (Selling Price)
AMOUNT	YCL_CH02_BILLI	Amount for the Item

With this specification of maintenance view, you proceed to create the maintenance view.

Create Maintenance View

On the opening screen of transaction code SE11, click on the 'View' radio button. Enter the name of the maintenance view to be created as YCL_CH14_BIIT_MV. Click the Create button or press the function key F5. The system will prompt for the type of view to be created. Select the 'Maintenance view' radio button.

The maintenance view creation screen appears. Enter appropriate short text. Under the column 'Tables', enter either name of the secondary table YCL_CH02_BILLI or select this table from the filtered (YCL_CH02*) selection list. To select the primary table, click on the 'Relationships' button. Select the table relationship of YCL_CH02_ITEMM & YCL_CH02_BILLI from the list. The screen after selection of table relationship is as shown in Figure 14-98.

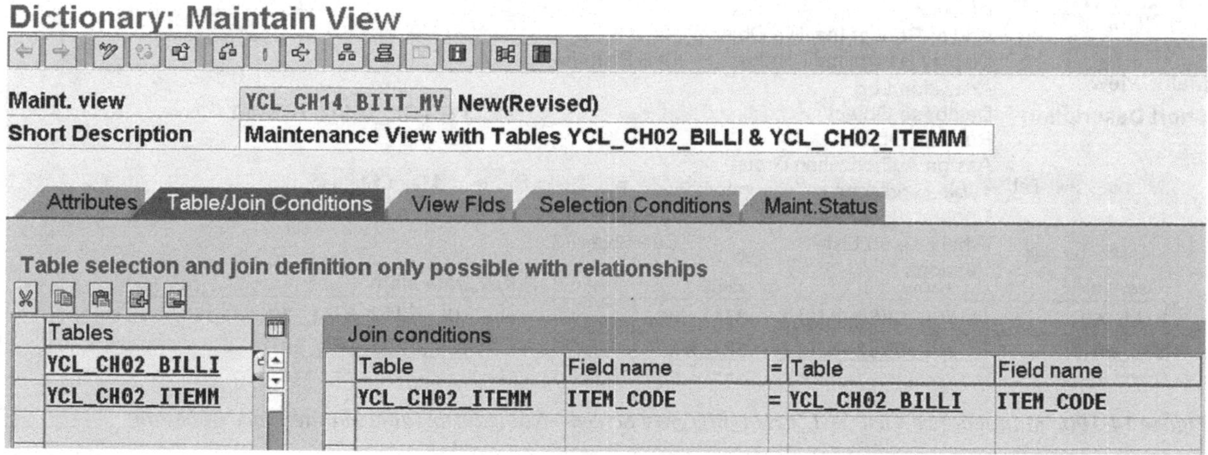

Figure 14-98. *Create Maintenance View YCL_CH14_BIIT_MV, Tab - Table/Join Conditions*

Click on the 'View Flds' tab. Select all the fields of the table YCL_CH02_BILLI. Select the field 'ITEM_DESC' from the table YCL_CH02_ITEMM. The screen after ordering the fields as per the specifications will look like those in Figure 14-99.

Dictionary: Maintain View

Maint. view YCL_CH14_BIIT_MV New

Short Description Maintenance View with Tables YCL_CH02_BILLI & YCL_CH02_ITEMM

Attributes | Table/Join Conditions | View Flds | Selection Conditions | Maint.Status

Table fields

View field	Table	Field	P	Key	Data elem.	Mod	DTyp	Length	Short description
BILL_NO	YCL_CH02_BILLI	BILL_NO		☑	YCL_CH02_BILL_NO	☐	NUMC	8	Bill number
SRL_NO	YCL_CH02_BILLI	SRL_NO		☑	YCL_CH02_SRL_NO	☐	NUMC	6	Srl No.
ITEM_CODE	YCL_CH02_BILLI	ITEM_CODE		☐	YCL_CH02_ITEM_CODE	☐	NUMC	4	Item Code
ITEM_DESC	YCL_CH02_ITEMM	ITEM_DESC		☐	YCL_CH02_ITEM_DESC	☐	CHAR	30	Item Desc
QNTY	YCL_CH02_BILLI	QNTY		☐	YCL_CH02_QNTY	☐	DEC	3	Quantity
RATE	YCL_CH02_BILLI	RATE		☐	YCL_CH02_RATE	☐	DEC	7	Rate
AMOUNT	YCL_CH02_BILLI	AMOUNT		☐	YCL_CH02_AMOUNT	☐	DEC	8	Amount

Figure 14-99. *Create Maintenance View YCL_CH14_BIIT_MV, Tab – View Fields*

Save, perform a consistency check, and activate the maintenance view. Now you need to create the *table maintenance dialog*. To generate the *table maintenance dialog*, make the following menu selection in the maintenance view screen: Utilities (M ➤ Table Maintenance Generator). This is shown in Figure 14-100.

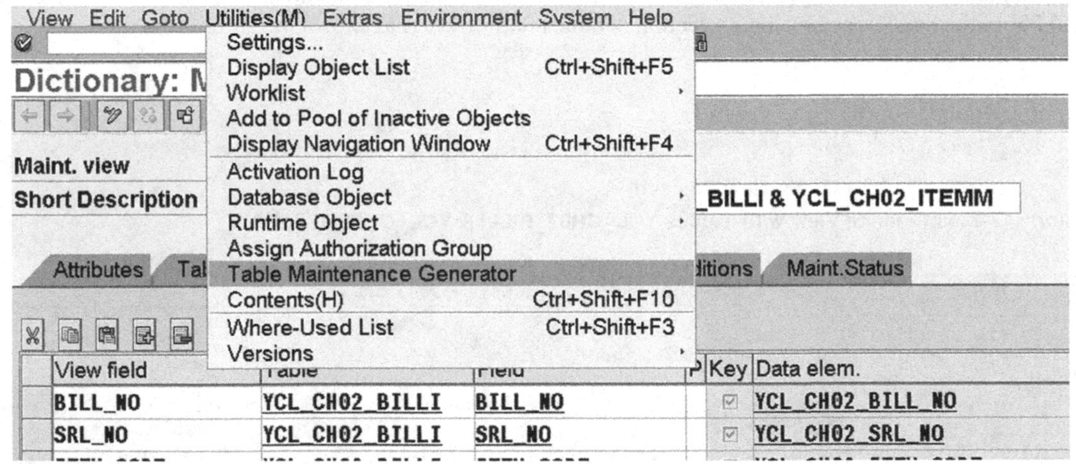

Figure 14-100. *Maintenance View YCL_CH14_BIIT_MV Screen – Navigate to Table Maintenance Generator*

Generate Table Maintenance Dialog

The *generate table maintenance dialog* screen will appear like in Figure 14-101.

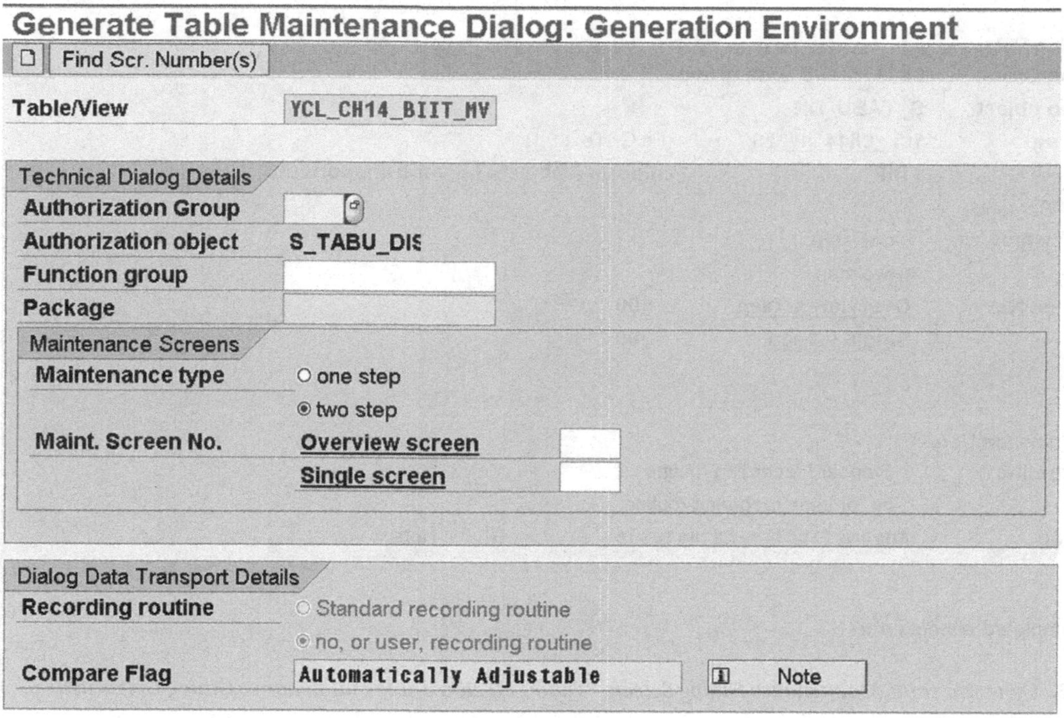

Figure 14-101. *Maintenance View YCL_CH14_BIIT_MV Screen – Generate Table Maintenance Dialog Screen*

Enter the 'Authorization Group' as '&NC&' (no authorization) from the selection list. 'Authorization object' is automatically assigned as 'S_TABU_DIS.'

Enter the 'Function group' value as YCL_CH14_MV_FG. This function group should not exist. The *table maintenance generator* will automatically create this function group and related function modules.

Select the 'Maintenance Type' as a 'two step.' With this option, there will be an overview screen displaying multiple rows. There will be a single screen in which all the fields of a selected row from the overview screen will appear. In case you select 'one step,' on a single screen, multiple rows will appear. Enter 'Overview screen' value as 100 and 'Single screen' value as 200.

For multiple maintenance views created with the same set of table/s, these screen numbers should be unique.

After the values have been entered, click on the create button on the application toolbar.

The screen with the entered values and the table maintenance generated will appear as in Figure 14-102.

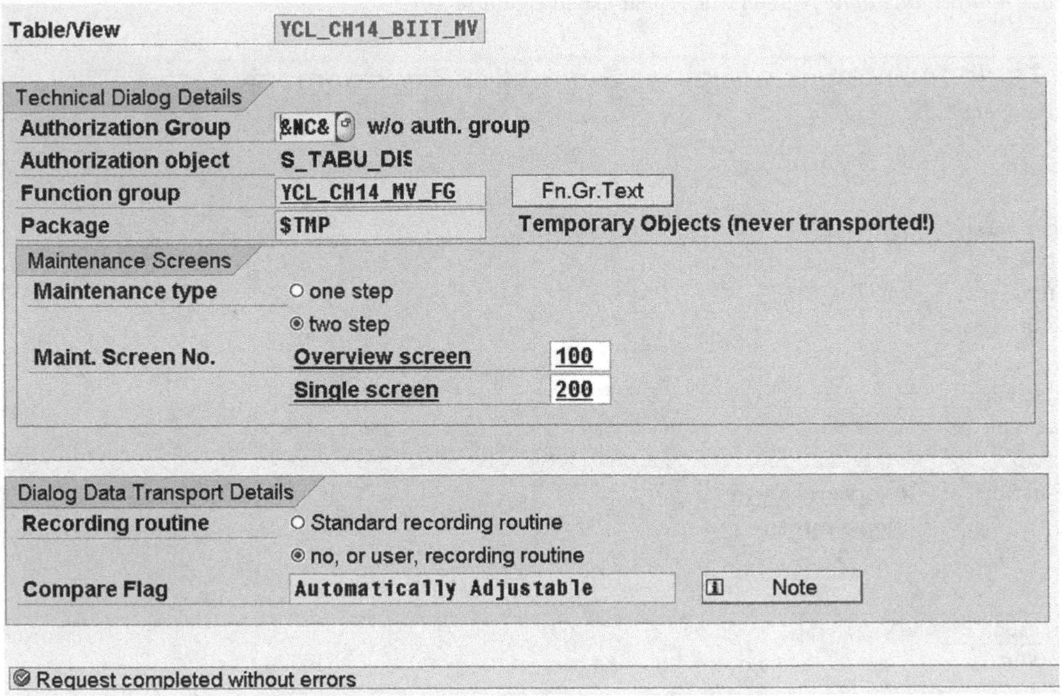

Table/View YCL_CH14_BIIT_MV

Technical Dialog Details
Authorization Group &NC& w/o auth. group
Authorization object S_TABU_DIS
Function group YCL_CH14_MV_FG Fn.Gr.Text
Package $TMP Temporary Objects (never transported!)

Maintenance Screens
Maintenance type ○ one step
◉ two step
Maint. Screen No. Overview screen 100
Single screen 200

Dialog Data Transport Details
Recording routine ○ Standard recording routine
◉ no, or user, recording routine
Compare Flag Automatically Adjustable Note

Request completed without errors

Figure 14-102. *Generate Table Maintenance Dialog Screen – Values Filled & Table Maintenance Dialog Generated*

Now that a *table maintenance dialog* has been created, you will use it to operate the data of table YCL_CH02_BILLI.

Operate Table YCL_CH02_BILLI Data Using Maintenance View Table Maintenance Dialog

With the *table maintenance dialog* generated, go back to the maintenance view screen. Click on the contents button of the application toolbar. The overview screen of the *table maintenance dialog* appears. It displays the first four fields of the maintenance view. This data was created in Chapter 2. If you click on the toggle button change on the application tool bar of the overview screen of the *table maintenance dialog*, an information alert appears as your table is cross-client (Client independent). This is shown in Figure 14-103.

Display View "Maintenance View with Tables YCL_CH02_BILLI & YCL_CH02_I

Maintenance View with Tables YCL_CH02_BILLI & YCL_CH02_ITEMM

Bill No.	Srl No.	Item Code	Item Desc
1	1	5	Vegetarian Supreme Medium
1	2	1005	Special Lemonade
2	1	5	Vegetarian Supreme Medium
2	2	10	Barbeque Chicken Regular
2	3	1005	Special Lemonade

Information

Caution: The table is cross-client

Figure 14-103. Table Maintenance Dialog Overview Screen-Alert for Cross-Client

With the select all button on the application toolbar, select all the rows. The overview screen interface with all the rows selected is shown in Figure 14-104.

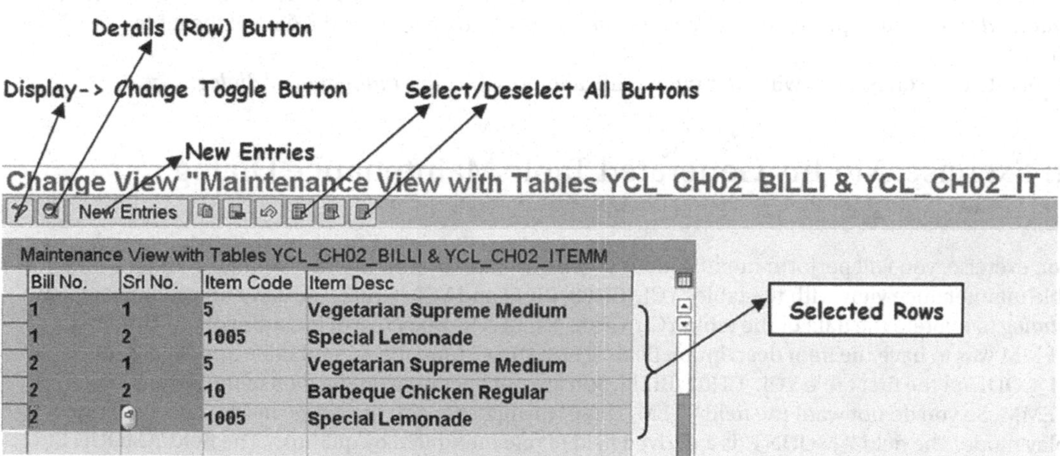

Figure 14-104. Table Maintenance Dialog – Overview Screen & Its Interface

If you click on the Details button, the screen will present each row's contents as shown in Figure 14-105.

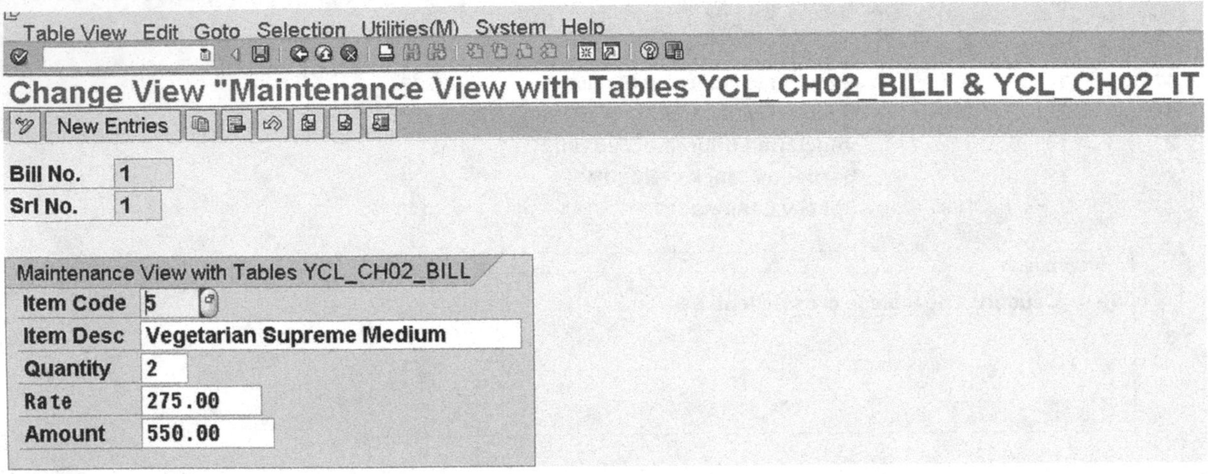

Figure 14-105. *Table Maintenance Dialog – Single Screen with Data*

There are buttons to create new rows and navigate to other rows (previous, next, etc.).

As an exercise, use the *table maintenance dialog* to create new rows, edit existing rows, and delete rows.

To recapitulate, you first defined a scenario for a maintenance view using tables YCL_CH02_BILLI and YCL_CH02_ITEMM. The scenario envisaged usage of the maintenance view for data operation of the table YCL_CH02_BILLI. You created a maintenance view as per the scenario. You used the maintenance view to generate a *table maintenance dialog*. You deployed the *table maintenance dialog* to operate on the data of the table YCL_CH02_BILLI.

In the next hands-on exercise, you will carry out modifications to the *table maintenance dialog*.

Hands-on Exercise. Modify Generated Table Maintenance Dialog

Scenario

In this hands-on exercise, you will perform modifications to the objects of preceding hands-on exercise in which you created the table maintenance view with the tables YCL_CH02_BILLI and YCL_CH02_ITEMM and generate a *table maintenance dialog* to operate the data of the table YCL_CH02_BILLI. The objective of including the second table YCL_CH02_ITEMM was to have the item description field 'ITEM_DESC' from the second table appear alongside the field 'ITEM_CODE' of the first table YCL_CH02_BILLI. You are not operating on the data of the second table YCL_CH02_ITEMM. So you do not want the field 'ITEM_DESC' to appear in edit or change mode. This field must appear in display mode. The field 'AMOUNT' is a derived field of rate multiplied by quantity. The field 'AMOUNT' should be set to display mode. It should be derived by multiplying the rate and quantity in a PAI module: that is, when you click on the save button or press the <Enter> key, (triggering a PAI event) on the *table maintenance dialog*, the field 'AMOUNT' should be derived by executing a PAI module.

To sum up, in the present hands-on exercise, you will perform the following:

- Set the field 'ITEM_DESC' in display mode in both screens of the *table maintenance dialog*: the overview screen (screen no. 100) as well as the single screen (screen no. 200).
- Set the 'AMOUNT' field to display mode in the single screen (screen no. 200) and derive the field 'AMOUN' by multiplying 'RATE' and 'QNTY' in a PAI module.

Modifications as per Scenario

To carry out these listed modifications in the *table maintenance dialog*, navigate to the *generate table maintenance dialog* screen of the maintenance view YCL_CH14_BIIT_MV (Figure 14-102) Double click on screen 200. (Single screen), and the system will navigate to the screen painter. Click on the layout editor button on the application tool bar. In the layout editor of screen 200, double click on the screen element 'YCL_CH14_BIIT_MV-ITEM_DESC' to bring up the properties dialog box of this screen element. On the property dialog box, click on the 'Program' tab, and disable the 'Input Field' checkbox. This is shown in Figure 14-106.

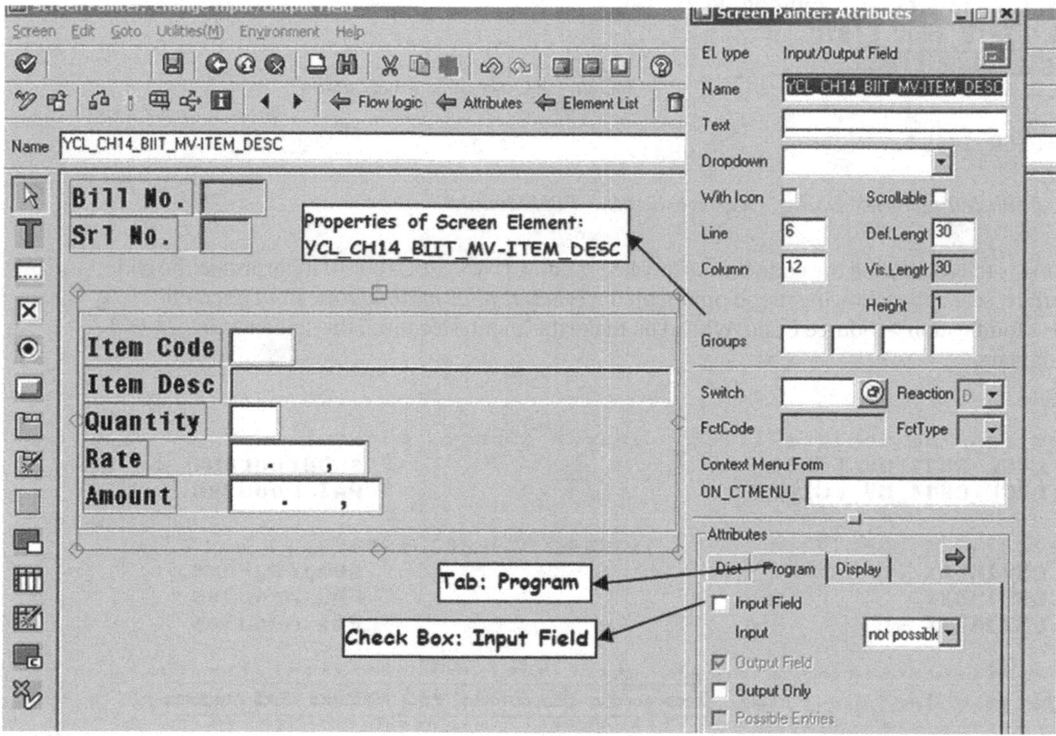

Figure 14-106. *Table Maintenance Dialog. Single Screen - Change Properties*

Carry out a similar procedure for the screen element 'YCL_CH14_BIIT_MV-AMOUNT'. Save, activate screen no. 200, and exit the layout editor. Return to the *generate table maintenance dialog* screen. This will ensure that the fields 'ITEM_DESC' and 'AMOUNT' on the single screen or screen no. 200 will appear in display mode when operating the *table maintenance dialog*.

To ensure that the field 'ITEM_DESC' on the overview screen or screen no. 100 appears in display mode, you have to execute a PBO module (dynamic setting of properties from the *flow logic* area of screen no. 100). This is so because the *table maintenance dialog* is manipulating the properties of this screen element in its PBO module. If you want to set the properties of this screen element, it should override the setting by PBO module of the *table maintenance dialog*. So your PBO module invocation should follow the *table maintenance dialog* invocation of PBO modules.

On the generate *table maintenance dialog* screen, double click on screen 100. The system will navigate to the *flow logic* area of screen no. 100. Insert a module invoking a statement like MODULE OWN_PBO100. This statement is just preceding the ENDLOOP statement in the PBO area. Perform syntax and activate the screen. The *flow logic* area with invocation of your PBO module after activation is shown in Figure 14-107.

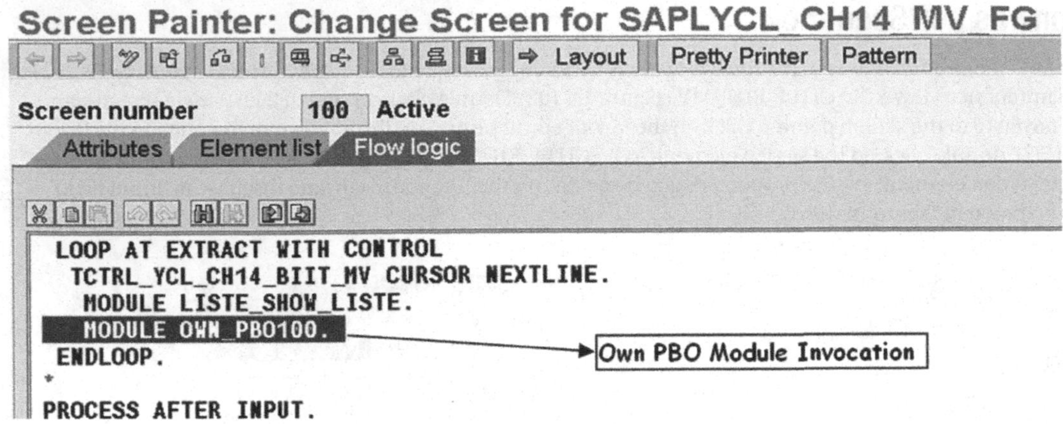

Figure 14-107. *Table Maintenance Dialog. Overview Screen – PBO Module*

The next step is to incorporate the code for the invoked module OWN_PBO100. To incorporate the code for invoked module, select the following menu option on the *generate table maintenance dialog* screen. Environment ➤ Modification ➤ Source Code. When you make this menu selection, the screen as in Figure 14-108 appears.

```
*       view related include-files    (never change, please)         *
  INCLUDE LYCL_CH14_MV_FGF00                        . " subprograms
  INCLUDE LYCL_CH14_MV_FGI00                        . " PAI modules

*       general include-files         (never change, please)         *
  INCLUDE LSVIMFXX                                  . " subprograms
  INCLUDE LSVIMOXX                                  . " PBO modules
  INCLUDE LSVIMIXX                                  . " PAI modules

**********************************************************************
*    User-defined Include-files  Incorporate Subroutines, PBO Modules, PAI Modules
**********************************************************************
* INCLUDE LYCL_CH14_MV_FGF...                    " Subprograms
* INCLUDE LYCL_CH14_MV_FGO...                    " PBO-Modules
* INCLUDE LYCL_CH14_MV_FGI...                    " PAI-Modules
```

Figure 14-108. *Table Maintenance Dialog. Overview Screen – Incorporate Source*

In Figure 14-108, at the bottom are commented INCLUDE source lines. They are a provision to create your own PBO and PAI modules. There is provision to create your own subroutines or subprograms. The subroutines get executed for events. There are over thirty events available in the *table maintenance dialog*. A list of these events can be found in SAP documentation on maintenance views and *table maintenance dialog*.

In the present scenario, you have to code a PBO module that will set the property of the screen element 'YCL_CH14_BIIT_MV-ITEM_DESC' to display mode: that is, SCREEN-INPUT = 0. So, de-comment the line

```
* INCLUDE LYCL_CH14_MV_FGO...
```

as INCLUDE LYCL_CH14_MV_FGO01.

Save and then double click on the include program name 'LYCL_CH14_MV_FGO01.' The system will alert that the program does not exist, should the program be created? This alert appears on the status bar and not as a pop-up. Press the <Enter> key. Then enter the following lines:

```
MODULE OWN_PBO100 OUTPUT.

LOOP AT SCREEN.
 IF SCREEN-NAME = 'YCL_CH14_BIIT_MV-ITEM_DESC'. "name of the screen element
  SCREEN-INPUT = 0.
  MODIFY SCREEN.
ENDIF.
ENDLOOP.

ENDMODULE.
```

Save, perform a syntax check, and activate the include program. Navigate to the previous screen in which the include program is being invoked. Activate this main program. Navigate back to the *generate table maintenance dialog* screen.

You have carried out the required modifications to make the field 'ITEM_DESC' appear in display mode in both the overview screen and the single screen. Next, you will incorporate a PAI module for the single screen (screen no. 200), which will calculate the field `YCL_CH14_BIIT_MV-AMOUNT = YCL_CH14_BIIT_MV-QNTY * YCL_CH14_BIIT_MV-RATE`.

To invoke its own PAI module and create code for its own PAI module for the single screen (screen no. 200), follow the same procedure you followed for invoking and creating its own PBO module.

In the *generate table maintenance dialog* screen, double click on the single screen (screen no. 200). The system will navigate to the *flow logic* area of screen no. 200. Scroll down the PAI area. The screen will look like Figure 14-109.

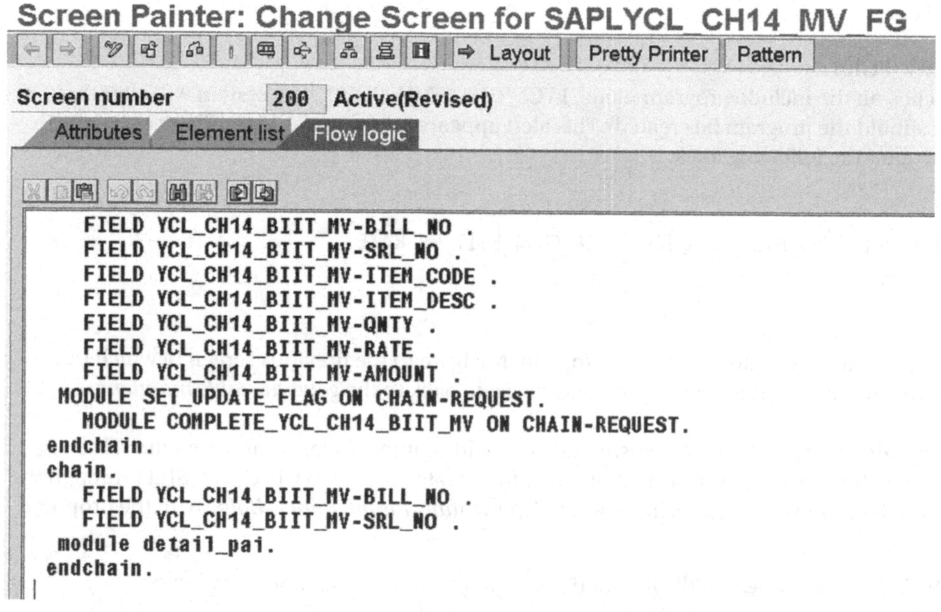

Figure 14-109. *Table Maintenance Dialog. Single Screen – PAI Module*

At the end of the existing PAI statements (after the statement 'endchain'), incorporate the PAI module invoking statement.

```
FIELD YCL_CH14_BIIT_MV-AMOUNT MODULE CALC_AMT.
```

Save, perform a syntax check, and activate the screen. Return to the *generate table maintenance dialog* screen. You have to create the code of invoked PAI module CALC_AMT. To incorporate the code for invoked PAI module, select the following menu option on the *generate table maintenance dialog* screen: Environment ➤ Modification ➤ Source Code. When you make this menu selection, the screen as in Figure 14-110 appears.

```
*      general include-files        (never change, please)         *
  INCLUDE LSVIMFXX                                  . " subprograms
  INCLUDE LSVIMOXX                                  . " PBO modules
  INCLUDE LSVIMIXX                                  . " PAI modules

*********************************************************************
*   User-defined Include-files (if necessary).                      *
*********************************************************************
* INCLUDE LYCL_CH14_MV_FGF...                   " Subprograms
  INCLUDE LYCL_CH14_MV_FGO01.                   " PBO-Modules
* INCLUDE LYCL_CH14_MV_FGI...                   " PAI-Modules
```

Figure 14-110. *Table Maintenance Dialog. Single Screen – Incorporate PAI Module Source*

You have to code a PAI module that will calculate the field 'AMOUNT.' So, de-comment the line:

```
* INCLUDE LYCL_CH14_MV_FGI...
```

as INCLUDE LYCL_CH14_MV_FGI01.

Save and then double click on the include program name 'LYCL_CH14_MV_FGI01.' The system will alert that the program does not exist, should the program be created? This alert appears on the status bar and not as a pop-up. Press the <Enter> key. Then enter the following lines:

```
MODULE CALC_AMT INPUT.
YCL_CH14_BIIT_MV-AMOUNT = YCL_CH14_BIIT_MV-QNTY * YCL_CH14_BIIT_MV-RATE.

ENDMODULE.
```

Save, perform a syntax check, and activate the include program. Navigate to the previous screen in which the include program is being invoked. Activate this (main) program. Navigate back to the *generate table maintenance dialog* screen.

On the *generate table maintenance dialog* screen, ensure that the field 'Compare Flag' is assigned the value 'Automatically Adjustable.' Press the save button. You are now ready to operate the table YCL_CH02_BILLI through the *table maintenance dialog* with the proposed changes incorporated in the *table maintenance dialog* with the proposed changes.

- The field 'ITEM_DESC' will appear in display mode both in overview screen and single screen.
- The field 'AMOUNT' will appear in display mode in the single screen.
- The field 'AMOUNT' is derived by multiplying the fields 'RATE' and 'QNTY.'

You will proceed to test these modifications to the original *table maintenance dialog.*

Operate Table YCL_CH02_BILLI after Modifications

Let the operation on the table YCL_CH02_BILLI with the modified *table maintenance dialog* be tested in transaction code SE16. On the screen of transaction code SE16, enter the name of the maintenance view as YCL_CH14_BIIT_MV. Click on the table contents button on the application tool bar. Switch to change the mode of the screen. The overview screen will appear as shown in Figure 14-111.

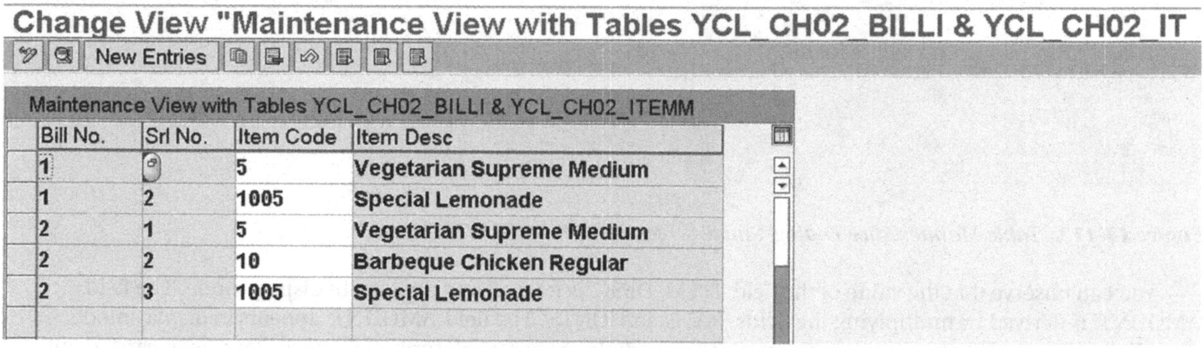

Change View "Maintenance View with Tables YCL_CH02_BILLI & YCL_CH02_IT

New Entries

Maintenance View with Tables YCL_CH02_BILLI & YCL_CH02_ITEMM

Bill No.	Srl No.	Item Code	Item Desc
1		5	Vegetarian Supreme Medium
1	2	1005	Special Lemonade
2	1	5	Vegetarian Supreme Medium
2	2	10	Barbeque Chicken Regular
2	3	1005	Special Lemonade

Figure 14-111. *Table Maintenance Dialog. Overview Screen - With Modifications*

As per the modifications, the field 'ITEM_DESC' appears in display mode on the overview screen. Select one or more rows on the overview screen and navigate to the single screen as shown in Figure 14-112.

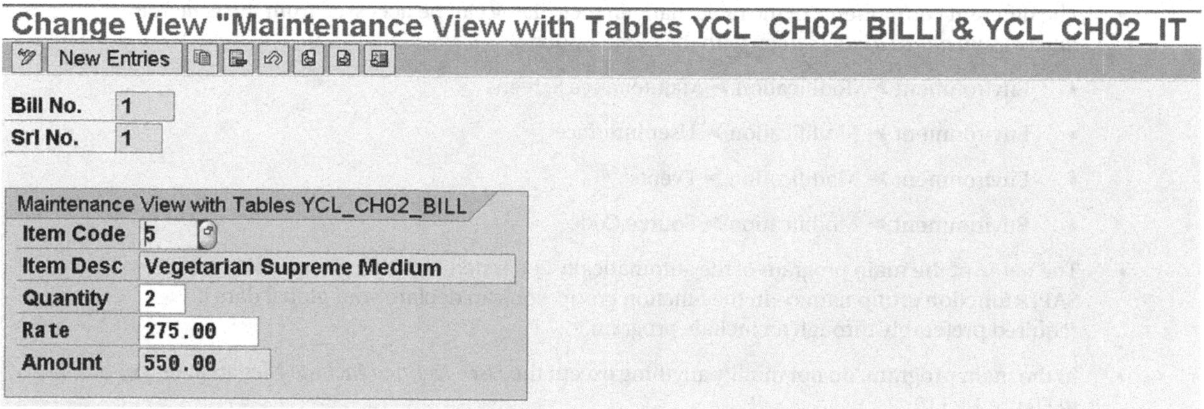

Change View "Maintenance View with Tables YCL_CH02_BILLI & YCL_CH02_IT

New Entries

Bill No.	1
Srl No.	1

Maintenance View with Tables YCL_CH02_BILL

Item Code	5
Item Desc	Vegetarian Supreme Medium
Quantity	2
Rate	275.00
Amount	550.00

Figure 14-112. *Table Maintenance Dialog. Single Screen - With Modifications*

You can observe that the fields 'ITEM_DESC' and 'AMOUNT' appear in display mode on the single screen.

To test whether the field 'AMOUNT' is derived by multiplying the fields 'RATE' and 'QNTY', you can either assign another value to the field 'ITEM_CODE' and/or change the contents of the field 'QNTY' of an existing row. Or you can create a new row and test the derivation of the field 'AMOUNT'.

In the following screen, the testing of derivation of 'AMOUNT' is demonstrated by creating a new row. You can create a new row by clicking the 'New Entries' button either on the overview screen or the single screen. When you click on the 'New Entries' button, a blank single screen appears. Click on the field 'ITEM_CODE'. Press function key F4 and make a selection from the selection list. Enter a value in the field 'QNTY'. Press the <Enter> key. This will trigger the PAI event, and a single screen will appear like in Figure 14-113.

Figure 14-113. *Table Maintenance Dialog. Single Screen – Field 'AMOUNT' Derived*

You can observe that the value of the field 'ITEM_DESC' is fetched and appears in display mode. The field 'AMOUNT' is derived by multiplying the fields 'RATE' and 'QNTY'. The field 'AMOUNT' appears in display mode.

All the proposed changes to the *table maintenance dialog* as per the described scenario have been carried out and tested.

Maintenance View, Table Maintenance Dialog, Miscellanea

The following should be borne in mind when modifying the *table maintenance dialog*.

- The different components of the table maintenance dialog can be accessed from the *generate table maintenance dialog* screen with the menu options.
    - Environment ➤Modification ➤ Maintenance Screens
    - Environment ➤ Modification ➤ User Interface
    - Environment ➤ Modification ➤ Events
    - Environment ➤ Modification ➤ Source Code
- The name of the main program of the automatically generated function group is as usual: SAPL<function group name>. In the function group, you can declare your global data if required preferably through an include program.
- In the main program, do not modify anything except the *User-Defined Include-files* area. Refer to Figure 14-110.
- If you want to make modifications to the function group in transaction code SE37, ensure that you are not on the *generate table maintenance dialog* screen. After carrying out modification to function group in transaction code SE37, activate all program components of the function group before exiting. If the function group is not active, you cannot access it from *generate table maintenance dialog* screen for modification.
- You can modify the *table maintenance dialog* screens in terms of layout, changing screen element properties, and inserting statements in the *flow logic* area.
- If things go wrong, delete the entire (all components) *table maintenance dialog*. Re-create the *table maintenance dialog* again.

This concludes maintenance views and *table maintenance dialog*.

Conclusion

The chapter began with a recapitulation of the screen painter basics that you were introduced to in Chapter 12. This was followed by the hands-on exercise that handles a database table data (i.e., display, change, create, and delete a row making use of multiple screens with screen navigations.

While performing the hands-on exercise, you were introduced to the object navigator - transaction code SE80. In the object navigator, you can create all workbench objects from a single point. With the object navigator, you can view all the workbench objects used in the ABAP program in a hierarchical tree-like structure.

The second hands-on exercise demonstrated the import parameters of a DDIC search help. While demonstrating the use of import parameters of a DDIC search help, you used the function modules: F4IF_FIELD_VALUE_REQUEST and DYNP_VALUES_UPDATE.

The third hands-on exercise involved the screen elements *Subscreen Area* and *Sub Screens* to simulate a tab strip element.

Having been exposed to the screen elements *Subscreen Area* and *Sub Screens,* you used a tab strip element in the fourth hands-on exercise. The tab strip is implemented using the screen elements *Subscreen Area* and *Sub Screens.*

The screen presentation of data of most business documents requires multiple rows to be displayed. The table screen element is used for presenting multiple rows data on the screen. The fifth hands-on exercise uses the table screen element to present the billing document data on the screen.

Some miscellanea are covered: creating custom transaction codes, a brief overview of the DDIC lock objects, and placing a tab strip on a selection screen.

The chapter concludes with a brief on maintenance views and table maintenance dialog.

Conclusion

APPENDIX A

Description of the SAP-Delivered Tables Used in the Hands-On Exercises

SAP-Delivered Tables Used in the Hands-On Exercises of the Book – Categories and Subcategories

This appendix contains descriptions of *SAP-delivered tables*, which you will use in the hands-on exercises of the book. Using an *SAP-delivered table* means that (i) some feature of the table is being highlighted in the book; (ii) the table is being used in the creation of ABAP dictionary objects such as views or search helps, etc., as part of hands-on exercise/s; and (iii) the table is used to access data in hands-on exercises on ABAP program/s (SELECT...).

You will relate better to the *SAP-delivered table* descriptions in this appendix after studying the two chapters on the ABAP dictionary – Chapters 2 and 3.

The phrase "*SAP delivered"* is being dropped from the subsequent text in the appendix because it is implicit. The tables described in this appendix are *SAP-delivered tables* only.

You will be using the following categories and subcategories of tables:

- The "T" series tables. The table names start with the letter "T." The "T" series tables contain:
    1. Universal nature of data such as country codes, country texts, currency codes, currency texts, etc. When SAP is installed, these tables are automatically populated with the universal data.
    2. Configuring data. In a real-life scenario, the configuring data tables get populated when configurations are performed by functional consultants. A simple example of configuring a table is the table T001 storing company codes. When company codes are created, typically by a finance functional module consultant, the table T001 gets populated.

The "T" series tables containing universal data or configuring data are client dependent. That is, the first field in these tables is of DDIC data type *CLNT*.

3. There are tables whose names start with the letter "T," containing other than universal or configuring information. These tables are cross client or client independent. An example of this table subcategory: TRDIRT storing ABAP source program title.

- The *master data* tables: These tables contain customer, vendor, material, and other information. Each of the *master data* information resides mostly in multiple tables. The customer, vendor, and material tables contain many fields; you will confine yourself to using a few essential fields.

The *master data* tables are client dependent. That is, the first field in these tables is of DDIC data type *CLNT*.

- The *transaction data* tables: The *transaction data* tables contain business document information. You will use these in most hands-on exercises – in the four business document tables relating to sales. You will use, for the most part, the tables related to billing. Only once will you will use tables related to the sales document (sales order). The *transaction data* tables also contain many fields; however, you will be confined to using a few essential ones.

The *transaction data* information of each business document is typically stored in two tables: the header table containing the header information and the item table containing item information.

The transaction data tables are also client dependent. That is, the first field in these tables is of DDIC data type *CLNT*.

- Cross client (client independent) tables. Examples of this table subcategory: DD02L storing table names, DD03l storing table field names, etc.

The *master data* and *transaction data* table categories are mentioned in any business application software context. The other categories and subcategories ("T" series and cross client, etc.) are specific to our present context and only for making the present context of table descriptions clearer. A diagrammatic representation of the categories and subcategories of tables used in the hands-on exercises of the book is shown in Figure A-1:

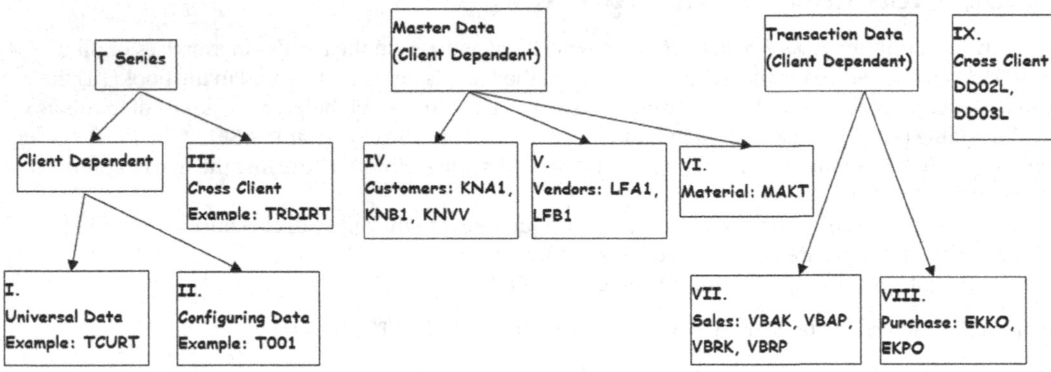

Figure A-1. *Tables used in hands-on exercises - categories and subcategories*

The table subcategories are numbered as I, II ... IX in Figure A-1.

One of the tables BUT000_TD does not fit into any of the neatly defined nine subcategories!

Out of the very large number of tables in the SAP application, very few - 29 - are being used in the hands-on exercises of the book.

If you are logged into the SAP IDES server, it is already configured for multiple dummy company codes and contains substantial dummy data in the configuring, *master data,* and *transaction data* tables. The IDES server is ideal to perform the hands-on exercises of the book. The hands-on exercises in the book produced results using the IDES server.

When describing tables, the fields are marked as PK for primary key fields and FK for foreign key fields. The table descriptions follow:

"T" Series - Universal Data Tables

Table A-1. *T005T (Country names)*

Field Name	DDIC Data Type	Length, Decimals	Description
MANDT (PK, FK)	CLNT	3	Client
SPRAS (PK, FK)	LANG	1	Language key
LAND1 (PK, FK)	CHAR	3	Country key
LANDX	CHAR	15	Country name
NATIO	CHAR	15	Nationality
LNADX50	CHAR	50	Country name (Max 50 characters)
NATIO50	CHAR	50	Nationality (Max 50 characters)
PRQ_SPREGT	CHAR	30	Super region per country text

Table A-2. *T005U (Taxes: Region key texts)*

Field Name	DDIC Data Type	Length, Decimals	Description
MANDT (PK,FK)	CLNT	3	Client
SPRAS (PK,FK)	LANG	1	Language key
LAND1 (PK,FK)	CHAR	3	Country key
BLAND (PK,FK)	CHAR	3	Region (State, Province, County)
BEZEI	CHAR	20	Description

Table A-3. *TCURT (Currency code names)*

Field Name	DDIC Data Type	Length, Decimals	Description
MANDT (PK,FK)	CLNT	3	Client
SPRAS (PK,FK)	LANG	1	Language key
WAERS (PK,FK)	CUKY	5	Currency key
LTEXT	CHAR	40	Long text
KTEXT	CHAR	15	Short text

"T" Series - Configuring Data Tables

■ **Note** For brevity, other fields of this table are not mentioned.

Table A-4. *T000 (Clients installed on the system)*

Field Name	DDIC Data Type	Length, Decimals	Description
MANDT (PK)	CLNT	3	Client
MTEXT	CHAR	25	Client name
ORT01	CHAR	25	City

■ **Note** For brevity, other fields in this table are not mentioned.

Table A-5. *T001 (Company codes)*

Field Name	DDIC Data Type	Length, Decimals	Description
MANDT (PK, FK)	CLNT	3	Client
BUKRS (PK)	CHAR	4	Company code
BUTXT	CHAR	25	Name of company code
ORT01	CHAR	25	City
LAND1 (FK)	CHAR	3	Country key
WAERS (FK)	CUKY	5	Currency key
SPRAS (FK)	LANG	1	Language key

A company code - BUKRS - is associated with a country, currency, and language.

Table A-6. *TVKO (Organization unit: Sales organizations)*

Field Name	DDIC Data Type	Length, Decimals	Description
MANDT (PK,FK)	CLNT	3	Client
VKORG (PK)	CHAR	4	Sales organization
WAERS (FK)	CUKY	5	Statistics currency
BUKRS (FK)	CHAR	4	Company code of the sales organization

Table A-7. *TVKOT (Organization unit: Sales organization texts)*

Field Name	DDIC Data Type	Length, Decimals	Description
MANDT (PK,FK)	CLNT	3	Client
SPRAS (PK,FK)	LANG	1	Language key
VKORG (PK,FK)	CHAR	4	Sales organization
VTEXT	CHAR	20	Name

Table A-8. *TVTW (Organization unit: Distribution channels)*

Field Name	DDIC Data Type	Length, Decimals	Description
MANDT (PK,FK)	CLNT	3	Client
VTWEG (PK)	CHAR	2	Distribution channel

Table A-9. *TVTWT (Organization unit: Distribution channel texts)*

Field Name	DDIC Data Type	Length, Decimals	Description
MANDT (PK,FK)	CLNT	3	Client
SPRAS (PK,FK)	LANG	1	Language key
VTWEG (PK,FK)	CHAR	2	Distribution channel
VTEXT	CHAR	20	Name

Table A-10. *TSPA (Organization unit: Sales divisions)*

Field Name	DDIC Data Type	Length, Decimals	Description
MANDT (PK,FK)	CLNT	3	Client
SPART (PK)	CHAR	2	Division

Table A-11. *TSPAT (Organization unit: Sales division texts)*

Field Name	DDIC Data Type	Length, Decimals	Description
MANDT (PK,FK)	CLNT	3	Client
SPRAS (PK,FK)	LANG	1	Language key
SPART (PK,FK)	CHAR	2	Division
VTEXT	CHAR	20	Name

'T' Series - Cross Client Tables

Table A-12. *TRDIRT (Title texts for programs in TRDIR)*

Field Name	DDIC Data Type	Length, Decimals	Description
NAME (PK)	CHAR	40	ABAP Program Name
SPRSL (PK, FK)	CHAR	1	Language key
TEXT	CHAR	40	Report Title

Table A-13. *T247 (Month name and short text)*

Field Name	DDIC Data Type	Length, Decimals	Description
SPRAS (PK, FK)	LANG	1	Language key
MNR (PK)	NUMC	2	Month number
KTX	CHAR	3	Month short text
LTX	CHAR	10	Month long text

Master Data Tables - Customers

Table A-14. *KNA1 (General data in customer master)*

Field Name	DDIC Data Type	Length, Decimals	Description
MANDT (PK,FK)	CLNT	3	Client
KUNNR (PK)	CHAR	10	Customer number/code
NAME1	CHAR	35	Name
STRAS	CHAR	35	Street
ORT01	CHAR	35	City
PSTLZ	CHAR	10	Postal code
LAND1 (FK)	CHAR	3	Country code
ANRED	CHAR	10	Title
TELF1	CHAR	16	Telephone
SPRAS (FK)	CHAR	1	Language key

Table A-15. *KNB1 (Customer master - company code)*

Field Name	DDIC Data Type	Length, Decimals	Description
MANDT (PK,FK)	CLNT	3	Client
KUNNR (PK,FK)	CHAR	10	Customer number/code
BUKRS (PK,FK)	CHAR	4	Company code
AKONT (FK)	CHAR	10	Reconciliation account

Table A-16. *KNVV (Customer master sales data)*

Field Name	DDIC Data Type	Length, Decimals	Description
MANDT (PK,FK)	CLNT	3	Client
KUNNR (PK,FK)	CHAR	10	Customer number/code
VKORG (PK,FK)	CHAR	4	Sales organization
VTWEG (PK,FK)	CHAR	2	Distribution channel
SPART (PK,FK)	CHAR	2	Division

Master Data Tables - Vendors

Table A-17. *LFA1 (Vendor master – general section)*

Field Name	DDIC Data Type	Length, Decimals	Description
MANDT (PK,FK)	CLNT	3	Client
LIFNR (PK)	CHAR	10	Vendor number/code
NAME1	CHAR	35	Name
STRAS	CHAR	35	Street
ORT01	CHAR	35	City
PSTLZ	CHAR	10	Postal Code
LAND1 (FK)	CHAR	3	Country code
ANRED	CHAR	10	Title
TELF1	CHAR	16	Telephone
SPRAS (FK)	CHAR	1	Language key

Table A-18. *LFB1 (Vendor master - company code)*

Field Name	DDIC Data Type	Length, Decimals	Description
MANDT (PK,FK)	CLNT	3	Client
LIFNR (PK,FK)	CHAR	10	Vendor number/code
BUKRS (PK,FK)	CHAR	4	Company code
AKONT (FK)	CHAR	10	Reconciliation account

Master Data Tables – Material

Table A-19. *MAKT (Material descriptions)*

Field Name	DDIC Data Type	Length, Decimals	Description
MANDT (PK,FK)	CLNT	3	Client
MATNR (PK,FK)	CHAR	18	Material number/code
SPRAS (PK,FK)	CHAR	1	Language key
MAKTX	CHAR	40	Material description
MAKTG	CHAR	40	Material description in upper case for matchcodes

Material descriptions or texts (field MAKTX) are maintained in multiple languages.

The material master table is MARA. The hands-on exercises in this book are not using any fields of this table. Hence, for simplicity and expediency, the table MARA is being bypassed. Normally, you will access material description table MAKT through the material master table MARA.

Transaction Data Tables - Sales

Table A-20. *VBAK (Sales document: Header data)*

Field Name	DDIC Data Type	Length, Decimals	Description
MANDT (PK,FK)	CLNT	3	Client
VBELN (PK, FK)	CHAR	10	SD document number
AUDAT	DATS	8	Document date
VBTYP	CHAR	1	SD document category
KUNNR (FK)	CHAR	10	Sold-to party
NETWR	CURR	15,2	Net value of sales order in document currency
WAERK (FK)	CUKY	5	SD document currency
BUKRS_VF (FK)	CHAR	4	Company code to be billed
VKORG (FK)	CHAR	4	Sales organization
VTWEG (FK)	CHAR	2	Distribution channel
SPART (FK)	CHAR	2	Division

Table A-21. *VBAP (Sales document: Item data)*

Field Name	DDIC Data Type	Length, Decimals	Description
MANDT (PK, FK)	CLNT	3	Client
VBELN (PK, FK)	CHAR	10	SD document number
POSNR (PK)	NUMC	6	Sales document Item
MATNR (FK)	CHAR	18	Material number/code
ZMENG	QUAN	13,3	Target quantity in sales units
ZIEME (FK)	UNIT	3	Target quantity UOM (unit of measure)
NETWR	CURR	15,2	Net value of the order item in document currency
WAERK (FK)	CUKY	5	Sales document currency

Table A-22. *VBRK (Billing document: Header data)*

Field Name	DDIC Data Type	Length, Decimals	Description
MANDT (PK, FK)	CLNT	3	Client
VBELN (PK, FK)	CHAR	10	Billing document number
FKDAT	DATS	8	Billing date
VBTYP	CHAR	1	SD document category
KUNAG (FK)	CHAR	10	Sold-to party
NETWR	CURR	15,2	Net value- in document currency
WAERK (FK)	CUKY	5	Document currency
BUKRS (FK)	CHAR	4	Company code
KURRF	DEC	9,5	Exchange rate
VKORG (FK)	CHAR	4	Sales organization
VTWEG (FK)	CHAR	2	Distribution channel
SPART (FK)	CHAR	2	Division

The table VBRK is linked to the *header status and administrative data* table VBUK. For this reason the field VBELN is marked as FK or foreign key. For simplicity and expediency, this relationship is being ignored. The table VBUK is not featuring in the sales functionality ER diagram in Figure A-2.

Fields Requiring Further Explanation

WAERK

A billing document can be generated in any currency. This field contains the currency code of the billing document.

KUNAG

The field KUNAG is a categorization of the customer. In an enterprise, you will ship the material to a particular customer authority and address; send the billing document to a different customer authority and address. Authority in an enterprise is distributed. For your purposes, you can treat the field KUNNR in tables KNA1, KNB1, and the field KUNAG in table VBRK as equivalent.

NETWR

This field contains the amount for all the items of a billing document. A billing document can contain zero or n number of items.

Each billing document amount value can be of a different currency. The billing document amount values can be converted to a single currency, the currency of the company code by multiplying the field NETWR with the exchange rate field KURRF.

The field NETWR can contain negative values. The following scenario will elucidate why a billing document can contain a negative value.

Suppose an enterprise sells 1,000 bolts at $ 1 apiece to a customer. The 1,000 bolts are dispatched to the customer along with a billing document of value $ 1,000. This billing document is categorized as a bill or an invoice. At the customer site, it is discovered that 5 bolts are defective or broken or short. In this situation, the customer must be charged only for 995 bolts. The typical accounting procedure that is followed to ensure that the customer is charged for 995 bolts only does not involve cancellation of the original billing document of $ 1,000 and reissuing of a new billing document of $ 995. A document category *Credit Memo* is generated with an amount value of $ -5. The net of these two billing documents will charge the customer $995. Since credit is to be given to the customer for $ 5, the document category is called a *Credit Memo*. You can have a scenario of customer receiving excess of quantity over the billing document say 1005 bolts. Then the customer needs to be charged for the extra 5 bolts. The extra charge of 5 bolts worth $ 5 will be adjusted through another document category: the *Debit Memo*.

To take care of minor adjustments to a generated billing document such as described in the previous paragraph, a debit or a credit memo is generated. Consider a scenario where all the dispatched goods get damaged during transportation. In such a situation, a complete cancellation of the invoice/bill is warranted. This kind of major adjustment is taken care by a document category *Invoice cancellation*. The document category (called the SD document category) is stored in the field VBTYP. Look up *Value Range* tab of the domain VBTYP for viewing all the SD document categories.

While accumulating the converted values of the field NETWR to obtain total sales of customers, materials, etc., it is to be ensured that only the document categories that contribute to the actual sales are retrieved. (WHERE VBTYP = ... etc.) Document categories such as *Performa Invoice* do not generate actual sales. Such document categories should be omitted when accumulating sales for customers, materials, etc. This has not been done in the hands-on exercises in the book. In the training and teaching paradigm, this can be overlooked, but you must still be aware of this issue.

Since the billing tables can contain not just the invoices/bills but multiple document categories, the tables are called billing document tables.

Table A-23. *VBRP (Billing document: Item data)*

Field Name	DDIC Data Type	Length, Decimals	Description
MANDT (PK, FK)	CLNT	3	Client
VBELN (PK, FK)	CHAR	10	Billing document number
POSNR (PK)	NUMC	6	Billing document Item
MATNR (FK)	CHAR	18	Material number
FKIMG	QUAN	13,3	Sold quantity in sales units
VRKME (FK)	UNIT	3	Sales unit of measure
NETWR	CURR	15,2	Net value of item in document currency

The table VBRP is not directly linked to the table VBRK. The table VBRP linked to the table VBRK through the *header status and administrative data* table VBUK. You can check this out by opening the foreign key dialog box for the field VBELN of table VBRP. For simplicity and expediency, the two tables VBRK and VBRP are linked directly for the hands-on exercises in the book. The sales functionality ER diagram in Figure A-2 reflects the direct linkage.

Fields Requiring Further Explanation

VRKME

sales unit of measure. For the same material, different units of measure can be used in different situations. A simple example: an enterprise may purchase a material in dozens and sell the same material in numbers/units.

NETWR

If you want to accumulate sales material wise, you will use the field NETWR of this table - that is, VBRP: multiply it with the corresponding exchange rate field KURRF of the table VBRK. For a billing document, you might end up with the total of individual amounts (NETWR) from the table VBRP multiplied by the exchange rate not exactly equal to that of the field NETWR of table VBRK multiplied by the exchange rate. There could be a slight difference between the two.

Tables of Sales Functionality - ER Diagram

An ER diagram of tables of sales functionality used in the hands-on exercises in the book is shown in Figure A-2:

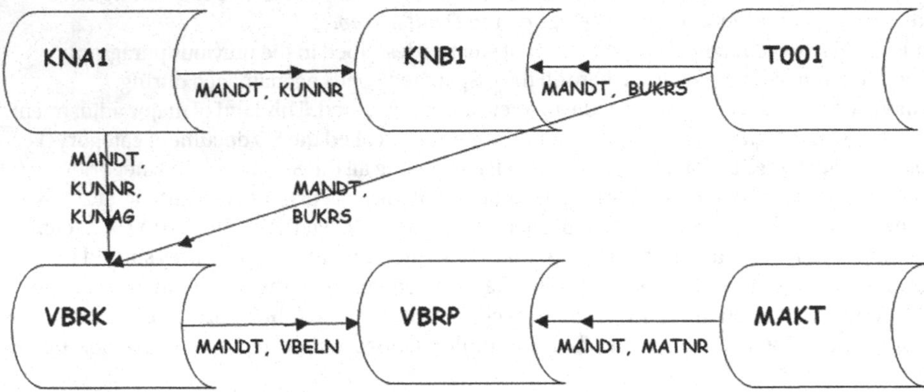

Figure A-2. *Sales functionality tables - ER diagram*

The ER diagram shown in Figure A-2 is not a comprehensive ER diagram as such, depicts and shows only the table relationships used in the hands-on exercises in the book.

Contextual ER diagrams are available in the chapters.

Transaction Data Tables - Purchase

For most programming hands-on exercises in the book, we have used the tables from the sales functionality. If you want to perform independently programming hands-on exercises on a parallel basis, you can use the tables from the purchase functionality.

While using the tables from the purchase functionality, you must bear in mind the following:

- The purchasing document tables contain data for different categories of purchasing documents such as purchase orders (POs) and request for quotation (RFQs), etc. This is similar to the billing documents tables containing different categories of billing documents such as invoices/bills, credit memos, debit memos, etc. You are summing the NETWR converted values for the different categories of billing documents. This made sense as described in the scenario of field NETWR of table VBRK. With the purchasing document tables, it does not make sense to sum converted amounts of different categories of purchasing documents such as purchase orders, request for quotation, etc. So while retrieving data from the purchasing document table; filter out the purchase orders data from the header table. The purchasing document category is contained in the field BSTYP. Refer to the *Single Values* tab of domain of this name for values of categories for purchasing documents.
- Unlike in the billing document tables, the total amount for a document is not available in the purchasing document header table. That is, the field NETWR is not available in the purchasing document header table EKKO. This field is available only in the purchasing document item table EKPO.

Table A-24. *EKKO (Purchasing document header)*

Field Name	DDIC Data Type	Length, Decimals	Description
MANDT (PK, FK)	CLNT	3	Client
EBELN (PK,)	CHAR	10	Purchasing document number
BEDAT	DATS	8	Purchasing document date
BSTYP	CHAR	1	Purchasing document category
LIFNR (FK)	CHAR	10	Vendor number/code
WAERS (FK)	CUKY	5	Currency key
WKURS	DEC	9,5	Exchange rate
BUKRS (FK)	CHAR	4	Company code
EKORG (FK)	CHAR	4	Purchasing organization

Table A-25. *EKPO (Purchasing document item)*

Field Name	DDIC Data Type	Length, Decimals	Description
MANDT (PK, FK)	CLNT	3	Client
EBELN (PK, FK)	CHAR	10	Purchasing document number
EBELP (PK)	NUMC	5	Item number of purchasing document
MATNR (FK)	CHAR	18	Material number/code
BUKRS (FK)	CHAR	4	Company code
MENGE	QUAN	13,3	Purchase order quantity
MEINS (FK)	UNIT	3	Purchase order UOM
NETWR	CURR	13,2	Net order value in document currency

ER Diagram of Tables of Purchase Functionality

An ER diagram of tables of purchase functionality is shown in Figure A-3:

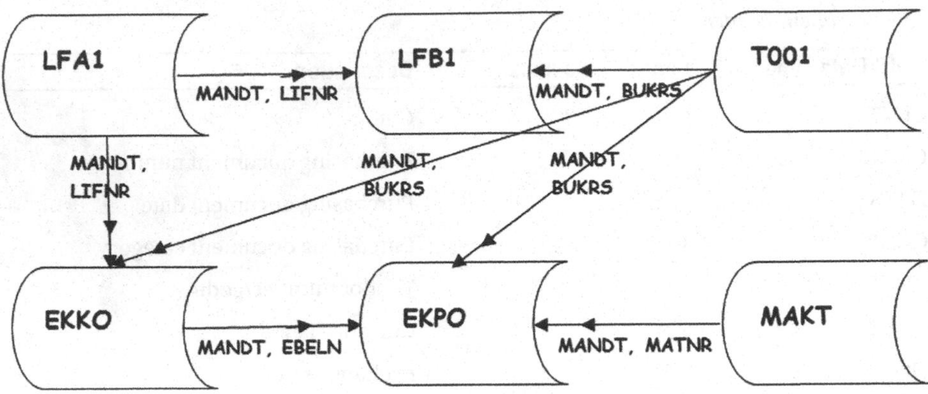

Figure A-3. *Purchase functionality tables - ER diagram*

The ER diagram shown in Figure A-3 is not a comprehensive ER diagram as such; it depicts and shows only the table relationships to be used in the independent hands-on exercises by the reader.

X. Cross client (Client independent) tables

A few non - 'T' series cross client (client independent) tables have been used in hands-on exercises in the book. The description of these tables follows:

Table A-26. *ICON (Icons table)*

Field Name	DDIC Data Type	Length, Decimals	Description
ID (PK)	CHAR	4	Icon in text fields (Icon Code)
NAME	CHAR	30	Name of an Icon

Table A-27. *DD02L (SAP tables)*

Field Name	DDIC Data Type	Length, Decimals	Description
TABNAME (PK)	CHAR	30	Table name
TABCLASS (PK)	CHAR	8	Table class

Table A-28. *DD03L (Table fields)*

Field Name	DDIC Data Type	Length, Decimals	Description
TABNAME (PK, FK)	CHAR	30	Table name
FIELDNAME (PK)	CHAR	30	Field name
POSITION (PK)	NUMC	4	Position of the field in the table

Non-categorized Table

The client dependent table BUT000_TD does not fit into any of our subcategories. This table was introduced in Chapter 2 to highlight in the *foreign key field* dialog box, the column *generic key field*. That is all. This table has not been referred to or used in any other place in the book. The table's fields are not listed since this table is not being processed in any of the hands-on exercises in the book.

Conclusion

This appendix was a description of all the tables used in the hands-on exercises in the book. Instead of using hypothetical tables, real-life application tables have been used to perform the hands-on exercises. The table descriptions give you technical as well as functional insights. And they also give you a fair perspective of the complexities of the real-life SAP application tables.

Index

A, B

C

D

E

F

G, H

I, J, K

L

M

N

O

P, Q

R

S

T, U, V

W, X, Y, Z

Printed in the United States
By Bookmasters